FIFTH EDITION
THE COMPLETE
ANTIQUES PRICE LIST

Cover illustration
courtesy of the Smithsonian Institution

Books by Ralph M. and Terry H. Kovel

The Complete Antiques Price List

Know Your Antiques

American Country Furniture 1780–1875

Dictionary of Marks—Pottery and Porcelain

The Official Bottle Price List

FIFTH EDITION
THE COMPLETE

ANTIQUES PRICE LIST

**A guide to the 1972–1973 market
for professionals, dealers, and collectors**

by Ralph M. and Terry H. Kovel
ILLUSTRATED

CROWN PUBLISHERS, INC., NEW YORK

© 1972 by Crown Publishers, Inc.
All rights reserved. No part of this book may be reproduced
or utilized in any form or by any means, electronic or mechanical,
including photocopying, recording, or by any information storage
and retrieval system, without permission in writing from the Publisher.
Inquiries should be addressed to Crown Publishers, Inc.,
419 Park Avenue South, New York, N.Y. 10016.
Library of Congress Catalog Card Number: 72-84290
ISBN: 0-517-500833
Printed in the United States of America
Published simultaneously in Canada by General Publishing Company Limited
Second Printing, March, 1973

GUIDE TO USE

The interest in collecting antiques continues to expand each year. THE COMPLETE ANTIQUES PRICE LIST is our attempt to report the current prices offered for antiques and collectibles in the United States. All prices listed are actual reports from auctions, antique shows, shops, sales, flea markets, and other sale sources. The prices included are those for items sold or offered for sale between June 1971 and June 1972. Prices can vary from one section of the country to another, so many items have a range of price. Whenever our staff has reported several sales at a variety of prices, the highest and lowest have been listed to show the price range. Illustrated items are accompanied by their actual sales prices as reported by the seller.

The book is compiled and printed by computer, so there is a limit to the amount of description possible for any single item. We have tried to include as much pertinent data as possible.

There are just a few simple rules to follow in using this book. Listing is arranged in this manner: category (such as pressed glass, silver, or furniture); the object (such as vase, spoon, table); the description, which includes as much information as possible about size, age, color, and pattern. All items are perfect unless otherwise noted. Leaf through the book and examine the various category headings. You can readily see that most of them are as expected. A few, such as "store," "wooden," "commemorative," "porcelain," and "household," include a varied assortment of antiques. Most porcelain pieces are listed by the factory name, but those of interest without a maker's name are included in the catchall category. In this year's edition we have added several new categories such as: "Indian"; "maize"; "trunk"; "lightning rod"; and many sections under celebrity names for those fictitious characters such as "Buck Rogers," "Orphan Annie," "Charlie McCarthy," etc. The many types of collector plates, including Christmas plates, are listed in a new category: "collector plate." This new large category includes all recent limited edition plates, because many antique collectors and antique publications are interested in these prices. The section on bottles includes primarily old bottles. Some new limited edition bottles have been included but there has been no attempt to make a comprehensive listing because this is long enough to make a book. They are listed in full in *The Official Bottle Price List*.

There are many new paragraph headings explaining the history of the factories and antiques mentioned. There are also about 40 additional cross-references, which should make the search for a specific antique easier.

The changing antique market in the United States can be readily seen by comparing this edition of THE COMPLETE ANTIQUES PRICE LIST with the four earlier editions. Collector plates and bottles are the two fastest rising categories. Barbed wire and telephone insulators have been gaining in popularity. Store advertising, especially on tin boxes, has risen sharply in price. Celebrity items, Big Little books, and comic books have become so popular that special antiques shows have been organized for these items. American furniture and American silver are rising in price whereas English furniture and silver have remained near last year's range. Art Deco items seem to have gained in price, and there is a growing interest in fine late Victorian furniture and American Art pottery. Mission furniture is starting to appear in the sales. Centennial items have gained in price and will probably continue to grow in demand through 1976. French bronzes of the late nineteenth century are higher priced. The market seems to show two distinct trends:

1. Prices of the very finest or rarest American or European antiques, such as Paul Revere silver or unique pieces of Meissen, continue to rise.

2. The very bottom of the market, or the inexpensive memorabilia that are not old enough to be true antiques, is also rising in price.

Other staple items of the antique trade such as art glass, pressed glass, good furniture, pewter, porcelains, etc., are rising in value by approximately 12 percent each year.

We can take no responsibility for any confusion or losses resulting from errors in the book. It is as accurate as possible but human errors can sometimes occur.

ACKNOWLEDGMENTS

Antique collectors from all over the country have written to make suggestions and offer price information through lists of sales. To all of you we say thank you. To those who suggest that the prices are too high or too low we can only say again that this is an actual report and not an appraisal. To our staff who keep tabs on all the sales from California to Maine, thank you. To

Debby Herman, Connie Dankulic, and the computer staff, more thanks. To Eleanor Dion, once again an extra helping of gratitude for the daily grind of seeing to it that the book made it out on time.

PICTURE ACKNOWLEDGMENTS

The color pictures used in this book are from the Smithsonian Institution in Washington, D.C. The Smithsonian's collection is vast, including Americana both old and new. Its rooms are filled with toys, musical instruments, political memorabilia, examples of fine arts, ceramics, silver, folk art, furniture, costumes, tools, clocks, glass, and period rooms from different parts of the United States. Washington, D.C., abounds in historic sites, and a visit there should include time at the Smithsonian Institution, where you can learn more about your own country's antiques.

The color picture used for the cover of this book was specially photographed at the Smithsonian Institution. Special thanks to Mr. Jim Pinkney and his staff who finally found a way to "get the shot" by removing a full wall.

The black-and-white pictures were taken in many parts of the country. The dealers who helped with this chore and loaned items to be pictured were:

Ada's Treasure Vault; Floyd & Barbara Adkins; Ampersand; The Ancestor Shop; Angela's Antiques; Antique Caravan; Antique Galleries, East; Twyla E. Barron; Bergman's Antiques; Barbara Bertsch; Betty's Antiques; Bill-Robbs; Blueberry Hill Antiques; Bliss Antiques; Blue Door Antiques; Bobby-Lynn; The Blue Plate Antiques; George Bolton, Books; Barbara Brown, Bryant's Antiques; Buddy's Antiques; Buterbaugh's This & That Shop; Bygones & Buttons; Chris-Cross Antiques; Mrs. Consilio; Continental Clutter; Conwag Antiques; Covered Bridge Antiques; Curiosity Corner; Cushman Antiques; Danbar's Distant View Farm Antiques; Dave's Antiques; Richard Davis, Antiques; Patricia B. DeMond; Nadine DePalmo; Dornhecker's Curiosity Shop; Roger Durflinger; East Eden Antiques; Et. Cetera; Mrs. Ferrini; Jeanne Fishman; Forest Hills Furnishings; Dixie Franklin; Gable Galleries; The Galerie; Glasshouse Antiques; Grandma's Attic; Granny's Rolling Pin; June Greenwald, Antiques; Koby Grond; Gwen's Antiques; Hanna Enterprise; Hawkins Antiques; Heritage House; Hillcrest Corn Sales; His n' Her Antiques; House of Antiques; I. J. & N. K. Antiques; Imperial Antiques; Irene's Antiques;

Louis Jindra; Kaytlersch Antiques; Mary Kempf; Kennedy Galleries; Bernice Kent; Kent House Antiques; Nell M. Kesson; Kitten's Antiques; Ray Klug; Knights Tiny Shop; Dorothy Lerner, Antiques; Lewallen Antiques; Lou Gay Antiques; Lyons Antiques; Male Room; Mardon Antiques; Margaret's Antiques; Margo Antiques; Martin's Antiques; Mary Jean Antiques; Mary "L" Antiques; Marge McDonald; Mitchell Antiques; Michael Morosko Antiques; Naomi's Fine Antiques; Now & Then; Oak Tree Antiques; The Old Store; Dale T. Orr; Our House; Painesville Antiques; William L. Perdue, Antiques; Albie Pink; R & C Antiques; Red House Antiques; Mary Rehker; Road Runner Antiques; James L. Roush; Ruby & Roy's Antiques; Rural Retreat; Ruth Antiques; S & S Jewelry Antiques; Opal Sallee; Seaway Antiques; Larry A. Selman; Sharon Center Antiques; Wayne Siddens, Inc.; Peter J. Sidlow; Siegferth Antiques; Paul Speyser; Mary Jo Spitz, Stephens Antiques; Lewis Stotz Antiques; Summit House Antiques; Swanks Antiques; Timely Treasure Antiques; Toonerville Junction; Walden Hill Antiques; Florence West; Whitman-Crafford Antiques; Wideman Antique Loft; Anne Wichert Antiques; John Coleman Wilcox; Viola R. Wollpert; Woodruff Antiques; A. Wolf and Don & Eloise Young.

DEDICATION

TO
Grace Jenkins
Albert J. Olson
Bernice Golden
Bernie Nathanson
Jack Dymond
Chuck Zappola
Elizabeth Caplinger
our "special associates" who really know
which is more important.
AND TO
KIM and LEE

ABC Plates or Children's Alphabet Plates were popular from 1780 to 1860. The letters on the plate were meant as teaching aids for the children who were learning to read. The plates were made of pottery, porcelain, metal, or glass.

Abc, Butter Chip, Fish Center, Alphabet Rim	8.50
Abc, Cup, Marked Germany, Children & Pets	4.50
Abc, Plate, Alphabet Border, Beaded Scalloped Rim, Star Center, Glass	15.00
Abc, Plate, American Sports, Baseball Caught On The Fly, Porcelain	20.00
Abc, Plate, Boy On Rocking Horse, Dachshund Pulling Tail	12.00
Abc, Plate, Caruso Rescues Friday, Tunstall, England, 8 In.	20.00
Abc, Plate, Cat, Yarn, Ohio Art, 4 In.	10.00
Abc, Plate, Chickens	20.00
Abc, Plate, Chickens, Rooster, Alphabet Border, Porcelain, 7 In.Diameter	15.00
Abc, Plate, Clear Glass, Clock Center, 6 In.	20.00
Abc, Plate, Clock	15.25
Abc, Plate, Clock Center, Clear, Stippled, Scalloped Edge	25.00
Abc, Plate, Cobalt Blue, 8 In.	12.50
Abc, Plate, Cock Robin, Tin	18.50
Abc, Plate, Dutch Scene	18.00
Abc, Plate, Elephant Center, Raised Letter Border, Tin, 6 In.	12.50
Abc, Plate, Five Pigs In Action Marching, 6 In.	15.50
Abc, Plate, Frosted Child's Head, Blue, Raised Letters, 8 In.Diameter	30.00
Abc, Plate, Germany, Child, Clowns, Animals, 7 1/2 In.	16.00
Abc, Plate, Hen & Chicks, Clear	20.00
Abc, Plate, Hey Diddle Diddle, Dancing Children Border, 6 1/2 In.	18.00
Abc, Plate, Hey Diddle Diddle, Tin	6.50
Abc, Plate, Iowa City, Frosted Stork Center	50.00
Abc, Plate, Ironstone, Transfer Print, The New Pony, Embossed Alphabet	22.50
Abc, Plate, Jack & Jill, 7 In.	16.00
Abc, Plate, Mother Reads To Children, 5 In.	17.50
Abc, Plate, Numbers, Inches, Roman Numerals	25.00
Abc, Plate, Picture Of Children & Verse	18.00
Abc, Plate, Scene, Man On Fence, Basket At Side, Church, C.1860	15.00
Abc, Plate, Sioux Indian Chief Center, 6 3/4 In.	22.50
Abc, Plate, Stork, Marigold, Glass	34.00
Abc, Plate, Sunbonnet Babies, Ring-Around-The-Rosy, Silver Plate	50.00
Abc, Plate, The Fox & Tiger, China	17.50

Adams China was made by William Adams and Sons of Staffordshire, England.The firm was founded in 1769 and is still working.

Adams, Bowl, Blue Chinese Pattern, Signed Wm.Adams On Bottom, 8 In.	18.00
Adams, Bowl, Oriental Design, Blue, Signed	15.00
Adams, Bowl, Sweet Oranges, Cries Of London, 9 In.Square	22.50
Adams, Box, White Figures, Blue, Tunstall Mark, 2 X 2 3/4 In.	50.00
Adams, Cup & Saucer, Milk Maid, Matchgirl, Marked, Circa 1890	32.50
Adams, Dish, Jelly, Classical Figures, Blue, White, Tray, Cover	35.00
Adams, Pitcher, Dark Blue Jasperware, White Crest, Says Ross's Ginger Ale	40.00
Adams, Plate, Black & White, Caledonia, 7 1/2 In.	20.00
Adams, Plate, Commemoration, Jamestown, Va., Blue & White	18.50
Adams, Plate, Dickens, Christmas Eve At Mr.Wardles, Rust Orange	20.00
Adams, Plate, Dickens, First Appearance Of Samuel Weller, Rust Orange	20.00
Adams, Plate, Monte Video, Conn., Pink, 7 In.	38.00
Adams, Plate, Pattern, 8 1/4 In.Diameter	40.00
Adams, Plate, Scenic, Lorna Doone & John Ridd, Tunstall, England, 6 In.	19.00
Adams, Plate, Sprig Pattern, Impressed Adams, 7 1/2 In.Diameter	2.00
Adams, Plate, Strawberries, Scarlet, C.1890	17.50
Adams, Platter, Blue & White, Bologna, 17 In.Long	10.00
Adams, Platter, Blue & White, Views Of Palestine, 15 In.Long	17.50
Adams, Platter, Fountain Scene, Blue, White, Marked, 12 X 15 In.	30.00
Adams, Spillholder, Blue Jasperware, White Figures, 6 In.Tall	25.00
Adams, Spillholder, Medium Blue, White Classic Figures, Jasperware, 6 In.	25.00

Advertising Card, see Card, Advertising

Agata Glass was made by Joseph Locke of the New England Glass Company of Cambridge, Massachusetts, after 1885.A metallic stain was applied to New England Peachblow and the mottled design characteristic of Agata appeared.

Agata, Bunch Of Grapes, Rust, Tan, Beige, Stone	15.00
Agata, Tumbler, Acid Coloring	475.00
Agate, Box, Blue, Four Lapis Ball Feet, Gold Dore Trim	135.00
Agate, Figurine, Horse, Galloping, Blue Gray, Black Striations, Pair	375.00
Agate, Rose Bowl, French, Moss, Clear Over Green, Signed Degue	85.00

Akro Agate Glass was made in Clarksburg, West Virginia, from 1932 to 1951. Before that time the firm made children's glass marbles.Most of the glass is marked with a crow flying through the letter A.

Akro Agate, Ashtray, Pair In Octagon Holder, Blue & White	8.00
Akro Agate, Ashtray, Shell, Orange & White	5.00
Akro Agate, Dish Set, Child's, Green & White, 16 Piece	19.50
Akro Agate, Dish, Children, Play Time, Green, White, 7 Piece Set	10.50
Akro Agate, Figurine, Colonial Lady, Blue	27.50
Akro Agate, Flowerpot, Blue, 2 1/2 In.High	4.00
Akro Agate, Flowerpot, Green	3.00
Akro Agate, Holder, Match, Cornucopia, Red, White	10.00
Akro Agate, Jar, Mexicali, Cream, Pumpkin, Hat Cover	15.00
Akro Agate, Marble, 1 In.Diameter	3.00
Akro Agate, Pitcher, Child's, Green, Clear	2.00
Akro Agate, Planter, Blue & White With Red Band	8.00
Akro Agate, Planter, Green & White, Embossed Floral, 5 X 3 In.	7.00
Akro Agate, Shaving Mug, Black, Covered, J.V.& Co.	12.00
Akro Agate, Sugar, Child's, Green	1.25
Akro Agate, Tea Set, Child's, Marbleized, 16 Piece	19.50 To 30.00
Akro Agate, Tumbler, Child's, Caramel	1.25
Akro Agate, Vase, Blue, 6 In., Pair	10.00
Akro Agate, Vase, Reddish Brown & White, 6 In.High	7.00
Akro Agate, Water Set, Child's, Green & White, 7 Piece	10.50 To 15.00
Alabaster, Figure, Young Girl, Round Pedestal Base, 13 In.High	22.50
Alabaster, Vase, 7 In.	50.00

Albums were popular in victorian times to hold the myriad pictures and cutouts favored by the collectors.All sorts of scrapbooks and albums can still be found.

Album, Card, Greeting, Victorian, 50	7.00
Album, German Graphic Art, Eckstein Costumes, 1930, 258 Cards	35.00
Album, German Graphic Art, Kaugummi Sitting Bull, 2nd, 1950, 64 Cards	10.00
Album, Miniature, Tintypes	8.50
Album, Photo, Gibson Girl In Canoe	29.50
Album, Photo, White Bead Studs, With 50 Tin Pictures, 5 1/2 X 4 In.	10.00
Album, Photograph, Family, Maroon Velvet Cover, Lock & Key, Leaf Shape	15.00
Album, Photograph, Musical, 2 Melodies, Picture Of Children On Cover	75.00
Album, Photograph, Western American, Leather, 110 Photographs, C.1870	295.00
Album, Photography, Daguerreotype, Gutta Percha, Octagon, Hinged	9.50
Album, Photography, White Bead Studs, 50 Tin Pictures	10.00
Album, Postcard, Black, Used & Unused, Scenic, Holiday, 396 Cards	32.50
Album, Postcard, C.1910	5.00
Album, Postcard, Greeting Cards, 204	19.50
Album, Postcard, Pre-War, Comics, Colored, 100	12.50
Album, Postcard, Pre-1910, 600 Cards	90.00
Album, Postcard, Teddy Bears With Beehive, Empty	12.00
Album, Postcard, 1909-15, Cancelled Stamps, 50	32.00
Album, Valentine, 100 In Album	25.00
Album, Velvet, Green, Floral Brass Corners, Mirror, Brass Clasp	15.00

Amber Glass is the name of any glassware with the proper yellow-brown shade.It was a popular color after civil war.

Amber, Basket, 6 In.	10.00
Amber, Beads, 60 Graduated	75.00
Amber, Beads, 90 Graduated	85.00
Amber, Bottle, see Bottle, Amber	
Amber, Bowl, Finger, Daisy & Button, Pair	19.50

Amber, Bowl, Rose, Enamel, Man Sitting, Bench	45.00
Amber, Butter, Covered, Beaded Medallions	35.00
Amber, Candlestick, Dolphin, Pair	75.00
Amber, Canoe, Daisy & Button, 1i In.	25.00
Amber, Castor, Pickle, Decorated, Double	200.00
Amber, Celery, Diamond Pattern, Two Handles	12.00
Amber, Compote, Painted Floral, Handles Are Winged Dragons, France	87.50
Amber, Compote, Stemmed, Silver Deposit Lily Of The Valley, Marked Sterling	27.50
Amber, Compote, Willow Oak, 6 1/2 In.High	22.50
Amber, Compote, Willow Oak, 7 1/2 In.High	25.00
Amber, Compote, 7 In.High	5.00
Amber, Creamer, Daisy & Button With X	35.00
Amber, Creamer, Willow Oak	22.00
Amber, Cruet, Applied Handle, Blown, Square, Teardrop Stopper, 7 1/2 In.Tall	30.00
Amber, Cruet, Flattened Hobnail	35.00
Amber, Cup, Candle, Fasten To Christmas Tree	4.50
Amber, Decanter, Deer, Castle, Six Glasses With Leaves & Stems, Bohemia	125.00
Amber, Dish, Butter, Clock	57.50
Amber, Dish, Butter, Hobnail, Footed, Cover	30.00
Amber, Dish, Candy, Drum Shape, Cat Finial On Lid, Portieux	15.00
Amber, Dish, Round Hobnail Pattern, Bone, Set Of 6	39.00
Amber, Dish, Soap	27.00
Amber, Dog, Holds Vase, Button & Daisy	36.50
Amber, Goblet, Diamond Cut, Leaf Pattern	20.00
Amber, Goblet, Diamond Point, Knop Stem	8.00
Amber, Goblet, Flashed, Etched Deer	20.00
Amber, Goblet, Hummingbird	22.50 To 35.00
Amber, Goblet, Inverted Thumbprint With Star	10.00
Amber, Goblet, Spirea Band	15.00
Amber, Goblet, Wheat & Barley	12.50
Amber, Hen, Frosted, 5 In.	35.00
Amber, Holder, Match, Hanging, Figural, Elephant	28.00
Amber, Jug, Syrup, Inverted Thumbprint, Collared Base, Pewter Top	45.00
Amber, Mug, Bead & Scroll	9.50
Amber, Mug, Bird, Open Rose, Leaves	13.50
Amber, Perfume, 6 In., Stopper	7.00
Amber, Pitcher, Herringbone & Iris	24.50
Amber, Plate, Hexagon Shape	3.00
Amber, Platter, Bread, Daisy & Button	22.00
Amber, Salt & Pepper, Holder With Ringed Handle In Center, Daisy	45.00
Amber, Salt Dip, Squirrel Sitting By Tree Stump	7.50
Amber, Salt Dip, Turtle On Back	8.50
Amber, Shaker, Salt, Inverted Thumbprint, Enamel, Sandwich Glass	28.00
Amber, Shoe *Illus*	5.00
Amber, Shoe, Wall Pocket For Matches, Daisy Pattern On Back	18.00
Amber, Slipper, Cane, Harem Style, 4 1/2 In.	17.50
Amber, Slipper, Daisy & Button	12.00
Amber, Spooner, Leaf & Flower, Clear	40.00
Amber, Stein, Child's, Quilted, Pewter & Clear Top	25.00
Amber, Sugar, Cover, Inverted Thumbprint, Collared Base	28.00
Amber, Toothpick, Hand Holding Cornucopia, 5 In.High	25.00
Amber, Toothpick, 2 Cupids Holding Cup, 4 In. High	22.00
Amber, Tub & Washboard	24.00
Amber, Tumbler, Daisy & Button	12.00
Amber, Tumbler, Herringbone & Iris, Footed	5.50
Amber, Tumbler, 1, 000-Eye, 4 In.High	27.50
Amber, Vase, Flowers, Butterfly, Leaves, Enamel, Blue, Footed, 7 In., Pair	95.00
Amber, Vase, Golden Band With Classical Figures Under Rim, Signed Walthers	85.00
Amber, Vase, Hand, 14 In. *Illus*	48.50
Amber, Vase, Rose Bowl Type, Applied Blue Glass At Rim, 3 1/2 In.Tall	30.00
Amber, Vase, Shape Of Hand Holding Torch, 11 1/2 In.High	38.00
Amber, Vase, Swirl Pattern, Steuben Mark, 10 In.	150.00
Amber, Vase, Thorn, 4 1/2 In.	15.00
Amber, Water Set, Ribbed Pattern, Applied Handle, Circa 1890, 5 Tumblers	85.00
Amber, Wine Set, Bottle, Five Pedestal Glasses, Tray	35.00

Amber, Shoe
See Page 3

Amber, Vase, Hand, 14 In.
See Page 3

Amber, Witch Ball, Hole For Hanging, 3 In. 155.00

Amberina is a two-toned glassware made from 1883 to about 1900.It was patented by Joseph Locke of the New England Glass Company.The glass shades from red to amber.

Amberina, see also Mt.Washington, Baccarat, Plated Amberina, Bluerina

Amberina, **Basket**, Boat Shape, Hanging, Daisy & Button	85.00
Amberina, **Bell**, 5 3/4 In.Tall	9.75
Amberina, **Bell**, 6 In.Tall	9.50
Amberina, **Boat**, Fuchsia, Daisy & Button, By Hobbs, Brockunier, 8 In.	225.00
Amberina, **Bottle**, Perfume, Stopper, Swirl, 5 1/2 In.High, 3 1/4 In.Diameter	45.00
Amberina, **Bowl & Plate**, Stevens & Williams, Ruffled, Swirled Airtrap Satin	170.00
Amberina, **Bowl**, Diamond Thumbprint, Light Amber Bottom	235.00
Amberina, **Bowl**, Finger, Inverted Thumbprint, Swirl, Deep Color	75.00
Amberina, **Bowl**, Finger, Inverted Thumbprint, 5 1/4 In.Diameter	20.00
Amberina, **Bowl**, Fuchsia, Rolled-Over Top, Round	150.00
Amberina, **Butter Pat**, Fuchsia, Daisy & Button	57.00
Amberina, **Canoe**, Daisy & Button, 8 X 3 In.	150.00
Amberina, **Carafe & Tumbler**, Reverse Diamond-Quilted	65.00
Amberina, **Castor**, Pickle, Decorated	250.00
Amberina, **Castor**, Pickle, Fuchsia, Inverted Thumbprint, Silver Holder, Tongs	225.00
Amberina, **Castor**, Pickle, Hobs	250.00
Amberina, **Celery**, Amber To Cranberry, Flared & Scalloped, 10 Sided, 7 In.	90.00
Amberina, **Celery**, Diamond Quilted, Red To Amber, Scalloped Edge, 6 1/4 In.	190.00
Amberina, **Celery**, Fuchsia At Top To Golden Amber, Inverted Baby Thumbprint	140.00
Amberina, **Compote**, Ruffled Edge, Brass & Silver Base, 6 1/2 In.High	150.00
Amberina, **Cruet**, Blown, Amber Handle	95.00
Amberina, **Cruet**, Heat Mark On Handle, Silver Plate Holder	825.00
Amberina, **Cup**, Punch, Amber Applied, Handle	42.00
Amberina, **Cup**, Punch, Diamond Quilted, Paneled Body, Applied Handle, Amber	85.00
Amberina, **Cup**, Punch, Drape Pattern, Applied Amber Handle	45.00
Amberina, **Cup**, Punch, Inverted Thumbprint	45.00
Amberina, **Cup**, Punch, Pan	45.00
Amberina, **Cup**, Ribbed Pattern	65.00
Amberina, **Cup**, Vichy Mark, Straw Carrying Case	150.00
Amberina, **Creamer**, Inverted Thumbprint, Fuchsia	195.00
Amberina, **Dish**, Signed Cambridge, Ohio, 9 In.	150.00
Amberina, **Glass**, 5 1/2 In.High	15.00
Amberina, **Goblet**, Fuchsia, Engraved Hollyhocks, Signed J.Locke, 1883	895.00
Amberina, **Goblet**, Mt.Washington, Paneled	135.00
Amberina, **Jar**, Hot Toddy, Clear Reeded Handle On Lid, Opening For Ladle	500.00
Amberina, **Mustard**, Fuchsia, Cover, Ivory Spoon, Clear Handle	115.00
Amberina, **Pitcher**, Amber, Reeded Handle, 5 1/2 In.	155.00
Amberina, **Pitcher**, Diamond Quilted, Scalloped Top, Clear Reeded Handle	165.00
Amberina, **Pitcher**, Inverted Thumbprint, Amber Handle, 11 In.	150.00

Amberina, **Pitcher**, Inverted Thumbprint, Applied Corn & Vine In Silver	225.00
Amberina, **Pitcher**, Milk, Fuchsia At Top Shading To Amber At Bottom	115.00
Amberina, **Pitcher**, Reverse Inverted Thumbprint, Square Top, Ribbed Handle	80.00
Amberina, **Pitcher**, Rope Handle, 7 1/2 In.	450.00
Amberina, **Pitcher**, Ruby Top, Inverted Thumprint, Swirled Rib, Amber Handle	125.00
Amberina, **Pitcher**, Water, Crackle Glass, Clear, 7 3/4 In.Tall	150.00
Amberina, **Pitcher**, Water, Inverted Thumbprint, Bulbous, Amber To Fuchsia	285.00
Amberina, **Plate**, Dessert, Comblike Quilting, 6 1/2 In.Diameter, Set Of 8	425.00
Amberina, **Plate**, Diamond-Quilted, Fuchsia Coloring, 7 In.	55.00
Amberina, **Salt Shaker**, Enamel, Pewter Top	32.50
Amberina, **Salt Shaker**, Inverted Thumbprint	45.00
Amberina, **Sauce**, Daisy & Button, 5 In.Square	57.50
Amberina, **Shade**, Gas, Fuchsia, Diamond-Quilted, 5 In.High	160.00
Amberina, **Shaker**, Pepper, Floral Pattern, Pewter Stopper, 3 3/4 In.High	30.00
Amberina, **Sugar & Creamer**, Fuchsia, Mt.Washington, Libbey	395.00
Amberina, **Syrup**, Fuchsia, Silver Plate Top	275.00
Amberina, **Tieback**, 3 1/4 In., Pair	49.50
Amberina, **Toothpick**, Daisy & Button	110.00
Amberina, **Toothpick**, Diamond-Quilted	115.00
Amberina, **Toothpick**, Inverted Thumbprint	80.00 To 110.00
Amberina, **Tumbler**, Diamond-Quilted, Blown, Fuchsia	70.00
Amberina, **Tumbler**, Diamond-Quilted, Reversed	45.00
Amberina, **Tumbler**, Fuchsia To Amber, Diamond Pattern, Venetian, Pair	80.00
Amberina, **Tumbler**, Fuchsia, Diamond Pattern	60.00
Amberina, **Tumbler**, Inverted Thumbprint	48.00
Amberina, **Tumbler**, Pan	45.00
Amberina, **Tumbler**, Quilted, Set Of 6	300.00
Amberina, **Tumbler**, Red At Base Shading To Amber At Top, Diamond-Quilted	70.00
Amberina, **Vase**, Blue, 10 In.High	60.00
Amberina, **Vase**, Enameled Decor, Flowers, Bird, 11 In.Tall	450.00
Amberina, **Vase**, Five Feet, Swirled, Cylindrical, Gold Enamel, Applied Snake	80.00
Amberina, **Vase**, Fuchsia, Libbey, 10 1/2 In.High	425.00
Amberina, **Vase**, Fuchsia, Mushroom, Signed Libbey	450.00
Amberina, **Vase**, Fuchsia, Trumpet Shape, 9 In.Tall	150.00
Amberina, **Vase**, Girl With Bonnet, Bulbous, 9 In.	210.00
Amberina, **Vase**, Honeycomb Pattern, 5 Applied Amber Glass Feet, Blown	75.00
Amberina, **Vase**, Inverted Thumbprint, Finished Acid, 10 1/2 In.High	295.00
Amberina, **Vase**, Libbey, Turned Over Top, 5 In.High	250.00
Amberina, **Vase**, Paneled, Bulbous, Flaring Rim, Amber, Signed, 5 1/4 In.	350.00
Amberina, **Vase**, Rigaree Around Neck, Reeded Amber Scroll Feet, 6 1/2 In.	155.00
Amberina, **Vase**, Swirls, Enameled Insects, Gold Leaves, Ruffled Top, 11 In.	175.00

American Crystal, see Collector Plate

*Amethyst Glass is any of the many glasswares made in the proper dark purple
shade.It was a color popular after the civil war.*

Amethyst, **Banana Boat**, Grape & Cable	85.00
Amethyst, **Basket**, Open, 6 1/2 In.Tall	10.00
Amethyst, **Basket**, Scalloped Rim, Gold Designs, Pink Bead In Each Design	15.00
Amethyst, **Bottle**, Cologne, Stopper, Flint	20.00
Amethyst, **Bottle**, Vinegar, Circa 1830, Ohio	200.00
Amethyst, **Bowl & Four Sauce Dishes**, Scroll Pattern, Gilded	20.00
Amethyst, **Bowl**, Finger	5.00
Amethyst, **Bowl**, Flared Top, 8 1/2 In.	15.00
Amethyst, **Bowl**, Medallion & Garland, 9 In.Diameter, 3 3/4 In.High	38.00
Amethyst, **Bowl**, Rose, Ribbed, Crimp Top, Gold, 3 In.Diameter	35.00
Amethyst, **Bowl**, Steuben, Unsigned, 9 In.Across	70.00
Amethyst, **Bowl**, Stretch, 10 In.Diameter	35.00
Amethyst, **Decanter**, Wine, Raised Grape & Leaf Design, Stopper	10.00
Amethyst, **Dish**, Candy, Cover, Silver Deposit	25.00
Amethyst, **Dish**, Fan, Daisy & Button	18.00
Amethyst, **Glass**, Whiskey	9.50
Amethyst, **Goblet**, Cut Panel, Gold Decoration, Embossed Enameled Base	45.00
Amethyst, **Goblet**, Diamond-Quilted	17.50
Amethyst, **Goblet**, Gold Border	40.00
Amethyst, **Jar**, Biscuit, Floral, Enamel, Brass Cover & Handle, 8 1/2 In.	60.00
Amethyst, **Mug**, Monkey	45.00

Amethyst, Mug, Stork & Rushes	35.00
Amethyst, Planter, Dancing Figures, Nudes, Horns, Veils, White, 3 1/2 In.	7.50
Amethyst, Plate, Grape & Cable, Footed, 9 In.Diameter	69.00
Amethyst, Salt Dip, Swan	7.50
Amethyst, Salt, Master, Sandwich Ivy	55.00
Amethyst, Salt, Standing, Late 18th Century	85.00
Amethyst, Swan, Cambridge Mark, 12 In.Long	165.00
Amethyst, Tieback, Drapery, Petal Shape, 4 1/2 In.Diameter, Two Pair	28.00
Amethyst, Toothpick, Chick By Basket	23.50
Amethyst, Tumbler, Enameled Daisies	28.00
Amethyst, Tumbler, Paneled, Enamel Floral, Gold Trim	22.00
Amethyst, Tumbler, Ribbed, Enameled Daisies	20.00
Amethyst, Tumbler, Snow Scene, Arched Panel	28.50
Amethyst, Vase, Handkerchief, Clear To Amethyst, 9 1/4 In.High	40.00
Amos & Andy, Ashtray, Plaster	12.00

Amphora, see Teplitz
Andiron, many related fireplace items are under fire

Andy Gump, Cigar Label	4.50
Ansbach, Chocolate Pot, Ovoid, Gilt Scroll Handle, Mask Spout, Harbor, C.1765	200.00
Ansbach, Coffeepot, Pear Shape, Female Mask Spout, Birds, Tree, C.1765	80.00

Apothecary jar, see Bottle
Apple Peeler, see Kitchen, Peeler, Apple

*Art Deco or Art Moderne is a style started at the Paris Exposition
of 1925. All types of furniture, and decorative arts, jewelry, bookbindings, and
even games were designed in this style.*

Art Deco, Buckle, Belt, Enamel & Glass, C.1930	30.00
Art Deco, Clock, Desk, Bronze & Cloisonne, Orb Form, E.Gubelin, Lucerne	60.00
Art Deco, Clock, Desk, Enameled Pewter, Leaf Motifs, 8 In.High	350.00
Art Deco, Clock, Desk, Nephrite, Onyx Stand, Cartier, Diamonds On Jade	600.00
Art Deco, Clock, Silver, Cartier *Illus*	575.00
Art Deco, Dressing Table Set, Cameo Glass, Dolphins & Dancers, 3 Piece	80.00
Art Deco, Earrings, 14k Gold & Rubies, Margarete Goldschmiedemeister	75.00
Art Deco, Figurine, Diana, Bronze, Kneeling, Nude, Roman Bronze Works, N.Y.	475.00
Art Deco, Figurine, Monkey, Bronze, Seated, 14 In.High	100.00
Art Deco, Figurine, Mother & Child, French, Glass, 14 In.Tall	20.00
Art Deco, Figurine, Young Woman Center, Bronze, French, Marble Base, 16 In.	200.00
Art Deco, Figurine, Young Woman, Bronze & Ivory, Signed D.H.Chiparus	400.00
Art Deco, Lamp, French, Bronze, H.Molins, Kneeling Dancer, Black Marble Base	110.00
Art Deco, Lamp, Pewter, Nude Girl Reclining, Pressed Glass Shade, 1923	32.00
Art Deco, Rug, Hooked, Red & Blue, Geometrical, Joseph Schillinger, C.1935	125.00
Art Deco, Sugar & Creamer, Covered, Butterflies, Gold Trim, Hand-Painted	6.00
Art Deco, Torchere, Copper & Walnut, Round Base, C.1930, Pair	30.00
Art Deco, Vase, Silver Design, Black Glass, Mark Czechoslovakia, 10 1/2 In.	55.00
Art Deco, Vase, Sterling Silver, Tiffany & Co., Applied Birds In Copper	250.00

*Art Glass means any of the many forms of glassware made during the late
nineteenth century or early twentieth century.These wares were expensive and
made in limited production.Art Glass is not the typical commercial
glassware that was made in large quantities, and most of the Art Glass was
produced by hand methods.*

Art Glass, see also Schneider, Nash
Art Glass, see also separate headings such as Burmese, etc.

Art Glass, Basket, Peachblow Cased Glass, Stourbridge, Circa 1890	95.00
Art Glass, Basket, Pink Opalescent Stripes & Swirls, Applied Flowers	95.00
Art Glass, Bottle, Green-Blue, Pinched, Brass Trim, Long Neck, 10 In.High	35.00
Art Glass, Bowl, Fruit, Pointed Rim, 10 In.Diameter	29.50
Art Glass, Bowl, Signed Sinclair, Purple, Polished Pontil	25.00
Art Glass, Compote, Wrought Iron Base, Clear To Lavender Opalescent	65.00
Art Glass, Ewer, Fishscale, Pink, Wittman & Roth, Eng. *Illus*	350.00
Art Glass, Inkwell, Rainbow Iridescence, 4 In.Square, Brass Lid, Milk Glass	35.00
Art Glass, Sauce, Tiffany Type, Ruffled, Iridescent Green, 5 1/4 In.Diameter	25.00
Art Glass, Shade, Luster Art, Gold & Green, Signed	42.00
Art Glass, Shade, Tulip, Green Iridescent Feathers, Gold Outline	26.00
Art Glass, Syrup, Leaves, Green, White, Silver Plated Lid & Handle, 6 In.	165.00
Art Glass, Vase, Vase Basket Type, Iridescent Gold, Clear Handle, 15 1/2 In.	175.00

Art Deco, Clock, Silver, Cartier
See Page 6

Art Glass, Ewer, Fish Scale, Pink, Wittman & Roth, Eng.
See Page 6

Art Glass, Vase, Bud, Victorian, Flared, Silver Plate Holder, Green, Pair	120.00
Art Glass, Vase, Cased Yellow Glass, Hand-Painted Swallows, Sterling Rim	15.00
Art Glass, Vase, Gold Enamel, Amber Ovals, 6 In.Tall, Pair	50.00
Art Glass, Vase, Green Cased, White, Czechoslovakia	37.50
Art Glass, Vase, Steuben Style, 4 1/4 In.Tall	20.00
Art Glass, Vase, Swirled, Blue, Aqua, Violet, 5 1/2 In.Tall	100.00
Art Glass, Vase, Twisted Neck, Green, Gold, Iridescent	50.00
Art Nouveau, see also Glass, Furniture, etc.	
Art Nouveau, see also Royal Dux, Schneider, Faberge	
Art Nouveau, Bookend, Iron, Nudes, Pair	10.00
Art Nouveau, Bookmark, Female Form, Sterling, Unger Brothers, N.Y., C.1900	40.00
Art Nouveau, Bookshelf, Brass, Ladies & Flower Wreath	12.00
Art Nouveau, Bowl, Flower, Lalique Type, Birds, Deep	40.00
Art Nouveau, Bowl, Fruit, Lily Design, Fluted, By Mt.Vernon, 12 In.	95.00
Art Nouveau, Bowl, Iridescent Amber Interior, Opalescent White Exterior	40.00
Art Nouveau, Box, Jewelry, Sterling Silver, Footed, Oval, 7 In.	18.50
Art Nouveau, Box, Powder, Brass	5.00
Art Nouveau, Brooch, Female Profile, Gold Plate, William B.Kerr, N.J., C.1900	120.00
Art Nouveau, Buckle, Belt, Enameled, Gold, Marked Paris, France, C.1930	40.00
Art Nouveau, Buckle, Woman's Head, Sterling, William B.Kerr, N.J., C.1900	200.00
Art Nouveau, Bust Of Girl, Gilded Bronze, T.Causse, 9 In.High, Signed	130.00
Art Nouveau, Bust, Young Woman, Pottery, Military Dress, Green & Gilt	130.00
Art Nouveau, Buttonhook, Hallmarked, Woman's Head	12.50
Art Nouveau, Candelabra, Gilt Metal, Maiden, Torso Wrapped In Leafage	120.00
Art Nouveau, Case, Cigarette, Silver, Cushion Shape, Enamel, Birmingham, 1902	60.00
Art Nouveau, Chandelier, Opalescent Glass, Copper, Pair	175.00
Art Nouveau, Chandelier, Tiffany Type, Iridescent Brown Bowl, Copper, Pair	80.00
Art Nouveau, Chandelier, Tiffany Type, Pierced Dome, Lustres, Pair	350.00
Art Nouveau, Chandelier, Tiffany Type, White Opalescent Glass, Copper, Pair	175.00
Art Nouveau, Clock, Gilt Metal, Meyer & Levy, Paris, Round, Signed Fesyeur	110.00
Art Nouveau, Clock, Seminude Female, Compo & Brass, 21 In.High	130.00
Art Nouveau, Coffret, Brass & Wood, Quadrilateral Form, Brass Roses	80.00
Art Nouveau, Desk Pad, Silver & Leather, Russian, Rectangular, 6 In.	15.00
Art Nouveau, Dresser, Lady's, Mirror & Brush, Mark G	28.00
Art Nouveau, Dressing Table Set, Silver, Repousse, Maiden, Floral, 9 Piece	200.00
Art Nouveau, Figurine, Basalt, Jackdaw, C.1910	395.00
Art Nouveau, Figurine, Girl, Ivory & Gilt Bronze, Striding, Signed Bofil	180.00
Art Nouveau, Figurine, Nude Female, Dresden Porcelain, Crossed Swords Mark	110.00
Art Nouveau, Figurine, Nude Nymph, Gilded Bronze, Raoul Larche, Signed	110.00

Art Nouveau, Figurine, Nymph, Standing, Nude, Signed Ricelle, 12 1/2 In.High 180.00
Art Nouveau, Figurine, Woman, Flowing Robes, White Metal, 8 In.High 5.00
Art Nouveau, Humidor, Clear Paneled Glass Base, Silver Plate Lid, Floral 22.00
Art Nouveau, Inkstand, Gilded Bronze, Pen Tray, Cover, Curschner-Signed 250.00
Art Nouveau, Inkwell, Bronze, Young Woman, Signed Ch.Korschann, Glass Liner 294.00
Art Nouveau, Inkwell, Cast Iron, Figure Of Dante, Flowing Robe 12.50
Art Nouveau, Lamp Shade, Tiffany Type, Iridescent Purple & Blue, Swags 1000.00
Art Nouveau, Lamp, Amber Iridescent Bell Shape Shade, Spherical Base 160.00
Art Nouveau, Lamp, Bronze, Glass, 24 In.High .... *Illus* 1400.00
Art Nouveau, Lamp, Stained Glass & Bronze, Duffner & Kimberley Type, 26 In. 1500.00
Art Nouveau, Locket, Figural, Female Profile, Gold, Marked F.& E. 170.00
Art Nouveau, Medallion, Pendant, Glass, Round, G.Argy-Rousseau, France, C.1930 ...... 70.00
Art Nouveau, Mirror, Hand, Sterling Silver 15.00
Art Nouveau, Nude, Bisque, Reclining, Light Brown Hair, 4 3/4 In.Long 17.00
Art Nouveau, Paperweight, Bronze, Bust Of Young Girl, Reverie & Extase, Pair 80.00
Art Nouveau, Pin, Bat, Tiffany Type, Iridescent Glass, 9k Gold, Marked 225.00
Art Nouveau, Pin, Female Head, Turquoise, Enamel, Gilded Silver, Rene Lalique 1400.00
Art Nouveau, Pin, Figural, Female Head, Enameled, Silver, Marked 80.00
Art Nouveau, Pin, Figural, Female Profile, 15k Gold, C.1900 .... 140.00
Art Nouveau, Pitcher-Vase, Green, Gold, Amphora, Seminude Forms 40.00
Art Nouveau, Pitcher, Silver, Footed, Rockford Silver Co., 3 3/4 In.High 22.00
Art Nouveau, Plaque, Oval, Young Girl Profile, Enamel On Gilt Metal, M.Carus 225.00
Art Nouveau, Print, Ballets Leonidoff, Color 100.00
Art Nouveau, Print, Boutin D'or, Nouveau Theatre, L.Lopes Silva, 1893 .... 70.00
Art Nouveau, Print, Folies-Bergere, Maurice Baisis 70.00
Art Nouveau, Print, Loie Fuller, Folies-Bergere, Jules Cheret, 1897 .... 150.00
Art Nouveau, Print, Mistinguett Succes, Gesmar, 1928 .... 225.00
Art Nouveau, Print, The Ault & Wiborg Company, Printing Inks, Will Bradley 40.00
Art Nouveau, Print, Victor Bicycles, Will Bradley, Framed 200.00
Art Nouveau, Purse, Change, Tooled Leather, Enamel Plaque, C.1900 .... 50.00
Art Nouveau, Purse, Change, Tooled Leather, Metal Female Form, C.1900 .... 80.00
Art Nouveau, Purse, Lady's Face, High Relief, Silver 12.50
Art Nouveau, Purse, Leather & Silver, Flying Fish & Lilies Of The Valley 40.00
Art Nouveau, Ring, Scarab, Tiffany Type, Iridescent Glass, 14k Gold 120.00
Art Nouveau, Sconce, Tiffany Type, Favrile Glass, Metal, Lustres, Pair 150.00
Art Nouveau, Seal, Silver, Orchid Design, France, 3 1/2 In. 22.00
Art Nouveau, Stein, Embossed Actress Head, Floral, Porcelain, Pewter Top 95.00
Art Nouveau, Syrup, Pewter Top .... *Illus* 36.00
Art Nouveau, Tazza, Bronze, Nude Nymph Holding Bowl, Signed 400.00
Art Nouveau, Tazza, Tiffany Type, Iridescent Amber Bowl, White Stem, 5 .... 300.00
Art Nouveau, Tongs, Sugar, Hallmarked 12.00
Art Nouveau, Tray, Brass, Open Border 10.00
Art Nouveau, Tray, Pewter, Round, Repousse, Laiden, Applied Iris & Leaves 160.00
Art Nouveau, Tray, Pin, Cherub, Flowers, Embossed 15.00
Art Nouveau, Tray, Pin, Heart Shape, Woman In Center, Fluted Rim 20.00
Art Nouveau, Tray, Pin, Petal Shape, Nude Woman, Dragonfly In Relief 25.00
Art Nouveau, Vase, Bisque, Painted, Nymph, Baluster Shape 80.00
Art Nouveau, Vase, Cantaloupe Color, White Lining, Overlay, Silver Deposit 30.00
Art Nouveau, Vase, Gilt Metal, Handle Is Flowing Seminude Girl 35.00
Art Nouveau, Vase, Glass, Flowers, Leaves, Sterling, 10 In.Tall 20.00
Art Nouveau, Vase, Green Iridescent, Cobalt Lining, Purple Top & Base 65.00
Art Nouveau, Vase, Iridescent Pottery, Three Handles, Signed Heliosin 33.00
Art Nouveau, Vase, Massier, Pottery, Peacock, Feathers, Green, Blue, & Lavender 260.00
Art Nouveau, Vase, Nash Type, Vertical Stripes, Swags, Iridescent Amber 50.00
Art Nouveau, Vase, Pewter, Open Ended, Baluster, Repousse Lily Of The Valley 30.00
Art Nouveau, Vase, Pottery, French, Bulbous, Floral, Green To Brown, Silver 60.00
Art Nouveau, Vase, Ruby Red Glass, Floral In Silver Overlay, Milk Lining 37.50
Art Nouveau, Vase, Sterling, Water Nymph & Applied Poppies Over Ceramic 400.00
Art Nouveau, Vase, Tiffany Type, Baluster Shape, Iridescent Amber, Bronze 160.00
Art Nouveau, Vase, Tiffany Type, Sapphire Blue, Leaf Striations, Ocher, Green 350.00

Aurene Glass was made by Frederick Carder of New York about 1904.
It is an iridescent gold glass, usually marked Aurene or Steuben.
Aurene, see also Steuben
Aurene, Atomizer, Gold Iridescence, Carder 85.00
Aurene, Atomizer, Perfume 22.50

Art Nouveau, Lamp, Bronze, Glass, 24 In.High
See Page 8

Art Nouveau, Syrup, Pewter Top
See Page 8

Aurene, Basket, Blue, On Calcite, Steuben, Carder 750.00
Aurene, Bowl, Centerpiece, Calcite, Footed, 7 In.Diameter, 2 3/4 In.Tall 95.00
Aurene, Bowl, Flower, Iridescent, Amber, Inscribed Aurene, 2851 .... 50.00
Aurene, Bowl, Fluted, Bulbous, Blue, Signed, Numbered, 3 1/2 In.Tall 125.00
Aurene, Bowl, Gold Iridescent, Red, Green, & Blue Tints, Ruffled Top, Signed 225.00
Aurene, Bowl, Gold, Signed, Numbered 2687 .... 155.00
Aurene, Bowl, With Calcite, Gold, No Mark, 10 In.Diameter, 2 1/4 In.High 90.00
Aurene, Candlestick, Gold With Amethyst Iridescent, Signed, 9 1/2 In., Pair 300.00
Aurene, Candlestick, Gold, On Calcite, Steuben, Carder, Pair 300.00
Aurene, Candlestick, Iridescent, Urn Shape Socket, Green-Amber, Signed, Pair 175.00
Aurene, Candlestick, Signed, 8 1/4 In.Tall 125.00
Aurene, Champagne, Silvery Iridescent Amber, Bell Shape Bowl, Spiral Stem, 5 .... 280.00
Aurene, Compote, Calcite, Gold, 9 3/4 In.Diameter 185.00
Aurene, Cordial, Gold, Signed, Set Of Six 395.00
Aurene, Darner, Sock, Blue 95.00
Aurene, Perfume, Gold Iridescent, Gold Washed Bronze Cap, 6 In. 110.00
Aurene, Shot Glass, Blue, Signed 140.00
Aurene, Vase, Blue, Iridescent, Signed Steuben, 6 1/2 In.Tall 350.00
Aurene, Vase, Blue, Mirrored Inside, Flared Top, Signed, 5 1/2 In.Tall 300.00
Aurene, Vase, Blue, Purple, Red & Green Highlights, Footed, Steuben, 6 3/4 In. 145.00
Aurene, Vase, Blue, Signed Steuben, 5 In.High 225.00
Aurene, Vase, Blue, Stretched Ruffled Rim, Signed, 5 In. 285.00
Aurene, Vase, Blue, 6 In.High, Steuben 200.00
Aurene, Vase, Cabinet, No.2640, Fluted Rim, Blue, 2 1/2 In.High 195.00
Aurene, Vase, Fan, Gold, Green, Vine, Leaves, Signed, 8 1/2 In.High 400.00
Aurene, Vase, Fan, Signed, Bluish Metallic Base, Green Vines & Leaves 400.00
Aurene, Vase, Gold, Red, Paper Label, Signed, 8 1/2 In.Tall 275.00
Aurene, Vase, Signed, Gold Iridescent, Footed, 6 In.Tall 135.00
Aurene, Vase, Stick, Blue, Signed, 7 In.Tall 155.00
    Austria, see Royal Dux, Kauffmann, Porcelain

Auto Parts and Accessories are collectors' items today.
Auto, Carrier, Luggage, Accordion Type, For Running Board 5.75
Auto, Cover, Battery, Edison 3.00
Auto, Emblem, Buick, Blue Cloisonne 10.00
Auto, Handle, Door, Kaiser-Frazer, Crest, Pair 9.00
Auto, Horn, Bulb Type, Brass, Curved, 17 In.Long 25.00

Auto, Horn, Brass, Bulb Type, 18 In.	37.50
Auto, Horn, Bugle Type, Marked Condor, Brass, 10 In.Long	20.00
Auto, Horn, Klaxon & Sparton, A-Ogg-Ah	7.50
Auto, Hub Cap, Model T	4.00
Auto, Hub Cap, Model T Ford, Nickel Plated, Pair	2.50
Auto, Key, Ignition, Model T	2.50
Auto, Key, Model T Ford	2.00
Auto, Kitchenette, To Fit On Running Board, Metal	15.00
Auto, Lamp, Eureka Mfg., Pat.1908 & 1910	15.00
Auto, Lamp, Side, Model T Ford, Pair	29.50
Auto, Lap Robe, Plaid, Fringed Ends, Chase & Co.Label	23.00
Auto, License Plate, Alaska, 1968, The Great Land Motto, Set	2.50
Auto, License Plate, Alaska, 1969, The Great Land Motto, Set	2.50
Auto, License Plate, California, Says World's Fair, 1939, Pair	15.00
Auto, License Plate, Connecticut, 1914, Porcelain	7.50
Auto, License Plate, Massachusetts, 1915	8.00
Auto, License Plate, Michigan, 1932, Pair	6.00
Auto, License Plate, Michigan, 1933, Commercial, Pair	6.00
Auto, License Plate, Michigan, 1933, Pair	6.00
Auto, License Plate, Michigan, 1933, Trailer	3.50
Auto, License Plate, We Demand Repeal, 1932	8.00
Auto, Light, Kerosene, Warsaw, N.Y., Duplex	16.00
Auto, Luggage Rack, Running Board	12.00
Auto, Ornament, Hood, Flags, 5 Fringed American Flags, Shield, Boxed, 1927	12.00
Auto, Ornament, Hood, Ram	9.50
Auto, Plate, 1911, Massachusetts, Porcelain	7.50
Auto, Plate, 1924, New Hampshire, Porcelain	5.00
Auto, Pump, Ford, Brass, Tire, Ford In Script	12.50
Auto, Rack, Luggage, Accordion	12.50
Auto, Radiator Cap, Goose In Flight, For 1928 Ford	25.00
Auto, Radiator Cap, Model T	4.00
Auto, Radiator Cap, Ornament, Eagle, Bronze, Marked	10.00
Auto, Radiator Ornament, Woman's Head, Glass, Frosted	25.00
Auto, Radiator, Model T, Honeycomb Style, 1916	25.00
Auto, Spark Plug Wrench, Model T	4.00
Auto, Vase, Cut Glass, Lily Shape, Turning Purple, Pair	5.00
Auto, Vase, Flower, Pressed Glass, 1916, 7 In.Long	4.50
Auto, Vase, Flower, Ribbed, Pink Glass, Pair	25.00
Auto, Vase, Limousine, Tiffany Type, Mauve, Striated Leaf, 2	80.00
Aventurine, Vase, Oval, Green Applied Handles, Teardrops, 9 In.High	100.00
Avon, see Bottle, Avon	
Babe Ruth, Watch, Memorial	75.00
Baby Carriage, Wicker	65.00

Baccarat Glass was made in France by La Compagnie Des
Cristalleries De Baccarat, located about 150 miles from Paris. The
factory was started in 1765. The firm went bankrupt and began operating about
1822. Famous Cane and Millefiori paperweights were made there during the
1860-1880 period. The firm is still working near Paris making paperweights
and glasswares.

Baccarat, Atomizer, Signed, Green, Gold	39.00
Baccarat, Bottle, Cologne, Swirled, Ruby To Clear, 7 In.Tall	25.00
Baccarat, Bowl, Finger, Amberina Swirl, 4 3/4 In.Diameter	27.00
Baccarat, Bowl, Wash, Pitcher, Swirls, Amberina, Signed	150.00
Baccarat, Box, Dresser, Signed, Silver Lid, Diagonal Amber & Diamond Point	25.00
Baccarat, Buddha	35.00
Baccarat, Candlestick, Swirled Glass, Pedestal Base, 7 In.Tall	19.50
Baccarat, Compote, Candy, Pedestal, Blue, Swirl Pattern	10.00
Baccarat, Compote, Diagonal Block, Amber, Clear, Signed, 8 In.Tall	150.00
Baccarat, Compote, Ribbon Pattern, 9 1/2 In.Diameter, 7 In.High	75.00
Baccarat, Compote, Scalloped, Clear With Raised Amber Diamonds	115.00
Baccarat, Compote, Swirl, Green, 4 In.	20.00
Baccarat, Decanter, Swirled Rubena, Swirled Stopper, 8 1/2 In.Tall	65.00
Baccarat, Dish, Celery, France	25.00
Baccarat, Dish, Relish, Rubena, Swirl, Diamond Points, 9 1/2 In.	37.50
Baccarat, Paperweight, Adlai E.Stevenson	60.00 To 75.00

Baccarat, Paperweight, Anemone, 6 Petaled White Flower, Red, Green, Faceted 885.00
Baccarat, Paperweight, Canes, Intertwined 185.00
Baccarat, Paperweight, Church With Zodiac, Millefiori 110.00
Baccarat, Paperweight, Clematis & Garland, Red, Green, Canes, Faceted 745.00
Baccarat, Paperweight, Concentric Circles Of Canes 35.00
Baccarat, Paperweight, Double Concentric Rows Of Canes 125.00
Baccarat, Paperweight, Dwight D.Eisenhower, 1952 .... 300.00
Baccarat, Paperweight, Eleanor Roosevelt 78.00
Baccarat, Paperweight, Faceted Millefiori, 2 Rows Of Windows, Canes 130.00
Baccarat, Paperweight, Herbert Hoover ....:........................... 50.00 To 78.00
Baccarat, Paperweight, Herbert Hoover, Sulfide, Blue Ground, Faceted 500.00
Baccarat, Paperweight, James Monroe .... 60.00 To 95.00
Baccarat, Paperweight, John F. Kennedy, Blue Ground, White Overlay, Sulfide 650.00
Baccarat, Paperweight, John F.Kennedy, Overlay, Cameo, Sulfide, Blue, Ruby 600.00
Baccarat, Paperweight, Millefiori, Zodiac Symbols, Canes, Signed 200.00
Baccarat, Paperweight, Miniature, Concentric, Stardust Canes, Florette 60.00
Baccarat, Paperweight, Mushroom, Millefiori Tuft, Blue Spiral, Star Cut 500.00
Baccarat, Paperweight, Pansy, 2 Mauve & 3 Yellow Petals, Green, Bud 375.00
Baccarat, Paperweight, Pansy, 2 Mauve & 3 Yellow Petals, Star Cut Base 350.00
Baccarat, Paperweight, Patterned Circles, Blue & White 325.00
Baccarat, Paperweight, Pompon, Star Cut Base 750.00
Baccarat, Paperweight, Pope John XXIII 95.00
Baccarat, Paperweight, Rings Of Canes, Miniature, 1 1/2 In.Diameter 175.00
Baccarat, Paperweight, Rock, Beige Sand, Green Glass 60.00
Baccarat, Paperweight, Scattered Magnum, Canes, Lacy Ground, Dated B1847 .... 850.00
Baccarat, Paperweight, Theodore Roosevelt 105.00
Baccarat, Paperweight, Zodiac Series, Leo 35.00
Baccarat, Perfume, Rubena Swirl, Bulbous, 5 In.High 25.00
Baccarat, Ring Tree, Swirls, Amberina, Signed 27.50
Baccarat, Sherry, Etched & Gold Leaf, Faceted Stem, 12 .... 120.00
Baccarat, Toilet Set, Depose, Amberina, Pinwheel, 7 Piece, C.1914, Signed 200.00
Baccarat, Tumbler, Clear To Cranberry, Signed, 5 In.Tall 40.00
Baccarat, Tumbler, Rubena Swirl, Signed 18.00
Baccarat, Vase, Bud, Blue, Enamel, Signed, 6 In.High 50.00
Baccarat, Vase, Cameo Glass, Strawberries & Vines, Pink & Gold, Signed, 1915 .... 160.00
Baccarat, Vase, Cameo, Blue Frosted, Leaves, Purple Carvings, 9 3/4 In. 135.00
Baccarat, Vase, Cameo, Frosted, Pink, Leaves, Berries, Enamel, Gold, Signed 225.00
Baccarat, Wine, Nancy 6.00
 Bag, Beaded, see Beaded Bag
Bank, Apollo, U.S.A., Cast Iron, Painted Gold, Black Letters, 4 1/2 In.Tall 4.00
Bank, Arabian Safe, Scenes In Panels, Still, 4 1/2 In.High 25.00
Bank, Bank Building, Cast Iron, 3 X 3 X 4 In. 18.00
Bank, Bank Building, Cast Iron, 6 X 5 1/2 X 4 1/2 In. 30.00
Bank, Bank Building, Grill Work On Doors & Windows, Cupola, Iron 30.00
Bank, Bank Building, Iron, Still, 2 1/2 In. 15.00
Bank, Bank Building, Iron, Still, 3 1/2 In.Tall 20.00
Bank, Bank Building, Iron, Still, 4 In.Tall 25.00
Bank, Bank Building, Iron, 2 X 3 In. 12.00
Bank, Bank Building, Whiting No.421, Cast Iron 7.00
Bank, Barrel, Chein, Tin, Happy Days, 2 Square & 1 Round Trap .... 5.00 To 10.00
Bank, Barrel, Dated 1923 .... 8.00
Bank, Bear, Sitting, Iron, Black, 6 1/2 In.Tall .... 20.00 To 29.50
Bank, Bear, Standing, Iron, 5 1/2 In.High 26.50
Bank, Bears At Beehive, Whiting No.168, Cast Iron 35.00
Bank, Beer Barrel, China 10.00
Bank, Bison, Cast Iron 40.00
Bank, Bisque, 2 Girls .... Illus   15.00
Bank, Black Beauty, Cast Iron 20.00
Bank, Book, Tin, Lithographed 5.00
Bank, Bosco, Tin, Children At Play 9.00
Bank, Bottle, Figural, Clown, 7 1/4 In.Tall 2.95
Bank, Bottle, Figural, Elephant, 7 1/4 In.Tall 2.95
Bank, Bottle, Lincoln .... 2.00 To 4.00
Bank, Boy Scout, Cast Iron, No.14 .... 30.00
Bank, Bronze Metal, Lincoln Head, Gary, Indiana 5.00
Bank, Buffalo, Iron 22.50

Bank, Buick Fireball Eight, Red, Tin	27.00
Bank, Building, A Century Of Progress, 1933, Metal, Paint	16.50
Bank, Building, Brass, Silver Dollar In Steeple	75.00
Bank, Building, Cast Iron, Whiting No.413	12.00
Bank, Building, Red & White, 3 1/4 X 3 5/8 In.	3.95
Bank, Building, Six Towers	18.50
Bank, Building, Two Chimneys, Iron, 3 1/4 In.Tall	16.00
Bank, Building, 6-Cornered, Birds, Cast Iron	25.00
Bank, Bull, Standing, Brass, Still	30.00
Bank, Bulldog & Cat, Sitting, Cast Iron	18.00
Bank, Buster & Tige, Iron, Still	40.00 To 75.00
Bank, Cab, Yellow, Cast Iron	150.00
Bank, Campbell Kids, Cast Iron	75.00
Bank, Canister, Register, Blue, Sun, Children, 3 1/2 In.	10.00
Bank, Cape Cod House, Dormer, Shrubs, Marked American Art Works, Key	15.00
Bank, Carnival Glass, Marigold, Eagle In Relief	9.50
Bank, Cash Register, Chein	5.00 To 6.00
Bank, Cash Register, Tin, Security, 7 In.Tall	28.00
Bank, Cat Playing With Ball, Black Paint, Iron	32.00
Bank, Cat, Grapette	3.00
Bank, Charlie McCarthy, Metal, Charlie With Suitcase, 8 In.	35.00
Bank, Chest Of Drawers, Pottery, Swirl, Bennington Type, 7 In.High	20.00
Bank, Church, Tin, Chein	*Illus* 9.50
Bank, Clock, Cast Iron, Says Save It	28.00
Bank, Clown, Cast Iron, No.29	28.00
Bank, Clown, Chein, Painted	4.00 To 12.00

Bank, Bisque, 2 Girls
See Page 11

Bank, Church, Tin, Chein

Bank, Clown, Glass, 7 In.Tall	2.95
Bank, Clown, Grapette	1.50
Bank, Collier Encyclopedia, Registering, Calendar, Bakelite & Tin	7.00
Bank, Combination, Marked Star Safe, Embossed Flowers In Pots, Iron	20.00
Bank, Coronation Crown, 1953, Cast Iron	25.00
Bank, Cow, Dairy	40.00
Bank, Deer With Antlers, Cast Iron, 6 In.Tall	20.00 To 25.00
Bank, Dog Head, Finial, Cast Iron	28.00
Bank, Dog With Collar, Fido On Collar	15.00 To 35.00
Bank, Dog With Pack	45.00
Bank, Dog, Newfoundland, Iron, 4 In.Tall	18.00
Bank, Dog, Pottery, Pennsylvania, Green, Yellow & Brown Glaze, 6 1/4 In.High	125.00
Bank, Dog, With Pack, Cast Iron, No.106	15.00
Bank, Donald Duck, Nabisco, 10 In.	5.50
Bank, Door Marked Safe Deposit, Key, Iron, 2 3/4 X 2 1/2 X 3 5/8 In.Tall	15.00

Bank, Door Marked Safe, Dated June 2, 1896, Iron, 2 1/2 X 3 1/4 In.High 20.00
Bank, Drum, Chein, Tin, Round Trap 10.00
Bank, Duck, Soft Paste, Cream Ground 25.00
Bank, Eagle On Front, Glass 3.00
Bank, Ear Of Corn, Pottery 13.00
Bank, Eisenhower Bust 16.00
Bank, Elephant On Tub, Circus, Painted 28.00
Bank, Elephant On Tub, Whiting No.60, Cast Iron 24.00
Bank, Elephant With Howdah, Cast Iron 12.00
Bank, Elephant, Glass, 7 In. 2.95
Bank, Elephant, Grapette 1.50
Bank, Elephant, Standing 20.00
Bank, Elephant, Whiting No.67, Gold Paint 15.00
Bank, Elephant, Whiting No.68, Iron 12.00
Bank, English Crown, Coronation 1953, Cast Iron 28.00
Bank, Excelsior, Hall's 55.00
Bank, Farmhouse, Hand-Carved Wood, Rustic, Still, 4 3/4 X 5 3/4 In.Wide 4.00
Bank, Foxy Grandpa 12.50
Bank, Garbage Can, Metal 4.00
Bank, General Pershing, Cast Iron 45.00
Bank, George Washington, Iron 13.00
Bank, Globe In Arc, Moving, Iron, Penny, Painted 55.00
Bank, Globe Of The World, Glass 9.50
Bank, Globe On Claw Feet 60.00
Bank, Globe, Chein, Tin, Colored .... 3.50 To 10.00
Bank, Globe, World, Embossed Clear Glass, 4 In.High 9.00
Bank, Greyhound, Head Nods When Coin Is Inserted 2.50
Bank, Home, Red & Black Lithograph, Chein, Tin 8.00
Bank, Horse, Beauty, Cast Iron 20.00
Bank, Horse, Prancing, Cast Iron .... 9.50 To 12.00
Bank, Horse, Prancing, Rectangular Base, Cast Iron 22.00
Bank, Horse, Prancing, Whiting No.77, Cast Iron 23.00
Bank, Hot Water Heater, Tin, Rex 23.50
Bank, House, Advertising Pittsburgh Paints, Glass 9.50
Bank, House, Cast Iron 30.00
Bank, House, Wooden 8.00
Bank, Ice Cream Freezer, Whiting No.156, Cast Iron 55.00
Bank, Ice Wagon, Iron, One Horse, Painted 49.50
Bank, Independence Hall, Cast Iron, American, C.1876 .... *Illus* 90.00
Bank, Indian Chief, White Metal, 4 In.High 12.50
Bank, Indian Head, Iron 6.00
Bank, Indian Tepee, Embossed Indian Signs, Copper Sheeting Over Pot Metal 28.00
Bank, Indian With Tomahawk, Cast Iron 35.00
Bank, Irish Cop 35.00
Bank, Iron Box With Handle, W.F.Burns Co., Dated Jan.1, 1901 .... 15.00
Bank, Joe & Dinah, Mechanical, Pair 120.00
Bank, Jolly Nigger, Cast Iron, Shepard Hardware Co. 75.00
Bank, Liberty Bell '1776' & Washington Bust In Relief, Cast Iron 16.00
Bank, Liberty Bell Centennial, Cast Iron, 1776-1876, 4 1/2 In.High 50.00
Bank, Liberty Bell, Bronze, C.1920 .... 8.00
Bank, Liberty Bell, Glass 4.00
Bank, Liberty Bell, Glass, Nash's Mustard 6.50
Bank, Liberty Bell, Marked Patented September 27, 1885, Milk Glass 30.00
Bank, Liberty Bell, Metal, C.1919 .... 5.50
Bank, Liberty Bell, Patent Feb.18, 1919, Still 15.00
Bank, Liberty Bell, Sebewaing, Mich., Patent 1919, Metal 12.00
Bank, Lion, Cast Iron, No.90 .... 14.00
Bank, Lion, Cast Iron, 5 In.Long, 3 In.Tall 15.00
Bank, Lion, Standing, Iron, Still, 6 In.Long X 4 1/2 In.Tall 50.00
Bank, Lion, Standing, 6 1/2 In. 20.00
Bank, Log Cabin, Hand-Carved Wood, Hand-Painted, Still, 9 X 6 1/4 In.High 8.00
Bank, Mailbox, Hanging, Cast Iron, Whiting No.13 .... 22.00
Bank, Mailbox, Novelty Padlock, 1899 .... 8.00
Bank, Mailbox, Wall Type 15.00
Bank, Mailbox, Whiting No.122, Red Paint 15.00
Bank, Mammy With Spoon, Cast Iron 40.00

Bank, Independence Hall, Cast Iron,
American, C.1876
See Page 13

Bank, Mechanical, Punch & Judy

Bank, Mammy With Spoon, Whiting No.17, Cast Iron 20.00

> *Mechanical Banks were first made about 1870. Any bank with moving parts is considered mechanical, although those most collected are the metal banks made before World War I. Reproductions are being made.*

Bank, Mechanical, Always Did Spise A Mule	75.00
Bank, Mechanical, Cabin, Dated 1885	110.00
Bank, Mechanical, Cabin, Painted, Cast Iron	85.00
Bank, Mechanical, Clown Head, Chein, Tin	15.00
Bank, Mechanical, Creedmore, Painted, Cast Iron	100.00
Bank, Mechanical, Eagle & Eaglets, Painted	95.00
Bank, Mechanical, Elephant, Marked Gar-Ru, Metal, Trunk Deposits Coin	17.00
Bank, Mechanical, Hall's Excelsior, Cast Iron	50.00
Bank, Mechanical, Jolly Nigger	40.00 To 75.00
Bank, Mechanical, Jolly Nigger, By Stevens	75.00
Bank, Mechanical, Little Joe, Wiggles His Ears	50.00
Bank, Mechanical, Log Cabin, Hamm's	35.00
Bank, Mechanical, Log Cabin, Negroes Play Banjo, Dance, Chein, Tin	15.00
Bank, Mechanical, Mickey Mouse	100.00
Bank, Mechanical, Monkey On Tree Throwing Coconut At Lion	150.00
Bank, Mechanical, Monkey Tips Hat, Tin, Chein	10.00 To 15.00
Bank, Mechanical, Owl, Turns Head	65.00 To 67.50
Bank, Mechanical, Punch & Judy	*Illus* 235.00
Bank, Mechanical, Reno Slot Machine	6.95
Bank, Mechanical, Rocket Ship, Fires Coin Into Moon	8.00
Bank, Mechanical, Soldier, Confederate, Southern Comfort Whiskey	22.00
Bank, Mechanical, Stump Speaker, Painted	312.00
Bank, Mechanical, Tammany, Politician, Nods Head	55.00 To 120.00
Bank, Mechanical, Trick Dog	45.00 To 150.00
Bank, Mechanical, Trick Pony	145.00
Bank, Mechanical, Two Frogs	40.00
Bank, Mechanical, William Tell, Cast Iron, Paint	125.00 To 145.00
Bank, Mechanical, World's Fair, Cast Iron	50.00
Bank, Miami Beach Federal Savings Bldg., White Metal	15.00
Bank, Mother's Oats	2.50
Bank, Monkey, Chein, Tips Hat	6.50

Bank, **Owl**, Glass, 'be Wise, 'marigold 20.00
Bank, **Owl**, On Log, 'be Wise & Save' 22.50
Bank, **Owl**, Staffordshire, 5 In.Tall, Pair 50.00
Bank, **Pail**, Prosperity, Pink, Chein, Tin 6.00
Bank, **Pig**, Carnival .... 1.50 To 4.75
Bank, **Pig**, Chalk 15.00
Bank, **Pig**, Sitting Position, Iron .... 9.00 To 25.00
Bank, **Pig**, Standing 45.00
Bank, **Pig**, 3 1/4 In.High, 7 In.Wide 35.00
Bank, **Poodle**, Head, Black, Staffordshire 35.00
Bank, **Poor Pitiful Pearl**, 18 In. 12.00
Bank, **Popeye**, Dime Registering, Copyright, 1929 .... 20.00
Bank, **Post Office**, Painted 15.00
Bank, **Pressed Glass**, Blue, Flint, Barn, 1888 .... 21.00
Bank, **Rabbit**, Cast Iron, No.98 .... 15.00
Bank, **Radio**, Glass 6.50
Bank, **Radio**, Kenton, Floor Model, Cast Iron 12.00
Bank, **Red Circle Coffee**, Yellow 2.50
Bank, **Refrigerator**, Servel 10.00
Bank, **Rival**, Tin .... 5.00 To 11.00
Bank, **Rudolph The Red Nosed Reindeer** 25.00
Bank, **Safe**, Arabian, Cast Iron, 4 1/2 In.High, Scenes In Panels 25.00
Bank, **Safe**, Arabian, Scenes In Panels, Iron, Still, 4 1/2 In.High 25.00
Bank, **Safe**, Combination, Marked Aug.24, 1897, Iron 20.00
Bank, **Safe**, Home, Double Combination, Cast Iron 17.00
Bank, **Safe**, Iron .... 8.50 To 15.00
Bank, **Safe**, Ixl, Patent 1881, Cast Iron 30.00
Bank, **Safe**, Patent 1898, Replacement Key, Cast Iron 20.00
Bank, **Semimechanical**, Merry-Go-Round, Cast Iron 55.00
Bank, **Sheep**, Iron 16.75
Bank, **Skeleton**, Cast Iron 16.00
Bank, **Slot In Side**, Savings, 1878 .... 10.00
Bank, **Snow White**, Dime Register, 1938 .... 9.50
Bank, **Sport**, Cast Iron, Pat.1882, 3 In.High 30.00
Bank, **St.Bernard With Pack**, Metal, Still, 8 X 5 1/2 In. .... 14.50 To 25.00
Bank, **Statue Of Liberty**, Iron .... 20.00 To 22.00
Bank, **Steer**, Iron, Horned, Painted 37.50
Bank, **Stove**, Cast Iron, Black, 3 1/2 X 4 1/4 In. 2.95
Bank, **Tank**, World War I 32.50
Bank, **Tank**, 1918, Cast Iron, No.162 .... 29.00
Bank, **Taxi**, Pristine, Arcade Green 95.00
Bank, **Teddy Roosevelt**, Cast Iron 30.00
Bank, **The Sport**, Iron, Still 40.00
Bank, **Three Little Pigs**, J.Chein & Co., Tin 55.00
Bank, **Time Lock Safe**, Tin 9.00
Bank, **Tin**, 8 O'clock Coffee 4.00
Bank, **Tower Of Independence Hall**, Cast Iron, Painted, Centennial Bank, 1876 .... 90.00
Bank, **Treasure Chest**, Embossed Pirates, Skull, Bones, Place For Padlock 15.00
Bank, **Two-Faced Woman**, Painted 45.00
Bank, **U.S.Government Building**, Columbian Exposition, Chicago, 1892 .... 37.50
Bank, **U.S.Mailbox**, Cast Iron, Green, 3 1/2 In.High 20.00
Bank, **U.S.Mailbox**, Iron, Still, 3 1/2 In.Tall 20.00
Bank, **Woman**, 2-Faced, Cast Iron, Gold, 3 In.High 30.00
Bank, **Woolworth Building**, Cast Iron 25.00
Bank, **World**, Tin, Made By Ohio Art Co. 10.00
Barometer, **Banjo**, George Ii, Mahogany, 18th Century 150.00
Barometer, **Banjo**, Inlaid Mahogany, Floral Inlay 100.00
Barometer, **Banjo**, Mahogany, B.Rines, Gloucester, Shell & Wheel Inlay Case 250.00
Barometer, **Dorrer & Co.**, Croydon, Pa., 18th Century, Mahogany Case 300.00
Barometer, **Stick**, Rosewood, Signed Dublin, Ireland 45.00
Barometer, **Victorian**, German, Walnut Frame, Banjo Type, 18 In.Long 30.00
    Barr, see Worcester
    Barsottini, see Bottle, Barsottini

*Basalt is a black stoneware made by mixing iron and oxides into a basic
clay. It is very hard and can be finished on a lathe. Wedgwood developed*

his famous black basalt in 1769, which was an improvement on a similar ware made in Staffordshire, England, as early as 1740. Basalt is still being made in England and on the continent.

Basalt, Urn, Ovoid, Classical Frieze, Female Mask Handle, Adams & T.C., Pair	225.00
Basket, Made From Strung Beads, Hanging, Green, Clear & White	50.00
Batman, Comic, No.43	3.50
Batman, Mug	3.00

Battersea Enamels are enamels painted on copper and made in the Battersea District of London from about 1750 to 1756. Many similar enamels are mistakenly called Battersea.

Battersea, Box, A Trifle From Buxton, Lover's Leap	200.00
Battersea, Box, Couple In Field With 3 Cows, Maid Milking	300.00
Battersea, Box, Heart Shape, Enamel, The Tighter The Knot, The Farther Apart	160.00
Battersea, Box, Oval, Lafayette In Blue Uniform On Cover, Blue Enamel Base	275.00
Battersea, Box, Pretty Dick	200.00
Battersea, Box, Snuff, Mauve Enamel, Black Sailing Ship, Oval	140.00
Battersea, Plaque, Scene After Boucher, Enamel, 18th Century, 4 1/2 In.	195.00

Bavaria was a district where many types of pottery and porcelain were made for centuries. The word Bavaria appears on many pieces of nineteenth century china. The words Bavaria, Germany, appeared after 1871.

Bavarian, see also Rosenthal

Bavarian, Bowl & Leaf Shape Dish, Signed F.Brown, Footed, Scalloped	35.00
Bavarian, Bowl, Beet Design, Hand-Painted, Green Band, 6 1/2 In.Diameter	8.00
Bavarian, Bowl, Berry, Pink Blossoms, Gilt Trim, Hand-Painted, Set Of 5	10.00
Bavarian, Candlestick, Double, White, Gold Trim, 5 In.High, 6 1/2 In.Wide	18.00
Bavarian, Celery, Green Mark, Crown, Wreath, Rm Bavaria, White, Orange Poppies	11.00
Bavarian, Chocolate Pot, Plum To Brown, Angel, Warrior, Nude Man & Woman	55.00
Bavarian, Chocolate Pot, Rose Design, Pink, Mignon	15.00
Bavarian, Chocolate Pot, Rose Design, Prince Regent	17.50
Bavarian, Chocolate Pot, Signed, Hand-Painted Grapes & Leaves, Beige, Green	55.00
Bavarian, Chocolate Set, Roses, Medallion, White, Black, 6 Cup & Saucer	49.00
Bavarian, Chocolate Set, Tea Rose Pattern, Z.S.& Co., Bavaria	150.00
Bavarian, Coffeepot, Green & Tan Ground, Hand-Painted Grapes, Gold Trim	55.00
Bavarian, Creamer, Roses, Prince Regent	9.00
Bavarian, Cup & Saucer, Baker's Chocolate Lady Portrait, Cream & Maroon	12.50
Bavarian, Cup & Saucer, Bouillon, Black Knight, Red & Gold, Yellow Flower	12.50
Bavarian, Cup & Saucer, Bouillon, Chrysanthemum Design	10.00
Bavarian, Cup & Saucer, Coffee, Gold & Yellow Bands, White & Pink Flowers	12.00
Bavarian, Cup & Saucer, Flowers, Pink, White, Mark Kingston	12.00
Bavarian, Cup & Saucer, Swag Design, Blue, Gold Rim	6.50
Bavarian, Cup, Chocolate, Red Roses On White, 6	32.00
Bavarian, Demitasse Set, Black Band With Fruit, Floral On White, 16 Piece	40.00
Bavarian, Dessert Set, Rosebud Center, 7 Piece	10.00
Bavarian, Dessert, Zs Bavaria, Ruffled Rim, Gold On Green, Violets	12.50
Bavarian, Dish, Bone, Ps Bavaria, Kidney Shape, Gold Rim, Floral	10.00
Bavarian, Dish, Open Edge, Tulips, Gold, 5 1/2 In.	6.00
Bavarian, Dish, Relish, Pink, Lilies, Marked, 11 1/2 In.Long	27.50
Bavarian, Jar, Cracker, Floral Design, Pink, Green, White, 5 1/2 In.High	28.00
Bavarian, Mug, Scene Of Union Station, Providence, R.I., Old Cars, 3 In.High	5.00
Bavarian, Mug, 1971	20.00
Bavarian, Pansy Ring, Footed, Scrolled	4.50
Bavarian, Pitcher, Pink Orchids, Green, Marked P.S.A.G.Inside Crown, Signed	9.00
Bavarian, Plate, Autumn Leaf, Grape, Schwartzenhammer, 9 1/2 In.Diameter	14.50
Bavarian, Plate, Black Knight, Eldorado Pattern, Gold Decoration	4.25
Bavarian, Plate, Black Knight, Vendome Pattern, Green & Gold, Square	4.75
Bavarian, Plate, Cake, Flowers, Pink, Gold, Signed Poole, Handle, 10 In.	12.50
Bavarian, Plate, Cake, Hand-Painted Pink Flowers	7.50
Bavarian, Plate, Daisy, Signed 1909, 9 1/8 In.Diameter	10.00
Bavarian, Plate, Fish, Four Designs, 7 1/4 In.Diameter, Set Of 12	60.00
Bavarian, Plate, Floral Festoons, Bouquet Center, Pierced Edge, Schumann	8.50
Bavarian, Plate, Fruit, Hand-Painted, Gold, Signed, 12 In.Diameter, Pair	70.00
Bavarian, Plate, Fruit, Purple, Pink, Blue, Wide Gold Border, 12 1/2 In., Pair	85.00
Bavarian, Plate, Game, Quail, Rock, Moss, Branches, Pierced, 9 5/8 In.	38.00
Bavarian, Plate, George & Martha Washington, Circa 1903, 9 In.Diameter	35.00

Bavarian, Plate, Gold & Yellow Bands, White & Pink Flowers, Marked 7.00
Bavarian, Plate, Hand-Painted Pink & Yellow Roses, Green & Brown, 7 3/4 In. 12.50
Bavarian, Plate, Hand-Painted Rose, Light & Dark Green, 7 3/4 In. 14.00
Bavarian, Plate, Hand-Painted, Signed 12.00
Bavarian, Plate, Lacy, Fruit Edge, Gold Trim, Pedestal 17.50
Bavarian, Plate, Pink & White Tulips, Gold Trim, Signed Doufreux, 11 1/2 In. 32.00
Bavarian, Plate, Pink Rose Swags, 9 1/2 In. 4.00
Bavarian, Plate, Pink Roses, Green Ground, Signed Artist J.Braun, 9 In. 13.00
Bavarian, Plate, Poppies, Gold Rim, Hand-Painted, 8 1/2 In.Diameter 7.50
Bavarian, Plate, Serving, Black Knight, Olivia Pattern, Green & Gold 12.50
Bavarian, Plate, Three Bunches Of Grapes, 8 1/2 In. 5.00
Bavarian, Plate, White, Autumn Leaves, Fruit, Gold Edge, 6 .... 15.00
Bavarian, Plate, Wildflowers, 10 In. 4.00
Bavarian, Salt, Forget-Me-Not, Hand-Painted 6.00
Bavarian, Salt, Pepper & Toothpick, Hand-Painted 18.00
Bavarian, Soup, Made For Kansas City Athletic Club, 1923, Bauscher, Bavaria 15.00
Bavarian, Tea Set, Green Ground, Pink & White Mums, Gold, Z.S.& Co., 3 Piece 37.50
Bavarian, Tea Set, Mother-Of-Pearl Eggshell, Black Band, 19 Piece 49.00
Bavarian, Tea Set, Schumann, Garlands Of Flowers, Gold, 3 Piece 75.00
Bavarian, Tile, Rose Sprays, Pink 7.50
Bayonet, see Weapon, Bayonet
Beaded Bag, Gray Jet Beads On Blue Crochet, Drawstring, Tassel On Bottom 10.00
Beaded Bag, Iridescent Beads, Blue, Bronze .... *Illus*   17.50
Beaded Bag, Jets, Etched Gunmetal Frame, 9 1/4 X 6 3/4 In. 7.00
Beaded Bag, Silver & Gold Beads, 3 1/2 In. 8.50
Beaded Bag, Suede Back 18.50
Beaded Bird, Dated 1899 .... *Illus*   8.50
Beam, see Bottle, Beam
Beck, Plate, Game, Deer At Watering Hole, Signed, 12 In. 25.00

Beehive, Austria, or Beehive, Vienna, China includes all the many types
of decorated porcelain marked with the famous Beehive mark, The mark has
been used since the eighteenth century.
Beehive, Candlestick, Push Up, Square Step-Up Base, 10 In., Pair 45.00
Beehive, Cup & Saucer, Demitasse, Marked, Magenta, Gold Handle & Scrolls 18.00
Beehive, Cup & Saucer, Medallion, Cobalt Blue 67.50
Beehive, Dish, Cake, Handles, 10 Plates, Overall Blue Decor, Germany 95.00
Beehive, Dish, Honey, Paneled Thistle, Square, 4 Feet, Bee Mark 14.00
Beehive, Pitcher, Portrait, Bulbous, Blue Mark 125.00
Beehive, Plate, Angelus, Maroon & Gold 185.00
Beehive, Plate, Dancing Figures, Red, Gold, Signed, 8 1/2 In.Diameter 24.50
Beehive, Plate, Lovers In A Boat, Des Meeres Und Der Siebe Wogen, 14 In. 350.00
Beehive, Plate, Portrait Kaiser Wilhelm In Center 35.00
Beehive, Vase, Musician & Dancer, Blue, Maroon, Gold Trim, 3 In. 12.50
Beehive, Vase, Portrait, Maroon, Gold, Signed, 10 In.Tall 35.00

Bells have been made of china, glass, or metal. All types are collected.
Bell, Brass, Bevin, No.177, Riveted, 88 On Strap 40.00
Bell, Brass, Cow, 4 1/2 In.High 10.00
Bell, Brass, Hames, 4 Graduated, Not Riveted 25.00
Bell, Brass, Pull Clang, Mounted On Board, 8 In.Diameter 35.00
Bell, Brass, Puritan, 1492 .... *Illus*   10.00
Bell, Brass, Round, Pat.Date On Bottom, 1876-78, Riveted, 11 On String 20.00
Bell, Brass, String Of 12, Graduated Size, Clip On 30.00
Bell, Brass, Dated 1848, Saignelier, 3 3/4 In.Diameter 10.00
Bell, Brass, 12 Graduated, Leather Handle 94.50
Bell, Brass, 24 Graduated On Strap, Not Riveted, Design On Top Of Bells 200.00
Bell, Brass, 5 In.Diameter, 9 In.High 20.00
Bell, Bronze, Cast, Wrought Iron Hanger, Marked U.S.N. 29.50
Bell, Bronze, Form Of Queen Elizabeth I, Legs For Clappers, 7 In.High 45.00
Bell, Bronze, Ornate, 4 1/2 In.High 20.00
Bell, Bronze, Spanish, Dated 1828 .... 30.00
Bell, Bronze, 3 In. 5.00
Bell, Bronze, 5 In. 5.00
Bell, Call, Gnomelike Figure On Pedestal Base, 9 In.High 42.50
Bell, Camel, Embossed, Birds, Brass, Iron Clobber, 8 In.Tall 55.00

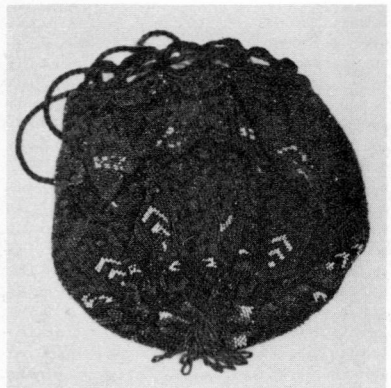

Beaded Bag, Iridescent Beads, Blue, Bronze
See Page 17

Bell, Brass, Puritan, 1492
See Page 17

Beaded Bird, Dated 1899
See Page 17

Bell, Cast Bronze, Wrought Iron Hanger, 10 In.Across, 15 Lbs., Marked U.S.N.	29.50
Bell, Cast Iron, Dinner, Yoke	25.00
Bell, Cast Iron, Patio, Wrought Iron Bracket, 8 In., 13 Lbs.	12.50
Bell, Chow, Wagon Train, Triangle	6.00
Bell, Church, 26 In.	125.00
Bell, Church, 28 In.	125.00
Bell, Cow, Brass, 4 1/2 In.High	10.00
Bell, Cow, Clapper, Wooden	25.00
Bell, Cow, New England, 6 In.High	4.95
Bell, Cow, Spanish, Iron, 11 In.	11.00
Bell, Cow, Spanish, Iron, 7 In.	11.00
Bell, Cow, Spanish, Iron, 9 In.	11.00
Bell, Cow, Strap & Buckle	9.50
Bell, Cow, Wood Clapper, Small	5.50
Bell, Cow's, Brass, 4 1/2 In.High	10.00
Bell, Dinner, Signed Star On Swirl Handle, Etched Scene, Columbus Landing	55.00
Bell, Elephant, Brass	10.00
Bell, Elephant, Engraved, Brass	10.00
Bell, Farm, Yard, Hanger	27.50
Bell, Fish, Brass, Marked China, 3 3/4 In.High	3.95
Bell, Four Graduated On 14 In.Brass Strap, Buffed, Polished	22.00
Bell, Four On Strap .... Illus	20.00
Bell, Glass, Cranberry To Clear, Myriad Bubbles, 6 X 10 In.	95.00
Bell, Glass, Cranberry, Clear Handle, Hand Blown, 12 In.	95.00

Bell, Glass, Green, Clear Handle, Hand Blown, 12 In.	95.00
Bell, Glass, Opaline, Blue, White, French	135.00
Bell, Gong, Brass Stand, Mallet, 7 In.	12.50
Bell, Gong, Oak Stand, Mallet, 5 In.	14.50
Bell, Hand, Brass, Fish Shape Handle, Mark China	3.95
Bell, Hand, Embossed Floral, Marked 1878, Brass, 3 1/4 In.	7.00
Bell, Hand, Embossed Floral, Marked 1878, Brass, 4 In.	9.00
Bell, Hand, Embossed Floral, Marked 1878, Brass, 5 In.	12.00
Bell, Hand, Victorian, Opaque White, Glass Handle, Cranberry, 12 In., Pair	50.00
Bell, Handshaker, Brass, Geisha On Handle, 7 In.Tall	20.00
Bell, Iron, Bevin, 7 Ft.Strap, Riveted, 30	25.00
Bell, Iron, Sheep, 4 In.High	10.00
Bell, Iron, 5 Lbs., 11 In.Long	8.50
Bell, Lady, Brass, 3 In. _Illus_	8.50
Bell, Lady, Long Gown, High Bonnet, Holds Fan, Bronze, 4 1/2 In.High	30.00
Bell, Locomotive, Brass, Framed, 28 In.Tall, 18 In.Diameter	525.00
Bell, Locomotive, Brass, N.Y.Central, Replaced Hanger & Support, 11 In.	165.00
Bell, Mexican, Iron _Illus_	7.50
Bell, Monkey & Coconut On Log, Gong Bell Co., 1880s, Painted, Cast Iron	275.00
Bell, Opaque White, Clear Cased, Ruby Handle, White Knob On Top, 12 1/2 In.	135.00
Bell, Ox	11.00
Bell, Patio, Cast Iron, Wrought Iron Bracket, 8 In.Across, 13 Lbs.	12.50
Bell, Patio, Hanger, 8 1/2 In.Diameter	17.50
Bell, Plantation, Embossed, Brass	30.00
Bell, School, Brass _Illus_	18.00

Bell, Four On Strap
See Page 18

Bell, Lady, Brass, 3 In.

Bell, School, Brass   Bell, Mexican, Iron

Bell, School, Brass, Heavy, Black Handle, 8 1/2 In.Tall	20.00
Bell, School, Hand, Copper	20.00
Bell, School, Nickel, Black Wooden Handle, 3 1/2 In.Diameter	8.50
Bell, School, Wood Handle, 10 In.High, 6 In.Diameter	15.00
Bell, School, 7 3/4 In.Tall	12.50
Bell, Schoolmarm's, Brass, Wooden Handle, 2 1/4 In.Diameter, 3 1/2 In.Tall	4.50
Bell, Schoolmarm's, Floral, Embossed, Brass, 5 In.Tall	12.00
Bell, Schoolmarm's, Wood Handle, 4 In.Tall	2.50
Bell, Sheep, Iron, 4 In.High	10.00
Bell, Ship Horn, Brass, Burnished, Engraved Candida, 6 1/4 X 18 In.Long	95.00
Bell, Ship's, Brass, 9 In.Diameter	45.00
Bell, Ship's, Bronze, 'russo', 12 1/2 In.Diameter	175.00
Bell, Ship's, Cast Iron, Mounting Arm	48.00
Bell, Ship's, Mounting Bracket, Bronze, 8 In.Diameter, 7 In.High	55.00
Bell, Signed Delft, Pipes Mark, Windmill Scene, Blues	29.00
Bell, Sleigh, Brass, Brass Link Belt, 15	70.00
Bell, Sleigh, Brass, Dated, 20	35.00
Bell, Sleigh, Brass, Engraved	1.50
Bell, Sleigh, Brass, Graduated String Of 22, Embossed	65.00
Bell, Sleigh, Brass, Leather Strap, 30 Bells	50.00
Bell, Sleigh, Brass, Padded Strap, 1 1/2 In.Diameter	15.00
Bell, Sleigh, Brass, String Of 30 Graduated	35.00 To 50.00
Bell, Sleigh, Brass, String Of 36	50.00
Bell, Sleigh, Brass, 14	38.50
Bell, Sleigh, Brass, 24 On Double Strap, Graduated, Design On Bells	200.00
Bell, Sleigh, Brass, 24 On 7 Ft.Strap, 1 1/2 In.Diameter	25.00
Bell, Sleigh, Brass, 25	48.50
Bell, Sleigh, Brass, 30 On Strap	45.00
Bell, Sleigh, Iron, Strap, Shaft	5.00
Bell, Sleigh, Nickel Plated, String Of 30 On 7 1/2 Ft.Leather Strap	79.50
Bell, Sleigh, Nickel Plated, 30 Bells, 1 1/2 In.Diameter	20.00
Bell, Sleigh, Nickel Plated, 30 On 7 Ft.Strap, Buckle	8.75 To 20.00
Bell, Sleigh, Shaft, Brass, Strap	10.00
Bell, Sleigh, String Of 16 Graduated	70.00
Bell, Sleigh, String Of 29	60.00
Bell, Sleigh, Swedish, Brass, 6 Way Slit, Set Of 4	18.00
Bell, Sleigh, Swedish, 4 Way Slit, Set Of 4	17.50
Bell, Sleigh, Swedish, 6 Way Slit, Set Of 6	30.00
Bell, Sleigh, 1 1/4 In., Leather Strap, 30	35.00
Bell, Sleigh, 24 On 48 In.Strap, Dated May 14, 1878	45.00
Bell, Sleigh, 24 On 88 In.Strap, Brass, 1 1/4 In.	40.00
Bell, Sleigh, 26, Swiss, 80 In.Strap, Buckle	45.00
Bell, Sleigh, 48 On 7 Ft.Strap, Dated May 14, 1878	85.00
Bell, Sleigh, 6 Way Slit, Set Of 4	19.50
Bell, Smoke, Blown Glass, Clear, Turned-Over Rim	15.00
Bell, Spreader Strap, 10 Ring, Colored, Pair	10.00
Bell, Store, Strap Spring, Brass	8.75
Bell, Table, India, Brass	10.00
Bell, Teacher's, Brass, Wood Handle, 8 In.	10.00
Bell, Teacher's, Embossed Floral, Brass, Marked 1878, 3 1/4 In.	7.00
Bell, Teacher's, Embossed Floral, Brass, Marked 1878, 4 In.	9.00
Bell, Teacher's, Embossed Floral, Brass, Marked 1878, 5 In.	12.00
Bell, Teacher's, Nickel Finish	7.00
Bell, U.S.Navy, Brass, 9 1/2 In.Diameter	50.00
Bell, Victorian Lady In Bouffant Court Dress, Brass, 4 In.High	18.00
Bell, Woman In Full Skirts, Leg Clapper, English, 5 1/2 In.	8.00
Bell, Yard, With Hanger	28.75

Belleek China was made in Ireland, other European countries, and the
United States. The glaze is creamy yellow and appears wet. The first
Belleek was made in 1857.

Belleek, see also Lenox

Belleek Pitcher, Iris, Leaves, Signed Ada C.Higgins, 14 In.Tall	165.00
Belleek, Basket, Heart Shape, Iridescent, Ireland	60.00
Belleek, Bowl & Plate, Bacchus Head, Black Mark	25.00
Belleek, Bowl, Basket Weave, Shamrock, Pierced Rim, Black Mark, Pair	145.00

Belleek, Bowl, Cooking-Pot Shape, Footed, Handles, 2 1/2 In.High, Marked 28.00
Belleek, Bowl, Enamel Floral, Two Handles, Willet, 7 1/2 In. 27.50
Belleek, Bowl, Shell Shape, Shell Feet, Red Mark 30.00
Belleek, Bowl, Signed Willet Belleek, Luster, Entwined Serpents 75.00
Belleek, Candlestick, American, White, 10 3/4 In.High 24.50
Belleek, Chocolate Set, White, Gold Trim, Square Base, Palette Mark, 18 Piece 225.00
Belleek, Compote, Embossed Paneling, 6 3/4 X 8 1/4 In.Diameter, Mark L 30.00
Belleek, Compote, Flowers, Blue, 6 5/8 In.Diameter 32.50
Belleek, Creamer & Open Sugar, Gypsy Kettle Shape, Footed, Shamrocks 30.00
Belleek, Creamer & Sugar, Floral Design, Gold, Footed, 4 In.Tall 70.00
Belleek, Creamer & Sugar, Hound & Harp, Green Mark 50.00
Belleek, Creamer & Sugar, Shell Pattern, Shell Feet, Black Mark 45.00
Belleek, Creamer, Embossed Bacchus Head, Black Mark 20.00
Belleek, Creamer, Gold Design, Signed, 5 In.High 55.00
Belleek, Creamer, Pink, Gold Trim, 3 3/4 In.High 16.00
Belleek, Creamer, Raised Floral, Green Handle, Harp House Tower, Fermanagh 22.00
Belleek, Creamer, Shamrock, Basket Weave, Brown & Green Twig Handle 30.00
Belleek, Creamer, Shell Pattern, Green Trim, Black Mark 22.00
Belleek, Creamer, Sugar, Shell, Green Mark 25.00
Belleek, Creamer, Swan, Black Mark, 6 In.Long 75.00
Belleek, Cup & Saucer, Basket Weave, Shamrocks, Ireland, Black Mark 17.00
Belleek, Cup & Saucer, C.A.C., Palette, American, Signed, Portrait Heads 40.00
Belleek, Cup & Saucer, Demitasse, C.A.C., Palette, American, Signed, Green 30.00
Belleek, Cup & Saucer, Demitasse, Green, Gold, Flowers 12.00
Belleek, Cup & Saucer, Green, Hexagon, Second Black Mark 35.00
Belleek, Cup & Saucer, Harp Shamrock, Second Black Mark 22.00
Belleek, Cup & Saucer, Hexagon Pattern, Pink, White, Gold Trim 35.00
Belleek, Cup & Saucer, Neptune Pattern, Green Trim 22.00
Belleek, Cup & Saucer, Neptune, Pink Trim, Black Mark 35.00
Belleek, Cup & Saucer, Pinecone, Pink 35.00
Belleek, Cup & Saucer, Serpent, Gold Handle 35.00
Belleek, Cup & Saucer, Shell Feet, Black Mark 25.00
Belleek, Cup & Saucer, Shell Pattern, Black Mark 10.00
Belleek, Cup & Saucer, Shell, Green Mark 16.00
Belleek, Cup, Saucer, Pie Plate, Coral Pattern 30.00
Belleek, Dessert Set, Shell Pattern, Dolphin Base, Compote, 8 Plates, Set 350.00
Belleek, Dish, Candy, Holly Motif, Two Handle, Oval, Footed 22.50
Belleek, Dish, Heart Shape, Green Edge, Black Mark 32.50
Belleek, Dish, Shell, Green Mark, Green Handle & Shamrocks 7.50
Belleek, Figurine, Swan, First Mark Irish, 6 In.Tall 75.00
Belleek, Jar, Cookie, Shamrock Pattern, Silver Cover 48.50
Belleek, Jar, Cracker, Enamel Floral, Shells, American 28.00
Belleek, Jug, Wine, Green, Monk Scene, Lenox, Palette Mark 65.00
Belleek, Mug, Blackberry Design, Green, Gold, Hand-Painted, 6 In.Tall 35.00
Belleek, Mug, Dutch Fishing Scene, Marked, Handled, 4 1/2 In. 35.00
Belleek, Mug, Grapes, Pink, Green, Ivory, Signed, 5 1/2 In. 55.00
Belleek, Pig, Ballymaclinton On Back, Green, White, 2nd Black Mark, 3 1/4 In. 42.00
Belleek, Pitcher, Stylized Decor, Enamel, Lenox, 6 In. 17.50
Belleek, Pitcher, Tankard, Hand-Painted, Signed, 14 In.Tall 77.50
Belleek, Plate, Cake, Basket Weave, Green Shamrocks, Twig Handles 25.00
Belleek, Plate, Plate, Pastoral, River Scene, Impressed Harp & Crown, Ireland 225.00
Belleek, Plate, Shamrock Pattern, 1st Black Mark, 6 1/4 In.Diameter 25.00
Belleek, Salt Dip, Flowers, Pink 8.50
Belleek, Salt Dip, Shell, Ball Feet, Gold Inside, Pink & White Outside 6.00
Belleek, Salt, Flowers, Hand-Painted, Heart Shaped, Gold Edge, Set Of 10 .... 50.00
Belleek, Salt, Individual, Blue, Gold, Serpent Mark 4.50
Belleek, Salt, Master, Gold Top Rim, 3 Gold Ball Feet, Set Of 6 .... 37.50
Belleek, Salt, Master, Neptune Pattern, Pink Accents, Black Mark 28.00
Belleek, Salt, Open, Blue & White, Enameled, Willet, Signed 5.00
Belleek, Salt, Open, Flowers, Blue, Individual, Pair 12.50
Belleek, Salt, Open, Shamrock, Black Mark 15.00
Belleek, Sugar, Open, Pink Trim, Shell Pattern, Yellow Luster Interior, Mark 22.00
Belleek, Tankard, C.A.C., Palette, American, Signed, Gold, Artist Higgins 155.00
Belleek, Tea Service, Shell Pattern, Shell Feet, Black Mark, 13 Piece 200.00
Belleek, Tea Set, Basket Weave, Shamrock, Green Mark, 4 Cup, Saucer, Plate 175.00
Belleek, Tea Set, Black Mark, Hexagon Pattern, Green Trim, 19 Pieces 290.00

Belleek, Tea Set, C.A.C., Palette, American, Signed Perlee Belleek, 5 Piece 85.00
Belleek, Tea Set, Hexagon, Green, White, Creamer, Sugar, Cup, Saucer, Teapot 190.00
Belleek, Tea Set, Shamrock, Black Mark 155.00
Belleek, Teakettle, Grass Pattern, Bird Spout, Second Black Mark 125.00
Belleek, Teapot, Basket Weave, Flowers 50.00
Belleek, Teapot, Colored Wheat Pattern, Bird Spout, Gold Trim On Handle 125.00
Belleek, Teapot, Creamer, Sugar, Coral Pattern 115.00
Belleek, Teapot, Creamer, Sugar, Neptune Pattern, Footed 125.00
Belleek, Teapot, Irish, Tridacna Green Trim 75.00
Belleek, Teapot, Miniature, Shamrock 55.00
Belleek, Teapot, Shamrock, Basket Weave, Brown & Green Twig Handle & Finial 65.00
Belleek, Tumbler, Gold, Flower Trim, Signed L. 12.50
Belleek, Tumbler, Green, Yellow, Tulip, Straight Side, 3 1/2 In. 25.00
Belleek, Vase, Bamboo, White, First Mark 100.00
Belleek, Vase, Coral Poppies, Green Ground, Artist-Signed, Willet, 8 In.Tall 55.00
Belleek, Vase, Flying Fish, Green, Mark 42.00
Belleek, Vase, Irish, Cornucopia Shape, Yellow Iridescent Inside 35.00
Belleek, Vase, Irish, Embossed Leaf Pattern, Black Mark 46.00
Belleek, Vase, Irish, Rathmore, Green & Gold, Green Mark 30.00
Belleek, Vase, Leaf, Flower, Cream, White, Green Mark, 7 In.Tall 18.00
Belleek, Vase, Lily, Salamander, Gold Trim, Black Mark, 9 In.Tall 200.00
Belleek, Vase, Morning Glories, Rose, White, Purple, Hand-Painted, 13 1/4 In. 50.00
Belleek, Vase, Poppies, Foliage, Green, Pink, Serpent Shape, Signed, 10 In. 50.00
Belleek, Vase, Rack, Second Mark Irish, Green, 5 1/2 In.Tall, Pair 90.00
Belleek, Vase, Roses, Pink, Hand-Painted, 11 1/4 In. 55.00
Belleek, Vase, Sea Horse, Yellow, Mark B 75.00
Belleek, Vase, White, Blue, Black, Geometric Design, 10 In., Pair 125.00
Bells, Iron Strips, Four Large Bells, 14 In.Long, Pair 35.00

*Bennington Ware was the product of two factories working in Bennington,
Vermont. Both firms were out of business by 1896. The wares include the
brown and yellow mottled pottery, Parian, Scroddle, Stoneware, Graniteware,
Yellowware, and Staffordshire-like vases.*
Bennington, see also Rockingham
Bennington, Bottle, Coachman, Signed Lyman & Fenton .... *Illus* 295.00
Bennington, Bowl, Mixing, 9 1/2 In.Diameter 5.00
Bennington, Bowl, Mottled, 4 In.Diameter 6.00
Bennington, Bowl, Paneled, Maroon Glaze, Signed Norton, Oblong, 10 In. 47.50
Bennington, Candleholder, Vermont, Signed, Brown With Black Decor 65.00
Bennington, Crock, Blue Floral, Marked E.& L.P.Norton 25.00
Bennington, Crock, Miniature, 3 In.Tall 10.00
Bennington, Dish, Pudding, Flaring, 9 1/2 In.Diameter 55.00
Bennington, Dish, Soap 16.50
Bennington, Doorknob, Pair 7.50
Bennington, Figurine, Lion, Flint, Enamel, Brown & Green Glaze, 9 1/2 In. 800.00
Bennington, Figurine, Lion, Flint, Enamel, Brown Glaze, 11 1/4 In. 1400.00
Bennington, Figurine, Woman Carrying Grapes, Flowing Robe, 12 In.High 65.00
Bennington, Jug, Blue & Gray, Stoneware, Gallon, Flower, E.& L.P.Norton 25.00
Bennington, Jug, Three Blue Feathers, Norton, Bennington 60.00
Bennington, Lion, Flint Enamel, 9 1/2 In.Long .... *Illus* 800.00
Bennington, Pickle, Maroon, Signed Norton 27.50
Bennington, Pitcher, Hunter & Dog, Hound Handle 125.00
Bennington, Plate, Pie, 8 1/4 X 1 1/4 In. 35.00
Bennington, Shaving Mug 50.00
Bennington, Teapot & Sugar, Flint Enamel, Marked .... *Illus* 575.00
Bennington, Teapot, Rebecca At Well 49.50
Bennington, Vase, Parian, Blue & White, Victoria, Albert Portrait, Grapes 35.00
Bennington, Vase, Parian, Plaster, 2 Dogs 35.00
Bennington Type, Bowl, 9 In.Diameter 12.50
Bennington Type, Crock, Open, Miniature 10.00
Bennington Type, Flask, Pretzel 45.00
Bennington Type, Pitcher, Raised Head On Side, 7 In.Diameter 4.00
Bennington Type, Teapot, Tan Glaze, Rebecca-At-The-Well Raised Design 35.00
Berlin, Cup & Saucer, Gold Fused Into Enamel Decoration, C.1870 .... 60.00
Berlin, Jar, Covered, Cylindrical, Gilt Grapevine, Greek Fret Border, C.1815 .... 80.00
Berlin, Tea & Coffee Pots, Covered, Barrel Form, Gilt Bands & Floral, C.1810 .... 70.00

Berlin, Tea & Coffee Set, Puce, Sprigs Of Deutsche Blumen, C.1770, 13 Piece 240.00
Berlin, Tete-A-Tete, Portraits Classical Figures, C.1780-1800, 15 Piece 125.00
Bicycle, Boneshaker, Wooden Wheel, 1864, France 475.00
Bicycle, Cast Iron & Wood, High-Wheel, 57 In.High .... *Illus* 600.00
Bicycle, High Wheel, Wooden Wheels, Iron Tires, Openwork Seat, Frame, 1870 .... 145.00

Bennington, Bottle, Coachman,
Signed Lyman & Fenton
See Page 22

Bennington, Lion, Flint Enamel, 9 1/2 In.Long
See Page 22

Bennington, Teapot &
Sugar, Flint Enamel,
Marked
See Page 22

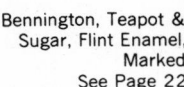

Bicycle, Cast Iron & Wood,
High-Wheel, 57 In.High

Bicycle, High Wheeler, 1881	525.00
Bicycle, Iron, 26 In.Front Wheel, Rubber Tires, 38 In.High	109.50
Bicycle, Wooden, Hand Carved, Mythological Figure, Circa 1890	750.00

Bing and Grondahl is a famous Danish factory making fine porcelains from 1853 to the present. Their Christmas Plates are especially well known.

Bing & Grondahl, see also Collector Plate

Bing & Grondahl, Figurine, Girl & Her Brother	30.00
Bing & Grondahl, Figurine, Poultry Girl, 9 1/2 In.High, Signed	65.00
Bing & Grondahl, Plaque, Poster	3.00
Binoculars, Bausch & Lomb, 50 X 7 In.Case	55.00
Binoculars, Royal Air Force, Aeroplane Engraved On Barrel, Foch, Paris	15.00

Bisque is an unglazed baked porcelain. Finished Bisque has a slightly sandy texture with a dull finish. Some of it may be decorated with various colors. Bisque gained favor during the late victorian era when thousands of Bisque figurines were made.

Bisque, Baby, Kewpie Type, With Ice Skates, Holes For Diaper Pins	15.00
Bisque, Baby, Kewpie Type, With Tennis Racquet	15.00
Bisque, Candlestick, Boy, Girl, White, Black Decor, Floral On Base, 7 In., Pair	125.00
Bisque, Dog, Gold String & Tassel Around Neck, 4 1/4 In.High	15.00
Bisque, Doll, Potty, Pink Trim, 3 1/2 In.	8.50
Bisque, Figurine, Bagel Seller, Gardner Decorated, 19th Century, 7 1/2 In.	200.00
Bisque, Figurine, Boy On Stump, Brown Shades	20.00
Bisque, Figurine, Boy Standing, Playing Harp, Brown, Gold, & Green	20.00
Bisque, Figurine, Boy, Girl, Dancing Position, Native Costume, 8 1/2 In., Pair	38.00
Bisque, Figurine, Boy, Girl, Germany, 4 In.High, Pair	24.00
Bisque, Figurine, Boy, Girl, On Tree Stump, Gold, German, 14 1/4 In., Pair	59.00
Bisque, Figurine, Circus, Clown, Girl, Trapeze, German, Marked	125.00
Bisque, Figurine, Dancing Position, Native Costume, Boy & Girl, Pair	38.00
Bisque, Figurine, Duck, Green, Iron Red, & Brown, 11 1/2 In.High, Pair	425.00
Bisque, Figurine, Elf, Painted Red, Stocking Hat, White Beard, Germany	10.00
Bisque, Figurine, Europe As Crowned Woman In Blue Gown, Painted	48.00
Bisque, Figurine, Gibson Girl With Umbrella, Pastel Colors, 9 1/2 In.Tall	22.50
Bisque, Figurine, Girl In High Chair, White, C.1895, 4 1/2 In.	18.00
Bisque, Figurine, Girl With Fruit In Apron, Pastels, Gold, 7 3/4 In.Tall	20.00
Bisque, Figurine, Girl, Empire-Style Dress, Bonnet, Holds Fan, 2 1/2 In.	20.00
Bisque, Figurine, Hansel & Gretel & The Witch, Tinted, 3	10.00
Bisque, Figurine, Lady, 7 1/2 In.Tall	15.00
Bisque, Figurine, Maiden In Victorian Dress, 7 3/4 In.Tall	16.00
Bisque, Figurine, Negro Baby On Potty, Watermelon, Coin, 3 1/2 In.Tall	10.00
Bisque, Figurine, Negro Boy Eating Watermelon, 3 1/2 In.High	7.50
Bisque, Figurine, Negro Man With Melon, Seated, Painted, 4 In.	12.00
Bisque, Figurine, Negro Potty Baby, 3 1/4 In.	5.00
Bisque, Figurine, Nude Woman Riding Tiger, Matte, White, 5 In.High	28.00
Bisque, Figurine, One Of The Wise Men, Signed In Blue, Crown & Initials	10.00
Bisque, Figurine, Small Boy, Girl, France, 1o In.Tall, Pair	350.00
Bisque, Figurine, Vase Type, Boy Clings To Side Of Basket, Lizard On Basket	24.00
Bisque, Figurine, Woman, Dancing, Gardner Decorated, 19th Century	190.00
Bisque, Figurine, Woman, Man, Tambourine, Horn, French, 14 1/2 In.Tall, Pair	105.00
Bisque, Figurine, Young Boy & Girl, 15 In.High, Pair	30.00
Bisque, Fountain, Holy Water, Made In Germany, No.4087, Painted	10.00
Bisque, Hair Receiver, Urn, Medallions Of Lady On Rust, 4 In.High	15.00
Bisque, Hen On Nest	4.75
Bisque, Holder, Match, Beggar Dog, Top Hat, Striker On Back	28.00
Bisque, Holder, Perfume, Germany, Felix The Cat, 1 In.	4.00
Bisque, Match Holder, Girl In Blue Bonnet, Lavender Curtains, Striker	12.50
Bisque, Napkin Ring, Miniature, Cluster Of Flowers	12.50
Bisque, Piano Baby .... *Illus*	60.00
Bisque, Piano Baby, Dressed, Lying On Stomach, Germany	25.00
Bisque, Pitcher, Hound Handle, Embossed Hunt Scene, Signed J.D.Bagster	45.00
Bisque, Planter, Raised Figure, 9 1/2 In.High	8.00
Bisque, Pot, Pink, Green, Pig, Boston Baked Beans, Germany	12.50
Bisque, Swan, White, 3 3/4 In.Long, 2 1/4 In.High	15.00

Black Amethyst Glass appears black until it is held to the light, and a dark purple can be seen. It was made in many factories from 1860 to the present time.

Black Amethyst, Bowl, Pair Candlesticks, Gold Encrusted	75.00
Black Amethyst, Bowl, Raised Geometric & Forget-Me-Not Design, 3 Feet	22.00
Black Amethyst, Goblet, Footed, Etched Clear	8.00
Black Amethyst, Goblet, Honeycomb Pattern	15.00
Black Amethyst, Plaque, Tiffin, U.S.Glass Co., On Base	22.00
Black Amethyst, Saucer, Silver Overlay, Marked Sterling	1.25
Black Amethyst, Sugar, Handled, Silver Overlay, Marked Sterling	12.50
Black Amethyst, Swan	32.50
Black Amethyst, Tray, Centerpiece, Oval, Pierced Handle, Candleholders	22.00
Black Amethyst, Vase, Bud	5.00
Black Amethyst, Vase, Bud, Enamel Flower Decor, 10 In.Tall	12.00
Black Amethyst, Vase, Dancing Nymphs, Embossed, 7 In.Tall	12.00
Black Amethyst, Vase, Pedestal, Urn Shape, 7 1/2 In.Tall	28.50

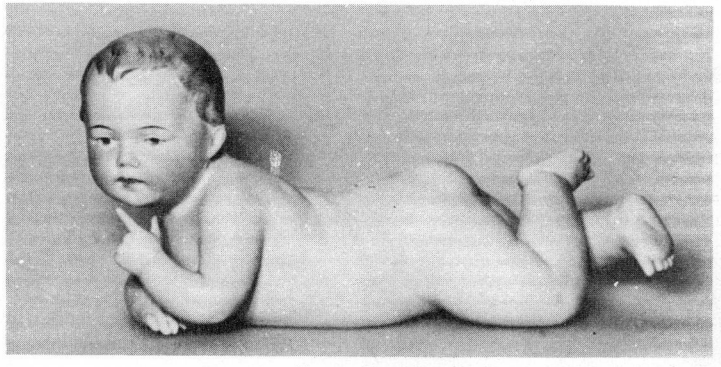

Bisque, Piano Baby
See Page 24

Black Amethyst, Vase, 2 Handled, Fluted Top, Embossed Girls Dancing, Pair	17.00
Black Amethyst, Vase, 2 Handles, 7 In.Tall, Raised Heart, Dancing Girls	20.00
Black Amethyst, Vase, 6 In.High	15.00
Blanc-De-Chine, Cup, Molded Figures, Schwarzlot Decoration, C.1725	170.00
Blanc-De Chine, Deity Seated On Reclining Elephant, Teak Stand	150.00

Blown Glass was formed by forcing air through a rod into molten glass. Early glass and some forms of Art Glass were hand blown. Other types of glass were molded or pressed.

Blown Glass, Basket, Amber, Free-Blown	17.50
Blown Glass, Basket, Frosted, White, Hand Blown, 7 In.High	8.00
Blown Glass, Bell, Dinner, Orange Luster, 5 In.Tall, Clapper On Gold Chain	3.00
Blown Glass, Bowl, English, Silver Holder, Cranberry, Spider Webbing	27.50
Blown Glass, Bowl, Marbleized, Dark Red & Brown, 6 In.Diameter	5.00
Blown Glass, Bowl, Mckearin G I-6, 3 Mold, 6 In., Flint	85.00
Blown Glass, Bowl, Midwestern, Folded Rim, Crooked, 9 In.Diameter, Aqua	125.00
Blown Glass, Bowl, Rose, Palm Tree Scene, Hand-Painted, Green	58.00
Blown Glass, Bowl, Rose, Ribbed Edge	40.00
Blown Glass, Bowl, Swirled, Applied Blue Rim, 5 In.Diameter, Clear	30.00
Blown Glass, Bucket, Ice, Amber, Silver Plate Handle	10.00
Blown Glass, Bulb, nt, Hand Blown, 3	14.50
Blown Glass, Candle ck, Flat Base, Amber, 10 In., Pair	32.00
Blown Glass, Comp e Clear, Flaring Sides, Hollow Sten	95.00
Blown Glass, Comp tsbur h Clear Standard, White Bowl, Blue Loops	275.00
Blown Glass, Comp ttsbur e-Blown, Folded Rim, Flint	95.00
Blown Glass Cove 2 Aqua	25.00

Blown Glass, Cruet, Amber, Blue Handle, Cut Stopper 45.00
Blown Glass, Cruet, Clear, Teardrop Stopper 16.00
Blown Glass, Cruet, Diamond-Quilted, Stopper 10.75
Blown Glass, Cup, Crimped, Applied Handle, Pittsburgh 18.00
Blown Glass, Decanter, Amelung Type 36.00
Blown Glass, Decanter, Clear, Swags & Vertical Ribs, Stopper 30.00
Blown Glass, Decanter, Emerald Green, Clear Handle & Stopper, Gold & White 60.00
Blown Glass, Decanter, Green, Enameled Flower, Hollow Stopper, 15 In. 29.50
Blown Glass, Decanter, Green, Hand Blown, Clear Stopper, 10 1/2 In.High 15.00
Blown Glass, Decanter, Hobnail 20.00
Blown Glass, Decanter, Molded Pattern, 1/2 Pint, Flint 30.00
Blown Glass, Decanter, Neck Rings, C.1800, Flint 30.00
Blown Glass, Decanter, Stoddard-Type, Sunburst & Diamond Cutting, 9 In.High 60.00
Blown Glass, Decanter, Vinegar, Mckearin G I-7, Deep Blue 110.00
Blown Glass, Glass, Cocktail, Clear, 5 1/2 In. 4.00
Blown Glass, Goblet, Clear, 7 1/2 In. 6.00
Blown Glass, Goblet, Plain 4.00
Blown Glass, Goblet, Twist Stem, 18th Century, English .... *Illus* 90.00

Blown Glass, Goblet, Twist Stem, 18th Century, English

Blown Glass, Jar, Powder, Ruby & Frosted, Free-Blown, Lid, Finial 15.00
Blown Glass, Jug, Applied Handle, Clear, Polished Pontil 15.00
Blown Glass, Jug, Zanesville, Strap Handle, Citron, 5 3/4 In.High 235.00
Blown Glass, Lamp, Free-Blown, Applied Handle, Whale Oil Burner, Flint 35.00
Blown Glass, Liqueur Set, Frosted, Enameled, Bottle & 2 Glasses 20.00
Blown Glass, Mug, Free-Blown, Handled, Enameled, 'remember Me' 45.00
Blown Glass, Mug, Friendship, Enameled Flowers & To My Daughter 25.00
Blown Glass, Pan, Folded Rim, Green, 7 In.Diameter 95.00
Blown Glass, Pen, Clear, Blue & White Threading, Amber Hobs On Top 2.00
Blown Glass, Pitcher, Hand-Blown, Victorian, White, Lavender Band, Green 14.00
Blown Glass, Pitcher, Milk, Opalescent, White To Clear, Coin Spot, 6 3/4 In. 30.00
Blown Glass, Pitcher, Rough Pontil, Enamel Blueberries, Gold, 6 In.Tall 10.50
Blown Glass, Pitcher, Swirl, Cobalt Blue, Applied Handle, 9 1/2 In.Tall 50.00
Blown Glass, Pitcher, Syrup, Hand Blown, Applied Handle, Pewter Top, Flint 125.00
Blown Glass, Plate, Clear, 7 1/4 In. 2.50
Blown Glass, Shaker, Castor, Mckearin G I-7, Flint 20.00
Blown Glass, Sherry Set, Floral Painted 10.00
Blown Glass, Syrup, Clear, Tin Hinged Lid, Mold Blown 14.75
Blown Glass, Syrup, Paneled, Clear To Wine 42.50
Blown Glass, Tumbler, Pink, Frosted Hobnail 35.00
Blown Glass, Vase, Amber, Applied Handle, Ribbed, 6 In. 12.00
Blown Glass, Vase, Amethyst, South Jersey, Clear Handle, 9 In. 15.00
Blown Glass, Vase, Castle, Trees, Pink, Aqua, Hand-Painted, 13 In.Tall, Pair 65.00
Blown Glass, Vase, Clear, Enameled Spring Flower, White Decor 25.00
Blown Glass, Vase, Clear, Ribbed, 6 1/4 In.Diameter At Base To 3 In.At Top 16.00
Blown Glass, Vase, Enamel, Amber, Green, Gold, Airplane, 9 In. 50.00
Blown Glass, Vase, Enameled Pansy Decoration, Clear To Purple 35.00
Blown Glass, Vase, Footed, Jade Green & Black Curtain Pattern, Flecks 45.00
Blown Glass, Vase, Milk White, Ruffled Top, Pink Interior, Coralene Floral 35.00

Blown Glass, Vase, Milk White, 8 3/4 In.High 35.00
Blown Glass, Water Set, Frosted, Hand-Painted, 5 Piece 29.75
Blown Glass, Wine, White Air Twist Stem, 18th Century 60.00
  Blue Amberina, see Bluerina
  Blue Glass, see Cobalt Blue
  Blue Onion, see Onion

  Blue Willow Pattern has been made in England since 1780. The pattern
  has been copied by factories in many countries, including Germany, Japan, and
  the United States. It is still being made. Willow was named for a
  pattern that pictures a bridge, birds, willow trees, and a chinese landscape.
Blue Willow, Bowl & Pitcher, Scenic, Porcelain 60.00
Blue Willow, Bowl, Fruit, Pedestal, Round, 2 Handles, Hulse, Nixon & Adderley 45.00
Blue Willow, Bowl, Fruit, Stevenson & Sons, Six Small Bowls, Set 15.00
Blue Willow, Bowl, Soup, Allerton's, 8 In. 9.00
Blue Willow, Butter, Three Piece, Ridgway 50.00
Blue Willow, Creamer, Allerton 20.00
Blue Willow, Cup & Saucer, Bread & Milk, Buffalo Pattern 32.00
Blue Willow, Dish, Doll's, 14 Pieces 12.00
Blue Willow, Dish, Vegetable, Covered, Allerton's, England, 1903-12 .... 25.00
Blue Willow, Gravy Boat, Buffalo Pottery 16.50
Blue Willow, Gravy Boat, Marked Staffordshire, W.Adams & Sons, England 25.00
Blue Willow, Gravy Boat, Ridgway, 1879 .... 15.00
Blue Willow, Jar, Ginger, Signed W. 12.50
Blue Willow, Pepper Pot 15.00
Blue Willow, Plate, Allerton's, 9 In. 4.00
Blue Willow, Plate, Blue, White, 6 In.Diameter, Set Of 4 .... 60.00
Blue Willow, Plate, Marked Staffordshire, W.Adams & Sons, England 6.00
Blue Willow, Plate, No Mark, 8 In. 2.00
Blue Willow, Plate, 9 In. 1.75
Blue Willow, Platter, Allerton's, 9 X 11 In. 15.00
Blue Willow, Platter, Buffalo Pottery, No.1109 .... 14.00
Blue Willow, Platter, Deep, Dark Blue, Unmarked, 15 1/2 X 12 1/2 In. 35.00
Blue Willow, Platter, Deep, Made In England, 11 X 14 In. 15.00
Blue Willow, Platter, England Mark, 17 In. 38.50
Blue Willow, Platter, English, 11 1/2 X 9 1/2 In. 6.00
Blue Willow, Sugar & Creamer, Stevenson & Sons 12.00
Blue Willow, Tea Set, Child's, Japan 15.00
Blue Willow, Teapot, Sadler, England 20.00
Bluerina, Cruet, Amber To Cobalt Blue, Baby Thumbprint, Blown, Bulbous 37.50
Bluerina, Tumbler, Amber To Cobalt Blue, Baby Thumbprint 27.50
Bluerina, Tumbler, Inverted Thumbprint, 5 1/2 In.High 50.00
Bluerina, Bowl, Centerpiece, Amber Base To Blue Top, Enamel Floral 750.00
Bluerina, Vase, Cambridge 90.00

  Edward Marshall Boehm made pottery in Trenton, New Jersey, starting
  in 1949. His bird figurines have achieved worldwide recognition.
Boehm, Bust, Madonna, White, 5 In.Tall 100.00
Boehm, Bust, Pope Pius XII, Square Plinth, Parian 250.00
Boehm, Figurine, Angel, White, Parian, 5 1/4 In. 48.00
Boehm, Figurine, Baby Bird, 4 In. 80.00
Boehm, Figurine, Brother & Sister Angel 175.00
Boehm, Figurine, Catbird 2450.00
Boehm, Figurine, Cocker Spaniel, Brown & White 425.00
Boehm, Figurine, Little Angel, White, Boy & Girl, Pair 175.00
Boehm, Figurine, Parula Warblers & Mourning Doves 3300.00
Boehm, Figurine, Tufted Titmice 1750.00

  Bohemian Glass is an ornate, overlay, or flashed glass made during the
  victorian era. It has been reproduced in Bohemia, which is now a part of
  Czechoslovakia. Glass made from 1875 to 1900 is preferred by collectors.
Bohemian Glass, Beaker, Cut & Etched, Dated 1842 .... 55.00
Bohemian Glass, Bell, Blue, Deer & Castle, Patent Dated 1904 .... 18.50
Bohemian Glass, Bottle, Barber, Ruby, Deer & Castle, Patent Dated 1900 .... 22.50
Bohemian Glass, Bottle, Barber, Ruby, Stopper 16.00
Bohemian Glass, Butter, Covered, Blue, Dome Shaped, Deer & Castle 21.00

Bohemian Glass, **Candy**, Covered, Ruby, Deer & Castle, Patent Date 1904 .... 22.50
Bohemian Glass, **Castor**, Pickle, Red, Silver Frame 35.00
Bohemian Glass, **Compote**, Scalloped, Enameled Scrolls & Flowers, Pedestal 40.00
Bohemian Glass, **Cordial Set**, Ruby, Deer & Castle, Patent Dated 1891, 7 Piece 59.00
Bohemian Glass, **Cruet**, Vinegar, Red, Leaf & Grape Pattern 18.00
Bohemian Glass, **Decanter**, Grape Design, Ruby, Clear Handle, Cut Stopper 48.00
Bohemian Glass, **Decanter**, Ruby, Stopper, Etched Vintage, Silver Label, Pair 105.00
Bohemian Glass, **Dish**, Two Way, Village & Sea Scenes 10.00
Bohemian Glass, **Glass**, Friendship, Red, Deer & Castle 15.00
Bohemian Glass, **Goblet**, Red, Etched Vintage Pattern, Knob Stem 42.50
Bohemian Glass, **Goblet**, Ruby, Etched Vintage 25.00
Bohemian Glass, **Inkwell**, Deer & Castle, Amber, 7 X 12 In. 195.00
Bohemian Glass, **Jar**, Amber, Overlay, Round, Cover, 3 In.Diameter 14.00
Bohemian Glass, **Jar**, Powder, Covered, Ruby, Frosted, Gold 12.00
Bohemian Glass, **Jug**, Syrup, Ruby 14.75
Bohemian Glass, **Perfume**, Engraved Floral On Deep Amber 38.00
Bohemian Glass, **Perfume**, Red, Stopper 15.00
Bohemian Glass, **Pokal**, Ruby, Etched Scenes, Deer, Pair 275.00
Bohemian Glass, **Shade**, Hexagonal Shape, 5 1/4 In. 20.00
Bohemian Glass, **Shaker**, Sugar, Ruby 14.00
Bohemian Glass, **Shaker**, Sugar, Ruby, Deer & Castle, Patent Dated 1906 .... 22.50
Bohemian Glass, **Tankard**, Engraved Neoclassical Runs, Flowers, C.1780 .... 60.00
Bohemian Glass, **Tankard**, Pewter Mounts, Engraved Leaves, Trellises, C.1780 .... 80.00
Bohemian Glass, **Toothpick**, Blue, Deer & Castle, Patent Dated 1900 .... 12.50
Bohemian Glass, **Toothpick**, Red, Gold Trim 15.00
Bohemian Glass, **Toothpick**, Ruby, Deer & Castle, Patent Dated 1904 .... 12.50
Bohemian Glass, **Tumbler**, Ruby, Deer & Castle, Patent Dated 1890 .... 12.50
Bohemian Glass, **Tumbler**, Ruby, Etched Building & Inscription 20.00
Bohemian Glass, **Tumbler**, Ruby, Footed, Etched Running Deer 25.00
Bohemian Glass, **Urn**, Forest Scene, Deer, Etched, Amber, Cover 95.00
Bohemian Glass, **Vase**, Bird Decoration .... *Illus* 55.00

Bohemian Glass, Vase, Bird Decoration

Bohemian Glass, **Vase**, Floral Decoration, Frosted Band, 8 3/4 In.High 7.00
Bohemian Glass, **Vase**, Frosted Ground, Vintage Pattern, Red Blown Pontil 18.00
Bohemian Glass, **Vase**, Portrait Of Lady, Green, Gold, 12 3/4 In.Tall 200.00
Bohemian Glass, **Vase**, Ruby, Bird & Leaves, 6 In.High .... 12.50 To 18.00
Bohemian Glass, **Vase**, Ruby, Footed, Etched Deer Scene, 7 1/2 In.High 45.00
Bohemian Glass, **Vase**, 10 X 4 1/2 In., Pair 65.00
Bohemian Glass, **Wine Set**, Amber, Cut, Decanter & 6 Wines 148.00
Bohemian Glass, **Wine**, Red Flashed, Grape Design, Blown, 4 1/2 In.High 22.00
Bone, **Carving**, Water Bird, Teakwood Stand, 4 In.Long 45.00
Bone, **Teaspoon**, Zigzag Handle, 5 1/4 In. 5.00
Book, **Boehm Limited**, 1970 .... 175.00
Book, **Brick Barton & The Winning Eleven**, Better Little Books 4.00
Book, **Centennial**, Exhibition, Phila., 1876 .... 10.00
Book, **Famous Stars Cookbook**, 1938 .... 5.00

Book, Grandma's Game Of Riddles, Copy.1898, Mcloughlin Bros.	2.00
Book, Jim Craig, State Trooper, Big Little Book	4.25
Book, Mutt & Jeff Cartoon Book, Bud Fisher, 1910	16.50
Book, Red Barry, Big Little Book	4.00
Book, Snow White & The Seven Dwarfs, Walt Disney, Big Little Book	8.00
Book, Speaking Picture, 1880	85.00
Book, The Dream City, Columbian Exposition, 1893	9.50
Book, The World's Fair Via Baltimore & Ohio Railroad, 1893	4.00
Book, What I Saw At The World's Fair, 1851	8.00
Book, World's Columbian Exposition, Illustrated 1892	2.00
Boston & Sandwich Co., see Sandwich, Fireglow, Lutz	
Bottger, Beaker, Armorial, Oriental Flowers, Ludwig Wilhelm, C.1715	800.00
Bottger, Dish, Pickle, Leaf Shape, Raised & Tooled Gilding, C.1720	1400.00

Bottle collecting has become a major american hobby.There are several general categories of bottles such as historic flasks, bitters, household, figural and others.

Bottle, Acid, Green, Sheared Neck, 22 In.High	22.50
Bottle, Amber, Pewter Collar, Kelly For Brickwork, Labeled	850.00
Bottle, Amberina Type, Oval, Stopper, 9 In.Tall	12.00
Bottle, Apothecary Jar, Blown Glass, 11 In.	18.00
Bottle, Apothecary Jar, Clear Glass, Gold Label, Largemouth, 9 1/2 In.Tall	8.50
Bottle, Apothecary Jar, Gold & Red Panels, Enameled Flowers	65.00
Bottle, Apothecary Jar, Statue Of Liberty, 12 1/2 In. High	125.00
Bottle, Apothecary, Beaker, 7 In.	2.50
Bottle, Apothecary, Blown Glass, Stopper, Amethyst	10.00
Bottle, Apothecary, Blue, Teardrop Stopper, Mounted As Lamp, Pair	60.00
Bottle, Apothecary, Calzpreac, Ground Stopper, Glass Label, Quart	5.50
Bottle, Apothecary, Cobalt Blue	3.50
Bottle, Apothecary, Cobalt Blue, Three-Piece Mold, Stopper	22.50
Bottle, Apothecary, E.S.Reeds Sons, Milk Glass, Atlantic City, Paper Label	15.00
Bottle, Apothecary, Emil Cermak Pharmacist, Omaha, 4 Oz.	1.25
Bottle, Apothecary, Etched Flamingo Habitat, Round, Pint	25.00
Bottle, Apothecary, Ground Glass Stopper, 8 In.	2.50
Bottle, Apothecary, Painted Episcopal Crest, White Crackle Glaze, 4	50.00
Bottle, Apothecary, South Carolina Dispensary, Clear	22.50
Bottle, Apothecary, South Carolina Dispensary, Pint, Monogram Scd	14.50
Bottle, Apothecary, Statue Of Liberty, Clear, Paneled, 12 1/2 In.High	125.00
Bottle, Apothecary, W.B.Jerons, Chemist Market, Rasen, 8 In.	3.00
Bottle, Avon, Alpine Flask, Full & Boxed	45.00
Bottle, Avon, Apothecary Soap Jar, 1965, Full & Boxed	12.50
Bottle, Avon, Apple, Amber	14.00
Bottle, Avon, Apple, Frosted	10.00
Bottle, Avon, Apple, Gold	8.00
Bottle, Avon, Apple, Red	12.00
Bottle, Avon, Barber Bottle, 1963	14.00
Bottle, Avon, Barometer	5.50
Bottle, Avon, Bay Rum After Shave Lotion, 1964	5.00
Bottle, Avon, Bay Rum Jug, 1962	4.50 To 9.00
Bottle, Avon, Bay Rum Keg, 1965	8.50 To 12.50
Bottle, Avon, Blue Blazer After Shave, 1963	6.00 To 16.00
Bottle, Avon, Boot, Amber, Gold Top, 1965 .... *Illus*	3.95
Bottle, Avon, Boot, Gold Top, Label	4.95
Bottle, Avon, Boot, Silver Top	6.00
Bottle, Avon, Boot, Silver Top, Label	4.95
Bottle, Avon, Bowl, Wassail	8.00
Bottle, Avon, Boxing Gloves, 1960, Pair	9.95
Bottle, Avon, Brilliantine, 1936	17.95
Bottle, Avon, Buffalo Nickel	3.00
Bottle, Avon, Caddy, Wood Carved	9.95
Bottle, Avon, Candle, Amber, 1965	1.00
Bottle, Avon, Candlestick, Silver	18.00
Bottle, Avon, Cannon, Label	11.95
Bottle, Avon, Cannon, 1966	11.50
Bottle, Avon, Captain's Choice, Label	8.95
Bottle, Avon, Captain's Choice, 1964	5.00

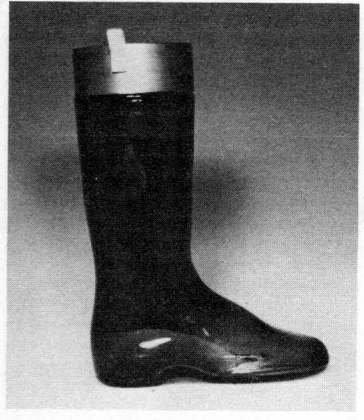

Bottle, Avon, Boot, Amber, Gold Top, 1965
See Page 29

Bottle, Avon, Car, Sterling 6, Label	6.95
Bottle, Avon, Car, Straight 8, Label	6.95
Bottle, Avon, Christmas Award, 1964	30.00
Bottle, Avon, Christmas Tree, Green, Label	3.95
Bottle, Avon, Christmas Tree, Red, Label	3.95
Bottle, Avon, Christmas, First	18.00
Bottle, Avon, Classic Book, Amber, 1969	6.50
Bottle, Avon, Classic Car, Amber	5.00
Bottle, Avon, Clock, Clear	5.00
Bottle, Avon, Cobalt Warrior	15.00
Bottle, Avon, Cotillion Cream Lotion	5.00
Bottle, Avon, Cotillion Powder Box, 1954	6.00
Bottle, Avon, Cotillion Talc, 1957	4.00
Bottle, Avon, Cotillion, Cologne, 2 Oz., 1968	2.00
Bottle, Avon, Cotillion, Cologne, 4 Oz.1957	5.00
Bottle, Avon, Cotillion, Toilet Water, 1957	4.00
Bottle, Avon, Crystal Cologne, Label	5.95
Bottle, Avon, Crystal Glory	12.00
Bottle, Avon, Danish Modern	3.00
Bottle, Avon, Daphne Talcum, 1936, Cpc & Avon, Full	10.50
Bottle, Avon, Decisions	18.00
Bottle, Avon, Decisions, 1965	14.50
Bottle, Avon, Deodorant For Men, 1951, 2 Oz.	2.25
Bottle, Avon, Dollars & Scents	17.95
Bottle, Avon, Dollars & Scents, Label	21.95
Bottle, Avon, Dolphin, Label	4.00
Bottle, Avon, Duck, Label	6.95
Bottle, Avon, Duck, 1967	5.00
Bottle, Avon, Dueling Pistol, Red	25.00
Bottle, Avon, First Class Male	2.00
Bottle, Avon, First Down	2.00
Bottle, Avon, First Edition, Label	7.50
Bottle, Avon, Floral Medley	4.00
Bottle, Avon, Forever Spring Cologne, 1950	8.50
Bottle, Avon, Fragrance Jar, Frosted	22.50
Bottle, Avon, Frosted Vigorate, 1960	8.95
Bottle, Avon, Futura	12.00 To 18.00
Bottle, Avon, Gavel, 1967, Full & Boxed	11.00
Bottle, Avon, Gentlemen's Collection, 1968	11.95
Bottle, Avon, Gold Apple, Label	5.95
Bottle, Avon, It's A Blast	5.00
Bottle, Avon, Just Two, Tags & Labels	49.50
Bottle, Avon, Keynote, Label	7.50
Bottle, Avon, Lady Slipper	10.00

Bottle, Avon, Lavender Sachet, Label	7.50
Bottle, Avon, Lincoln Decanter	3.00
Bottle, Avon, Lotion Lovely, Full & Boxed	8.95
Bottle, Avon, Mallard	10.00
Bottle, Avon, Man's World	5.00
Bottle, Avon, Marionette Sachet, 1 1/4 Oz., 1936	16.50
Bottle, Avon, Nesting Dove	7.00
Bottle, Avon, Perfume Jewel Pin, 1965	5.99
Bottle, Avon, Perfumed Deodorant, 1943, Montreal Label	3.50
Bottle, Avon, Persian Wood Beauty Dust, Glass, Label	9.50
Bottle, Avon, Petti Point	10.00
Bottle, Avon, Pipe Dream, 1967	10.50 To 12.95
Bottle, Avon, Pony Post, Short, Label	3.50
Bottle, Avon, Pony Post, Tall, Label	6.50
Bottle, Avon, Pot Belly Stove	3.00
Bottle, Avon, Red Lantern, 1966	5.00
Bottle, Avon, Red Lantern, 1966, Handle	10.00
Bottle, Avon, Rose Fragrance Jar, 1952, Frosted Stopper	17.50
Bottle, Avon, Rosewater, Glycerine, Benzoin, 1936	11.95
Bottle, Avon, Royal Orb, Full & Boxed	22.50
Bottle, Avon, Ship In Bottle, 1970, Full & Boxed	4.00
Bottle, Avon, Silver Dollar	3.00
Bottle, Avon, Small Pony Decanter	4.00
Bottle, Avon, Snail, Boxed, Label	6.95
Bottle, Avon, Sonnet Toilet Water	12.95
Bottle, Avon, Spicy After Shave, 1965	4.00
Bottle, Avon, Spiral Cologne, Label	4.95
Bottle, Avon, Steer Horns, Label	13.95
Bottle, Avon, Steer Horns, 1967	13.50
Bottle, Avon, Stein, 6 Oz., Label	5.95
Bottle, Avon, Stein, 6 Oz., Silver, 1968 *Illus*	4.00
Bottle, Avon, Stein, 8 Oz.	6.95 To 7.50
Bottle, Avon, Stein, 8 Oz., 1965	6.00
Bottle, Avon, Sterling Six, Full & Boxed	3.50
Bottle, Avon, Structured For Man	12.00
Bottle, Avon, Swinger	4.00
Bottle, Avon, Tall Pony Decanter	5.00
Bottle, Avon, Telephone	5.00
Bottle, Avon, Telephone, 1969, Full & Boxed	6.00
Bottle, Avon, Three Hearts On Glass Tray, Label	13.95
Bottle, Avon, Topaze Cream Lotion, Label	2.50
Bottle, Avon, Touring Tee	4.00
Bottle, Avon, Town Pump	4.00
Bottle, Avon, Tribute After Shave, 1963	4.00

Bottle, Avon, Stein, 6 Oz., Silver, 1968

Bottle, Avon, Trilogy	8.00
Bottle, Avon, Tub Talk	3.50
Bottle, Avon, Vase, Bud, Ruby	3.50
Bottle, Avon, Viking Horn	8.00
Bottle, Avon, Viking Horn, Label	10.95
Bottle, Avon, Volkswagen, Full & Boxed	2.50
Bottle, Avon, Warrior, Frosted, Label	4.75
Bottle, Avon, Washington Decanter	3.00
Bottle, Avon, Weather Or Not	5.00
Bottle, Avon, Windjammer, Painted Label	6.50
Bottle, Avon, Wise Choice	5.00
Bottle, Avon, World's Greatest Dad	2.00
Bottle, Avon, 4-A	14.00
Bottle, Avon, 4-A, Mirror Top, Full & Boxed	19.95
Bottle, Balloon, Captive, Dated 1878, Case	40.00
Bottle, Bar, Back, Fluted, Quart, Emerald Green	35.00
Bottle, Bar, Douglas Club, Decanter, Fifth	32.00
Bottle, Bar, Grapes, Leaves, Pewter Overlay & Stopper, Green	22.50
Bottle, Bar, Pressed Glass, Smocking, Quart	45.00
Bottle, Barber, Bay Rum, Label	11.50
Bottle, Barber, Cobalt Blue, Enamel Floral	40.00
Bottle, Barber, Cranberry With Opalescent Hobnails	38.00
Bottle, Barber, Embossed Flowers, Stopper	25.00
Bottle, Barber, Green, Melon Ribbed, Cobalt Blue Enamel	35.00
Bottle, Barber, Hand Blown, Applied Lip, Pair	125.00
Bottle, Barber, Hobnail, Cranberry	65.00
Bottle, Barber, Midmill Scene, Purple, White	48.50
Bottle, Barber, N.Wampler, Eight Sided	16.00
Bottle, Barber, Porcelain, Stoppers, 9 3/4 In.Tall, Set Of 4	9.75
Bottle, Barber, Purple, Painted, Vegederma	55.00
Bottle, Barber, Water, Clambroth	17.50
Bottle, Barrel, Chapin & Gore, Sour Mash 1867	39.00

*Beam Bottles are made to hold Kentucky Straight Bourbon made by the
James B. Beam Distilling Company. The Beam series of ceramic
bottles began in 1953.*

Bottle, Beam, Alaska Star, Original Issue	84.95
Bottle, Beam, Antioch	9.50
Bottle, Beam, Arizona	6.95
Bottle, Beam, Baseball	16.00
Bottle, Beam, Bell Ringer, Plaid	8.95
Bottle, Beam, Bell, Scotch	8.95
Bottle, Beam, Bing Crosby, 30th Anniversary	16.00
Bottle, Beam, Binion's Horseshoe	11.50 To 12.95
Bottle, Beam, Blackhills	16.00
Bottle, Beam, Blue Jay	8.95
Bottle, Beam, Buffalo Bill	8.95
Bottle, Beam, Cable Car	2.50
Bottle, Beam, California Derby, In Bag	24.95
Bottle, Beam, California Mission	24.95
Bottle, Beam, Cameo, Blue	4.95
Bottle, Beam, Cannon	2.95 To 4.50
Bottle, Beam, Cardinal	39.95
Bottle, Beam, Cat, Tabby	10.95
Bottle, Beam, Centennial, Alaska Purchase	19.95
Bottle, Beam, Centennial, Armanetti Vase	8.95
Bottle, Beam, Centennial, Armanetti, Bacchus	19.95
Bottle, Beam, Centennial, Armanetti, 1st Award	14.95
Bottle, Beam, Centennial, Ashtray, Ivory	24.95
Bottle, Beam, Centennial, Cheyenne	12.95
Bottle, Beam, Centennial, China Jug, Turquoise	6.95
Bottle, Beam, Centennial, Churchill Downs, 19th, Pink	4.95
Bottle, Beam, Centennial, Churchill Downs, 95th, Red	8.95
Bottle, Beam, Centennial, Churchill Downs, 96th, Red	8.95
Bottle, Beam, Centennial, Churchill Downs, 96th, Red, Double Rose Stopper	14.95
Bottle, Beam, Centennial, Churchill Downs, 97th	8.95

Bottle, Beam, Centennial, Civil War, North 37.50
Bottle, Beam, Centennial, Civil War, South 39.95
Bottle, Beam, Centennial, Harold's Club, VIP, 1967 .... 59.95
Bottle, Beam, Centennial, Harold's Club, VIP, 1968 .... 64.95
Bottle, Beam, Centennial, Harold's Club, VIP, 1970 .... 74.95
Bottle, Beam, Centennial, Hemisfair 12.95
Bottle, Beam, Centennial, Katz Cat, Black 8.95
Bottle, Beam, Centennial, Katz Cat, Yellow 27.50
Bottle, Beam, Centennial, Marina City 44.95
Bottle, Beam, Centennial, New York World's Fair 24.95
Bottle, Beam, Centennial, Ponderosa 6.95
Bottle, Beam, Centennial, Portula Trek 2.50
Bottle, Beam, Centennial, Richard's New Mexico 8.95
Bottle, Beam, Centennial, Santa Fe 225.00
Bottle, Beam, Centennial, St.Louis Arch 22.50
Bottle, Beam, Centennial, Yosemite 7.95
Bottle, Beam, Centennial, Yuma Rifle 37.50
Bottle, Beam, Cherub, Salmon 8.00
Bottle, Beam, Coffee Warmer, 1954 .... 14.95
Bottle, Beam, Coffee Warmer, 1956, Black Handle 3.95
Bottle, Beam, Coffee Warmer, 1956, Gold Handle 3.95
Bottle, Beam, Collector's Volume I 30.00
Bottle, Beam, Collector's Volume II 30.00
Bottle, Beam, Colorado 45.00
Bottle, Beam, Convention Bottle 16.50
Bottle, Beam, Dancing Scot, Tall .... 6.00 To 7.95
Bottle, Beam, Delft, Blue 3.95
Bottle, Beam, Denver 16.95
Bottle, Beam, Doe 34.95
Bottle, Beam, Doe, 1963 .... 37.50
Bottle, Beam, Doe, 1967 .... 33.00
Bottle, Beam, Dog .... 60.00 To 69.95
Bottle, Beam, Donkey 16.00
Bottle, Beam, Duck 37.50
Bottle, Beam, Eagle .... 14.50 To 15.95
Bottle, Beam, Emerald Crystal 4.95
Bottle, Beam, Executive, 1955 .... 225.00
Bottle, Beam, Executive, 1956 .... 137.50
Bottle, Beam, Executive, 1957 .... 62.50
Bottle, Beam, Executive, 1958 .... 155.00
Bottle, Beam, Executive, 1959 .... 62.50
Bottle, Beam, Executive, 1961 .... 65.00
Bottle, Beam, Executive, 1962 .... 47.50
Bottle, Beam, Executive, 1963 .... 50.00
Bottle, Beam, Executive, 1964 .... 45.00 To 49.00
Bottle, Beam, Executive, 1965 .... 65.00
Bottle, Beam, Executive, 1966 .... 37.50
Bottle, Beam, Executive, 1967 .... 19.75
Bottle, Beam, Executive, 1968 .... 9.95
Bottle, Beam, Executive, 1969 .... 7.95
Bottle, Beam, Executive, 1970, Case .... 15.00 To 30.00
Bottle, Beam, Fish, 1965 .... 20.00 To 36.50
Bottle, Beam, Florida Shell .... 6.95 To 16.00
Bottle, Beam, Flower Basket, 1962 .... 47.00
Bottle, Beam, Fox, Blue Coat 145.00
Bottle, Beam, Fox, Gold 80.00
Bottle, Beam, Fox, Green .... 25.00 To 48.00
Bottle, Beam, Fox, Orange Coat 85.00
Bottle, Beam, Fox, White Coat .... 43.00 To 47.50
Bottle, Beam, Franklin Mint 16.00
Bottle, Beam, Genie 4.95
Bottle, Beam, Germany .... 5.95 To 16.00
Bottle, Beam, Golden Chalice, 1961 .... 50.00 To 65.00
Bottle, Beam, Golden Gate, 1970 .... 11.50 To 12.95
Bottle, Beam, Goose, Blue 20.00
Bottle, Beam, Grecian .... 4.95 To 6.50

Bottle, Beam, Harold's Club Covered Wagon .... 17.50 To 20.00
Bottle, Beam, Harold's Club, Silver 175.00
Bottle, Beam, Harold's Club, Vip, 1967 .... 65.00
Bottle, Beam, Harold's Club, Vip, 1968 .... 69.00
Bottle, Beam, Harold's Club, Vip, 1970 .... 75.00
Bottle, Beam, Harvey's, In Bag 14.95
Bottle, Beam, Hawaii, Original Issue 72.50
Bottle, Beam, Hawaii, Reissue 49.95
Bottle, Beam, Hemisfair, Regal China, 1968 .... *Illus* 17.50
Bottle, Beam, Honorary Kentucky Colonel 16.00
Bottle, Beam, Horse 22.50
Bottle, Beam, Humboldt County Fair, In Bag 19.95
Bottle, Beam, Idaho 69.95
Bottle, Beam, Illinois 8.95
Bottle, Beam, Indiana 16.00
Bottle, Beam, Indianapolis Centennial, Blue & Gold 8.50
Bottle, Beam, International Pet 8.95
Bottle, Beam, Jackalope .... 7.95 To 8.95
Bottle, Beam, Kansas State .... 50.00 To 75.00
Bottle, Beam, Katz Kat, Black 11.50
Bottle, Beam, Katz Kat, Yellow 25.00
Bottle, Beam, Kentucky Colonel 7.95
Bottle, Beam, Kentucky Derby, Black Head 12.95
Bottle, Beam, Lilac .... 3.95 To 5.95
Bottle, Beam, Maine 8.95
Bottle, Beam, Majestic, 1966, Case 38.00
Bottle, Beam, Man On Horse, De Keyser 4.00
Bottle, Beam, Marbled Fantasy, 1965 .... 68.00
Bottle, Beam, Marina City 45.00
Bottle, Beam, Mark Antony 20.00
Bottle, Beam, Mint 400, Metal Car Stopper 8.95
Bottle, Beam, Mint 400, Motorcycle Top 12.95
Bottle, Beam, Mission Club 29.00
Bottle, Beam, Montana .... 89.00 To 95.00
Bottle, Beam, Mt.Rushmore .... *Illus* 9.00
Bottle, Beam, Musician On Wine Cask 11.95
Bottle, Beam, National Convention 12.95

Bottle, Beam, Hemisfair, Regal China, 1968

Bottle, Beam, Mt.Rushmore

Bottle, Beam, Nevada 69.95
Bottle, Beam, New Jersey, Gold .... 40.00 To 65.00
Bottle, Beam, New Jersey, Gray 85.00
Bottle, Beam, North Dakota 85.00
Bottle, Beam, Oatmeal 45.00
Bottle, Beam, Ohio .... 12.00 To 12.95
Bottle, Beam, Olympian .... 4.95 To 6.50
Bottle, Beam, Oregon 45.00
Bottle, Beam, Paul Bunyan .... 7.95 To 16.00
Bottle, Beam, Pga 16.00
Bottle, Beam, Pheasant, Reissue 15.00
Bottle, Beam, Pheasant, 1961 .... 20.00
Bottle, Beam, Pin Bottle, Pint, Wood Stopper 4.95
Bottle, Beam, Pin Bottle, 1/5, Wood Stopper 10.95
Bottle, Beam, Political, 1956 .... 14.50
Bottle, Beam, Political, 1960 .... 14.50
Bottle, Beam, Political, 1964 .... 14.50
Bottle, Beam, Ponderosa 25.00
Bottle, Beam, Poodle 8.95
Bottle, Beam, Preakness 16.00
Bottle, Beam, Rabbit 16.00
Bottle, Beam, Ram 112.00
Bottle, Beam, Reno 5.95
Bottle, Beam, Riverside Centennial 19.95
Bottle, Beam, Robin 8.95
Bottle, Beam, Rocky Mountain Club, Denver .... 20.00 To 29.00
Bottle, Beam, Royal Crystal 5.95
Bottle, Beam, Royal Dimonte, 1957 .... 67.00
Bottle, Beam, Royal Emperor 5.95
Bottle, Beam, Royal Opal 6.50
Bottle, Beam, St.Louis Arch 20.00
Bottle, Beam, Scotch, Clear, 1966 .... 8.95
Bottle, Beam, Shriners .... 5.95 To 7.95
Bottle, Beam, Slot, Gray 6.50
Bottle, Beam, Smoked Crystal 6.50
Bottle, Beam, South Carolina 8.95
Bottle, Beam, Telephone 11.50
Bottle, Beam, Texas Rabbit .... 8.00 To 10.00
Bottle, Beam, Thailand 5.00
Bottle, Beam, Tombstone 7.95
Bottle, Beam, Uncle Sam Fox .... 17.95 To 18.50
Bottle, Beam, Village Of Lombard, Ill. 12.50
Bottle, Beam, West Virginia Centennial .... 135.00 To 150.00
Bottle, Beam, Western Golf Tournament .... 7.95 To 9.00
Bottle, Beam, Woodpecker 8.95
Bottle, Beam, Wyoming .... 65.00 To 75.00
Bottle, Beam, Zimmerman 'z' Bottle 14.00
Bottle, Beam, Zimmerman, Blue Daisy 7.95
Bottle, Beer, A.B.G.M. Co., Cobalt 33.50
Bottle, Beer, A.H.Smith & Co., Ltd., Don Brewery, Sheffield, 8 In. 3.00
Bottle, Beer, Acme, Miniature, San Francisco, Calif., Pair 4.00
Bottle, Beer, Arnas, 3 Mold, Whittled, Double Applied Lip, Honey Amber ... 3.50
Bottle, Beer, C.Conrad Co., Embossed Patent No.6376, 9 3/4 In. 10.00
Bottle, Beer, English, Screw In Stopper, Embossed 5.00
Bottle, Beer, German, Wire Harness, Porcelain Top, Amber 1.75
Bottle, Beer, Goebel's Old Stag, Stone, Embossed Barley Vines, Tan & Brown ... 19.00
Bottle, Beer, Hanley, Lawton, & Crews, Youngs Botanic Brewery, Ltd., 7 In. 3.00
Bottle, Beer, L.G.Co., Bubbly, Applied Lip & Ring, 9 3/4 In., Blue 3.00
Bottle, Beer, Liquid Bread, Cobalt Blue, Circa 1885 .... 35.00
Bottle, Beer, Melchers, Detroit, Pint 2.00
Bottle, Beer, Milk Glass, 6 In. 4.00
Bottle, Beer, Minster Brewery, Ohio, Regular 1.75
Bottle, Beer, Minster Brewery, Ohio, Tall 2.25
Bottle, Beer, Paul Polh, Chicago, Ill., Pony, Square Blob, Honey Amber ... 10.00
Bottle, Beer, Royal Ruby Bottom, Ruby Red Top 8.00
Bottle, Beer, Royal Ruby Red, Quart 7.50

Bottle, Beer, Royal Ruby, Thin Neck, Long 25.00
Bottle, Beer, Royal Ruby, 12 Oz., Nonreturnable 22.00
Bottle, Beer, Schemm Brewing, Saginaw, Mich., Quart 2.25
Bottle, Beer, Schlitz, Royal Ruby, Label, 7 Oz. 18.00
Bottle, Beer, Schwartzenbach Brewing Co. 2.50
Bottle, Beer, Stoneware, Brown, 10 In. 7.50
Bottle, Bitters, Angostura Bark, Eagle 55.00
Bottle, Bitters, Atwood's, Five Star, Watson No.15, Aqua, 6 3/4 In.Tall 20.00
Bottle, Bitters, Atwood's Genuine, Aqua, 99 Percent Label 12.00
Bottle, Bitters, Atwood's, Sample 10.00
Bottle, Bitters, Baker's Orange Grove, Amber 98.50
Bottle, Bitters, Baxter's Mandrake, Label, Aqua 15.00
Bottle, Bitters, Bitterquelle, Dark Green 5.00
Bottle, Bitters, Bitterquelle, 90 Percent Label 6.50
Bottle, Bitters, Browns Iron 22.00
Bottle, Bitters, Burdock, Aqua 16.00
Bottle, Bitters, Carpathian Herb, Amber, Square, 9 In. 50.00
Bottle, Bitters, Carter's Atwood's Bitters, Aqua 7.00
Bottle, Bitters, Damiana, Aqua 45.00
Bottle, Bitters, Doyle's Hop, Amber .... 25.00 To 35.00
Bottle, Bitters, Doyle's Hop, Yellow Amber 23.00
Bottle, Bitters, Dr.Baxter's Mandrake, 12 Sided, Clear 8.00
Bottle, Bitters, Dr.Fisch's, Amber .... 165.00 To 175.00
Bottle, Bitters, Dr.Gould's, Label 15.00
Bottle, Bitters, Dr.Henleys, Wild Grape, Aqua 50.00
Bottle, Bitters, Dr.Hoofland's, German, Aqua, 8 In.Tall 22.50
Bottle, Bitters, Dr.J.G.B.Siegert & Hijas, 3 Mold, Whittled, Green 5.00
Bottle, Bitters, Dr.J.Hostetter's Stomach, Amber 17.50
Bottle, Bitters, Dr.Job Sweets, Aqua, Label 55.00
Bottle, Bitters, Dr.Miles Restorative Tonic 8.00
Bottle, Bitters, Dr.Pierce's, Dated 1908 .... 18.50
Bottle, Bitters, Dr.R.F.Hibbard, Wild Cherry, Round, Aqua, 7 In.Tall 60.00
Bottle, Bitters, Dr.Siegert's, 3 Piece Mold, Embossed, Olive Green 5.00
Bottle, Bitters, Dr.Von Hopf's Curacao, Chamberlain Co., Amber 65.00
Bottle, Bitters, Drake's Plantation, 4 Log, Amber .... 32.00 To 42.00
Bottle, Bitters, Drake's Plantation, 6 Log, Light Amber 37.00
Bottle, Bitters, Drake's Plantation, 6 Log, Amber .... 38.00 To 40.00
Bottle, Bitters, Duffy's, Baltimore, Md., Crude, Yellow Amber 10.00
Bottle, Bitters, E.Baker's Premium, Clear 40.00
Bottle, Bitters, E.E.Hall's, Barrel, Amber 95.00
Bottle, Bitters, Electric Brand, Amber 16.00
Bottle, Bitters, Figural, Lady's Leg, Schroeder's 190.00
Bottle, Bitters, Globe Tonic, Amber 60.00
Bottle, Bitters, Goff's Herb 8.00
Bottle, Bitters, Greeley's Bourbon, Barrel, Puce 100.00
Bottle, Bitters, H.Lakes Indian Specific, Open Pontil 65.00
Bottle, Bitters, Hall's, Barrel, Amber 95.00
Bottle, Bitters, Hartwig Kantorowicz, Embossed Fish In Star, Amber 225.00
Bottle, Bitters, Herb, Aqua 14.00
Bottle, Bitters, Horn Of Plenty, H.E.Swan, 7 In.High 26.66
Bottle, Bitters, Horn Of Plenty, H.E.Swan, 11 In.High 45.00
Bottle, Bitters, Hostetter, Amber 8.00
Bottle, Bitters, Hostetter's, Crude, C.1868, Citron Yellow 20.00
Bottle, Bitters, Hostetter's, Crude, Green 65.00
Bottle, Bitters, Hostetter's Stomach Bitters, Amber, Label 17.00
Bottle, Bitters, Keg Shape, Brass Spout & Knob, Deep Green 45.00
Bottle, Bitters, Kilmer's Swamp Root 3.00
Bottle, Bitters, L.F.Atwood's, Aqua, 99 Percent Label 12.00
Bottle, Bitters, Langley's, Aqua 25.00
Bottle, Bitters, Litthauer Stomach, Milk Glass 75.00
Bottle, Bitters, Mishler's, Amber 50.00
Bottle, Bitters, Mishler's, Yellow Amber 30.00
Bottle, Bitters, Morning Call Bitters 150.00
Bottle, Bitters, Morning Star, Amber 160.00
Bottle, Bitters, Old Sachem Bitters & Wigwam Tonic, Amber 110.00
Bottle, Bitters, Phoenix, Olive Green 135.00

Bottle, Bitters, Phoenix, Open Pontil 40.00
Bottle, Bitters, Pierce's Indian Restorative, 9 In., Aqua 28.75
Bottle, Bitters, Polo Club, Amber 85.00
Bottle, Bitters, Poorman's 20.00
Bottle, Bitters, Quaker, Embossed, Aqua 22.50
Bottle, Bitters, Russ St.Domingo, Amber 55.00
Bottle, Bitters, S.B.Goff's, Herb Camden, New Jersey, Aqua, 5 3/4 In.Tall 10.00
Bottle, Bitters, S.O.Richardson, Aqua, Plain Base 20.50
Bottle, Bitters, Sanborn's Kidney & Liver Vegetable Laxative, 10 In. 70.00
Bottle, Bitters, Sockalexic Indian Blood Elixir 20.00
Bottle, Bitters, Spiller's Golden Balsam 5.50
Bottle, Bitters, Stephen Jewett's, Aqua 75.00
Bottle, Bitters, Stewart's, Paper Label 35.00
Bottle, Bitters, The Fish, Amber 100.00
Bottle, Bitters, Tippecanoe, Amber 60.00
Bottle, Bitters, Union, E.Wormer's & Co., Pittsburgh, Pa., Quart 45.00
Bottle, Bitters, Wahoo & Calisaya, Amber 150.00
Bottle, Blob Top, Bridgeton Glass Works, N.H., Graphite Pontil, Green 20.00
Bottle, Blob Top, Embossed Whyte & Mackay, Glasgow 15.00
Bottle, Blown, Black Glass 30.00
Bottle, Blown, Chestnut, Aquamarine, Fold-Down Lip, 12 In.Tall 55.00
Bottle, Blown, Chestnut, New England, Olive Green, Open Pontil, 12 In.Tall 60.00
Bottle, Blown, Pontil, Olive Amber 30.00
Bottle, Blown, Silver Vintage Top & Gin Stopper, Amber 17.50
Bottle, Blown, 7 1/2 In. Long .... *Illus* 70.00

Bottle, Blown, 7 1/2 In. Long

Bottle, Bugine, Iron City Chemical Co., Applied Lip, Clear 4.00
Bottle, Carafe, Wine, Blue, Pewter Top & Handle, 12 In. Tall 65.00
Bottle, Case Gin, Taper, Quart, Green 10.00
Bottle, Case Gin, V.Hoytema & Co., Black Glass 18.00
Bottle, Chemical, Ammonium Hydroxide, Nh-40h 4.00
Bottle, Chemical, Con Acid Hydrochloric, Glass Stopper 5.00
Bottle, Chemical, Dioviburnia Dios Chemical Co., Label 5.00
Bottle, Chemical, Dioxogen, The Oakland Chemical Co., Amber 4.00
Bottle, Chemical, Keasbey & Mattison Co., Chemists, Ambler, Pa., Light Blue 5.00
Bottle, Chemical, Spt Ammon Arom, Glass Stopper 5.00
Bottle, Chemical, W.B.Jerons, Chemist Market, Rasen, 8 In. 3.00
Bottle, Clear, Amber Stopper, Basket Weave, 10 In.Long 15.00
Bottle, Clear, C.1900-1910, Stopper 1.25
Bottle, Clear, 15 Ribs, Swirl, Blown Pontil, Flared Top, 5 1/2 In.High 32.00
Bottle, Clinton Bottling Company, Marked, 6 Oz., Dated 1944-49 .... 1.25
Bottle, Cobalt Blue, Bubbly, Wavy, 7 1/2 In. 6.00
    Bottle, Coca-Cola, see Cola-Cola
Bottle, Coca Mariana, Paris, Green 6.00
Bottle, Codd, American, Marble Stopper 7.50
Bottle, Codd, Constricted Neck, Marble Stopper 6.00
Bottle, Codd, E.P.Shaw & Co., Wakefield, Hound Trademark, Marble In Neck 5.00
Bottle, Codd, Embossed C.N.Ballinger, Monmouth, Marble Stopper, Bimal 4.95
Bottle, Codd, Glass Ball Stopper, Aqua Green 6.50
Bottle, Codd, Marble Inside, 5 1/2 Oz., Sample, 12 .... 5.00

Bottle, Codd, Soda Water, Sunken & Pinched Neck, Aqua 6.00
Bottle, Cognac, Applied Scroll, Fleur-De-Lis, Signed Baccarat, Clear 28.00
Bottle, Cologne, Crystal With Sterling Silver Overlay, Ground Pontil, 3 In. 12.00
Bottle, Cologne, Dresden Type, Embossed & Enameled Flowers, Stopper, 7 In. 15.00
Bottle, Cologne, Green, Silver Overlay, Marked Alvin Co., 3 In. 22.00
Bottle, Cologne, Scrolls, Pear Shape, Gold, Ruby, Stopper, 9 In.Tall 25.00
Bottle, Cologne, Wheat Design, Copperwheel Cut, Stopper, 5 In.Tall 18.00
Bottle, Cosmetic, Ayer's Hair Vigor, Peacock Blue, Stopper 20.00
Bottle, Cosmetic, Hall's Hair Renewer, Cobalt, Embossed, Paper Label, Stopper 20.00
Bottle, Cosmetic, Jar, Cherry Toothpaste, Lid, Woman & Lion, C.1840 .... 21.00
Bottle, Cosmetic, Richard Hudnut, Emerald Green, Preston, N.H. 5.00
Bottle, Cosmetic, Rubifoam For The Teeth, Embossed, Sample, Label, Clear 2.50
Bottle, Cosmetic, Shaw's Dressing For Hair & Face, Glass Label 17.50
Bottle, Crockery, Finger Painted, Squat, 9 In. 7.50
Bottle, Crockery, Finger Painted, 10 In. 12.50
Bottle, Crockery, Finger Painted, 11 In. 12.50
Bottle, Dant, Alamo .... *Illus* 7.75

Bottle, Dant, Alamo

Bottle, Decanter, Blown In Mold, Ring Neck, Clear 25.00
Bottle, Decanter, Clear Glass, 13 In.High 40.00
Bottle, Decanter, Cut Glass, Stopper, Clear 15.00
Bottle, Decanter, Deep Blue Cut To Clear, 14 In. 65.00
Bottle, Decanter, Grapes, Vines, Bulbous, Mushroom Stopper, 7 In.Tall 35.00
Bottle, Decanter, Green, Ribbed Body, Clear Cut Stopper 26.00
Bottle, Decanter, Green, Square, Applied Collar, Cut Corners, 9 1/2 In. Tall 6.00
Bottle, Decanter, Impressed Star Pattern, 13 1/2 In.High 17.50
Bottle, Decanter, Lily Of The Valley, Pewter Rim, Green, Enamel 65.00
Bottle, Decanter, Pillar Mold 6.25
Bottle, Decanter, Ribbed Green Glass, Bellflower, Decorated, Stopper 50.00
Bottle, Decanter, Stork, Etched, Blown, Circa 1880 .... 25.00
Bottle, Decanter, Three Applied Rings, Polished Pontil, Blown, Flint 28.50
Bottle, Decanter, Victorian, 8 In.High, Pair 60.00
Bottle, Decanter, Waffle Pattern, Pint, No Stopper 10.00
Bottle, Decanter, Wine, Amethyst, Crystal Stopper 37.50
Bottle, Decanter, Wine, Green Glass, Silver Overlay, Pair 25.00
Bottle, Decanter, Wine, Green Ovoid, Enamel Lily-Of-The-Valley, Clear Stopper 50.00
Bottle, Demijohn, Cobalt Blue, Applied Top, 15 In.Tall 150.00
Bottle, Dresser, Block & Sawtooth, Cut Stopper 10.00
Bottle, Dresser, Cut Glass, Floral, Leaves, Bird Stopper, 5 1/2 In.Tall 27.50
Bottle, Dresser, Ribbon & Bow Design, White, Gold, Mushroom Stopper, 10 In. 45.00
Bottle, Enamel Decor, Medallion, Birds, Signed Damon & Deleute-Paris, Pair 45.00
Bottle, Encased In Repousse Silver, Engraved Decor, Stopper, Sinclaire 325.00
Bottle, Error, Mason's Patent, Nov.30th, 1858, Backward S In Mason, Amber 8.00
Bottle, Error, Try Me Rock, Tarde Mark Registered, Pint, Green 10.00

Bottle, Ezra Brooks, Antique Cannon 7.00
Bottle, Ezra Brooks, Antique Slot Machine 19.95
Bottle, Ezra Brooks, Arizona .... 8.00 To 8.50
Bottle, Ezra Brooks, Big Bertha 22.50
Bottle, Ezra Brooks, Big Daddy 14.50
Bottle, Ezra Brooks, Big Red 35.00
Bottle, Ezra Brooks, Bird Dog .... 12.45 To 12.95
Bottle, Ezra Brooks, Border Town Fun 14.95
Bottle, Ezra Brooks, Bucket Of Blood .... 18.00 To 25.00
Bottle, Ezra Brooks, Buffalo Hunt .... 19.95 To 20.95
Bottle, Ezra Brooks, Cable Car 4.95
Bottle, Ezra Brooks, California Quail 8.00
Bottle, Ezra Brooks, Ceremonial Indian .... 22.00 To 24.00
Bottle, Ezra Brooks, Cheyenne Frontier Days 18.00
Bottle, Ezra Brooks, Distillery Club Bottle 55.00
Bottle, Ezra Brooks, Dueling Pistol 8.00
Bottle, Ezra Brooks, Dueling Pistol, Japan 90.00
Bottle, Ezra Brooks, Duesenberg 12.00
Bottle, Ezra Brooks, Eagle 24.95
Bottle, Ezra Brooks, Fire Engine .... 10.95 To 12.95
Bottle, Ezra Brooks, Fordson Tractor 16.25
Bottle, Ezra Brooks, Foremost Astronaut 13.50
Bottle, Ezra Brooks, Fresno Grape .... 22.00 To 24.00
Bottle, Ezra Brooks, Gold Prospector .... 8.00 To 10.50
Bottle, Ezra Brooks, Golden Eagle .... 24.95 To 30.00
Bottle, Ezra Brooks, Golden Horseshoe .... 30.00 To 45.00
Bottle, Ezra Brooks, Golden Rooster, No.1 .... 95.00
Bottle, Ezra Brooks, Golden Rooster, No.2 .... 25.00
Bottle, Ezra Brooks, Hambletonian .... 11.50 To 12.95
Bottle, Ezra Brooks, Indian 4.95
Bottle, Ezra Brooks, Iowa State House .... 14.95 To 16.45
Bottle, Ezra Brooks, Iron Horse Train 9.00
Bottle, Ezra Brooks, Jack Of Diamonds 9.50
Bottle, Ezra Brooks, Kansas Wheatshocker 13.50
Bottle, Ezra Brooks, Katz Philharmonic 12.95
Bottle, Ezra Brooks, King Of Clubs 9.50
Bottle, Ezra Brooks, Lion On Rock .... 11.50 To 12.95
Bottle, Ezra Brooks, Lobster 32.00
Bottle, Ezra Brooks, Maine Lobster .... 32.00 To 35.00
Bottle, Ezra Brooks, Mr.Foremost 22.50
Bottle, Ezra Brooks, New Hampshire Statehouse 22.00
Bottle, Ezra Brooks, Nugget Classic .... 22.50 To 32.50
Bottle, Ezra Brooks, Oil Derrick 10.95
Bottle, Ezra Brooks, Ontario Racer .... 9.50 To 11.50
Bottle, Ezra Brooks, Phoenix Bird 15.00
Bottle, Ezra Brooks, Phonograph .... 11.50 To 13.50
Bottle, Ezra Brooks, Pirate 11.50
Bottle, Ezra Brooks, Pot Belly Stove 10.40
Bottle, Ezra Brooks, Queen Of Hearts 9.50
Bottle, Ezra Brooks, Red Dice 10.50
Bottle, Ezra Brooks, Reno Arch .... 12.95 To 16.00
Bottle, Ezra Brooks, Sailfish 12.45
Bottle, Ezra Brooks, Silver Spur 19.95
Bottle, Ezra Brooks, South Carolina Fighting Cock ... 16.95 To 17.50
Bottle, Ezra Brooks, Sprint Racer 13.00
Bottle, Ezra Brooks, Stage Coach 8.50
Bottle, Ezra Brooks, Telephone 12.45
Bottle, Ezra Brooks, Texas Longhorn .... 24.00 To 28.50
Bottle, Ezra Brooks, Ticker Tape 9.95
Bottle, Ezra Brooks, Trout & Fly 9.95
Bottle, Ezra Brooks, Water Tower 11.50
Bottle, Ezra Brooks, West Virginia Mountaineer 160.00
Bottle, Ezra Brooks, Wheat Shocker .... 14.50 To 16.45
Bottle, Ezra Brooks, White Turkey .... 16.50 To 17.95
Bottle, Ezra Brooks, Winston Churchill 4.95
Bottle, Ezra Brooks, Zimmerman Old Hat 15.95

Bottle, Fernet Branca Milano, Green	5.00
Bottle, Ferro China Bisleri Milano, Bright Green	11.00
Bottle, Ferro China, Light Olive Amber	6.00
Bottle, Figural, Alarm Clock	4.00
Bottle, Figural, American Eagle, Mid-America Wine Co.	12.50
Bottle, Figural, Angelica Globe	19.50
Bottle, Figural, Bear, Black, Amethyst	33.00
Bottle, Figural, Bird, Milk Glass, 8 In.Tall, From Spain	10.00
Bottle, Figural, Bird, Milk Glass, 10 In.Tall, From Spain	12.00
Bottle, Figural, Charlie Chaplin, Ceramic	45.00
Bottle, Figural, Child & Cornucopia, 5 1/2 In.	17.50
Bottle, Figural, Clock, Bininger, Amber	300.00
Bottle, Figural, Cuckoo Clock	23.50
Bottle, Figural, Ear Of Corn, C.1885, 6 1/2 In.	65.00
Bottle, Figural, Ear Of Corn, Ivory, 3 1/2 In.Tall	45.00
Bottle, Figural, El Lorito Parot, 4 In.	20.00
Bottle, Figural, Fortunate Fisherman	17.50
Bottle, Figural, Girl, 3 1/2 In.	10.00
Bottle, Figural, Horse & Horseshoe, Milk Glass, Japan, Red Paint, 3 1/2 In.	7.00
Bottle, Figural, Insulator, Cobalt Blue, 5 In.Tall, Handmade	8.00
Bottle, Figural, Lady's Leg, Turn Mold, Dark Green	30.00
Bottle, Figural, Lady's Shoe, High Top, 4 1/2 In., Clear	4.50
Bottle, Figural, Madonna, Amber, Hand Blown, Dated 1932, 13 In.Tall	4.00
Bottle, Figural, Madonna, Hand Blown, Dated 1932, Amber, 13 In.Tall	4.00
Bottle, Figural, Madonna, Hand Blown, Pontil, Dated 1932, Cobalt Blue	4.00
Bottle, Figural, Mermaid, Paper Belt, Brandle & Smoth Co., 10 In.	3.50
Bottle, Figural, Monk, Milk Glass, Holland *Illus*	18.00
Bottle, Figural, Monkey, 13 1/2 In., Green	5.00
Bottle, Figural, Moon Bottle, Mid-America Wine Co.	11.00
Bottle, Figural, Mr.Pickwick, Clear, 9 In.High	4.75 To 7.00
Bottle, Figural, Negro Boy, Miniature, 1 In.	2.75
Bottle, Figural, Porcelain, Mermaid, Silver Neck, 9 1/2 In.Long	125.00
Bottle, Figural, Queen Anne Long Clock	22.50
Bottle, Figural, Romeo	21.00
Bottle, Figural, Scroll, Sheared Lip, Aqua, Half Pint	48.00
Bottle, Figural, Shakespeare Folio	22.50
Bottle, Figural, Shoe, Bimal, Applied Lip, 4 3/4 In.Long, Clear	7.50
Bottle, Figural, Sitting Bear, Amber	40.00
Bottle, Figural, Sitting, Elephant, Clear	18.50
Bottle, Figural, Stanley, Frosted *Illus*	24.00
Bottle, Figural, Statue Of Liberty, Clear, 12 1/2 In.High	125.00
Bottle, Figural, Violin, Blue, Holder, 9 1/2 In.Tall	12.00
Bottle, Figural, Violin, Cobalt Blue, 10 In.Tall	1.25
Bottle, Figural, Violin, West Pittsburgh, Amber	50.00
Bottle, Figural, Violin, 7 1/4 In., Aqua	5.00
Bottle, Figural, Washington, Bimal, Clear	7.00

Bottle, Figural, Monk,
Milk Glass, Holland

Bottle, Figural,
Stanley, Frosted

Bottle, Figural, Zorro, Royal Doulton, 10 1/2 In.High .... 17.50 To 35.00
Bottle, Fire Extinguisher, Carbona, 12 Sided, Amber 10.00
Bottle, Flask, Aqua, Glass, Initials D.F., Pint 18.00
Bottle, Flask, Bininger, Pint, Green 48.00
Bottle, Flask, Bull's-Eye, Applied Mouth, Dark Green 12.00
Bottle, Flask, Centennial, Dr.Livingstone I Presume 7.95
Bottle, Flask, Chestnut, Pontil, 6 In., Olive Amber 45.00
Bottle, Flask, Chestnut, 9 1/2 In., Aqua 35.00
Bottle, Flask, Cornucopia & Urn, 1/2 Pt., Olive Green 45.00
Bottle, Flask, Cornucopia, Amber 65.00
Bottle, Flask, Crude, Pint, C.1830, Dark Olive Green 35.00
Bottle, Flask, Diamond Pattern, Clear, 1/2 Pint 8.50
Bottle, Flask, Double Eagle, Pint, Aqua 40.00
Bottle, Flask, Double Eagle, Pint, Olive Amber 62.00
Bottle, Flask, Double Eagle, 1/2 Pint, Olive Amber 65.00
Bottle, Flask, Double Eagle, Pittsburgh, Pa., Deep Green, Quart 65.00
Bottle, Flask, Drum Prohibition, Full Label 35.00
Bottle, Flask, Eastern, 1/2 Pint, Olive Green 300.00
Bottle, Flask, Floral & Scrolls Decor, Silver 14.00
Bottle, Flask, Geometric Design, Brass Screw Cap, 1/2 Pint, Clear 12.00
Bottle, Flask, Hand Blown, Embossed, Corker 1.00
Bottle, Flask, J.P.Masonic, Eagle, Open Pontil, Mckearin Giv-I, Green, Pint 200.00
Bottle, Flask, Jenny Lind, Eisterville Glass Works, Embossed, Amber 15.00
Bottle, Flask, Jenny Lind, Open, 5 In., Embossed Flowers 20.00
Bottle, Flask, Jenny Lind, Solid Smoke Turns Left, Green 16.00
Bottle, Flask, Jos.A.Magnus & Co., Cincinnati 13.50
Bottle, Flask, Ladies', Sterling Silver, Floral Overlay, One Shot 18.00
Bottle, Flask, Lynche & Clarke, Saratoga Type, Pontil, Pint, Olive 48.00
Bottle, Flask, Mckearin G II-70, Eagle, Coventry, Dark Olive 125.00
Bottle, Flask, Mckearin G III-12, Blown In Mold, Miniature, Clear, 2 5/8 In. 35.00
Bottle, Flask, Mckearin G IV-17, Keene, Masonic, Olive Green 185.00
Bottle, Flask, Mckearin G IX-10, Scroll, Pint, Aqua 35.00
Bottle, Flask, Miniature, Milk Glass, 2 In., Stars & Banner 20.00
Bottle, Flask, Obverse Hunter, Reverse Laurel Wreaths, Aqua, Half Pint 125.00
Bottle, Flask, Open Pontil, Applied Top, Quart, Aqua 45.00
Bottle, Flask, Paul Jones, Amber 13.00
Bottle, Flask, Pewter & Glass, Marked M.Vlory's Patent 1866 .... 6.95
Bottle, Flask, Pewter & Glass, Olry & Co., Circa 1866, Pint 6.95
Bottle, Flask, Picnic, Merry Christmas & Happy New Year, Embossed 23.00
Bottle, Flask, Picture Of Kaiser, First World War 65.00
Bottle, Flask, Pike's Peak, Eagle, Pint, Aqua 65.00
Bottle, Flask, Pike's Peak, Quart, Aqua 60.00
Bottle, Flask, Pitkin, Midwestern, 20 Vertical & Swirled Ribs, Green 305.00
Bottle, Flask, Pitkin, Swirled To Left, New England, Open Pontil, Olive Green 180.00
Bottle, Flask, Pocket, Leather Top Initials N.S.G. 7.75
Bottle, Flask, Pocket, Silver, Initials H.A. 9.75
Bottle, Flask, Pocket, Silver, Top, Leather, Bottom 6.00
Bottle, Flask, Pumpkin Seed, Amethyst 6.00
Bottle, Flask, Pumpkin Seed, Flattish, 4 3/4 In., Clear 4.00
Bottle, Flask, Ravenna, 8-Pointed Star 75.00
Bottle, Flask, Redware, 4 3/4 In. 12.00
Bottle, Flask, Regimental, Kaiser Photo, Germany 65.00
Bottle, Flask, S.Mckee & Co., 1/2 Pint 15.00
Bottle, Flask, Scent, Ribbed, Embossed Heart & Star, 1/2 Pint, Clear 135.00
Bottle, Flask, Scroll, 1/2 Pint, Aqua 36.00
Bottle, Flask, Stoddard Eagle, Amber, 7 1/2 In.Tall 85.00
Bottle, Flask, Stoddard, Double Eagle, Amber, Open Pontil, Pint, Unmarked 80.00
Bottle, Flask, Stoddard, Double Eagle, Amber, Open Pontil, Quart, Unmarked 80.00
Bottle, Flask, Stoddard, Three-Part Mold, Embossed Week's Glass Works 92.50
Bottle, Flask, Success To The Railroad 55.00
Bottle, Flask, Taylor Never Surrenders, Aqua .... 45.00 To 58.00
Bottle, Flask, Union, Aqua 45.00
Bottle, Flask, Warranted Oval, Squarish, 14 Oz., Amethyst 3.00
Bottle, Flask, Warranted, Oval, 10 Oz., Squarish, Amethyst 3.00
Bottle, Flask, Washington, Taylor, Aqua 65.00
Bottle, Flask, Whiskey, Pewter, Glass, Leather, C.1866 .... 11.00

Bottle, Food, Charles Gulden, Sauce, Bulbous, Amethyst 3.00
Bottle, Food, Chico's Spanish Peanut Jar, Metal Cover & Base .... 10.00 To 22.50
Bottle, Food, Gebhardt Eagle Chili Powder, Embossed Eagle 1.00
Bottle, Food, Horlick's Malted Milk, Racine, Wis., Clear, Lid 5.00
Bottle, Food, Horlick's Malted Milk, Racine, Wis., Clear, 99 Percent Label 5.00
Bottle, Food, Horlick's Malted Milk, Racine, Wis., Light Green 4.00
Bottle, Food, Horsford's Baking Powder, Embossed, 5 In.Tall, Green 7.50
Bottle, Food, Ketchup, Heinz, Red, Original Label, 26 1/2 In.Tall 225.00
Bottle, Food, Log Cabin Extract, 6 1/2 In., Amber 60.00
Bottle, Food, Olives .... Illus .50
Bottle, Food, Peanut Butter, Jumbo 2.00
Bottle, Food, Strawberry Flavor, California Perfume Co., Label 25.00
Bottle, Food, Wan-Eta Cocoa, Label, Quart 10.00
Bottle, Fruit Jar, A.Kline, Glass Stopper, Quart 22.00
Bottle, Fruit Jar, Acme, Pint 3.00
Bottle, Fruit Jar, Acme, Quart, Clear .... 2.00 To 3.00
Bottle, Fruit Jar, Acme, 1/2 Gallon 5.00
Bottle, Fruit Jar, Anchor Hocking, Lightning, Quart 4.00
Bottle, Fruit Jar, Atlas E-Z Seal, Amber, Milk Glass Lid, Quart 22.00
Bottle, Fruit Jar, Atlas E-Z Seal, Aqua, Half Pint 6.00
Bottle, Fruit Jar, Atlas E-Z Seal, Aqua, Pint .... 2.50 To 3.50
Bottle, Fruit Jar, Atlas E-Z Seal, Aqua, Quart 3.50
Bottle, Fruit Jar, Atlas E-Z Seal, Clear, Pint 2.00
Bottle, Fruit Jar, Atlas E-Z Seal, Clear, Quart 2.00
Bottle, Fruit Jar, Atlas E-Z Seal, Copper, Aqua, Half Pint 4.00
Bottle, Fruit Jar, Atlas E-Z Seal, Quart, Amber 15.00
Bottle, Fruit Jar, Atlas E-Z Seal, Squatty, Pint, Aqua 2.00
Bottle, Fruit Jar, Atlas E-Z Seal, Vaseline, Quart 15.00
Bottle, Fruit Jar, Atlas E-Z Seal, 1/2 Pint, Clear 8.00
Bottle, Fruit Jar, Atlas Good Luck 2.50
Bottle, Fruit Jar, Atlas Ha Mason 1.75
Bottle, Fruit Jar, Atlas Improved, Quart 3.00
Bottle, Fruit Jar, Atlas Mason 2.00
Bottle, Fruit Jar, Atlas Strong Shoulder, Aqua 1.75
Bottle, Fruit Jar, Atlas, Amber, Quart 25.00
Bottle, Fruit Jar, Atlas, Glass Top, 1/2 Pint, Aqua 7.50
Bottle, Fruit Jar, Atlas, Good Luck, Pint 4.00
Bottle, Fruit Jar, Atlas, Good Luck, Quart 3.00
Bottle, Fruit Jar, Atlas, Good Luck, 2 Quart 6.00
Bottle, Fruit Jar, Atlas, Mason's Patent, Quart 3.00
Bottle, Fruit Jar, Atlas, Mason's Patent, Quart, Apple Green 4.50
Bottle, Fruit Jar, Atlas, Strong Shoulder, Quart, Aqua 2.00
Bottle, Fruit Jar, Atlas, Wholefruit, Quart, Clear 2.00
Bottle, Fruit Jar, Atlas, 1858, Aqua, Half Gallon 4.00
Bottle, Fruit Jar, Automatic Sealer, Quart, Aqua 50.00
Bottle, Fruit Jar, Ball Deluxe 2.50
Bottle, Fruit Jar, Ball Eclipse 1.75
Bottle, Fruit Jar, Ball Ideal, 1/2 Gallon, Blue 7.50
Bottle, Fruit Jar, Ball Sure Seal, Aqua, Quart 2.50
Bottle, Fruit Jar, Ball, Ideal, 1/2 Pint 3.00
Bottle, Fruit Jar, Ball, Improved Mason, Aqua, Pint 3.00
Bottle, Fruit Jar, Ball, Improved, Quart, Aqua 2.00
Bottle, Fruit Jar, Ball, Mason, 1858, Quart, Clear 2.00
Bottle, Fruit Jar, Ball, Standard, Quart, Aqua 2.00
Bottle, Fruit Jar, Ball, Sure Seal, Quart, Aqua 2.00
Bottle, Fruit Jar, Ball, 1/2 Pint, Clear 2.00
Bottle, Fruit Jar, Ball, 1/3 Pint, Clear 3.00
Bottle, Fruit Jar, Ball, 2 Quart, Amber 20.00
Bottle, Fruit Jar, Ball, 1858, Quart 5.00
Bottle, Fruit Jar, Banner, Pat'd Feb.9th, 1864, Reissue Jan.22, 1867, Aqua 40.00
Bottle, Fruit Jar, Banner, Quart .... 6.00 To 9.00
Bottle, Fruit Jar, Barrel, Figural, Quart, Clear 2.00
Bottle, Fruit Jar, Beaver 35.00
Bottle, Fruit Jar, Beechnut, Pint 3.00
Bottle, Fruit Jar, Best Fruitkeeper, Clear, Quart 35.00
Bottle, Fruit Jar, Boyd Mason, Quart 3.50

Bottle, Fruit Jar, Boyd's Perfect Mason, Quart 4.00
Bottle, Fruit Jar, Brockway, Quart, Clear 2.00
Bottle, Fruit Jar, C.S.& Co., Pint 1.00
Bottle, Fruit Jar, C.S.& Co., Quart 12.00
Bottle, Fruit Jar, Canadian Jewel, Pint 2.50
Bottle, Fruit Jar, Champion, The, Aqua, Quart 65.00
Bottle, Fruit Jar, Clark's Peerless, Aqua, Pint .... 4.95 To 6.00
Bottle, Fruit Jar, Clark's Peerless, Pint 1.00
Bottle, Fruit Jar, Clark's Peerless, Quart, Aqua 4.95
Bottle, Fruit Jar, Clarke, Cleveland, Ohio .... *Illus* 25.00

Bottle, Food, Olives
See Page 42

Bottle, Fruit Jar, Clarke,
Cleveland, Ohio

Bottle, Fruit Jar, Clyde In Circle, Pint 5.00
Bottle, Fruit Jar, Clyde In Circle, Quart 5.00
Bottle, Fruit Jar, Clyde In Script, Pint 5.00
Bottle, Fruit Jar, Clyde, N.Y. 3.50
Bottle, Fruit Jar, Cohansey, Aqua, 1 /2 Pint 40.00
Bottle, Fruit Jar, Cohansey, Quart 12.00
Bottle, Fruit Jar, Conserve, Pint 4.00
Bottle, Fruit Jar, Conserve, Quart 6.00
Bottle, Fruit Jar, Crandall & Codley Co., 2 Quart 8.00
Bottle, Fruit Jar, Crown Cordial & Extract Co., 2 Quart 8.00
Bottle, Fruit Jar, Crown Imperial, Aqua, Quart 3.00
Bottle, Fruit Jar, Crown Imperial, Clear, Pint 2.50
Bottle, Fruit Jar, Crown Imperial, Midget, Aqua 20.00
Bottle, Fruit Jar, Crown Imperial, Midget, Clear 20.00
Bottle, Fruit Jar, Crown Midget, Aqua 12.00
Bottle, Fruit Jar, Crown, Midget, Clear 12.00
Bottle, Fruit Jar, Crown, Pint 3.00
Bottle, Fruit Jar, Crown, Quart, Clear 2.00
Bottle, Fruit Jar, Crown, 2 Quart 6.00
Bottle, Fruit Jar, Cunningham Co., Aqua, Kline Stopper, 1/2 Gallon 18.00
Bottle, Fruit Jar, Dandy 9.00
Bottle, Fruit Jar, Doolittle, Aqua 20.00
Bottle, Fruit Jar, Double Safety, Quart, Clear 2.00
Bottle, Fruit Jar, Drey, Mason, Quart, Clear 2.00
Bottle, Fruit Jar, Drey, Perfect Mason, Quart, Clear 2.00
Bottle, Fruit Jar, Drey, Square Mason, Quart, Clear 2.00
Bottle, Fruit Jar, Eagle, Quart 40.00
Bottle, Fruit Jar, Eagle, 2 Quart 50.00
Bottle, Fruit Jar, Economy, Quart, Clear 2.00
Bottle, Fruit Jar, Electric, World Globe, Aqua 40.00
Bottle, Fruit Jar, Empire, Half Pint 18.00
Bottle, Fruit Jar, Empire, Pint .... 4.00 To 12.00
Bottle, Fruit Jar, Empire, Quart 5.00
Bottle, Fruit Jar, Empire, 2 Quart 8.00
Bottle, Fruit Jar, Eureka, Pint 8.00
Bottle, Fruit Jar, Eureka, Quart 8.00

Bottle, Fruit Jar, F.& J.Bodine, Aqua, Quart	55.00
Bottle, Fruit Jar, F.C.G.Co., Wax Sealer, Quart, Aqua	12.00
Bottle, Fruit Jar, F.Dexter, 2 Quart, Aqua	25.00
Bottle, Fruit Jar, Flaccus Bros.Table Delicacies, Wheeling, Square, Clear	75.00
Bottle, Fruit Jar, Flaccus, Glass Stopper, Clear	90.00
Bottle, Fruit Jar, Flaccus, Pint, No Lid	21.00
Bottle, Fruit Jar, Foster, Sealfast, Pint	4.00
Bottle, Fruit Jar, Foster Sealfast, Quart	2.50
Bottle, Fruit Jar, Four Seasons Mason, Pint	5.00
Bottle, Fruit Jar, Franklin Dexter, Quart, Aqua	35.00
Bottle, Fruit Jar, Franklin Dexter, 1/2 Gallon	30.00
Bottle, Fruit Jar, Franklin, Quart	35.00
Bottle, Fruit Jar, Franklin, 2 Quart	40.00
Bottle, Fruit Jar, Fruitkeeper, Quart	25.00
Bottle, Fruit Jar, Gayner, Glass Top, Quart	4.00
Bottle, Fruit Jar, Gayner Mason, Quart, Clear	10.00
Bottle, Fruit Jar, Gayner, Quart	3.00
Bottle, Fruit Jar, Gem, Midget	18.00
Bottle, Fruit Jar, Gem, Quart	4.00 To 8.00
Bottle, Fruit Jar, Gem, Reverse Shield, 2 Quart	12.00
Bottle, Fruit Jar, Gem, 2 Quart	6.00
Bottle, Fruit Jar, Gilberd's Import, Clear, Quart	95.00
Bottle, Fruit Jar, Gilchrist, Quart	22.00
Bottle, Fruit Jar, Glass Lid, Wire Clamp, 2 Gallon	5.50
Bottle, Fruit Jar, Glassboro Improved, Quart	20.00
Bottle, Fruit Jar, Glassboro, Pint	20.00
Bottle, Fruit Jar, Globe Lightning Top, 2 Quart	8.00
Bottle, Fruit Jar, Globe, Quart, Aqua	13.00
Bottle, Fruit Jar, Globe, 2 Quart, Aqua	17.50
Bottle, Fruit Jar, Golden State	9.00
Bottle, Fruit Jar, Good Housekeepers, Half Pint	4.50
Bottle, Fruit Jar, Greek Key, Safety Valve, 2 Quart, Aqua	25.00
Bottle, Fruit Jar, GWH Monogram, Quart	8.00
Bottle, Fruit Jar, H.W.Pettit, Quart	5.00
Bottle, Fruit Jar, Hartell, Letchworth, 3 Lug Base, Quart, Aqua	45.00
Bottle, Fruit Jar, Hartell, Lid Date Only, 2 Quart, Aqua	25.00
Bottle, Fruit Jar, Harvest Mason, Quart, Clear	8.00
Bottle, Fruit Jar, Hazel Preserve Jar, H Over A Mono, Quart	6.00
Bottle, Fruit Jar, Hazel Preserve Jar, 1/2 Pint	6.00
Bottle, Fruit Jar, Hero, Aqua, Quart	14.00
Bottle, Fruit Jar, Hero, Improved, 2 Quart, Aqua	17.50
Bottle, Fruit Jar, Hero, Whittled, Quart	20.00
Bottle, Fruit Jar, Hero, 2 Quart	15.00
Bottle, Fruit Jar, Hompak, Mason, Quart	3.00
Bottle, Fruit Jar, Hormel, Pint	3.00
Bottle, Fruit Jar, Hwp, Pint, Aqua	12.00
Bottle, Fruit Jar, Improved Gem, Pint	3.00
Bottle, Fruit Jar, Ivanhoe, Pint	3.00
Bottle, Fruit Jar, Ivanhoe, Quart	3.00
Bottle, Fruit Jar, J.Ellwood Lee Co., Amber, Quart	30.00
Bottle, Fruit Jar, Jeanette, Quart, Clear	2.00
Bottle, Fruit Jar, Johnson & Johnson, Amber	15.00
Bottle, Fruit Jar, Johnson & Johnson, 1/2 Pint.Amber, Embossed, Label	15.00
Bottle, Fruit Jar, Jos.Middleby, Jr., Inc., 2 Quart	8.00
Bottle, Fruit Jar, Jumbo Peanut Butter, Keystone, Pint	3.00
Bottle, Fruit Jar, Jumbo Peanut Butter, Pint	2.00
Bottle, Fruit Jar, Kerr Mason, Quart, Amber	7.50
Bottle, Fruit Jar, Kerr, Self-Sealer, 1915, Clear	1.50
Bottle, Fruit Jar, Kerr, 2 Quart	5.00
Bottle, Fruit Jar, Keystone Trademark, Registered, Quart	5.00
Bottle, Fruit Jar, Keystone, Quart	4.00
Bottle, Fruit Jar, King, Oval, Quart, Aqua	10.00
Bottle, Fruit Jar, King, Pint	8.00
Bottle, Fruit Jar, Kinsella, Clear, 1874, Quart	5.50
Bottle, Fruit Jar, Kline, 2 Quart, Aqua	20.00
Bottle, Fruit Jar, Knowlton Vacuum, Pint	25.00

Bottle, Fruit Jar, Knowlton Vacuum, Quart, Aqua 20.00
Bottle, Fruit Jar, Knowlton, 1903, 1/2 Gallon 12.50
Bottle, Fruit Jar, Knox Mason, Half Pint 3.00
Bottle, Fruit Jar, Knox, Half Pint 4.00
Bottle, Fruit Jar, Lafayette, Aqua 75.00
Bottle, Fruit Jar, Lamb, Quart, Clear 2.00
Bottle, Fruit Jar, Leader, The, Aqua, Quart 29.00
Bottle, Fruit Jar, Leotric, Pint 5.00
Bottle, Fruit Jar, Leotric, Quart .... 4.00 To 6.50
Bottle, Fruit Jar, Lightning, Amber, Quart 17.00
Bottle, Fruit Jar, Lightning, Clear, 2 Quart 6.00
Bottle, Fruit Jar, Lightning, Mason, 1858, Quart, Aqua 2.00
Bottle, Fruit Jar, Lightning, Pint, Aqua .... 1.00 To 2.00
Bottle, Fruit Jar, Lightning, Putnam, Aqua, Quart 6.50
Bottle, Fruit Jar, Lightning, Putnam, Clear, Pint 6.50
Bottle, Fruit Jar, Lightning, Quart, Aqua 2.00
Bottle, Fruit Jar, Lightning, Quart, Cornflower Blue 20.00
Bottle, Fruit Jar, Lightning, Wire Basket, Quart, Amber 27.50
Bottle, Fruit Jar, Lightning, 1/2 Gallon 5.00
Bottle, Fruit Jar, Lightning, 1/2 Pint 10.00
Bottle, Fruit Jar, Liquid Carbonic 2.50
Bottle, Fruit Jar, Lockport Improved, Quart 4.00
Bottle, Fruit Jar, Lockport, Improved, Pint 4.00
Bottle, Fruit Jar, Lustre, Pint 5.00
Bottle, Fruit Jar, Lustre, Quart 3.00
Bottle, Fruit Jar, Mason C.F.J.Co.Clyde N.Y., 1858, Pint 3.00
Bottle, Fruit Jar, Mason Jar Of 1872, Quart 20.00
Bottle, Fruit Jar, Mason Midget, C.F.J.Co. 15.00
Bottle, Fruit Jar, Mason Midget, C.F.J.Co., Improved Tm 18.00
Bottle, Fruit Jar, Mason Midget, Half Pint 8.00
Bottle, Fruit Jar, Mason, Amber, Pint 30.00
Bottle, Fruit Jar, Mason, Aqua, 1858, Half Gallon 5.50
Bottle, Fruit Jar, Mason, Cfj, 1858, Quart, Aqua 2.00
Bottle, Fruit Jar, Mason, Pint, Amber 15.00
Bottle, Fruit Jar, Mason, Quart, Aqua 2.00
Bottle, Fruit Jar, Mason, Trademark On Slant, Quart, Aqua 10.00
Bottle, Fruit Jar, Mason, 1858, Cross, Quart, Aqua 2.00
Bottle, Fruit Jar, Mason's Cfg Co., Pat.Nov.30, 1858, Cobalt Blue, 1/2 Gallon 15.00
Bottle, Fruit Jar, Mason's Cfj Improved Reverse, Clyde, N.Y., Clear, Pint 5.00
Bottle, Fruit Jar, Mason's Cfj Improved Reverse, Clyde, N.Y., Clear, Quart 5.00
Bottle, Fruit Jar, Mason's Cfj Improved, 1/2 Gallon, Amber 20.00
Bottle, Fruit Jar, Mason's Cfj, Patent, Nov.30th, 1858, Vaseline, Quart 25.00
Bottle, Fruit Jar, Mason's GLW Imperial, Pint 8.00
Bottle, Fruit Jar, Mason's Improved, Clyde, N.Y., Reverse, 2 Quart 6.00
Bottle, Fruit Jar, Mason's Improved, Cross 3.50
Bottle, Fruit Jar, Mason's Improved, Monogram, Ground Top, Aqua 3.50
Bottle, Fruit Jar, Mason's Improved, Patent, 1870, Quart 4.00
Bottle, Fruit Jar, Mason's Improved, Pint 3.00
Bottle, Fruit Jar, Mason's Improved, Whittled, Midget 6.50
Bottle, Fruit Jar, Mason's Lgw, Improved, Pint 12.00
Bottle, Fruit Jar, Mason's Midget 8.50
Bottle, Fruit Jar, Mason's Patent, Aqua, Quart 2.00
Bottle, Fruit Jar, Mason's Patent Cfj, Quart, Blue 35.00
Bottle, Fruit Jar, Mason's Patent, Cross, Amber, Quart 35.00
Bottle, Fruit Jar, Mason's Patent, Embossed, Ground Top, 1/2 Gallon, Aqua 4.50
Bottle, Fruit Jar, Mason's Patent, Lightning, Pint 3.00
Bottle, Fruit Jar, Mason's Patent, Nov.30, 1858, Amber, Quart 35.00
Bottle, Fruit Jar, Mason's Patent, Nov.30, 1858, U.G.Co., Rev., Quart, Clear 12.50
Bottle, Fruit Jar, Mason's Patent, Nov.30th, 1858, Ball Reverse, Pint 5.00
Bottle, Fruit Jar, Mason's Patent, Nov.30th, 1858, Keystone, Whittled 6.50
Bottle, Fruit Jar, Mason's 1858, Embossed, Quart 2.95
Bottle, Fruit Jar, Mason's 1858, Embossed, 1/2 Gallon 2.95
Bottle, Fruit Jar, Mcdonald New Perfect Seal, Quart, Aqua 4.50
Bottle, Fruit Jar, Metre Easi-Pak 2.50
Bottle, Fruit Jar, Midget, 1-Piece Top 7.00
Bottle, Fruit Jar, Midget, 2-Piece Top 6.00

Bottle, Fruit Jar, Miller's Fine Flavors, Square, 2 Quart, Aqua 17.50
Bottle, Fruit Jar, Millville Atmospheric, Embossed, Quart 20.00
Bottle, Fruit Jar, Millville Atmospheric, 1/2 Gallon 15.00
Bottle, Fruit Jar, Millville, Half Pint, No Lid 32.00
Bottle, Fruit Jar, Milville, Quart, Aqua 20.00
Bottle, Fruit Jar, Milville, Pint 25.00
Bottle, Fruit Jar, Model Mason, Clear, Quart 10.00
Bottle, Fruit Jar, Monarch, Lion's Head, Quart 3.00
Bottle, Fruit Jar, Moore's Patent, Millville Clamp, Quart 25.00
Bottle, Fruit Jar, National, 1/2 Gallon, Clear 5.00
Bottle, Fruit Jar, Ohio Quality Mason, Pint 3.00
Bottle, Fruit Jar, Old Judge, Coffee, Quart, Clear 2.00
Bottle, Fruit Jar, Opler Brothers, Clear, Quart 6.00
Bottle, Fruit Jar, Pearl, 3 Dates At Base, Aqua, Quart 40.00
Bottle, Fruit Jar, Peerless, Quart 50.00
Bottle, Fruit Jar, Perfect Seal, Pint 4.00
Bottle, Fruit Jar, Perfection, 1/2 Gal., Lid 40.00
Bottle, Fruit Jar, Plain, Slender, 1/2 Pint, Clear 2.00
Bottle, Fruit Jar, Protector, 2 Quart, Aqua 30.00
Bottle, Fruit Jar, Putnam On Base, 1/2 Pint 6.00
Bottle, Fruit Jar, Quality Mason, Ohio, Clear, Pint 6.00
Bottle, Fruit Jar, Queen, Clear, Half Pint 4.00
Bottle, Fruit Jar, Queen, GLWB, Victory, 1/2 Pint 6.00
Bottle, Fruit Jar, Queen, Pint 3.00
Bottle, Fruit Jar, Queen, Quart, Clear 2.00
Bottle, Fruit Jar, Queen, 1/2 Gallon 14.00
Bottle, Fruit Jar, Quick Seal, Pint 3.00
Bottle, Fruit Jar, Quick Seal, Quart, Clear 2.00
Bottle, Fruit Jar, Rath's, Quart 3.00
Bottle, Fruit Jar, Red Key Mason, Lid, Aqua 7.50
Bottle, Fruit Jar, Red Key, Quart 8.00
Bottle, Fruit Jar, Root Mason, Green, Half Gallon 15.00
Bottle, Fruit Jar, Root Mason, Pint 5.00
Bottle, Fruit Jar, Root, Quart 4.00
Bottle, Fruit Jar, Roth, Quart 4.00
Bottle, Fruit Jar, Royal Of 1876, Quart, Aqua 85.00
Bottle, Fruit Jar, Royal, Pint 4.00
Bottle, Fruit Jar, Royal, Quart 4.00
Bottle, Fruit Jar, Royal, Quart, Clear 2.00
Bottle, Fruit Jar, Royal, 1/2 Gallon, Aqua 90.00
Bottle, Fruit Jar, S.Mc Kee Co.Wax, Aqua, Quart 8.00
Bottle, Fruit Jar, Safety Valve, Amethyst, Quart 13.00
Bottle, Fruit Jar, Safety Valve, Bubbly, 1/2 Pint 20.00
Bottle, Fruit Jar, Safety Valve, Green 12.00
Bottle, Fruit Jar, Safety Valve, Pint 15.00
Bottle, Fruit Jar, Samco, Quart, Clear 2.00
Bottle, Fruit Jar, Schram, Automatic Sealer, Pint, B 5.00
Bottle, Fruit Jar, Schram, Pint 3.00
Bottle, Fruit Jar, Security Seal, Quart 5.00
Bottle, Fruit Jar, Sko Queen 2.50
Bottle, Fruit Jar, Smalley, Full Measure, Pint 5.00
Bottle, Fruit Jar, Smalley, Ground Top, Aqua 3.50
Bottle, Fruit Jar, Smalley, Ground Top, 1/2 Gallon, Aqua 4.50
Bottle, Fruit Jar, Smalley, Pint 4.00
Bottle, Fruit Jar, Smalley, Quart, Clear 2.00
Bottle, Fruit Jar, Smalley, 2 Quart 8.00
Bottle, Fruit Jar, Smalley, Self Sealer, Widemouth, Pint 3.50
Bottle, Fruit Jar, Smalley, Self Sealer, Widemouth, Quart 4.00
Bottle, Fruit Jar, Smalley, Self Sealer, Widemouth, 1/2 Gallon 5.00
Bottle, Fruit Jar, Smith & Son Co., Wax, Clear, Quart 8.00
Bottle, Fruit Jar, Spencer's Patent, Quart, Aqua 40.00
Bottle, Fruit Jar, Sterling, Mason, Quart, Clear 2.00
Bottle, Fruit Jar, Sterling, Pint 3.00
Bottle, Fruit Jar, Sun, Aqua, Pint 45.00
Bottle, Fruit Jar, Sun, Quart 40.00
Bottle, Fruit Jar, Sun, Safety Valve Clamp, Quart .... 12.50 To 22.50

Bottle, Fruit Jar, Sure Seal, Pint, Clear .... 2.00 To 4.00
Bottle, Fruit Jar, Swayzie's, Quart 4.00
Bottle, Fruit Jar, Telephone, Pint .... 5.00 To 9.00
Bottle, Fruit Jar, Telephone, Quart 5.00
Bottle, Fruit Jar, Texas Mason, Pint 10.00
Bottle, Fruit Jar, Texas Mason, Quart 10.00
Bottle, Fruit Jar, Tf 1.75
Bottle, Fruit Jar, Tight Seal, Pint 3.00
Bottle, Fruit Jar, Tight Seal, Quart, Clear 2.00
Bottle, Fruit Jar, Trademark Climax 4.75
Bottle, Fruit Jar, Trademark, Banner, Warranted, Pint 5.00
Bottle, Fruit Jar, Trademark, Lightning, Quart 2.00
Bottle, Fruit Jar, Triomphe, 1/2 Pint 5.00
Bottle, Fruit Jar, True's Imperial Brand, Pint 5.00
Bottle, Fruit Jar, Vacuum Tite, Metal Lid, Rubber Dome & Pump, Quart, Clear 60.00
Bottle, Fruit Jar, Veteran, Quart 12.00
Bottle, Fruit Jar, Victory, Pint 6.00
Bottle, Fruit Jar, Victory, Quart 8.00
Bottle, Fruit Jar, Victory, 1, 1864-1867, Quart 15.00
Bottle, Fruit Jar, W.W.Lyman, Half Gallon, No Lid 16.00
Bottle, Fruit Jar, Wallaceburg Gem, Clear, Half Gallon 5.50
Bottle, Fruit Jar, Wan-Eta Cocoa, Embossed, 1/2 Pt., Amber 15.00
Bottle, Fruit Jar, Wan-Eta Cocoa, Quart, Amber 3.50
Bottle, Fruit Jar, Wan-Eta Cocoa, Quart, Aqua 4.00
Bottle, Fruit Jar, Wan-Eta Cocoa, Quart, Label, Amber 6.00
Bottle, Fruit Jar, Wan-Eta Cocoa, 1/2 Pint, Amber 6.00
Bottle, Fruit Jar, Wears, On Banner Below Crown 8.00
Bottle, Fruit Jar, Weideman, Quart 4.00
Bottle, Fruit Jar, Weir Stone, Brown & Tin, C.1892, Bail 8.50
Bottle, Fruit Jar, Weir, Brown & White, Quart 7.00
Bottle, Fruit Jar, Weir, The, Crockery, Amber Top, Quart 20.00
Bottle, Fruit Jar, Whitall-Tatum, Pontil, Pint 28.00
Bottle, Fruit Jar, White Bear, Quart 15.00
Bottle, Fruit Jar, White Crown, Milk Glass Insert Band, Quart 8.00
Bottle, Fruit Jar, Whitney, Quart 3.00
Bottle, Fruit Jar, Whitney, 1858 .... 4.75
Bottle, Fruit Jar, Widemouth, Telephone, Empire, Pint 5.00
Bottle, Fruit Jar, Widemouth, Telephone, Pint .... 5.00 To 8.00
Bottle, Fruit Jar, Widemouth, Telephone, Quart .... 4.00 To 5.00
Bottle, Fruit Jar, Winslow Jar, 2 Quart 35.00
Bottle, Fruit Jar, Wire Closure, Glass Lid, Pint 1.00
Bottle, Fruit Jar, Woodbury, Quart 20.00
Bottle, Fruit Jar, Yeoman's, Quart, Aqua 32.00
Bottle, Fruit Jar, 1908, Pint, Blue .... .95
Bottle, Fruit Jar, 1908, Quart, Blue .... .95
Bottle, Fruit, Drey Ever Seal, Dated 1858 With Cross 1.75
Bottle, Fruit, Jar, Keystone, Quart 10.00
Bottle, Fruitkeeper, Pint 25.00
Bottle, Gar Canteen, Lincoln Portrait, China 24.00
Bottle, Gar Canteen, Raised Emblem, Brass & Cork Stopper, Quart 35.00
Bottle, Garnier, Red Rooster, Labeled 35.00
Bottle, Gemel, Pedestal Base, Necks Curve Outward, 7 In.Tall 35.00
Bottle, Gemel, 1885, M, Bland .... Illus   78.00
Bottle, George Washington, Clear, Centennial 1732-1932, 7 1/2 X 5 1/2 In. 9.98
Bottle, Gin, Binninger, Old London Dock 40.00
Bottle, Gin, Case, Free-Blown, Squashed Lip, Olive Amber 35.00
Bottle, Gin, Case, Olive Green, 10 1/2 In.Tall 4.00
Bottle, Gin, Case, Olive Green, 9 1/2 In.Tall 4.00
Bottle, Gin, Case, Quart, Emerald 6.00
Bottle, Gin, Case, Taper, Amber 20.00
Bottle, Gin, Slant Sided, Machine Mold 2.75
Bottle, Gin, Square Face, Open Pontil, Olive Green 25.00
Bottle, Ginger, Stoneware, Screw Stopper, English 4.00
Bottle, Green & Amber, 10 In.High, Pair 4.00
Bottle, Grenadier Soldier, Captain, U.S.Infantry, Union Army 12.95
Bottle, Grenadier Soldier, Confederate Captain 12.95

Bottle, Grenadier Soldier, General George A.Custer	14.95
Bottle, Grenadier Soldier, General Jeb Stuart	14.95
Bottle, Grenadier Soldier, King's African Rifle Corps, Qt.	29.95
Bottle, Groft's Swiss Milk Cocoa, Pint	10.00
Bottle, H.Gardner, West Bromwick, 7 1/2 In.High	3.00
Bottle, Hayner Whiskey, Troy, Ohio, 1897	10.00
Bottle, Herb, Fluting Waterfall, Free Cut, Square Base, 4 In.	38.00
Bottle, Hog-Type, Inscribed Fultonham, Ohio	55.00
Bottle, Household, Blacking, Olive Amber	40.00
Bottle, Household, Bluing, Cone-Shaped, Amber, Label	5.00
Bottle, Household, Clorox, Elephant Figural, 1930s, Amber	35.00
Bottle, Household, Elysian Mfg.Co., 6 In., Round, Cobalt	8.00
Bottle, Household, F.E.Morgan, Oval, 3 3/4 In., Cobalt, Sloped Shoulders	6.00
Bottle, Household, Hand Blown, Embossed, Corker	1.00
Bottle, Household, Keasby & Mattison, 5 In., Rectangular, Cobalt	6.00
Bottle, Household, Keasby & Mattison, 6 In., Round, Cobalt	3.00
Bottle, Household, Larkin Soap Co., Emerald Green, Preston, N.H.	4.00
Bottle, Household, Mouse Exterminator, Embossed, Dated 1918, Wire Legs	7.50
Bottle, Household, Puritana, Oval, 6 1/2 In., Cobalt, 1 1/2 In.Letters	7.00
Bottle, Household, Sawyers Bluing, Emerald, 8 In.	10.00
Bottle, Indiana, Clear, Stopper, 1900-1910	1.25
Bottle, Ink, Aqua, Umbrella, 2 3/4 In.	8.00
Bottle, Ink, Arnold, Pottery, Quart, 75 % Label	9.00
Bottle, Ink, Beveled Edge, Aqua, Marked, Square, 2 1/2 In.Tall	23.50
Bottle, Ink, Billing's Mauve, Domed, Sheared Top, Aqua	15.00
Bottle, Ink, Carter's, Cathedral, Quart, Cobalt	40.00
Bottle, Ink, Carter's, Figural, Ma Carter, China, Germany	10.00 To 30.00
Bottle, Ink, Caw's	6.00
Bottle, Ink, Caw's, Schoolhouse, Bimal, Aqua	3.50
Bottle, Ink, Cone, Amber	3.50 To 5.00
Bottle, Ink, Cone, Blown, Amber	60.00
Bottle, Ink, Cone, L.H.Thomas, Embossed, Label, Aqua	11.50
Bottle, Ink, Cucumber	4.00
Bottle, Ink, Haley Ink Co., Quart, Sheared Lip, Tin Pour Lip, Bimal, Aqua	25.00
Bottle, Ink, Harrison's Columbian, Octagon, Aqua, 1 3/4 In.Tall	63.50
Bottle, Ink, House Shape, Blue	15.00
Bottle, Ink, J.& I.E.M., Turtle, Dated, Aqua	17.00
Bottle, Ink, Keene Geometric	85.00
Bottle, Ink, Master, Pat.1886, Cobalt, Spout, 9 In.High	22.00
Bottle, Ink, Pomeroy's, 1/2 Pint, Bimal, Aqua	8.00
Bottle, Ink, Pottery, Single Lip, Embossed Notts Langley Mill	25.00
Bottle, Ink, Pour Lip, Bimal, 16 Oz., Cobalt	4.50
Bottle, Ink, Sanford's, Milk Glass	3.00
Bottle, Ink, Sanford's, Quart, Round, Amber	6.00
Bottle, Ink, Signot, Cobalt, 6 In.	8.00
Bottle, Ink, Square, Cobalt	1.00
Bottle, Ink, Stafford's, 6 In.Tall, Cobalt	10.00
Bottle, Ink, Swirls, Cover, Square	4.98
Bottle, Ink, The Oliver Typewriter, Bimal, Clear	7.00
Bottle, Ink, Umbrella Shape, Amber, Stoddard, Pontil	75.00
Bottle, Ink, Umbrella, Bubbly, Green	15.00
Bottle, Ink, W.E.Bonney, Barrel, Aqua	17.50
Bottle, Ink, White Friars, Candied End, Stopper, Signed	55.00
Bottle, Jar, Hathorn Springs, Black Glass, Quart	15.00
Bottle, Jar, Honey, Clear, Amethyst, Beehive & Bees	9.00
Bottle, Jar, Measuring, Clear, Rochester Tumbler Co., Pat.1880	3.95
Bottle, Jar, Molded, 11 1/2 In.High, Blue	20.00
Bottle, Jar, Pickle, Amber, Bunker Hill	13.50
Bottle, Jar, Pickle, Bunker Hill, Aqua	15.00
Bottle, Jar, Pickle, Cathedral, Five Panel, 13 In.	18.00
Bottle, Jar, Pickle, Paneled Forget-Me-Not, Cover	25.00
Bottle, Jar, Pickle, Panels & Flowers, Clear, 13 In.Tall	50.00
Bottle, Jar, Pickle, Skilton Foote Bunker Hill, Amber	15.50
Bottle, Jar, Planter's Peanut, Lid, Square	20.00
Bottle, Jar, Snuff, P.Lorillard & Co.	11.50
Bottle, Jar, Tan Glaze, Brown, Cover, 12 In.Tall	35.00

Bottle, Jar, Tobacco, Amber, Globe, No Lid 6.00
Bottle, Jar, Tobacco, Rust & Green, Signed Handel 150.00
Bottle, Jar, Widemouth, Molded, Signed On Bottom, Aqua 7.50
Bottle, Jug, Amber, Cork Stopper, Iron & Wooden Handle, 2 Gallon 3.75
Bottle, Jug, Holtz Freystadt Co., Amber, Handled, Round 20.00
Bottle, Jug, Macy & Jenkins, Amber, Handled, Round 20.00
Bottle, Jug, Seal Chestnut Grove, C.W., Flat Chestnut, Original Label 150.00
Bottle, Jug, Syrup, Libbey, Maize, Spring Lid 135.00
Bottle, Jug, Syrup, Mt.Washington, Fern Decor 95.00
Bottle, Jug, Vinegar, White House, Handle, Aqua 12.00
Bottle, Kahlua, Bum 38.00
Bottle, Keystone, 1854, Malt Whiskey, Applied Mouth, Amber 15.00
Bottle, L'abee Francois, Choir Boy 25.00
Bottle, Lionstone, Johnny Lightning 23.00
Bottle, Lionstone, Stp Racer 18.00
Bottle, Liqueur, Galliano, 1 Gallon, Labels, 27 In.High 22.00
Bottle, Liqueur, Lemon Horehound Rock & Rye, Oblique Embossing, Amethyst 5.00
Bottle, Liqueur, Pons's Rock & Rye With Horehound, Oval, Amethyst 5.00
Bottle, Loft's Pure Candies, Quart 3.00
Bottle, Mcallister's Mocking Bird Food, N.Y., Pint 10.00
Bottle, Medicine, Alexander's Cure, Labels, Contents 15.00
Bottle, Medicine, Allenrhu For Rheumatism & Neuritis, Pint, Clear 5.00
Bottle, Medicine, Armour's Vigoral, Chicago, Squat, Widemouth, Amber 3.00
Bottle, Medicine, Ayer's, Cobalt, Paper Label 8.00
Bottle, Medicine, Baver's Cough Cure, Aqua 2.50
Bottle, Medicine, Benne's Pain Killing Magic Oil, Slug Plate, Aqua 5.00
Bottle, Medicine, Buxton's Rheumatic, Embossed, Label, Aqua 10.00
Bottle, Medicine, Chamberlain's Cough Remedy 3.00
Bottle, Medicine, Chinese, Hand Blown, 3 In.Tall 2.25
Bottle, Medicine, Cobalt Blue, Eyecup Stopper 15.00
Bottle, Medicine, Cobalt, Free Blown, Rough Pontil, Stopper, 12 1/4 In. 25.00
Bottle, Medicine, Coltsfoote Expectorant, Label, Box, & Circular 5.00
Bottle, Medicine, Crownford, 8 In.Tall 15.00
Bottle, Medicine, Cuticura, For Curing Constitutional Humors 4.00
Bottle, Medicine, Dr.D.Jayne's Tonic Vermifuge, The Strength Giver 3.00
Bottle, Medicine, Dr.D.Kennedy's Favorite Remedy, Applied Lip, Clear 3.00
Bottle, Medicine, Dr.Daniel's Oster-Cocus Liniment .... *Illus* 5.00
Bottle, Medicine, Dr.Daniel's Wonder Worker, Wonder Misspelled, Clear ... 7.00
Bottle, Medicine, Dr.Jayne's Expectorant, Embossed, Aqua, 5 1/2 In. 2.50
Bottle, Medicine, Dr.Kilmer's Kidney, Liver, & Bladder Cure 6.00
Bottle, Medicine, Dr.Kilmer's Swamp Root Kidney, Liver, & Bladder Cure, Aqua 9.00
Bottle, Medicine, Dr.Kilmer's Swamp Root Kidney Remedy, Sample Bottle 3.00
Bottle, Medicine, Dr.Kilmer's U & O Anointment, Ground Lip, Aqua 5.00
Bottle, Medicine, Dr.King's New Discovery For Coughs & Colds, Aqua 4.00
Bottle, Medicine, Dr.Miles New Heart Cure, Aqua 5.00
Bottle, Medicine, Dr.Pierce, 8 1/2 In.High, Embossed R.V.Pierce, M.C., Aqua 4.00
Bottle, Medicine, Dr.Pierce's, Embossed, Whittled, 8 1/2 In.High, Aqua 4.00
Bottle, Medicine, Dr.Rumbaugh, Chicago, Ohio .... *Illus* 25.00
Bottle, Medicine, Dr.Sage's Buffalo Catarrh Remedy, 2 In. 3.00
Bottle, Medicine, Dr.Shoop's Family Medicines, Square 3.00

Bottle, Medicine, Dr.Daniel's
Oster-Cocus Liniment

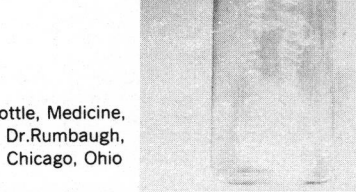

Bottle, Medicine,
Dr.Rumbaugh,
Chicago, Ohio

Bottle, Medicine, Dr.Thompson's Eye Water		3.00
Bottle, Medicine, Electric Brand Laxative, Amber, Label & Contents		8.00
Bottle, Medicine, Elepizone Cure		30.00
Bottle, Medicine, Embossed, Hand Blown, Corker		1.00
Bottle, Medicine, Eno's Fruit Salts, Glass Stopper		5.00
Bottle, Medicine, Foley's Kidney Cure, Sample		8.00
Bottle, Medicine, Garget Cure, C.T.Whipple, Aqua		7.00
Bottle, Medicine, Glover's Imperial Mange Cure, Amber		5.00
Bottle, Medicine, Gold Medal Harlem Oil, Label, Embossed		2.00
Bottle, Medicine, Granular Citrate Magnesia, 6 1/4 In., Cobalt		7.00
Bottle, Medicine, Grove's Chill Tonic		3.00
Bottle, Medicine, Grover Graham's Dyspepsia, Clear		5.00
Bottle, Medicine, Hall's Catarrh Cure, Aqua		2.50
Bottle, Medicine, Harper Method Tonic For The Hair, Martha Matilda Harper		4.00
Bottle, Medicine, Hart's Swedish Asthma Cure, Amber		3.00
Bottle, Medicine, Hayner's, Quart, Amber		12.00
Bottle, Medicine, Hayner's, Quart, Clear		3.50
Bottle, Medicine, Herring's Catarrh Cure, Cork, Box & Label		6.50
Bottle, Medicine, Himalaya, Kola Compound, Asthma Cure, Square, Amber		7.00
Bottle, Medicine, Hood's Pills, Liver Ills, Flask		4.00
Bottle, Medicine, Humphrey's Homeopathic Veterinary, Embossed Horse's Head		4.00
Bottle, Medicine, John Bull, Eye Cup, Clear		6.00
Bottle, Medicine, Ka Ton Ka, The Great Indian Remedy, Applied Lip, Clear		6.00
Bottle, Medicine, Kalish, 3 1/2 In., Square, Cobalt		5.00
Bottle, Medicine, Kendall's Spavin Cure, 12 Sided, Amber		4.00
Bottle, Medicine, Kendall's Spavin, Amber		2.50
Bottle, Medicine, Kennedy's Medicinal Discovery		4.00
Bottle, Medicine, Kickapoo Oil		4.00
Bottle, Medicine, Kidney Cure, Forestine, Label		16.50
Bottle, Medicine, Lactopeptine, 8 In., Cobalt		10.00
Bottle, Medicine, Liver Invigorator, Aqua		3.00
Bottle, Medicine, Log Cabin Cough & Consumption Remedy		95.00
Bottle, Medicine, Lydia Pinkham, 1906, 95 Percent Label		4.50
Bottle, Medicine, M.Fenner's People's Remedies, Usa, 1872, 1898		3.00
Bottle, Medicine, Mange Cure, Amber		3.00
Bottle, Medicine, Medicinal Solution Of Pyrozone, Glass Stopper		7.00
Bottle, Medicine, Mexican Mustang Liniment, Brooklyn, N.Y., Amethyst		5.00
Bottle, Medicine, Mrs.Winslow's Soothing Syrup	1.50 To	3.00
Bottle, Medicine, One Minute Cough Cure, Aqua		2.50
Bottle, Medicine, Opium, Open Pontil, Aqua		6.00
Bottle, Medicine, Ozomulsion, Dark Amber		3.00
Bottle, Medicine, Paine's Celery Compound, Amber		4.00
Bottle, Medicine, Parker's Hair Balm, Amber		5.00
Bottle, Medicine, Peptoenzyme, Cobalt, Label & Contents, 3 In.		7.00
Bottle, Medicine, Piso's Consumption Cure, Aqua		2.50
Bottle, Medicine, Piso's Consumption Cure, Emerald Green	5.00 To	7.00
Bottle, Medicine, Pitcher's, The Kind The Baby Cries For, Castoria, Aqua		3.00
Bottle, Medicine, Portus Cure Of Pain, Aqua		2.00
Bottle, Medicine, Portus Cure Of Pain, Clear		2.00
Bottle, Medicine, Psychine, Greatest Of Tonics, Label, Box, & Circular		5.00
Bottle, Medicine, Radam's, The Water Of Life, Embossed Man & Skeleton, Quart		25.00
Bottle, Medicine, Reed's Gilt Edge Tonic, 1878, Rectangular, Bimal, Amber		28.00
Bottle, Medicine, Round, Aqua		4.00
Bottle, Medicine, Royal Gall Remedy, 7 1/2 In., Amber		8.00
Bottle, Medicine, Sal Eminant, Rectangular, 5 In., Cobalt		6.00
Bottle, Medicine, Sanford's Radical Cure, Cobalt		20.00
Bottle, Medicine, Saymen's Vegetable Liniment, Catarrh & Colds		30.00
Bottle, Medicine, Schenck's Pulmonic Syrup, 8 Sided		6.50
Bottle, Medicine, Scott's Emulsion Cod Liver Oil, Raised Fisherman, Aqua		4.75
Bottle, Medicine, Scott's Emulsion With Lime & Soda		3.00
Bottle, Medicine, Sloan's Sure Colic Cure, Aqua		3.50
Bottle, Medicine, Smelling Salts, Bullet Shape, Eight Sided, Emerald Green		4.00
Bottle, Medicine, Spavin Cure, Amber		4.00
Bottle, Medicine, Spohn's Distemper Cure, Epizotic & Glut		4.00
Bottle, Medicine, Swanson's Rheumatic Cure, Aqua		6.00
Bottle, Medicine, United States Medicine Co., N.Y., Aqua		4.00

Bottle, Medicine, Wakefield's Blackberry Balsam 3.00
Bottle, Medicine, Warner's Kidney & Liver Cure 12.00
Bottle, Medicine, Warner's Safe Cure Co., Sample, Embossed, Dug, Amber 20.00
Bottle, Medicine, Warner's Safe Cure, Small Size, Amber 25.00
Bottle, Medicine, Warner's Safe Kidney & Liver Cure, C.1880, Amber 10.00
Bottle, Medicine, Warner's Safe Nervine, Amber 43.00
Bottle, Medicine, Warner's Safe Nervine, 90 Per Cent Label 18.00
Bottle, Medicine, Warner's Safe Remedy, Clear 25.00
Bottle, Medicine, Warner's Safe Rheumatic Cure, Amber 40.00
Bottle, Medicine, Warner's, Dose Cap, 6 In., Cobalt 6.00
Bottle, Medicine, Warner's Log Cabin Hops & Buchi Remedy 14.00
Bottle, Medicine, Warner's Safe Diabetes Cure, Embossed 38.00
Bottle, Medicine, Warner's Safe Remedies, 12 1/2 Oz. 25.00
Bottle, Medicine, Warner's Safe Nervine, Rochester, N.Y., Amber, Pint 37.50
Bottle, Medicine, Whipple Garget Cure, Aqua 3.50
Bottle, Medicine, Whipple Garget Cure, Clear 3.50
Bottle, Medicine, Wolfstirn's Rheumatic & Gout Remedy, Embossed, N.J., Aqua 7.25
Bottle, Medicine, Wyeth, Dose Bottle With Cap 12.00
Bottle, Medicine, Wyeth, Dose Cap, Cobalt 5.00
Bottle, Midwestern, Club Shape, Swirled & Vertical Ribs, 8 In.High, Aqua 55.00
Bottle, Midwestern, Globular, Aqua, 11 In.High 110.00
Bottle, Milk Glass, Champlin's .... *Illus* 10.00

Bottle, Milk Glass, Champlin's

Bottle, Milk Glass, Senorita With Tiara, Miniature 20.00
Bottle, Milk, Ags & Co.1898, Metal Band, Clamp, Handle 45.00
Bottle, Milk, Borden's, Picture & Date, 1/2 Gallon, Amber 1.90
Bottle, Milk, Borden's, Quart, Amber 8.00
Bottle, Milk, Brown 1.75
Bottle, Milk, Duluth, Embossed, Tintop, 1/2 Pt. 1.50
Bottle, Milk, Milk Glass, A In Triangle, Japan, 3 In. 6.00
Bottle, Milk, Minnesota, Quart, Amber 4.00
Bottle, Milk, Missouri Pacific 2.00
Bottle, Milk, Orange Lettering, Pint, Clear 1.00
Bottle, Milk, Orange Lettering, Quart, Amber 1.75
Bottle, Milk, Parkside Dairy, East Rochester, N.Y., Painted, Amber, Quart 3.00
Bottle, Milk, Round, Amber, Embossed 14.00
Bottle, Milk, Special Dairy, 1914, Widemouth 3.50
Bottle, Milk, 1930s, Amber 1.75
Bottle, Miniature, Figural, Camel, Stopper On Howdah, German Crown, 2 In. 10.00
Bottle, Miniature, Sprite, Case Of 24, Filled & Capped 9.90
Bottle, Musical, Panel Cut, Faceted Stopper, Plays Two Tunes, 11 1/2 In.Tall 125.00
Bottle, Napoleon, Folding Fan 15.00
Bottle, Nursing, Embossed 4.00
Bottle, Nursing, Embossed Lyric, 10 Oz. 4.00

Bottle, Nursing, Franklin 4.50
Bottle, Nursing, Happy Baby 3.50
Bottle, Nursing, Safe Grip Ovale, Armstrong, 8 Oz. 2.50
Bottle, Obr, Titanic 12.00
Bottle, Obr, 5th Avenue Bus 12.00
Bottle, Oil & Vinegar, Pressed Glass, 7 1/2 In.Tall, Pair 22.00
Bottle, Old Crow, Chess 10.00
Bottle, Old Fitzgerald, O.S.U.Centennial 25.00
Bottle, Owl, Mortar & Pestle On Front, Says Owl Drug Co., White Milk Glass 20.00
Bottle, Paperweight Base, Cypriote, Leaves, Feathers, Heat Check At Bottom 295.00
Bottle, Parrot, White Milk Glass, Marked Destilereas El Lorito, 10 In.Tall 15.00
Bottle, Paul Jones, Blob Seal, Quart 9.00
Bottle, Pepper Sauce, Gothic Arch, Octagonal, Aqua Blue 30.00
Bottle, Pepper Sauce, Gothic, Six-Sided, Aqua 17.00
Bottle, Pepper Sauce, Ridges, E.R.Durkee, Green 19.00
Bottle, Pepper Sauce, 8 1/2 In., Aqua 9.50
Bottle, Pepper Sauce, 15 Ridges, C.C.O.Pat.Sept.28, 1875 .... 12.00
Bottle, Pepper Sauce, 20 Ring, Aqua 10.00
Bottle, Perfume, Amber, Stopper 8.00
Bottle, Perfume, Atomizer, Iridescent, Marked Devilbiss 6.75
Bottle, Perfume, Blue, Pressed Glass, Oblong, Stopper 15.00
Bottle, Perfume, Bubbles, Stopper, Pairpoint 38.00
Bottle, Perfume, Cameo Cut, Signed V & S, Green Acid Cut Ground, Flowers 95.00
Bottle, Perfume, Cranberry Overlay 22.00
Bottle, Perfume, Cranberry, Cut, Stopper 25.00
Bottle, Perfume, Crystal, Brass Frame With Miniature Of Lady 15.00
Bottle, Perfume, Embossed Circle For Label, Bulbous, Emerald Green 7.00
Bottle, Perfume, Facet Cut, Ground Stopper, Pyralin Holder, French 2.50
Bottle, Perfume, Floral Design, Amber, 4 1/2 In.High 10.00
Bottle, Perfume, Floral, Gold, Porcelain, Pair 25.00
Bottle, Perfume, Francis Whittemore, Stopper Enclosing Blue Rose 225.00
Bottle, Perfume, Hobnail, White, Opalescent 8.50
Bottle, Perfume, Imperial Crown, Stopper & Label 2.50
Bottle, Perfume, Lalique, Dancing Nudes, Signed, 3 1/2 In.High 35.00
Bottle, Perfume, Mellier's, Stopper & Label 2.50
Bottle, Perfume, Pairpoint, Paperweight Style, Stopper, 7 1/2 In. 15.00
Bottle, Perfume, Paperweight, Pink Floral, Stopper, Signed St.Clair 20.00
Bottle, Perfume, Portrait, Cobalt, Gold Trim 15.00
Bottle, Perfume, Purse Size, Striped Glass, Marked Germany, 3 In. 18.50
Bottle, Perfume, Satin Glass, Pink, 4 1/2 In.High 23.00
Bottle, Perfume, Silver Deposit, Glass, Round, 2 In.Tall 9.00
Bottle, Perfume, Silver Overlay, Engraved Initials G.E.H., Emerald Green 40.00
Bottle, Perfume, Silver Overlay, Engraved Initials, M.S., Emerald Green 15.00
Bottle, Perfume, Square, Porcelain, Germany, 5 In.Tall 9.00
Bottle, Perfume, Vantine's Indian Perfume, Label, 4 3/4 In.Tall 2.25
Bottle, Perfume, White Opaline, Burgundy & Gold Trim 35.00
Bottle, Pickle, Blown, Panel, Ringed Neck, Square Base 33.50
Bottle, Pickle, Bunker Hill, Pint, Embossed, Amber 14.00
Bottle, Pickle, The M.A.Gedney Pickling Co., Pint, Amethyst 3.00
Bottle, Poison, Amber, Says Poison, Not To Be Taken, Ribbed, Hexagon 10.00
Bottle, Poison, Cobalt, Says Poison, Owl, Mortar & Pestle On Front, 5 In.Tall 18.00
Bottle, Poison, Dug, Embossed, Amber 2.00
Bottle, Poison, Eight Sided, Dug, Embossed, Cobalt 6.00
Bottle, Poison, Embossed, 6 In.Tall, Glass Lid, Clear 4.00
Bottle, Poison, In Round Wood Screw Cap Box, 5 In. 5.00
Bottle, Poison, Lattice, Round, 3 1/2 In., Cobalt 6.00
Bottle, Poison, Moberly Lade, B.C., Canada, Cobalt 10.00
Bottle, Poison, Owl, 2 7/8 In., Cobalt 8.00
Bottle, Poison, Skull & Crossbones, Dug, Embossed, Amber 5.00
Bottle, Poison, Trilets, Cobalt Blue 4.00
Bottle, Poison, Wyeth, 4 In., Oval, Cobalt, Hobnails 6.00
Bottle, Pushup Base, Dark Green 3.50
Bottle, Raised Letters, This Bottle Filled By Dudenhofer Bottling Co. 5.00
Bottle, Rev.J.B.Melhuisk, Sealed, Open Pontil, Olive Green 60.00
Bottle, Root Beer, Knapp, Colonial Man Holding Foaming Goblet, Aqua 12.00
Bottle, Royal Doulton, Sandeman, 1937, Coronation Crest 27.00

Bottle, Rubena, Crystal Faceted Stopper, 12 Panels Around, 5 In.Tall 32.50
Bottle, Rum, Carioca, Three Pirates & Chest, 1938 .... 20.00
Bottle, Safe Kidney & Liver Cure, Warner's, Embossed Front, Amber, 9 3/4 In. 10.00
Bottle, Sapphire Blue Glass, Metal Top 10.00
Bottle, Sarsaparilla, Ayer's Compound, Applied Mouth 12.00
Bottle, Sarsaparilla, Belfast, Maine, Label, Aqua, 9 In.Tall 12.00
Bottle, Sarsaparilla, Bristol's Genuine, Embossed, Dug, Bimal, Aqua 25.00
Bottle, Sarsaparilla, Brown, Aqua 8.00
Bottle, Sarsaparilla, Dalton's Sarsaparilla & Nerve Tonic, Aqua 12.00
Bottle, Sarsaparilla, Dalton's, Label 9.00
Bottle, Sarsaparilla, Dana's, Belfast, Maine, Aqua, 9 In.Tall 6.00
Bottle, Sarsaparilla, Dr.Green's 23.00
Bottle, Sarsaparilla, Foley's, Amber 12.50
Bottle, Sarsaparilla, John Bull, Deep Aqua 30.00
Bottle, Sarsaparilla, Masury's, Cloudy 47.00
Bottle, Sarsaparilla, Warner's Log Cabin 85.00
Bottle, Sarsaparilla, World's Columbian, Clear 38.00
Bottle, Sarsaparilla, Yager's, Amber 30.00
Bottle, Seltzer, Blue, 12 In. 5.00
Bottle, Seltzer, Green, 13 In. 5.75
Bottle, Seltzer, Harris Home Service, Brooklyn, Sapphire Blue 16.00
Bottle, Seltzer, Maiden Blush, Pink, 12 In. 5.00
Bottle, Shaker, Talc, Frosted, Brass Top, Patented 4.00
Bottle, Snuff, Blue & White Porcelain, Agate Top, Hexagon 50.00
Bottle, Snuff, Blue & White Porcelain, Two-Men Design, Blue Tiger Eye 75.00
Bottle, Snuff, Blue & White Procelain, Scenes, Carnelian Top 80.00
Bottle, Snuff, Blue & White, 6-Sided, Porcelain, Agate Top 50.00
Bottle, Snuff, Carved Ivory, Scenic 37.50
Bottle, Snuff, Carved Stone, Jade Top, Stand 155.00
Bottle, Snuff, Carved Translucent Mutton Jade Circle, Medallion, On Stand 85.00
Bottle, Snuff, Carved, Turquoise & Coral Insets, Tibetan, 4 In. 40.00
Bottle, Snuff, Chinese, Coral & Turquoise Inlay, 3 1/4 In.Tall 150.00
Bottle, Snuff, Chinese, Painted Inside, Peking Glass Trim 37.50
Bottle, Snuff, Chinese, Teakwood, Silver Inlay, 2 3/4 In.Tall 35.00
Bottle, Snuff, Crackle Blue & Gray Porcelain, Fisherman Design, Coral Top 95.00
Bottle, Snuff, Dr.Marshall's, Paper Label, Embossed, Contents 5.00
Bottle, Snuff, Emerald Green, Cut Glass, Germany 55.00
Bottle, Snuff, Figural, Fantail Fish, Jade 60.00
Bottle, Snuff, Figures In Relief, Porcelain, Green 40.00
Bottle, Snuff, Fisherman Design, Crackle Blue & Gray Porcelain, Coral Top 95.00
Bottle, Snuff, Fossilized Mammoth Tooth, Chinese 375.00
Bottle, Snuff, Ivory, Head Form, 2 1/2 In. 75.00
Bottle, Snuff, Ivory, Panels, Figures, On Stand, 19th Century, China 85.00
Bottle, Snuff, Jade & Silver, Coral Top & Center 200.00
Bottle, Snuff, Jade, Carved, Gray & Brown, Medallion, Stand 135.00
Bottle, Snuff, Jade, Heart Shape, Green 60.00
Bottle, Snuff, Jade, Mutton, Carved, Translucent, Medallion, Stand 85.00
Bottle, Snuff, Jade, Silver, Mongolian, Coral Top & Center 200.00
Bottle, Snuff, Mother-Of-Pearl, Ivory Panel On Each Side, Carved Tiger 65.00
Bottle, Snuff, Porcelain, Blue & White, Square, 2 Men Design, Tiger-Eye Top 75.00
Bottle, Snuff, Porcelain, Round, Blue & White, Orange, Carnelian Top 80.00
Bottle, Snuff, Rectangular, Crude, Green 20.00
Bottle, Snuff, Red On White, White Jade Stopper, Carved Horses, Trees, Peking 50.00
Bottle, Snuff, Round, Pontil, Olive Amber 35.00
Bottle, Snuff, Russian Malachite, Carved Stalking Tiger, Green 150.00
Bottle, Snuff, Square, Round Top, Green 40.00
Bottle, Snuff, Yellow Overlay, Painted Lining, Stopper, 2 1/8 In. 65.00
Bottle, Snuff, 4 1/2 In., Black 15.00
Bottle, Soda, A.J.Nevers, Norway, Me., Blob Top, Fluted Bottom, Aqua 6.00
Bottle, Soda, Aunt Ida, Embossed, Green 4.00
Bottle, Soda, C.C.& Co., Blob Top, Aqua 6.00
Bottle, Soda, C.R.Wigert, Burlington, Ia., C.1870, Aqua 4.00
Bottle, Soda, Canada Dry, Dated 1923, Marigold, Label 22.00
Bottle, Soda, Canada Dry, Dated 1923, White Carnival Glass, Label 22.00
Bottle, Soda, Canada Dry, Dated 1926, Marigold, Label 22.00
Bottle, Soda, Canada Dry, Dated 1926, White Carnival Glass, Label 22.00

Bottle, Soda, Canada Dry, Ginger Ale, Carnival Glass, Marigold 7.50
Bottle, Soda, Embossed Seltz Bros., Easton, Pa., Blob Top, Green 12.50
Bottle, Soda, Embossed, Aqua 3.00
Bottle, Soda, Embossed, Squat, Aqua 7.00
Bottle, Soda, English, Screw In Stopper, Embossed 5.00
Bottle, Soda, Eye-Se, Embossed, Clear 4.00
Bottle, Soda, Fanta, Miniature, Coca-Cola Product, Threaded Design, Label .... .50
Bottle, Soda, Fanta, Miniature, Threaded Design, 3 In.Tall .... .40
Bottle, Soda, Ginger Beer, Pottery 3.00
Bottle, Soda, Hippo, 1926, Embossed 5.00
Bottle, Soda, Hires Root Beer, Cobalt 8.00
Bottle, Soda, Hutchinson, Aqua, Rubber Gasket 4.50
Bottle, Soda, Hutchinson, Hand Blown, Wire Loop, Rubber Gasket, Aqua 4.50
Bottle, Soda, Hutchinson, Jos.Allgair, Sayreville, N.J., Aqua 5.00
Bottle, Soda, Hutchinson's, Blob Top, Canal, Dover, Aqua 5.00
Bottle, Soda, John Ryan, Cobalt, Graphite Pontil, Iridescent 26.00
Bottle, Soda, John Ryan, 1866, Cobalt Blue 25.00
Bottle, Soda, Lime Cola, Embossed, Clear 4.00
Bottle, Soda, Miniature, Sprite, Hobnail, Green, Emblem .... .50
Bottle, Soda, Moxie, Inscribed On Front & Back, 7 Oz., 8 In.Tall, Aqua 2.00
Bottle, Soda, Murray Bottling Works, Muncy, Pa., Blob Top, Aqua 6.00
Bottle, Soda, Nu-Icy, Embossed, Clear 4.00
Bottle, Soda, Pepsi Cola 4.95
Bottle, Soda, Round Bottom, Crown Top 1.00
Bottle, Soda, Rounded Bottom, 12 In. 2.98
Bottle, Soda, Schmuck's Ginger Ale, Cleveland, Ohio, Aqua 5.00
Bottle, Soda, Sprite, Miniature, Hobnail, Green, Filled & Capped .... .50
Bottle, Soda, Sprite, Miniature, Hobnail, Green, 3 In.Tall .... .50
Bottle, Soda, Star Boy, Cathedral, Dated, 7 Oz., Aqua 2.25
Bottle, Soda, Star Boy, Cathedral, Dated, 7 Oz.Green 2.25
Bottle, Soda, Star Boy, Cathedral, Dated, 9 Oz., Aqua 2.25
Bottle, Soda, Star Boy, Cathedral, Dated, 9 Oz., Green 2.25
Bottle, Soda, Uncle Jo, Embossed, Amber 4.00
Bottle, Soda, 5 Points, Embossed, Clear 4.00
Bottle, Sonnet Toilet Water, Full & Boxed 19.95
Bottle, Souvenir, World's Fair, 1939, White, Bulbous 6.50
Bottle, Square, Boy & Girl On Lid, Clear 7.50
Bottle, Stoddard, Free-Blown 15.00
Bottle, Stoneware, Ginger, English, Screw In Stopper 4.00
Bottle, Stoneware, Gray, 10 In. 6.00
Bottle, Stoneware, 3 Liters, 14 In.High 11.50
Bottle, Syrup, Swirl Ribs & Stripes, Blue, Opalescent 60.00
Bottle, Syrup, Thousand Eye, Amber, Dated 58.00
Bottle, Syrup, Torpedo, Stopper 27.50
Bottle, Talcum, Rubina, Red, Sterling Silver Cap, 8 In.High 39.00
Bottle, Toilet Water, Swirl Pattern, Metal Filigree Encased, C.1890 .... 7.50
Bottle, Vial, Wooden, 2 1/2 In.High, Stopper 1.25
Bottle, Vinegar, White House, Green 8.00
Bottle, Vinegar, White House, Green, Dancing Girl Design 18.00
Bottle, Vinegar, Whitehouse, Crackle Design, Flowers 5.50
Bottle, Vino Banderia, Woman From Spain, Ceramic 35.00
Bottle, Water, Buffalo Lithia, Embossed, Figure Of Woman, Aqua 16.00
Bottle, Water, E.P.Shaw & Co., Highest Award, Gold Medal, Table Water 3.00
Bottle, Water, Mineral, Bedford Springs Co., Aqua, Embossing Misspelled 15.00
Bottle, Water, Mineral, E.P.Shaw, Wakefield, Gold Medal Award, London, 1903 .... 3.00
Bottle, Water, Mineral, E.P.Shaw, Wakefield, 7 In. 3.00
Bottle, Water, Mineral, E.P.Shaw, Wakefield, 9 1/2 In. 3.00
Bottle, Water, Mineral, Hammond Mineral Water Co., Embossed, Blob Top, Amber 3.95
Bottle, Water, Mineral, Madden Co., Clarendon Springs, Derby, Round Bottom 3.00
Bottle, Water, Mineral, Madden Co., Clarendon Springs, Round Bottom, 7 In. 3.00
Bottle, Water, Mineral, Sweetwater Springs, Cal., 1/2 Gallon 4.50
Bottle, Water, Mineral, Veronica Medicinal Spring Water, Quart, Amber 6.00
Bottle, Water, Sno-Top Distilled, Clear, Label 4.00
Bottle, Water, Spring, Middletown Springs, Amber 38.00
Bottle, Water, Teepee 15.00
Bottle, Wheaton Nuline, Andrew Jackson 5.00

Bottle, Wheaton Nuline, Andrew Jackson, Green	5.00
Bottle, Wheaton Nuline, Apollo Ii	20.00
Bottle, Wheaton Nuline, Charles Evans, Light Blue	5.00
Bottle, Wheaton Nuline, Hughes	5.00
Bottle, Wheaton Nuline, Paul Revere, Blue	5.00
Bottle, Whiskey, A & Dh Chambers, Amber, Dated, Thread Glass Stopper, Quart	37.50
Bottle, Whiskey, A.J.Wintles & Sons, Bill Mill, Mr.Ross, 7 In.	3.00
Bottle, Whiskey, A.J.Wintles & Sons, Bill Mills, Mr.Ross, 6 1/2 In., Amber	3.00
Bottle, Whiskey, Ashburton, 10 1/2 In.Tall	30.00
Bottle, Whiskey, Bar, Lincoln Club Lettering, Enameled, Clear	15.00
Bottle, Whiskey, Benedictine, Green, Label, Miniature	7.00
Bottle, Whiskey, Bonnel & Co., Ky., 1 1/4 Quart, Glass Stopper, Clear	6.00
Bottle, Whiskey, Bourbon, Pig, Clear, 7 In.	35.00
Bottle, Whiskey, Brown-Forman Co., Distillers, Louisville, Ky., 1/2 Pint	9.50
Bottle, Whiskey, Cabin Still, Deer	11.00
Bottle, Whiskey, Cabin Still, Fleur-De-Lis	7.50
Bottle, Whiskey, Cabin Still, Pheasant	11.00
Bottle, Whiskey, Coco Marjieni, Paris, 3 Mold, Whittled, Squat, Deep Green	8.00
Bottle, Whiskey, Colebrook & Co., Rye, 9 In.	3.00
Bottle, Whiskey, Dallemond & Co., Inc., Chicago, Quart, Amber	7.00
Bottle, Whiskey, Dewar & Sons, Quart, Label, Olive	12.00
Bottle, Whiskey, Duffy's Malt Whiskey, Quart, Amber	4.00
Bottle, Whiskey, Dunbar's, Quart, Green	8.00
Bottle, Whiskey, Embossed Black & White, Quart, 3 Mold, Green	15.00
Bottle, Whiskey, Etched Leaves, Stopper	15.00
Bottle, Whiskey, Flask, Fifth, Deep Amethyst	4.00
Bottle, Whiskey, Flask, Pint, Deep Amethyst	3.00
Bottle, Whiskey, Four Roses, Embossed, Dug, Miniature, Amber	4.00
Bottle, Whiskey, George Holley, Ltd., Nottingham, Raised Sheaf Of Wheat	3.00
Bottle, Whiskey, German, Pretzel Shape, 7 In.	17.00
Bottle, Whiskey, Gibbs Special, Quart, Amethyst	16.50
Bottle, Whiskey, Golden Wedding, 1/2 Pint, Carnival Glass	7.00 To 10.00
Bottle, Whiskey, Green River	4.00
Bottle, Whiskey, Hand Blown, Embossed, Corker	1.00
Bottle, Whiskey, Hayner's, Amethyst, Quart	12.50
Bottle, Whiskey, Hayner's, Embossed, Label	6.75
Bottle, Whiskey, Hayner's, Pat.Date 1879, Embossed, Amber	10.00
Bottle, Whiskey, Held By Composition Old Man In Four Parts	15.00
Bottle, Whiskey, Hollywood, Amber	3.75
Bottle, Whiskey, Hollywood, Quart, Amber	7.50
Bottle, Whiskey, Imperial, Quart, Bubbles, Applied Mouth, Dark Green	12.00
Bottle, Whiskey, Inside Screw, 1/2 Pint, Amber	25.00
Bottle, Whiskey, J.Rieger & Co., Quart, Amethyst	7.00
Bottle, Whiskey, Jaranson, Full Measure, Seattle, Wash., Quart, Amber	21.00
Bottle, Whiskey, L.Greenbaum Crescent Club, Quart, Flask, Amber	20.00
Bottle, Whiskey, Lady's, 4 1/2 In.	1.75
Bottle, Whiskey, Little Corn, Blue, Iridescent	135.00
Bottle, Whiskey, Macy & Jenkins, Dark Amber	23.00
Bottle, Whiskey, Macy & Jenkins, Honey Amber	31.00
Bottle, Whiskey, Old Fitzgerald, White, Decanter	2.50
Bottle, Whiskey, Old Kentucky Distillers Co., Covington, Ky., Clear, Quart	5.00
Bottle, Whiskey, P.Chapman, P.C., Kirkstall, 9 In.	3.00
Bottle, Whiskey, Paper Label, Sold For Medicinal Purposes Only, Screw Cap	4.50
Bottle, Whiskey, Paul Jones, Amber	15.00
Bottle, Whiskey, Paul Jones, Bimal, Dug, Miniature, Amber	8.00
Bottle, Whiskey, Personal Service, Sherman Hotel, Chicago, Etched, 1870s	1.00
Bottle, Whiskey, Pierce Arrow Sport Phaeton, 1932, Mccoy Pottery, 1969	4.25
Bottle, Whiskey, Pretzel Shape, German, 7 In.High	17.00
Bottle, Whiskey, Rams Head Rye, Quart	3.00
Bottle, Whiskey, Ribbed, Amber, Labels, Cap, 1916 Stamp	15.00
Bottle, Whiskey, Rye, Colebrook & Co., 9 In.	3.00
Bottle, Whiskey, Sacks Sons, Quart, Amber	7.00
Bottle, Whiskey, Sam Bass, Baltimore, Md., Square, Indented Panels, Amber	22.00
Bottle, Whiskey, Smuggler, Old Gaelic, Black Glass	12.00
Bottle, Whiskey, Union, Rye, A & Dhc, Pittsburgh, Quart, Aqua	45.00
Bottle, Whiskey, W.Harper, Wicker Windows, Amber	15.00

Bottle, Whiskey, White Horse, Quart, Green 6.50
Bottle, Whiskey, Whyte & Mackay, Glasgow, 3 Mold, Quart, Aqua 7.50
Bottle, Whiskey, Wright & Taylor, Amber, Label, Quart 4.00
Bottle, Wine Tester, Turn Mold, Olive Green 15.00
Bottle, Wine, Blob Top, Spun, Quart, Cobalt 65.00
Bottle, Wine, Brocton, Quart, Square Collar, Embossed Grape Cluster, Clear 5.00
Bottle, Wine, Clear, Enamel Flowers, Glass, 11 In.Tall 15.00
Bottle, Wine, Dug, Crooked Whittley, Olive Green, Stopper, Grantsville, Nevada 10.00
Bottle, Wine, Eight-O-Eight 10.00
Bottle, Wine, France, Cupid With Clock On His Shoulders, 14 In. 2.75
Bottle, Wine, Garrett, Sample 12.00
Bottle, Wine, Hyde In Script, Seattle, Wash., Full Measure, Quart, Amber 22.50
Bottle, Wine, James & Co., Wine Merchants, Bascomb, 9 In. 3.00
Bottle, Wine, Mascotte 8.00
Bottle, Wine, Star In Honeycomb 8.50
Bottle, Wine, 8 In., Light Brown 4.75
Bottle, Zanesville, Globular, Broken Swirl, 8 In.High, Deep Aqua 1700.00
Bottle, Zanesville, Globular, Plain, 9 1/2 In.High, Deep Amber 150.00
Bottle, Zanesville, Globular, Swirled To Left, 7 In.High, Aquamarine 175.00
Bottle, Zanesville, Globular, Swirled To Left, 7 1/2 In.High, Amber 375.00
Bottle, Zanesville, Globular, Swirled To Left, 7 3/4 In.High, Black Amber 450.00
Bottle, Zanesville, Globular, Swirled To Left, 7 3/4 In.High, Red Amber 400.00
Bottle, Zanesville, Globular, Swirled To Left, 7 5/8 In.High, Amber 275.00
Bottle, Zanesville, Globular, Swirled To Left, 8 In.High, Honey Amber 400.00
Bottle, Zanesville, Globular, Swirled To Left, 8 1/4 In.High, Amber 275.00
Bottle, Zanesville, Globular, Swirled To Left, 8 1/4 In.High, Black Amber 550.00
Bottle, Zanesville, Globular, Swirled To Left, 8 3/4 In.High, Aquamarine 120.00
Bottle, Zanesville, Globular, Swirled To Left, 8 3/8 In.High, Red Amber 200.00
Bottle, Zanesville, Globular, Swirled To Right, 7 3/4 In.High, Aquamarine 175.00
Bottle, Zanesville, Globular, Swirled To Right, 8 In.High, Yellow Amber 600.00
Bottle, Zanesville, Globular, Swirled To Right, 8 1/4 In.High, Amber 475.00
Bottle, Zanesville, Globular, Swirled, 7 1/2 In.High, Golden Amber 1100.00
Bottle, Zanesville, Globular, Swirled, 8 In.High, Green 700.00
Bottle, Zanesville, Globular, 12 In.High, Honey Amber 1300.00
Bottle, Zanesville, Globular, 24 Ribs, Swirl To Left, 7 1/2 In.High, Aqua 125.00
Bottle, Zanesville, Globular, 24 Ribs, Swirl To Right, 8 In.High, Amber 200.00
Bottle, Zanesville, Globular, 24 Ribs, Swirled To Left, 7 1/2 In.High, Aqua 120.00
Bottle, Zanesville, Globular, 8 In.High, Deep Amber 350.00
Bottles, Jug, Syrup, Signed Bennington 135.00
Bow, Basket, Oval, Recticulated, Applied Flowers & Rope Handle, C.1765 .... 140.00
Bow, Bowl, Famille Rose, Peonies, Central Blue Floral, C.1755 .... 90.00
Bow, Candlestick, Figure Of Peacock, C.1760, 10 1/2 In.High 425.00
Bow, Figurine, Bird Group, Birds, Nest, In Apple Tree, C.1760, 9 In.High 70.00
Bow, Figurine, Bunting, C.1760, 3 1/2 In.High .... *Illus* 350.00
Bow, Figurine, Bunting, C.1760, 3 1/4 In.High, Pair .... *Illus* 600.00
Bow, Figurine, Liberty, Bocage, Gilt, C.1765, 8 1/2 In.High 175.00
Bow, Figurine, New Dancer, Boy & Girl, C.1765, 8 In.High, Pair 225.00
Bow, Figurine, Pheasant, C.1760, On Tree Stump, 6 1/2 In.High 250.00
Bow, Pot Of Flowers, C.1760, Ribbed Tub, Floral Bouquet 150.00
Bow, Tureen, Stand, Covered, Blue & White, Oriental Landscape Panels, C.1760 .... 250.00

*Boxes of all kinds are collected. They were made of thin strips of inlaid
wood, metal, tortoiseshell, embroidery, or other material.*
Box, see also Porcelain, Store, Tin
Box, Battersea, see Battersea, Box
Box, Bible, Oak, Brown Paint, Cotter Key Hinges, Dated 1795 .... 45.00
Box, Bible, Red Paint, New Jersey Newspaper On Lid Dated 1795 .... 22.50
Box, Black, Gold, Red Floral, Lacquered, Wooden, Marked C.C.C.P., Russia, 4 In. 10.00
Box, Bonbonniere, Birmingham, C.1765, 3 In. .... *Illus* 425.00
Box, Bonbonniere, Carved, Flora Macdonald, C.1770 .... *Illus* 575.00
Box, Bonbonniere, Head Of Duchess Of Argyle, C.1780 .... *Illus* 575.00
Box, Brass, Covered, Rectangular, 18th Century 27.50
Box, Bread, Baker's, Green Paint, 'W.A.Fullerton, Bakery, Tuscola, Ill.' 12.50
Box, Bride's, Blue Ground, Lady Watching Man In Tree Decorated 155.00
Box, Bride's, Pennsylvania Dutch, C.1800, German Words, Flowers 225.00
Box, Bride's, Pennsylvania, Figure Of Girl, 'What I Love That Is Beautiful' 250.00

Bow, Figurine, Bunting,
C.1760, 3 1/2 In.High
See Page 56

Bow, Figurine, Bunting, C.1760, 3 1/4 In.High, Pair
See Page 56

Box, Bonbonniere, Head Of Duchess Of Argyle, C.1780
See Page 56

Box, Bonbonniere, Carved,
Flora Macdonald, C.1770
See Page 56

Box, Bonbonniere, Birmingham, C.1765, 3 In.
See Page 56

Box, Bride's, Wood, Oval, Painted Man & Woman, Penna., 19th Century	225.00
Box, Button, Brown Metal, Oval	2.00
Box, Candle, Cherry, Hanging, Lift Lid, Drawer, Dovetailed	125.00
Box, Candle, Painted Birds & Floral, Edward Hicks, Penna., C.1800	750.00
Box, Case, Vernis Martin, Louis XVI, Tortoiseshell Framework, Gold, C.1750	80.00
Box, Case, Vernis Martin, Round, Boucher Figures, Perfume Flask	80.00
Box, Casket, German, Gold Mounted Boxwood, Jewel, Rectangular, C.1745	2500.00
Box, Casket, Rectangular, Enamel, Couple, Boy, & Girl, Metal Mounts, C.1755	475.00
Box, Celluloid, Embossed Design Of Flowers, Acorns, Leaves, Basket Weave Top	8.00
Box, Celluloid, Harbor Scene, Ships, 6 X 8 In.	10.00
Box, Celluloid, Inside Has Mirror, Comb, Button Hook, Nail Buffer, Jar	20.00
Box, Celluloid, Lady On Green Background, 10 X 7 X 4 In.	15.00
Box, Celluloid, Man & Woman On Cream Background	10.00
Box, Celluloid, Outdoor Harbor Scene	
Box, Celluloid, Pink Satin Lining, Mirror Inside, Cream Ground, Violets	8.00
Box, Celluloid, Pink, Matching File, Buffer, Scissors	4.98
Box, Celluloid, Rose Satin Lining, Picture Mother & Child, 4 X 6 In.	8.00
Box, Celluloid, Violets On Top, Pink Lining & Mirror Inside Lid, 4 X 6 In.	8.00
Box, Chinese, Camphorwood, Carved, Brass Hasp, 8 3/4 X 4 3/4 X 5 In.	50.00
Box, Cigarette, Green, Covered	16.00

Box, Clear, Inset Porcelain Of Woman's Head, Ormolu Lid, Ribbed, 4 1/2 In.	55.00
Box, Cobbler's, 14 Tools	25.00
Box, Document, Chippendale, Walnut, Pennsylvania, C.1760, Scrolled Feet	375.00
Box, Document, Wood, Oval, Hinged, Painted Tulips, Penna.Dated 1868	140.00
Box, Dome Top, Covered With Blue Paper, Inscribed Inside, 7 1/2 In.Wide	35.00
Box, Dovetailed, Hanging, 2 Doors	37.50
Box, Egg Shape, Two Color Gold, Swirling Panels Of Flutes & Leaves, C.1780	130.00
Box, French, Enameled, Painting On Top, Silver With Gold Wash	115.00
Box, Hand-Painted Sailboat Scene, Aqua, 2 1/2 In.	35.00
Box, Hanging, Pennsylvania, 2 Drawers, Upside-Down Paintings Of Birds	225.00
Box, Hinged Lid, Inlay, Fruitwood, 4 1/2 X 6 X 2 1/2 In.High	16.50
Box, Inlaid, Fans & Star On Lid	55.00
Box, Italian, Paper & Straw, 18th Century, Diamond Medallion, Floral	170.00
Box, Jewel, Figure Medallion, Lift-Off Dome Cover, Signed Delaumoy	58.00
Box, Jewel, Gold, Figural, Lined, Splay Legs	34.00
Box, Jewel, Hinged, Opalescent	29.00
Box, Jewel, Man's, Rosewood, Dog House, Brass Fittings, Brass Dog	38.50
Box, Jewel, Oak, Painted Interior, Carved, 11 1/2 X 7 1/2 In.	24.00
Box, Jewel, Ormolu, Hinged Cover Set With Color Jewels, Velvet Lined	75.00
Box, Knife, Georgian, Inlaid Mahogany, Serpentine Case, Hinged, C.1780, Pair	500.00
Box, Knife, Mahogany, Brass Bound, Star Inlaid Interior, Shaped Front	45.00
Box, Knife, Mahogany, Slant Lid, Ogee Front, 18th Century, Pair	375.00
Box, Knife, Pine, Dovetail Corners	14.00
Box, Knife, Pine, 11 3/4 X 7 3/8 In.	8.00
Box, Knife, Sheraton, Inlaid Mahogany, C.1780, Serpentine Case, Pair	600.00
Box, Knife, Sheraton, Mahogany, C.1780, Oval Insert Of Urn & Leaves, Pair	500.00
Box, Lacquer, Oriental, Black, Gold Design, 10 1/2 In.Diameter	15.00
Box, Leather, Covered, Pincushion Top, Brass Nail Decoration & Feet	20.00
Box, Leather, Tooled, Brown	17.50
Box, Letter, Mahogany, Ogee Front, Checkered Inlaid Edge, Brass Handles	145.00
Box, Lift Top, Compartmented, Pine, Red, Dovetailed	30.00
Box, Lift Top, Decorated On Red Ground, Carved, Eagle, Birds, & Animals	55.00
Box, Lift Top, Green, 30 In.Wide	5.00
Box, Lift Top, Red Grained, Floral, 'for Ana Catharine Alder, 1830'	175.00
Box, Liquor Chest, Federal, Inlaid Mahogany, C.1790 .... *Illus*	350.00
Box, Mahogany Inlaid, Lift Lid, 2 Doors, Pigeonholes	150.00
Box, Mahogany, Brass Bound, Escutcheons, Handle	105.00
Box, Mahogany, Fitted Drawer, 9 In.Wide, 8 1/2 In.High	25.00
Box, Make-Up, Celluloid, Country Scene, Flowers On Sides, Mirror In Top	7.00
Box, Marble, Covered, 4 X 6 1/2 In.	5.00

Box, Liquor Chest, Federal,
Inlaid Mahogany, C.1790

Box, **Metal**, Enamel Top, Rural Scenery, Church & Bridge, 5 In.Diameter 35.00
Box, **Money**, European, Wrought Iron Lock, Hinges, & Chain 17.50
Box, **Mother-Of-Pearl Inlay At Key Hole & Cover**, 8 X 11 X 5 In. 22.00
Box, **New England**, Stenciled, Yellow Ground, Red & Brown Lines, Bird On Lid 100.00
Box, **Patch**, Ivory Miniature Under Glass, Viking Man & Woman, Silver Frame 65.00
Box, **Pencil**, Child's, 1915, Pen, Pencil, Eraser, Ruler, Chalk 8.00
Box, **Pencil**, Four Color Woods, Geometric Mosaic, 9 3/4 In.Long 22.00
Box, **Pennsylvania**, Cardboard, Red & Green Decoration, 'sarah Grays 1828' 95.00
Box, **Pill**, Enamel On Black Ground, Greek Head, Greek Key On Sides, France 45.00
Box, **Pill**, Enamel On Silver, Fantailed Fish, China 25.00
Box, **Pill**, Engraved Silver, Jade Stone On Top, China 25.00
Box, **Pine**, Dovetailed, Dome Top, Brown Marbelized Paint, 12 1/2 In.Wide 35.00
Box, **Pine**, Dovetailed, Lift Top, Till, 24 In.Wide, 9 In.High 25.00
Box, **Pine**, Dovetailed, Painted, 6 In.High, 17 In.Wide 30.00
Box, **Pine**, Dovetailed, 2 Compartments, Disk Handle, 5 X 9 In. 27.50
Box, **Pine**, Lift Top, Dovetailed, Green Paint 17.50
Box, **Pine**, Oval, Covered, American, C.1820, Bentwood Sides, Lock 90.00
Box, **Pine**, Slant Lid, Initials 'd.S.M.', 14 1/2 In.Wide 37.50
Box, **Pine**, Slant Top, Dovetailed, 19 In.Square 25.00
Box, **Pipe**, Cherry, Scroll Carved, Connecticut, C.1750, Upright, Drawer 900.00
Box, **Powder**, Art Nouveau, Satin Finish, Red, Pewter Decor Signed M.Hess 65.00
Box, **Powder**, Celluloid, White, Cover 3.98
Box, **Powder**, French, Gold Flashed, Enameled, Applied Porcelain Flowers 39.50
Box, **Powder**, The Cat & The Drum, Signed Porteiux, 4 1/2 In.Diameter 100.00
Box, **Ring**, Victorian, Mandolin, Horn, Music Box On Cover, Footed 17.50
Box, **Rose Center**, Two Views, Decor On Lid, China, Circa 1820, 3 3/4 In. 140.00
Box, **Rosebud**, Drawer On End, Brass Inlay 35.00
Box, **Rosewood**, Canted Sides, Ring Feet 40.00
Box, **Russian Lacquer**, Horsemen, Troikas, Peasants, Noble Ladies, 4 .... 239.50
Box, **Salt**, Pine, Hanging, Dovetailed, 2 Compartments 40.00
Box, **Salt**, Pine, Hanging, Wedge Shape, 16 1/2 In.High, 7 3/4 In.Wide 18.00
Box, **Salt**, Stave, Red 10.00
Box, **Salt**, Tin, Hanging, Pine Lid, Gold Bands, Word Salt, Germany 12.00
Box, **Salt**, Wooden, Hanging, Word Salt Across Front 12.00
Box, **Scent**, Enamel, 3 Cut Glass Bottles, South Staffordshire, C.1770 .... 160.00
Box, **Seed**, Compartments, Slide Lid, Heart Carving On Lid, Dated '1835, S-K' 150.00
Box, **Sewing**, Burl, Inlays Of Mother-Of-Pearl 45.00
Box, **Sewing**, Chinese, Lacquered, Writing Case Drawer, C.1840 .... 175.00
Box, **Sewing**, Compartments, Slide Lid, Figured Maple, 7 X 4 1/2 X 2 In. 65.00
Box, **Sewing**, Federal, Inlaid Mahogany, C.1790-1810, Drawer, 13 In.Long 175.00
Box, **Sewing**, Veneered, Tray, Bun Feet 17.50
Box, **Sewing**, Wood, Brown & Green Painted & Decorated, American, C.1850 .... 120.00
Box, **Simulating A Shelf Of Leather-Bound Books** 27.50
Box, **Snuff**, Carved Wood, Foot Shape, Hinged 22.50
Box, **Snuff**, Dutch Shoe, Wooden 10.00
Box, **Snuff**, Engraved Jockey On Horse, Race Track, Pat.1869, Metal 28.00
Box, **Snuff**, Figure On Horseback, Brass, Silver Plate, Handmade, 18th Century 38.00
Box, **Snuff**, Lacquered, Inlaid Mother-Of-Pearl Top, 3 X 1 1/2 In. 10.00
Box, **Snuff**, Made Of Horn 20.00
Box, **Snuff**, Mahogany, Brass Trim, Hinged, Inlaid, Full 20.00
Box, **Snuff**, Red Lacquer, Gold Flower Spray, Butterfly On Lid, Oriental 9.50
Box, **Snuff**, Victorian, Silver Gilt, Marked F.M., Birmingham, 1854, Engraved 150.00
Box, **Snuff**, Wooden, Puzzle, English, C.1810 .... 17.50
Box, **Soap**, Engraved Owl Amid Foliage, Silver 22.00
Box, **Spice**, Hanging, 8 Drawers, Porcelain Knobs 35.00
Box, **Stamp**, Pan-American Exposition, Buffalo, Aluminum 4.00
Box, **Tea Caddy**, Regency, Satinwood, Apple, C.1850 .... *Illus* 200.00
Box, **Tea Caddy**, Regency, Satinwood, Keyhole Escutcheon .... *Illus* 175.00
Box, **Tea Caddy**, Regency, Satinwood, Pear, C.1850 .... *Illus* 120.00
Box, **Tea Caddy**, Regency, Satinwood, 19th Century 200.00
    Box, **Tea Caddy, see also Furniture, Tea Caddy**
Box, **Tobacco**, Rectangular, Enamel, Gilt Mounts, South Staffordshire, C.1765 .... 500.00
Box, **Tobacco**, Silver & Tortoiseshell, Oval, Engraved Armorials, 18th Century 100.00
Box, **Trinket**, White, Cherub On Top 35.00
Box, **Trinket**, White, Ribbed With Grapes 35.00
Box, **Tunbridge Ware**, Fitted Interior, English, 19th Century 30.00

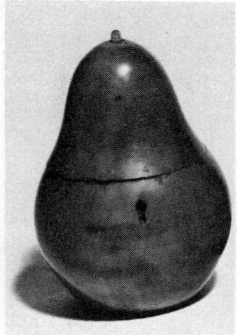

Box, Tea Caddy, Regency, Satinwood, Pear, C.1850
See Page 59

Box, Tea Caddy, Regency,
Satinwood, Apple, C.1850
See Page 59

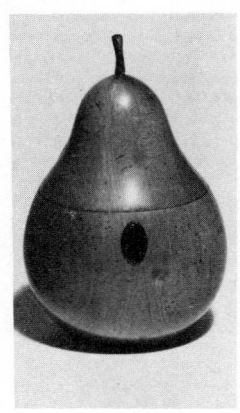

Box, Tea Caddy, Regency, Satinwood, Keyhole Escutcheon
See Page 59

Box, Vanity, Parquetry Inlaid, Two-Drawer Interior, Mirror In Top	70.00
Box, Wall, Hanging, Pine, Gray Paint, 'made With A Knife By Rev.Joel Winch'	450.00
Box, Walnut, Star Inlaid Top	35.00
Box, Watteau Scene, Cobalt & Gold, Hinged, Molded Feet	55.00
Box, Wood, Dome Top, Painted, Stippled Decoration, 10 1/2 In.Wide	55.00
Box, Wooden, Cylindrical, Inlaid Sterling Sunburst In Lid, Pierced	12.50
Box, Work, Chippendale, Mahogany, Bracket Feet, Brasses	70.00
Box, Writing, Federal, Bird's-Eye Maple, Traveling, Boston, C.1800, 4 Drawers	250.00
Box, Writing, Inlaid Mahogany, Traveling, 19th Century, 19 In.Long	120.00
Boy Scout, Book, Corley Of The Wilderness Trails, 1937	2.00
Boy Scout, Book, Year, 1929	3.00

Brass has been used for decorative pieces and useful tablewares since ancient times. It is an alloy of copper, zinc, and other metals.

Brass, see also Bells, Bronze, Miniature, Tools, Trivet, etc.

Brass, Andiron, Miniature, Pair	7.50
Brass, Angel, Painted Gold, 9 1/2 In.High	25.00
Brass, Basin, Signed, Flared Rim, 12 In.	48.00
Brass, Bed Warmer, Engraved Lid, Iron Handle, Queen Anne Period	130.00
Brass, Bed Warmer, Flower Stenciling, Maple Handle	100.00
Brass, Bed Warmer, Iron Handle	25.00
Brass, Bed Warmer, Iron Handles, Hand Forged, Brass Lid	25.00
Brass, Bed Warmer, Pierced & Engraved	45.00
Brass, Bed Warmer, Pierced & Etched	35.00
Brass, Bed Warmer, Wood Handle, Embossed, 42 In.Long	85.00
Brass, Bee Smoker, Plated	2.75
Brass, Bell, Cow, Leather Neck Strap, Brass Buckle, 4 In.Diameter	8.50
Brass, Bell, Cow, Leather Neck Strap, Brass Buckle, 5 In.Diameter	12.50
Brass, Bell, Disciples	42.50
Brass, Bell, Fur Trade, C.1855, St.Louis	3.00
Brass, Bell, Hand, Figure Of Napoleon On Handle	12.00
Brass, Bell, Roman Soldier	15.00
Brass, Bell, School, Maple Handle	35.00
Brass, Bell, School, Wooden Handle	27.50

Brass, Bell, School, 4 In. 8.00
Brass, Bell, Sleigh, String Of 35, Etched, Leather Strap 65.00
Brass, Bell, String Of 30 Alternating 45.00
Brass, Bell, Tugboat, Hanger, Clapper, 10 In.Diameter 150.00
Brass, Bell, Turkey 12.50
Brass, Belt Plate, British Cross, 8th Regt., War Of 1812, Rectangular 325.00
Brass, Birdcage, Wire, 9 X 12 X 11 In. 15.00
Brass, Blow Torch 3.50
Brass, Bob, Plumb, Carpenter's 7.50
Brass, Bookend, Monk Figure, Floral Design, 7 In.Tall, Set 32.00
Brass, Bootjack, Beetle, 10 In. 35.00
Brass, Bottle, Miniature, Screw Brass Top, 2 In., Pair 5.00
Brass, Bowl, Dragon Design, Etched, Teak Stand, 9 In.Diameter 8.50
Brass, Bowl, Marked China, Etched, Teakwood Stand 10.00
Brass, Bowl, Openwork, 7 In. 12.50
Brass, Bowl, Scalloped, Footed, Mark China 4.95
Brass, Bowl, Shallow, 10 In. Diameter 22.00
Brass, Bowl, Sifting, Apothecary, Late 18th Century, Set Of 4 Graduated 22.00
Brass, Box, Copper & Silver Panels, Repousse Elephant On Lid, India, 4 In. 11.00
Brass, Box, Jewelry, Portraits On Cover, Ivory, Signed, Plays Tunes 165.00
Brass, Box, Match, Advertising, Est.1866, Curtis Bros., Brass, Hinged Top 10.50
Brass, Box, Match, Gott Mit Uns, Imperial Germany Crown & Wreath 12.50
Brass, Box, Medallion, Enamel, Insects, Floral, China, 6 1/2 X 4 1/2 In. 35.00
Brass, Box, Octagonal, Pierced, Handle, Ball Feet 25.00
Brass, Box, Patch, Enamel, Marked China, 1 1/2 X 1 In. 7.00
Brass, Box, Porcelain Insert, Echo, Signed Wagner, 2 1/2 In.Across 150.00
Brass, Box, Stamp, Chinese, Enamel, Hand-Painted Scene, 4 Feet, Marked 29.00
Brass, Box, Stamp, Footed, 3-Section, Hinged Cover 18.00
Brass, Box, Trinket, Victorian, Hinged, 4 Feet, Orse Casting, Blue Lines 9.00
Brass, Bridle Rosette, Glass Covers, 1889, Pair 50.00
Brass, Bridle Rosette, U.S.Cavalry, Pair 10.00
Brass, Bucket, Ansonia, 1851, 11 In.High 45.00
Brass, Bucket, Hammered, 15 In.Diameter 55.00
Brass, Bucket, Signed Waterbury, 12 In. 45.00
Brass, Bucket, Spun, Signed & Dated, 12 In.Diameter 40.00
Brass, Bucket, Wrought Iron Bail Handle, American, 19th Century, Nest Of 5 ...... 210.00
Brass, Buckle, Belt, U.S.Dragoon, Oval, C.1840-50, Marked U.S. 27.50
Brass, Bust, Abraham Lincoln, Wall, 6 In. 18.00
Brass, Candelabrum, 3 Branch, Enamel Embossing, 11 1/2 In.High 38.00
Brass, Candelabrum, 3 Branch, Enameled Flowers, 9 In.Spread, 10 In.High 16.50
Brass, Candelabrum, 5 Branch, Glass Bobeches, Fleur De Lis & Leaves, 11 In. 24.50
Brass, Candelabrum, 5 Branch, Gothic Stem, 31 In.High 75.00
Brass, Candelabrum, 5 Branch, Leaves, Wheat, Grapes, Claw Feet, 29 In.High 75.00
Brass, Candelabrum, 5 Branch, Lion Paw Feet, 22 1/2 In., Pair 59.50
Brass, Candelabrum, 5 Branch, Urn Holders, Saucer Bobeches, Pair 50.00
Brass, Candelabrum, 7 Branch, Dolphin Feet, 25 In.High 75.00
Brass, Candelabrum, 10 Branch, 37 In.High, Pair 75.00
Brass, Candleholder, Religious, 18 In.High, Pair 42.00
Brass, Candleholder, Saucer, Push-Up, Thumb Grip, Burnished 27.50
Brass, Candlesnuffer, Bird Finial, 12 In.Handle, Marked China 30.00
Brass, Candlesnuffer, Footed, Tray, Scalloped & Embossed 23.50
Brass, Candlestick, Beehive, Push-Up, Cut Corner Base, 8 In., Pair 35.00
Brass, Candlestick, Beehive, Push-Up, 9 In.Tall 45.00
Brass, Candlestick, Beehive, Push-Up, 10 In.Tall, Pair 38.00
Brass, Candlestick, Beehive, Push-Up, 10 1/2 In.Tall, Pair 45.00
Brass, Candlestick, Beehive, 8 3/4 In.High, 4 Matching 60.00
Brass, Candlestick, Bell Base, 5 In. 65.00
Brass, Candlestick, C.1910, 28 1/2 In.High 125.00
Brass, Candlestick, Capstan, Engraved, 4 1/2 In.High 75.00
Brass, Candlestick, Chamber, Ring Handle, Thumb Rest, Marked China 4.75
Brass, Candlestick, Drum Base, 17th Century, 5 In.High, Pair 120.00
Brass, Candlestick, Ejector, 7 In.High 17.50
Brass, Candlestick, English, Octagonal Base, 11 In., Pair 65.00
Brass, Candlestick, Engraved, 17th Century, 6 Sided Drip Pan, Pair 160.00
Brass, Candlestick, Flat Base, Twisted Stem, 5 1/4 In.High 50.00
Brass, Candlestick, Georgian, Square Base, 9 1/2 In.High, Pair 57.50

Brass, Candlestick, Gothic, Footed, Spiked Top, 18 In.High, Pair	29.50
Brass, Candlestick, Grape Design, 7 1/2 In.High	12.50
Brass, Candlestick, Hexagonal, Spikes, 13 In.High, Pair	17.50
Brass, Candlestick, Incised Designs, 25 In.High	100.00
Brass, Candlestick, Inverted Saucer Base, C.1690, 9 In.High	65.00
Brass, Candlestick, Louis XVI, 11 In.Tall, Pair	168.00
Brass, Candlestick, Miniature, Pair	7.50
Brass, Candlestick, Octagonal Base, 5 1/2 In.High, Pair	95.00
Brass, Candlestick, Push-Up Rod, 12 In., Pair	22.50
Brass, Candlestick, Push-Up, Bell Pattern, Square Base, 8 1/8 In.High	12.75
Brass, Candlestick, Push-Up, C.1850, 8 1/2 In.Tall, Pair	50.00
Brass, Candlestick, Push-Up, Diamond Knops, Hand Polished, 10 In., Pair	45.00
Brass, Candlestick, Push-Up, Etched Globe, 17 In.Tall	45.00
Brass, Candlestick, Push-Up, 12 In., Pair	60.00
Brass, Candlestick, Queen Anne, Scalloped Base, 7 3/4 In.High, Pair	225.00
Brass, Candlestick, Queen Anne, 9 1/4 In.High, Pair	425.00
Brass, Candlestick, Queen Anne, 18th Century	24.00
Brass, Candlestick, Ribbed Circular Base, 5 1/2 In.High	45.00
Brass, Candlestick, Saucer Base, Ring Turned Stem, Pair	50.00
Brass, Candlestick, Saucer, Glass Chimney, 5 X 8 In.	10.00
Brass, Candlestick, Saucer, Ring Handle	19.00
Brass, Candlestick, Saucer, Side Handle	9.50
Brass, Candlestick, Scroll Feet, Spiked Tops, 15 In.High, Pair	29.50
Brass, Candlestick, Scrolls, Leaves, Prisms, Brass, Marble Base, Pair	25.00
Brass, Candlestick, Spooled, Octagonal Base With Raised Circle, C.1750, Pair	50.00
Brass, Candlestick, Square Base, C.1700	35.00
Brass, Candlestick, Square Base, Footed, Taper Hole, 3 3/4 In.Tall, Pair	18.00
Brass, Candlestick, Square Base, Modified Paw Feet, 10 In.High, Pair	90.00
Brass, Candlestick, Square Base, Paw Feet, 8 1/2 In.High, Pair	70.00
Brass, Candlestick, Square Base, Push-Up, 11 3/4 In., Pair	59.00
Brass, Candlestick, Square-Footed Base, 18 In.High, Pair	85.00
Brass, Candlestick, Square, Notched Corner Base, 18th Century, Pair	95.00
Brass, Candlestick, Three Arms, Marked China, 6 3/4 In.High	4.95
Brass, Candlestick, Three Legs On Stand, Dated 1880, 20 1/2 In.High, Pair	65.00
Brass, Candlestick, Tripod, Incised Religious Designs, Pair	35.00
Brass, Candlestick, Victorian, Push-Up, Diamond Pattern, 12 In.High, Pair	45.00
Brass, Candlestick, Victorian, Push-Up, Beehive Pattern, 10 1/2 In.High, Pair	30.00
Brass, Candlestick, Wall, Scroll Arm, China, Pair	21.00
Brass, Candlestick, Winged Dragon, China, Pair	22.50
Brass, Candlestick, 3 Legged Stand, Dated 1880, 20 1/2 In.High, Pair	65.00
Brass, Candlestick, 7 3/4 In., Round Base, Baluster Stem, Pair	12.50
Brass, Candlestick, 9 1/4 In.High, Pair	30.00
Brass, Chamberstick, French	35.00
Brass, Chamberstick, Saucer Base, Push-Up, 6 1/2 In.Base	27.50
Brass, Chamberstick, Square Saucer, Handle, Circa 1840	30.00
Brass, Chamberstick, 3 3/4 In.Base	21.00
Brass, Chandelier, Church, Eight-Light, Electric	125.00
Brass, Chandelier, Georgian, 12 Light, Baluster, Upright, Dutch, C.1750	1300.00
Brass, Change Dispenser, San Francisco Trolley, Nickel Plated, Johnson Co.	37.50
Brass, Coal Box, Ball Feet, Slant Front, Embossed Decor, Shovel In Pocket	86.00
Brass, Coffee Server	195.00
Brass, Compass, Like Closed Faced Watch, 2 In.Diameter	18.00
Brass, Compass, Surveyor's, Scottish, C.1820-40, Glass Pane, Mahogany Box	135.00
Brass, Cooler, Champagne, Ring Handles In Lion's Mouth	20.00
Brass, Cover, Spittoon	9.00
Brass, Cross, Figure Of Christ, Incised Designs, C.1880, 28 In.High	50.00
Brass, Cuspidor, Lady's Size	19.00
Brass, Cuspidor, Weighted Base, 7 1/2 In.Diameter	20.00
Brass, Dipper, Iron Handle	9.00
Brass, Dipper, Wrought Handle	5.95
Brass, Dish, Devil Laying On Back, Holding Net, 4 In.Wide, 6 In.Long	9.75
Brass, Dish, Painted Black, Incised Lion Of Venice, Gondola	12.00
Brass, Door Knocker, Shape Of Ornate Handle	15.00
Brass, Doorbell, Brownstone, 1884	9.50
Brass, Drawer Pull, Sheraton Style, Lion's Head	4.00
Brass, Eagle, From Bank In Pennsylvania, 25 In.Wing Spread	200.00

Brass, Easel Mirror, Beveled Glass, 12 X 16 In.	27.50
Brass, Figurine, Beehive, Russian Bear Finial, Signed P.Tereszazuk, 6 In.	75.00
Brass, Figurine, Boy Holding Weight, 1903, 4 1/4 In.High	18.00
Brass, Figurine, Cherub, Marble Base, 17th Century, 5 In.High	28.00
Brass, Figurine, Cocks, Fighting, Feathery Tail, Pair	12.50
Brass, Figurine, Eagle, Full Body, 7 In.Wingspread	28.00
Brass, Figurine, Frog, 4 In.Long	4.95
Brass, Figurine, Man With Chisel & Hammer, Marble Base, 7 3/4 In.High	45.00
Brass, Figurine, Nude Lady, Arms Up	18.00
Brass, Figurine, Policeman, 5 3/4 In.High	18.00
Brass, Figurine, Woman With One Hand Up, 4 In.High	8.00
Brass, Fire Extinguisher, 2 1/2 Gallon Size	12.50
Brass, Fixture, Light, 1903, 13 In.Long	7.50
Brass, Flag, American, Lapel, Mechanical, 'to Hell With Spain'	25.00
Brass, Flashlight, Dated 1912	2.50
Brass, Font, Holy Water, Mother-Of-Pearl, Christ On Cross, C.1850	8.00
Brass, Foo Dog, Pair	50.00
Brass, Fork & Spoon, Serving, Horn & Fancy Handle, 11 In.	15.00
Brass, Fork, Toasting, Victorian, 16 In.	7.00
Brass, Frame, Standing, Ornate, 9 In.	10.00
Brass, Gong, Mounted On Metal Plate, 15 In.Diameter	35.00
Brass, Grater, Food, Handle, 7 X 18 In.	7.50
Brass, Harness Knob	25.00
Brass, Head Of Man, Mounted On Plexiglas Stand, 2 In.High	8.00
Brass, Helmet, Painted	9.75
Brass, Holder, Match, Two Compartments, Banjo, 15 In.High	25.00
Brass, Holder, Pencil, Spring Type	4.00
Brass, Hook, Bracket, Wall, Screw In Type, Extends 8 In.From Wall	2.00
Brass, Hook, Ceiling, Screw-In Type, Dolphin Design, For Lantern, 9 In.Long	4.75
Brass, Horn, Car, Bulb	22.00
Brass, Horn, For Car, Bulb, Black Paint	22.00
Brass, Humidor, Glass Liner, Tobacco In Raised Script On Front	15.00
Brass, Incence Burner, Chinese, Foo Dog On Lid, Open Scrollwork, 3 Legs	47.50
Brass, Incense Burner, Hanging Type, Hand Embossing, Piercing, Chains	85.00
Brass, Incense Burner, Kettle, Three Legs, Two Open Handles, China	6.00
Brass, Inkstand, Continental, 18th Century, Sander, Bell, & Seal Box	200.00
Brass, Inkstand, Continental, 18th Century, Urn-Shape Wells, Sander, Holders	150.00
Brass, Inkwell, Double, Ornate, 8 X 7 1/2 In.	32.00
Brass, Inkwell, Pen Rack, Calendar, Glass Insert, Pat.1914	8.75
Brass, Inkwell, Square, Footed Base, Groved For Pens, Hinged Lid, Porcelain	29.00
Brass, Jardiniere, Allover Relief Embossing, Men, Pyramids, Palm Trees	35.00
Brass, Jardiniere, Cast, 7 In.Deep, 9 In.Diameter At Top	12.50
Brass, Jardiniere, Handles, 8 In.High, 8 In.Diameter	9.75
Brass, Jardiniere, 8 In.High, 8 1/2 In.Diameter, Lattice Top	9.75
Brass, Kettle, Gypsy, Footed, Bail, Small	8.50
Brass, Kettle, Jelly, Cast, Iron Handles, 11 In.Diameter	18.50
Brass, Kettle, Jelly, Cast, Iron Handles, 12 In.Diameter	18.50
Brass, Kettle, Round, 7 1/2 In.High	15.00
Brass, Key, Ship, 4 In.	1.00
Brass, Key, Ship, 5 In.	1.00
Brass, Key, Ship's Stateroom	1.00
Brass, Lamp, Heater, Ruby Globe, 16 In.	57.50
Brass, Lamp, Minor, Burn Carbide, Hook	14.50
Brass, Lamps, Oil, Small	7.00
Brass, Lantern, Ship's Cabin, Etched Beveled Glass, Pair	165.00
Brass, Letter Opener, Acrobat Handle, 8 1/4 In.	7.50
Brass, Letter Opener, Knight Handle, 9 1/2 In.	12.50
Brass, Letter Opener, Oriental Figures On Top, Marked China	3.75
Brass, Light, Search, Ship's, Carbide, Brass Fuel Tank	175.00
Brass, Lighter, Cigarette, Ministers Of England	9.50
Brass, Lock, Eagle Lock Co., Embossed International Harvester Co.	6.00
Brass, Lock, J H W Climax, Newark, N.J.	6.00
Brass, Lock, Pagoma, 1908	4.00
Brass, Lock, Slaymaker, Lancaster, Pa., Patent Aug.5, '73	6.00
Brass, Match Safe, Figural, Cat With Mouse In Paws	25.00
Brass, Mortar & Pestle, Heavy, 4 In.Diameter	20.00

Brass, Mortar & Pestle, Spain	13.00
Brass, Mortar & Pestle, Spanish, 16th Century	85.00
Brass, Mortar & Pestle, Wooden Frame, Hangs, Drawer At Bottom	22.00
Brass, Mortar & Pestle, 17th Century, Incised Designs, 6 1/2 In.High	45.00
Brass, Mortar & Pestle, 3 In.High	15.00
Brass, Mortar & Pestle, 4 In.High	15.00
Brass, Muffin Stand, Three Tiers, Pierced Apron With Green Stone At Top	48.00
Brass, Nozzle, Thumbscrew, Pointed, For Hose	2.00
Brass, Nutcracker, Figural, Dragon	12.50
Brass, Opener, Bottle, Elephant, Mouth Removes Cap, 3 1/4 In.	5.00
Brass, Opener, Bottle, Marked Kinsey	4.50
Brass, Ornament, Dagger, Incised Designs, 18th Century, 10 1/2 In.High	20.00
Brass, Ornament, Wall, Diana Hunting, 7 1/2 In.Diameter	24.00
Brass, Ornament, Wall, Lamb Lying On Cross, 18th Century, 4 In.High	20.00
Brass, Pail, Spun Brass, Iron Bail, 9 In.Diameter, 4 1/4 In.High	35.00
Brass, Pan, Bed Warming, Pierced & Engraved	125.00
Brass, Pan, Handles, 9 In.Diameter	11.50
Brass, Pan, Handles, 12 In.Diameter	11.50
Brass, Pan, Iron Handle, 10 In.Diameter, 4 In.Deep	12.50
Brass, Pan, Round, High Handles 4 In.Deep	9.75
Brass, Pan, Round, Iron Handle, 9 In.Diameter	9.75
Brass, Pan, Round, 6 In.Deep, 16 In.Diameter	14.50
Brass, Pan, Wrought Iron Handle, 13 1/2 In.Diameter	17.50
Brass, Paper Clip, Horseshoe Shape, M.Myers & Son, Good Luck 1870, 4 In.Long	6.50
Brass, Paperweight, Flat, Chalmers Motor Car Co., Detroit	10.00
Brass, Picture, Easel Stand, Grecian Woman On Chariot In Relief	50.00
Brass, Pipe, Soap Bubble	4.00
Brass, Planter, Hanging, Signed England, Embossed, Copper Rivets, 8 In.Deep	50.00
Brass, Plaque, Eagle, Pressed, Spread Wings, 36 In.Long	225.00
Brass, Plaque, Wall, 2 Grecian Boys, Holding Flowers In Vase, Incised	30.00
Brass, Plate, Hand-Painted, Yellow, Red, Roses, 10 In.Diameter	7.00
Brass, Plate, On Stand, Chinese, Dragon Design	20.00
Brass, Plate, White House, Washington, D.C., Flowers In Relief On Rim	15.00
Brass, Pot, Hand Hammered, Footed, Cover, 14 In.High, 11 In.Diameter	22.00
Brass, Pot, Jelly, Signed Reiss, May 24, 1870, 9 1/2 In.Diameter, 6 In.Tall	35.00
Brass, Pump, Beer	35.00
Brass, Rattle, Child's, Ivory Handle, 19th Century, 6 1/2 In.	11.00
Brass, Razor, Gillette, Box	1.25
Brass, Salter, Spit Jack, 13 In.	80.00
Brass, Samovar, Russian, Signed	39.00 To 200.00
Brass, Scale, Wood Platform, 1/2 To 8 Oz.Weights	90.00
Brass, Scales, Gold Coin, Marked H.Maranville's Patent, Jan.1857, Ohio	115.00
Brass, Scales, Gold Miner's, California, Oval Tin Box, Orange Paint, 2 Pans	84.50
Brass, Sconce, Gaslight, Two Arms, Glass Shade, 11 1/2 In., Pair	25.00
Brass, Screen, Embossed Lady Sitting By Fireplace, Splayed Feet, 25 In.High	48.00
Brass, Server, Coffee, Turkish, Engraved	11.50
Brass, Shelf, Expandable, Two Ladies With Streaming Tresses, Art Nouveau	7.50
Brass, Shoe Horn, Advertising Brandt's, St.Louis	2.00
Brass, Shoe, Man's, Peeping Mice	15.00
Brass, Shoulderboard, Artillery Officer, Pair	10.00
Brass, Shovel, Coal, Wooden Handles	3.75
Brass, Spigot, Wine-Barrel	10.00
Brass, Spittoon, Burnished, 7 1/2 X 3 In.	15.00
Brass, Spittoon, Copper Bottom, Ornate Brass Handles	45.00
Brass, Spittoon, 6 In.High, 8 1/2 In.Diameter	22.50
Brass, Spoon, Caddy, Horn Of Ulphus	27.62
Brass, Spoon, Caddy, Lincoln Imp	27.62
Brass, Spoon, Tea Caddy	8.50
Brass, Spurs, Union Cavalry Officer's, Shape Of American Eagle, Pair	125.00
Brass, Stand, Kettle, Pierced Daisylike Design, 13 In.Long, 6 1/2 In.High	27.50
Brass, Stand, Umbrella, Lions' Heads Handles, Polished, 22 In.Tall	35.00
Brass, Stick, Columnar, Georgian, Hurricane Shade, 18th Century, Pair	225.00
Brass, Stomach Warmer, Filagree Top, Iron Pan & Handles	19.50
Brass, Strainer, Nickel Plated	5.00
Brass, Tape Measure, Figural, Pig	16.50
Brass, Taperstick, Flat Circular Base, 3 1/4 In.High	50.00

Brass, Tazza, Circular Revolving, Porcelain Plaque, Eagle, Mountain Goat	37.50
Brass, Tea Caddy, Basket Weave, Sailing Vessel	18.50
Brass, Teakettle, Amber Grip, Bun Feet, 8 In.High	38.00
Brass, Teakettle, Gooseneck Spout, Stationary Handle, Four Splayed Feet	45.00
Brass, Teakettle, Lacquered, On Stand	10.00
Brass, Teapot, Burnished, Tin Lined, England, Circa 1840	65.00
Brass, Teapot, Wooden Insulated Swing Handle, 8 In.	15.00
Brass, Telescope, Ship, Wooden Barrel, Signed W.Hogg, London	75.00
Brass, Telescope, Wooden Tripod Stand, 2 Eyepieces, 7 Ft.Long	950.00
Brass, Tray, American, Round, Raised Side, 12 1/2 In.Diameter	48.00
Brass, Tray, China, Etched Scene, 9 X 11 In.	22.00
Brass, Tray, Chinese, Incised Dragons, Handled, 5 1/2 In.Diameter	25.00
Brass, Tray, Egyptian Figures, Handle, 15 In.	5.50
Brass, Tray, Hallmarked Russian, 2 Handles, Oval	45.00
Brass, Tray, Russian, Round, 2 Handled	45.00
Brass, Tray, Square, 1 In.Deep, 13 X 13 In.	6.00
Brass, Trivet, Black, 4 In.Leg	8.00
Brass, Trivet, For Crane	30.00
Brass, Trivet, Queen Anne Legs, 12 In.High	15.00
Brass, Vase, India, Enameled, 11 1/2 In.High	17.00
Brass, Vase, Russian, Corset Shape, 2 Ring Handles, Hand Hammered, Signed	30.00
Brass, Vase, 2 Handles, Incised Designs, Art Nouveau, C.1870	20.00
Brass, Weight, Butcher, 2 Lb.	5.00
Brass, Weight, Scale, 5	2.75
Brass, Weights, Scale, Hatbox-Shape Container	15.00
Brass, Whistle, Police, Victorian Type, 3 1/2 In.Long	10.00
Brass, Whistle, Railroad	35.00
Brass, Whistle, Steamboat, Crane Valve Co.	50.00
Brass, Whistle, Water Bird	3.00 To 12.00

Brides' Baskets of glass were usually one-of-a-kind novelties made in American and European glass factories. They were especially popular about 1880 when the decorated basket was often given as a wedding gift. Cut-glass baskets were popular after 1890. All Brides' Baskets lost favor about 1905.

Bride's Basket, Cranberry Glass, Rigaree Decor, Silver Holder, 1820	35.00
Bride's Basket, Cranberry To Pink Overlay, Ornamented Silver Stand	65.00
Bride's Basket, Cranberry To Pink, Rippled & Fluted Edge, Silver Holder	75.00
Bride's Basket, Opalescent Blue Bowl, Silver Plate Holder, Bow On Top	50.00
Bride's Basket, Purple, Enamel Floral, Gold Trim, Bristol, Plated Frame	150.00
Bride's Basket, Silver Holder, Footed, Meriden Co., 11 In.Tall	28.00
Bride's Basket, Threaded Glass, Oval, 13 X 6 In.	12.50
Bride's Basket, White, Pink, Ruffled, Applied Clear Edge, No Holder	38.00
Bride's Bowl, Cranberry & Opalescent, Ruffled, Fluted, Hobs In & Out	70.00
Bride's Bowl, Deep Pink Overlay On White	30.00
Bride's Bowl, Ruffled, Green Inside, White Outside, 11 In.	50.00
Bride's Bowl, Satin Glass, Burnt Orange To Apricot, Diamond-Quilted	275.00
Bridle Rosette, Horse's Head	4.00
Bridle, Rosette, U.S.Cavalry, Brass, Pair	10.00

Bristol Glass was made in Bristol, England, after the 1700s. The Bristol Glass most often seen today is a victorian, lightweight opaque glass that is often blue. Some of the glass was decorated with enamels.

Bristol, Basket, Flowers, Egg Shape, Pedestal Base, Enamel, Opalescent	45.00
Bristol, Basket, Purple, Bride, Flowers, Gold Trim, 10 1/2 In.Diameter	150.00
Bristol, Bottle, Blue	*Illus* 25.00
Bristol, Box, Blue, Covered, Enameled Top, Shape Of Door Knob	17.50
Bristol, Cream Jug, Enameled, English, C.1760	*Illus* 100.00
Bristol, Glass, Amber & Blue, 7 In.High	2.00
Bristol, Jar, Biscuit, Flower, Stork, Blue, Bail Handle, Cover, 6 In.Tall	45.00
Bristol, Jar, Cookie, Pansy Design, Green, Silver Plated Top	72.50
Bristol, Jar, Cracker, Storks, Palm Trees, Hand-Painted, Green, Tan, Cover	78.50
Bristol, Jar, Pink, Enamel Birds, Floral, Cased, White Lining, Steeple Finial	75.00
Bristol, Jar, Satin Finish, Enameled Flower, Stopper, 12 In.	21.50
Bristol, Jug, Cream, Enameled Roses, Opaque White, English, C.1760	100.00
Bristol, Mug, Blue, White, Enamel, 4 1/2 In.Tall	22.00

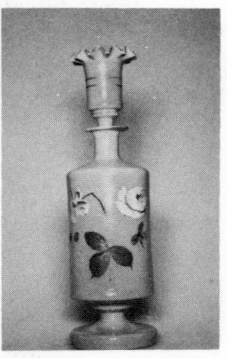

Bristol, Bottle, Blue
See Page 65

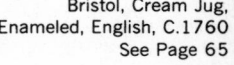

Bristol, Cream Jug,
Enameled, English, C.1760
See Page 65

Bristol, Mug, Flowers & Leaf Design, Blue, White, Applied Handle	28.00
Bristol, Mug, 'remember Me, 'white, Gold, 4 1/4 In.Tall	22.00
Bristol, Paperweight, Green, Six Flowers	50.00
Bristol, Plate, Bird, Flowers, Enamel, 11 1/2 In.Diameter	45.00
Bristol, Plate, Concave, Hand-Painted Rose, 8 In.	5.00
Bristol, Saucer, Enameled, Puce, Yellow, Green, & Rose, Flowers, C.1775	30.00
Bristol, Shaker, Sugar, Flowers, Ivy, Green, Pink, Brown, 5 In.High	20.00
Bristol, Tea Caddy, Ovoid, Green Floral, C.1775, 5 3/4 In.High	70.00
Bristol, Vase, Bird & Floral, Blue, Tangerine, 16 In.	45.00
Bristol, Vase, Bird, Flowers, Yellow, White, Brown	32.50
Bristol, Vase, Blue, Blown, Painted Grapevine, 12 In.High	30.00
Bristol, Vase, Bud, Lily Of The Valley, Lavender, Gold, 4 1/2 In.High	24.50
Bristol, Vase, Custard Color, Opalescent, Ruffled Top, Gold, Pair	60.00
Bristol, Vase, Dancing Children, Bluebells, 10 1/2 In.Tall	35.00
Bristol, Vase, Floral Design, Blue, Enamel, 10 In.Tall	16.50
Bristol, Vase, Floral Design, Bulbous, Enamel, 8 1/4 In.High, Pair	45.00
Bristol, Vase, Floral Design, Gold, White, Hand-Painted, 8 In.Tall, Pair	25.00
Bristol, Vase, Floral Design, Hand-Painted, Blown, Blue, 6 In.Tall	22.50
Bristol, Vase, Floral Design, Pink, White Lining, Enamel, 9 1/2 In.Tall, Pair	37.50
Bristol, Vase, Floral Design, White, Lavender, Pedestal Base, 12 1/2 In.Tall	55.00
Bristol, Vase, Floral Design, Yellow, Blue, Pink, Enamel, 4 X 12 In.	16.50
Bristol, Vase, Frosted, Hand-Painted, 10 In.	15.00
Bristol, Vase, Frosted, Wheat Decoration In Gold, 11 In.High	12.50
Bristol, Vase, Gray Ground, Bird, Berries, Floral, Enameled, 12 1/2 In.	21.00
Bristol, Vase, Hand-Painted Dahlias	52.00
Bristol, Vase, Hand-Painted, Blue Flowers, Orange, Green, Gold, Signed	17.50
Bristol, Vase, Oatmeal, Floral Enamels, Pair	43.00
Bristol, Vase, Orange Beading, Green, White, 9 In.Tall	15.00
Bristol, Vase, Pale Blue, Ruffled Top, Enameled Daisies	17.50
Bristol, Vase, Pink Satin, Enameled Decoration, 9 In.High, Pair	75.00
Bristol, Vase, Pink, White, Flowers, 6 1/2 In.High	23.00
Bristol, Vase, Roses, American, 12 1/2 In.High	10.00
Bristol, Vase, Smoky, 9 In.	17.50
Bristol, Vase, Stag Design, White, Brown, 11 1/4 In.High	20.00
Bristol, Vase, Stick, Pink, Enameled Gold & White Decor, White Lining	42.50
Bristol, Vase, Turquoise, Flared & Fluted Top, Blown	25.00
Bristol, Vase, White Background, Embossed Scene Of Horse, Water, Pair	49.50
Bristol, Vase, White Cased, Enamel Daisies, Leaves, 6 1/4 In.High	45.00
Bristol, Vase, White, Satin Finish, Collar, Ground Pontil, 7 In., Pair	16.50
Bristol, Vase, White, Scene, Boy & Girl Dancing, Floral Sprays, 10 1/2 In.	37.50
Bristol, Wine, Blown, Green, 19th Century, Flute Cut, Knop Stem	25.00
Bromley, Pitcher, Embossed Silver Luster Vine On Putty	30.00
Bronze, Appeal To The Great Spirit, Signed Cyrus E.Dallin, Foundry Mark	575.00
Bronze, Ashtray, Scottie Dog	30.00
Bronze, Bear, Scratching Foot, Signed Barye, 5 X 4 In.	90.00
Bronze, Bookend, Chinese & Japanese Boy, Signed, 7 In.Tall, Pair	135.00
Bronze, Bookend, Fish, Bartoli, 1930, 7 1/2 In.High, Pair	25.00
Bronze, Bookend, Fish, Onyx Bases, Brass Curling Waves, C.1930, Pair	25.00

Bronze, Bookend, Indian Chief, Full Headdress, Pair 22.50
Bronze, Bookend, Tinker, Pair 40.00
Bronze, Box, Jewel, Musical, Marble Top, Cast, Bombe French Chest 25.00
Bronze, Bust Of Napoleon, French 75.00
Bronze, Bust, Armor Bronze, 7 In. .... *Illus* 20.00
Bronze, Bust, Napoleon, Brown Patina, 23 1/2 In.Tall, 11 In.Wide 350.00
Bronze, Bust, Rip Van Winkle, Jefferson Island 18.00
Bronze, Bust, Wagner, Signed H.Muller, 3 1/4 In.Tall 45.00
Bronze, Camel, Victorian Mark, 1870, 3 3/4 In.High 50.00
Bronze, Candelabra, Empire, French, Pair 750.00
Bronze, Candelabra, 5 Candle, Buds, Leaves, French, Gold, 18 In., Pair 85.00
Bronze, Candlestick, Charles X, Ormolu, Blackamoor, 18th Century, Pair 325.00
Bronze, Candlestick, Tiffany Type, Iridescent Glass Shade, Rod Standard 190.00
Bronze, Chamberstick, Enameled, Blue, Ivory, Raspberry, France 50.00
Bronze, Chinese, Vase, Champleve, Fish-Scale Molded 75.00
Bronze, Desk Set, Gilt, Chased Floral, Impressed Geschutzt, 5 Piece 110.00
Bronze, Desk Set, Marble, Empire, French, 4 Piece 148.00
Bronze, Earth, On Stand, Moon Rotating 175.00
Bronze, Figurine, Alassant, Signed E.Fontaine, 26 In.High 675.00
Bronze, Figurine, Allegorical Figure, Industria, Signed E.Drouot 200.00

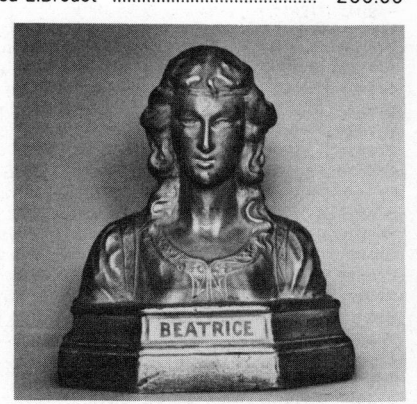

Bronze, Bust, Armor Bronze, 7 In.

Bronze, Figurine, Ballerina, Onyx Base, 10 In.Tall 35.00
Bronze, Figurine, Basset, Barye, Standing, Head Left, 1830-40 .... 550.00 To 750.00
Bronze, Figurine, Bear Lying On Back, Signed Barye, 5 In.Long, 4 In.High 290.00
Bronze, Figurine, Bear, Marble Base, Signed Gardet, 4 1/2 In. X 7 In.High 325.00
Bronze, Figurine, Bear, Relaxing, Signed Barye, 5 In.Long, 4 In.High 425.00
Bronze, Figurine, Bear, Signed Barye, Cire Perdue 500.00
Bronze, Figurine, Bird, Coral & Yellow Feathers, Orange Collar, 13 In.Long 175.00
Bronze, Figurine, Bird, Signed F.Pautrot, 6 In.High 215.00
Bronze, Figurine, Buck, Antlers, In Resting Position, P.J.Mene, 5 X 3 1/2 In. 155.00
Bronze, Figurine, Bull Dog, English, 3 1/4 In.Long 60.00
Bronze, Figurine, Bull Dog, French, 4 1/2 In.Long 85.00
Bronze, Figurine, Bull, Charging, Vienna, 8 In.Long, 6 1/2 In.High 325.00
Bronze, Figurine, Burmese Foot Soldier, 9 In.High 60.00
Bronze, Figurine, Burmese Warriors On Horseback, 9 In.High, Pair 150.00
Bronze, Figurine, Camel, A.Barye, 6 X 5 1/4 In. 150.00
Bronze, Figurine, Cocker Spaniel, Vienna, 2 3/4 In.Long, 2 In.High 48.00
Bronze, Figurine, Cocker Spaniel, 2 In.High, 2 1/2 In.Long 45.00
Bronze, Figurine, Cossack By Horse, Lighting Pipe, Russia, Wolf, 10 1/2 In. 750.00
Bronze, Figurine, Cossack, Malachite Base, Russian, 7 In.Tall 245.00
Bronze, Figurine, Couple, Bobo, Wooden Block, 19th Century, 3 3/4 In.Tall 325.00
Bronze, Figurine, Dachshund, Signed Jarl, 7 X 5 In. 125.00
Bronze, Figurine, Dark Skin Man, White Hair, Blue Jacket, Red Pants, Vienna 45.00
Bronze, Figurine, Deer, Signed Barye, Doe & Fawn, 1832, 8 1/2 X 10 In. 1200.00
Bronze, Figurine, Deer, Signed Barye, On Alert, 1830-40, 7 1/2 X 6 3/4 In. 900.00
Bronze, Figurine, Deer, Standing, Signed P.J.Mene, 11 X 11 In.High 450.00
Bronze, Figurine, Doe & Fawn, Signed Barye, Recumbent, 1820-30 .... 375.00

Bronze, Figurine, Dog Pawing Snail, Signed Le Blanc	195.00
Bronze, Figurine, Dog, Signed Barye, Hunting, 1820-30, 3 3/4 X 6 In.	325.00
Bronze, Figurine, Dog, Signed Barye, Hunting, 1820-30, 4 X 6 5/8 In.	325.00
Bronze, Figurine, Dog, Signed J.Mene	400.00
Bronze, Figurine, Dog, Standing, Marble Base, Green, 6 In.High	60.00
Bronze, Figurine, Dog, Vienna, Whippet, Marked	45.00
Bronze, Figurine, Dogs, Sitting, 5 1/2 In.	18.00
Bronze, Figurine, Dromedary, Barye, 9 1/8 In. _Illus_	950.00
Bronze, Figurine, Eagle Fighting Snake, 7 In.High, 7 3/4 In.Long	175.00
Bronze, Figurine, Egyptian Woman, Nude, Bird Wing, Signed Moore, 9 In.Tall	80.00
Bronze, Figurine, Elephant, Burmese, Driver, Pulling Log, 5 1/2 In.High	100.00
Bronze, Figurine, Elephant, Signed Barye, African, Running, 1830-40	1400.00
Bronze, Figurine, Elephant, Signed Barye, Asian, Walking, 1833	800.00
Bronze, Figurine, Elephant, Signed Peggy Holder & Cire Perdue	35.00
Bronze, Figurine, Elephant, Upraised Trunk, 11 1/2 In.Long, 9 3/4 In.Tall	125.00
Bronze, Figurine, Elk, Reclining, Signed Fratin, 8 X 18 1/2 In.	360.00
Bronze, Figurine, Falconer, Standing, Signed P.J.Mene, Dated 1873, 25 In.High	700.00
Bronze, Figurine, Female Nude In Repose Holding Flower Tray, Signed Maxime	75.00
Bronze, Figurine, French Soldier, Bugle, Signed C.Anfrie	150.00
Bronze, Figurine, French Soldier, Signed Gaudez, 14 1/2 In.	165.00
Bronze, Figurine, Gazelle, Signed Barye, 7 X 6 In.	160.00
Bronze, Figurine, Girl, Country, Carved Ivory Hands, Signed Chiparus	300.00
Bronze, Figurine, Girl, Slender, Silvered, Green, Signed Lorenzl, 11 1/2 In.	175.00
Bronze, Figurine, Gladiator Driving 3 Lions, Signed F.Corinle, Marble Base	300.00
Bronze, Figurine, God Of Longevity, Chinese, On Animal, 16th Century, 10 In.	70.00
Bronze, Figurine, Greyhound, Signed, 5 1/2 In.High	95.00
Bronze, Figurine, Horse, Signed Barye, Attacked By Lion, 1833	1600.00
Bronze, Figurine, Indian Warrior On Horse, Headdress, Hollow Base	39.50
Bronze, Figurine, Infant Hercules & Serpent, Signed Ercole Tillice, 1900	35.00
Bronze, Figurine, Irish Setter, Signed Dubucand, 5 In. X 6 1/2 In.Long	145.00
Bronze, Figurine, Joan Of Arc, Signed Gaudez, 18 In.Tall	275.00
Bronze, Figurine, Kevel Antelope, Signed Barye, 1820-30, 3 3/8 X 3 1/4 In.	325.00
Bronze, Figurine, Kevel, Signed Barye, Poised, 1820-30, 3 7/8 X 5 1/4 In.	400.00
Bronze, Figurine, Kitten, Vienna, Striped Gray, 7 In.Long, 4 1/2 In.Tall	105.00
Bronze, Figurine, Knight On Horseback, Rectangular Pedestal Base	325.00
Bronze, Figurine, Lady Standing, Dead Bird In Hand, Signed Paul Duboy	225.00
Bronze, Figurine, Les Animaliers, P.J.Mene, 15 In.Long, 8 In.High	500.00
Bronze, Figurine, Lion Holds Rabbit In Jaws, Delabriere, 22 In.Long	750.00
Bronze, Figurine, Lion, Reclining, 1 1/4 X 2 3/4 In.	15.00
Bronze, Figurine, Lion, Signed Barye, Crushing Serpent, 1832, 10 X 14 In.	1050.00
Bronze, Figurine, Lion, Standing, Signed Barye, 8 1/2 In.Long, 4 1/2 In.High	500.00
Bronze, Figurine, Lion, Striking A Serpent, Barye _Illus_	850.00
Bronze, Figurine, Lioness Protecting Cub, A.Cain, 25 In.Long, 18 In.High	500.00
Bronze, Figurine, Man & Woman, French, Signed, Pair	450.00
Bronze, Figurine, Monkey, 6 1/2 In.High	85.00
Bronze, Figurine, Mouse Eating Cheese, Signed C Masson, 3 1/2 In.Tall	175.00
Bronze, Figurine, Mule With Pack & Tribesman, Russian, Lanceroy, Dated 1875	425.00
Bronze, Figurine, Napoleon, Hands Behind Back, Hat Sword, Medals, 5 In.Tall	55.00
Bronze, Figurine, Nude, Dancer, Signed Lorenzl, 9 In.	95.00
Bronze, Figurine, Panther Stalking Two Rabbits, Delabriere, 7 X 4 In.	150.00
Bronze, Figurine, Panther, Signed A.L.Barye, Surprising Civet Cat, 1830-40	525.00
Bronze, Figurine, Panther, Signed Barye, Indian, Reclining, C.1933	650.00
Bronze, Figurine, Panther, Signed Barye, Seizing Civet Cat, 1830-40	900.00
Bronze, Figurine, Peacock, Foundry Mark & Geschutzt, Enameled, Viennese	160.00
Bronze, Figurine, Pig, Miniature, On Oval Beaded Base	35.00
Bronze, Figurine, Pointer, Signed Barye, On Alert, 1820-30, 3 1/2 X 6 7/8 In.	500.00
Bronze, Figurine, Polar Bear, Sitting, Ice, Crystal, Russian	250.00
Bronze, Figurine, Rabbit, Miniature, Signed Gesonizi, 1 1/2 X 1 3/4 In.	75.00
Bronze, Figurine, Rabbit, Signed Barye, 2 1/2 In.Long, 1 3/4 In.High	110.00
Bronze, Figurine, Reindeer, Vienna, Signed, 8 X 10 In.	185.00
Bronze, Figurine, Seated Lady, F.Barbedienne, Fondeur, R.Chapu, 14 In.Tall	325.00
Bronze, Figurine, Setter, E.Fremiet, 6 1/2 X 6 1/4 In.	170.00
Bronze, Figurine, Shepherd Herding A Ram, Russia, Lanceroy	1000.00
Bronze, Figurine, Soldier, En Avant, 11 1/2 In. High	125.00
Bronze, Figurine, Spaniel, Sleeping, Black Marble Base, 8 In.Long, 3 In.Tall	185.00
Bronze, Figurine, Stag, Walking, Barye _Illus_	550.00

Bronze, Figurine, Dromedary, Barye, 9 1/8 In.
See Page 68

Bronze, Figurine, Stag, Walking, Barye
See Page 68

Bronze, Figurine, Lion,
Striking A Serpent, Barye
See Page 68

Bronze, Figurine, Three Deer, Signed Barye, 9 1/2 In.Long, 9 In.High	695.00
Bronze, Figurine, Tiger, Signed Barye, Devouring Gavial, 1831, 7 3/4 X 20 In.	1050.00
Bronze, Figurine, Turtle With Smaller Turtle On Back, Oriental	55.00
Bronze, Figurine, Turtle, Signed Barye, 3 1/2 In.	115.00
Bronze, Figurine, Two Dogs Pointing Pheasants, Signed Barye, 1820-30	775.00
Bronze, Figurine, Two Turkeys, Bayre, 4 X 3 1/2 In.	155.00
Bronze, Figurine, Warrior Holding Torch, Signed E.Picault, 12 1/2 In. High	65.00
Bronze, Figurine, Winged Moths, Vienna, Wings 5 In. Span, Pair	165.00
Bronze, Figurine, Woman, Classical, Draped, Standing, 6 1/2 In.High	35.00
Bronze, Figurine, Young Girl, Signed Rolners, 18 1/2 In.High	250.00
Bronze, Group, Cow, Calf & Milkmaid, Signed I.Bonheur	450.00
Bronze, Group, Deer, Signed Barye, 9 1/2 In.Long, 9 In.High	550.00
Bronze, Group, French, Dancing Muse With Satyr, Signed Clodion	600.00
Bronze, Group, Whippet & King Charles, Spaniel, Signed P.J.Mene	325.00
Bronze, Incense Burner, Elephant Handles, Foo Dog Finial, China, 10 In., Pair	145.00
Bronze, Incense Burner, Foo Dog, Handles, Footed, 6 In.High	25.00
Bronze, Incense Burner, France, 6 1/2 In.High	18.50
Bronze, Incense Burner, Hanging, Lost Wax Method	38.00
Bronze, Incense Burner, Oriental, 15 In.	48.00
Bronze, Inkwell, Deer, Standing, Rocky Mound, 18 In.Long, 8 In.Wide	100.00
Bronze, Light, French, Peacock, Marble Base, Crystals, Pair	400.00
Bronze, Lighter, King Of Hearts *Illus*	85.00
Bronze, Mirror, Japanese, Signed, 7 X 11 In. To End Of Handle	50.00

Bronze, Nut Cracker, Dog Shape, 12 In.Long 35.00
Bronze, Opium Weight, Cat, China 18.00
Bronze, Opium Weight, Figure Of Duck, China 10.00
Bronze, Opium Weight, Foo Dog, China 10.00
Bronze, Ornament, Winged Griffon, Rectangular Platform, 11 In.Long 70.00
Bronze, Paperweight, Bird, Wings Spread 40.00
Bronze, Paperweight, Boar's Ear, 5 1/2 In.Long 6.50
Bronze, Pitcher, Pompeii Form 35.00
Bronze, Plaque, Bust Of Washington, First In The Hearts Of His Countrymen 3.75
Bronze, Plaque, Charles Dickens, By Ralph Goddard, 10 X 7 In. 85.00
Bronze, Plaque, Face Of Elderly Woman, Round Cherry Frame 20.00
Bronze, Plaque, Gettysburg Address, Floral Relief, Signed S.Klaber 300.00
Bronze, Plaque, Nurse Cavell, Killed October 12, 1915, In Brussels 24.00
Bronze, Plaque, Young Woman Wearing Fancy Hat, Round Walnut Frame 20.00
Bronze, Relief, Leopard, Signed Barye, Walking, 1831, Wood Frame 300.00
Bronze, Relief, Panther, Signed Barye, Walking, 1831, Wood Frame 250.00

Bronze, Lighter,
King Of Hearts
See Page 69

Buffalo Pottery, Deldare,
Candleholder, Emerald

Bronze, Seal, Owl, Full Figure, 21/4 In.High 30.00
Bronze, Vase, Chinese, C.1850, 5 1/2 In.Tall 20.00
Bronze, Vase, Chinese, Trees, Birds & Ornamentations, 13 1/2 In.Tall 65.00
Bronze, Vase, Dark Patina, Dragon Handles, China, 8 1/2 In.High 90.00
Bronze, Vase, Serpent Circling Body, 12 1/2 In. 45.00
Bronze, Vase, Slender Neck, Bulbous Bottom, Circa 1840, 6 3/4 In., Pair 50.00
Bronze, Vase, Sterling Silver Applique Of Daisies, 12 In.High 17.50
Buck Rogers, Gun, Sonic Ray, Signaling, Plastic, 1940s, Cipher Booklet 20.00
Buck Rogers, Holster & Belt, 1930s, Picture Of Buck Rogers, Leather, 9 In. 12.00
Buck Rogers, Pistol, Space 60.00
Buck Rogers, Puzzle, 1951, 10 X 14 In. 7.50
Buck Rogers, Space Ship 6.00

*Buffalo Pottery was made in Buffalo, New York, after 1902. The
company was established by the Larkin Company, famous manufacturers of soap.
The wares are marked with a picture of a buffalo and the date of manufacture.
Deldare ware is the most famous pottery made at the factory. It is a
khaki-colored transfer decorated ware.*

Buffalo Pottery, Chocolate Pot, Signed, 11 1/2 In.High 45.00
Buffalo Pottery, Crane, 7 1/2 In.Diameter 17.50
Buffalo Pottery, Deldare, Bowl, Soup, Village Street, 9 In. 79.00
Buffalo Pottery, Deldare, Bowl, Village Tavern, Dated 1908, 9 In.Diameter 146.50
Buffalo Pottery, Deldare, Bowl, Ye Village Inn, Signed W.Foster, Dated 1908 .... 140.00
Buffalo Pottery, Deldare, Candleholder, Emerald .... *Illus* 300.00
Buffalo Pottery, Deldare, Creamer, Village Life 69.00
Buffalo Pottery, Deldare, Dish, Powder, 1911, Artist Initial 29.50
Buffalo Pottery, Deldare, Eggcup, Old English Scene, Artist-Signed, Whar 42.50
Buffalo Pottery, Deldare, Mug, Fallowfield Hunt, Breaking Cover 80.00
Buffalo Pottery, Deldare, Pitcher, 'To Demand My Annual Rent', 8 In.Tall 160.00
Buffalo Pottery, Deldare, Pitcher, Old Soldier, Initial M.B., 7 3/4 In.High 167.50

Buffalo Pottery, Deldare, Plate, At Ye Lion Inn, 6 1/4 In. 50.00
Buffalo Pottery, Deldare, Plate, Dr.Syntax Disputing His Bill, Blue 100.00
Buffalo Pottery, Deldare, Plate, Dr.Syntax Making Discovery, Emerald, 10 In. 200.00
Buffalo Pottery, Deldare, Plate, Dr.Syntax Soliloquising, Emerald, 7 1/4 In. 115.00
Buffalo Pottery, Deldare, Plate, Fallowfield Hunt, Breaking Cover 65.00
Buffalo Pottery, Deldare, Plate, Fallowfield Hunt, The Death, 8 1/2 In. 80.00
Buffalo Pottery, Deldare, Plate, Fallowfield Hunt, 1908, 10 In.Diameter 95.00
Buffalo Pottery, Deldare, Plate, Fallowfield Hunt, 6 1/4 In. 59.00
Buffalo Pottery, Deldare, Plate, Fallowfield Hunt, 7 1/4 In. 75.00
Buffalo Pottery, Deldare, Plate, Fallowfield Hunt, 9 1/2 In. 85.00
Buffalo Pottery, Deldare, Plate, Niagara Falls, Blue-Green, 7 1/2 In. 17.50
Buffalo Pottery, Deldare, Plate, Niagara Falls, Blue, 10 1/4 In. 17.00
Buffalo Pottery, Deldare, Plate, Old Times, 9 1/2 In. 80.00
Buffalo Pottery, Deldare, Plate, Store Ad .... *Illus* 175.00
Buffalo Pottery, Deldare, Plate, The Start, 9 1/4 In. 70.00
Buffalo Pottery, Deldare, Plate, Town Crier, 8 1/4 In. 78.00

Buffalo Pottery, Deldare, Plate, Store Ad

Buffalo Pottery, Deldare, Plate, Village Gossips, 10 In. 100.00
Buffalo Pottery, Deldare, Plate, Village Street, 7 1/4 In. 69.00
Buffalo Pottery, Deldare, Plate, Ye Olden Times, 9 1/4 In. 75.00
Buffalo Pottery, Deldare, Plate, Ye Town Crier, 1908, 8 1/4 In. 60.00
Buffalo Pottery, Deldare, Plate, Ye Village Street, 7 1/4 In. 75.00
Buffalo Pottery, Deldare, Sugar, Fallowfield Hunt 75.00
Buffalo Pottery, Deldare, Sugar, Scene Village Days In Ye Olden Days, Mark 150.00
Buffalo Pottery, Deldare, Sugar, Village Life 69.00
Buffalo Pottery, Deldare, Tankard, At The Three Pigeons, Signed N.Sheenan 75.00
Buffalo Pottery, Deldare, Tankard, Ye Lion Inn, Signed M.S., 4 1/2 In. 65.00
Buffalo Pottery, Deldare, Teapot, Dr.Syntax, 5 In. 115.00
Buffalo Pottery, Deldare, Teapot, Village Life In Ye Olden Day ....80.00 To 150.00
Buffalo Pottery, Deldare, Teapot, Village Life, Four Sided ....95.00 To 165.00
Buffalo Pottery, Deldare, Tray, Dresser, Minuet, 12 In. 185.00
Buffalo Pottery, Dish, Child's, Campbell Kids 10.00
Buffalo Pottery, Dish, Vegetable, Blue Willow, Cover, 9 X 7 1/2 In. 18.50
Buffalo Pottery, Fish Set, 15 In.Platter, Five 9 In.Plates, Green Edge 45.00
Buffalo Pottery, Gravy Boat, White, Pink Floral Band, Gold Rim 5.00
Buffalo Pottery, Inkwell, Butterfly Design, Emeraldware, Square, Pair 150.00
Buffalo Pottery, Pitcher, Geo.Washington Decoration, Dated 1907 .... 135.00
Buffalo Pottery, Pitcher, Holland 75.00
Buffalo Pottery, Place Setting, For 8, Rose & Fern, 100 Piece 150.00
Buffalo Pottery, Plate, American Woodcock, 1908, 9 In.Diameter 12.50
Buffalo Pottery, Plate, Capitol Building, 10 In.Diameter 18.50
Buffalo Pottery, Plate, Child's, Buffalo China Co., Bluebird Decor 10.00
Buffalo Pottery, Plate, Christmas, 1952 .... 18.50
Buffalo Pottery, Plate, Marked Souvenir Of Savenburg, Kansas, 1907 .... 15.00
Buffalo Pottery, Plate, New Bedford, 1908, Commemorative, Blue & White 40.00
Buffalo Pottery, Plate, Niagara Falls, 7 1/2 In. 15.00
Buffalo Pottery, Plate, White House, Washington, D.C., 7 1/2 In.Diameter 17.50
Buffalo Pottery, Plate, Wild Ducks, Gold Rim, Dated 1907 .... 22.00
Buffalo Pottery, Plate, Wild Ducks, 1908, 9 In.Diameter 12.50
Buffalo Pottery, Platter, Blue Willow, 1909, 11 1/2 X 9 1/2 In. 8.00

Buffalo Pottery, Sauce, Blue Willow, Set Of 5 .... 18.00
Buggy, Doctor's, 1 Horse 300.00
Buggy, Doctor's, 2 Horse 250.00

Burmese Glass was developed by Frederick Shirley at the Mt.
Washington Glass Works in New Bedford, Massachusetts, in 1885. It
is a two-tone glass, shading from peach to yellow. Some have a pattern mold
design. A few Burmese pieces were decorated with pictures or applied glass
flowers of colored Burmese Glass.

Burmese, Bowl, Rose, Miniature, Mt.Washington, Fluted Rim, 3 1/2 In.High 180.00
Burmese, Bowl, Sugar, Hobnail 975.00
Burmese, Cabinet Piece, Fairy Lamp, Clark Cricklite Holder, Candleholder 450.00
Burmese, Creamer & Sugar, Ribbed, Matte Finish, Ivy Decor 465.00
Burmese, Creamer, Salmon Pink, Yellow Handle, Mt.Washington 385.00
Burmese, Egg, Daisies, Unfired Glass, Pat.May 28, 1889, Mt.Washington 550.00
Burmese, Jar, Biscuit, Flowers, Stems, Silver Collar, Rope Bail, Mt.Washington 200.00
Burmese, Lamp, Fairy, Cut Glass Inset, Signed Clarke 500.00
Burmese, Lamp, Fairy, Flowered, Skirted, Beaded Decor 450.00
Burmese, Lamp, Fairy, Signed Clarke Base, Blue 175.00
Burmese, Lamp, Fairy, Signed, Acid Queens, Yellow, Ruffled Rim, 3 Piece, 6 In. 450.00
Burmese, Lamp, Fairy, Yellow, Ruffled Rim, Deep Cut, Signed, 6 In.Tall 450.00
Burmese, Pitcher, Egg Shape, Pink To Yellow, Footed, Mt.Washington, 3 1/2 In. 220.00
Burmese, Pitcher, 4 1/2 In.High 300.00
Burmese, Sconce, Berry Pontil Candleholders, Signed Fairy Lamp 650.00
Burmese, Shade, Lamp, Refired Edge, Mt.Washington, 5 3/4 In.High 60.00
Burmese, Shaker, Salt, Ribbed 87.50
Burmese, Toothpick, Diamond-Quilted, Fold In Tricorn Rim, Mt.Washington 325.00
Burmese, Toothpick, Mum Design, Ribbed, Mt.Washington 67.50
Burmese, Toothpick, Top-Hat Shape, Glossy, 3 1/2 In. X 3 1/4 In. 250.00
Burmese, Tumbler, Acid Finish 135.00
Burmese, Tumbler, Gunderson 100.00
Burmese, Tumbler, Mt.Washington, Refired Rim, Shiny 150.00
Burmese, Vase, Ball-Shape Body, Flared Pleated Top, Salmon Pink To Yellow 300.00
Burmese, Vase, Bulbous, Glossy, Pink, Mt.Washington, 4 3/4 In.Tall 225.00
Burmese, Vase, Five-Petal Rose, No Mark, 6 In.High 200.00
Burmese, Vase, Fluted, Ruffled Top, 3 1/2 In.Tall, 3 In.Across 300.00
Burmese, Vase, In Holder, Mt.Washington 135.00
Burmese, Vase, Lily, Three-Petal Top, Yellow Edge, Mt.Washington, 12 In.Tall 265.00
Burmese, Vase, Queen's, Signed Webb .... *Illus* 675.00
Burmese, Vase, Red, Berry Decoration, Hand Painted, 3 In. 250.00
Burmese, Vase, Scalloped Refired Top, Mt.Washington, 4 3/4 In.High 95.00
Burmese, Vase, Scalloped, Straight Sided, Bulbous, Mt.Washington, 7 In.Tall 275.00
Burmese, Vase, Single Rose, 6 In.High 250.00
Burmese, Vase, Tricorn, 5 In.Diameter, 2 In.Tall 200.00
Burmese, Vase, Trumpet, Curved Rim, 5 1/2 In.Base, 16 1/2 In.Tall 575.00
    Burmese, Webb, see Webb
Buster Brown, Book, Experiences With Pond's Extract, Signed 12.50
Buster Brown, Button, Pin, Picture, Tige 4.00
Buster Brown, Dictionary 9.00
Buster Brown, Dish, Child's, Feeding 30.00

Burmese, Vase, Queen's, Signed Webb

Buster Brown, Noise Maker, Cricket 12.00
Buster Brown, Postcard, 1903, Signed Outcault, 3 .... 1.00
Buster Brown, Shoe, Button, Size 5, Pair 18.50
Buster Brown, Toothpick, Bisque, Green Basket 8.50
Buster Brown, Yo-Yo, Tin 4.50

Butter Chips, or Butter Pats, were small individual dishes for butter.
They were in the height of fashion from 1880 to 1910. Earlier as well as
later examples are known.
Butter Chip, Chinese Enamel, Pink Ground, Blue, Gold & Pink, Porcelain 15.00
Butter Chip, Embossed Border, Gold Scrolls, Porcelain, 4 .... 5.00
Butter Chip, Heads Of Ladies, Gold Ground, Porcelain, 8 .... 88.00
Butter Chip, White With Gold Flower Center, Porcelain, 8 .... 6.00
   Buttermilk Glass, see Custard

Buttons have been known through the centuries, and there are millions of
styles. Only a few of the most common types are listed for comparison.
Button, Adams Express Co., Copper, 10 .... 12.00
Button, Advertising, National Lead Co., Dutch Boy 3.50
Button, Brass, Crown & Wreath, E.R.M.E., 3/4 In., 18 .... 5.50
Button, Brass, Raised Deer, The Herfordshire Regiment, 3/4 In., 24 .... 7.50
Button, Brass, Raised Horse, Berkshire, 3/4 In., 16 .... 4.50
Button, Brass, Uniform, Adams Express Co., 7/8 In.Diameter 2.50
Button, Brass, Uniform, Colt Firearms, 7/8 In.Diameter 2.50
Button, Brass, Uniform, Indian Service, 7/8 In.Diameter 2.50
Button, Brass, Uniform, Wells Fargo Guard, 7/8 In.Diameter 2.50
Button, Bridle, 2 Layer, Metal Design 2.50
Button, Carnival Glass, Deer In Forest, Purple Hilites On Gold 5.00
Button, Carnival Glass, Oval Butterfly, 1 3/4 In., Green, Purple 20.00
Button, Carnival Glass, Rooster, Blue With Purple 10.00
Button, Carnival Glass, Rooster, Purple With Blue & Gold 10.00
Button, Carnival Glass, 3 Bees, Green Iridescence, 1 1/2 In. 15.00
Button, Chicago City Palace, Brass, 1 In., Set Of 12 .... 9.00
Button, Chicago City Palace, Brass, 5/8 In.15 .... 7.50
Button, Collar, Gold Plate, Jewel 2.00
Button, Colt Fire Arms Factory Guard, 10 .... 15.00
Button, Crown & Initial R.Y.C., Brass, 1 In. 1.00
Button, Crystal, 40 .... 9.00
Button, Csn, Blockade, 10 .... 12.00
Button, Cuff, Paperweight Glass 5.00
Button, Grapes, Leaves & Bug, 1 1/4 In. 2.50
Button, Horse Yoeman Lothian & Border, Brass, 1 In., 7 .... 7.50
Button, Indian Service, Federal Eagle, New York Made, 10 .... 15.00
Button, Ivory, Dragon, Black Eyes, Carved, 1 7/8 In.Diameter, Set Of 4 .... 24.00
Button, Knight Head, 1 1/2 In. 4.00
Button, Lapel, Pearl, Signed Muenchen 10.00
Button, Military, Crown, & Cannon, Brass, 1 In. 1.00
Button, Navy, 'i Have Joined The Navy, 'pat.1899 .... 3.00
Button, Oxfordshire, Brass, 1 In., 3 .... 3.00
Button, Pierrot & Pierrette, 1 3/4 In. 1.00
Button, Silver Coin, Shank Soldered, 3/4 In. 8.75
Button, Uniform, Civil War 1.00
   Buttonhook, see also Store, Buttonhook
Buttonhook, Celluloid Handle, Amber & Pink 7.00

Calendar Plates were very popular in the United States from 1906 to
1929. Since then plates have been made every year. A calendar, the name of a
store, a picture of flowers, a girl, or a scene was featured on the plate.
Calendar Plate, 1908, Santa At Chimney 18.00
Calendar Plate, 1909, Cherubs, Advertising 15.00
Calendar Plate, 1909, Dresden China, Advertising 6.00
Calendar Plate, 1909, Fruit 12.00
Calendar Plate, 1909, Girl Holds Roses In Apron, Advertising 18.00
Calendar Plate, 1909, Months Around Border, Bird, Ribbon Center 10.00
Calendar Plate, 1909, Soup Bowl, Berries 15.00
Calendar Plate, 1909, Soup Bowl, Fruits, 8 1/4 In.Diameter 10.00

Calendar Plate, 1909, Young Girl		10.00
Calendar Plate, 1910, Amland Cigars, San Francisco, 9 In., Roses		22.00
Calendar Plate, 1910, Bust Of Indian Chief In Center, Months In Feathers		9.00
Calendar Plate, 1910, Cherubs In Center, Months Around Border		10.00
Calendar Plate, 1910, Cherubs, Advertising		15.00
Calendar Plate, 1910, Dog Holding Banner	*Illus*	9.50
Calendar Plate, 1910, Dog Holding Calendar, Yellow Border, 6 1/2 In.		18.00
Calendar Plate, 1910, Fruit Center		25.00
Calendar Plate, 1910, Girl & Horse		11.50
Calendar Plate, 1910, Holly Sprays, Gilt Edge		11.25
Calendar Plate, 1910, Holly, The Old Swimming Hole, Green Luster, Beaded		28.00
Calendar Plate, 1910, Horseshoe, Waterfall, 7 1/4 In.		12.50
Calendar Plate, 1910, Leaf & Flower Design		15.00
Calendar Plate, 1910, Making American Flag		10.00
Calendar Plate, 1910, Mission Grocer, San Francisco, 8 In., Green, Red, Girl		22.00
Calendar Plate, 1910, Months On Border, Floral, Gibson Girl Center		15.00
Calendar Plate, 1910, Niagara Falls		13.50
Calendar Plate, 1910, Portrait Of Girl, Wearing Hat With Roses, 9 In.		18.00
Calendar Plate, 1910, River Scene, Verse, 9 1/4 In.Diameter		19.00
Calendar Plate, 1910, Roses, Apples, 8 1/2 In.Diameter		12.00
Calendar Plate, 1911, Birds, Animals & Months Border, Three Deer Center		15.00
Calendar Plate, 1911, Deer Scene		23.00
Calendar Plate, 1911, Floral		14.00
Calendar Plate, 1911, Victorian Couple Center, 'Should Auld Acquaintance'		14.50
Calendar Plate, 1912, Draped Nude, 8 In.Diameter		16.00
Calendar Plate, 1912, Fruit & Flower, 9 1/2 In.		25.00
Calendar Plate, 1912, Girl & Cherub Look Into Pond, Advertising		15.00
Calendar Plate, 1912, Hunter, Turkey, Woods, Ford & Clarke, Druggists, 7 3/4		12.00
Calendar Plate, 1912, Pear Branch		16.00
Calendar Plate, 1912, Portrait Girl Holding Towel, Full-Length, Pink Dress		28.00
Calendar Plate, 1913, Old Mill Center		25.00
Calendar Plate, 1913, Phillips' Mercantile, Laton, 8 In., Farm Scene		24.00
Calendar Plate, 1914, Cape Girardeau		12.00
Calendar Plate, 1914, Floral & Bird Design		14.50
Calendar Plate, 1914, Grant's Tomb, 9 1/4 In.Diameter		18.00
Calendar Plate, 1914, Wild Geese In Flight, Signed Beck		18.00
Calendar Plate, 1915, Map Of Panama Canal, Green, Gold		25.00
Calendar Plate, 1915, Panama Canal		18.00
Calendar Plate, 1915, Panama Canal, People's Store, Chancellor, S.D.		28.00
Calendar Plate, 1920, Advertising, Flag, Eagle, Says Victory		19.50
Calendar Plate, 1924, Dog, Pheasant, 9 In.Diameter		17.00
Calendar Plate, 1940, Golden Gate International Exposition, 10 In., Blue		16.00
Calendar Plate, 1970, Wedgwood		7.50
Calendar Plate, 1971, Wedgwood		12.50
Calendar Plate, 1972, Wedgwood		12.00
Calendar, Bowl, Roses, Rabbits, Crackle Glaze, Gold, 10 In.Diameter, 1911		35.00
Calendar, Plate, Chop, 1911, Roses		27.50

*The Cambridge Glass Company made Pressed Glass in Cambridge,
Ohio. It was marked with a C in a triangle about 1902. The words near-
cut were used after 1906.*

Cambridge, Ashtray, Crown Tuscan	*Illus*	35.00
Cambridge, Ashtray, Pistachio, Apple Green		8.00
Cambridge, Basket, Georgian Pattern, Amethyst, Crystal Handle, Paper Label		35.00
Cambridge, Bell, Clear, 6 In.		35.00
Cambridge, Bell, Crystal, Engraved, Paper Label, 5 In.		15.00
Cambridge, Bonbon, Pink		4.50
Cambridge, Bottle, Urn, Floral Swag, Etched, Oil & Vinegar, Clear		19.00
Cambridge, Bowl, Azurite, 7 1/2 In.		35.00
Cambridge, Bowl, Black Amethyst, Shaped Like Wide Brim Hat, Signed		40.00
Cambridge, Bowl, Blue, Cleo Pattern, Handles, Ten-Sided, Signed		15.00
Cambridge, Bowl, Clear, Seashell, Footed, 8 In.		30.00
Cambridge, Bowl, Console, Ram's Head		250.00
Cambridge, Bowl, Flowers, Cobalt Blue, Silver Overlay, Signed, 10 In.Diameter		45.00
Cambridge, Bowl, Fruit, Caprice Pattern, Triangular, Footed, Handle		11.50
Cambridge, Bowl, Fruit, Clear With Silver Overlay, 12 In.Diameter		45.00

Cambridge, Bowl, Helio, Flat Rim, 6 1/2 In.Diameter	32.50
Cambridge, Bowl, Helio, Footed, 7 In.Diameter	24.50
Cambridge, Bowl, Helio, 10 In.Diameter	59.00
Cambridge, Bowl, Primrose, Ebony, Stand, Signed, 6 In.	30.00
Cambridge, Bowl, Ram's Head, Lavender *Illus*	300.00
Cambridge, Bowl, Seashell, 3-Toed, Signed, 9 In.	85.00
Cambridge, Bowl, Shell Shape, Crown, Tuscan, Footed, 5 X 8 In.	32.50
Cambridge, Box, Cigarette, Nude Lady, Clear	45.00
Cambridge, Bucket, Ice, Amber	24.00
Cambridge, Bucket, Ice, Amethyst, Signed, Hammered Handle, Scalloped Rim	18.50
Cambridge, Bucket, Ice, Peach-Blo, Patent On Handle	9.50
Cambridge, Candelabra, 2-Light, Elaine Etched, Pair	32.00

Calendar Plate, 1910, Dog Holding Banner
See Page 74

Cambridge, Ashtray, Crown Tuscan
See Page 74

Cambridge, Bowl, Ram's Head, Lavender

Cambridge, Candlestick, Caprice, Three Light, Clear, Pair	25.00
Cambridge, Candlestick, Clear Loop, Pair	17.50
Cambridge, Candlestick, Doric Column, Ivory, Flashed Caramel, 9 1/2 In.Tall	32.00
Cambridge, Candlestick, Ebony, Enameled Roses, 7 1/2 In.	15.00
Cambridge, Candlestick, Etched Floral, Gold, 3 Light, 6 1/2 In., Pair	24.00
Cambridge, Candlestick, Jade Color, Twisted Stem, 8 1/2 In.Tall	17.50
Cambridge, Candlestick, Lily Design, Clear, Pair	12.00
Cambridge, Candlestick, Mulberry, 7 In., Pair	40.00
Cambridge, Candlestick, Three-Light, Caprice, Clear, Pair	15.00
Cambridge, Candlestick, Three-Light, Crown Tuscan, 5 1/2 In.Tall, Pair	49.50
Cambridge, Candlestick, 2-Light, Light Blue Milk, 6 In.	125.00
Cambridge, Candy, Covered, Seashell, Signed, 6 In.	50.00
Cambridge, Center Bowl, Inverted Thumbprint, Amberina, Signed	150.00
Cambridge, Centerpiece, Amber, 3 Piece	58.00
Cambridge, Centerpiece, Crown Tuscan, Snail Shape, Footed	45.00
Cambridge, Cocktail Set, Chrome Shaker, Amethyst Glass Inserts, 7 Piece	40.00
Cambridge, Compote, Apple Green, C Mark	6.50
Cambridge, Compote, Azurite, Footed, 7 1/2 In.Tall	24.50
Cambridge, Compote, Carmen Nude Stem	65.00
Cambridge, Compote, Crown Tuscan, Flesh Color, Gold Design, Nude Lady Stem	65.00

Cambridge, **Compote**, Crown Tuscan, Nude Figure Stem, Gold Decor, Marked 165.00
Cambridge, **Compote**, Crown Tuscan, Nude Stem, Seashell 110.00
Cambridge, **Compote**, Flying Lady, Crown Tuscan, 9 1/2 In.High 110.00
Cambridge, **Compote**, Pink, Signed, Nude Holding Dish 65.00
Cambridge, **Compote**, Seashell, Flared, Footed, Blue Milk, Signed, 10 In. 145.00
Cambridge, **Compote**, Shell, Crown Tuscan 22.50
Cambridge, **Creamer & Sugar**, Caprice, Blue, Footed 15.00
Cambridge, **Creamer & Sugar**, Heatherbloom 25.00
Cambridge, **Cup**, Nut, Cobalt, Footed, 3 In., Set Of 6 .... 85.00
Cambridge, **Dish**, Candy, Gadroon Pattern, Cover 23.00
Cambridge, **Dish**, Candy, Pink, Handled 8.00
Cambridge, **Dish**, Center, Signed, Amberina, Ohio Cambridge Glass Co. 150.00
Cambridge, **Dish**, Cigarette, Shell, Crown Tuscan, Footed, Cover, 4 X 5 In. 37.50
Cambridge, **Dish**, Clear, Mark, Swan, 4 1/2 In.Diameter 15.00
Cambridge, **Dish**, Covered, Crown Tuscan .... *Illus* 45.00
Cambridge, **Dish**, Relish, Three-Compartment, Handles, Crown Tuscan 22.50
Cambridge, **Dish**, Seashell Pattern, Crown Tuscan 26.00
Cambridge, **Dish**, Shell Shape, Crown Tuscan, Footed, 4 In.Diameter 12.00
Cambridge, **Dish**, Shell, Milk Glass, Scalloped Rim, 7 1/2 In. 6.50
Cambridge, **Figurine**, Swan, Clear, 5 In. 12.00
Cambridge, **Figurine**, Swan, Milk Glass, Black, Marked, 8 1/2 In.Long 35.00
Cambridge, **Glass**, Ice Tea, Chantilly 4.50
Cambridge, **Goblet**, Blue, Caprice 12.00
Cambridge, **Goblet**, Cobalt Blue, Clear Stem, 24 Piece Set 225.00
Cambridge, **Goblet**, Cobalt Blue, Ivy Gall, Clear Stem 35.00
Cambridge, **Goblet**, Hunt Etched, Schooner Bowl, 7 In., Clear 35.00
Cambridge, **Goblet**, Water, Chantilly 4.50
Cambridge, **Holder**, Flower, Clear, 6 In. 15.00
Cambridge, **Holder**, Flower, Figur, Pistachio, Apple Green, 13 In.Tall 75.00
Cambridge, **Holder**, Flower, Sea Gull, Clear, 8 In. 27.50
Cambridge, **Ice Bucket**, 12 In., Clear 45.00
Cambridge, **Ice Bucket**, Ebony, Clear 60.00
Cambridge, **Icer**, Cocktail, Footed, Floret Cut, 2 Piece, Clear 12.50
Cambridge, **Ivy Ball**, Footed, Crown Tuscan 30.00
Cambridge, **Jar**, Candy, Honeycomb, Clear 14.00
Cambridge, **Jug**, Syrup, Metal Top & Thumb Lift, Sunburst, Fan & Stars 42.50
Cambridge, **Pitcher & Six Tumblers**, Moonlight, Caprice 32.00
Cambridge, **Plate**, Chantilly, Etched, Clear, 6 1/4 In. 3.50
Cambridge, **Plate**, Hunting Scene, Green, Gold Border, 8 In. 12.00
Cambridge, **Plate**, Salad, Chantilly 4.50
Cambridge, **Plate**, Salad, Rose Point Etched, Clear 7.50
Cambridge, **Plate**, Serving, Apple Green, Round, 11 In., C Mark 17.00
Cambridge, **Plate**, Shell Shape, Pink, Crown Tuscan 17.50
Cambridge, **Plate**, Swan, Pink, 8 1/2 In.Diameter 22.00
Cambridge, **Relish**, Divided, Blue, Capri, 7 In. 8.50
Cambridge, **Relish**, Wildflower Pattern, 3 Part 11.00
Cambridge, **Salt & Pepper**, Chantilly Etched, Handled, Clear, Pair 15.00
Cambridge, **Sherbet**, Chantilly, Long Stemmed 4.50
Cambridge, **Squirrel** .... *Illus* 12.00
Cambridge, **Sugar & Creamer**, Blue, Capri 12.50
Cambridge, **Sugar & Creamer**, Caprice, Clear, Blue, Frosted, Tray 8.50
Cambridge, **Sugar & Creamer**, Chantilly 5.75
Cambridge, **Sugar & Creamer**, Clear, Tray 14.00
Cambridge, **Sugar**, Cascade, Gold, Open, Handles 5.00
Cambridge, **Swan**, Clear, Signed, 12 1/2 In. 60.00
Cambridge, **Swan**, Ebony, Plant Liner, Signed, 12 In. 60.00
Cambridge, **Swan**, Pistachio, Apple Green, 6 1/4 In. 33.00
Cambridge, **Swan**, Pistachio, Apple Green, 6 1/2 In. 38.00
Cambridge, **Toothpick**, Cane Medallion, Red & Clear, Notched Scalloped Top 25.00
Cambridge, **Tumbler**, Caprice, Blue 7.50
Cambridge, **Vase**, Bird, Berries, Leaves, Butterfly, 8 1/2 In. 20.00
Cambridge, **Vase**, Bud, Chantilly 5.00
Cambridge, **Vase**, Cobalt Blue, Clear Stem, 12 In. 56.00
Cambridge, **Vase**, Cornucopia, Footed, Single, Clear 9.00
Cambridge, **Vase**, Cornucopia, Seashell Base, Clear 18.00
Cambridge, **Vase**, Cornucopia, Shell Base, Crown Tuscan, 9 1/2 In.Tall 27.50

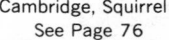

Cambridge, Squirrel
See Page 76

Cambridge, Dish, Covered, Crown Tuscan
See Page 76

Cambridge, Vase, Crown Tuscan, Seashell	65.00
Cambridge, Vase, Ebony, Enameled Roses, 14 In.	35.00
Cambridge, Vase, Footed, Ebony, Enameled Roses, 8 In., Handled	18.50
Cambridge, Vase, Ivy Ball, Ringed Stem, Crown Tuscan, 9 In.Tall	48.00
Cambridge, Vase, Nautilus, 12 In., Crown Tuscan	35.00
Cambridge, Vase, Snail Shell Shape, Crown Tuscan, 8 In.High	45.00
Cambridge, Vase, Urn, Clear Standard, Amber Bowl, 11 1/2 In.High	23.00
Cambridge, Wine, Heatherbloom Bowl, Regency Stem, Clear	35.75
Cambridge, Wine, Heatherbloom Bowl, Pair	52.00
Cambridge, Wine, Heatherbloom Bowl, Stem, Clear	17.00

Cameo Glass was made in layers in much the same manner as a cameo in jewelry. Part of the top layer of glass was cut away to reveal a different colored glass beneath. The most famous cameo glass was made during the nineteenth century.

Cameo, see also Galle, De Vez, Le Verre Francais

Cameo, Bowl, Iridescent, Signed Cristallerie De Pantin, 4 1/2 In.	350.00
Cameo, Bowl, Oval, Amethyst & Green On White	375.00
Cameo, Plate, Purple, Art Deco Pattern, Signed Charder, 11 1/2 In.Diameter	110.00
Cameo, Vase, Amethyst Iris On Yellow, 2 1/2 In.High	125.00
Cameo, Vase, Amethyst Jonquils On White, 3 In.High	145.00
Cameo, Vase, Arsall, Four Colors, 8 In.Tall	165.00
Cameo, Vase, Blossoms, Leaves, Orange, Purple Handles, Signed Richard, France	145.00
Cameo, Vase, Brown & Gold On White, Iron Oxide Base, Wheel Cut Leaves	550.00
Cameo, Vase, Burnt Orange On White, Floral, 2 In.High	100.00
Cameo, Vase, Green & Blue On Pink, White Hydrangea Wheel Cut Edges	275.00
Cameo, Vase, Pink, Purple, Blue, Floral, Signed, 7 In.	145.00
Cameo, Vase, Red To Clear, Trumpet Shape, Silver Base, 7 1/2 In.High	75.00
Cameo, Vase, Sailboats, Lake, Blue, Pink, Green, Slender Neck, 8 In.High	265.00
Cameo, Vase, Signed Weis, Tumbler Shaped, Yellow & Amber, 5 1/2 In.High	125.00
Cameo, Vase, Stick, Amethyst Jonquils On White, Silver Rim, Applied Leaves	155.00
Cameo, Vase, Yellow, Frosted, Gold Gilding, Signed Honesdale, 12 In.Tall	145.00
Cameo, Vase, Yellow, Red, Orange, Flowers, Bulbous, Arsall, Signed, 6 1/2 In.	375.00

Cameo, Webb, see Webb
Campaign, see Political Campaign

Campbell Kids, Salt & Pepper, Celluloid, 4 1/2 In.Tall	15.00
Campbell Kids, Spoon, Boy	6.00
Campbell Kids, Spoon, Girl	6.00
Campbell Kids, Spoon, Silver Plate, Pair	12.00

Camphor Glass is a cloudy white glass that has been blown or pressed. It was made by many factories in the midwest during the mid-nineteenth century.

Camphor Glass, Bookends, Grecian, Column Shape, White, Pair	55.00
Camphor Glass, Bowl, Butter, Duck With Eggs	45.00
Camphor Glass, Bowl, Flared, Scalloped Top, Footed, 7 1/2 In.Diameter	7.50
Camphor Glass, Candlestick, Bell Shape, Bottoms, Turquoise, Pair	25.00

Camphor Glass, **Dog**, Begging, 2 1/2 In.	2.00
Camphor Glass, **Donkey Head Down**, 2 1/2 In.	4.00
Camphor Glass, **Figurine**, Bulldog, Diamond Eyes, 2 1/2 In.Tall	22.50
Camphor Glass, **Figurine**, Hat, Daisy & Button	5.00
Camphor Glass, **Figurine**, Topless Maiden Sitting On Stump, 5 1/2 In.High	15.00
Camphor Glass, **Flask**, Liquor, Silver Deposit, Hunting Scene	12.00
Camphor Glass, **Hen On Nest**, 6 X 9 In.	12.00
Camphor Glass, **Plate**, Cake, Center Handle, Painted Florals	12.50
Camphor Glass, **Plate**, Sailing Scene, Fleur-De-Lis Rim, 7 1/2 In.Diameter	14.00
Camphor Glass, **Plate**, Three Kittens, Black, Gold	8.50
Camphor Glass, **Rooster**, 2 In.	4.00
Camphor Glass, **Salt**, Master, Pink, Duckling	10.00
Camphor Glass, **Squirrel**, Standing, 2 In.	5.00
Camphor Glass, **Sugar & Creamer**, Leaf Pattern, Tray, Cover	20.00
Camphor Glass, **Toothpick**, Child Resting, Bucket, 5 In.Long, 3 In.Tall	40.00
Camphor Glass, **Topiary**, Enamel Trim	10.00
Camphor Glass, **Torche**, Hand, Marked Philadelphia, 1876, Pair	75.00
Camphor Glass, **Vase**, Bud, Footed, Scalloped Edge, Green Enamel Decoration	7.50
Camphor Glass, **Vase**, Floral Design, Bulbous, 9 In.Tall	12.00
Camphor Glass, **Vase**, Imperial's Grape, Bulbous, Signed	32.50
Camphor Glass, **Vase**, Pink	6.50
Canary Glass, see Vaseline Glass	
Candelabra, **Empire**, Bronze, Ormolu, Malachite, 1850, Pair .... *Illus*	1300.00
Candelabra, **Georgian**, Crystal & Bronze, C.1810-20, Amber Glass Drops, Pair	300.00
Candelabra, **Louis XV**, Ormolu, 4-Light, Baluster Shape, C.1750, Pair	2200.00
Candelabra, **Louis XVI Style**, Ormolu, 3 S Scroll Stems, Pair	750.00
Candelabra, **Louis XVI**, Ormolu, Figural, Falconet, Nude Figures, C.1750, Pair	7200.00
Candelabra, **Miniature**, 3-Branch	17.00
Candelabra, **Porcelain**, Boys On Movable Teeter, Two Branches, 8 In., Pair	87.50
Candelabra, **Porcelain**, German Marks, 4 Candles, Raised Flowers, Pair	135.00
Candelabra, **Regency**, Table, Gilt Metal & Cut Glass, 19th Century, Pair	2000.00
Candelabra, **Victorian**, Gilded Metal, 3-Light, Lustres, C.1845, Marble, Pair	90.00
Candelabra, **Victorian**, Gilded Metal, 5-Branch, Applied Grapevine, Pair	450.00
Candelabra, **7 Candle**, Onyx Stem & Bobeches, 14 In.Spread, 17 In.High	37.50
Candelabra, **7 Candle**, Regency, Ormolu, 32 In.High	2600.00
Candle Sconce, **Two-Branch**, Adam, Gilt Gesso, Leaves & Flowers, 18th Century	500.00
Candleholder, **Alabaster**, Brass Fittings, 8 1/2 In., Pair	17.50
Candleholder, **Hogscraper**, Push-Up & Hook	22.50
Candleholder, **Porcelain**, Germany, Hotel Astor, N.Y., Floral, Painted, Pair	7.50
Candleholder, **Porcelain**, Pipe Resting On Pink & White Leaf	6.00
Candleholder, **Porcelain**, Saucer Type, Hall's China, Blue Green, Gold Bands	8.50
Candleholder, **Turned Wood & Pewter**, 10 In., Pair	18.00
Candlestand, **Walnut**, Adjustable, American, C.1750, 32 In.	900.00
Candlestand, **Wrought Iron**, American, C.1750, 27 3/4 In. .... *Illus*	525.00
Candlestick, see also Brass, Candleholder, Pewter, Pressed Glass	
Candlestick, **Brass**, Spiral, Pair .... *Illus*	32.50
Candlestick, **Brass**, Traveling, Folds Into Book Form	135.00
Candlestick, **Cut Glass**, 19th Century, 22 In.High .... *Illus*	375.00
Candlestick, **Empire Style**, Gilt Metal, Foliate Nozzle, Pair	100.00
Candlestick, **Empire**, Ormolu, Chinoiserie, Oriental Figure, C.1850, Pair	275.00
Candlestick, **Footed**, Spiked Top, 16 In. High, Pair	32.00
Candlestick, **Iron**, Winged Dragon, 6 3/4 In.High, Pair	15.95
Candlestick, **Louis XVI**, Ormolu & Marble, 18th Century, 9 In.High, Pair	275.00
Candlestick, **Onyx**, Columnar Support, Square Step Base, 11 1/2 In.High, Pair	7.50
Candlestick, **Queen Anne**, 8 In.High, Pair	100.00
Candlestick, **Silver**, Tongue & Petal & Elongated Flower Bud Band, 4	500.00
Candlestick, **Traveling**, Screw Nested, Olive Wood, Pair	60.00
Candlestick, **Victorian**, Round Base, Pair	40.00
Candlestick, **Victorian**, Square Base, 9 In.High, Pair	45.00

*Candy Containers, especially those made of glass, were popular during the
late victorian era.*

Candy Container, **Aeroplane**	6.00 To 9.00
Candy Container, **Army Tank**	9.00
Candy Container, **Auto**, Label	8.50 To 9.00
Candy Container, **Auto**, Original Candy	6.50

Candelabra, Empire, Bronze, Ormolu,
Malachite, 1850, Pair
See Page 78

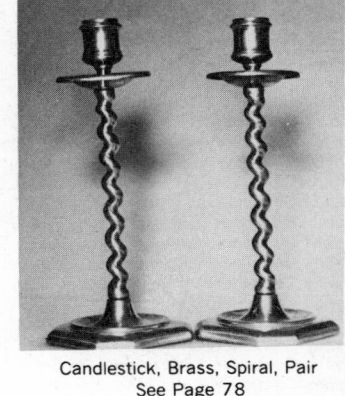

Candlestick, Brass, Spiral, Pair
See Page 78

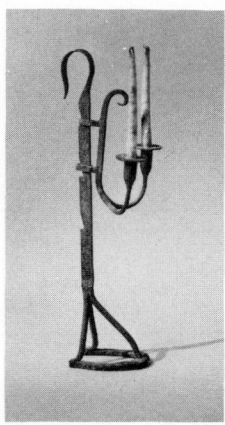

Candlestand, Wrought Iron,
American, C.1750,
27 3/4 In.
See Page 78

Candlestick, Cut Glass, 19th Century,
22 In.High
See Page 78

Candy Container, Auto, Streamlined, Cardboard Closure, Victory Glass Co.	4.25
Candy Container, Baby Chick, No.145	25.00
Candy Container, Babyface Character, Porcelain, Cover	75.00
Candy Container, Battleship	9.00
Candy Container, Billiken, The God Of Things As They Ought To Be, Glass	15.00
Candy Container, Bomber, Army	8.00
Candy Container, Bottle Carrier & Bottles, No.3	30.00
Candy Container, Bottle, Baby's, Label Jeannette, Pa.	3.00
Candy Container, Bull Dog, Round Tin Bottom Closure	18.00
Candy Container, Bulldog, Sitting, Round Base, Hand-Painted	20.00
Candy Container, Cap, Military	9.00
Candy Container, Chicken On Nest	11.00 To 25.00
Candy Container, Chicken, Clear	12.50
Candy Container, Clown Dog, No.42, J.C.Crosetti Co., Jeannette, Pa.	4.00

Candy Container, **Cruiser** 6.00
Candy Container, **Doll Nurser**, No.7, J.C.Crosetti Co., Jeannette, Pa. 4.00
Candy Container, **Drum Mug** 26.00
Candy Container, **Drum Mug**, No.543 .... 20.00
Candy Container, **Fire Engine** .... 6.00 To 12.50
Candy Container, **Fire Engine**, Clear, Cardboard Closure, Victory Glass Co. 6.50
Candy Container, **Fire Engine**, Painted 25.00
Candy Container, **Fire Truck** 4.50
Candy Container, **Fire Truck**, Label 8.50
Candy Container, **French Telephone**, No.21, J.C.Crosetti Co., Jeannette, Pa. 4.00
Candy Container, **Frog Holding Leaf Cup** 17.50
Candy Container, **Girl With Geese** .... 11.00 To 16.50
Candy Container, **Gun**, Large 15.00
Candy Container, **Hen On Nest** 4.50
Candy Container, **Horse & Cart** .... 3.00 To 6.00
Candy Container, **Hound Pup** .... 4.00 To 9.00
Candy Container, **Jack-O-Lantern** 24.00
Candy Container, **Jumbo Pencil**, No.567 .... 25.00
Candy Container, **Lantern** .... 6.00 To 16.00
Candy Container, **Lantern Shape**, Flint Globe 20.00
Candy Container, **Lantern**, Barn, Clear 20.00
Candy Container, **Lantern**, Beaded Globe 8.00
Candy Container, **Lantern**, Glass & Tin 7.00
Candy Container, **Lantern**, Red Flashed 10.00
Candy Container, **Lantern**, Tin Shade 6.00
Candy Container, **Liberty Bell**, Green, E & A No.85 .... 15.00
Candy Container, **Liberty Bell**, Tin Screw On Lid, 2 1/2 In. 5.00
Candy Container, **Little Man**, 3 In. 6.00
Candy Container, **Locomotive**, Clear, Cardboard Closure, Victory Glass Co. 8.50
Candy Container, **Locomotive**, No.1025 .... 6.50
Candy Container, **Mug** 10.00
Candy Container, **Naked Child** 8.50
Candy Container, **Old Santa**, No.671 .... 25.00
Candy Container, **Opera Glasses**, No, 558 .... 40.00
Candy Container, **Pencil** 25.00
Candy Container, **Pencil & Chicken On Nest** 25.00
Candy Container, **Pierce Arrow**, Tin Top 25.00
Candy Container, **Pistol**, Clear 9.50
Candy Container, **Pistol**, Glass, 7 1/2 In.Long 15.00
Candy Container, **Rabbit Eating Carrot** 10.00
Candy Container, **Rabbit Emerging From Egg**, No.638 .... 16.75
Candy Container, **Rabbit In Eggshell**, No.608 .... 35.00
Candy Container, **Rabbit With Basket**, Tin Bottom .... *Illus* 15.00
Candy Container, **Rabbit**, Digging, Basket On Arm, Tin Top 12.00
Candy Container, **Rabbit**, Ears Back, 6 1/2 In.High 10.00
Candy Container, **Rabbit**, On Egg 15.00
Candy Container, **Rabbit**, Sitting, Round 12.50
Candy Container, **Record Player With Horn**, No.575, Inkwell 40.00
Candy Container, **Santa At Chimney** 35.00
Candy Container, **Santa Claus**, Fat, Celluloid Head, Label 45.00
Candy Container, **Santa Claus**, Leaving Chimney, Red, White, 5 1/2 In.Tall 30.00
Candy Container, **Santa Claus**, Paint, Label 15.00
Candy Container, **Santa Leaving Chimney**, No.673 .... 25.00
Candy Container, **Santa's Boot** 6.00
Candy Container, **Santa's Head**, Plastic 30.00
Candy Container, **Scottie** .... *Illus* 4.00
Candy Container, **Scottie Dog**, Open Top .... 5.00 To 8.00
Candy Container, **Snowman** 12.00
Candy Container, **Spirit Of Goodwill**, No.8 .... 35.00
Candy Container, **Station Wagon** .... 6.00 To 10.00
Candy Container, **Suitcase** .... 7.00 To 30.00
Candy Container, **Suitcase & Santa Head** 30.00
Candy Container, **Tank**, Label .... 8.50 To 10.00
Candy Container, **Tank**, U.S.A., Man In Turret, Khaki Paint 6.50
Candy Container, **Telephone** .... 6.00 To 25.00
Candy Container, **Telephone**, Clear, Cardboard Closure, Victory Glass Co. 7.50

Candy Container, Telephone, Desk, Candy, Closure, Wood Receiver 11.00
Candy Container, Telephone, Dial, Candy, Closure .... 11.00 To 15.00
Candy Container, Train 9.00
Candy Container, War Tank, Clear, Cardboard Closure, Victory Glass Co. 6.50
Candy Container, Wheelbarrow, No.842 .... 35.00
Candy Container, Willy's Jeep .... *Illus* 8.50
Candy Container, Windmill 22.00

Candy Container, Rabbit With Basket, Tin Bottom
See Page 80

Candy Container, Scottie
See Page 80

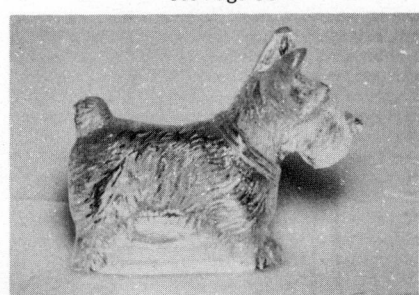

Candy Container, Willy's Jeep

Candy Container, Windmill, Glass, 5 In.High 24.00
Candy Container, Windmill, Metal Blades, No.843 .... 30.00
Candy, Container, Fat Puppy, Sitting, Copper 13.00
Cane, Ivory Handle, Carved 9.00

Canton China is a blue-and-white ware made near Canton, China, from about 1785 to 1895. It has hand-decorated chinese scenes.
Canton, Basket & Underplate, Blue & White, Openwork, 8 1/2 In.High 80.00
Canton, Basket, Reticulated, Blue & White, Ovoid, Oriental Landscape, C.1820 .... 80.00
Canton, Bowl, Blue Decorated, 9 1/2 X 13 In. 55.00
Canton, Bowl, 4 1/2 In.Diameter, 2 3/8 In.High 16.00
Canton, Creamer, Human Figure, Channel Mouth, 3 In.High 40.00
Canton, Cruet, Open, Blue & White, 5 1/2 In.High 45.00
Canton, Cup & Saucer, Wishbone Handle 38.00
Canton, Cup, Handleless, Blue & White, 3 In.High 4.00
Canton, Dish, Beefsteak, Cover, 18th Century 250.00
Canton, Dish, Leaf, Blue & White, 8 In.Long 35.00
Canton, Dish, Serving, Blue & White, Square 60.00
Canton, Dish, Vegetable, Rectangular, Acorn Finial, 10 In.Long, Pair 75.00
Canton, Jar, Ginger, Blue, Domed Lid, Blue Mountain Scene, Fishing Figure 15.00
Canton, Jar, Ginger, Covered, House & Trees, Blue Lines, Bulbous 37.00
Canton, Jar, Rose, 6 In.High 15.00
Canton, Jar, Spice, Lock & Key 350.00
Canton, Pitcher, Blue & White, Barrel Shape, Woven Branch Handle, 8 In.High 120.00
Canton, Pitcher, Covered, Blue & White, Branch Handle, Foo Dog Finial 160.00
Canton, Pitcher, Water, Blue & White, 6 In.Tall 95.00
Canton, Pitcher, Water, Strap Handle 225.00
Canton, Plate, Blue & White, Deep, 9 1/2 In.Diameter 55.00
Canton, Plate, Blue & White, 8 1/4 In.Diameter 8.00
Canton, Plate, Blue & White, 9 In.Diameter 15.00
Canton, Plate, Blue, White, Scene, Landscape, Bridge, Houses, People 18.00

Canton, Plate, Dinner, 9 3/4 In.	28.00
Canton, Plate, Hand-Painted Scene, Circa 1840, 3 3/8 In.	4.00
Canton, Plate, Polychrome, Pair	55.00
Canton, Plate, Wide Border, 7 In., 6	110.00
Canton, Platter, Blue & White, Oval, 18 In.	80.00
Canton, Platter, Blue & White, 19th Century, 20 In.	375.00
Canton, Platter, Blue, Cut Corners, 14 1/2 X 11 1/2 In.	62.00
Canton, Platter, Blue, 7 X 10 In.	30.00
Canton, Platter, Blue, 7 X 10 1/4 In.	35.00
Canton, Tazza, Blue Decorated, Set Of 4	45.00
Canton, Tea & Coffee Service, Blue & White, 64 Piece	475.00
Canton, Teapot, Blue & White, Wicker Handle	25.00
Canton, Teapot, Blue, White	45.00
Canton, Tureen, Covered, Blue & White, Feathered Finial, Rhinoceros Handles	275.00

*Capo-Di-Monte Porcelain was first made in Naples, Italy, from 1743 to
1759. The factory moved near Madrid, Spain, and reopened in 1771 and worked
to 1834. Since that time the Doccia factory of Italy acquired the molds
and style, even using the N and crown mark, which was made famous by the
factory.*

Capo-Di-Monte, Box, Children At Play, Raised, Hinged, 5 1/2 X 4 1/2 In.	125.00
Capo-Di-Monte, Box, Embossed Group Scene, Flowers Inside, 18th Century	95.00
Capo-Di-Monte, Candlestick _Illus_	125.00

Capo-Di-Monte, Candlestick

Capo-Di-Monte, Cup & Saucer, Demitasse	70.00
Capo-Di-Monte, Cup & Saucer, Demitasse, Gold Ground	30.00
Capo-Di-Monte, Cup & Saucer, People, Horses, Chariots, Twig Handle, Mark	50.00
Capo-Di-Monte, Cup & Saucer, Raised Figures, Demitasse, Italy	8.00
Capo-Di-Monte, Dish, Covered, Flaring, Gilt Framed Classical Panels, C.1850	60.00
Capo-Di-Monte, Figure, Lady, Colonial, Blue, 4 In., Crown Over N	12.00
Capo-Di-Monte, Figurine, Bust, Man, Woman, 14 In.Tall, Pair	350.00
Capo-Di-Monte, Jar, Powder, Footed, Marked	22.50
Capo-Di-Monte, Plaque, Battle Scene, Blue Crown & N Mark, 9 X 5 In.	175.00
Capo-Di-Monte, Stein, Mythological Figures, Lion On Lid	55.00
Capo-Di-Monte, Urn, Cupids, Blue Underglaze Crown & N Mark, 9 1/2 In.High	325.00
Captain Marvel, Tie Clip	17.50
Captain Midnight, Decoder, 1945	38.00
Captain Midnight, Decoder, 1946	38.00
Captain Midnight, Medal, 1940, Flight Patrol, Brass	14.00
Captain Midnight, Mug, Plastic	8.00
Caramel Slag, see Slag	
Card, see also Postcard	
Card, Advertising, Arm & Hammer Baking Soda, Bird Series, 60	6.00
Card, Advertising, Arm & Hammer Soda, 12	3.75
Card, Advertising, Cibil Meat Extract, 35	3.75
Card, Advertising, Cigar, German, 1, 450	20.00
Card, Advertising, Cigarette, Wings Airplane, World War II, 50	5.00
Card, Advertising, Currier & Ives	10.00
Card, Advertising, Duke Yacht Colors, 50	9.00

Card, Advertising, Great Form, Corsets, Girl Modeling Warp, 9 3/4 X 12 In.	7.00
Card, Advertising, Gum, Antique Auto, 45	4.00
Card, Advertising, Gum, Bowman, W.West, 154	10.50
Card, Advertising, Gum, Heroes, Pearl Harbor, 6	6.00
Card, Advertising, Gum, U.S.Warships, 8	4.75
Card, Advertising, Gum, Welch Comics, 50	6.00
Card, Advertising, Gum, World War I, Goudey, 78	18.50
Card, Advertising, Kinney Tobacco, Family, Horses, 25	6.50
Card, Advertising, Liebig Meat Extract, 1898, Pack Animals Of The World, 6	5.00
Card, Advertising, Liebig Meat Extract, 1900, Making Of Salt, 6	5.00
Card, Advertising, Liebig Meat Extract, 53	4.75
Card, Advertising, Moxie, 1906, Cardboard, Boy & Carton	5.00
Card, Advertising, Murad Cigarettes, Colleges, 41	3.75
Card, Advertising, Oliver Chilled Plow Works, Color	.35
Card, Advertising, Robbins Education, Picture, Indians, 24	5.00
Card, Advertising, Wings Cigarettes, 150	6.50
Card, Advertising, 1938 Pontiac Six	1.00
Card, Comic, Pre-1920, 100	7.50
Card, Comic, Signed Dwig	1.00
Card, Easter, 1880	.70
Card, Fortune Telling, Tarot	15.50
Card, Fortune Telling, 1897-1904, 53 Cards With Directions	7.50
Card, Fortune Telling, 1919, Candelabra On Backs	5.50
Card, Greeting, Christmas, Pre-1925, 30	1.00
Card, Greeting, Christmas, Victorian, Fringed, 1884, L.Prang, Color	.75
Card, Greeting, Easter, Pre-1925, 30	10.00
Card, Greeting, Easter, Raphael Tuck, 1907	1.00
Card, Greeting, New Year's, Pre-1925, 30	1.00
Card, Greeting, Pre-1920, 100	6.50
Card, Greeting, Valentine, Foldout Type, 2	3.50
Card, Lion Coffee, Lithograph, Knapp, 1891, Color, Christmas	1.00
Card, Lion Coffee, Lithograph, Knapp, 1891, Color, Easter	1.00
Card, Lion Coffee, Lithograph, Knapp, 1891, Color, Midsummer	1.00
Card, Mechanical, 2 View, 1882	1.00
Card, Playing, Advertising, Calco	1.00
Card, Playing, Advertising, Schering Medical	17.00
Card, Playing, Austria, 1850, Tarot, 50	10.00
Card, Playing, Avon	4.00
Card, Playing, Belgian, Eros, By Chas Pry, 1968	12.75
Card, Playing, Belgium, 1850, Hand-Stenciled	25.00
Card, Playing, Belgium, 1870, Single Face	2.00
Card, Playing, Belgium, 1870, 52	10.00
Card, Playing, Belgium, 1880, Export Singapore	12.00
Card, Playing, Belgium, 1900, Paris Exposition, 52	15.00
Card, Playing, Belgium, 1910, Fancy Aces & Courts, Joker	12.00
Card, Playing, Belgium, 1910, Jumbo, No.5, Joker	3.00
Card, Playing, Belgium, 1945, World War II, Allied Air Insurance	8.00
Card, Playing, Columbian Exposition	9.00 To 25.00
Card, Playing, Crook, Black, Boston Theatre 100th Performance, 1892	7.00
Card, Playing, Danish, The Royal, 1914	95.00
Card, Playing, England, 1918, Miniature, Tobacco	10.00
Card, Playing, English, By Bancks Brothers, 1840	36.00
Card, Playing, English, Coronation, 1953	3.75
Card, Playing, France, 1800, Life Of Christ, 24	15.00
Card, Playing, France, 1800, Roman History, 48	35.00
Card, Playing, France, 1890, Transportation	50.00
Card, Playing, French, Jeu Louis XV, 1890	35.00
Card, Playing, German, By Lattman, 1891	30.00
Card, Playing, German, 1900, Dondorf, 52	12.00
Card, Playing, Giant Cards, Austrian, 4 1/2 X 7 In.	3.95
Card, Playing, Instructive Game Of Authors	4.00
Card, Playing, Italian, Rotondi, 1912	9.00
Card, Playing, Italy, 1900, Modiano, 28	4.00
Card, Playing, Italy, 1945, Ferrero Chocolate, Comic Courts, 52	12.00
Card, Playing, Japanese, Young Men	9.25
Card, Playing, Kennedy Kards, Printed In 1963, Pictures Of J.F.Kennedy	3.00

Card, Playing, Klm Airline 3.75
Card, Playing, La Carte Toilee 4.50
Card, Playing, Lady In Car, Congress .... *Illus* 6.00
Card, Playing, Mexican, Bullfighter 3.00
Card, Playing, Mexico, La Cubana, 40 .... 8.00
Card, Playing, Miniature, Austrian, Piatnik, 1960, 1 3/4 X 2 5/8 In. 1.50
Card, Playing, Souvenir, Columbian Exposition At Chicago, 1893 .... 19.00
Card, Playing, Souvenir, Montana 4.00
Card, Playing, Souvenir, Washington Monument 10.00
Card, Playing, Spain, 1840, Hand-Stenciled, 40 .... 25.00
Card, Playing, Spanish, By Hiji De Torras Y Lleo, 1890 .... 13.00
Card, Playing, Swiss, Album 75.00
Card, Playing, U.S., 1865, Civil War 35.00
Card, Playing, U.S., 1893, Columbian Exposition 14.00
Card, Playing, U.S., 1896, Stage Star Courts 25.00
Card, Playing, U.S., 1900, Panama Canal, Scenic, Joker 6.00
Card, Playing, U.S., 1901, Pan-American Exposition, Joker 10.00
Card, Playing, Winston Cigarettes 2.50
Card, Playing, World War II, Hitler & Mussolini Joker, 1943 .... 22.00
Card, Playing, Yellowstone National Park, 1906 .... 5.50
Card, Playing, Zolar's Astrological Fortune, 1945 .... 4.00
Card, Trade, Lion Coffee, Boy In Sailor Suit Doll 2.00
Card, Trade, Lion Coffee, Palmer Cox Brownie Doll, Policeman, 1892 .... 3.75
Card, Trade, Mclaughlin's Coffee, Girl, Green Dress 2.00
Card, Valentine, Beaded Border, Cutout Roses Center, Gold Foil Paper 4.00
Card, Valentine, Carriage, Pop-Up, 10 In.Tall .... *Illus* 4.00
Card, Valentine, Dolly Dingle, Three Figures In Touring Car, 9 X 6 In. 5.00
Card, Valentine, Easel, Cherubs, 4 1/2 In. .... .25

Card, Playing,
Lady In Car, Congress

Card, Valentine, Carriage, Pop-Up, 10 In.Tall

Card, Valentine, Easel, Rocking Horse, 9 In. 2.00
Card, Valentine, Easel, Tuck, 11 In. 2.00
Card, Valentine, Hearts, Colored Tissue, 8 In. 3.00
Card, Valentine, Lace Front Folder, Embossed Envelope, Whitney, C.1860 .... 7.50
Card, Valentine, Mechanical, German, 5 .... 3.00
Card, Valentine, Pink Satin, Lacy, Birds, Floral, Mansell, Frame, 9 X 7 In. 35.00
Card, Valentine, Pre-1900, Howland, 90 .... 200.00
　　Carder, see Steuben, Aurene

　　　Carlsbad, Germany, is a mark found on china made by several factories in
　　　Germany. Most of the pieces available today were made after 1891.
Carlsbad, Chocolate Pot, Daisy Design, Multicolor, 10 In.Tall 30.00
Carlsbad, Chocolate Pot, Roses, Foliage, Bulbous 22.00
Carlsbad, Cup & Saucer, Maroon Luster, Green, Petal Shaped Saucer, Demitasse 10.00
Carlsbad, Dish, Bone, Flowers, White, Gold, Pink, Austrian 4.00

Carlsbad, Plate, Chrysanthemum & Rose, Lattice, Victoria, Austria	17.50
Carlsbad, Platter, Wall, Yellow Morning Glory	20.00
Carlsbad, Shoe, High Button, Marked Victoria	12.50
Carlsbad, Smoking Set, Signed Victoria, Figural, Jester, 4 Piece	65.00
Carlsbad, Tray & Pitcher, Marked Victoria, Austria, Pink Floral	22.50

*Carnival, or Taffeta, Glass was an inexpensive, pressed, iridescent glass
made from about 1900 to 1920. Carnival Glass is currently being reproduced.
Over 200 different patterns are known.*

Carnival Glass, see also Northwood

Carnival Glass, Banana Boat, Fenton's Thistle, Cobalt, Footed	97.50
Carnival Glass, Banana Boat, Grape & Cable, Blue	325.00
Carnival Glass, Banana Boat, Grape & Cable, Green	165.00
Carnival Glass, Banana Boat, Grape & Cable, Ice Blue, Oval, Footed	175.00
Carnival Glass, Banana Boat, Grape & Cable, Ice Green	225.00
Carnival Glass, Banana Boat, Grape & Cable, Purple	125.00
Carnival Glass, Banana Boat, Thistle, Cobalt Blue	115.00
Carnival Glass, Banana Boat, Wreathed Cherry, Purple 95.00 To	110.00
Carnival Glass, Bank, Standing Pig, Orange	4.50
Carnival Glass, Basket, Basket Weave, Green, High Handle	16.50
Carnival Glass, Basket, Bride's, Fruits, Orange, 14 X 10 In.	75.00
Carnival Glass, Basket, Honeycomb, Amber, 10 In.High	23.00
Carnival Glass, Berry Set, Beaded Heart, Peach, Petal & Fan Inside, 7 Piece	125.00
Carnival Glass, Berry Set, Butterfly & Berry, Marigold, 7 Piece	95.00
Carnival Glass, Berry Set, Jeweled Heart, Peach, Bowl & Four Sauce	165.00
Carnival Glass, Bonbon, Butterflies, Green	29.50
Carnival Glass, Bonbon, Butterfly, Amethyst	29.00
Carnival Glass, Bonbon, Lotus & Grape, Green	26.00
Carnival Glass, Bonbon, Strawberry, Marigold	15.00
Carnival Glass, Bottle, Water, Imperial Grape, Purple	88.00
Carnival Glass, Bowl & Base, Punch, Wreathed Roses, Green	165.00
Carnival Glass, Bowl, Acorn, Amethyst, 7 In.Diameter	35.00
Carnival Glass, Bowl, Acorn, Red, 6 1/2 In.Diameter	145.00
Carnival Glass, Bowl, Acorn, Scalloped Edge, Marigold, 7 1/2 In.	12.75
Carnival Glass, Bowl, Acorns & Leaves, Blue, Fluted Edge	42.00
Carnival Glass, Bowl, Acorns, Marigold, Small	15.00
Carnival Glass, Bowl, Advertising, John H.Brand Co.Furniture, Marigold	32.00
Carnival Glass, Bowl, Arch, Grape Interior, Marigold, 9 In.	25.00
Carnival Glass, Bowl, Banana, Cherry Wreath, Purple	75.00
Carnival Glass, Bowl, Banana, Grape & Cable, Marigold, Footed	92.00
Carnival Glass, Bowl, Banana, Kittens, Marigold	45.00
Carnival Glass, Bowl, Banana, Wreathed Cherry, Marigold, Oval	50.00
Carnival Glass, Bowl, Basket Weave, Amethyst, Grape & Cable Inside, 9 In.	32.00
Carnival Glass, Bowl, Basket Weave, Amethyst, Ribbon & Rays In, Northwood	35.00
Carnival Glass, Bowl, Basket Weave, Grape & Cable, Purple, 9 In.	40.00
Carnival Glass, Bowl, Basket Weave, Marigold, Miller's Furniture, Lace Edge	35.00
Carnival Glass, Bowl, Basket Weave, Purple, Mark N, 10 1/2 In.	65.00
Carnival Glass, Bowl, Basket Weave, Purple, 9 In., Marked N	35.00
Carnival Glass, Bowl, Basket Weave, Red, Open Edge, 5 1/2 In.Diameter	125.00
Carnival Glass, Bowl, Bearded Berry, Green, Captive Rose Inside, Shallow	42.00
Carnival Glass, Bowl, Bearded Berry, Marigold, Orange Tree Inside, 9 In.	24.00
Carnival Glass, Bowl, Bearded Berry, Marigold, Peacock & Grape Inside	24.00
Carnival Glass, Bowl, Bearded Berry, Marigold, Peacock At Fountain Inside	29.00
Carnival Glass, Bowl, Bearded Berry, Purple, Peacock & Grape Inside, 9 In.	39.00
Carnival Glass, Bowl, Berry, Cherry Thumbprints, Clear, Gold, Signed N	28.00
Carnival Glass, Bowl, Berry, Diamond Lace, Marigold, Claw Feet	37.00
Carnival Glass, Bowl, Berry, Diamond Lace, Purple, 5 In.Diameter	15.00
Carnival Glass, Bowl, Berry, Grape & Gothic Arches, Blue	11.00
Carnival Glass, Bowl, Berry, Holly, Purple, 9 In.Diameter	30.00
Carnival Glass, Bowl, Berry, Little Flowers, Purple	12.50
Carnival Glass, Bowl, Berry, Marigold, Paneled Peacock & Grape Inside	35.00
Carnival Glass, Bowl, Berry, Ribbed With Flowers, Marigold	8.00
Carnival Glass, Bowl, Berry, Two Flower, Marigold, Claw Feet	35.00
Carnival Glass, Bowl, Berry, Windmill, Marigold, Footed, 9 In.	40.00
Carnival Glass, Bowl, Bird & Bee, White, Iridescent	95.00
Carnival Glass, Bowl, Blackberry Bramble, Green, 8 1/2 In.	37.50

Carnival Glass, Bowl, Butterfly & Berry, Marigold, 3 Ball & Claw Feet	39.00
Carnival Glass, Bowl, Butterfly, Amethyst, 2 Handles, 7 In.Diameter	34.00
Carnival Glass, Bowl, Cactus, Amethyst, Rays & Ribbons Inside	25.00
Carnival Glass, Bowl, Captive Rose, Blue, 9 In.Diameter	45.00
Carnival Glass, Bowl, Center, Butterfly & Berry, Cobalt, Footed	49.50
Carnival Glass, Bowl, Cereal, Bouquet & Lattice, Marigold, 6 1/2 In.	1.95
Carnival Glass, Bowl, Cereal, Kittens, Blue	58.50
Carnival Glass, Bowl, Cereal, Lattice & Bouquet, Marigold	3.00
Carnival Glass, Bowl, Cherry Panels, Peach, Dome, Footed, . In.	35.00
Carnival Glass, Bowl, Cherry Panels, Peach, Piecrust Edge	45.00
Carnival Glass, Bowl, Cherry, Purple, Amethyst, Marked N, Footed, 8 1/2 In.	33.00
Carnival Glass, Bowl, Cobblestones, Marigold, Flat, 9 In.	28.00
Carnival Glass, Bowl, Coin Dots, Green, Shallow, 8 1/2 In.Diameter	34.00
Carnival Glass, Bowl, Comet, Blue, 9 In.Diameter	36.00 To 45.00
Carnival Glass, Bowl, Cosmos, Amethyst, 10 In.	37.00
Carnival Glass, Bowl, Cosmos, Marigold, 9 1/2 In.	24.00
Carnival Glass, Bowl, Cosmos, Purple, Amethyst, 10 In.	28.00
Carnival Glass, Bowl, Diamond Lace, Marigold	15.00
Carnival Glass, Bowl, Double Dutch, Smoky, Footed, 9 In.Diameter	42.50
Carnival Glass, Bowl, Double Stemmed Rose, Marigold, Footed, Crimped	15.00
Carnival Glass, Bowl, Double Stemmed Rose, Purple	32.50
Carnival Glass, Bowl, Dragon & Lotus, Amethyst, 9 In.Diameter	39.00
Carnival Glass, Bowl, Dragon & Lotus, Blue, 3 Feet	29.00
Carnival Glass, Bowl, Dragon & Lotus, Green, 3 Feet, 8 In.Diameter	42.00
Carnival Glass, Bowl, Dragon & Lotus, Marigold	28.50
Carnival Glass, Bowl, Dragon & Lotus, Marigold, Footed, 7 In.	30.00
Carnival Glass, Bowl, Dragon & Lotus, Marigold, 8 In.	25.00 To 27.00
Carnival Glass, Bowl, Dragon & Lotus, Marigold, 8 1/2 In.Diameter	24.00
Carnival Glass, Bowl, Dragon & Lotus, Marigold, 9 In.Diameter	25.00
Carnival Glass, Bowl, Dragon & Lotus, Purple, Amethyst, Footed, 8 1/2 In.	25.00
Carnival Glass, Bowl, Dragon & Lotus, Red, Fluted	125.00
Carnival Glass, Bowl, Dragon & Rose, Green, Footed, 7 1/2 In.Across	40.00
Carnival Glass, Bowl, Dragon Lotus, Marigold, Flared, 9 In.Diameter	25.00
Carnival Glass, Bowl, Drapery, White, Signed N	45.00
Carnival Glass, Bowl, Embossed Mums, Ice Blue	50.00
Carnival Glass, Bowl, Embossed Mums, Purple, 9 1/2 In.	85.00
Carnival Glass, Bowl, Fanciful, White, Ruffled, 8 1/2 In.	59.50
Carnival Glass, Bowl, Fashion Pattern, Marigold, Fluted Edge, 9 In.Diameter	25.00
Carnival Glass, Bowl, Feathered Serpent, Green, 10 In.Diameter	40.00 To 50.00
Carnival Glass, Bowl, Fenton Lion, Marigold, 7 In.	95.00
Carnival Glass, Bowl, File, Amethyst, Scroll Embossed Inside	30.00
Carnival Glass, Bowl, File, Marigold, Ruffled, 9 In.	25.00
Carnival Glass, Bowl, Fish Scale & Beads, Marigold, 6 1/2 In.Diameter	12.75
Carnival Glass, Bowl, Fishes, Marigold, 6 In.Diameter	50.00
Carnival Glass, Bowl, Five Open Flowers, Amethyst, 6 In.Diameter	24.00
Carnival Glass, Bowl, Flowering Almond, Amethyst, 2 Handles, 7 In.Diameter	27.00
Carnival Glass, Bowl, Flowering Almond, Green, 7 In.Diameter	22.00
Carnival Glass, Bowl, Flowering Almond, Marigold, 8 1/2 In.Diameter	24.00
Carnival Glass, Bowl, Flowering Almond, Purple, 9 In.	34.00
Carnival Glass, Bowl, Footed, Question Mark, Marigold *Illus*	20.00
Carnival Glass, Bowl, Four Flowers, Emerald Green, 8 1/2 In.	25.00
Carnival Glass, Bowl, Fruit, Rose Pattern, Marigold, Footed	37.50
Carnival Glass, Bowl, Fruit, Stretch, Marigold, Footed, 10 In.Diameter	35.00
Carnival Glass, Bowl, Garden Path, Marigold, 8 In.Diameter	42.50
Carnival Glass, Bowl, Geometric, Marigold, 9 In.	12.00
Carnival Glass, Bowl, Good Luck, Blue, Flat, Stippled Ground	85.00
Carnival Glass, Bowl, Good Luck, Marigold, 8 1/2 In.	29.00 To 45.00
Carnival Glass, Bowl, Good Luck, Purple, Flat Basket Weave, N	85.00 To 95.00
Carnival Glass, Bowl, Good Luck, Purple, Ruffled Edge, 8 1/2 In.	50.00 To 75.00
Carnival Glass, Bowl, Gooseberry, White, Orange Tree Inside, Ruffled	67.50
Carnival Glass, Bowl, Grape & Cable, Amethyst, Shallow, Crimped Edge	32.50
Carnival Glass, Bowl, Grape & Cable, Amethyst, 8 In.	33.50 To 40.00
Carnival Glass, Bowl, Grape & Cable, Basket Weave Exterior, Green, Northwood	48.50
Carnival Glass, Bowl, Grape & Cable, Blue, Spatulated Feet	39.50 To 58.00
Carnival Glass, Bowl, Grape & Cable, Blue, 3 Legs, 7 3/4 In.	25.00
Carnival Glass, Bowl, Grape & Cable, Green, Ruffled Edge, Signed N	95.00

Carnival Glass, Bowl, Footed, Question Mark, Marigold
See Page 86

Carnival Glass, Bowl, Grape & Cable, Green, 7 In.Diameter .... 27.00 To 32.50
Carnival Glass, Bowl, Grape & Cable, Marigold, 3 Scroll Feet .... 22.00 To 24.00
Carnival Glass, Bowl, Grape & Cable, Persian Medallion, Green, 10 In. 115.00
Carnival Glass, Bowl, Grape & Cable, Persian Medallion, Marigold, Footed 68.00
Carnival Glass, Bowl, Grape & Cable, Purple, Footed, 8 In.Diameter 40.00
Carnival Glass, Bowl, Grape, Green, Marked N, 7 1/2 In. 28.00
Carnival Glass, Bowl, Grape, Purple, Amethyst, Marked N, 9 In. 34.00
Carnival Glass, Bowl, Grape, Purple, 7 In.Diameter 37.50
Carnival Glass, Bowl, Grape, Wild Rose, Amethyst, Ruffled Rim, N Mark 28.00
Carnival Glass, Bowl, Greek Key With Sunflowers, Marigold, Footed, Marked N 25.00
Carnival Glass, Bowl, Hattie, Marigold, 8 In. .... 20.00 To 24.00
Carnival Glass, Bowl, Hattie, Smoky, 9 In.Diameter 32.00
Carnival Glass, Bowl, Heart & Vine, Blue, 9 1/2 In. 87.50
Carnival Glass, Bowl, Heart & Vine, Green, 7 1/2 In. 35.00
Carnival Glass, Bowl, Hearts & Fern, Marigold, Fluted, 8 1/2 In.Diameter 30.00
Carnival Glass, Bowl, Hearts & Flowers, White 45.00
Carnival Glass, Bowl, Helios, Green 35.00
Carnival Glass, Bowl, Herringbone, Marigold, 9 3/4 In.Diameter 12.00
Carnival Glass, Bowl, Holly & Berry, Amethyst, 9 In.Diameter 39.00
Carnival Glass, Bowl, Holly & Berry, Green, Ruffled Edge, 9 In. 27.00
Carnival Glass, Bowl, Holly & Berry, Marigold, 9 In.Diameter 24.00
Carnival Glass, Bowl, Holly, Blue, 8 3/4 In.Across 37.50
Carnival Glass, Bowl, Holly, Marigold, Ruffled, 9 In. 27.00
Carnival Glass, Bowl, Holly, Marigold, Scalloped Border, Shallow .... 9.50 To 14.75
Carnival Glass, Bowl, Holly, Purple, 8 3/4 In.Across 37.50
Carnival Glass, Bowl, Holly, White, Gold, Iridescent, 8 In.Diameter 89.00
Carnival Glass, Bowl, Honeycomb & Bead, Marigold 15.00
Carnival Glass, Bowl, Horses' Heads, Marigold, Footed 35.00
Carnival Glass, Bowl, Horses' Heads, Marigold, Ruffled 42.50
Carnival Glass, Bowl, Horses' Heads, Green, 6 1/2 In. 62.00
Carnival Glass, Bowl, Horses' Heads, Marigold .... 48.00 To 55.00
Carnival Glass, Bowl, Ice Cream, Grape, White, Marked N, 10 5/8 In. 178.00
Carnival Glass, Bowl, Ice Cream, Maple Leaf, Marigold 35.00
Carnival Glass, Bowl, Ice Cream, Persian Garden, White, 12 In., Northwood 110.00
Carnival Glass, Bowl, Imperial Grape, Marigold 11.50
Carnival Glass, Bowl, Imperial Jewels, Deep Red .... 45.00 To 95.00
Carnival Glass, Bowl, Imperial Jewels, Sapphire Blue, 9 1/2 In.Diameter 17.00
Carnival Glass, Bowl, Imperial Jewels, Vaseline, Gold Band On Rim 23.00
Carnival Glass, Bowl, Jewels, White, Imperial Mark 25.00
Carnival Glass, Bowl, Keyhole, Peach, Raindrops Inside, Footed 35.00
Carnival Glass, Bowl, Kittens, Marigold 60.00
Carnival Glass, Bowl, Lattice & Grape, Amethyst, 8 1/2 In. 35.00
Carnival Glass, Bowl, Leaf & Beads, Green, Opalescent Ruffled Rim, Pedestal 25.00
Carnival Glass, Bowl, Leaf Chain, White 45.00
Carnival Glass, Bowl, Lion, Marigold, 6 1/2 In. 47.00

Carnival Glass, Bowl, Lion, Marigold, 7 In. 65.00
Carnival Glass, Bowl, Little Fishes, Amethyst, Footed, 6 In.Diameter 75.00
Carnival Glass, Bowl, Little Flowers, Blue, 10 In.Diameter 50.00
Carnival Glass, Bowl, Lotus & Dragon, Amethyst, 8 In.Diameter 75.00
Carnival Glass, Bowl, Lotus & Grape, Marigold, 3 Scroll Feet, 6 In. 22.00
Carnival Glass, Bowl, Louisa Rose, Green 45.00
Carnival Glass, Bowl, Louisa, Marigold, Silver Luster 10.00
Carnival Glass, Bowl, Luster Rose, Green, Three Scroll Feet, 9 In. 39.50
Carnival Glass, Bowl, Luster Rose, Marigold, 3 Scroll Feet, 7 1/2 In. 32.00
Carnival Glass, Bowl, Luster Rose, Purple, Three Scroll Feet 29.00
Carnival Glass, Bowl, Millersburg Cherry, Peach Overlay, 3 Feet 40.00
Carnival Glass, Bowl, Nut, Fenton Flowers, Marigold, Footed 26.00
Carnival Glass, Bowl, Nut, Vintage, Marigold, Footed 21.00
Carnival Glass, Bowl, Orange Tree, Blue 35.00
Carnival Glass, Bowl, Orange Tree, Marigold, Footed 50.00
Carnival Glass, Bowl, Orange Tree, Royal Blue, Footed, 10 In. 125.00
Carnival Glass, Bowl, Orange, Three Reeded Feet, Marigold, 8 1/2 In. 72.50
Carnival Glass, Bowl, Pansy, Ice Green, 9 In. 32.00
Carnival Glass, Bowl, Panther Berry, Marigold 85.00
Carnival Glass, Bowl, Panther, Marigold, Footed, Ruffled, 6 In. 27.00
Carnival Glass, Bowl, Peacock & Grape, Blue, 8 In. 45.00
Carnival Glass, Bowl, Peacock & Grape, Green, Footed 29.50
Carnival Glass, Bowl, Peacock & Grape, Green, Three Feet, 7 1/2 In. 27.00
Carnival Glass, Bowl, Peacock & Grape, Marigold, Flat 21.00
Carnival Glass, Bowl, Peacock & Grape, Marigold, 3 Feet, 8 In.Diameter 22.00
Carnival Glass, Bowl, Peacock & Grape, Marigold, 9 In. 22.00
Carnival Glass, Bowl, Peacock & Grape, Orange 18.00
Carnival Glass, Bowl, Peacock & Grape, Purple, 8 1/2 In. 32.00
Carnival Glass, Bowl, Peacock & Urn, Amethyst, Deep 65.00
Carnival Glass, Bowl, Peacock & Urn, White, N Mark, 11 In.Diameter 150.00
Carnival Glass, Bowl, Peacock At Fountain, Cobalt Blue, Marked N 20.00
Carnival Glass, Bowl, Peacock At Urn, Marigold, 8 1/2 In. 42.00
Carnival Glass, Bowl, Peacock At Urn, White, Low 70.00
Carnival Glass, Bowl, Peacock Eye, Purple, 8 In. 27.00
Carnival Glass, Bowl, Peacock Eye With File, Purple 27.50
Carnival Glass, Bowl, Peacock Grape, Blue, Fluted, 9 In. 35.00
Carnival Glass, Bowl, Peacock On Fence, Ruffled Edge, Marigold, 9 In. 40.00
Carnival Glass, Bowl, Peacock On Fence, White, N Mark 125.00
Carnival Glass, Bowl, Peacock On The Fence, Marigold, Ruffled 47.50
Carnival Glass, Bowl, Peacock, Aqua, Opalescent 185.00
Carnival Glass, Bowl, Peacock, Blue 125.00
Carnival Glass, Bowl, Peacock, Marigold, 9 In., Marked N 45.00
Carnival Glass, Bowl, Peacock, Stippled Background, Purple 95.00
Carnival Glass, Bowl, Persian Medallion, Blue 15.00
Carnival Glass, Bowl, Persian Medallion, Green, 7 In.Diameter 22.00
Carnival Glass, Bowl, Persian Medallion, Marigold, Small 19.50
Carnival Glass, Bowl, Pinecone, Marigold, 7 In.Diameter 17.50
Carnival Glass, Bowl, Pony Head, Marigold, Fluted 40.00
Carnival Glass, Bowl, Pony, Marigold, 8 1/2 In.Diameter 37.50
Carnival Glass, Bowl, Pony, Purple, Satin Iridescence 89.50
Carnival Glass, Bowl, Poppy Show, Blue 175.00
Carnival Glass, Bowl, Poppy Show, White 140.00
Carnival Glass, Bowl, Punch, Base, Stork & Rushes, Marigold 97.50
Carnival Glass, Bowl, Punch, Grape & Cable, Green 45.00
Carnival Glass, Bowl, Punch, Grape & Cable, Marigold, 2 Piece 700.00
Carnival Glass, Bowl, Punch, Grape & Cable, Purple, 2 Piece .... 265.00 To 350.00
Carnival Glass, Bowl, Punch, Imperial Grape, Marigold, Base 65.00
Carnival Glass, Bowl, Punch, Marigold, Stand, Six Cups, Set 130.00
Carnival Glass, Bowl, Punch, Orange Tree, Marigold, Four Cups 95.00
Carnival Glass, Bowl, Punch, Persian Medallion, Wreath Of Roses, Green, 3 Cup 265.00
Carnival Glass, Bowl, Purple, Ruffled Rim, Pedestal Base, 4 1/2 In.Tall 32.50
Carnival Glass, Bowl, Question Mark, Footed, Handles, Marigold 20.00
Carnival Glass, Bowl, Reindeer, Holly Leaves, Orange, Three Clear Feet 35.00
Carnival Glass, Bowl, Rib & Wild Rose, Openwork Edge With Hearts, Amethyst 20.00
Carnival Glass, Bowl, Ribbon & Rays, Marigold, 9 1/2 In. 22.00
Carnival Glass, Bowl, Ribbon Tie, Amethyst, 8 In.Diameter 30.00

Carnival Glass, Bowl, Rosalind, Amethyst, Scalloped Rim, 10 In.Diameter 45.00
Carnival Glass, Bowl, Rose Show, Opalescent, Aqua 150.00
Carnival Glass, Bowl, Rose Show, White 145.00
Carnival Glass, Bowl, Roses & Loops, Amethyst, Footed, 8 In.Diameter 39.00
Carnival Glass, Bowl, Rosette, Ruffles & Rings, Amethyst, Footed, N Mark 22.00
Carnival Glass, Bowl, Ruffled Rib, Amethyst, 9 In. 17.50
Carnival Glass, Bowl, Scale Band, Red 75.00
Carnival Glass, Bowl, Sea Lane's, Marigold, Footed, 6 In. 50.00
Carnival Glass, Bowl, Show, Poppy, Blue 160.00
Carnival Glass, Bowl, Ski Star, Peach, Ruffled, 11 In. 65.00
Carnival Glass, Bowl, Stippled Ray, Purple, 7 1/2 In. 22.00
Carnival Glass, Bowl, Soup, Herringbone, Marigold, 8 In.Diameter 3.95
Carnival Glass, Bowl, Soup, Iris & Herringbone, Marigold 3.75
Carnival Glass, Bowl, Soup, Kittens, Marigold 57.50
Carnival Glass, Bowl, Stag & Holly, Marigold, Footed .... 70.00 To 90.00
Carnival Glass, Bowl, Stag & Holly, Marigold, Footed, 10 In. 47.00
Carnival Glass, Bowl, Stag & Holly, Marigold, Footed, 8 In. 39.00
Carnival Glass, Bowl, Stag & Holly, Marigold, Scroll Feet, 9 In. .... 45.00 To 55.00
Carnival Glass, Bowl, Star & File, Marigold 12.50
Carnival Glass, Bowl, Star Medallion, Marigold, 7 1/2 In. 20.00
Carnival Glass, Bowl, Star Of David & Bows, Purple, Marked N 45.00
Carnival Glass, Bowl, Star Of David, Purple, Green Luster, Signed N 60.00
Carnival Glass, Bowl, Stippled Rays, Green, 9 In.Diameter 24.00
Carnival Glass, Bowl, Stippled Rays, Marigold, Northwood, 9 1/2 In. 27.00
Carnival Glass, Bowl, Stippled Rays, Purple, Marked N 22.50
Carnival Glass, Bowl, Stippled Three Fruits, Blue 43.00
Carnival Glass, Bowl, Stork In Rushes, Purple 15.00
Carnival Glass, Bowl, Strawberry, Basket Weave, Green 35.00
Carnival Glass, Bowl, Strawberry, Green, Signed N 60.00
Carnival Glass, Bowl, Strawberry, Marigold, Basket Weave Back, 8 1/2 In. 21.50
Carnival Glass, Bowl, Strawberry, Marigold, Basket Weave Back, 9 In. 27.00
Carnival Glass, Bowl, Strawberry, Purple, 8 1/2 In., Marked N 45.00
Carnival Glass, Bowl, Strawberry, Purple, 9 In., Marked N 45.00
Carnival Glass, Bowl, Swirl, Orange, 10 X 4 In. 15.00
Carnival Glass, Bowl, Ten Mums, Blue, Ribbon Edge 70.00
Carnival Glass, Bowl, Thistle & Lotus, Marigold, 6 1/2 In.Diameter 22.50
Carnival Glass, Bowl, Thistle, Amethyst, 7 1/2 In. 45.00
Carnival Glass, Bowl, Three Fruit, Green, Basket Weave Dome, Footed, 9 In. 35.00
Carnival Glass, Bowl, Three Fruits, Amethyst, 3 Feet, 9 In.Diameter 45.00
Carnival Glass, Bowl, Three Fruits, Amethyst, 8 1/2 In. 36.00
Carnival Glass, Bowl, Three Fruits, Green, Footed 35.00
Carnival Glass, Bowl, Three Fruits, Ice Blue, 9 In.Diameter 42.00
Carnival Glass, Bowl, Three Fruits, Purple, Footed, 2 Handles, 7 In. 39.00
Carnival Glass, Bowl, Three Fruits, White, Fluted 60.00
Carnival Glass, Bowl, Tree Of Life, Marigold, 9 1/2 In.Diameter 9.00
Carnival Glass, Bowl, Tree Of Life, Purple, Footed, 4 1/4 In.Diameter 20.00
Carnival Glass, Bowl, Trout & Fly, Green 150.00
Carnival Glass, Bowl, Trout & Fly, Purple, 9 In.Diameter 200.00
Carnival Glass, Bowl, Victorian, Purple, Ruffled 125.00
Carnival Glass, Bowl, Vintage, Amethyst, 9 In.Diameter 37.00
Carnival Glass, Bowl, Vintage, Green, 9 In. 28.00
Carnival Glass, Bowl, Vintage, Marigold, 9 In.Diameter 25.50
Carnival Glass, Bowl, Vintage, Purple, Collar Base, 7 In.Diameter 18.00
Carnival Glass, Bowl, Vintage, Purple, Footed 37.50
Carnival Glass, Bowl, Vintage, Purple, 8 In.Diam., Scalloped Top 45.00
Carnival Glass, Bowl, Whirling Leaves, Green 28.00
Carnival Glass, Bowl, Wild Strawberry, Purple, Amethyst, Marked N, 9 1/2 In. 39.00
Carnival Glass, Bowl, Windflower, Marigold, 8 1/2 In. 24.00
Carnival Glass, Bowl, Windflower, Purple, 8 1/2 In. 27.00
Carnival Glass, Bowl, Windmill, Marigold .... 18.00 To 18.50
Carnival Glass, Bowl, Windmill, Marigold, Scalloped Edge, 7 In.Diameter 13.75
Carnival Glass, Bowl, Windmill, Purple, 7 In.Across 37.50
Carnival Glass, Bowl, Wishbone, Green, Mark N, Footed, 9 In. .... 45.00 To 60.00
Carnival Glass, Bowl, Wishbone, Purple, Northwood, 3 Feet, Fluted 50.00
Carnival Glass, Bowl, Wreathed Cherry, Amethyst, Oval, 6 In. 20.00
Carnival Glass, Bowl, Zig Zag Pattern, Green, 9 In. Diameter 29.50

Carnival Glass, Box, Powder, Imperial Grape, Marigold, Covered 20.00
Carnival Glass, Box, Powder, Vintage, Marigold 31.50
Carnival Glass, Brooklyn Bridge, Marigold 195.00
Carnival Glass, Butter, Dahlia, White, Gold Trim 157.00
Carnival Glass, Butter, Geometrics Hobstar, Blue-Green Turquoise 125.00
Carnival Glass, Butter, Peacock At Fountain, Cobalt Blue, Marked N 68.00
Carnival Glass, Butter, Peacock At Fountain, Marigold, Marked N 95.00
Carnival Glass, Butter, Pineapple & Fan, Marigold, Covered 35.00
Carnival Glass, Candleholder, Grape & Cable, Marigold, Mark N 70.00
Carnival Glass, Candlestick, Colonial, Marigold, 10 1/2 In.High, Pair 35.00
Carnival Glass, Candlestick, Grape & Cable, Purple 85.00
Carnival Glass, Candlestick, Imperial Jewels, Green, Pair 40.00
Carnival Glass, Candlestick, Lydia, Red To Amberina, Pair 79.50
Carnival Glass, Candlestick, Paneled, Marigold, Pair 38.50
Carnival Glass, Carafe, Imperial Grape, Purple 90.00
Carnival Glass, Carafe, Water, Green 65.00
Carnival Glass, Carafe, Water, Helios, Marigold 40.00
Carnival Glass, Carafe, Water, Imperial Grape, Green 90.00
Carnival Glass, Carafe, Water, Imperial Grape, Marigold 40.00
Carnival Glass, Carnival Glass, Compote, Poppy, Marigold 25.00
Carnival Glass, Compote, Acanthus, Amber, Tulip Shape 27.50
Carnival Glass, Compote, Acanthus, Teal Blue, Tulip Shape 38.50
Carnival Glass, Compote, Blackberry, Blue, Miniature .... 29.00 To 42.50
Carnival Glass, Compote, Blackberry, Purple, Tripod Feet, 8 In. 42.00
Carnival Glass, Compote, Blossom Time, Purple, Ribbed Stem, Signed N 47.50
Carnival Glass, Compote, Daisy & Plume, Green, Fluted, Mark N, 5 In. 30.00
Carnival Glass, Compote, Daisy & Plume, Marigold, 6 In. 20.00
Carnival Glass, Compote, Daisy & Plume, Ruffled, Marigold, N Mark 18.00
Carnival Glass, Compote, Double Star, Marigold 32.00
Carnival Glass, Compote, Flower, Leaves, White, Footed, 9 1/2 In.Diameter 35.00
Carnival Glass, Compote, Grape & Cable, Clear, Open 30.00
Carnival Glass, Compote, Hearts & Flowers, Marigold 18.00
Carnival Glass, Compote, Hearts & Flowers, White, Footed .... 45.00 To 75.00
Carnival Glass, Compote, Holly, Blue 18.00
Carnival Glass, Compote, Iris Pattern, Amethyst 30.00
Carnival Glass, Compote, Iris, Marigold, 7 In. 32.50
Carnival Glass, Compote, Jelly, Birds & Cherries, Marigold 25.00
Carnival Glass, Compote, Jelly, Holly, Marigold 13.00
Carnival Glass, Compote, Marigold 32.50
Carnival Glass, Compote, Mikado, Cherry, Blue 165.00
Carnival Glass, Compote, Mikado, Purple, 8 5/8 In.High 165.00
Carnival Glass, Compote, Panel & Thumbprint, Marigold, Ruffled Edge 18.50
Carnival Glass, Compote, Peacock At Urn, Blue, 5 In. 55.00
Carnival Glass, Compote, Peacock At Urn, Marigold, 6 In. 40.00
Carnival Glass, Compote, Peacock Feather, Footed, Scalloped Rim, 2 1/4 In. 18.50
Carnival Glass, Compote, Peacock Tail, Green 16.50
Carnival Glass, Compote, Persian Gardens, Marigold 15.00
Carnival Glass, Compote, Persian Medallion, Blue 30.00
Carnival Glass, Compote, Persian Medallion, Marigold, Footed 28.50
Carnival Glass, Compote, Stippled Rays, Marigold, 6 In. 9.50
Carnival Glass, Compote, Stippled Rose Panels, Marigold, 9 1/2 In.Tall 29.50
Carnival Glass, Compote, Thin Rib, Marigold, Marked N 7.50
Carnival Glass, Compote, Three Fruits, Purple, Handles, Marked N 50.00
Carnival Glass, Compote, Wildflower, Marigold, Primrose Inside, Marked N 22.50
Carnival Glass, Compote, Wreath Of Roses, Green, Two Handles 24.75
Carnival Glass, Creamer, Acorn & Burr, Marigold, Mark N .... 35.00 To 38.00
Carnival Glass, Creamer, Basket Weave, Marigold 15.00
Carnival Glass, Creamer, Bird & Strawberry, Blue 35.00
Carnival Glass, Creamer, Butterfly & Berry, Marigold 24.00
Carnival Glass, Creamer, Flute, Purple 40.00
Carnival Glass, Creamer, Maple Leaf, Purple 29.00
Carnival Glass, Creamer, Pansy Spray, Stippled, Green 24.50
Carnival Glass, Creamer, Peacock At The Fountain, Purple, Signed 43.00
Carnival Glass, Creamer, Pineapple, Marigold 28.00
Carnival Glass, Creamer, Split Diamond, Marigold 25.00
Carnival Glass, Creamer, Thistle & Thorn, Marigold, Footed 25.00

Carnival Glass, Creamer, Thumbprint & Spear, Marigold 9.00
Carnival Glass, Cruet, Buzz Saw, Marigold 175.00
Carnival Glass, Cup & Saucer, Imperial Grape, Marigold 15.00
Carnival Glass, Cup, Loving, Orange Tree, Flowering Almond, Amber 100.00
Carnival Glass, Cup, Orange Tree, Marigold 7.00
Carnival Glass, Cup, Punch, Grape & Cable, Amethyst, Marked N 15.00
Carnival Glass, Cup, Punch, Acorn & Burr, Cobalt, Signed N 25.00
Carnival Glass, Cup, Punch, Acorn & Burr, Green 22.00
Carnival Glass, Cup, Punch, Fashion, Marigold 8.00
Carnival Glass, Cup, Punch, Grape & Cable, Amethyst, Marked N 17.00
Carnival Glass, Cup, Punch, Grape & Cable, Blue, Stippled, Set Of 6 .... 100.00
Carnival Glass, Cup, Punch, Hobstar & Feather, Marigold 17.00
Carnival Glass, Cup, Punch, Orange Peel, Marigold 12.00
Carnival Glass, Cup, Punch, Orange Tree, Blue 12.50
Carnival Glass, Cup, Punch, Orange Tree, Marigold 6.50
Carnival Glass, Cup, Punch, Peacock At Fountain, Marigold 12.00
Carnival Glass, Cup, Punch, S Repeat, Purple 15.00
Carnival Glass, Cup, Punch, Star Medallion, Marigold 8.00
Carnival Glass, Cup, Punch, Stippled Grape & Cable, Marigold 20.00
Carnival Glass, Cup, Punch, Stork & Rushes, Amethyst 15.00
Carnival Glass, Cup, Punch, Stork & Rushes, Marigold .... 6.00 To 15.00
Carnival Glass, Cup, Punch, Vintage, Marigold 6.00
Carnival Glass, Cuspidor, Tree Of Life, Marigold 17.00
Carnival Glass, Decanter, Grapes, Smoky 135.00
Carnival Glass, Decanter, Imperial Grape, Green, Stopper 59.50
Carnival Glass, Decanter, Imperial Grape, Purple 85.00
Carnival Glass, Decanter, Wine, Diamond & Sunburst, Purple 90.00
Carnival Glass, Decanter, Wine, Imperial Grape, Marigold 45.00
Carnival Glass, Dish, Acorn, Greeb, Ruffled, 7 In. 30.00
Carnival Glass, Dish, Banana, Water Lily & Cattail, Thistle, Marigold 85.00
Carnival Glass, Dish, Bark, Marigold, 9 In. 28.00
Carnival Glass, Dish, Basket Weave, Red, Open Edge, Turned-Down Front 75.00
Carnival Glass, Dish, Berry, Bouquet & Lattice, Marigold, 5 In. 1.95
Carnival Glass, Dish, Berry, Bouquet & Lattice, Marigold, 6 In. 1.95
Carnival Glass, Dish, Berry, Peacock At Fountain, White, N Mark 30.00
Carnival Glass, Dish, Bonbon, Amethyst 25.00
Carnival Glass, Dish, Bonbon, Brocaded Acorns, Pink, Handle 10.00
Carnival Glass, Dish, Bonbon, Butterfly, Marigold 20.00
Carnival Glass, Dish, Bonbon, Grape, Marigold, Ruffles, Handles 16.00
Carnival Glass, Dish, Bonbon, Persian Medallion, Green, Pedestal Base 34.00
Carnival Glass, Dish, Bonbon, Three Fruits, Purple, Handle, N Mark 35.00
Carnival Glass, Dish, Butter, Grape & Cable, Purple 145.00
Carnival Glass, Dish, Butter, Pineapple, Marigold 15.00
Carnival Glass, Dish, Butter, Stork & Rushes, Marigold, Cover, Beaded Edge 15.00
Carnival Glass, Dish, Butterfly, Berry, & Panther, Marigold, 5 1/4 In. 25.67
Carnival Glass, Dish, Butterfly, Berry, & Panther, Marigold, 5 1/4 In. 25.67
Carnival Glass, Dish, Candy, Cut & Roses, Amethyst, 3 Legs, Marked N 31.00
Carnival Glass, Dish, Candy, Draper, Blue, Mark N 50.00
Carnival Glass, Dish, Candy, Form Of Duck, Marigold, Covered 16.00
Carnival Glass, Dish, Candy, Heart & Vine, Amethyst, Ribbon Edge 35.00
Carnival Glass, Dish, Candy, Kookaburra, Purple 35.00
Carnival Glass, Dish, Candy, Lacy Edge, Red 110.00
Carnival Glass, Dish, Covered Hen, Purple 8.00
Carnival Glass, Dish, Covered Turkey, Orange 8.50
Carnival Glass, Dish, Dahlia, Marigold 12.00
Carnival Glass, Dish, Drapery, Ice Blue, Triangular 45.00
Carnival Glass, Dish, Egyptian Band, White, Fluted, 9 In. 80.00
Carnival Glass, Dish, Fine Cut & Roses, Dark Green, Footed, Marked N 30.00
Carnival Glass, Dish, French Poodle, Marigold, Covered 7.00
Carnival Glass, Dish, Holly, Berry, Red, Hat Shape 110.00
Carnival Glass, Dish, Holly, Marigold, 9 In. .... Illus 30.00
Carnival Glass, Dish, Ice Cream, Grape & Cable, Purple, Footed, Marked N 29.00
Carnival Glass, Dish, Kittens, Marigold, Four Sides Up 50.00
Carnival Glass, Dish, Kittens, Marigold, Two Sides Up 55.00
Carnival Glass, Dish, Leaf & Beads, White Opalescent, Northwood 28.00
Carnival Glass, Dish, Looped Rim, Purple, Footed, Signed N, 3 In.Tall 40.00

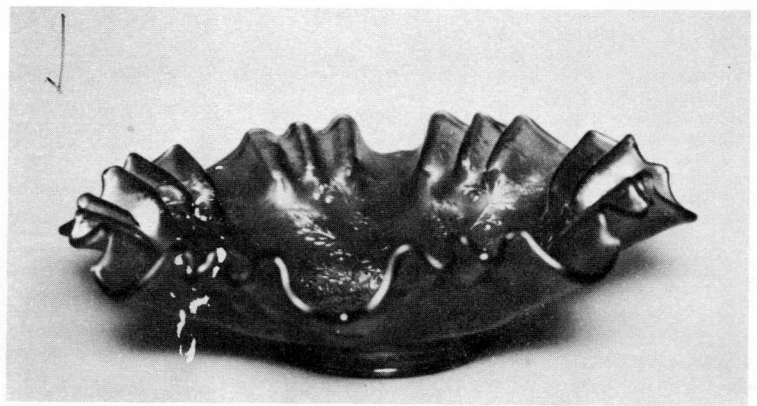

Carnival Glass, Dish, Holly, Marigold, 9 In.
See Page 91

Carnival Glass, Dish, Lotus & Dragon, Marigold, 9 In.	25.00
Carnival Glass, Dish, Meat, Tree Of Life, Orange, Cover	12.00
Carnival Glass, Dish, Relish, Pansy Spray, Orange	12.50
Carnival Glass, Dish, Ruffled, Footed, White, 7 In.Tall	35.00
Carnival Glass, Dish, Shell, Purple, 3 Feet	40.00
Carnival Glass, Dish, Stag, Blue, Footed, 10 1/2 In.	100.00
Carnival Glass, Dish, Stippled Flower, Peach	20.00
Carnival Glass, Dish, Three Fruits, Purple, Pedestal Base, Signed N	15.00
Carnival Glass, Dish, Trout & Fly, Purple, 6 1/2 In.Square	120.00
Carnival Glass, Dish, Wild Rose, Dark Green, Open, Lacy Edge, Marked N	30.00
Carnival Glass, Duck, Marigold	20.00
Carnival Glass, Epergne, Vintage, Blue	95.00
Carnival Glass, Fernery, Luster Rose, Marigold, Footed	15.00
Carnival Glass, Fernery, Open Rose, Footed, Marigold	16.50
Carnival Glass, Fernery, Vintage, Blue, Three Footed	29.50 To 85.00
Carnival Glass, Figurine, Duck, Marigold	15.00
Carnival Glass, Figurine, Swan, Green, Blue	30.00
Carnival Glass, Goblet, Octagon Pattern, Marigold, Set Of 6	95.00
Carnival Glass, Goblet, Sailboat, Purple	65.00
Carnival Glass, Goblet, Water, Imperial Grape, Marigold	12.50
Carnival Glass, Hair Receiver, Persian Medallion, Marigold	37.50
Carnival Glass, Hat, Advertising Miller's Furniture, Marigold, Lattice Edge	29.50
Carnival Glass, Hat, Advertising, John H.Brand, Marigold, Lattice Edge	29.50
Carnival Glass, Hat, Basket Weave, Blackberries, Cobalt, Millersburg	32.50
Carnival Glass, Hat, Grape, Marigold, Marked N	22.00
Carnival Glass, Hat, Holly, Amethyst To Green, Millersburg	32.50
Carnival Glass, Hat, Holly, Blue	16.00
Carnival Glass, Hat, Holly, Green	15.00
Carnival Glass, Hat, Top, Stork & Rushes, Marigold	15.00
Carnival Glass, Hat, Triplets, Marigold, 3 1/4 In.High	12.00
Carnival Glass, Hat, Waffle & Band, Marigold, Signed N	35.00
Carnival Glass, Hatpin Holder, Grape & Cable, Purple, N Mark	65.00 To 10.00
Carnival Glass, Holder, Hatpin, Orange Tree, Blue, Footed	75.00
Carnival Glass, Holder, Hatpin, Purple, Grape 2 Cable	79.50
Carnival Glass, Holder, Spoon, Kittens, Marigold	60.00
Carnival Glass, Jar, Bambi, Marigold, Covered	5.00
Carnival Glass, Jar, Cracker, Grape & Cable, Marigold	175.00
Carnival Glass, Jar, Cracker, Grape & Cable, Thumbprint, Marigold	165.00
Carnival Glass, Jar, Cracker, Inverted Feather, Green	135.00
Carnival Glass, Jar, Powder, Bambi, Marigold	4.00 To 6.00
Carnival Glass, Jar, Powder, Grape & Cable, Green, Mark N	15.00
Carnival Glass, Jar, Powder, Grape & Cable, Purple, N Mark	35.00 To 65.00

Carnival Glass, Jar, Powder, Inverted Strawberry, Marigold 15.00
Carnival Glass, Jar, Powder, Orange Tree, Blue 40.00
Carnival Glass, Jar, Powder, Poodle, Marigold 6.00
Carnival Glass, Jar, Powder, Scottie Dog, Marigold 4.00
Carnival Glass, Jar, Powder, Vintage, Marigold 35.00
Carnival Glass, Jar, Tobacco, Fashion, Marigold, Covered 60.00
Carnival Glass, Light Shade, White, Set Of 4 .... 15.00
Carnival Glass, Mug, Dandelion Pattern, Aqua, Signed N 107.00
Carnival Glass, Mug, Dandelion, Marigold, Signed N 87.00
Carnival Glass, Mug, Dandelion, Purple, Mark N 63.00
Carnival Glass, Mug, Fisherman, Purple 60.00
Carnival Glass, Mug, Orange Tree, Blue 20.00
Carnival Glass, Mug, Orange Tree, Cobalt, Fenton, Silver Iridescence 50.00
Carnival Glass, Mug, Orange Tree, Red To Amberina 85.00
Carnival Glass, Mug, Singing Bird, Amethyst, Marked N .... 38.00 To 45.00
Carnival Glass, Mug, Singing Bird, Blue, N Mark 40.00
Carnival Glass, Mug, Singing Bird, Marigold, Mark N .... 20.00 To 22.00
Carnival Glass, Mug, Singing Bird, Marigold, Stippled Background 26.00
Carnival Glass, Mug, Singing Bird, Orange, Northwood 22.00
Carnival Glass, Nappy, Grape & Lotus, Green, 2 Handles 29.00
Carnival Glass, Nappy, Leaf Rays, Amethyst 20.00
Carnival Glass, Nappy, Leaf Rays, Frosty White, Handle 33.00
Carnival Glass, Nappy, Persian Medallion, Red, Two Handle 145.00
Carnival Glass, Nappy, Stippled Holly & Berry, Peach 35.00
Carnival Glass, Nappy, Swan On Nest, Red 450.00
Carnival Glass, Occasional Piece, Raspberry, Purple, Marked N, Footed 43.00
Carnival Glass, Perfume, Grape & Cable, Marigold, Marked N, Stopper 175.00
Carnival Glass, Pitcher, Banded Drape, Amethyst, Tankard 115.00
Carnival Glass, Pitcher, Grape, Marigold 65.00
Carnival Glass, Pitcher, Hobstar, Marigold 125.00
Carnival Glass, Pitcher, Imperial Stippled Rays, Amethyst, 9 In. 39.50
Carnival Glass, Pitcher, Milk, Star Medallion, Marigold 19.00
Carnival Glass, Pitcher, Stork & Rushes, Amethyst 250.00
Carnival Glass, Pitcher, Vineyard, Marigold 50.00
Carnival Glass, Pitcher, Water, Blackberry, Purple, Basket Base, Marked N 150.00
Carnival Glass, Pitcher, Water, Butterfly & Berry, Marigold 60.00
Carnival Glass, Pitcher, Water, Butterfly, Plume, Green 170.00
Carnival Glass, Pitcher, Water, Coin Dot, Marigold, Bulbous, Ruffled Top 50.00
Carnival Glass, Pitcher, Water, Dahlia, White 350.00
Carnival Glass, Pitcher, Water, Diamond Lace, Purple .... 140.00 To 150.00
Carnival Glass, Pitcher, Water, Fashion, Marigold 55.00
Carnival Glass, Pitcher, Water, Herringbone, Paneled, Emerald 35.00
Carnival Glass, Pitcher, Water, Maple Leaf, Amber, 4 Tumblers, Set 225.00
Carnival Glass, Pitcher, Water, Orange Tree Orchard, White 160.00
Carnival Glass, Pitcher, Water, Paneled Dandelion, Green 170.00
Carnival Glass, Pitcher, Water, Peacock At Fountain, White 350.00
Carnival Glass, Pitcher, Water, Tiger Lily, Bronze Iridescent 125.00
Carnival Glass, Pitcher, Water, Tree Bark, Marigold, Tankard Type, 8 3/4 In. 9.75
Carnival Glass, Pitcher, Water, Water Lily & Cattails, Marigold 175.00
Carnival Glass, Pitcher, Windmill, Marigold, Frosted Panels, 8 1/2 In.Tall 900.00
Carnival Glass, Pitcher, Windmill, Marigold, Rubigold Carnival, 3 Pint 900.00
Carnival Glass, Plate, Acanthus, Marigold, 10 In.Diameter 125.00
Carnival Glass, Plate, Advertising, 'eat Paradise Soda, 'purple, 6 In. 82.50
Carnival Glass, Plate, Bouquet & Lattice, Divided, Marigold, 11 In. 2.95
Carnival Glass, Plate, Caroline, White, 9 In. 37.50
Carnival Glass, Plate, Chop, Grape & Cable, Green, Basket Weave Back, Mark N ... 195.00
Carnival Glass, Plate, Chop, Zipper, Marigold, 11 In. 65.00
Carnival Glass, Plate, Diamond-Quilted, Ice Green, Dolphin Handle, 11 In. 35.00
Carnival Glass, Plate, Diamond-Quilted, Pink, Dolphin Handle, 11 In. 39.50
Carnival Glass, Plate, Dutch Windmill, Marigold 9.50
Carnival Glass, Plate, Fanciful, White, 9 In. 93.00
Carnival Glass, Plate, File, Marigold, 7 In. 12.50
Carnival Glass, Plate, Floral & Optic, Purple, Imperial, Stretch 35.00
Carnival Glass, Plate, Fluted Edge, Orange, 6 1/4 In.Diameter 12.00
Carnival Glass, Plate, Good Luck, Cobalt Blue 85.00
Carnival Glass, Plate, Good Luck, Green 85.00

Carnival Glass, Plate, Good Luck, Purple 75.00
Carnival Glass, Plate, Grape & Cable, Green, Collar Base, Mark N .... 70.00 To 85.00
Carnival Glass, Plate, Grape & Cable, Marigold, Footed .... 35.00 To 40.00
Carnival Glass, Plate, Grape & Cable, Marigold, Iridescent, Checkerboard 28.00
Carnival Glass, Plate, Grape, Purple, Amethyst, Marked N, Handgrip, 8 1/4 In. 45.00
Carnival Glass, Plate, Holly & Berry, Marigold, 9 In.Diameter 39.00
Carnival Glass, Plate, Imperial Jewels, Aqua, 9 In. 15.00
Carnival Glass, Plate, Imperial Jewels, Green, 12 In. 15.00
Carnival Glass, Plate, Iris & Herringbone, Marigold, 6 1/4 In. 2.50
Carnival Glass, Plate, Iris & Herringbone, Marigold, 9 1/2 In. 3.95
Carnival Glass, Plate, Lattice & Bouquet, Marigold, Divided, Scalloped 5.00
Carnival Glass, Plate, Orange Tree, White 85.00
Carnival Glass, Plate, Paneled Rose, Marigold, 9 In. 25.00
Carnival Glass, Plate, Peacock & Grape, Marigold, Bearded Berry On Back 75.00
Carnival Glass, Plate, Peacock On Fence, Blue 90.00
Carnival Glass, Plate, Peacock On Fence, Cobalt Blue, Show, 9 In. 95.00
Carnival Glass, Plate, Peacock On Fence, Green 80.00
Carnival Glass, Plate, Peacock On Fence, Ice Green, N Mark .... 125.00 To 148.50
Carnival Glass, Plate, Peacock On Fence, White, N Mark 150.00
Carnival Glass, Plate, Peacock, Mark N 90.00
Carnival Glass, Plate, Peacock, White 165.00
Carnival Glass, Plate, Peacock, White, Marked N 175.00
Carnival Glass, Plate, Persian Garden, White, Flat, 6 In. 55.00
Carnival Glass, Plate, Persian Garden, White, 7 In. 50.00
Carnival Glass, Plate, Persian Medallion, Marigold, 6 1/2 In.Diameter 40.00
Carnival Glass, Plate, Pine Cone, Marigold, 6 In.Diameter 31.00
Carnival Glass, Plate, Pods & Poppies, Peach, Opalescent, 6 1/2 In. 25.00
Carnival Glass, Plate, Poppy Show, Cobalt .... Illus 285.00

Carnival Glass, Plate, Poppy Show, Cobalt

Carnival Glass, Plate, Ribbon Tie, Blue, 9 In. 45.00
Carnival Glass, Plate, Rose Show, Marigold, 9 1/2 In. 140.00
Carnival Glass, Plate, Round-Up, Amethyst, Basket Weave Back 65.00
Carnival Glass, Plate, Scale Band, Red, 6 1/2 In. 75.00
Carnival Glass, Plate, Ship & Stars, Amber, 8 In.Diameter 5.00
Carnival Glass, Plate, Ship & Stars, Marigold 18.00
Carnival Glass, Plate, Single Flower Framed, Peach, 8 In., Pleated 65.00
Carnival Glass, Plate, Strawberry, Marigold, Marked N, 9 In. 40.00
Carnival Glass, Plate, Three Fruits, Blue, 9 In. 50.00
Carnival Glass, Plate, Three Fruits, Marigold, 9 In., Marked N .... 22.50 To 42.50
Carnival Glass, Plate, Three Fruits, Purple, 9 In.Diameter 55.00
Carnival Glass, Plate, Windflower, Amethyst, Ruffled, 9 In. 70.00
Carnival Glass, Plate, Windmill, Marigold, 8 In. 10.00
Carnival Glass, Plate, Wishbone & Spades, 6 In.Diameter 39.00
Carnival Glass, Poppy Show, Blue 175.00
Carnival Glass, Pump, Town, Ivy, Purple, N Mark 500.00
Carnival Glass, Punch Set, Amber, Red Highlights, 8 Piece 250.00
Carnival Glass, Punch Set, Fashion Pattern, Marigold, 6 Cups 115.00

Carnival Glass, **Punch Set**, Fashion, Marigold, 6 Cups 115.00
Carnival Glass, **Punch Set**, Grape, Green, Stand, Hangers, Six Cups, Bowl 150.00
Carnival Glass, **Punch Set**, Imperial Grape, Green, Stippled, 7 Piece 150.00
Carnival Glass, **Punch Set**, Orange Tree, Marigold, 10 Piece 120.00
Carnival Glass, **Punch Set**, Rose, Marigold, Vintage Grape Inside, 7 Piece 175.00
Carnival Glass, **Punch Set**, Waffle Block, Marigold, Base & 10 Cups 130.00
Carnival Glass, **Relish**, Pansy Spray, Amber, 9 In. 27.50
Carnival Glass, **Rose Bowl**, Beaded Cable, Aqua, Opalescent 70.00
Carnival Glass, **Rose Bowl**, Beaded Cable, Marigold 40.00
Carnival Glass, **Rose Bowl**, Beaded Cable, Purple, Footed, Mark N 35.00
Carnival Glass, **Rose Bowl**, Daisy & Plume, Marigold 37.50
Carnival Glass, **Rose Bowl**, Daisy & Plume, Purple, N .... *Illus* 19.50
Carnival Glass, **Rose Bowl**, Drapery, Blue, Opalescent .... 70.00 To 95.00
Carnival Glass, **Rose Bowl**, Fenton Flowers, Blue, Footed 45.00
Carnival Glass, **Rose Bowl**, Floral Diamond Point, Green, Footed 75.00
Carnival Glass, **Rose Bowl**, Garland, Blue, Footed 50.00
Carnival Glass, **Rose Bowl**, Garland, Marigold 32.00
Carnival Glass, **Rose Bowl**, Grape, Blue, Footed 59.00
Carnival Glass, **Rose Bowl**, Grape Delight, White 75.00
Carnival Glass, **Rose Bowl**, Grape, Marigold, Footed 45.00
Carnival Glass, **Rose Bowl**, Grape, Purple, Footed .... 48.00 To 59.00
Carnival Glass, **Rose Bowl**, Grape, White, Iridescent 87.50
Carnival Glass, **Rose Bowl**, Green, Footed, 7 1/2 In.Diameter 37.50
Carnival Glass, **Rose Bowl**, Inverted Fan & Feather, Footed 26.50
Carnival Glass, **Rose Bowl**, Leaf & Bead, Aqua 55.00
Carnival Glass, **Rose Bowl**, Leaf & Bead, Blue, Marked N 55.00
Carnival Glass, **Rose Bowl**, Leaf & Bead, Green 57.50
Carnival Glass, **Rose Bowl**, Leaf & Bead, Marigold 39.50

Carnival Glass, Rose Bowl, Daisy & Plume, Purple, N

Carnival Glass, **Rose Bowl**, Leaf & Bead, Marigold, Mark N, Footed 57.50
Carnival Glass, **Rose Bowl**, Louisa, Green 35.00
Carnival Glass, **Rose Bowl**, Louisa, Purple 32.50
Carnival Glass, **Rose Bowl**, Persian Medallion, Marigold 30.00
Carnival Glass, **Sauce Set**, Acorn & Burr, Green, Marked N, 4 Piece 119.00
Carnival Glass, **Sauce Set**, Diamond Ring, Marigold, 6 Piece 40.00
Carnival Glass, **Sauce**, Beaded Shell, Marigold, Footed, 4 1/2 In. 12.00
Carnival Glass, **Sauce**, Butterfly & Berry, Footed, Marigold, Set Of 6 .... 60.00
Carnival Glass, **Sauce**, Feathered Serpent, Green 15.00
Carnival Glass, **Sauce**, Fountain With Fence, Marigold, Marked N 10.00
Carnival Glass, **Sauce**, Fruit & Flower, Amethyst, Signed N 16.00
Carnival Glass, **Sauce**, Kingfisher, Marigold 47.00
Carnival Glass, **Sauce**, Millersburg Peacock At Urn, Purple 23.00
Carnival Glass, **Sauce**, Panther, Blue 45.00
Carnival Glass, **Sauce**, Panther, Marigold, Footed .... 25.00 To 30.00
Carnival Glass, **Sauce**, Panther, Red 90.00
Carnival Glass, **Sauce**, Peacock At Fountain, Ice Blue 28.50
Carnival Glass, **Sauce**, Persian Garden, White, 5 3/4 In. 29.00
Carnival Glass, **Sauce**, Persian Garden, White, 6 In. 29.00
Carnival Glass, **Sauce**, Pinecone, Purple 20.00
Carnival Glass, **Sauce**, Singing Bird, Marigold 15.00
Carnival Glass, **Sauce**, Stork In Rushes, Amethyst 18.00

Carnival Glass, Sauce, Thunderbird, Marigold 47.00
Carnival Glass, Sauce, Windmill, Marigold .... 9.50 To 15.00
Carnival Glass, Shade, August Flower, Marigold 15.00
Carnival Glass, Shade, Fall Wildflowers, Amethyst 30.00
Carnival Glass, Shade, White, Nuart, Signed, 5 1/2 In. 20.00
Carnival Glass, Shaker, Salt, Heavy Rib, Marigold 33.00
Carnival Glass, Sherbet, Beads, Turquoise, Footed 12.50
Carnival Glass, Sherbet, Rays, Amberina Color, Footed 19.50
Carnival Glass, Sherbet, Ribbed, Marigold, Clear Stem 3.50
Carnival Glass, Spooner, Acorn & Burr, Green, Mark N 52.00
Carnival Glass, Spooner, Bird & Strawberry, Blue 30.00
Carnival Glass, Spooner, Grape & Cable, Green 55.00
Carnival Glass, Spooner, Grape & Cable, Purple 55.00
Carnival Glass, Spooner, Kittens, Blue 95.00
Carnival Glass, Spooner, Kittens, Marigold .... 52.50 To 65.00
Carnival Glass, Spooner, Springtime, Purple 50.00
Carnival Glass, Stand, Punch, Grape & Cable, Purple, Mark N 125.00
Carnival Glass, Sugar & Creamer, Grape & Cable, Green, Marked N 75.00
Carnival Glass, Sugar & Creamer, Pansy, Purple 55.00
Carnival Glass, Sugar, Cattail & Water Lily, Marigold, Cover 25.00
Carnival Glass, Sugar, Flute, Purple, Mark N 37.50
Carnival Glass, Sugar, Grape & Cable, Green, Cover 75.00
Carnival Glass, Sugar, Luster Flute, Green, Open, Signed N 22.50
Carnival Glass, Sugar, Peacock At Fountain, Ice Blue, Cover 10.00
Carnival Glass, Sugar, Peacock At Fountain, Marigold, Signed N, Covered 70.00
Carnival Glass, Sugar, Peacock At Fountain, White, Cover 73.00
Carnival Glass, Sugar, Peacock On Fence, Amethyst, Covered 38.50
Carnival Glass, Sugar, Shell & Jewel, Marigold, Covered 25.00
Carnival Glass, Swan Nesting, Millersville, Purple 125.00
Carnival Glass, Swan, Amethyst 95.00
Carnival Glass, Swan, Green 20.00
Carnival Glass, Table, Luster Rose, Marigold, 4 Piece, Spooner, Butter 150.00
Carnival Glass, Tankard, Paneled Dandelion, Amethyst 225.00
Carnival Glass, Tankard, Swirl, Marigold, Marked N 75.00
Carnival Glass, Toothpick, Flute, Amethyst 55.00
Carnival Glass, Toothpick, Indian Chief, Marigold 6.50
. Carnival Glass, Toothpick Holder, see Toothpick
Carnival Glass, Tray, Dresser, Grape & Cable, Purple .... 165.00 To 195.00
Carnival Glass, Tray, Dresser, Spider Web & Beads, Marigold 25.00
Carnival Glass, Tray, Dresser, Windmill, Marigold 39.50
Carnival Glass, Tray, Sandwich, Grapes, Clambroth, Center Handle 27.00
Carnival Glass, Tumbler, Acorn & Burr, Green 30.00
Carnival Glass, Tumbler, Acorn & Burr, Purple, N Mark 30.00
Carnival Glass, Tumbler, Banded Drape, Marigold, Pitcher & Tumbler, Set 100.00
Carnival Glass, Tumbler, Blueberry, Blue 40.00
Carnival Glass, Tumbler, Bouquet, Marigold 15.00
Carnival Glass, Tumbler, Butterfly & Berry, Blue .... 18.35 To 20.00
Carnival Glass, Tumbler, Butterfly & Berry, Marigold .... 12.50 To 15.00
Carnival Glass, Tumbler, Butterfly & Berry, Orange 12.00
Carnival Glass, Tumbler, Butterfly & Fern, Amethyst, Set Of 6 .... 115.00
Carnival Glass, Tumbler, Butterfly & Fern, Green .... 23.50 To 29.50
Carnival Glass, Tumbler, Butterfly, Green 9.00
Carnival Glass, Tumbler, Butterfly, Purple 9.00
Carnival Glass, Tumbler, Cattail & Water Lily, Marigold 13.50
Carnival Glass, Tumbler, Cherry & Rope, Green, Signed Northwood 14.00
Carnival Glass, Tumbler, Cherry Lattice, Signed Northwood 10.00
Carnival Glass, Tumbler, Crab Claw, Marigold 22.00
Carnival Glass, Tumbler, Crackle, Marigold, Footed 6.50
Carnival Glass, Tumbler, Dahlia, White, Blue Trim 69.00
Carnival Glass, Tumbler, Feather & Heart, Marigold 25.00
Carnival Glass, Tumbler, Fentonia, Blue 35.00
Carnival Glass, Tumbler, Fleur-De-Lis, Blue 8.50
Carnival Glass, Tumbler, Floral & Grape, Amethyst 22.00
Carnival Glass, Tumbler, Floral & Grape, Purple .... 18.00 To 19.00
Carnival Glass, Tumbler, Floral & Grape, White 40.00
Carnival Glass, Tumbler, Fruit Luster, Marigold 5.00

Carnival Glass, Tumbler, Grape & Cable With Thumbprint, Marigold 12.50
Carnival Glass, Tumbler, Grape & Cable, Green 12.50
Carnival Glass, Tumbler, Grape & Cable, Mark N 20.00
Carnival Glass, Tumbler, Grapes & Leaves, Marigold 10.00
Carnival Glass, Tumbler, Greek Key, Marigold 38.00
Carnival Glass, Tumbler, Hand-Painted Cherries, Purple, Iridescent, 8 .... 70.00
Carnival Glass, Tumbler, Maple Leaf, Purple 26.00
Carnival Glass, Tumbler, Oriental Poppy, Green .... 15.00 To 30.00
Carnival Glass, Tumbler, Oriental Poppy, Purple .... 29.00 To 32.00
Carnival Glass, Tumbler, Paneled Dandelion, Marigold 17.00
Carnival Glass, Tumbler, Peacock At Fountain, Marigold, Mark N 19.00
Carnival Glass, Tumbler, Peacock At Fountain, Purple .... *Illus* 20.00

Carnival Glass, Tumbler, Peacock At Fountain, Purple

Carnival Glass, Tumbler, Rambler Rose, Purple 18.00
Carnival Glass, Tumbler, Singing Birds, Green, Signed N .... 24.00 To 30.00
Carnival Glass, Tumbler, Singing Birds, Purple, Signed N 32.00
Carnival Glass, Tumbler, Spring Flowers, Blue 37.00
Carnival Glass, Tumbler, Star & File, Marigold 15.00
Carnival Glass, Tumbler, Stork & Rushes, Amethyst 16.50
Carnival Glass, Tumbler, Stork & Rushes, Blue 18.00
Carnival Glass, Tumbler, Stork, Marigold 12.50
Carnival Glass, Tumbler, Sunflower & Wheat, Marigold, Dark 18.00
Carnival Glass, Tumbler, Ten Mums, Marigold 30.00
Carnival Glass, Tumbler, Tree Bark, Marigold 4.00
Carnival Glass, Tumbler, Water Lily & Cattail, Marigold, N Mark 15.00
Carnival Glass, Tumbler, White Oak, Marigold 150.00
Carnival Glass, Tumbler, Windmill, Purple 42.00
Carnival Glass, Tumbler, Wishbone, Green 35.00
Carnival Glass, Tumbler, Wisteria, Blue 75.00
Carnival Glass, Vase, Auto, Cobalt Blue, Holder 25.00
Carnival Glass, Vase, Bark, Green, Signed Northwood, 8 In.High 30.00
Carnival Glass, Vase, Car, Tree Of Life, Holder 16.00
Carnival Glass, Vase, Corn, Dark Green 175.00
Carnival Glass, Vase, Corn, Ice Green, N Mark 160.00
Carnival Glass, Vase, Corn, White, Marked N 135.00
Carnival Glass, Vase, Daisy & Drape, Aqua, Opalescent 85.00
Carnival Glass, Vase, Daisy & Drape, Gold 65.00
Carnival Glass, Vase, Daisy & Drape, White, Marked N 85.00
Carnival Glass, Vase, Diamond Point, Blue 25.00
Carnival Glass, Vase, Diamond, Purple, Marked N, 10 In. 32.00
Carnival Glass, Vase, Feathers, Marigold 14.00
Carnival Glass, Vase, Helio, Blue, 10 1/4 In. 18.00
Carnival Glass, Vase, Imperial Jewels, Sapphire Blue, Ribbed Swirl 30.00
Carnival Glass, Vase, Jack-In-The-Pulpit, Marigold, 8 In. 20.00
Carnival Glass, Vase, Jack-In-The-Pulpit, Orange, 8 In.Tall 14.00
Carnival Glass, Vase, Kittens, Orange 75.00
Carnival Glass, Vase, Knobby, Green, Pointed Scalloped Top, 9 1/2 In. 20.00

Carnival Glass, Vase, Knotted Beads, Blue, 10 1/2 In. 20.00
Carnival Glass, Vase, Loganberry, Green 72.00
Carnival Glass, Vase, Long Thumbprints, Green, 10 3/4 In. 20.00
Carnival Glass, Vase, Mary Ann, Marigold 40.00
Carnival Glass, Vase, Mitered, Purple, Oval 250.00
Carnival Glass, Vase, Paneled, Orange, 8 In. 7.50
Carnival Glass, Vase, Pulled Loop, Amethyst, 9 1/2 In. 20.00
Carnival Glass, Vase, Ribbed, Purple, Signed N, 10 1/2 In. 32.00
Carnival Glass, Vase, Ripple, Marigold, 8 3/4 In.Tall 12.00
Carnival Glass, Vase, Ripple, Orange, Ruffled Top, 11 In. 12.00
Carnival Glass, Vase, Ripple, Orange, Ruffled Top, 11 1/2 In. 12.00
Carnival Glass, Vase, Ripple, Green, Ruffled Top, 12 1/2 In.High 18.00
Carnival Glass, Vase, Rose Column, Green 195.00
Carnival Glass, Vase, Rustic, Purple, 23 In. 79.50
Carnival Glass, Vase, Stork, Marigold 15.00
Carnival Glass, Vase, Thin, Blue, Silver Luster, 10 1/2 In. 19.00
Carnival Glass, Vase, Tornado, Purple 90.00
Carnival Glass, Vase, Tornado, Purple, Marked 98.00
Carnival Glass, Vase, Tree Bark, Blue, 20 In.Tall 45.00
Carnival Glass, Vase, Tree Bark, Marigold, 7 1/2 In.Tall 4.95
Carnival Glass, Vase, Tree Trunk, Purple, Northwood, 10 1/4 In. .... 20.00 To 22.00
Carnival Glass, Vase, Trumpet, Marigold, Signed Northwood 15.00
Carnival Glass, Water Set, Floral & Grape, Blue 275.00
Carnival Glass, Water Set, Floral Grape, Purple, 7 Piece .... Illus 175.00
Carnival Glass, Water Set, Imperial Grape, Marigold, 7 Piece 90.00
Carnival Glass, Water Set, Inverted Diamond, Blue 300.00
Carnival Glass, Water Set, Lattice & Grape, Marigold, 6 Piece 185.00
Carnival Glass, Water Set, Orange Tree Orchard, Blue, 7 Piece 400.00
Carnival Glass, Water Set, Peacock At Fountain, Blue, 7 Piece 325.00
Carnival Glass, Water Set, Singing Birds, Green, 5 Piece 275.00
Carnival Glass, Water Set, Treebark, Marigold, Six Glasses 45.00
Carnival Glass, Water Set, Vineyard, Marigold, Seven Piece 150.00
Carnival Glass, Water, Set, Wreathed Cherry, Purple, 7 Piece 285.00
Carnival Glass, Wine Set, Golden Harvest, Marigold, 7 Piece 130.00
Carnival Glass, Wine, Grape Pattern, Marigold 22.00
Carnival Glass, Wine, Imperial Grape, Marigold 15.00
Carnival Glass, Wine, Vintage, Marigold 15.00
Carousel Horse, Carved, Painted, 43 In.High, 48 In.Long 300.00
Carousel Horse, Wooden, Gustave Dentzel, Pa., 55 In.High .... Illus 950.00
Carousel Pig, Carved & Painted Wood, 58 In.Long, Pair 1500.00

Castor Sets have been known as early as 1705. Most of those that have
been found today date from victorian times. A castor set usually consists of
a silver-plated frame that holds three to seven condiment bottles. The
Pickle Castor was a single glass jar about six inches high and held in a
silver frame. A cover and tongs were kept with the jar. They were popular
from 1890 to 1900.

Castor Set, Five Bottles, Engraved Lazy Susan, Dated 1871, Resilvered 98.00
Castor Set, Five Bottles, Etched, Silver Frame, Revolving 55.00
Castor Set, Five Bottles, Revolving, Rose Cut To Clear, Silver Plate 75.00
Castor Set, Five Bottles, Silver Plate .... Illus 55.00
Castor Set, Five Bottles, Silver Plate Frame .... Illus 40.00
Castor Set, Five Bottles, Silver Plate Frame, Birds & Filigree Handle 67.50
Castor Set, Five Bottles, Silver Plate, Pedestal, Floral, Birds 40.00
Castor Set, Five Bottles, Silver Turn Table, Pedestal Base 65.00
Castor Set, Four Bottles, Cable Pattern, Silver Holder, Marked, 9 10i In. 46.00
Castor Set, Four Bottles, Leaf Design, Pewter, Revolving 40.00
Castor Set, Four Bottles, Pewter Frame 28.50
Castor Set, Four Bottles, Resilvered Frame 50.00
Castor Set, Four Bottles, Silver Frame, 9 1/4 In. 16.00
Castor Set, Four Cut Glass Bottle, Hall Mark, Sterling Silver Holder 100.00
Castor Set, Hallmarked, Silver Plate, Bottles Turning Purple 50.00
Castor Set, Miniature, Clear Pattern Glass, Silver Holder, 4 Bottles 25.00
Castor Set, Salt & Pepper, 2-Hole, Silver, Ruby Red Cut To Rose Design 22.50
Castor Set, Six Bottles, Cut Glass, English, Silver Plate Frame, C.1850 .... 45.00
Castor Set, Six Bottles, Silver Frame 37.50

Castor Set, Six Bottles, Sheffield Silver Holder, England	55.00
Castor Set, Six Bottles, 3 Metal Covers, Spoon, Rectangular Holder	45.00
Castor Set, Three Bottles, Gothic Arch, Flint	24.00
Castor Set, Three Bottles, Pewter	24.00
Castor, Condiment, Silver Plate Stand, Center Handle, 4 Crystal Bottles	37.50
Castor, Pickle.Moss Rose, White Satin Glass, Pink Lining, Silver Plate	67.50
Castor, Pickle, Amber, Daisy & Button, Silver Plate Frame	69.00
Castor, Pickle, Amberina, Thumbprint, Silver Frame With Drawer	300.00
Castor, Pickle, Block Pattern, Blue, Lid, Tongs	70.00
Castor, Pickle, Blue, Footed, Tongs, Rogers Frame	75.00
Castor, Pickle, Cranberry Glass, Decorated, Silver Plate Frame	125.00
Castor, Pickle, Cranberry Glass, Inverted Thumbprint	60.00
Castor, Pickle, Cranberry, Daisies, Bulbous, Squatty, Wilcox Frame	89.00
Castor, Pickle, Daisy & Button Insert, Silver Plate Tongs	85.00
Castor, Pickle, Daisy & Button, Clear, Silver Plate Holder	45.00
Castor, Pickle, Dark Blue, Maltese Cross, Silver Frame & Tongs	137.22
Castor, Pickle, Frosted Glass Insert, Silver Frame, Lid, & Tongs, C.1890	90.00

Carnival Glass, Water Set, Floral Grape, Purple, 7 Piece
See Page 98

Castor Set, Five Bottles, Silver Plate Frame
See Page 98

Castor Set, Five Bottles, Silver Plate
See Page 98

Carousel Horse, Wooden, Gustave Dentzel, Pa., 55 In.High
See Page 98

Castor, Pickle, Medallion Head, Ruby Glass .... *Illus*   65.00
Castor, Pickle, Pressed Glass Insert, Silver Frame 30.00
Castor, Pickle, Purple Slag, Silver Frame 225.00
Castor, Pickle, Satin Glass, Flowers, Leaves, Tufts Frame 110.00
Castor, Pickle, Silver Plate, Enameled Light Green To Clear Inserts ... 175.00
Castor, Pickle, Silver Stand, Pickle Fork, Cover 19.50
Castor, Pickle, Swirl Clear, Silver Plate Holder 35.00
Castor, Pickle, Tongs, Etched Insert 80.00
Castor, Pickle, Water Wheel, Castle, Bridge, Lake, Man, Silver Frame ... 65.00
Castor, Relish, Clear, Hobnail, Pewter Cap, Glass, Spoon 20.00
Catalogue, Homer Laughlin China, 1926 .... 7.00
Catalogue, Peerless Water Closets, 1910 .... 6.00
Catalogue, Sears Roebuck, 1908 .... 30.00
Catalogue, Sears, 1935-36 .... 3.50
Catalogue, Starrett Tools, 1924 .... 8.00
Catalogue, Stewart Electrical Supplies, C.1900 .... 10.00
Catalogue, Ward, Bicycling For Ladies, Illustrated, 1896 .... 11.00
Caughley, Bowl, Blue & White, Transfer Printed Bell Toy Chinoiserie, C.1755 ... 140.00
Caughley, Coffeepot, Blue & White, Transfer Printed Fisherman Pattern, 1780 ... 200.00
Caughley, Dish, Blue & White, C.1790, Scalloped Edge, Temple Pattern ... 110.00
Caughley, Dish, Transfer Printed Full Nanking Pattern, Blue, C.1785, Oval ... 70.00
Caughley, Jug, Cabbage Leaf, Mask Head Pattern, Gilt & Blue, Floral, C.1770 ... 140.00
Caughley, Tea & Coffee Set, Blue & White, Pagoda Pattern, C.1780, 23 Piece ... 375.00

Cauldon is an English pottery factory working after 1905.
Cauldon, Plate, England, Painted Flowers On Border, Gothic Arches 6.00

Celadon is a chinese porcelain having a velvet-textured green-gray glaze.
Japanese and Korean factories also made a celadon-colored glaze.
Celadon, Bowl, Dragon In Center, Blue, White, 8 1/2 In.Diameter 28.00
Celadon, Creamer, 3 In.High 8.50
Celadon, Plate, Birds, Butterflies, Roses, 6 In.Diameter 35.00
Celadon, Plate, 6 In. 25.00
Celadon, Teapot, Miniature, Bamboo Handle, 3 In.Tall 10.00
Celadon, Vase, Green, Raised Floral, 6 Sided, Rose, White & Blue, Pair 150.00
Centennial, Medal, Philadelphia, Wooden, Fairmount Park, 1876 .... 20.00
Centennial, Tray, Pickle, 1776-1876, Bear Paw Handles 29.00

Chalkware is really plaster of paris decorated with watercolors. The
pieces were molded from known Staffordshire and other porcelain models and
painted and sold as inexpensive decorations. Most of this type of Chalkware
was made from about 1820 to 1870.
Chalkware, Bird, Color 37.50
Chalkware, Cat, Mouth Open, Sitting 30.00
Chalkware, Compote, Fruit, Painted 350.00
Chalkware, Dog, Staffordshire, Glass Eyes 28.00
Chalkware, Figure, Pigeon, Pouter, Green Paint, 5 1/2 In.High 275.00
Chalkware, Figurine, Poodle, Standing, Brown & Ocher, 6 1/2 In. High, Pair ... 130.00
Chalkware, Figurine, Pug Dog, 13 In.Long 15.00
Chalkware, Figurine, Whistling Sailor, Dated 1923 .... 20.00
Chalkware, Statue, Indian, Full Length, Ceremonial Dress, 22 In.High 40.00
Chalkware, Vase, White, 2 Handles, Embossed Colored Roses, 11 In.High, Pair ... 20.00
Charles Lindbergh, Tapestry, Spirit Of St.Louis, Reg.No. 35.00
Charlie Chaplin, Box, Pencil, Tin, Painted On Top 8.00
Charlie Chaplin, Figure, Lead, Paint, 2 1/2 In. 4.00
Charlie McCarthy, Book, Big Little Book 5.00
Charlie McCarthy, Book, Charlie McCarthy Meets Snow White, 1938 ...... 6.00
Charlie McCarthy, Bottle, Perfume, 3 In. 6.00

Chelsea Grape Pattern was made before 1840, probably at the Coalport
Factory in England and at other firms. A small bunch of grapes in a
raised design, colored with purple or blue luster, is on the border of the white
plate. Most of the pieces are unmarked. The pattern is sometimes called
aynsley or grandmother.
Chelsea Grape, Creamer, Purple Luster 15.00
Chelsea Grape, Cup & Saucer, Purple Luster 14.00

Chelsea Grape, Plate, Purple Luster, 7 In.Diameter	8.00
Chelsea Grape, Ramekin, Signed Addersley, England, 12	50.00
Chelsea Grape, Sugar, Purple Luster, Covered	35.00

Chelsea Porcelain was made in the Chelsea area of London from about 1745 to 1784. Recent copies of this work have been made from the original molds.

Chelsea, Basket, Fruit & Floral, Pierced Rim, Rectangular, Gold Anchor	250.00
Chelsea, Bowl, Covered, Hans Sloane, Applied Scroll Handles, Red Anchor	275.00
Chelsea, Bowl, Covered, Potpourri, Basketwork, Painted Flowers, Brown Anchor	325.00
Chelsea, Creamer, Thistle Design, Violet, Blue	22.50
Chelsea, Cup & Saucer, Blue Spray	15.00
Chelsea, Cup & Saucer, Blue, Basket, Flowers, Paneled	20.00
Chelsea, Dish, Cabbage Leaf, Stalk Handle, Floral Bouquet, Red Anchor, Pair	800.00
Chelsea, Dish, White, Leaf, Red Anchor Period, Pair	150.00
Chelsea, Figurine, Cat, White, Black Spots, Gold Anchor Period, C.1750, Pair	95.00
Chelsea, Figurine, Four Seasons, Red Anchor, 9 In.High, 4 ...... *Illus*	1400.00

Castor, Pickle,
Medallion Head,
Ruby Glass
See Page 100

Chelsea, Figurine, Four Seasons, Red Anchor, 9 In.High, 4

Chelsea, Figurine, Gentleman On Horse, Green Colonial Cloak, White Horse	200.00
Chelsea, Figurine, Girl & Boy, Gold Anchor, 7 1/2 In.High, Pair	50.00
Chelsea, Plate, Bouquets, Puce, Yellow, Red, & Green, Red Anchor, Pair	100.00
Chelsea, Plate, Cake, Grapes & Leaves, Mark Ns & D	9.00
Chelsea, Plate, Floral, Blue & Gilt Scroll Rim, Gold Anchor Period	90.00
Chelsea, Plate, Roses & Flowers, Puce, Rust, Yellow, & Green, Red Anchor, Pair	75.00
Chelsea, Plate, Thistle Design, Violet, Blue, 8 1/2 In.Diameter	9.50
Chelsea, Tea Service, 44 Piece	140.00
Chelsea, Tea Set, 25 Piece	130.00
Chelsea, Teapot, Lavender Decor	75.00
Chelsea, Teaset, Child's, White Paneled, Blue Flowers, 15 Piece	35.00
Chelsea, Urn, Beige, Floral, England, 9 In.	22.00
Chelsea, Vase, Potpourri, Covered, 2 Handles, Painted, Gold Anchor, Pair	375.00

*Chinese Export Porcelain is all the many kinds of porcelain made in
China for export to America and Europe in the 18th and 19th centuries.
Included in the category are Nanking, Canton, Chinese Lowestoft,
Armorial, Jesuit, and other types of the ware.*

Chinese Export, see also Canton, Nanking

Chinese Export, Beaker, Black & Gold, Flower Vases, C.1750, Pair	80.00
Chinese Export, Bowl & Saucer, Gold Stars On Blue Band Rim, C.1790	150.00
Chinese Export, Bowl, Armorial, Peonies & Floral, C.1755	250.00
Chinese Export, Bowl, Blue & Red Floral, Rose Medallion Interior	60.00
Chinese Export, Bowl, Blue & White, Sages & Palm Trees, 15 1/4 In.	175.00
Chinese Export, Bowl, Crested, Landscape Central Medallion, C.1750	225.00
Chinese Export, Bowl, Eggshell, Rose Peonies, Black Border, 5 In.Diameter	85.00
Chinese Export, Bowl, Famille Rose Palette With Floral & Roses, C.1765	80.00
Chinese Export, Bowl, Famille Rose, Peony Decor, Yung Cheng Period	125.00
Chinese Export, Bowl, Famille Verte, Birds & Flowers, 8 3/4 In.Diameter	35.00
Chinese Export, Bowl, Footed, Chinese Domestic Scenes, Red Ground, C.1800	175.00
Chinese Export, Bowl, Goats In Landscape, Green Trellis Band, C.1760	400.00
Chinese Export, Bowl, Iron Red Flowers, 19th Century	120.00
Chinese Export, Bowl, Lotus Leaf, Gold Outline, C.1750	425.00
Chinese Export, Bowl, Medallion With Initials, Shallow, 10 In.Diameter	75.00
Chinese Export, Bowl, Oval, Four Shell Feet, 12 1/2 In.	500.00
Chinese Export, Bowl, Portrait Of Willem & Consort Of Orange-Nassau, 1747	225.00
Chinese Export, Bowl, Punch, Armorial Decoration, 10 In.Diameter	15.00
Chinese Export, Bowl, Punch, Blue & White, Vases Of Flowers, 18th Century	200.00
Chinese Export, Bowl, Punch, Famille Rose Floral, Seal Of United States	100.00
Chinese Export, Bowl, Punch, Famille Rose, Panels Of Chinese Figures, C.1790	325.00
Chinese Export, Bowl, Punch, Floral & Animal Devices, Red & Gold, C.1820	700.00
Chinese Export, Bowl, Punch, Mauve Landscape, C.1790, 11 In.Diameter	225.00
Chinese Export, Bowl, Punch, Panels Of Figures & Phoenix Birds, C.1760	200.00
Chinese Export, Bowl, Punch, Swags & Floral In Famille Rose, C.1790, Pair	175.00
Chinese Export, Bowl, Punch, Swags Or Roses Of Floral In & Out, C.1785	600.00
Chinese Export, Bowl, Rose Sprigs Outside, Husk Motifs Inside, C.1750	100.00
Chinese Export, Bowl, Rose, Oriental Landscape, Chien Lung, 5 1/4 In.	125.00
Chinese Export, Bowl, Sailor's Farewell, C.1780, 10 1/2 In.Diameter	300.00
Chinese Export, Bowl, Shallow, Floral Center & Reserves, 6 In.Diameter	25.00
Chinese Export, Bowl, Shaving, Famille Rose, Landscape, C.1790	375.00
Chinese Export, Bowl, Soup, Famille Rose, C.1760, Scalloped Edge, Floral, 6	300.00
Chinese Export, Bowl, Swirled, Floral Decoration, 6 In.Diameter	75.00
Chinese Export, Box, Covered, Famille Rose Palette, Floral, Buddhist, C.1820	125.00
Chinese Export, Box, Covered, Rectangular, Celadon Ground, Buddhist, C.1820	85.00
Chinese Export, Box, Stamp, Flowers, Green, Pink, Brass, Enamel, 4 X 1 1/2 In.	35.00
Chinese Export, Brushpot, Lotus Bud, Famille Rose, Green & Pink, C.1800	85.00
Chinese Export, Brushpot, Lotus Bud, Famille Rose, Pink Petals, C.1800	30.00
Chinese Export, Butter & Strainer, Covered, Famille Rose Figures, C.1820	100.00
Chinese Export, Cachepot, Gilded Floral Panel On Caramel, C.1850, Pair	375.00
Chinese Export, Charger, Blue & Gold Border, C.1790, 17 In.Diameter	300.00
Chinese Export, Charger, Famille Rose, Octagonal, Central Lotus, C.1760	275.00
Chinese Export, Charger, Famille Rose, Peonies, C.1760	275.00
Chinese Export, Creamer, Helmet Shape, Blue & Gold Medallion, Floral, C.1790	80.00
Chinese Export, Creamer, Helmet Shape, Pedestal, White With Off-Pink, Flower	95.00
Chinese Export, Creamer, Writing Decoration	40.00
Chinese Export, Cup & Saucer, Blue & White, Woman By Fence, C.1750, 3	100.00

Chinese Export, Cup & Saucer, Blue Band, Floral Decoration 40.00
Chinese Export, Cup & Saucer, Blue Enamel Sprays, Gold Border, C.1750, Pair 80.00
Chinese Export, Cup & Saucer, Coffee, Watteau Decoration, C.1780 .... 200.00
Chinese Export, Cup & Saucer, Handleless, Rosebud Pattern 30.00
Chinese Export, Cup & Saucer, Handleless, Sepia Geometric Border, Porcelain 40.00
Chinese Export, Cup & Saucer, Jesuit Decorated, Landscape, C.1760 .... 70.00
Chinese Export, Cup & Saucer, Ruby Ground, Landscapes In Reserve, C.1750, 2 .... 70.00
Chinese Export, Cup & Saucer, Sepia, Floral, Gold, C.1790, Pair 100.00
Chinese Export, Cup, Fitzhugh, En Grisaille Flowers, C.1800 .... 140.00
Chinese Export, Dinner Set, Fitzhugh Type, Blue & White, C.1820, 52 Piece 1600.00
Chinese Export, Dinner Set, Floral & Leaf Swags, Lavender, C.1780, 146 Piece 4000.00
Chinese Export, Dish, Armorial, Famille Rose Oriental Birds, Flowers, C.1760 .... 325.00
Chinese Export, Dish, Berry, Serpentine Rim, Floral Sprays, C.1780, Pair 230.00
Chinese Export, Dish, Blue & White, Cavettos With Floral, C.1750, 8 .... 160.00
Chinese Export, Dish, Blue & White, Fitzhugh, Quatrefoil, C.1790 .... 160.00
Chinese Export, Dish, Deep, Peonies In Famille Rose, 19th Century 150.00
Chinese Export, Dish, Famille Rose Baskets Of Peony Blossoms, C.1790 .... 110.00
Chinese Export, Dish, Famille Rose Enamel Floral Swags, Scrolls, C.1790 .... 50.00
Chinese Export, Dish, Famille Rose Peony, Central Flowering Tree, C.1760 .... 500.00
Chinese Export, Dish, Famille Rose Tobacco Leaf Decoration, C.1760, Pair 250.00
Chinese Export, Dish, Famille Rose, Floral Bouquet, C.1770, 18 .... 625.00
Chinese Export, Dish, Fitzhugh, 9 3/4 In.Diameter, Pair 70.00
Chinese Export, Dish, Hot Water, Iron Red Fitzhugh, British Crest, C.1805, 2 .... 1000.00
Chinese Export, Dish, Leaf Shape, Green Fitzhugh, U.S.Arms, C.1810 .... 2000.00
Chinese Export, Dish, Lotus, Ruffled Rim, Carmine Sprigs Border, C.1760, Pair 350.00
Chinese Export, Dish, Monogrammed, Stars, Blue, Red & Gold, C.1790, 2 .... 175.00
Chinese Export, Dish, Serving, Iron Red Fitzhugh, British Crest, C.1805 .... 1200.00
Chinese Export, Dish, Vegetable, Blue & White, Covered, Leaf Finial 39.50
Chinese Export, Dish, Vegetable, Green Fitzhugh, Covered, C.1790 .... 600.00
Chinese Export, Ecuelle, Covered, Applied Double Twig Handles, C.1760 .... 90.00
Chinese Export, Ewer, Pear Shape, Loop Handle, Silver Cover, C.1740 .... 300.00
Chinese Export, Figurine, Dancers, C.1760, 6 In. .... *Illus* 2400.00
Chinese Export, Figurine, Dove, On Stump, 19th Century, 8 In.Long, Pair 150.00
Chinese Export, Jar, Ginger, Blue Decoration 25.00
Chinese Export, Jar, Rose, Blue Decoration, Pink Flowers, Inner Lid 25.00
Chinese Export, Jardiniere, Blue On White, Landscape, 10 In.High 100.00
Chinese Export, Jardiniere, Blue, Flowers & Trees On Side Panels, 15 In. 110.00
Chinese Export, Jardiniere, Famille Rose, Cylindrical, Figures Painted 150.00
Chinese Export, Jardiniere, Lotus, Coral Red Interior, C.1780, Pair 550.00
Chinese Export, Jug, Helmet Shape, Stalk Handle, Family Medallion, C.1770 .... 120.00
Chinese Export, Jug, Mexican Market, Pear Shape, Strap Handle, Dated 1790 .... 1800.00
Chinese Export, Mug, Armorial, Floral, Puce Rope Banding, C.1770 .... 150.00

Chinese Export, Figurine, Dancers,
C.1760, 6 In.

Chinese Export, Mug, Barrel Shape, C Scroll Handle, Famille Rose, C.1780 .... 175.00
Chinese Export, Mug, Bell Shape, Famille Rose Floral, C.1770 .... 125.00
Chinese Export, Mug, Blue & White, Famille Rose Panel, Strap Handles, C.1800 .... 130.00
Chinese Export, Mug, C Scroll Handle, Famille Rose Florals, C.1780 .... 150.00
Chinese Export, Mug, Famille Rose Aubergine Camaieu Landscape, C.1780 .... 175.00
Chinese Export, Mug, Famille Rose, Medallions Of Blossoms, C.1800 .... 120.00
Chinese Export, Mug, Oriental Design, Mandarin, Enamel, 5 1/2 In.High 100.00
Chinese Export, Pitcher, Birds, Flowers, Paneled, Polychrome, 5 1/4 In.Tall 60.00
Chinese Export, Pitcher, Covered, Gray With Floral Spray, Branch Handle 40.00
Chinese Export, Plate, Armorial, C.1750, 9 1/2 In.Diameter, 12 .... 1000.00
Chinese Export, Plate, Armorial, C.1790, Shield Center 70.00
Chinese Export, Plate, Armorial, Monogram J.A.T., Blue & Gold, C.1790 .... 150.00
Chinese Export, Plate, Black & Gold, Vases Of Oriental Flowers, Gilt, C.1740 .... 30.00
Chinese Export, Plate, Blue & White, Central Pagoda, C.1850, 12 .... 175.00
Chinese Export, Plate, Blue & White, Floral, Beaded Rim, C.1750, 6 .... 100.00
Chinese Export, Plate, Blue & White, Florals, Scalework, C.1750, 13 .... 225.00
Chinese Export, Plate, Blue & White, Peonies, Floral, Leaves, C.1750, 11 .... 200.00
Chinese Export, Plate, Blue Flowered Border, 9 3/4 In.Diameter 40.00
Chinese Export, Plate, Chop, Blue & White, Landscape Decoration 45.00
Chinese Export, Plate, Chop, Blue & White, Landscape Scene, 15 In. 40.00
Chinese Export, Plate, Chop, Blue & White, 13 In.Diameter 25.00
Chinese Export, Plate, Crest Medallion, Greyhound Head, C.1790, Pair 190.00
Chinese Export, Plate, Dinner, Dewitt Clinton & Wife Initials, 8 Gods, 1796 .... 900.00
Chinese Export, Plate, Dinner, Famille Rose, Floral Bouquet, C.1770, 18 .... 425.00
Chinese Export, Plate, Dinner, Green Fitzhugh, 18th Century, 10 In., 4 .... 850.00
Chinese Export, Plate, Dinner, Green Fitzhugh, 18th Century, 8 3/4 In., 4 .... 800.00
Chinese Export, Plate, Dinner, Iron Red Fitzhugh, British Crest, C.1805, 4 .... 1100.00
Chinese Export, Plate, Famille Rose Floral, Birds, Yung Cheng Period 50.00
Chinese Export, Plate, Famille Rose Tobacco Leaf Decoration, C.1760 .... 150.00
Chinese Export, Plate, Famille Rose, Center Floral, C.1740, Pair 125.00
Chinese Export, Plate, Famille Rose, Peonies, Garden Scene, C.1750 .... 20.00
Chinese Export, Plate, Famille Verte, Central Medallion, C.1710, 6 .... 225.00
Chinese Export, Plate, Famille Verte, Nubian With Cross Of Lorraine, C.1710 .... 100.00
Chinese Export, Plate, Fisherman In European Costume, C.1760, 8 In.Long 350.00
Chinese Export, Plate, Fitzhugh, Green, C.1800 .... 90.00
Chinese Export, Plate, Fitzhugh, 9 3/4 In.Diameter 35.00
Chinese Export, Plate, Floral Banded Border, 8 1/2 In.Diameter 40.00
Chinese Export, Plate, Green Fitzhugh, U.S.Arms, C.1810 .... 550.00
Chinese Export, Plate, Green Fitzhugh, 18th Century, 10 In.Diameter, 4 .... 800.00
Chinese Export, Plate, Irish Armorial, Shaw-Taylor Family, C.1730 .... 180.00
Chinese Export, Plate, Jesuit, The Embroideress, C.1760, European Woman 120.00
Chinese Export, Plate, Judgment Of Paris, Famille Rose Enamels, C.1740 .... 325.00
Chinese Export, Plate, Luncheon, Iron Red Fitzhugh, British Crest, C.1805 .... 225.00
Chinese Export, Plate, Octagonal, Enameled Tobacco Leaves, C.1770 .... 50.00
Chinese Export, Plate, Petal Shape Rim, Birds, Floral, C.1750, 8 .... 600.00
Chinese Export, Plate, Polychrome Decorated, Red Seal Mark, 8 3/4 In. 17.50
Chinese Export, Plate, Pseudo Tobacco Leaf Pattern, C.1740 .... 120.00
Chinese Export, Plate, Rose, Garland, Green, Blue, Pink, 10 In.Diameter 75.00
Chinese Export, Plate, Soup, Armorial, Octagonal, C.1790, 2 .... 125.00
Chinese Export, Platter, Armorial, Arms Of Aquitar, Impaling Husada, C.1790 .... 250.00
Chinese Export, Platter, Armorial, Oval, Gilt & Blue Border, C.1810 .... 950.00
Chinese Export, Platter, Famille Rose Tobacco Leaf Decoration, C.1760 .... 450.00
Chinese Export, Platter, Famille Rose, Oblong, C.1760 .... 100.00
Chinese Export, Platter, Green Fitzhugh, Well & Tree, 18th Century 1000.00
Chinese Export, Platter, Iron Red Fitzhugh, British Crest, C.1805, Pair 1200.00
Chinese Export, Platter, Oblong, Octagonal, Famille Rose, C.1770 .... 100.00
Chinese Export, Platter, Oval, Center Medallion, Pierced Mazarin, C.1780 .... 450.00
Chinese Export, Platter, Oval, Green Fitzhugh, U.S.Arms, C.1810 .... 1700.00
Chinese Export, Platter, Oval, Initials Rad, Flower Swags, Blue, Gilt, C.1780 .... 110.00
Chinese Export, Platter, Tobacco Leaf Type Decor, Peonies, C.1770 .... 325.00
Chinese Export, Platter, Well & Tree, Famille Rose Bouquets, C.1820 .... 160.00
Chinese Export, Pot, Cover, Bough, Double Handle, Famille Rose Enamel, C.1780 .... 225.00
Chinese Export, Pot, Crocus, Floral In Famille Rose Enamels, C.1750, Pair 675.00
Chinese Export, Salt, Octagonal, Crane Walking, Peonies, Floral, C.1750, Pair 275.00
Chinese Export, Sauceboat, Armorial, C.1780, Scalloped Rim, Pair 350.00
Chinese Export, Sauceboat, Rust & Gold Border, Boat Shape, C.1750, 3 .... 120.00

Chinese Export, Saucer, Black & Gold Border On Peach Ground, C.1800, 10 .... 400.00
Chinese Export, Saucer, Famille Rose, Peacocks, Peonies, C.1735 .... 140.00
Chinese Export, Saucer, Famille Rose, Potted Tree Center, C.1740 .... 60.00
Chinese Export, Saucer, Figural, Chinese Domestic Scene, C.1780, Pair 40.00
Chinese Export, Saucer, Theological Decoration, Calvin Portrait, C.1740 .... 140.00
Chinese Export, Seat, Garden, Barrel Shape, Famille Rose, Pierced, C.1850 .... 550.00
Chinese Export, Stand, Famille Rose, Floral Panels On Black Floral, C.1735 .... 80.00
Chinese Export, Stand, Teapot, Armorial, Hexagonal, C.1760 .... 90.00
Chinese Export, Stand, Teapot, Famille Rose, Hexagonal, Man & Woman, C.1760 .... 120.00
Chinese Export, Stand, Teapot, Famille Rose, Puce Ground, C.1750 .... 90.00
Chinese Export, Stand, Teapot, Hexagonal, Floral Sprigs, Medallion, C.1770 .... 160.00
Chinese Export, Tea Caddy, Enamel, Reserved Landscape, 18th Century 175.00
Chinese Export, Tea Caddy, Famille Rose, Rectangular, Coat-Of-Arms, C.1800 .... 120.00
Chinese Export, Tea Caddy, Square, Painted European Figures, 18th Century 225.00
Chinese Export, Teabowl & Saucer, Egg Shell, Famille Rose Enamels, C.1735 .... 70.00
Chinese Export, Teabowl & Saucer, Famille Rose Florals, C.1780, Pair 90.00
Chinese Export, Teabowl & Saucer, Marriage, Dated 1779, Coat Of Arms 170.00
Chinese Export, Teabowl & Saucer, Ruby Ground, Landscapes, C.1750, Pair 70.00
Chinese Export, Teabowl & Saucer, Seascape Medallion, C.1790, Pair 125.00
Chinese Export, Teabowl & Saucer, Sunburst Medallion, C.1790, Pair 225.00
Chinese Export, Teapot, Blue, Pseudo Armorial, Twisted Handle, Porcelain 265.00
Chinese Export, Teapot, Double Ogee Shape, Rose Sprigs, Blue Ribbons, C.1780 .... 175.00
Chinese Export, Teapot, Double Ribbon Handle, Berry Finial, Basket Flowers 130.00
Chinese Export, Teapot, Drum Shape, Black & Gold, Initials Tb, C.1790 .... 125.00
Chinese Export, Teapot, Dutch Decorated, Blue & White Body, Floral, C.1750 .... 125.00
Chinese Export, Teapot, Famille Rose Floral, Strap Handle, C.1800 .... 180.00
Chinese Export, Teapot, Famille Rose Landscapes, Applied Branches, C.1740 .... 100.00
Chinese Export, Teapot, Famille Rose, Globular, Flowers, Fruit, C.1740 .... 160.00
Chinese Export, Teapot, Globular, White Orange Peel Glaze, Floral, C.1760 .... 150.00
Chinese Export, Teapot, Ovoid, Applied Gilt Scrollwork, C.1765 .... 50.00
Chinese Export, Teapot, Spherical, Flower Filled Vase On Sides, C.1780 .... 80.00
Chinese Export, Teapot, Tobacco Leaf Decoration, Birds, Peonies, C.1760 .... 425.00
Chinese Export, Teapot, Valentine Pattern, Ovoid, Scroll Handle, C.1750 .... 250.00
Chinese Export, Tray, Spoon, Oriental Family Scene Center, Peonies, C.1770 .... 60.00
Chinese Export, Tray, Spoon, Sprigs Of Flowers Interior, Puce Band, C.1760 .... 80.00
Chinese Export, Tree, Flowering, Blanc De Chine, In Jardiniere, C.1750, Pair 150.00
Chinese Export, Tureen & Stand, Cover, Famille Rose Fruit & Floral, C.1760 .... 950.00
Chinese Export, Tureen & Stand, Covered, Oval, Famille Rose Floral, C.1760 .... 850.00
Chinese Export, Tureen & Stand, Covered, Oval, Medallions, Landscape, C.1770 .... 900.00
Chinese Export, Tureen, Covered, Stand, Oval, Sheep In Meadows, Floral, C.1760 .... 1000.00
Chinese Export, Tureen, Enameled, Round, Gadrooned Handles, Deer, C.1740 .... 425.00
Chinese Export, Tureen, Hot Water, Liner, C.1780, Pair .... *Illus* 325.00
Chinese Export, Tureen, Stand, Blue & White, Pomegranate, C.1790 .... 325.00
Chinese Export, Urn, Pottery, Battle Scene, Foo Dog Finial On Lid, Pair 90.00
Chinese Export, Vase, Baluster, Applied Orange & Gilt Chimera, C.1850 .... 125.00
Chinese Export, Vase, Baluster, Famille Rose, Floral, Fishing, C.1820, Pair 90.00
Chinese Export, Vase, Battle Scenes, Foo Dog Finial On Lid, Seal Mark, Pair 80.00
Chinese Export, Vase, Covered, Raised Panels Of Scenes On Turquoise, C.1850 .... 425.00
Chinese Export, Vase, Crackle Glaze, Blue Decoration Of Ladies, Pair 45.00

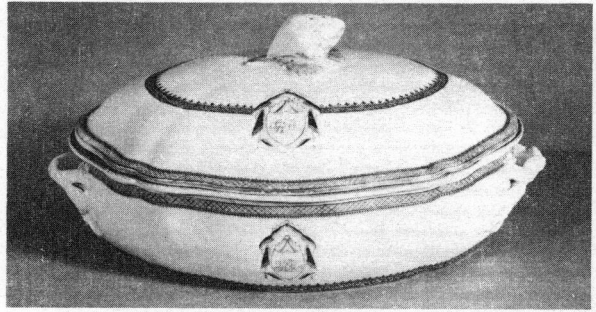

Chinese Export, Tureen, Hot Water, Liner, C.1780, Pair

Chinese Export, Vase, Cylindrical, White, Artist & Scribe Decoration, Pair	45.00
Chinese Export, Vase, Double Gourd, Blue & White, Hawthorn, K'ang Hsi Mark	175.00
Chinese Export, Vase, Famille Rose, Birds, Flowers, Seal Mark, 8 In.Tall	150.00
Chinese Export, Vase, Famille Rose, Light Green, Flowers & Birds, Pair	250.00
Chinese Export, Vase, Figural Decoration, Famille Rose, Scroll Handles, Pair	250.00
Chinese Export, Vase, Hexagonal, Famille Rose, Baluster, C.1850, Pair	200.00
Chinese Export, Vase, Mounted In Louis XVI Ormolu, Dark Blue, C.1750, Pair	2500.00
Chinese Export, Vase, Raised Blue & White On Turquoise, C.1850, Pair	250.00
Chinese Export, Vase, Ruffled Top, Polychrome Of Flowers & Birds, Pair	30.00
Chocolate Glass, see Slag, Caramel	
Christmas Plate, see Collector Plate	
Christmas Tree Candleholder, Clip-On, Tin, Set Of 12	8.00 To 10.00
Christmas Tree Candleholder, Snap-On, Tin, C.1900	.80
Christmas Tree Light, Diamond-Quilted, Amber	12.00
Christmas Tree Light, Diamond-Quilted, Blue	12.00
Christmas Tree Light, Diamond-Quilted, White	12.00
Christmas Tree Ornament, Handmade, Silk Trim, 4 1/2 In.Diameter	10.00
Christmas Tree Ornament, Handmade, Silk Trim, 6 In.Diameter	13.50
Christmas Tree Ornament, Handmade, Velvet Trim, 4 1/2 In.Diameter	12.75
Christmas Tree Ornament, Handmade, Velvet Trim, 6 In.Diameter	16.00
Christmas Tree Ornament, Spaniel In Belted Coat, Saluting, Staffordshire	25.00
Christmas Tree Ornament, Woman, Chalk, Arms & Legs Strung On Tin, Dressed	15.00
Christmas Tree Stand, Conical Shape, Tin, Dated Nov.5, 1915	14.50
Cigar Store Indian, see Wooden, Cigar Store Indian	

Cinnabar is a vermilion or red lacquer. Some pieces are made with hundreds of thicknesses of the lacquer that is later carved.

Cinnabar, Box, Chinese Men In Garden, 2 X 4 In.	16.00
Cinnabar, Box, Lacquer, Carved Lady In Garden On Top	90.00
Cinnabar, Clip, Oval, 1 1/4 X 1 3/4 In., Marked China	8.50
Cinnabar, Plate, Village Scene, Flowers, Geometric Design Back, 9 In.	145.00
Cinnabar, Tray, Lacquer, Deep Carving, Red, 12 X 8 In.	120.00
Cinnabar, Vase, Carved Trees, People, Mountains, Foliage, 9 In.High	42.50
Cinnabar, Vase, Dragon Design, High Relief, Red, 10 In.Tall, Pair	90.00
Cinnabar, Vase, Landscape, 8 People, 10 In.	175.00

Civil War Mementos are important collectors' items. Most of the pieces are military items used from 1861 to 1865.

Civil War, Bag, Saddle, Leather, Cavalry, Pair	29.50
Civil War, Belt, Bullet Case, Brass U.S.Buckle & Insignia	25.00
Civil War, Boot, Brass Toes, Child's, Pair	32.50
Civil War, Box, Bullet, Infantry, Tin Inserts, Impressed U.S., Brass Buckle	84.50
Civil War, Buckle, Belt, Brass, N.Y. On Face	15.00
Civil War, Bullet, Embedded In Portion Of A Tree	4.50
Civil War, Button, Excelsior	6.95
Civil War, Button, Lapel, Grand Army Of Republic, 1861-1866	6.95
Civil War, Button, State Of Iowa	6.95
Civil War, Cannon Level, U.S.Artillery, Brass, Pointer In Center, 1862	135.00
Civil War, Canteen, Metal, Bull's-Eye, Cork	15.00
Civil War, Canteen, Wool Covering, Shoulder Strap, Cork Stopper, Insignia	24.50
Civil War, Carpetbag	8.00
Civil War, Case, Dispatch & Map, U.S., Black Leather, Marked Penna.Vol.Unit	64.50
Civil War, Cup, Drinking, Tin, U.S.Army, Field Type, Loop Handle	5.95
Civil War, Emblem, Cap, Sixth Bugle Corps, Copper, Shape Of Bugle	22.50
Civil War, Holster, For Rogers & Spencer .44-Caliber Percussion Revolver	29.50
Civil War, Knapsack	8.00
Civil War, Knapsack, Confederate, Made In England, C.1860, Leather, Canvas	57.50
Civil War, Knapsack, Wooden Frame, Black Canvas, Patent March, 1862	97.50
Civil War, Knife, Bowie, Sheath, Fighting, Marked I.S.L.	87.50
Civil War, Knife, Pocket, Sailor's	18.00
Civil War, Medal, National Dames Of The Civil War, 1861-5, 2 Piece, Brass	17.50
Civil War, Medal, 9-Years Service, Mass., 1887-1886, Sgt.Briggs, Ribbon	8.00
Civil War, Plate, Confederate, Open Edge, Flag, Gold Rim	3.00
Civil War, Poster, Recruiting, Philadelphia, American Eagle	145.00
Civil War, Poster, Union Recruiting, Black Letters, Pennsylvania Legion	155.00
Civil War, Pouch, Bullet, Infantry, Black Leather, Impressed U.S.	44.50

Civil War, Pouch, Bullet, Infantry, Black Leather, Impressed U.S.Arsenal 37.50
Civil War, Pouch, Bullet, Infantry, Black Leather, Impressed U.S.Ordnance 69.50
Civil War, Pouch, Cap, Black Leather, Infantry 14.50
Civil War, Pouch, Cartridge, Infantry, Leather, Brass Plate On Front, U.S. 42.50
Civil War, Pouch, Cartridge, Leather, For Colt Or Remington Cartridges 14.50
Civil War, Pouch, For Fuses, Tools & Accessories, Artilleryman's, Brown 57.50
Civil War, Record, Voting, Pennsylvania Soldiers, 3 Books 13.00
Civil War, Revolver, Tranter, Percussion, English Oak Cased 550.00
Civil War, Ribbon Badge, G.A.R., 44th Regiment, Indiana, 1906, Silk 7.50
Civil War, Saber-Bayonet 12.00
Civil War, Sidearm, Percussion, Johnson 125.00
Civil War, Suitcase, Officer's, Leather, Brass Lock, 4th Regt., N.Y. 59.50
Civil War, Surgeon's Kit, Field, Brassbound Box, British Markings, Tools 295.00
Civil War, Sword, Sheath, Presentation, Virginia, June, 1864, Brass Hilt 550.00
Civil War, Waistbelt, Infantryman's, Black Buff Leather, Brass Buckle 39.50

Clambroth Glass, popular in the victorian era, is a grayish color and is
semiopaque like the soup.
Clambroth, Dish, Relish, Bird 48.50
Clambroth, Pitcher, Pink, 2 Swans, 2 1/2 In.Tall 20.00
Clewell, Vase, Blue, 4 1/2 X 4 1/2 In.High 60.00
Clewell, Vase, Ohio, Blue, 4 1/2 In.High 30.00

Clews Pottery was made by George Clews & Co. of Brownhills
Pottery, Tunstall, England, from 1906 to 1961.
Clews, see also Flow Blue
Clews, Plate, Escape Of The Mouse, 10 In. 80.00
Clews, Plate, Staffordshire Black Transfer, Scalloped Edge 7.00
Clews, Plate, States, 8 3/4 In. 150.00
Clews, Platter, Blue, Landing Of Lafayette At New York, 1824, 15 1/4 In. 325.00
Clews, Platter, Blue, Landing Of Lafayette At New York, 1824, 19 In. 500.00
Clock, Aaron Willard, Boston, Label Inside Door, 7 Ft.8 In.Tall 5000.00
Clock, Advertising, 'general Tire-Use Our Easy-Pay Plan, 'glass Face 27.00
Clock, Advertising, Shape Of Refrigerator 27.50
Clock, Alarm, Big Ben, 1927 .... 25.00
Clock, Alarm, Exterior Bell 9.00
Clock, Alarm, Porcelain, Cream, Green, Pansy Design 37.50
Clock, Alcott Cheney, Wooden Works, Stenciling On Case, Painted, Label 160.00
Clock, Animated, Lincoln, Roosevelt, Washington .... *Illus* 65.00
Clock, Anniversary, 400-Day, Wind, Needs Pendulum Wire, Under Glass Dome 55.00
Clock, Ansonia, Carriage, Alarm 32.50
Clock, Ansonia, China Case, Royal Bonn 150.00
Clock, Ansonia, China, Tecumseh Case, Purple, Flowers 120.00

Clock, Animated, Lincoln, Roosevelt, Washington

Clock, **Ansonia**, Schoolhouse, 8 Day, 7 In.Dial 90.00
Clock, **Ansonia**, 8 Day, Bluebird On Tablet 45.00
Clock, **Ansonia**, 8 Day, Iron, Lady's Face On Each Side, Scrollwork 300.00
Clock, **Banjo**, Gold Numeral Dial, Mahogany, 27 In. 45.00
Clock, **Banjo**, Inlaid Mahogany, Boston Massacre View, New England, C.1815 .... 850.00
Clock, **Banjo**, Inlaid Mahogany, New England, C.1825, Brass Eagle Finial 800.00
Clock, **Banjo**, Mahogany, New England, C.1825, Drum Movement, Lafayette Bust 550.00
Clock, **Banjo**, Mahogany, Parcel Gilt, Simon Willard, C.1810, Brass 725.00
Clock, **Banjo**, Mahogany, Signed Hull, Eagle Finial, Painted Metal Face 200.00
Clock, **Banjo**, Mahogany, Simon Willard, Boston, C.1820 .... *Illus* 950.00
Clock, **Banjo**, Sessions, 35 In. 95.00
Clock, **Banjo**, Simon Willard Patent, American, Nov.11, 1839, Eagle Finial 2000.00
Clock, **Banjo**, Wall, Mahogany, Weight Driven 450.00
Clock, **Birdcage**, Spring Driven, Removable Cage, Minute & Hour Dial Inside 11.50
Clock, **Birge & Peck**, Triple Decker, Strap, Brass 275.00
Clock, **Boudoir**, Cut Glass, Harvard Pattern, 5 1/2 X 4 X 3 In. 110.00
Clock, **Boudoir**, Three Color, Gold & Onyx, 18th Century Style, Upright 1100.00
Clock, **Bracket**, 8 Bell 315.00
Clock, **Brass**, Porcelain Dial, Square 29.50
Clock, **Brass**, Round, Abercrombie & Fitch, Case 100.00
Clock, **Brass**, Works In Round Compartment, Snake-Shape Hands, Cherubs, Ladies 450.00
Clock, **Brass**, 21 In.High Urns, Marble Base, 3 Pieces 500.00
Clock, **Carlsbad**, Picture Fallstaff & Mrs.Ford 75.00
Clock, **Carriage**, Brass, Alarm Bell, 7 In.High 25.00
Clock, **Carriage**, Brass, Glass On Four Sides, France 75.00
Clock, **Carriage**, Musical Alarm 45.00
Clock, **Carriage**, Shelf, C.1860, Brass, Alarm, 7 In.High 37.50
Clock, **Carriage**, Waterbury, Brass, Porcelain Face, Pat.Jan.1901 .... 25.00
Clock, **Case**, George III, Lacquered, 18th Century, 8 Ft.Tall 1200.00
Clock, **Ceramic**, Double Handles, Arabic Scene, England, 9 1/2 In.High 23.00
Clock, **China Case**, 10 In.High .... *Illus* 65.00
Clock, **China**, Pheasants On Front 22.00
Clock, **Chippendale**, Cherry, Tall Case, Jacob Stein, Penna., C.1810 .... 1600.00
Clock, **Chippendale**, Cherry, Tall Case, Odessa, Del., C.1760, Arched Hood 3750.00
Clock, **Chippendale**, Cherry, Tall Case, Pennsylvania, C.1760, Arched Hood 1300.00
Clock, **Chippendale**, Mahogany, Tall Case, H.Copden, Halifax, C.1790 .... 550.00
Clock, **Chippendale**, Mahogany, Tall Case, Simon Willard, Mass., C.1780 .... 3500.00
Clock, **Chippendale**, Maple & Curly Maple, Tall Case, Isaac Doolittle, C.1760 .... 1200.00
Clock, **Chippendale**, Walnut, Frederick Dominick, C.1770 .... *Illus* 3500.00
Clock, **Cut Glass**, Boudoir, Russian Pattern, Strawberry, Diamond, Buttons 125.00
Clock, **Cut Glass**, Harvard & Flowers, Miter-Cut Leaves 50.00
Clock, **Desk**, French, Silver, Circular Case, White Enamel Dial, C.1900 .... 50.00
Clock, **Dog & Child Scene**, Eli Terry, Wooden Works, Glass Door 400.00
Clock, **E.N.Welch**, 30 Hour, Balloon Carrying American Flags 29.50
Clock, **E.N.Welch**, 8 Day, New Opera House, New Orleans On Tablet 45.00
Clock, **E.N.Welch**, 8 Day, Picture Of Iodine Springs On Tablet 45.00
Clock, **Edwardian**, 4 Bar Chime, 30 In. 37.50
Clock, **Electric**, Schaefer Beer, Light 12.00
Clock, **Eli Terry**, Inlaid Mahogany, Pillar & Scroll, Conn., C.1825 .... 1400.00
Clock, **Empire**, Mahogany, Shelf, Brass Works, Sunburst Pendant 150.00
Clock, **Empire**, Wall, Wooden Works, Painting On Glass, Circa 1815 .... 185.00
Clock, **Enameled**, Green Marble Base, Signed Henri Blane, Geneva 450.00
Clock, **Federal**, Cherry & Walnut, Tall Case, American, C.1815, 3 Brass Finials 850.00
Clock, **Figural**, Gold, 12 X 14 In. 49.50
Clock, **Figural**, Metal, Bronze Finish, Scroll Design, By Gilbert, 11 1/2 In. 250.00
Clock, **Figure 8** 10.00
Clock, **Forestville Mfg.Co.**, Conn., C.1835, Mahogany .... *Illus* 200.00
Clock, **Free Swinger**, 34 In. 110.00
Clock, **French**, Picture Frame, Miniature, Mother-Of-Pearl Inlay, Signed 85.00
Clock, **French**, Square, Black Lacquer, 10 In.Dial 59.00
Clock, **George III**, Mahogany, Tall Case, Thomas Draper, London, C.1750 .... 325.00
Clock, **George III**, Mantel, Gilt Metal & Porcelain, Vulliamy, London, C.1750 .... 2900.00
Clock, **German**, Brass, Anniversary 10.00
Clock, **Gilbert**, Cathedral, Chime, Painted Landscape, 13 In.High 25.00
Clock, **Gilbert**, Tin Case, Mantel, Dated June, 1872 .... 45.00

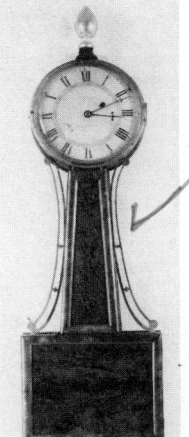

Clock, Banjo, Mahogany, Simon Willard, Boston, C.1820
See Page 108

Clock, China Case, 10 In.High
See Page 108

Clock, Chippendale, Walnut,
Frederick Dominick, C.1770
See Page 108

Clock, Forestville Mfg.Co., Conn., C.1835, Mahogany
See Page 108

Clock, Gilt Metal & Enamel, Curved Colonnade, Urn Finial, 19th Century 425.00
Clock, Grandfather, English, Early 1800 .... 285.00
Clock, Grandfather, German, Circa 1920 .... 275.00
Clock, Grandfather, German, Oak Case, 4 Bar Chime, 6 Ft. 6 In. 179.00
Clock, Grandfather, German, Oak Case, Beveled Glass In Door, 6 Ft.5 In. 179.00
Clock, Grandfather, German, Oak Case, Matched Brass Weights & Pendulum 179.00
Clock, Grandfather's, Musical Organ, Black Forest, C.1797, Cherry Case 2200.00
Clock, Grandfather's, Philadelphia, Mahogany, Carved, Brass Works 4000.00
Clock, Grandfather's, Robert Logie, Edinburgh, 1784-1872, Mahogany 600.00
Clock, Grandfather's, Wooden, Miniature, 2 Names & 1902 Cut In Front 25.00
Clock, Grandmother's, Federal, Inlaid Mahogany, Peter H.Cushing, C.1790 .... 2500.00
Clock, Grandmother's, J.Wilder, Hingham, Mass., Pine Case, Mahogany Graining 7750.00
Clock, Grandmother's, 8-Day, Striker, Pine Case, Forestville Mfg.Co. 135.00
Clock, Gudrun, China, Ivory, Floral 20.00
Clock, Herschedehall, Mantel, Key Wind 20.00
Clock, Howard, No.20 .... 350.00
Clock, Ingraham, Calendar, Wall 95.00
Clock, Ingraham, Mantel, Eagle Pendulum, Oak Case, General Grant Figure 135.00
Clock, Inlaid Mother-Of-Pearl, 27 In. 57.50
Clock, Ithaca, Calendar, Bank Model, Weight Driven, Double Dial, 48 In. 900.00
Clock, Ithaca, Double Dial, Walnut Case 385.00

Clock, Ithaca, Parlor, Calendar, Patent Date 1876 .... 1500.00
Clock, Jerome, 8 Day, Pansies On Tablet 45.00
Clock, Junghans, Brass Face, Quarter-Hour Strike, 5 Bar Chime, 19 In. 89.50
Clock, Kewpie, Signed Rose O'Neill, Blue Jasper 125.00
Clock, Kitchen, Shelf 105.00
Clock, Lighthouse, Mahogany, Simon Willard, Mass., C.1825, Glass Dome 3250.00
Clock, Lindbergh, June 12, 1928, 7 In.Tall .... *Illus*   35.00
Clock, Louis XV, Ormolu, Chantilly Porcelain Figure, Chinaman, C.1750 .... 6200.00
Clock, Louis XVI, Marble & Ormolu, Mantel, Francois A Paris, 1766-89 .... 1800.00
Clock, Louis XVI, Ormolu & Marble, Allegorical, Lepaute, H.Du Roi, Dated 1764 .... 3400.00
Clock, Mantel, Alarm, E.Ingraham, Pendulum & Key 35.00
Clock, Mantel, Beehive Shape, 8 Day, Alarm, Seth Thomas 60.00
Clock, Mantel, Cast Iron, Black Paint, Gold Decoration, 11 In.High 20.00
Clock, Mantel, Empire, Ormolu & Cut Glass, F.D.Huguinin Lardy A.Namur, 1850 .... 350.00
Clock, Mantel, Empire, Ormolu, Bacchante, Grapes, Child Satyr, C.1850 .... 600.00
Clock, Mantel, French, Bronze, Dore, Chopin A Paris, C.1808, Washington Figure 1300.00
Clock, Mantel, French, Bronze, Dore, Leroy A Paris, C.1810, Allegorical Figure 110.00
Clock, Mantel, George IV, Mahogany, Minute Dial, 19th Century, 14 1/2 In.Tall 160.00
Clock, Mantel, Gingerbread, Painting On Glass Door, Carved, Oak 39.00
Clock, Mantel, Jacob Pettit, Porcelain, 19th Century, Silvered Dial 700.00
Clock, Mantel, Louis XVI Style, Ormolu, White Enameled Dial 350.00
Clock, Mantel, Marble, 3 Piece 32.50
Clock, Mantel, Oak, Cut Crystal Pendulum 107.00
Clock, Mantel, Outside Escapement, Round Beveled Glass, Wendell Albany, N.Y. 50.00
Clock, Mantel, Quarter Hour Strike, Five Coils, 19 X 12 In. 89.00
Clock, Mantel, Spaulding & Company, Marble & Gilt Bronze, Electric 65.00
Clock, Mantel, Tin, Painted Arabian Scene 20.00
Clock, Mantel, Waterbury 22.00
Clock, Mantel, William IV, Satinwood, Plinth Base, 19th Century 350.00
Clock, Mantel, 2 Candelabra, 20 In.High, 3 Pieces 49.50
Clock, Michel-Victor Acier, Ormolu Mounted Monument, C.1777 .... 350.00
Clock, Miniature, Tall Case, Chinese Chippendale Style, Red Paint, Gilt 35.00
Clock, Mirror, Simon Willard, Green & Gilt, 17 In.Wide, 34 In.High 2500.00
Clock, Musical, Alarm 50.00
Clock, Musical, Automaton Sailing Ship In Shadow Box Base 795.00
Clock, Musical, Bracket, Prior, London, 18th Century .... *Illus* 1500.00
Clock, Musical, French, Ormolu, Music Box In Base 595.00
Clock, Musical, Painting, Watch In Tower Appears As Part Of Scene 495.00
Clock, Naval Observatory Time Western Union, Battery Operated, Square 49.50
Clock, Naval Observatory Time, Western Union, Battery Operated, Round 49.50
Clock, New Haven, Iron Case, Mantle 22.00
Clock, New Haven, Schoolhouse, 8 Day, 7 In.Dial 90.00
Clock, O.G., 30 Hour, Painted Black, Gold Trimmed Door, Fruit 29.50
Clock, O.G.Forestville Mfg. Co., 8 Day, Flower Print On Glass Door 45.00

Clock, Lindbergh, June 12, 1928, 7 In.Tall

Clock, Musical, Bracket, Prior, London, 18th Century

Clock, O.G.Jerome, 30 Hour, Flowers, Gold Trim 29.50
Clock, Oak, Runs On Dry Cell Battery, 9 X 11 In. 27.50
Clock, Pillar & Scroll, Eli Terry, Eglomise Tablet Of White House 1400.00
Clock, Pillar & Scroll, Inlaid Mahogany, Shelf, Eli Terry, C.1825 .... 650.00
Clock, Pillar & Scroll, Shelf, Inlaid Mahogany, Eli Terry, Conn., C.1825 .... 400.00
Clock, Portrait On Door, Patent Eli Terry & Sons, Made By Henry Terry 395.00
Clock, Queen Anne 185.00
Clock, Regulator, Waterbury, Oak Case, Ornate, 38 In.Tall 57.50
Clock, Royal Bonn, 11 In.High 49.00
Clock, Schoolhouse, Carved, Sample Size 100.00
Clock, Schoolhouse, Chauncey Jerome, Single Fusee 165.00
Clock, Schoolhouse, English, Mahogany, Mother-Of-Pearl Inlaid, Marked 150.00
Clock, Schoolhouse, Fusee, Walnut Case, 30 In. 57.00
Clock, Schoolhouse, Inlaid, 28 Inches 49.00
Clock, Schoolhouse, Miniature, Octagon Face, Chimes, Rosewood Finish 120.00
Clock, Schoolhouse, 30 Day 195.00
Clock, Schoolhouse, 8 Day, Regulator, Wall, Octagon Shape, Bristol, Conn. 85.00
Clock, Schoolhouse, 8 Day, Wall, Octagon Shape, Striking 85.00
Clock, Sessions, Mantel 35.00
Clock, Seth Thomas, Banjo 10.00
Clock, Seth Thomas, Brass Keywind, Carriage, Roman Numerals 75.00
Clock, Seth Thomas, Inlaid Rosewood, Shelf, Conn., C.1850, Painted Dial 200.00
Clock, Seth Thomas, Mahogany, Pillar & Scroll, Conn., C.1815, Painted Dial 650.00
Clock, Seth Thomas, Mantel, 30 Day 175.00
Clock, Seth Thomas, Ogee, 30 Hr. 40.00
Clock, Seth Thomas, 30 Hour, Weight, Label 55.00
Clock, Seth Thomas, 8 Day, Weight Driven, Reverse Painting, Strikes Hour 225.00
Clock, Shelf, Ephraim Downs, Bristol, Conn. 120.00
Clock, Shelf, Forestville Manufacturing Co., Conn., Eagle Finial 140.00
Clock, Shelf, Inlaid Mahogany, Forestville Mfg., Co., Conn., C.1835, Upright 200.00
Clock, Shelf, Inlaid Mahogany, James Doull, Mass., C.1800, Kidney Dial 2900.00
Clock, Shelf, Inlaid Mahogany, Simon Willard, Mass., C.1800, 2 Parts 3250.00
Clock, Shelf, Mahogany, E.C.Brewster, Conn., C.1825, Molded Cornice 200.00
Clock, Shelf, Mahogany, Pillar & Scroll, Connecticut, C.1825, Upright Case 375.00
Clock, Shelf, Samuel Terry, Bristol, Conn., Brass Eagle & Urn Finial 250.00
Clock, Shelf, Victorian, Carved Wood Side Columns, 16 In.High 45.00
Clock, Steeple, Ansonia, Brass, Copper, Eagle Painting, C.1840 .... 250.00
Clock, Steeple, Chime Strike, Hand-Painted Roses On Door, E.N.Welch 68.50
Clock, Steeple, Walnut 58.00
Clock, Sunburst, 'Pepsi The Light Refreshment', Metal, 18 In.Diameter 15.00
Clock, Tall Case, Cherry, A.W.Carpenter, Pa., C.1830, Moon Phases 550.00
Clock, Tall Case, Chippendale, Cherry & Mahogany, Rhode Island, C.1770 .... 650.00
Clock, Tall Case, Chippendale, Walnut, Carved, William Hudson, N.J., C.1780 .... 5000.00
Clock, Tall Case, John Chambley, West Hampton, 7 Ft.10 In. 375.00
Clock, Tall Case, Sheraton, Inlaid Mahogany, C.1825, Moon Phases 250.00
Clock, Tall Case, Thomas Lands Of Tiverton, 18th Century, 6 Ft.9 In.Tall 475.00
Clock, Tall Case, Warner Of Shrewsbury, 7 Ft.4 In.Tall 400.00
Clock, Tiffany & Co., Candelabra, 20th Century 1995.00
Clock, Tiffany, Anniversary, Battery Operated, Signed 85.00
Clock, Tiffany, Oak Case, Intricate Metal Ornaments, 24 In.Tall 425.00
Clock, Tower, Three Train, Quarter Strike, Pinwheel Escapement 325.00
Clock, Victorian, Steeple, Welsh Manufacturing Co., Walnut Case, 15 In.High 60.00
Clock, Vienna, Wall, 1 Weight, 44 In. 85.00
Clock, Vienna, 2 Weights 65.00
Clock, Wag-On-Wall, Floral Decorated, Scalloped Wooden Face 75.00
Clock, Wag-On-Wall, Wood & Brass Works, Painted Face, 14 X 10 In. 50.00
Clock, Wall, Ansonia, Brass, Copper, 1875 .... 425.00
Clock, Wall, Brass Works, Exposed Iron Weights, Pendulum, Joseph Rembach 210.00
Clock, Wall, Brass, Nickel Plate, One-Day Works, Ansonia 30.00
Clock, Wall, Calendar, Octagonal 110.00
Clock, Wall, Free Swinger, Dark Finish, 27 In. 64.50
Clock, Wall, French, Acorn Weights, Embossed Face, 8 X 11 In. 50.00
Clock, Wall, Fusee, Pendulum, Bezel 12 In. 35.00
Clock, Wall, German, 1880 .... 150.00
Clock, Wall, Inlaid Mahogany, Aaron Willard, Mass., C.1800, Drum 900.00
Clock, Wall, Octagonal, 30 Hour 38.00

Clock, Wall, Waterbury, Oak Case, 1889 .... 425.00
Clock, Wall, Waterbury, Schoolhouse, 1895 .... 150.00
Clock, Wall, Weight Driven, Walnut Case, Brass Weight & Pendulum 200.00
Clock, Wall, 3 Weights, Austria 245.00
Clock, Wall, 30 Day, Patent Feb.25, 1897 .... 435.00
Clock, Waltham, Pedestal, Key Wind, Honduras & Santo Domingo Mahogany 25.00
Clock, Waterbury, Carriage 23.00
Clock, Waterbury, Carriage, Repeater 35.00
Clock, Waterbury, Regulator, Oak Case, Ornate 57.50
Clock, Waterbury, Rosewood, Steeple, Mantel, Reverse Painting Of Ships 59.00
Clock, Waterbury, 30 Hour, Woman's Picture On Tablet 32.50
Clock, Welch, Schoolhouse, 8 Day, 7 In.Dial 90.00
Clock, Western Union Naval Observatory Time, Battery Operated, Round 50.00
Clock, Western Union Naval Observatory Time, Battery Operated, Square 50.00
Clock, William & Mary, Brass, Lantern, Joseph Buckingham, London, C.1650 .... 300.00
Clock, Wooden Works, Original Label, Case, By Alcott Cheney 160.00
Clock, 3 Piece Set, Gilded Metal Frame, 3 Branch Candelabra 175.00

*Cloisonne Enamel was developed during the nineteenth century. A glass
enamel was applied between small ribbon-like pieces of metal on a metal base.
Most Cloisonne is Japanese.*
Cloisonne, Ashtray, 3 In.Diameter .... *Illus* 25.00

Cloisonne, Ashtray, 3 In.Diameter

Cloisonne, Bottle, Snuff, Heart Shape, Brown Ground, Floral 110.00
Cloisonne, Bottle, Snuff, Oriental Design, 4 1/4 In.Tall 65.00
Cloisonne, Bowl, Blue Ground 35.00
Cloisonne, Bowl, Bulb, Shallow, Yellow, Blue Band Around Top, Floral 65.00
Cloisonne, Bowl, Chinese, Stand, Multicolored Floral, 2 1/4 In.High 15.00
Cloisonne, Bowl, Covered, Black Ground 12.50
Cloisonne, Bowl, Covered, Cream Ground 30.00
Cloisonne, Bowl, Covered, Foo Dog Finial, Red Ground 45.00
Cloisonne, Bowl, Floral Design, Multicolor, Goldstone, 5 1/2 In.Tall 48.00
Cloisonne, Bowl, Floral, Transparent, Footed, 3 1/2 In.Diameter, 2 In.Tall 295.00
Cloisonne, Bowl, Fruit, Flowers, Multicolored, Cover, 9 In.Diameter 60.00
Cloisonne, Bowl, Goldstone, Butterflies, Phoenixes, Floral, Teak Stand 85.00
Cloisonne, Bowl, 1000 Flowers, Teak Stand, Cover 140.00
Cloisonne, Box, Black Multicolor Floral, Butterflies, Compartments, China 30.00
Cloisonne, Box, Cigar, Blue, Floral, Matching Ashtray, Set 18.50
Cloisonne, Box, Cigarette, Covered 18.00
Cloisonne, Box, Covered, Square, For Cards, Black Ground 30.00
Cloisonne, Box, Dark Blue, Enameled Golf Sticks, Footed 18.00
Cloisonne, Box, Dome Top, Red Ground 25.00
Cloisonne, Box, Fishscale Design, Floral, Cover, ... 32.50
Cloisonne, Box, Flowers On Black, Foo Dog Finial, 5 In.Diameter 45.00
Cloisonne, Box, Flowers, Butterflies, Fighting Cock, Round, 2 1/2 In.Diameter 27.00
Cloisonne, Box, French, Blue, Yellow, Red, Pink & White, 4 X 4 X 6 In. 350.00
Cloisonne, Box, Match, Green, Red, Blue, Pink, Floral, Cover 9.50
Cloisonne, Box, Round, Black 18.00
Cloisonne, Box, Signed China, Turquoise, Flowers, Round, 3 In.High 18.00
Cloisonne, Box, Signed China, Turquoise, Oblong, 3 3/4 In.High 10.00
Cloisonne, Box, Stamp, Blue Ground, Floral 8.00

Cloisonne, Box, Stamp, Flowers, Red, Blue, White, Yellow, 1 1/2 X 3 1/2 In.	22.00
Cloisonne, Box, Tobacco, Green Leaves, Pink & Blue Firs, Butterflies	55.00
Cloisonne, Box, Trinket, Floral & Fruit, Hinged, Covered, Footed	27.00
Cloisonne, Dish, Boat Shape, Green, Amber & Rose Petal Flowers, Jade Tree	275.00
Cloisonne, Fernery, Butterflies, Floral, Green, Enamel Lining, Footed	135.00
Cloisonne, Figurine, Horse, 11 X 11 1/2 In.	475.00
Cloisonne, Holder, Matchbox, Floral Pattern	8.00
Cloisonne, Humidor, Round, Green Ground, Flowers, Butterflies, Flat Finial	75.00
Cloisonne, Incense Burner, Floral Insets, Tripod Feet, Japan	45.00
Cloisonne, Incense Burner, Yellow, Fish & Sea Creatures, 18th Century	120.00
Cloisonne, Jar, Cover, Birds & Dragons, Japan, 3 1/2 In.High	75.00
Cloisonne, Jar, Covered, Flowers, Gold Mica	35.00
Cloisonne, Jar, Ginger, Hawthorn Blossoms, Black, 7 1/2 In.Tall, Pair	135.00
Cloisonne, Jar, Ginger, 14 In.Tall	195.00
Cloisonne, Jar, Lid, Dragon, Birds, Butterflies, Animals, Japan, 3 1/2 In.High	75.00
Cloisonne, Jar, 1, 000-Flower, Brown, Cover, 7 In.High, Pair	90.00
Cloisonne, Jardiniere, Blue, Green, & Black Ground, Butterflies, 10 In.	575.00
Cloisonne, Jardiniere, Peonies & Birds, 18 In.Tall	175.00
Cloisonne, Jug, Blue, Floral, Circa 1820, 3 3/4 In.Tall	68.00
Cloisonne, Jug, Wine, Dragon Design	38.00
Cloisonne, Lamp Base, 38 In.High, 18 Lbs.	425.00
Cloisonne, Napkin Ring, Blue, Aqua Inside, Set Of 6	55.00
Cloisonne, Napkin Ring, Blue, Dragon All Around, Light Blue Inside	10.50
Cloisonne, Pin Tray, Fan Shape, Floral & Butterfly Decor	24.00
Cloisonne, Planter, Circa 1850, France, 8 In.Long, 5 In.High	240.00
Cloisonne, Plaque, Bird, Flowers, Foliage, Green, Pink, 11 1/2 In.Diameter	85.00
Cloisonne, Plate, Birds & Flowers, 12 In.Diameter	85.00
Cloisonne, Plate, Blue Ground, On Brass, White Flowers, Leaves, Blue Birds	80.00
Cloisonne, Plate, Crane Standing In Water, Lily Pads & Blossoms, Birds	135.00
Cloisonne, Plate, Floral Design, Pink, Yellow, White, 12 In.Diameter	90.00
Cloisonne, Plate, Geometric Design Border, Center Scene, Mountains	95.00
Cloisonne, Plate, Geometric Design Border, Flowers & Birds In Center	85.00
Cloisonne, Platter, Blue Ground, Brown Border, Gray Birds, Flowers	185.00
Cloisonne, Pot, Butterflies, Goldstone, Cover, 4 1/2 In.Tall, Pair	150.00
Cloisonne, Pot, Miniature, Footed, Black Ground, 5 Toed Imperial Dragon, Pair	38.00
Cloisonne, Pot, Wine, Chien Lung Period, Circa 1785, 3 1/2 In.Tall	225.00
Cloisonne, Rabbit, Stand, 3 1/2 X 5 1/2 In., Pair	385.00
Cloisonne, Rooster, Carved Stand, 7 In.Long, 5 In.High	340.00
Cloisonne, Salt & Pepper, Dragon Motif, Set	18.00
Cloisonne, Salt & Pepper, Flowers, Enamel, White, Pink, Green	22.00
Cloisonne, Salt & Pepper, Open, Blue, White, Royal, Black, Floral, Set	18.00
Cloisonne, Teapot, Flowers & Butterflies, Pedestal Base, Black, 4 1/2 In.	75.00
Cloisonne, Teapot, Miniature, China, C.1800, 2 1/4 In.	75.00
Cloisonne, Tray, Black Ground, Yellow Dragons, Circa 1820, 11 X 7 1/2 In.	92.00
Cloisonne, Tray, Flowers & Butterflies On Yellow	12.50
Cloisonne, Tray, Light Green, Pink & Blue Floral, Oblong	45.00
Cloisonne, Tray, Pin, Yellow With Blue	8.00
Cloisonne, Tray, Scene, Yellow Bird On Flowering Tree Branch, 12 X 8 In.	135.00
Cloisonne, Tumbler, Turquoise, Miniature Cloisons Form Pattern	27.50
Cloisonne, Umbrella Handle, Green Ground, Dragon, Floral On Knob	35.00
Cloisonne, Urn, Japanese, Peacock & Dragon Design, 15 1/2 In.High	150.00
Cloisonne, Vase, Black Ground, Blue, Green, Pink Floral, 5 In.High	35.00
Cloisonne, Vase, Blue Ground, Dragon Decoration, 10 In.High, Pair	60.00
Cloisonne, Vase, Blue Ground, Lavender Iris, Japan, 6 In.High, Pair	100.00
Cloisonne, Vase, Blue Ground, Pink & Blue Floral, Flared Top, 9 In.High	45.00
Cloisonne, Vase, Blue, Maroon, Pink, Lemon, Black, White, Turquoise, Brass Rim	55.00
Cloisonne, Vase, Blue, Medallions, Goldstone, Flowers, Butterflies, 2 1/4 In.	20.00
Cloisonne, Vase, Blue, Pink, Green, Black, 7 In.Tall	38.00
Cloisonne, Vase, Blue, White, 5 In.Tall	25.00
Cloisonne, Vase, Brass, 13 In.High, Birds, Flowers	175.00
Cloisonne, Vase, Chien Lung, 18th Century, 8 In.High, Pair	195.00
Cloisonne, Vase, Crystallized, Stand, 7 In.Tall	285.00
Cloisonne, Vase, Dark Blue, Maroon Band, Floral, 5 In.High	39.50
Cloisonne, Vase, Dragon Encircles Body Of Vase, Green & Blue Stones, 4 In.	25.00
Cloisonne, Vase, Elephant Head Handles, Brass Bands, 9 1/2 In.Tall	20.00
Cloisonne, Vase, Floral Design, Blue, 7 In.Tall	48.00

Cloisonne, Vase, Flowers, Tassels, Blue, 4 1/2 In.Tall	20.00
Cloisonne, Vase, Geometric Design, Floral, Red, Brass Rim, 10 In.Tall, Pair	150.00
Cloisonne, Vase, Goldstones, Butterflies, Birds, 6 1/2 In.	45.00
Cloisonne, Vase, Green Medallions, Goldstone, 11 In.High, Pair	125.00
Cloisonne, Vase, Iridescent, Green, Blue, Dragon, 4 In.	25.00
Cloisonne, Vase, Lady From Orient, 9 3/4 In.High	49.00
Cloisonne, Vase, Leaves, Flowers, Multicolor, 9 1/2 In., Pair	180.00
Cloisonne, Vase, Pigeon Blood, Wisteria, Melon Shape, Silver Base, 7 In.	130.00
Cloisonne, Vase, Purple & White Scaled Dragon On Black	95.00
Cloisonne, Vase, Red, Mums, Leaves, 9 In.	65.00
Cloisonne, Vase, Stick, Chinese On Porcelain, Brown, Red, C.1750	85.00
Cloisonne, Vase, Thousand Flower, Stand, 8 1/2 In., Pair	130.00
Cloisonne, Vase, Wisteria, Birds, Rust-Red Ground, Japan, 6 In.High, Pair	95.00
Cloisonne, Vase, Yellow, Floral, Brass Trim, Marked, 9 1/4 In.High, Pair	65.00

Cluthra Glass is a two-layered glass with small air pockets that form white spots. The Steuben Glass Works of Corning, New York, made it after 1903. Kimball Glass Company of Vineland, New Jersey, made Cluthra from about 1925.

Cluthra, see also Steuben

Cluthra, Bowl, Green, 5 X 3 1/2 In.	21.00
Cluthra, Rose Bowl, Smoky Rose, 4 1/2 In.Tall	68.50
Cluthra, Vase, Amethyst, Steuben, 11 In.	435.00
Cluthra, Vase, Paper Label, Monart Scotch, Pink, Amethyst Neck	65.00
Coalbrookdale, Bowl, Covered, Applied Flowers, Footed, C.1830, Pair	80.00
Coalbrookdale, Bowl, Covered, Applied Flowers, Footed, Pair	175.00

Coalport Ware has been made by the Coalport Porcelain Works of England from 1795 to the present time.

Coalport, Bowl, Shell Shape, White, 7 X 4 In.	10.00
Coalport, Cup & Saucer, Blue, White, Gold Lining	7.50
Coalport, Cup & Saucer, Cobalt & Gold	45.00
Coalport, Cup & Saucer, Demitasse, Tree Of Life	8.00
Coalport, Cup & Saucer, Flower Cluster, Two Handled, Set Of 9	65.00
Coalport, Dessert Set, Flowers, Gilt Scrolls, Yellow Ground, C.1835, 14 Piece	175.00
Coalport, Mug, Gold & Corals, C.1810	12.00
Coalport, Plate, Cafe Au Lait Border, Scrolls, Floral, C.1737, 12	150.00
Coalport, Plate, Flowerpot Pattern, Marked England & Crown, Ad1750	10.00
Coalport, Plate, Indian Tree, J.Maddock & Son	11.50
Coalport, Plate, White & Gold, Sevres Style, 9 1/2 In.Diameter, C.1830, 24	150.00
Coalport, Ruler, Poodle Finial, Flowers, 8 1/2 In.Long, C.1830	80.00
Coalport, Tea & Coffee Set, Blue Ground, Floral, C.1820, 22 Piece	50.00
Coalport, Tea & Coffee Set, Imari Decorated, C.1810, 46 Piece	650.00
Coalport, Tea Set, Iron Red & Gold Banded Borders, C.1815, 38 Piece	220.00

Cobalt Blue Glass was made using oxide of cobalt. The characteristic bright dark blue identifies it for the collector. Most Cobalt Glass found today was made after the Civil War.

Cobalt Blue, see also Shirley Temple

Cobalt Blue, Ashtray, Hat Shape, 2 1/4 In.Square	4.00 To 7.00
Cobalt Blue, Beaker, White Cut To Cobalt, Overlay, Footed, Enameled Scene	75.00
Cobalt Blue, Beaker, White To Cobalt, Cut Overlay, Enameled Hunting Scene	75.00
Cobalt Blue, Bottle, Cologne, Blown, Ribbed, Clear Tam-O'-Shanter Stopper	75.00
Cobalt Blue, Bottle, Violin	4.50
Cobalt Blue, Bowl, Bride's, Grapes & Leaves, Ruffled	50.00
Cobalt Blue, Bowl, Bride's, Ruffled, Grape	35.00
Cobalt Blue, Bowl, Finger, Free Blown, 4 3/4 In.Diameter, 2 3/4 In.Tall	15.00
Cobalt Blue, Bowl, Powder, Hinged Cover Has Floral Enamel Decor	36.00
Cobalt Blue, Bowl, Spittoon Shape, Blown, Gold Decoration	12.50
Cobalt Blue, Bowl, Tricorn Top, Striped Marbleized Design	10.00
Cobalt Blue, Box, Patch, Leaves, Butterfly, Enamel, Round, 1 1/4 In.Tall	45.00
Cobalt Blue, Bucket, Ice, Sailboats	5.00
Cobalt Blue, Carafe & Tumbler, Blown, Gold Decoration	25.00
Cobalt Blue, Castor, Pickle, Decorated	125.00
Cobalt Blue, Compote, Blackberry Design, Small	26.00
Cobalt Blue, Console Set, Gold Trim, Germany, 4 Piece	55.00

Cobalt Blue, Cruet	13.75
Cobalt Blue, Cup & Saucer, Demitasse, Sponged Border	15.00
Cobalt Blue, Cup, Candle, For Christmas Tree	4.50
Cobalt Blue, Decanter & Glasses, Mariner's	45.00
Cobalt Blue, Dish, Owl	22.00
Cobalt Blue, Eyecup, On Rubber, Marked Wyeth	6.50
Cobalt Blue, Goblet, Cobalt To White To Clear, Triple Overlay	55.00
Cobalt Blue, Goblet, Double Wedding Ring	4.50
Cobalt Blue, Goblet, Printed Medallion	60.00
Cobalt Blue, Hat, Daisy & Button	35.00
Cobalt Blue, Inkwell, Hand Blown, Bubble Glass, School Desk Type	1.50
Cobalt Blue, Jar, Cracker, Diamond-Quilted, Metal Top & Handles	58.50
Cobalt Blue, Jar, Honey, Flashed	5.00
Cobalt Blue, Jug, Claret, Silver Handle & Lid, England, 8 In.Tall	45.00
Cobalt Blue, Mug, Child's, Hobnail	8.00
Cobalt Blue, Mustard Jar, Ornate Silver Holder, Cover, Spoon	8.50
Cobalt Blue, Pitcher, Water, Lily Design, Enamel, Gold Rim, 5 Tumblers	72.50
Cobalt Blue, Rose Bowl, Cut To Clear	35.00
Cobalt Blue, Salt, Individual, Open	14.50
Cobalt Blue, Salt, White Enamel Lacy Decoration, Signed 'S.Salbista' ...	57.50
Cobalt Blue, Sugar, Colonial	125.00
Cobalt Blue, Toothpick	4.75
Cobalt Blue, Toothpick, Hand-Painted	7.50
Cobalt Blue, Tumbler, Enamel, Yellow, White, Flowers	8.00
Cobalt Blue, Tumbler, Pittsburgh Eight Panel, 3 1/4 In.High	15.00
Cobalt Blue, Tumbler, Pittsburgh Six Panel, 3 In.High	17.50
Cobalt Blue, Tumbler, Shell & Jewel	10.00
Cobalt Blue, Urn, Covered, 11 In.Tall, Pair	50.00
Cobalt Blue, Vase, Blue Cut To Clear, Overlay, Gold Decoration, 5 In.High	25.00
Cobalt Blue, Vase, Bud, Clear, Footed, 8 In.Tall	8.00
Cobalt Blue, Vase, Bud, 5 1/2 In., Pair	6.00
Cobalt Blue, Vase, Conical, Blown, 6 3/4 In.High, Pair	10.00
Cobalt Blue, Vase, Silver Overlay, Floral Design, 8 1/2 In.High	32.00
Cobalt Blue, Water Set, Clear Applied Handle, 7 Piece .... 35.00 To 45.00	

Coca-Cola Advertising Items have become a special field for collectors.

Coca-Cola, Ad, 1905, Passengers In Car Served Coke, Black & White	5.00
Coca-Cola, Amber .... *Illus*	12.00
Coca-Cola, Bookcover, Copyright 1930, 3	2.00
Coca-Cola, Bottle Top, Baseball, 125	7.50
Coca-Cola, Bottle Top, Family, People, 12	1.50
Coca-Cola, Bottle Top, Football, 225	12.50
Coca-Cola, Bottle, Amber, Chattanooga	13.50
Coca-Cola, Bottle, Amber, Huntsville, Ala.	7.50
Coca-Cola, Bottle, Amber, Memphis	22.50

Coca-Cola, Amber

Coca-Cola, **Bottle**, Aqua, Coke, Birmingham, Ala.	7.50
Coca-Cola, **Bottle**, Augusta, Me., Raised Name, Green	3.00
Coca-Cola, **Bottle**, Baltimore, Md., Raised Name, Green	3.00
Coca-Cola, **Bottle**, Bangor, Me., Raised Name, Green	3.00
Coca-Cola, **Bottle**, Big Chief Embossed	3.50
Coca-Cola, **Bottle**, Case Of 24, Miniature, Filled & Capped	11.50
Coca-Cola, **Bottle**, Columbia, Ind., Raised Name, Green	3.00
Coca-Cola, **Bottle**, Cuero Turkey, Embossed Four Sides	25.00
Coca-Cola, **Bottle**, Green, Portland, Me.	3.00
Coca-Cola, **Bottle**, Green, Providence, R.I.	3.00
Coca-Cola, **Bottle**, Miniature, Capped, Marked, 3 In.Tall	.75
Coca-Cola, **Bottle**, Miniature, Filled, Capped, 12	5.00
Coca-Cola, **Bottle**, Miniature, 2 In.Tall, Original Coke	5.00
Coca-Cola, **Bottle**, Miniature, 3 In.Tall, 6	2.95
Coca-Cola, **Bottle**, Paper Label, 1920s	12.50
Coca-Cola, **Bottle**, Portland, Me., Raised Name, Green	3.00
Coca-Cola, **Bottle**, Providence, R.I., Raised Name, Green	3.00
Coca-Cola, **Bottle**, Soda Water, Dated 1923, Green	3.50
Coca-Cola, **Bottle**, Soda Water, Dated 1926, Green	4.50
Coca-Cola, **Bottle**, Soda Water, 5 Stars, Square Middle	1.25
Coca-Cola, **Bottle**, Standard Size, Raised Lettering	2.00
Coca-Cola, **Bottle**, Two Gallon, Clear, 20 In.Tall	20.00
Coca-Cola, **Bottle**, 1 1/2 In.	.25
Coca-Cola, **Calendar**, 1918	20.00
Coca-Cola, **Calendar**, 1928, Bathing Beauty	30.00
Coca-Cola, **Calendar**, 1940, Copyright 1939	12.50
Coca-Cola, **Calendar**, 1953-54	7.50
Coca-Cola, **Card**, Aeroplane, 20	5.25
Coca-Cola, **Card**, Birds, 20	6.50
Coca-Cola, **Card**, Favorite Flowers, 20	6.50
Coca-Cola, **Card**, Nature Study, 96	5.75
Coca-Cola, **Card**, Pushout Picture, 14	5.00
Coca-Cola, **Cards**, Playing	9.50
Coca-Cola, **Carrier**, Bottle, Plastic, 6 Oz.Bottles	10.75
Coca-Cola, **Carrier**, Metal	4.50 To 8.50
Coca-Cola, **Carrier**, Metal, 12 Bottle	11.00
Coca-Cola, **Carrier**, Wood, Six Pack	4.95
Coca-Cola, **Carton**, Wooden, 1920s	4.95
Coca-Cola, **Case & Bottles**, Miniature, Hubley	2.50
Coca-Cola, **Case With Bottles**	2.50
Coca-Cola, **Case**, Display, Miniature, Holds 24 Bottles, 6 1/2 X 4 1/4 In.	1.00
Coca-Cola, **Case**, 24 Gold Bottles, Miniature	10.75
Coca-Cola, **Case**, 24 Green Bottles, Miniature	8.75
Coca-Cola, **Cigarette Case**, Frosted, 50th Anniversary	85.00
Coca-Cola, **Cigarette Lighter**, Butane, Dispos-A-Lite	4.95
Coca-Cola, **Cigarette Lighter**, Coke Bottle Shape, 1940	2.50
Coca-Cola, **Clock**, Green Background, 15 X 15 In.	19.50
Coca-Cola, **Cuff Links**, Blue, Pearl	50.00
Coca-Cola, **Dish**, Ice, Aluminum, Dated 1935, Supported By 3 Bottles	37.50
Coca-Cola, **Flashlight**, Bottle Shape, Plastic, White Letters, Drink Coca-Cola	2.50
Coca-Cola, **Folder**, Souvenir, Bottling Plant	5.00
Coca-Cola, **Glass**, C.1900 *Illus*	35.00
Coca-Cola, **Glass**, C.1920 *Illus*	12.50
Coca-Cola, **Glass**, Coke On One Side, Coca-Cola On Other, 10 Oz.	5.50
Coca-Cola, **Glass**, 6 Oz., Star On Bottom	2.50
Coca-Cola, **Holder**, Aluminum	5.00
Coca-Cola, **Ice Pick**	2.00
Coca-Cola, **Ice Pick**, Dated 1939	6.00
Coca-Cola, **Key Chain**, Gold	.50
Coca-Cola, **Key Ring**, Drink Coca-Cola, Plastic Disk, Chain	1.95
Coca-Cola, **Knife On Key Chain**, Enjoy Coca-Cola	4.50 To 6.00
Coca-Cola, **Knife**, Fishing	5.75
Coca-Cola, **Knife**, Pocket, Gold	8.75
Coca-Cola, **Knife**, Yellow Handle, 'drink Coca-Cola' In Red, 2 Blades	3.00
Coca-Cola, **Lighter**, Cigarette, Bottle Shape, 2 1/2 In.Tall	3.50
Coca-Cola, **Lighter**, Musical	17.00

Coca-Cola, Glass, C.1900
See Page 116

Coca-Cola, Glass, C.1920
See Page 116

Coca-Cola, **Lighter**, Plays Dixie 14.75
Coca-Cola, **Mirror**, Pocket, C.1905-10 .... 17.50
Coca-Cola, **Mirror**, Pocket, Celluloid, Red Background, White Letters 4.50
Coca-Cola, **Mirror**, Pocket, Round, Girl Holding Glass, 1918 .... 3.00
Coca-Cola, **Mirror**, Pocket, Round, Marked 'everybody Drinks Coca-Cola' 2.50
Coca-Cola, **Mirror**, Pocket, Round, 1918 Calendar Girl Holding Glass 3.50
Coca-Cola, **Mirror**, Purse, 50th Anniversary, 1886-1936, 2 1/4 X 3 1/4 In. 2.00
Coca-Cola, **Opener**, Bottle, Cap Catcher, Wall Type 3.50
Coca-Cola, **Opener**, Bottle, Hand .... .35
Coca-Cola, **Opener**, Bottle, Stationary 1.50
Coca-Cola, **Paperweight**, Coke Is Coca-Cola .... 35.00 To 60.00
Coca-Cola, **Paperweight**, Union Glass Works, Somerville, Mass. 45.00
Coca-Cola, **Pen**, Ballpoint 1.25
Coca-Cola, **Pencil**, Ballpoint, Gold Bond, Nickel Cap, 'drink Coca-Cola' .... .75
Coca-Cola, **Plate**, Advertising 27.00
Coca-Cola, **Plate**, Bottle & Glass Center, 'refresh Yourself'on Edge 60.00
Coca-Cola, **Playing Cards**, Girl, Picnic 3.00
Coca-Cola, **Poster**, Woman In Blue Turban, White Fox Stole 10.00
Coca-Cola, **Radio**, Drink Box 75.00
Coca-Cola, **Ring**, Black With Gold Bottle, Hinged Box 4.95
Coca-Cola, **Ruler**, 5 Cents, Wood, 12 In. 1.25
Coca-Cola, **Sign**, 'Coke Refreshes You Best, '20 X 28 In. 17.50
Coca-Cola, **Sign**, Dark Haired Girl Holding Coke, 1940, Cardboard 8.00
Coca-Cola, **Sign**, Embossed, Christmas Coke, 34 X 12 In. 22.00
Coca-Cola, **Sign**, Girl, 1944, Cardboard, 36 X 20 In. 5.00
Coca-Cola, **Sign**, Girls Dancing, Sailboat, Two Sided, Cardboard, 1953, 50 X 36 .... 20.00
Coca-Cola, **Sign**, Metal, 1947 .... 17.00
Coca-Cola, **Sign**, Porcelain, Brown, 15 In. 12.00
Coca-Cola, **Sign**, Tin, Shape Of Coke Bottle, Thermometer, 17 In. 23.00
Coca-Cola, **Sign**, 1929, Standup, Cardboard, Bathing Beauty, 'just A Drink' 50.00
Coca-Cola, **Thermometer**, Bottle 4.50
Coca-Cola, **Thermometer**, Bottle Shape, Dec.25, 1923, 17 In. 12.50
Coca-Cola, **Thermometer**, 15 In.Tall 12.50
Coca-Cola, **Tieback**, Bottle 5.50
Coca-Cola, **Toy**, Vending Machine 10.95
Coca-Cola, **Tray**, Change, Scene Of Mexico City, 1860 Street Scene, Tin 10.00
Coca-Cola, **Tray**, Change, Tin, Oval, 1893 .... 150.00
Coca-Cola, **Tray**, Change, 1914 .... 75.00
Coca-Cola, **Tray**, Coke Bottle, Tin, 13 In. Round 2.00
Coca-Cola, **Tray**, Fanta Soda Water, Boy Drinking Fanta, Tin, 13 In.Round 2.00
Coca-Cola, **Tray**, Fanta, Tin, Round, Boy & Dog 2.00
Coca-Cola, **Tray**, Fruit, Food, 5 Coke Bottles, 18 X 13 In. 5.50
Coca-Cola, **Tray**, Girl Holding Coke, 'thirst Knows No Seasons' 17.00
Coca-Cola, **Tray**, Girl Rests Chin In Hand, Holds Bottle With Other Hand 8.00
Coca-Cola, **Tray**, Girl With Bottle, Sports & Animals On Rim, 13 X 10 1/4 In. 15.00
Coca-Cola, **Tray**, Girl With Menu, Pre-1940 .... 12.50
Coca-Cola, **Tray**, Girl, 'the Four Seasons' 12.00
Coca-Cola, **Tray**, Tip, Girl In Bonnet 45.00

Coca-Cola, Tray, Tip, Oval, World War I, Girl 55.00
Coca-Cola, Tray, Weissmuller 125.00
Coca-Cola, Tray, 1914, Betty, Oval 125.00
Coca-Cola, Tray, 1914, Oval, Betty, Change 75.00
Coca-Cola, Tray, 1917, Girl With Wide Hat Drinking Coke .... 70.00 To 85.00
Coca-Cola, Tray, 1925, Girl Wearing Turban & Fox Stole, Tin 37.00
Coca-Cola, Tray, 1929, Nude Girl, 13 X 10 1/2 In. 28.00
Coca-Cola, Tray, 1930, Girl On Telephone 25.00
Coca-Cola, Tray, 1933, Frances Dee Picture 25.00
Coca-Cola, Tray, 1935 .... 25.00
Coca-Cola, Tray, 1935, Madge Evans 24.00
Coca-Cola, Tray, 1936 .... 18.00
Coca-Cola, Tray, 1937 .... 17.50
Coca-Cola, Tray, 1937, Girl In Bathing Suit Running Along Beach 35.00
Coca-Cola, Tray, 1938, Girl In Yellow .... 15.00 To 18.00
Coca-Cola, Tray, 1939, Bathing Beauty .... 15.00 To 18.00
Coca-Cola, Tray, 1939, Girl On Diving Board .... 10.00 To 14.00
Coca-Cola, Tray, 1940, Girl Sitting On Pier Drinking Coke .... 15.00 To 24.00
Coca-Cola, Tray, 1959, Hand Pouring Coke, Pansies .... 4.00 To 7.95
Coca-Cola, Tray, 1961, Flowers 5.00
Coca-Cola, Tray, 1968, Canadian 14.50
Coca-Cola, Tray, 1969, Canadian 10.50
Coca-Cola, Tray, 1969, French Opera Star, Lillian Nordica, Red Ground 20.00
Coca-Cola, Tray, 1941, 10 1/2 X 13 In. .... 12.00 To 20.00
Coca-Cola, Tray, 1942, Two Girls & Car .... 18.00 To 26.00
Coca-Cola, Tray, 1950, 'have A Coke' 16.00
Coca-Cola, Tray, 1956, 18 1/2 In. X 13 1/2 In. 6.50
Coca-Cola, Tray, 1971 .... 20.00
Coca-Cola, Truck & Bottles, 1934 .... 32.50
Coca-Cola, Truck, Route, Metal 7.90
Coca-Cola, Truck, White, C.1936 .... 50.00
Coca-Cola, Truck, White, 1936 .... 50.00
Coca-Cola, Watch Fob, Coke 5 Cents, Shape Of Swastika Good Luck Symbol 45.00

Coffee Grinders, home size, were first made about 1894. They lost favor by the 1930s.
Coffee Grinder, Arcade, Wall 20.00
Coffee Grinder, Brass Cup, Dovetailed, Drawer 13.00
Coffee Grinder, Brass Top, 6 In. .... *Illus* 35.00
Coffee Grinder, Double Wheel, 24 In.Diameter, Stencil, 1873, Enterprise, Iron 195.00
Coffee Grinder, Enterprise .... *Illus* 35.00
Coffee Grinder, Iron, Marked Koffee Krusher 12.00
Coffee Grinder, Iron, Wall, China Jar At Top, Glass Measuring Cup 11.75
Coffee Grinder, Lap, American 17.50
Coffee Grinder, Wall Hanging, Glass Jar 22.50
Coffee Grinder, Wall Type, Glass 20.00
Coffee Grinder, Wall Type, Tin & Iron 15.00

Coffee Grinder,
Brass Top, 6 In.

Coffee Grinder,
Enterprise

Coffee Grinder, Wall Type, Tole & Iron, Regal	14.50
Coffee Grinder, Wall, Blue Windmill	38.50
Coffee Grinder, Wall, Cast Iron, Universal 1905	13.00
Coffee Grinder, Wood, Cast Iron Handle	12.95
Coffee Grinder, Wood, Metal Top, Lap	16.50
Coffee Grinder, Wooden, Pewter Top	35.00
Coffee Mill, Elgin National, Double Wheel, 25 In.Diameter Wheels	150.00
Coffee Mill, Iron, Wheel 9 1/2 In.	24.00
Coffee Mill, Two Wheel, Iron, 12 1/2 In. Wheels	57.50
Coffee Mill, Wheel 11 In.	24.00
Coffee Mill, Wheel 13 In.	27.50
Coffee, Roaster, Iron, Ball Shaped, 17 In.	75.00
Coin Silver, see Silver, American, and Silver, Coin	
Collector Bell, Crown Delft, Christmas, 1970, 1st Issue	4.00
Collector Bell, Crown Delft, Christmas, 1971	4.00
Collector Bell, Seven Seas, Historical, 1970, Innitzer Peace, 1st Issue	20.00
Collector Bell, Seven Seas, Historical, 1971, Glory To God	20.00
Collector Bell, Spode, Christmas, 1971, Hammersley, 1st Issue	18.50 To 25.00
Collector Bell, Wittig, New Year's, 1972, Cranberry, Crystal, 1st Issue	18.50
Collector Decanter, Wheaton Nuline, Christmas, 1971, 1st Issue	5.00
Collector Figurine, Royale, Easter, 1972, Rabbit	20.00
Collector Fork, Michelsen, Christmas, 1940	38.00
Collector Fork, Michelsen, Christmas, 1941	38.00
Collector Fork, Michelsen, Christmas, 1942	38.00
Collector Fork, Michelsen, Christmas, 1943	38.00
Collector Fork, Michelsen, Christmas, 1944	38.00
Collector Fork, Michelsen, Christmas, 1945	38.00
Collector Fork, Michelsen, Christmas, 1946	38.00
Collector Fork, Michelsen, Christmas, 1947	38.00
Collector Fork, Michelsen, Christmas, 1948	38.00
Collector Fork, Michelsen, Christmas, 1949	38.00
Collector Fork, Michelsen, Christmas, 1950	32.00
Collector Fork, Michelsen, Christmas, 1951	32.00
Collector Fork, Michelsen, Christmas, 1952	32.00
Collector Fork, Michelsen, Christmas, 1953	32.00
Collector Fork, Michelsen, Christmas, 1954	32.00
Collector Fork, Michelsen, Christmas, 1955	32.00
Collector Fork, Michelsen, Christmas, 1956	32.00
Collector Fork, Michelsen, Christmas, 1957	32.00
Collector Fork, Michelsen, Christmas, 1958	32.00
Collector Fork, Michelsen, Christmas, 1959	32.00
Collector Fork, Michelsen, Christmas, 1971, Sterling, Gold-Plated, Enamel	24.00
Collector Mug, Berlin, Annual, 1971, Callenberg Castle, 1st Issue	40.00
Collector Mug, Blue Delft, Father's Day, 1971, Lana's Air-Ship	9.00
Collector Mug, Blue Delft, Father's Day, 1972, Dr.Jonathan's Balloon	10.00
Collector Mug, Bygdo, Christmas, 1969, Shepherdess & Chimney Sweep, 1st	15.00
Collector Mug, Bygdo, Christmas, 1970, Clumsy Hans	12.50
Collector Mug, Bygdo, Christmas, 1971, Flying Trunk	10.00
Collector Mug, Frankoma, G.O.P., 1968, White, 1st Issue	12.50 To 15.00
Collector Mug, Hans Christian Andersen, 1969	8.00
Collector Mug, Hans Christian Andersen, 1970	8.00
Collector Mug, Kera, Christmas, 1967, Kobenhavn, 1st Issue	14.00
Collector Mug, Kera, Christmas, 1968, Forste	11.50
Collector Mug, Kera, Christmas, 1969, Andersen's House	10.00
Collector Mug, Kera, Christmas, 1970, Pa Langelinie	8.50
Collector Mug, Kera, Christmas, 1971	8.50
Collector Mug, Kosta, Annual, 1971, Heraldic Lion, 1st Issue	22.50 To 30.00
Collector Mug, Mueller, 1971	20.00
Collector Mug, Porsgrund, Christmas, 1970, 1st Issue	12.50 To 15.00
Collector Mug, Porsgrund, Christmas, 1971, A Child Is Born	12.50 To 15.00
Collector Mug, Royal Copenhagen, Faience, 1967, 6 Oz.	49.50
Collector Mug, Royal Copenhagen, Faience, 1967, 24 Oz.	49.50
Collector Mug, Royal Copenhagen, Faience, 1968, 6 Oz.	17.50
Collector Mug, Royal Copenhagen, Faience, 1968, 24 Oz.	30.00
Collector Mug, Royal Copenhagen, Faience, 1969, 6 Oz.	12.00
Collector Mug, Royal Copenhagen, Faience, 1969, 24 Oz.	22.50

Collector Mug, Royal Copenhagen, Faience, 1970, 6 Oz.	10.00
Collector Mug, Royal Copenhagen, Faience, 1970, 24 Oz.	21.00
Collector Mug, Royal Copenhagen, Faience, 1971, 6 Oz.	8.00
Collector Mug, Royal Copenhagen, Faience, 1971, 24 Oz.	20.00
Collector Mug, Schmid Design, Christmas, 1971	20.00
Collector Mug, Stromberg, 1968, 1st Issue	60.00
Collector Mug, Stromberg, 1969, Moon Craft	50.00
Collector Mug, Stromberg, 1970, Jingo Ji	27.50
Collector Mug, Stromberg, 1971, Freden	25.00
Collector Mug, Veneto Flair, Van Gogh, 1970, Drawbridge	11.00
Collector Mug, Veneto Flair, Van Gogh, 1971, Night Cafe	11.00
Collector Mug, Wedgwood, Christmas, 1971, Piccadilly, 1st Issue	17.50 To 30.00
Collector Plaque, Bing & Grondahl, Easter, 1910	39.50
Collector Plaque, Bing & Grondahl, Easter, 1911	39.50
Collector Plaque, Bing & Grondahl, Easter, 1912	39.50
Collector Plaque, Bing & Grondahl, Easter, 1913	39.50
Collector Plaque, Bing & Grondahl, Easter, 1914	39.50
Collector Plaque, Bing & Grondahl, Easter, 1915	39.50
Collector Plaque, Bing & Grondahl, Easter, 1916	39.50
Collector Plaque, Bing & Grondahl, Easter, 1917	39.50
Collector Plaque, Bing & Grondahl, Easter, 1918	39.50
Collector Plaque, Bing & Grondahl, Easter, 1919	39.50
Collector Plaque, Bing & Grondahl, Easter, 1920	39.50
Collector Plaque, Bing & Grondahl, Easter, 1921	39.50
Collector Plaque, Bing & Grondahl, Easter, 1922	39.50
Collector Plaque, Bing & Grondahl, Easter, 1923	39.50
Collector Plaque, Bing & Grondahl, Easter, 1924	39.50
Collector Plaque, Bing & Grondahl, Easter, 1925	39.50
Collector Plaque, Bing & Grondahl, Easter, 1926	42.50
Collector Plaque, Bing & Grondahl, Easter, 1927	50.00
Collector Plaque, Bing & Grondahl, Easter, 1928	50.00
Collector Plaque, Bing & Grondahl, Easter, 1929	50.00
Collector Plaque, Bing & Grondahl, Easter, 1930	100.00
Collector Plaque, Bing & Grondahl, Easter, 1931	100.00
Collector Plaque, Bing & Grondahl, Easter, 1932	100.00
Collector Plaque, Bing & Grondahl, Easter, 1933	100.00
Collector Plaque, Bing & Grondahl, Easter, 1934	300.00
Collector Plaque, Bing & Grondahl, Easter, 1935	500.00
Collector Plate, American Coin Glass, Silver Dollar, Carnival, Amethyst	10.00
Collector Plate, American Crystal, Astronaut, 1968	95.00
Collector Plate, American Crystal, Astronaut, 1969	73.00 To 90.00
Collector Plate, American Crystal, Christmas, 1970	40.00 To 65.00
Collector Plate, American Crystal, Christmas, 1971	15.00 To 30.00
Collector Plate, American Crystal, Christmas, 1972	32.00
Collector Plate, American Crystal, First Flight, 1971, Iceberg	45.00 To 115.00
Collector Plate, American Crystal, Mother's Day, 1971	20.00 To 65.00
Collector Plate, American, First Flight, 1971	110.00 To 115.00
Collector Plate, Andrew Wyeth, The Kuerner Farm, 1st Issue	50.00
Collector Plate, Anri, Birthday, 1972, Boy	15.00
Collector Plate, Anri, Birthday, 1972, Girl	15.00
Collector Plate, Anri, Christmas, 1970, 1st Issue	45.00
Collector Plate, Anri, Christmas, 1971, 1st Issue	45.00
Collector Plate, Anri, Father's Day, 1971	35.00
Collector Plate, Anri, Father's Day, 1972, Father With Children	35.00
Collector Plate, Anri, Mother's Day, 1971	35.00
Collector Plate, Anri, Mother's Day, 1972	35.00
Collector Plate, August, Columbus, 1971, Pewter	30.00
Collector Plate, August, Kennedy, 1971, Pewter	30.00

*Christmas Plates were made by several firms. The most famous were made by
The Bing & Grondahl Factory of Denmark, after 1895, and the Royal
Copenhagen Factory, after 1908. Each of these plates has a blue-and-white
glaze with a scene in the center, the date, and the word jule.*

Collector Plate, Bareuther, Christmas, 1967, 1st Issue	50.00 To 100.00
Collector Plate, Bareuther, Christmas, 1968	17.00 To 35.00
Collector Plate, Bareuther, Christmas, 1969	6.75 To 24.00

Dr Pepper fountain syrup
dispenser used in 1900.

Beautiful hand-painted picture, typical of
the art used in Dr Pepper point-of-sale
advertising between 1900 and 1910.

An old regulator calendar clock used as
an advertising medium by Dr Pepper in
early 1900.

Serving tray used by Dr Pepper in the '30s.

Beautiful hand-painted plate used in 1900 as a souvenir premium by Dr Pepper.

Sugarloaf and sugar snipper. Belgium, 1758.

Log-cabin sugar tureen. English Staffordshire, 1840.

Blue and white Canton platter. Chinese export. G. Washington.

Burmese plate and vase. Mt. Washington Glass Co., New Bedford, Mass.

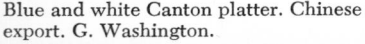

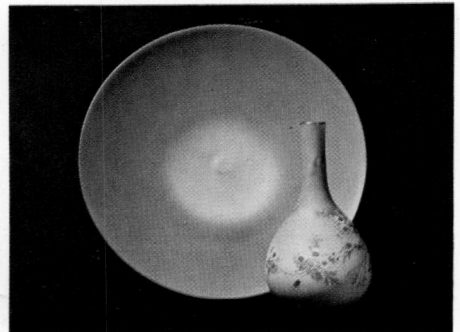

Three Etruscan majolica pieces by
Griffen, Smith & Hill, Phoenixville,
Pa. (1879–1890)

Staffordshire plate. Red transfer design,
Franklin's Experiment with Electricity.

Campaign buttons, 1895.

Campaign bandanna. Candidates James A. Garfield, Chester A. Arthur.

"Mary Louise McCully wrought this in the ninth year of her age. Patterson. 1840."

Campaign buttons, 1876.

Pieced-work crib quilt, Log Cabin pattern in wool and cotton. Made near Harrisburg, Pa., ca. 1860–1870. 43" X 30".

Double-woven cover. Let, Pa., 1846.

1870 ad for spouted water can for kerosene.

Paisley shawl, nineteenth century.
Owned by J. Buchanan's niece.

Andrew Jackson sewing box, 1828.

Embroidered mourning picture, ca. 1800.

Harrison, Morton, cigar box.

Tobacco cards. American, nineteenth century.

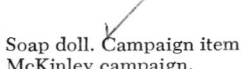

Soap doll. Campaign item,
McKinley campaign.

Tammany mechanical bank, 1872.

Carousel figure, nineteenth century. Gous.

China-head doll. Germany
ca. 1880.

Figurine, "Roman Charity," by
Ralph Wood. Staffordshire,
England, ca. 1750.

Lunette-shaped housing from steamboat *Neptune*. Ca. 1850.

Weathervane rooster, nineteenth century.

Eagle by Wilhelm Schimmel (1817–1890), Pennsylvania.

Collector Plate, **Bareuther**, Christmas, 1970 .... 6.70 To 13.50
Collector Plate, **Bareuther**, Christmas, 1970, 4th Issue .... 6.75 To 13.00
Collector Plate, **Bareuther**, Christmas, 1971 .... 8.50 To 10.50
Collector Plate, **Bareuther**, Christmas, 1971, 5th Issue .... 10.00 To 12.50
Collector Plate, **Bareuther**, Father's Day, 1969, 1st Issue .... 35.00 To 55.00
Collector Plate, **Bareuther**, Father's Day, 1970, 2nd Issue .... 6.25 To 12.50
Collector Plate, **Bareuther**, Father's Day, 1971, 3rd Issue .... 8.00 To 12.00
Collector Plate, **Bareuther**, Mother's Day, 1969 .... 35.00 To 50.00
Collector Plate, **Bareuther**, Mother's Day, 1970 .... 6.25 To 12.50
Collector Plate, **Bareuther**, Mother's Day, 1971 .... 11.00 To 13.00
Collector Plate, **Bareuther**, Thanksgiving, 1971, 1st Issue .... 10.75 To 13.00
Collector Plate, **Barlin**, Christmas, 1971 .... 14.00
Collector Plate, **Barlin**, Father's Day, 1971 .... 14.75
Collector Plate, **Bavaria**, Pope Paul 100.00
Collector Plate, **Belleek**, Castle Caldwell, 1970 .... 60.00
Collector Plate, **Belleek**, Celtic Cross, 1971 .... 50.00
Collector Plate, **Belleek**, Christmas, 1970 .... 63.00 To 100.00
Collector Plate, **Belleek**, Christmas, 1971 .... 42.00
Collector Plate, **Berlin**, Christmas, 1970, Bernkastel, 1st Issue .... 16.00 To 25.00
Collector Plate, **Berlin**, Christmas, 1971, 2nd Issue .... 10.50 To 14.50
Collector Plate, **Berlin**, Father's Day, 1971, 1st Issue .... 10.00 To 14.50
Collector Plate, **Berlin**, Mother's Day, 1971, Poodles, 1st Issue .... 14.50 To 22.50
Collector Plate, **Berlin**, Mother's Day, 1972, Fledglings 15.00
Collector Plate, **Berlin**, Munich Olympic, 1972 .... 15.00
Collector Plate, **Berta Hummel**, Christmas, 1971, 1st Issue 15.00
Collector Plate, **Berta Hummel**, Mother's Day, 1971 .... 15.00
Collector Plate, **Berta Hummel**, Mother's Day, 1972 .... 15.00
Collector Plate, **Bing & Grondahl**, Christmas, 1900 .... 600.00
Collector Plate, **Bing & Grondahl**, Christmas, 1901 .... 220.00
Collector Plate, **Bing & Grondahl**, Christmas, 1902 .... 160.00
Collector Plate, **Bing & Grondahl**, Christmas, 1903 .... 155.00
Collector Plate, **Bing & Grondahl**, Christmas, 1904 .... 90.00
Collector Plate, **Bing & Grondahl**, Christmas, 1905 .... 90.00
Collector Plate, **Bing & Grondahl**, Christmas, 1906 .... 65.00
Collector Plate, **Bing & Grondahl**, Christmas, 1907 .... 90.00
Collector Plate, **Bing & Grondahl**, Christmas, 1908 .... 45.00
Collector Plate, **Bing & Grondahl**, Christmas, 1909 .... 65.00
Collector Plate, **Bing & Grondahl**, Christmas, 1910 .... 65.00
Collector Plate, **Bing & Grondahl**, Christmas, 1911 .... 60.00
Collector Plate, **Bing & Grondahl**, Christmas, 1912 .... 60.00
Collector Plate, **Bing & Grondahl**, Christmas, 1913 .... 60.00
Collector Plate, **Bing & Grondahl**, Christmas, 1914 .... 50.00
Collector Plate, **Bing & Grondahl**, Christmas, 1915 .... 84.00
Collector Plate, **Bing & Grondahl**, Christmas, 1916 .... 54.00
Collector Plate, **Bing & Grondahl**, Christmas, 1917 .... 54.00
Collector Plate, **Bing & Grondahl**, Christmas, 1918 .... 54.00
Collector Plate, **Bing & Grondahl**, Christmas, 1919 .... 54.00
Collector Plate, **Bing & Grondahl**, Christmas, 1920 .... 50.00
Collector Plate, **Bing & Grondahl**, Christmas, 1921 .... 50.00
Collector Plate, **Bing & Grondahl**, Christmas, 1922 .... 50.00
Collector Plate, **Bing & Grondahl**, Christmas, 1923 .... 50.00
Collector Plate, **Bing & Grondahl**, Christmas, 1924 .... 45.00
Collector Plate, **Bing & Grondahl**, Christmas, 1925 .... 50.00
Collector Plate, **Bing & Grondahl**, Christmas, 1926 .... 50.00
Collector Plate, **Bing & Grondahl**, Christmas, 1927 .... 60.00
Collector Plate, **Bing & Grondahl**, Christmas, 1928 .... 50.00
Collector Plate, **Bing & Grondahl**, Christmas, 1929 .... 60.00
Collector Plate, **Bing & Grondahl**, Christmas, 1930 .... 70.00
Collector Plate, **Bing & Grondahl**, Christmas, 1931 .... 50.00
Collector Plate, **Bing & Grondahl**, Christmas, 1932 .... 54.00
Collector Plate, **Bing & Grondahl**, Christmas, 1933 .... 40.00
Collector Plate, **Bing & Grondahl**, Christmas, 1934 .... 50.00
Collector Plate, **Bing & Grondahl**, Christmas, 1935 .... 50.00
Collector Plate, **Bing & Grondahl**, Christmas, 1936 .... 50.00
Collector Plate, **Bing & Grondahl**, Christmas, 1937 .... 60.00
Collector Plate, **Bing & Grondahl**, Christmas, 1938 .... 90.00

Collector Plate, **Bing & Grondahl**, Christmas, 1939 .... 120.00
Collector Plate, **Bing & Grondahl**, Christmas, 1940 .... 100.00
Collector Plate, **Bing & Grondahl**, Christmas, 1941 .... 240.00
Collector Plate, **Bing & Grondahl**, Christmas, 1942 .... 110.00
Collector Plate, **Bing & Grondahl**, Christmas, 1943 .... 110.00
Collector Plate, **Bing & Grondahl**, Christmas, 1944 .... 60.00
Collector Plate, **Bing & Grondahl**, Christmas, 1945 .... 80.00
Collector Plate, **Bing & Grondahl**, Christmas, 1946 .... 52.50
Collector Plate, **Bing & Grondahl**, Christmas, 1947 .... 60.00
Collector Plate, **Bing & Grondahl**, Christmas, 1948 .... 50.00
Collector Plate, **Bing & Grondahl**, Christmas, 1949 .... 50.00
Collector Plate, **Bing & Grondahl**, Christmas, 1950 .... 60.00
Collector Plate, **Bing & Grondahl**, Christmas, 1951 .... 57.50
Collector Plate, **Bing & Grondahl**, Christmas, 1952 .... 55.00
Collector Plate, **Bing & Grondahl**, Christmas, 1953 .... 50.00
Collector Plate, **Bing & Grondahl**, Christmas, 1954 .... 60.00
Collector Plate, **Bing & Grondahl**, Christmas, 1955 .... 57.50
Collector Plate, **Bing & Grondahl**, Christmas, 1956 .... 82.50
Collector Plate, **Bing & Grondahl**, Christmas, 1957 .... 85.00
Collector Plate, **Bing & Grondahl**, Christmas, 1958 .... 65.00
Collector Plate, **Bing & Grondahl**, Christmas, 1959 .... 110.00
Collector Plate, **Bing & Grondahl**, Christmas, 1960 .... 110.00
Collector Plate, **Bing & Grondahl**, Christmas, 1961 .... 72.50
Collector Plate, **Bing & Grondahl**, Christmas, 1962 .... 30.00
Collector Plate, **Bing & Grondahl**, Christmas, 1962 .... 40.00
Collector Plate, **Bing & Grondahl**, Christmas, 1963 .... 79.50
Collector Plate, **Bing & Grondahl**, Christmas, 1964 .... 35.00
Collector Plate, **Bing & Grondahl**, Christmas, 1965 .... 35.00
Collector Plate, **Bing & Grondahl**, Christmas, 1966 .... 20.00 To 70.00
Collector Plate, **Bing & Grondahl**, Christmas, 1967 .... 24.00 To 27.00
Collector Plate, **Bing & Grondahl**, Christmas, 1968 .... 16.50 To 25.00
Collector Plate, **Bing & Grondahl**, Christmas, 1969 .... 10.00 To 21.00
Collector Plate, **Bing & Grondahl**, Christmas, 1970 .... 11.00 To 18.00
Collector Plate, **Bing & Grondahl**, Christmas, 1971 .... 10.00 To 15.00
Collector Plate, **Bing & Grondahl**, Commemorative, May 4th 18.50
Collector Plate, **Bing & Grondahl**, Jubilee, 1915 .... 79.50
Collector Plate, **Bing & Grondahl**, Jubilee, 1920 .... 75.00
Collector Plate, **Bing & Grondahl**, Jubilee, 1925 .... 100.00
Collector Plate, **Bing & Grondahl**, Jubilee, 1930 .... 150.00
Collector Plate, **Bing & Grondahl**, Jubilee, 1935 .... 600.00
Collector Plate, **Bing & Grondahl**, Jubilee, 1940 .... 1000.00
Collector Plate, **Bing & Grondahl**, Jubilee, 1945 .... 300.00
Collector Plate, **Bing & Grondahl**, Jubilee, 1950 .... 150.00
Collector Plate, **Bing & Grondahl**, Jubilee, 1955 .... 140.00
Collector Plate, **Bing & Grondahl**, Jubilee, 1960 .... 100.00
Collector Plate, **Bing & Grondahl**, Jubilee, 1965 .... 60.00
Collector Plate, **Bing & Grondahl**, Jubilee, 1970 .... 13.75 To 25.00
Collector Plate, **Bing & Grondahl**, Mother's Day, 1969 .... 135.00 To 185.00
Collector Plate, **Bing & Grondahl**, Mother's Day, 1969, Dog, Puppies, 1st Issue 185.00
Collector Plate, **Bing & Grondahl**, Mother's Day, 1970 .... 18.00 To 22.50
Collector Plate, **Bing & Grondahl**, Mother's Day, 1971 .... 8.00 To 11.00
Collector Plate, **Bing & Grondahl**, Mother's Day, 1972, 4th Issue .... 9.50 To 10.50
Collector Plate, **Bing & Grondahl**, Olympics, 1972, 1st Issue 15.00
Collector Plate, **Bing & Grondahl**, 100th Year, 1970 .... 25.00
Collector Plate, **Blue Delft**, Christmas, 1969 .... 21.50
Collector Plate, **Blue Delft**, Christmas, 1970, 1st Issue .... 11.00 To 14.00
Collector Plate, **Blue Delft**, Christmas, 1971, St.Laurens Church 11.00
Collector Plate, **Blue Delft**, Commemorative, 1972, Olympiade Munchen 13.50
Collector Plate, **Blue Delft**, Father's Day, 1971, Lana's Air-Ship, 1st Issue 11.00
Collector Plate, **Blue Delft**, Father's Day, 1972, Dr.Jonathan's Balloon 12.00
Collector Plate, **Blue Delft**, Mother's Day.1971, 1st Issue 11.00
Collector Plate, **Blue Delft**, Mother's Day, 1972, Isle Of Urk, Mother, Child 12.00
Collector Plate, **Bridge**, Crystal, 1970 .... 75.00
Collector Plate, **Bygdo**, Christmas, 1969, Shepherdess & Chimney Sweep, 1st 15.00
Collector Plate, **Bygdo**, Christmas, 1970, Clumsy Hans 12.50
Collector Plate, **Bygdo**, Christmas, 1971, Flying Trunk 10.00

Collector Plate, Church, Christmas, 1968 .... 18.00
Collector Plate, Church, Christmas, 1969 .... 12.00
Collector Plate, Church, Christmas, 1970 .... 9.00
Collector Plate, Coalport, Mayflower, 1970 .... 35.00
Collector Plate, Coronation Plate, Edward VII, Queen Alexandria, Blue, Gold 16.50
Collector Plate, Count Agazzi, Children's Hour, 1970, Owl, 1st Issue 14.50
Collector Plate, Count Agazzi, Children's Hour, 1971, Cat 12.50
Collector Plate, Count Agazzi, Commemorative, Apollo II 17.00
Collector Plate, Count Agazzi, Easter, 1971, Cherubs, Violin, 1st Issue 12.50
Collector Plate, Crown Delft, Christmas, 1969, Man By Fire, 1st Issue 18.00
Collector Plate, Crown Delft, Christmas, 1970, Sleigh & 2 Riders 10.00
Collector Plate, Crown Delft, Christmas, 1971, Tree On Market Square 9.25
Collector Plate, Crown Delft, Father's Day, 1970, Ship, 1st Issue 12.50
Collector Plate, Crown Delft, Father's Day, 1971, Ship 9.25
Collector Plate, Crown Delft, Mother's Day, 1970, Sheep, 1st Issue 12.50
Collector Plate, Crown Delft, Mother's Day, 1971, Storks 9.25
Collector Plate, Danish Church, Christmas, 1968, 1st Issue 18.00
Collector Plate, Danish Church, Christmas, 1969 .... 12.00
Collector Plate, Danish Church, Christmas, 1970 .... 9.00
Collector Plate, Danish Church, Christmas, 1971 .... 9.00
Collector Plate, Daum, Four Seasons, 1971 .... 600.00
Collector Plate, Dawn's House Of Ceramics, Thanskgiving, 1971, Mayflower 12.50
Collector Plate, Delft, Apollo II, 1969 .... 18.00
Collector Plate, Delft, Apollo 8, 1968 .... 18.00
Collector Plate, Delft, Christmas, 1969 .... 10.50
Collector Plate, Delft, Christmas, 1970, Blue 11.00
Collector Plate, Delft, Father's Day, 1970 .... 5.50
Collector Plate, Delft, Father's Day, 1971, Blue 11.00
Collector Plate, Delft, Mother's Day, 1970 .... 5.50
Collector Plate, Delft, Mother's Day, 1971, Blue 11.00
Collector Plate, Delft, Thanksgiving, 1970, Pilgrim Fathers 16.00
Collector Plate, Dresden, Christmas, 1971, Shepherds, 1st Issue .... 14.50 To 25.00
Collector Plate, Ellard, Christmas, 1970, Winter At White House, 1st Issue 12.00
Collector Plate, Ellard, Christmas, 1971 .... 12.00
Collector Plate, Ellard, Father's Day, 1971, Lion & Cubs, 1st Issue 12.00
Collector Plate, Ellard, Mother's Day, 1971, Lioness & Cubs, 1st Issue 12.00
Collector Plate, Ellard, Thanksgiving, 1970, Mayflower, 1st Issue 12.00
Collector Plate, Ellard, Thanksgiving, 1971, Getting Ready 14.00
Collector Plate, Eschenbach, Christmas, 1971, Nuremberg, 1st Issue 13.00
Collector Plate, Eschenbach, Christmas, 1971, 1st Issue .... 10.00 To 12.00
Collector Plate, Fenton, Blacksmith, 1972, Carnival Glass 10.00
Collector Plate, Fenton, Christmas, 1970, Blue Marble, 1st Issue .... 6.50 To 12.50
Collector Plate, Fenton, Christmas, 1970, Carnival, 1st Issue .... 6.50 To 12.50
Collector Plate, Fenton, Christmas, 1971, Blue Marble 12.50
Collector Plate, Fenton, Christmas, 1971, Blue Marble, 2nd Issue 12.50
Collector Plate, Fenton, Christmas, 1971, 2nd Issue, Carnival Glass 12.50
Collector Plate, Fenton, Commemorative, 1970, Glassmaker, 1st Issue 10.00
Collector Plate, Fenton, Great Lovers, 1971, Blue Marble, 1st Issue 15.00
Collector Plate, Fenton, Great Lovers, 1971, Carnival Glass, 1st Issue 15.00
Collector Plate, Fenton, Mother's Day.1971, 1st Issue, Blue Marble 12.50
Collector Plate, Fenton, Mother's Day, 1971, Madonna & Child, Carnival, 1st 12.50
Collector Plate, Fenton, Mother's Day, 1972 .... 12.50
Collector Plate, Fenton, Printer Press, 1971 .... 8.00 To 10.00
Collector Plate, Fenton, Valentine's Day, 1972, Romeo & Juliet, Blue, 1st 15.00
Collector Plate, Fenton, Valentine's Day, 1972, Romeo & Juliet, Carnival, 1st 15.00
Collector Plate, Fostoria, American Milestones, 1971, The Flag, 1st Issue 12.00
Collector Plate, Franklin Mint Christmas, 1970, 1st Issue 250.00
Collector Plate, Franklin Mint, Christmas, 1971 .... 150.00
Collector Plate, Franklin Mint, Christmas, 1972, Norman Rockwell, Sterling 100.00
Collector Plate, Franklin Mint, Rockwell, 1970 .... 400.00 To 500.00
Collector Plate, Franklin Mint, Rockwell, 1971 .... 100.00 To 175.00
Collector Plate, Frankoma, Christmas, 1965, Goodwill Towards Men, 1st 175.00
Collector Plate, Frankoma, Christmas, 1966, Bethlehem Shepherds 65.00
Collector Plate, Frankoma, Christmas, 1967, Gifts For The Christ Child 50.00
Collector Plate, Frankoma, Christmas, 1968, Flight Into Egypt .... 10.00 To 20.00
Collector Plate, Frankoma, Christmas, 1969, Laid In A Manger .... 5.00 To 6.00

Collector Plate, **Frankoma**, Christmas, 1970, King Of Kings .... 5.00 To 6.00
Collector Plate, **Frankoma**, Christmas, 1971, No Room In The Inn 5.00
Collector Plate, **Fuerstenberg**, Christmas, 1971, 1st Issue .... 12.00 To 15.00
Collector Plate, **Fuerstenberg**, Easter, 1st Issue .... 25.00 To 30.00
Collector Plate, **Fuerstenberg**, Mother's Day, 1972 .... 15.00
Collector Plate, **Gorham**, Artists, 1971, Rembrandt's Man In Gilt Helmet, 1st 50.00
Collector Plate, **Gorham**, Barrymore Etching, 1972 .... 25.00
Collector Plate, **Gorham**, Four Seasons, 1971, Boy & Dog, 1st Issue, Set 50.00
Collector Plate, **Gorham**, Four Seasons, 1972, Boy & Girl, Set 60.00
Collector Plate, **Gorham**, Lionel Barrymore, 1971, Quiet Waters, 1st Issue 25.00
Collector Plate, **Grandma Moses**, Jack & Jill, Signed, 1st Issue 150.00
Collector Plate, **Grandma Moses**, The Red Checkered House, Signed, 1st Issue 150.00
Collector Plate, **Greentree**, Mt.Rushmore, 1970, 1st Issue 7.50
Collector Plate, **Hans Christian Andersen**, Christmas, 1969 .... 8.00
Collector Plate, **Haviland & Company**, President Grant 100.00
Collector Plate, **Haviland Christmas**, Partridge, 1970 .... 35.00
Collector Plate, **Haviland Tapestry**, Start Of The Hunt, 1972 .... 35.00
Collector Plate, **Haviland**, Christmas, 1970, Partridge .... 25.00 To 40.00
Collector Plate, **Haviland**, Christmas, 1971, Two Turtledoves .... 22.50 To 25.00
Collector Plate, **Haviland**, Christmas, 1972, Tapestry 35.00
Collector Plate, **Haviland**, Presidents, Abraham Lincoln 150.00
Collector Plate, **Haviland**, Presidents, Grant, 1970 .... 100.00
Collector Plate, **Haviland**, Presidents, Hayes, 1971 .... 110.00
Collector Plate, **Haviland**, Presidents, Lincoln 150.00
Collector Plate, **Haviland**, Presidents, Martha Washington .... 50.00 To 80.00
Collector Plate, **Haviland**, Presidents, Rutherford B.Hayes 110.00
Collector Plate, **Haviland**, Presidents, Ulysses S.Grant .... 110.00 To 125.00
Collector Plate, **Hummel**, Commemorative, 1971, 100th Anniversary 40.00
Collector Plate, **Hummel**, Mother's Day, 1972 .... 15.00
Collector Plate, **Hummel**, Story Book, 1972 .... 5.50
Collector Plate, **Imperial**, America, 1969, Capitol, Red Carnival, 1st Issue 20.00
Collector Plate, **Imperial**, Christmas, 1970, Blue Carnival, 1st .... 10.00 To 19.00
Collector Plate, **Imperial**, Christmas, 1970, Crystal, 1st Issue .... 18.50 To 20.00
Collector Plate, **Imperial**, Christmas, 1970, White Satin, 1st Issue 15.00
Collector Plate, **Imperial**, Christmas, 1971, Carnival Glass 12.00
Collector Plate, **Imperial**, Christmas, 1971, Crystal 16.00
Collector Plate, **Imperial**, Christmas, 1971, Two Turtledoves, Green Carnival 12.00
Collector Plate, **Imperial**, Christmas, 1971, 2nd Issue, White Satin 15.00
Collector Plate, **Imperial**, Coin, 1971, 1964 Coins, 9 In., 1st Issue 15.00
Collector Plate, **Imperial**, Coin, 1972, Crystal 15.00
Collector Plate, **Israel**, Annual, 1969, Rachael 10.00
Collector Plate, **Israel**, Annual, 1970, Galilee 7.50
Collector Plate, **Kaiser**, Anniversary, 1972, Doves In Park, 1st Issue 16.50
Collector Plate, **Kaiser**, Christmas, 1970, 1st Issue .... 20.00 To 30.00
Collector Plate, **Kaiser**, Christmas, 1971, Silent Night 13.50
Collector Plate, **Kaiser**, Great Yachts, 1972, Pair 100.00
Collector Plate, **Kaiser**, Mother's Day, 1971, Mare & Foal, 1st Issue 17.50
Collector Plate, **Kaiser**, Mother's Day, 1972 .... 10.75
Collector Plate, **Kaiser**, Toronto Horse Show, 1970 .... 16.00
Collector Plate, **Kate Greenaway**, Mother's Day, 1971, 1st Issue 14.95
Collector Plate, **Kera**, Astronaut, 1969, Wrong Date 13.00
Collector Plate, **Kera**, Christmas, 1967, Kobenhavn, 1st Issue .... 14.50 To 24.00
Collector Plate, **Kera**, Christmas, 1968, Forste .... 12.50 To 20.00
Collector Plate, **Kera**, Christmas, 1969, Andersen's House .... 10.25 To 18.00
Collector Plate, **Kera**, Christmas, 1970, Pa Langelinie 10.00
Collector Plate, **Kera**, Christmas, 1971 .... 10.00
Collector Plate, **Kera**, Father's Day, 1970, 1st Issue 10.50
Collector Plate, **Kera**, Father's Day, 1971 .... 10.00
Collector Plate, **Kera**, Mother's Day, 1970, 1st Issue 10.50
Collector Plate, **Kera**, Mother's Day, 1971 .... 10.00
Collector Plate, **Kosta**, Annual, 1971, Madonna & Child, 1st Issue .... 22.50 To 25.00
Collector Plate, **Kosta**, Christmas, 1971, Madonna 29.00
Collector Plate, **Kosta**, Christmas, 1971, 1st Issue 17.50
Collector Plate, **Kosta**, Christmas, 1971, 1st Issue, Crystal, Blue 27.50
Collector Plate, **Lalique**, Annual, 1965 .... 850.00

Collector Plate, **Lalique**, Annual, 1966 .... 225.00
Collector Plate, **Lalique**, Annual, 1967 .... 170.00 To 175.00
Collector Plate, **Lalique**, Annual, 1968 .... 75.00 To 90.00
Collector Plate, **Lalique**, Annual, 1969 .... 70.00 To 75.00
Collector Plate, **Lalique**, Annual, 1970 .... 70.00
Collector Plate, **Lalique**, Annual, 1971 .... 45.00 To 70.00
Collector Plate, **Lenox**, Boehm Bird, 1971 .... 35.00
Collector Plate, **Lenox**, Boehm, Wood Thrush, 1970 .... 95.00 To 165.00
Collector Plate, **Lenox**, Christmas, 1970, Boehm .... 49.50 To 65.00
Collector Plate, **Lenox**, Christmas, 1971, 2nd Issue 35.00
Collector Plate, **Lincoln Mint**, Annual, 1971 .... 100.00 To 135.00
Collector Plate, **Lincoln Mint**, Annual, 1972, Platinum 4000.00
Collector Plate, **Lincoln Mint**, Annual, 1972, Sterling Silver .... 100.00 To 250.00
Collector Plate, **Lincoln Mint**, Annual, 1972, 18k Gold 1000.00
Collector Plate, **Lincoln Mint**, Christmas, 1971, Dali, Sterling .... 100.00 To 200.00
Collector Plate, **Lincoln Mint**, Dali Annual, 1971, 18k Gold 1000.00
Collector Plate, **Lincoln Mint**, Easter, 1972, Dali, Gold Plated Sterling 200.00
Collector Plate, **Lincoln Mint**, Easter, 1972, Dali, Sterling Silver 150.00
Collector Plate, **Lincoln Mint**, Mother's Day, 1971, Sterling Silver 125.00
Collector Plate, **Lincoln Mint**, Mother's Day, 1972, Franzen, Silver 125.00
Collector Plate, **Lincoln Mint**, Mother's Day, 1972, Gold On Silver 150.00
Collector Plate, **Lladro**, Christmas, 1971, Navidad, 1st Issue .... 25.00 To 27.50
Collector Plate, **Lladro**, Mother's Day, 1971, 1st Issue .... 25.00 To 30.00
Collector Plate, **Llardo**, Christmas, 1971 .... 27.50
Collector Plate, **Lourioux**, Chateau 1971, Fontainebleau, 1st .... 12.00 To 16.00
Collector Plate, **Lourioux**, Chateaux Of France, 1972, Versailles 12.50
Collector Plate, **Lund & Clausen**, Apollo 13, 1971 .... 13.50
Collector Plate, **Lund & Clausen**, Astronaut, 1969 .... 13.00
Collector Plate, **Lund & Clausen**, Christmas, 1971 .... 8.50
Collector Plate, **Lund & Clausen**, Christmas, 1971, 1st Issue .... 9.50 To 13.50
Collector Plate, **Lund & Clausen**, Mother's Day, 1970, Rose, 1st Issue 15.00
Collector Plate, **Lund & Clausen**, Mother's Day, 1971 .... 11.50 To 14.50
Collector Plate, **Mabel Hesper**, Steam Engine Days, Hand-Decorated, White 5.00
Collector Plate, **Mallek**, Christmas, 1971, Navajo, 1st Issue 15.00
Collector Plate, **Marmot**, Christmas, 1970, Polar Bear, 1st Issue .... 12.50 To 18.00
Collector Plate, **Marmot**, Christmas, 1971, Buffalo .... 10.63 To 14.50
Collector Plate, **Marmot**, Father's Day, 1970, 1st Issue .... 13.75 To 20.00
Collector Plate, **Marmot**, Father's Day, 1971, 2nd Issue .... 12.50 To 16.00
Collector Plate, **Marmot**, Presidents, Washington 25.00
Collector Plate, **Marmot**, Presidents, Washington, 1st Issue 25.00
Collector Plate, **Marmot**, Presidents, Washington, 1st Issue 25.00
Collector Plate, **Marmot**, Presidents, 1971, Washington 25.00
Collector Plate, **Marnot**, Father's Day, 1970 .... 22.50
Collector Plate, **Mayflower**, 1970, 10 1/2 In. 15.00
Collector Plate, **Meakin**, Calendar, 1971, Blue, 1st Issue 2.50
Collector Plate, **Meakin**, Calendar, 1971, Brown, 1st Issue 2.50
Collector Plate, **Meakin**, Calendar, 1971, Red, 1st Issue 2.50
Collector Plate, **Meissen**, Annual, 1971, 1st Issue 50.00
Collector Plate, **Metlox**, Christmas, 1971, Partridge In Pear Tree, 1st Issue 15.00
Collector Plate, **Moser**, Annual, 1971, Crystal 100.00
Collector Plate, **Moser**, Christmas, 1970, Crystal, 1st Issue .... 450.00 To 600.00
Collector Plate, **Moser**, Christmas, 1970, 1st Issue 150.00
Collector Plate, **Moser**, Christmas, 1971, Crystal .... 75.00 To 100.00
Collector Plate, **Moser**, Mother's Day, 1971, Crystal .... 150.00 To 400.00
Collector Plate, **Mothers Day 1972**, James Franzen 150.00
Collector Plate, **Mueller**, Christmas, 1971, Tyrol, 1st Issue .... 10.00 To 13.00
Collector Plate, **Naaman**, Commemorative, 1967, Tower Of David, 1st Issue 15.00
Collector Plate, **Naaman**, Commemorative, 1967, Wailing Wall, 1st Issue 15.00
Collector Plate, **Naaman**, Commemorative, 1968, Masada 10.00
Collector Plate, **Naaman**, Commemorative, 1969, Rachel's Tomb 8.00
Collector Plate, **Naaman**, Commemorative, 1970, Tiberias 8.00
Collector Plate, **Naaman**, Commemorative, 1971, Nazareth 8.00
Collector Plate, **Navajo**, Christmas, 1971 .... 35.00 To 99.50
Collector Plate, **Nidaros**, Christmas, 1970, Cathedral, Blue, 1st Issue 12.50
Collector Plate, **Nidaros**, Christmas, 1970, Cathedral, Green, 1st Issue 12.50

Collector Plate, **Nidaros**, Christmas, 1970, Cathedral, Red, 1st Issue	12.50
Collector Plate, **Nidaros**, Christmas, 1971, Stave Church, Blue	12.50
Collector Plate, **Nidaros**, Christmas, 1971, Stave Church, Green	12.50
Collector Plate, **Nidaros**, Christmas, 1971, Stave Church, Red	12.50
Collector Plate, **Oberammergau**, Christmas, 1970, Passion Play	22.00
Collector Plate, **Orrefors**, Annual, 1970, Notre Dame, 1st Issue	45.00 To 50.00
Collector Plate, **Orrefors**, Annual, 1971, Westminster Abbey	37.50 To 50.00
Collector Plate, **Orrefors**, Mother's Day, 1971, Flowers For Mother, 1st	25.00
Collector Plate, **Palisander**, Christmas, 1971, Red Robin On Holly, 1st Issue	40.00
Collector Plate, **Peanuts**, Mother's Day.1972	10.00
Collector Plate, **Pickard**, Lockhart, 1970, Game Birds, 1st Issue, Pair	150.00
Collector Plate, **Pickard**, Lockhart, 1971, Song Birds, Pair	150.00
Collector Plate, **Pickard**, Presidential, Harry Truman, 1st Issue	35.00
Collector Plate, **Porcelana Granada**, Annual, 1971	12.00
Collector Plate, **Porcelana Granada**, Christmas, 1971, Annunciation, 1st	12.00
Collector Plate, **Porsgrund**, Castle, 1970, Hamlet's, 1st Issue	6.50
Collector Plate, **Porsgrund**, Castle, 1971, Rosenborg Slot	6.00
Collector Plate, **Porsgrund**, Christmas, 1968, Church, 1st Issue	37.50 To 50.00
Collector Plate, **Porsgrund**, Christmas, 1969	9.00 To 10.00
Collector Plate, **Porsgrund**, Christmas, 1969, Three Kings	11.00
Collector Plate, **Porsgrund**, Christmas, 1970, Road To Bethlehem, Deluxe, 1st	35.00
Collector Plate, **Porsgrund**, Christmas, 1970, 3rd Issue	6.25 To 12.00
Collector Plate, **Porsgrund**, Christmas, 1971, A Child Is Born	8.00 To 12.00
Collector Plate, **Porsgrund**, Christmas, 1971, A Child Is Born, Deluxe	35.00
Collector Plate, **Porsgrund**, Father's Day, 1970, Father & Son Fishing, 1st	7.50
Collector Plate, **Porsgrund**, Father's Day, 1971, 1st Issue	5.00 To 7.50
Collector Plate, **Porsgrund**, Father's Day, 1972	7.50
Collector Plate, **Porsgrund**, Jubilee, 1970, Femboringer, 1st Issue	14.00 To 20.00
Collector Plate, **Porsgrund**, Mother's Day, 1970, 1st Issue	12.00 To 17.00
Collector Plate, **Porsgrund.Mother's Day**, 1971	7.00
Collector Plate, **Porsgrund**, Mother's Day, 1971, Boy & Geese	6.50 To 7.50
Collector Plate, **Porsgrund**, Mother's Day, 1972	7.50
Collector Plate, **Portmeirion**, Mother's Day, 1971, 1st Issue	7.00 To 10.00
Collector Plate, **Reed & Barton**, Audubon, 1970, 1st Issue	70.00 To 75.00
Collector Plate, **Reed & Barton**, Audubon, 1971	55.00 To 60.00
Collector Plate, **Reed & Barton**, Christmas, 1970, 1st Issue	100.00 To 125.00
Collector Plate, **Rorstrand**, Christmas, 1968, 1st Issue	85.00 To 100.00
Collector Plate, **Rorstrand**, Christmas, 1969, Vaggtallrik Jul	12.00 To 18.00
Collector Plate, **Rorstrand**, Christmas, 1970, Nils With His Gees	11.00 To 14.50
Collector Plate, **Rorstrand**, Christmas, 1971, Nils In Lapland	10.00 To 15.00
Collector Plate, **Rorstrand**, Father's Day, 1971, 1st Issue	8.50 To 13.50
Collector Plate, **Rorstrand**, Mother's Day, 1971, 1st Issue	8.50 To 14.00
Collector Plate, **Rosenthal**, Christmas, 1910	45.00
Collector Plate, **Rosenthal**, Christmas, 1911	45.00
Collector Plate, **Rosenthal**, Christmas, 1912	45.00
Collector Plate, **Rosenthal**, Christmas, 1913	45.00
Collector Plate, **Rosenthal**, Christmas, 1914	45.00
Collector Plate, **Rosenthal**, Christmas, 1915	45.
Collector Plate, **Rosenthal**, Christmas, 1916	45.
Collector Plate, **Rosenthal**, Christmas, 1917	45.00
Collector Plate, **Rosenthal**, Christmas, 1918	45.00
Collector Plate, **Rosenthal**, Christmas, 1919	45.00
Collector Plate, **Rosenthal**, Christmas, 1920	45.00
Collector Plate, **Rosenthal**, Christmas, 1921	45.00
Collector Plate, **Rosenthal**, Christmas, 1922	45.00
Collector Plate, **Rosenthal**, Christmas, 1923	45.00
Collector Plate, **Rosenthal**, Christmas, 1924	45.00
Collector Plate, **Rosenthal**, Christmas, 1925	45.00
Collector Plate, **Rosenthal**, Christmas, 1926	45.00
Collector Plate, **Rosenthal**, Christmas, 1927	45.00
Collector Plate, **Rosenthal**, Christmas, 1928	45.00
Collector Plate, **Rosenthal**, Christmas, 1929	45.00
Collector Plate, **Rosenthal**, Christmas, 1930	45.00
Collector Plate, **Rosenthal**, Christmas, 1931	45.00
Collector Plate, **Rosenthal**, Christmas, 1932	45.00
Collector Plate, **Rosenthal**, Christmas, 1933	45.00

Collector Plate, Rosenthal, Christmas, 1934	45.00
Collector Plate, Rosenthal, Christmas, 1935	45.00
Collector Plate, Rosenthal, Christmas, 1936	45.00
Collector Plate, Rosenthal, Christmas, 1937	45.00
Collector Plate, Rosenthal, Christmas, 1938	45.00
Collector Plate, Rosenthal, Christmas, 1939	45.00
Collector Plate, Rosenthal, Christmas, 1940	45.00
Collector Plate, Rosenthal, Christmas, 1941	45.00
Collector Plate, Rosenthal, Christmas, 1942	45.00
Collector Plate, Rosenthal, Christmas, 1943	45.00
Collector Plate, Rosenthal, Christmas, 1944	45.00
Collector Plate, Rosenthal, Christmas, 1945	45.00
Collector Plate, Rosenthal, Christmas, 1946	45.00
Collector Plate, Rosenthal, Christmas, 1947	45.00
Collector Plate, Rosenthal, Christmas, 1948	45.00
Collector Plate, Rosenthal, Christmas, 1949	45.00
Collector Plate, Rosenthal, Christmas, 1950	45.00
Collector Plate, Rosenthal, Christmas, 1951	45.00
Collector Plate, Rosenthal, Christmas, 1952	45.00
Collector Plate, Rosenthal, Christmas, 1953	45.00
Collector Plate, Rosenthal, Christmas, 1954	45.00
Collector Plate, Rosenthal, Christmas, 1955	45.00
Collector Plate, Rosenthal, Christmas, 1956	45.00
Collector Plate, Rosenthal, Christmas, 1957	45.00
Collector Plate, Rosenthal, Christmas, 1958	45.00
Collector Plate, Rosenthal, Christmas, 1959	45.00
Collector Plate, Rosenthal, Christmas, 1960	45.00
Collector Plate, Rosenthal, Christmas, 1961	45.00
Collector Plate, Rosenthal, Christmas, 1962	45.00
Collector Plate, Rosenthal, Christmas, 1963	45.00
Collector Plate, Rosenthal, Christmas, 1964	45.00
Collector Plate, Rosenthal, Christmas, 1965	45.00
Collector Plate, Rosenthal, Christmas, 1966	45.00
Collector Plate, Rosenthal, Christmas, 1967	45.00
Collector Plate, Rosenthal, Christmas, 1968	45.00
Collector Plate, Rosenthal, Christmas, 1969	45.00
Collector Plate, Rosenthal, Christmas, 1970	45.00 To 48.00
Collector Plate, Rosenthal, Christmas, 1971	35.00 To 42.00
Collector Plate, Roskilde, Danish Church, 1968, Roskilde Cathedral, 1st	15.00
Collector Plate, Roskilde, Danish Church, 1969, Ribe	7.50 To 11.00
Collector Plate, Roskilde, Danish Church, 1970, Marmorkirken	10.00
Collector Plate, Roskilde, Danish Church, 1971, Ejby Church	12.00
Collector Plate, Royal Copenhagen, Christmas, 1909	90.00
Collector Plate, Royal Copenhagen, Christmas, 1910	85.00 To 90.00
Collector Plate, Royal Copenhagen, Christmas, 1911	110.00
Collector Plate, Royal Copenhagen, Christmas, 1912	110.00
Collector Plate, Royal Copenhagen, Christmas, 1913	105.00
Collector Plate, Royal Copenhagen, Christmas, 1914	90.00
Collector Plate, Royal Copenhagen, Christmas, 1915	75.00 To 90.00
Collector Plate, Royal Copenhagen, Christmas, 1916	60.00
Collector Plate, Royal Copenhagen, Christmas, 1917	57.50
Collector Plate, Royal Copenhagen, Christmas, 1918	57.50 To 82.50
Collector Plate, Royal Copenhagen, Christmas, 1919	57.50
Collector Plate, Royal Copenhagen, Christmas, 1920	60.00
Collector Plate, Royal Copenhagen, Christmas, 1921	50.00
Collector Plate, Royal Copenhagen, Christmas, 1922	50.00
Collector Plate, Royal Copenhagen, Christmas, 1923	50.00
Collector Plate, Royal Copenhagen, Christmas, 1924	55.00
Collector Plate, Royal Copenhagen, Christmas, 1925	50.00
Collector Plate, Royal Copenhagen, Christmas, 1926	50.00
Collector Plate, Royal Copenhagen, Christmas, 1927	70.00
Collector Plate, Royal Copenhagen, Christmas, 1928	55.00
Collector Plate, Royal Copenhagen, Christmas, 1929	50.00 To 60.00
Collector Plate, Royal Copenhagen, Christmas, 1930	60.00
Collector Plate, Royal Copenhagen, Christmas, 1931	60.00
Collector Plate, Royal Copenhagen, Christmas, 1932	60.00

Collector Plate, Royal Copenhagen, Christmas, 1933 .... 80.00
Collector Plate, Royal Copenhagen, Christmas, 1934 .... 80.00
Collector Plate, Royal Copenhagen, Christmas, 1935 .... 85.00
Collector Plate, Royal Copenhagen, Christmas, 1936 .... 90.00
Collector Plate, Royal Copenhagen, Christmas, 1937 .... 110.00
Collector Plate, Royal Copenhagen, Christmas, 1938 .... 200.00
Collector Plate, Royal Copenhagen, Christmas, 1939 .... 200.00
Collector Plate, Royal Copenhagen, Christmas, 1940 .... 300.00
Collector Plate, Royal Copenhagen, Christmas, 1941 .... 220.00
Collector Plate, Royal Copenhagen, Christmas, 1942 .... 275.00
Collector Plate, Royal Copenhagen, Christmas, 1943 .... 350.00
Collector Plate, Royal Copenhagen, Christmas, 1944 .... 115.00
Collector Plate, Royal Copenhagen, Christmas, 1945 .... 245.00
Collector Plate, Royal Copenhagen, Christmas, 1946 .... 90.00
Collector Plate, Royal Copenhagen, Christmas, 1947 .... 127.50
Collector Plate, Royal Copenhagen, Christmas, 1948 .... 85.00
Collector Plate, Royal Copenhagen, Christmas, 1949 .... 89.50
Collector Plate, Royal Copenhagen, Christmas, 1950 .... 95.00
Collector Plate, Royal Copenhagen, Christmas, 1951 .... 220.00
Collector Plate, Royal Copenhagen, Christmas, 1952 .... 70.00
Collector Plate, Royal Copenhagen, Christmas, 1953 .... 70.00
Collector Plate, Royal Copenhagen, Christmas, 1954 .... 89.50
Collector Plate, Royal Copenhagen, Christmas, 1955 .... 140.00
Collector Plate, Royal Copenhagen, Christmas, 1956 .... 95.00
Collector Plate, Royal Copenhagen, Christmas, 1957 .... 72.50
Collector Plate, Royal Copenhagen, Christmas, 1958 .... 80.00
Collector Plate, Royal Copenhagen, Christmas, 1959 ....75.00 To 100.00
Collector Plate, Royal Copenhagen, Christmas, 1960 .... 80.00
Collector Plate, Royal Copenhagen, Christmas, 1961 .... 80.00
Collector Plate, Royal Copenhagen, Christmas, 1962 ....35.00 To 110.00
Collector Plate, Royal Copenhagen, Christmas, 1963 .... 35.00 To 45.00
Collector Plate, Royal Copenhagen, Christmas, 1964 .... 28.00 To 45.00
Collector Plate, Royal Copenhagen, Christmas, 1965 .... 25.00 To 42.50
Collector Plate, Royal Copenhagen, Christmas, 1966 .... 25.00 To 36.00
Collector Plate, Royal Copenhagen, Christmas, 1967 .... 24.00 To 27.00
Collector Plate, Royal Copenhagen, Christmas, 1968 .... 18.00 To 24.00
Collector Plate, Royal Copenhagen, Christmas, 1969 .... 15.00 To 21.00
Collector Plate, Royal Copenhagen, Christmas, 1970 .... 11.00 To 16.00
Collector Plate, Royal Copenhagen, Christmas, 1971 .... 9.75
Collector Plate, Royal Copenhagen, Moon Landing, 1969 .... 15.00 To 16.00
Collector Plate, Royal Copenhagen, Mother's Day, 1971, 1st Issue ....59.00 To 100.00
Collector Plate, Royal Crystal, Annual, 1971 .... 200.00
Collector Plate, Royal Delft, Christmas, 1968, Schreierstoren, 10 In. 60.00
Collector Plate, Royal Delft, Christmas, 1968, Walmolen Mill Schiedam, 7 In. 35.00
Collector Plate, Royal Delft, Christmas, 1969, Church In Dordrecht, 10 In. 60.00
Collector Plate, Royal Delft, Christmas, 1969, Mill Near Gorkum .... 20.00 To 35.00
Collector Plate, Royal Delft, Christmas, 1970, Cathedral In Veere, 10 In. 60.00
Collector Plate, Royal Delft, Christmas, 1970, Mill Near Haarlem, 7 In. 35.00
Collector Plate, Royal Delft, Christmas, 1971, Canal In Utrecht, 10 In. 60.00
Collector Plate, Royal Delft, Christmas, 1971, Towngate Of Zierkee, 7 In. 35.00
Collector Plate, Royal Delft, Mother's Day, 1971, Volendam, 1st Issue 40.00
Collector Plate, Royal Rockwood, Christmas, 1970 .... 15.00 To 45.00
Collector Plate, Royal Rockwood, Christmas, 1971 .... 8.00 To 20.00
Collector Plate, Royal Rockwood, Father's Day, 1970, 1st Issue .... 15.00 To 35.00
Collector Plate, Royal Rockwood, Father's Day, 1971 .... 10.00 To 30.00
Collector Plate, Royale, Annual, 1970, Crystal, 1st Issue .... 450.00 To 575.00
Collector Plate, Royale, Annual, 1971, Crystal 200.00
Collector Plate, Royale, Astronaut, Landing On The Moon .... 65.00 To 75.00
Collector Plate, Royale, Christmas, 1969, 1st Issue .... 55.00 To 90.00
Collector Plate, Royale, Christmas, 1970 .... 8.50 To 40.00
Collector Plate, Royale, Christmas, 1971 .... 9.50 To 11.00
Collector Plate, Royale, Father's Day, 1970 .... 14.50 To 36.00
Collector Plate, Royale, Father's Day, 1971 .... 9.50 To 13.00
Collector Plate, Royale, Mother's Day, 1970 .... 25.00 To 65.00
Collector Plate, Royale, Mother's Day, 1971 .... 9.50 To 19.00
Collector Plate, Royale, Mother's Day, 1971, Crystal .... 350.00 To 400.00

Collector Plate, **Royale**, Mother's Day, 1972 .... 15.00
Collector Plate, **Sabino**, Annual, 1970, 1st Issue 65.00
Collector Plate, **Santa Clara**, Christmas, 1970, 1st Issue .... 10.00 To 15.00
Collector Plate, **Santa Clara**, Christmas, 1971, Three Wise Men .... 12.00 To 15.00
Collector Plate, **Santa Clara**, Mother's Day, 1970 .... 10.00
Collector Plate, **Santa Clara**, Mother's Day, 1971 .... 10.00 To 12.00
Collector Plate, **Schumann**, Christmas, 1971, Snow Scene, 1st Issue .... 12.00 To 13.00
Collector Plate, **Schumann**, Composers, 1970, Beethoven, 1st Issue .... 10.00 To 12.50
Collector Plate, **Schumann**, Composers, 1971, Mozart 16.00
Collector Plate, **Sebring Heritage**, Easter, 1971 .... 14.50
Collector Plate, **Sebring Heritage**, Father's Day, 1971 .... 13.00
Collector Plate, **Sebring Heritage**, Fourth Of July, 1971 .... 14.50
Collector Plate, **Sebring Heritage**, Mother's Day, 1971 .... 9.00 To 13.00
Collector Plate, **Seven Seas**, Astronaut, 1969 .... 15.00
Collector Plate, **Seven Seas**, Christmas, 1971, Tannenbaum 14.50
Collector Plate, **Seven Seas**, Moon, 1969, Flag 15.00
Collector Plate, **Seven Seas**, Moon, 1969, No Flag 33.00
Collector Plate, **Seven Seas**, Mother's Day, 1970, 1st Issue .... 15.00 To 18.00
Collector Plate, **Seven Seas**, Mother's Day, 1971, Scandinavian Girl 14.50
Collector Plate, **Seven Seas**, New World, 1971 .... 14.50
Collector Plate, **Silver City**, Christmas, 1969, Winter Scene, 1st Issue 20.00
Collector Plate, **Silver City**, Christmas, 1970, Water Mill 17.50
Collector Plate, **Silver City**, Christmas, 1971, Skating Scene 17.50
Collector Plate, **Smith Glass**, Christmas, 1971 .... 10.00
Collector Plate, **Smith Glass**, Coin, 1971 .... 10.00 To 12.00
Collector Plate, **Smith Glass**, Kennedy, 1971 .... 15.00 To 20.00
Collector Plate, **Smith Glass**, Lincoln, 1971 .... 12.00 To 20.00
Collector Plate, **Smith**, Mayflower, 1971, Pewter, 1st Issue 30.00
Collector Plate, **Spode**, Annual, 1970, Beaton 30.00
Collector Plate, **Spode**, Annual, 1970, Partridge 22.50
Collector Plate, **Spode**, Annual, 1971 .... 25.00
Collector Plate, **Spode**, Christmas, 1970, Partridge, 1st Issue .... 18.50 To 35.00
Collector Plate, **Spode**, Churchill 110.00
Collector Plate, **Spode**, Dickens .... 60.00 To 70.00
Collector Plate, **St.Amand**, Annual, 1970, 1st Issue .... 8.50 To 15.00
Collector Plate, **St.Amand**, Annual, 1971 .... 6.00 To 7.50
Collector Plate, **Stumar**, Christmas, 1970, Angel, 1st Issue .... 7.50 To 10.00
Collector Plate, **Stumar**, Christmas, 1971, 2nd Issue .... 7.50 To 8.00
Collector Plate, **Stumar**, Mother's Day, 1971, Amish Mother & Daughter, 1st 7.95
Collector Plate, **Svend Jensen**, Christmas, 1970, 1st Issue .... 11.75 To 16.00
Collector Plate, **Svend Jensen**, Christmas, 1971 .... 12.50 To 15.00
Collector Plate, **Svend Jensen**, Father's Day, 1971, 1st Issue 11.50
Collector Plate, **Svend Jensen**, Father's Day, 1972, Father's Joy, 1st 15.00
Collector Plate, **Svend Jensen**, Mother's Day, 1970, 1st Issue .... 8.50 To 15.50
Collector Plate, **Svend Jensen**, Mother's Day, 1971, Mother's Love .... 10.00 To 15.00
Collector Plate, **Tirschenreuth**, Christmas, 1969, 1st Issue .... 20.00 To 22.00
Collector Plate, **Tirschenreuth**, Christmas, 1970, 2nd Issue .... 13.00 To 14.00
Collector Plate, **Tirschenreuth**, Christmas, 1971, Star Of Bethlehem 12.00
Collector Plate, **Ulmer Keramik**, Christmas, 1971, 1st Issue 15.00
Collector Plate, **Val St.Lambert**, Artist, 1968, 1st Issue, Pair .... 65.00 To 75.00
Collector Plate, **Val St.Lambert**, Artist, 1969, Van Gogh, Vandyke, Pair 50.00
Collector Plate, **Val St.Lambert**, Artist, 1970, Da Vinci, Michelangelo, Pair 50.00
Collector Plate, **Val St.Lambert**, Artist, 1971, Pair .... 45.00 To 50.00
Collector Plate, **Val St.Lambert**, Thanksgiving, 1970, Pilgrim .... 25.00 To 30.00
Collector Plate, **Veneto Flair**, Christmas, 1970, Madonna & Child, 1st Issue 60.00
Collector Plate, **Veneto Flair**, Christmas, 1971, 3 Kings 45.00
Collector Plate, **Veneto Flair**, Deer 45.00
Collector Plate, **Veneto Flair**, Elephant, 1971 .... 35.00 To 45.00
Collector Plate, **Veneto Flair**, Mother's Day, 1971 .... 60.00
Collector Plate, **Veneto Flair**, Mother's Day, 1972, Mother & Child, 1st Issue 45.00
Collector Plate, **Veneto Flair**, Owl, 1972 .... 37.50
Collector Plate, **Veneto Flair**, Van Gogh, 1971, Night Cafe 11.00
Collector Plate, **Veneto Flair**, Wildlife, 1971, Stag, 1st Issue 35.00
Collector Plate, **Veneto Flair**, Windlife, 1971, Elephant 35.00
Collector Plate, **Washington Mint**, Annual, 1972, 4th Of July, Wyeth, Sterling 150.00
Collector Plate, **Washington Mint**, Mother's Day, 1972, Whistler's Mother 150.00

Collector Plate, Wedgwood, Apollo, 1969 .... 12.50 To 21.00
Collector Plate, Wedgwood, Apollo, 1970 .... 20.00 To 21.75
Collector Plate, Wedgwood, Calendar, 1971 .... 10.00 To 12.50
Collector Plate, Wedgwood, Calendar, 1972 ....   12.50
Collector Plate, Wedgwood, Child's Day, 1971, 1st Issue .... 7.50 To 14.50
Collector Plate, Wedgwood, Christmas, 1969, 1st Issue .... 62.00 To 82.50
Collector Plate, Wedgwood, Christmas, 1970, 2nd Issue .... 12.50 To 22.50
Collector Plate, Wedgwood, Christmas, 1971, Picadilly Circus .... 24.50 To 30.00
Collector Plate, Wedgwood, Mother's Day, 1971, 1st Issue .... 12.50 To 20.00
Collector Plate, Wendell August, Columbus, 1971 ....   30.00
Collector Plate, Wendell August, Kennedy, 1971 ....   30.00
Collector Rabbit, Royale, Easter, 1972 ....   20.00
Collector Spoon, Blue Delft, Christmas, 1970, Drawbridge Near Binnenhof, 1st 7.00
Collector Spoon, Blue Delft, Christmas, 1971, German, Boy With Trumpet 6.00
Collector Spoon, Blue Delft, Father's Day, 1971, Lana's Air-Ship, 1st Issue 6.00
Collector Spoon, Blue Delft, Mother's Day, 1972, Isle Of Urk, Mother, Child 6.00
Collector Spoon, Crown Delft, Christmas, 1970, 1st Issue 2.00
Collector Spoon, Crown Delft, Christmas, 1971 ....   2.00
Collector Spoon, Meka, Mother's Day, 1970, 1st Issue 10.00
Collector Spoon, Meka, Mother's Day, 1971 ....   10.00
Collector Spoon, Michelsen, Christmas, 1940 ....   38.00
Collector Spoon, Michelsen, Christmas, 1941 ....   39.00
Collector Spoon, Michelsen, Christmas, 1942 ....   38.00
Collector Spoon, Michelsen, Christmas, 1943 ....   38.00
Collector Spoon, Michelsen, Christmas, 1944 ....   38.00
Collector Spoon, Michelsen, Christmas, 1945 ....   38.00
Collector Spoon, Michelsen, Christmas, 1946 ....   38.00
Collector Spoon, Michelsen, Christmas, 1947 ....   38.00
Collector Spoon, Michelsen, Christmas, 1948 ....   38.00
Collector Spoon, Michelsen, Christmas, 1949 ....   38.00
Collector Spoon, Michelsen, Christmas, 1950 ....   32.00
Collector Spoon, Michelsen, Christmas, 1951 ....   32.00
Collector Spoon, Michelsen, Christmas, 1952 ....   32.00
Collector Spoon, Michelsen, Christmas, 1953 ....   32.00
Collector Spoon, Michelsen, Christmas, 1954 ....   32.00
Collector Spoon, Michelsen, Christmas, 1955 ....   32.00
Collector Spoon, Michelsen, Christmas, 1956 ....   32.00
Collector Spoon, Michelsen, Christmas, 1957 ....   32.00
Collector Spoon, Michelsen, Christmas, 1958 ....   32.00
Collector Spoon, Michelsen, Christmas, 1959 ....   32.00
Collector Spoon, Michelsen, Christmas, 1971, Sterling, Gold-Plated, Enamel 24.00
Collector Spoon, Michelsen, Commemorative, 1960 ....   30.00
Collector Spoon, Michelsen, Commemorative, 1961 ....   30.00
Collector Spoon, Michelsen, Commemorative, 1962 ....   30.00
Collector Spoon, Michelsen, Commemorative, 1963 ....   30.00
Collector Spoon, Michelsen, Commemorative, 1964 ....   30.00
Collector Spoon, Michelsen, Commemorative, 1965 ....   30.00
Collector Spoon, Michelsen, Commemorative, 1966 ....   30.00
Collector Spoon, Michelsen, Commemorative, 1967 ....   30.00
Collector Spoon, Michelsen, Commemorative, 1968 ....   30.00
Collector Spoon, Michelsen, Commemorative, 1969 ....   30.00
Collector Spoon, Michelsen, Commemorative, 1970 ....   30.00
Collector Spoon, Michelsen, Commemorative, 1971 ....   26.00
Collector Tankard, Stromberg, Christmas, 1970 ....   50.00
Collector Tankard, Stromberg, Christmas, 1971 ....   20.00
Collector Tile, Blue Delft, Christmas, 1967, Winter Scene, 1st Issue 35.00
Collector Tile, Blue Delft, Christmas, 1968, Admiring The Tree .... 12.00 To 15.00
Collector Tile, Blue Delft, Christmas, 1969, Windmill .... 8.00 To 10.00
Collector Tile, Blue Delft, Christmas, 1970, Drawbridge Near Binnenhof 6.00
Collector Tile, Blue Delft, Christmas, 1971, St.Laurens Chruch 4.50
Collector Tile, Crown Delft, Christmas, 1969, Man By Fire, 1st Issue 7.50
Collector Tile, Crown Delft, Christmas, 1970, Sleigh & 2 Riders 4.25
Collector Tile, Crown Delft, Christmas, 1971, Tree On Market Square 4.25
Collector Tile, Crown Delft, Father's Day, 1970, Ship, 1st Issue 4.25
Collector Tile, Crown Delft, Mother's Day, 1970, Sheep, 1st Issue 4.25
Collector Tile, Crown Delft, Mother's Day, 1971, Storks 4.25

Commemoration items have been made to honor members of royalty and those of great national fame. World's Fairs and important historical events are also remembered with commemoration pieces.

Commemoration, see also Coronation

Commemoration, Beaker, George V, Jubilee	12.50
Commemoration, Beaker, George V, 4 1/2 In.	10.00
Commemoration, Cup & Saucer, Elizabeth Ii	9.00
Commemoration, Jar, King George, Queen Mary, 1910-1935, Crown Shape Lid	34.00
Commemoration, Match Safe, Pocket, Queen Victoria 1837-1887, Advertising	14.50
Commemoration, Medal, Mine Workers, 1898, 8 Hour Day	7.00
Commemoration, Mug, George VI, 3 1/2 In.	9.00
Commemoration, Mug, George Washington, Centennial, 1776-1876, W.T.Copeland	25.00
Commemoration, Mug, King Edward VII, Queen Alexandra, 1902, Royal Doulton	32.50
Commemoration, Mug, U.S.Maine, Blown Up In Havana Harbor, Feb.15, 1898	22.00
Commemoration, Pitcher, Dewey & Flagship, Eagle Spout, Black Transfer, 4 In.	32.00
Commemoration, Plate, Admiral George Dewey, Stars, Picture, Milk Glass	18.00
Commemoration, Plate, Elizabeth II, 1954, Australia Visit, Pottery, Blue	17.50
Commemoration, Plate, French, English, Russian Flags, Gloire Aux Allies 1914	10.00
Commemoration, Plate, Mckinley, Clear Glass, Oval	17.00
Commemoration, Plate, Patrick Henry Addressing Virginia Assembly	16.00
Commemoration, Plate, Queen Victoria, Glass, 9 In., Pair	20.00
Commemoration, Plate, 'remember The Maine, 'eagle's Talons Clutch Flags	25.00
Commemoration, Plate, Roosevelt & Churchill, England, 9 In.Diameter, Pair	28.00
Commemoration, Plate, Star Spangled Banner, 1814-1914, Flag, Portrait, Tin	34.00
Commemoration, Plate, Ulysses Grant, Star, Beaded Decor, 9 1/2 In.Square	35.00
Commemoration, Platter, Liberty Bell	34.00
Commemoration, Platter, Three Presidents, 'in Remembrance'	32.00

W.T.Copeland & Sons, Ltd., ran the Spode Works in Staffordshire, England, from 1847 to the present. Copeland & Garrett was the firm name from 1833 to 1847.

Copeland, see also Spode

Copeland Spode, Bowl, Hand-Painted Pheasants In A Tree, 5 1/2 In., Set Of 4	10.00
Copeland Spode, Creamer, Blue Oriental Decoration	20.00
Copeland Spode, Cup & Saucer, Demitasse, Gray, Purple Decor, Circa 1943	4.00
Copeland Spode, Pitcher, Milk, Hunters, Horses, Dogs, Brown Ground, Circa 1891	38.00
Copeland Spode, Plate, Dessert, Blue, Tower, England, Set Of 6	25.00
Copeland Spode, Plate, Dessert, Japanese Pattern, C.1870, Cobalt, Orange, 6	40.00
Copeland Spode, Saucer, Japanese Pattern, C.1870, Cobalt, Orange, Gold	3.00
Copeland Spode, Sugar, Japanese Pattern, C.1870, Cobalt, Orange, Gold, Open	15.00
Copeland Spode, Vase, Transfer, Italian Series, Handles, Staffordshire, Pair	95.00
Copeland, Bust, Young Woman, Music, Parian, Signed, Dated 1874	125.00
Copeland, Cake Set, Shamrock Pattern, 9 In.Plate, 6 Servers, Marked	35.00
Copeland, Creamer, Blue, Italian, Marked	16.00
Copeland, Creamer, Figural, Oriental Man, Sitting, White	20.00
Copeland, Cup & Saucer, Flowers, Scrolls, Coin Gold	39.50
Copeland, Dish, Botanical, Oval, Green, White, C.1833, Copeland & Garrett, Pair	100.00
Copeland, Dish, Cheese, Cover, Agateware, Brown, Ocher, White, & Blue, C.1833	225.00
Copeland, Gravy Boat, Blue & White Border, Red Roses, 1847 Mark	17.50
Copeland, Jug, Parian, Morning Glory, Twisted Limb Handle, 1846, 8 1/2 In.	60.00
Copeland, Pitcher, Hunting Scene, Green, Twig Handle, 4 1/4 In.High	18.00
Copeland, Pitcher, Roses, Pink, England, 2 1/4 In.Tall	5.00
Copeland, Plate, Birds, Flowers, Blue, Green, Red, Yellow, Signed, Set Of 12	125.00
Copeland, Plate, Soup, White With Gold Rope Edge, 8 In.Diameter, 12	60.00
Copeland, Platter, Bird On Branch, Floral Border, 10 X 14 In.	10.00
Copeland, Platter, Flowers, Beaded Edge, Rectangular, Yellow, Red, 11 X 21 In.	55.00
Copeland, Platter, Indian Tree, 17 X 13 In.	25.00
Copenhagen, Plaque, Oval, Watteau Figural Scenes, C.1780, Pair	175.00
Copenhagen, Sauceboat, Leaf Shape, Named Botanical Flower, C.1775	150.00
Copper, Bed Warmer, Brass Cap	9.00
Copper, Bed Warmer, Brass Stopper, 8 1/2 In.Diameter	20.00
Copper, Bed Warmer, Pan, Engraved	50.00
Copper, Bed Warmer, Wooden Handle	49.50
Copper, Boiler, Cover	12.50
Copper, Bowl, Flared, 8 3/4 In.Diameter, 2 1/4 In.High	7.50
Copper, Box, Stamp, Art Nouveau Design, Hinged, Two Compartments	12.00

Copper, Candlestick, Queen Anne, 8 1/2 In.High, Pair	110.00
Copper, Desk Set, Hand Hammered, Five Piece	140.00
Copper, Ewer, Engraved, China, 7 1/2 In.High	12.00
Copper, Flask, Powder, Embossed Shell, 7 1/2 In.Tall	27.00
Copper, Holder, Letter, Indian & Quill Pens, Victorian	15.00
Copper, Incense Burner, Three Brass Cherubs' Heads, Brass Flame Finial	65.00
Copper, Jardiniere, Footed, 7 1/2 In.Deep, 9 In.Diameter	12.50
Copper, Kettle, Apple Butter, 12 In.Deep, 18 In.Diameter, Wooden Stirrer	87.50
Copper, Kettle, Candy Making, Round Bottom Iron Handles, 15 1/2 In.Diameter	65.00
Copper, Kettle, Cooking, Handmade, Dovetailed Tin Liner, Iron Handle	65.00
Copper, Kettle, Embossed, Marked Made In China, Round, 8 In.Tall	30.00
Copper, Kettle, Handle Turned Upright, 10 In.Diameter	25.00
Copper, Kettle, On Burner Stand	10.00
Copper, Kettle, Round, Straight Sided, Iron Handles, 12 In.Deep, 14 In.	
Copper, Kettle, Signed I.Witman, 6 In.Diameter	850.00
Copper, Kettle, Three Iron Feet, 10 1/2 In.Diameter	22.50
Copper, Kettle, 10 1/2 In.High, 5 3/4 In.Diameter	50.00
Copper, Kettle, 2 Brass Ring Handles, 6 In.Diameter, 5 In.Deep	12.00
Copper, Kovsh, Russian, Enamel Designs, R Shaped Handle, 19th Century	1200.00
Copper, Mold, Bunch Of Flowers, 7 1/4 In.Diameter	32.50
Copper, Mold, Bunch Of Grapes, 10 In.Diameter	42.50
Copper, Mold, Cheese, Removable Rim, 15 In.Diameter	22.00
Copper, Mold, Fluted Sides, 8 In.	22.50
Copper, Mold, Marked Kreamer, Oval, Fruits, Brass Hanging Ring	13.50
Copper, Mold, Marked Kreamer, Round, Ladyfinger Edge, Brass Hanging Ring	13.50
Copper, Mold, Ring, 6 1/2 In.Diameter	22.50
Copper, Mold, Squirrel Eating Nut, 8 1/2 In.Diameter	35.00
Copper, Mug, Two Handles, 5 1/2 In.High	12.50
Copper, Owl, American, C.1850, 45 In.High	375.00
Copper, Pan, Warming, Pierced Edge, Engraved Strutting Cock, Turned Handle	75.00
Copper, Pitcher, Marked W.S., Hollow Riveted Handle, 6 3/4 In.Tall	25.00
Copper, Pitcher, Water, Handmade, 7 5/8 In.	20.00
Copper, Pull, Hammered, 2 X 3 In.Plates, 8	15.00
Copper, Salt & Pepper, Pierced Rim, Tray, 12 In.	13.50
Copper, Scuttle, Coal, Helmet Shape, Opalescent Milk Glass Handles	60.00
Copper, Skillet, Brass Handle, Tin Lined, 9 In. Diameter	14.50
Copper, Skillet, 8 1/2 In.Diameter	15.00
Copper, Stomach Warmer, Wooden Handle, 40 In., 11 In. Diameter	39.50
Copper, Stomach Warmer, 16 In.Handle, 9 In.Diameter	24.50
Copper, Strainer, Iron Feet & Handle, 8 In. Deep, 8 In.Diameter	17.50
Copper, Teakettle, Brass Handle, Large	27.50
Copper, Teakettle, Brass Lid, Pewter Spout, Handle & Finial	27.50
Copper, Teakettle, Brass Reliefs & Handle, Frame, Alcohol Burner	145.00
Copper, Teakettle, Burnished, 7 In.Diameter, 6 In.High	32.50
Copper, Teakettle, Dovetailed, Signed P.Blada, Handle, Gooseneck	250.00
Copper, Teakettle, Goose Necked	39.50
Copper, Teakettle, Norwegian, Signed	50.00
Copper, Teakettle, On Frame, Porcelain Handles, 15 In.High	50.00
Copper, Teakettle, On Standard, English, 19th Century	50.00
Copper, Teakettle, Strap Handle, 12 In.Diameter	27.50
Copper, Teakettle, Wooden Handle & Finial, Stand With Spirit Warmer, 1892	22.00
Copper, Teapot, 1 1/2 Quart	23.00
Copper, Thermometer, Candy Maker's, Brass Gauge Plate, 12 In.Long	12.50
Copper, Thermometer, Dairy, 12 In.High	7.00
Copper, Tray & Brush, Crumb, Elephant Decor, Marked Germany	18.00
Copper, Tray, Oval, Hammered, Raised Handles, Marked R In Circle	28.00
Copper, Tray, Round, 12 In.Diameter	5.00
Copper, Tray, Wood Handles, 14 In.	15.00
Copper, Urn, Coffee, Pedestal Base, Ball Feet, Tin Lined, England, 20 In.Tall	95.00
Copper, Wash Boiler	6.50
Copper, Wine Taster, South African, Twin Handles, 5 In.Tall	50.00

*Coralene Glass was made by firing many small colored beads on the outside
of glassware. It was made in many patterns in the United States and
Europe in the 1880s. Reproductions are made today.*

Coralene, Bowl, Rose, 6 In.Wide, 5 1/2 In.High	275.00

Coralene, Tumbler	350.00
Coralene, Vase, Blue Ground, Beaded Pussy Willows, Dated 1909, Japan	48.00
Coralene, Vase, Celery, Mother-Of-Pearl, Red To Pink, Yellow Branches	450.00
Coralene, Vase, White Diamond-Quilted Mother-Of-Pearl, Yellow Flowerettes	225.00

Coronation Cups have been made since the 1800s. Pieces of pottery or glass with a picture of the monarch and the date have been made as souvenirs for many coronations.

Coronation, Bust, Queen Elizabeth & Prince Philip, 1953, Guiterman, Pair	30.00
Coronation, Cup & Saucer, Elizabeth II, June 2, 1953, Brown, Bone China	15.00
Coronation, Cup & Saucer, George IV & Elizabeth, 1937	10.00 To 12.00
Coronation, Dish, King Edward VIII, 1939, 6 X 4 In.	6.95
Coronation, Dish, Nut, George IV, Metal	7.50
Coronation, Eggcup, George V, 1935	8.00
Coronation, Glass, Elizabeth II, Crown, Enamel & Gold, 3 1/2 In.	1.50
Coronation, Mug, Edward VII, 1902, 3 1/2 In.	12.00
Coronation, Mug, Elizabeth II	9.00
Coronation, Mug, George & Mary, 1911, Green Transfer, 3 In.	9.00
Coronation, Mug, George V, Queen Mary, Accession May 7, 1910, Tuscan	27.50
Coronation, Mug, George V, 1911, 3 3/4 In.	12.00
Coronation, Mug, George VI, 1937	9.00
Coronation, Mug, King George & Queen Elizabeth, 1937	6.95
Coronation, Mug, King George VI & Queen Elizabeth	6.50
Coronation, Mug, Queen Elizabeth II, 1953	5.95
Coronation, Mug, Queen Elizabeth, Photo In Sepia, Color Shield	8.00
Coronation, Pitcher, Edward VIII, 1937, 7 1/2 In.	23.00
Coronation, Pitcher, King George V, Pink, 6 1/2 In.Tall	38.00
Coronation, Pitcher, Queen Mary, 2 In.	6.00
Coronation, Plaque, Edward VII, Hanging, 7 X 8 In.	15.50
Coronation, Plate, Bread, George IV, 1917, 'God Save The King,' Shell Rim	20.00
Coronation, Plate, Bread, George VI	19.50
Coronation, Plate, Cake, George VI, May 12, 1937	21.00
Coronation, Plate, Edward VII, China, 8 In.	16.00
Coronation, Plate, King Edward VIII, 1937, 6 X 4 In.	6.95
Coronation, Plate, King George VI, & Queen Elizabeth	8.00
Coronation, Plate, Portrait, King George, Queen Mary, Copper Luster, Pair	50.00
Coronation, Plate, Queen Elizabeth II, 1953, 4 3/4 In.Square	4.95
Coronation, Plate, Queen Elizabeth, Black & Gold Border, 13 In.Wide	32.50
Coronation, Plate, Tea, Elizabeth II	7.50
Coronation, Teaspoon, George VI & Queen Elizabeth, Silver Plate	4.50
Coronation, Tray, Pin, George & Elizabeth, 1937, Aynsley Bone	8.00
Coronation, Tray, Pin, Queen Mary, 1911	10.00
Coronation, Tray, Queen Elizabeth, 12 X 16 In.	10.00

Cosmos Pattern Glass is a pattern of pressed milk glass with colored flowers.

Cosmos, Bowl, Green, Low, 6 In.Diameter	10.00
Cosmos, Dish, Butter	140.00
Cosmos, Lamp Base, Miniature, Pink Band	30.00
Cosmos, Lamp, Blue, Milk Glass, 22 In.High	190.00
Cosmos, Lamp, Table, Pink, Brass Base	150.00
Cosmos, Pitcher, Water, Pink Band	110.00 To 125.00
Cosmos, Shaker, Salt	12.00
Cosmos, Spooner	65.00
Cosmos, Syrup, Pink Band	175.00
Cosmos, Tumbler, Pink Band	25.00 To 32.50
Country Store, see Store	

Cowan Pottery was made in Cleveland, Ohio, from 1913 to 1920. Most pieces of the art pottery were marked with the name of the firm in various ways.

Cowan, Figurine, Man, Blue, Iridescent Gold, Maroon, 9 In.	*Illus*	35.00

Crackle Glass was originally made by the Venetians, but most of the ware found today dates from the 1800s. The glass was heated, cooled, and refired so

Cowan, Figurine, Man, Blue, Iridescent Gold, Maroon, 9 In.
See Page 133

that many small lines appeared inside the glass. It was made in many
factories in the United States and Europe.

Crackle Glass, **Bowl**, Finger, Amber, 5 In.Diameter	1.00
Crackle Glass, **Bowl**, Green, 5 X 4 In.High	15.00
Crackle Glass, **Pitcher**, French, Cranberry, Applied Sandwich Handle, Gold	275.00
Crackle Glass, **Pitcher**, Milk, Straw Color, Applied Blue-Green Reeded Handle	22.50
Crackle Glass, **Vase**, Blue, Applied Looping, Flared Top	18.00
Crackle Glass, **Vase**, Blue, 5 In.	5.00
Crackle Glass, **Vase**, Canary, Enamel Floral & Butterlfy Decoration	75.00

Cranberry Glass is an almost transparent yellow red glass. It resembles
the color of cranberry juice.
Cranberry Glass, see also Cruet, Toothpick, Rubena Verde, etc.

Cranberry Glass, **Basket**, Clear Applied Handle, Rim, & Base, Rosettes	87.50
Cranberry Glass, **Basket**, Hanging, Decorated, Scalloped Top	20.50
Cranberry Glass, **Basket**, Opalescent To Vaseline, Footed Frame, Silver Plate	55.00
Cranberry Glass, **Basket**, Overshot, Twist Handle, 6 In.Long	90.00
Cranberry Glass, **Bell**, Crystal Clapper & Handle, Blown, 11 In.Tall	65.00
Cranberry Glass, **Bell**, Crystal Steeple Handle, 10 In.Tall	55.00
Cranberry Glass, **Bell**, Dinner, Feathered, Luster, Hand Blown, 5 In.Tall	3.00
Cranberry Glass, **Bell**, Dinner, Hand Blown, Feather Pattern, Gold Chain	3.00
Cranberry Glass, **Bell**, Hand, Graduated Knobs On Top, Clear Handle, 13 In.	115.00
Cranberry Glass, **Boot**, Clear Applied Rose On Toe, Ruffle Around Top, 5 In.	85.00
Cranberry Glass, **Bottle**, Barber, Opalescent Hobs	50.00
Cranberry Glass, **Bottle**, Barber, Satin, Enemel Ivory Color Flowers	37.50
Cranberry Glass, **Bottle**, Bitters, Cut To Clear	22.50
Cranberry Glass, **Bottle**, Cut, Overlay, White To Cranberry, 8 1/2 In.High	85.00
Cranberry Glass, **Bottle**, Overlay, Cut, Diamond Pattern, 10 In.Tall	75.00
Cranberry Glass, **Bottle**, Water, Inverted Thumbprint, Square Top	37.50
Cranberry Glass, **Bottle**, Wine	65.00
Cranberry Glass, **Bowl**, Acorn, Scroll, Harry Northwood, 263 Ware, 5 In.	75.00
Cranberry Glass, **Bowl**, Berry, Wild Roses, 4 Sauces, Signed Northwood	37.50
Cranberry Glass, **Bowl**, Candy, Blown, Clear Applied Ornate Rim	42.00
Cranberry Glass, **Bowl**, Deep, 8 In.Diameter	17.50
Cranberry Glass, **Bowl**, Finger, Inverted Thumbprint, 4 3/4 In.Diameter	18.50
Cranberry Glass, **Bowl**, Finger, Swirled Inverted Rib	32.00
Cranberry Glass, **Bowl**, Fleur-De-Lis, Divided, Handles	25.75
Cranberry Glass, **Bowl**, Fruit, Boat Shape, Delaware, Gilt Rim & Flowers	50.00
Cranberry Glass, **Bowl**, Opalescent, Clear Applied Top, 4 In.High	35.00
Cranberry Glass, **Bowl**, Ruffled Top, Satin, White Threading, Frosted Feet	45.00
Cranberry Glass, **Bowl**, Stag & Holly, Blue, Footed	100.00
Cranberry Glass, **Bowls**, Finger, Clear, Cut Back, Set Of 10	225.00
Cranberry Glass, **Box**, Brass Bound, Hinged Lid, Enameled White Daisies, Blue	50.00
Cranberry Glass, **Box**, Powder, Enamel Daisies, Violets, Gold Bands	50.00
Cranberry Glass, **Box**, Powder, Gold	40.00
Cranberry Glass, **Butter**, Covered, Frosted, Royal Oak	110.00
Cranberry Glass, **Butter**, Thumbprint, Covered	75.00
Cranberry Glass, **Candleholder**, Double Twist Stem, 7 1/2 In., Pair	45.00
Cranberry Glass, **Candlestick**, Clear Ball Knob, Bubbles, Pair	35.00
Cranberry Glass, **Candlestick**, Tree Of Life, Corset Shape, 6 1/4 In.High	65.00

Cranberry Glass, Castor, Pickle, Applied Trim 125.00
Cranberry Glass, Castor, Pickle, Decorated 125.00
Cranberry Glass, Castor, Pickle, Enamel, Silver Stand, Lid & Tongs 130.00
Cranberry Glass, Castor, Pickle, Enameled Floral, Ornate Frame & Fork 115.00
Cranberry Glass, Castor, Pickle, Enameling On Insert, Resilvered 140.00
Cranberry Glass, Castor, Pickle, Insert With Enamel 75.00
Cranberry Glass, Castor, Pickle, Relief Frame, Bulbous Insert 175.00
Cranberry Glass, Compote, Clear Stem & Foot, 8 1/4 X 6 In.High 45.00
Cranberry Glass, Compote, Raised Leaf Pattern, Silver Plate Base & Stem 45.00
Cranberry Glass, Creamer & Sugar, Clear, Applied Handle & Feet 68.00
Cranberry Glass, Creamer, Bulbous, Swirls, Clear Handle 45.00
Cranberry Glass, Creamer, Clear Applied Handle & Foot, 4 In.High 22.50
Cranberry Glass, Creamer, Clear, Applied Handle, 4 1/4 In.High 25.00
Cranberry Glass, Cruet, Ball-Shape, Clear Handle, Stopper, 8 1/2 In. 37.50
Cranberry Glass, Cruet, Clear Stopper & Handle 48.00
Cranberry Glass, Cruet, Cross Ribs, Swirls, Cut Stopper 48.00
Cranberry Glass, Cruet, Fluted Vine Pattern 27.50
Cranberry Glass, Cruet, Inverted Thumbprint, 6 1/2 In.High .... 15.00 To 30.00
Cranberry Glass, Cruet, Swirl, 6 1/2 In.Tall .... 13.75 To 15.00
Cranberry Glass, Cruet, Thumbprint, Clear Handle & Stopper, 10 In.Tall 75.00
Cranberry Glass, Cup & Saucer, Clear Handle 10.00
Cranberry Glass, Cup, Punch, Fluted Inside, Clear Applied Handle 3.50
Cranberry Glass, Cup, Punch, Opalescent, Blue, Swags, Threading 45.00
Cranberry Glass, Cup, Punch, Thumbprint, Enameled Flowers, Threaded Handle 22.50
Cranberry Glass, Decanter, Applied Handle, Clear, Stopper, 11 1/2 In.High 49.50
Cranberry Glass, Decanter, Gold Flowers & Insects, 8 In. 35.00
Cranberry Glass, Dish, Finger Grip, Gold Leaf Decoration, Pair 22.50
Cranberry Glass, Dish, Powder, Covered, Flash & Clear, Seaweed, Shells, Snails 12.00
Cranberry Glass, Epergne, Four Trumpet Vases, Crimped Tops, Matching Bowl 125.00
Cranberry Glass, Epergne, Lily, Ruffled Edge, Pinched Spirals, 9 In.Square 135.00
Cranberry Glass, Epergne, Ribbed Bowl, Ruffled Border, 15 In. 95.00
Cranberry Glass, Epergne, Three Trumpet, Ruffled Top, Silver Stand, 6 In. 55.00
Cranberry Glass, Ewer, Applied Crystal Leaf, Ribbed Stem 42.00
Cranberry Glass, Glass, Juice, Swirled, Threaded, Enameled Floral 25.00
Cranberry Glass, Glass, Old Fashioned, Cut To Clear 6.00
Cranberry Glass, Goblet, Bull's-Eye, Flashed, Gold 25.00
Cranberry Glass, Goblet, Inverted Thumbprint, Cone Shape, 6 In.High 18.00
Cranberry Glass, Holder, String, Cut Overlay, Cranberry To Clear 20.00
Cranberry Glass, Jar, Biscuit, Threaded, Silver Cover, Bail, 8 1/2 In. 58.00
Cranberry Glass, Jar, Cracker, Pale To Dark 85.00
Cranberry Glass, Jar, Jam, Panel, Silver Plate Cover, Bail 50.00
Cranberry Glass, Jar, Pickle, Floral & Daisy, Enamel 58.00
Cranberry Glass, Lamp, Hanging, Frosted, Gold Decoration 110.00
Cranberry Glass, Lamp, Hanging, Hall, Birds In Stipples Panels 110.00
Cranberry Glass, Lamp, Hanging, Satin Finish, Milk Glass, Brass Frame 150.00
Cranberry Glass, Muffineer, Silver Pierced Top, Paneled Body 28.00
Cranberry Glass, Mug, Floral, Enamel, 'a Present For A Good Boy, 'handle 62.50
Cranberry Glass, Perfume, Enameled Leaves, Butterflies, Clear Stopper 40.00
Cranberry Glass, Pipe, Loop Decoration 125.00
Cranberry Glass, Pitcher, Baby Thumbprint, Clear Handle, 5 In. 35.00
Cranberry Glass, Pitcher, Bulbous, Applied Handle, Blown, 6 In.Tall 45.00
Cranberry Glass, Pitcher, Bulbous, Enameled Flowers, Ribbed, 8 In. 65.00
Cranberry Glass, Pitcher, Crimped Top, Ribbed Base, Applied Clear Handle 78.00
Cranberry Glass, Pitcher, Fluted Top, Applied Handle, Clear, 5 In.Tall 48.50
Cranberry Glass, Pitcher, Frosted, Hobnail, 7 1/2 In.Tall 135.00
Cranberry Glass, Pitcher, Ground Pontil, Bulbous, Clear Reeded Handle 72.50
Cranberry Glass, Pitcher, Hand-Painted Flowers, Clear Applied Handle 55.00
Cranberry Glass, Pitcher, Milk, Bulbous 50.00
Cranberry Glass, Pitcher, Milk, Clear, Ribbed, Shell Handle 55.00
Cranberry Glass, Pitcher, Milk, Melon Rib, Bulbous, Applied Reed Handle 75.00
Cranberry Glass, Pitcher, Miniature, Gold Enamel Decoration, 2 In.High 20.00
Cranberry Glass, Pitcher, Quilted Pattern, Clear Applied Handle, 7 1/2 In. 87.50
Cranberry Glass, Pitcher, Ruffled Top, Clear Handle, 8 1/2 In.High 75.00
Cranberry Glass, Pitcher, Swirls, Applied Clear Handle, 7 3/4 In.High 74.50
Cranberry Glass, Pitcher, Thumbprint 35.00
Cranberry Glass, Pitcher, Water, Bulbous, Diamond Quilted, Square Mouth 85.00

Cranberry Glass, Pitcher, Water, Clear, Inverted Thumbprint 95.00
Cranberry Glass, Pitcher, Water, Hobnail, Bulbous, Square Mouth 145.00
Cranberry Glass, Pitcher, Water, Inverted Thumbprint, Molded 30.00
Cranberry Glass, Pitcher, Water, Inverted Thumbprint, Ruffled Edge 45.00
Cranberry Glass, Pitcher, Water, Overshot 60.00
Cranberry Glass, Pitcher, Water, Tankard, Clear Handle 55.00
Cranberry Glass, Plate, Leaf Design, 9 In.Diameter 35.50
Cranberry Glass, Plate, Roman Key, 7 3/4 In.Diameter 21.00
Cranberry Glass, Rose Bowl, Diamond-Quilted, Clear 65.00
Cranberry Glass, Rose Bowl, Inverted Melon Mold, Applied Milk Glass Base 65.00
Cranberry Glass, Rose Bowl, Inverted Thumbprint, 4 In.Diameter 10.00
Cranberry Glass, Rose Bowl, Overshot, Crimped Top, 3 1/2 In.High 45.00
Cranberry Glass, Rose Bowl, Overshot Enamel, 6 In.Diameter 72.50
Cranberry Glass, Rose Bowl, Three Applied Scroll Feet, 4 In.Tall 48.00
Cranberry Glass, Salt & Pepper, Inverted Thumbprint, Opalescent, Pair 50.00
Cranberry Glass, Salt, Applied Clear Feet 27.50
Cranberry Glass, Salt, Clear Vaseline Applied Edge .... *Illus* 50.00
Cranberry Glass, Salt, Individual, Open, Clear Glass Foot & Base 14.50
Cranberry Glass, Salt, Master, Clear Rigaree, Footed Silver Holder 42.00
Cranberry Glass, Shade, Electric, Leaves & Flowers, Blue 22.00
Cranberry Glass, Shade, Hobnail 17.50
Cranberry Glass, Shaker, Salt, Opalescent, Coin Spot, Pewter Top 25.00
Cranberry Glass, Shaker, Sugar, Cut Paneled, Pierced Top, 6 In. .... 2 .50
Cranberry Glass, Shaker, Sugar, English 45.00
Cranberry Glass, Shaker, Sugar, Panels, Silver Plate Top 40.00
Cranberry Glass, Shaker, Sugar, Ribbed Pattern, 6 X 7 In. 29.00
Cranberry Glass, Shoe, Threaded On Clear Glass 25.00
Cranberry Glass, Spittoon, White Edge .... *Illus* 65.00

Cranberry Glass, Salt, Clear Vaseline Applied Edge

Cranberry Glass, Spittoon, White Edge

Cranberry Glass, Spooner, Delaware, Footed 30.00
Cranberry Glass, Sugar, Covered, Applied Clear Rigaree Foot 42.50
Cranberry Glass, Sugar, Covered, Frosted, Royal Oak 98.00
Cranberry Glass, Syrup, Bulbous Body, Applied Crystal Handle, Hand Blown 45.00
Cranberry Glass, Syrup, Clear To Cranberry, Dated March 28, 1882 .... 55.00
Cranberry Glass, Syrup, Opalescent Swirl Stripes, Plated Lid, Clear Handle 42.50
Cranberry Glass, Toothpick, Flower Form, Silver Holder 45.00
Cranberry Glass, Tray, Pin, Gold, Flowers, 6 1/4 X 3 1/4 In. 20.00
Cranberry Glass, Tumbler, Baby Inverted Thumprint 40.00
Cranberry Glass, Tumbler, Cut Overlay, White To Cranberry, Gold Decoration 50.00
Cranberry Glass, Tumbler, Cut To Clear 6.00
Cranberry Glass, Tumbler, Diamond-Quilted, Opalescent .... 15.00 To 35.00
Cranberry Glass, Tumbler, Enameled Floral, Leaves, Vines 40.00
Cranberry Glass, Tumbler, Gilded & Enameled 50.00
Cranberry Glass, Tumbler, Gold Scrolls, White Enamel Reserves, Floral 45.00
Cranberry Glass, Tumbler, Inverted Thumbprint 35.00
Cranberry Glass, Tumbler, Inverted Toothpick, Enameled Daisy Decoration 20.00

Cranberry Glass, Tumbler, Lace Pattern, Opalescent	35.00
Cranberry Glass, Tumbler, Mottled White To Cranberry, Cut Overlay	12.50
Cranberry Glass, Tumbler, Opalescent Swirls	17.50 To 25.00
Cranberry Glass, Tumbler, Opalescent, Thumbprint	20.00
Cranberry Glass, Tumbler, Thumbprint, Lily-Of-The-Valley, Daisy, Enamel	45.00
Cranberry Glass, Vase, Applied Ruffle Edge, Amber, Blown, Footed, 10 In.Tall	55.00
Cranberry Glass, Vase, Bud, Vaseline Rigaree Top, Silver Holder, Child, Dog	65.00
Cranberry Glass, Vase, Bulbous Bottom, Narrow Neck, Crimped Top, Pair	60.00
Cranberry Glass, Vase, Concave Sides, Flared Top, 7 1/2 In.High, Pair	75.00
Cranberry Glass, Vase, Cut, Overlay, White To Cranberry, 7 1/4 In.High, Pair	85.00
Cranberry Glass, Vase, Cylindrical, Clear Rigaree Feet, Opalescent Drapery	30.00
Cranberry Glass, Vase, Gem Cameo, Enameled, White Floral	45.00
Cranberry Glass, Vase, Melon Shape, 4 In.High, Pair	60.00
Cranberry Glass, Vase, Narrow Neck, Four Concave Sides, 7 1/2 In., Pair	75.00
Cranberry Glass, Vase, Opalescent Streaks, Mica Flecks, 11 In.	49.50
Cranberry Glass, Vase, Shading To Clear Frosted At Bottom, Enameled	90.00
Cranberry Glass, Vase, Tapered, Scalloped Top, Gold Decor, 12 1/2 In.High	45.00
Cranberry Glass, Vase, Thorn, Footed	29.00
Cranberry Glass, Vase, Thorn, Shell Base, Footed	27.50
Cranberry Glass, Vase, Trumpet, Knob At Base, Teardrop In Clear Stem	35.00
Cranberry Glass, Vase, Victorian Shape, Enameled	27.00
Cranberry Glass, Vase, White Enameled Flowers, 9 3/4 In.High	35.00
Cranberry Glass, Water Set, Daisy Design, Tankard Pitcher, 4 Tumbler	105.00
Cranberry Glass, Water Set, Gold Stripes, Clear Applied Handle, 7 Piece	22.50
Cranberry Glass, Wine, Blue-Red Color, Applied Stem, 5 In.Tall	16.00
Cranberry Glass, Wine, Clear Stem, Set Of 12	150.00
Cranberry Glass, Wine, Cranberry To Clear, Overlay, Cut	8.00
Cranberry Glass, Wine, Cut To Clear, Stemmed	9.00
Cranberry Glass, Wine, Inverted Thumbprint, Clear Stem, 7 In.Tall	30.00

Creamware, or Queensware, was developed by Josiah Wedgwood about 1765.
It is a cream-colored Earthenware that has been copied by many factories.

Creamware, Bowl, English, Oval, Ribbon Sides	22.50
Creamware, Bowl, English, Pierced Ribbon Sides, Ruffled Top, 4 1/2 In.High	20.00
Creamware, Bowl, English, Pierced Sides, 3 1/2 In.High	25.00
Creamware, Cup, Handleless, Black Transfer Of Man Fishing, Wedgwood, C.1800	45.00
Creamware, Dessert Set, Shell, Gilt Outlined, Wedgwood, 1893, 14 Piece	250.00
Creamware, Dish, Scalloped Border, Chinese Painted, C.1780, Pair	70.00
Creamware, Dish, Wedgwood, Oval, Open Ribbon Sides	40.00
Creamware, Hatpin Holder, Armorial, Miniature, Renfrewshire	5.50
Creamware, Jug, Toby, 4 In.Tall	10.00
Creamware, Plate, Blue & White, Chinese Style Painted, English, C.1765	70.00
Creamware, Plate, French, Creil, Scalloped Edge, 18th Century, Pair	70.00
Creamware, Sauceboat, Brown Transfer Harbor Scenes, C.1820, Wedgwood	10.00

Croesus Glass is a special pattern of Pressed Glass made about 1897.
It was made in clear glass, emerald green, or amethyst. Each piece was
decorated with gold.

Croesus, Amethyst, Butter, Gold, Covered	105.00
Croesus, Amethyst, Celery	60.00
Croesus, Amethyst, Compote, Jelly	60.00
Croesus, Amethyst, Creamer, Miniature	70.00
Croesus, Amethyst, Cruet, Small	115.00
Croesus, Amethyst, Dish, Butter, Cover	90.00
Croesus, Amethyst, Dish, Sauce	35.00
Croesus, Amethyst, Spooner	70.00
Croesus, Amethyst, Sugar & Creamer, Covered, 5 1/2 In.High	140.00
Croesus, Amethyst, Sugar, Cover	70.00 To 75.00
Croesus, Amethyst, Tray	38.00
Croesus, Amethyst, Tumbler	35.00
Croesus, Clear, Celery	47.50
Croesus, Clear, Compote, 7 In.	25.00
Croesus, Clear, Cruet	25.00
Croesus, Clear, Sugar	47.50
Croesus, Clear, Tumbler	10.00
Croesus, Green, Bowl, Berry	55.00

Croesus, Green, Butter, Covered 95.00
Croesus, Green, Compote, Jelly 50.00
Croesus, Green, Creamer .... 65.00 To 80.00
Croesus, Green, Creamer, Miniature 55.00
Croesus, Green, Cruet, Large 90.00
Croesus, Green, Cruet, Small 90.00
Croesus, Green, Dish, Pickle 30.00
Croesus, Green, Dish, Sauce 25.00
Croesus, Green, Pitcher, Footed, Three Tumblers, Set 255.00
Croesus, Green, Pitcher, Milk 65.00
Croesus, Green, Pitcher, Water ....70.00 To 165.00
Croesus, Green, Pitcher, 5 1/2 In. 67.50
Croesus, Green, Salt & Pepper 55.00
Croesus, Green, Sauce 26.00
Croesus, Green, Sauce, Footed 32.50
Croesus, Green, Spooner .... 38.00 To 70.00
Croesus, Green, Spooner, Gold, Footed 43.00
Croesus, Green, Sugar, Cover .... 65.00 To 85.00
Croesus, Green, Sugar, Open, Gold 39.00
Croesus, Green, Toothpick .... 45.00 To 75.00
Croesus, Green, Tray 35.00
Croesus, Green, Tumbler .... 28.00 To 32.00
Croesus, Purple, Creamer, Gold, Footed, 3 In.Tall .... 80.00 To 82.50
Croesus, Purple, Sauce 32.00
Croesus, Purple, Spooner, Gold .... 77.50 To 95.00
Croesus, Purple, Sugar, Cover, Footed .... 69.50 To 82.50
Croesus, Purple, Toothpick, Gold, Footed .... 78.50 To 89.50
Croesus, Purple, Tumbler, Gold .... 55.00 To 75.00
Croesus, Purple, Water Set, 7 Piece 500.00

Crown Derby is the nickname given to the works of the Royal Crown Derby factory, which began working in England in 1859. An earlier and more famous English Derby factory existed from 1750 to 1848. The two factories were not related. Most of the porcelain found today with the Derby mark is the work of the later Derby factory.
Crown Derby, see also Royal Crown Derby
Crown Derby, Jar, Rose, Cream Ground, Hand-Painted Firs, Melon Rib, Gold 65.00
Crown Derby, Pitcher, Blue, Red, & Gilt Floral 50.00
Crown Derby, Plate, Blue & Orange Allover Pattern, 10 1/2 In.Diameter, 12 .... 276.00
Crown Derby, Plate, Floral, Hand-Painted, L Mark, Circa 1878, Set Of 6 .... 100.00
Crown Derby, Pot, Three Ball Feet, Miniature 17.50
Crown Devon, Coffeepot, Fluted Footing, Medallions In Relief, Gold Handle 45.00
Crown Devon, Vase, Mallards In Flight, Gold Feet, 10 In. 45.00
Crown Ducal, Compote, Footed, Floral On Cream, 4 In.High 15.00
Crown Ducal, Dresser Set, 5 Piece, Birds, Butterflies & Flowers On Cream 35.00
Crown Ducal, Plate, Spirit Of '76, Mulberry Color 13.00

Crown Milano Glass was made by Frederick Shirley about 1890. It had a plain biscuit color with a satin finish. It was decorated with flowers, and often had large gold scrolls.
Crown Milano, Box, Floral Design, Green, Rose, Signed, Cover, 4 1/2 In.Square 650.00
Crown Milano, Jar, Biscuit, Signed M.W., Yellow, Tan, Jeweled, Silver Mounts 450.00
Crown Milano, Jar, Biscuit, Silver Plate Bail & Cover, Applied Gilt, 'M.W.' 425.00
Crown Milano, Jar, Cover, Swirled Ribbing, Bamboo Leaf Decor 135.00
Crown Milano, Jar, Cracker, Blue, Beige, Gold, Roses, Signed, 7 1/2 In. 550.00
Crown Milano, Jar, Cracker, Green, Red, Yellow, Enamel, Signed, Mark P 200.00
Crown Milano, Jardiniere, Floral Design, Pink, White, Gold Trim, Signed 350.00
Crown Milano, Pitcher, Syrup, Leaves & Crown, Marked 195.00
Crown Milano, Salt & Pepper, Melon 80.00
Crown Milano, Vase, Flowers, Scrolls, Raised, Gold, Marked 120.00
Crown Milano, Vase, Orchid, Pink, White, Brown, Bulbous, Signed, 5 3/4 In.Tall 650.00
Crown Tuscan, Bowl, Flared Rim, 12 In. 85.00
Crown Tuscan, Compote, Hobnail, Ruffled, 5 1/2 In.Tall, 7 1/2 In.Diameter 32.00
Crown Tuscan, Dessert, Dolphin 25.00
Crown Tuscan, Figurine, Lady, Nude, Cocktail, Mandarin Gold Top, 6 1/2 In. 40.00
Crown Tuscan, Plate, Shell, 5 In. 20.00

Crown Tuscan, Plate, Shell, 7 In. 30.00
Crown Tuscan, Vase, Cornucopia, Gold Trim, Footed, 9 1/2 In.Tall .... 28.00 To 32.00
Crown Worcester, Creamer, Girffon Handle, Matte Finish, Gold 25.00
Crown Worcester, Vase, 2 Handles, Matte Finish, Floral Decoration, 6 In.High 75.00

Cruets of glass or porcelain were made to hold vinegar or oil. They were
especially popular during victorian times.
Cruet, see also other sections, Amber, Pressed Glass, etc.
Cruet, Alaska, Blue, Opalescent, Stopper ....42.00 To 45.00
Cruet, Amber, Blue Handle & Stopper, Square Shaped 52.50
Cruet, Ball Shape, Blue, Slim Neck, Clear Handle & Stopper, Pink Floral 45.00
Cruet, Blue, Applied Amber-Reeded Handle, Panels, Amber, Stopper 65.00
Cruet, Blue, Opal Threaded, Clear Stopper, Blown 35.00
Cruet, Blue, Opalescent, Threaded, Stopper 45.00
Cruet, Blue, Panels, Enameled Orange Floral, Cut Stopper 35.00
Cruet, Bull's-Eye In Heart, Stopper 38.00
Cruet, Clear, Crimped Handle, Blown, Circa 1850 .... 45.00
Cruet, Cobalt, Swirl, 6 1/2 In.Tall 9.75
Cruet, Diamond Pattern, Amber, Blown, Stopper 45.00
Cruet, Engraved Galley Frame, 5 Cut Glass Bottles 95.00
Cruet, Fern Pattern, Clear, Bulbous, 7 In.High 15.00
Cruet, Hobnail, Opalescent, Stopper, 4 1/2 In.Tall 15.00
Cruet, Hunt Scene, Cobalt Blue, Silver, Clear Stopper 42.50
Cruet, Inverted Rib, Opalescent, Vaseline, Stopper 42.50
Cruet, Miniature, Blue Opaque, 5 In. 30.00
Cruet, Paddle Wheel, Faceted Stopper 9.50
Cruet, Paneled, Dark Green, Clear Stopper 20.00
Cruet, Paneled, Green, Steeple Stopper, 3 1/2 In.Tall 18.00
Cruet, Pink, Clear, 3 Piece Set, Handled Tray, Ground Stoppers 8.00
Cruet, Pink, Opaline, Quilted, Frosted Applied Handle 18.50
Cruet, Portland, Stopper 11.00
Cruet, Red, Gold, Clear Handle 25.00
Cruet, Spanish Lace, Opalsecent, Tricornered Lip, Stopper 28.00
Crystal, Rock, Palm Tree, Ormolu, Pair .... *Illus* 900.00

Cup Plates are small glass or china plates that held the cup, while a
gentleman of the mid-nineteenth century drank his coffee or tea from the
saucer. The most famous Cup Plates were made of glass at the Boston and
Sandwich Factory located in Massachusetts.
Cup Plate, Henry Clay 95.00
Cup Plate, Henry Clay, Pontil 145.00
Cup Plate, Lacy, Fort Pitt Glass Works 135.00
Cup Plate, Midwestern, Lacy 40.00

Currier & Ives made the famous American Lithographs marked with their
name from 1857 to 1907.
Currier & Ives, A Bare Chance 40.00
Currier & Ives, A Midnight Race On The Mississippi, F.F.Palmer, 1860 .... 900.00
Currier & Ives, A Sure Thing, Comic 22.50
Currier & Ives, Abraham Lincoln, The Nation's Martyr, Small Folio 25.00
Currier & Ives, Africa, Framed 35.00
Currier & Ives, An Anxious Moment, Brook Trout Fishing, Charles Parsons 525.00
Currier & Ives, Arabian Horse, Alexander, Lithograph, Color 35.00
Currier & Ives, Beauty Asleep, Framed 30.00
Currier & Ives, Between Two Fires 45.00
Currier & Ives, Bombardment Of Ft.Pulaski, Cockspur, April, 1862 .... 35.00
Currier & Ives, Bothwell Castle, Oval, Color 50.00
Currier & Ives, Bothwell Castle, 7 3/4 X 10 In. 50.00
Currier & Ives, Brook Trout Fishing, Parsons, 1863 .... *Illus* 525.00
Currier & Ives, Chancellorsville, 1863, Color 20.00
Currier & Ives, Charles Sumner 18.00
Currier & Ives, Deer In Wooded Landscape In Early Morning Mist 275.00
Currier & Ives, Eliza, Cross Frame 35.00
Currier & Ives, Family Register, No.74, Dated From 1852 To 1914, Names 27.00
Currier & Ives, Fashionable Turn-Outs In Central Park, Thomas Worth, 1869 .... 750.00

Currier & Ives, Flushed, American Field Sports, Charles Parsons, 1857 .... 350.00
Currier & Ives, Funeral Of Lincoln, Black & White, Walnut Frame 40.00
Currier & Ives, General Scott's Entry, Mexico, 1847, No.549, Color 35.00
Currier & Ives, Hon.Stephen A.Douglas, Small Folio, Gilt Frame 12.50
Currier & Ives, In Memory Of Thomas Boston, Died 1841 .... 15.00
Currier & Ives, James K.Polk, Small Folio, Framed 27.50
Currier & Ives, Little Brothers, Framed 20.00
Currier & Ives, Little David, Cross Frame 35.00
Currier & Ives, Little Sisters, Framed 20.00
Currier & Ives, Monitor & Merrimac Hampton Roads, 1862 .... 100.00
Currier & Ives, Morning Prayer, Evening Prayer, Frames, Pair 48.00
Currier & Ives, My Little Playfellow, Medium Folio 35.00
Currier & Ives, Night Scene At American R.R.Junction .... *Illus* 2500.00

Crystal, Rock, Palm Tree, Ormolu, Pair
See Page 139

Currier & Ives, Brook Trout Fishing, Parsons, 1863
See Page 139

Currier & Ives, Night Scene At American R.R.Junction
See Page 140

Currier & Ives, On A Point, American Field Sports, Charles Parsons, 1857 .... 225.00
Currier & Ives, Out For A Day's Shooting, Louis Maurer, 1859 .... 600.00
Currier & Ives, Starting Out, Life In The Woods, Louis Maurer, 1860 .... 425.00
Currier & Ives, Summer In The Country 50.00
Currier & Ives, The Angel Gabriel, Frame 20.00
Currier & Ives, The Darktown Brigade, The Last Shake, Comic 22.50
Currier & Ives, The Killeries, Connemara, Frame, 13 X 17 In. 37.50
Currier & Ives, The Last Shot, 1867, 11 X 16 .... 25.00
Currier & Ives, The Little Beggar, 13 X 8 In. 12.50
Currier & Ives, The Old Homestead, Original, 1855, Frame, 10 X 15 .... 130.00
Currier & Ives, The Old Oaken Bucket, Frame 70.00
Currier & Ives, The Queen Of Beauty & The Girl I Love, Frame, Pair 27.50
Currier & Ives, The Rose Of May, Oval, Walnut Frame 35.00
Currier & Ives, The Scales Of Justice, Frame 25.00
Currier & Ives, The Soldier's Home, The Vision, Small Folio 15.00
Currier & Ives, The Tomb Of Kosciusko, West Point 50.00
Currier & Ives, Trenton High Falls 55.00
Currier & Ives, Trotting Cracks On Snow, Large Folio, Maple Frame 650.00
Currier & Ives, Trotting For A Great Stake, Lithograph, N.Y., 1890, L.Maurer 110.00
Currier & Ives, Washington, Mahogany Frame 17.50
Currier & Ives, Washington's Reception By The Ladies 25.00
Currier & Ives, Winter In Country, Old Grist Mill, Large Folio 1300.00
Currier & Ives, Wooding Up On The Mississippi, F.F.Palmer, 1863 .... 1300.00
Currier & Ives, Yound Blood In An Old Body, Small Folio 50.00
Currier, The Road—Winter, Lithograph, Hand-Colored, 1853, ... Illus 2700.00

Custard Glass is an opaque glass sometimes known as Buttermilk Glass.
It was first made after 1886 at the La Belle Glass Works,
Bridgeport, Ohio.
Custard Glass, Banana Boat, Louis XV 135.00
Custard Glass, Bell, Smoke, Lemon, Metal Handle 15.00
Custard Glass, Bowl, Banana, Louis IV, Footed, Scalloped 115.00
Custard Glass, Bowl, Berry, Chrysanthemum Sprig, Gold, Oval .... 145.00 To 155.00
Custard Glass, Bowl, Berry, Inverted Fan & Feather 165.00
Custard Glass, Bowl, Berry, Little Gem 70.00
Custard Glass, Bowl, Grapes & Leaves In Center, N In Circle 25.00
Custard Glass, Bowl, Inverted Fan, Feather Berry 165.00
Custard Glass, Bowl, Louis XV, Footed, 10 In.Diameter 125.00
Custard Glass, Bowl, Sugar, Cover, Red Wild Roses, Blue Bowknots 58.00
Custard Glass, Butter, Argonaut Shell, Cover 200.00

Currier, The Road—Winter, Lithograph, Hand Colored, 1853
See Page 141

Custard Glass, Butter, Beaded Circle	130.00
Custard Glass, Butter, Beaded Swag, Buttermilk Color, Covered, Gold, Roses	88.00
Custard Glass, Butter, Covered, Little Gem, Apple Blossoms	110.00
Custard Glass, Butter, Geneva, Raised Flange	87.50
Custard Glass, Butter, Intaglio Pattern	45.00
Custard Glass, Butter, Inverted Fan & Feather, Covered	165.00
Custard Glass, Celery, Chrysanthemum Sprig, Signed, Northwood	130.00
Custard Glass, Compote, Intaglio, 8 1/2 In.Diameter, 6 In.Tall	125.00
Custard Glass, Compote, Jelly, Chrysanthemum Sprig	60.00
Custard Glass, Compote, Jelly, Raised Strawberries On Upper Edge	28.50
Custard Glass, Creamer, Arched Thumbprint, Mother, 1912, Red Roses	38.00
Custard Glass, Creamer, Argonaut Shell, Signed, Gold	50.00 To 85.00
Custard Glass, Creamer, Beaded, Stockton, Ill.	15.00
Custard Glass, Creamer, Beaver Dam, Wisconsin, Notched Base	18.00
Custard Glass, Creamer, Chrysanthemum Sprig, Signed Northwood, Script	85.00
Custard Glass, Creamer, Diamond Peg, Marked Krystol, Hand-Painted Roses	55.00
Custard Glass, Creamer, Fan, Northwood	55.00
Custard Glass, Creamer, Gold, Scalloped Top	18.00
Custard Glass, Creamer, Jackson	60.00
Custard Glass, Creamer, Louis XV	65.00
Custard Glass, Creamer, Miniature, Souvenir, Arch Rock, Mackinac Island	10.00
Custard Glass, Creamer, Souvenir, Clear Lake, Iowa	25.00
Custard Glass, Cup, Art Nouveau	*Illus* 15.00
Custard Glass, Dish, Banana, Louis XV, Gold	160.00
Custard Glass, Dish, Berry, Delaware, Green	25.00
Custard Glass, Dish, Bonbon, Grape & Cable, N Mark, 7 In.	35.00
Custard Glass, Dish, Butter, Cover, Chrysanthemum Sprig, Northwood	165.00
Custard Glass, Dish, Relish, Scales Pattern, Rope Handle	9.00
Custard Glass, Figurine, Hat, Grape & Lattice, Mark N	50.00
Custard Glass, Goblet, Embossed Grapes	30.00
Custard Glass, Goblet, Grape & Gothic Arches	25.00 To 35.00
Custard Glass, Goblet, Rose Design, Six Sided, Stemmed	40.00
Custard Glass, Hair Receiver, Red Roses	33.00
Custard Glass, Hat, Grape Arbor, Ruffled, Tan Ground	37.00
Custard Glass, Mug, Pudding, Rose Design, Paneled Bottom, 3 1/2 In.Tall	27.00
Custard Glass, Mug, Woodward, Okla., Floral Painted, Gold	10.00
Custard Glass, Nappy, Lotus & Grape, Scalloped, Handled	24.00
Custard Glass, Nappy, Prayer Rug, Two Handled, Marigold	32.00
Custard Glass, Pitcher, Pineapple & Fan, Fargo, N.D., 4 1/4 In.Tall	20.00
Custard Glass, Pitcher, Souvenir Of Coney Island, Diamond Peg Pattern	30.00

Custard Glass, Cup, Art Nouveau
See Page 142

Custard Glass, Pitcher, Victoria, Green, Blue, Orange, Flowers	150.00
Custard Glass, Pitcher, Water, Argonaut Shell	200.00
Custard Glass, Pitcher, Water, Chrysanthemum Sprig	85.00 To 170.00
Custard Glass, Pitcher, Water, Fluted, Scrolls	125.00
Custard Glass, Pitcher, Water, Ivorina Verde, Six Tumbler, Set	365.00
Custard Glass, Pitcher, Water, Jackson, Gold Trim	150.00
Custard Glass, Pitcher, Water, Winged, Scroll Pattern, Bulbous	75.00
Custard Glass, Plate, Berry, Marked Mckee	12.00
Custard Glass, Plate, Prayer Rug, 7 1/2 In.	14.00
Custard Glass, Rose Bowl, Alabaster, Fluted, Inverted Rim, Gold Spatters	37.50
Custard Glass, Rose Bowl, Persian Medallion, Green	75.00
Custard Glass, Salt & Pepper, Chrysanthemum Sprig, Gold, Pair	95.00
Custard Glass, Salt & Pepper, Flower Medallion, Gold Leaves, Flowers	65.00
Custard Glass, Salt & Pepper, Maize Pattern, 3 3/4 In.High, Set	45.00
Custard Glass, Sauce, Argonaut Shell	42.50
Custard Glass, Sauce, Beaded Circle	32.50
Custard Glass, Sauce, Cherry Scale, Footed	35.00
Custard Glass, Sauce, Intaglio, Green Trim	35.00
Custard Glass, Sauce, Inverted Fan, Feather	55.00
Custard Glass, Sauce, Little Gem, Blue & Green Trim	32.50
Custard Glass, Sauce, Louis XV, Gold, Footed	30.00
Custard Glass, Sauce, Maple Leaf	85.00
Custard Glass, Shaker, Intaglio, Green & Gold, Pair	90.00
Custard Glass, Shaker, Salt, Floral, Kiowa, Kansas	10.00
Custard Glass, Shot, Flowers, Raised Enamel, 2 1/2 In.High	18.00
Custard Glass, Spooner, Beaded Swag, Buttermilk Color, Gold, Roses, Marked	45.00
Custard Glass, Spooner, Diamond Peg, Rose Design, Yellow	35.00
Custard Glass, Spooner, Geneva	45.00
Custard Glass, Spooner, Inverted Fan, Feather	90.00
Custard Glass, Spooner, Louis XIV, Gold Trim	55.00
Custard Glass, Spooner, Louis XV	55.00
Custard Glass, Spooner, Red & Green, Geneva	40.00
Custard Glass, Spooner, Red Wild Roses, Blue Bowknots	48.00
Custard Glass, Spooner, Ribbed Drape, Rose Design	35.00
Custard Glass, Spooner, Wild Rose & Bowknot	48.00
Custard Glass, Sugar & Creamer, Beaded Swag, Buttermilk Color, Gold, Roses	78.00
Custard Glass, Sugar, Argonaut Shell, Cover	115.00
Custard Glass, Sugar, Creamer, & Butter, Argonaut Shell, Covered	265.00
Custard Glass, Sugar, Creamer, Spooner, & Butter, Covered, Winged Scroll	290.00
Custard Glass, Sugar, Geneva, Green, Gold, No Lid	50.00
Custard Glass, Sugar, Grape & Cable, Open, Cinnamon Color, Northwood	48.00
Custard Glass, Sugar, Grape & Gothic, Pearl, Cover	42.00
Custard Glass, Sugar, Inverted Fan, Feather, Cover	125.00
Custard Glass, Sugar, Louis XV, Cover	72.50
Custard Glass, Sugar, Open, Ivorina Verde, Gold	52.50
Custard Glass, Table Set, Intaglio, Green, Butter, Sugar, Creamer, Spooner	400.00

Custard Glass, Toothpick, Argonaut Shell 200.00
Custard Glass, Toothpick, Beaded Edge, Flowers, 4 Footed 14.00
Custard Glass, Toothpick, Beaded, Souvenir, Clinton, Ia. 22.50
Custard Glass, Toothpick, Diamond Peg, Rose Design 37.50
Custard Glass, Toothpick, Diamond With Peg Pattern, Marked Krystol 60.00
Custard Glass, Toothpick, Diamond, Hand-Painted Roses, Souvenir Michigan 34.50
Custard Glass, Toothpick, French Lick Springs Hotel 12.00
Custard Glass, Toothpick, Inverted Fan & Feather .... 300.00 To 325.00
Custard Glass, Toothpick, Inverted Oval Arches, Red Chrysanthemums, Gold 25.00
Custard Glass, Toothpick, Souvenir, Seminary, Northwood Ridge, N.H., Gold 19.00
Custard Glass, Toothpick, Wild Bouquet 210.00
Custard Glass, Tumbler, Bottoms-Up, Amber, 3 1/2 In.Tall 35.00
Custard Glass, Tumbler, Chrysanthemum Sprig .... 30.00 To 47.50
Custard Glass, Tumbler, Chrysanthemum Sprig, Blue 95.00
Custard Glass, Tumbler, Chrysanthemum Sprig, No Paint Or Gold 22.50
Custard Glass, Tumbler, Diamond Peg, Rose, Leaves, Red 25.00
Custard Glass, Tumbler, Everglades 32.50
Custard Glass, Tumbler, Grape, Amber .... Illus 25.00

Custard Glass, Tumbler, Grape, Amber

Custard Glass, Tumbler, Honeycomb, Apple Blossoms, Flower Rim, Pink 25.00
Custard Glass, Tumbler, Intaglio Pattern 45.00
Custard Glass, Tumbler, Inverted Fan, Feather 50.00
Custard Glass, Tumbler, Ivorina Verde 32.50
Custard Glass, Tumbler, Louis XV 48.50
Custard Glass, Tumbler, Souvenir, Doylestown, Wisconsin, Catholic Church 20.00
Custard Glass, Vase, Birds, Flowers, Blue, Brown, Green, Amber, 14 1/4 In.Pair 250.00
Custard Glass, Vase, Grape & Gothic, Arches Sweet Pea 45.00
Custard Glass, Vase, Jack-In-The-Pulpit, Hand-Painted Florals, Gold 48.00
Custard Glass, Vase, Rosebud, Flared, Scalloped, Panels, Drapery, 9 1/2 In. 18.00
Custard Glass, Vase, Souvenir, Pawnee, Oklahoma, 7 In. 29.50
Custard Glass, Water Set, Green, Simplicity Pattern, 7 Piece 200.00
Custard Glass, Water Set, Ivorina Verde, 6 Piece 250.00
Custard Glass, Water Set, Panel Drape Pattern, Hand-Painted Roses, 7 Piece 250.00
Custard Glass, Wine, Souvenir Of Sangerville, Maine 12.50

Cut Glass has been made since ancient times, but the large majority of the
pieces now for sale date from the brilliant period of glass design, 1880 to
1905. These pieces had elaborate geometric designs with a deep miter cut.
   Cut Glass, see also Cruet, Toothpick, etc.
Cut Glass, Bowl, Hobstars, 8 In. 110.00
Cut Glass Carafe, Signed J.B.M.Co., Sherbrooke 25.00
Cut Glass Decanter, Clear, Shallow Cut 7.50
Cut Glass, Applique, Scandinavian, Gilt Metal Banding, 19th Century, Pair 275.00
Cut Glass, Atomizer, Clear Vesicas Framed By Cane Bands, Star On Base 85.00
Cut Glass, Banana Boat, Hobstar & Fan, Cut Base, 9 X 6 In. 55.00
Cut Glass, Basket, Hobstars, Panels, 7 7/8 In.Long, 12 In.High 325.00
Cut Glass, Basket, Hobstars, Pinwheels, Notched Prisms, 6 In.Long, 5 In.High 200.00
Cut Glass, Bear, Solid Crystal, 5 Lbs., 4 1/2 In.High, Pair 100.00
Cut Glass, Bell, Engraved Floral & World's Fair 1893, Frosted Handle 65.00
Cut Glass, Bell, Etched, Facet-Cut Handle 16.50

Cut Glass, Bell, Etched, 4 3/8 In.High 10.00
Cut Glass, Bell, Fans & Crosses, 5 In.Tall 18.00
Cut Glass, Bell, Hobstars, Fans, Cut Handle, 4 1/2 In.High 85.00
Cut Glass, Bottle, Back Bar, Hill & Hill 22.50
Cut Glass, Bottle, Back Bar, Hudson Rye 22.50
Cut Glass, Bottle, Claret, Clear, Diamond Stopper, Long Neck & Handle 25.00
Cut Glass, Bottle, Cologne, Flowers & Leaves, 6 In.Tall, Pair 75.00
Cut Glass, Bottle, Cologne, Pointed Panel, Notched Ribs, Faceted Stopper 39.50
Cut Glass, Bottle, Dresser, Ball Shape, Pair 100.00
Cut Glass, Bottle, Dressing, Engraved, Dated 1914, Townsende M.Hawke 88.00
Cut Glass, Bottle, Holy Water, 5 In., Cross Cut Stopper 12.50
Cut Glass, Bottle, Honeycomb Pattern, 11 1/2 In.Tall, Pair 49.00
Cut Glass, Bottle, Oil & Vinegar, Signed Hawkes, Sterling Top, June 20, 1916 ...... 65.00
Cut Glass, Bottle, Perfume, Faceted Stopper, 4 3/4 In. 22.50
Cut Glass, Bottle, Perfume, Icicle Shaped, Allover Sharp Cut, 5 In. 25.00
Cut Glass, Bottle, Perfume, Strawberrry & Fan, Pinched Waist, Amber Button 28.00
Cut Glass, Bottle, Perfume, 5 In.High 5.00
Cut Glass, Bottle, Water, Diamond & Fan Pattern 25.00
Cut Glass, Bottle, Water, Hobstars, Flat Bottom 59.00
Cut Glass, Bottle, Water, Hobstars, Wide Body 31.00
Cut Glass, Bottle, Water, Strawberry, Diamond, Fan, 8 1/2 In.Tall 30.00
Cut Glass, Bottle, Wine, Harvard, Hobstar, Cane, Harvard Teardrop Stopper 175.00
Cut Glass, Bowl, Allover Cut, Scalloped Edge, Oval, 10 1/2 In.Long 110.00
Cut Glass, Bowl, Allover Cut, Signed Clark, 7 In.Diameter, 3 In.Tall 49.50
Cut Glass, Bowl, Allover Cutting, 8 In. 65.00
Cut Glass, Bowl, Allover Harvard 75.00
Cut Glass, Bowl, Amber Bottom 165.00
Cut Glass, Bowl, American, Deep Cut 75.00
Cut Glass, Bowl, Banana, Hobstar & Petals, 8 X 4 7/8 In. 165.00
Cut Glass, Bowl, Block Pattern, Rose 12.00
Cut Glass, Bowl, Brilliant Period, Pinwheels & Hobstars 55.00
Cut Glass, Bowl, Buzz Star, Shallow, 6 In. 12.00
Cut Glass, Bowl, Canoe Shape, 8 1/2 In. 63.00
Cut Glass, Bowl, Cherries & Butterfly, Shallow, 6 In. 12.00
Cut Glass, Bowl, Clark, 8 In.Diameter 75.00
Cut Glass, Bowl, Daisy & Leaf, 6 In.Diameter 7.50
Cut Glass, Bowl, Dessert, Encore Pattern, Hobstar Base, 5 In.Diameter, Pair 30.00
Cut Glass, Bowl, English, Hobnail & Bull's-Eye 26.00
Cut Glass, Bowl, Fans, Hobstar, Geometrics, Signed Libbey, 8 1/4 In. 60.00
Cut Glass, Bowl, Fern, Double X Cut Vesica, Footed, 4 3/4 In. 95.00
Cut Glass, Bowl, Finger, Diamond Cut, Set Of 6 .... 100.00
Cut Glass, Bowl, Finger, Fan, Hobstar, Star Base, 4 1/2 In.Diameter 28.00
Cut Glass, Bowl, Finger, On Tray 22.00
Cut Glass, Bowl, Finger, Signed Alfred, Fan, Crosshatch & Hobstar 24.00
Cut Glass, Bowl, Flute Pattern, Signed J.Hoare & Co., 1853, 9 In.Diameter 195.00
Cut Glass, Bowl, Fruit, Hobstar, Medallion, Ruffled Edge, 8 In.Diameter 44.00
Cut Glass, Bowl, Fruit, Hobstars, Strawberry Diamond, 3 In.Tall 45.00
Cut Glass, Bowl, Fruit, Serrated Ruffles, Hobstars, 8 In. 47.00
Cut Glass, Bowl, Heart, Hobstar, 8 In.Diameter 100.00
Cut Glass, Bowl, Hobstar, Crosshatch, Footed, 3 1/4 In.Tall 28.00
Cut Glass, Bowl, Hobstar, Rosettes, Russian Daisy Centers, 10 In. 65.00
Cut Glass, Bowl, Hobstars, Crosshatching, Stars, Signed Libbey, 11 In.Long 225.00
Cut Glass, Bowl, Hobstars, Fans, & Vintage Grape, 9 In.Diameter 65.00
Cut Glass, Bowl, Hobstars, Starred Button, Canoe Shape, 12 1/2 In.Long 95.00
Cut Glass, Bowl, Hobstars, Stars, Scalloped, Star Bottom, 8 3/4 In.Diameter 45.00
Cut Glass, Bowl, Ice, Hobstars, Fans, Stars, 4 1/2 X 6 In.Diameter 38.00
Cut Glass, Bowl, Lead Crystal, Sterling Silver Edge 15.00
Cut Glass, Bowl, Mayonnaise, Pedestal, Matching Plate, Maple City Glass Co. 145.00
Cut Glass, Bowl, Medallions, Deep 66.50
Cut Glass, Bowl, Middlesex Pattern, Signed Libbey, 7 In.Diameter 60.00
Cut Glass, Bowl, Oval, Ruby Cased, English 55.00
Cut Glass, Bowl, Pairpoint Standard 47.50
Cut Glass, Bowl, Pinwheel, Cane, Button, Hobstar, Crosshatch 95.00
Cut Glass, Bowl, Punch, Base, Hobstars, Canes, 12 X 11 1/2 In.High 465.00
Cut Glass, Bowl, Punch, Base, Tulip Shape, Pinwheels, Sunburst, 12 1/4 In.Tall 550.00
Cut Glass, Bowl, Punch, Buzz Hobstars, Two Pieces 550.00

Cut Glass, Bowl, Punch, Corinthian, Two Part, 14 1/2 In.Diameter 475.00
Cut Glass, Bowl, Punch. Crosshatch, Sawtooth Edge, 9 1/2 In.Diameter, 11 In. 135.00
Cut Glass, Bowl, Punch, Fan, Hobstar, Bulbous, Pedestal, 11 In.Diameter, 12 In. 295.00
Cut Glass, Bowl, Punch, Flower Form, C.1880-1915 .... 875.00
Cut Glass, Bowl, Punch, Signed Libbey, 15 In. 385.00
Cut Glass, Bowl, Punch, Signed Libbey, 2 Piece, Star & Feather 600.00
Cut Glass, Bowl, Punch, Signed Pitkin & Brooks, Cut Roses, Rolled Edge 250.00
Cut Glass, Bowl, Punch, Two Piece, Eight Cups, Ladle, Pitkin & Brooks 1800.00
Cut Glass, Bowl, Punch, Two Piece, Star & Feather, Signed Libbey 800.00
Cut Glass, Bowl, Signed Clark, Jewel Pattern, 3 1/2 In.High 57.50
Cut Glass, Bowl, Signed Hawkes, Pale Green Intaglio Leaf & Vine, Footed 40.00
Cut Glass, Bowl, Signed Hawkes, Pinwheel With Hobstars, 8 In.Diameter 125.00
Cut Glass, Bowl, Signed Hawkes, Queen's Pattern, 8 In.Diameter 95.00
Cut Glass, Bowl, Signed Hawkes, 9 In. 60.00
Cut Glass, Bowl, Signed Hoare, 8 1/4 In.Diameter 80.00
Cut Glass, Bowl, Signed Irving, 11 In.Long X 6 1/2 In.Wide 220.00
Cut Glass, Bowl, Signed Libbey, 5 1/4 In.Diameter, 3 In.High 30.00
Cut Glass, Bowl, Signed, Libbey, 8 1/2 In.Diameter 68.50
Cut Glass, Bowl, Signed Tuthill, 9 In. 75.00
Cut Glass, Bowl, Snowflake, Shallow, 6 In. 12.00
Cut Glass, Bowl, Star, Shallow, 6 In. 12.00
Cut Glass, Bowl, Waterford, Footed 95.00
Cut Glass, Bowl, 8 In.Diameter 27.50
Cut Glass, Box, Cigarette, Hobstar, Fan, Cover, 8 In.Long, 3 In.Wide 80.00
Cut Glass, Box, Collar & Cuff, Hobstar, Crosscut, Diamond, Fan, 7 1/2 In. 250.00
Cut Glass, Box, Handkerchief, Intaglio Floral, Notched Sides, 7 In.Square 175.00
Cut Glass, Box, Hinged, Hobstar Lid, Notched Prisms, Thumbprints 60.00
Cut Glass, Box, Jewelry, Victorian, Hinged, Brass Feet 25.00
Cut Glass, Box, Powder, Jeweled Silver Plate Cover 45.00
Cut Glass, Box, Puff, Amber Fans & Stars, Signed Hawkes 37.50
Cut Glass, Box, Star, Prism, Meteor Cutting, Cover, 5 1/2 In. 55.00
Cut Glass, Bucket, Ice, Hobstars, Flashed Fans, Crosshatching, Handles 145.00
Cut Glass, Bucket, Ice, Hobstars, Strawberry Diamonds, Handles, Silver Rim 235.00
Cut Glass, Bucket, Ice, Strawberry Diamond & Fan, Silver Rim & Handle 75.00
Cut Glass, Bucket, Ice, 3 Feet, Hobstars, Pinwheels, Hobnail & Fans 55.00
Cut Glass, Butter, Covered, Hobstar, Cross Diamond, Fan 150.00
Cut Glass, Butter, Facet Cut Knob, Hobstars & Flashed Fans, Covered 175.00
Cut Glass, Butter, Hobstar, Strawberry, Diamond Point, & Fan 150.00
Cut Glass, Butter, Thistle Pattern 125.00
Cut Glass, Candelabra, Regency, 2 Branch Arms, 19th Century, Pair 150.00
Cut Glass, Candlestick, Ball, Bar, Flowers, 10 In., Pair 60.00
Cut Glass, Candlestick, Cranberry Threading, Tulip Candle Cup, Pair 125.00
Cut Glass, Candlestick, George III, Faceted Cylindrical Standard, C.1765, 4 .... 700.00
Cut Glass, Candlestick, Honeycomb, Teardrop, Hex Base, 8 1/2 In. Pair 145.00
Cut Glass, Candlestick, Pairpoint Wilton Pattern, 10 1/2 In.High, Pair 125.00
Cut Glass, Candlestick, Signed Libbey, 8 In.High, Pair 115.00
Cut Glass, Candlestick, Signed Nash, Gold Iridescent, Bobeche Diamond, Pair 185.00
Cut Glass, Carafe, Hobstar, Fans, Notched Prisms & Crosshatching 35.00
Cut Glass, Carafe, Signed Libbey, 10 Panels, Cane & Zipper 60.00
Cut Glass, Carafe, Water, Hobstars, Strawberry Diamond, Stars, Fan, 8 1/4 In. 95.00
Cut Glass, Carafe, Water, Straus Imperial Pattern, Hobstar Base 65.00
Cut Glass, Carafe, Water, Strawberry, Diamond & Fan 32.00
Cut Glass, Celery, Flat, Deep Cut 22.50
Cut Glass, Celery, Hobstar Medallions, Starfish, Harvard, 11 1/4 In. 35.00
Cut Glass, Celery, Hobstar, Cane & Fan, 10 In. 45.00
Cut Glass, Celery, Hobstar, Hobnail, Strawberry Diamond, Cane 52.00
Cut Glass, Celery, Oblong, Harvard, Intaglio Cut Flowers 28.00
Cut Glass, Celery, Signed Clark 90.00
Cut Glass, Chalice, Crosscut Diamond, Strawberry, Diamond & Fan 50.00
Cut Glass, Champagne, Engraved Genia 8.00
Cut Glass, Cheese, Buzz Diamond Filled Vesica, Cane & Hobstar 275.00
Cut Glass, Clock, Pedestal Base, Running 65.00
Cut Glass, Coaster, Diamond Pattern, Hawks, 5 1/2 In. 30.00
Cut Glass, Coffeepot, Cut Handle & Spout 650.00
Cut Glass, Cologne, Hobstar & Pinwheel, 5 1/2 In.High 45.00
Cut Glass, Cologne, 112 Facets In Stopper, Signed Libbey, 7 In.High 110.00

Cut Glass, Compote, Chair Cane, Hobstar, Floral, Notched Pedestal, 9 In.Tall 55.00
Cut Glass, Compote, Crystal Wedding, Covered, 13 In. 60.00
Cut Glass, Compote, Diamond, Hobstars, Stars & Fans, Teardrop Stem 80.00
Cut Glass, Compote, Divided Into 3 Sections, C.1880-1915 .... 395.00
Cut Glass, Compote, Firs & Leaves, Etched Petals, 16 Point Star Base 20.00
Cut Glass, Compote, Hobstar Base, 6 X 10 In.Tall 90.00
Cut Glass, Compote, Hobstar, Cane, Fan, & Diamond Point, 20 Point Star Base 95.00
Cut Glass, Compote, Hobstar, Fan, Notched Stem Point Star, 9 In.Tall 95.00
Cut Glass, Compote, Hobstar, Roses, Signed Fry, 8 In.Tall 110.00
Cut Glass, Compote, Hobstars, Fans, Notched Stem, 9 In.Tall, 5 1/2 In.Across 95.00
Cut Glass, Compote, Hobstars, Medallions, 8 3/4 In. 61.00
Cut Glass, Compote, Hobstars, Strawberry, & Feathered Stars, Notched Stem 70.00
Cut Glass, Compote, Intaglio Butterflies & Leaves, Star Base 55.00
Cut Glass, Compote, Jelly, Hobstars, Stars, Diamond Point, Paperweight Base 60.00
Cut Glass, Compote, Jelly, Signed Libbey, Hobstar, Diamond Point, & Fan 70.00
Cut Glass, Compote, Leaves & Flowers 10.00
Cut Glass, Compote, Panel, Buttons, Intaglio Flowers, 6 In.Diameter, 5 1/2 In 42.50
Cut Glass, Compote, Ribbon & Star, Fluted Stem, Hobstar Base 155.00
Cut Glass, Compote, Rose Pattern, Rayed Base, 6 In.High, 6 In.Diameter 35.00
Cut Glass, Compote, Sawtooth, 11 In.High, Covered, Pair 130.00
Cut Glass, Compote, Signed Hawkes, Three Fruit, Gravic, 8 In.Tall 225.00
Cut Glass, Compote, Star Petal, Star Point, Clear, 6 In.High 35.00
Cut Glass, Compote, Strawberry Diamond, Flashed Star, Two Notched Handles 35.00
Cut Glass, Compote, Sunburst Pattern, Teardrop Stem, 10 1/2 X 9 1/2 In.High 400.00
Cut Glass, Compote, Teardrop Stem, Scalloped & Cut Base 95.00
Cut Glass, Compote, Teardrop, Post Ribbed, 8 In.Tall 45.00
Cut Glass, Compote, Waterford, Covered, Square Base, 12 In.High, Pair 275.00
Cut Glass, Console Set, Vintage Pattern, Signed Sinclaire, Candlesticks 595.00
Cut Glass, Cordial, Signed Libbey, Saber Mark, Stemmed, Hobstars, Set Of 4 .... 120.00
Cut Glass, Cordial, Strawberry, Diamond, & Fan 12.00
Cut Glass, Creamer & Sugar, Allover Cut 48.00
Cut Glass, Creamer & Sugar, Chrysanthemums, Hobstars, Hobnails, Fans 85.00
Cut Glass, Creamer & Sugar, Diamond, Allover Cut 65.00
Cut Glass, Creamer & Sugar, Florence Pattern 40.00
Cut Glass, Creamer & Sugar, Frosted Rose Cut, Cut Leaves, Feathered Edge 22.50
Cut Glass, Creamer & Sugar, Hobstar, Fan & Star, Star Cut Base 179.00
Cut Glass, Creamer & Sugar, Hobstars, Crosshatching, Fans, Star Bases 275.00
Cut Glass, Creamer & Sugar, Hobstars, Pinwheels, Cut Handles 47.50
Cut Glass, Creamer & Sugar, Intaglio, Havard 27.50
Cut Glass, Creamer & Sugar, Pinwheel, Star Base 27.50
Cut Glass, Creamer & Sugar, Poinsettia, Signed Clarke 42.50
Cut Glass, Creamer, Cluster Variation, Russian Cutting, Signed Unger 35.00
Cut Glass, Creamer, Harvard 10.00
Cut Glass, Creamer, Silsbee Pattern, Double Notched Handles, Star Base 35.00
Cut Glass, Cruet, Allover Thumbprint Cuts 38.00
Cut Glass, Cruet, Crosscut Diamond & Fan, Blown Bubble Stopper 35.00
Cut Glass, Cruet, Diamond & Fan, Stopper, 6 3/4 In.High 24.50
Cut Glass, Cruet, Fan, Radiant, Crosshatch, Stopper, 6 1/2 In.Tall 28.00
Cut Glass, Cruet, Hobstars, Flutes 38.00
Cut Glass, Cruet, Meteor Pattern, 9 In.High 37.50
Cut Glass, Cruet, Signed J.Hoare, Ship's, Hobstar & Notched Panel 80.00
Cut Glass, Cruet, Star Cut 19.50
Cut Glass, Cruet, Stopper, Inverted Thumbprint 38.00
Cut Glass, Cruet, Stopper, Irish, Pair 27.50
Cut Glass, Cruet, Stopper, Mark Three Birds In Clover, Hawkes 75.00
Cut Glass, Cruet, Strawberry, Fan, Tankard Shape, Lapidary Stopper, 7 1/2 In. 22.50
Cut Glass, Cruet, Three Lips, Star In Diamond & Fan, Panel Neck, Hawkes 75.00
Cut Glass, Cruet, Thumbprint, Mushroom Stopper, Squat, Notched Handle 17.00
Cut Glass, Cruet, Vinegar, Heavy Cut 12.00
Cut Glass, Cruet, Vinegar, Red Cut To Crystal, Stopper 18.50
Cut Glass, Cruet, Vinegar, Star 19.50
Cut Glass, Cup, Egg, Double, Hobnail, Clear 5.00
Cut Glass, Cup, Loving, Notching, Rounded Flutes, Two Handles, Silver Top 235.00
Cut Glass, Cup, Punch, Butterflies & Floral 15.00
Cut Glass, Cup, Punch, Frost Crystal, Clear 4.50
Cut Glass, Cup, Punch, Gorham Sterling Silver Rim, Hobstars & Prisms, 6 .... 150.00

Cut Glass, Cup, Punch, Handled	8.50
Cut Glass, Cup, Punch, Hobstar, Feather, Fan	18.00
Cut Glass, Cup, Punch, Lozenge Pattern	15.00
Cut Glass, Cup, Punch, Monarch Pattern	15.00
Cut Glass, Cup, Punch, Prism & Hobstars	15.00
Cut Glass, Cup, Punch, Star Cut Base	3.00
Cut Glass, Cup, Punch, Strawberry, Diamond, & Fan, Handled, Star Cut Base, 8	90.00
Cut Glass, Cup, Punch, Strawberry, Diamond, & Fan, Set Of 8	140.00
Cut Glass, Cuspidor, Hobstars, 12 In.Diameter	195.00
Cut Glass, Cuspidor, Lady's, Cut Hobstar At Bottom, Cornflowers At Rim	145.00
Cut Glass, Decanter, Amethyst Cut To Clear, Tapered, 14 In.	75.00
Cut Glass, Decanter, Button Pattern, Silver Lock, Stopper	95.00
Cut Glass, Decanter, Diamond Cut, Stopper, 11 In.High, Pair	110.00
Cut Glass, Decanter, Diamond Pattern, Sterling Rim, English	55.00
Cut Glass, Decanter, Emerald Green Cut To Clear, 15 In.	50.00
Cut Glass, Decanter, Engraved Initials	40.00
Cut Glass, Decanter, George Iv, Octagonal, Flared Rim, 19th Century, Pair	130.00
Cut Glass, Decanter, Harvard Bands, Flowers, Star Base, Bull's-Eye Neck	95.00
Cut Glass, Decanter, Intaglio Cut Floral, Strawberry Diamond, 11 In.	50.00
Cut Glass, Decanter, Lapidary, Stopper, 12 In.High	150.00
Cut Glass, Decanter, Matching Stopper	85.00
Cut Glass, Decanter, Pinwheels, Double Fan, St.Louis, Stopper, 11 1/2 In.Tall	145.00
Cut Glass, Decanter, Pitcher Shape, Allover Cut, Stopper, 16 In.Tall	52.50
Cut Glass, Decanter, Polished Pontil, Pittsburgh, Stopper, 13 In.Tall	65.00
Cut Glass, Decanter, Prismatic & Honeycomb With Prismatic Stoppers, Pair	250.00
Cut Glass, Decanter, Prismatic Cut, Honeycomb Neck, Stopper, Pair	275.00
Cut Glass, Decanter, Signed Tiffany & Co., Intaglio Bluebells, 16 1/2 In.	300.00
Cut Glass, Decanter, Sunburst, 7 1/2 In.High	45.00
Cut Glass, Decanter, Triple Notched Strawberry, Diamond & Fan, 13 In.Tall	95.00
Cut Glass, Decanter, Vertical Grooving, Knob Stem, Stopper, Pair	40.00
Cut Glass, Decanter, Waterford, Stopper, 9 In.High, Pair	110.00
Cut Glass, Decanter, Wine, Pinwheel, Panel Stopper, Handle, 14 In.Tall	55.00
Cut Glass, Decanter, 12 1/2 In.Tall	25.00
Cut Glass, Demitasse Set, French, Gold Rim, Ribbed, Set Of 8	64.00
Cut Glass, Dish, Bonbon, Star, Sawtooth, Cover	20.00
Cut Glass, Dish, Butter, Harvard Pattern, Cover, 8 In.Diameter	195.00
Cut Glass, Dish, Butter, Hobstar, Russian Cut, Dome Shape Cover	35.00
Cut Glass, Dish, Butter, Pinwheel	150.00
Cut Glass, Dish, Butter, Rayed Blossoms, Buds, Foliage, Faceted Knob	125.00
Cut Glass, Dish, Candy, Daisy & Leaf, Footed, 5 In.High	17.50
Cut Glass, Dish, Candy, Footed, Signed R With Rampant Lion, 6 In.Diameter	48.00
Cut Glass, Dish, Candy, Four Sections, Cut Handles, 10 3/4 In.	82.00
Cut Glass, Dish, Candy, Hobstars, Variants, Sectioned, Two Handles	75.00
Cut Glass, Dish, Candy, Honeycomb, Diamond & Fan Border, Pedestal	95.00
Cut Glass, Dish, Candy, Pinwheel, 6 X 7 1/2 In.	28.00
Cut Glass, Dish, Celery, Hobstar, Strawberry Diamond, Ovals, Pair	145.00
Cut Glass, Dish, Celery, Hobstars, Vesicas	40.00
Cut Glass, Dish, Cheese, Allover Cut, Signed Newark	455.00
Cut Glass, Dish, Cheese, Cluster Pattern, 9 3/4 X 7 1/2 In.High	300.00
Cut Glass, Dish, Cheese, Diamond Point Cutting, Squared Flutes, Cut Knop	45.00
Cut Glass, Dish, Cheese, Diamond, Star	21.50
Cut Glass, Dish, Desert, Flower Spray Cut, Signed International, Set Of 4	60.00
Cut Glass, Dish, Dessert, Hobstar, Fan, Scalloped Edge, 5 1/2 In.	20.00
Cut Glass, Dish, Diamond Cut, Leaf, 8 In.Diameter	30.00
Cut Glass, Dish, Heart Shape, 5 1/2 In.Long	46.00
Cut Glass, Dish, Hobstar, Diamond, Sawtooth Edge, Footed	30.00
Cut Glass, Dish, Hobstars, Crosscut Diamond, Leaf Shape, 7 X 6 In.	55.00
Cut Glass, Dish, Ice Cream, Hobstars, Fans, Scalloped Top, Set Of 8	160.00
Cut Glass, Dish, Leaf Shape, Hobstars, Crosscut Diamond, Notched Handle	55.00
Cut Glass, Dish, Olive, Hunt's Royal Pattern, 5 In.Wide	40.00
Cut Glass, Dish, Olive, Signed R With Rampant Lion, 7 X 3 1/2 In.	30.00
Cut Glass, Dish, Oval, Diamond Cut, 9 In.Long, Pair	40.00
Cut Glass, Dish, Relish, Waffle Pattern, Handle, 5 In.Diameter	12.50
Cut Glass, Dish, Relish, 8 In.Diameter	12.50
Cut Glass, Dish, Ruffle Serrated, Hobstars, Oval, 5 1/2 In.	22.00
Cut Glass, Dish, Sauce, Comet Variation, Turned Sides, Signed Hoare, Set Of 4	150.00

Cut Glass, Dish, Swan	18.50
Cut Glass, Dish, Sweetmeat, Covered, Diamond Cutting, 6 In.Diameter	60.00
Cut Glass, Dish, Triangular, Pineapple & Fan, 6 In.	22.00
Cut Glass, Fernery, Footed, 7 1/2 In.Diameter	38.00
Cut Glass, Fernery, Harvard Prism, Star Bottom, Round	42.00
Cut Glass, Fernery, Hobstar & Fan, 3 Feet, 4 1/2 In.High	64.50
Cut Glass, Fernery, Hobstar & Buzz, Footed, 7 1/2 In.Diameter	25.00
Cut Glass, Fernery, Punwheel, 3 3/4 In.High	68.50
Cut Glass, Fernery, 8 In.Diameter	30.00
Cut Glass, Flower Center, Signed Hoare, Monarch Pattern	225.00
Cut Glass, Flower Centerpiece, Hobstars, Strawberry Diamond, Rosette Base	195.00
Cut Glass, Flute, Engraved Row Of Beads & Feather, Square Foot, 7 In.	40.00
Cut Glass, Goblet, Barrel Shape, Pale Blue To Clear, Square Block Base	10.00
Cut Glass, Goblet, Bell Shape, Hobstar Rosettes, Notched Prism, Panel Stem, 3	100.00
Cut Glass, Goblet, Buckle Pattern	12.00
Cut Glass, Goblet, Diamond Pattern, Silhouette On Sides	45.00
Cut Glass, Goblet, Diamond, Fan	35.00
Cut Glass, Goblet, Double Lozenge Pattern	40.00
Cut Glass, Goblet, Encore Pattern, Hobstar Base, 6 1/2 In., Set Of 6	40.00
Cut Glass, Goblet, Engraved Rose & 2 Buds, Conical Foot, C.1760, English	200.00
Cut Glass, Goblet, Greek Key & Laurel, Signed Sinclaire, Set Of 6	185.00
Cut Glass, Goblet, Hobstar	45.00
Cut Glass, Goblet, Louisiana Pattern	10.00
Cut Glass, Goblet, Monarch Pattern	40.00
Cut Glass, Goblet, Signed Hawkes, Hobstar, Fan & English Strawberry Diamond	50.00
Cut Glass, Goblet, Strawberry, Fan, Notched Stem, 7 In.Tall	28.50
Cut Glass, Goblet, Strawberry, Fan, Point Star, Notched Stem, 7 In.	25.00
Cut Glass, Goblet, Swirl, Pedestal, Pale Green, Gold Design Around Rim	18.00
Cut Glass, Goblet, Teardrop Stem, English Strawberry Diamond & Fan	65.00
Cut Glass, Goblet, White To Clear, Gilt & Enamel Floral Decoration	25.00
Cut Glass, Holder, Toothbrush, Hobstars, Signed, Sterling Top	55.00
Cut Glass, Humidor, Silver Top Marked Black, Starr & Frost	130.00
Cut Glass, Ice Cream Set, American, Strawberry, Diamond, & Fan, 10 Piece	165.00
Cut Glass, Inkwell, Lid, Gilt Tray Frame, Double Handle	30.00
Cut Glass, Inkwell, Sapphire Blue, Covered	27.50
Cut Glass, Inkwell, Square Base, Intaglio Cut, Laurel Wreath, Sterling Top	58.00
Cut Glass, Inkwell, Sterling Silver Top	30.00
Cut Glass, Jar, Biscuit, Diamond & Thumbprint	49.50
Cut Glass, Jar, Blue To Clear, Over Lay, Silver Tray, Ring Rack, Set	150.00
Cut Glass, Jar, Cookie, Cover	22.00
Cut Glass, Jar, Cookie, Silver Rim, Handle, & Cover	22.00
Cut Glass, Jar, Cracker, Barrel Shape, Diagonal Ferns & Leaves, Silver Bail	45.00
Cut Glass, Jar, Dresser, Sterling Top, Poppies	23.00
Cut Glass, Jar, English Cut, Ground Cut Stopper	35.00
Cut Glass, Jar, Leaves, Butterflies, Flowers, Sterling Silver Cover, 7 In.	195.00
Cut Glass, Jar, Mayonnaise, Pinwheel, Star, Panels	20.00
Cut Glass, Jar, Mustard, Hobstar, Sunburst, Cover, Spoon	19.00
Cut Glass, Jar, Mustard, Russian Pattern, Silver Cover	45.00
Cut Glass, Jar, Powder, Allover Cut, Beaded Rim, Sterling Silver Top	50.00
Cut Glass, Jar, Powder, Diamond, Fan, Sterling Lid, Floral Design	35.00
Cut Glass, Jar, Powder, Floral Cut, 4 1/2 In.Diameter, Cover	34.00
Cut Glass, Jar, Powder, International Sterling Lid	15.00
Cut Glass, Jar, Powder, Repousse Sterling Lid	30.00
Cut Glass, Jar, Powder, Sharp Cuttings, Deep, Sterling Silver Cover	35.00
Cut Glass, Jar, Relish, Spoon, 4 1/2 In.High	4.00
Cut Glass, Jar, Signed Hawkes, Gravic, Thistle Pattern	195.00
Cut Glass, Jar, Tobacco, Hobstar Cover, Arcadia Pattern	145.00
Cut Glass, Jardiniere, Harvard, 8 In.Diameter, 6 In.High	150.00
Cut Glass, Jelly, Stemmed, Tall, 7 1/4 In.Diameter	32.00
Cut Glass, Jug, Water, Strawberry Diamonds, 5 Vertical Prisms, 19th Century	50.00
Cut Glass, Jug, Water, 7 In.High	17.50
Cut Glass, Jug, Whiskey, Applied Rosette Decor, Square Handle	225.00
Cut Glass, Knife Rest, Ball Ends, Crosscut Diamond & Stars, Notched Prism	25.00
Cut Glass, Knife Rest, Dumbell, Ends, Notched Prism, 5 1/2 In.	22.00
Cut Glass, Knife Rest, Dumbbell Shape, Allover Cut, 4 1/4 In.Long, Pair	25.00
Cut Glass, Knife Rest, Dumbbell, 6 In.Long	90.00

Cut Glass, Knife Rest, Faceted Ends, 6 In.Long	25.00
Cut Glass, Knife Rest, Fan & Serrated, Sterling Silver Ends, Pair	25.00
Cut Glass, Knife Rest, Individual, Rod Shape	3.50
Cut Glass, Knife Rest, Notched Shank, Dumbbell Ends Cut In Vesica, Prism	22.00
Cut Glass, Knife Rest, Prism Type, 4 1/2 In.Long	15.00
Cut Glass, Knife Rest, Prismatic Center, Ball Ends, 4 In.Long	15.00
Cut Glass, Knife Rest, Prisms, 6	12.00
Cut Glass, Knife Rest, Square Ends, Sevres, 3 In., Pair	15.00
Cut Glass, Knife Rest, Star	12.50
Cut Glass, Knife Rest, Strawberry Diamonds, Sterling Rims On Ends, Pair	35.00
Cut Glass, Knife Rest, Strawberry Diamonds On Shank & Dumbbell Ends	28.00
Cut Glass, Knob, Dresser, Cut Star Center, 1 3/4 In.Diameter, Set Of 5	18.00
Cut Glass, Lamp, Hobstar, Pinwheel, Flashed Star, 32 Cut Prisms, 17 In.Tall	550.00
Cut Glass, Lamp, Mushroom Shade, Allover Cut, 19 In.High	100.00
Cut Glass, Lamp, Mushroom, Allover Cut, 12 In.	79.50
Cut Glass, Lamp, Mushroom, Allover Cut, 15 In. High	79.50
Cut Glass, Lamp, Round Shade, Allover Cut, 12 In. High	79.50
Cut Glass, Lamp, Round Shape, Allover Cut, 16 In.	79.50
Cut Glass, Lighter, Cigarette, Table, Block Cut, Pair	8.00
Cut Glass, Mug, Fan & Diamonds, Applied Handle, 3 In.Tall	25.00
Cut Glass, Mug, Handled, Middlesex Pattern	45.00
Cut Glass, Napkin Ring, Buzz, Fans, Pair	80.00
Cut Glass, Napkin Ring, Diamond & Star Design	18.50
Cut Glass, Napkin Ring, Diamond Cut, Oval	21.00
Cut Glass, Napkin Ring, Hobstar, Diamond, Herringbone Border	35.00
Cut Glass, Nappy, Allover Cut, Scalloped Top, Handle	32.00
Cut Glass, Nappy, Divided, Double Handled, Pansy Pattern, 8 1/2 In.	45.00
Cut Glass, Nappy, Floral, Leaves & Stems, Ring Handle, Toothed Edge	14.00
Cut Glass, Nappy, Handled Scalloped Edge, 5 In.	10.00
Cut Glass, Nappy, Handled, 5 In.	20.00
Cut Glass, Nappy, Handled, 6 In.	20.00
Cut Glass, Nappy, Hobstars, Geometrics, Cut Handle, Scalloped Notched Top	30.00
Cut Glass, Nappy, Hobstars, Notched, Scalloped, Cut Handle	25.00
Cut Glass, Nappy, Pinwheel, Hobstar, Feather, Ring Handle, 5 In.Diameter	27.50
Cut Glass, Nappy, Russian Cut, 6 In.	32.50
Cut Glass, Nappy, Signed Corning, 7 In.	37.50
Cut Glass, Nappy, Signed Hawkes, Hobstar, Fan, & Split Vesicas, Handle	45.00
Cut Glass, Nappy, Signed Hawkes, 6 In.Wide	37.50
Cut Glass, Nappy, Signed Hunt, Copper Wheel Engraved, Intaglio Floral	90.00
Cut Glass, Nappy, Signed J.Hoare & Co., Corning Handled	5.00
Cut Glass, Nappy, Signed Tuthill, Fully Cut, 6 In.Diameter	70.00
Cut Glass, Nappy, Stars, Notched Handle, 6 In.Diameter	24.00
Cut Glass, Paperweight, Diamond Facets, Beveled Lines, Star Cut In Base	20.00
Cut Glass, Paperweight, Facet Corners, Bevels, Hexagon	25.00
Cut Glass, Perfume, Atomizer, Hobstars, Leaves, Cosmos, Pedestal, 10 In.	37.00
Cut Glass, Perfume, Harvard, Sterling Silver Top, Floral Design	20.00
Cut Glass, Perfume, Heart Shape Cutting, Signed Czechoslovakia	45.00
Cut Glass, Perfume, Hobstar Rosettes, X Cut Vesicas, Strawberry Diamond, Fan	30.00
Cut Glass, Perfume, Horn Shape, Hinged Sterling Top	15.00
Cut Glass, Perfume, Icicle Shape, Sterling Silver Top, 5 In.Tall	18.50
Cut Glass, Perfume, Russian Pattern, Clear, Silver Cap, Lying Down	45.00
Cut Glass, Perfume, Signed Tuthill, Etched Flowers, Stopper, 3 1/2 In.High	35.00
Cut Glass, Perfume, Teardrop Paneled, Relief Diamond, Atomizer, 7 In.High	55.00
Cut Glass, Pitcher & Tumbler Set, Signed Libbey, 7 Piece	325.00
Cut Glass, Pitcher, Applied Handle, Hobstars, Fans, & Finecut	60.00
Cut Glass, Pitcher, Buzz Wheel, 9 In.High	75.00
Cut Glass, Pitcher, Chrysanthemums, Notched Handle, 10 1/2 In.High	128.00
Cut Glass, Pitcher, Cider, Encore Pattern, Hobstar Base, 10 In.	95.00
Cut Glass, Pitcher, Cider, Four Tumblers & Coasters, J.Hoare & Co., 1853	132.50
Cut Glass, Pitcher, Diamond & Fan, Notched Handle, 9 1/2 In.Tall	50.00
Cut Glass, Pitcher, Diamond Cut, Ball Shape, 6 In.High	60.00
Cut Glass, Pitcher, Diamond Hobstar, Notched Prisms, Signed, Tankard	165.00
Cut Glass, Pitcher, Flowers, Crosshatching, Tankard Shaped, 10 In.Tall	65.00
Cut Glass, Pitcher, Graduated Harvard Pattern, Floral Insert	110.00
Cut Glass, Pitcher, Hawkes, Signed	250.00
Cut Glass, Pitcher, Hobstar, Strawberry Diamond, Cane, Notched Prism, Tankard	185.00

Cut Glass, Pitcher, Hobstars, Fans, Crosshatching, Notching, Notched Handle 185.00
Cut Glass, Pitcher, Hobstars, Variants, 12 In.High 69.00
Cut Glass, Pitcher, Intaglio Cut 32.00
Cut Glass, Pitcher, Meteor Pattern, 6 Matching Glasses 120.00
Cut Glass, Pitcher, Milk, Hobstar Base, Pinwheel, Fan, Triple Notched Handle 45.00
Cut Glass, Pitcher, Milk, Strawberry, Diamond, & Fan, Ball Shape 25.00
Cut Glass, Pitcher, Milk, 8 In.High 50.00
Cut Glass, Pitcher, Notched Handle, Star Cut Bottom, 10 In.High 85.00
Cut Glass, Pitcher, Overlay Pink & White Glass, Cut Pineapple & Florals 350.00
Cut Glass, Pitcher, Pedestal, Intaglio Grape & Leaves, 11 In.High 200.00
Cut Glass, Pitcher, Pinwheel, Hobstar, Diamond, Star, 9 1/2 In.Tall 85.00
Cut Glass, Pitcher, Signed Hawkes, 14 In.Tall 250.00
Cut Glass, Pitcher, Silver Handle, Cover, & Spout, 11 1/2 In.High 35.00
Cut Glass, Pitcher, Silver Overlay Grapes, Intaglio Cut Grapes, 9 1/2 In. 175.00
Cut Glass, Pitcher, Star Base, Crosscut Diamond, Notched Rim, 10 In. 35.00
Cut Glass, Pitcher, Strawberry Diamond, Hobstar, Fan, Tankard Type, 12 In. 135.00
Cut Glass, Pitcher, Strawberry Diamond, Hobstars, Fan, 12 In. 135.00
Cut Glass, Pitcher, Syrup, Prism Pattern, Lid & Handle Silver Plate 35.00
Cut Glass, Pitcher, Tankard Shape, Hobstars, Fans, Cross-Hatching 85.00
Cut Glass, Pitcher, Tankard Shape, Meteor Pattern 57.50
Cut Glass, Pitcher, Tankard, Allover Flattened Hobnails, Honeycomb Handle 175.00
Cut Glass, Pitcher, Tankard, Meteor Pattern 57.50
Cut Glass, Pitcher, Water, Cross Block 75.00
Cut Glass, Pitcher, Water, Engraved Fruits On Body, Signed P & B 325.00
Cut Glass, Pitcher, Water, Florals 45.00
Cut Glass, Pitcher, Water, Hobstar, Thumbprint Cutting On Handle, 10 1/2 In. 40.00
Cut Glass, Pitcher, Water, Hobstars, 9 In. 59.00
Cut Glass, Pitcher, Water, Middlesex, 8 In.High, 8 In.Diameter 80.00
Cut Glass, Pitcher, Water, Pinwheel 50.00
Cut Glass, Pitcher, Water, Star, Pinwheel, Applied Handle, Tankard Shape 55.00
Cut Glass, Pitcher, Water, Tankard Shape, Bergen, 11 1/2 In. 135.00
Cut Glass, Pitcher, Water, Tankard Shape, Hobstars, Cane, Diamond Point, Fans 95.00
Cut Glass, Pitcher, Water, Tankard, Hobstar, Thumbprint Cut On Handle 40.00
Cut Glass, Pitcher, Water, Tankard, Signed C In Shamrock 65.00
Cut Glass, Pitcher, Water, Three Star Decoration, 8 1/2 In.High 15.00
Cut Glass, Pitcher, Water, Tulip, Fern, Vesica, Hobstars, Fans, Cut Handle 60.00
Cut Glass, Plate, Butterflies & Flowers, Star, 12 1/2 In.Diameter 55.00
Cut Glass, Plate, Butterflies, Honeycomb, 10 In.Diameter 35.00
Cut Glass, Plate, Cake, Pedestal, Hobstars, Fans, Diamond Point & Stars 80.00
Cut Glass, Plate, Cake, Russian Pattern, Footed, Star Cut Base 125.00
Cut Glass, Plate, Chop, Hobstar, Buzz, Star, Fan 125.00
Cut Glass, Plate, Diamond Cut, Star Bottom, 7 In.Diameter, 12 .... 84.00
Cut Glass, Plate, Dorflinger's Strawberry Pattern, 7 1/4 In. 45.00
Cut Glass, Plate, Engraved, Flowers, Pink, Octagonal, Footed, 8 In.Diameter 20.00
Cut Glass, Plate, Hobstar, Strawberry Diamond, Fan, Signed Hawkes, Pair 50.00
Cut Glass, Plate, Pink, Gold Trim, Fostoria 3.00
Cut Glass, Plate, Wisteria, Signed Libbey, 8 In. 175.00
Cut Glass, Receptacle, Dresser, Oval, Sterling Silver Lid, 5 In.Long 25.00
Cut Glass, Relish, Signed Hawkes, 10 3/4 X 4 1/2 In. 60.00
Cut Glass, Relish, 1890, Silver Plate Holder & Fork 10.00
Cut Glass, Rose Bowl, Block & Fan, Glass Insert 12.00
Cut Glass, Rose Bowl, Block Pattern 12.00
Cut Glass, Rose Bowl, Brilliant, Hobstar Cut Base 55.00
Cut Glass, Rose Bowl, Fan, Diamond Point, 5 X 6 In. 75.00
Cut Glass, Rose Bowl, Fans, Hobstars, Crosscut, Dorflinger, Unsigned 240.00
Cut Glass, Rose Bowl, Hobstar, Sunburst, Miniature, 3 1/8 In.Diameter, 3 In. 55.00
Cut Glass, Rose Bowl, Hobstars, Vesicas, Fans, 24-Point Hobstar Base 160.00
Cut Glass, Rose Bowl, Pinwheel, Zipper, Hobstar, Notched Rim, 4 1/4 In. 27.50
Cut Glass, Rose Bowl, Strawberry Diamond, Pineapple 75.00
Cut Glass, Rose Bowl, Tall Standard, Hobstar, 10 In.Tall 275.00
Cut Glass, Salad Set, Waterford, Clear, 11 Piece 11.00
Cut Glass, Salt & Pepper, Allover Cut, Sterling Silver Tops 7.50
Cut Glass, Salt & Pepper, Allover Cut, Sterling Tops, Signed Hawkes 32.00
Cut Glass, Salt & Pepper, Clear, Pair 3.50
Cut Glass, Salt & Pepper, Frosted Rose Cut, Sterling Tops 6.50
Cut Glass, Salt & Pepper, Sterling Tops 15.00

Cut Glass, Salt & Pepper, Zipper Cuttings, Set	12.50
Cut Glass, Salt Dip, Star Cut, Six Sided, Pink	2.25
Cut Glass, Salt Dip, Strawberry Diamond, Fan, Set Of 6	65.00
Cut Glass, Salt, Open	3.00
Cut Glass, Shaker, Salt, Signed Hawkes, Sterling Silver Top	11.00
Cut Glass, Shaker, Salt, Sterling Base	7.00
Cut Glass, Shaker, Sugar, Green To Clear, Crosscut Diamond, Stars, Fans	90.00
Cut Glass, Shaker, Sugar, Pear Shape	25.00
Cut Glass, Sherbet, Signed Hawkes, Cleopatra Pattern, 6	120.00
Cut Glass, Sherry, Encore Pattern, Hobstar Base, 4 3/8 In., Pair	35.00
Cut Glass, Shot Glass, Strawberry Diamond & Fan, Star In Base	14.50
Cut Glass, Spooner, Arcadian Pattern, Applied Handle, 4 1/2 In.Tall	23.00
Cut Glass, Spooner, Buzz Star	38.00
Cut Glass, Spooner, Hobstars, Cane, Crosscut Diamond & Fans, Hobstar Base	35.00
Cut Glass, Spooner, Panels Of Fruit, Eight Sided, 5 In.High	33.00
Cut Glass, Sugar & Creamer, Child's, Strawberry, Diamond, & Fan, Clear	12.00
Cut Glass, Sugar & Creamer, Flashed Hobstars, Notched Handle, Pedestal	175.00
Cut Glass, Sugar & Creamer, Flowers & Leaves, Miniature	12.50
Cut Glass, Sugar & Creamer, Flowers, Crosshatch Button, 3 3/4 In.Tall	95.00
Cut Glass, Sugar & Creamer, Footed, Hobstars, Crosscuts & Fans	110.00
Cut Glass, Sugar & Creamer, Hobstar & Buzz, Deep Vesica, Star Bottom	45.00
Cut Glass, Sugar & Creamer, Hobstar & Diamond Point, Hobstar In Bottom	65.00
Cut Glass, Sugar & Creamer, Hobstar, Fan, Buzz, Pedestal Base, 4 In.Tall	135.00
Cut Glass, Sugar & Creamer, Hobstar, Strawberry Diamond, Intaglio Cut Roses	35.00
Cut Glass, Sugar & Creamer, Hobstars, 2 Rows Notching On Handles	75.00
Cut Glass, Sugar & Creamer, Pedestal, Bird Motif	125.00
Cut Glass, Sugar & Creamer, Pinwheel, Etched Handles	50.00
Cut Glass, Sugar & Creamer, Rose Pattern With Intaglio Leaves & Hobstars	55.00
Cut Glass, Sugar & Creamer, Signed C In Shamrock	45.00
Cut Glass, Sugar & Creamer, Signed Libbey	65.00
Cut Glass, Sugar & Creamer, Signed Libbey, Hobstar & Notched Pillar	90.00
Cut Glass, Sugar & Creamer, Split Vesicas, Hobstars, Cane, Harvard Borders	110.00
Cut Glass, Sugar & Creamer, Strawberry Pattern	35.00
Cut Glass, Sugar, Hobstar & Fan, 3 In.High	28.00
Cut Glass, Sugar, Pinwheel, Handles	10.00
Cut Glass, Sugar, Signed Wright, Hobstars	20.00
Cut Glass, Sugar, Wheeler Pattern, Hobstar Base, Two Notched Handles	25.00
Cut Glass, Syrup, Intaglio Cut, Underplate, Signed Clark	40.00
Cut Glass, Syrup, Sterling Top, Strawberry, Baby Cane, Hobstar, & Crosscut	85.00
Cut Glass, Toothpick, Fan & Star, Faceted Bottom, Bulbous	17.50
Cut Glass, Toothpick, Footed, Stemmed	22.50
Cut Glass, Toothpick, Signed Hawkes	14.75
Cut Glass, Toothpick, Three Notched Handles, Rayed Bottom	55.00
Cut Glass, Tray, Bread, Hobstars, Crosscuts Without Open Space	75.00
Cut Glass, Tray, Bun, Hobstars, Harvard Sides, Oval	225.00
Cut Glass, Tray, Clear, Inserts, 13 1/2 In.	7.50
Cut Glass, Tray, Delphos, Signed Libbey, 1i In.Diameter	350.00
Cut Glass, Tray, Encore Pattern, 14 In. Long, 8 3/4 In.Wide	175.00
Cut Glass, Tray, Extended Butterfly Handles, Strawberry, Diamond & Fan	95.00
Cut Glass, Tray, Green To Clear, Overlay, Round	65.00
Cut Glass, Tray, Harvard, Flower, Hobstars, 14 1/2 X 7 1/2 In.	80.00
Cut Glass, Tray, Ice Cream, Clear Buttons, Cut Handles, Russia	275.00
Cut Glass, Tray, Ice Cream, Harvard, Daisy Insets, Printed Buttons	135.00
Cut Glass, Tray, Ice Cream, Hobstars, Cane, Buzz, & Fans, 8 X 14 In.	55.00
Cut Glass, Tray, Ice Cream, Hobstars, Stars, Diamond Point & Fans	80.00
Cut Glass, Tray, Kohinoor Pattern, Signed Hawkes, 9 X 12 In.	225.00
Cut Glass, Tray, Open Handle, Black & Gold Edge, Hand-Painted Flowers, Clear	25.00
Cut Glass, Tray, Pink, Embossed Floral	4.00
Cut Glass, Tray, Russian Pattern, 11 In.Long, 4 1/4 In.Wide	110.00
Cut Glass, Tray, Sandwich, Hobstar, Fan, Sawtooth Edge, 12 1/2 In.Round	175.00
Cut Glass, Tray, Signed Hawkes, Oval, Iris Pattern, Serrated Edge	75.00
Cut Glass, Tray, Signed Libbey, Round, 5 1/4 In.Diameter	35.00
Cut Glass, Tray, Spoon Drip, 7 1/2 In.	40.00
Cut Glass, Tray, Straus Imperial Pattern, 11 1/2 X 7 3/4 In.	80.00
Cut Glass, Tub, Ice, Brilliant	54.00
Cut Glass, Tumbler, Allover Geometric Cuts, Signed Hawkes	25.00

Cut Glass, Tumbler, Crosby Pattern, Signed Hoare 1853 Corning 17.00
Cut Glass, Tumbler, Diamond & Fan, 3 1/8 In., Set Of 6 ....45.00 To 95.00
Cut Glass, Tumbler, Floral & Leaf Pattern, Rayed Bottom 6.00
Cut Glass, Tumbler, Georgian, Amber, 4 In. 4.00
Cut Glass, Tumbler, Grapes In Relief, Clear 4.50
Cut Glass, Tumbler, Heart Pattern, Set Of 6 .... 150.00
Cut Glass, Tumbler, Hobstar, Fan, Crosshatch 18.00
Cut Glass, Tumbler, Hobstar, Signed Libbey, Set Of 6 .... 185.00
Cut Glass, Tumbler, Hobstar, Star, Fan 10.00
Cut Glass, Tumbler, Ice Tea, Fan & Hobstar, Ray Bottom, 6 In., Set Of 6 .... 125.00
Cut Glass, Tumbler, Pinwheel 12.50
Cut Glass, Tumbler, Satin Wheels, Geometric Cuts, Signed Hawkes 25.00
Cut Glass, Tumbler, Signed Hawkes, Prism, Fans, & Stars 25.00
Cut Glass, Tumbler, Signed Hoare, Brilliant Cut 17.50
Cut Glass, Tumbler, Strawberry Diamond 50.00
Cut Glass, Tumbler, Strawberry Diamond & Fan, Set Of 8 .... 100.00
Cut Glass, Tumbler, Strawberry, Pineapple 37.00
Cut Glass, Tumbler, Water, Encore Pattern, Hobstar Base, 3 3/4 In. 25.00
Cut Glass, Tumbler, Whiskey, Flute, Oval Thumbprint, & Fan, 3 In.High 10.00
Cut Glass, Urn, Footed, Covered, Oval Panels With Diamond Cutting, Pair 80.00
Cut Glass, Vase, Allover Cut, 14 In. 75.00
Cut Glass, Vase, Bucket Shape, Emerald Green, Diamond-Quilted, Floral Cut 18.00
Cut Glass, Vase, Bud, Crosscut Diamond, Diamond Point, 9 1/2 In.Tall, Pair 55.00
Cut Glass, Vase, Bull's Eye, Hobstars, 10 In.Tall 45.00
Cut Glass, Vase, Butterflies, Honeycomb, Oval, 10 1/2 In.High 55.00
Cut Glass, Vase, Buzz Saw, Hobstar, Fan & Splits, 12 In. 75.00
Cut Glass, Vase, Chalice, Hobstar Notched Base, Howard, 14 In.High 455.00
Cut Glass, Vase, Creswick Pattern, Signed Eggington, Fluted Lip 185.00
Cut Glass, Vase, Cut Floral, 10 In. 22.00
Cut Glass, Vase, Embossed Sterling Base, Russia, 11 3/4 In.High 265.00
Cut Glass, Vase, Etched Flowers, 12 In.Tall 25.00
Cut Glass, Vase, Fern, Leaves, Floral, Scalloped, Heavy, 12 In.Tall 40.00
Cut Glass, Vase, Floral, Engraved, Corset Shape, 11 In. 45.00
Cut Glass, Vase, Floral, Ferns, Leaves, Scalloped Top, Star On Bottom, 12 In. 40.00
Cut Glass, Vase, Flower, 10 In. 30.00
Cut Glass, Vase, Harvard & Floral, 15 In.High 200.00
Cut Glass, Vase, Harvard With Intaglio Cut Flowers, 12 In. 40.00
Cut Glass, Vase, Hobstar, Crosscut Diamond, Star Base, 6 In.Tall 90.00
Cut Glass, Vase, Hobstar, Cross-Hatching, Notched Fluted, 9 1/4 In. 70.00
Cut Glass, Vase, Hobstar, Fan, Hatching & Strawberry Diamond, 9 In. 75.00
Cut Glass, Vase, Hobstars, Notched Base, 7 In. 18.00
Cut Glass, Vase, Intaglio Flowers & Harvard Bands, 12 In.Tall 50.00
Cut Glass, Vase, Jewel Pattern, Flowers Cut Like Diamonds 37.50
Cut Glass, Vase, Leaf Cutting, Engraved Lotus, 13 1/2 In.High 45.00
Cut Glass, Vase, Leaf Cuttings, 12 In.High 100.00
Cut Glass, Vase, Modified Pinwheel Pattern, Hourglass Shape, 11 In.High 95.00
Cut Glass, Vase, Notched Prism, Pinwheel, Bulbous, 8 In.Tall 42.50
Cut Glass, Vase, Pinwheel Pattern, 12 In.Tall 125.00
Cut Glass, Vase, Prism & Bull's-Eye, 2 Panels Of Hobstars, Rayed Bottom 38.00
Cut Glass, Vase, Rayed Star, Allover Cut, Corset Shape, 7 In.Tall 45.00
Cut Glass, Vase, Signed Hawkes & E.Palme, Vintage, 12 In.Tall 350.00
Cut Glass, Vase, Signed Hawkes, Millicent Pattern, 10 In. 70.00
Cut Glass, Vase, Signed Hawkes, 17 X 9 In.Diameter 285.00
Cut Glass, Vase, Signed Hawkes, 9 In.High 95.00
Cut Glass, Vase, Signed Libbey, Lily Of The Valley, Ruffled Edge, 4 1/2 In. 32.00
Cut Glass, Vase, Signed Tuthill, Intaglio Daisies & Brilliants, 12 In.Tall 195.00
Cut Glass, Vase, Silver Thread, Signed Sinclaire, 11 In. ....180.00 To 300.00
Cut Glass, Vase, Square Cut, Cobalt, Clear, 9 In.Tall 25.00
Cut Glass, Vase, Sterling Silver Rim, Marked 1914, Round, 8 3/4 In.Tall 40.00
Cut Glass, Vase, Tapering Sides, Short Pedestal Stem, Stalks, Stars, Libbey 125.00
Cut Glass, Vase, Thistle, 4 1/2 In. 9.00
Cut Glass, Vase, Three Pieces, Screws Into Center Ring, 3 1/2 Ft.High 2500.00
Cut Glass, Vase, Trumpet, Allover Cut, Hobstars, Inverted Fans, Faceted Knob 75.00
Cut Glass, Vase, Trumpet, Signed J.Hoare, Hobstar & Notched Pillar 150.00
Cut Glass, Vase, 10 In.High .... *Illus* 42.50
Cut Glass, Vase, 16 In. 48.00

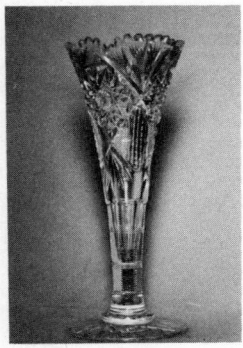

Cut Glass, Vase, 10 In.High
See Page 153

Cut Glass, Vial, Perfume, Purse, Sterling Top, 4 In.Long	12.00
Cut Glass, Water Set, American, Strawberry, Diamond, & Fan, 6 Piece	165.00
Cut Glass, Water Set, Floral, 5 Pieces	70.00
Cut Glass, Water Set, Intaglio, Star Bottom, 5 Piece	60.00
Cut Glass, Water Set, Meteor Pattern, 7 Pieces	40.00
Cut Glass, Water Set, 5 Piece, Intaglio Cut Flowers, Star Base	80.00
Cut Glass, Whiskey Glass, Double Shot, Hobstars, Fan, Set Of 6	180.00
Cut Glass, Whiskey Set, Star, Six Shot Glasses, Silver Rims	27.00
Cut Glass, Whiskey Set, Teardrop, Mushroom Stopper, 4 Piece	135.00
Cut Glass, Wine, Cut Conical Bowl, 6	20.00
Cut Glass, Wine, Hobstar, Diamond Point, & Fan, 24 Stars In Base, 6 Panels	30.00
Cut Glass, Wine, Hobstar, Sunburst, Pedestal Base, 4 1/2 In.Tall, Pair	21.50
Cut Glass, Wine, Ogee Bowl, Engraved Floral Band, C.1760, English, Pair	90.00
Cut Glass, Wine, Signed Hawkes, Middlesex Pattern, Notched Stem, 10	250.00
Cut Glass, Wine, Star & Pineapple, Green & Clear	45.00

Cut Velvet is a special type of Art Glass made with two layers of Blown Glass, which shows a raised pattern. It usually had an acid finish or velvetlike texture. It was made by many glass factories during the late victorian years.

Cut Velvet, Bowl, Satin, Diamond-Quilted, Blue, 5 In.Tall	95.00
Cut Velvet, Vase, Blue, 4 In.High	90.00
Cut Velvet, Vase, Purple To White, Satin, 10 In.Tall	350.00
Cut Velvet, Vase, Robin, Sitting, Blue, White, Green, Enamel, 11 3/4 In.Tall	250.00
Cut Velvet, Vase, To Deep Pinks	47.50
Cybis, Bust, Madonna, Lace, White, Bisque, 5 In.Tall	100.00

Daguerreotype, see Album, Photography
Danish Christmas Plates, see Collector Plates
Dant, see Bottle, Dant

D'Argental was a french cameo glassmaker of the late victorian period.

D'argental, Vase, Cameo, Maroon, Slender Neck, Bird Acid Cut, 17 In.Tall	275.00
D'argental, Vase, Castle Scene, Hand-Carved, Violet To Lavender, White, 5 In.	265.00
D'argental, Vase, Foliage Scene, Maroon, Amber, Black, 7 In.	165.00
D'argental, Vase, Sweet Peas, Frosted, Purple, Signed, 12 In.Tall	145.00

Daum Nancy is the mark used by Auguste and Antonin Daum on pieces of French Cameo Glass made after 1875.

Daum Nancy, see also Cameo Glass

Daum Nancy, Ashtray, Cameo, Emerald Green Cut To Clear, Enamel Floral	85.00
Daum Nancy, Bottle, Cameo, Flask Shape, Pedestal, Daisies, Gold Enamel	125.00
Daum Nancy, Bowl, Cameo Glass, Peacock Feathers, Signed	160.00
Daum Nancy, Bowl, Footed, Clear To Green, Flowers & Writing In Relief	105.00
Daum Nancy, Bowl, Green Mottled In Brown & Black, 5 In.Diameter	100.00
Daum Nancy, Bowl, Rose, Cameo, Scenic, Carved Trees, Foliage, Water, Castle	175.00
Daum Nancy, Bowl, Silveria, Orange Mottle, Gold, Signed, 4 1/2 In.Diameter	45.00
Daum Nancy, Bowl, Star Of Lorraine, Amber, Brown, Green, Oblong, 5 In.High	125.00
Daum Nancy, Bowl, Winter Scene, Signed, 8 In.	350.00

Daum Nancy, Box, Cameo, Enamel Purple & Pink Foral, Lid, 6 In.Diameter 285.00
Daum Nancy, Box, Cover, Green, Cameo, 7 X 3 1/2 In.Tall 295.00
Daum Nancy, Box, Floral Design, Red, Gold, Cameo, Signed, 3 1/4 In.Diameter 85.00
Daum Nancy, Box, Round, Blue & White, 2 3/4 In.Diameter, 2 In.High 45.00
Daum Nancy, Glass, Shot, Berries, Leaves, Green, Gold, Cameo, Signed, 2 In.Tall 45.00
Daum Nancy, Lamp, Pewter Floral, Yellow To Beige Ground, Electrified 550.00
Daum Nancy, Lamp, Table, Lavender, Green, Mottled Shade, Signed 87.50
Daum Nancy, Lamp, Winter Scene, Original Wiring & Hardware 300.00
Daum Nancy, Liqueur Set, Berries, Gold, Red, Six Wines, Stopper, 10 In., Set 250.00
Daum Nancy, Liqueur Set, Crystal Ribbed Blown, Intaglio Cut Thistles, Gold 175.00
Daum Nancy, Perfume, Clear Shading To Deep Green, Carved Cameo Floral 140.00
Daum Nancy, Plate, Boat Shape, Signed 225.00
Daum Nancy, Tumbler, Cameo Cut, Acid Cut On Surface, Berries, Gold 85.00
Daum Nancy, Tumbler, Cameo, Enamel, Floral Design, 4 1/2 In.Tall 125.00
Daum Nancy, Tumbler, Cameo, Green, Floral, Enamel, Gold Trim, Signed 45.00
Daum Nancy, Tumbler, Custard Color, Signed, Red & Brown Casing 40.00
Daum Nancy, Tumbler, Enameled Floral, Vines In Gold, Signed, 5 In. 110.00
Daum Nancy, Vase, Acid Cut Back, Green, Urn Shape, Signed, 10 In.Tall 90.00
Daum Nancy, Vase, Art Deco, Mottled Green, Bronze Framework, 4 Handles 200.00
Daum Nancy, Vase, Autumn Scene, Corset Shape, Orange, Red, Yellow, Gold, 12 In. 395.00
Daum Nancy, Vase, Bud, Cameo, Flowers, Leaves, White, Green, Signed, 7 3/4 In. 150.00
Daum Nancy, Vase, Cameo Cut, Orange To Light At Top, Green, Red, Signed 425.00
Daum Nancy, Vase, Cameo Cut, Rust Color Flowers, Orange Background 875.00
Daum Nancy, Vase, Cameo, Baluster, Relief Grapevines On Purple To Amber 250.00
Daum Nancy, Vase, Cameo, Enameled, Green, Yellow, & Red, Leaves & Flowers 295.00
Daum Nancy, Vase, Cameo, Flowers, Foliage, Amethyst, Signed, 15 1/2 In.Tall 225.00
Daum Nancy, Vase, Cameo, Globular, Purple & Green, Blossoming Vine On Gray 120.00
Daum Nancy, Vase, Cameo, Gourd Shape, Honeysuckle Pattern, Yellow To Purple 325.00
Daum Nancy, Vase, Cameo, Green Thistle Pattern, Square, Gold Leaf Signed 100.00
Daum Nancy, Vase, Cameo, Lakeside Scene, Orange, Green, Pink, Signed, 12 In. 280.00
Daum Nancy, Vase, Cameo, Ovoid, Green Iris On Frosted Pink, Signed 275.00
Daum Nancy, Vase, Cameo, Sailboats, Trees, Brown, Orange, 11 3/4 In.Tall 230.00
Daum Nancy, Vase, Cameo, Swelling, Amber & Green Foliage On Yellow, Signed 70.00
Daum Nancy, Vase, Cameo, Tapering, Ocher Hibiscus On Gray To Pink To Brown 300.00
Daum Nancy, Vase, Cameo, Tulip Blossoms, Green & Amber, Signed, 7 1/2 In.High 210.00
Daum Nancy, Vase, Cameo, Urn Shape, Leafy Branches In Ocher On Gray, Signed 180.00
Daum Nancy, Vase, Crocus, Leaves, Green, Purple, Sawtooth Cut, 8 1/2 In.Tall 125.00
Daum Nancy, Vase, Emerald Green Cut, Greek Urn Fashion, Signed 265.00
Daum Nancy, Vase, French Cameo, Footed, Pink Roses, Signed, 6 1/2 In.High 175.00
Daum Nancy, Vase, Frosted Ground, Red Flowers, Green Leaves, Says Noel 395.00
Daum Nancy, Vase, Green & Brown At Bottom, Acid Cut, Enameled, Signed 215.00
Daum Nancy, Vase, Hammered, Black, Brown, Signed 75.00
Daum Nancy, Vase, Lake Scene, Tree, Sailboat, Signed, 10 In.High 275.00
Daum Nancy, Vase, Oblong, Mottled Blue Scenic, Signed 65.00
Daum Nancy, Vase, Purple Hydrangeas, Butterflies, Six Jewels 450.00
Daum Nancy, Vase, Scenic Trees, Cameo, Enamel, Brown To Pink, 13 In.Tall 150.00
Daum Nancy, Vase, Signed, 4 In.Square, Cameo 125.00
Daum Nancy, Vase, Summer Scene, Woods, Water, Sun, Amber Black, Maroon 300.00
Daum Nancy, Vase, Winter Cameo Scene, Unsigned, 8 1/2 In.Tall 195.00
Daum Nancy, Vase, Winter Scene, Yellow, Green, Brown, Signed, 3 1/2 In.Tall 225.00

*Davenport Pottery and Porcelain were made at the Davenport Factory in
Longport, Staffordshire, England, from 1793 to 1887. Earthenwares,
Creamwares, Porcelains, Ironstone Wares, and other products were made.
Most of the pieces are marked with a form of the word Davenport.*

Davenport, Creamer, Tan Jasperware, Basket Weave, Incised With Anchor 42.00
Davenport, Cup & Saucer, Oriental Pattern, Circa 1870 .... 27.50
Davenport, Dish, Footed, Three Corner, Belvoir Castle 75.00
Davenport, Dish, Vegetable, Floral Border, Oblong 27.50
Davenport, Plate, Blue & Orange, Chinese Figures, 8 In.Diameter 20.00
Davenport, Plate, Blue & White, Scenic, Impressed Anchor Mark, 10 1/2 In. 15.00
Davenport, Plate, Floral Spray, Cobalt, Gold, Hand-Painted, 9 In., Pair 45.00
Davenport, Plate, Raised Border, Gold, 9 In.Diameter 9.00
Davenport, Platter, Dark Blue Border, Circa 1835, Impressed Anchor 30.00
Davenport, Tea Set, Pink Luster, C.1825, 3 Piece 225.00
Davenport, Toby Mug, The Gin Woman Of Brighton, C.1825 .... 100.00

Davenport, Urn, White, Gold, 17 In.Tall 150.00

De Vez is a name found on special pieces of French Cameo Glass made by the Cristallerie de Pantin about 1890. Monsieur de Varreux was the art director of the glassworks and he signed pieces 'De Vez'.

De Vez, Lamp, Cameo, Venice Scenes, Blue, Pink Tinge, Signed, 20 In.High 700.00
De Vez, Vase, Cameo, Blue, Pink, Scene, Tapered, 7 1/4 In. 250.00
De Vez, Vase, Cameo, Scenic, Buildings, Ships, Gondola, & A Man, Signed, 3 .... 265.50
De Vez, Vase, Cameo, Scenic, Floral, 6 In.High 150.00
De Vez, Vase, Forest & Lake Scene, Green, Rose, Gold, Signed, 5 In.Tall 165.00
De Vez, Vase, Iridescent, Signed, 3 In. 225.00

Decoys are carved or turned wooden copies of birds. The decoy was placed in the water to lure flying birds to the pond for hunters.

Decoy, Black Duck, Sleeping Position, Hollow Construction 160.00
Decoy, Brown, Glass Eyes 10.00
Decoy, Canada Goose, Hollow Construction, Tuckerton, New Jersey, C.1850 .... 160.00
Decoy, Canvas, Mason, Challenge, Painted 39.00
Decoy, Canvasback, Drake, Mason's Decoy Factory Of Detroit 160.00
Decoy, Coot, Wooden 11.50
Decoy, Crow, American, Carved Wood & Metal, 3 .... *Illus* 50.00
Decoy, Crow, Wood 45.00
Decoy, Duck, Black, Silver, Red Head, Silver Bill, Glass Eyes, Repainted 12.00
Decoy, Duck, Crude 10.00
Decoy, Duck, Painted, Initial 'm, ' 22 In.Long 35.00
Decoy, Duck, Papier-Mache, Glass Eyes, C.1930 .... 2.00 To 7.00
Decoy, Duck, Wooden, Color 12.50
Decoy, Duck, Wooden, Painted .... 40.00 To 65.00
Decoy, Duck, Wooden, 2 Section Type, Glass Eyes 15.00
Decoy, Great Blue Heron, White Cedar 325.00
Decoy, Greater Scaup, Harry Von Nockson, N.J., 1915 .... *Illus* 110.00

Decoy, Crow, American,
Carved Wood & Metal, 3

Decoy, Plover,
Jess Birdsall Type
See Page 157

Decoy, Greater Scaup,
Harry Von Nockson,
N.J., 1915

Decoy, Merganser, Hen,
Rhoades Troux, N.J.
See Page 157

Decoy, Mallard, Drake, Mason's Decoy Factory Of Detroit	170.00
Decoy, Merganser, Drake, American, Long Island Origin, Painted	80.00
Decoy, Merganser, Hen, Rhoades Troux, N.J. *Illus*	60.00
Decoy, Plover, Jess Birdsall Type *Illus*	70.00
Decoy, Shore Bird, Wooden, Long Bill, Pair	35.00
Decoy, Snipe, Turned Head, Painted, Wooden, Pair	70.00

The Dedham Pottery Company of Dedham, Massachusetts, started making pottery in 1866. It was reorganized as the Chelsea Pottery Company in 1891, and became the Dedham Pottery Company in 1895. The factory was famous for its crackleware dishes, which picture blue outlines of animals, flowers, and other natural motifs.

Dedham Pottery, Bowl & Plate Set, Turkey, 7 1/2	145.00
Dedham Pottery, Bowl, Rabbit, 5 1/4 In.Diameter	38.00
Dedham Pottery, Cup & Saucer, Azalea Pattern	58.00
Dedham Pottery, Cup & Saucer, Rabbit, Magnolia	23.50
Dedham Pottery, Jar, Marmalade	150.00
Dedham Pottery, Plate, Bird, Orange Tree, 6 In.	75.00
Dedham Pottery, Plate, Cup, Saucer, Duck	145.00
Dedham Pottery, Plate, Grape, 8 In.	50.00
Dedham Pottery, Plate, Rabbit, 6 In.	28.00
Dedham Pottery, Plate, Rabbit, 8 In.	35.00
Dedham Pottery, Plate, Rabbit, 8 1/2 In.	32.50
Dedham Pottery, Plate, Rabbit, 10 In.	47.50
Dedham Pottery, Plate, Swan, 8 In.Diameter	95.00
Dedham, Pitcher, Milk, Rabbits & Fruit, Marked, 5 In.	67.50
Delatte, Bowl, Yellow Frosted Decor, Oval	36.00
Delatte, Pitcher, Silveria, Signed, Yellow, Pink, & White	110.00
Delatte, Vase, Cameo, Red Roses, Apricot Color Ground, 7 1/2 In.Tall	145.00
Delatte, Vase, Floral Design, Frosted Orange, Cameo, Signed, 6 3/4 In.Tall	110.00
Delatte, Vase, Peacock Design, Cameo, Purple, White, 12 In.Tall	275.00
Delatte, Vase, Yellow, Brown Spatterings, Signed F.Delatte Nancy	97.50

Delaware, see Pressed Glass, bowl
Deldare, see Buffalo Pottery

Delft is a tin-glazed pottery that has been made since the seventeenth century. It is decorated with blue on white or with colored decorations. Most of the pieces sold today were made after 1891, and the name Holland appears with the Delft Factory marks.

Delft, Bowl, Blue & White, Dutch, 17th Century, Chinese Figures, Round	125.00
Delft, Charger, 15 1/2 In.Diameter	22.50
Delft, Creamer, Cow, Reclining	18.00
Delft, Dish, Cheese, Shape Of Dutch House, Blue & White, Signed Script F	85.00
Delft, Jar, Tobacco, Amphora, Brass Lid	15.00
Delft, Knife Rests, Pair	22.00
Delft, Lamp, Banquet, Blue & White, Pear Shaped, Ball Shade, 23 In.	75.00
Delft, Pitcher, Cobalt, Figures & Dutch Girl	12.50
Delft, Pitcher, Holland Scene, Blue, White, Hand-Painted, 3 In.Tall	6.00
Delft, Pitcher, Scene, Signed, Blue, White, 6 In.	10.00
Delft, Plaque, Blue & White, Windmill & Boat, Impressed, 12 In.	30.00
Delft, Plaque, Blue, Boch, Windmill & Sailboat Scene, 12 1/4 In.	27.50
Delft, Plate, Blue & White, Oriental Scene, Lambeth, C.1775, Pair	100.00
Delft, Plate, Blue, Oriental Shrubs, Fence, Lambeth, C.1740	80.00
Delft, Plate, Blue, Plants, Bamboo, & Fence, Lambeth Of Bristol, C.1750, Pair	80.00
Delft, Plate, German, Octagon, Boating Scene, Crossed Pipes Mark	10.00
Delft, Plate, Polychrome, Fazackerly Colors, Circa 1760, Liverpool, 9 In.	115.00
Delft, Plate, Prince Of Orange, Dutch, C.1770, Portraits Of Prince & Wife	110.00
Delft, Plate, Windmill Scene, 8 1/2 In.	7.00
Delft, Platter, Blue, Hanging, Farm Scenery, 15 1/2 In.Diameter	40.00
Delft, Shoe, Basket Weave, Two Scroll Reserves At Sides, Boats, Windmills	25.00
Delft, Stein, Blue & White Floral, Medallion, Pewter Lid, Royal Bonn, 4 Liter	295.00
Delft, Tile, Scene Of St.Laurens Church, Blue & White	4.50
Delft, Tile, Sea, Buildings, Ships, Swans, 18th Century, 6 In.Square	10.00
Delft, Tile, Tea, Water, Boats, Birds, Houses, Pair	.25.00
Delft, Tile, Windmill, Blue, Hand-Painted, 4 In.	4.00
Delft, Tile, Windmill, Boat Scene, Pair	12.00

Delft, Tray, Water, Boats, Scrolled Edge, Crossed Pipes Mark, 8 1/2 In.	25.00
Delft, Vase, Blue, Artist Marked, 8 In.High	75.00

Depression Glass was an inexpensive glass manufactured in large quantities during the 1920s and early 1930s. It was made in many colors and patterns by dozens of factories in the United States. The name Depression Glass is a modern one.

Depression Glass, Ashtray, Adam, Pink	3.00
Depression Glass, Ashtray, Princess, Pink	1.25
Depression Glass, Berry Set, Coronation, Pink, 7 Piece	10.00
Depression Glass, Berry Set, Doric, Green, 7 Pieces	15.00
Depression Glass, Berry Set, Sandwich, Pink, 7 Pieces	15.00
Depression Glass, Bottle, Moonstone, Stopper	4.00
Depression Glass, Bottle, Vinegar, Whitehouse	9.00
Depression Glass, Bowl & Underplate, Doric, Green	2.00
Depression Glass, Bowl, Adam, Pink, Covered, 9 In.	9.00
Depression Glass, Bowl, American Sweetheart, Pink, Oval, 13 In.	5.50
Depression Glass, Bowl, Berry, Bubble, Blue	1.00
Depression Glass, Bowl, Berry, Coronation, Pink	1.00
Depression Glass, Bowl, Berry, Cube, Green	1.25
Depression Glass, Bowl, Berry, Normandie, Pink	1.25
Depression Glass, Bowl, Berry, Patrician, Amber, 5 In.	2.00
Depression Glass, Bowl, Berry, Patrician, Green, 5 In.	2.00
Depression Glass, Bowl, Berry, Sharon, Amber	1.25
Depression Glass, Bowl, Bubble, Blue, 5 1/2 In.	1.00
Depression Glass, Bowl, Bubble, Blue, 8 1/2 In.	2.50
Depression Glass, Bowl, Cabbage Rose, Pink, 4 In.	1.25
Depression Glass, Bowl, Cameo, Green, 8 1/4 In. .... 3.00 To	5.00
Depression Glass, Bowl, Centerpiece, Madrid, Amber, 9 1/2 X 4 1/2 In.	7.50
Depression Glass, Bowl, Cereal, Miss America, Green	5.00
Depression Glass, Bowl, Cereal, Sharon, Amber	1.50
Depression Glass, Bowl, Cherry Blossom, Pink, Handled, 9 In. .... 6.00 To	7.00
Depression Glass, Bowl, Cherry Blossom, Pink, Handled, 9 1/2 In.	5.00
Depression Glass, Bowl, Cherry Blossom, Pink, 8 1/2 In.	6.00
Depression Glass, Bowl, Colonial, Green, 9 In.	6.00
Depression Glass, Bowl, Console, Floragold-Louisa, Ruffled, 11 In.	9.50
Depression Glass, Bowl, Coronation Royal Ruby, 4 1/4 In.	2.00
Depression Glass, Bowl, Coronation Royal Ruby, 8 In.	6.00
Depression Glass, Bowl, Cream Soup, Cabbage Rose, Pink, 4 Handles	2.25
Depression Glass, Bowl, Cream Soup, Moderntone, Blue	2.25
Depression Glass, Bowl, Cream Soup, Royal Lace, Blue, 5 In.	6.00
Depression Glass, Bowl, Diamond Block, Pink, Handle, 5 In.	1.25
Depression Glass, Bowl, Diana, Clear, 5 In.	1.00
Depression Glass, Bowl, Diana, Pink, 5 In.	2.00
Depression Glass, Bowl, Dutch Rose, Amber, 5 In.	1.00
Depression Glass, Bowl, Floragold, 9 In.	3.75
Depression Glass, Bowl, Floragold, 12 In.	4.50
Depression Glass, Bowl, Floral, Green, 7 1/2 In.	4.50
Depression Glass, Bowl, Florentine, Covered, 9 In., Green	12.50
Depression Glass, Bowl, Fruit, Cherry Blossom, Pink, 3 Legs, 10 1/2 In.	12.00
Depression Glass, Bowl, Fruit, Cherry, Pink, 3 Feet	10.00
Depression Glass, Bowl, Fruit, Manhattan, Clear	2.75
Depression Glass, Bowl, Fruit, Manhattan, Pink, Handles, 9 1/2 In.	5.00
Depression Glass, Bowl, Fruit, Mayfair, Green, Flared, 12 In.	14.00
Depression Glass, Bowl, Fruit, Mayfair, Pink, Flared	10.00
Depression Glass, Bowl, Fruit, Mayfair, Pink, 12 In.	7.00
Depression Glass, Bowl, Fruit, Miss America, Pink, 8 1/2 In.	15.00
Depression Glass, Bowl, Fruit, Royal Lace, Cobalt Blue	22.50
Depression Glass, Bowl, Georgian, Green 4 1/2 In.	1.50
Depression Glass, Bowl, Green, Pedestal	7.50
Depression Glass, Bowl, Hairpin, Pink, 4 3/4 In.	2.00
Depression Glass, Bowl, Herringbone, Clear, Ruffled, 9 In.	3.75
Depression Glass, Bowl, Herringbone, Clear, Ruffled, 13 In.	4.50
Depression Glass, Bowl, Holiday, Pink, 5 In.	1.50
Depression Glass, Bowl, Irish, Crystal, Fluted, 5 In.	2.00
Depression Glass, Bowl, Irish, Crystal, Fluted, 9 1/2 In.	5.00

Depression Glass, Bowl, Lace Edge, Pink, 8 In. 3.25
Depression Glass, Bowl, Lydia Ray, Green, 4 1/2 In. 1.00
Depression Glass, Bowl, Madrid, Amber, Console, Flared-Out 6.50
Depression Glass, Bowl, Madrid, Green, 5 1/2 In. 1.35
Depression Glass, Bowl, Madrid, Oval, Amber 5.50
Depression Glass, Bowl, Mayfair Hocking's, Pink, Handled, 10 In. 4.00
Depression Glass, Bowl, Mayfair, Blue, Handled 8.00
Depression Glass, Bowl, Miss America, Pink, 6 1/4 In. 3.00
Depression Glass, Bowl, Miss American, Crystal, 6 1/4 In. 2.50
Depression Glass, Bowl, Moderntone, Cobalt Blue, 5 In. 1.50
Depression Glass, Bowl, Moderntone, Cobalt Blue, 9 In. 6.00
Depression Glass, Bowl, Nut, Floragold-Louisa, Oval, Footed 3.50
Depression Glass, Bowl, Old Cafe, Pink, Round 2.75
Depression Glass, Bowl, Open Rose, Green, Flared 6.50
Depression Glass, Bowl, Parrot, Green, Oval 9.00
Depression Glass, Bowl, Patrician, Green, 5 In. 1.75
Depression Glass, Bowl, Patrician, Green, 8 1/2 In. 5.00
Depression Glass, Bowl, Pink, Footed, 7 In. 2.00
Depression Glass, Bowl, Pink, Footed, 10 In. 2.75
Depression Glass, Bowl, Princess, Green, Hat Shape 6.00
Depression Glass, Bowl, Princess, Green, Oval, 10 In. 4.00
Depression Glass, Bowl, Princess, Green, 5 1/2 In. 1.00
Depression Glass, Bowl, Ribbed, Pink, Lace Edge 5.00
Depression Glass, Bowl, Rope, Green, 7 3/4 In. 2.50
Depression Glass, Bowl, Round.American Sweetheart, 9 In. 5.00
Depression Glass, Bowl, Royal Lace, Blue, 10 In., 3 Legs 20.00
Depression Glass, Bowl, Royal Lace, Pink, 10 In. 5.00
Depression Glass, Bowl, Royal Lace, Pink, 10 In., 6 Legs, Ruffled 10.00
Depression Glass, Bowl, Royal Ruby 3.50
Depression Glass, Bowl, Salad, Madrid, Amber, Deep, Round, 9 In. 11.00
Depression Glass, Bowl, Sharon, Amber, Round, 8 In. 3.00
Depression Glass, Bowl, Sharon, Amber, 8 1/2 In. 2.50
Depression Glass, Bowl, Sharon, Amber, Round, 10 1/2 In. 5.00
Depression Glass, Bowl, Sharon, Yellow, 8 1/2 In. 3.00
Depression Glass, Bowl, Soup, American Sweetheart, Milk Glass 4.00
Depression Glass, Bowl, Soup, Bubble, Blue 1.25
Depression Glass, Bowl, Soup, Cameo, Green, Flanged Rim, 9 In. 4.50
Depression Glass, Bowl, Soup, Daisy, Amber, Two Handle, 4 1/2 In. 2.00
Depression Glass, Bowl, Soup, Florentine, Green, 4 3/4 In. 3.50
Depression Glass, Bowl, Soup, Moderntone, Cobalt Blue, Ruffled 3.00
Depression Glass, Bowl, Soup, Moderntone, Milk Glass, Two Handle 1.75
Depression Glass, Bowl, Soup, Normandie, Sunburst 3.50
Depression Glass, Bowl, Strawberry, Clear, 7 1/2 In. 3.00
Depression Glass, Bowl, Vegetable, Adam, Pink, Covered 10.00
Depression Glass, Bowl, Vegetable, Cameo, Green, Oval, 10 In. 4.25
Depression Glass, Bowl, Vegetable, Cherry, Green, Oval 4.00
Depression Glass, Bowl, Vegetable, Doric, Pink, Oblong 4.50
Depression Glass, Bowl, Vegetable, Floral, Green, Oval 4.00
Depression Glass, Bowl, Vegetable, Floral, Pink, Covered 8.50
Depression Glass, Bowl, Vegetable, Floral, Pink, Oval 4.00
Depression Glass, Bowl, Vegetable, Madrid, Amber, Oval 5.00
Depression Glass, Bowl, Vegetable, Miss American, Pink, Oval 6.00
Depression Glass, Bowl, Vegetable, Open Lace, Pink, Vertical Ribbed Sides 7.50
Depression Glass, Bowl, Vegetable, Patrician, Amber, Oval 5.00
Depression Glass, Bowl, Vegetable, Princess, Green 3.25
Depression Glass, Bowl, Vegetable, Sharon, Amber, Round 3.00
Depression Glass, Bowl, Vegetable, Sharon, Pink 7.50
Depression Glass, Box, Powder, Panel Optic, Green, Oval, Flat Top 7.50
Depression Glass, Bread & Butter, American Sweetheart, Monax 2.50
Depression Glass, Bread & Butter, Bubble, Blue .... .75
Depression Glass, Bread & Butter, Madrid, Amber 1.25
Depression Glass, Bread & Butter, Normandie, Amber 1.25
Depression Glass, Bread & Butter, Normandie, Sunburst 1.75
Depression Glass, Bread & Butter, Patrician, Amber 1.25
Depression Glass, Bread & Butter, Petalware, Pink 1.10
Depression Glass, Butter, Adam, Pink .... 8.00 To 12.50

Depression Glass, Butter, Block Optic, Green, Covered	7.50
Depression Glass, Butter, Cabbage Rose, Amber, Covered	17.00
Depression Glass, Butter, Cabbage Rose, Green	22.00
Depression Glass, Butter, Cherry, Green	28.00
Depression Glass, Butter, Colonial, Green	18.00
Depression Glass, Butter, Cover, Sandwich, Clear	8.00
Depression Glass, Butter, Cube, Green, Covered	12.00
Depression Glass, Butter, Florentine, Green	7.50
Depression Glass, Butter, Holiday, Pink	12.00 To 12.50
Depression Glass, Butter, Holiday, Pink, Lid	15.50
Depression Glass, Butter, Iris, Clear	5.50
Depression Glass, Butter, Lace Edge, Pink	17.00
Depression Glass, Butter, Lovebird, Green	12.00
Depression Glass, Butter, Madrid, Amber	6.00
Depression Glass, Butter, Mayfair, Pink	7.50
Depression Glass, Butter, Mayfair, Pink, Lid	18.75
Depression Glass, Butter, Miss America, Clear	7.50
Depression Glass, Butter, Miss America, Pink	9.75
Depression Glass, Butter, Patrician, Amber, Cover	17.50
Depression Glass, Butter, Princess, Green	4.50
Depression Glass, Butter, Sharon, Amber, Covered	20.00
Depression Glass, Butter, Sharon, Green	14.50 To 15.00
Depression Glass, Butter, Sharon, Pink	10.75 To 15.00
Depression Glass, Butter, Sharon, Pink, Lid	21.50
Depression Glass, Butter, Sharon, Yellow	15.00
Depression Glass, Butter, Swirl, Pink	9.75
Depression Glass, Cake Stand, Doric, Pink, Footed	4.25
Depression Glass, Cake Stand, Princess, Green, Footed, 10 In.	6.00
Depression Glass, Candleholder, Adam, Pink	4.00
Depression Glass, Candleholder, Adam, Pink, Pair	10.00
Depression Glass, Candleholder, Herringbone, Clear, Double	6.75
Depression Glass, Candleholder, Irish, Crystal, 2 Branch	3.75
Depression Glass, Candleholder, Madrid, Amber, Pair	9.00
Depression Glass, Candleholder, Madrid, Pink, Pair	9.00
Depression Glass, Candleholder, Oyster & Pearls, Pink	4.50
Depression Glass, Candleholder, Princess, Green, Twisted Optic	4.50
Depression Glass, Celery, Miss America, Crystal	4.50
Depression Glass, Celery, Miss America, Pink	6.00
Depression Glass, Celery, Open Rose, Blue, Divided	15.00
Depression Glass, Celery, Ruby Block, Red, 4 3/4 In.	16.00
Depression Glass, Champagne, Diana, Clear Crystal, Green Base, Stemmed, 7 In.	9.50
Depression Glass, Champagne, Iris, Clear, Stemmed	3.50
Depression Glass, Coaster, Doric, Clear, Star & Grapes, 4 In.	1.00
Depression Glass, Coaster, Floral, Green, 3 1/4 In.	2.00
Depression Glass, Compote, Candy, Floral, Green	6.00
Depression Glass, Compote, Candy, Mayfair, Pink, Covered	8.00
Depression Glass, Compote, Diana, Pink, Twisted	2.50
Depression Glass, Compote, Manhattan, Pink	2.25
Depression Glass, Compote, Mayfair, Pink	9.00
Depression Glass, Compote, Miss America, Pink	4.50 To 6.50
Depression Glass, Compote, Miss American, Crystal	5.00
Depression Glass, Compote, Pineapple & Floral, Clear	1.50
Depression Glass, Compote, Sharon, Pink, Cover	9.50
Depression Glass, Console Set, Madrid, Amber, 3 Pieces	12.50
Depression Glass, Console Set, Oyster & Pearl, Ruby, 3 Pieces	17.50
Depression Glass, Creamer, American Sweetheart, Milk Glass	4.50
Depression Glass, Creamer, Cabbage Rose, Pink	3.00
Depression Glass, Creamer, Cameo, Cobalt Blue, Round, Cover	2.50
Depression Glass, Creamer, Cameo, Green, 3 In.	2.50
Depression Glass, Creamer, Cherry Blossom, Green	3.50
Depression Glass, Creamer, Colonial, Crystal, 5 In.	3.50
Depression Glass, Creamer, Colonial, Green	5.50
Depression Glass, Creamer, Cube, Green	5.00
Depression Glass, Creamer, Floragold	3.00
Depression Glass, Creamer, Florentine, Amber, No.2	2.75
Depression Glass, Creamer, Iris, Amber	2.50

Depression Glass, Creamer, Miss American, Clear	4.00
Depression Glass, Creamer, Moonstone	3.00
Depression Glass, Creamer, Queen Mary, Pink	3.50
Depression Glass, Creamer, Ribbon, Green	1.00
Depression Glass, Creamer, Sharon, Amber	2.25
Depression Glass, Creamer, Sharon, Pink	3.00
Depression Glass, Creamer, Winsor, Pink, Diamond	3.00
Depression Glass, Cup & Saucer, American Sweetheart	3.50
Depression Glass, Cup & Saucer, American Sweetheart, Monax	6.50
Depression Glass, Cup & Saucer, American Sweetheart, Pink	3.00
Depression Glass, Cup & Saucer, Ballerina, Green	3.00
Depression Glass, Cup & Saucer, Block, Pink, Stippled Band	2.00
Depression Glass, Cup & Saucer, Bubble, Blue	2.00
Depression Glass, Cup & Saucer, Cherry Blossom, Pink	5.00
Depression Glass, Cup & Saucer, Child's, Diana, Cobalt Blue	4.00
Depression Glass, Cup & Saucer, Colonial Rope, Green	2.15
Depression Glass, Cup & Saucer, Colonial, Green	1.50
Depression Glass, Cup & Saucer, Crystal	2.00
Depression Glass, Cup & Saucer, Cube, Pink	3.00
Depression Glass, Cup & Saucer, Doric, Pink	3.50
Depression Glass, Cup & Saucer, Hairpin, Pink	3.00
Depression Glass, Cup & Saucer, Iris & Herringbone, Clear	2.00
Depression Glass, Cup & Saucer, Iris & Herringbone, Marigold	2.50
Depression Glass, Cup & Saucer, Lorain, Milk Glass, Yellow, Aster	3.00
Depression Glass, Cup & Saucer, Madrid, Amber	3.75
Depression Glass, Cup & Saucer, Moderntone, Blue	3.10
Depression Glass, Cup & Saucer, Moderntone, Milk Glass	3.00
Depression Glass, Cup & Saucer, Moonstone	1.50
Depression Glass, Cup & Saucer, New Century, Green	2.00
Depression Glass, Cup & Saucer, Normandie, Pink, Carnival	3.50
Depression Glass, Cup & Saucer, Princess, Green	3.00
Depression Glass, Cup & Saucer, Rope, Green	2.50
Depression Glass, Cup & Saucer, Royal Lace, Cobalt Blue	14.00
Depression Glass, Cup & Saucer, Sharon, Amber	3.50
Depression Glass, Cup & Saucer, Winsor, Clear	3.00
Depression Glass, Cup, American Sweetheart, Milk Glass	5.00
Depression Glass, Cup, American Sweetheart, Pink	1.80
Depression Glass, Cup, Block Optic, Pink	2.00
Depression Glass, Cup, Bowknot, Green	2.50
Depression Glass, Cup, Bubble, Blue	1.50
Depression Glass, Cup, Cabbage Rose, Pink	1.75 To 2.50
Depression Glass, Cup, Cameo, Green	1.50 To 2.50
Depression Glass, Cup, Cameo, Yellow	2.00
Depression Glass, Cup, Child's, Cherry, Pink	3.00
Depression Glass, Cup, Coronation, Pink	1.50
Depression Glass, Cup, Custard, Cherry Blossom, Green	1.25
Depression Glass, Cup, Demitasse, Iris & Herringbone, Clear	2.00
Depression Glass, Cup, Dogwood, Pink, Thick	2.50
Depression Glass, Cup, Dogwood, Pink, Thin	2.50
Depression Glass, Cup, Floral, Pink	2.50
Depression Glass, Cup, Florentine, Yellow	2.50
Depression Glass, Cup, Hairpin, Pink	1.50
Depression Glass, Cup, Hobnail, Clear	2.50
Depression Glass, Cup, Holiday, Pink	2.00
Depression Glass, Cup, Lydia Ray, Green	1.50
Depression Glass, Cup, Madrid, Amber	2.00 To 2.50
Depression Glass, Cup, Madrid, Blue	3.75
Depression Glass, Cup, Manhattan, Clear	1.50
Depression Glass, Cup, Miss America, Crystal	3.50
Depression Glass, Cup, Miss America, Green	5.00
Depression Glass, Cup, Miss America, Pink	.88 To 3.00
Depression Glass, Cup, Moderntone, Cobalt Blue	2.50
Depression Glass, Cup, Normandie, Amber	2.50
Depression Glass, Cup, Normandie, Pink	2.00
Depression Glass, Cup, Normandie, Sunburst	3.00
Depression Glass, Cup, Octagonal, Pink	2.50

Depression Glass, Cup, Patrician, Amber	2.50
Depression Glass, Cup, Patterns, Yellow	2.00
Depression Glass, Cup, Poppy, Yellow	2.25
Depression Glass, Cup, Princess, Green	2.15 To 2.25
Depression Glass, Cup, Princess, Yellow	2.00
Depression Glass, Cup, Punch, Cameo, Green	.50
Depression Glass, Cup, Punch, Lorain, Milk Glass, Clear, Thumbprint	1.00
Depression Glass, Cup, Royal Ruby, Round	1.50
Depression Glass, Cup, Royal Ruby, Square	1.50
Depression Glass, Cup, Sandwich, Clear	.25
Depression Glass, Cup, Sharon, Amber	2.00
Depression Glass, Custard, Moderntone, Cobalt Blue	2.50
Depression Glass, Dipper, Frosted, Pink, Miniature	3.00
Depression Glass, Dish, Berry, Iris & Herringbone, Clear	1.25
Depression Glass, Dish, Candy, Cabbage Rose, Pink, Covered	9.00
Depression Glass, Dish, Candy, Floral, Green, Covered	7.50
Depression Glass, Dish, Candy, Mayfair Hocking's, Pink, Cover	8.50
Depression Glass, Dish, Candy, Open Rose, Pink, Covered	10.00
Depression Glass, Dish, Ice Cream, Royal Ruby, Stemmed	3.25
Depression Glass, Dish, Princess, Pink, Boat Shape, 11 In.	4.00
Depression Glass, Dish, Relish, Cameo, Green	2.00
Depression Glass, Dish, Relish, Old Cafe, Pink, Clear Handles, Oval	2.50
Depression Glass, Dish, Square, Floragold, 5 1/2 In.	1.10
Depression Glass, Dish, Sweetmeat, Miss America, Pink	20.00
Depression Glass, Dish, Vegetable, Cabbage Rose, Amber, Oval	5.00
Depression Glass, Dish, Vegetable, Cabbage Rose, Amber, Round	4.00
Depression Glass, Dish, Vegetable, Cabbage Rose, Pink, Oval	5.00
Depression Glass, Dish, Vegetable, Cherry Blossom, Pink, Oval	6.00
Depression Glass, Dish, Vegetable, Cherry, Green, Round	5.50
Depression Glass, Dish, Vegetable, Rosemary, Amber, Oval	4.50
Depression Glass, Dish, Vegetable, Royal Lace, Cobalt Blue, Oval	15.00
Depression Glass, Glass, Adam, Pink, Footed, 4 1/2 In.Tall	4.75
Depression Glass, Glass, Cherry Blossom, Pink, Footed, 4 1/2 In.	4.25
Depression Glass, Glass, Floral, Green, Footed, 4 3/4 In.	4.25
Depression Glass, Glass, Floral, Green, Footed, 5 1/4 In.	4.50
Depression Glass, Glass, Sharon, Green, Footed, 6 1/2 In.	6.50
Depression Glass, Glass, Spoke, Amber, Footed, 5 In.	5.00
Depression Glass, Glass, Water, Miss America, Green	5.00
Depression Glass, Glass, Windsor Diamond, Clear, 5 In.	3.50
Depression Glass, Goblet, Cameo Ballerina, Green, Stemmed, 6 In.	10.00
Depression Glass, Goblet, Colonial, Green	7.50
Depression Glass, Goblet, Iris, Clear, Stemmed	3.50
Depression Glass, Goblet, Miss America, Clear, Footed	4.50
Depression Glass, Goblet, Miss America, Pink, 10 Oz.	5.00
Depression Glass, Goblet, Optic Block, Green	4.50
Depression Glass, Goblet, Princess, Clear	4.00
Depression Glass, Grill, Cameo, Green	1.85 To 2.50
Depression Glass, Grill, Madrid, Amber	2.50
Depression Glass, Grill, Normandie, Sunburst	4.50
Depression Glass, Grill, Patrician, Amber	2.00
Depression Glass, Jar & Cover, Cubist, Green	4.00
Depression Glass, Jar, Candy, Adam, Pink, Flat Rim	7.50
Depression Glass, Jar, Candy, Floral, Green, Covered	8.00
Depression Glass, Jar, Candy, Floral, Pink, Lid	7.50
Depression Glass, Jar, Cookie, Cameo, Green, Covered	8.00
Depression Glass, Jar, Cookie, Holiday, Pink, Lace Edge	10.00
Depression Glass, Jar, Cookie, Madrid, Covered, Amber	14.50
Depression Glass, Jar, Cookie, Mayfair Hocking's, Pink, Cover	8.50
Depression Glass, Jar, Cookie, Royal Lace, Cobalt Blue	14.00
Depression Glass, Jar, Cracker, Frosted, Pink	3.00
Depression Glass, Jar, Cracker, Mayfair, Pink	3.50 To 14.50
Depression Glass, Jar, Cracker, Royal Lace, Covered, Green	15.00
Depression Glass, Jar, Mayfair, Pink, Candy, Cover	8.50
Depression Glass, Jar, Mustard, Petal, Cobalt, Attached Liner	4.00
Depression Glass, Juice Set, Fine Ribbed, Cobalt Blue, Tilt Pitcher	17.50
Depression Glass, Juice, Cameo, Green	4.25

Depression Glass, Juice, Cherry, Green	3.00
Depression Glass, Juice, Cherry Blossom, Pink, Footed	2.35
Depression Glass, Juice, Cherry Blossom, Pink, Footed	3.50
Depression Glass, Juice, Holiday, Pink	4.00
Depression Glass, Juice, Miss America, Clear	3.25
Depression Glass, Juice, Poppy, Green, Footed	3.00
Depression Glass, Juice, Poppy, Yellow, Footed, 5	2.75
Depression Glass, Juice, Royal Ruby	2.00
Depression Glass, Mayonnaise, Petalware, Cobalt Blue, Covered, Metal Cover	7.50
Depression Glass, Mint Tray, Pink	1.10
Depression Glass, Mold, Jello, Madrid, Amber	4.00
Depression Glass, Nappy, Adam, Pink, 4 3/4 In.	1.00
Depression Glass, Nappy, Herringbone, Clear, Ruffled, 5 In.	1.50
Depression Glass, Nappy, Miss America, Green	5.00
Depression Glass, Nappy, Oyster & Pearl, Handled	2.50
Depression Glass, Nappy, Oyster & Pearls, Pink, Applied Handle, Heart Shape	2.50
Depression Glass, Nappy, Pink, Handled	1.15
Depression Glass, Nappy, Rosemary, Amber, 5 In.	1.25
Depression Glass, Pitcher, Adam, Pink	12.50
Depression Glass, Pitcher, Adam, Pink, 32 Oz., Cone Shape	10.00 To 13.50
Depression Glass, Pitcher, Cameo, Clear, Rib Tilt	3.00
Depression Glass, Pitcher, Cameo, Green, 36 Oz.	6.00
Depression Glass, Pitcher, Cherry Blossom, Green	12.00
Depression Glass, Pitcher, Cherry Blossom, Pink	12.00
Depression Glass, Pitcher, Colonial, Crystal, 7 In., 54 Oz.	12.50
Depression Glass, Pitcher, Dogwood, Green	8.00
Depression Glass, Pitcher, Dutch Rose, Pink, 2 Cup	2.00
Depression Glass, Pitcher, Floral, Green, 8 In., Cone Shape	8.50
Depression Glass, Pitcher, Floral, Pink *Illus*	10.00
Depression Glass, Pitcher, Florentine, Pink, Juice	3.00
Depression Glass, Pitcher, Florentine, Yellow, Cone Shape	10.00
Depression Glass, Pitcher, Herringbone, Clear	6.50
Depression Glass, Pitcher, Irish, Crystal	9.00
Depression Glass, Pitcher, Juice, Manhattan, Clear	3.00
Depression Glass, Pitcher, Juice, Mayfair, Pink	6.75
Depression Glass, Pitcher, Juice, Princess, Pink	8.50
Depression Glass, Pitcher, Mayfair Hocking's, Pink, 8 In.	9.00
Depression Glass, Pitcher, Mayfair, Pink, 37 Oz.	6.00
Depression Glass, Pitcher, Mayfair, Pink, 60 Oz.	8.50
Depression Glass, Pitcher, Milk, Holiday, Pink	6.00
Depression Glass, Pitcher, Panel Optic, Green, 60 Oz.	7.50
Depression Glass, Pitcher, Poppy, Yellow	8.00
Depression Glass, Pitcher, Princess, Green, 8 In.	12.00
Depression Glass, Pitcher, Royal Lace, Clear, 80 Oz.	17.50
Depression Glass, Pitcher, Royal Ruby	8.00
Depression Glass, Pitcher, Sharon, Green	20.00
Depression Glass, Pitcher, Water, Cameo, Green	12.00
Depression Glass, Pitcher, Water, Cherry, Green	18.00

Depression Glass, Pitcher, Floral, Pink

Depression Glass, Pitcher, Water, Diamond, Pink 7.00
Depression Glass, Pitcher, Water, Floral, Green 9.00
Depression Glass, Pitcher, Water, Holiday, Pink 8.00
Depression Glass, Pitcher, Water, Mayfair, Pink 14.00
Depression Glass, Pitcher, Water, Optic Block, Green 10.00
Depression Glass, Pitcher, Water, Spoke, Green 18.00
Depression Glass, Pitcher, Water, Wreath, Pink 6.00
Depression Glass, Plate, Adam, Pink, 6 In. 1.25
Depression Glass, Plate, American Sweetheart, Milk Glass 5.00
Depression Glass, Plate, American Sweetheart, Monax, 12 In. 6.50
Depression Glass, Plate, American Sweetheart, Monax, 6 In. 2.50
Depression Glass, Plate, American Sweetheart, Monax, 9 In. 4.00
Depression Glass, Plate, American Sweetheart, Pink, 6 In. .... 1.00 To 1.15
Depression Glass, Plate, American Sweetheart, Pink; 8 In. 1.35
Depression Glass, Plate, American Sweetheart, Pink, 10 In. 2.10
Depression Glass, Plate, Block Optic, Green, 6 In. 1.50
Depression Glass, Plate, Block Optic, Pink, 8 In. 1.75
Depression Glass, Plate, Block, Green, 8 In. 1.00
Depression Glass, Plate, Block, Green, 9 1/4 In. 1.75
Depression Glass, Plate, Block, Yellow, 6 In. .... .75
Depression Glass, Plate, Block, Yellow, 8 In. 1.00
Depression Glass, Plate, Bread, Madrid, Blue, 6 In. 2.00
Depression Glass, Plate, Bubble, Blue, Dinner 1.50
Depression Glass, Plate, Bubble, Blue, 9 1/2 In. 1.50
Depression Glass, Plate, Cake, Adam, Pink, Footed .... 6.50 To 8.00
Depression Glass, Plate, Cake, Cherry, Green 9.00
Depression Glass, Plate, Cake, Cherry, Pink 4.00
Depression Glass, Plate, Cake, Dogwood, Pink, 12 In. 7.00
Depression Glass, Plate, Cake, Doric, Green 4.00
Depression Glass, Plate, Cake, Hobstar, Clear, 11 In.Diameter 7.50
Depression Glass, Plate, Cake, Madrid, Amber 6.00
Depression Glass, Plate, Cake, Open Rose, Pink 4.00
Depression Glass, Plate, Cake, Princess, Green, Footed .... 4.00 To 6.00
Depression Glass, Plate, Cake, Windsor, Pink 4.00
Depression Glass, Plate, Cameo Girl, Green, 8 In. 1.50
Depression Glass, Plate, Cameo Girl, Green, 9 1/2 In. 1.75
Depression Glass, Plate, Cherry Blossom, Pink 3.00
Depression Glass, Plate, Cherry, Green, 9 In. 2.25
Depression Glass, Plate, Cherry, Pink 2.50
Depression Glass, Plate, Chop, American Sweetheart, Monax, 11 In. 6.00
Depression Glass, Plate, Chop, American Sweetheart, Pink, 11 In. 4.00
Depression Glass, Plate, Clover Leaf, Green, 8 In. 1.00
Depression Glass, Plate, Colonial Rope, Green, 6 In. .... .75
Depression Glass, Plate, Colonial, Pink, 8 1/2 In. 2.00
Depression Glass, Plate, Coronation, Pink, 8 1/2 In. 2.00
Depression Glass, Plate, Dessert, Doric, Pink 1.50
Depression Glass, Plate, Diamond, Pink, 8 In. 1.50
Depression Glass, Plate, Dinner, American Sweetheart, Milk Glass 6.00
Depression Glass, Plate, Dinner, American Sweetheart, Pink 2.00
Depression Glass, Plate, Dinner, Bubble, Blue 1.60
Depression Glass, Plate, Dinner, Cherry Blossom, Pink, 9 In. 3.00
Depression Glass, Plate, Dinner, Doric, Green 2.50
Depression Glass, Plate, Dinner, Doric, Pink 1.85
Depression Glass, Plate, Dinner, Floral, Green 2.50
Depression Glass, Plate, Dinner, Iris & Herringbone, Clear 2.50
Depression Glass, Plate, Dinner, Iris & Herringbone, Marigold 3.50
Depression Glass, Plate, Dinner, Madrid, Amber 2.25
Depression Glass, Plate, Dinner, Madrid, Blue 4.50
Depression Glass, Plate, Dinner, Manhattan, Clear 1.50
Depression Glass, Plate, Dinner, Mayfair, Rose 1.50
Depression Glass, Plate, Dinner, Miss America, Pink .... 3.50 To 5.00
Depression Glass, Plate, Dinner, Moderntone, Blue .... 1.90 To 2.50
Depression Glass, Plate, Dinner, Moderntone, Milk Glass 2.00
Depression Glass, Plate, Dinner, Normandie, Sunburst 4.50
Depression Glass, Plate, Dinner, Parrot, Green, Divided 4.00
Depression Glass, Plate, Dinner, Patrician, Amber 2.00

Depression Glass, Plate, Dinner, Poppy, Green	1.75
Depression Glass, Plate, Dinner, Poppy, Yellow	2.50
Depression Glass, Plate, Dinner, Princess, Green	2.00
Depression Glass, Plate, Dinner, Princess, Pink	2.00
Depression Glass, Plate, Dinner, Royal Lace, Cobalt Blue	8.00
Depression Glass, Plate, Dinner, Sharon, Amber	2.00
Depression Glass, Plate, Dinner, Windsor Diamond, Pink	1.90
Depression Glass, Plate, Divided, Cameo, Yellow	1.75
Depression Glass, Plate, Dogwood, Green, 8 In.	2.00
Depression Glass, Plate, Doric, Pink, 6 In.	.80 To 2.50
Depression Glass, Plate, Florentine, Yellow, 6 In.	1.25
Depression Glass, Plate, Grill, Cameo, Green, Stippled Outer Edge, 11 In.	1.00
Depression Glass, Plate, Grill, Cameo, Yellow, Closed Handle	2.00 To 2.50
Depression Glass, Plate, Grill, Dogwood, Pink	2.50
Depression Glass, Plate, Grill, Miss America, Crystal	4.00
Depression Glass, Plate, Grill, Miss America, Pink, 10 In.	3.75
Depression Glass, Plate, Grill, Princess, Green, Handled	2.10
Depression Glass, Plate, Grill, Princess, Pink	2.00
Depression Glass, Plate, Grill, Princess, Yellow	2.00
Depression Glass, Plate, Hairpin, Cobalt	2.00
Depression Glass, Plate, Hairpin, Pink, 9 In.	2.00
Depression Glass, Plate, Hobnail, Pink, Sectional *Illus*	9.00

Depression Glass, Plate,
Hobnail, Pink, Sectional

Depression Glass, Plate, Leaf, Pink, 8 In.	1.00
Depression Glass, Plate, Lorain, Yellow, 8 3/4 In.	1.75
Depression Glass, Plate, Luncheon, Block, Pink	1.25
Depression Glass, Plate, Luncheon, Block, Pink, Stippled Band	1.50
Depression Glass, Plate, Luncheon, Cameo, Green	1.50
Depression Glass, Plate, Luncheon, Cube, Pink	1.75
Depression Glass, Plate, Luncheon, Dogwood, Pink	2.00 To 5.00
Depression Glass, Plate, Luncheon, Florentine, Green	1.75
Depression Glass, Plate, Luncheon, Georgian, Green	1.75
Depression Glass, Plate, Luncheon, Leaf, Pink	1.25
Depression Glass, Plate, Luncheon, Lydia Ray, Green	1.50
Depression Glass, Plate, Luncheon, Madrid, Amber	1.50
Depression Glass, Plate, Luncheon, Madrid, Blue, 9 In.	4.25
Depression Glass, Plate, Luncheon, Miss America, Pink	3.25
Depression Glass, Plate, Luncheon, Moderntone, Blue	1.45
Depression Glass, Plate, Luncheon, New Century, Green	1.25
Depression Glass, Plate, Luncheon, Patrician, Amber	1.75
Depression Glass, Plate, Luncheon, Patrician, Green	1.75
Depression Glass, Plate, Luncheon, Poppy, Yellow	1.75
Depression Glass, Plate, Luncheon, Rope, Green	1.25
Depression Glass, Plate, Madrid, Amber, 6 In.	1.25
Depression Glass, Plate, Madrid, Green, 9 In.	2.25
Depression Glass, Plate, Miss America, Green, 7 In.	3.00

Depression Glass, Plate, Moderntone, Blue, 7 In. 1.10
Depression Glass, Plate, Moonstone, 8 1/2 In. 1.75
Depression Glass, Plate, No.612, Green, 11 1/4 In. 2.50
Depression Glass, Plate, Normandie, Pink, 8 In. 1.50
Depression Glass, Plate, Octagonal, Pink, 8 In. 4.50
Depression Glass, Plate, Patrician, Amber, 9 In. .... 1.50 To 1.75
Depression Glass, Plate, Pie, Cherry Blossom, Pink 2.00
Depression Glass, Plate, Pie, Cube, Pink 1.25
Depression Glass, Plate, Pie, Diana, Clear 1.25
Depression Glass, Plate, Pie, Diana, Pink 1.25
Depression Glass, Plate, Pie, Doric, Green 1.25
Depression Glass, Plate, Pie, Doric, Pink 1.50
Depression Glass, Plate, Pie, Floral, Green 1.25
Depression Glass, Plate, Pie, Hairpin, Pink 1.00
Depression Glass, Plate, Pie, Madrid, Amber .... .35 To 1.00
Depression Glass, Plate, Pie, Manhattan, Clear .... .75
Depression Glass, Plate, Pie, Miss America, Clear 1.50
Depression Glass, Plate, Pie, Moderntone, Blue 1.15
Depression Glass, Plate, Pie, Poppy, Yellow 1.15
Depression Glass, Plate, Pie, Princess, Pink 1.25
Depression Glass, Plate, Pie, Rope, Green 1.00
Depression Glass, Plate, Pie, Royal Lace, Cobalt Blue 4.50
Depression Glass, Plate, Pie, Winsor, Green, Diamond 1.25
Depression Glass, Plate, Princess, Pink, Tab Handle, 10 In. 1.50
Depression Glass, Plate, Rosemary, Amber, 9 1/2 In. 2.00
Depression Glass, Plate, Queen Mary, Clear, 6 3/4 In. 1.50
Depression Glass, Plate, Queen Mary, Clear, 12 In. 4.50
Depression Glass, Plate, Queen Mary, Pink, 10 In. 4.50
Depression Glass, Plate, Raindrop, Green, 8 In. 1.00
Depression Glass, Plate, Ribbon, Green, 6 In. 1.50
Depression Glass, Plate, Rope, Green, 8 1/2 In. 1.50
Depression Glass, Plate, Rosemary, Amber, 6 1/2 In. 1.50
Depression Glass, Plate, Royal Ruby, Dinner, Square 1.50
Depression Glass, Plate, Royal Ruby, 9 In. 3.50
Depression Glass, Plate, Ruby, Red, Square, 8 1/2 In. 2.00
Depression Glass, Plate, Salad, Adam, Pink, 7 3/4 In. 1.50
Depression Glass, Plate, Salad, American Sweetheart, Pink, 8 In. 1.50
Depression Glass, Plate, Salad, Bubble, Blue 1.00
Depression Glass, Plate, Salad, Cloverleaf, Green, 8 In. 1.50
Depression Glass, Plate, Salad, Dutch Rose, Amber 1.00
Depression Glass, Plate, Salad, Floral, Pink 2.00
Depression Glass, Plate, Salad, Madrid, Amber 1.75
Depression Glass, Plate, Salad, Miss America, Crystal, 8 1/2 In. 4.00
Depression Glass, Plate, Salad, Moderntone, Cobalt Blue 2.00
Depression Glass, Plate, Salad, Moonstone 1.50
Depression Glass, Plate, Sandwich, Cameo, Green, 10 In. 3.50
Depression Glass, Plate, Sandwich, Clear, 9 In. 1.00
Depression Glass, Plate, Sharon, Amber, 6 In. 2.00
Depression Glass, Plate, Sharon, Amber, 7 1/2 In. 1.50
Depression Glass, Plate, Sharon, Pink, 9 In. 3.25
Depression Glass, Plate, Sherbet, Adam, Pink, 6 In. 1.00
Depression Glass, Plate, Sherbet, Cameo, Green 1.50
Depression Glass, Plate, Sherbet, Floral, Green 1.50
Depression Glass, Plate, Sherbet, Florentine, Yellow 1.25
Depression Glass, Plate, Sherbet, Georgian, Green 1.25
Depression Glass, Plate, Sherbet, Mayfair Hocking's, Pink 2.50
Depression Glass, Plate, Sherbet, Miss America, Green 5.00
Depression Glass, Plate, Sherbet, Miss American, Pink 2.00
Depression Glass, Plate, Sherbet, Moderntone, Cobalt Blue 1.25
Depression Glass, Plate, Sherbet, Pink, Block .... .75
Depression Glass, Plate, Sherbet, Princess, Yellow 1.00
Depression Glass, Plate, Spoke, Green, 7 1/2 In. 1.25
Depression Glass, Plate, Waterford, Clear, 9 1/2 In. 2.00
Depression Glass, Platter, Adam, Pink 6.00
Depression Glass, Platter, American Sweetheart, Pink, 13 In. 5.50
Depression Glass, Platter, Bubble, Blue, 12 In. 2.00

Depression Glass, Platter, Cabbage Rose, Amber 5.00
Depression Glass, Platter, Cabbage Rose, Pink 5.00
Depression Glass, Platter, Cameo, Green 5.00
Depression Glass, Platter, Cherry Blossom, Pink, 11 In. .... 5.00 To 5.50
Depression Glass, Platter, Doric, Pink .... 4.00 To 6.50
Depression Glass, Platter, Floral Green 4.00
Depression Glass, Platter, Floral, Pink .... 3.00 To 4.00
Depression Glass, Platter, Florentine, Amber, No.2 .... 3.50
Depression Glass, Platter, Hairpin, Cobalt 2.00
Depression Glass, Platter, Hairpin, Pink, 12 In. 4.50
Depression Glass, Platter, Honeycomb, Green, 10 3/4 In. Long 4.00
Depression Glass, Platter, Honeycomb, Pink, Floral, 10 3/4 In. Long 4.00
Depression Glass, Platter, Madrid, Amber 5.00
Depression Glass, Platter, Mayfair, Green, 12 1/2 In. 12.00
Depression Glass, Platter, Miss America, Pink, 12 In. .... 7.00 To 7.50
Depression Glass, Platter, Normandie, Sunburst 6.00
Depression Glass, Platter, Open Rose, Blue 7.00
Depression Glass, Platter, Parrot, Green 9.00
Depression Glass, Platter, Patrician, Amber 4.00
Depression Glass, Platter, Poppy, Yellow 4.00
Depression Glass, Platter, Princess, Green 5.00
Depression Glass, Platter, Royal Lace, Cobalt 15.00
Depression Glass, Platter, Royal Lace, Pink, 13 In. 4.75
Depression Glass, Platter, Sharon, Amber 4.00
Depression Glass, Punch Set, Royal Ruby, 2 Piece Bowl, 10 Cups 67.50
Depression Glass, Reamer, Juice, Diana, Green, Large 3.00
Depression Glass, Reamer, Juice, Diana, Green, Medium 1.50
Depression Glass, Relish, Cameo, Green, 3 Part .... 3.00 To 3.50
Depression Glass, Relish, Clear .... .90
Depression Glass, Relish, Floral, Green, Section 4.00
Depression Glass, Relish, Floral, Pink, Section .... 3.00 To 4.00
Depression Glass, Relish, Lace Edge, Pink, Section 3.25
Depression Glass, Relish, Miss America, Pink, 4 Part, 8 1/2 In. .... 5.00 To 6.00
Depression Glass, Relish, No.612, Yellow 3.00
Depression Glass, Salt & Pepper, Cube, Green 6.00
Depression Glass, Salt & Pepper, Doric, Green, Pair 5.00
Depression Glass, Salt & Pepper, Florentine, Green, Pair 10.00
Depression Glass, Salt & Pepper, Lydia Ray, Green 6.00
Depression Glass, Salt & Pepper, Miss America, Pink, Set 12.00
Depression Glass, Salt & Pepper, Moderntone, Blue .... 6.50 To 7.00
Depression Glass, Salt & Pepper, Moderntone, Cobalt Blue 4.50
Depression Glass, Salt & Pepper, Moderntone, Milk Glass 6.00
Depression Glass, Salt & Pepper, Royal Lace, Pink, Set 9.00
Depression Glass, Salt & Pepper, Sharon, Amber, Pair 10.00
Depression Glass, Salt & Pepper, Waterford, Clear 4.00
Depression Glass, Salver, American Sweetheart, Monax, 12 In. 6.00
Depression Glass, Sauce, Adam, Pink, ... .60
Depression Glass, Sauce, Normandie, Pink 1.00
Depression Glass, Sauce, Ribbed, Pink 1.00
Depression Glass, Saucer, Adam, Pink .... 1.00 To 1.50
Depression Glass, Saucer, American Sweetheart, Milk Glass 1.50
Depression Glass, Saucer, American Sweetheart, Monax 2.50
Depression Glass, Saucer, Block Optic, Pink 1.50
Depression Glass, Saucer, Bubble, Blue ....75 To 1.00
Depression Glass, Saucer, Cameo Green 1.00
Depression Glass, Saucer, Cherry Blossom, Pink 1.75
Depression Glass, Saucer, Cherry Blossom, Pink, Child's 2.00
Depression Glass, Saucer, Colonial Rope, Green .... .75
Depression Glass, Saucer, Colonial, Green 1.50
Depression Glass, Saucer, Diana, Pink 1.25
Depression Glass, Saucer, Dogwood, Pink 1.50
Depression Glass, Saucer, Doric, Green 1.50
Depression Glass, Saucer, Doric, Pink .... .90
Depression Glass, Saucer, Floral, Green 1.50
Depression Glass, Saucer, Florentine, Pink 1.00
Depression Glass, Saucer, Florentine, Yellow 1.50

Depression Glass, Saucer, Georgian, Green	1.50
Depression Glass, Saucer, Hairpin, Pink	1.00
Depression Glass, Saucer, Madrid, Amber	.60 To 1.50
Depression Glass, Saucer, Manhattan, Clear	.75
Depression Glass, Saucer, Mayfair Hocking's, Pink	1.50
Depression Glass, Saucer, Miss America, Crystal	1.50
Depression Glass, Saucer, Miss America, Pink	1.50 To 2.00
Depression Glass, Saucer, Moderntone, Cobalt Blue	1.50
Depression Glass, Saucer, Normandie, Amber	1.50
Depression Glass, Saucer, Normandie, Pink	1.00
Depression Glass, Saucer, Normandie, Sunburst	2.00
Depression Glass, Saucer, Octagonal, Pink	2.00
Depression Glass, Saucer, Patrician, Amber	1.50
Depression Glass, Saucer, Patrician, Green	1.50 To 2.00
Depression Glass, Saucer, Patterns, Yellow	1.00
Depression Glass, Saucer, Petalware, Milk Glass	1.15
Depression Glass, Saucer, Royal Lace, Cobalt Blue	4.50
Depression Glass, Saucer, Royal Lace, Pink	1.50
Depression Glass, Saucer, S Pattern, Yellow	8.00
Depression Glass, Saucer, Sharon, Amber	1.00 To 2.00
Depression Glass, Saucer, Sherbet, Coronation, Pink	1.00
Depression Glass, Saucer, Waterford, Clear	1.00
Depression Glass, Server, Mayfair, Pink, Center Glass Handle	8.00
Depression Glass, Sherbet, Adam, Pink	2.25
Depression Glass, Sherbet, American Sweetheart, Pink	1.75
Depression Glass, Sherbet, Cabbage Rose, Pink	2.50
Depression Glass, Sherbet, Cameo Rose, Green	2.50
Depression Glass, Sherbet, Cameo, Green, Stemmed	2.50 To 4.75
Depression Glass, Sherbet, Cameo, Green, 3 In.	2.50 To 3.00
Depression Glass, Sherbet, Cherry Blossom, Pink, Footed	2.50 To 3.50
Depression Glass, Sherbet, Coronation, Pink	1.10
Depression Glass, Sherbet, Cube, Green, Footed	1.50
Depression Glass, Sherbet, Daisy, Amber	1.50
Depression Glass, Sherbet, Daisy, Green	1.50
Depression Glass, Sherbet, Doric Delfite, Blue	4.00
Depression Glass, Sherbet, Floral, Green	2.00
Depression Glass, Sherbet, Florentine, Green	2.00
Depression Glass, Sherbet, Florentine, Yellow	2.00
Depression Glass, Sherbet, Green, Mark F6	.75
Depression Glass, Sherbet, Holiday, Pink	2.50
Depression Glass, Sherbet, Iris, Clear, 4 In.	3.00
Depression Glass, Sherbet, Lorain, Milk Glass, Clear, Crackle	.75
Depression Glass, Sherbet, Madrid, Amber	1.30
Depression Glass, Sherbet, Madrid, Amber, 2 1/2 In.	1.50 To 2.00
Depression Glass, Sherbet, Madrid, Amber, 3 In.	2.00
Depression Glass, Sherbet, Mayfair, Pink, 2 1/4 In.	1.50 To 2.00
Depression Glass, Sherbet, Miss America, Crystal	3.00
Depression Glass, Sherbet, Miss America, Pink	2.75 To 3.50
Depression Glass, Sherbet, Moderntone, Cobalt Blue	2.00
Depression Glass, Sherbet, New Century, Green	1.00 To 1.50
Depression Glass, Sherbet, Normandie, Amber	1.50
Depression Glass, Sherbet, Normandie, Pink	1.35 To 1.50
Depression Glass, Sherbet, Open Rose, Pink, Footed	2.00
Depression Glass, Sherbet, Patrician, Amber	1.75
Depression Glass, Sherbet, Patrician, Amber, Footed	2.00
Depression Glass, Sherbet, Patrician, Green, Footed	3.50
Depression Glass, Sherbet, Princess, Green	2.15
Depression Glass, Sherbet, Roulette, Madrid, Green	2.00
Depression Glass, Sherbet, Swirl, Pink	1.50
Depression Glass, Soup, Royal Lace, Cobalt Blue, 2 Handles	10.00
Depression Glass, Squeezer, Sunkist, Green	5.50
Depression Glass, Squeezer, Sunkist, Milk Glass	4.00
Depression Glass, Sugar & Creamer, Cameo, Green	4.00
Depression Glass, Sugar & Creamer, Dogwood, Pink	6.00
Depression Glass, Sugar & Creamer, Iris, Clear	5.00
Depression Glass, Sugar & Creamer, Madrid, Amber	4.00 To 6.00

Depression Glass, Sugar & Creamer, Madrid, Blue, Open	11.00
Depression Glass, Sugar & Creamer, Manhattan, Clear	3.75
Depression Glass, Sugar & Creamer, Moderntone, Blue	7.50
Depression Glass, Sugar & Creamer, Moderntone, Milk Glass	5.00
Depression Glass, Sugar & Creamer, Pineapple & Floral, Clear	5.00
Depression Glass, Sugar & Creamer, Princess, Pink, Frosted	9.50
Depression Glass, Sugar & Creamer, Royal Lace, Cobalt Blue	15.00
Depression Glass, Sugar & Creamer, Royal Ruby, Open	4.50
Depression Glass, Sugar & Creamer, Waterford, Clear, Cover	4.50
Depression Glass, Sugar, American Sweetheart, Milk Glass	4.50
Depression Glass, Sugar, American Sweetheart, Monax, Open	3.00
Depression Glass, Sugar, Cameo, Green, 3 In.	2.50
Depression Glass, Sugar, Cherry, Green, Covered	4.00
Depression Glass, Sugar, Cube, Green, Covered	5.00
Depression Glass, Sugar, Doric, Pink	2.50
Depression Glass, Sugar, Iris & Herringbone, Clear, Open	2.00
Depression Glass, Sugar, Madrid, Blue, Open	6.00
Depression Glass, Sugar, Miss America, Clear	7.50
Depression Glass, Sugar, Moderntone, Cobalt Blue	2.50
Depression Glass, Sugar, Octagonal, Pink, Pedestal, Open	3.50
Depression Glass, Sugar, Open, Adam, Pink	2.75
Depression Glass, Sugar, Open, Madrid, Amber	2.00
Depression Glass, Sugar, Patrician, Amber, Open	3.00
Depression Glass, Sugar, Petalware, Milk Glass, Gold Band	3.00
Depression Glass, Sugar, Pink, No.1, Cover	3.50
Depression Glass, Sugar, Ribbon, Green	1.00
Depression Glass, Sugar, Royal Ruby, Handled	1.75
Depression Glass, Sugar, Sharon, Amber	3.50
Depression Glass, Sugar, Waterford, Clear, Cover	2.00
Depression Glass, Tray, Cherry Blossom, Pink, 10 1/2 In.	4.00 To 5.00
Depression Glass, Tray, Floral, Pink, 6 In.Square, Handles	5.00
Depression Glass, Tray, Mayfair, Green, Handled	10.00
Depression Glass, Tray, Winsor, Clear, Diamond, 10 In.	2.50
Depression Glass, Tray, Winsor, Pink, Diamond	3.00
Depression Glass, Tumbler, Adam, Pink, Flared Rim	8.50
Depression Glass, Tumbler, Adam, Pink, Footed, 4 1/2 In.	3.00 To 4.00
Depression Glass, Tumbler, Block, Green, Footed Cone	2.25
Depression Glass, Tumbler, Bowknot, Green, Footed, 5 In.	3.00 To 4.50
Depression Glass, Tumbler, Cameo, Rose, Footed	3.00
Depression Glass, Tumbler, Cameo, Yellow, 5 In., 6 Feet	4.00
Depression Glass, Tumbler, Cherry Blossom, Pink	1.00
Depression Glass, Tumbler, Cloverleaf, Green, Footed, 10 Oz.	3.50
Depression Glass, Tumbler, Coronation, Pink, 5 In.	3.00
Depression Glass, Tumbler, Daisy, Amber, 9 Oz., Footed	4.00
Depression Glass, Tumbler, Dogwood, Pink, Hand Decorated, 5 In.	5.00
Depression Glass, Tumbler, Doric, Flat, 4 In., Pink	4.00
Depression Glass, Tumbler, Floragold	4.50
Depression Glass, Tumbler, Floral, Green, Footed, 4 3/4 In.	3.50
Depression Glass, Tumbler, Floral, Green, 7 Oz.	3.00
Depression Glass, Tumbler, Floral, Green, 9 Oz.	3.50
Depression Glass, Tumbler, Floral, Pink, 4 3/4 In., 4 Feet	4.00
Depression Glass, Tumbler, Florentine, Flat, 4 In., Green	4.00
Depression Glass, Tumbler, Georgian, Green	1.25
Depression Glass, Tumbler, Herringbone, Clear, Cone, 6 In.	2.75
Depression Glass, Tumbler, Holiday, Flat, 4 In., Pink	4.00
Depression Glass, Tumbler, Homespun, Flat, 4 In., Pink	4.00
Depression Glass, Tumbler, Honeycomb, Green	1.50
Depression Glass, Tumbler, Irish, Crystal, Footed, 6 In.	3.50
Depression Glass, Tumbler, Juice, Cherry Blossom, Pink, 3 1/2 In.	5.75
Depression Glass, Tumbler, Juice, Honeycomb, Green	1.00
Depression Glass, Tumbler, Madrid, Flat, 4 1/2 In., Amber	4.00
Depression Glass, Tumbler, Manhattan, Clear, Footed	1.50
Depression Glass, Tumbler, Manhattan, Pink, Footed	7.00
Depression Glass, Tumbler, Miss America, Clear	3.00
Depression Glass, Tumbler, Normandie, Amber, 4 In.	3.00
Depression Glass, Tumbler, Old Florentine, Green, 5 In., Footed	4.00

Depression Glass, Tumbler, Open Lace, Pink, Vertical Ribbed, Flare Top 1.25
Depression Glass, Tumbler, Patrician, Amber, 4 In. 3.50
Depression Glass, Tumbler, Princess, Pink, Footed, 5 1/4 In. 4.00
Depression Glass, Tumbler, Princess, Pink, Footed, 5 1/2 In. 4.00
Depression Glass, Tumbler, Princess, Pink, 4 In. 2.50
Depression Glass, Tumbler, Princess, Pink, 5 In. 3.00
Depression Glass, Tumbler, Princess, Yellow, Footed, 5 1/4 In. 4.00
Depression Glass, Tumbler, Queen Mary, Pink, 3 1/2 In. 1.50
Depression Glass, Tumbler, Queen Mary, Pink, 4 In. 2.00
Depression Glass, Tumbler, Rose Cameo, Footed, 4 1/2 In., Green 4.00
Depression Glass, Tumbler, Rose Cameo, Green.Footed, 6 In. 2.50
Depression Glass, Tumbler, Rosemary, Amber 4.00
Depression Glass, Tumbler, Royal Lace, Clear, 3 1/2 In. 1.50
Depression Glass, Tumbler, Royal Lace, Cobalt Blue 9.50
Depression Glass, Tumbler, Royal Lace, Flat, 4 In., Pink 4.00
Depression Glass, Tumbler, Royal Ruby 5.50
Depression Glass, Tumbler, Waterford, Footed, 5 1/2 In., Clear 4.00
Depression Glass, Tumbler, Windsor, Flat, 5 In., Pink 4.00
Depression Glass, Tumbler, Yellow, Footed, 10 Oz. 4.00
Depression Glass, Vase, Blue Pea, Pink 23.00
Depression Glass, Vase, Cameo Girl, Green, 8 In., Bulbous 5.50
Depression Glass, Vase, Cameo, Green, 8 1/2 In. 9.00
Depression Glass, Vase, Herringbone, Clear 4.25
Depression Glass, Vase, Manhattan, Clear, 8 In. Tall 2.50
Depression Glass, Vase, Poppy, Green 4.00
Depression Glass, Vase, Princess, Green 7.00
Depression Glass, Vase, Ruby, Globular, 3 1/2 In. 1.00
Depression Glass, Vase, Sweetpea, Open Rose, Blue 19.00
Depression Glass, Water Set, Banded Ribbon, Cobalt, 7 Pieces 30.00
Depression Glass, Water Set, Cherry, Pink, 7 Piece 37.50
Depression Glass, Water Set, Florentine, Green, 7 Piece, Cone-Shaped Jug 35.00
Depression Glass, Water Set, Patrician, Amber, 6 Piece 50.00
Depression Glass, Water Set, Sailboat, Cobalt, 7 Piece 25.00
Depression Glass, Wine, Cameo, Green, Stemmed 1.75
Depression Glass, Wine, Iris, Clear, Stemmed 3.50
Depression Glass, Wine, Miss America, Clear 3.50
Depression Glass, Wine, Panel Optic, Pink, Stemmed, 5 In.Tall 7.50

*Derby Porcelain was made in Derby, England, from 1756 to the present.
The factory changed names and marks several times. Chelsea Derby (1770-
1784), Crown Derby (1784-1811), and the modern Royal Crown Derby are
some of the most famous periods of the factory.*

Derby, see also Crown Derby, Royal Crown Derby, Chelsea
Derby, Bowl, Soup, Flowers, Blue, Gold, Hand-Painted, Marked, 10 In.Across 180.00
Derby, Candelabra, Figures Of Liberty & Matrimony, C.1770, Pair 45.00
Derby, Candlestick, Figure, Chelsea, Bocage, C.1775, Pair 275.00
Derby, Cup & Saucer, Flowers, Green, Red Mark, Circa 1810 .... 150.00
Derby, Figurine, Boy Holds Goat, Chelsea, Circa 1770, 5 1/2 In.High 250.00
Derby, Figurine, Cow Group, C.1790, Gray & White Spotted Cow, 5 3/4 In.High 120.00
Derby, Figurine, Girl With Basket Of Grapes, 18th Century, 6 In.High 250.00
Derby, Figurine, Maiden Dressed In Armor, Pedestal, C.1765, 2 Piece 75.00
Derby, Figurine, Poet Holds Scrap Of Paper, Dog At Side, 18th Century 275.00
Derby, Figurine, The Seasons, Woman-Autumn, Winter-Man, 19th Century, Pair 200.00
Derby, Pitcher, Salmon Color, Gilt Handle & Borders, Marked, Dated 1885 .... 25.00
Derby, Pitcher, White & Gold, 1870, Puce Mark 150.00
Derby, Vase Of Flowers, Scroll Shape, Birds, C.1760, 6 In.High, Pair 125.00
Derby Vase, Flower Encrusted, Shield Shape, Trumpet Neck, D Mark, C.1825 .... 125.00
Derby, Vase, Miniature, Chinoiserie, Ovoid Form, William Watson, C.1830, Pair 100.00
Derby, Vase, White, Dark Blue Band Of Scenes, Serpent Handles, Bloor, Pair 150.00
Dick Tracy, Book, Big Little Book 5.00
Dick Tracy, Book, Dick Tracy & The Mad Killer, Better Little Books 4.00
Dick Tracy, Book, Dick Tracy And The Spider Gang, Big Little Book, 1937 .... 10.00
Dick Tracy, Booklet, Advertising Gum, Goudey, 3 .... 12.00
Dick Tracy, Doll, 19 In.Tall 6.00
Dionne Quintuplets, Calendar, 1937 .... 5.00
Dionne Quintuplets, Calendar, 1943, Andrew Loomis Paintings 10.00

Doll, A.M., Baby, No.990, Dressed, Dutch Cut Wig, 14 In.Tall 47.50
Doll, A.M., Bisque Head, Sleeping Eyes, Wig, Dressed, Jointed Body, 22 In.Tall 65.00
Doll, A.M., Bisque Head, Stationary Eyes, Wig, Jointed Body, 18 In.Tall 55.00
Doll, A.M., Dream Baby, Dressed, Composition Body, 11 In.Tall 85.00
Doll, A.M., Dream Baby, 14 In.Tall 85.00
Doll, A.M., Dressed, 20 In.Tall 45.00
Doll, A.M., Human Hair, Dressed, 24 In.Tall 80.00
Doll, A.M., Mabel, Germany, Bisque, Marked, Blue Eyes, Blonde Wig, 16 In.Tall 40.00
Doll, A.M., Marked, 24 In.Tall, Bisque Head Marked No.390, Dressed 60.00
Doll, A.M., 390 N, Dressed, 21 In.Tall 50.00
Doll, Advertising, Lee Overall Boy, Composition, Overalls, Lee Buttons 55.00
Doll, Agnes, Blonde, China Head, 8 1/2 In.Tall 38.00
Doll, Alexander, Bride, 18 In.Tall 15.00
Doll, Alexander, Composition, Dressed, Sleep Eyes, Long Hair, 17 In. 35.00
Doll, Alexander, Dionne Quintuplet, 7 1/2 In.Tall 20.00
Doll, Alexander, Wendy Ann, Wig, Sleep Eyes, 13 In.Tall 20.00
Doll, Alexander, 1960, Bent Leg, Dark Hair, 12 In.Tall 10.00
Doll, Amasandra 12.00
Doll, American, Yellow Hair, Moving Eyes, White Dress, 25 In.Tall 20.00
Doll, Ann Shirley, Composition, Brown Eyes, Blonde Wig, 14 In.Tall 25.00
Doll, Armand Marseille, Bisque Head, Marked Grgm, Composition, 10 1/2 In. 25.00
Doll, Armand Marseille, Blonde Human Hair, Blue Sleep Eyes, Dressed, 32 In. 185.00
Doll, Armand Marseille, Boy, Germany, Character 125.00
Doll, Armand Marseille, Jointed Body, Blue Eyes, Germany, 23 In. 69.50
Doll, Armand Marseille, Jointed, Blonde Hair, Brown Eyes, 21 In. 79.50
Doll, Baby Majic, Sleep Eyes, Blonde, Thimble, Bottle, 18 In.Tall 18.00
Doll, Baby Sandy 60.00
Doll, Baby Stewart, Bonnet, Blue Velvet Suit, 12 In. 350.00
Doll, Baby, Bald, Pierced Nostrils, Sleep Eyes, Franz Schilling, 22 In. 175.00
Doll, Baby, Bent Legs, Open Mouth, Human Hair Wig, Dressed, J.D.K., 17 In. 100.00
Doll, Baby, Bent Limb Body, Open Mouth, Fir Wig, Jdk Character 250.00
Doll, Baby, Character, Unis France 251, Sleeping Eyes, 17 In. 275.00
Doll, Baby, Cloth Body, 6 In.Around Head 85.00
Doll, Baby, Human Hair Wig, 16 In.Head, Dressed In Rompers, K R, 24 In. 200.00
Doll, Baby, K Star, Dress & Bonnet, No.126, 15 In.Tall 125.00
Doll, Baby, Lori, Sleeping Blue Eyes, 23 In. 350.00
Doll, Baby, Marked S In W Sweet, Bald Head, Blue Glass Eyes 22.50
Doll, Baby, Schoenhut, Character Face, Dressed Closed Mouth, Mark, 13 1/2 In. 165.00
Doll, Baby, Sleep Eye, Mohair Wig, Open Mouth, Marked Jdk, 18 In. 85.00
Doll, Baby, 13 In.Tall, 3-Faced, Crying, Smiling & Sleeping, Dressed 35.00
Doll, Baby, 9 In.Tall, Composition, Colored, Dressed 20.00
Doll, Ball Jointed, Closed Mouth, 19 In. 150.00
Doll, Ball Jointed, Human Hair Wig, Closed Mouth, 28 In. 375.00
Doll, Ball Jointed, Lashes, Sleep Eyes, Bergman, 30 In.Tall 95.00
Doll, Bang, Bisque, 25 In.Tall 135.00
Doll, Bergman, Marked, Toddler, Blonde, Dressed, 16 In.Tall 55.00
Doll, Betsy Mccall, 8 In.Tall .... 5.00 To 7.00
Doll, Bisque Head, Albert Levy, Tanagra, 26 In.Tall 200.00
Doll, Bisque Head, Blue Glass Eyes, Kyser, Jointed Body, Marked No.2, 13 In. 165.00
Doll, Bisque Head, Carl Bergman, 24 In.Tall, Dressed 175.00
Doll, Bisque Head, Character Baby, Marked G.B.-A.M.12 In. 55.00
Doll, Bisque Head, Closed Mouth, Pierced Ears, Jumeau Medaille Dor Paris 395.00
Doll, Bisque Head, Fulper Baby, Wobbly Tongue, Dressed, Marked, 1910, 14 In. 95.00
Doll, Bisque Head, Fur Eyebrows, Teeth, Pink Kid Body, Germany, 20 1/2 In. 87.50
Doll, Bisque Head, Glass Eyes, Gibson Girl Hairdo, Jointed Limbs, Germany 325.00
Doll, Bisque Head, Googly Eyes, Composition Body, Marked Germany, Crown 145.00
Doll, Bisque Head, Googly Eyes, Papier-Mache Body, Glass Eyes, 8 In.Tall 135.00
Doll, Bisque Head, Handwerch-Halbig, 25 In.Tall, Dressed 200.00
Doll, Bisque Head, Incised No.5, 23 In.Tall, Goe.Vinchy 175.00
Doll, Bisque Head, Incised No.9, 26 In.Tall, Jumeau Type Body 200.00
Doll, Bisque Head, Incised 5-0, 16 In.Tall, Dressed, Edmund Steiner 45.00
Doll, Bisque Head, J.Verlingue, 25 In.Tall, Inance, Voice Box 225.00
Doll, Bisque Head, Jointed Kid Body, Blonde Wig, Dressed, 17 In.Tall 95.00
Doll, Bisque Head, Lanternier, Limoges, 27 In.Tall, Favorite 225.00
Doll, Bisque Head, Marked Floradora A3/om, Kid Body, Blue Eyes, 17 In.Tall 50.00
Doll, Bisque Head, Marked Germany, Kid Body, Blue Eyes, 17 In.Tall 47.50

Doll, Bisque Head, Marked Germany, Kid Body, Brown Eyes, 13 In.Tall 40.00
Doll, Bisque Head, Marked Queen Louise, Jointed Body, Blue Eyes, 28 In.Tall 90.00
Doll, Bisque Head, Marked Sh With Pb In Star, Jointed Body, 23 In.Tall 65.00
Doll, Bisque Head, Marked Sh 1079 Dep, Jointed Body, Blue Eyes, 24 In.Tall 97.50
Doll, Bisque Head, Painted Eyes, Tongue, Dressed, Open Mouth, Mark 33-5, 11 In 85.00
Doll, Bisque Head, Pull Cord & Throws Kiss, Walks, Bru Jne, Dressed, 23 In. 850.00
Doll, Bisque Head, Schoneau-Hoffmeister, 24 In.Tall, Dressed 200.00
Doll, Bisque Head, Simon Halbig, 26 In.Tall, Dressed 200.00
Doll, Bisque Head, Sleep Eyes, Human Hair Wig, A.M.Mark, No Clothes, 34 In. 225.00
Doll, Bisque Head, Sleep Eyes, Open Mouth, Human Hair Braids, Germany 135.00
Doll, Bisque Head, Stick & Paper Body, Snow Baby 30.00
Doll, Bisque Head, Unis France, 27 In.Tall, Voice Box 225.00
Doll, Bisque Head, White Dress, 17 In.Tall 40.00
Doll, Bisque Shoulder Head, Bonnet Molded, Girl, Closed Mouth, 15 In.Tall 85.00
Doll, Bisque Shoulder Head, Dressed, Street Vendors, Wooden Yokes, Pair 82.00
Doll, Bisque Shoulder Head, French Kid Body, Glass Eyes, 21 In.Tall 75.00
Doll, Bisque Shoulder Head, Glass Eyes, Open Mouth, Kid Body, Celluloid Arms 52.50
Doll, Bisque Shoulder Head, Kid Body, Mohair Wig, Dressed, Parian, 16 In. 385.00
Doll, Bisque Shoulder Head, Pierced Ears, Kid Body, Marked D.E.P. L&h 65.00
Doll, Bisque Shoulder Head, Sleep Eyes, Kid Body, Celluloid Arms, Marked 48.00
Doll, Bisque Shoulder Head, Stationary Glass Eyes, Kid Body, Wig, Undressed 42.00
Doll, Bisque Shoulder Head, Stationary Glass Eyes, Open Mouth, Wig, Kid Body 70.00
Doll, Bisque Socket Head, Sleep Eyes, Lashes, Composition, Marked Floradora 65.00
Doll, Bisque Socket Head, Stationary Eyes, Composition Body, Marked Germany 40.00
Doll, Bisque Socket Head, Stationary Glass Eyes, Marked R.A., Dated 1909 .... 35.00
Doll, Bisque Socket Type Head, Bahr & Proschild, Germany, 6 1/2 In.Tall 60.00
Doll, Bisque Swivel Head, Glass Eyes, Open Nostrils, Heubach Kopplesdorf 65.00
Doll, Bisque, Angel, German, 3 1/4 In. 2.00
Doll, Bisque, Baby, Brown Eyes & Hair, Horsman, Nippon, 21 1/2 In.Tall 125.00
Doll, Bisque, Baby, Crying, 5 In.Tall 35.00
Doll, Bisque, Baby, Glass Eyes, Composition, Heubach Kopplesdorf, Germany 65.00
Doll, Bisque, Baby, Head Marked 682/4, Germany, 7 In.Tall 35.00
Doll, Bisque, Baby, Smiling, Rattle, French, 8 1/2 In.Tall, Pair 350.00
Doll, Bisque, Bathing Beauty, Reclining, Applied Bisque Flakes, Gray Suit 13.50
Doll, Bisque, Blue Eyes, Mohair Wig, Brocade Costume, French Fashion 345.00
Doll, Bisque, Boy Holding Rabbit, German, 1 1/2 In. 5.00
Doll, Bisque, Boy, Dressed, 5 1/2 In.Tall 10.00
Doll, Bisque, Brown Eyes, Paris, Marked Sfbj-60, 19 In. 69.00
Doll, Bisque, Brown Hair & Eyes, Dressed, Quivering Tongue, 11 In.Tall 85.00
Doll, Bisque, Fat, Painted Eyes, 5 In.Tall 7.00
Doll, Bisque, Flapper, 3 1/4 In., Pair 17.50
Doll, Bisque, German, Jointed At Hips & Shoulders, Blonde Wig, 5 In.Tall 28.50
Doll, Bisque, German, Marked R.A., Sleep Blue Eyes, 14 In.Tall 55.00
Doll, Bisque, Gibson Girl, 24 In.Tall 235.00
Doll, Bisque, Girl, Sleep Eyes, Jointed, 4 1/2 In.Tall 32.00
Doll, Bisque, Girl, Sleep Eyes, O.M., Dressed, Wig, 8 In.Tall 60.00
Doll, Bisque, Glass Eyes, Blonde Hair, Marked 1910, 12 In.Tall 28.00
Doll, Bisque, Heubach, Bonnet Baby, Piano Doll 120.00
Doll, Bisque, Japan, Movable Arms, Closed Legs, 3 1/2 In.High 5.00
Doll, Bisque, Japan, Movable Arms, Open Legs, 3 1/2 In.High 6.00
Doll, Bisque, Jointed Shoulders & Hips, Painted Shoes & Socks, Wig, 4 In. 22.50
Doll, Bisque, Man, Molded Head, Beard, Mustache 45.00
Doll, Bisque, Marked R 12/0 A, Composition Body, Blue Eyes, Blonde Wig 30.00
Doll, Bisque, Negro, 4 In.Tall 2.25
Doll, Bisque, Orange Blossoms Entwined Through Hair, French Fashion 335.00
Doll, Bisque, Paris, Brown Eyes, 19 In. 69.50
Doll, Bisque, Piano Baby, Sitting, Playing With Toes, Blonde, Blue Eyes, 8 In. 28.00
Doll, Bisque, Queen Louise, Dressed, 25 In.Tall 68.00
Doll, Bisque, Signed Germany, Dressed, 3 In.Tall, Boy & Girl, Pair 25.00
Doll, Bisque, Storybook, 6 In.Tall 10.00
Doll, Bisque, Swivel Head, Sleep Eyes, Open Mouth, Mark K.H.Walkure, 14 In. 40.00
Doll, Blonde, Says Dorothy On Molded Blouse, Porcelain, 21 In. 125.00
Doll, Blue Painted Eyes, Four Molded Teeth, Marked Schoenhut, 17 In. 125.00
Doll, Bonnet, Painted Features, Molded Hair, Swing Arms & Legs, 10 In.Tall 28.00
Doll, Bonnie Braids, Dick Tracy 15.00

Doll, Boudoir, Fashion, 30 In.Tall, Dressed, Composition Head, Arms, Feet	30.00
Doll, Boy, Bisque Head, Composition Body, Dressed, Marked Halbig, 7 1/4 In.	45.00
Doll, Boy, Bisque Head, Jointed Body, English, 21 In.	89.50
Doll, Boy, Character, Bisque Shoulder Head, Painted Eyes, Kid Body, Germany	125.00
Doll, Boy, Flirty Eyes, Bisque Head, Composition Body, 6 1/2 In.Tall	112.00
Doll, Boy, Girl, Bisque, Marked Nippon, 3 1/2 In.Tall, Pair	85.00
Doll, Boy, Human Hair Wig, Brown Eyes, S.F.B.J.236, 27 In.	350.00
Doll, Boy, J.D.K., Dressed, Brushed Hair, Open, Closed Mouth, 23 1/2 In.Tall	140.00
Doll, Boy, Mechanical, Dressed Stars & Stripes, Bell, Flag, 7 In.Tall	16.00
Doll, Boy, S.F.B.J., Open & Closed Mouth, Marked 236, Dressed, 27 In.	350.00
Doll, Boy, Schoenhut, Wooden, Dressed, Marked, Blue Eyes, Teeth, 11 In.Tall	125.00
Doll, Boy, Toddler, Bisque Head, Brown Eyes & Hair, 12 In.	75.00
Doll, Bread Dough, Hobo Clown, Handmade, 8 In.Tall	20.00
Doll, Bride, Blonde, Swing Arms, 4 1/2 In.Tall	9.00
Doll, Bride, Closed Mouth, Human Hair, Wired Fingers, E.J.Jumeau, 15 In.	395.00
Doll, Bru, Human Hair Wig, Mechanical Limbs, 22 In.	850.00
Doll, Bruckney, 11 In.Tall, 2 Headed, One White, One Colored, Cloth, Dressed	8.00
Doll, Butterick Mannequin, Junior Miss, Patterns, 14 In.Tall	6.00
Doll, Bye-Lo, Baby, By Grace Storey Putnam, Turtle Mark	225.00
Doll, Bye-Lo Baby, Sleep Eyes, Grace S.Putnam, Germany, 13 In.Tall	285.00
Doll, Bye-Lo, Baby, 14 In.Tall	375.00
Doll, Bye-Lo, Bisque, Movable Legs & Arms, Marked Copy By Grace S.Putnam	100.00
Doll, Bye-Lo, Composition Head, Cloth Body, Signed Grace Putnam, 13 In.	140.00
Doll, Bye-Lo, Composition, Grace Storey Putnam	75.00
Doll, Bye-Lo, Composition, Sleeping Eyes, Cloth Body, 12 In.Tall	65.00
Doll, Bye-Lo, Mapan	35.00
Doll, Bye-Lo, Marked Grace S.Putnam, Bisque Head, 11 1/2 In.Tall	155.00
Doll, C.O.D.930 Dep. Marks, Leather Body, 18 In.Tall	85.00
Doll, Callerfelder Puppen Tabrik, Bisque Head, Boy, Dressed, 14 In.Tall	35.00
Doll, Campbell Kid, Girl, Ideal, 8 In.Tall	10.00
Doll, Cardboard, Germany, C.1890, Ballet Lady	2.00
Doll, Cardboard, Germany, C.1890, Bloomer Lady	2.00
Doll, Cardboard, Germany, C.1890, Colored Children, 4	6.00
Doll, Carnival, Hat & Cane, 12 In.	5.00
Doll, Celluloid Head, Boy, Cloth Body, Swedish Costume, Marked Germany	20.00
Doll, Celluloid Head, Molded Hair, Painted Eyes, Molded Teeth, Cloth Body	20.00
Doll, Celluloid, Baby In Bath Tub, 1 1/2 In.	4.00
Doll, Celluloid, Baby, Jointed Arms, Blue Eyes, Bootees, Hong Kong	5.00
Doll, Celluloid, Boy, C.1925, 4 1/2 In.Tall	3.00
Doll, Celluloid, Boy, Miniature, C.1922, 6 1/2 In.Tall	1.50
Doll, Celluloid, Boy, Turtle Mark, 13 In.Tall	30.00
Doll, Celluloid, Girl, C.1925, 5 1/2 In.Tall	3.50
Doll, Celluloid, Girl, Miniature, C.1922, 6 In.Tall	1.50
Doll, Celluloid, Girl, Turtle Mark, 17 In.Tall	30.00
Doll, Celluloid, Glass Eyes, Molded Hair, Marked No.41, 15 In.Tall	25.00
Doll, Character, Baby Otto, 12 In.Tall, Composition Body	135.00
Doll, Character, Boy, Bisque Shoulder Head, Molded Hair, Mark Heubach 1724	165.00
Doll, Character, Boy, Blue Intaglio Eyes, Molded Hair, Mark Am No.600	150.00
Doll, Character, Composition, Germany	60.00
Doll, Character, Signed E.S.Dubois, Paris, C.1745, Dressed, 20 In.Tall	500.00
Doll, Charlie Chaplin	90.00
Doll, Charlie Mccarthy, Dressed	38.50
Doll, Charlie Mccarthy, Marked Effanbee, Dressed, 15 In.Tall 20.00 To 25.00	
Doll, Chatty Kathy, Blonde Hair, Mumbles, 20 In.Tall	18.00
Doll, China Head & Limbs, Dressed, 11 In.	58.00
Doll, China Head, Auburn Hair, 10 In.Tall	22.50
Doll, China Head, Black Hair, Cloth Body, Dressed	30.00
Doll, China Head, Blonde Hair, Name Ruth	35.00
Doll, China Head, Brunette, White Dress, 16 In.Tall	35.00
Doll, China Head, Cloth Body, Blonde Painted Hair, Dressed As Boy, 18 In.	150.00
Doll, China Head, Feet, & Arms, 7 In.Tall	10.00
Doll, China Head, Kid Body, Dressed, 32 In.Tall	35.00
Doll, China Head, Lady, Blonde, Dressed, German, 12 In.Tall	37.50
Doll, China Head, Negro, Closed Mouth, 10 In.Tall	85.00
Doll, China Head, Yellow Hair, Black Dress, 12 In.Tall	40.00

Doll, China Head, 32 In.Tall, 1890, Dressed, Silk Bustle Dress 135.00
Doll, China Head, 5 In.Tall, Dressed, Blue Eyes 29.50
Doll, China Lady, Dressed, Blue Eyes, C.1870, 19 In.Tall 75.00
Doll, China, Blonde, Calico Dress, Slip, Pantalettes, 32 In.Tall 35.00
Doll, China, Brown Peasant Dress, 8 1/2 In.Tall 10.00
Doll, China, Marked 9-13, Leather Hands, Cloth Body, Black Hair, 30 In.Tall 125.00
Doll, China, Painted Black Hair, Dressed 45.00
Doll, China, Short Hair, 11 In.Tall 38.00
Doll, China, 7 In.Tall, Black Hair, China Legs & Arms 20.00
Doll, Chinese Boy, 16 In.Tall, Composition 45.00
Doll, Chinese, Red Dress, 19 In.Tall 20.00
Doll, Christopher Robin, Vinyl Head, Cloth Body, Walt Disney, 18 In.Tall 15.00
Doll, Chubby, Painted Features, Molded Hair, Swing Legs, 6 1/2 In.Tall 30.00
Doll, Closed Mouth, Blue Eyes, Dressed, E.J., 26 In. 535.00
Doll, Closed Mouth, Blue Eyes, French, Belton, Dressed, 12 In. 295.00
Doll, Closed Mouth, Brown Eyes, Human Hair, Dressed, Mark R2d, 23 In. 400.00
Doll, Closed Mouth, Dome Head Toddler, J.D.K., 17 In. 165.00
Doll, Closed Mouth, French, 18 In. 195.00
Doll, Closed Mouth, Human Hair Wig, Dressed, E.J., 16 In. 500.00
Doll, Cloth, Marked Exposition Internationale, Paris 1937 .... 70.00
Doll, Clothespin, Betty & Jimmy, Painted Face, Yarn Wig, Movable Arms, Pair 3.00
Doll, Clown, Body, Music Box, Wood Legs 45.00
Doll, Composition Head, Glass Eyes, Composition Hands & Feet, Made In China 35.00
Doll, Composition Head, Sawdust Filled, Cloth Body, 30 In. 129.50
Doll, Composition Shoulder Head, Man, Glass Eyes, Closed Mouth, 11 In.Tall 40.00
Doll, Composition, Baby, Swivel Head, 9 In.Tall 7.00
Doll, Composition, Baby, 15 In.Tall, Bentlimb 35.00
Doll, Composition, Cloth Body, Kopplesdorf, Germany, 12 In.Tall 95.00
Doll, Composition, Cloth Body, Open Mouth, Glass Eyes, 19 In.Tall 12.00
Doll, Composition, Cloth Body, Painted Eyes, 17 In.Tall 6.00
Doll, Composition, Cloth Body, Tin Open & Close Eyes, 18 In.Tall 8.00
Doll, Composition, Flapper, Painted Shoes & Hair, Dressed, 14 In.Tall 16.00
Doll, Composition, Marked J.D.12, 16 In.Tall 175.00
Doll, Composition, Marked Patsy Ann, Dressed, 20 In.Tall 45.00
Doll, Composition, Negro, Baby, C.1931 .... 8.00
Doll, Composition, Open & Close Glass Eyes, Pigtails, 16 In.Tall 15.00
Doll, Composition, Open & Close Glass Eyes, 16 In.Tall 12.00
Doll, Composition, Open Mouth, Painted Eyes, Pigtails, 16 In.Tall 8.00
Doll, Composition, Painted Eyes, Dressed, 8 In.Tall 5.00
Doll, Composition, Painted Eyes, Dressed, 12 In.Tall 5.00
Doll, Composition, Toddler, 15 In.Tall 35.00
Doll, Dainty Dorthy, Twins, Leather Bodies, Composition Arms & Legs 150.00
Doll, Deanna Durbin, 16 In.Tall 45.00
Doll, Deanna Durbin, 23 In.Tall 75.00
Doll, Dick Clark 30.00
Doll, Dionne Quintuplet, 20 In.Tall, Alexander, Dressed, Composition 60.00
Doll, Dionne, Toddler, Wig, Dressed, 16 In.Tall 75.00
Doll, Doctor's, Carved Ivory, Laying On Base, Teakwood, 6 In.Tall 100.00
Doll, Dream Baby, Bisque Head, Dressed, Open Mouth, Teeth, 10 3/4 In.Tall 58.00
Doll, Dutch, Black Pants, 10 In.Tall 15.00
Doll, Effanbee, Ann Shirley, Brown Sleep Eye, Blond 35.00
Doll, Effanbee, Baby Tinette, 7 In.Tall 15.00
Doll, Effanbee, Emily Ann, Puppet, Dressed, 14 In.Tall 10.00
Doll, Effanbee, Patsyette, 9 1/2 In.Tall 15.00
Doll, Effanbee, Toddler, Marked, Flirty Eyes, Lamb's Wool Hair, 23 In.Tall 15.00
Doll, Ei Horsman, Baby, Blue Tin Sleep Eyes, Dressed, 21 In.Tall 27.50
Doll, Emmet Kelly, Carved, Wooden, 15 In.Tall, Dressed 17.00
Doll, Eugene, Composition, Cloth Body, Tin Eyes, Open & Close, 15 In.Tall 8.00
Doll, Fanny Brice 75.00
Doll, Fanny Brice, Wooden, 12 In.Tall 15.00
Doll, Fashion, Wax, Glass Eyes, Wig, Cloth Body, Dressed, 36 In.Tall 75.00
Doll, Floradora, Doll Of The Month, Germany, 13 1/2 In.Tall 35.00
Doll, Floradora, 13 1/2 In.Tall, Composition Body, Dressed 36.50
Doll, French Artist, Label Says Cocher Qu Cois, Vers 1888, Dressed 250.00
Doll, French Fashion, Bisque Shoulder Swivel Head, Kid Body, Marked Fg 375.00
Doll, French Fashion, Swivel Neck, Kid Body, Bisque Arms, 18 In. 550.00

Doll, French, Boy, 12 In.Tall	10.00
Doll, French, Fashion, Gesland Body, F.G.Head	650.00
Doll, French, Steiner, Cardboard Torso, Bisque Head, 12 In.Tall, Dressed	65.00
Doll, Frozen Charlotte, Bisque, Negro Luster, 16 In.Tall	12.00
Doll, Frozen Charlotte, Bisque, 3 In.Tall	9.50
Doll, Frozen Charlotte, Black Hair, 2 In.High	5.00
Doll, Frozen Charlotte, Boy, Blonde Hair, Blue Eyes, 16 1/2 In.Tall	395.00
Doll, Gans & Seyfarth, Dressed, 23 In.Tall	125.00
Doll, Gem, Marked, Composition, Colored, C.1935, Dressed, 9 In.Tall	15.00
Doll, General Macarthur, Composition, Dressed In Uniform, 20 1/2 In.Tall	40.00
Doll, General Macarthur, Composition, 17 In.Tall	45.00
Doll, Gesland	495.00
Doll, Girl, A.M., Scotch Outfit, Teeth, Blue Eyes, Auburn Wig, 21 In.	65.00
Doll, Girl, B.J., Body O.M., Brown Eyes, Marked France, 12 In.Tall	78.00
Doll, Girl, Braided Brown Hair, Closing Eyes, Germany, 26 In.	69.50
Doll, Girl, Celluloid, Sleep Eyes, Dressed	12.50
Doll, Girl, French Fashion, 15 In.Tall	169.00
Doll, Girl, Hand-Sewn Body, Goats'-Hair Wig, French, 16 In.Tall	330.00
Doll, Girl, Lenci, Original Dress	50.00
Doll, Girl, Schoenhut, Intaglio Eyes, All Original, 13 In.Tall	125.00
Doll, Girl, Swivel Neck, Jointed Body, Brown Eyes, 16 In.	42.50
Doll, Girl, Swivel Neck, Jointed Body, German, Hair Wig	59.50
Doll, Girl, Toddler, Flirty, J.D.K., Blue Eyes, Blonde Hair, 19 In.Tall	175.00
Doll, Goo-Goo, Sleep Eyes, Watermelon Mouth, Marked No.165-2/0	310.00
Doll, Grace Kelly, Blonde, Blue Eyes, Dressed, 20 In.Tall	12.00
Doll, Handwerck, Bisque Head, Sleep Eyes, Wig, Dressed, 23 In.Tall	85.00
Doll, Handwerck, Dressed, 26 In.Tall	100.00
Doll, Handwerck, Marked 14-99-Dep., Sleep Eyes, Pierced Ears, 26 In.Tall	125.00
Doll, Hawaiian Dancer, Brown Bisque Head, Sleep Eyes, Mohair Wig, Germany	60.00
Doll, Hawaiian, Windup	10.00
Doll, Hebee Shebee, Composition, Jointed, 13 In.Tall	95.00
Doll, Heinrich Handwerck, Marked Germany, Simon Halbig, Jointed, 30 In.Tall	150.00
Doll, Herbuck Negro Hindo, Turned-Up Shoes In Rings	50.00
Doll, Heubach Kopplesdorf, Bisque Head, Felt Tongue, Dressed, 25 In.Tall	225.00
Doll, Heubach Kopplesdorf, Dressed, 23 In.Tall	250.00
Doll, Heubach Kopplesdorf, 26 In.Tall	125.00
Doll, Heubach, Boy, German, Intaglio Eyes, 10 1/2 In.Tall	290.00
Doll, Hilda, Marked Jdk, Baby, Solid Dome, Sleep Eyes, 14 In.Tall	49.00
Doll, Horseman, Mama, 24 In.	15.00
Doll, Howdy Doody, Composition Head	10.00
Doll, Ideal, D-20-1, Rooted Hair, Mouth Opens, 23 In.Tall	10.00
Doll, Ideal, Giggles, Vinyl, Dressed, 18 In.Tall	10.00
Doll, Ideal, Kissy, Vinyl, Dressed, 22 In.Tall	10.00
Doll, Ideal, Marked Patsy Ann, 1959, Vinyl, 15 In.Tall	10.00
Doll, Indian Papoose, Koasati	1.25
Doll, Indian, Papier-Mache, Human Hair Wig, Clothes, Germany, 12 In.	20.00
Doll, Jackie Kennedy, Horseman, Vinyl, Dressed, Marked J.K., 1961, 25 In.Tall	10.00
Doll, Japanese Girl, Dressed, Molded Hair, 4 In.Tall	10.00
Doll, Japanese Woman, Papier-Mache Face, Kimono, Human Hair, 13 In.Tall	14.00
Doll, Jenny Lind, Molded Hair, Cloth Body, Bisque Arms & Legs, 15 In.	35.00
Doll, Jumeau, Bebe Tete Dep., Bisque Head, Paperweight Eyes, Heavy Brows	475.00
Doll, Jumeau, Bride, Gray Eyes, Wired Fingers, 15 In.	395.00
Doll, Jumeau, Child, Stockinette Body, Bisque Feet & Hands	75.00
Doll, Jumeau, Closed Mouth, Clothes, Human Hair, Pierced Ears, 14 In.	375.00
Doll, Jumeau, Closed Mouth, Human Hair, Blue Eyes, Dressed, 26 In.	535.00
Doll, Jumeau, Closed Mouth, Unjointed Wrists, Clothes, Mark No.7, 14 In.	375.00
Doll, Jumeau, Cork Pate, Composition Body, Paperweight Eyes, 24 In.	450.00
Doll, Jumeau, Dressed, Marked S.F.B.J., 14 In.Tall	78.00
Doll, Jumeau, E.J., Girl, Closed Mouth, Dressed, Blue Eyes, Marked, 27 In.Tall	950.00
Doll, Jumeau, Marked O.M., Brown Paperweight Eyes, Dressed, 28 In.Tall	325.00
Doll, Jumeau, Marked 1907, Brown Eyes, 5 Piece Body, 14 In.Tall	138.00
Doll, Jumeau, Marked, French	350.00
Doll, Jumeau, Open Mouth, Brown Eyes, Human Hair, Dressed, Marked, 25 In.Tall	300.00
Doll, Jumeau, Paperweight Blue Eyes, Human Hair Wig, 1917, 33 In.Tall	375.00
Doll, Jumeau, Tete, Blue Eyes, Blonde Wig, Dressed, 21 In.Tall	210.00
Doll, Jumeau, Tete, Open Mouth, Blown Glass Eyes, Pierced Ears, 27 In.Tall	225.00

Doll, Jumeau, Tete, Open Mouth, Blue Eyes, Human Hair Wig, Dressed, 26 In.Tall	300.00
Doll, Just Me, Closed Mouth, 9 1/2 In.	150.00
Doll, K Star R, 30 In.Tall	375.00
Doll, Kestner, Baby, Bisque Head, Sleeping Eyes, Wig, 25 In.Tall	300.00
Doll, Kestner, Bisque Head, Marked Made In Germany-167, Jointed, 23 In.Tall	97.50
Doll, Kestner, Bisque Shoulder Head, Molded Teeth, 10 In.	65.00
Doll, Kestner, Bisque, Glass Eyes, Closed Mouth, Colored, Box, 5 In.	95.00
Doll, Kestner, Bisque, Sleep Eyes, Human Hair, 5 In.Tall	65.00
Doll, Kestner, Brown Eyes, Blonde, Signed, 24 In.Tall	125.00
Doll, Kestner, Character, No.220	250.00
Doll, Kestner, Composition, Sleep Eyes, Raised Eyebrows, Dressed, 19 In.Tall	65.00
Doll, Kestner, J.D., Bisque, No.257, Composition Baby Body, 24 In.Tall	145.00
Doll, Kestner, 11 In.Tall, Century, Baby, Bisque, Dressed	85.00
Doll, Kestner, 168, Dressed, 22 In.Tall	75.00
Doll, Kestner, 23 In.Tall, Bisque Head, Kid Body, Blue Eyes, Brown Hair	85.00
Doll, Kewpie, Bisque, Signed O'neill, Dressed, Paper Sticker On Back	65.00
Doll, Kewpie, Bisque, Signed O'neill, 4 1/2 In.Tall	25.00
Doll, Kewpie, Bisque, Star	35.00
Doll, Kewpie, Composition, Blue Wings, 6 In. Tall	5.00
Doll, Kewpie, Composition, Rose O'neill, Talcum Powder, 7 In.Tall	35.00
Doll, Kewpie, Composition, 13 In.Tall	17.00
Doll, Kewpie, Signed Rose O'neill, The Thinker, Bisque, 4 3/4 In.	55.00
Doll, Kid Body, Brown Eyes, Bobbed Hair, German	69.00
Doll, Kid Body, 13 In.Tall, Bisque Arms	25.00
Doll, Kid Body, 14 In.Tall, Bisque Arms	25.00
Doll, Kochina, God, 18 In.Tall	69.50
Doll, Kochina, Wolf, 14 In.Tall	39.50
Doll, Lady, Feathered Hat, Satin & Lace Dress, French	240.00
Doll, Lady, Umbrella, Bisque, German, 2 In.Tall	8.00
Doll, Lenci, Boudoir, Raquel Miller, Dancer, Dressed	60.00
Doll, Lenci, 12 In.Tall, Boy	35.00
Doll, Linda Williams, Vinyl, Marked, 14 In.Tall	5.00
Doll, Lone Ranger	60.00
Doll, Ludwig Greiner, Philadelphia, Patent, 1858	90.00
Doll, M.B.Japan, Shoulder Head, Dressed, 19 In.Tall	60.00
Doll, Madame Alexander, Little Genius, Composition	25.00
Doll, Madame Alexander, 12 In.Tall, Princess Elizabeth, Dressed	30.00
Doll, Madame Hendron, Baby, Composition, 17 In.Tall	25.00
Doll, Made Of Shells, Shell Purse, 5 In.Tall	4.50
Doll, Majestic, Marked, 26 In.Tall, Bisque Face & Hands, Blue Eyes	74.50
Doll, Marionette, On Strings, Boy, Blonde, Wood, Carved, Dressed, 20 In.Tall	20.00
Doll, Marionette, On Strings, Girl, Blonde, Wood, Carved, Dressed, 16 1/2 In.	20.00
Doll, Mary Hartland	25.00
Doll, Mechanical, Walks, Pierced Ears, Dressed, France	250.00
Doll, Mickey Mouse, Sun Rubber, 11 In.Tall	8.50
Doll, Milliner, Greiner Hairdo, Clothes, 8 1/2 In.	155.00
Doll, Miss Candy Fashion, Mannequin	12.00
Doll, Mm Wonder-Marked, Boy, Composition, Gray Eyes, 11 In.Tall	5.00
Doll, Molded Porcelain Head, Painted Eyes, Cloth Body, Dressed, 11 In.	38.00
Doll, Mon Cheri, Paris, Open Mouth, Human Hair Wig, Dressed, 26 In.	225.00
Doll, My Girl, Open Mouth, Brown Eyes, Human Hair Wig, Dressed, 25 In.Tall	135.00
Doll, My Girlie, Open Mouth, Human Hair, Dressed, Brown Eyes, 25 In.	135.00
Doll, Natural Doll Co., Composition, Tin Open & Close Eyes, 16 In.Tall	20.00
Doll, Negro, Dated 1895	35.00
Doll, Negro, Man, 7 1/2 In.Tall	50.00
Doll, Nippon, Bisque, Molded Hair, Painted Eyes, Moves Arms, Oriental, 5 In.	20.00
Doll, Nippon, Marked F.Y.Nippon, Blue Eyes, Blonde Wig, O.M., Kid Body, 22 In.	50.00
Doll, Nippon, Movable Arms, Painted Features, 6 In.	10.00
Doll, Nippon, Painted Features, Shoes, Blue Cap	7.00
Doll, No.150, Dressed, 18 In.Tall	50.00
Doll, Novelty Doll & Toy Co., Composition, Cloth Body, 16 In.Tall	8.00
Doll, O.M., Bisque, Jointed, Brown Glass Sleep Eyes, 6 In.Tall	45.00
Doll, O.M., Character, Toddler, Marked 152-1, Bisque Head, German	65.00
Doll, O.M., Fashion, Bisque Head, Kid Body, Marked L.H.B., German, 23 In.Tall	95.00
Doll, O.M., Girl, Colored, French, Brown Eyes, Marked Uris	135.00
Doll, O.M., Girl, German, Blonde Wig, Kid Body, Bisque Hands, 23 In.Tall	75.00

Doll, O.M., Marked S & H, Bisque Head, Blonde, Dressed, 27 In.Tall 145.00
Doll, O.M., Marked 3-148, Bisque Head, Kid Body, Dressed, 15 In.Tall 62.00
Doll, Occupied Japan, Baby, Painted, Bisque, Dressed, 9 In.Tall 18.00
Doll, Open Mouth, Blue Eyes, Human Hair Wig, Dressed, Unis France 251, 25 In. 350.00
Doll, Open Mouth, Blue Eyes, Human Hair, Mark Unis France 251, 25 In. 350.00
Doll, Open Mouth, French, 18 In. 100.00
Doll, Open Mouth, Human Hair Wig, Dressed, Tenara Pearl, 20 In. 350.00
Doll, Oriental Lady, Bisque Head, Teeth, Composition Body, 10 In.Tall 165.00
Doll, Oriental Princess, Original Clothing, Made In China 75.00
Doll, Oriental Woman, Composition Head, Hands, Feet, Silk Clothes, China 50.00
Doll, Painted Eyes, Molded Hair, Cloth Body, Kid Arms, France, 19 In. 365.00
Doll, Painted Eyes, Skin Wig, Swivel Neck, Kid Body, French Fashion 220.00
Doll, Pansy, Open Mouth, Brown Eyes, Dressed, 23 In. 125.00
Doll, Paper, Betty Bonnet's Sister's Baby, 1916, Magazine Sheet 6.00
Doll, Paper, Bobby Blake In His New Sunday Suit, 1919, Magazine Sheet 5.00
Doll, Paper, Carnival, No.2488, 1944, Saalfield 20.00
Doll, Paper, Circus For The Children, Ladies' Home Journal, July, 1913 .... 4.00
Doll, Paper, Dolly Dingle Show How To Keep Well, Pictorial Review, 1923 .... 5.00
Doll, Paper, Dolly Dingle, Boy, Uncut, Grace Drayton, 1931 .... 4.75
Doll, Paper, Dolly Dingle, Uncut Page From Magazine, January 1927 .... 6.00
Doll, Paper, Dolly Dingle's Trip Around The World, 1917, Magazine Sheet 5.00
Doll, Paper, Hollywood Dollies, First Series, Douglas Maclean, 1925 .... 10.00
Doll, Paper, Lettie Lane's World Party, Chinese, Ladies' Home Journal, 1910 .... 6.00
Doll, Paper, Overall Boys Camping Out, Uncut Page From Magazine, 1909 .... 60.00
Doll, Paper, Tiny In Tinytown, The Delineator, 1915 .... 3.75
Doll, Papier-Mache Head, Boy, Original Clothes .... *Illus* 29.00

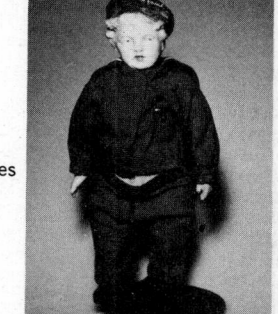

Doll, Papier-Machie Head, Boy, Original Clothes

Doll, Papier-Mache Shoulder Head, Bulge Eyes, Cloth Body, Composition Hands 20.00
Doll, Papier-Mache, Brown Eyes, Roller Skates, Felt Dress, 13 In.Tall 7.00
Doll, Papier-Mache, Dated 1830, Boy 145.00
Doll, Papier-Mache, Toddler, 15 In.Tall 6.00
Doll, Parian Head, Cloth Body, Molded Blonde Hair, 9 1/2 In.Tall 20.00
Doll, Parian Head, Dresden Ruffle Around Head, 5 3/4 In.Tall 225.00
Doll, Parian, Hair Parted In Center, Cloth Body, Dressed, 22 In.Tall 300.00
Doll, Parsons-Jackson, Baby, Dressed, 10 In.Tall 85.00
Doll, Patsy Baby, Effanbee Composition, Label, 11 In.Tall 20.00
Doll, Patsy, Composition, Dressed 13.00
Doll, Patsy, Composition, Sleeping Eyes, 19 In.Tall 30.00
Doll, Penny-Wooden, Hand-Carved, 12 In.Tall 2.50
Doll, Penny-Wooden, Hand-Painted, Dutch, Dressed, 12 In.Tall 4.00
Doll, Performer, Lady Acrobat, Bisque Head, Schoenhut 67.50
Doll, Performer, Ringmaster, Bisque Head, Schoenhut 67.50
Doll, Petit Frere, French, Anatomically Correct 27.95
Doll, Pincushion, Dresden-Type, Porcelain, 4 1/2 In.Tall 8.00
Doll, Pincushion, German 2.00
Doll, Pincushion, German, Blonde, Hair Ribbon 8.00
Doll, Pincushion, Senorita, Black Hair, Blue Comb, Crepe Paper Dress, Germany 15.00

Doll, Pinocchio, Jointed, Wooden, 11 In.	50.00
Doll, Pm Harmus, Boy, 20 In.Tall	85.00
Doll, Pm, Character	175.00
Doll, Popeye, Wooden, Jointed, 6 In.Tall	15.00
Doll, Porcelain Head, Arms, Legs, Closed Mouth, 17 In.Tall	98.00
Doll, Porcelain Head, Leather & Cloth Body, Marked Germany No.2, 12 In.	35.00
Doll, Porcelain Head, Marked Made In Germany, Cloth Body, Dressed, 14 In.	35.00
Doll, Porcelain Head, Shoulders, Hands, Feet, Molded Hair, Germany	30.00
Doll, Porcelain Head, Victorian Dress, Blonde Hair, 19th Century, 9 In.Tall	160.00
Doll, Porcelain Shoulder Head, Painted Eyes, Cloth Body, Molded Hair, 18 In.	48.00
Doll, Porcelain, Blonde, Dorothy, 21 In.	100.00
Doll, Princess Elizabeth, Dressed, 14 In.Tall	28.00
Doll, Puppet, Composition, Dressed	17.00
Doll, Puppet, Emily Ann, Effanbee, Composition	14.00
Doll, Queen Louise, Bisque, Dressed, Marked Germany, Jointed Body, 24 In.Tall	100.00
Doll, Queen Louise, Original Clothes, Black Wig, Blue Eyes, Marked, 27 In.	125.00
Doll, Rag, Brownie, Highlander, Palmer Cox, Copyright 1892, 7 In.	30.00
Doll, Rag, Brownie, Soldier, Palmer Cox, Copyright 1892, 7 In.	30.00
Doll, Rag, Handmade By Hopis, 6 In.Tall	1.50
Doll, Rag, Indian, Belt, Bracelet, Necklace	5.00
Doll, Rag, Printed, Dutch Girl, Dressed	4.75
Doll, Rag, Sam Farmer, Embroidered Face, Blonde Wool Wig, Dressed, 18 In.	9.50
Doll, Rag, Sue Farmer, Embroidered Face, Blonde Wool Wig, Dressed, 18 In.	9.50
Doll, Raggedy Ann, 25 In.Tall, Handmade	15.00
Doll, Roma, Austria-Marked, Bisque, Blue Eyes, Dark Wig, 26 In.Tall	60.00
Doll, Rubber Face, Cloth Body, Holland Garb, Marked D.R.G.M.	40.00
Doll, Rubber, Amosandra, Painted Eyes, 9 1/2 In.Tall	6.00
Doll, Rubber, Boy, Composition Head, Imperial Crown Toy, 28 In.Tall	25.00
Doll, Rubber, Cry Baby, Composition Head, Uneeda Doll Co., 16 In.Tall	15.00
Doll, Rubber, Cry Baby, Plastic Head, Glass Eyes, E.E.-G.E.E., 16 In.Tall	15.00
Doll, Rubber, Cry Baby, Plastic Head, Imperial Crown Toy, 15 In.Tall	10.00
Doll, Rubber, Cry Baby, Plastic Head, Imperial Crown Toy, 19 In.Tall	15.00
Doll, Rubber, Dopey, Signed, 5 1/2 In.Tall	10.00
Doll, Rubber, Girl, Composition Head, Imperial Crown Toy, 28 In.Tall	25.00
Doll, Rubber, Ideal, Blue Eyes, Blonde Hair, Cloth Body, 21 In.	6.00
Doll, Rubber, So Wee, Horseman Rubber Body, Composition Head, 10 1/2 In.	20.00
Doll, Rubber, So Wee, Painted Eyes, 1941, 9 1/2 In.Tall	6.00
Doll, Russian, Tea Cozy, 20 In.Tall	10.00
Doll, Samurai Warrior, On Plaque, Dressed, 8 1/2 In.Tall	35.00
Doll, Scarlet O'hara, Composition, Dressed, 14 In.Tall	40.00
Doll, Scarlet O'hara, Composition, 11 In.Tall	35.00
Doll, Schoenhut, Boy, Marked, Molded Hair, Painted Eyes, 14 1/2 In.Tall	80.00
Doll, Schoenhut, Wooden, Spring Hinge Joints, Sleep Eyes, 16 1/2 In.	200.00
Doll, Shirley Temple, Jointed, Original Clothes, 22 In.	37.50
Doll, Shirley Temple, White Dress, Red Heart Design, Marked, 17 In.	45.00
Doll, Shoulder Head, Kid Body, Dressed, 14 In.Tall	55.00
Doll, Simon & Halbig, Bisque Head & Tongue, Dressed, New Wig, 23 In.Tall	200.00
Doll, Simon & Halbig, Bisque Head, 22 In.Tall	77.00
Doll, Simon & Halbig, Bisque Socket Head, Composition Body, Dressed, 18 In.	85.00
Doll, Simon & Halbig, Bisque, Composition Body, Dressed, 31 In.Tall	145.00
Doll, Simon & Halbig, Bisque, Papier-Mache Jointed Body, 9 In.Tall	58.00
Doll, Simon & Halbig, Bisque, 1909, 5 3/4 In.Tall	72.00
Doll, Simon & Halbig, Blonde Hair, Blue Eyes, Pierced Ears, 22 In.Tall	79.50
Doll, Simon & Halbig, Closed Mouth, Human Hair, Brown Eyes, Marked 949	400.00
Doll, Simon & Halbig, Composition, Dressed, Brown Eyes, 24 In.Tall	75.00
Doll, Simon & Halbig, Girl, Dressed, 43 In.Tall	550.00
Doll, Simon & Halbig, K Star R, Jointed Body, Pierced Ears, 25 In.Tall	79.50
Doll, Simon & Halbig, Marked K Star R, Girl, Bisque Head, 10 In.Tall	32.00
Doll, Skippy, Character, 5 In.Tall, Made In Japan, Bisque	25.00
Doll, Snow Baby, Marked Germany, 1 In.Tall	12.50
Doll, Snow White, 2 Dwarf Figurines, Boxed	90.00
Doll, Socket Head, Marked Ra Dep, 1907, Set Eyes	17.00
Doll, Socket Head, Open Mouth, Tongue, Kaiser Character, 10 In.	55.00
Doll, Sonja Henie, Composition, Dressed, 15 In.Tall	55.00
Doll, Sonja Henie, Dressed, 18 In.	65.00
Doll, Sonja Henie, Human Hair Wig, Original Attire	65.00

Doll, Stand-Up, R.Tuck, Red Riding Hood, 18 In.High	12.00
Doll, Swiss, Bone Handle White Parasol, 7 In.Tall	7.00
Doll, Swivel Neck, Kid Body, Hair Wig, Marked J On Breastplate, 17 In.	365.00
Doll, Swivel Neck, Pierced Ears, Kid Body, French Fashion	285.00
Doll, Terri Lee, Blonde, Drum Majorette, Skating Outfit, 16 In.Tall	22.00
Doll, Terri Lee, Colored	40.00
Doll, The New Interchangeable, French, Original Box, Three Heads	1200.00
Doll, Tin Head, Minerva, Kid Body, Bisque Arms, Jointed Hips, 17 In.	55.00
Doll, Tiny Tears, Dressed	7.00
Doll, Toddler, Dressed, Crossed Nail Mark, German, Colored, 9 1/2 In.	85.00
Doll, Toddler, Jointed Body, Paper Label's.F.B.J.', Clothes, 27 In.	350.00
Doll, Toddler, Marked Bavaria 120, Dressed, Jointed, Sleep Eyes, 13 In.Tall	85.00
Doll, Toddler, Pouty, Human Hair Wig, Blue Eyes, Marked F.France, 10 1/2 In.	150.00
Doll, Toddler, Swivel Head, Jointed Composition Body	12.00
Doll, Toddler, Wooden, Schoenhut, Dressed, Marked, 14 In.	125.00
Doll, Tonto	60.00
Doll, Twin Babies, Painted Faces, Original Clothes, Pink, Blue, Pair	20.00
Doll, Unis, France, Blue Eyes, Blonde Wig, B.J.Body, Marked, 23 In.Tall	125.00
Doll, Victorian Dressed, S.F.B.J., 5 In.Tall	125.00
Doll, Vogue, Ginny, Dressed	10.00
Doll, W.C.Fields	90.00
Doll, Walterhausen, Germany, 23 In.	75.00
Doll, Wax & Cloth, Italian, C.1810-13 *Illus*	350.00
Doll, Wax, Mrs.Kattenburg	8.00
Doll, Wax, Scottish Garb, Man, 12 In.	89.00
Doll, Wax, Shoulder Head, Lady, Glass Eyes, Dressed	65.00
Doll, Wax, Wire Eye, Dressed, Dated 1820	185.00
Doll, Wendy Ann, Alexander, 10 In.Long	22.50
Doll, 12-154 Dep.H Made In Germany Marks On Head, Blue Eyes, 24 In.Tall	90.00
Donald Duck, Bank, Plastic, 19 In.Tall	20.00
Donald Duck, Book, Walt Disney, 1944	3.00
Donald Duck, Bowl & Tumbler, Plastic, Pictures Of Disney Characters	2.50
Donald Duck, Jar, Cookie, Signed Disney	13.00
Donald Duck, Jar, 4 In.	4.00
Donald Duck, Mug, China	12.00
Donald Duck, Pull Toy, Wood	3.00
Donald Duck, Watch	45.00
Doorstop, see Iron, Doorstop	

Doughty Birds were made by Dorothy Doughty for the Royal Worcester Porcelain Company of England from 1936 to 1962. They have become very collectible.

Doughty, Bird, Crowned Kinglets, Noble Pin, 1951 Edition, Pair	1200.00
Doughty, Figurine, Apple Blossom Sprays & Bee, 1942 Edition, Pair	500.00
Doughty, Hummingbirds, Rubythroat, Pair *Illus*	2100.00

Doulton Pottery and Porcelain were made by Doulton and Co. of Burslem, England, after 1882. The name Royal Doulton appeared on their wares after 1902.

Doulton, see also Royal Doulton

Doulton, Bowl, English, Blue & White, 17 In.Long	35.00
Doulton, Foot Warmer, Improved Pottery	10.00
Doulton, Jar, Biscuit, Blue, Gold, Flowers, Butterflies, Ribbed, 7 1/2 In.	40.00
Doulton, Jar, Owl, Cover, Signed, 7 1/2 In.High	190.00
Doulton, Jardiniere, Blue Floral Decoration, Stippled Gold	27.50
Doulton, Jug, Silver Rim, Dogs, Three Handles, 1873, 7 In.High	125.00
Doulton, Pitcher, Brown, Tan, White, Relief Figures, Mark, 1 3/4 In.	22.00
Doulton, Pitcher, David Garrick	45.00
Doulton, Pitcher, Matte Finish, Floral Decoration	25.00
Doulton, Pitcher, Scenes, Signed W.Munn, Brown & Light Blue, 6 3/4 In.	42.50
Doulton, Pitcher, Water, Cream & Brown, Bearded Face, Nude Boys, Lambeth	75.00
Doulton, Plate, Dickensware, Barkis, 10 1/2 In.	31.00
Doulton, Plate, Dickensware, Sam Weller, Signed Noke, 10 1/2 In.	35.00
Doulton, Plate, Dickensware, Tom Pinch, 10 1/2 In.	32.00
Doulton, Plate, Floral, Gold, Porcelain, Signed C.Bilton	45.00

Doll, Wax & Cloth, Italian, C.1810-13
See Page 179

Doughty, Hummingbirds, Rubythroat, Pair
See Page 179

Doulton, Plate, Flowers, Scalloped Edge, Gold, 9 In.Diameter	30.00
Doulton, Tray, Dickensware, Mr.Squeers, Signed Noke, 5 1/2 X 11 In.	44.00
Doulton, Urn, Cuspidor Shape, White & Gold, Blue Floral, 7 1/4 In.Tall, Pair	50.00
Doulton, Vase, Artist George Tinworth, 11 1/2 In.High	55.00
Doulton, Vase, Brown Background, White Iris, Signed Mary Mitchell, Lambeth	250.00
Doulton, Vase, Flambe, Man On Horse, Reflecting In Water, 9 In.	95.00
Doulton, Vase, Flambe, Plow Scene & Field Of Flowers, 8 1/2 In.	95.00
Doulton, Vase, Floral Design, Hand-Painted, Artist Signed, 5 In.Tall	75.00
Doulton, Vase, Salt Glaze Decor, Liverpool, 1886, Signed Aep, Lambeth	75.00
Doulton, Vase, Signed Hanna B.Barlow, 1878, Lambeth, 12 In.High, Pair	375.00
Doulton, Vase, Tapestry, Green, Beige, Aqua, Gold, 10 1/2 In.Tall	55.00

*Dresden China is any china made in the town of Dresden, Germany. The
most famous factory in Dresden is the Meissen Factory.*

Dresden, see also Meissen	
Dresden, Bowl, Blue, Hand-Painted Grapes	10.00
Dresden, Bowl, Chowder, Indian Tree, 10 In.Diameter	14.00
Dresden, Bowl, Embossed Gold Decoration, Blue Crossed Swords Mark	30.00
Dresden, Bowl, Oval, Embossed Gold Vine, Blue Crossed Swords Mark	25.00
Dresden, Bowl, Oval, Handles, Floral Decoration, Pierced Edge	45.00
Dresden, Caddy, Tea, Hand-Painted Flowers, Gilt Trim, Marked	38.00
Dresden, Chocolate Pot, Multicolored Bouquets, Helmet Shape Cover	30.00
Dresden, Dish & Pin Box, Leaf Shape Dish, Crossed Swords Mark	17.50
Dresden, Figurine, Cavalier, Lady, Impressed & Incised 24, C.1760, Pair	600.00
Dresden, Figurine, Girl & Boy, Flowers, Mark Germany, 12 In.	26.00
Dresden, Figurine, Pierrot, Impressed Numeral 24, C.1760, 5 In.High	125.00
Dresden, Figurine, Polichinelle, Impressed Numeral 24, C.1760, 5 1/2 In.	450.00
Dresden, Figurine, Young Girl, C.1760, 5 In.High	30.00
Dresden, Jardiniere, Double Mask Handles, Bouquet Of Flowers, 4 1/4 In.	40.00
Dresden, Painting Of Porcelain, Victorian Woman, Oval, 5 X 4 In.	50.00
Dresden, Pitcher, Hot Water, Commemorative, Conservation Exposition, 1918	15.00
Dresden, Plate, Baroque Flower Border Encrusted With Gold, 11 In., 8	65.00
Dresden, Plate, Floral & Gilt, Mark, 7 1/4 In.Diameter, Set Of 12	75.00
Dresden, Plate, Floral Design, Pink, White, 12 In.Diameter	53.00
Dresden, Plate, Green Border, Grape Center By Toulon, 10 In.	20.00
Dresden, Plate, Picture, Sailing Close, Christy, 7 In.Diameter	18.00
Dresden, Plate, Soup, Armorial, Neu Brandenstein Pattern, C.1830	30.00
Dresden, Salt Dip, Encrusted Flowers, Marked Dresden, Saxony, 6	37.50
Dresden, Urn, Snake Handles, Floral Decoration, Crossed Swords Mark, Pair	80.00
Dresden, Vase, Cobalt Blue, Gold, Romantic Scenes, Crossed Swords Mark, Pair	75.00
Dresden, Vase, Rose Decoration, 6 In.High, Crossed Swords Mark, Pair	15.00
Du Paquier, Beaker & Saucer, Black, Gilding, C.1725 .... *Illus*	1250.00

*Durand Glass was made by Victor Durand from 1879 to 1935 at several
factories. Most of the iridescent Durand Glass was made by Victor*

Du Paquier, Beaker & Saucer
Black, Gilding, C.1725
See Page 180

Durand, Jr., from 1912 to 1924 at the Durand Art Glass Works in Vineland, New Jersey.

Durand, Bowl, Rose, Leaves & Trailings, Blue Luster, White, Signed, 6 In.Tall	550.00
Durand, Cordial, Dark Green Overlay Cut To Clear, Set Of 4	75.00
Durand, Lamp Base, Green & White Feather On Yellow Iridescent, Gold	95.00
Durand, Lamp Base, Iridescent, Trumpet Shape, Green On Ivory, 15 1/2 In.	170.00
Durand, Lamp, Red Crackle Shade, White Lining, Bronze Metal Column & Base	125.00
Durand, Plate, Cobalt, Opalescent, Blue Five Leaf Clover, Feather Decor	125.00
Durand, Plate, Feather Pattern, Cranberry, Intaglio Cut Border	150.00
Durand, Plate, King Tut Feather Decor In Center, Cut Rose Border	125.00
Durand, Vase, Blue, Opalescent, Ambergris, Signed, 6 1/2 In.	195.00
Durand, Vase, Chocolate Brown, Signed, 10 In.Tall	275.00
Durand, Vase, Crackle, Iridescent, Unsigned	260.00
Durand, Vase, Cranberry, Amethyst With Blue On Outside, 14 In., Pair	150.00
Durand, Vase, Emil Larsen, White, Blue Lotus, Burnt Orange Interior	225.00
Durand, Vase, Flaring, Footed, Cranberry Border, Striated Leaves, 11 3/4 In.	180.00
Durand, Vase, Floral Design, Pink, Gray, Yellow, Bulbous Middle, 12 In.High	135.00
Durand, Vase, Gold Iridescent, Signed, 10 In.	165.00
Durand, Vase, Gold Threaded, Signed, 8 1/2 In.Tall	300.00
Durand, Vase, Iridescent Blue, Cobweb Threads, Signed, 5 1/2 In.	195.00
Durand, Vase, Iridescent, Ovoid, Coral, Amber Swirls, 12 1/4 In.	200.00
Durand, Vase, King Tut, Blue, Signed, 7 1/2 In.Tall	385.00
Durand, Vase, Orange & Pink With Green & Blue Swirl, Signed, Stick Neck	625.00
Durand, Vase, Urn Shape, Iridescent Orange, Striated Feathers, Gold, Signed	250.00
Enamel, Belt Buckle, On Brass, Two Pieces Held Together With Dagger, Russia	48.00
Enamel, Buckle, Multicolor, Dagger Pin Closing, Turquoise, Russia	350.00
Enamel, Ladle, Russia, Artist Signed, 3 1/4 In.Long	195.00
Enamel, Plaque, Madonna & Child In Garden, Silver Foil Ground, France, 4 In.	175.00
Enamel, Russian, Spoon, 4 1/2 In.Long	65.00
Enamel, Tongs, Sugar, G.Klingart, Russia	195.00
Enamel, Tray, Viennese, Lapis Lazuli, Medallions Of Gemstones, C.1850	1500.00
Enamel, Vase, Cabinet Size, Blue Ground, Holly Leaves, Red Berries, France	135.00

End-of-Day glass is now an out-of-fashion name for Spattered Glass. The glass was made of many bits and pieces of colored glass. Traditionally, the glass was made by workmen from the odds and ends left from the glass used during the day. Actually it was a deliberately manufactured product popular about 1880 to 1900, and some of it is still being made.

End-Of-Day, Basket, Blown In Mold, Clear Thorn Handle	42.50
End-Of-Day, Basket, Pink, Basket Weave, Twisted Clear Handle	65.00
End-Of-Day, Basket, Thorn Handle, White Interior, Large	110.00
End-Of-Day, Bowl, Finger, Swirl Pattern, Pink Opaque, White Lining	20.00
End-Of-Day, Bowl, Green, White, Mahogany Color, C.1820, 3 1/4 X 2 In.	22.50
End-Of-Day, Epergne, Ruffled Edge, Pedestal, 1 Lily, 12 In.High	95.00
End-Of-Day, Paperweight, Sandwich Glass	225.00
End-Of-Day, Pitcher, Water, Cranberry & White, Melon Shape, 8 In.Tall	55.00

End-Of-Day, Pitcher, Water, Pink, White	85.00
End-Of-Day, Pitcher, Water, Yellow, Swirled Body, Cased In Yellow	85.00
End-Of-Day, Rolling Pin	35.00
End-Of-Day, Rolling Pin, 11 In.Long	35.00
End-Of-Day, Rose Bowl, Crimped Top, Colored Spatter	55.00
End-Of-Day, Toothpick	50.00
End-Of-Day, Tumbler, Cased, Swirled	15.00
End-Of-Day, Vase, Crimped Top, Blown Glass, Cased, 8 In.High	12.50
End-Of-Day, Vase, Green, White, Clear Swags, Footed	45.00
End-Of-Day, Vase, Pink, Opaque, Amber, White Lining, 5 3/4 In.Tall	40.00
End-Of-Day, Vase, Rainbow Spatter, Ruffled Top	35.00
End-Of-Day, Vase, Stick, Pink, Overlay	15.00
End-Of-Day, Vase, Yellow, Pink, Oranges, White Lining, 10 In.	45.00
Erickson, Ashtray, Amber & Clear, Bubbles	25.00
Erickson, Ashtray, Bubbles, Champagne, Signed, 5 In.Diameter	25.00
Erickson, Ashtray, Bubbles, Helio, Signed	30.00
Erickson, Ashtray, Cased, Ruby With Clear, 6 1/2 In.Diameter	35.00
Erickson, Ashtray, Emerald Green & Clear, 5 1/2 In.Diameter	17.50
Erickson, Ashtray, Emerald Green, Bubbles, 9 In.Diameter	20.00
Erickson, Ashtray, Emerald Green, Clear Holder, 6 1/2 In.Diameter	15.00
Erickson, Ashtray, Gold Ruby & Clear, Signed	50.00
Erickson, Ashtray, Sunlight, Petal Edge, Bubbles	40.00
Erickson, Basket, Bubbles, Smoke Handle, 7 In.High	27.50
Erickson, Bottle, Teardrop Stopper, Sunlight Yellow	100.00
Erickson, Bowl, Emerald Green, Bubbles, 7 In.Diameter	20.00
Erickson, Bowl, Salad, Bubbles, Signed Erickson	30.00
Erickson, Bowl, Sapphire Blue, Turned Up Rim, 8 1/2 In.Diameter	20.00
Erickson, Compote, Smoke, Paperweight, Signed, 7 1/2 In.Tall	55.00
Erickson, Decanter, Clear & Sunlight Yellow Flames, Hollow Stopper	35.00
Erickson, Ewer, Emerald Green, Clear Handle, Bubbles, 7 In.High	25.00
Erickson, Glass, Iced Tea, Smoke, 6	36.00
Erickson, Glass, Martini, Smoke Base, Bubbles	15.00
Erickson, Lamp, Hurricane, Turquoise, Signed, Labeled	85.00
Erickson, Pitcher, Amethyst, Clear Handle, 5 In.High	10.00
Erickson, Pitcher, Charcoal, Signed	55.00
Erickson, Pitcher, Smoke, Signed	45.00
Erickson, Pitcher, Turquoise, Signed, Labeled	75.00
Erickson, Plate, Sandwich, Conical Base, Smoke Color, Label	25.00
Erickson, Vase, Clear, Cylindrical, 11 In.High	17.50
Erickson, Vase, Clear, Signed, 8 In.Tall	25.00
Erickson, Vase, Crackle, Clear, Signed	55.00
Erickson, Vase, Emerald Green, Elongated Bubbles, 30 3/4 In.High	22.50
Erickson, Vase, Emerald, Signed	70.00
Erickson, Vase, Green, Cylindrical, Bubbled Paperweight Base, Signed	45.00
Erickson, Vase, Paperweight Base, Amethyst Top, 10 In.High	30.00
Erickson, Vase, Periwinkle Blue, Bubbles, 5 In.High	10.00
Erickson, Vase, Periwinkle Blue, Bubbles, 9 3/4 In.High, 9 In.Diameter	5.00
Erickson, Vase, Pinched, Signed	35.00
Erickson, Vase, Red, 2 Clear Handles, 9 1/2 In.High	20.00
Erickson, Vase, Round, Amethyst, Bubbles	12.50
Erickson, Vase, Smoke, Cylindrical, Bubbled Paperweight Base, Signed	35.00
Erickson, Vase, Smoke, Signed	35.00

Etruscan Majolica, see Majolica
Ezra Brooks, see Bottle, Ezra Brooks

Faberge, Carl Gustavovich, was a goldsmith and jeweler to the Russian Imperial Court from about 1870 to 1914.

Faberge, Bracelet, Bangle, Gold, Emerald, Diamonds, August Hollming, C.1900	950.00
Faberge, Case, Cigarette, Gold, Rectangular, Michael Perchin, C.1900	1400.00
Faberge, Case, Cigarette, Silver, Anders Nevalainen, C.1900	800.00
Faberge, Figurine, Cossack On Horse, Bronze, Artist Signed, 6 1/2 In.Long	700.00
Faberge, Figurine, Frog, Carved Bowenite, Garnet Eyes, Diamonds, C.1900	425.00
Faberge, Holder, Cigar, 2 Color Gold, Translucent Enamel, Ivory, C.1900	550.00
Faberge, Pillbox, 2 Color Gold, Translucent Enamel, August Holstrom, C.1900	2300.00
Faberge, Pin, Gold, Translucent Enamel, Diamonds, Pearls, C.1900	750.00
Faience, Bowl, Roses, Pink, Paneled, Scalloped Rim, 9 In.Diameter	15.00

Faience, Figurine, Italian, C.1800 .... *Illus*   85.00
Faience, Pot, Bulb, French, D Shape, Painted Flowers, C.1760, Pair 170.00
Faience, Spittoon, White, Red Floral 27.50
Faience, Vase, Tulip Design, Blue, Yellow, Hand-Painted, 7 In.Tall 48.00

> *Fairings are small souvenir china boxes sold at country fairs during the*
> *nineteenth century.*

Fan, Advertising, Cafe Martin, N.Y., Air Races 7.50

Faience, Figurine, Italian, C.1800

Fan, Advertising, Knickerbocker Restaurant, Auto, Woman, Men 4.50
Fan, Black Feathers 9.00
Fan, Black Lace, 18th Century Lady In Garden, Tortoiseshell Sticks, Tiffany 22.50
Fan, Carved Ivory Sticks, Chantilly Lace 20.00
Fan, Gray, Blue & Black Stripes, Silver Inlay On Gray Sticks 7.50
Fan, Ivory, Hand-Painted 2.00
Fan, Oriental, Carved Ivory Frame, Embroidered Flowers 35.00
Fan, Ostrich Feather 5.00
Fan, Ostrich Feather, Wooden Sticks, Incised Silver Decor 18.00
Fan, Pastoral Scene, Hand-Painted, Gold, Silver, Signed 35.00
Fan, Rose Color Ostrich Feathers, Tortoiseshell Sticks, 20 X 21 In. 20.00
Fan, Silk, Strutting Peacock, Both Sides 24.00
Fan, Tortoiseshell Ribs, Orange Ostrich Feathers 6.00
Fan, Turkey Feather 12.50
Fan, Wedding, Ivory Sticks, Feathers, White To Smoke 35.00
Fan, White Lace, Flying Bird, Ivory Sticks 15.00
Fan, White Satin, Painted Pink & Blue Morning Glories, Ivory Sticks 15.00
Fenton, Frame, Single Flower, Peach, Opalescent, Ruffled Edge, 6 3/4 In. 21.00
Fenton, Plate, Antique Ballads, Frank Beardman & Co., Fenton, C.1903 ....   22.50
Fenton, Plate, Dust-O, Copyright, Frank Beardman & Co., Fenton, C.1903 ....   22.50
Fenton, Plate, Fresh Cabbage, Copyright, Frank Beardman & Co., Fenton, C.1903 ....   22.50
Fenton, Plate, Great News, Copyright, Frank Beardman & Co., Fenton, C.1903 ....   22.50
Fenton, Plate, O Clo, Copyright, Frank Beardman & Co., Fenton, C.1903 ....   22.50

> *Findlay, or onyx, glass was made using three layers of glass. It was*
> *manufactured by the Dalzell Gilmore Leighton Company about 1889 in*
> *Findlay, Ohio. The silver, ruby, or black pattern was molded into the glass.*
> *The glass came in several colors, but was usually white or ruby.*

Findlay Onyx, Bowl, Double Beetle Band, Blue, Flat 48.50
Findlay Onyx, Goblet, Mitered Frieze 15.00
Findlay Onyx, Muffineer, Platinum, Metal, White 250.00
Findlay Onyx, Pitcher, Peach Color, 4 1/2 In.High 225.00
Findlay Onyx, Spooner, Silver Inlay, 4 1/4 In.High 180.00
Findlay Onyx, Sugar, Covered 325.00
Findlay Onyx, Sugar, Platinum On White, Cover 460.00
Findlay Onyx, Vase, 6 1/4 In.High 105.00
Fire Extinguisher, Mitchell, Tin, Tube Type 7.50
Fire, Andiron, Ball Top, Snake Feet, Signed John Molineux, Boston, Pair 400.00

Fire, Andiron, Brass & Wrought Iron, Knife Blade Andiron, Penny Feet, Pair 150.00
Fire, Andiron, Brass, Acorn Finial, Branch Feet, Round Knobbed Columns, Pair 200.00
Fire, Andiron, Brass, Acorn Top, American, C.1760, Penny Feet, Pair 175.00
Fire, Andiron, Brass, Ball Top, C.1810, Hexagonal Standard, Pair 130.00
Fire, Andiron, Brass, Ball Top, Knopped Standard, American, C.1810, Pair 225.00
Fire, Andiron, Brass, Double, Lemon Top, Ball Feet, Pair 275.00
Fire, Andiron, Brass, Lemon Top, C.1800, Columnar Standard, Pair 220.00
Fire, Andiron, Brass, Steeple Top, American, C.1750, Pair .... *Illus* 450.00
Fire, Andiron, Brass, Steeple Top, Hexagonal Standard, Pair 125.00
Fire, Andiron, Brass, Urn Finial, Knopped Standard, American, C.1850, Pair 100.00
Fire, Andiron, Brass, Urn Top, American, 18th Century, Pair 300.00
Fire, Andiron, Brass, Urn Top, Colonial Style, Pair 100.00
Fire, Andiron, Brass, Urn Top, Knopped Standard, American, C.1800, Pair 225.00
Fire, Andiron, Brass, Urn Top, R.Wittingham, N.Y., C.1790, Pair 750.00
Fire, Andiron, Brass, Urn, Bracket Feet, 20 In.High, Pair 150.00
Fire, Andiron, Brass, Urns Mounted On Square Footed Bases, 19 In.High, Pair 100.00

Fire, Andiron, Brass, Steeple Top,
American, C.1750, Pair

Fire, Andiron, Brick Oven, Wrought Iron, Ring Top, 9 In.High, Pair 65.00
Fire, Andiron, Bronze & Iron, C.1925, Pair 12.00
Fire, Andiron, Cast Iron, Form Of Squatting Black Man, Pair 30.00
Fire, Andiron, Iron, Christmas Tree, Brass Cannon Ball Finial, 1840, Pair 30.00
Fire, Andiron, Wrought Iron, Knife Blade, Brass Flame & Diamond Finial, Pair 600.00
Fire, Andiron, Wrought Iron, Knife Blade, Brass Urn Finial, Penny Feet, Pair 350.00
Fire, Andiron, Wrought, Brass Finials, Spit Rack, Pair 85.00
Fire, Andirons & Tools, Brass, Chippendale, 18th Century 99.00
Fire, Bellows, Fireplace, Brass Nailheads, Leather, Stencil 15.00
Fire, Bellows, Fireplace, New England, Red, Cornucopia Decoration 150.00
Fire, Bellows, Fireplace, New England, Yellow Ground, Red Fruit 65.00
Fire, Bellows, Fireplace, New England, Yellow With Gilt 40.00
Fire, Bellows, 18 In.Long 18.50
Fire, Box, Coal, Oak, Brass Handle .... 21.00 To 22.00
Fire, Box, Coal, Wood, Brass Hinge & Handle 22.00
Fire, Box, Coal, Wood, Carving On Door 22.00
Fire, Box, Coal, Wood, Cast Iron Hinges & Handle 29.50
Fire, Box, Coal, Wood, Metal Hinge & Handle 22.00
Fire, Bucket, Coal, Brass, Helmet Shape 90.00
Fire, Bucket, Leather, Red With Gold & Black 95.00
Fire, Cabinet, Coal, Beveled Mirror At Top 39.50
Fire, Coal Hod, Brass, 14 In.High 30.00
Fire, Crane, Fireplace 30.00
Fire, Crane, Fireplace, Iron 27.50
Fire, Crane, Fireplace, Wrought Iron 20.00
Fire, Extinguisher, Manrille, Tin, Tube Type 7.50
Fire, Extinguisher, Phoenix, Tin, Tube Type 7.50
Fire, Extinguisher, Standard, Tin, Tube Type 7.50

Fire, Fender, Brass & Mesh, 18th Century, Three Ball Finials, 37 In.Wide 120.00
Fire, Fender, Brass, Pierced, Rope Band, Paw Feet, Spark Pan, 48 In.Long 50.00
Fire, Fender, Brass, Rail, 41 In.Long 50.00
Fire, Fender, Fireplace, Iron, Brass Ball Finials, 14 In.Wide 5.00
Fire, Fender, Fireplace, Iron, Pierced, 44 In.Wide 10.00
Fire, Fire Back, Iron, C.1730, Arched, Dolphins & Shell Crest, Dragon, Female 60.00
Fire, Fireplace Set, Brass Finish On Iron, Franklin, Galleon Heads, 6 Piece 42.50
Fire, Fireplace, Oak, Beveled Mirror, Ornate Iron Door 250.00
Fire, Fireplace, Victorian, Gray Marble, Sculpted & Intaglio Design 300.00
Fire, Fork, Fireplace, Brass, 3 Tines, Rope Effect Handle, Scrolls At Top 21.00
Fire, Fork, Fireplace, Colonial, Wrought Iron, Cannon Ball Finial, Silver 165.00
Fire, Fork, Hand Forged, Twisted, Iron 16.00
Fire, Garniture, Hearth, Brass, Pierced Screen, Serpentine Fender, 5 Piece 200.00
Fire, Garniture, Hearth, Brass, 19th Century, 5 Pieces 275.00
Fire, Garniture, Hearth, Brass, 19th Century, 8 Pieces 140.00
Fire, Grate, George Iii, Brass & Steel, Serpentine Pierced Front, C.1750 .... 50.00
Fire, Grate, Scrolling Foliage, Steel, Brass, George Ii, 18th Century 175.00
Fire, Grate, Trellis Design, Steel, Brass, George Ii, 18th Century 20.00
Fire, Grenade, Auto Frystop, Glass, Holder 8.50
Fire, Grenade, Red Comet, Glass, Holder 8.50
Fire, Hanger, Fireplace, Wrought Iron, 2 & 3 Hooks 10.00
Fire, Hat, Fire Chief, White, Eagle 20.00
Fire, Helmet, Leather, Brass Department Plate, Syas No.21, Boston 30.00
Fire, Hod, Coal, Cast Iron, Covered 37.50
Fire, Hod, Coal, Cast Iron, Embossed, Hinged Lid 75.00
Fire, Hod, Coal, Frog Style, Green Enameled Serpent, Pinecones On Cover 37.50
Fire, Hod, Coal, Galvanized, Corrugated, Wire Bound Top & Bottom 4.75
Fire, Hod, Coal, Iron, Blue Tile With Raised Pink Flowers, Porcelain Handles 32.50
Fire, Hod, Coal, Iron, Enameled Insert With Blue Flowers 29.50
Fire, Hod, Coal, Iron, Frog Style, Covered, White Paint 37.50
Fire, Hod, Coal, Iron, Ivory & Green Tile In Cover 32.50
Fire, Hod, Coal, Nickel Over Iron, Enameled Insert 29.50
Fire, Hod, Coal, Nickel Plate, Green Enamel Inserts 29.50
Fire, Holder, Shovel, & Poker, Brass 80.00
Fire, Holder, Wood, Brass, Oval, 4 Urn Finials, Scroll Feet 170.00
Fire, Hose Nozzle, Leather Bound, C.1800 .... 30.00
Fire, Pan, Dust, Copper Base, Wood Handle, Handmade 7.00
Fire, Peel, Fireplace, Iron, Handwrought, Twisted Handle, Loop End 15.00
Fire, Rack, Fireplace, Wrought Iron, 18th Century 7.50
Fire, Screen, Brass, Fan, Pierced, 9 Connecting Segments, Urn & Torch Finial 200.00
Fire, Screen, Brass, Threefold 90.00
Fire, Screen, Fireplace, Wire, Brass Top Rail, 24 In.High, 28 1/2 In.Wide 100.00
Fire, Screen, Mahogany Finish, Watercolor, Glass 34.00
Fire, Screen, Mahogany, Embroidery, 33 X 23 In. 39.00
Fire, Screen, Mezzotint Accompagne D'une Femme, Nicolas Lancret, 1690 .... 4000.00
Fire, Scuttle, Coal, Lid, Flowers, Hand-Painted, Iron 13.00
Fire, Shelf, Warming, Fireplace, Iron & Brass 12.50
Fire, Shovel & Tongs, Fireplace, Turned Handles 65.00
Fire, Shovel & Tongs, 18th Century 27.00
Fire, Siren, Champion, 12 Volt 20.00
Fire, Stove Piece, Cast Iron, Picture Of Hunter With Hound Shooting Deer 24.50
Fire, Tongs & Shovel, Fireplace, Brass, Ball Top 60.00
Fire, Tongs & Shovel, Fireplace, Polished Iron 17.50
Fire, Tongs, Ember, Hand Forged, Scissor Type, 15 In. 7.50
Fire, Tongs, Ember, Hand-Carved, Hand-Forged, Iron, Scissor Type 7.50
Fire, Tongs, Fireplace, Iron .... 1.25 To 6.00
Fire, Tools, Brass, 6 Pieces 110.00
Fire, Trammel, Fireplace, Engraved, 18th Century 65.00
Fire, Trammel, Fireplace, Wrought Iron, Ratchet, Hanging Rod 15.00
Fire, Trammel, Fireplace, Wrought Iron, Sawtooth 10.00
Fire, Trammel, Fireplace, Wrought Iron, 2 .... 12.00
Fire, Trivet, Fireplace, Hand-Forged, Pot Handle Rest 12.50
Fire, Trivet, Iron, Hand-Forged 12.50
Fire, Trivet, Iron, Hand-Forged, Fireplace 12.50
Fire, Trivet, Square Top, Inset Tile, 12 In.High 24.50

Fireglow Glass resembles English Bristol Glass. But a reddish-brown color can be seen when the piece is held to the light. It is a form of Art Glass made by the Boston and Sandwich Glass Co. of Massachusetts, and other companies.

Fireglow, Vase, Crackle, Apricot, Squatty, Acid Finish	62.50
Fireglow, Vase, Floral Design, Pedestal, Acid Finish, 10 In.High	95.00
Fireglow, Vase, Flower Design, Red, Hand-Painted, 5 1/2 In.Tall	40.00
Fireglow, Vase, Hand-Painted Plums, Pears, Yellow Leaf Decor, Round	35.00
Fireglow, Vase, Tan Ecru, Enameled Florals, Acid Finish, Pedestal Base	88.50
Fireman, Hat, White, Eagle, Marked Engineer Auburn F.D.	50.00
Fireman, Hose Nozzle, Brass, Sacramento Fire Fighters, 1880, Burnished	10.00
Fireplace Tools, see Fire, Tongs, etc.	
Fischer, Pitcher, Blue, White, Flowers, Hand-Painted, Signed, 14 1/2 In.Tall	59.00
Fischer, Urn, Art Nouveau Floral, Gold Handles, Budapest	55.00
Fischer, Vase, Flowers, Pink, Yellow, Brown, Openwork, Signed, 9 In.Tall	35.00
Flash Gordon, Book, Big Little Books	10.00
Flash Gordon, Puzzle, King Features, 1951, 10 X 14 In.	7.50

Flow Blue, or Flo Blue, was made in England about 1830 to 1900. The plates were printed with designs using a cobalt blue coloring. The color flowed from the design to the white plate so the finished plate had a smeared blue design. The plates were usually made of Ironstone China.

Flow Blue, see also Staffordshire	
Flow Blue, Bowl Soup, Lucania	7.50
Flow Blue, Bowl, Conway, 9 In.Diameter	13.95
Flow Blue, Bowl, Mareschal Neil, Scalloped Edge & Base, Underplate	18.00
Flow Blue, Bowl, Marked Maastricht, Holland, Footed, 5 1/2 In.	16.00
Flow Blue, Bowl, Pekin, Davenport, 10 1/4 In.Diameter	45.00
Flow Blue, Bowl, Soup, Eclipse	8.00
Flow Blue, Bowl, Soup, Kyber	25.00
Flow Blue, Bowl, Vegetable, Clover	13.50
Flow Blue, Bowl, Vegetable, La Belle, Open	36.00
Flow Blue, Butter Pat, Argyle	7.50
Flow Blue, Butter Pat, Scenic	4.50
Flow Blue, Compote, Cabbage Rose, Marked Ironstone, Staffordshire	17.50
Flow Blue, Compote, Messina, Footed, Leaf Handles, Acorn Finial	50.00
Flow Blue, Cup & Saucer, Argyle	25.00
Flow Blue, Cup & Saucer, Brooklyn Pattern	35.00
Flow Blue, Cup & Saucer, Burgess & Leigh, Middleport	12.50
Flow Blue, Cup & Saucer, Celtic Pattern, Demitasse, Scalloped Rim	10.00
Flow Blue, Cup & Saucer, Cinde	25.00
Flow Blue, Cup & Saucer, Handleless, Chapoo	35.00
Flow Blue, Cup & Saucer, Handleless, Doburg, Panels, Gothic Castle, Fisherman	18.00
Flow Blue, Cup & Saucer, Handleless, Leaf Design At Top, Copper Luster Band	37.50
Flow Blue, Cup & Saucer, Lakewood Pattern	22.00
Flow Blue, Cup & Saucer, Red Decoration, 6 1/2 In. *Illus*	75.00
Flow Blue, Cup & Saucer, 'remember Me' In Gold	10.00
Flow Blue, Cup & Saucer, Touraine 19.00 To	32.00
Flow Blue, Cup & Saucer, Wheel Pattern	22.50

Flow Blue, Cup & Saucer, Red Decoration, 6 1/2 In.

Flow Blue, Cup Plate, Chusan Pattern By Clementson, Staffordshire 12.00
Flow Blue, Cup, Custard, Dr.Syntax, Blue 68.00
Flow Blue, Dish, Bone, Touraine, Crescent-Moon Shape .... 8.50 To 15.00
Flow Blue, Dish, Cheese, Cabbage Rose, 7 X 9 1/2 In. 29.50
Flow Blue, Dish, Deep 18.00
Flow Blue, Dish, Oyster, Cabbage Rose, Marked, 5 X 8 3/4 In. 15.95
Flow Blue, Dish, Sauce, Waldorf, 5 1/2 In.Diameter 7.50
Flow Blue, Hatpin Holder, Cabbage Rose, 5 In.Tall 9.95
Flow Blue, Hatpin Holder, Staffordshire 11.50
Flow Blue, Holder, Ring, Cabbage Rose, Marked, 3 3/4 X 4 5/8 In. 7.95
Flow Blue, Jardiniere, 7 1/2 In.High, 8 1/2 In.Diameter 43.00
Flow Blue, Luncheon Set, Grindley's Argyle, 20 Piece 25.00
Flow Blue, Mug, Scuttle, Marked England 14.00
Flow Blue, Pitcher, Blue & Gilded Trees & Flowers, Ironstone, 7 In.High 30.00
Flow Blue, Pitcher, Cabbage Rose, Marked, 8 1/2 In.Tall 17.50
Flow Blue, Pitcher, Gold Trim, Flowers, Solid Blue Panels .... 32.50 To 35.00
Flow Blue, Pitcher, Gold Trim, Flowers, Solid Blue Panels, 8 3/4 In.High 37.50
Flow Blue, Pitcher, Milk, Scenic, Nonpareil, Quart 40.00
Flow Blue, Plate, Alaska, Grindley, 10 In. 12.00
Flow Blue, Plate, Althea, 7 In. 10.00
Flow Blue, Plate, Amoy, 9 1/4 In.Diameter 26.00
Flow Blue, Plate, Ayr, N & E Corn, 9 1/4 In. 10.00
Flow Blue, Plate, Blue, 8 1/2 In.Diameter, Set Of 8 .... 90.00
Flow Blue, Plate, Brooklyn Pattern, Gold-Scalloped Edge, 7 In. 15.00
Flow Blue, Plate, Burgess & Leigh, Middleport, 9 In. 4.00
Flow Blue, Plate, Chapoo, 9 In.Diameter 22.00
Flow Blue, Plate, Cinde, 9 In. 17.50
Flow Blue, Plate, Conway, 10 In.Diameter .... 14.50 To 18.50
Flow Blue, Plate, Dinner, Waldorf, 9 In.Diameter 12.50
Flow Blue, Plate, Fairy Villas, Adams, 8 In. 12.50
Flow Blue, Plate, Festoon, Adams, 9 In. 10.00
Flow Blue, Plate, Gironde, 9 3/4 In. 8.50
Flow Blue, Plate, H.W.P.England, Watteau, 9 In.Diameter 11.00
Flow Blue, Plate, Hindustan, 7 1/2 In.Diameter 21.00
Flow Blue, Plate, Hong Kong, 9 1/2 In.Diameter 24.50
Flow Blue, Plate, Indian Pattern, 7 In.Diameter 14.50
Flow Blue, Plate, Ivy, Leaves, Flowers, Blue, White, Green, 12 In.Diameter 45.00
Flow Blue, Plate, Labelle, 9 1/2 In. 9.50
Flow Blue, Plate, Navy, T.Till, 9 1/4 In. 10.00
Flow Blue, Plate, Oriental Decoration, 8 3/4 In. 12.50
Flow Blue, Plate, Oriental Pattern, 8 In. 14.00
Flow Blue, Plate, Osborne, Grindley, 9 In. 10.00
Flow Blue, Plate, Sancho Panza Boar Hunt, Clews, 10 In.Diameter 85.00
Flow Blue, Plate, Scinde, 10 1/2 In.Diameter 32.00
Flow Blue, Plate, Shell, 9 1/2 In.Diameter 25.00
Flow Blue, Plate, Soup, Don Quixote, Sancho Panza At The Boar Hunt, Blue 88.00
Flow Blue, Plate, Soup, Nonpareil 16.50
Flow Blue, Plate, Soup, Oriental Pattern, Set Of 6 .... 68.00
Flow Blue, Plate, Temple, 7 In.Diameter 15.00
Flow Blue, Plate, Touraine, 6 1/2 In.Diameter 7.50
Flow Blue, Plate, Touraine, 6 3/4 In. 9.00
Flow Blue, Plate, Touraine, 7 3/4 In. 13.50
Flow Blue, Plate, Touraine, 8 In. 16.50
Flow Blue, Plate, Wagon Wheel Pattern, Staffordshire 15.00
Flow Blue, Plate, Waldorf Pattern, 10 In.Diameter, Set Of 6 .... 58.00
Flow Blue, Platter, Acanthus 15.00
Flow Blue, Platter, Blue, Cumberland Territory Regents Park, C.1783-1790 .... 275.00
Flow Blue, Platter, Constance Pattern, W.A.A.& Co. 30.00
Flow Blue, Platter, Conway, Oval, 7 3/4 X 10 1/2 In. 15.00
Flow Blue, Platter, Florida Pattern 15.00
Flow Blue, Platter, Lugano, 11 1/2 X 7 In. 48.00
Flow Blue, Platter, Malvern Pattern, 12 In. 9.00
Flow Blue, Platter, Scinde, 11 X 8 1/2 In. 22.00
Flow Blue, Platter, Shanghai, 16 X 11 1/2 In. 42.50
Flow Blue, Platter, Touraine, Gold, 15 X 10 1/2 In. 38.50
Flow Blue, Platter, Waldorf Pattern, Diamond Shape, 10 1/2 In.Long 27.50

Flow Blue, **Ring Tree**, Staffordshire	28.50
Flow Blue, **Sauce**, Burgess & Leigh, Middleport	6.00
Flow Blue, **Saucer**, Touraine	6.00
Flow Blue, **Saucer**, Waldorf	6.50
Flow Blue, **Syrup**, Pewter Lid	12.50
Flow Blue, **Toothpick**	5.75
Flow Blue, **Tureen**, Rural Village, Tray	195.00
Flow Blue, **Urn**, Covered, Victorian, Gilded, 9 In.High	10.00
Flow Blue, **Vase**, Gold, Flask Shape, Mark, Round, Handle, 8 1/2 In.Tall	30.00
Flow Blue, **Vegetable**, Alaska, Grindley, Round, Covered	35.00
Flow Blue, **Vegetable**, Leon, Meakin, Oval, Open	16.00
Flow Blue, **Vegetable**, Touraine, H.Alcock, Oval, Open	25.00
Flow Blue, **Wash Set**, Clayton Johnson Bros., 5 Piece	50.00
Flow Blue, **Wash Set**, Signed Hancock & Sons, England, 2 Piece	375.00

Foo Dogs are mythical chinese figures, part dog and part lion. They were made of pottery, porcelain, carved stone, and wood.

Foo Dog, **Amber**, Standing, Carved, 3 1/2 In.	35.00
Foo Dog, **Bronze**, Chinese, 14 In.High	150.00
Foo Dog, **Porcelain**, Cobalt Blue, 10 In.High	27.50

Fostoria Glass, made in Fostoria, Ohio, is a twentieth century product.

Fostoria, **Candlestick**, Bell Bottom, Double Candelabrum, Pair	11.00
Fostoria, **Candlestick**, Pink Etched, Pair	15.00
Fostoria, **Tray**, Relish, Satinized, Signed	12.50
Fountain Pen, see Store, Fountain Pen	
Foval, see Fry	
Frame, see Furniture, Frame	

Francisware is an amber hobnail glassware.
Francisware, see also Hobnail

Francisware, **Berry Set**, Eight Small Bowls, 9 In.Square Large	140.00
Francisware, **Bowl**, Frosted Hobnail, Ribbon Top, Pontil, 8 In.Square	54.00
Francisware, **Bowl**, Frosted, Amber, Crimped Ruffled Rim, 3 1/4 In.Tall ...	48.50
Francisware, **Celery**, Frosted Swirl, Flared Ruffled Amber Band, Dated	52.00
Francisware, **Celery**, Hobnail, Frosted, Clear, Amber	85.00
Francisware, **Celery**, Hobs In Bottom	36.50
Francisware, **Dish**, Oval, 9 X 6 In.	49.50
Francisware, **Dish**, Sauce, Frosted Hob, Amber Band	20.00
Francisware, **Sauce**, Square	22.50
Francisware, **Spooner**, Crimped Top, Amber	35.00
Francisware, **Toothpick**, Frosted Swirl	32.00
Francisware, **Toothpick**, Hobnail .... 35.00 To	37.50
Francisware, **Toothpick**, Swirl, Fluted Top, Amber	32.00
Frankenthal, **Cup & Saucer**, Coffee, Painted Turnips, Floral Festoons, C.1775	130.00
Frankenthal, **Plate**, Soup, C.1775, Kakiemon Style Center, Petal Shape Rim	190.00
Frankenthal, **Tea Service**, Oval Medallions, Harbor View, C.1765-1770, 4 Piece	275.00
Frankenthal, **Teacup & Saucer**, Chinoiserie Figures, C.1772	100.00
Frankenthal, **Vase**, Covered, Potpourri, Ovoid, Double Handles, C.1775, Pair	375.00
Frankoma, **Bowl**, Rose, Incised, Green, Brown, Signed	9.00
Frankoma, **Mug**, Elephant Shape, Red, White, Blue	25.00
Frankoma, **Mug**, Nixon-Agnew, 1967	18.00
Frankoma, **Mug**, Nixon-Agnew, 1968	12.00

Fry Glass was made by the famous H.C.Fry Glass Company of Rochester, Pennsylvania. It includes Cut Glass, but the famous Fry Glass today is the Foval, or Pearl, Art Glass. This is an opal ware decorated with colored trim. It was made from 1922 to 1933.

Fry, see also Cut Glass

Fry Foval, **Basket**, Fiery Opal, Cobalt Handle & Top Rim.1i In.	235.00
Fry Foval, **Bowl**, Fruit, Flared Rim, Footed, 9 1/2 In.Wide, 4 1/2 In.Tall ...	135.00
Fry Foval, **Bowl**, Green Foot	125.00
Fry Foval, **Candleholder**, White, Blue, Unsigned, 11 In.Tall, Pair	135.00
Fry Foval, **Candlestick**, Opalescent, Applied Blue Threading, 12 In.High	85.00
Fry Foval, **Candlestick**, Stripes, Buttons, Blue, Matching Match Holder, Pair	185.00
Fry Foval, **Casserole**, Covered, 8 1/2 In.	12.50

Fry Foval, **Compote**, Jade Base, Oval 59.00
Fry Foval, **Cup**, Measuring, Ovenware 8.50
Fry Foval, **Jug**, Hot Water, Covered,•Delft Handle & Knob, 6 1/4 In.High 185.00
Fry Foval, **Lid**, Baking Dish, Opalescent Knob Finial, Dated 1920 .... 10.00
Fry Foval, **Paperweight**, Figural, Snail 85.00
Fry Foval, **Perfume**, Fiery Opal Base, Red Curled Feather Stopper, 7 In.Tall 95.00
Fry Foval, **Pitcher Set**, Cranberry To Amber To Clear, 3 Piece 79.00
Fry Foval, **Plate**, Opalescent Edge, 8 1/2 In. 7.50
Fry Foval, **Plate**, Opalescent, Divided, Signed, 10 1/2 In.Diameter 10.00
Fry Foval, **Shell On Pedestal**, 6 1/2 X 7 In. 150.00
Fry Foval, **Sherbet**, Clear, Blue Stem 30.00
Fry Foval, **Sherbet**, Clear, Green Stem 30.00
Fry Foval, **Tumbler**, Clear, Blue Stem, Footed 30.00
Fry Foval, **Tumbler**, Lemonade, Green Handle 29.00
Fry, **Fernery**, Cut Flowers, Leaves, Footed, 7 3/4 In.Diameter, 4 1/2 In.Tall 65.00
Fry, **Pitcher**, Crackle Glass, Green Applied Handle & Knob On Lid, 9 1/2 In. 60.00
Fry, **Shot Glass**, Crystal & Green Stripe, Gold Rim 15.00
Fry, **Sugar & Creamer**, Grape Design, Ground Pontil 9.50
Fry, **Tumbler**, Lemonade, Crackle Glass, Blue Applied Berries On Base 7.00
Fry, **Vase**, Cobalt Blue, Rolled Edge, Footed, 7 In.Diameter, 4 1/2 In.Tall 110.00
Fry, **Vase**, Star Shaped Opening, 8 In.Tall, Pair 25.00
Fulda, **Coffeepot**, Covered, Painted Landscape Panels, C.1765 .... 450.00
Fulda, **Coffeepot**, Covered, Pear Shape, Scroll Handle, Bouquets, C.1765 .... 175.00
Fulda, **Cup & Saucer**, Covered, Iron Red Monochrome Decor, C.1770 .... 360.00
Fulda, **Tankard**, Cylindrical, Scroll Handle, Portrait Medallion, C.1775 .... 300.00

Fulper is the mark used by the American Pottery Company of
Flemington, New Jersey. The art pottery was made from 1910 to 1929.
The firm had been making bottles, jugs, and housewares from 1805. Doll heads
were made about 1928. The firm became Stangl Pottery in 1929.

Fulper, **Bowl**, Brown To Butterscotch, 3 1/2 In.High, Verticle Fulper Mark 35.00
Fulper, **Bowl**, Green Glazed, 8 1/2 In.Diameter, 2 3/4 In.High 25.00
Fulper, **Box**, Dresser, Covered, Figure Of Young Lady, Marked, Artist-Signed 28.50
Fulper, **Candlestick**, Chamber Style, Green Glaze, Signed 65.00
Fulper, **Candlestick**, Twist Stem, Green, 8 In.Tall, Pair 20.00
Fulper, **Compote**, Metal Nude Stem, Pottery Dish, Art Nouveau 35.00
Fulper, **Lamp**, Perfume, Figural Ballerina, Signed 50.00
Fulper, **Lamp**, Perfume, Kneeling Ballerina, 6 In.High, Incised Signature 27.50
Fulper, **Pitcher**, Green & Purple, Signed, 4 1/2 In. 10.00
Fulper, **Vase**, Green To Turquoise, Three Handles 32.50
Furniture, **Armchair**, Art Nouveau, Inlaid Mahogany, Cartouches Of Tulips, 2 .... 120.00
Furniture, **Armchair**, Cherry, Banister Back, New England, C.1700, Rush Seat 700.00
Furniture, **Armchair**, Child's, Maple, Mushroom, Black Paint, C.1725 .... 800.00
Furniture, **Armchair**, Child's, Queen Anne Style, Wing, Cabriole Legs 375.00
Furniture, **Armchair**, Chinese, Chippendale, Mahogany, Soho Tapestry 5500.00
Furniture, **Armchair**, Chippendale, Mahogany, Carved, Mass., C.1760 .... 1500.00
Furniture, **Armchair**, Chippendale, Mahogany, Carved, Massachusetts, C.1760 .... 4500.00
Furniture, **Armchair**, Chippendale, Mahogany, Carved, Wing, New York, C.1760 .... 3500.00
Furniture, **Armchair**, Chippendale, Mahogany, Chinese, Open, 19th Century 350.00
Furniture, **Armchair**, Chippendale, Mahogany, Philadelphia, C.1760, Pair 1300.00
Furniture, **Armchair**, Chippendale, Mahogany, Scroll Ears, Square Legs 125.00
Furniture, **Armchair**, Chippendale, Mahogany, Wing, Massachusetts, C.1760 .... 1300.00
Furniture, **Armchair**, Chippendale, Mahogany, Wing, Massachusetts, C.1770 .... 1300.00
Furniture, **Armchair**, Chippendale, Mahogany, Wing, Philadelphia, C.1760 .... 1000.00
Furniture, **Armchair**, Chippendale, Mahogany, 18th Century 170.00
Furniture, **Armchair**, Chippendale, Walnut, Carved, Philadelphia, C.1750 .... 4500.00
Furniture, **Armchair**, Chippendale, Walnut, Shell Carved, Philadelphia, C.1760 .... 4750.00
Furniture, **Armchair**, Chippendale, 18th Century, Pierced Slat, Square Legs 150.00
Furniture, **Armchair**, English, C.1775 .... *Illus* 650.00
Furniture, **Armchair**, Federal, Inlaid Mahogany, Martha Washington, C.1790 .... 2700.00
Furniture, **Armchair**, Federal, Mahogany, Martha Washington, Mass., C.1790 .... 1900.00
Furniture, **Armchair**, George II, Mahogany, Cartouche Back, 18th Century 4000.00
Furniture, **Armchair**, George II, Mahogany, Carved, Library, Needlework, Pair 4500.00
Furniture, **Armchair**, George III, Beechwood, Painted, Shield Back, C.1750 .... 175.00
Furniture, **Armchair**, George III, Black Japanned, Rectangular Back, Pair 750.00
Furniture, **Armchair**, George III, Black Japanned, Wheel Back, C.1750, 4 .... 2700.00

Furniture, Armchair, George III, Floral, Hand-Painted, 18th Century, Pair 800.00
Furniture, Armchair, George III, Hand-Painted, Cherry Design, 18th Century 250.00
Furniture, Armchair, George III, Mahogany, Arched Top Rail, 18th Century 550.00
Furniture, Armchair, George III, Mahogany, Caned, Arched Back, 18th Century 800.00
Furniture, Armchair, George III, Mahogany, Ladder Back, 18th Century 375.00
Furniture, Armchair, George III, Painted, C.1750, 4 .... *Illus* 475.00
Furniture, Armchair, George III, Painted, 18th Century, Green Silk 400.00
Furniture, Armchair, George III, Painted, 18th Century, Pair 650.00
Furniture, Armchair, Hepplewhite, Mahogany, Lady's, New England, C.1790 .... 350.00
Furniture, Armchair, Hepplewhite, Mahogany, Martha Washington, N.E., C.1790 .... 1000.00
Furniture, Armchair, Hepplewhite, Mahogany, Pierced Splat 80.00
Furniture, Armchair, Italian, Walnut, Pierced Splats, C.1750, Pair 140.00
Furniture, Armchair, Library, George III, Mahogany, 18th Century 225.00
Furniture, Armchair, Louis XII, Walnut, Carved, Rectangular Back, 1650, Pair 475.00
Furniture, Armchair, Maple, Slat Back, Painted, C.1720 .... *Illus* 1500.00
Furniture, Armchair, New England, Arrow Back, Rush Seat, Signed Wm.White 350.00
Furniture, Armchair, Pilgrim, Carver, Turned, Painted, Rhode Island, C.1680 .... 3750.00
Furniture, Armchair, Queen Anne, Cherry, Wing, Rhode Island, C.1740 .... 2000.00
Furniture, Armchair, Queen Anne, Maple, C.1740, Spooned Back, Crest Rail 3500.00
Furniture, Armchair, Queen Anne, Walnut, Wing, Massachusetts, C.1750 .... 6750.00
Furniture, Armchair, Queen Anne, Walnut, Wing, Rhode Island, C.1740 .... 6250.00
Furniture, Armchair, Queen Anne, Walnut, Wing, 18th Century, Serpentine Sides 500.00
Furniture, Armchair, Sheraton, Mahogany, Martha Washington, Mass., C.1790 .... 2000.00
Furniture, Armchair, Sheraton, Painted Green, Gilding, N.Y., C.1820, Pair 200.00
Furniture, Armchair, Venetian, Painted, 18th Century, Hooped Backrest, Pair 1400.00
Furniture, Armchair, Victorian, Rosewood, Belter Style, Cartouche Back, Pair 1300.00
Furniture, Armchair, Victorian, Rosewood, Carved, New York, C.1850, Pair 325.00
Furniture, Armchair, Walnut, Open Back, Heart Shaped Top, Oval Seat 100.00
Furniture, Armchair, William & Mary Transitional, Curly Maple, N.E., C.1710 .... 1100.00
Furniture, Armchair, Windsor, Bamboo, Turned, Saddle Seat, Penna., C.1800 .... 225.00
Furniture, Armchair, Windsor, Bow Back 400.00
Furniture, Armchair, Windsor, Brace Back, Continuous Arm, Signed E.B.Tracy 1000.00
Furniture, Armchair, Windsor, Brace Back, Rhode Island, C.1780 .... 525.00
Furniture, Armchair, Windsor, Comb Back, New England, C.1750 .... 100.00 To 575.00
Furniture, Armchair, Windsor, Continuous Arm, Black Paint 475.00
Furniture, Armchair, Windsor, Ebenezer Tracy, Conn., 1780 .... *Illus* 700.00
Furniture, Armchair, Windsor, Fanback, Made Into Potty Chair 70.00
Furniture, Armchair, Windsor, Fanback, Penna., C.1750 .... 575.00
Furniture, Armchair, Windsor, Fanback, Pennsylvania, 18th Century 850.00
Furniture, Armchair, Windsor, Hoop Back, I.Sproson, New York, C.1790 .... 600.00
Furniture, Armchair, Windsor, Hoop Back, New England, C.1790, Spliced Feet 175.00
Furniture, Armchair, Windsor, Hoop Back, Wallace Nutting, 6 .... 800.00
Furniture, Armchair, Windsor, Maple, Ash, & Chestnut, New England, C.1750 .... 850.00
Furniture, Armchair, Windsor, Maple, Saddle Seat, Knuckle, Comb Back 525.00
Furniture, Armchair, Windsor, New England, Black Paint, Comb Back 900.00
Furniture, Armchair, Windsor, New England, C.1780, Bow Back 160.00
Furniture, Armchair, Windsor, New York State, Saddle Seat, Black Paint, Pair 1100.00
Furniture, Armchair, Windsor, Pennsylvania, Bow Back, Knuckle Arms, Pair 2000.00
Furniture, Armchair, Windsor, Spindle Back, Wood Seat, Bamboo Turned Legs 110.00
Furniture, Armchair, Windsor, Step Down, Spool Turned Spindles, Saddle Seat 130.00
Furniture, Armchair, Windsor, Writing, Arrow Back, C.1820 .... *Illus* 325.00
Furniture, Armchair, Windsor, Yewwood, English, 19th Century, Hoop Back 275.00
Furniture, Armchair, Windsor, 7 Spindles, Shaped Saddle Seat 600.00
Furniture, Armchair, Writing, Arrow Back, Levi Yodur, Allentown, Candleholder 400.00
Furniture, Armoire, Empire, French, Mahogany, Double Mirrored Doors 225.00
Furniture, Bar, Back, Framed Cherry Mirror, 8 Ft.Long 200.00
Furniture, Bar, Front & Back, Framed Mirror, 12 Ft.Long 400.00
Furniture, Bar, Oak, Marble Top, Church Glass End Cabinets, 14 In.Back 800.00
Furniture, Bar, Towel, Pine, Scalloped, 36 In.Wide 12.50
Furniture, Bassinette, Wicker, Hood, Wheels 40.00
Furniture, Bed, Baby's, Stripped Bentwood 55.00
Furniture, Bed, Bird's-Eye Maple, Single, Vanity With Cabriole Legs 50.00
Furniture, Bed, Brass, Double 125.00
Furniture, Bed, Brass, Flat Knob Top, Cylindrical Bars, 62 In.High 115.00
Furniture, Bed, Brass, Flat Knob Top, Full Size, 55 In.Headpost 110.00
Furniture, Bed, Brass, Polished 195.00

Furniture,
Armchair,
English,
C.1775
See Page 189

Furniture,
Armchair,
Maple,
Slat Back,
Painted,
C.1720
See Page 190

Furniture, Armchair, George III,
Painted, C.1750, 4
See Page 190

Furniture, Armchair, Windsor,
Ebenezer Tracy, Conn., 1780
See Page 190

Furniture, Armchair, Windsor,
Writing, Arrow Back, C.1820
See Page 190

Furniture, Bed, Brass, Poster	145.00
Furniture, Bed, Brass, Queen, Head 92 In., Foot 51 In.	1050.00
Furniture, Bed, Brass, Tubular, Full Size, Casters	65.00
Furniture, Bed, Cannon Ball, Twin Size, Maple, Iron Side Rails, Posts	225.00
Furniture, Bed, Canopy, C.1830	595.00
Furniture, Bed, Cherry, Acanthus Carved, High Post, Single	225.00
Furniture, Bed, Cherry, Canopy, Rope Turned & Blocked Posts, Arched Canopy	675.00
Furniture, Bed, Cherry, Turned, Low, American, 19th Century, Ball Finials	225.00
Furniture, Bed, Chippendale, Mahogany, Tester, Carved, Reifsnyder, C.1790	7000.00
Furniture, Bed, Curly Maple, Canopy, Cut Panel Headboard, Pencil Posts	750.00
Furniture, Bed, Curly Maple, Pencil Post, Pine Headboard, Square Canopy	600.00
Furniture, Bed, Day, Rope	20.00
Furniture, Bed, Empire, Bird's-Eye Maple, Turned, American, C.1830	425.00
Furniture, Bed, Empire, French, Mahogany, Canopied, Caryatids & Wreaths Decor	1000.00
Furniture, Bed, Empire, Mahogany, Low Post, Three Quarter, C.1830	220.00
Furniture, Bed, Federal, Cherrywood, Tester, American, C.1815	375.00
Furniture, Bed, Federal, Curly Maple, Tester, C.1820, American	550.00
Furniture, Bed, Federal, Pine, Tester, Painted, Pennsylvania, C.1800	475.00
Furniture, Bed, George III, Mahogany, 4 Post, Tester, 18th Century	925.00
Furniture, Bed, Hepplewhite, Cherry, Turned, Mass., C.1790, 6 Ft.5 In.	625.00
Furniture, Bed, Hired Man's, American, Maple, Square Posts With Mushroom Top	75.00
Furniture, Bed, Hired Man's, New England, Tapered Posts	175.00
Furniture, Bed, Louis XV, American Revival Period, Mahogany & Cherry, C.1860	2100.00
Furniture, Bed, Low Post, Rope, Red Paint, Acorn Finials	55.00
Furniture, Bed, Mahogany, High Post, Double, Ball & Claw Foot	750.00
Furniture, Bed, Maple, Arched Canopy, Turned & Blocked Posts	325.00
Furniture, Bed, Maple, Rope, Ball Finish, 44 In.Posts	55.00
Furniture, Bed, Maple, Rope, Trundle, Wooden Rollers	50.00
Furniture, Bed, Oak, Plain	45.00 To 51.00
Furniture, Bed, Pencil Post, New England, Maple, Red Finish	900.00
Furniture, Bed, Pencil Post, Red Paint, Black Feather Graining, C.1800	1600.00
Furniture, Bed, Pine, Low Post, 3/4, Acorn Turned Posts, Carved	200.00
Furniture, Bed, Rope, Cannonball, Black & Red Graining	175.00
Furniture, Bed, Rope, Walnut, 4 1/2 Ft.Posts	275.00
Furniture, Bed, Sheraton, Mahogany, Carved Eagles On Posts, C.1757	2750.00
Furniture, Bed, Sheraton, Rope, Melon Fluted Posts, Maple, Pine Headboard	100.00
Furniture, Bed, Spool, No Paint, Maple	22.50
Furniture, Bed, Trundle, Rope Style, Poplar, Turned Posts	75.00
Furniture, Bed, Walnut, Poster	25.00
Furniture, Bed, Walnut, Rope Posts, 4 1/2 Feet Tall	175.00
Furniture, Bed, Yard, C.1820, Handmade Side Rails, Red Paint	25.00
Furniture, Bench, Box, 2 Lift Lids, Red Paint, Dovetailed, Ball Feet	125.00
Furniture, Bench, Bucket, Pennsylvania, Bootjack Ends, Brown Paint	275.00
Furniture, Bench, Bucket, Pennsylvania, Pine, 3 Shelves, 39 X 14 X 48 In.	60.00
Furniture, Bench, Bucket, Pine, Three Shelf, Top Rail, 42 In.Wide	110.00
Furniture, Bench, Church, Windsor, Slab Seat, 8 Bamboo Turned Legs	625.00
Furniture, Bench, Cobbler, Farmer, Drawer, Crude	75.00
Furniture, Bench, Cobbler, Without Drawer	185.00
Furniture, Bench, Deacon, Pine Seat, Maple Spindled Back, 7 Ft.Long	84.50
Furniture, Bench, Deacon's, 8 Legs, 8 Ft.Long	125.00
Furniture, Bench, Fireside, Mahogany, Square Legs, H Stretcher, 18 X 28 In.	65.00
Furniture, Bench, Louis XVI, Painted Gray, Rectangular, Pair	350.00
Furniture, Bench, Mammy, Windsor Style, Poplar Seat, Rockers & Side Rail	265.00
Furniture, Bench, Milk, Pine Slab, Peg Leg, 69 In.High	25.00
Furniture, Bench, Milk, Pine, Board Sides, 16 In.Long	12.50
Furniture, Bench, Oak, 36 In.Long	10.00
Furniture, Bench, Pine, Straight Skirt, Scalloped Legs, 58 In.Long	50.00
Furniture, Bench, Prayer, Cabriole Legs, Plush Cover	39.50
Furniture, Bench, Prayer, Plush Cover	35.00
Furniture, Bench, Water	52.00
Furniture, Bergere A Oreille, Petite, Louis XV, Walnut, Carved, C.1750, Pair	1000.00
Furniture, Bergere, Louis XV Style, Carved Gilt Wood, Cartouche Back, C.1850	200.00
Furniture, Bergere, Louis XV-XVI, Painted Cream, Tub Form Back, C.1750	450.00
Furniture, Bergere, Louis XV, Provincial, Walnut, Carved, Tub Back, C.1750	425.00
Furniture, Bergere, Louis XV, Provincial, Walnut, Tub Form Back, C.1780	225.00
Furniture, Bergere, Louis XVI, Beechwood, C.L.Hutel, 1750	*Illus* 1300.00

Furniture, **Bergere**, Louis XVI, Beechwood, Carved, Signed C.L.Hutel, 1750, Pair 1300.00
Furniture, **Bergere**, Louis XVI, Beechwood, 18th Century, Upholstered 550.00
Furniture, **Bonheur Du Jour**, George III Style, Satinwood, Painted Oval 450.00
Furniture, **Bookcase**, Black Walnut, Slant Lid, Carved, 7 Ft.2 In. 275.00
Furniture, **Bookcase**, Breakfront, George III, Mahogany, 19th Century 1400.00
Furniture, **Bookcase**, George III, Mahogany, Breakfront, Mallett & Son, C.1750 .... 2600.00
Furniture, **Bookcase**, Glass Shelves, 42 In.Wide, 7 Ft.6 In.High, Pair 150.00
Furniture, **Bookshelf**, George III, Pine & Mahogany, Rosewood, Standing, C.1750 .... 500.00
Furniture, **Bookshelf**, Regency, Mahogany, Standing, Open, 4 Graduated Tiers 400.00
Furniture, **Bottle Carrier**, Mahogany, C.1760 .... *Illus* 750.00
Furniture, **Box**, Bible, William & Mary, Ball Feet, Iron Heart Escutcheon 1600.00
Furniture, **Box**, Document, Dovetailed, Walnut, 4 1/2 In.Tall, 11 In.Long 15.00

Furniture, Bergere, Louis XVI,
Beechwood, C.L.Hutel, 1750
See Page 192

Furniture, Bottle Carrier, Mahogany, C.1760

Furniture, **Box**, Hanging, Compartment, Walnut, Heart Decoration, 10 In.High 50.00
Furniture, **Box**, Knife, George II, Mahogany, 18th Century, 15 In.High 400.00
Furniture, **Box**, Knife, Sheraton, Mahogany, C.1780, Pair .... *Illus* 600.00
Furniture, **Box**, Work, George III, Satinwood & Eglomise, Octagonal Top, C.1750 .... 1300.00
Furniture, **Box**, Work, George III, Satinwood & Eglomise, Oval Panel, C.1750 .... 1000.00
Furniture, **Box**, Writing, Mahogany, Slant Lid, Inlaid Top 30.00
Furniture, **Bracket**, Corner, Victorian, Rosewood, 19th Century, Pair 60.00
Furniture, **Buffet**, Oak, 1865, Concave Glass, China Top, Plate Glass Mirrors 1500.00
Furniture, **Bureau A Cylindre**, Louis XV, Kingwood & Purpleheart, C.1750 .... 3250.00
Furniture, **Bureau A Cylindre**, Louis XVI, Mahogany, White Marble Top, C.1750 .... 500.00
Furniture, **Bureau A Cylindre**, Mahogany, Kolping, C.1850 .... *Illus* 950.00
Furniture, **Bureau Bookcase**, George I, Walnut, Mirrored Doors, C.1750 .... 5000.00
Furniture, **Bureau Bookcase**, George III, Mahogany, 18th Century 850.00
Furniture, **Bureau Bookcase**, Sicilian, Painted, C.1750 .... *Illus* 3500.00
Furniture, **Bureau Desk**, Sheraton, Mahogany, C.1830, Splay Legs 550.00
Furniture, **Bureau Plat**, Louis XV, Kingwood, Signed J.Stumpff Jme, C.1750 .... 6000.00
Furniture, **Bureau**, Bracket Foot, C.1800, Four Drawers, Escutcheon Brassed 200.00
Furniture, **Bureau**, Cherry, Bracket Foot, 4 Graduated Drawers, Brass 300.00
Furniture, **Bureau**, Cherry, 18th Century, 4 Drawers 550.00
Furniture, **Bureau**, Cottage, Child's, 2 Drawers On Top Support Mirror 130.00
Furniture, **Bureau**, Doll's, 3 Drawers, White Knobs 17.50
Furniture, **Bureau**, Massachusettes, C.1820, Bowfront, 4 Drawers, Mahogany Top 700.00
Furniture, **Bureau**, Oak, Miniature, Three Drawers, Mirror Frame 10.00
Furniture, **Bureau**, Walnut, 4 Drawers, Bracket Foot, Escutcheon Brasses 375.00
Furniture, **Butcher Block**, Round, Cut From Tree, 45 1/2 In.Diameter, 3 Legs 350.00
Furniture, **Cabinet Desk**, Victorian, Label 'harmon's Hotel, Sheldon, N.Y.' 200.00
Furniture, **Cabinet**, American, 2 Part Hutch, Red Paint, Cupboard Base 325.00

Furniture, Box, Knife, Sheraton,
Mahogany, C.1780, Pair
See Page 193

Furniture, Bureau Bookcase,
Sicillian, Painted, C.1750
See Page 193

Furniture, Bureau A Cylindre,
Mahogany, Kolping, C.1850
See Page 193

Furniture, Cabinet, Bedside, Federal, Inlaid Mahogany, New York, C.1800	375.00
Furniture, Cabinet, China, Maple Finish, 65 X 32 X 12 In.	60.00
Furniture, Cabinet, Chuck Wagon	250.00
Furniture, Cabinet, Collector's, Pine, Upright, 12 Velvet Lined Drawers	90.00
Furniture, Cabinet, Combination, Lower Shelves, 45 X 15 X 72 In.	160.00
Furniture, Cabinet, Continental, 17th Century, 38 In.Wide, 39 In.High	200.00
Furniture, Cabinet, Corner, Cherry, 12 Paneled Glass Door, Bracket Feet	650.00
Furniture, Cabinet, Corner, George III, Oak, 18th Century, 6 Ft.Tall	750.00
Furniture, Cabinet, Corner, Hanging, Pine, 3 Shelves, 27 In.High	25.00
Furniture, Cabinet, Corner, Hepplewhite, Inlaid Mahogany, Hanging, C.1780	325.00
Furniture, Cabinet, Corner, Oak, Multipanel Door, Bracket Foot	120.00
Furniture, Cabinet, Corner, One Piece, Arch Door With 15 Panes, Ogee Top	600.00
Furniture, Cabinet, Corner, Walnut, 4 Shelves, Bracket Base & Top	80.00
Furniture, Cabinet, Curio, Mahogany, French	550.00
Furniture, Cabinet, Curio, Mahogany, Leaded Glass Door & Sides	275.00
Furniture, Cabinet, Dentist's, Marble Base, Porcelain Top, Mahogany	400.00
Furniture, Cabinet, Display, Regency, Rosewood, 19th Century, 39 In.Tall	425.00
Furniture, Cabinet, German, Ebonized Wood, Tortoiseshell, Brass Inlaid, 1650	250.00
Furniture, Cabinet, Hanging, Pine, Erie, Pa., Paneled Door & Undershelf	300.00
Furniture, Cabinet, Hanging, Pine, 2 Shelves, Panel Doors, 31 In.High	30.00
Furniture, Cabinet, Hanging, 3 Shelves, Oak Finish, 28 X 24 X 6 In.	39.50

Furniture, Cabinet, Hutch, Pine, Open, 2 Part, 3 Shelves At Top, Cabinet Base 175.00
Furniture, Cabinet, Italian, Walnut, Ivory Inlaid, Rectangular, C.1750 .... 50.00
Furniture, Cabinet, Jam, Poplar, Wooden Knobs 165.00
Furniture, Cabinet, Medicine, Pine, Glass Door, Towel Bar 20.00
Furniture, Cabinet, Music Box, Walnut, Imperial Symphonion Mark, 80 In.Tall 3250.00
Furniture, Cabinet, Oak, For Long Loaves Of French Bread, Lift Cover 37.50
Furniture, Cabinet, Pie, Pennsylvania, Punched, 2 Doors Of 3 Panels 150.00
Furniture, Cabinet, Pine, 1 Door, 30 X 31 In. 35.00
Furniture, Cabinet, Pine, 2 Doors On Hutch 175.00
Furniture, Cabinet, Side, George III, Satinwood, D Shaped 950.00
Furniture, Cabinet, Side, George III, Satinwood, Rectangular Top, C.1750 .... 475.00
Furniture, Cabinet, Side, George III, Satinwood, Rosewood, Late 18th Century 1200.00
Furniture, Cabinet, Side, George IV, Mahogany, 2 Shelves, 2 Door, 19th Century 825.00
Furniture, Cabinet, Side, Regency, Rosewood, C.1850, Pair .... *Illus* 675.00

Furniture, Cabinet, Side, Regency,
Rosewood, C.1850, Pair

Furniture, Cabinet, Side, Regency, Rosewood, 19th Century, Brass Gallery 200.00
Furniture, Cabinet, Side, Rosewood, Regency, Rectangular, 19th Century 450.00
Furniture, Cabinet, Smoking, Edwardian, Glass Door, Brass Fittings 35.00
Furniture, Cabinet, Smoking, 1 Drawer, Pipe Rack, Tobacco Jar 29.50
Furniture, Cabinet, Smoking, 4 Drawers, Beveled Glass In 2 Doors 29.50
Furniture, Cabinet, Spice, Eight Drawers, White Wooden Knobs 40.00
Furniture, Cabinet, Spice, Hanging, Harry E.Wentz, Dec., 1882, 13 Drawers 310.00
Furniture, Cabinet, Spool, Walnut, 3 Drawers, Glass Inserts, Reverse Painted 39.00
Furniture, Cabinet, Wall, Hanging, 1 Shelf, Beveled Mirror In Door 29.50
Furniture, Cabinet, Writing, Victorian, Zebrawood, Drawer, 19th Century 325.00
Furniture, Caddy, Tea, Rosewood, Canted Sides, Silver Inlays 40.00
Furniture, Caddy, Tea, Two Part, Painted Black & Gold, Bombay Sides 50.00
Furniture, Canape, Louis XVI Style, Walnut, Carved Back Crest 90.00
Furniture, Candleholder, Wall, Two Compartments, Wooden, 15 1/2 In.High 50.00
Furniture, Candlestand, American, Paint Over Decoupage, 16 In.Diameter 110.00
Furniture, Candlestand, Cherry, Pennsylvania, Dish Top, Urn Pedestal 1900.00
Furniture, Candlestand, Cherry, Snake Leg, 18 In.Square Top, D Corners 375.00
Furniture, Candlestand, Cherry, 18th Century, Rectangular Top, Splay Legs 160.00
Furniture, Candlestand, Chippendale, Mahogany, Circular, Tilt Top, Penna.1760 .... 750.00
Furniture, Candlestand, Chippendale, Mahogany, Tilt Top, Pennsylvania, C.1770 .... 1200.00
Furniture, Candlestand, Dish Top, Turned Support, Snake Legs, 28 In.High 140.00
Furniture, Candlestand, Federal, Mahogany, N.Y., C.1810, Clover Top 500.00
Furniture, Candlestand, Federal, Mahogany, Oblong, Penna., C.1790 .... 250.00
Furniture, Candlestand, Federal, Mahogany, Tilt Top, N.Y., C.1810, Clover Leaf 200.00
Furniture, Candlestand, Federal, Mahogany, Tilt Top, Oblong, Penna., C.1790 .... 325.00
Furniture, Candlestand, Hepplewhite, Cherry, New England, C.1790, Oval Top 350.00
Furniture, Candlestand, Hepplewhite, Cherry, New England, C.1790, Round Top 225.00
Furniture, Candlestand, Hepplewhite, Mahogany, New England, C.1790, Square 475.00

Furniture, Candlestand, Hepplewhite, Mahogany, Tilt Top, Mass., C.1760, Oval	500.00
Furniture, Candlestand, Hepplewhite, Tiger Maple, D Shape Corners	650.00
Furniture, Candlestand, Hepplewhite, Tilt Top, New England, C.1790, Round Top	275.00
Furniture, Candlestand, Hepplewhite, Tilt Top, Painted, Shell Graining	700.00
Furniture, Candlestand, Mahogany & Curly Maple, American, Dish Top	80.00
Furniture, Candlestand, Mahogany, Tilt Top, Carved Knees	45.00
Furniture, Candlestand, Mahogany, Tilt Top, Snake Feet, 25 In.Diameter	175.00
Furniture, Candlestand, Maple, Snake Leg, Varnish Over Red Paint	300.00
Furniture, Candlestand, New England, Birch, Spider Foot, C.1790	60.00
Furniture, Candlestand, Oak & Maple, Turned, New England, 18th Century	300.00
Furniture, Candlestand, Walnut, Tilt Top, Snake Feet With Pad	175.00
Furniture, Canterbury, George IV, Mahogany, Drawer, Rectangular, 19th Century	400.00
Furniture, Canterbury, Mahogany, American, C.1830, Pull Drawer, 4 Open Slots	300.00
Furniture, Canterbury, 2 Shelf, Drawer, Casters	70.00
Furniture, Case, Gun, American, Walnut, C.1880-90, 12 X 29 In.	375.00
Furniture, Cellarette, George III, Mahogany, Octagonal, 18th Century	750.00
Furniture, Cellarette, George III, Mahogany, Sarcophagus Shape, C.1750	400.00
Furniture, Chair, Balloon Back, Set Of 5	195.00
Furniture, Chair, Bentwood, Cane Bottom, 2	48.00
Furniture, Chair, Bentwood, Cane, High Back, Arm, Victorian	95.00
Furniture, Chair, Bentwood, Marked Fishler, 6	125.00
Furniture, Chair, Bentwood, Painted	6.00
Furniture, Chair, Bentwood, Signed Josepf Kohn, Wein, Austria, Pair	58.00
Furniture, Chair, Captain's, English, 8	520.00
Furniture, Chair, Captain's, Small Size, Pair	40.00
Furniture, Chair, Captain's, Telegrapher's Chair In Brookston Depot	150.00
Furniture, Chair, Captain's, Victorian, Burl Walnut Inlay, 4	225.00
Furniture, Chair, Carved Grape & Leaf, Walnut	37.50
Furniture, Chair, Child's, Pine, Four Board	22.50
Furniture, Chair, Child's, Shaker, Slat Back	25.00
Furniture, Chair, Child's, Walnut, Folding	22.50
Furniture, Chair, Child's, Windsor, Arrow Back, Mule Ears, Pine & Maple	60.00
Furniture, Chair, Chippendale Style, Wing, Ball & Claw Feet, Carved Knees	300.00
Furniture, Chair, Chippendale, Mahogany, Carved, Lolling, N.Y., C.1760	1700.00
Furniture, Chair, Chippendale, Mahogany, Carved, Tassel Back, C.1760, Pair	4200.00
Furniture, Chair, Chippendale, Mahogany, Lolling, Massachusetts, C.1760	8500.00
Furniture, Chair, Chippendale, Mahogany, Upholstered Seat, Square Legs	55.00
Furniture, Chair, Chippendale, Mahogany, Urn Shaped Splat, Fan & Grooved Ears, Pair	340.00
Furniture, Chair, Chippendale, Walnut, Carved, Balloon Seat, Mass., 1760, Pair	3500.00
Furniture, Chair, Chippendale, Wing, N.H., Red-Brown Paint, Upholstered	3000.00
Furniture, Chair, Church, Victorian, Walnut, Gothic Style, Hinged Seat	45.00
Furniture, Chair, Corner, Chippendale, Cherry, Connecticut, C.1780	300.00
Furniture, Chair, Corner, Chippendale, Mahogany, C.1760, American	7000.00
Furniture, Chair, Corner, Chippendale, Mahogany, Rhode Island, C.1760	4000.00
Furniture, Chair, Corner, Mahogany, Country, Upholstered Back	35.00
Furniture, Chair, Corner, Oak, 18th Century	*Illus* 750.00
Furniture, Chair, Curly Maple, Rush Seat, Pillow Back, 4	340.00
Furniture, Chair, Dining, Bird's-Eye Maple, C.1830, 4	135.00
Furniture, Chair, Dining, Chippendale, Mahogany, English, 19th Century, 8	1000.00
Furniture, Chair, Dining, Chippendale, Mahogany, Massachusetts, C.1770, 6	1600.00
Furniture, Chair, Dining, Continental, Beechwood, 19th Century, Carved, 6	1000.00
Furniture, Chair, Dining, Empire, Mahogany, Gondola, N.Y., C.1825, 6	550.00
Furniture, Chair, Dining, George III, Black Japanned, Armchairs, C.1780, 6	2100.00
Furniture, Chair, Dining, George III, Mahogany, C.1750, Set Of 4	425.00 To 650.00
Furniture, Chair, Dining, Regency, Mahogany, Inlaid Satinwood, C.1850, 4	450.00
Furniture, Chair, Dining, Venetian, 18th Century Style, Painted, Gilt, 6	300.00
Furniture, Chair, Empire, Curly Maple, Saber Leg, Set Of 6	300.00
Furniture, Chair, Federal, Painted, Decorated, C.1820, 4	*Illus* 225.00
Furniture, Chair, Folding, Carpet Back & Seat	26.50
Furniture, Chair, Folding, Green, Velvet, Signed Hunzinger, Dated 1868	125.00
Furniture, Chair, Half Arrow Back, Plank Seat, Pillow Top Rail, 5	175.00
Furniture, Chair, Hand Carved, 19th Century	40.00
Furniture, Chair, High, Gray Paint	19.00
Furniture, Chair, High, Oak	18.00
Furniture, Chair, Hitchcock, C.1840	65.00
Furniture, Chair, Hitchcock, Half Spindle, Plank Seat, Beveled Ears, 6	90.00

Furniture, Chair, Federal, Painted, Decorated, C.1820, 4
See Page 196

Furniture, Chair,
Corner, Oak, 18th Century
See Page 196

Furniture, Chair, Hitchcock, Rush Seat, Pair 100.00
Furniture, Chair, Hitchcock, Stenciled Decoration, 3 .... 82.00
Furniture, Chair, Hitchcock, Stenciled, Connecticut, C.1845, Pair 175.00
Furniture, Chair, Hitchcock, Wood Seat, Fruit Stenciling, 4 .... 180.00
Furniture, Chair, Hitchcock, Wood Seat, Pillow Back, Arms, Pair 140.00
Furniture, Chair, Ice Cream, Child's 20.00
Furniture, Chair, Ladder Back, George III, Mahogany, 18th Century, Set Of 6 .... 1200.00
Furniture, Chair, Ladder Back, Scroll, Rush Seat, 6 .... 1020.00
Furniture, Chair, Ladder Back, 3 Slats, Rush Seat 35.00
Furniture, Chair, Lady's, Walnut, Finial At Top In Back 79.50
Furniture, Chair, Lady's, Walnut, Rose Carved 79.50
Furniture, Chair, Low, Rush Seat With High Back 22.50
Furniture, Chair, Lyre Shaped Back, Mahogany, 19th Century, Set Of 6 .... 2100.00
Furniture, Chair, Mahogany, C.1775, Set Of 6 .... *Illus* 2000.00
Furniture, Chair, Mahogany, Phila., C.1760 .... *Illus* 2700.00
Furniture, Chair, Maple Inlay In Back, Cabriole Legs, Covered Seat 22.00
Furniture, Chair, Maple, Cane Seat 11.50
Furniture, Chair, New Hampshire, Wing, Green Velvet, C.1790 .... 1450.00
Furniture, Chair, Oak, Cane Back & Seat 22.00
Furniture, Chair, Oak, Covered Seat, Carving On Back 16.50
Furniture, Chair, Oak, Turned Spindles, Square Legs, 18th Century, 4 .... 60.00
Furniture, Chair, Pillow Back, Painted, Stencil, Paper Rush Seat, 6 .... 120.00
Furniture, Chair, Pine, Rush Seat, Painted Black 11.50
Furniture, Chair, Pine, Stained Walnut, Rattan Seat 11.50
Furniture, Chair, Plank Seat, Arrow Back, 2 .... 35.00
Furniture, Chair, Plank Seat, Half Back, Green Finish, Yellow, Floral, 6 .... 250.00
Furniture, Chair, Potty, Rocking, Child's, Mahogany, Shaped Sides & Skirt 65.00
Furniture, Chair, Potty, Spindle Back, Half Arrow 70.00
Furniture, Chair, Potty, Windsor, Comb Back, Black Paint 55.00
Furniture, Chair, Prayer, Green Velvet, Brass Name Plate At Top 37.50
Furniture, Chair, Queen Anne Chippendale, Cherry, C.1755 .... *Illus* 400.00
Furniture, Chair, Queen Anne, Country, American, Spanish Feet .... 50.00 To 30.00
Furniture, Chair, Queen Anne, Mahogany, English, Carved Knees, Duck Feet 200.00
Furniture, Chair, Roundabout, Walnut, Massachusetts, 1770 .... 900.00
Furniture, Chair, Shaker, Rock Maple, Ladder Back, Cane Seat 125.00
Furniture, Chair, Side, Arrow Back, Painted Green, Stenciled, Plant Seat, 6 .... 770.00
Furniture, Chair, Side, Arrow Back, Saddle Seat, Arrow Stretcher 35.00
Furniture, Chair, Side, Arrow Back, Wood Seat 20.00
Furniture, Chair, Side, Banister Back, Black Paint, Paper Rush Seat 85.00
Furniture, Chair, Side, Chippendale, American, Country, Rush Seat 40.00

Furniture, Chair, Mahogany,
C.1775, Set Of 6
See Page 197

Furniture, Chair, Mahogany,
Phila., C.1760
See Page 197

Furniture, Chair, Queen Anne Chippendale,
Cherry, C.1755
See Page 197

Furniture, Chair, Side, Chippendale, Cedar, Country	50.00
Furniture, Chair, Side, Chippendale, Cherry, Connecticut, C.1760, Pair	800.00
Furniture, Chair, Side, Chippendale, Cherry, Connecticut, C.1780, Crest Rail	425.00
Furniture, Chair, Side, Chippendale, English, 18th Century, Slip Seat	55.00
Furniture, Chair, Side, Chippendale, Mahogany, American, 18th Century, Pair	350.00
Furniture, Chair, Side, Chippendale, Mahogany, Carved Cupid's Bow, C.1750	200.00
Furniture, Chair, Side, Chippendale, Mahogany, Carved, Mass., C.1760	550.00
Furniture, Chair, Side, Chippendale, Mahogany, Carved, Penna., C.1760	2700.00
Furniture, Chair, Side, Chippendale, Mahogany, Carved, Phila., C.1760, Pair	4500.00
Furniture, Chair, Side, Chippendale, Mahogany, Carved, Phila., 176	450.00 To 4000.00
Furniture, Chair, Side, Chippendale, Mahogany, Carved, Quincy Family, C.1760, 3	4750.00
Furniture, Chair, Side, Chippendale, Mahogany, Carved, R.I., C.1760, Pair	6000.00
Furniture, Chair, Side, Chippendale, Mahogany, Carved, Rhode Island, C.1760	2500.00
Furniture, Chair, Side, Chippendale, Mahogany, New England, C.1760	275.00
Furniture, Chair, Side, Chippendale, Mahogany, Pennsylvania, C.1790, Pair	500.00
Furniture, Chair, Side, Chippendale, Mahogany, Philadelphia, C.1760-80	1600.00
Furniture, Chair, Side, Chippendale, Mahogany, Philadelphia, C.1760, Pair	2200.00
Furniture, Chair, Side, Chippendale, Mahogany, Philadelphia, C.1790, Pair	1000.00
Furniture, Chair, Side, Chippendale, Mahogany, Pierced Back, Red Chinoiserie	150.00
Furniture, Chair, Side, Chippendale, Mahogany, Rhode Island, C.1760	800.00
Furniture, Chair, Side, Chippendale, Mahogany, Serpentine Rail, Mass., 1760, 4	2500.00
Furniture, Chair, Side, Chippendale, Open Vase Splat, Pair	140.00
Furniture, Chair, Side, Chippendale, Ribbonback, Square Tapering Legs	80.00
Furniture, Chair, Side, Chippendale, Square Legs, Upholstered	175.00
Furniture, Chair, Side, Chippendale, Walnut, Philadelphia, 18th Century, Pair	600.00
Furniture, Chair, Side, Chippendale, 18th Century	175.00

Furniture, Chair, Side, Duncan Phyfe, Mahogany, Slat Back, Pair 300.00
Furniture, Chair, Side, Empire, Curly Maple, Slat Back, Pair 180.00
Furniture, Chair, Side, English, 3 Slat Back, Wood Seat, Square Legs, 5 .... 75.00
Furniture, Chair, Side, Federal, Inlaid Mahogany, Mass., C.1790, Pair 575.00
Furniture, Chair, Side, Federal, Inlaid Mahogany, Shield Back, Mass., C.1790, 4 .... 1600.00
Furniture, Chair, Side, Federal, Mahogany, Black Leather, Mass., C.1810 .... 600.00
Furniture, Chair, Side, Federal, Mahogany, Carved, N.Y., 1810, Pair .... 275.00 To 300.00
Furniture, Chair, Side, Federal, Mahogany, Carved, New York, C.1815, Cane Seat 1800.00
Furniture, Chair, Side, Federal, Mahogany, Carved, Philadelphia, C.1785 .... 1200.00
Furniture, Chair, Side, Federal, Mahogany, Carved, Philadelphia, C.1790 .... 300.00
Furniture, Chair, Side, Federal, Mahogany, Carved, Rhode Island, C.1790, 5 .... 2000.00
Furniture, Chair, Side, Federal, Mahogany, Carved, Stephen Badlam, Mass., 1790 .... 5000.00
Furniture, Chair, Side, Federal, Painted & Decorated, New York, C.1810, Pair 1800.00
Furniture, Chair, Side, Flemish, Walnut, Bobbin Turned Legs, C.1650, 8 .... 1300.00
Furniture, Chair, Side, George I Style, Carved Front Rail In Shell Motif 90.00
Furniture, Chair, Side, George III, Mahogany, Cut Velvet Cover, 18th Century 130.00
Furniture, Chair, Side, George III, Mahogany, Floral Silk Cover, 18th Century 80.00
Furniture, Chair, Side, George III, Mahogany, Shield Shape Back, C.1750, 6 .... 1300.00
Furniture, Chair, Side, George III, Mahogany, Shield Shape Back, 18th Century 300.00
Furniture, Chair, Side, George III, Mahogany, 18th Century, Serpentine Rail, 5 .... 900.00
Furniture, Chair, Side, George III, Mahogany, 18th Century, Set Of 5 .... 500.00
Furniture, Chair, Side, Hepplewhite, Cherry, Carved, American, C.1790 .... 200.00
Furniture, Chair, Side, Hepplewhite, Mahogany, Carved, Philadelphia, C.1790 .... 175.00
Furniture, Chair, Side, Hepplewhite, Mahogany, Rhode Island, C.1790, Carved 225.00
Furniture, Chair, Side, Louis XV, Walnut, Hand Carved, 19th Century, Pair 300.00
Furniture, Chair, Side, Louis XVI, Style, Dark Brown Velvet, 8 .... 1400.00
Furniture, Chair, Side, Louis XVI Style, Painted Cream, Caned Back, 6 .... 700.00
Furniture, Chair, Side, Maple, Banister Back 50.00
Furniture, Chair, Side, Maple, Bootjack, Signed 'edwards, '6 .... 210.00
Furniture, Chair, Side, Oak, English, Duck Feet, Rush Seat, Spindle Back 35.00
Furniture, Chair, Side, Pa., 19th Century, Set Of 6 .... *Illus* 425.00

Furniture, Chair, Side, Pa., 19th Century, Set Of 6

Furniture, Chair, Side, Painted & Decorated, Pennsylvania, 19th Century, 6 .... 425.00
Furniture, Chair, Side, Painted, Decorated, Crest Rail, New England, C.1815, 4 .... 150.00
Furniture, Chair, Side, Pennsylvania, Birdcage, Brown Paint, Stenciled, 6 .... 120.00
Furniture, Chair, Side, Queen Anne, Black Japanned, 18th Century, 8 .... 1800.00
Furniture, Chair, Side, Queen Anne, Cherry, Carved Crest, N.Y., C.1700, Pair 800.00
Furniture, Chair, Side, Queen Anne, Cherry, Connecticut, Balloon Seat, Pair 2500.00
Furniture, Chair, Side, Queen Anne, Cherry, Rhode Island, C.1740, Spoon Back 1400.00
Furniture, Chair, Side, Queen Anne, Cherry, William Ellery, R.I., C.1750 .... 2250.00
Furniture, Chair, Side, Queen Anne, English, Oak, Duck Feet With Pads 75.00
Furniture, Chair, Side, Queen Anne, Japanned Side, Vase Decorated Splat, Pair 250.00

Furniture, Chair, Side, Queen Anne, Mahogany, 18th Century 400.00
Furniture, Chair, Side, Queen Anne, Maple, Rush Seat, New England, C.1740, 4 .... 550.00
Furniture, Chair, Side, Queen Anne, Walnut, Rhode Island, C.1740 .... 2750.00
Furniture, Chair, Side, Queen Anne, Walnut, Spoon Back, Penna., C.1740 .... 2500.00
Furniture, Chair, Side, Rosewood, Balloon Back 35.00
Furniture, Chair, Side, Sheraton, Bamboo Turned, Rush Seat, Black Paint, 6 .... 150.00
Furniture, Chair, Side, Sheraton, Curly Maple, Ring Turnings, Splayed Legs 42.50
Furniture, Chair, Side, Sheraton, Red & Black Paint, Stencil, Pillow Back 30.00
Furniture, Chair, Side, Sheraton, Satinwood, Painted, C.1790, 3 .... 300.00
Furniture, Chair, Side, Sheraton, Tiger Maple, Rush Seat 140.00
Furniture, Chair, Side, Slat Back, Upholstered Seat 22.50
Furniture, Chair, Side, Spindle Back, Rush Seat, Black Paint, Pair 35.00
Furniture, Chair, Side, Victorian, Mahogany, Carved, American, C.1840, Pair 175.00
Furniture, Chair, Side, William & Mary, Carved, Painted, Caned, R.I., C.1685 .... 600.00
Furniture, Chair, Side, William & Mary, Maple, Turned, Conn., C.1720, Pair 275.00
Furniture, Chair, Side, William & Mary, Maple, Turned, Rush Seat, Conn., 1710, 3 .... 675.00
Furniture, Chair, Splint Seat, Serpentine Slat Back, Chippendale 195.00
Furniture, Chair, Teakwood, Embossed With Mother-Of-Pearl, Marble Seat, Silk 500.00
Furniture, Chair, Victorian, Curly Maple, Cane Seat 75.00
Furniture, Chair, Victorian, Rosewood, Slipper, Carved, Belter, C.1850, Pair 1100.00
Furniture, Chair, Victorian, Upholstered, Lion Head Under Arm 95.00
Furniture, Chair, Victorian, Walnut, Lady's, Open, Finger Carved Arms 90.00
Furniture, Chair, Walnut, Double Brace Between Legs 22.00
Furniture, Chair, Walnut, Rose Carved 24.50
Furniture, Chair, Windsor, Bamboo Turned, Chicken Coop Back, Black Paint 100.00
Furniture, Chair, Windsor, Bamboo Turned, Saddle Seat, 17th Century, Pair 149.00
Furniture, Chair, Windsor, Bamboo Turnings 85.00
Furniture, Chair, Windsor, Bent Back, Saddle Seat, Pair 100.00
Furniture, Chair, Windsor, Bent Back, Step Down, Bamboo Turned Legs, 4 .... 240.00
Furniture, Chair, Windsor, Birdcage 45.00
Furniture, Chair, Windsor, Birdcage With Duck's Bill, Black, Stencil, 6 .... 1500.00
Furniture, Chair, Windsor, Bow Back, Curved Stretcher, 8 Spindle 925.00
Furniture, Chair, Windsor, Butterfly, Bamboo Turned, Painted Green, Pair 140.00
Furniture, Chair, Windsor, Butterfly, Bamboo Turnings, 6 .... 420.00
Furniture, Chair, Windsor, Butterfly, Pair 200.00
Furniture, Chair, Windsor, Child's, Butterfly 90.00
Furniture, Chair, Windsor, Desk, Yellow Paint, Stencil 89.00
Furniture, Chair, Windsor, Fanback, American, 18th Century, 2 .... 325.00
Furniture, Chair, Windsor, Fanback, Bamboo Turnings 100.0
Furniture, Chair, Windsor, Fanback, Pennsylvania, 18th Century, Painted 250.00
Furniture, Chair, Windsor, Fanback, Slant Arms, Cane Seat, Pair 70.00
Furniture, Chair, Windsor, Hoop Back, New England, 18th Century, 2 .... 200.00
Furniture, Chair, Windsor, Joseph Hensey, Phila. 175.00
Furniture, Chair, Windsor, New England, C.1790, Fanback 50.00
Furniture, Chair, Windsor, New England, 18th Century, Fanback 50.00
Furniture, Chair, Windsor, Pistol Grip Arms, Stretcher Base 375.00
Furniture, Chair, Windsor, Saddle Seat, New England, C.1750, 2 .... 150.00
Furniture, Chair, Windsor, Step Down, Bamboo Turnings 60.00
Furniture, Chair, Windsor, Step Down, Bamboo Turnings, Black Paint 45.00
Furniture, Chair, Wing, American Queen Anne, Mahogany 1950.00
Furniture, Chair, Youth, Pine, Wooden Seat, Red Stain, Slat Back, Pair 30.00
Furniture, Chaise Longue, Louis XV, Walnut, Carved, Shell Motif, C.1750 .... 500.00
Furniture, Chaise Longue, Recamier, Rose Upholstered, Cushion 100.00
Furniture, Chest, Apothecary, Mahogany, 13 1/2 X 16 1/4 X 12 In. 148.00
Furniture, Chest, Apothecary, Maple, Twelve Drawers, Oval Loop Brasses 230.00
Furniture, Chest, Apothecary, Soft Wood, 16 Drawers, Bracket Feet 200.00
Furniture, Chest, Apothecary, 14 Drawers, White Porcelain Knobs 200.00
Furniture, Chest, Apothecary, 16 Drawers 260.00
Furniture, Chest, Art Nouveau, Inlaid Mahogany, Leaves & Buds 50.00
Furniture, Chest, Art Nouveau, Inlaid Mahogany, 5 Drawers 150.00
Furniture, Chest, Bachelor's, Walnut, 7 Drawers, 50 In.High 70.00
Furniture, Chest, Birch, New England, 42 In.Long 325.00
Furniture, Chest, Bird's-Eye Maple & Cherry, C.1820 .... 245.00
Furniture, Chest, Blanket, Cherry, Bracket Foot, 32 X 17 X 22 In. 80.00
Furniture, Chest, Blanket, Cherry, Drawer In Bottom 77.00
Furniture, Chest, Blanket, Cherry, Lift Lid, Cut Bracket Foot, 2 Drawers 80.00

Furniture, Chest, Chippendale, Walnut, Pennsylvania, C.1760 .... 275.00 To 300.00
Furniture, Chest, Blanket, Chippendale, Walnut, Thumb Molded, Penna., C.1770 .... 325.00
Furniture, Chest, Blanket, Curly Maple, Lift Top, 2 Drawer, 18 X 37 X 38 In. 350.00
Furniture, Chest, Blanket, New England, Red Ground, Black Graining 110.00
Furniture, Chest, Blanket, Painted Decoration, Jars Of Flowers On Panels 550.00
Furniture, Chest, Blanket, Penna.Dutch, Dovetail, Pine, 26 X 14 X 16 In. 100.00
Furniture, Chest, Blanket, Pennsylvania Dutch, Dovetailed, Stippled, Pine 100.00
Furniture, Chest, Blanket, Pennsylvania, Dovetailed, Red & Yellow Decoration 170.00
Furniture, Chest, Blanket, Pennsylvania, Ephrata Fraktur On Lid Dated 1803 .... 1350.00
Furniture, Chest, Blanket, Pennsylvania, Miniature, Painted, Webber, C.1851 .... 1400.00
Furniture, Chest, Blanket, Pennsylvania, Painted, Brown & Yellow Graining 75.00
Furniture, Chest, Blanket, Pine, Bracket Foot, 41 X 17 X 21 In. 110.00
Furniture, Chest, Blanket, Pine, Dovetail Sides, Breadboard Top, 42 In.Long 90.00
Furniture, Chest, Blanket, Pine, Green Paint, 44 X 20 X 23 In. 90.00
Furniture, Chest, Blanket, Pine, Painted, Pennsylvania, C.1790, Hinged Top 300.00
Furniture, Chest, Blanket, Pine, Pennsylvania Dutch, Stippled 100.00
Furniture, Chest, Blanket, Pine, Two Drawer, Two False Drawers 200.00
Furniture, Chest, Blanket, Queen Anne, Three Drawer, Red 195.00
Furniture, Chest, Blanket, 2 Drawer, Sunburst Painted, Mustard Graining, Red 800.00
Furniture, Chest, Bowfront, George Iii, Mahogany, Satinwood, 19th Century 600.00
Furniture, Chest, Bowfront, George Iii, Mahogany, 5 Drawer, 19th Century 325.00
Furniture, Chest, Bowfront, Four Drawers, Hepplewhite, Mahogany, New Brasses 650.00
Furniture, Chest, Camphorwood, Chinese Lock, Hand Carved, 8 In.Long 10.95
Furniture, Chest, Cherry, Inlaid, High, French Feet, 67 In.High 1150.00
Furniture, Chest, Cherry, Wicket Band Line Inlay Around Top 600.00
Furniture, Chest, Cherry, 4 Drawers, Chamfered Fluted Corners 750.00
Furniture, Chest, Cherry, 4 Drawers, Eagle Pulls, Splay Feet 450.00
Furniture, Chest, Child's, Cedar, 17 X 9 X 8 In. 20.00
Furniture, Chest, Child's, 3 Drawers, Tin Pulls, 5 1/4 X 4 1/2 In. 13.50
Furniture, Chest, Chippendale, Cherry, Serpentine, Conn., C.1760 .... 1600.00
Furniture, Chest, Chippendale, Curly Maple, Connecticut, C.1760 .... 1800.00
Furniture, Chest, Chippendale, Mahogany, Bowfront, Ogee Feet 1700.00
Furniture, Chest, Chippendale, Mahogany, Phila., C.1760, 43 In. 3500.00
Furniture, Chest, Chippendale, Mahogany, Philadelphia, Ogee Feet 4500.00
Furniture, Chest, Chippendale, Mahogany, Thumb Molded, Pa., C.1760 .... 1800.00
Furniture, Chest, Chippendale, Maple, Mahogany Feet, Mass. 1160.00
Furniture, Chest, Chippendale, Maple, New Hampshire, 18th Century 800.00
Furniture, Chest, Chippendale, Molded Mahogany Top, 4 Drawers, C.1770 .... 1300.00
Furniture, Chest, Chippendale, Pennsylvania, 40 X 20 X 21 In. 600.00
Furniture, Chest, Chippendale, Sunburst Carving, 9 Drawers, 18th Century 1100.00
Furniture, Chest, Chippendale, Tall, 5 Drawers, Conn., C.1760 .... 600.00
Furniture, Chest, Chippendale, Walnut Veneer, New England, C.1750 .... 4800.00
Furniture, Chest, Chippendale, Walnut, Pennsylvania, C.1760 .... 2000.00
Furniture, Chest, Chippendale, Walnut, Pennsylvania, C.1775 .... 470.00
Furniture, Chest, Chippendale, Walnut, Pennsylvania, 18th Century 525.00
Furniture, Chest, Chippendale, Walnut, Tall, Pennsylvania, C.1780 .... 650.00
Furniture, Chest, Country, Red Paint, 2 Overlapping Drawers 205.00
Furniture, Chest, Decorated, 1811 .... 175.00
Furniture, Chest, Dower, Pennsylvania, Red & Black Dovetailed Bracket Feet 120.00
Furniture, Chest, Empire, Cherry, Maple, 1820 .... *Illus* 475.00
Furniture, Chest, Empire, Tiger Maple, 4 Drawers, Walnut Mushroom Pulls 350.00
Furniture, Chest, Federal, Curly Walnut, Tall, Penna., C.1790 .... 1100.00
Furniture, Chest, Federal, Inlaid Mahogany, Bowfront, Conn., 1800 .... 1400.00
Furniture, Chest, Federal, Inlaid Mahogany, New England, C.1810 .... 300.00
Furniture, Chest, Federal, Inlaid Mahogany, Penna., C.1790 .... 575.00
Furniture, Chest, Federal, Inlaid Mahogany, Serpentine, Pa., 1790 .... 2500.00
Furniture, Chest, Federal, Inlaid Mahogany, Tall, American, C.1820 .... 225.00
Furniture, Chest, Federal, Mahogany, Bowfront, Penna., C.1850 .... 600.00
Furniture, Chest, Federal, Mahogany, New England, C.1820 .... 200.00
Furniture, Chest, Federal, Mahogany, Serpentine, Conn., C.1790 .... 700.00
Furniture, Chest, Federal, Mahogany, Tall, Pennsylvania, C.1800 .... 650.00
Furniture, Chest, George Ii, Burr Elmwood, Rectangular Top, 1750 .... 1400.00
Furniture, Chest, George Ii, Walnut & Elmwood, 18th Century 900.00
Furniture, Chest, George Iii, Mahogany, Bowfront, Fruitwood Edge 475.00
Furniture, Chest, George Iii, Mahogany, 4 Drawer, 18th Century 950.00
Furniture, Chest, George Iii, Mahogany, 1850 .... *Illus* 1400.00

Furniture, Chest, George III, Mahogany, 1850
See Page 201

Furniture, Chest, Empire, Cherry, Maple, 1820
See Page 201

Furniture, Chest, Hepplewhite, Birch Case, N.H., C.1800	1600.00
Furniture, Chest, Hepplewhite, Cherry Case, Curly Maple Drawers, Penna.	1350.00
Furniture, Chest, Hepplewhite, Cherry, New England, C.1790	500.00
Furniture, Chest, Hepplewhite, Cherry, Pennsylvania, C.1790	450.00
Furniture, Chest, Hepplewhite, Cherry, Tall, Pennsylvania, C.1800	650.00
Furniture, Chest, Hepplewhite, Cherry, 4 Drawer, Banding On Apron	415.00
Furniture, Chest, Hepplewhite, Cherrywood, Philadelphia, C.1780	700.00
Furniture, Chest, Hepplewhite, Inlaid Walnut, Penna., C.1800	300.00
Furniture, Chest, Hepplewhite, Inlaid Walnut, Tall, Penna., C.1790	950.00
Furniture, Chest, Hepplewhite, Mahogany & Bird's-Eye Maple, Conn., C.1790	575.00
Furniture, Chest, Hepplewhite, Pine, American, 5 Drawers	250.00
Furniture, Chest, Hepplewhite, Walnut, Pennsylvania, C.1800	400.00
Furniture, Chest, Jewelry, Curly Maple, French Bracket Foot, 8 Drawers	175.00
Furniture, Chest, Lift Top, European, Carved Paw Feet, 17th Century	200.00
Furniture, Chest, Lift Top, 17th Century, 23 X 31 In.	105.00
Furniture, Chest, Mahogany, Divided Top Drawer, 3 Overlapping Drawers	425.00
Furniture, Chest, Mahogany, Lift Lid, Inlaid Top, Brass Cupid Handles	300.00
Furniture, Chest, Mahogany, Miniature, 5 Drawers, Pine Secondary	150.00
Furniture, Chest, Mahogany, Oxbow Front, 4 Drawer, 40 X 20 X 35 In.	275.00
Furniture, Chest, Mahogany, Philadelphia, Carved, C.1760-70	3500.00
Furniture, Chest, Mahogany, R.I., C.1760	*Illus* 4750.00
Furniture, Chest, Mahogany, Swell Front, Five Drawers, Splay Feet	400.00
Furniture, Chest, Mahogany, 7 Drawers, 58 In.High	110.00
Furniture, Chest, Maple, Bracket Foot, Four Drawers, Escutcheon Brasses	225.00
Furniture, Chest, Medicine, Mahogany, C.1750	95.00
Furniture, Chest, Miniature, 4 Drawers, 10 1/2 In.High	45.00
Furniture, Chest, Near East, Mother-Of-Pearl	*Illus* 575.00
Furniture, Chest, New England, Pine, Solid End, 4 Drawers, 37 In.High	125.00
Furniture, Chest, Oak, Miniature, 3 Drawers, 19 In.High	45.00
Furniture, Chest, Pennsylvania, Cherry, Ogee Feet, Cock Beaded Drawers	800.00
Furniture, Chest, Pine, Country, 4 Drawers, Bracket Feet	55.00
Furniture, Chest, Pine, Miniature, 20 1/2 X 13 In.	165.00
Furniture, Chest, Pine, Paneled, Guilford, Connecticut, 17th Century	3300.00
Furniture, Chest, Pine, 3 Drawers, Brass Loop Pulls, 28 X 15 X 28 In.	90.00
Furniture, Chest, Pine, 3 Large & 2 Small Drawers	175.00
Furniture, Chest, Pine, 4 Cock Beaded Drawers, 36 In.High	230.00
Furniture, Chest, Pine, 4 Drawer, Plank End, Graduated Drawers, C.1830	335.00
Furniture, Chest, Pine, 4 Drawers, 1/2 Turned Pilasters, Dovetailed	80.00

Furniture, Chest, Pine, 6 Drawers, 14 X 13 X 24 In. 90.00
Furniture, Chest, Queen Anne, Cherry, Tall, New England, C.1720 .... 1300.00
Furniture, Chest, Rod Lock, 2 Drawers, 20 X 11 X 11 In. 45.00
Furniture, Chest, Sheraton, Cherry, 4 Drawers, 39 1/2 X 43 1/2 In. 140.00
Furniture, Chest, Sheraton, Cherry, 6 Drawers, Carved Top Post 175.00
Furniture, Chest, Sheraton, Curly Maple, High, Inlaid Mahogany Veneer 160.00
Furniture, Chest, Sheraton, Walnut, Reeded Top Edge & Posts, Turned Legs 225.00
Furniture, Chest, Spanish, Pine, Painted, Carved, C.1650 .... *Illus* 600.00
Furniture, Chest, Spice, Nine Drawers, Handle At Top, Pine, 8 X 11 In. 59.00
Furniture, Chest, Spice, Oak, 7 Drawer, 10 In.High 65.00
Furniture, Chest, Spice, Pine, 10 Drawers, Ring Feet, Dovetailed Case 70.00
Furniture, Chest, Spice, Queen Anne, Pennsylvania, C.1760, Ogee Feet 7000.00
Furniture, Chest, Spirit, Continental, Oak, 18th Century, Iron Mounts 225.00
Furniture, Chest, Spool, Oak, Three Drawer, 21 X 16 In., 9 In.Tall 60.00
Furniture, Chest, Tea, Chinese, Handmade, 3 Lift-Out Compartments 43.50
Furniture, Chest, Tool, 22 X 11 1/2 X 9 1/2 In. 20.00
Furniture, Chest, Victorian, Walnut, Carved Wood Drawer Pulls 145.00
Furniture, Chest, Victorian, Walnut, 6 Drawers, Patented Hinge Side Lock 375.00
Furniture, Chest, Walnut, Pennsylvania, High, Overlapping Drawers, Ogee Feet 1200.00
Furniture, Chest, Walnut, Solid End, 3 Drawers, 2 Handkerchief Drawers 75.00
Furniture, Chest, Wellington, George IV, Mahogany, 19th Century, Rectangular 525.00
Furniture, Chest, William & Mary, Pennsylvania, C.1720 .... 1700.00

Furniture, Chest, Mahogany, R.I., C.1760
See Page 202

Furniture, Chest, Near East,
Mother-Of-Pearl
See Page 202

Furniture, Chest, Spanish, Pine,
Painted, Carved, C.1650

Furniture, Chest, William & Mary, Walnut, Geometric, 4 Drawer, 17th Century 250.00
Furniture, Chest-On-Chest, Chippendale, Mahogany, Carved, Phila., C.1760 .... 6250.00
Furniture, Chest-On-Chest, Chippendale, Mahogany, Maryland, C.1760 .... 1800.00
Furniture, Chest-On-Chest, Chippendale, Walnut, Carved, Philadelphia, C.1760 .... 8250.00
Furniture, Chest-On-Chest, Chippendale, Walnut, Philadelphia, C.1760 .... 3500.00
Furniture, Chest-On-Chest, Curly Maple, Bonnet Top, Bracket Feet 700.00
Furniture, Chest-On-Chest, English, Mahogany, C.1780, Chinese Hardware 1750.00
Furniture, Chest-On-Chest, George III, Mahogany, 18th Century, 6 Ft.Tall 1300.00
Furniture, Chest On Frame, Pine, New England, 18th Century, 5 Drawers 1400.00
Furniture, Chiffonnier, Louis XV-XVI, Kingwood, Ormolu, C.1780 .... 1700.00
Furniture, Chiffonnier, Louis XVI, Kingwood, Rectangular, 18th Century 450.00
Furniture, Closet, China, Quarter Oak, Plate Glass Mirror Back, Hand-Carved 600.00
Furniture, Commode, Bedside, Victorian, Walnut, Circular, Lift Top, C.1850 .... 20.00
Furniture, Commode, George III, Mahogany, Satinwood Inlay, 18th Century 3800.00
Furniture, Commode, George III, Satinwood & Rosewood, D Shape Top, C.1750 .... 1500.00
Furniture, Commode, Louis XV Provincial, Walnut, Liege .... *Illus* 2400.00
Furniture, Commode, Louis XV Style, Kingwood, Petite, Ormolu Rimmed Top 400.00
Furniture, Commode, Louis XV-XVI Style, Marquetry, Mercier Freres, C.1850 .... 1300.00
Furniture, Commode, Louis XV, Kingwood, C.Revault, C.1750 .... *Illus* 7250.00
Furniture, Commode, Louis XVI, Inlaid Kingwood, D Shape, Signed Lardin, 1750 .... 3000.00
Furniture, Commode, Louis XVI, Mahogany, Signed P.Garn, Jme, C.1780 .... 1200.00
Furniture, Commode, North Italian, Walnut, 18th Century .... *Illus* 1500.00
Furniture, Commode, Petite, Louis XV-XVI, Kingwood, Signed A.Hericourt, 1750 .... 2500.00
Furniture, Commode, Petite, Louis XV-XVI, Provincial, Walnut, Marble, C.1750 .... 425.00
Furniture, Console, Chippendale, Chinese, England, 19th Century, Sideboard 1300.00
Furniture, Console, Hepplewhite Style, Inlaid Walnut, Demilune, Pair 250.00
Furniture, Console, Louis XV Style, Carved Gilt Wood, Marble Top, Pair 300.00
Furniture, Console, Louis XV, Provincial, Oak, Carved, Corner, C.1750, Pair 400.00
Furniture, Console, Petit, Louis XVI, Carved Gilt Wood, D Shape, C.1750, Pair 3100.00
Furniture, Couch, Queen Anne, Country 495.00
Furniture, Counter, Side, Walnut, Double, 2 Drawers, 2 Doors 120.00
Furniture, Cradle & Doll, Wooden 59.00
Furniture, Cradle, Boat Shape, Wheels, Handle, Red Paint, Dated 10/17/76 .... 250.00
Furniture, Cradle, Doll's, Heart Cut Out On Headboard & Footboard 35.00
Furniture, Cradle, Doll's, Pine 65.00
Furniture, Cradle, Pennsylvania Dutch, C.1800 .... 150.00
Furniture, Cradle, Pine, Cheese Cutter Rockers, 4 Posters 225.00
Furniture, Cradle, Pine, Original Finish 125.00
Furniture, Cradle, Pine, Painted, Pennsylvania, 18th Century, Arched Panels 300.00
Furniture, Cradle, Pine, 14 X 23 In. 69.50
Furniture, Cradle, Pine, 31 X 19 X 19 In. 32.00
Furniture, Cradle, Pine, 33 X 20 X 19 In. 32.00
Furniture, Cradle, Queen Anne, Walnut, Shaped Hood, Penna., C.1750 .... 180.00
Furniture, Cradle, Rocking, Blue Paint 45.00
Furniture, Cradle, Wicker, White, 45 In.Long, Spider Caned, Swings 150.00
Furniture, Cradle, Windup 52.00
Furniture, Cupboard, Cherry, Corner, Brass 300.00
Furniture, Cupboard, Child's, Pine, Porcelain Pulls, 24 In.High 70.00
Furniture, Cupboard, Child's, Spiral Turned Columns, Ogee Feet 200.00
Furniture, Cupboard, China, Pennsylvania Dutch, Glass, Red Stain, C.1800 .... 450.00
Furniture, Cupboard, Corner, Cherry & Mahogany, Double Glass Door 750.00
Furniture, Cupboard, Corner, Cherry, 12 Pane Door, Bracket Feet 425.00
Furniture, Cupboard, Corner, Cherry, 12 Panes In Top Door, Ogee Molding 750.00
Furniture, Cupboard, Corner, Chippendale, Curly Maple, Pennsylvania, C.1760 .... 3500.00
Furniture, Cupboard, Corner, Chippendale, Curly Maple, Pennsylvania, C.1780 .... 1200.00
Furniture, Cupboard, Corner, Chippendale, Mahogany, Cathedral Door 950.00
Furniture, Cupboard, Corner, Curly Maple, Ogee Molding Top, 12 Pane Doors 1100.00
Furniture, Cupboard, Corner, Federal, Cherry, Pa., C.1810 .... *Illus* 500.00
Furniture, Cupboard, Corner, Federal, Cherrywood, Pennsylvania, C.1810-20 .... 500.00
Furniture, Cupboard, Corner, One Piece, Bowfront, One Paneled Door 165.00
Furniture, Cupboard, Corner, Pennsylvania, Brown, Grapes & Floral 1200.00
Furniture, Cupboard, Corner, Pennsylvania, Cherry, 7 Ft.10 In. High 1000.00
Furniture, Cupboard, Corner, Pennsylvania, One Piece, 41 X 25 X 77 In. 325.00
Furniture, Cupboard, Corner, Pine, C.1800, Glass 350.00
Furniture, Cupboard, Corner, Pine, 2 Piece, 18 Pane Doors, 6 Ft.11 In.High 900.00
Furniture, Cupboard, Curly Maple, One Piece, 8 Pane Doors, Ohio, Half Columns 350.00

Furniture, Commode, Louis XV Provincial,
Walnut, Liege
See Page 204

Furniture, Commode, Louis XV
Kingwood, C.Revault, C.1750
See Page 204

Furniture, Cupboard,
Corner, Federal,
Cherry, Pa., C.1810
See Page 204

Furniture, Commode, North Italian,
Walnut, 18th Century
See Page 204

Furniture, Cupboard, Dutch, Glass Doors, Spice Drawers, Walnut, 2 Piece 3100.00
Furniture, Cupboard, Dutch, Miniature, Two Glass Doors With 6 Panes 120.00
Furniture, Cupboard, Dutch, Pine, Open Shelf, 3 Drawers, Cabinet Base 125.00
Furniture, Cupboard, English Oak, Hanging, Corner, Raised Panel Door, 36 In. 60.00
Furniture, Cupboard, Floor, Waist High, Leaded Stained Glass Doors 2.00
Furniture, Cupboard, Hanging, Blue-Green Paint, Glass Door, 16 In.High 15.00

Furniture, **Cupboard**, Hanging, Walnut, Pennsylvania, C.1740, 34 In.High 1100.00
Furniture, **Cupboard**, Hanging, 6 Pane Door, Brown Paint, 30 X 31 In. 85.00
Furniture, **Cupboard**, Hutch, Doll's, Hickory, 18 X 22 In. 19.50
Furniture, **Cupboard**, Hutch, Pine .... 265.00 To 350.00
Furniture, **Cupboard**, Jelly, Pennsylvania Dutch, Walnut 130.00
Furniture, **Cupboard**, Oak, Roll Top, The Queen, Dated 1885, 4 Drawers 250.00
Furniture, **Cupboard**, Pennsylvania Dutch, Red Stain 275.00
Furniture, **Cupboard**, Pennsylvania Dutch, Walnut, China, Double Door 625.00
Furniture, **Cupboard**, Pennsylvania Dutch, 2 Paneled Doors, Cabinet Base 750.00
Furniture, **Cupboard**, Pennsylvania Dutch, 2 Section, Glass Doors, Ball Feet 1900.00
Furniture, **Cupboard**, Pennsylvania, Walnut, 2 Glass Doors With 9 Panes 1700.00
Furniture, **Cupboard**, Pewter, Maple & Pine, New England, C.1760 .... 575.00
Furniture, **Cupboard**, Pewter, Pine, Open, Shoe Feet, Brown Graining 275.00
Furniture, **Cupboard**, Pewter, Pine, Painted Red, Pennsylvania, C.1780 .... 600.00
Furniture, **Cupboard**, Pewter, Vermont, Red Paint, 6 Ft.6 1/2 In.High 900.00
Furniture, **Cupboard**, Pie, Tin, Punched, Red & Black, 9 Drawers 500.00
Furniture, **Cupboard**, Pine & Maple, Catherine Wheel, New England, C.1850 .... 475.00
Furniture, **Cupboard**, Pine, American, Corner, 6 Ft.7 1/2 In.X 32 In. 225.00
Furniture, **Cupboard**, Pine, Corner, 2 Arched Doors, Cabinet Base, Ogee Top 1100.00
Furniture, **Cupboard**, Pine, Hanging, Drawer At Bottom, Rope Cornice Molding 50.00
Furniture, **Cupboard**, Pine, Hanging, Paneled Door, 15 Drawers Inside 200.00
Furniture, **Cupboard**, Pine, Hanging, Red & Floral Decoration, Butterfly Hinge 200.00
Furniture, **Cupboard**, Pine, Hanging, Yellow Paint, Dovetailed Case 110.00
Furniture, **Cupboard**, Pine, Hanging, 2 Shelves, Plate Rail 100.00
Furniture, **Cupboard**, Pine, One Piece, Pie Shelf, Blind Door, Red Stain 155.00
Furniture, **Cupboard**, Pine, One Piece, Raised Panel Doors Above & Below 140.00
Furniture, **Cupboard**, Pine, 18th Century, Open, Architectural, Painted 2250.00
Furniture, **Cupboard**, Pine, 2 Piece, Stepped Ribbed Top Molding 350.00
Furniture, **Cupboard**, Pine, 2 Shelf, 26 In.Long 50.00
Furniture, **Cupboard**, Press, Chippendale, Walnut, Pennsylvania, C.1760 .... 2400.00
Furniture, **Cupboard**, Wall, Hanging, Lower Shelf, Red Stain, 25 X 36 In. 180.00
Furniture, **Cupboard**, Wall, One Piece, Cherry, Walnut Upper Doors & Frame 50.00
Furniture, **Cupboard**, Walnut & Ash, 2 Piece, Pie Shelf, Silver Drawers, 2 Door 150.00
Furniture, **Cupboard**, Walnut, Corner, Glass Doors, 2 Piece, 1 Drawer 165.00
Furniture, **Cupboard**, 2 Part, Arched Door At Top, Glass Panes, Ogee Feet 850.00
Furniture, **Cupbord**, Corner, Glass Door, Fluted, Carved, Footed 900.00
Furniture, **Daybed**, Child's, Pine 15.00
Furniture, **Desk & Seat**, School, Pine, Adjustable Writing Board 65.00
Furniture, **Desk**, Art Deco, Walnut, Fall Front, C.1930, Bookcase Top 200.00
Furniture, **Desk**, Birch, Mass., 1780, Serpentine Front, Fall Front 900.00
Furniture, **Desk**, Birch, New England, C.1780, Slant Lid, French Feet 475.00
Furniture, **Desk**, Block Front, Mahogany, Mass., C.1760 .... *Illus* 6500.00
Furniture, **Desk**, Butler's, Federal, Inlaid Mahogany, Oblong, Penna., C.1800 .... 275.00
Furniture, **Desk**, Cherry, American, 18th Century, Fall Front, Bracket Feet 1000.00
Furniture, **Desk**, Cherry, Crotch Mahogany Veneer Front, Slant Top 400.00
Furniture, **Desk**, Cherry, Lift Top 65.00
Furniture, **Desk**, Cherry, School Master's, Secretary Top, 6 Pane Doors 175.00
Furniture, **Desk**, Cherry, Slant Lid, 18th Century, 4 Graduated Drawers 1200.00
Furniture, **Desk**, Cherry, Slant Top, Ogee Feet, Reeded Quarter Columns 1000.00
Furniture, **Desk**, Child's, Lift Top 18.50
Furniture, **Desk**, Chippendale Style, Mahogany, 37 In.Wide, 44 In.Tall 275.00
Furniture, **Desk**, Chippendale, Cherry, Slant Front, New England, C.1780 .... 700.00
Furniture, **Desk**, Chippendale, Curly Maple, Pennsylvania, C.1760, Slant Front 1600.00
Furniture, **Desk**, Chippendale, Curly Maple, Slant Front, Hinged, Mass., C.1760 .... 2300.00
Furniture, **Desk**, Chippendale, Inlaid Mahogany, Miniature, Slant Front, C.1780 .... 500.00
Furniture, **Desk**, Chippendale, Mahogany, Benjamin Frothingham, C.1770 .... 900.00
Furniture, **Desk**, Chippendale, Mahogany, Block Front, Mass., C.1760 .... 3250.00
Furniture, **Desk**, Chippendale, Mahogany, Carved, Slant Front, R.I., C.1760 .... 3500.00
Furniture, **Desk**, Chippendale, Mahogany, Serpentine Front, Mass., C.1760 .... 2500.00
Furniture, **Desk**, Chippendale, Mahogany, Slant Front, New Hampshire, C.1760 .... 1000.00
Furniture, **Desk**, Chippendale, Santo Domingo Mahogany, Massachusetts, C.1760 .... 6500.00
Furniture, **Desk**, Chippendale, Slant Front, Rhode Island, C.1760, 43 In.High 5500.00
Furniture, **Desk**, Chippendale, Walnut, Serpentine Front, New England, C.1760 .... 2500.00
Furniture, **Desk**, Chippendale, Walnut, Slant Front, New England, C.1760 .... 1200.00
Furniture, **Desk**, Clerk's, Pine, 1 Drawer, Pigeonholes, Dovetailed 275.00
Furniture, **Desk**, Counting, Federal, Inlaid Mahogany, Baltimore, C.1790 .... 1000.00

Furniture, Desk, Block Front,
Mahogany, Mass., C.1760
See Page 206

Furniture, Desk, Federal,
Curly Maple, Pa., 19th Century

Furniture, Desk, Knee Hole, England, 18th Century

Furniture, Desk,
Mahogany, Salem, Mass., C.1740

Furniture, Desk, Empire, French, Marble Top, Drop Front	250.00
Furniture, Desk, Empire, Lady's, French, Brass Molding On 2 Drawers, Marble	130.00
Furniture, Desk, Federal, Curly Maple, Pa., 19th Century *Illus*	900.00
Furniture, Desk, Federal, Curly Maple, Slant Front, Pennsylvania, C.1850	400.00
Furniture, Desk, Federal, Inlaid Burl Maple & Mahogany, Boston, C.1790	1800.00
Furniture, Desk, Federal, Inlaid Mahogany, Slant Front, Pennsylvania, C.1790	950.00
Furniture, Desk, Federal, Inlaid Mahogany, 2 Parts, Boston, C.1790	1000.00
Furniture, Desk, Federal, Inlaid Walnut, Slant Front, Pennsylvania, C.1790	1350.00
Furniture, Desk, Field, Confederate, Walnut, 12 X 18 X 7 1/2 In., 1863	295.00
Furniture, Desk, Governor Winthrop	850.00
Furniture, Desk, Grocer's, Pine, Lift Top	50.00
Furniture, Desk, Hepplewhite, Inlaid Mahogany, Slant Front, Penna., C.1790	650.00
Furniture, Desk, Hepplewhite, Mahogany, Slant Front, New England, C.1790	400.00
Furniture, Desk, Italian, Olivewood, Slant Front, Sandalwood Inlay	195.00
Furniture, Desk, Kneehole, England, 18th Century *Illus*	850.00
Furniture, Desk, Lap, Burled Walnut, 9 X 13 1/2 X 5 1/2 In.	32.00
Furniture, Desk, Lap, Curly Maple	30.00
Furniture, Desk, Lap, 8 1/2 X 12 1/2 X 4 In.	29.00
Furniture, Desk, Made From Organ	35.00
Furniture, Desk, Mahogany, C.1830, Slant Front, Bracket Feet	650.00
Furniture, Desk, Mahogany, Oxbow, Pine & Cedar Secondary Wood, 41 In.Wide	3000.00
Furniture, Desk, Mahogany, Salem, Mass., C.1740 *Illus*	3250.00

Furniture, Desk, Miniature, Walnut, Block Front, Hinged Slant Front 700.00
Furniture, Desk, New England, Maple, Slant Top, Ogee Feet, 31 In.Lid 500.00
Furniture, Desk, Oak, Ball & Claw Feet, Turned Legs 97.50
Furniture, Desk, Pine & Cherry, Flat Top, 19th Century, 15 Small Drawers 280.00
Furniture, Desk, Pine, Slant Top 220.00
Furniture, Desk, Portable, Black Lacquer, Decorated, Chinese, C.1815 .... 50.00
Furniture, Desk, Queen Anne, Cherry, On Frame, Connecticut, C.1740-1750 .... 6750.00
Furniture, Desk, Queen Anne, Walnut, Slant Front, Pennsylvania, C.1710 .... 2800.00
Furniture, Desk, Rolltop .... 250.00 To 400.00
Furniture, Desk, Rolltop, Oak, 42 In. 180.00
Furniture, Desk, School, Dated 1888 .... 75.00
Furniture, Desk, Schoolmaster's, Birch, Tapered Legs 90.00
Furniture, Desk, Schoolmaster's, Pine 85.00
Furniture, Desk, Secretary, Cabinet Top, 18th Century, 4 Graduated Drawers 1400.00
Furniture, Desk, Secretary, Cherry, Broken Arch Top, Walls Of Troy Molding 1900.00
Furniture, Desk, Stenciled, C.1840, One Drawer 25.00
Furniture, Desk, Three Drawers, Yellow Paint, Stencil, C.1810, Brasses 179.00
Furniture, Desk, Treaty, Louis XV, Black Leather Top, Bronze Dore Fittings 4100.00
Furniture, Desk, Victorian, English, Leather Top, Glass Doors, 52 In.High 395.00
Furniture, Desk, Walnut, Cylinder Top, Secretary 500.00
Furniture, Desk, Walnut, English, 19th Century, 2 Pedestal, 7 Drawers 325.00
Furniture, Desk, Walnut, Roll Top, 60 In.Long, 52 In.High, Holland, C.1890 .... 750.00
Furniture, Desk, Walnut, Slant Top 285.00
Furniture, Dough Bin, Pine, Covered, Breadboard Top, 34 X 19 X 28 1/2 In. 40.00
Furniture, Dough Box, Pennsylvania Dutch 99.00
Furniture, Dough Box, Pine, Cabinet Base, One Piece, 37 In.High 325.00
Furniture, Dough Box, Pine, Lift Lid, 25 X 19 X 31 In. 25.00
Furniture, Dresser & Washstand, Victorian, Walnut, Marble Top, Mirror 310.00
Furniture, Dresser, Chippendale, Walnut, Penna., C.1790 .... *Illus* 2600.00
Furniture, Dresser, Doll's, Mirror, 1930s 4.75
Furniture, Dresser, Mahogany, American, C.1830, Serpentine Front 350.00
Furniture, Dresser, Makes Into Hide-A-Bed 55.00

Furniture, Dresser, Chippendale,
Walnut, Penna., C.1790

Furniture, Dresser, Marble Top 100.00
Furniture, Dresser, Oak, Plain 38.00
Furniture, Dresser, Victorian, Four Drawers, Inlaid Parquetry & Marquetry 175.00
Furniture, Dressing Glass, Federal, Inlaid Mahogany, 5 Drawers, Penna.1790 .... 160.00
Furniture, Dry Sink, Cupboard, Pennsylvania Dutch 365.00
Furniture, Dry Sink, Door In Base, Pine 120.00
Furniture, Dry Sink, Maple, 1 Side Drawer, Double Door Cabinet 130.00
Furniture, Dry Sink, Pennsylvania, Maple, Lift Top, 2 Drawers 150.00
Furniture, Dry Sink, Pine 145.00

Furniture, **Dry Sink**, Pine, Plank Ends, Porcelain Knobs, 2 Door, 37 X 20 X 33 .... 175.00
Furniture, **Dry Sink**, Pine, Single, Paneled Door, Bracket Feet 110.00
Furniture, **Dry Sink**, Pine, 1 Drawer, 3 Panel Door, Cabinet Base 110.00
Furniture, **Dry Sink**, Walnut, 48 In.Wide, 32 In.High 145.00
Furniture, **Dumbwaiter**, George III, Mahogany, 18th Century, 47 In.High 275.00
Furniture, **Etagere**, Louis XVI Style, Kingwood, Ormolu Galleries 150.00
Furniture, **Etagere**, Victorian, Rosewood, Carved, Pierced Rail, N.Y., C.1850 .... 250.00
Furniture, **Fainting Couch**, Walnut, Victorian, Opens To Double Bed, C.1860 .... 110.00
Furniture, **Fauteuil**, Directoire, Beechwood, Carved, Spade Back, C.1750, Pair 400.00
Furniture, **Fauteuil**, Directoire, Beechwood, Carved, Vase Form Supports, 1750 .... 175.00
Furniture, **Fauteuil**, Directoire, Beechwood, 18th Century, Pair 700.00
Furniture, **Fauteuil**, Directoire, Walnut, Signed G.Jacob, C.1750, Pair 775.00
Furniture, **Fauteuil**, Louis XV Style, Beechwood, Carved, Cartouche Back, Pair 600.00
Furniture, **Fauteuil**, Louis XV Style, Painted Gray, Cartouche Back, Pair 400.00
Furniture, **Fauteuil**, Louis XV, Beechwood, Cartouche Back, Carved, C.1750, Pair 750.00
Furniture, **Fauteuil**, Louis XV, Beechwood, Carved, Cartouche, 1750 .... 400.00 To 475.00
Furniture, **Fauteuil**, Louis XV, Beechwood, Carved, Signed I.Chenevat, C.1750 .... 475.00
Furniture, **Fauteuil**, Louis XV, Carved Gilt Wood, Cartouche Back, C.1750 .... 175.00
Furniture, **Fauteuil**, Louis XV, Walnut, Carved Crest, C.1750 .... 750.00
Furniture, **Fauteuil**, Louis XV, Walnut, Carved, Parcel Gilt, Needlework, Pair 1700.00
Furniture, **Fauteuil**, Louis XVI, Carved Gilt Wood, Rectangular Back, C.1750 .... 1000.00
Furniture, **Fauteuil**, Louis XVI, Painted Gray, Carved, C.1750, 4 .... 1200.00
Furniture, **Fireplace Screen**, Carved, Needlepoint Under Glass, England 225.00
Furniture, **Footstool**, George I, Elmwood, Floral Needlework, 18th Century 1200.00
Furniture, **Footstool**, Mahogany, Turned Side Handles, Purple Velvet Cushion 25.00
Furniture, **Footstool**, Round, 3 Legs 8.00
Furniture, **Footstool**, Splayed Legs 20.00
Furniture, **Footstool**, Victorian, Mahogany, Upholstered 90.00
Furniture, **Footstool**, Walnut, Canted Ends, Scalloped 12.50
Furniture, **Frame**, Crisscross, Leaf Corner, 8 X 10 In. 6.50
Furniture, **Frame**, Curly Maple Frame, 15 X 19 In. 12.50
Furniture, **Frame**, Easel, Miniature, Silver Gilt, Rubies, Sapphires, Emeralds 600.00
Furniture, **Frame**, Hand-Carved, 8 X 10 In. 6.50
Furniture, **Frame**, Handmade, 1860, 5 3/4 X 4 1/2 In. 8.00
Furniture, **Frame**, Oval, Plaster, 8 X 10 In. 7.50
Furniture, **Frame**, Picture, Curly Maple, 5 X 6 In. 3.00
Furniture, **Frame**, Picture, Oak, Oval, Fruit Print, 12 X 16 In. 12.00
Furniture, **Frame**, Picture, Walnut, Deep, 4 .... 39.00
Furniture, **Frame**, Shadow Box, 20 X 33 In. 50.00
Furniture, **Frame**, Walnut Finish, 8 X 10 In. 9.75
Furniture, **Frame**, Walnut, 12 X 14 In. 15.00
Furniture, **Frame**, White Plaster, Raised Leaves And Flowers 7.50
Furniture, **Girandole**, Federal, Gilded Wood, Convex, Eagle, C.1800, Pair 1500.00
Furniture, **Girandole**, Louis XV Style, Carved Gilt Wood, 2 Branch Arm, Pair 80.00
Furniture, **Girandole**, Regency, Carved Gilt Wood, 2 Light, Eagle, C.1850, Pair 900.00
Furniture, **Glass**, Dressing, Federal, Mahogany, C.1810-30 .... *Illus* 375.00
Furniture, **Gueridon**, Directoire, Mahogany, Signed C.Gauduel, C.1750 .... 1300.00
Furniture, **Gueridon**, Louis XVI Style, Mahogany, Round St.Anne Marble Top 225.00
Furniture, **Gueridon**, Louis XVI, Burr Chestnut, 18th Century, Marble Top 650.00
Furniture, **Highboy Base**, Queen Anne, Maple, 3 Drawers, Mass., C.1740 .... 475.00
Furniture, **Highboy**, Curly Maple, Essex County, Mass., C.1730 .... 3250.00
Furniture, **Highboy**, Curly Maple, Mass., C.1740 .... *Illus* 4400.00
Furniture, **Highboy**, Curly Maple, Mass., C.1760 .... *Illus* 5750.00
Furniture, **Highboy**, Queen Anne, Cherry, Carved, Bonnet Top, Conn., C.1730 .... 6000.00
Furniture, **Highboy**, Queen Anne, Curly Maple, New York, C.1740, 2 Parts 5500.00
Furniture, **Highboy**, Queen Anne, Maple, Fan Carved, Samuel Dunlap Ii, C.1775 .... 2500.00
Furniture, **Highboy**, Queen Anne, Maple, New Hampshire, C.1730 .... 2100.00
Furniture, **Highboy**, Queen Anne, Walnut, Flat Top, 2 Parts, Mass., C.1740 .... 1700.00
Furniture, **Highboy**, William & Mary, Inlaid Walnut, 2 Parts, New England, 1690 .... 850.00
Furniture, **Highchair**, Child's, Cane Seat & Back 75.00
Furniture, **Highchair**, Child's, Cane Seat, Carved Back, Dated 1890, Wheels 95.00
Furniture, **Highchair**, Child's, Painted Red, Yellow Trim 12.00
Furniture, **Highchair**, Child's, Rabbit Ear, Painted, Stenciled In Green 225.00
Furniture, **Highchair**, Child's, Wicker 25.00
Furniture, **Highchair**, New England, Arrow Back, Black Paint 50.00
Furniture, **Huntboard**, Federal, Cherry, Concave Center, Virginia, C.1810 .... 1800.00

Furniture, Glass, Dressing, Federal,
Mahogany, C.1810-30
See Page 209

Furniture, Highboy,
Curly Maple, Mass., C.1740
See Page 209

Furniture, Highboy, Curly Maple,
Mass., C.1760
See Page 209

Furniture, Huntboard, Queen Anne		415.00
Furniture, Hutch Table, Pine & Maple, 6 Ft.		295.00
Furniture, Hutch, Doors, Drawers, Dovetailed, Pine		495.00
Furniture, Hutch, Paneled Doors, Drawers, Circa 1840, Pine, 48 X 81 In.High		275.00
Furniture, Ice Cream Set, Child's, Handmade, Painted White, 3 Piece		29.50
Furniture, Ice Cream Set, Child's, Handmade, Painted White, 5 Piece		39.50
Furniture, Ice Cream Set, Heart Back Chairs, 5 Piece		100.00
Furniture, Jardiniere, George III, Mahogany, Cylindrical, 19th Century		350.00
Furniture, Kas, Painted Red With Black Graining, 2 Doors, Bracket Feet		225.00
Furniture, Kas, Walnut, Raised Panels In Door & Ends, Drawer Below		75.00
Furniture, Kennel, Dog, Louis XVI Style, Carved Gilt Wood, Beading		325.00
Furniture, Lectern, Mahogany		22.50
Furniture, Linen Press, Curly Maple, Splay Feet, Cabinet Top, 4 Drawers		1000.00
Furniture, Lit A La Polonaise, Louis XVI, Beechwood	*Illus*	1800.00
Furniture, Lit De Repos, Directoire, Beechwood, Damask, 18th Century		475.00
Furniture, Love Seat, Duncan Phyfe, Mahogany Back Rail, Green Striped Silk		600.00
Furniture, Love Seat, Victorian, Walnut, Cabriole Leg, 46 In.Long		325.00
Furniture, Lowboy, Burl Walnut, English, C.1720, Cabriole Legs		475.00
Furniture, Lowboy, Chippendale, Stepped Top, 1 Drawer, Brass Pull		625.00
Furniture, Lowboy, Mahogany, New England, 18th Century, Cabriole Legs		4000.00
Furniture, Lowboy, Mahogany, Philadelphia, C.1740, Drake Feet		2000.00
Furniture, Lowboy, Queen Anne Style, Curly Maple, 3 Drawers		475.00

Furniture, Lowboy, Queen Anne, Cherry, 3 Drawers In Apron, Turned Legs 850.00
Furniture, Lowboy, Queen Anne, Curly Maple, C.1730-40, Cabriole Legs 6000.00
Furniture, Lowboy, Queen Anne, Inlaid Cherry, The Lockwood, Mass., C.1725 .... 8000.00
Furniture, Lowboy, Queen Anne, Mahogany, Oblong Top, 3 Drawers, Penna., C.1740 .... 6250.00
Furniture, Lowboy, Queen Anne, Mahogany, 3 Drawers, Duck Feet, Molded Top 550.00
Furniture, Lowboy, Queen Anne, Walnut, Philadelphia, C.1720, 4 Drawers 3000.00
Furniture, Lowboy, Queen Anne, Walnut, Philadelphia, C.1740 .... 5000.00
Furniture, Lowboy, Walnut, New England, C.1750, Cabriole Legs 5400.00
Furniture, Mirror Frame, Florentine, Walnut, Carved, Tabernacle Form, 1550 .... 250.00
Furniture, Mirror Frame, Florentine, Walnut, Carved, 10 Satyr Masks, C.1550 .... 300.00
Furniture, Mirror, Adam, Gilt Wood, Carved, Oval, 18th Century, Pair 4000.00
Furniture, Mirror, Bird's-Eye Maple, Frame, 29 X 37 In. 90.00
Furniture, Mirror, Bull's-Eye, Ogee Frame, Winged Horse Finial 325.00
Furniture, Mirror, Chippendale Style, American 90.00
Furniture, Mirror, Chippendale Style, Eagle Finial, Bonnet Top, 45 In.High 225.00
Furniture, Mirror, Chippendale Style, Walnut Frame, 39 In.High 60.00
Furniture, Mirror, Chippendale, Chinese, Oval Top, Black & Gold Decor 90.00
Furniture, Mirror, Chippendale, Chinese, 18th Century, Gilt Frame, Lakeside 6000.00
Furniture, Mirror, Chippendale, Mahogany, Carved, Parcel Gilt, Phila., C.1750 .... 2000.00
Furniture, Mirror, Chippendale, Mahogany, Cut Frame, Gilt Oak Leaf 210.00
Furniture, Mirror, Chippendale, New York, Carved & Gilded Draperies 2750.00
Furniture, Mirror, Chippendale, Scalloped Crest, 24 In.High 100.00
Furniture, Mirror, Chippendale, Scroll, Carved, Etched Glass, 20 In.High 700.00
Furniture, Mirror, Colonial, Gilded, 2 Part, Basket Of Fruit At Top 250.00
Furniture, Mirror, Colonial, Gilded, 2 Part, Top, Spode Tower, 39 In.High 170.00
Furniture, Mirror, Continental, Flowers, Birds, 18th Century, Pair 250.00
Furniture, Mirror, Convex, Gilded Frame With Applied Balls, Eagle Finial 1800.00
Furniture, Mirror, Convex, Regency, Gilt Wood, Carved, Circular, 19th Century 350.00
Furniture, Mirror, Courting, Ivory Corner Mounts, In Box, Paper Covered 150.00
Furniture, Mirror, Dowry, Carved Wood, Gilded, Etched Grapes, Pair 500.00
Furniture, Mirror, Dresser, Brass Frame, Flowers & Leaves, Pedestal Base 37.00
Furniture, Mirror, Dressing Table, Federal, Inlaid Mahogany, N.E., C.1800 .... 200.00
Furniture, Mirror, Dressing, Mahogany, Ogee Drawer 30.00
Furniture, Mirror, Edge Of Cut Bull's-Eye, Round 25.00
Furniture, Mirror, Empire, Picture, 2 Part, Reverse Painting, Black & Gold 90.00
Furniture, Mirror, Empire, 2 Part, Reverse Painting Of House On Glass 130.00
Furniture, Mirror, English, C.1775 .... *Illus* 950.00
Furniture, Mirror, Federal, Gilded, Picture, Ball Drops, Reverse Painting 300.00
Furniture, Mirror, Federal, Mahogany, Eagle Finial, 23 X 61 In. 350.00

Furniture, Lit A La Polonaise,
Louis XVI, Beechwood
See Page 210

Furniture, Mirror, English, C.1775

Furniture, Mirror, Federal, Mahogany, Reverse Painting 55.00
Furniture, Mirror, Federal, 2 Part, Picture, Reverse Of Church, Gilt 125.00
Furniture, Mirror, French Style Decorated, 24 X 39 In. 30.00
Furniture, Mirror, French, Gold Leaf, 3 Part Glass, Carved, 18th Century 200.00
Furniture, Mirror, George II, Gilt Gesso, Arched Plate, 18th Century 600.00
Furniture, Mirror, George III Style, Gilt Wood, Oval Plate, Pair 85.00
Furniture, Mirror, George III, Bird On Flowering Tree, 18th Century, Pair 225.00
Furniture, Mirror, George III, Carved Gilt Wood, Pier, Oblong Plate, C.1750 .... 600.00
Furniture, Mirror, George III, Eglomise & Gilt Wood, Wall, Rectangular Plate 450.00
Furniture, Mirror, George III, Gilt Wood, Carved, 18th Century 1800.00
Furniture, Mirror, George III, Gilt Wood, Mantel, Rectangular Plate, C.1750 .... 500.00
Furniture, Mirror, George III, Gilt, Carved, 18th Century, Oval Plate, Pair 1800.00
Furniture, Mirror, George III, Mallards In Pond, Trees, 18th Century, Pair 375.00
Furniture, Mirror, Georgian, 18th Century, Gilded & Mahogany 2200.00
Furniture, Mirror, Gilded Frame, Eagle Finial, Wheat Molding, 35 In.High 90.00
Furniture, Mirror, Gilt Wood, Oval, Applied Ribbon Twists, Pair 90.00
Furniture, Mirror, Gold Leaf, 48 In.Long 425.00
Furniture, Mirror, Hall, Oak, Hooks, Bench, 2 Piece Set 90.00
Furniture, Mirror, Italian, Carved Gilt Wood, Rectangular Plate, C.1780 .... 180.00
Furniture, Mirror, Italian, Pier, Gilt Wood, 18th Century 250.00
Furniture, Mirror, Italian, 18th Century, Carved, Gilded Frame, Pierced 600.00
Furniture, Mirror, Louis XV, Carved Gilt Wood, Rectangular, C.1780 .... 250.00
Furniture, Mirror, Mahogany & Pine, Ogee, 20 X 26 In. 35.00
Furniture, Mirror, Mahogany & Walnut, Ogee Frame, 23 X 33 1/2 In. 45.00
Furniture, Mirror, Mahogany, Cut Frame, Line Inlay, 39 In.High 250.00
Furniture, Mirror, Mahogany, Ogee Frame, 17 X 29 In. 20.00
Furniture, Mirror, Mahogany, Ogee Frame, 31 X 22 In. 50.00
Furniture, Mirror, Mahogany, Ogee, 13 X 18 In. 45.00
Furniture, Mirror, Mahogany, Ogee, 22 X 33 In. 40.00
Furniture, Mirror, Mahogany, Ogee, 28 X 42 In. 65.00
Furniture, Mirror, Mahogany, Stepped Top, Turned & Rope Sides, Block Corners 90.00
Furniture, Mirror, Mantel, American, Gilt Wood, Rectangular Plate, C.1850 .... 160.00
Furniture, Mirror, Pine Frame, Ogee, 18 X 24 In. 40.00
Furniture, Mirror, Plateau, Copper Footed Base, 10 In. 25.00
Furniture, Mirror, Plateau, 12 In. 10.00
Furniture, Mirror, Queen Anne, Gilt, Gesso, Pier, Rectangular Vauxhall Plate 1500.00
Furniture, Mirror, Queen Anne, Parcel Gilt, Candle Branches, C.1760 .... 4750.00
Furniture, Mirror, Queen Anne, 12 1/2 In.Wide, 26 In.High 350.00
Furniture, Mirror, Queen Anne, 18th Century, Gilded Eagle Top, Burled Glass 300.00
Furniture, Mirror, Regency, Gilt Wood, Carved, Rectangular, 19th Century 250.00
Furniture, Mirror, Rococo Style, Gilt, 33 X 54 In. 160.00
Furniture, Mirror, Shaving, Curly Maple, 2 Drawers, Bowfront, Bracket Feet 90.00
Furniture, Mirror, Shaving, Federal, Inalid Mahogany, Phila., C.1810 .... 180.00
Furniture, Mirror, Shaving, Mahogany, Bowfront, Ogee Feet 65.00
Furniture, Mirror, Shaving, Mahogany, Ogee Bracket Feet 45.00
Furniture, Mirror, Shaving, Mahogany, 2 Drawers, Rolled Front, Carved 70.00
Furniture, Mirror, Shaving, Mahogany, 3 Drawers 60.00
Furniture, Mirror, Shaving, Sheraton, 3 Drawers In Base, Fluted Column 70.00
Furniture, Mirror, Shaving, Walnut 27.50
Furniture, Mirror, Sheraton, Tabernacle, Reverse Painting Naval Engagement 325.00
Furniture, Mirror, Venetian, Gilt Wood, Carved, Pier, 18th Century 2100.00
Furniture, Mirror, Victorian, Oval, Fretwork Frame, 27 X 23 In. 125.00
Furniture, Mirror, Victorian, Walnut, Oval, 16 X 23 1/2 In. 15.00
Furniture, Mirror, Wall, Chippendale Style, Mahogany, Scrolled Top 325.00
Furniture, Mirror, Wall, Chippendale, Carved, Parcel Gilded, C.1760 .... 1150.00
Furniture, Mirror, Wall, Chippendale, Mahogany, C.1760, Carved 150.00
Furniture, Mirror, Wall, Chippendale, Mahogany, Carved, Parcel Gilt, Pa., 1760 .... 950.00
Furniture, Mirror, Wall, Chippendale, Mahogany, Carved, Penna., C.1760 .... 575.00
Furniture, Mirror, Wall, Chippendale, Mahogany, Carved, Scrolled Crest, C.1760 .... 700.00
Furniture, Mirror, Wall, Chippendale, Mahogany, Inlaid, Parcel Gilt, C.1790 .... 300.00
Furniture, Mirror, Wall, Chippendale, Mahogany, Parcel Gilt, 1760 .... 250.00 To 1000.00
Furniture, Mirror, Wall, Chippendale, Walnut, Carved, Parcel Gilt, C.1750 .... 1050.00
Furniture, Mirror, Wall, Federal, Carved & Gilded Wood & Gesso, N.Y., C.1800 .... 850.00
Furniture, Mirror, Wall, Federal, Carved & Gilded Wood, Eagle, Convex, C.1810 .... 225.00
Furniture, Mirror, Wall, Federal, Carved & Gilded Wood, Gesso, C.1820 .... 125.00
Furniture, Mirror, Wall, Federal, Carved & Gilded, Eagle, Convex, C.1815 .... 800.00

Furniture, Mirror, Wall, Federal, Carved & Painted Wood, Pennsylvania, C.1810 .... 475.00
Furniture, Mirror, Wall, Federal, Carved, Gilded, Eagle, Eglomise, N.Y., C.1800 .... 3500.00
Furniture, Mirror, Wall, Federal, Eagle, Carved & Gilded, Convex, C.1815 .... 450.00
Furniture, Mirror, Wall, Federal, Gilded Wood & Gesso, Eglomise, N.E., C.1800 .... 225.00
Furniture, Mirror, Wall, Federal, Gilded Wood, Eglomise Decor, American, 1800s 300.00
Furniture, Mirror, Wall, Federal, Gilt, Eglomise, Cermenati & Monfreno, Boston 200.00
Furniture, Mirror, Wall, George II, Mahogany, Gilt, 18th Century, Carved 950.00
Furniture, Mirror, Wall, George III, Gilt Wood, Rectangular, C.1750, Pair 600.00
Furniture, Mirror, Wall, Georgian, Gilded, Center Medallion, Urn & Scroll 200.00
Furniture, Mirror, Wall, Italian, Gilt Wood, Rectangular Plate, C.1780 .... 150.00
Furniture, Mirror, Wall, Louis XV, Painted & Parcel Gilt, 18th Century 650.00
Furniture, Mirror, Wall, Queen Anne, Gilt Wood, Rectangular Plate, C.1750 .... 800.00
Furniture, Mirror, Wall, Queen Anne, Japanned & Parcel Gilt, C.1720 .... 900.00
Furniture, Mirror, Wall, Queen Anne, Walnut, Rhode Island, C.1740, Ogee Frame 1600.00
Furniture, Mirror, Wall, Walnut, Carved, Parcel Gilt, 18th Century 375.00
Furniture, Mirror, Walnut, Carved, Scrolled, Victorian, 5 X 7 In. 250.00
Furniture, Mirror, Walnut, Parcel Gilt, American, C.1760 .... *Illus* 2500.00
Furniture, Mixing Board, Hepplewhite, Inlaid Mahogany, Marble Insert, C.1790 .... 3250.00
Furniture, Music Stand, N.Y., C.1800 .... *Illus* 1900.00

Furniture, Mirror, Walnut, Parcel Gilt, American, C.1760

Furniture, Music Stand, N.Y., C.1800

Furniture, Nightstand, Cherry, Drop Leaf, 3 Drawers, Brass Pulls 80.00
Furniture, Nightstand, Cherry, One Drawer, Brass, Knob, Turned Legs 140.00
Furniture, Nightstand, Cherry, One Drawer, Breadboard Top, Square Legs 1000.00
Furniture, Nightstand, Cherry, One Drawer, Square Tapered Legs 45.00
Furniture, Nightstand, Cherry, One Drawer, Turned Leg, Button Foot 80.00
Furniture, Nightstand, Cherry, One Drawer, Turned Legs, 28 1/2 In.High 30.00
Furniture, Nightstand, Cherry, Three Drawers, Tiger Maple Drawer Fronts 150.00
Furniture, Nightstand, Cherry, Two Drawers, Shaped Drawer Fronts 115.00
Furniture, Nightstand, Cherry, Two Drawers, Turned Knobs & Legs 130.00
Furniture, Nightstand, Curly Maple, 1 Drawer, Breadboard Top 160.00
Furniture, Nightstand, Federal, Mahogany, New England, C.1790, 2 Drawers 180.00
Furniture, Nightstand, Hepplewhite, Cherry, Corner, 1 Drawer 90.00
Furniture, Nightstand, Mahogany, Drop Leaf, Duncan Phyfe Legs 170.00
Furniture, Nightstand, Mahogany, One Drawer, Cabinet Base, Fitted Interior 70.00
Furniture, Nightstand, Mahogany, Two Drawers, Brass Pulls, Turned Legs 90.00
Furniture, Nightstand, Maple, One Drawer, Scalloped Curl Aprons 70.00
Furniture, Nightstand, One Drawer, Smoke Decorated, Tapered Legs 250.00
Furniture, Nightstand, One Drawer, Yellow Paint, Stencil 325.00
Furniture, Nightstand, One Drawer, 16 1/2 In.Wide 105.00
Furniture, Nightstand, Pine, Breadboard Top, Square Tapered Legs 50.00
Furniture, Nightstand, Sheraton, Checkerboard Top 190.00
Furniture, Nightstand, Sheraton, Mahogany, Satinwood Drawer Fronts, C.1800 .... 550.00

Furniture, **Nightstand**, Tiger Maple, Three Drawers, Mahogany Pulls 175.00
Furniture, **Nightstand**, Walnut On Oak, White Marble Top, 3 Drawers 45.00
Furniture, **Nightstand**, Walnut, Drop Leaf, Two Drawers, 16 X 25 X 28 1/2 In. 110.00
Furniture, **Nightstand**, Walnut, Tapered Legs 45.00
Furniture, **Parlor Suite**, Rosewood, N.Y., C.1850, 4 Piece .... *Illus* 2800.00
Furniture, **Pew**, Church, Oak, Gothic, 11 Ft.Long 35.00
Furniture, **Pew**, Church, 6 Ft.Long 35.00
Furniture, **Pew**, Pine, 43 In.Long 45.00
Furniture, **Pie Safe**, Pennsylvania Dutch, Pierced Tin Ends, Wood Doors 120.00
Furniture, **Poudreuse**, Louis XV, Provincial, Kingwood, Parquetry, C.1750 .... 150.00
Furniture, **Press**, Linen, Cherry, Two Doors, Three Shelves, Brass Pulls 1100.00
Furniture, **Prie-Dieu**, Venetian, Painted White, Gold Trim, Green Velvet, 1750 .... 300.00
Furniture, **Rack**, Blanket, Folding, 3 Section 17.50
Furniture, **Rack**, Coat, Mahogany, Paw Feet, Finial At Top 65.00
Furniture, **Rack**, Hanging, Magazine, Walnut, Carved, Leaves, Victorian 14.50
Furniture, **Rack**, Hat, Accordion, Brass Buttons On Each Post 14.50
Furniture, **Rack**, Hat, Accordion, Maple, Ten Enamel Pegs, 18 In.Long 15.00
Furniture, **Rack**, Hat, Hanging, Wooden Hooks, Bentwood 27.50
Furniture, **Rack**, Hat, Wood, Folding 4.00
Furniture, **Rack**, Linen, Shoe Feet 45.00
Furniture, **Rack**, Magazine, Victorian, Wall, Hanging, Glass Drop Front, White 18.00
Furniture, **Rack**, Spice, Hanging, Pine, 17 X 8 1/2 X 5 In. 55.00
Furniture, **Rack**, Spoon, English 42.00
Furniture, **Rack**, Utensil, Queen Anne Scallops, Pine, Wrought Iron Hooks 30.00
Furniture, **Rack**, Wall, Hanging, Blue Delft Tile With Sailboats 22.00
Furniture, **Rocker**, Arrow Back 30.00
Furniture, **Rocker**, Balloon Back, Painted, Decorated 30.00
Furniture, **Rocker**, Bentwood 45.00
Furniture, **Rocker**, Boston, Arrow Back 70.00
Furniture, **Rocker**, Boston, Painted & Stenciled, 19th Century, Graining 350.00
Furniture, **Rocker**, Boston, Painted, Stenciled, 19th Century 200.00
Furniture, **Rocker**, Boston, Stenciled House On Top Rail 65.00
Furniture, **Rocker**, Boston, Yellow, Stenciled 59.00
Furniture, **Rocker**, Child's, Boston, Painted, Stencil 80.00
Furniture, **Rocker**, Child's, Captain's Chair Back, Dark Stain 20.00
Furniture, **Rocker**, Child's, Maple 27.50
Furniture, **Rocker**, Child's, Wicker .... 30.00 To 35.00
Furniture, **Rocker**, Child's, Wicker, 25 In.High 45.00
Furniture, **Rocker**, Maple, Ladder Back, Red, Rush Seat 35.00
Furniture, **Rocker**, Maple, Slat Back, New England, 18th Century, Rush Seat, 2 .... 175.00
Furniture, **Rocker**, Oak 39.00
Furniture, **Rocker**, Painted, Decorated, Penna., C.1850 .... *Illus* 175.00
Furniture, **Rocker**, Polished Steel & Leather, Peter Cooper, C.1850 .... 700.00
Furniture, **Rocker**, Shaker ....75.00 To 150.00
Furniture, **Rocker**, Shaker, Signed Lebanon 125.00
Furniture, **Rocker**, Shaker, Stamped, Impressed No.7 .... 170.00
Furniture, **Rocker**, Victorian, Platform, Velvet Seat 45.00
Furniture, **Rocker**, Walnut, Platform 49.50
Furniture, **Rocker**, Walnut, Platform, Upholstered 59.00
Furniture, **Rocker**, Windsor, Arm, Comb Back, Black Paint, Stencil Of Village 275.00
Furniture, **Rocker**, Windsor, Arrow Back, Rabbit Ear, Green 99.00
Furniture, **Rocker**, Windsor, Country 15.00
Furniture, **Safe**, Pie, Ash, 2 Drawers At Top, Pierced Tin Doors 50.00
Furniture, **Safe**, Pie, Pine, Pierced Tin Doors & Ends 45.00
Furniture, **Sconce**, Wall, Louis XVI Style, Ormolu, 3 Scrolling Arms, Pair 400.00
Furniture, **Sconce**, Wall, Louis XVI Style, 3 Light, Ormolu, Scrolling, Pair 1500.00
Furniture, **Screen**, Chinese, Carved & Gilded Wood, 4 Fold, 19th Century 200.00
Furniture, **Screen**, Chinese, Coromandel, Lacquer, 8 Fold, 19th Century 2000.00
Furniture, **Screen**, Chinese, Painted & Lacquered, C.1750 .... *Illus* 2500.00
Furniture, **Screen**, Chinese, Red Lacquer, 4 Fold, Figures, C.1850 .... 350.00
Furniture, **Screen**, Coromandel, Seal Of K'ang Hsi, Carved, 4 Fold 1950.00
Furniture, **Screen**, Flemish, Floral On Oatmeal Tapestry, 3 Fold, C.1650 .... 150.00
Furniture, **Screen**, Japanese Lacquer, Landscape, Gold, Silver, & Red, 4 Panels 120.00
Furniture, **Screen**, Japanese, Kabuki Dancer & Onlooker, Painted On Gold Leaf 140.00
Furniture, **Screen**, Painted Canvas, Birds, 4 Fold, 7 Ft.6 In.High 180.00
Furniture, **Screen**, Pole, Continental, Walnut, Carved, 19th Century, Pair 325.00

Furniture, Parlor Suite,
Rosewood, N.Y.,
C.1850, 4 Piece
See Page 214

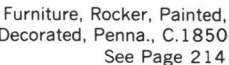

Furniture, Rocker, Painted,
Decorated, Penna., C.1850
See Page 214

Furniture, Screen, Chinese,
Painted & Lacquered, C.1750
See Page 214

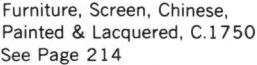

Furniture, Screen, Pole, Federal, Inlaid Mahogany, Mass., C.1780, Urn Finial 4250.00
Furniture, Screen, Pole, George III Style, Mahogany, Octagonal, Needlework 50.00
Furniture, Screen, Spanish, Painted Harbor Scene, 4 Fold, C.1780 .... 675.00
Furniture, Seat, Buggy, 42 In.Wide, 25 In.High 24.50
Furniture, Seat, Deacon, Spindle Back, Signed, Pine 85.00
Furniture, Seat, Sleigh, Empire, Mahogany, Lyre Supports, Lion Head Terminals 250.00
Furniture, Seat, Wagon, Child's, 10 1/2 X 20 In. 8.00
Furniture, Seat, Wagon, Mushroom Turnings On Posts, 18th Century 450.00
Furniture, Seat, Wagon, Spring, 40 In.Wide, 20 In.High 22.50

Furniture, Seat, Window, Federal, Mahogany, Carved, New York, C.1810, Pair 600.00
Furniture, Seat, Window, George III, Beechwood, Painted, 18th Century 325.00
Furniture, Seat, Window, George III, Mahogany, Square Legs, 18th Century 500.00
Furniture, Seat, Window, Louis XV, Beechwood, Carved, 18th Century, Pair 2250.00
Furniture, Secretaire A Abattant, Charles X, Fruitwood, 19th Century, Marble 475.00
Furniture, Secretaire A Abattant, Louis XVI, Provincial, Marble Top, C.1750 .... 900.00
Furniture, Secretaire A Abattant, Louis XVI, Tulipwood, Ormolu, C.1750 .... 1700.00
Furniture, Secretaire Bookcase, George III, Satinwood, 18th Century 6750.00
Furniture, Secretaire Cabinet, George III, Satinwood & Sabicu, 18th Century 6000.00
Furniture, Secretaire Commode, Petite, Louis XVI, Fruitwood, Lacquer, C.1750 .... 500.00
Furniture, Secretary Bookcase, Cherry, Mid-Victorian 275.00
Furniture, Secretary Bookcase, Chippendale, Cherry, Carved, R.I., C.1750 .... 8000.00
Furniture, Secretary Bookcase, Queen Anne, Inlaid Mahogany, R.I., C.1740 .... 3750.00
Furniture, Secretary Bookcase, Slant Top Desk, Pine 275.00
Furniture, Secretary Cabinet, Chippendale, Curly Maple, Connecticut, C.1760 .... 1200.00
Furniture, Secretary Cabinet, Chippendale, Mahogany, Carved, New York, C.1760 .... 2500.00
Furniture, Secretary Cabinet, Chippendale, Mahogany, New York, C.1760, 2 Part 2600.00
Furniture, Secretary, Butternut, Glass Doors On Top, Pigeonholes 500.00
Furniture, Secretary, Cylinder Front, Glass Door, Walnut, Victorian 290.00
Furniture, Secretary, Lady's, Federal, Curly Maple, New England, C.1800 .... 300.00
Furniture, Secretary, Oak, Curved Glass 50.00
Furniture, Secretary, Pilgrim, Pine 1650.00
Furniture, Secretary, Pine, Drop Front, Glass Doors Top, 4 Drawers 165.00
Furniture, Secretary, Pine, Lift Front, 2 Doors With 6 Panes, Signed 250.00
Furniture, Secretary, Sheridan, Ringed Brassed, Reeded Side Columns, Glass 350.00
Furniture, Semainier, Louis XV-XVI, Kingwood, Signed Reizel, C.1750 .... 1500.00
Furniture, Server, Mahogany, English, Reeded Legs, Gallery Top, 25 In.Wide 150.00
Furniture, Server, Mahogany, Inlaid, Square Top, 32 X 21 X 30 In. 250.00
Furniture, Server, Pennsylvania, Pine, 1 Drawer, 1 Shelf, Scalloped Rail 80.00
Furniture, Server, Pine, One Drawer, 48 X 19 1/2 X 30 In. 70.00
Furniture, Server, Sheraton, Mahogany, New York, C.1820, Duncan Phyfe Style 275.00
Furniture, Settee, Arrow Back 485.00
Furniture, Settee, Arrow Back, Painted, Decorated, Pennsylvania, C.1850 .... 250.00
Furniture, Settee, Art Nouveau, Walnut, Blue Velour Covering, 50 In.Long 300.00
Furniture, Settee, Banister Back, Rush Seat, Bamboo Turnings 240.00
Furniture, Settee, Belter, Rosewood, Chair Back, Serpentine Front 800.00
Furniture, Settee, Cherry, Victorian, Carved Back, Floral Upholstery, 62 In. 350.00
Furniture, Settee, Child's, Bentwood 125.00
Furniture, Settee, Chippendale, Mahogany, Carved, Serpentine Back 750.00
Furniture, Settee, Directoire, Beechwood, Carved, Scroll Terminals, C.1750 .... 450.00
Furniture, Settee, Directoire, Beechwood, White Floral Silk, C.1750 .... 300.00
Furniture, Settee, George II, Mahogany, Serpentine Top Rail, C.1750 .... 2000.00
Furniture, Settee, George III, Mahogany, Arched Back, Floral Satin, C.1750 .... 1000.00
Furniture, Settee, George III, Mahogany, Needlework Cover, 18th Century 675.00
Furniture, Settee, George III, Three Chair Back, Hand-Painted, 18th Century 250.00
Furniture, Settee, Hitchcock, Porch, Pillar Back, Stretcher Base 475.00
Furniture, Settee, Louis XV, Beechwood, Carved, Cartouche Back, C.1750 .... 1300.00
Furniture, Settee, Louis XV, Beechwood, 18th Century, Cartouche Shape Back 800.00
Furniture, Settee, Louis XV, Walnut, Carved, Parcel Gilt, Needlework, C.1750 .... 850.00
Furniture, Settee, Painted, Decorated, E.Ermentrout, Pennsylvania, C.1840 .... 275.00
Furniture, Settee, Windsor, American, C.1790 .... *Illus* 750.00
Furniture, Settle, Child's, Potty, Double Hole, Fretwork Back, Crest, 26 In. 30.00
Furniture, Settle, Four Panel Back, Painted, Forms Bed 125.00
Furniture, Settle, Pine, Paneled Back, Scalloped Ends, Forms Bed 205.00
Furniture, Sewing Stand, Two Drawers, Pedestal Base, Federal, Rosewood, 1850 .... 90.00
Furniture, Shelf, Corner, Pierced Decor, One Rounded Shelf, Walnut, 12 In. 8.00
Furniture, Shelf, Hanging, Burl Walnut, Mahogany, Regency, 19 Century, Pair 650.00
Furniture, Shelf, Hanging, George III, Mahogany, 3 Shelves, 18th Century 600.00
Furniture, Shelf, Hanging, Regency, Mahogany, 3 Tier, C.1810, Ball Finials 300.00
Furniture, Shelf, Hooks To Hold Utensils, 71 In. 15.00
Furniture, Shelf, Oak, For Telephone 2.00
Furniture, Shelf, Plate, Scalloped Molding, 18th Century, 45 1/2 In.Wide 75.00
Furniture, Shelf, Regency, Mahogany, 4 Tier, Hanging, 2 Drawers, C.1810 .... 190.00
Furniture, Shelf, Victorian, Walnut, Hanging, 2 Shelves, Cabinet With 2 Doors 45.00
Furniture, Shelf, Wall, Two Drawers, White Pine, 14 1/2 X 11 1/4 In. 35.00
Furniture, Shelves, Hanging, Pine, 19 In.Wide 160.00

Furniture, Shelves, Pewter & Pine, 18th Century, Shoe Feet, 6 Ft.2 In.High 90.00
Furniture, Shelves, Whatnot, Chinese Scenes, Four Shelf, 41 1/2 In.Tall 41.00
Furniture, Sideboard, Cherry, Three Drawers Above Two Cabinets 150.00
Furniture, Sideboard, Empire, Mahogany, Crotch Veneer, 43 In.High, C.1820 .... 300.00
Furniture, Sideboard, Federal, Inlaid Mahogany, Oblong, American, C.1800 .... 1600.00
Furniture, Sideboard, Federal, Inlaid Mahogany, Serpentine, New York, C.1790 .... 5500.00
Furniture, Sideboard, Federal, Mahogany, Carved, N.Y., C.1825, Brass Gallery 750.00
Furniture, Sideboard, Federal, Mahogany, Tambour, C.1790 .... *Illus* 1700.00

Furniture, Settee, Windsor, American, C.1790
See Page 216

Furniture, Sideboard, Federal, Mahogany, Tambour, C.1790

Furniture, Sideboard, George III, Mahogany, Bowfront, Ebony Inlay, C.1850 .... 350.00
Furniture, Sideboard, George III, Mahogany, Bowfront, 18th Century 500.00
Furniture, Sideboard, George III, Mahogany, D Shape Top, 18th Century 425.00
Furniture, Sideboard, George III, Mahogany, 18th Century .... *Illus* 2000.00
Furniture, Sideboard, Hepplewhite Style, Mahogany, Serpentine Front, Brass 175.00
Furniture, Sideboard, Hepplewhite, Inlaid Mahogany, Baltimore, C.1790 .... 3300.00
Furniture, Sideboard, Hepplewhite, Inlaid Mahogany, Serpentine, C.1790 .... 3000.00
Furniture, Sideboard, Sheraton, Mahogany With Pine, Lion Head Brasses 250.00
Furniture, Sideboard, Sheraton, Mahogany, American, C.1780, Bowfront 2000.00
Furniture, Sideboard, Sheraton, Mahogany, Gallery Top, Reeded Front 30.00
Furniture, Sideboard, Sheraton, Mahogany, Petite, American, Serpentine Front 350.00
Furniture, Sideboard, Victorian, Mahogany, Pierced Crests, C.1850 .... 80.00

Furniture, Sideboard, Walnut, Red Marble Top, Twisted Reed Decoration 275.00
Furniture, Sideboard, Walnut, White Marble Top, 46 In.Wide, 6 Ft.2 In.Tall 425.00
Furniture, Sideboard, Walnut, White Marble Top, 47 In.Wide, 7 1/2 Ft.Tall 750.00
Furniture, Sofa, Bird's-Eye Maple & Mahogany, Rolled Arm, Floral Tapestry 850.00
Furniture, Sofa, Carved, Inlaid, Salem, Mass., C.1800 .... *Illus* 5000.00

Furniture, Sideboard,
George III, Mahogany,
18th Century
See Page 217

Furniture, Sofa,
Carved, Inlaid,
Salem, Mass.,
C.1800

Furniture, Sofa, Chippendale, Mahogany, Pennsylvania, C.1780, Serpentine Back 1600.00
Furniture, Sofa, Chippendale, Walnut, Pennsylvania, C.1800, Square Legs 1600.00
Furniture, Sofa, Duncan Phyfe, Rolled Arm, Grooved Back Panel, Carved Eagles 650.00
Furniture, Sofa, Empire, C.1840 .... 350.00
Furniture, Sofa, Federal, Inlaid Mahogany, Carved, Massachusetts, C.1800 .... 5000.00
Furniture, Sofa, Federal, Mahogany, Carved, Baluster Supports, N.Y., C.1800 .... 1500.00
Furniture, Sofa, Federal, Mahogany, Carved, N.Y., C.1820 .... *Illus* 350.00
Furniture, Sofa, Federal, Mahogany, Carved, N.Y., C.1825, 6 Ft.7 In.Long 1300.00
Furniture, Sofa, Federal, Mahogany, Upholstered, 19th Century, 6 Ft.4 In. 400.00
Furniture, Sofa, Victorian, Upholstered, O Back, Carved Roses On Back 300.00
Furniture, Sofa, Walnut, Cameo Back, Grape Carved, Pink, Velvet, Victorian 295.00
Furniture, Stand, Basin, George III, Mahogany, 18th Century, Round 425.00
Furniture, Stand, Birch, Tilt Top, Spider Legs, Coffin Top 250.00
Furniture, Stand, Butler, George III, Mahogany, Rectangular, 18th Century 300.00
Furniture, Stand, Butler, George III, Mahogany, 18th Century, Tray, 17 1/4 In. 300.00
Furniture, Stand, Curly Maple, Drop Leaf, 1 Drawer, Queen Anne Tripod Foot 325.00
Furniture, Stand, Dressing, Directoire, Provincial, Mahogany, Marble Top, 1780 .... 400.00
Furniture, Stand, Empire, Mahogany, 2 Drawers, Pineapple Carved Legs & Posts 130.00
Furniture, Stand, Fruitwood, French, Drawer In Frieze, Signature 450.00
Furniture, Stand, Kettle, George III, Mahogany, Pull-Out Slide, 18th Century 650.00
Furniture, Stand, Kettle, George III, Mahogany, Square, Scallop, 18th Century 1600.00

Furniture, Stand, Mahogany, Bulbous Support, Queen Anne Tripod Foot 120.00
Furniture, Stand, Mahogany, Drop Leaf, 2 False Front Drawers 100.00
Furniture, Stand, Mahogany, X Stretcher, Oval Top, Reeded Bed 150.00
Furniture, Stand, Maple & Bird's-Eye Maple, 2 Drawers 65.00
Furniture, Stand, Muffin, Mahogany, Three Tier, Veneer 50.00

Furniture, Sofa, Federal, Mahogany, Carved, N.Y., C.1820
See Page 218

Furniture, Stand, Plant, George III, Mahogany, Drawer, 18th Century 475.00
Furniture, Stand, Regency, Mahogany, Turned Legs, Stretchers 45.00
Furniture, Stand, Sewing, Cherry, Drop Leaf, Two Drawers, Turned Legs 80.00
Furniture, Stand, Sewing, Cherry, Two Drawers, Duncan Phyfe Style Base 35.00
Furniture, Stand, Sewing, Empire, Lift Lid, Two Drawers, Brass Pulls 170.00
Furniture, Stand, Sewing, Hepplewhite, Two Drawers, Satinwood Inlaid 170.00
Furniture, Stand, Sewing, Martha Washington, Three Drawers, Inlaid 50.00
Furniture, Stand, Sewing, Rosewood Federal, Two, Drawer 365.00
Furniture, Stand, Sewing, Victorian, Walnut & Cherry, Lift Lid 100.00
Furniture, Stand, Sewing, Victorian, Walnut, Snake Legs 90.00
Furniture, Stand, Shaving, Oak, Drawer At Each End, Mug & Brush Holder 25.00
Furniture, Stand, Teakwood, Carved, Pink Marble Top, 13 In.High 80.00
Furniture, Stand, Three Drawers, Drop Leaf, Rope Legs, Sewing Bag 275.00
Furniture, Stand, Urn, George III, Mahogany, Concave Sides, Square Top, C.1750 .... 450.00
Furniture, Stand, Urn, George III, Mahogany, 18th Century, 26 1/2 In.Tall 125.00
Furniture, Stand, Whatnot, Maple, 5-Tier 60.00
Furniture, Step, Library, Mahogany, In Form Of Empire Chair, Cane Seat 275.00
Furniture, Stool, Burl Top, 9 In.High, 15 In.Diameter 17.50
Furniture, Stool, Charles II, Oak, Hinged Top, 17th Century, 20 In.Wide 725.00
Furniture, Stool, Continental, Fruitwood, Curule, 19th Century, Yellow Satin 175.00
Furniture, Stool, Empire, Curly Maple, C.1840, Needlepoint Slip Seat 160.00
Furniture, Stool, English, C.1750, 18 In.High .... *Illus* 1300.00

Furniture, Stool, English, C.1750, 18 In.High

Furniture, Stool, Foot, Large	22.50
Furniture, Stool, Foot, Pine, Scalloped Apron	10.00
Furniture, Stool, Foot, Pine, V Ends	10.00
Furniture, Stool, George III, Mahogany, Paneled Top, 18th Century, Pair	325.00
Furniture, Stool, George III, Mahogany, Rectangular, Drop In Seat, C.1750	275.00
Furniture, Stool, George III, Mahogany, Rectangular, Rose Pattern Cover	250.00
Furniture, Stool, Italian, Carved Gilt Wood, Serpentine Outline, C.1750, Pair	475.00
Furniture, Stool, Jointer's, Saddle Seat, Turned Legs	35.00
Furniture, Stool, Made Of Three Limbs & Tree.Trunk, Green Paint	6.00
Furniture, Stool, Mahogany, Needlepoint, X Legs, Needlepoint & Enamel Top	70.00
Furniture, Stool, Milk, Pine, Slab Seat, Octagonal Oak Legs, T Stretcher	40.00
Furniture, Stool, Organ, High Back	49.00
Furniture, Stool, Organ, Turn Up	16.00
Furniture, Stool, Piano, Claw Feet	10.50
Furniture, Stool, Piano, Miniature, 7 1/2 In.Round, For Schoenhut Piano	27.50
Furniture, Stool, Pine, Splay Legs, Mortised & Pin Construction	35.00
Furniture, Stool, Queen Anne, English, C.1710, Flame Stitch Upholstery	350.00
Furniture, Stool, Queen Anne, Walnut, Connecticut, C.1740, Scalloped Apron	2500.00
Furniture, Stool, Tyrolean, Oak Back, Oval Medallions Carved, C.1650, Pair	900.00
Furniture, Stool, Walnut, 5 Board	17.50
Furniture, Stool, 3 Legs, Blue Paint	9.00
Furniture, Stool, 4 Legs, 23 In.Long	45.00
Furniture, Stool, 4 Legs, 25 In.Long	45.00
Furniture, Stroller, Wooden	38.00
Furniture, Table De Chevet, Louis XVI, Provincial, Fruitwood	100.00 To 150.00
Furniture, Table, Architect, George III, Mahogany, 18th Century, 39 In.	1100.00
Furniture, Table, Banquet, Victorian, Mahogany, Dated Feb.12, 1856	495.00
Furniture, Table, Bed, Pine, Tapered Legs, 19 X 24 In.	15.00
Furniture, Table, Bedside, Louis XV, Provincial, Fruitwood, 18th Century	750.00
Furniture, Table, Bentwood, Oval Top, Walnut, 50 X 26 In.	375.00
Furniture, Table, Birch, Drop Leaf, Tapered Legs	225.00
Furniture, Table, Black Lacquer, Chinese, American Market, C.1820, Nest Of 3	250.00
Furniture, Table, Black Lacquer, Low, Rectangular Top, Square Legs	250.00
Furniture, Table, Book, George III, Satinwood, Rectangular Top, C.1750	1300.00
Furniture, Table, Bouillotte, Louis XVI Style, Mahogany, Circular, Marble Top	425.00
Furniture, Table, Brass Top, Round, 23 In.Diameter, Engraved	39.50
Furniture, Table, Brass, 24 In.Round Top, Engraved Egyptian Scene	49.50
Furniture, Table, Breakfast, Queen Anne, Walnut, New York, C.1750, Oblong	700.00
Furniture, Table, Breakfast, William IV, Mahogany, Round Top, Carved, C.1850	475.00
Furniture, Table, Butterfly, Cherry & Maple, American, Oval, Drop Leaf	1400.00
Furniture, Table, Canadian, Tilt Top, Round, Tuckaway Hinge Frame	90.00
Furniture, Table, Canadian, Tilt Top, 45 In.Diameter	100.00
Furniture, Table, Card, Chippendale, Mahogany, Carved, New York, C.1760, Oblong	2100.00
Furniture, Table, Card, Chippendale, Mahogany, Drawer In Front	275.00
Furniture, Table, Card, Chippendale, 34 1/2 In.Wide	150.00
Furniture, Table, Card, Empire, Mahogany, Bacon, Portsmouth, N.H., Carved	400.00
Furniture, Table, Card, Federal Style, Inlaid Mahogany, D Shape Top	275.00
Furniture, Table, Card, Federal, Inlaid Mahogany & Satinwood	500.00 To 750.00
Furniture, Table, Card, Federal, Inlaid Mahogany & Satinwood, Mass., C.1815	600.00
Furniture, Table, Card, Federal, Inlaid Mahogany, American, C.1790	950.00
Furniture, Table, Card, Federal, Inlaid Mahogany, C.1790, American	700.00
Furniture, Table, Card, Federal, Inlaid Mahogany, Goddard, C.1780, Demilune	2700.00
Furniture, Table, Card, Federal, Inlaid Mahogany, Mass., C.1790, Hinged Top	500.00
Furniture, Table, Card, Federal, Inlaid Mahogany, Reeded Edge, N.Y., C.1810	400.00
Furniture, Table, Card, Federal, Inlaid Mahogany, Rhode Island, C.1780	3000.00
Furniture, Table, Card, Federal, Inlaid Mahogany, Serpentine, Mass., C.1790	950.00
Furniture, Table, Card, Federal, Mahogany, Carved, New York, C.1815	275.00
Furniture, Table, Card, George III, Mahogany, 18th Century, Rectangular	400.00
Furniture, Table, Card, George III, Satinwood, Marquetry, 18th Century, Pair	3750.00
Furniture, Table, Card, Hepplewhite, Curly Maple, New England, C.1790	400.00
Furniture, Table, Card, Hepplewhite, Inlaid Mahogany, Baltimore, C.1790	400.00
Furniture, Table, Card, Hepplewhite, Inlaid Mahogany, C.1790, Serpentine Top	1100.00
Furniture, Table, Card, Hepplewhite, Inlaid, Center Leg Pulls Out, Drawer	275.00
Furniture, Table, Card, Hepplewhite, Mahogany With Inlay, Center Drawer	150.00
Furniture, Table, Card, Hepplewhite, Mahogany, Boston, C.1790-1800	1600.00
Furniture, Table, Card, Hepplewhite, Mahogany, Demilune, C.1790-1800	1100.00

Furniture, Table, Card, Hepplewhite, Mahogany, 19th Century, Tapered Legs 55.00
Furniture, Table, Card, Mahogany, C.1830, Rope Leg 135.00
Furniture, Table, Card, Mahogany, Directoire, C.1750 .... *Illus* 450.00
Furniture, Table, Card, Queen Anne, Mahogany, 19th Century, Demilune 150.00
Furniture, Table, Card, Queen Anne, Walnut, Oblong, Hinged, N.Y., C.1720 .... 1500.00
Furniture, Table, Card, Sheraton, American, Mahogany, Console, Stainwood Apron 625.00
Furniture, Table, Card, Sheraton, Mahogany, American, Console, Turret Corners 150.00
Furniture, Table, Center, Art Nouveau, Mahogany, Floral Carvings 325.00
Furniture, Table, Center, Federal, Mahogany, Carved, Philadelphia, C.1820 .... 375.00
Furniture, Table, Center, George III, Mahogany, Serpentine Top, 18th Century 1600.00
Furniture, Table, Center, Victorian, Marble Top, Oval, Carved Scroll Legs 250.00
Furniture, Table, Chairs, Six, Dining, Lion's Head, Paw Feet, C.1899 .... 600.00
Furniture, Table, Cherry & Tiger Maple, Turned Legs, Pegged Top 110.00
Furniture, Table, Cherry, Breadboard Top, Square, Tapered Legs 45.00
Furniture, Table, Cherry, Drop Leaf, Square Tapering Legs, 22 X 14 X 19 In. 70.00
Furniture, Table, Cherry, Drop Leaf, Tapered Legs, 18 X 40 In. Top 110.00
Furniture, Table, Cherry, Drop Leaf, Turned Legs, 39 In.Long, 19 In.High 100.00
Furniture, Table, Cherry, Drop Leaf, 1 Drawer, 21 In.Leaves 240.00
Furniture, Table, Cherry, Drop Leaf, 4 Legs, Sausage Turnings 90.00
Furniture, Table, Cherry, Drop Leaf, 6 Block & Turned Legs, 21 1/2 In.Leaves 300.00
Furniture, Table, Cherry, Turned, Gateleg, New England, C.1700, Oval Top 900.00
Furniture, Table, Cherry, 1 Drawer, Shelf 80.00
Furniture, Table, Cherrywood, Drop Leaf, Pennsylvania, C.1820 .... 250.00
Furniture, Table, Cherrywood, Inset With Cross-Stitch Sampler, Low, 1818 .... 180.00
Furniture, Table, Chess, Walnut, English, C.1850, Pedestal Base, Chessmen 130.00
Furniture, Table, Chinese Export, Black Lacquer, C.1850, Nest Of 4 .... 80.00
Furniture, Table, Chinese, Lacquer Panel, Pheasant, 18th Century, 17 In.Tall 350.00
Furniture, Table, Chinese, Lacquered, Polychrome Floral, Fruit, Pair 180.00
Furniture, Table, Chippendale, Cherry, Tilt Top, Tripod, C.1760, Square 80.00
Furniture, Table, Chippendale, Mahogany, Carved, Tilt Top, Penna., C.1760 .... 300.00
Furniture, Table, Chippendale, Mahogany, Carved, Tilt Top, Tripod, N.Y., C.1760 .... 1500.00
Furniture, Table, Chippendale, Mahogany, Carved, Tilt Top, Tripod, Phila., 1760 .... 2300.00
Furniture, Table, Chippendale, Mahogany, Chinese, England, 19th Century 275.00
Furniture, Table, Chippendale, Mahogany, Drop Leaf, Claw & Ball Feet 350.00
Furniture, Table, Chippendale, Mahogany, Pembroke, Philadelphia, C.1770 .... 750.00
Furniture, Table, Chippendale, Mahogany, Piecrust Edge, Tilt Top, N.Y., C.1760 .... 5250.00
Furniture, Table, Chippendale, Mahogany, Santo Domingo, Drop Leaf, C.1760-70 .... 1500.00
Furniture, Table, Chippendale, Mahogany, Tilt Top, C.1760 .... *Illus* 2400.00
Furniture, Table, Chippendale, Mahogany, Tilt Top, Philadelphia, C.1760 .... 2000.00
Furniture, Table, Chippendale, Mahogany, Tilt Top, Piecrust, New York, C.1760 .... 5250.00
Furniture, Table, Chippendale, Mahogany, Tilt Top, Tripod, New England, C.1780 .... 325.00

Furniture, Table, Card, Mahogany,
Directoire, C.1750

Furniture, Table, Chippendale, Mahogany,
Tilt Top, C.1760

Furniture, Table, Chippendale, Mahogany, Turned, Tripod, Philadelphia, C.1760 .... 1700.00
Furniture, Table, Chippendale, Pine, Country, Américan, Drop Leaf, Double Gate 175.00
Furniture, Table, Chippendale, Walnut, Carved, Tilt Top, Tripod, C.1760, Round 700.00
Furniture, Table, Chippendale, Walnut, Drop Leaf, American, 18th Century 450.00
Furniture, Table, Chippendale, 19th Century, Tilt Top, Birdcage 500.00
Furniture, Table, Coaching, Mahogany, English, 18th Century 90.00
Furniture, Table, Coffee, Art Deco, Walnut, Wrought Iron Tile Top, C.1920 .... 50.00
Furniture, Table, Coffee, Mahogany, Gallery Top, Smith & Watson, N.Y. 300.00
Furniture, Table, Coffee, Victorian, Walnut, Marble Top 69.00
Furniture, Table, Console, Empire, Mahogany, Petticoat, Rectangular Top 275.00
Furniture, Table, Console, George III, Satinwood, 18th Century, Pair 1600.00
Furniture, Table, Console, Hepplewhite, Mahogany, Inlaid, Oval Stretchers 1100.00
Furniture, Table, Console, Louis XV, Beechwood, Carved, Serpentine Top, C.1750 .... 400.00
Furniture, Table, Console, Louis XVI, Pine, Painted, Carved, 18th Century 750.00
Furniture, Table, Console, Regence, Carved Gilt Wood, Rectangular, C.1750 .... 2400.00
Furniture, Table, Console, South German, Walnut, D Shape Top, C.1720 .... 425.00
Furniture, Table, Console, Venetian, 18th Century Style, Mahogany 100.00
Furniture, Table, Dining, Directoire, Mahogany, Oval, Ormolu Rimmed, C.1750 .... 2400.00
Furniture, Table, Dining, Drop Leaf, Queen Anne, Oak, 18th Century ...., ... 300.00
Furniture, Table, Dining, Federal, Mahogany, Carved, Three Part, N.Y., C.1820 .... 600.00
Furniture, Table, Dining, Federal, Mahogany, N.Y., C.1815 .... *Illus* 4000.00
Furniture, Table, Dining, Louis XVI, Mahogany, Oval, Square Legs, C.1750 .... 1500.00
Furniture, Table, Dining, Mahogany, C.1820, 2 Pedestal, 90 In.Long Extended 650.00
Furniture, Table, Dining, Mahogany, Drop Leaf, C.1810 .... 99.00
Furniture, Table, Dining, Oak, Self-Storing Leaves, Spiral Legs, 43 X 49 In. 100.00
Furniture, Table, Dining, Queen Anne, Crotch Mahogany, Pad Foot 500.00
Furniture, Table, Dining, Queen Anne, Maple & Curly Maple, Drop Leaf, C.1740 .... 1300.00
Furniture, Table, Dining, Queen Anne, Maple, Drop Leaf, Rhode Island, C.1740 .... 1200.00
Furniture, Table, Dining, Queen Anne, Walnut, Drop Leaf, Oval, Delaware, C.1740 .... 1000.00
Furniture, Table, Dining, Victorian, Walnut, Oval, Extends To Eight Feet 195.00
Furniture, Table, Dining, Walnut & Mahogany, Gateleg, Massachusetts, C.1700 .... 1200.00
Furniture, Table, Dough, Five Leg, One Drop Leaf, Drawer, Pine 90.00
Furniture, Table, Dressing, Art Nouveau, Inlaid Mahogany, One Drawer 200.00
Furniture, Table, Dressing, Cherry & Mahogany, 3 Drawers, Oval Brass Pulls 100.00
Furniture, Table, Dressing, Chippendale, Mahogany, C.1760, One Drawer 200.00
Furniture, Table, Dressing, Curly Maple, One Drawer, Cabinet Base, Mirror 35.00
Furniture, Table, Dressing, Federal, Inlaid Mahogany, Serpentine, Salem, 1790 .... 300.00
Furniture, Table, Dressing, Hepplewhite, Kidney Shape, Roman Key Inlay 120.00
Furniture, Table, Dressing, Hepplewhite, Mahogany With Inlay, English, C.1780 .... 475.00
Furniture, Table, Dressing, Louis XV Style, Kingwood, Ormolu 450.00
Furniture, Table, Dressing, Mahogany, Carved Rose, One Drawer, Marked 'f R' 100.00
Furniture, Table, Dressing, New England, Yellow Paint, Stencil, Sandwich Knob 450.00
Furniture, Table, Dressing, Pine, Step-Down, Three Drawers, Turned Legs 70.00
Furniture, Table, Dressing, Queen Anne, Walnut, Drawer, 18th Century 750.00
Furniture, Table, Dressing, Queen Anne, Walnut, 18th Century, Rectangular Top 450.00
Furniture, Table, Dressing, Sheraton, Country 25.00
Furniture, Table, Dressing, Sheraton, Mahogany, Boston, C.1790-1800 .... 950.00
Furniture, Table, Dressing, Victorian, Decorated, Black Box Top, Floral 175.00
Furniture, Table, Dressing, William & Mary, Cherry, Oblong, New York, C.1690 .... 3250.00
Furniture, Table, Drop Leaf, Breadboard Top, Red Paint, 1 Drawer 550.00
Furniture, Table, Drop Leaf, Drawer, Rope Legs, Federal, Mahogany, 1820, 3o In. 150.00
Furniture, Table, Drop Leaf, George III, Mahogany, Pembroke, 18th Century 450.00
Furniture, Table, Drop Leaf, Pegged, Red Paint, Pine, 48 X 19 In. 42.50
Furniture, Table, Drop Leaf, Six Turned Legs, Cherry, 47 X 60 X 29 In.Tall 400.00
Furniture, Table, Drum Top, George III, Mahogany, Four Drawer, 18th Century 775.00
Furniture, Table, Duncan Phyfe, Drop Leaf, One Drawer, Brass Pulls, Claw Foot 110.00
Furniture, Table, Empire, Walnut 200.00
Furniture, Table, English Oak, Shoe Feet, Tilt Top, Tuckaway, 18th Century 175.00
Furniture, Table, English, Mahogany, Drop End, Lyre Leg, Two Drawers 475.00
Furniture, Table, Federal, Cherrywood, Pembroke, Pennsylvania, C.1815 .... 250.00
Furniture, Table, Federal, Inlaid Mahogany, Pembroke, Goddard, R.I., C.1760 .... 900.00
Furniture, Table, Federal, Mahogany, Drop Leaf, Oblong, Penna.C.1810 .... 325.00
Furniture, Table, Federal, Mahogany, Drop Leaf, Pennsylvania, C.1820 .... 250.00
Furniture, Table, Game, Cherry, Compartments To Hold Chips 40.00
Furniture, Table, Game, Directoire, Mahogany, C.1750 .... *Illus* 1050.00
Furniture, Table, Game, Duncan Phyfe, Mahogany, Lift Lid, American, C.1850 .... 350.00

Furniture, Table, Dining,
Federal, Mahogany,
N.Y., C.1815
See Page 222

Furniture, Table, Game, Directoire, Mahogany, C.1750
See Page 222

Furniture, Table, Game, George III, Mahogany, D Shape, 18th Century 625.00
Furniture, Table, Game, George III, Mahogany, Triple Top, 18th Century 1050.00
Furniture, Table, Game, Louis XV, Provincial, Fruitwood, Rectangular, C.1780 .... 550.00
Furniture, Table, Game, Mahogany & Curly Maple, 35 In.Long 800.00
Furniture, Table, Game, Mahogany & Satinwood, C.1780, Lift Lid, Inlaid 1000.00
Furniture, Table, Game, North Italian, Fruitwood, D Shape, Chess Board, C.1750 .... 575.00
Furniture, Table, Game, Pine Top, Maple Base, 36 In.Round 50.00
Furniture, Table, Game, Sheraton, Mahogany, Lift Lid, Fluted Leg 300.00
Furniture, Table, Gate Leg, George III, Mahogany, Drop Leaf, 18th Century 500.00
Furniture, Table, George II, Mahogany, Round, Tripod, 18th Century 1000.00
Furniture, Table, George II, Mahogany, Tripod, 18th Century, Round Top 130.00
Furniture, Table, George III, Burr Walnut, Rectangular Top, C.1750, Nest Of 3 .... 800.00
Furniture, Table, George III, Mahogany, Drawer, Rectangular, 18th Century 125.00
Furniture, Table, George III, Mahogany, Gateleg, Rectangular Top, C.1750 .... 450.00
Furniture, Table, George III, Mahogany, Rectangular Top, C.1750, Nest Of 4 .... 450.00
Furniture, Table, George III, Mahogany, Satinwood & Ebony, C.1750, Nest Of 3 .... 325.00
Furniture, Table, George III, Mahogany, Tilt Top, Rectangular, C.1750 .... 300.00
Furniture, Table, George III, Mahogany, Tilt Top, Tripod, Octagonal, C.1750 .... 250.00
Furniture, Table, George III, Mahogany, Tripod, Octagonal, 19th Century 325.00
Furniture, Table, George III, Mahogany, Tripod, Round, Piecrust Edge, C.1750 .... 550.00
Furniture, Table, George III, Tulipwood, Tilt Top, Octagonal, 18th Century 425.00
Furniture, Table, Harvest, Drop Leaf, Single Board Top, Pine, 6 Feet 400.00
Furniture, Table, Harvest, Pine, Two Drop Leaves, 8 Ft.Long, 31 In.High 125.00
Furniture, Table, Hepplewhite, Mahogany, Drop Leaf, One Drawer 175.00
Furniture, Table, Hepplewhite, Mahogany, Irish, 18th Century, Pembroke 375.00
Furniture, Table, Hutch, Pine, Storage Compartment Seat, 33 X 48 In. 250.00
Furniture, Table, Hutch, Sheraton, American, Red Paint, 40 In.Square Top 350.00
Furniture, Table, Iron, Nickel Plated, Engraved Portrait 29.50

Furniture, Table, Jade Top, Baroque Shape, Gold Colored Base 2375.00
Furniture, Table, Kidney Shape, One Drawer 65.00
Furniture, Table, Kitchen, Peasant, C.1670 .... 450.00
Furniture, Table, Lamp, White Marble Top 65.00
Furniture, Table, Library, Drum Top, George III, Mahogany, 18th Century 550.00
Furniture, Table, Library, Regency, Rosewood, 19th Century, Brass Inlaid 900.00
Furniture, Table, Louis XV, Parcel Gilt, Iron, C.1750 .... *Illus* 900.00

Furniture, Table, Louis XV,
Parcel Gilt, Iron, C.1750

Furniture, Table, Mahogany, Breadboard Top, One Drawer 80.00
Furniture, Table, Mahogany, Drop Leaf, Gateleg, Salesman's Sample 40.00
Furniture, Table, Mahogany, Drop Leaf, Shell Carved Knee, Claw & Ball Feet 300.00
Furniture, Table, Mahogany, Drop Leaf, Swing Leg, Chippendale Legs 325.00
Furniture, Table, Mahogany, Drop Leaf, Swing Leg, Tapered Legs, Spade Feet 80.00
Furniture, Table, Mahogany, Inset With Cross-Stitch Sampler, Low, Dated 1831 .... 250.00
Furniture, Table, Mahogany, Tier, On Rollers 42.50
Furniture, Table, Mahogany, Tilt Top, C.1830, Palette Top, 3 Scroll Feet 400.00
Furniture, Table, Mahogany, Tilt Top, Snake Feet, Box Birdcage 115.00
Furniture, Table, Mahogany, Tuckaway, Sausage Turned Legs, Brass Casters 100.00
Furniture, Table, Mahogany, 3 Drawers, Marlboro Feet, Rectangular Legs 200.00
Furniture, Table, Marble Top, Sewing Machine Legs 40.00
Furniture, Table, Nest Of 4, Black Lacquered, Glass Top, Oriental Figures 300.00
Furniture, Table, Night, Federal, Inlaid Cherry, Pennsylvania, C.1800 .... 300.00
Furniture, Table, Oak, Gateleg, Drop Leaf, 54 X 40 In. With Sides Up 49.50
Furniture, Table, Oak, Gateleg, Inlaid Top 45.00
Furniture, Table, Oak, Queen Anne Type, Round, 32 X 24 X 29 1/2 In. 68.50
Furniture, Table, Oak, Round 65.00
Furniture, Table, Oak, 4 Legs, Brass Outer Rim 39.50
Furniture, Table, Occasional Tilt Top, George Iii, Mahogany, 18th Century 950.00
Furniture, Table, Occasional, Art Nouveau, French, Inliad Mahogany, 2 Tier 275.00
Furniture, Table, Occasional, George I, Mahogany, 18th Century, Rectangular 1200.00
Furniture, Table, Occasional, George III, Style, Satinwood, Oval, X Stretcher 220.00
Furniture, Table, Occasional, George III, Mahogany, Square Top, 18th Century 500.00
Furniture, Table, Occasional, George III, Mahogany, Tilt Top, 18th Century 130.00
Furniture, Table, Occasional, George III, Mahogany, Tilt Top, 18th Century 375.00
Furniture, Table, Occasional, George III, Mahogany, 18th Century 250.00
Furniture, Table, Occasional, George III, Mahogany, 18th Century, Pair 80.00
Furniture, Table, Occasional, Louis Iii, Style, Kingwood, Parquetry, Kidney 200.00
Furniture, Table, Occasional, Louis XV, Kingwood, Marquetry, C.1780 .... 4000.00
Furniture, Table, Occasional, Louis XV, Kingwood, Signed P.Roussel, C.1750 .... 1900.00
Furniture, Table, Occasional, Louis XVI Style, Kingwood & Rosewood, Round 1100.00
Furniture, Table, Occasional, North Italian, Fruitwood, Oval, C.1850 .... 160.00
Furniture, Table, Occasional, North Italian, Fruitwood, Rectangular, C.1850 .... 260.00
Furniture, Table, Occasional, Tilt Top, George III, Mahogany, 18th Century 2100.00
Furniture, Table, One Drawer, Tapered & Grooved Legs, Black Base 35.00
Furniture, Table, Papier-Mache, Victorian, Mother-Of-Pearl Inlay, Set Of 2 .... 100.00
Furniture, Table, Papier-Mache, Victorian, Mother-Of-Pearl Inlay, Set Of 4 .... 400.00
Furniture, Table, Parlor, Black Walnut, Marble Top, 32 X 23 X 30 In. 175.00
Furniture, Table, Parlor, Walnut, Victorian, Pedestal, 37 In.Diameter 300.00
Furniture, Table, Pembroke, Birch, Tapered Legs, 19 1/2 X 35 1/2 In. 145.00

Furniture, Table, Pembroke, Cherry, American, C.1770, Rectangular Top 425.00
Furniture, Table, Pembroke, Cherry, One Drawer, 36 In. 95.00
Furniture, Table, Pembroke, Chippendale, Mahogany, Serpentine Top, 2 Leaves 325.00
Furniture, Table, Pembroke, Curly Maple, American, 18th Century 800.00
Furniture, Table, Pembroke, George III, Mahogany, Drop Leaf, 18th Century 575.00
Furniture, Table, Pembroke, George III, Mahogany, Oval Top, 18th Century 325.00
Furniture, Table, Pembroke, George III, Mahogany, Rectangular Top, C.1750 .... 400.00
Furniture, Table, Pembroke, George III, Mahogany, Rectangular, 18th Century 850.00
Furniture, Table, Pembroke, George III, Mahogany, Two Drawers, 18th Century 1000.00
Furniture, Table, Pembroke, George III, Oval, 18th Century 750.00
Furniture, Table, Pembroke, George III, Satinwood, Oval Top, C.1750, Pair 2200.00
Furniture, Table, Pembroke, George III, Satinwood, Rectangular, C.1750 .... 1200.00
Furniture, Table, Pembroke, Hepplewhite, Mahogany, Rhode Island, C.1780 .... 950.00
Furniture, Table, Pembroke, Mahogany, Bowfront, One Drawer, Oval Top 2000.00
Furniture, Table, Pembroke, Mahogany, Drawer, Square Legs, Inside Chamfer 175.00
Furniture, Table, Pembroke, Mahogany, New York, C.1790, One Drawer, Brass 500.00
Furniture, Table, Pembroke, Mahogany, Oval 185.00
Furniture, Table, Piecrust, George III, Mahogany, Circular, 18th Century 325.00
Furniture, Table, Piecrust, George III, Mahogany, Tilt Top, 18th Century 750.00
Furniture, Table, Pine & Maple, Swing Leg, Drop Leaf, Square Legs 150.00
Furniture, Table, Pine, Breadboard Top, 1 Drawer 180.00
Furniture, Table, Pine, Drawer On Front, 18 X 36 X 15 In. 34.50
Furniture, Table, Pine, Handmade, Wooden Pulls On Drawer, 17 X 23 In. 29.50
Furniture, Table, Pine, Work, H Stretched, Scrubbed Top 45.00
Furniture, Table, Poker, Pedestal Base, Shelf Each Player, 37 In. 110.00
Furniture, Table, Queen Anne Style, Oak, Round 140.00
Furniture, Table, Queen Anne Tea, Pine, Snake Foot 195.00
Furniture, Table, Queen Anne, Cherry & Maple, Drop Leaf, Mass., C.1740 .... 1200.00
Furniture, Table, Queen Anne, Cherry, Connecticut, Drop Leaf, Duck Feet 700.00
Furniture, Table, Queen Anne, Cherry, Drop Leaf, Rhode Island, C.1740 .... 800.00
Furniture, Table, Queen Anne, Curly Maple, Tilt Top, Circular, Penna., C.1750 .... 275.00
Furniture, Table, Queen Anne, Mahogany, Drop Leaf, American, C.1740 .... 450.00
Furniture, Table, Queen Anne, Mahogany, Drop Leaf, R.I., C.1740 .... 1300.00 To 1900.00
Furniture, Table, Queen Anne, Maple & Cherry, Drop Leaf, Oval, Mass., C.1740 .... 1000.00
Furniture, Table, Queen Anne, Maple, Drop Leaf, Oval, C.1740, Cabriole Legs 950.00
Furniture, Table, Queen Anne, Walnut, Drop Leaf, Philadelphia, C.1740 .... 1000.00
Furniture, Table, Queen Anne, 18th Century, Drop Leaf, Oval, Padded Feet 300.00
Furniture, Table, Reading, Regency, Mahogany, Kidney Shape, C.185 .... 200.00 To 225.00
Furniture, Table, Regency, Burr Yewwood, Low, Round Top, 19th Century 130.00
Furniture, Table, Regency, Mahogany, Rectangular Top, 19th Century, Nest Of 4 .... 300.00
Furniture, Table, Regency, Rosewood, Rectangular, 19th Century, Nest Of 3 .... 325.00
Furniture, Table, Renaissance Design, Marble Top, Walnut, Oval 125.00
Furniture, Table, Satinwood, Rosewood Crossbanding, Nest Of 4 .... 200.00
Furniture, Table, Sawbuck, 3 X 5 1/2 Feet 80.00
Furniture, Table, Serving, Federal, Inlaid Mahogany, New York, C.1810 .... 1000.00
Furniture, Table, Serving, Federal, Inlaid Mahogany, Rhode Island, C.1790 .... 3750.00
Furniture, Table, Serving, Federal, Mahogany, New York, C.1820, Marble Top 200.00
Furniture, Table, Sewing, Mahogany, New York, 1830, Stenciled, Two Drawers 600.00
Furniture, Table, Sewing, Maple & Mahogany, Salem, 1820, Lift Top 350.00
Furniture, Table, Sewing, Two Drawers, Spindles, Pedestal Base, Walnut 25.00
Furniture, Table, Sheraton Style, Circular, Galleried Top 55.00
Furniture, Table, Sheraton, Cherry, Drop Leaf, One Drawer, Square Legs 125.00
Furniture, Table, Sheraton, Drop Leaf, Curly Maple Base 150.00
Furniture, Table, Sheraton, Mahogany, Drop Leaf, Drawers, Turned Legs, English 110.00
Furniture, Table, Sheraton, Mahogany, Salem, Mass., C.1820 .... 385.00
Furniture, Table, Side, Cherry, Drawer, Brass Cup Casters, Turned Legs 225.00
Furniture, Table, Side, Federal, Mahogany, New York, C.1820, Marble Top 175.00
Furniture, Table, Side, George I, Walnut, Long Drawer, 18th Century 850.00
Furniture, Table, Side, George I, Yew Wood, Rectangular, 18th Century 275.00
Furniture, Table, Side, George III, Mahogany, Rectangular Top, C.1750 .... 425.00
Furniture, Table, Side, George III, Satinwood, D Shape Top, Metal Rim, C.1750 .... 4750.00
Furniture, Table, Side, George III, Satinwood, Serpentine, 18th Century 850.00
Furniture, Table, Side, Mahogany, 6 Ft.Long, 16 In.Wide, 26 In.Tall 80.00
Furniture, Table, Side, Spanish, Walnut, 17th Century, Rectangular Top 400.00
Furniture, Table, Sofa, George III, Mahogany, D Shape, Drop Leaf .... 425.00 To 1400.00
Furniture, Table, Sofa, George III, Mahogany, Rectangular Top, C.1750 .... 450.00

Furniture, Table, Sofa, Regency, Rosewood, 19th Century, Rectangular Top 400.00
Furniture, Table, Spanish, Walnut, Low, 17th Century, Rectangular Top 550.00
Furniture, Table, Splayed Legs, Mortised, 14 1/4 In.High 40.00
Furniture, Table, Square Top, Platform Halfway Up 24.50
Furniture, Table, Square, Carved Basket Weave Rim, Brass Ball & Claw Feet 29.50
Furniture, Table, Tavern, Drawer, Red Painted Base, Tapered Legs, 37 X 52 In. 150.00
Furniture, Table, Tavern, English, Oak, 18th Century, Block & Turned Legs 100.00
Furniture, Table, Tavern, Maple & Pine, Button Feet, C.1720-40 .... 575.00
Furniture, Table, Tavern, Pine & Ash, Oval, Mass., C.1720 .... 500.00
Furniture, Table, Tavern, Walnut & Pine, Turned, New England, C.1700 .... 1100.00
Furniture, Table, Tavern, Walnut, Pennsylvania, Bun Feet, 33 X 50 In. 400.00
Furniture, Table, Tavern, Walnut, Turned, Penna., C.1720, Oblong Top 450.00
Furniture, Table, Tea, Cherry, Rhode Island, Dish Top, C.1760 .... 2000.00
Furniture, Table, Tea, Chippendale, Mahogany, American, 18th Century 1200.00
Furniture, Table, Tea, Chippendale, Mahogany, Carved, Porringer Top, C.1750 .... 5000.00
Furniture, Table, Tea, Chippendale, Mahogany, Tilt Top, Circular, Conn., C.1760 .... 600.00
Furniture, Table, Tea, Mahogany, Chippendale, Tilt Top, English 225.00
Furniture, Table, Tea, Maple, New England, C.1730-40, Duck Feet 550.00
Furniture, Table, Tea, Maple, Porringer Top, Squared Cabriole Legs 7000.00
Furniture, Table, Tea, Pine, Painted, Circular, Tilt Top, Snake Legs 400.00
Furniture, Table, Tea, Queen Anne, Cherry, C.1780, Oblong, Dished Top 1300.00
Furniture, Table, Tea, Queen Anne, Cherry, Connecticut, C.1740, Oblong Top 3000.00
Furniture, Table, Tea, Queen Anne, Connecticut Country, Birdcage, Snake Feet 250.00
Furniture, Table, Tea, Queen Anne, Mahogany, New England, C.1730 .... 2400.00
Furniture, Table, Tea, Queen Anne, Mahogany, Tilt Top, Figured Top, Snake Feet 225.00
Furniture, Table, Tea, Queen Anne, Maple, R.I., C.1740, Oval Top .... 575.00 To 650.00
Furniture, Table, Tiger Maple, Drop Leaf, 1 Drawer, Turned, Grooved Legs 225.00
Furniture, Table, Tiger Maple, Tilt Top, Round Dish Top, Snake Feet 200.00
Furniture, Table, Tiger Maple, Tripod, Urn Support, Queen Anne Foot 200.00
Furniture, Table, Tilt Top, Cutout Corners, Three Legs, Cherry 225.00
Furniture, Table, Tilt Top, Swivel, Pedestal Base, Walnut, Circa 1850 .... 275.00
Furniture, Table, Tilt Top, Tuckaway, Circular, Canadian, 32 In.Diameter 50.00
Furniture, Table, Tilt Top, Walnut, 39 In.Diameter 175.00
Furniture, Table, Victorian, Satinwood, Marquetry, 19th Century, 2 Tiers 190.00
Furniture, Table, Victorian, Slate Top, Tripod, Round, Painted Floral, Pair 175.00
Furniture, Table, Victorian, Walnut, Marble Top, 2 X 3 Ft. 135.00
Furniture, Table, Victorian, Walnut, Marble Top, 24 X 32 In. 139.00
Furniture, Table, Victorian, Walnut, Oval, Marble, 32 In.High 265.00
Furniture, Table, Victorian, Walnut, Oval, 29 X 21 In. 65.00
Furniture, Table, Victorian, Walnut, Round, 3 Scroll Feet, 36 In.Diameter 80.00
Furniture, Table, Victorian, Walnut, Two Drawers, Turned Legs 80.00
Furniture, Table, Walnut & Mahogany, Mass., C.1700-20 .... *Illus* 1200.00
Furniture, Table, Walnut, Drop Leaf, Rectangular Top, One Drawer 140.00
Furniture, Table, Walnut, Drop Leaf, 6 Turned Legs, 45 X 20 X 29 In. 80.00
Furniture, Table, Walnut, English, Drop End, Two Drawers 325.00
Furniture, Table, Walnut, Gateleg, Drop Leaf, 18th Century 200.00
Furniture, Table, Walnut, One Drawer, Grooved Tapered Legs 52.50
Furniture, Table, Walnut, Victorian, Oval, 32 X 24 X 29 In. 65.00
Furniture, Table, William & Mary, Cherry, Slate Top, New York, C.1720 .... 3500.00
Furniture, Table, William & Mary, Pine & Maple, Gateleg, Pennsylvania, C.1690 .... 2100.00
Furniture, Table, Wine, Piecrust Top, George Iii, Mahogany, 18th Century 900.00
Furniture, Table, Work, Astragal End, N.Y., C.1810 .... *Illus* 1000.00
Furniture, Table, Work, Federal, Inlaid Mahogany & Curly Maple, Phila., 1800 .... 400.00
Furniture, Table, Work, Federal, Inlaid Mahogany & Satinwood, C.1800, Oblong 2000.00
Furniture, Table, Work, Federal, Inlaid Mahogany, Massachusetts, C.1810 .... 400.00
Furniture, Table, Work, Federal, Inlaid Mahogany, New York, C.1810, Oblong Top 275.00
Furniture, Table, Work, Federal, Inlaid Mahogany, 2 Drawers, American, C.1800 .... 550.00
Furniture, Table, Work, Federal, Mahogany, Astragal End, New York, C.1805 .... 850.00
Furniture, Table, Work, Federal, Mahogany, New England, C.1810 .... 225.00
Furniture, Table, Work, Federal, Mahogany, New York, C.1815, 2 Drawers 175.00
Furniture, Table, Work, George III, Mahogany, Rectangular, 18th Century 300.00
Furniture, Table, Work, Pine, Dovetailed, Joint Braces At Foot 39.50
Furniture, Table, Work, Pine, Square Legs, H Stretcher, Mortised 65.00
Furniture, Table, Writing, Carlton House, C.1790 .... 900.00
Furniture, Table, Writing, Directoire, Mahogany, 19th Century, Green Leather 625.00
Furniture, Table, Writing, George II, Walnut, 18th Century, Rectangular Top 500.00

Furniture, Table, Writing, George III, Mahogany, C.1850 .... *Illus* 550.00
Furniture, Table, Writing, George III, Mahogany, Carlton House, C.1750 .... 5250.00
Furniture, Table, Writing, George III, Mahogany, Library, Rectangular, Leather 2500.00
Furniture, Table, Writing, George III, Mahogany, Pedestal, 18th Century 725.00
Furniture, Table, Writing, George III, Satinwood, Carlton House, C.1750 .... 3250.00

Furniture, Table,
Walnut & Mahogany,
Mass., C.1700-20
See Page 226

Furniture, Table, Work,
Astragal End, N.Y., C.1810
See Page 226

Furniture, Table, Writing, George III,
Mahogany, C.1850

Furniture, Table, Writing, Kneehole, George III, Mahogany, 18th Century 650.00
Furniture, Table, Writing, Louis XV, Provincial, Fruitwood, Lady's, C.1750 .... 500.00
Furniture, Table, Writing, Mahogany, Leather Top, Gold Tooled, 29 1/2 In.High 170.00
Furniture, Table, Writing, Pedestal, George III, Mahogany, 19th Century 475.00
Furniture, Table, Writing, Tambour, George III, Mahogany, 18th Century 700.00
Furniture, Table, Writing, Tambour, George III, Mahogany, 18th Century 950.00
Furniture, Tallboy, Cherry, Philadelphia, C.1770, Molded Top, Ogee Feet 800.00
Furniture, Tea Caddy, Coffin Shape, Brass Feet & Handles, Mahogany 148.00
Furniture, Tea Caddy, Curly Maple, Sheffield Handle, 2 Compartments 150.00
Furniture, Tea Caddy, George II, Mahogany, Lion Design, 18th Century, 8 In. 150.00
Furniture, Tea Caddy, George III, Mahogany, Oval Sunburst Medallion On Top 75.00
Furniture, Tea Caddy, George III, Silver & Mahogany, Gillois, 1763, Pair 750.00
Furniture, Tea Caddy, Georgian, C.1790, Inlaid 55.00
Furniture, Tea Caddy, Regency, Inlaid Mahogany, Coffered Lid, C.1850 .... 70.00
Furniture, Tea Caddy, Regency, Satinwood, Apple, C.1850 .... 200.00
Furniture, Tea Caddy, Regency, Satinwood, Keyhole 175.00
Furniture, Tea Caddy, Regency, Stainwood, Pear, C.1850 .... 120.00
Furniture, Tea Caddy, Regency, Satinwood, 19th Century 200.00
Furniture, Tea Caddy, Rosewood Inlaid, 9 In.Long 40.00
Furniture, Tea Caddy, Rosewood, Spool Feet 40.00
Furniture, Tea Caddy, Sheraton, Inlaid Mahogany, C.1790, Medallions 200.00
Furniture, Tea Caddy, Victorian, Rosewood, Burl Walnut Inlay, Lion Handles 35.00
Furniture, Tea Cart, Oak 65.00

Furniture, **Tea Tray**, Stand, Tole, Victorian, Floral Design, 19th Century 225.00
Furniture, **Teapoy**, Regency, Rosewood, 19th Century, 29 In.High 200.00
Furniture, **Torchere**, George III, Painted, Parcel Gilt, Round, C.1750, Pair 300.00
Furniture, **Torchere**, Regency, Black Japanned, Round Top, 19th Century, Pair 800.00
Furniture, **Tray**, Butler's, Mahogany, Folding Base 40.00
Furniture, **Wardrobe & Bed Combination**, Child's, 2 Drawers In Bottom 25.00
Furniture, **Washstand**, Cherry, Single Cabinet Beneath, Batwing Splash Back 90.00
Furniture, **Washstand**, Child's, Fruit Pulls, Drawers, 31 X 24 X 12 In. 38.00
Furniture, **Washstand**, Curly Maple, Drawer At Bottom, Sandwich Knob 100.00
Furniture, **Washstand**, Drawer, Spool Towel Racks, Pine 32.50
Furniture, **Washstand**, Made At Zoar, Ohio 125.00
Furniture, **Washstand**, Marble Top, Pine, Mahogany 32.00
Furniture, **Washstand**, Painted, One Drawer 27.50
Furniture, **Washstand**, Pine & Maple, Drawer At Bottom, Dovetailed Gallery 45.00
Furniture, **Washstand**, Pine, C.1860 .... 95.00
Furniture, **Washstand**, Pine, One Drawer & Shelf, Turned Legs 90.00
Furniture, **Washstand**, Victorian, Oak, Marble Top, One Door & Drawer 80.00
Furniture, **Whatnot**, Mahogany, English, C.1775 .... *Illus* 600.00
Furniture, **Whatnot**, Sheraton, Mahogany, 4 Tier, New York, C.1790 .... 375.00
Furstenberg, Bust, Portrait, Biscuit, Voltaire, C.1780 .... 80.00
Furstenberg, Chocolate Pot, Cylindrical, Wood Handle, Medallion, C.1780 .... 200.00

*Galle Glass was made by the Galle Factory founded by Emile Galle of
France. The firm made Cameo Glass, furniture, and other art nouveau items
from 1879 to 1905.*
Galle, see also Cameo Glass, Furniture
Galle, **Atomizer**, Perfume, Cameo 225.00
Galle, **Basket & Tray**, Reticulated, Signed 95.00
Galle, **Bottle**, Scent, Onion Shape, Amber, Thistle Spray In Pink & Brown 140.00
Galle, **Bowl**, Cabinet, Signed, Purple Cut Flowers On Orange, Cameo 95.00
Galle, **Bowl**, Covered, Lake With Boat Scene, 6 1/2 In.High 275.00
Galle, **Bowl**, Flower, Royal Blue, Pink, Morning Glory, Cameo, 7 3/4 In. 235.00
Galle, **Box**, Ginko Leaves, Stems, Butterfly, Signed, Cameo, 5 1/2 In.Diameter 175.00
Galle, **Box**, Floral, Lavender, Blue, Purple, Signed, 4 In.Diameter, 3 In.High 175.00
Galle, **Box**, Flowers, Leaves, Purple, Lavender, Signed, Cover, 5 In.Diameter 165.00
Galle, **Box**, Powder, Base & Lid Signed, Amethyst & Blue On Pink 325.00
Galle, **Compote**, Dark & Light Chartreuse, Maple Leaves, Signed, Cameo 295.55
Galle, **Cruet**, Amber, Enameled Thistles, Sprial Shape Stopper, Signed, 9 In. 185.00
Galle, **Decanter**, Pastel Blue, Wafer Base, Panels, Chrysanthemums, 8 In.High 385.00
Galle, **Dish**, Bonbon, Enameled Buds, Handles, 4 Button Legs 150.00
Galle, **Lamp**, Cameo, 22 In.High .... *Illus* 1200.00
Galle, **Lamp**, Table, Rust & Brown Floral, Coolie Hat Shape Shade, 32 In.High 1350.00
Galle, **Lamp**, Tiger Lilies, Orange, Yellow, Signed Base & Shade, Cameo 750.00
Galle, **Liqueur Glass**, Amber, Enameled Floral, Signed, 2 In.High 30.00

Furniture, Whatnot,
Mahogany, English, C.1775

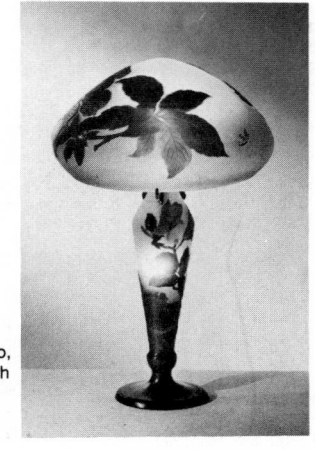

Galle, Lamp, Cameo,
22 In.High

Galle, Pitcher, Thistle Design, Amber, Enamel, Signed, 9 1/2 In.Tall 225.00
Galle, Plate, Birds, Blue, White, Pierced Edge, Signed, 7 1/2 In.Diameter 75.00
Galle, Plate, Blue, Gray, Floral, Dragon, Crown, Signed Galle, Nancy 42.00
Galle, Plate, Nancy, St.Clement Faience, Armorial Decor, 9 In. 35.00
Galle, Saucer, Green Leaves With White Cut To Pink, Frosted, Cameo 65.00
Galle, Tray, Horseman, Children, Wooden Inlay, Signed, 17 X 24 In. 185.00
Galle, Tray, Rosewood, Inlaid Art Nouveau Flowers, Butterflies, 18 In.Long 125.00
Galle, Vase, Acid Cut, Red Currants On White & Yellow, Signed, Cameo 95.00
Galle, Vase, Acorns, Leaves, Green, Rose, Cut, Signed, Cameo, 5 1/4 In.Tall 150.00
Galle, Vase, Amber, Maroon, Polished Surfaces, 6 In. 165.00
Galle, Vase, Berries, Leaves, Purple, Signed, Cameo, 5 In.Tall 125.00
Galle, Vase, Blackberries, Leaves, Green, Brown, Pink, Bulbous, Cameo, 6 1/2 In. 165.00
Galle, Vase, Blown In Mold, Frieze Of Cherries In Amber On Yellow, Signed 600.00
Galle, Vase, Blue, Rose, Morning Glories, Vines, Footed, 11 In.Tall 295.00
Galle, Vase, Brown, Tan, Trees, Lake, Birds, Stick Neck, Signed, 11 In.High 185.00
Galle, Vase, Bud, Signed, Cameo, 6 3/4 In.High 140.00
Galle, Vase, Bud, Signed, Dark Red, 6 In. 250.00
Galle, Vase, Buds, Leaves, Green, Flared Mouth, 24 1/2 In.Tall 300.00
Galle, Vase, Bulbous, Landscape In Green On Pink, Brown, Signed, Cameo 170.00
Galle, Vase, Bulbous, Pale Green, Polychrome Enamel Floral, Signed 80.00
Galle, Cabinet, Bottle Form, Leafy Sprays, Yellow Green, Signed, Cameo 160.00
Galle, Vase, Cabinet, Signed, Cut Berries & Leaves, Brown, Green, & Red, Cameo 115.00
Galle, Vase, Cabinet, Signed, Cut Brown Florals On Yellow 115.00
Galle, Vase, Cabinet, Signed, Cut Orange Nasturtiums, Yellow & Frosted 145.00
Galle, Vase, Cabinet, Signed, Cut, Purple Flowers, Cameo 105.00
Galle, Vase, Cabinet, Signed, Pink With Green Spidery Flowers, 4 In.High 110.00
Galle, Vase, Cabinet, Signed, 4 In.Tall 150.00
Galle, Vase, Camel, Enamel, Cylindrical, 13 1/4 In.High 300.00
Galle, Vase, Camel, Scenic, Mountains, Trees, Blue, Purple, 16 In.Tall 425.00
Galle, Vase, Cattails, Frogs, Insects, Birds, Flared Neck, Cameo 175.00
Galle, Vase, Clematis, Green & Lavender, White, Salmon Field, 29 In.High 895.00
Galle, Vase, Covered, Globular, Swirled Ribs, Tulips & Floral On Smoky Green 500.00
Galle, Vase, Cranberry Over Matte White, Nasturtium, Leaves, Cameo, 8 In.High 265.00
Galle, Vase, Cut, Green With Faint Orange, Cameo, 19 In.Tall 475.00
Galle, Vase, Cut, Lavender Flower, Relief, Signed, Cameo 175.00
Galle, Vase, Cylindrical, Flaring, Enameled, Flowering Branches, Signed 150.00
Galle, Vase, Cylindrical, Polychrome Scrolling Foliage, Applied Bosses 170.00
Galle, Vase, Cylindrical, Relief Amber Water Plants On White, Signed, Cameo 160.00
Galle, Vase, Deep Orange Flowers, Leaves, Frosted Ground, 6 1/2 In.High 145.00
Galle, Vase, Dragonfly Design, Signed, Cameo 425.00
Galle, Vase, Fern Design, Frosted, Green, Signed, Cameo, 13 1/2 In.Tall 275.00
Galle, Vase, Flattened Globular, Water Plants In Purple On Gray, Signed 150.00
Galle, Vase, Floral Design, Banjo Shape, Red, Signed, Cameo, 6 1/2 In.High 145.00
Galle, Vase, Floral, Lavender To White, Crescent Shape Top, Signed, 4 1/2 In. 120.00
Galle, Vase, Floral, Maroon On Cream Ground, Slender Neck, Cameo, 15 In.High 250.00
Galle, Vase, Floral, Purple & Yellow Design, Cameo, 10 In.High 170.00
Galle, Vase, Floral, Yellow To Brown, Flared Neck, Signed, 6 1/2 In.High 165.00
Galle, Vase, Flowers, Leaves, Banjo Shape, Maroon, Frosted, Signed, Cameo, 7 In. 150.00
Galle, Vase, Flowers, Leaves, Purple, Pink, White, Hand Carved, Signed 137.50
Galle, Vase, Flowers, Leaves, White, Gold, Signed, Cameo, 7 1/2 In.High 195.00
Galle, Vase, Forest Scene, Four Colors, Cameo, 10 In.Tall 185.00
Galle, Vase, Frosted Peach Ground, Nasturtium, Signed, Cameo, 5 1/8 In.High 210.00
Galle, Vase, Fruit, Leaves, Green, Footed, Signed, 15 1/2 In.High 175.00
Galle, Vase, Fruiting Plant, Amber To Green On Pink, Cameo, 5 In.High 60.00
Galle, Vase, Globular, Brown Lakeside View On Beige To Yellow, Signed, Cameo 425.00
Galle, Vase, Globular, Purple Daisy Pattern On Gray Green Forsted 375.00
Galle, Vase, Gray, Blue, Champagne Ground, 8 In.High 150.00
Galle, Vase, Green & Blue Ground, Tan Leaves & Pods, Bulbous Bottom, Signed 250.00
Galle, Vase, Green, Red, Frosted, Butterfly, Leaves, Cameo, 3 1/2 In.High 105.00
Galle, Vase, Iris & Leaves, Amber, Purple, Signed, 16 1/2 In.High 800.00
Galle, Vase, Iris Design, Light To Dark Blue, Signed 295.00
Galle, Vase, Lavender Ground, Purple Floral, Signed, 6 In.High 175.00
Galle, Vase, Lavender, Purple, Leaves, Flowers, Signed, Cameo, 4 In.High 95.00
Galle, Vase, Maroon On Yellow Ground, Signed, 8 In.High 350.00
Galle, Vase, Mauve, Gray, Water Lily Scene, 10 1/2 In.High 175.00
Galle, Vase, Molded, Yellow, 10 1/2 In.High .... *Illus* 1100.00

Galle, Vase, Molded, Yellow, 10 1/2 In.
See Page 229

Galle, Vase, Peonies, Leaves, Orange, Signed, 14 In.High 400.00
Galle, Vase, Pine Tree Foliage, Burrs, Pinecones, Brown, Champagne, Bronze 175.00
Galle, Vase, Pinecones, Pine Needles, Stems, Signed, Cameo, 6 In.Tall 135.00
Galle, Vase, Pink Ground, Lime Green Thistles, Signed, 4 In.High 125.00
Galle, Vase, Pink, Chartreuse Floral, Signed, 2 1/2 In.High 145.00
Galle, Vase, Pottery, Neo-Medieval French Armorial, Joan Of Arc, Signed 230.00
Galle, Vase, Red Shading Floral, Cameo, 16 In.High 425.00
Galle, Vase, Red, Yellow, Signed, Cameo, 4 In.High 235.00
Galle, Vase, Red, Yellow, Signed, Cameo, 6 In.High 175.00
Galle, Vase, Rust, Brown, Golden Tan, Morning Glories, Cameo, 15 1/2 In.High 850.00
Galle, Vase, Spherical, Translucent Yellow, Rhododendron Blossoms, Signed 1100.00
Galle, Vase, Sprays Of Berries & Leaves, Signed, Cameo 130.00
Galle, Vase, Squat, Blossoms, Purple, Signed, Cameo 90.00
Galle, Vase, Star, Amethyst, Frosted, Wheel Cut, Signed, Cameo, 9 In.High 145.00
Galle, Vase, Stick, Chartreuse, Variegated Shades Of Brown Leaves, 8 1/2 In. 228.00
Galle, Vase, Stick, Fern Leaves, Frosted Ground, Green Base, 11 1/4 In.High 149.00
Galle, Vase, Tapering, Blue Flowering Plants, Signed, Cameo, 15 In.High 120.00
Galle, Vase, Tapering, Ribbed Base, Etched Orchids & Fungi, Green, Signed 135.00
Galle, Vase, Teardrop Shape, Burnt Orange, Grapevine & Leaf, Signed, Cameo 140.00
Galle, Vase, Tree, Fruit, Leaves, Yellow, Brown, Bulbous, 7 1/4 In.High 825.00
Galle, Vase, Thin Neck, Pink & Pale Green Floral, Signed, 15 In.High 250.00
Galle, Vase, Trilobed, Phlox In Green To Lavender, Signed, Cameo 100.00
Galle, Vase, Vine Decor, Amber, Maroon, Champagne, 11 3/4 In.High 200.00
Galle, Vase, Wheat Design, Orange, Brown, Yellow, Cameo, 4 In.High 185.00
Galle, Vase, White, Orange Poppies, Signed, Cameo, 2 3/4 In.High 140.00
Galle, Vase, Wild Flowers & Leafage In Red On Frosted Green, Signed, Cameo 140.00
Galle, Vase, Wood Rose & Foliage Decor, Pink, Amber, Mahogany, 10 In.High 275.00
Galle, Vase, Yellow At Top, Blue Center, Cut Trees, Signed, 16 In.High 475.00
Galle, Vase, Yellow, Green, Leaf Design, Signed, Cameo, 6 1/2 In.High 175.00

Game Plates are any type of plate decorated with pictures of birds, animals,
or fish. The Game Plates usually came in sets consisting of twelve dishes
and a serving platter. These Games Plates were most popular during the
1880s.

Game Plate, Bird, Silver Ground, Blue Border 15.00
Game Plate, Bird, 8 In. 16.00
Game Plate, Birds Of America, John J. Audubon, Adams, Wall Hanger, 10 In. 20.00
Game Plate, Coronet, Artist-Signed 75.00
Game Plate, Deer At Watering Hole, Signed Beck, 12 In. 25.00
Game Plate, Deer, R.K.Beck, Signed, Water Scene, Green, Gold Edge, 9 1/4 In. 15.00
Game Plate, Duck, Bavarian, Roses Border, Autumn Landscape 22.00
Game Plate, Ducks In Flight & Water, Blue & Gold Border, Haviland Limoges 28.00
Game Plate, Elk, R.K.Beck, Signed, Water Scene, Green, Gold Edge, 9 1/4 In. 15.00
Game Plate, Flamingo, Floral Ground, Blue Border, Germany 25.00
Game Plate, Flying Turkey, 6 In. 3.00
Game Plate, Flying Turkey, 7 In. 3.50

Game Plate, Flying Turkey, 8 1/2 In.	4.50
Game Plate, Germany, Floral Border, 8 1/2 In.	22.00
Game Plate, Inscribed Oude Loosdrecht, Red Breasted Bird Center, C.1780	60.00
Game Plate, Moose, R.K.Beck, Signed, Water Scene, Green, Gold Edge, 9 1/4 In.	15.00
Game Plate, Quail, Beehive, Brown Ground, Gold, 10 In.	80.00
Game Plate, Quail, Registered Furnival, 1913	5.00
Game Plate, Snipes, Quail, Wild Geese, Grouse, Pheasant, France, Daudin, 5	55.00
Game Plate, Two Dogs & Bird, R.K.Beck-Signed, Browns & Greens, 10 In.	27.50
Game Plate, Wild Duck, Mignon Zs & Co., Bavaria	16.50
Game, Checkerboard, Folding, Form Of Vol.I-Ii Cooper's Works	5.00
Game, Chess Set, Staunton, French, Box & Board	25.00
Game, Cribbage, Iron Top	8.00
Game, Dart, Coth, Who Can Kill Teddy Bear, American Printing Co., 1906	12.50
Game, Dominoes, Picture Backs, To Double Nines	5.00
Game, Dominoes, Ebony & Ivory	15.00
Game, Flags, Copyright, 1896	2.50
Game, Game Of Fairy Tales, 1900, Parker Bros.	6.00
Game, Peter Coddle's Trip To N.Y., Parker Bros.	5.00
Game, Puzzle Peg, 1922	5.00
Game, Roodles, 1912	5.00
Game, Rook, 1924	5.00
Game, The Magic Rose	3.00
Game, Words & Sentences, Milton Bradley	3.50

*Gaudy Dutch Pottery was made in England for America from about 1810
to 1820. It is a white earthenware with Imari style decorations of red,
blue, green, yellow, and black.*

Gaudy Dutch, Cup & Saucer, King's Rose Pattern	150.00
Gaudy Dutch, Cup & Saucer, King's Rose With Oyster	250.00
Gaudy Dutch, Plate, Deep, Double Rose Pattern, 10 In.Diameter	325.00
Gaudy Dutch, Plate, Deep, Grape Pattern, 10 In.Diameter	120.00
Gaudy Dutch, Plate, Deep, Single Rose Pattern, 10 In.Diameter	250.00
Gaudy Dutch, Plate, Deep, War Bonnet Pattern, 8 10i In.Diameter	265.00
Gaudy Dutch, Plate, Grape Pattern, 7 In.Diameter	125.00
Gaudy Dutch, Plate, Oyster Pattern, 7 1/2 In.Diameter	110.00
Gaudy Dutch, Plate, Toddy, Flowers, Green, Rose, Yellow	65.00
Gaudy Dutch, Plate, Vine Pattern, Red, Blue, Green, Black, 9 In.	14.00
Gaudy Dutch, Saucer, Butterfly Pattern, 5 1/2 In.	200.00
Gaudy Ironstone, Cup & Saucer, Handleless, Seeing Eye Pattern	50.00
Gaudy Ironstone, Dish, Vegetable, Round, Cover	75.00
Gaudy Ironstone, Plate, Walley, Niagara Shape, Impressed On Back	40.00
Gaudy Ironstone, Platter, Well & Tree, Vesper, 17 X 21 In.	128.00
Gaudy Ironstone, Platter, Well & Tree, 17 X 21 In.	98.00

*Gaudy Welsh is an Imari decorated earthenware with red, blue, green, and
gold decorations. It was made after 1820.*

Gaudy Welsh, Bowl, Tulip Pattern, 9 In.	17.00
Gaudy Welsh, Creamer, Grape	40.00
Gaudy Welsh, Creamer, Oyster Pattern, 3 1/2 In.Tall	25.00
Gaudy Welsh, Cup & Saucer, Demitasse	36.50
Gaudy Welsh, Cup & Saucer, Flower Basket Pattern	35.00
Gaudy Welsh, Cup & Saucer, Grape Pattern	35.00
Gaudy Welsh, Cup & Saucer, Handled	45.00
Gaudy Welsh, Cup & Saucer, Matching Chocolate Cup	25.00
Gaudy Welsh, Cup & Saucer, Oyster Pattern	25.00 To 40.00
Gaudy Welsh, Cup & Saucer, Oyster Pattern, Pink Luster Trim	28.00
Gaudy Welsh, Cup & Saucer, Peacock Feather Pattern	30.00
Gaudy Welsh, Cup & Saucer, Traditional Pattern	18.50
Gaudy Welsh, Cup & Saucer, Tulip	22.00 To 30.00
Gaudy Welsh, Cup, Children, Oyster Pattern, Pair	22.00
Gaudy Welsh, Jar, Cracker, Silver Lid, Bail	55.00
Gaudy Welsh, Mug, Oyster Pattern, 3 In.	30.00
Gaudy Welsh, Pitcher & Bowl, Miniature, Pitcher 3 1/2 In.High	42.00
Gaudy Welsh, Pitcher, Oyster Pattern, 3 In.High	35.00
Gaudy Welsh, Pitcher, Oyster Pattern, 4 In.	25.00
Gaudy Welsh, Pitcher, Oyster, 5 In.	68.00

Gaudy Welsh, Pitcher, Signed, 3 1/2 In.High	25.00
Gaudy Welsh, Pitcher, White, Blue, Green, Orange, Copper Rim, 6 In.	35.00
Gaudy Welsh, Pitcher, White, Blue, Green, Orange, Copper Rim, 7 In.	40.00
Gaudy Welsh, Plate, Blue, Center Flower, Open Cartouches	7.50
Gaudy Welsh, Plate, Blue, Ironstone, Three Open Cartouches, Flower Center	7.50
Gaudy Welsh, Plate, Blue, Orange Flowers, 8 In.Diameter	30.00
Gaudy Welsh, Plate, Flower Basket Design, 8 In.Diameter	45.00
Gaudy Welsh, Plate, Oyster Pattern, 6 In.Diameter	15.00
Gaudy Welsh, Plate, Oyster Pattern, 6 3/4 In.	15.00
Gaudy Welsh, Plate, Oyster, 7 1/4 In.	48.00
Gaudy Welsh, Plate, Soup, Blackberry Pattern, Ironstone	65.00
Gaudy Welsh, Plate, Yellow Tulips, C.1840 .... *Illus*	30.00
Gaudy Welsh, Platter, Blue, Floral Decoration	35.00
Gaudy Welsh, Platter, Blue, Floral, Ironstone, 15 In.Long	35.00
Gaudy Welsh, Platter, Grape Pattern, Ironstone	150.00
Gaudy Welsh, Platter, Oval, Dark Blue Tree With Gold & Orange Flowers	40.00
Gaudy Welsh, Teapot, Blue & Orange Flowers, Paneled Sides, 8 1/2 In.High	50.00
Gaudy Welsh, Teapot, Dark Blue & Red Panels	17.50
Gera, Coffee Service, Garlands Of Puce Flowers, C.1785, 6 Piece	40.00

*Gibson Girl Plates were made in the early 1900s by the Royal Doulton
Pottery at Lambeth, England. There are twenty-four different plates
featuring a picture of the Gibson Girl by the artist Charles Dana
Gibson.*

Gibson Girl, Plate, She Becomes A Trained Nurse, 10 1/2 In.	40.00
Gibson Girl, Plate, She Decides To Die, 10 1/2 In.	40.00
Gibson Girl, Plate, She Goes Into Colors, Widow Series, Mark	58.00
Gibson Girl, Plate, She Goes To The Fancy Dress Ball	40.00
Gibson Girl, Plate, She Is The Subject Of More Criticism	37.50
Gibson Girl, Plate, She Longs For Seclusion, 10 1/2 In. .... 35.00 To 40.00	
Gibson Girl, Plate, They All Go Skating, 10 1/2 In.	40.00
Gibson Girl, Plate, Widow Series, No Rest In The Country	32.50
Gibson Girl, Tile, Hat & Hairdo	10.50
Ginori, Compote, Footed, Hand-Painted Flowers & Gold Cameos, Pierced Band	25.00
Girandole, Eagle, Carved Wood, American, C.1830, Gilded	950.00
Girandole, Elizabethan Figure On Marble Base, Crystal Prisms, Pair	45.00
Girandole, Gilt Wood, English, C.1775 .... *Illus*	1750.00
Girandole, Pair Singles, Three-Branch Center, Dog On Brass, Prisms	135.00
Girandole, Three Candle, Indian, Marble Base, Bronze, Three Piece, 18 1/2 In.	325.00
Girandole, Waterford Bobeches & Prisms, 2 Arm, C.1880, Pair	750.00
Glasses, Granny, Case	4.00
Glasses, Granny, Oval Silver Frames	3.50
Gold & Platinum, Compact, Powder, Rectangular, Enameled Peacock, Foliage	130.00
Gold, Badge, Russian, Order Of St.Stanislaus, Second Class, Enemeled, C.1850	160.00
Gold, Case, Cigarette, Russian, Sapphire Thumbpiece, C.1900	450.00
Gold, Case, Vanity, 14k, 1 1/2 In.Diameter	75.00
Gold, Cross, 24k, Ornate, Handmade, 1 1/2 In.Long	20.00
Gold, Crucifix, 24k, Handmade	22.00
Gold, Figurine, St.Peter & St.Catherine, Enameled, French, C.1850, Pair	700.00
Gold, Hairpin, Lady's, Chain To Hold Glasses	5.00
Gold, Lorgnette, 14k	45.00
Gold, Pen & Pencil Set	5.50
Gold, Pencil, Automatic, Hexagon, 14k, 3 1/3 In.Long	12.00
Gold, Quill, Feather Form, Inscribed With Name And Dates 1870-1920	80.00
Gold, Toilet Set, Traveling, G.Keller, Paris, 42 Piece	7250.00
Goldcrest, Figurine, Lady & Gentleman, Minuet, 8 1/2 In.High, Pair	20.00

*Goofus Glass was made from about 1900 to 1920 by many american factories,
it was originally painted gold, red, green, bronze, pink, purple, and other bright
colors.*

Goofus Glass, Bowl, Red, Gold Grapes, Leaves, Footed, 10 In.	6.00
Goofus Glass, Bowl, Roses, Gold, Red, 10 X 3 In.	20.50
Goofus Glass, Bowl, Roses, Leaves, Clear, 6 In.Diameter, 5 1/2 In.Tall	10.00
Goofus Glass, Bowl, Roses, Leaves, Red, Gold, 9 1/2 In.	10.00
Goofus Glass, Dish, Green, Painted, Marked N	10.00
Goofus Glass, Jar, Powder, Covered, Painted .... 2.25 To 9.00	

Goofus Glass, Plate, Fruits Pattern, Burgundy With Silver	12.00
Goofus Glass, Plate, 10 1/2 In.Diameter .... *Illus*	12.50
Goofus Glass, Vase, Cabbage Rose, Small	11.00
Goofus Glass, Vase, Grapes, Opalescent, 8 In.High	6.00
Goofus Glass, Vase, Roses, Clear, 5 1/4 In.High	5.00
Goofus Glass, Vase, Roses, Clear, 8 In.High	6.00
Goofus Glass, Vase, Roses, 12 In.	22.00
Goss, Bowl, 3 1/2 In.	8.00
Goss, Ewer, 2 1/2 In.	7.00
Goss, Vase, Gourd Shape, 2 1/2 In. .... *Illus*	4.00
Goss, Vase, High Neck, 3 In. .... *Illus*	4.00

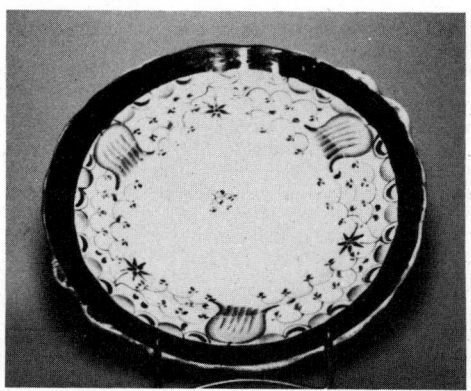

Gaudy Welsh, Plate,
Yellow Tulips, C.1840
See Page 232

Girandole, Gilt Wood, English, C.1775
See Page 232

Goofus Glass, Plate, 10 1/2 In.Diameter

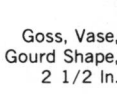

Goss, Vase,
Gourd Shape,
2 1/2 In.

Goss, Vase,
High Neck, 3 In.

Goss, Vase, 4 In.	10.00
Gotha, Cup & Saucer, Coffee, Silhouette Portraits, C.1775-80	90.00
Gouda, Ashtray, 2 1/2 In.Diameter, Colorful	10.00
Gouda, Base, Bud, Tulip & Flower Decoration, 6 In.	27.50
Gouda, Basket, Holland, Handled, Floral On Cream, Signed	12.50
Gouda, Holder, Letter, Zuid Pattern, 8 X 4 X 3 In.	35.00
Gouda, Jardiniere, Matte Finish, Marked 3f2, Dec 247, Made Holland, 9 In.High	85.00
Gouda, Plate, Ivora Pattern, 9 In.Diameter	40.00
Gouda, Urn, Rhoda Pattern, Flowers, Blue, Green, 11 1/2 In.Tall	55.00
Gouda, Vase, Coral Pattern, Black, Yellow, Green, Blue, 4 In.High	35.00
Gouda, Vase, Emo, 2 1/2 In.	18.00
Gouda, Vase, Flambe, Artist Signed, 8 1/2 In.Tall	40.00
Gouda, Vase, Flared, Art Deco Style, 5 In.	15.00
Gouda, Vase, Lydia, 8 In.	27.50
Gouda, Vase, 6 1/2 In.	27.00

Graniteware is an enameled tinware that has been used in the kitchen from the late nineteenth century to the present. Earlier Graniteware was green or turquoise blue, with white spatters. The later ware was gray with white spatters. Reproductions are being made in all colors.

Graniteware, Bed Pan, Blue	8.00
Graniteware, Boiler, Bail Handle, Lift-Out Rack, Cover Gray	9.00
Graniteware, Bottle, Flask, Screw Top	18.00
Graniteware, Can, Cream, Gray, Bail, Quart	6.00
Graniteware, Coffeepot, Blue & White	14.00
Graniteware, Coffeepot, Gray, Ribbed Handle, Dome Lid, 8 In.Tall	22.00
Graniteware, Coffeepot, Gray, Tin Lid, 7 In.	6.00
Graniteware, Coffeepot, Statue Of Liberty, Pewter Handle, Spout, Lid, Rim	65.00
Graniteware, Dish, Soap, Gray	3.00
Graniteware, Kettle, Lid, Cobalt Blue & White, 6 In.Tall, 11 In.Diameter	16.00
Graniteware, Pail, Blue, 7 1/2 In.Diameter	6.00
Graniteware, Platter, Blue, White, Lady, Man, River, Mountains, Lucerne, England	40.00
Graniteware, Teapot, Pewter Trim, Cover, 9 1/2 In.	21.00
Greentown, see also Pressed Glass;Slag, Caramel	
Greentown, Butter, Dewey, Amber, Covered	20.00
Greentown, Mug, Shuttle, Clear	15.00
Greentown, Stein, Dwarfs Scene, Opaque Blue, 5 In.	30.00
Greentown, Sugar, Wild Rose & Bowknot, Frosted, Covered	29.00
Greentown, Tumbler, Clear, Austrian	10.00
Grueby, Bowl, Green, Fluted Top, 2 1/2 In.High, Marked	55.00
Grueby, Lamp, Bigelow & Kinnard, White Tiles, Wreath Of Ivy Leaves On Green	500.00
Grueby, Vase, Signed, 7 In.	95.00
Grueby, Vase, Speckled Green, Artist Wilhelmina Post, 7 In.High	135.00
Gun, see Weapon, Gun	

Gunderson Glass was made at the Gunderson Pairpoint Works of New Bedford, Massachusetts, from 1952 to 1957. Gunderson Peachblow is especially famous.

Gunderson, see also Peachblow	
Gunderson, Burmese, Bowl, Rose, Crimped Edge, Miniature, 3 In.	99.00
Gunderson, Burmese, Bowl, Ruffled Top, Glossy, 8 In.Diameter	200.00
Gunderson, Burmese, Tumbler, 4 1/2 In.	76.50
Gunderson, Peachblow, Bowl, Miniature, Applied Prunties, Satin, Mt.Washington	90.00
Gunderson, Peachblow, Bowl, Pink & White	35.00
Gunderson, Peachblow, Bowl, Violet, Expanded Diamond Pattern	165.00
Gunderson, Peachblow, Chalice, Acid Finish, Lemon Base	225.00
Gunderson, Peachblow, Cup & Saucer, Applied Reeded Handle, Acid Finish	95.00
Gunderson, Peachblow, Cup & Saucer, Deep Raspberry, White Reeded Handle	200.00
Gunderson, Peachblow, Sherbet	195.00
Gunderson, Peachblow, Toothpick, Acid Finish, Mt.Washington	70.00
Gunderson, Peachblow, Vase, Diamond Shape Opening, 2 Camphor Handles	250.00
Gunderson, Peachblow, Vase, Two Applied Handle, 3 3/4 In.High	127.50
Gutta-Percha, see also Album, Photography	
Gutta-Percha, Match Holder, King Edward VII Portrait Front	10.00

Hampshire Pottery founded by J.S.Taft and Co. of Keene, New

Hampshire. The pottery started in 1871. Stoneware, Artware, and Majolica were among the many wares.

Hampshire Pottery, Bowl, Swastika Decoration, Green	27.50
Hampshire Pottery, Lamp, Oil, Green, Marked, 6 1/2 In.High	32.00
Hampshire Pottery, Vase, Figural, Avocado, Green Matte, Leaf Design, 4 In.	15.00
Hampshire, Vase, Green Matte, 9 1/2 In.High	16.50
Hampshire, Vase, Green, Signed, 5 In.Tall	22.00
Hampshire, Vase, Opalescent Green, Raised Petal Motif, Marked M In Circle	40.00

Philip Handel worked in Meriden, Connecticut, about 1885 and in New York City from about 1900 to the 1930s. His firm made Art Glass and other types of lamps.

Handel, Humidor, Elk, Upright Pipe On Lid	125.00
Handel, Lamp, Boudoir, Burnished Tree Base, Yellow & Green Shade, Signed	130.00
Handel, Lamp, Desk, Feather Decor, Pen Rack, Pen Well, Pin Cup In Base, Bronze	110.00
Handel, Lamp, Floor, Signed Quezal, Gold, Bell Shaped Frame, 56 In.Tall	225.00
Handel, Lamp, Hanging, Square Shade, Medieval Design, Caramel Glass, 22 In.	250.00
Handel, Lamp, Landscape Scene, Shade, Signed, 14 In.	125.00
Handel, Lamp, Rose Color, Signed	255.00
Handel, Lamp, Signed, Bronze, Open Filigree On Base, 30 In.High	75.00
Handel, Lamp, Signed, Desk, Bronze, Rectangular Green Flowered Glass Shade	125.00
Handel, Lamp, Signed, Table, Sunset Scene, Pine Trees, Pine-Needle Border	450.00
Handel, Lamp, Swirl, Green, Yellow, Tree Trunk Base, Signed, 18 In.Diameter	265.00
Handel, Lamp, Table, Mottled Yellow Domed Shade, Bronze Tree Trunk Base	135.00
Handel, Lamp, Table, Yellow, Green, Signed Base, 18 In.Shade	275.00
Handel, Lamp, Woodland Scene On Glass Shade	330.00
Handel, Lamp, Yellow Ground, Acorns, Oak Leaves, Green & Rust, 20 In.High	210.00
Handel, Shade, Tam, Leaves, Berries, Red, Signed, 10 In.Diameter	125.00
Harness Brass, Horseshoe With Horse's Head	9.50
Hatpin holder, see Porcelain	

Haviland China has been made in Limoges, France, since 1846. The factory was started by the Haviland Brothers of New York City. Other factories worked in the town of Limoges making a similar chinaware.

Haviland, see also Limoges

Haviland, Bowl, Cereal, Montebello, Pattern No.61	3.50
Haviland, Bowl, Covered, Pierced Lid, Rosebud Border, 9 1/2 In.Diameter	10.00
Haviland, Bowl, Soup, Ransom, White, 7 1/2 In.Diameter	4.00
Haviland, Butter Pat, Garlands Of Pink Roses, Scalloped Rim, Gold	4.75
Haviland, Chocolate Pot, Marked H & Co.	6.00
Haviland, Chocolate Pot, Marked Haviland & Co.	60.00
Haviland, Chocolate Pot, Violets & Leaf Design, Pink To Lavender, Signed	35.00
Haviland, Compote, Floral Center, Pink Edge, Footed, 8 1/2 In.Diameter	17.50
Haviland, Creamer & Sugar, Flowered, Red, Blue	15.00
Haviland, Creamer & Sugar, Roses & Scroll	22.50
Haviland, Cup & Saucer, Ardennes Pattern, Pink, Green, Set Of 6	75.00
Haviland, Cup & Saucer, Autumn Leaf Pattern	8.00
Haviland, Cup & Saucer, Bouillon, Lid, No.475g, 4	20.00
Haviland, Cup & Saucer, Bouillon, Silver, Pattern No.19	12.50
Haviland, Cup & Saucer, Demitasse, Filigree Design, Crimson Border	8.00
Haviland, Cup & Saucer, Demitasse, Forget-Me-Nots	10.00
Haviland, Cup & Saucer, Demitasse, Forget-Me-Nots, Gold Metal Stand, Cupid	10.00
Haviland, Cup & Saucer, Demitasse, Pink & Blue Floral, Green Leaves	30.00
Haviland, Cup & Saucer, Floral Design, Inside & Out	14.50
Haviland, Cup & Saucer, Montebello, Pattern No.61	12.50
Haviland, Cup & Saucer, No.267d	10.00
Haviland, Cup & Saucer, No.659a	15.00
Haviland, Cup & Saucer, Pattern No.100-A	12.50
Haviland, Cup & Saucer, Ransom, White, Demitasse, Set Of 8	50.00
Haviland, Cup & Saucer, Ransom, White, Set Of 7	75.00
Haviland, Cup & Saucer, Roses, Green, Brown, Scallop	6.50
Haviland, Cup & Saucer, Tea, Gold & Green Leaves & Flowers, 12	144.00
Haviland, Cup & Saucer, Troy, Pattern No.170	10.00
Haviland, Cup, Troy, Pattern No.170	6.00
Haviland, Dish, Bone, Lavender Floral, Leaves, Scalloped Edge, Set Of 4	16.00
Haviland, Dish, Bone, Rose Garlands	6.00

Haviland, Dish, Paradise Pattern, 7 1/2 In.Diameter	5.00
Haviland, Dish, Vegetable, Cover, Hand-Painted, Floral, Butterflies, Birds	30.00
Haviland, Dish, Vegetable, Covered, Oval, Conventional, Pattern No.618	22.50
Haviland, Dish, Vegetable, Covered, Pink Roses, Theodore Haviland	15.00
Haviland, Dish, Vegetable, Oval, Silver, Pattern No.19	10.00
Haviland, Dish, Vegetable, Round, Handled, Silver, Pattern No.19	10.00
Haviland, Fish Set, 12 Pieces, 23 1/2 X 8 1/2 In.Platter	100.00
Haviland, Gravy Boat, Attached Base, Pattern No.100-A	15.00
Haviland, Gravy Boat, Attached Tray, Floral, Gold	32.50
Haviland, Gravy Boat, Double Spout, Attached Underplate, Gold & White	15.00
Haviland, Gravy Boat, On Tray, No.19, Haviland & Co.	25.00
Haviland, Jelly, Handled, Silver, Pattern No.19	10.00
Haviland, Pitcher, Pink & Yellow Ground, Red Berries, 8 1/2 In.Tall	40.00
Haviland, Plate, Bread & Butter, Montebello, Pattern No.61	3.50
Haviland, Plate, Bread & Butter, Troy, Pattern No.170	3.00
Haviland, Plate, Chop, No.724	18.50
Haviland, Plate, Coupe, Silver, Pattern No.19	4.00
Haviland, Plate, Dinner, Gold Band, Pink Roses, Blue, Limoges, France	4.00
Haviland, Plate, Dinner, Marie, 9 3/4 In.Diameter	6.00
Haviland, Plate, Dinner, Musical Motif	15.00
Haviland, Plate, Dinner, No.19, Haviland & Co., 10 In.	9.00
Haviland, Plate, Dinner, No.19, Haviland & Co., 7 1/2 In.	6.00
Haviland, Plate, Dinner, No.19, Haviland & Co., 8 1/2 In.	8.00
Haviland, Plate, Dinner, Pink Carnations	10.00
Haviland, Plate, Dinner, Pink, Apple Blossoms, Set Of 8	35.00
Haviland, Plate, Dinner, Ransom, White	5.00
Haviland, Plate, Dinner, Royal Blue & Gold Border, Theodore Haviland, 10 In.	8.75
Haviland, Plate, Dinner, Silver, Pattern No.19	6.50
Haviland, Plate, Dinner, Troy, Pattern No.170	5.00
Haviland, Plate, Floral Design, Pink Border, Marked, 7 1/2 In.Diameter	6.50
Haviland, Plate, French, White, Gold, Scalloped, 7 1/2 In.	3.00
Haviland, Plate, French, White, Gold, Scalloped, 9 1/2 In.	4.00
Haviland, Plate, Hand-Painted, Birds, Green, Gold Band, 8 1/2 In.	18.50
Haviland, Plate, Hand-Painted, Roses, Signed, Dated 1902	30.00
Haviland, Plate, Luncheon, Montebello, Pattern No.61	6.00
Haviland, Plate, Luncheon, Pink Carnations	8.00
Haviland, Plate, Morning Glory Pattern	11.00
Haviland, Plate, Orange Poppies, Gold, Scalloped, 8 1/2 In.	14.00
Haviland, Plate, Oyster, White, Yellow, Floral Border	15.00
Haviland, Plate, Pie, Ransom, White, 6 In.Diameter	1.50
Haviland, Plate, Salad, Green & Gold Pattern	6.25
Haviland, Plate, Salad, Pink Carnations	8.00
Haviland, Plate, Toy, White With Yellow & Blue Floral, 4 1/2 In.	2.00
Haviland, Plater, Ransom, White, 18 In.	15.00
Haviland, Platter, Morning Glories, Green, Clipped Corner, 14 X 10 In.	20.00
Haviland, Platter, No.19, Haviland & Co., 14 In.	20.00
Haviland, Platter, No.270, 12 In.	12.00
Haviland, Platter, Ransom, White, 11 1/2 In.	10.00
Haviland, Platter, Ransom, White, 13 In.	12.00
Haviland, Platter, Silver, Pattern No.19, 16 X 12 1/4 In.	20.00
Haviland, Platter, Toy, Oval, White With Yellow & Blue Floral	5.00
Haviland, Ramekin	8.00
Haviland, Ramekin, Gold Edge, Saucer, Signed	75.00
Haviland, Relish, Oval, Pattern No.100-A	8.50
Haviland, Sauce, Montebello, Pattern No.61	2.00
Haviland, Sauce, Pink, Apple Blossoms, 4 3/4 In., Set Of 12	25.00
Haviland, Sauce, Pink, White Flowers	6.00
Haviland, Sauce, Ransom, White, 5 In.Diameter	1.50
Haviland, Sauce, Silver, Pattern No.19	2.50
Haviland, Sauceboat, Toy, Attached Plate, White With Yellow & Blue Floral	3.50
Haviland, Server, Covered, Toy, White With Yellow & Blue Floral, Handles	5.00
Haviland, Soup, Green & Gold Pattern	5.00
Haviland, Sugar & Creamer, Conventional, Pattern No.618	27.50
Haviland, Tea Set, Wedding Ring, Open Handle Cake Plate, 26 Piece	105.00
Haviland, Teapot, Roses & Scroll	16.50
Haviland, Tray, Dressed, Pin, Signed, Yellow Roses	10.00

Haviland, Tray, Dresser, Floral Design, Yellow, Open Handle, 8 X 11 In. 15.00
Haviland, Tray, Tea, Blue Forget-Me-Nots, Marked France 21.00
Haviland, Tureen, Oporto Pattern, Gold Handles & Cover Finial 35.00
Haviland, Tureen, Ransom, White, Cover 25.00
Haviland, Tureen, Soup, Covered, Toy, White With Yellow & Blue Floral, Ladle 6.50
Haviland, Tureen, Soup, Oval, Rope Design Handles, Gold Trim 65.00

T.G.Hawkes & Company of Corning, New York, was founded in 1880.
The firm cut glass made at other firms until 1962. Many pieces are marked
with the trademark, a trefoil ring enclosing a fleur-de-lis and two hawks.

Hawkes, Bottle, Fleur-De-Lis, Etched Wheat, Signed, Quart 85.00
Hawkes, Bottle, Water, Hobstars, Fan, Panels, Clear, Signed, 10 In. 120.00
Hawkes, Bowl, Blue Silver, Signed, 9 In.Diameter 50.00
Hawkes, Bowl, Finger, Etched, Signed 8.00
Hawkes, Bowl, Hobstar, Signed, 9 In.Diameter 70.00
Hawkes, Box, Fruit & Flowers, Signed, Cover, 9 In.Diameter 130.00
Hawkes, Butter, Tub, Cut Glass, Signed 95.00
Hawkes, Candlestick, Cut To Clear, Cut Birds, Pair 137.50
Hawkes, Compote, Berries, Leaves, Vines, Clear, Green Stem & Base, Signed 40.00
Hawkes, Cruet, Floral Design, Engraved Catsup, Double Lip, Marked 24.00
Hawkes, Cruet, Floral Design, Engraved Vinegar, Double Lip 24.00
Hawkes, Cruet, Vintage Design, Applied Handle, 3 Sided Spout, Signed, 7 In. 39.50
Hawkes, Cup, Loving, Pedestal, Three Handle, Signed, 6 1/2 In.High 350.00
Hawkes, Dish, Nut, Golf Course Scene, Clear, Cover, Footed, Signed, 6 In. 65.00
Hawkes, Dish, Relish, Button, Intaglio Flowers, Scallop Top, Signed, 8 In. 35.00
Hawkes, Goblet, Floral, Intaglio Cut, Signed, Set Of 8 .... 55.00
Hawkes, Goblet, Sherry, Etched, Signed 10.00
Hawkes, Goblet, Water, Etched, Signed 10.00
Hawkes, Goblet, Wine, Etched, Signed 10.00
Hawkes, Jar, Powder, Flowers, Engraved, Signed, No Cover 15.00
Hawkes, Nappy, Cut Glass, Signed, 6 In. 45.00
Hawkes, Nappy, Hobstar, Rosette, Thistle, Handle, Signed, 7 1/2 In. 37.50
Hawkes, Perfume, Amber, Gold Band, Dome Stopper, 6 In.Tall 20.00
Hawkes, Plate, Cut Glass, Rayed, Fruit, Signed, 10 1/2 In.Diameter 125.00
Hawkes, Salt, Intaglio Cut, Floral, Signed, Set Of 5 .... 30.00
Hawkes, Tray, Ice Cream, Cut Glass, Signed, C Mark, 15 In.Long, 9 In.Wide 125.00
Hawkes, Vase, Brunswick Pattern, Corset Shape, 11 1/2 In.Tall 100.00
Hawkes, Vase, Bud, Flowers, Leaves, Bulbous, Clear, 8 In.Tall 20.00
Hawkes, Vase, Fan Shape, Green Base, Clear Body, Intaglio Cut Leaves, Vines 45.00
Hawkes, Vase, Flute Cutting, Flare Top, Signed, 10 3/4 In.Tall 50.00
Hawkes, Vase, Grape Design, Rose To Clear, Footed, 9 1/2 In.Tall 45.00
Hawkes, Vase, Iris, Gravic, Signed, 8 In. 150.00
Hawkes, Vase, Trumpet, Engraved, 13 In. 85.00
Hawkes, Vase, Trumpet, Signed, 14 In.Tall 95.00
Hearse, Horse Drawn, 100 Years Old 1400.00

Heisey Glass was made from 1895 to 1958 in Newark, Ohio, by A.H.
Heisey and Co., Inc.

Heisey, Ashtray & Matchbook Holder, Crystal & Ruby Glass 30.00
Heisey, Ashtray, Crystolite, Square 3.25
Heisey, Ashtray, Queen Anne, Alexandrite, Signed 75.00
Heisey, Ashtray, Triangular, Polished Bottom 4.00
Heisey, Basket, Clear, Etched Border, Marked, 10 In. 40.00
Heisey, Basket, Clear, Rayed, Signed, Six Sided 40.00
Heisey, Basket, Cut, Etched, Large 85.00
Heisey, Basket, Green, Handled, Signed, 7 In.Tall 18.00
Heisey, Basket, Handle, Dark Apple Green, Flared Base, V Shape, Signed 22.50
Heisey, Basket, Paneled Base, Floral Band, Signed, 7 3/8 X 8 3/4 In.Tall 29.50
Heisey, Basket, Prism Cut In Flame Like Design 28.00
Heisey, Bell, Dinner, Jamestown, Etched In Minuet Pattern 24.00
Heisey, Boat, French Dressing 12.00
Heisey, Bowl, Centerpiece, Cornucopia, Clear, Signed, 10 1/2 In.Diameter 22.00
Heisey, Bowl, Colonial, 8 In.Diameter, Marked 12.50
Heisey, Bowl, Finger, Thumbprint & Panel, Signed, 4 1/2 In.Diameter, Set Of 6 .... 24.00
Heisey, Bowl, Flower, Etched, Paneled, Floral Decor, Signed, 8 In.Diameter 45.00
Heisey, Bowl, Fruit, Paneled Petals, Star Base, 11 In.Diameter, 3 1/2 In.Tall 15.00

Heisey, Bowl, Inverted Thumbprint, Green, Mark, Oval	24.00
Heisey, Bowl, Mayonnaise, Crystolite, Handled Plate, Clear	20.00
Heisey, Bowl, Oyster Cocktail, 9 In.Wide	8.35
Heisey, Bowl, Paneled Sides, Scalloped Top, 9 In.	16.50
Heisey, Bowl, Panels, Rayed Bottom, Pat.4/15/15, 8 1/4 In.Diameter	15.00
Heisey, Bowl, Pink	10.00
Heisey, Bowl, Pressed, 9 In.Diameter *Illus*	75.00
Heisey, Bowl, Punch, Signed	100.00
Heisey, Bowl, Ribbed, Scalloped Edge, Mark, 12 In.	15.00
Heisey, Box, Cigarette, Crystolite, Cover	20.00
Heisey, Box, Cigarette, Melon Rib, Covered, 4 In.	12.00
Heisey, Box, Cigarette, 4 X 3 X 2 In.	10.00
Heisey, Butter, Beaded Swag, Opal Milk, Rose Decoration, Cover	55.00
Heisey, Butter, Colonial, Cover	36.00
Heisey, Butter, Lid, Winged Scroll, Custard	85.00
Heisey, Candelabra, 2 Light, 20 Prisms, Pair	125.00
Heisey, Candlestick, Colonial, Clear, Marked, 7 1/2 In.Tall, Pair	20.00
Heisey, Candlestick, Lariat Pattern, Double	10.00
Heisey, Candlestick, Miniature, Clear, Signed, Pair	15.00
Heisey, Candlestick, Paneled, Sahara Base, Signed, 8 1/2 In., Pair	150.00
Heisey, Candlestick, Squat	12.00
Heisey, Celery, Sunburst, Diamond & Hobstars	17.50
Heisey, Champagne, Colonial, Pattern No.351, 4 Oz.	5.00
Heisey, Champagne, New Era, Footed, 6 Oz.	6.00
Heisey, Coaster, Ridgeleigh, Stacking, 3 1/2 In.Diameter, 2	7.50
Heisey, Compote, Candy, Gold Trim, Footed Cover, Marked, 9 1/2 In.Tall	18.00
Heisey, Compote, Clear Diamond-Quilted Bowl, Green Stem & Foot	15.00
Heisey, Compote, Etched, Amber, Signed, 6 In., Pair	50.00
Heisey, Compote, Greek Key, Marked	27.50
Heisey, Compote, Jelly, Colonial, Marked	15.00
Heisey, Compote, Pink, Paneled & Scalloped, Signed	14.00
Heisey, Compote, Victoria, Pink, Flared Top, Signed, 5 3/8 X 4 1/2 In.High	35.00
Heisey, Console Set, Moongleam, Marked	25.00
Heisey, Cordial, Puritan, Marked	6.00
Heisey, Creamer, Individual, Signed, Custard, Punty Band	35.00
Heisey, Creamer, Pineapple & Fan, Yellow, 5 In.	29.50
Heisey, Cruet, Panels, Pointed Stopper, Signed	14.50
Heisey, Cruet, Priscilla, Signed, Clear, Stopper	18.00
Heisey, Cruet, Queen Anne, Sahara	25.00
Heisey, Cruet, Williamsburg, Stopper	20.00
Heisey, Cup Plate, Marked	5.00
Heisey, Cup, Punch, Colonial, Clear	4.00
Heisey, Cup, Punch, Pinwheel & Pineapple, Clear, Marked, Set Of 10	27.50
Heisey, Cup, Punch, Ribbed, Clear, Marked, Set Of 8	24.00
Heisey, Cup, Punch, Wedding Band, Signed	2.50
Heisey, Dish, Bonbon, Clear, Hand-Painted, Ivory Fork, Set	10.00
Heisey, Dish, Butter, Colonial, Scalloped, Marked	20.00
Heisey, Dish, Candy, Dolphin Foot, Signed, Shell Pink	15.00
Heisey, Dish, Candy, Double, Crystolite, Center Handle	15.00
Heisey, Dish, Candy, Melon Rib, Covered, 7 In.	17.00
Heisey, Dish, Candy, Paneled, Itched Rim, Gold, Cover, Signed	18.50
Heisey, Dish, Candy, Pink, Two Handles, Signed	10.50
Heisey, Dish, Candy, Signed, Covered, Gold Trim, 8 In.	18.00
Heisey, Dish, Celery, Paneled Scalloped Edge, Marked, 12 In.Long	12.00
Heisey, Dish, Cheese & Cracker, Marked	15.00
Heisey, Dish, Dessert, Saucer, Beading, Pastel Apricot Color, Signed	10.50
Heisey, Dish, Handled, 3 Corner, Kalonyal, Clear, No.1776	45.00
Heisey, Dish, Jelly, Pleat & Panel, Flamingo Pink, 2 Handles	17.50
Heisey, Dish, Jelly, Twist Pattern, Green, 2 Handles	17.50
Heisey, Dish, Lariat Pattern *Illus*	6.50
Heisey, Dish, Nut, Handled, Green, 6	25.00
Heisey, Dish, Nut, Individual, Handles	5.00
Heisey, Dish, Pickle, Scallop Edge, Paneled, Star Base, Signed	12.00
Heisey, Dish, Relish, Scalloped Edge, 9 In.Long, Signed	8.00
Heisey, Dish, Relish, Star, Clear, Signed	17.50
Heisey, Dish, Triangular, Handled, Ribbed, Signed	12.00

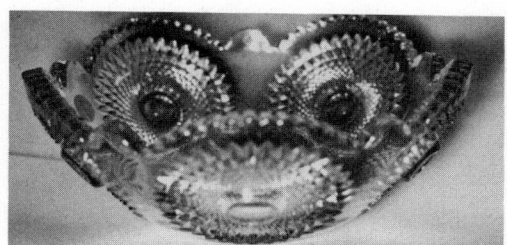

Heisey, Bowl, Pressed, 9 In.Diameter
See Page 238

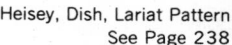

Heisey, Dish, Lariat Pattern
See Page 238

Heisey, **Dish**, Turned-Up Sides, Amber	15.00
Heisey, **Donkey**, Marked, 6 In.Tall	75.00
Heisey, **Elephant**, Crystal, Signed, 4 1/2 In.High	35.00
Heisey, **Geese**, Pair	95.00
Heisey, **Glass**, Ice Tea, Vertical Ribs Extending To Flare Top, Signed	6.50
Heisey, **Goblet**, Alexandrite, Diamond Optic, Twist	75.00
Heisey, **Goblet**, Colonial, Marked	9.50
Heisey, **Goblet**, Comet Pattern, Signed	5.00
Heisey, **Goblet**, Diamond Pattern, 5 1/4 In.Tall	8.00
Heisey, **Goblet**, Fluted Pattern, 6 Sided Base	12.50
Heisey, **Goblet**, New Era, 10 Oz.	10.00
Heisey, **Goblet**, Old Williamsburg, Signed	9.00
Heisey, **Goblet**, Sahara, Empress Pattern, Gold	7.50
Heisey, **Goblet**, Spanish, Cobalt, Clear Stem	45.00
Heisey, **Hair Receiver**, Colonial, Silver Plate Cover, Marked	20.00
Heisey, **Holder**, Match, Clear	12.00
Heisey, **Holder**, Match, Purple	17.50
Heisey, **Horn Of Plenty**, Alexandrite, 15 In.Long	17.50
Heisey, **Horse**, Sparky	25.00 To 35.00
Heisey, **Humidor**, Dated 1908, Signed	60.00
Heisey, **Humidor**, Diamond & Hobstars, Dated 1908	60.00
Heisey, **Ice Bucket**, Greek Key, Tabs On Side	16.50
Heisey, **Ice Cream Set**, 8 Piece	39.00
Heisey, **Jar**, Candy, Covered, Iridescent, 12 In.High	35.00
Heisey, **Jar**, Dresser, Sterling Lid	25.00
Heisey, **Jar**, Mustard, Clear, Signed	10.00 To 17.50
Heisey, **Jar**, Mustard, Ribbed, Clear, Signed	16.00
Heisey, **Jar**, Powder, Bull's-Eye Design, Art Nouveau Lid, Marked 1905, Signed	35.00
Heisey, **Jar**, Powder, Colonial, Cover, Signed	26.50
Heisey, **Jar**, Powder, Silver Plated Cover, Signed	17.50
Heisey, **Luncheon Set**, 20 Pieces, Etched, Yellow	35.00
Heisey, **Mustard Pot**, Pink, Swirled, Cover, Signed	10.00
Heisey, **Nutcup**, Green, Handled, 8 Sided, 8	25.00
Heisey, **Perfume**, Quilted, Pink	18.00
Heisey, **Pheasant**, Pair	130.00
Heisey, **Pitcher**, Colonial, Bulbous, Applied Handle, Marked, 7 In.Tall	35.00
Heisey, **Pitcher**, Milk, Greek Key, Marked	32.00
Heisey, **Pitcher**, Moongleam, Diamond Optic, Six Tumblers	42.00
Heisey, **Pitcher**, Roman Key, Signed, 6 1/2 In.High, 5 1/2 In.Diameter	40.00
Heisey, **Pitcher**, Roman Key, 6 1/2 In.Tall	48.50
Heisey, **Pitcher**, Round, Applied Handle, Marked	35.00

Heisey, Pitcher, Signed, 9 In.	20.00
Heisey, Pitcher, Syrup, Graphic Cut, Marked, Cover, Dated 1910	15.00
Heisey, Pitcher, Water, Sunburst, Signed	40.00
Heisey, Plate, Cake, Sunburst, Clear, 14 In.Diameter	23.00
Heisey, Plate, Colonial, Light Pink, 7 In.	4.00
Heisey, Plate, Cut Floral Border, Marked, 8 1/2 In.	5.00
Heisey, Plate, Dinner, Queen Anne, Clear, 10 1/2 In.	10.00
Heisey, Plate, Gold Rim, Marked	7.50
Heisey, Plate, Greek Key, 8 In.	25.00
Heisey, Plate, Ipswich Pattern	10.00
Heisey, Plate, Old Williamsburg, 10 In.	8.00
Heisey, Plate, Pied Piper, 6 1/4 In.Diameter	5.00
Heisey, Plate, Queen Anne, Alexandrite, Round, Signed	50.00
Heisey, Plate, Sahara, 6 In.	3.00
Heisey, Plate, Sahara, 7 1/2 In.	4.00
Heisey, Plate, Star Base, Pleated Effect, 5 3/4 In.Diameter, Marked	2.25
Heisey, Pony, Kicking	65.00
Heisey, Punch Set, Prince Of Wales Plume, Marked, 8 Piece	225.00
Heisey, Punch Set, Provincial Pattern, Signed, 18 Piece	225.00
Heisey, Punch Set, Ribbed, Clear, Tray, 12 Cups, Bowl, Ladle, Signed	135.00
Heisey, Relish, Divided, Crystolite, Signed, 6 In.	8.00
Heisey, Relish, Etched, Green, 3 Part, Signed	20.00
Heisey, Relish, Wheel Cut, Marked	13.00
Heisey, Rose Bowl, Ribbed, Paper Label	20.00
Heisey, Salt & Pepper, Pattern No.1225, Set	16.50
Heisey, Salt, Open, Figural, Swan, Paper Label, Pair	8.00
Heisey, Salt, Swan	5.00
Heisey, Sauce, Oceanic, No.1252, Green, Marked	8.50
Heisey, Scottie Dog	25.00
Heisey, Shaker, Custard, Ring Band, Marked, Souvenir Of White Lake, Michigan	19.50
Heisey, Shaker, Salt, Locket On Chain, Ruby Flashed, Gold Trim	22.00
Heisey, Sherbet, Crystolite	7.50
Heisey, Sherbet, Lariat, Knotted Stem, 6 Oz.	4.25
Heisey, Sherbet, Ridge & Panel, Pattern No.411, 5 Oz.	5.00
Heisey, Soda, Flamingo, Oceanic	6.25
Heisey, Spooner, Colonial, Marked	12.00
Heisey, Spooner, Prince Of Wales Plumes, Signed	18.00
Heisey, Sugar & Creamer, Clear, Mark, Tray	12.00
Heisey, Sugar & Creamer, Clear, Paneled, Ray Star Bottoms, Stacks	22.50
Heisey, Sugar & Creamer, Colonial, Petal Shape Bowls, Footed, Clear	35.00
Heisey, Sugar & Creamer, Crystolite	10.00 To 18.00
Heisey, Sugar & Creamer, Etched Flowers, Marked	15.00
Heisey, Sugar & Creamer, Etched, Square Shape, Marked	22.50
Heisey, Sugar & Creamer, Gold Trim	77.00
Heisey, Sugar & Creamer, Individual	12.00
Heisey, Sugar & Creamer, Open, Ribbed Pattern	6.00
Heisey, Sugar & Creamer, Panel, Ray Star, Clear, Signed, 3 1/2 In.High	15.00
Heisey, Sugar & Creamer, Queen Anne Pattern, Flamingo Pink	30.00
Heisey, Sugar & Creamer, Ridge & Panel, Pattern No.411	25.00
Heisey, Sugar & Creamer, Sandwich Pattern, Sahara	18.00
Heisey, Sugar & Creamer, Silver Overlay	30.00 To 32.50
Heisey, Sugar & Creamer, Sterling Overlay In Lacy Filigree, Signed	22.50
Heisey, Sugar & Creamer, Waffle Pattern	15.00
Heisey, Sugar & Creamer, Whirlpool, Footed, Marked, Green	19.00
Heisey, Sugar & Creamer & Tray, Ribbed Pattern, Signed	16.50
Heisey, Sugar, Colonial, Marked, Cover	20.00
Heisey, Sugar, Colonial, Open, 2 Handles, Signed & Dated	15.00
Heisey, Sugar, Empress, Open, 2 Handles, Marked Heisey, Sahara	15.00
Heisey, Sugar, Plunger Cut, Signed	8.00
Heisey, Sugar, Prince Of Wales Plumes, Cover, Signed	25.00
Heisey, Syrup, Paneled, Marked Heisey, Sahara	12.00
Heisey, Syrup, Sahara, Paneled, Signed, Small	22.50
Heisey, Syrup, Sanitary, Signed	12.50
Heisey, Tazza, Flamingo, Diamond Optic, 6 7/8 In.Diameter, 3 3/4 In.High	23.00
Heisey, Toothpick, Diamond Swag, Gold	16.00
Heisey, Toothpick, No.1225	8.00

Heisey, Toothpick, Prince Of Whales	35.00
Heisey, Toothpick, Ring Band, Custard, Souvenir	35.00
Heisey, Tray, Celery, Artic Ice, Queen Anne, Marked	30.00
Heisey, Tray, Celery, Boat Shape, Williamsburg, 9 In.	15.00
Heisey, Tray, Celery, Cut Fan & Etched, Marked, 12 1/2 In.Long	12.00
Heisey, Tray, Celery, Green, Wide Panels, 13 In., Marked	27.50
Heisey, Tray, Pickle, Oval, Pattern No.393	12.50
Heisey, Tray, Relish, Oval, Puritan Pattern, 7 In.	10.00
Heisey, Tray, Sugar Cube, Clear, Signed, 2 X 8 1/4 In.	17.00
Heisey, Tub, Butter, Signed, Greek Key Pattern	34.50
Heisey, Tumbler, Alexandrite, Footed, Diamond Optic Pattern, 5 In.Tall	38.00
Heisey, Tumbler, Beaded & Roses	30.00
Heisey, Tumbler, Diamond Optic Pattern, Footed, 5 In.Tall	38.00
Heisey, Tumbler, Domed, Paneled, 3 3/4 In.	6.50
Heisey, Tumbler, Prince Of Wales Plumes, Signed, Gold	22.00
Heisey, Tumbler, Rose Design, Star Cut Base, Signed	36.00
Heisey, Tumbler, Thumbprint, Ruby, Signed, 4 In.Tall	30.00
Heisey, Vase, Candle, Prisms, Clear, Ipswich, 10 In.High	75.00
Heisey, Vase, Clear, Panels, Marked, 10 In.High	7.95
Heisey, Vase, Colonial, 3 1/2 In.Tall, Pair	12.00
Heisey, Vase, Cornucopia, Clear, Signed, 5 In.Tall	8.50
Heisey, Vase, Fan, Lariat Pattern, 7 1/2 In.	10.00
Heisey, Vase, Fluted, Clear, 9 In.Tall	40.00
Heisey, Vase, Loop Design At Bottom, Flares To Wide Ruffled Top, 8 In.	13.00
Heisey, Vase, Orchid Pattern, Fan, 7	30.00
Heisey, Vase, Scalloped Top, 9 Paneled Sides, 13 In.High	30.00
Heisey, Water Set, Greek Key, Signed, 7 Piece	74.00
Heisey, Water Set, Paneled, 11 Piece	95.00

*Herend, Hungary, had a porcelain factory that was founded in 1839, and it has
continued working into the twentieth century. The firm was directed by
Moritz Fischer, and the wares are sometimes called Fischer China.*
Herend, see Fischer

*Higbee Glass was made by the J.B.Higbee Company of Bridgeville,
Pennsylvania, about 1900.*

Higbee, Bowl, Flower Embossed, Open Edge, Pierced Sides, Beehive Mark	17.50
Higbee, Bowl, Marked, Cut & Pressed, Footed, Scalloped Top, Hobstar, Fern	30.00
Higbee, Cake Stand, Paneled Thistle, 9 1/2 In.Diameter, Signed	19.00
Higbee, Dish, Paneled Thistle, Bee Mark	20.00
Higbee, Plate, China, Cobalt Blue Border, Children In Center, Beehive Mark	55.00
Higbee, Relish, Paneled Thistle, 10 In.Long, Signed	18.00
Higbee, Vase, Clear, Ribbed, 13 In.Tall, Signed	9.00
Historic Blue, see Staffordshire	

*Hobnail Glass is a pattern of Pressed Glass with bumps in an allover
pattern. Dozens of hobnail patterns and variants have been made.
Reproductioins of many types of Hobnail Glass can be found.*
Hobnail, see also Francisware

Hobnail, Bowl, Berry, Opalescent, Fluted	22.00
Hobnail, Creamer, Opalescent	20.00
Hobnail, Jar, Clear, Paneled, Cover, 5 In.High	9.00
Hobnail, Lamp, Ruby Fount, Pedestal Base, Bulbous Chimney, 21 In.Tall	55.00
Hobnail, Perfume, Opalescent, Stopper	3.50
Hobnail, Tumbler, Bluish Cast	12.50
Hobnail, Vase, Opalescent Blue, Fluted Top, 5 In.	12.00

*Hochst, or Hoechst, Porcelain was made in Germany from 1746 to 1796. It
was marked with a six-spoke wheel.*

Hochst, Basket, Nut, C.1760, Double Ogee Shape, Pierced Florette Apertures	250.00
Hochst, Figurine, Boy, Standing, C.1760, Wheel & D Marks, 5 In.High	100.00
Hochst, Figurine, Boy, Standing, Faience, 18th Century, Hochst Wheel Mark	100.00
Hochst, Figurine, Girl, Standing, C.1755, Wheel Mark, Incised 81, 6 1/4 In.	110.00
Hochst, Jug, Hot Water, C.1775, Stepped Shoulder & Foot, Sepia Tones	100.00
Hochst, Nut Basket, C.1760 .... *Illus*	250.00
Hochst, Plate, Soup, C.1785, Gilt Border, Blue Scalework, Scrolls	240.00

Hochst, Tete-A-Tete, Landscape Medallions, C.1770-1775, 6 Piece 525.00

Holly Amber, or Golden Agate, Glass was made by the Indiana Tumbler and Goblet Company from January 1, 1903, to june 13, 1903. It is a pressed glass pattern featuring holly leaves in the amber shaded glass.

Holly Amber, Compote, Jelly 750.00
Holly Amber, Spooner 450.00
Holly Amber, Toothpick .... *Illus* 175.00

Hochst, Nut Basket, C.1760
See Page 241

Holly Amber, Toothpick

Hopalong Cassidy, Mug 5.00
Hopalong Cassidy, Watch, Wrist, Band 42.00
Howdy Doody, Dummy 10.00
Howdy Doody, Figure, Puppet, Celluloid, 5 .... 5.00
Howdy Doody, Spoon 3.50
Howdy Doody, Tumbler 2.00

Hull Pottery is made in Crooksville, Ohio. The factory started in 1903 as the Acme Pottery Company. Art Pottery was first made in 1917.

Hull, Basket, Ivory Color, Green, Pink, Floral 7.00
Hull, Basket, 11 In.Tall 12.00
Hull, Bowl, Twig Handles, Pink Flowers 5.00
Hull, Planter, Oblong 4.50
Hull, Planter, Pink, Green, Flower, Leaves, Embossed, 8 3/4 In.Long 5.00
Hull, Vase, Flowers, Leaves, Cream, Brown, Pink, Bulbous, Handled, 7 1/2 In.Tall 7.50
Hull, Vase, Pink Shading To Blue, Floral, Ovoid, Two Handles 18.00
Hull, Vase, Tulips & Leaves, Blue, Matte Finish, 8 1/2 In.Tall 7.50
Hummel, Figurine, Bookworm, 8 1/2 In.Tall 130.00
Hummel, Figurine, Merry Wanderer, 10 1/2 In.Tall 130.00
Hummel, Figurine, Umbrella Boy, 8 In.Tall 175.00
Hummel, Figurine, Umbrella Girl, 7 1/2 In.Tall 175.00
Hummel, Group, 3 Boys Looking At Slate, 7 1/2 In.Base 105.00

Imari Patterns are named for the Japanese Ware decorated with orange and blue stylized flowers. The design on the Japanese Ware became so characteristic that the name Imari has come to mean any pattern of this type. It was copied by the European factories of the eighteenth and early nineteenth centuries.

Imari, Bowl, Cover, Underplate, 18th Century 125.00
Imari, Bowl, Allover Decor, Bamboo, Chrysanthemums, Four Reserves, Footed 43.00
Imari, Bowl, Chinese Decorated, 6 1/4 In.Diameter 37.50
Imari, Bowl, Chinese Decorated, 7 1/4 In.Diameter 37.50
Imari, Bowl, Cobalt & Reds, Black Decorations, Scalloped Edge 26.00
Imari, Bowl, Covered, Decorated, 8 In.Diameter 85.00
Imari, Bowl, Decorated, 7 In.Diameter 40.00
Imari, Bowl, Fish Decoration, 6 In.Diameter 20.00
Imari, Bowl, Floral & Figure Design, Blue, Orange, White, Green, 11 In. 75.00
Imari, Bowl, Fluted, 8 In.Diameter 40.00

Imari, Bowl, Octagonal, 7 In.Diameter	35.00
Imari, Bowl, Ormolu Mounts, Dragon Handle, 18th Century	350.00
Imari, Bowl, Panels, Pedestal Base, 7 In.	40.00
Imari, Bowl, Rice, Cover, Alternate Panels, Blue, Red, & Gold, Marked	40.00
Imari, Bowl, Rice, Panels, Cover	40.00
Imari, Bowl, Scalloped Edge, Footed, Gold, Green, Cobalt Blue, & Iron Red	75.00
Imari, Bowl, Terra-Cotta, Cobalt Design, Scalloped Edge, 12 In.	30.00
Imari, Bowl, White, Double Ring Base, 5 In.Diameter	15.00
Imari, Bowl, White, Polychrome Colors, Birds & Flowers	18.00
Imari, Bowl, White, Scalloped Edge, Double Ring Base, 6 In.Diameter	18.00
Imari, Brush Holder, Blue, White, Pierced Sides, 4 1/4 In.High	15.00
Imari, Butter Chip, Red, Blue, Green, Gold, Floral, Set Of 6	40.00
Imari, Charger, Blue, Green, Rust, Mark, 12 In.	48.00
Imari, Charger, Circa 1710, 12 1/2 In.	110.00
Imari, Charger, Flower & Carrot Design, Blue, 16 In.Diameter	85.00
Imari, Charger, Foo Lion, Prunus Blooms, Fans, 19th Century	100.00
Imari, Cup, Handleless, Blue, White, Butterfly & Flowering Branches, Pair	7.50
Imari, Cup, Handleless, Terra-Cotta, Red, Green Panels, Floral, C.1880	2.00
Imari, Dish, Blue & White, Fish Design, Pair	55.00
Imari, Jar, Blue, White, Miniature Scenes, Cover, 4 In.	37.50
Imari, Lamp, Bird Design, Red, Green, Silk Shade, Single Bulb, 20 In.Tall	85.00
Imari, Plaque, Chinese, Green Ground, Wood Frame, 11 1/2 In.Square	15.00
Imari, Plate, Blue & Red Flowers, 8 1/4 In.Diameter	10.00
Imari, Plate, Blue & White, Water, Island, Geese Flying, 18 In.Diameter	100.00
Imari, Plate, Blue, White, Landscape In Center, Square	45.00
Imari, Plate, Carp, Birds, Pool, Gold, Orange, White, Blue, 18 In.Diameter	120.00
Imari, Plate, Chicks, Flowers, Blue Orange, 11 In.Diameter	37.50
Imari, Plate, Chinese Decorated, 8 1/2 In.Diameter	20.00
Imari, Plate, Chop, Basket Of Flowers Center, 11 In.Diameter, Pair	70.00
Imari, Plate, Chop, Central Medallion, 18th Century, 5 Colors	140.00
Imari, Plate, Chop, Vase Of Flowers Center, 12 In.Diameter	55.00
Imari, Plate, Flower Design, Red, Blue, Green, 11 In.Diameter	25.00
Imari, Plate, Garden Wall, Tree, Birds, 12 In.Diameter	65.00
Imari, Plate, Gold, Blue, Red/rust, Green, Scalloped Border, 16 In.	120.00
Imari, Plate, Hand-Painted, 9 In.	9.50
Imari, Plate, Octagonal, Decorated, 6 1/2 In.	22.50
Imari, Plate, Panels With Artichokes, 8 1/2 In.Diameter, Pair	40.00
Imari, Plate, Red & Blue Floral, 12 In.Diameter	45.00
Imari, Plate, Urn Of Flowers In Center, 7 1/2 In.	6.25
Imari, Plate, White, Cobalt Scene, Circa 1830	9.50
Imari, Platter, Oval, Scalloped Rim, 11 In.Long	35.00
Imari, Sugar, Miniature, Covered, Decorated	10.00
Imari, Vase, Blue & White, 4 1/4 In.	8.00
Imari, Vase, Bud, Long Neck	35.00
Imari, Vase, Chinese Decorated, 6 1/2 In.High, Pair	25.00
Imari, Vase, Miniature, 8 Sided, 4 In.High	9.50
Imari, Vase, Red & Blue Flowers & Figures In Panel, 14 In.High, Pair	225.00
Imari, Vase, Stick, 8 In.High, Pair	45.00
Imperial, Bowl, Jewels, Purple, Signed, 5 In.Diameter	49.50
Imperial, Bowl, Stretch, Cut Stripes On Exterior, 12 In., Light Green	28.00
Imperial, Vase, Frosty Iridescent, Blue, Heart Shaped Leaves, 11 In.	95.00
Imperial, Vase, Iridescent Cobalt With White Hearts & Vines, 6 1/2 In.High	35.00
Imperial, Vine, Leaf, Cobalt Blue, Paper Label, Signed, 9 In.Tall	125.00

Indian Tree is a china pattern that was popular during the last half of the nineteenth century. It was copied from earlier patterns of English China that were very similar. The pattern includes the crooked branch of a tree and a partial landscape with exotic flowers and leaves. It is colored green, blue, pink, and orange. King's Rose Pattern of soft paste Staffordshire was made in England from about 1820 to 1830. It was decorated in pink, red, yellow, and green. The pattern featured a large roselike flower.

Indian Tree, Bowl, Cereal, 2 Handles, Johnson Brothers	2.50
Indian Tree, Bowl, Soup, Johnson Brothers	3.50
Indian Tree, Compote, Minton, Handles, C.1874, Low Standard	30.00
Indian Tree, Creamer, Johnson Brothers	6.00
Indian Tree, Creamer, 3 1/4 In.High	8.00

Indian Tree, Cup, Johnson Brothers .... 2.00 To 5.00
Indian Tree, Dish, Vegetable, Oval, Johnson Brothers, 9 In. 5.00
Indian Tree, Plate, Bread, Johnson Brothers 1.50
Indian Tree, Plate, Dinner, Johnson Brothers, 10 In. 5.00
Indian Tree, Plate, Luncheon, Octagonal, Johnson Brothers 3.50
Indian Tree, Platter, Blue Maddox 25.00
Indian Tree, Platter, Johnson Brothers, 12 1/2 In. 7.50
Indian Tree, Platter, Signed H.& C.Indian Tree, 18 X 14 1/2 In. 65.00
Indian Tree, Relish, Oval, Johnson Brothers, 8 In. 3.50
Indian Tree, Saucer, Johnson Brothers 1.00
Indian Tree, Sugar, Covered, Johnson Brothers 7.50
Indian Tree, Teapot, Sadler, England 12.50

*Indian Art from North America has attracted the collector for many
years. Each tribe has its own distinctive designs and techniques. Baskets,
jewelry, and leatherwork are of greatest collector interest.*
Indian, Arm Band, Quillwork, Metal, Red Feather, 23 In.Long, Sioux, Pair 110.00
Indian, Arrowhead, Apache, 4 .... 1.00
Indian, Ax, North American, Grooved, Fluted 10.00
Indian, Bag, Beaded, Geometric Floral Design, Black Velvet, Red Trim 15.00
Indian, Bag, Medicine, Body Of Skunk, Glass Beadwork, Arapaho, 25 In.Long 180.00
Indian, Bag, Medicine, Hide, Badger Body, Metal Stud, Quillwork, Plains Indian 550.00
Indian, Bag, Pipe, Hide, Glass, Quillwork, Metal & Feather Suspensions, Sioux 400.00
Indian, Bag, Pipe, Hide, Quillwork, Metal & Red Hair Suspensions, Sioux 650.00
Indian, Bark Vessel, Birch, Foliate Design, Rectangular, Algonquin 100.00
Indian, Bark Vessel, Geometric Design, Loop Handle, Lid, Algonquin, 6 1/4 In. 60.00
Indian, Bark Vessel, Round, Flat Base, Birch, Chippewa, 18 1/2 In.Diameter 30.00
Indian, Basket, Animal Design, Cylindrical, Lid, Red, Purple, Makah, 5 In. 160.00
Indian, Basket, Apache .... *Illus* 400.00
Indian, Basket, Arrow Head, Diamond, Geometric Motifs, Globular, Washo, 13 In. 6100.00
Indian, Basket, Ascending Step Motifs, Cylindrical, Pima, 2 3/4 In. 30.00
Indian, Basket, Concentric & Angular Design, Shallow, Round, Pima, 10 1/2 In. 190.00
Indian, Basket, Concentric Friezes, Hexagonal Motifs, Round, Maidu, 21 3/4 In 380.00
Indian, Basket, Concentric Friezes, Step Motifs, Round, Flared, Panamint 390.00
Indian, Basket, Conjoined Triangular, Panels, Globular, Washo, 10 In. 375.00
Indian, Basket, Crisscross Design, Feathers, Yellow, Black, Pomo, 8 1/4 In. 1750.00
Indian, Basket, Feathers, Beads, Shell, Round, Pomo, 6 1/2 In.Diameter 3200.00
Indian, Basket, Figures, Swastika, Cross, Geometric Design, Round, 11 In.Tall 450.00
Indian, Basket, Flame Motifs, Depressed Globular Body, Washo, 12 3/4 In. 2600.00
Indian, Basket, Flowerhead Tondo, Frieze, Animals, Zigzag, Apache, 22 1/4 In. 750.00
Indian, Basket, Frieze, Angular Foliate, Geometric, Round, Washo, 9 1/4 In. 375.00
Indian, Basket, Geometric & Angular Design, Feather Stitched, Kern 350.00
Indian, Basket, Geometric Design, Brown, Orange, Blue, Cylindrical, Tlingit 140.00
Indian, Basket, Geometric Design, Circular Tondo, Pima, 21 3/4 In. 270.00
Indian, Basket, Geometric Design, Flared Rectangular, Brown, Salish 190.00
Indian, Basket, Geometric Design, Glass Beads, Zoomorphic Motifs, 4 1/2 In. 430.00
Indian, Basket, Geometric Design, Hide Terminals, Yurok-Karok, 20 In.Long 350.00
Indian, Basket, Geometric, Equestrian Figures, Cylindrical, 21 1/2 In.Tall 1300.00
Indian, Basket, Human Figures, Reptiles, Flared Cylindrical, Pima, 15 In. 250.00
Indian, Basket, Leaf Shaped Motifs, Depressed Round Body, Pomo, 2 In. 90.00
Indian, Basket, Parallel Step Motifs, Concentric Tondo, Saboda, 8 1/2 In. 200.00
Indian, Basket, Rincon, California Mission Indian .... *Illus* 260.00
Indian, Basket, Running Frieze, Parallel Step Design, Round, Pomo, 5 1/2 In. 70.00
Indian, Basket, Shell & Glass Bead Design, Step Motifs, Round, Pomo, 3 In. 170.00
Indian, Basket, Spiral Design, Looped Rim, Coiled Vessel, Browns, 13 3/4 In. 80.00
Indian, Basket, Step Design, Depressed Hemispherical Body, Tulare, 11 In. 220.00
Indian, Basket, Stitched Feathers, Geometric Design, Round, Pomo, 2 1/4 In. 210.00
Indian, Basket, Three Eagles, Coiled Vessel, Shallow, Round, Browns, 11 1/2 In 160.00
Indian, Basket, Triangular, Geometric Design, Brown, Blue, Lid, Cylindrical 130.00
Indian, Basketry Cap, Angular Geometric Design, Indented Base, Round, 7 In. 80.00
Indian, Blanket, Woolen, Openwork Angular Stepped Motifs, Red To Brown 550.00
Indian, Blanket, Woolen, Parallel Friezes, Medallions, Geometric, Navajo 1800.00
Indian, Boots, Metal Buttons, Glass Beads, Geometric, Cheyenne, 21 In.Long 290.00
Indian, Bow & Arrow Set, Chippewa 500.00
Indian, Bow Guard, Silver, Engraved, Geometric, Turquoise In Center, Navajo 275.00
Indian, Bowl, Burl, Turned Rim, Seneca, 14 In.Diameter 125.00

Indian, Basket, Rincon, California Mission Indian
See Page 244

Indian, Basket, Apache
See Page 244

Indian, **Bowl**, Burl, 7 In.Diameter	100.00
Indian, **Box**, Tusk Shape, Eskimo, Hunting Scene, 2 In.Tall, 1 1/2 In.Wide	55.00
Indian, **Buckle**, Belt, Indian War	15.00
Indian, **Club**, Hide Handle, Tassel, Glass Beads, Metal, Hair, 23 1/2 In.	375.00
Indian, **Cradle Cover**, Hide, Geometric Design, Glass Beads, Red, Green, Sioux	950.00
Indian, **Doll**, Corn, Husk Face, Dance Mask, Pierced Eyes & Mouth, 12 1/2 In.	25.00
Indian, **Dress**, Hide, Glass Beads, Tassels, Geometric, Blue, Red, Sioux	3300.00
Indian, **Fetish**, Hide, Turtle Shape, Glass Beadwork, Geometric, 7 1/2 In.Long	170.00
Indian, **Hair Roach**, Stiched Horsehair, Metal Bell Suspension, 14 1/2 In.	425.00
Indian, **Head Ornament**, Silver, Engraved, Cross, Foliate, Thunderbird, 14 In.	675.00
Indian, **Headdress**, Feathers, Glass Beads, Geometric, 64 1/2 In.Long, Sioux	550.00
Indian, **Implement**, Bone, Carved Hunting Scenes, Eskimo, 9 In.Long	250.00
Indian, **Knife**, Wooden Handle, Metal Studs, Sheath, Glass Beads, 14 In.Long	225.00
Indian, **Leggings**, Geometric Design, Metal Buttons, Orange, Yellow, 16 3/4 In.	200.00
Indian, **Mask**, Dance, Wooden, Open Mouth, Pierced Eyes, Kwakiutl, 15 In.Tall	300.00
Indian, **Mat**, Navajo, Yellow, Green, & White Striped Flags	40.00
Indian, **Moccasins**, Geometric & Foliate Design, Glass Beads, 8 3/4 In.Long	90.00
Indian, **Necklace**, Dentalium Shell, Globular Beads, 30 In.Long, Sioux	170.00
Indian, **Necklace**, Horn Pendants, Painted Design, Hide Band, 21 In.Long	175.00
Indian, **Pipe**, Peace, Catlinite Stone	50.00
Indian, **Pipe**, Stone, Cylindrical Stem & Bowl, Inlaid Of Pewter, 6 1/2 In.	500.00
Indian, **Pipe**, Wooden, Cylindrical Catlinite Bowl, Flat Stem, Sioux, 23 1/4 In	125.00
Indian, **Pottery**, Birds, Flowers, Foliage, Globular, Brown, 8 3/4 In.Tall	200.00
Indian, **Pottery**, Bowl, Flower & Leaf Design, Red, Black, Pueblo, 6 1/2 In.	12.50
Indian, **Pouch**, Tobacco, Hide, Geometric, Glass Beads, Tassels, Metal Bells	325.00
Indian, **Robe**, Puberty, Tassels, Painted Center, Box Design, Arapaho	4600.00
Indian, **Rug**, see Textile, Rug, Navaho	
Indian, **Shell Vessel**, Conch, Concentric Design, Woven Cover, Makah, 5 In.	200.00
Indian, **Shirt**, Hide, Geometric Design, Beads, Feather, Mauve Hair, Crow	1300.00
Indian, **Spear**, North American, 8 In.Long	10.00
Indian, **Tomahawk**, North American, Flint	3.00
Indian, **Tomahawk**, Stone Blade, Rawhide Ties	45.00
Indian, **Tomahawk**, Trade	15.00
Indian, **Tomahawk**, Wooden, Blade Flared & Arrow Form, Metal Studs, 31 In.	1400.00
Indian, **Vest**, Beaded, American Plains Indian, Buckskin, 1890-1900	275.00
Inkstand, **Double**, Green Marble & Brass, 12 In.High	17.50
Inkstand, **George Ii**, Handle, 19th Century, Mahogany, Pair	110.00
Inkstand, **George Ii**, Rectangular, 19th Century, Mahogany, 4 1/4 In.	80.00
Inkstand, **George Ii**, Single Drawer, 19th Century, Mahogany, 3 In.	60.00
Inkstand, **George Ii**, 19th Century, Mahogany, 4 In.High	110.00
Inkstand, **Moose Foot**, Silver Top, Mt.Kineo On Moosehead Lake, Mo.	10.00

Inkstand, Russian, Copper & Silver Plate, Art Nouveau Style, 19th Century 150.00
Inkstand, Walnut & Brass, Continental, 18th Century, Urn Shape Sander 150.00
 Inkwell, see also Pewter, Inkwell
Inkwell, Apple Shape, Manzanita, 3 1/2 In.Long 10.00
Inkwell, Bear, Chained To Tree, Hinged Head, Bronze, 3 In. 50.00
Inkwell, Black Bakelite Cover, Marked Gem No.2, Pat.1912 .... 3.95
Inkwell, Blown In Mold, 1 3/4 In.High, Deep Olive Amber 70.00
Inkwell, Blown In Mold, 2 In.High, Olive Amber 100.00
Inkwell, Brass & Crystal, Father Reading With Children, 10 In.Long 55.00
Inkwell, Brass & Metal Boat, Rudder, Ropes, Mast, 2 Swirled Glass Wells 30.00
Inkwell, Brass & Pewter, Chinese, 3 In.Long, 2 In.Tall 22.00
Inkwell, Brass Hinged Lid, England, Circa 1850 .... 18.50
Inkwell, Brass, Stag's Head, 7 1/2 In.Long 35.00
Inkwell, Brown, Gold, Flower, Slater Patent, Circa 1885 .... 75.00
Inkwell, China, Hinged Top, Swirled, Blue With Daisies, 6 1/2 In.High 20.00
Inkwell, Cone Shape, Glazed Pottery 4.75
Inkwell, Cone Shape, Panels, Aqua .... 2.95 To 3.95
Inkwell, Cone Shape, Silver Top 8.00
Inkwell, Crystal, Cut Spray, Hinged Top, Brass, 4 In.Square 55.00
Inkwell, Double, White, Pewter, Sad & Happy Face 45.00
Inkwell, Eiffel Tower, Signed Ll Paris, Metal, 4 In. 15.00
Inkwell, Faceted Glass, Pink, White, Brass Lid 20.00
Inkwell, Figural, Bear's Head, Metal, Painted 35.00
Inkwell, Figural, Chair, Open Seat Holds Ink, Clear, Daisy & Button 17.50
Inkwell, Figural, Crab, Bronze, 7 In. 45.00
Inkwell, Figural, Dante, Flowing, Iron Cast, 2 1/4 In.Tall 12.50
Inkwell, Figural, Devil's Head, 4 1/2 X 3 1/2 In. 28.00
Inkwell, Figural, Jockey Hat & Horseshoe, Metal 10.00
Inkwell, Fine Rib, Marked Patented January 31, 1860, 3 In.High 32.00
Inkwell, Fish Shaped, Silver Plate Hinged Tops, Pressed 18.00
Inkwell, Flowers, Scrolls, Embossed, Sterling Silver Cover, Round 30.00
Inkwell, Glass & Bakelite, Marked David Automatic Ink Stand, Pat.1889 .... 4.95
Inkwell, Glass, Aqua, Marked, October 31, 1865, J & lem 10.00
Inkwell, Gold Leaf Platform Holder, Two Square Glass Inserts, Brass Covers 15.00
Inkwell, Ground Bottom, Round, Open Hole At Top 2.50
Inkwell, Iron, Camel, Colorful 16.50
Inkwell, Pair On Clear Glass Stand, Double Penholder In Front 5.95
Inkwell, Pewter Type Finish, Double, Good News & Bad News 45.00
Inkwell, Pewter, China Well, Round, 3 In.Diameter 38.00
Inkwell, Pink Medallions, Gold Trim, Classical Figures, Kauffmann 25.00
Inkwell, Pony's Hoof, Horseshoe Still On, Mounted On Silver, Engraved 45.00
Inkwell, School Desk, Black Bakelite Top 2.25
Inkwell, Shape Of Curling Stone, Pottery, Brass Handle 15.00
Inkwell, Tan, Cylindrical, Stoneware 7.50
Inkwell, Traveler's, Confederate Hat 17.50
Inkwell, Two Wells, Letter Holder, Bronze, France 145.00
Inkwell, White, Luster, Classical Figures, French, 3 In.Tall 25.00

Insulators of glass or pottery have been made for use on telegraph or
telephone poles since 1844.
Insulator, A.M., Telephone & Telegraph, Toll .... .50
Insulator, Agee, Tepee Shape, Purple 12.50
Insulator, American Insulator Co., Dated 1884, Bluish 5.00
Insulator, American Telegraph, Co 1900/1901, Aqua 6.00
Insulator, American Telephone & Telegraph, Toll 2.00
Insulator, Armstrong, Cd 214, No.10, Clear 3.00
Insulator, Armstrong, Cd 272, No.511a, Dark Amber 9.00
Insulator, Armstrong, D.P.1 .... 50 To 2.00
Insulator, Armstrong, D-510, Amber 8.00
Insulator, Armstrong, 51-C1, Cd 167, Dark Amber 6.00
Insulator, Armstrong, 51-C3, Deep Amber 7.50
Insulator, Armstrong, 511a, Amber 7.00
Insulator, B & O, Cd 136, Aqua 12.00
Insulator, B, No.44, Dark Aqua 8.00
Insulator, Bat Ears, 9 In. 40.00
Insulator, Beehive, Arizona 12.00

Insulator, Beehive, Dwight Pattern, Ice Blue	12.50
Insulator, Beehive, Flat Top, Porcelain	.50 To 2.00
Insulator, Beehive, Pleated, Aqua	22.00
Insulator, Black Rubber, Continental Rubber Works, W.U.Telephone Co.	1.00
Insulator, Brookfield, Aqua	5.00
Insulator, Brookfield, B, Olive Green	.50
Insulator, Brookfield, Cd 101, No.9, Aqua	3.00
Insulator, Brookfield, Cd 102, New York, Green	2.00
Insulator, Brookfield, Cd 102, Triple Patent Dates, Aqua	2.00
Insulator, Brookfield, Cd 126, Embossed, Light Blue	4.00
Insulator, Brookfield, Cd 152, Black Glass, Olive Green	8.00
Insulator, Brookfield, Cd 205	18.00
Insulator, Brookfield, Cd 205, No.3, Transposition, Dark Green	20.00
Insulator, Brookfield, Cd 427, 3 Patent Dates	25.00
Insulator, Brookfield, Hoopskirt, Olive Green	7.50
Insulator, Brookfield, Inner Skirt Clip	7.00
Insulator, Brookfield, Olive Green, B	2.00
Insulator, Brown's Pony, Patent Nov.23, 1886, Embossed, Aqua	6.00
Insulator, C.D.& P., Cd 121, Aqua	6.00
Insulator, C.D.& P.Telegraph To., Toll, Aqua	8.00
Insulator, C.E.L.Co., Cd 134, Green	75.00
Insulator, Cable, Cd 261, Norse Helmet, Dark Aqua	35.00
Insulator, Cable, Nm, Embossed 100	65.00
Insulator, Cable, No.2, Cd 252, Green	10.00
Insulator, Cal Electric	60.00
Insulator, California, Signal, Burgundy	12.50
Insulator, California, Signal, Pink	7.50
Insulator, Canadian, Pony, Purple	5.95
Insulator, Canadian, Signal, Embossed 1678, Aqua	18.00
Insulator, Canadian, Toll, Embossed B.T.C.Canada, Aqua	6.50
Insulator, Capacitator, Amber	8.00
Insulator, Cd 106, No.9, Aqua	2.00
Insulator, Cd 121, Toll, Diamond Embossed, Purple	8.00
Insulator, Cd 121, Toll, Diamond Embossed, Royal Purple	8.00
Insulator, Cd 134, Patent Dec.19, 1871 & May 2, 1893, Round, Aqua	5.00
Insulator, Cd 143, Vertical Ridged, Aqua Blue	30.00
Insulator, Cd 147, Patent Oct.8, 1907, Aqua	1.00
Insulator, Cd 194, 54a & B, 195, Sun Colored Amethyst	40.00
Insulator, Cd 433, Green, Patent, Dec.19, 1871	18.00
Insulator, Corning Pyrex, Cd 235, No.622, Brass	7.00
Insulator, Corning Pyrex, No.662, Carnival	20.00
Insulator, D In Diamond, Cd 154, Embossed On Both Sides, Straw Color	3.00
Insulator, Diamond, Pony, Amber	5.00
Insulator, Diamond, 2 Piece, Purple	37.50
Insulator, Dominion, Cd 154, No.42, Straw Color	1.00
Insulator, Dominion, Cd 155, No.42, Straw Color	1.00
Insulator, Double Diamond, Pony, Ice Blue	3.50
Insulator, Duquesne Glass Co., Aqua	22.00
Insulator, English, White Ceramic, 2 Piece	6.75
Insulator, Er, Cd 145, Aqua	7.00
Insulator, Fireplug, No.1002	6.50
Insulator, Fog Bowl, Porcelain, Brown	10.00
Insulator, Fog Bowl, Porcelain, Gray	7.00
Insulator, From Persian Desert, Crude, Bubbles	10.00
Insulator, G.E.Co., Cd 134	10.00
Insulator, G.N.W.Telephone Co.	30.00
Insulator, G.N.W.Telephone Co., Deep Purple	17.50
Insulator, Gaynor, No.530	15.00 To 22.00
Insulator, Glass Cutter, Nm	95.00
Insulator, H.G.Co., Beehive	.50 To 2.00
Insulator, H.G.Co., Beehive, Green	7.50
Insulator, H.G.Co., Cd 145, Green Milky Glass	7.00
Insulator, H.G.Co., 1893, Double, Petticoat	.50 To 2.00
Insulator, H.K.Porter	3.50
Insulator, Hemingray No.4, With Dp, 1893 Patent	5.00
Insulator, Hemingray/Lowex, Cd 168, No.D-510, Clear	1.00

Insulator, **Hemingray**, Amber .... 12.50 To 16.00
Insulator, **Hemingray**, Cd 120, No.5, Aqua 14.00
Insulator, **Hemingray**, Cd 124, No.4, 1893 Patent 5.00
Insulator, **Hemingray**, Cd 133, No.3, Aqua 8.00
Insulator, **Hemingray**, Cd 133, No.3, Lime Green 12.00
Insulator, **Hemingray**, Cd 137, No.D-990, Aqua 4.00
Insulator, **Hemingray**, Cd 137, No.D-990, Clear 3.00
Insulator, **Hemingray**, Cd 145, Aqua 3.00
Insulator, **Hemingray**, Cd 145, No.21, Blue 4.00
Insulator, **Hemingray**, Cd 145, Petticoat, Yellow Green 18.00
Insulator, **Hemingray**, Cd 152, No.40, Olive Green 2.00
Insulator, **Hemingray**, Cd 168, No.D-510, Amber .... 4.00 To 6.00
Insulator, **Hemingray**, Cd 168, No.D-510, Clear 1.00
Insulator, **Hemingray**, Cd 168, No.D-510, Deep Aqua 5.00
Insulator, **Hemingray**, Cd 194-195, 54, A & B, Sun Colored Amethyst 50.00
Insulator, **Hemingray**, Cd 201, No.2, Transposition, Aqua 5.00
Insulator, **Hemingray**, Cd 202, No.50, Ice Blue 6.00
Insulator, **Hemingray**, Cd 203, No.53, Clear 2.00
Insulator, **Hemingray**, Cd 257, No.60, Clear 6.00
Insulator, **Hemingray**, Cobalt 15.00
Insulator, **Hemingray**, Columbia 70.00
Insulator, **Hemingray**, D-510, Green 4.50
Insulator, **Hemingray**, D-512, Blue 9.50
Insulator, **Hemingray**, Green Milk Glass 3.50
Insulator, **Hemingray**, Mickey Mouse, Dated 1893 .... 17.50
Insulator, **Hemingray**, Mickey Mouse, No.60, Clear 11.00
Insulator, **Hemingray**, No.19 ....50 To 2.00
Insulator, **Hemingray**, No.25 .... 17.50
Insulator, **Hemingray**, No.25, Aqua 15.00
Insulator, **Hemingray**, No.40 .... .50
Insulator, **Hemingray**, No.42, Clear ....50 To .75
Insulator, **Hemingray**, No.42, Green 2.00
Insulator, **Hemingray**, No.43, Cable Top, Blue 5.00
Insulator, **Hemingray**, No.43, Green 9.50
Insulator, **Hemingray**, No.45 .... .50
Insulator, **Hemingray**, No.45, Aqua 3.00
Insulator, **Hemingray**, No.55 .... 7.00
Insulator, **Hemingray**, No.55, Aqua 8.00
Insulator, **Hemingray**, No.60, Mickey Mouse .... 9.50 To 12.50
Insulator, **Hemingray**, No.62, Aqua 8.00
Insulator, **Hemingray**, No.820, Clear 15.00
Insulator, **Hemingray**, Ts, Double Groove 3.50
Insulator, **Hemingray**, Ts, Double Groove, Dated 1907 .... 3.50
Insulator, **June 17**, 1890, Blue .... *Illus* 12.50
Insulator, **Kc-Gw**, Cd 145, Ice Blue 65.00
Insulator, **Kimble**, No.820, Clear 10.00
Insulator, **Lapp**, Dated, Porcelain Top 8.50
Insulator, **Lowex No.512**, Bug Eyes, Amber 12.50

Insulator, June 17, 1890, Blue

Insulator, Lynchburg, Cd 154, No.44, Aqua	3.00
Insulator, Lynchburg, Cd 205, No.530	22.00
Insulator, Lynchburg, No.53, Aqua	32.00
Insulator, Manhattan, Dated, Cd 256, Blue	75.00
Insulator, Manhattan, N.M.	60.00
Insulator, Manhattan, Vnm, Blue	75.00
Insulator, Maydwell, Cd 164, No.20, Clear	1.00
Insulator, Maydwell, Milk Glass	5.00
Insulator, Maydwell, No.20, Milk Glass	12.50
Insulator, Mclaughlin, Cd 106, No.9, Bubbly, Light Aqua	2.00
Insulator, Mclaughlin, No.16, Green	7.50
Insulator, Mclaughlin, No.20, Ice Blue	5.00
Insulator, Milk Glass	15.00
Insulator, Negm, Cd 145, Aqua	3.00
Insulator, Negm, Cd 162, Light Aqua	3.00
Insulator, New England Telegraph & Telephone Co.	2.00
Insulator, New England Telephone & Telegraph Co., Cd 104, Green	5.50
Insulator, New England Telephone & Telegraph Co., Cd 104, Ice Blue	3.00
Insulator, No.D-512, Bug Eyes	5.00
Insulator, No.670, Nm, Amber	40.00
Insulator, No.9, Aqua	2.00
Insulator, Orange, Pyrex, Carnival Glass	35.00
Insulator, Pacific Railroad	10.00
Insulator, Pacific Railroad, Cd 462, No.B, Dark Aqua	2.00
Insulator, Peacock, Mickey Mouse, Nm, Vnm	85.00
Insulator, Peak Top, Ice Blue	34.00
Insulator, Pony, Ceramic, Cobalt	5.00
Insulator, Pony, Diamond, Amber	5.00
Insulator, Pony, Double Diamond, Ice Blue	3.50
Insulator, Postal Telegraph Co., Cd 156, Patent Sept.13, 1881, Embossed	40.00
Insulator, Postal Telephone Co., Cd 138, Aqua	9.00
Insulator, Postal Telephone Co., Cd 145, Greenish Aqua	5.00
Insulator, Postal, Cd 210	3.00
Insulator, Pottery, Brown	1.50 To 2.00
Insulator, Pyrex No.662, Carnival	12.50
Insulator, Pyrex, Carnival Glass, Cd 235	9.00
Insulator, Pyrex, Carnival Glass, 10 In.	25.00
Insulator, Pyrex, Carnival Glass, 10 In., Dark Color	25.00
Insulator, Pyrex, No.63, Carnival Glass	13.50 To 20.00
Insulator, Pyrex, No.63, Carnival Glass, Aqua	9.50
Insulator, Pyrex, No.662, Carnival Glass	18.50
Insulator, Roman Helmet, White Porcelain	9.50
Insulator, Sombrero Type, Made In France, Green, 10 X 4 In.	75.00
Insulator, Sombrero Type, Made In France, Green, 11 1/4 X 5 In.	75.00
Insulator, Sombrero Type, Made In France, Green, 12 1/2 X 6 In.	75.00
Insulator, Sombrero, Metal, Green Glass	4.00 To 5.00
Insulator, Spiral	.50 To 2.00
Insulator, Spiral Groove, Dated 1907	3.50
Insulator, Star, Cd 145, Olive Green	3.00
Insulator, Surge, Cd 100, Clear	2.00
Insulator, Surge, Clear	2.00
Insulator, Suspended Transposition, Clear	2.00
Insulator, T.H.E.Co., Cd 134, Aqua	12.00 To 14.00
Insulator, U.S.Telegraph Co., Toll, Aqua	18.00
Insulator, W.Brookfield, Cd 102, Aqua	1.00
Insulator, W.Brookfield, Cd 126, Aqua	3.00
Insulator, W.Brookfield, Cd 145, Jan.25, 1870, Aqua	1.00
Insulator, W.E.Mfg.Co., Cd 426, Wu, Dark Aqua	10.00
Insulator, W.F.G.Co., Cd 121, Gray	7.00
Insulator, W.F.G.Co., Denver, Roman Helmet, Blue	9.50
Insulator, W.F.G.Co., Gray	7.00
Insulator, W.T., Cd 214, No.10	2.00
Insulator, W.T., No.1, Cd 154, Sun Colored Amethyst	7.50
Insulator, W.T., No.1, Cd 154, Sun Colored Amethyst	7.50
Insulator, Whitall Tatum, No.1	.50 To 2.00
Insulator, Whitall Tatum, No.1, Amethyst	7.50

Insulator, **Whitall Tatum**, No.3, Clear With Pink Tint 1.75
Insulator, **Whitall Tatum**, No.512-U, Cd 216, Amber 6.00
Insulator, **Whitall Tatum**, No.512-U, Deep Amber 7.50
Insulator, **Whitall Tatum**, 5120, Cd 216, Dark Amber .... 3.00 To 3.50
Insulator, **Wu 5**, Patent Date Dec.19, 1871 .... 6.00
Insulator, **Wu 5a**, Patent Date Dec.19, 1871 .... 5.00 To 6.00
Insulator, **Wu5**, Cd 125, Light Aqua 6.00

Invalid Feeders were made during the eighteenth and nineteenth centuries.
The feeder is a dish having a spout or beak that made it easier for a sick
person to be fed.
Invalid **Feeder**, Hand-Painted Violets On White, Gold, Ring Handle 7.00
Iron, see also Kitchen, Tool, Store
Iron, **Auger**, Fruit, Dated, 16 In.Long 35.00
Iron, **Basket**, White, Ornate, 2 1/2 X 2 Ft. 18.00
Iron, **Bell**, Dinner, Cast, Yoke 25.00
Iron, **Bell**, Patio, Cast, Wrought Iron Bracket, 8 In. 12.50
Iron, **Bird Spit**, Bell Shaped, Three Arched Feet, 26 In. 175.00
Iron, **Bookend**, Buccaneer, Paint, Pair 18.00
Iron, **Bookend**, Bust Of Henry W.Longfellow, Bronze Finish, Pair 3.95
Iron, **Bookend**, Cottage Shape, 4 3/4 X 3 5/8 In., Pair 4.75
Iron, **Bookend**, Figural, Wild Horses, Copyright 1926, 5 X 5 In., Pair 4.75
Iron, **Bookend**, Galleon Shape, Copyright 1930, 4 1/2 In.High, Pair 4.75
Iron, **Bookend**, Indian's Head, Pair 8.00
Iron, **Bookend**, Penguin, Hand-Painted, 6 1/2 In.High, Pair 30.00
Iron, **Bootjack**, Adjustable Prongs, Maple Cleat, Pat.1859 .... 20.00
Iron, **Bootjack**, Beetle Design, Variation 25.00
Iron, **Bootjack**, Beetle Design, 10 1/4 In. 25.00
Iron, **Bootjack**, Beetle Design, 10 1/2 In. 25.00
Iron, **Bootjack**, Cast, Double End 12.00
Iron, **Bootjack**, Cast, Maplewood, Pat.1859, Prongs Adjustable 20.00
Iron, **Bootjack**, Cast, Oval At Top, Geometric Design At Bottom, 20 1/2 In. 25.00
Iron, **Bootjack**, Cast, Try Me, 12 In. 25.00
Iron, **Bootjack**, Oval At Top, Geometric Design Bottom, 20 1/2 In. 25.00
Iron, **Bootjack**, Scroll Pattern, Ornate, 12 In.Long 9.95
Iron, **Bootjack**, Triple Heart, 9 1/2 In. 65.00
Iron, **Bootjack**, Try Me, 1i In. 25.00
Iron, **Bootjack**, Try Me, 12 In. 25.00
Iron, **Bootscraper**, Terrier Dog, 10 In.Long 15.00
Iron, **Box**, Frog, Brass Knob 25.00
Iron, **Box**, Tool, Planters 5.75
Iron, **Bracket**, Shelf, Lacy, 8 X 6 In., Pair 3.95
Iron, **Bracket**, Wall, Openwork Design, Extends 7 1/2 In.From Wall 2.50
Iron, **Branding Iron**, Hand-Forged, Socket End Handle .... 3.00 To 4.50
Iron, **Branding Iron**, Z-Y 7.50
Iron, **Broiler**, Cast, Drip Pan 4.00
Iron, **Broiler**, Stationary, Wrought, 3 Graduated 37.50
Iron, **Broiler**, Wrought, Folding Standard, Heart Design 45.00
Iron, **Broiler**, Wrought, Folding Standard, Squiggly Line Design 15.00
Iron, **Broiler**, Wrought, Rotary, 12 1/2 In.Diameter 65.00
Iron, **Broiler**, Wrought, Standing, 18th Century 40.00
Iron, **Broiler**, Wrought, Stationary, Handle 55.00
Iron, **Broiler**, Wrought, Stationary, Square, Handle 17.50
Iron, **Broiler**, Wrought, Swivel, Fancy Design In 14 In.Pan 75.00
Iron, **Caliper**, 25 In. 35.00
Iron, **Candle Light**, Wrought, Floor Model, Adjustable, Tripod Base 200.00
Iron, **Candleholder**, Forged From One Piece Iron, Sticking Tommy, 6 1/2 In. 55.00
Iron, **Candleholder**, Hand-Forged, American, Arched Shoe Foot, 3 Socket 150.00
Iron, **Candleholder**, Stand Holds Two Candles, Two Glass Chimneys, Snuffer 7.98
Iron, **Candleholder**, Wrought, Adjustable Candle In Wire Cage, Wood Base 65.00
Iron, **Candleholder**, Wrought, Adjustable, Floor Model, 18th Century, 4 Legs 550.00
Iron, **Candleholder**, Wrought, Hanging, Twisted, One Piece 30.00
Iron, **Candlesnuffer**, Copper Tray 20.00
Iron, **Candlestick**, Hog Scraper, 7 In.High 17.50
Iron, **Candlestick**, Miniature 2.00
Iron, **Chain**, Log, Cast, 12 Ft.Ring At One End, Hook At Other 25.00

Iron, Chair, Fireplace, Hooks, Wrought 2.50
Iron, Chandelier, Wrought, Circular, Scrolls, 5 Candle Sockets, 18th Century 300.00
Iron, Charcoal Iron, Smokestack 9.75
Iron, Cherry Stoner, Enterprise, Cast 5.00
    Iron, Cigar Store Indian, see also Wooden, Cigar Store Indian
Iron, Coal Hod, Brass Bail, Advertising, 3 1/2 In.Long, 3 3/4 In.High 7.00
    Iron, Coffee Grinder, see Coffee Grinder
Iron, Coffer, Tobacco, Cast, Coffin Shape, Covered, 18th Century, Claw Feet 55.00
Iron, Counter Standard, Cobbler's, 6 Lasts 17.50
Iron, Cup, Nail, Shoe Coffer, 8 Compartment 15.00
Iron, Cuspidor, Turtle Shape, Head Lifts, 14 In.Long, 4 1/2 In.High 40.00
Iron, Cutter, Sugar, Wrought, Brass Standard, Wood Base & Handle 55.00
Iron, Cutter, Tobacco, Marked Brown's Mule, R.J.Reynolds Tob.Co. 125.00
Iron, Deer, Cast, 17 1/2 In.High, 15 1/2 In.Long 350.00
Iron, Dish, Flower Design, Two Section, 2 3/4 In.Wide, 6 1/4 In.Long 3.75
Iron, Door Knocker, 'mather, '4 X 8 In. 12.50

*Iron Doorstops have been made in all types of designs. The vast majority
of the doorstops sold today are cast iron and were made from about 1890 to
1930. Most of them are shaped like people, animals, flowers, or ships.*

Iron, Doorstop, Basket Of Flowers .... 5.00 To 6.95
Iron, Doorstop, Basket Of Nasturtiums, 7 In. .... *Illus* 8.50

Iron, Doorstop, Basket Of Nasturtiums, 7 In.

Iron, Doorstop, Bird Of Paradise, 3 1/2 X 13 In.Tall 10.00
Iron, Doorstop, Blonde Southern Belle, Blue Dress, Pink Hat & Flowers 18.00
Iron, Doorstop, Boston Terrier, 9 In.Long, 8 In.High 12.75
Iron, Doorstop, Bulldog, Boston, Painted 20.00
Iron, Doorstop, Bulldog, Cast .... 14.00 To 25.00
Iron, Doorstop, Clown 19.50
Iron, Doorstop, Colonial Girl Carrying Flowers, 11 5/8 In.High 7.95
Iron, Doorstop, Colonial Lady 8.00
Iron, Doorstop, Cottage 6.95
Iron, Doorstop, Dutch Figure, Man, Dog, Axe, Pipe, 15 In.Tall 45.00
Iron, Doorstop, Floral Bouquet 3.50
Iron, Doorstop, Flowerpot, 7 In. 8.50
Iron, Doorstop, Flowers In Vase, 7 1/2 In.High 10.00
Iron, Doorstop, Flowers, Basket, Ribbon, 10 1/2 In.High 10.00
Iron, Doorstop, Gordon Pasha 7.50
Iron, Doorstop, Large Dog, 12 1/2 In.High 12.95
Iron, Doorstop, Mayflower Type Ship 6.95
Iron, Doorstop, Peter Rabbit 6.00
Iron, Doorstop, Terrier, 8 3/4 In.High 12.95
Iron, Doorstop, Three Iris 12.00
Iron, Doorstop, Windmill, 7 In.High 6.75
Iron, Dryer, Corn .... 2.00 To 3.00
Iron, Dryer, Corn, 1 Piece, 10 Prong 2.00
Iron, Dryer, Corn, 1 Piece, 14 Prong 2.50
Iron, Eagle, Cast, Hook To Hold Lantern 85.00
Iron, Eagle, Cast, 23 In.Wing Spread 22.50
Iron, Figure, Garden, Child Sitting On Jug Holding Oar, 29 In.High 125.00

Iron, **Figurine**, Cat, Standing, Smoking Pipe 17.00
Iron, **Figurine**, Dog, Spaniel, 6 3/4 In.Long, 4 3/4 In.Tall 9.95
Iron, **Fire Carrier**, Pierced, Club Design 65.00
Iron, **Flatiron**, Charcoal 17.50
Iron, **Flatiron**, Wooden Handle 6.00
Iron, **Foot Scraper**, Cast, Fancy Pan 25.00
Iron, **Foot Scraper**, Cast, Octagonal Pan, Pair 30.00
Iron, **Foot Scraper**, Wrought, Diamond Ball Finial 20.00
Iron, **Fork**, Wrought, Becket, 2 Tined, 17 In. 17.50
Iron, **Fork**, Wrought, In Frame For Fireplace Use 12.50
Iron, **Fork**, Wrought, 2 Tines, 27 1/2 In.Long 12.50
Iron, **Frame**, Picture, Easel, Art Nouveau, Flowers, Painted Gold, 6 X 8 In.High 6.95
Iron, **Frame**, Picture, Easel Type, Gold Leaf, Cutout Lacy 18.00
Iron, **Funnel**, Anchor, Miniature 2.00
Iron, **Gate**, American Navy Yard, Set 400.00
Iron, **Griddle**, For Kitchen Stove 6.00
Iron, **Griddle**, Handle, 14 In.Diameter 3.00
Iron, **Griddle**, Pancake, Swedish, Patent, 1884 .... 15.00
Iron, **Grill**, Charcoal, Pat.1885 .... 17.50
Iron, **Hatchet**, Miniature 2.00
Iron, **Heater**, Charcoal, Perforated At Top, 6 X 8 X 10 In. 12.50
Iron, **Hinge**, Strap, Wrought, Fancy Tips, 43 In., Pair 12.50
Iron, **Hinge**, Strap, Wrought, Pair 6.00
Iron, **Hinge**, Wrought, H & L, 9 X 9 In., Pair 35.00
Iron, **Hinge**, Wrought, Pennsylvania, 18th Century, Tulip Terminals, Pair 425.00
Iron, **Hitching Post**, Cast, Negro Groom With Top Hat, Painted, 26 In.High 175.00
Iron, **Hitching Post**, Horse's Head, Cast, Tie Rings, Signed J.C. 150.00
Iron, **Hitching Post**, Iron Mounting Block, M.Dyer, Elmira, N.Y. 350.00
Iron, **Holder**, For Goffering Irons 5.00
Iron, **Holder**, Match, Cast, Dated 1899 .... 3.45
Iron, **Holder**, Match, Cast, Wall Type, Urn Shape, Dated 1867 .... 10.00
Iron, **Holder**, Match, Footed, Slotted For Hanging, Gold Finish 17.50
Iron, **Holder**, Match, Open Pocket, Openwork Design Of Scrolls On Back 9.75
Iron, **Holder**, Match, Table, Acorn Shape, Gilt Finish, Pedestal Frame 24.00
Iron, **Holder**, Match, Wall Type, Box With Self-Closing Lid, Dated 1864 .... 10.00
Iron, **Holder**, Match, Wall, 2-Tier, Lower Self-Closes 17.50
Iron, **Holder**, Rush & Candle, Wrought, Floor Model, Crown Base, 35 In.High 90.00
Iron, **Holder**, Rush & Candle, Wrought, Twisted Standard, Ring Base, 11 1/2 In. 70.00
Iron, **Holder**, Rush & Candle, Wrought, Wooden Block Box, 33 In.High 35.00
Iron, **Holder**, Spittoon, Turtle Shape, Shell Raises 42.00
Iron, **Holder**, Spool, Three Tiers, Holds 18 Spools, Pin Cushion On Top, Footed 35.00
Iron, **Holder**, String, Beehive, 6 1/4 In.Tall 17.00
Iron, **Hook**, Ceiling, For Hall Lantern, Screw-In Type, 10 In.Long 2.75
Iron, **Hook**, For Crane, Wrought, S 7.50
Iron, **Hook**, Harness, Shelf Bracket, Pair 40.00
Iron, **Hook**, Kettle, Wrought, Shaped Like Hay Hook 25.00
Iron, **Hook**, Log, Wooden Handle, Marked Davis 4.00
Iron, **Hook**, S, Wrought, For Use On Crane 4.50
Iron, **Hook**, Singletree 1.00
Iron, **Hook**, Wrought, Vertical To Go In Beam 3.00
Iron, **Horse Head**, Cast, Painted Black, Fits On 3 1/2 In. Pipe 8.50
Iron, **Horse Head**, Cast, 13 In.High, 15 Lbs., Painted Black 5.75
Iron, **Horse Head**, Cast, 15 Lbs., Painted Black, Fits On 3 1/2 In.Pipe 8.50
Iron, **Horse Weight**, No.22 .... 6.50
Iron, **Horse**, Ives, Cast, Galloping, 8 In.Long, 6 In.High 18.00
Iron, **Ice Tongs** .... *Illus* 5.00
Iron, **Inkwell**, Cast, Crane, 1915 .... 20.00
Iron, **Kettle**, Bail Handle, 3 Feet 12.50
Iron, **Kettle**, Cast, Black, 3 Legs, Wire Bale, Porcelain Lined 14.00
Iron, **Kettle**, Flat Bottom, Bail Handle 9.00
Iron, **Kettle**, Gypsy, Cast, Covered, 3 Legs 65.00
Iron, **Kettle**, Gypsy, Cast, 12 1/4 In.Diameter 20.00
Iron, **Kettle**, Gypsy, Cast, 9 In.Diameter 20.00
Iron, **Kettle**, Gypsy, Cover, Bail, 4 1/2 In.Legs, 15 In.High 65.00
Iron, **Kettle**, Gypsy, Footed, Cover 24.00
Iron, **Kettle**, Gypsy, Removable Handle 12.50

Iron, Kettle, Three Gallon	12.50
Iron, Kettle, Three 4 1/2-In.Legs, Lid, Iron, Bail, 12 X 13 In.	65.00
Iron, Knocker, Door, Bunch Of Grapes	15.00
Iron, Knocker, Door, Cast, Hand, Wreaths, & Lion Head	15.00
Iron, Knocker, Door, Hand, Back Plate	17.50
Iron, Knocker, Door, Wrought, Pennsylvania, Serpent Ornament On Back Plate	225.00
Iron, Ladle, Wrought, For Pouring Lead	5.00
Iron, Lamp, Kitchen, Weights, Bristol Shade, Peg Font	89.50
Iron, Letter Holder, Cast, Wall Mount, John Deere, Dated 1847	45.00
Iron, Light, Candle & Rush, Wrought, 18th Century, Ring Base, 10 1/2 In.High	65.00
Iron, Lock, Box	3.00
Iron, Lock, Cast, Fancy Designs	20.00
Iron, Lock, Hacienda, Spanish *Illus*	150.00
Iron, Mailbox, Wall Type	3.50 To 6.50
Iron, Mammy, Cast, 4 In.Tall, Painted	5.50
Iron, Mark, Firehouse, Hydrant & Hose	60.00
Iron, Match Holder, see also Match Holder	
Iron, Match Safe, Shape Of Boot, Cast, 4 In.Tall	12.00
Iron, Match Safe, Wall, General Grant, Cast	40.00
Iron, Mold, Bullet, Scissor Type	7.50
Iron, Mold, Cake, Santa Claus, 12 In.	25.00
Iron, Mold, Cornbread, Dated 1920 *Illus*	6.50

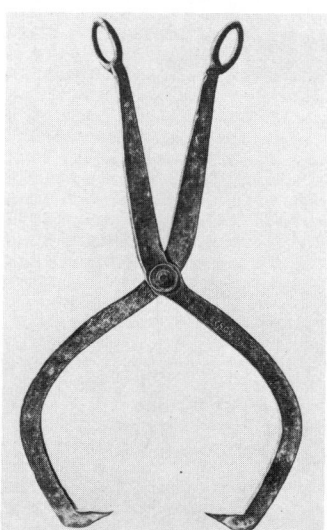

Iron, Ice Tongs
See Page 252

Iron, Lock, Hacienda, Spanish

Iron, Mold, Cornbread, Dated 1920

Iron, Mortar & Pestle, Cast	12.50
Iron, Mortar & Pestle, Cast, 12 Lbs., 7 In.High	12.50

Iron, Mortar & Pestle, Cast, 7 In.Diameter, 7 In.High, 12 Lbs.	12.50
Iron, Nutcracker, Dog, Brass Pan Catcher	12.50
Iron, Nutcracker, Dog, Cast	8.50
Iron, Nutcracker, Dog, Cast, Painted	16.50
Iron, Nutcracker, Dog, Harper Supply Co., Pat.1900, 13 In.Long, 6 In.High	12.50
Iron, Ornament, Wrought, 18th Century, 10 Ft. Tall, Bird & Scrolls	1110.00
Iron, Pan, Muffin, Case, Cutout Triangles, Marked R.& G.Mfg.Co., Patent	17.00
Iron, Peel, American, Handwrought, One Piece Of Iron, Round Ball End	39.00
Iron, Peel, Wrought, Ring Terminal, 5 Ft.1 1/2 In.Long	35.00
Iron, Peel, Wrought, 4 Ft.3 In.Long	65.00
Iron, Peeler, Wrought, Wood Handle, Lumberman's	15.00
Iron, Pen Rack, Double Sided, Holds Ten Pens, 5 1/4 In.Long	3.95
Iron, Plane, Grooving, Set Of Blades	6.00
Iron, Plane, Guide, 1 In.Blade	4.50
Iron, Porringer, Heart Center, Pierced Handle, 6 1/2 In.Tall	18.00
Iron, Porringer, Porcelain Lining	47.50
Iron, Pot, Bean, Cast, Footed, 9 In.High, 9 1/2 In.Diameter	12.00
Iron, Pot, Cast, Iron Handle, Label, 10 1/4 In.Diameter	10.00
Iron, Pot, Cast, Oval, Tin Cover, Label, 12 1/2 In.Diameter	15.00
Iron, Pot, Cast, Oval, Tin Cover, Label, 14 In.Diameter	15.00
Iron, Pot, Rosin, For Cooking Potatoes	6.75
Iron, Pot, Spice Grinding, Cast, Oval, 3 Legs, Handle	20.00
Iron, Pulley, Well	3.50 To 10.00
Iron, Rack, Bonnet, Wall, Five Pegs, Folds, Dated 1864	19.00
Iron, Rack, Utensil, Hand Forged	18.00
Iron, Rack, Utensil, Wrought	22.50 To 30.00
Iron, Rack, Utensil, Wrought, 16 1/2 In.Wide	65.00
Iron, Register Floor Plate, Stove Pipe, Cast	4.50
Iron, Rod, Spit, Fork For Holding Meat, Wrought	15.00
Iron, Ropemaker, Cast, Crank Handle	15.00
Iron, Ropemaker, Hand Crank, Gear Drive, Cast	15.00
Iron, Rushlight & Candle, Wrought, Crown Base, 11 1/2 In.High	60.00
Iron, Rushlight & Candle, Wrought, Twisted Parts, Flat Circular Base	65.00
Iron, Rushlight, Wrought, Crown Base, 14 In.High	30.00
Iron, Sadiron *Illus*	9.00

Iron, Sadiron

Iron, Sadiron, Charcoal	2.50
Iron, Sadiron, Child's	.50
Iron, Sadiron, Child's, Cast Handle	1.00
Iron, Sadiron, Child's, Wire Handle	1.00
Iron, Sadiron, Raised Design Of Anchor, Marked Trademark	3.95
Iron, Sadiron, Trivet, Salesman's Sample	10.00
Iron, Scale, Balancing, Iron Weight, Brass Pan	19.50
Iron, Scale, Hand-Forged, Balance, 13 In.	10.00
Iron, Scales, Balance, Copper & Porcelain Pans, 20 In.High	50.00
Iron, Sconce, Candle, Wrought	85.00
Iron, Scraper, Foot, Handwrought, For Wall	32.50

Iron, Scraper, Foot, Unicorn, Pennsylvania	400.00
Iron, Scraper, Foot, Wrought, Ram's Horn Terminals	17.50
Iron, Seat, Cast, Champion	8.00
Iron, Seat, Cast, Deering	8.00
Iron, Seat, Cast, Hoosier	14.00
Iron, Seat, Cast, Mccormick	10.00
Iron, Seat, Cast, Milwaukee	10.00
Iron, Seat, Cast, Stoddard	12.00
Iron, Seat, Machinery, Cast	5.75
Iron, Seat, Machinery, Cast, Massey, Toronto	15.00
Iron, Seat, Machinery, Cast, Mccormick	9.00
Iron, Seat, Machinery, Cast, No.79	10.00
Iron, Seat, Machinery, Cast, Toronto, No.3	15.00
Iron, Seat, Machinery, Cast, Walter A.Wood	12.50
Iron, Shelf Bracket, Lacy, 8 X 6 In., Pair	3.95
Iron, Shoe, High Button, 8 X 10 In., Pair	50.00
Iron, Skewer Set, Wrought Holder & 6 Twisted Skewers, Heart Shape	950.00
Iron, Skewer, For Roasting, Handwrought, 21 In.	35.00
Iron, Skillet, Pancake, Flat	4.00
Iron, Skimmer, Cooking, Handwrought, Hook End Handle	7.50
Iron, Snow Eagle, Cast, Pair	28.00
Iron, Spatula, Hand Forged	7.00
Iron, Spatula, Wrought	20.00
Iron, Spatula, Wrought, Pierced Heart Handle	22.50
Iron, Spatula, Wrought, Round Pan, Pierced Clover Leaf In Handle	12.50
Iron, Spike, Marlin	7.50
Iron, Spoon, Hand Forged	7.00
Iron, Spoon, Handwrought, Ring Tip Handle, 15 In.Long	15.00
Iron, Spoon, Handwrought, Ring Tip Handle, 27 In.Long	25.00
Iron, Spoon, Wrought, 17 In.Long	12.50
Iron, Spurs, Heavy Rowels	4.50
Iron, Spurs, South American, 1750-1850, Hand-Forged, Inlaid Silver & Copper	115.00
Iron, Spurs, Spanish, 2 1/2 In.Rowels	1.75 To 3.50
Iron, Squeezer, Juice	3.50
Iron, Stamper, For Wax Seals, Cast, Lion Head, Black, Red, & Gold Paint	12.50
Iron, Stirrup, Cast, Spanish, Pair	12.50
Iron, Stirrup, Pair	4.00
Iron, Stirrup, Spanish, Heavy	12.50
Iron, Teakettle, Bent Wire Handle, Cover	11.50
Iron, Teakettle, Black, 8 Quart, Sliding Cover, Goodell & Co.	15.00
Iron, Teakettle, Cast, Brass Handle, Signed 'kirk'	80.00
Iron, Teakettle, Cast, 5 Graduated	100.00
Iron, Teakettle, Gooseneck Spout	22.50
Iron, Teakettle, Gooseneck, 5 Quart	37.50
Iron, Toaster, Wrought, Swivel, Turned-Out Feet, Fleur-De-Lis & Loops	165.00
Iron, Tongs, Blacksmith's, Handmade	3.00
Iron, Tongs, Wrought, Twisted Handles, 2	6.00
Iron, Tool, Cutting, Wrought, Signed	15.00
Iron, Trammel, Cast, Saw-Type, Adjustable, 31 In.	50.00
Iron, Trammel, Ring, Wrought Iron	7.00 To 20.00
Iron, Trammel, Ring, Wrought, Twisted	15.00
Iron, Trap, Bear, Triumph 415-X, Toothed Jaws	45.00
Iron, Trap, Deer, Handmade	9.75
Iron, Trap, Newhouse, Double Spring, 19 In.	5.75
Iron, Tray, Card, Eagle Claw, Leaf, 8 In.Long	14.00
Iron, Tray, Pin, Figural, Turtle, Lid	5.00
Iron, Trivet, Plain, 3 X 6 In.	1.00
Iron, Utensils, Royal Cookstove, Salesman's Sample	55.00
Iron, Waffle Iron, Handles, Heart Pattern	7.50
Iron, Waffle Iron, Hearth Type, Spring Handle With Clip	25.00
Iron, Waffle Iron, 2 Handles	6.50
Iron, Weight, Scale, 2 Kilograms To 100 Grams, 5	3.75

Ironstone China was first made in 1813. It gained its greatest popularity during the mid-nineteenth century. The heavy, durable, off-white pottery was made in white or was colored with any of hundreds of patterns. Much Flow

Blue Pottery was made of Ironstone. Some of the pieces had raised decorations.

Ironstone, see also Chelsea Grape, Gaudy Ironstone

Ironstone, Basket, Openwork, 9 1/2 In.	17.50
Ironstone, Bowl & Pitcher Set, White, Raised Wheat Design	35.00
Ironstone, Bowl, Chamber, Jenny Lind, Colored	25.00
Ironstone, Bowl, Chowder, American Marine, Mason's, England	15.00
Ironstone, Bowl, Soup, Arcadia Pattern, Marked A.J.Wilkinson Ltd., England	4.25
Ironstone, Chamber Pot, Blue & White, Dragon Center, Mason's	20.00
Ironstone, Chamber Pot, Brown & White, Cover	12.00
Ironstone, Chamber Pot, Pail, White	22.00
Ironstone, Chamber Set, Lily Of The Valley	39.00
Ironstone, Compote, Covered, Lady Peel, 11 In.Diameter, Pair	35.00
Ironstone, Creamer & Sugar, Acorn Finial, White, Cover	35.00
Ironstone, Cup & Saucer, Adams	1.75
Ironstone, Cup & Saucer, Pink & White, Tendril Pattern	8.50
Ironstone, Cup & Saucer, Rosaline Pattern	7.50
Ironstone, Cup, Apothecary, White, Blue Trim, 4 1/2 In.High	4.50
Ironstone, Cup, Egg, Ribbed	2.50
Ironstone, Dish, Soap, Open	4.00
Ironstone, Dish, Vegetable, Covered, Imari Decoration, Mason's	30.00
Ironstone, Dish, Vegetable, Covered, Oak Leaf & Flower, 2 Handles	18.00
Ironstone, Eggcup, Pair	8.00
Ironstone, Funnel, With Sieve	4.00
Ironstone, Gravy Boat, Imari Colors	22.00
Ironstone, Invalid Feeder, J.M.& Co., White	7.00
Ironstone, Jar, Cracker, Oriental Design, Silver Bail & Lid, Mason's, England	47.50
Ironstone, Ladle, White, Large	10.00
Ironstone, Mortar & Pestle	10.00
Ironstone, Mug, Blue Willow, 3 1/4 In.Tall	5.00
Ironstone, Mug, Roses, White, Blue, Marked	22.50
Ironstone, Pitcher & Washbowl, Wheat Pattern	39.00
Ironstone, Pitcher, Blue Willow, Hexagonal Shape, 5 In.	22.50
Ironstone, Pitcher, Blue, Pink, Rust & Green Floral, Mason's Patent	45.00
Ironstone, Pitcher, Chamber, Mulberry, Morning Glory	25.00
Ironstone, Pitcher, Cypress Pattern, 5 1/2 In.High	22.50
Ironstone, Pitcher, Grecian Scene, Purple, 5 In.High	5.00
Ironstone, Pitcher, Imari Decorated, Swans, 7 1/4 In.High	40.00
Ironstone, Pitcher, Milk, Pink & Light Blue, 5 In.High	12.50
Ironstone, Pitcher, Milk, Pink, Blue, 5 In.High	12.50
Ironstone, Pitcher, Oriental Design, C.1850, Hand-Painted, Staffordshire	20.00
Ironstone, Pitcher, Purple, Grecian Scene, Small	5.00
Ironstone, Pitcher, White, Alfred Meakin, England, 8 In.	9.00
Ironstone, Pitcher, White, Oval, Ribbon & Leaves, J & G Meakin, England	16.00
Ironstone, Pitcher, White, Sheaf Of Wheat	22.50
Ironstone, Pitcher, White, Sheaf Of Wheat Design, 12 1/2 In.High	22.50
Ironstone, Pitcher, 9 In.	8.75
Ironstone, Plate, Altarino Pattern, Blue, 8 1/4 In.	7.50
Ironstone, Plate, Blue & White, Burleigh, 9 1/2 In.Set Of 6	12.50
Ironstone, Plate, Blue & White, Daffodil Pattern, W.H.Grindley & Co., 1882	6.00
Ironstone, Plate, Castle Pattern, Pink, 9 In.	8.50
Ironstone, Plate, Chop, Imari Colors	22.00
Ironstone, Plate, Dinner, Boote Sydenham	7.00
Ironstone, Plate, Feather, Red, 9 In.Diameter	9.00
Ironstone, Plate, Flower Urn, Orange & Cobalt, Mason's	7.50
Ironstone, Plate, Footed, Rural Blue Scenery, 11 1/2 In.Diameter	22.50
Ironstone, Plate, Green Floral, 10 1/2 In.Diameter, Pair	7.50
Ironstone, Plate, Imari Decoration, Deep, 10 1/2 In.Diameter, Mason's, 6	120.00
Ironstone, Plate, Imari Decoration, Gold, Impressed Mark, Mason's, Pair	50.00
Ironstone, Plate, Mason's Patent, Persiana Pattern, Oriental Colors	12.50
Ironstone, Plate, Mulberry, 7 1/2 In.Diameter	12.00
Ironstone, Plate, Soup, Willow Pattern, Brown, 8 In.Diameter	8.00
Ironstone, Platter, Blue Decoration, Octagonal, Mason's, 19 In.	22.50
Ironstone, Platter, Blue, Scenic View, 16 In.Long	17.50
Ironstone, Platter, Chinese Pattern, Mason's-Ashworth Bros., 12 X 9 1/2 In.	22.00
Ironstone, Platter, English, Imari Decoration In Blue & Brick	50.00

Ironstone, Platter, Gold Band, 12 In.Diameter, 2	5.00
Ironstone, Platter, Grecian Scene, Triple, 15 In.Long	10.00
Ironstone, Platter, Imari Decorated, Blue Dragon Center, 17 In.Diameter	50.00
Ironstone, Platter, Imari Decorated, Mason's, 17 In.Diameter	35.00
Ironstone, Platter, J.& G.Meakin, Dated 1869, Oval	5.00
Ironstone, Platter, Lavender Border, Chinese River Scene, 14 In.Long	10.00
Ironstone, Platter, Lily Of The Valley, 15 In.	7.50
Ironstone, Platter, Mason's Gypsy Pattern, Mounted As Table, English, C.1850	150.00
Ironstone, Platter, Meat, Blue & White, Transfer Peacocks, C.1815, Mason's	70.00
Ironstone, Platter, Oriental Decor, Mason, Patent 1820, 9 In.Long	57.20
Ironstone, Platter, Tea Leaf, Luster	18.00
Ironstone, Platter, Vincennes, Alcock Mulberry	50.00
Ironstone, Platter, White, 14 X 9 1/4 In.	5.98
Ironstone, Soup, Boote Sydenham	7.00
Ironstone, Soup, Wheat Pattern, Anthony Shaw	7.50
Ironstone, Spittoon, Two Piece, Mason, 8 In.Diameter	25.00
Ironstone, Sugar & Creamer, Gold Band, 5 In.High	4.00
Ironstone, Tea Leaf, Bone Dish, Alfred Meakin	16.50
Ironstone, Tea Leaf, Bowl, Square, Wedgwood	14.00
Ironstone, Tea Leaf, Butter Chip, Alfred Meakin, Royal Ironstone, Luster	7.00
Ironstone, Tea Leaf, Butter Pat, Square	5.00
Ironstone, Tea Leaf, Compote, Wilkinson	95.00
Ironstone, Tea Leaf, Cup & Saucer, Handleless, Anthony Shaw, Burslem	20.00
Ironstone, Tea Leaf, Dish, Bone, Wilkinson	15.00
Ironstone, Tea Leaf, Dish, Soap, Oblong, 3 Piece, Johnson Bros.	46.00
Ironstone, Tea Leaf, Dish, Vegetable, A.J.Wilkinson, Open, Oblong	12.50
Ironstone, Tea Leaf, Gravyboat, Meakin	22.50
Ironstone, Tea Leaf, Pitcher, Gravy, Alfred Meakin, Light Brown Inside	16.00
Ironstone, Tea Leaf, Plate, Dinner, 8 In.	9.00
Ironstone, Tea Leaf, Plate, Salad, 7 In.	6.00
Ironstone, Tea Leaf, Plate, Serving, 9 1/2 In.Diameter	10.00
Ironstone, Tea Leaf, Plate, 8 In.Diameter	8.00 To 9.00
Ironstone, Tea Leaf, Plate, 9 In.Diameter	9.50
Ironstone, Tea Leaf, Plate, 9 3/4 In.Diameter, Meakin	7.00
Ironstone, Tea Leaf, Plate, 10 In.Diameter, A.Shaw	12.50
Ironstone, Tea Leaf, Plate, 10 In.Diameter, Wedgwood	12.50
Ironstone, Tea Leaf, Platter, Meakin, 14 In.	15.00
Ironstone, Tea Leaf, Platter, 15 In.	15.00
Ironstone, Tea Leaf, Sauce, Anthony Shaw, Square	6.00
Ironstone, Tea Leaf, Saucer, A.J.Wilkinson	5.00
Ironstone, Tea Leaf, Soup, 8 3/4 In.	7.00
Ironstone, Tea Leaf, Soup, 10 In.	7.00
Ironstone, Tea Leaf, Tray, Alfred Meakin, 6 1/4 X 4 1/2 In.	8.00
Ironstone, Tea Set, Blue, Staffordshire, England, 15 Piece	70.00
Ironstone, Tea Set, Lavender, Deer & Hunter Design, 3 Piece	30.00
Ironstone, Tea Set, Miniature, Blue Sheaf Of Wheat, 14 Piece	35.00
Ironstone, Tea Set, White, Gold Scrolls & Buds, 42 Piece	250.00
Ironstone, Tea Set, 5 Piece	22.50
Ironstone, Teapot, Acorn Finial, White, Cover, 9 In.High	29.00
Ironstone, Teapot, Excelsior Pattern	10.00
Ironstone, Teapot, Turner & Goddard	24.00
Ironstone, Teapot, White, Rosebuds & Bluebells, Ott & Brewer, C.1875	28.50
Ironstone, Teapot, 9 1/2 In. _Illus_	32.00
Ironstone, Tureen On Plate, Open, Imari Decorated, Mason's	20.00
Ironstone, Tureen, Covered, White, Impressed Boots & Registry Mark	50.00
Ironstone, Tureen, Gravy, Lily Of The Valley, Cover & Tray, White	18.00
Ironstone, Tureen, Liner, & Ladle, Sauce, Ribbed, Twig Handles, Edwards, 1844	45.00
Ironstone, Tureen, Soup, Red, White, Flowers, Johnson Brothers, Cover, England	65.00
Ironstone, Vase, White, Blue, Dragon, Mason Patented, 5 1/2 In.Tall	15.00
Ironstone, Washbowl, Imari Decorated, Mason's	25.00
Ivory, see also Bottle, Snuff, Netsuke	
Ivory, Back Scratcher, Hand, Terminates With Head Swallowing Fish	70.00
Ivory, Bald-Headed Man Holding Staff & Gourd, Carved, 3 In.High	30.00
Ivory, Bear, Brown, By Brisson, 4 1/2 In.Long, 2 In.Tall	130.00
Ivory, Bearded Man With Bow & Arrows, Carved, 7 In.High	120.00
Ivory, Binoculars, Doll's	7.50

Ironstone, Teapot, 9 1/2 In.
See Page 257

Ivory, **Box**, Carved, Japanese, Figures, 7 3/4 In.High	350.00
Ivory, **Box**, Leopard Decorated, Round, China	25.00
Ivory, **Buckle**, Dragon Design, Carved	24.00
Ivory, **Buttonhook**	2.50
Ivory, **Candlestick**, Polar Bear, 7 In., Pair	150.00
Ivory, **Card Case**, Book Shape, Leather-Lined, Chased Silver Trim, 3 X 4 In.	24.00
Ivory, **Chinese Figure Holding Scroll**, Carved, 3 1/2 In.High	30.00
Ivory, **Chinese Fisherman With Spear & Basket**, Carved, 3 In.High	45.00
Ivory, **Chinese Gentleman Seated**, Eating Rice & Drinking, Signed In Red	80.00
Ivory, **Cigarette Holder**, Carved	4.00
Ivory, **Cigarette Holder**, Carved Dragon, 10 In.	76.00
Ivory, **Coolie Holding Staff & Bag**, Carved, 3 1/2 In.High	35.00
Ivory, **Dance Program**	9.50
Ivory, **Doctor's Lady**, In Case, 5 1/2 In.	105.00
Ivory, **Dog**, Sheep, Carved, White	8.00
Ivory, **Drummer With Infant**, Dancer, Signed, Carved, 4 In.High	170.00
Ivory, **Elephant**, Carved, Mounted On Ebony Pedestal, Glass Dome	160.00
Ivory, **Elephant**, Carved, Walking With Trunk Outstretched, 8 1/2 In.Long	175.00
Ivory, **Elephant**, Set Of Three, Graduated From 2 In.To 1 1/2 In.	45.00
Ivory, **Fan**, 5 1/2 In.Long	3.50
Ivory, **Father**, Two Sons & Crane, Carved, 4 3/4 In.High	80.00
Ivory, **Foolish Man Seated**, Playing With Turtle, Carved, 2 1/4 In.High	70.00
Ivory, **Four Men Performing**, Red Insert, Carved, 2 3/4 In.High	70.00
Ivory, **Frame**, Picture, French, Easel Back, Oval, 6 3/4 X 8 1/2 In.	6.50
Ivory, **Frog Being Suffocated By Snake**, Carved, 2 In.High	60.00
Ivory, **Holder**, Needle, Umbrella Form, 4 In.Long	10.00
Ivory, **Jar**, Powder, Repousse Flowers, 2 1/2 In.Diameter	5.00
Ivory, **Junk**, Hand Carved, 7 Immortals, Dragon Head	250.00
Ivory, **Lady Holding Rooster**, Oriental, 16th Century, Hand Carved	375.00
Ivory, **Letter Opener**, Elephant Head Handle, Hand Carved	12.50
Ivory, **Letter Opener**, Fish Handle, 12 In.	25.00
Ivory, **Man Holding Falcon & Staff**, Carved, 3 1/2 In.High	50.00
Ivory, **Man Holding Turtle & Shell**, Red Insert Mark, Carved, 5 1/2 In.High	80.00
Ivory, **Man Resting On Mat Disturbed By Rat**, Red Insert, Carved, 4 In.Long	90.00
Ivory, **Man Riding Fish With Horns**, Carved, 11 In.Long	225.00
Ivory, **Man With Gun**, Carved, 3 In.High	30.00
Ivory, **Man**, Carved, 5 In.Tall	35.00
Ivory, **Napkin Ring**, Inlaid Frogs	11.00
Ivory, **Penguin**, By Brisson, 4 1/4 In.Tall	125.00
Ivory, **Plaque**, Carved, German, 18th Century, St.George & Dragon, Tole Insert	185.00
Ivory, **Plaque**, French, Carved Cherubs Playing, 19th Century	300.00
Ivory, **Queen Elizabeth I**, Triptych, 14 In.Tall	410.00
Ivory, **Rats Attacking Snake**, Carved, 4 In.Long	30.00
Ivory, **Rats Devouring Fish Caught With Hook**, Carved, 2 In.High	65.00
Ivory, **Tankard**, Carved, Renaissance, Gold Base, Lid, & Handle, Rubies, Emeralds	3000.00
Ivory, **Three Monkeys Playing**, Carved, 4 In.Long	35.00
Ivory, **Tusk With Wolf Howling At Moon**	29.00
Ivory, **Two Dancers Playing Drum**, Signed In Red, Carved, 3 1/2 In.High	90.00

*Jack-in-the-Pulpit Vases were named for their odd trumpetlike shape that
resembles the wild plant called Jack-in-the-Pulpit. The design originated
in the late victorian years.*

Jack-in-the-Pulpit, see also under specific Art Glass headings

Jack-In-The-Pulpit, **Bowl**, Flower, Smoky Opalescent, Pink Rim, 4 In.Tall	37.50
Jack-In-The-Pulpit, **Bowl**, Horse Head Medallion, Blue, Footed	95.00
Jack-In-The-Pulpit, **Rose Bowl**, Amberina, Inverted Thumbprint	125.00
Jack-In-The-Pulpit, **Vase**, Amber & Custard, Swirls, Blown, 11 In.Tall	62.00
Jack-In-The-Pulpit, **Vase**, Amethyst, Opalescent, Blown, 4 1/2 In.Tall	35.00
Jack-In-The-Pulpit, **Vase**, Apricot, Gold, Bulbous, 5 In.	42.00
Jack-In-The-Pulpit, **Vase**, Blown, Opalescent Pastel Stripes, Applied Amber	45.00
Jack-In-The-Pulpit, **Vase**, Blue, Red, Pink, White Spatter, Blown, 7 1/2 In.	35.00
Jack-In-The-Pulpit, **Vase**, Cranberry Edge, Opalescent Body, Teardrop Decor	35.00
Jack-In-The-Pulpit, **Vase**, Cranberry, Green Glass Loops, Crystal Petal Feet	38.00
Jack-In-The-Pulpit, **Vase**, Cranberry, Ruffled Top, Clear Base, 9 In., Pair	61.00
Jack-In-The-Pulpit, **Vase**, Diamond, Opalescent, Green Band, 8 1/2 In.High	45.00
Jack-In-The-Pulpit, **Vase**, Fiery Opalescent, Vaseline, Applied Rigaree	145.00
Jack-In-The-Pulpit, **Vase**, Floral, White, Red, Green, Footed	65.00
Jack-In-The-Pulpit, **Vase**, Green, Opalescent, Red Stripe, 9 In.	22.50
Jack-In-The-Pulpit, **Vase**, Green, 6 1/2 In.Tall	19.00
Jack-In-The-Pulpit, **Vase**, Marigold, 6 1/2 In.Tall	25.00
Jack-In-The-Pulpit, **Vase**, Pink, White, Blue, Red Spatter, Ruffled Flower Top	30.00
Jack-In-The-Pulpit, **Vase**, Pink, White, Clear, Stripes, 9 1/2 In.	55.00
Jack-In-The-Pulpit, **Vase**, Vaseline Glass, Hand-Blown, Ruffled	35.00
Jack-In-The-Pulpit, **Vase**, Vaseline, Opalescent Rim, In Silver Plate Base	20.00

Jackfield Ware was originally a black glazed pottery made in Jackfield, England, since 1630. A yellow glazed ware has also been called Jackfield Ware. Most of the pieces referred to as Jackfield are black pieces made during the victorian era.

Jackfield, **Creamer**, Cow .... *Illus* 40.00

Jackfield, Creamer, Cow

Jackfield, **Dog**, 12 In.High, Pair	35.00
Jackfield, **Jug**, Floral Design, Green Panels, Pewter Lid, 8 In.	32.00
Jackfield, **Teapot**, Hot Water Pot, Tray, Green & Gold Enamel	89.50
Jacob Petit, **Inkstand**, King Charles Spaniel	3200.00
Jacob Petit, **Jardiniere**, Stand, Rectangular, Scroll & Foliate, C.1840, Pair	525.00
Jacob Petit, **Pot**, Crocus, Cover, Claret, Florals, C.1830, Pair	70.00
Jade, **Ashtray**, 3 X 3 X 1 In., Square	60.00
Jade, **Bowl**, Pale Green, Round, Carved Buddhist Symbols, Lotus Leaf Base	550.00
Jade, **Bull**, 5 In.Long	250.00
Jade, **Camel**, Spinach Green, Carved, Wood Base, 6 1/4 In.	200.00
Jade, **Carved**, Mutton Fat, 4 X 3 In.	55.00
Jade, **Case**, Card, Signed Cartier, Paris, Platinum Hinge, Diamonds, Coral	275.00
Jade, **Figurine**, Boy, Basket Of Apples, Soo Chow, 4 1/2 X 5 1/2	35.00
Jade, **Figurine**, Mutton, White & Pale Green, Serpent, 2 3/4 In.Long, 2 In.High	225.00
Jade, **Figurine**, Rooster, Coral Eyes, 3 In.Tall	28.00
Jade, **Figurine**, Spinach Jade, On Teak Stand, 10 In.High	500.00
Jade, **Figurine**, Woman, Carved, Teak Stand, 9 1/2 In.High	550.00
Jade, **Fish**, Carved, Fins Standing On Fitted Stands, 3 1/2 X 2 1/2 In., Pair	110.00
Jade, **Fish**, 5 1/4 In.Long	115.00

Jade, Foo Dog, Gray, Massive Carving, Curly Matted Head, Teak Stand, Pair	800.00
Jade, God Of Longevity, 6 1/2 In.Tall	390.00
Jade, Horse, Running, Light Green, Teak Stand, Pair	250.00
Jade, Hoti, 2 5/8 In.Tall	75.00
Jade, Hoti, 8 In.Tall	275.00
Jade, Jar, Cover, Loose Ring Handles, Foo Dog Finial, Carved Stand	700.00
Jade, Kuan-Yin, Green, 8 1/2 In.Tall	320.00
Jade, Kuan-Yin, 5 1/4 In.Tall	60.00
Jade, Ming Dog, 5 In.Tall	275.00
Jade, Statue, Green & White Coloration, 8 In.Tall	575.00
Jade, Tang Horse, 5 1/4 In.Tall	325.00

Jasperware is a fine-grained pottery developed by Josiah Wedgwood in 1775. The jasper was made in many colors including the most famous, a light blue. It is still being made.

Jasperware, Barrel, Biscuit, Figures, White, Blue, Silver Lid & Handle	115.00
Jasperware, Bowl, Urn Shape, Black, White Classic Figures	50.00
Jasperware, Box, Cupids, Blue, White, Cover, Round, Marked England, 2 In.	45.00
Jasperware, Dish, Green & Black, Octagonal, Ram's Heads & Floral Swags	30.00
Jasperware, Jar, Biscuit, Blue, Silver Plate Top, Adams, England	50.00
Jasperware, Jar, Powder, Covered, Portrait	20.00
Jasperware, Pitcher, Green, Embossed Medallions, Washington & Franklin	35.00
Jasperware, Pitcher, Miniature, Blue & White, 3 In.	4.00
Jasperware, Pitcher, White, Blue, Marked 'paxton, '7 3/4 In.	75.00
Jasperware, Plaque, Acorns, Indian, Green, Pierced For Hanging	25.00
Jasperware, Plaque, Green, White Lady, Cupid, Floral Border, 6 In.Diameter	35.00
Jasperware, Plaque, Lady, Green, Floral Border, 6 In., Pair	40.00
Jasperware, Plaque, Wall, Green, White Medieval Lady With Bonnet, 1 1/4 In.	15.00
Jasperware, Plate, Chief High Hawk, Green & White, 5 1/2 In.Diameter	38.00
Jasperware, Plate, Hanging, Green & White, Stork & Babies Border	12.50
Jasperware, Shaker, Sugar, Dark Green, White Classical Figures	35.00
Jasperware, Toothpick, Blue, Footed, Number On Bottom, 3 X 2 1/2 In.	15.00
Jasperware, Urn, Ovoid, Applied White Frieze On Green, Tan Floral, Wedgwood	350.00
Jasperware, Vase, Blue	28.50
Jasperware, Vase, Covered, Potpourri, Dip, Green, Ovoid, Classical, C.1820, Pair	250.00
Jefferson Glass, Basket, 5 In.Diameter *Illus*	30.00

Jefferson Glass, Basket, 5 In.Diameter

Jewelry, Beads, Baroque, 244 Gem Peridots, 14k Gold Clasp	255.00
Jewelry, Beads, Garnet	20.00
Jewelry, Beads, Ivory, Rose Carved	14.00
Jewelry, Beads, Jade, 10 Mm., Hand Knotted, 14k Gold Clasp, 16 In.	75.00
Jewelry, Beads, Russian Cut Crystal, 16 In.Strand	25.00
Jewelry, Beads, Sterling Silver, 17 In.Strand	7.00
Jewelry, Beads, String Of 68, Choker	50.00
Jewelry, Beads, Venetian, 26 In.	40.00
Jewelry, Beads, 30 In.Long, Turquoise Color	6.00
Jewelry, Bracelet, Amethyst	150.00
Jewelry, Bracelet, Bangle, Opals & Rose Diamonds	150.00
Jewelry, Bracelet, Blue Enamel	65.00
Jewelry, Bracelet, Charm, Lock & Key For Fastener, Gold	65.00

Jewelry, Bracelet, Coin, Soldered Coins 70.00
Jewelry, Bracelet, Coin, 14 Netherlands Dimes, Dated 1919-1938 .... 15.00
Jewelry, Bracelet, Cord Band, Braided With Iron Charms, Gold Clasp 25.00
Jewelry, Bracelet, Crystal Center, Fox Hunting Scene, Gold, Flexible 225.00
Jewelry, Bracelet, Cutout 50.00
Jewelry, Bracelet, Double Link Chain, 14k Gold 48.00
Jewelry, Bracelet, Gold, Enameled, Safety Chain, Pair 150.00
Jewelry, Bracelet, Gold, Flexible Links 90.00
Jewelry, Bracelet, Gold, Link 12.50
Jewelry, Bracelet, Heart, Ann Shirley, Effanbee 30.00
Jewelry, Bracelet, Jade, Blue, Six Stones, Gold Mount 195.00
Jewelry, Bracelet, Jade, Gold Clasp 130.00
Jewelry, Bracelet, Lady's, Gold Filled, Ornate, Rigid 20.00
Jewelry, Bracelet, Leg, African Tribesman's, Silver 40.00
Jewelry, Bracelet, Opal & Diamond 65.00
Jewelry, Bracelet, Polished Seashells, Cut Steel Beads, Amber, Silver 10.00
Jewelry, Bracelet, Purple Stones, Pearls Between 15.00
Jewelry, Bracelet, Silver & Turquoise, Indian 20.00
Jewelry, Bracelet, Silver, Turquoise Setting, Navajo 57.50
Jewelry, Bracelet, Silver, Turquoise Settings, Handmade, Navajo Indians 69.50
Jewelry, Bracelet, Whiting Davis, Mesh, Slide & Tassel 10.00
Jewelry, Bracelet, 14k Gold, Opals Set In Rectangular Filigree 125.00
Jewelry, Brooch, Brass, Picture, Glass Front, Pin On Back, Portrait 2.50
Jewelry, Brooch, Cameo, Can Be Worn As Pendant, Gold Setting 95.00
Jewelry, Brooch, Cameo, Gold, Lattice Edge, Woman's Face 27.50
Jewelry, Brooch, Cameo, Lady's Head, 14k Lacy Gold Setting, 1 3/8 In. 35.00
Jewelry, Brooch, Cameo, Rebecca-At-The-Well, Beaded Gold Frame, 1 3/4 In. 52.50
Jewelry, Brooch, Cameo, Woman's Face, Gold 22.50
Jewelry, Brooch, Carved Lava Stone Set In Silver, Gold Twisted Wire Trim 28.50
Jewelry, Brooch, Chatelaine, Swivel Drop, Gold-Filled 15.00
Jewelry, Brooch, Cinnabar Set In Silver, Oval 22.00
Jewelry, Brooch, Crescent, Garnets 65.00
Jewelry, Brooch, Enamel Portrait, Dutch Girl, 14k Gold Frame, France 135.00
Jewelry, Brooch, Enameled Birds On Wire, Moon, 14k Gold Frame, France 125.00
Jewelry, Brooch, Enameled Portrait, Amber Ground, 14k Gold Frame, France 135.00
Jewelry, Brooch, Enameled Wild Swans, 14k Gold Frame, France 135.00
Jewelry, Brooch, English, Cameo .... *Illus* 285.00
Jewelry, Brooch, English, Cameo, Diamonds .... *Illus* 300.00

Jewelry, Brooch,
English, Cameo

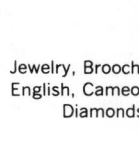

Jewelry, Brooch,
English, Cameo,
Diamonds

Jewelry, Brooch, French, Gold, Agate, Swan Carved Cameo, 19th Century 250.00
Jewelry, Brooch, Gold Plated, Wm.Kerr .... *Illus* 120.00
Jewelry, Brooch, Gold, Onyx Center, Pearl Cluster, Chase Work 87.50
Jewelry, Brooch, Lava Cameo, Woman's Head, Matching Earrings 35.00
Jewelry, Brooch, Miniature Painting On Ivory, Court Lady, Signed, Red Stones 35.00
Jewelry, Brooch, Mosaic, Scene, Ancient Ruins, Gold Filled Frame 50.00
Jewelry, Brooch, Scalloped, Oval, Mourning, Contains Hair 15.00
Jewelry, Brooch, Silver, Gold, & Rose Diamond, Russian, Griffon, 19th Century 3600.00
Jewelry, Brooch, Silver, Turquoise, Handmade, Navajo Indians 42.50

Jewelry, Buckle, Art Deco, C.1930 .... *Illus* 30.00
Jewelry, Buckle, Belt, Silver, Cutout Work Of Flowers, French 10.00
Jewelry, Buckle, Sterling, Wm.Kerr .... *Illus* 200.00
Jewelry, Cameo, Gray Agate, Profile, Classical Figure, Gilt Metal, C.1750 .... 1200.00
Jewelry, Cameo, Hand-Carved, Shell, C.1930, Lady's Head 12.00
Jewelry, Chain & Hook, Watch, 14k Gold, 62 In.Long 45.00
Jewelry, Chain & Slide, Watch, Lady's, Gold Filled 35.00
Jewelry, Chain & Slide, 14k Gold, Jewel 16.00
Jewelry, Chain, Gold Slide, Diamond Chip 25.00
Jewelry, Chain, Gold Slide, Opal & 2 Pearls 25.00
Jewelry, Chain, Man's, Gold & Platinum, Matching Round Fob, Diamond 110.00
Jewelry, Chain, Neck, Silver, Heavy 25.00
Jewelry, Chain, Rope, 14k Gold, 18 In.Long 75.00
Jewelry, Chain, Rope, 14k Gold, Clasp, 30 1/4 In.Long 125.00
Jewelry, Chain, Slide, Lady's, Gold Filled, Pearl Ruby Slide 35.00
Jewelry, Chain, Slide, Lady's, Gold Filled, Solid Gold Slide, Opal, 20 Pearls 57.00
Jewelry, Chain, Slide, Lady's, Green Gold, 7 Ruby Slide 75.00
Jewelry, Chain, Slide, Lady's, Yellow Gold, Heart Slide, Blue Sapphire 85.00
Jewelry, Chain, Slide, Lady's, Yellow Gold, Round Slide, Green Jade 85.00
Jewelry, Chain, Slide, Lady's, 14k Gold, Diamond Shape Slide, 3 Sapphires 155.00
Jewelry, Chain, Slide, Lady's, 14k Gold, Shield Type Slide, 7 Garnets 165.00
Jewelry, Chain, Slide, Lady's, 14k Gold, Star Shape Slide, Turquoise Setting 165.00
Jewelry, Chain, Watch, Gold Nuggets, Ivory, Nugget Fob, Gold Pick, Shovel, Pan 320.00
Jewelry, Chain, Watch, Gold, Lady's, Two Rubies, 48 In.Long 50.00
Jewelry, Chain, Watch, Gold, Watch Hook, 13 1/2 In. 35.00
Jewelry, Chain, Watch, Man's, Gold 75.00
Jewelry, Chain, Watch, 2 Bladed Penknife, 10k Gold, C.1900 .... 50.00
Jewelry, Charm, Heart, Flowers, Amethyst Center, Sterling Silver 12.95
Jewelry, Charm, Heart, Sterling Silver, Enamel, Blue, Butterfly, Flower 15.95
Jewelry, Charm, Monkey On A Potty With Fan, Sterling Silver 5.00
Jewelry, Charm, Rabbit, Platinum, Diamond, Ruby Eye, 1/2 In.Tall 165.00
Jewelry, Chatelaine, Gold, Dated 1792, 3 Oval Gouache Miniatures Of Girls 200.00
Jewelry, Chatelaine, Shield Shape, Scalloped Edges, Chain 22.00
Jewelry, Chatelaine, Snowflake Design, Double Chain 40.00
Jewelry, Comb, Hair, Rhinestones 8.50
Jewelry, Comb, Horn, Flared Rim 3.50
Jewelry, Cross & Chain, Sterling Silver & Turquoise, Zuni Indians Made 4.95
Jewelry, Cross, Enamel & Silver, 3 In. 25.00
Jewelry, Cross, Persian, Enamel, Hand-Painted, Copper, 1 5/8 In.Long 2.00
Jewelry, Cross, 14k Gold, 2 X 1 1/8 In. 28.00
Jewelry, Crucifix, Ebony, France Impressed On Back, 3 In.Tall 6.00
Jewelry, Cuff Link, Pair 1.25
Jewelry, Cuff Links, Gold Nugget, Emeralds Set In Platinum Bezel 185.00
Jewelry, Cuff Links, Sterling Silver, Blue Underglaze, Link Type 9.50
Jewelry, Earring, Silver, Zuni, Handmade 22.50
Jewelry, Earrings & Pin, Cloisonne, Enameled Rose, 14k Gold 25.00
Jewelry, Earrings, Amber, Dangle, Prehistoric Inclusions, 14k Gold, Pair 55.00
Jewelry, Earrings, Coral & Pearl In Sterling, Marcasite, Pierced 28.00
Jewelry, Earrings, Enameled, Pink Roses, 14k Open Lace Setting, France, Pair 125.00
Jewelry, Earrings, Gold Nuggets, Pair 90.00
Jewelry, Earrings, Jade, Chinese, Hoop, Emerald Green, Carved, 14k Gold 350.00
Jewelry, Earrings, Jade, Dangle, Pair 285.00
Jewelry, Earrings, Lapis & Chased Gold Ball, Long, Pierced 85.00
Jewelry, Earrings, Leaf Shape, Gold, Paved With Turquoise & Pearls, Pair 200.00
Jewelry, Earrings, Opal, Flower Design, Hanging 30.00
Jewelry, Earrings, Opal, Post Back 17.50
Jewelry, Earrings, Opal, Teardrop, 14k Gold, Blue Points, Pair 250.00
Jewelry, Earrings, Silver, Turquoise Setting, Handmade, Navajo Indians 24.00
Jewelry, Earrings, Silver, Turquoise, Handmade, Navajo Indians 24.00
Jewelry, Earrings, Silver, Zuni Indians 24.00
Jewelry, Earrings, 4 Graduated Diamonds, Rubies, White Gold, Pierced 325.00
Jewelry, Hatpin, Glass Tube, Fringe Of Magenta Beads, Gilt Filigree Band 8.00
Jewelry, Hatpin, Gold Filled Metal Top, Insignia K Of C 2.95
Jewelry, Holder, Comb, Silver 5.00
Jewelry, Lavaliere, Gold, 2 Fire Opals 35.00
Jewelry, Lavaliere, Pink Cameo, Four Pearls, Gold Hasp 29.00

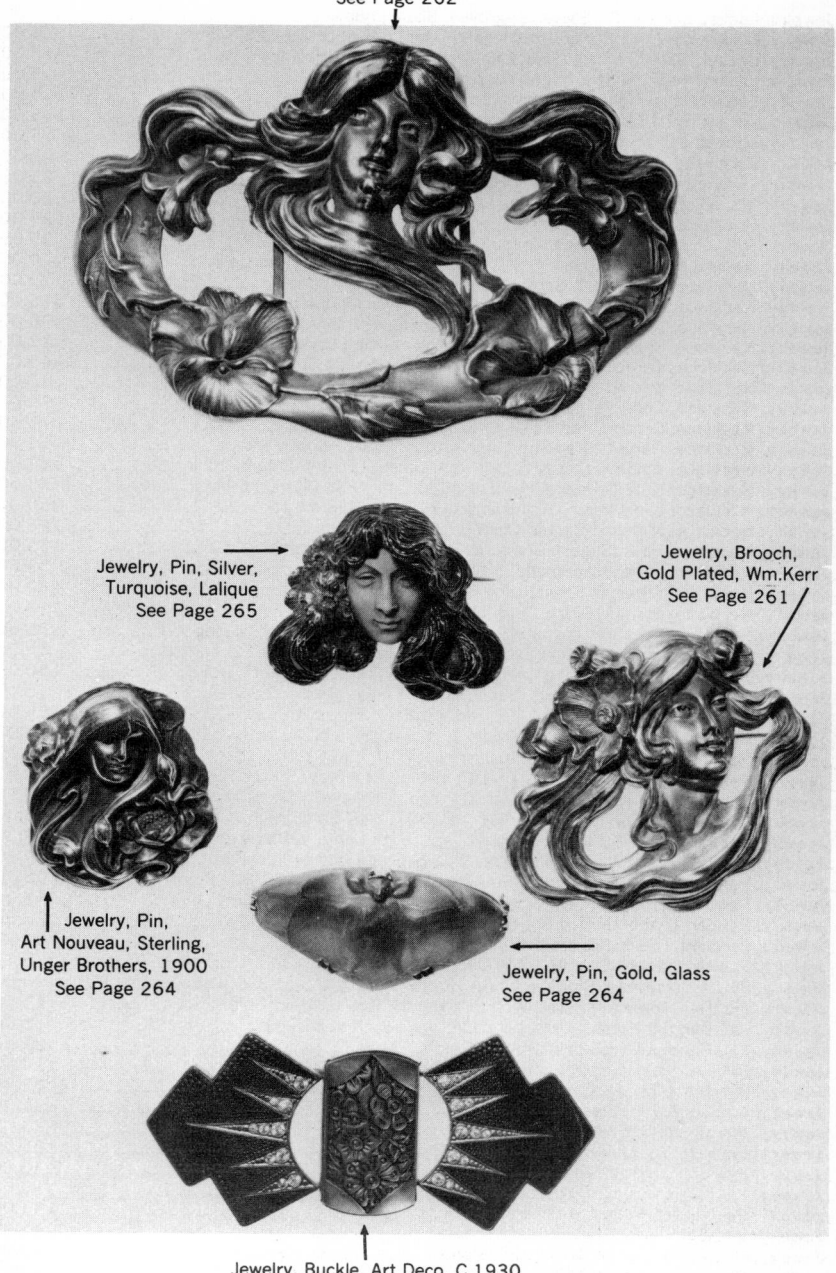

Jewelry, Buckle, Sterling, Wm.Kerr
See Page 262

Jewelry, Pin, Silver,
Turquoise, Lalique
See Page 265

Jewelry, Brooch,
Gold Plated, Wm.Kerr
See Page 261

Jewelry, Pin,
Art Nouveau, Sterling,
Unger Brothers, 1900
See Page 264

Jewelry, Pin, Gold, Glass
See Page 264

Jewelry, Buckle, Art Deco, C.1930
See Page 262

Jewelry, Locket, Double, On Swivel, Engraved, Black Enamel, Gold 75.00
Jewelry, Locket, Form Of Curled-Up Dragon, Emerald Eye, Diamond In Mouth 85.00
Jewelry, Locket, Gold, B.Mfg.Co., Rectangular, Oval Picture Holder Inside 10.00
Jewelry, Locket, Heart Shape, Engraved, Gold-Filled, Chain 5.00
Jewelry, Locket, Mosaic, Beatle Scarab, Gold, 1 1/2 In.Diameter 165.00
Jewelry, Locket, Oval, Six Diamonds, Engraved, Gold 195.00
Jewelry, Locket, 20 Small Pearls, Framed Glass Inside, Gold Filled 15.00
Jewelry, Lorgnette, Tortoiseshell, Gold Trim, Silver Chain 22.00
Jewelry, Lorgnette, 14k Gold Rims & Handle 35.00
Jewelry, Medallion, Lotus Carving, Red 20.00
Jewelry, Necklace, African Goldstone Interspersed With Topazes, 25 In.Long 125.00
Jewelry, Necklace, Amber Beads, Graduated, Sterling Clasp, 17 In.Long 35.00
Jewelry, Necklace, Amber, Russian, Single Strand, Graduated, 19th Century 70.00
Jewelry, Necklace, Amber, 87 Graduated Faceted Beads 75.00
Jewelry, Necklace, Amethyst, Pearl, & Diamond, Silver Mounted, 19th Century 575.00
Jewelry, Necklace, Angelskin Coral, Matched, White With Pink Flecks 135.00
Jewelry, Necklace, Brown Beads Alternating With Faceted Crystal Beads 12.00
Jewelry, Necklace, Carnelian, Marcasites, Art Deco, Sterling Silver 45.00
Jewelry, Necklace, Carved Ivory 20.00
Jewelry, Necklace, Coral Beads, Graduated, 18 1/2 In.Long, Gold Clasp 25.00
Jewelry, Necklace, Coral, Three Strands, Graduated, Gold Clasp 75.00
Jewelry, Necklace, Garnet, Graduated, 16 In. 19.00
Jewelry, Necklace, Gold Nugget & Fossil Ivory, Dated 1909, Pendant, 11 In. 550.00
Jewelry, Necklace, Jade & Pearls, Hand Knotted, 14k Gold Clasp, 16 In. 77.00
Jewelry, Necklace, Lapis Lazuli, Afghanistan, 39 Balls, Gold Clasp 250.00
Jewelry, Necklace, Matched Carved Coral 185.00
Jewelry, Necklace, Pawn Squash Blossom, Silver, Turquoise Stones 185.00
Jewelry, Necklace, Silver, Handmade, Navajo Indians 39.50
Jewelry, Necklace, Silver, 5 Turquoise Around Mother-Of-Pearl Stone 130.00
Jewelry, Necklace, Sterling Silver, Turquoise, Handmade 225.00
Jewelry, Necklace, 40 Lapis Lazuli Beads, Silver Overlay Floral, 32 In.Long 105.00
Jewelry, Pendant, Amethyst, Gold Setting, Chain 55.00
Jewelry, Pendant, Black Opal, Lightning Ridge, Gold Frame & Chain 150.00
Jewelry, Pendant, Calla Lily, Pearls, Blue Enamel, Fringe, Gold 65.00
Jewelry, Pendant, Chased Leaves & Filigree, 40 Point Emerald 65.00
Jewelry, Pendant, Cross, Set With Garnets 25.00
Jewelry, Pendant, Devotional, Gold, Spanish, C.1700 .... *Illus* 150.00
Jewelry, Pendant, Enamel Leaf Center, Garnet Bud, Openwork, Silver Gilt 75.00
Jewelry, Pendant, Enameled Gold, South German, Monkey On Horseback, C.1600 .... 2500.00
Jewelry, Pendant, English Gold Sovereign Of 1907, 14k Gold Chain 45.00
Jewelry, Pendant, Gold & Mother-Of-Pearl, Fish, 19th Century, Diamond Eyes 550.00
Jewelry, Pendant, Gold Wash, Triangular, Blue & Green Enamel, London 70.00
Jewelry, Pendant, Gold, Blue, White, Pearl Border, Wedgwood, 1 1/8 In.Diameter 95.00
Jewelry, Pendant, Horseshoe Of Pearls Edged With Blue Enamel & Gold 45.00
Jewelry, Pendant, Jade, Carved Both Sides, Chain Jade & Pearl Beads 125.00
Jewelry, Pendant, Pierced Carved White Jade, Circular 65.00
Jewelry, Pendant, Silver, Enamel, 16th Century .... *Illus* 275.00
Jewelry, Pin, Art Nouveau, Sterling, Unger Brothers, 1900 .... *Illus* 90.00
Jewelry, Pin, Bar, Three Enameled Women's Heads, Flowing Hair, Gold, 2 In. 55.00
Jewelry, Pin, Bar, 10 Faceted Jets, Loop On Hinge For Chain, Gold 18.00
Jewelry, Pin, Cameo, Coral Pink Ground, Gold 27.50
Jewelry, Pin, Cameo, Head Of Woman, Oval, Gold Frame 30.00
Jewelry, Pin, Carved Ivory, Eagle With Spread Wings 12.50
Jewelry, Pin, Carved Mother-Of-Pearl, Scene, Silver, Enamel, China 35.00
Jewelry, Pin, Circle, Set With Garnets 20.00
Jewelry, Pin, Clip On Back, Gold Dove, Ruby Eye, 1 3/8 In.Long 125.00
Jewelry, Pin, Clip, Carved, Chinese Lapis, Bow Shape, Set In Beaded Silver 45.00
Jewelry, Pin, Eagle & Flag, Columbian Exposition 10.00
Jewelry, Pin, Flower, Pearl Center, Pair Earrings, Gold, Velvet Lined Box 195.00
Jewelry, Pin, Garnet, Bird 45.00
Jewelry, Pin, Garnet, Moon & Star, 29 Stones 25.00
Jewelry, Pin, Gold Horseshoe, 1 1/2 In. 20.00
Jewelry, Pin, Gold, Glass .... *Illus* 225.00
Jewelry, Pin, Jade, Carved Floral Design, Silver Mount, Seed Pearls 35.00
Jewelry, Pin, Label, French, Silver, Enameled, Lavender & Pink On Green 17.50
Jewelry, Pin, Lapel, Brass, Al Smith, Derby 12.00

Jewelry, Pin, Lingerie, Engraved, Gold Filled, Pair 10.00
Jewelry, Pin, Mountains, Wisteria, Silver Back, Satsuma 32.00
Jewelry, Pin, Mourning, Gold, Hair 38.50
Jewelry, Pin, Painted Enamel 12.50
Jewelry, Pin, Seven Cabochon Moonstones, Gold, 1 In.Diameter 165.00
Jewelry, Pin, Shell Cameo, Gold Frame, Nymphs In Grecian Costume, Ruins 200.00
Jewelry, Pin, Silver, Turquoise, Lalique .... *Illus* 1400.00

Jewelry, Pendant, Devotional,
Gold, Spanish, C.1700
See Page 264

Jewelry, Pendant, Silver,
Enamel, 16th Century
See Page 264

Jewelry, Pin, Stick, Circle With Triangle K Of L, Gold 4.75
Jewelry, Pin, Victorian, Pearl Center, Gold, Flower Shape 15.00
Jewelry, Pin, Wedgwood, Blue Cameo, 10k Gold Rim 85.00
Jewelry, Pin, White Gold Filigree, 32k Diamond, 2 Blue Sapphires 55.00
Jewelry, Riding Crop With Lorgnette, Sterling Repousse Handle 70.00
Jewelry, Ring.Lady's, Diamond, Prong Mount, Solitaire, Gold, 1/2 Carat 250.00
Jewelry, Ring, Band, Five Opals 35.00
Jewelry, Ring, Black Onyx, Diamond, White Gold, Rectangular 35.00
Jewelry, Ring, Black Opal, Doublet, Seed Pearls 15.00
Jewelry, Ring, Black Opal, Lightning Ridge, Openwork Setting, 14k Gold 150.00
Jewelry, Ring, Cameo, Lady's Head, 14k Gold 95.00
Jewelry, Ring, Cinnabar, Chinese, Carved Lotus Blossoms, Cherry Red 27.00
Jewelry, Ring, Coral Cameo, 14k Gold, Diamonds, Pearls 50.00
Jewelry, Ring, Enameled Wild Swans, 14k Gold, France 140.00
Jewelry, Ring, Engraved, Pierced, Faceted Aquamarine, 14k Gold 25.00
Jewelry, Ring, Garnet Cluster, Gold Mount 195.00
Jewelry, Ring, Garnet Cluster, Seven Stones 22.50
Jewelry, Ring, Garnet, 14k Yellow Gold, Crown Style, 7 Garnets 17.50
Jewelry, Ring, German, Ss.Viking Head, Sterling Silver 12.95
Jewelry, Ring, Gold, Elk Head 15.00
Jewelry, Ring, Hair, Gold, Inscribed 'remember The Giver, 'c.1860 .... 25.00
Jewelry, Ring, Himmler Death Head, Sterling Silver 12.95
Jewelry, Ring, Jade, Gold Setting, Four 10 Pt.Diamonds 375.00
Jewelry, Ring, Jade, Marquise, Full-Cut Diamond, Set In 14k Gold 95.00
Jewelry, Ring, Lady, Diamond, Solitaire, Yellow Gold, 30 Points 125.00
Jewelry, Ring, Lady, Sapphire, Raised Setting, Two Side Diamonds 85.00
Jewelry, Ring, Lady's, Amethyst, Opals, Tiffany Setting, Gold 90.00
Jewelry, Ring, Lady's, Angelskin, Pink Coral, Gold 70.00
Jewelry, Ring, Lady's, Coral, Rose, Carved, Gold Setting 45.00
Jewelry, Ring, Lady's, Eight Teardrop Opals, Seventeen Rubies, Gold Setting 90.00
Jewelry, Ring, Lady's, Gold, Amethyst Setting 20.00
Jewelry, Ring, Lady's, Gold, Set With Garnets 15.00
Jewelry, Ring, Lady's, Garnets, Red, Tiffany Setting, Gold 78.00
Jewelry, Ring, Lady's, Lapis, Roped Gold Setting, 14 Carat, Engraved 95.00
Jewelry, Ring, Lady's, Opal, Tiffany Setting 32.00

Jewelry, Ring, Lady's, Pink Coral, Gold Setting 55.00
Jewelry, Ring, Lady's, Rubies, Tiffany, Birdcage Setting, Gold Setting 90.00
Jewelry, Ring, Lady's, Tiffany, 2 Diamonds & 1 Pearl In Center 500.00
Jewelry, Ring, Lady's, White Gold Filigree, 3 Diamonds 150.00
Jewelry, Ring, Lady's, 10k Gold, Australian Opal, Tiffany Setting 50.00
Jewelry, Ring, Lady's, 15 Fire Opals, 14 Amethysts, Tiffany Setting 125.00
Jewelry, Ring, Man's, Gold, Green Stone, 2 Small Diamonds 20.00
Jewelry, Ring, Man's, Turquoise & Coral, Sterling Silver Setting 24.00
Jewelry, Ring, Man's, 14k Gold, Red Stone 29.00
Jewelry, Ring, Moonstone, Fish Shape 35.00
Jewelry, Ring, Opal Cluster 45.00
Jewelry, Ring, Opal In Center, Six Smaller Opals, Flower Setting 25.00
Jewelry, Ring, Opal, Australian, 2 Diamonds, Carved Sides 22.50
Jewelry, Ring, Opal, Butterfly & Shadow, Gold Setting 150.00
Jewelry, Ring, Opal, Gold Mount, Two Diamonds 500.00
Jewelry, Ring, Opal, Oval Shape Opal 35.00
Jewelry, Ring, Platinum, 35-Point Diamond, 6 1-Point Diamonds 245.00
Jewelry, Ring, Silver, Handmade, Rope Design, Turquoise, Navajo Indians 18.50
Jewelry, Ring, Silver, Turquoise & Coral Setting, Handmade, Navajo Indians 24.00
Jewelry, Ring, Six-Carat Andamooka Black Opal, Two 18-Pt.Diamonds, Gold 400.00
Jewelry, Ring, Turquoise, Oval 10.00
Jewelry, Ring, Victorian, Garnets, C.1860, 9k Gold 22.00
Jewelry, Ring, Victorian, Rectangular Sardonyx Inlay, Bird, Flower, Gold 75.00
Jewelry, Ring, Wedding Band, Initials, Dated 1871 .... 12.00
Jewelry, Ring, Wedding Band, White Gold, 5 Diamonds 350.00
Jewelry, Ring, Wedding, Carved, Wide 7.00
Jewelry, Ring, Wedding, Plain, Narrow 2.00
Jewelry, Ring, Wedding, Quilt Top, Handmade 14.00
Jewelry, Ring, Wedding, 18k Gold, Inscribed November 25, 1873 .... 7.50
Jewelry, Ring, 4k Peridot, Two 8-Point Diamonds, 14k White Gold Mount 175.00
Jewelry, Ring, 12 Carat Blue Star Sapphire, Platinum Mount 1900.00
Jewelry, Seal, King Form Handle, Baroque Pearl, Diamond, Turquoise, C.1850 .... 350.00
Jewelry, Slide, Gold, Geometric, Heart Shape, Engraved, Ruby 25.00
Jewelry, Slide, Gold, Round, Engraved, Emerald 25.00
Jewelry, Slide, Gold, Three Sections, Engraved, Fiery Opals 20.00
Jewelry, Slide, Heart Shape, Engraved, Pearls, Gold 20.00
Jewelry, Slide, Opal, Four Pearls 25.00
Jewelry, Slide, 23 In.Chain, Opals 35.00
Jewelry, Stick Pin, Advertising, Haines Brothers, Brass, 2 In.Long 5.00
Jewelry, Stickpin, Amethyst, Diamond Shape Cabochon, Seed Pearls 18.00
Jewelry, Stickpin, Art Nouveau Flower End, Gold 15.00
Jewelry, Stickpin, Cameo, 14k Gold 25.00
Jewelry, Stickpin, Figural, Hand Holds Small Blue Stone 2.95
Jewelry, Stickpin, Fish, Enamel, Sterling Silver Trim 1.50
Jewelry, Stickpin, Four-Leaf-Clover Shape, Diamond Chip Each Leaf 40.00
Jewelry, Stickpin, Gold, Pearl Studded Leaves, Ruby 24.50
Jewelry, Stickpin, Heart Shape, Small Blue Stone 2.95
Jewelry, Stickpin, Horseshoe, Pearl, Gold 18.00
Jewelry, Stickpin, Jet Flower Petals, Pearl In Center, Gold 25.00
Jewelry, Stickpin, Lacywork, Small Set Diamond, Gold 37.50
Jewelry, Stickpin, Made From Gold Nugget, Animal Face, Diamond Chip Eyes 45.00
Jewelry, Stickpin, Mosaic On Onyx 15.00
Jewelry, Stickpin, Paperweight End, Horse's Head Inside, Gold Filled 9.50
Jewelry, Stickpin, Pea-Size Opal, Andamooka, Gold Prongs 32.00
Jewelry, Stickpin, Rose Diamond, Pearls, England, Gold 27.50
Jewelry, Stickpin, Rose, Diamond, Gold, English 45.00
Jewelry, Stickpin, Satanic Head, Garnet Eyes, Pearl Collar, Gold 22.50
Jewelry, Stickpin, Sterling & Enamel Top, Shield Shape Coat Of Arms, Crown 3.75
Jewelry, Stickpin, Sterling Horse's Head At Top 3.75
Jewelry, Stickpin, Top Made From 1875 Silver Dime, Initial 3.75
Jewelry, Tiepin, Pearl, Gold, Mono B 2.00
Jewelry, Tiepin, Raised Dog's Head On Mother-Of-Pearl 4.50
Jewelry, Vinaigrette, Enameled Gold, Chestnut Form, 19th Century 225.00
Jewelry, Vinaigrette, Scottish, Barrel Shape, Hard Stones, Gold, 19th Century 850.00
    Jewelry, Watch, see Watch
Jewelry, Watch Chain & Slide, Gold, Lady's, 5 Opals 45.00

Jewelry, Watch Chain & Slide, Lady's, Gold Filled	32.50
Jewelry, Watch Chain & Slide, Man's, Gold	35.00
Jewelry, Watch Chain, Gold, Wheat Link, 14k	40.00
Jewelry, Watch Chain, Silver, Double, Hallmarked	35.00
Jewelry, Watch Chain, Silver, Single	17.50
Jewelry, Watch Chain, Sterling Silver	10.00
Jewelry, Watch Chain, 10k Gold	35.00
Jewelry, Watch Fob Charm, Order Of Elks, Tooth Set In 14k Gold, Enamel Star	8.50
Jewelry, Watch Fob Charm, Sardonyx, Gold	28.00
Jewelry, Wedding Band, White Gold, 5 Diamonds	385.00

John Rogers Statues were made from 1859 to 1892. The originals were bronze. But the thousands of copies made by Rogers Factory were of painted plaster. Eighty different figures were made.

John Rogers, Group, Coming To The Parson, Bronze Paint	175.00
John Rogers, Group, Council Of War	500.00
John Rogers, Group, 'speak For Yourself, John'	450.00
John Rogers, Group, Taking The Oath & Drawing Rations, Bronze Paint, 1866	225.00
John Rogers, Group, 'why Don't You Speak For Yourself, '22 In.High	225.00
Johnson Brothers, Cup & Saucer, Cream, Gold Trim	35.00
Judaica, Belt, Bridal, Wrought Silver, Double Linked, Polish, C.1750	500.00
Judaica, Binding, Prayer Book, Silver Relief, Hebrew Text, Italian, C.1820	400.00
Judaica, Bottle, Rosewater, Silver, Repousse, Pear Shape, Persian, C.1750	80.00
Judaica, Box, Charity, Silver, Engraved, Quadrangular, Moscow, 1856	350.00
Judaica, Circumcision Set, Silver Handle Knife, C.1850 *Illus*	325.00
Judaica, Container, Silver, Ajoure & Engraved, Turret Form, Pierced, C.1750	1000.00
Judaica, Contract, Marriage, On Paper, Illuminated, Damascus, 1860	210.00
Judaica, Cup, Holiday, Silver, Repousse, Chased, 12 Tribes, Italian, C.1750	650.00
Judaica, Cup, Kiddush, Silver, Chased, Octagonal, Augsburg, 1737	375.00
Judaica, Cup, Kiddush, Silver, Repousse, Hexagonal, Europe, C.1850	130.00
Judaica, Engraving, The Holy City, Hand Colored, Sebastian Munster, C.1550	80.00
Judaica, Goblet, Kiddush, Silver, Repousse, Inscribed, Persian	60.00
Judaica, Keter, Silver, Repousse & Ajoure, I.Perlman, St.Petersburg, C.1850	550.00
Judaica, Lamp, Hanukkah, Brass, Pierced, Engraved, 8 Oil Fonts	130.00
Judaica, Lamp, Hanukkah, Cast Brass, Serpentine Back, Grotesque, C.1850	70.00
Judaica, Lamp, Hanukkah, Silver, Engraved, Parcel Gilt, Stones, Europe, C.1800	400.00
Judaica, Lamp, Hanukkah, Silver, Repousse, Ajoure & Engraved, German, C.1750	600.00
Judaica, Lamp, Sabbath, Silver, Dutch, C.1800 *Illus*	900.00
Judaica, Map, Canaan, Engraving, English, 17th Century	35.00
Judaica, Matzah Cover, Gold Embroidered Red Velvet & Gray Silk, C.1750	300.00
Judaica, Menorah & Hanukkah Lamp, Brass, Poland, C.1750 *Illus*	850.00
Judaica, Menorah, Hanukkah, Terra-Cotta, Dish Form, Libya, 18th Century	475.00
Judaica, Picture, Silk & Crewel Embroidery, Moses, English, C.1850	100.00
Judaica, Plaque, The Sacrifice Of Isaac, Carved Wood, C.1800	400.00
Judaica, Plate, Festival, Copper, Engraved Mogen David Center, Persian, 1750	40.00
Judaica, Plate, Passover, Brass, Inscribed Center, Moscow, 1891	30.00
Judaica, Plate, Passover, Limoges, Moses & Israelites At Red Sea	200.00
Judaica, Pointer, Torah, Floral Design, Sterling Silver, 13 3/4 In.Long	125.00
Judaica, Print, Purim Celebration, Hand Colored, French, 18th Century	210.00
Judaica, Ring, Marriage, Gold, Filigree, Applique & Enamel, Venice, C.1650	800.00
Judaica, Ring, Marriage, Wrought Filigree Gold & Enamel, Italian, C.1650	3500.00
Judaica, Scroll, Ha-Melech-Megillah, Parchment, Silver Case, Italian, C.1650	3300.00
Judaica, Scroll, Megillah, Parchment, Chased Silver Case, Mediterranean, 1700	350.00
Judaica, Scroll, Megillah, Parchment, Repousse Gold & Silver, Jeweled, 1850	575.00
Judaica, Spice Container, Silver, Filigree, Turret Form, Floral, Europe, 1750	170.00
Judaica, Spice Container, Silver, Turret Form, Chased Scrolls, Moscow, 1867	175.00
Judaica, Tass, Silver, Repousse, Parcel Gilt, Cartouche Shape, Moscow, 1892	325.00
Judaica, Tray, Passover, Silver, Engraved, Round, Scenes, Dutch, C.1750	1100.00
Judaica, Yad, Engraved Silver, North Africa, C.1750, Hand Pointing Finger	70.00
Judaica, Yad, Silver, Flat Spatulated, Inscribed Holy To G'd, C.1850	130.00
Jugtown Pottery, Plate, Green, Navy, Leaf Decoration	24.00

Kate Greenaway, who was a famous illustrator of children's books, drew pictures of children in high-waisted empire dresses. She lived from 1846 to 1901. Her designs appear on china, glass, and other pieces.

Kate Greenaway Type, Tape Measure, Figural, Girl Holds Muff	16.00

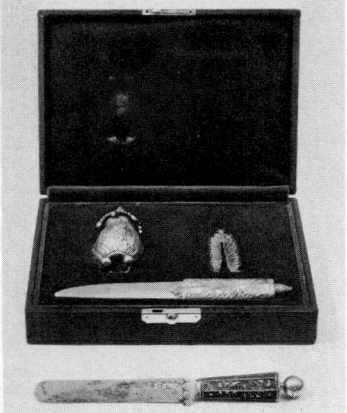

Judaica, Circumcision Set, Silver Handle Knife, C.1850
See Page 267

Judaica, Lamp, Sabbath,
Silver, Dutch, C.1800
See Page 267

Judaica, Menorah & Hanukkah Lamp, Brass, Poland, C.1750
See Page 267

Kate Greenaway, Book, Marigold Garden, Signed	38.00
Kate Greenaway, Book, Under The Window	23.50
Kate Greenaway, Box, Jewelry, Wooden, Stenciled K.G., Children On Front	25.00
Kate Greenaway, Cup & Saucer, Child's	15.00
Kate Greenaway, Doorstop	22.00
Kate Greenaway, Figurine, Little Girl In Mother's Clothes, Bronze	80.00
Kate Greenaway, Holder, Match, Girls, Bonnets, Blue, White, 3 1/2 In.	25.00
Kate Greenaway, Napkin Ring, Boy Holding Books	55.00
Kate Greenaway, Napkin Ring, Boy Rolling Ring	40.00
Kate Greenaway, Napkin Ring, Girl, Holding Drum	55.00
Kate Greenaway, Picture, Two Little Girls, Frame	7.50
Kate Greenaway, Plate, Girls In Hoops, Blue, Fluted Edge, 7 1/2 In.Diameter	15.00
Kate Greenaway, Plate, Mother Hubbard, Girl, Fruit, 8 1/4 In.	14.00
Kate Greenaway, Plate, 2 Little Girls & Toys, 8 In.	15.00
Kate Greenaway, Print, We Wish You A Merry Xmas, Girl Dressed In Fur, 1840	30.00
Kate Greenaway, Salt & Pepper, Boy & Girl In Baskets, Set	40.00
Kate Greenaway, Salt Dip, Bisque, Girl Sitting By Each End Of Dip	17.50
Kate Greenaway, Salt, Head Resting On Arm, White, 2 3/4 In.High	12.50
Kate Greenaway, Toothpick, Parian, 3 1/2 In., Pair	48.00
Kate Greenaway, Whistle, Figure Of Girl, Cream Color, Porcelain, 3 In.	11.50

Kauffmann, Box, Jewel, Figures, Medallion, Blue Border, Signed 55.00
Kauffmann, Box, Jewel, Hinged Lid, Signed, 3 In. 50.00
Kauffmann, Box, Jewel, Medallion, Allover Paintings, Dome Lid 65.00
Kauffmann, Box, White To Green, Gold Feet, Decor, Hinged Lid, 2 1/2 In. 67.50
Kaufmann, Butter Chip, Green & Gold, Portrait, Signed 6.50
Kauffmann, Butter Pat, Crazed, Signed 6.00
Kauffmann, Cup, Portrait Scene, Pink Border, Signed 10.00
Kauffmann, Jar, Cracker, Garden Scene, Maidens, Silver Plated Bail, Handle 69.00
Kauffmann, Plate, Blue Border, Gold Tracery, Classical Scene Center 15.00
Kauffmann, Plate, Classical Women & Cupid On Cobalt, Gold, Signed 15.00
Kauffmann, Plate, Ivory, Green, Gold Design Profusion, Figures Medallion 58.00
Kauffmann, Plate, Lady & Man, Ivory & Green, Marked, 8 1/4 In. 55.00
Kauffmann, Plate, Signed, Light Blue Ground, Gold, 3 Dancing Maidens, Handles 55.00
Kauffmann, Tray, Pin, Maroon & Gold Border, Classical Figure Center 65.00
Kauffmann, Vase, Figure Medallion, Gold Design, Blue Border, Bulbous, Signed 25.00
 Kayserzinn, see Pewter

 Kaziun Glass has been made by Charles Kaziun since 1942. His
 paperweights have been gaining fame steadily. Most of his glass and all of
 the paperweights are signed with A K designed cane worked into the design.
 He makes buttons, earrings, perfume bottles, and paperweights.
Kaziun, see also Paperweight
Kaziun, Bottle, Perfume, Upright Pink Lily, Blue Ground, Cut Facets 285.00
Kaziun, Paperweight, Pedestal, Yellow Lily, Lavender & Goldstone, 2 In.High 175.00
Kaziun, Salt, Paperweight, Yellow Rose In Base, Signed 325.00

 Kelva Glassware was made by the C.F. Monroe Company of Meriden,
 Connecticut, about 1904. It is a pale pastel painted glass decorated with
 flowers, designs, or scenes.
Kelva, Bowl, Signed 75.00
Kelva, Box, Flowers, Blue, Pink, Cover, 4 In. 175.00
Kelva, Box, Gray, Lavender .... *Illus* 167.00
Kelva, Box, Jewel, Sterling Rim, Gray-Green Tapestry Floral Decoration 395.00
Kelva, Box, Silver Collar, Signed, 8 In.Diameter 275.00
Kelva, Sweetmeat, Signed 125.00
Kelva, Vase, Pink & White Hand-Painted Floral On Green, Metal Holder 185.00

 Kew Blas is the name used by the Union Glass Company of Somerville,
 Massachusetts. The name refers to an iridescent golden glass made from the
 1890s to 1924.
Kew Blas, Pitcher, Gold Iridescent, Reverses Handle, Signed 110.00
Kew Blas, Vase, Green & Gold Leaves, White Opal Border, 4 In.High 375.00
Kew Blas, Vase, Green, Amber, 4 In. .... *Illus* 350.00
Kew Blas, Vase, Pearl Background, 4 Gold Open Feathers, 6 3/4 In.Tall 350.00

 Kewpies were first pictured in the Ladies' Home Journal by Rose
 O'Neill. The pixie-like figures became an immediate success, and Kewpie
 dolls started appearing in 1911. Kewpie pictures and other items soon
 followed.
Kewpie, Album, Signed Rose O'Neill, 4 Kewpies On Cover 20.00
Kewpie, Bell, Metal, Handle, 4 In. 25.00
Kewpie, Bell, Silver, Kewpie Stands On Top Of Bell, Signed, 2 3/4 In. 45.00

Kelva, Box,
Gray, Lavender

Kew Blas, Vase,
Green, Amber, 4 In.

Kewpie, Bisque, The Traveler, Rose O'Neill, Paper Label, 3 1/2 In.Tall 50.00
Kewpie, Book, Scrap, 1909-1928 .... 85.00
Kewpie, Bowl, Signed Rose O'Neill, Rose Banded, 7 Kewpies, 8 1/2 In. 35.00
Kewpie, Bowl, Vegetable, Kewpie Decor, Copyrighted Rose O'Neill, Germany 55.00
Kewpie, Box, Jewel, Silver, Signed Rose O'Neill, 5 In.Long, 2 In.Tall 10.00
Kewpie, Candy Container, Kewpie Stands Beside Container, 3 In.Tall 30.00
Kewpie, Card, Signed Rose O'Neill 10.50
Kewpie, Charm, Silver, Signed Kewpie & Rose O'Neill 35.00
Kewpie, Clock, Blue Jasperware, White Kewpies, Signed, 4 In. ....95.00 To 155.00
Kewpie, Creamer, Cut Roses, Signed Rose O'Neill 60.00
Kewpie, Creamer, Green Jasper, Floral Edge, Rose O'Neill, Germany 102.00
Kewpie, Creamer, Signed Rose O'Neill, Playing Kewpies, Royal Rudolstadt 45.00
Kewpie, Creamer, Signed Rose O'Neill, 2 1/2 In.Tall 15.00
Kewpie, Cup & Saucer, Signed Rose O'Neill, 4 Kewpies On Cup, 3 On Saucer 47.50
Kewpie, Cup & Saucer, Signed Rose O'Neill, 7 Kewpies 60.00
Kewpie, Dish, Kewpie Design, Signed Rose O'Neill, Wilson, Matching Bowl, Set 150.00
Kewpie, Dish, Signed Rose O'Neill, 5 In., 5 Kewpies 45.00
Kewpie, Doll, Bisque, Jointed Arms, Signed O'Neill, 5 In.High 45.00
Kewpie, Doll, Bisque, Jointed Arms, Signed O'Neill, 7 1/2 In.High 75.00
Kewpie, Doll, Bisque, Label, Rose O'Neill, 1913, Made In Japan 35.00
Kewpie, Doll, Bisque, Lying On Back, Right Foot Up, 4 1/2 In. 160.00
Kewpie, Doll, Bisque, Lying On Stomach, Feet & Arms Out, Label, 3 1/2 In. 195.00
Kewpie, Doll, Bisque, Rose O'Neill, Signed, 4 1/2 In.Tall 45.00
Kewpie, Doll, Bisque, Signed, 4 1/2 In. 47.00
Kewpie, Doll, Bisque, Sits On Letter, Holds Pen, Says Love From Rose O'Neill 225.00
Kewpie, Doll, Bisque, Sitting With Black Cat In Lap 180.00
Kewpie, Doll, Bisque, With Turkey, 1 3/4 In. 97.50
Kewpie, Doll, Cameo Rubber, Signed Kewpie, Rose O'Neill, 12 In.Tall 50.00
Kewpie, Doll, Celluloid, Hands Molded On Chest, Pin On Back, 1 1/4 In. 6.00
Kewpie, Doll, Celluloid, Movable Arms, Japan, 3 1/2 In. 4.00
Kewpie, Doll, Cloth, Uncut, To Be Stuffed, 3 1/2 In. 10.00
Kewpie, Doll, Composition, Dressed, 14 In.Tall 20.00
Kewpie, Doll, Composition, Movable Arms & Legs, Boy, 13 In.Tall 29.50
Kewpie, Doll, Composition, Scootles, 13 In.Tall 40.00
Kewpie, Doll, Farmer, Bisque, Molded Hat, Signed O'neill, 4 In.Tall 145.00
Kewpie, Doll, Head, Composition 18.00
Kewpie, Doll, Metal, Standing, 6 3/4 In. 175.00
Kewpie, Doll, Plaster, 13 In.Tall 15.00
Kewpie, Doll, Ragsy, Vinyl, 1964, 11 In.Tall 8.00
Kewpie, Doll, Rose O'Neill, Bisque, Arms Move, 5 1/2 In.Tall 50.00
Kewpie, Doll, Rose O'Neill, Bisque, 6 In.Tall 80.00
Kewpie, Doll, Rubber, Signed Rose O'Neill .... *Illus* 40.00

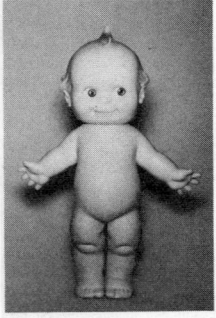

Kewpie, Doll, Rubber, Signed Rose O'Neill

Kewpie, Doll, Signed Rose O'Neill, Cameo, Red Plush Body 50.00
Kewpie, Doll, Thinker, Bisque, Signed Rose O'Neill, 6 In. 150.00
Kewpie, Doll, Traveler, Umbrella, Walking Dog, Bisque, 3 In.Tall 250.00
Kewpie, Doll, Two Kewpies Hugging, Bisque, Rose O'Neill Sticker, 2 1/2 In. 55.00
Kewpie, Doll, Two Kewpies Hugging, Red Heart Shape Label, Germany, 3 1/2 In. 65.00
Kewpie, Doll, Two Kewpies Hugging, Signed Nippon, 2 1/2 In.Tall 30.00
Kewpie, Doll, Vinyl, 11 In.Tall 7.00

Kewpie, Flannel, Copyright 1914, Flying, Red Nightcap 12.00
Kewpie, Flannel, Copyright 1914, Marching, Army Cap, Rifle 12.00
Kewpie, Flannel, Kewpie With American Flag 9.75
Kewpie, Flannel, Leap Frog, 1914, Signed Rose O'Neill 16.00
Kewpie, Flannel, Smelling Rose, 1914, Signed Rose O'Neill 16.00
Kewpie, Hair Receiver, Signed Rose O'Neill 35.00
Kewpie, Hugger, Bisque, Germany, 3 In.High 50.00
Kewpie, Knocker, Brass, 3 In. 20.00
Kewpie, Knocker, Brass, 5 In., Made In England 25.00
Kewpie, Mirror, Rose O'Neill 2.50
Kewpie, Mold, Doll Head, Bronze, 4 1/2 In. 15.00
Kewpie, Mold, Metal, 6 In. 50.00
Kewpie, Mug, Soldier, Wag The Chief, Mark Rose O'Neill, Wilson 50.00
Kewpie, Page, Rose O'Neill, Kewpieville, 4 .... 16.00
Kewpie, Pin, Three Kewpies Sitting On Fence, Sterling Silver 25.00
Kewpie, Pitcher, Cream, Signed Rose O'Neill, 4 1/2 In.High 60.00
Kewpie, Plate, Signed O'Neill, 5 1/2 In. 47.50
Kewpie, Plate, Signed Rose O'Neill, Germany, Pink Luster Border 30.00
Kewpie, Postcard, Clock, Gibson Art 12.50
Kewpie, Postcard, New Years Greeting, Gibson Art 12.50
Kewpie, Postcard, Signed Rose O'Neill, Christmas Greeting, Gibson Art Co. 8.00
Kewpie, Postcard, Signed Rose O'Neill, Hanging Stocking, Fireplace 8.00
Kewpie, Postcard, Signed Rose O'Neill, Kicking Ball, On Hobbyhorse 8.00
Kewpie, Postcard, Signed Rose O'Neill, On Roof Pulling Santa 8.00
Kewpie, Postcard, Signed Rose O'Neill, 5 Kewpies On Tree Limb, Singing 8.00
Kewpie, Postcard, Tis Christmas, Dear, Gibson Art 12.50
Kewpie, Print, Eating Ice Cream, Rose O'Neill-Signed, Framed, 11 X 15 In. 22.50
Kewpie, Print, Kewpie Eating Ice Cream Sundae, Color On Light Blue, C.1922 .... 8.50
Kewpie, Print, Kewpie In Baseball Cap, Bat, Color On White, C.1922 .... 7.50
Kewpie, Print, Kewpie In Baseball Cap, Bat, Eating, Color On Blue, C.1922 .... 8.50
Kewpie, Print, Kewpie Running With Spoon, Color In White, C.1922 .... 7.50
Kewpie, Print, Kewpie With Pharmacy Equipment, Color On Blue, C.1922 .... 8.50
Kewpie, Rose O'Neill, 12 In.Tall, Box & Clothes 60.00
Kewpie, Sheet, Signed Rose O'Neill, Dotty Darling & The Kewpies, 1910 .... 8.00
Kewpie, Sheet, Signed Rose O'Neill, The Kewpies & The Wealthy Child, 1910 .... 8.00
Kewpie, Sheet, Signed Rose O'Neill The Kewpies Christmas Dog, 1913 .... 8.00
Kewpie, Spoon, Sterling Silver, Kewpie On Handle 20.00
Kewpie, Thinker, Blue Porcelain 40.00
Kewpie, Tray, Scene, Signed Rose O'Neill, 10 In.Diameter 125.00
Kewpie, Tray, Signed Rose O'Neill 100.00
Kewpie, Vase, Blue Jasper, Wag The Chief, Rose O'Neill, 4 1/4 In. 95.00
Kewpie, Vinyl, Jointed, 20 In.Tall 15.00
Key, Iron, Flat, Handmade From Carpenter's Square 10.00
Key, Iron, 5 In. 1.50
Key, Iron, 5 In., 17th Century 4.50
Key, Iron, 6 In. 1.50
Key, Pattern, Brass, 6 In.Long 8.50

*Kimball Glass Company of Vineland, New Jersey, worked in the early
1900s. The firm was managed by Colonel Ewan Kimball, who had worked with
several other glass firms, including the company of Kimball and Durand.
His glass was made through the 1930s.*
Kimball, see Cluthra
King's Rose, see also Soft Paste
King's Rose, Plate, Flower Border, Yellow 55.00
King's Rose, Plate, Oyster, Pink Border, Swags, 7 1/8 In.Diameter 35.00
King's Rose, Plate, Pink Border, 8 1/4 In.Diameter 80.00
Kitchen, see also Store, Tool, Wooden, Iron
Kitchen, Apple Peeler, White Mt., By Goodell 15.00
Kitchen, Basket Spoon, Wicker, Marked Chinese Manufacturer 3.00
Kitchen, Board, Cutting, Slaw, Sliding Box, 12 In.Wide, 30 In.Long 12.50
Kitchen, Board, Dough, Slate Slab 15.00
Kitchen, Bowl, Burl, American, 13 In.Diameter 175.00
Kitchen, Bowl, Butter, Oval, Wooden, 20 1/2 X 11 In. 12.00
Kitchen, Bowl, Butter, Wooden, 24 In.Diameter, 7 1/2 In.High 100.00
Kitchen, Bowl, Butter, Wooden, 9 In.Diameter 6.00

Kitchen, **Bowl**, Dough, Handles, Oblong 40.00
Kitchen, **Box**, Candle, Slide Top, Dovetailed, Pine, Pennsylvania Dutch 50.00
Kitchen, **Box**, Knife, Dovetailed, Cutout, Walnut 30.00
Kitchen, **Box**, Knife, High Center Handle, Pine, 14 X 10 In. 12.50
Kitchen, **Box**, Salt, Pennsylvania Dutch 75.00
Kitchen, **Breadboard**, Pine, 10 X 19 In. 8.50
Kitchen, **Bucket**, Stove, Ironbound, Conical, 11 1/2 In.High 15.00
Kitchen, **Butter Melter**, Wooden Handle, Circa 1920 .... 6.00
Kitchen, **Butter Paddle**, Wooden, 3 X 11 In. 6.50
Kitchen, **Butter Stamp**, Daisy 12.00
Kitchen, **Butter Stamp**, Sheaf Of Wheat, Wooden, 4 3/8 In.Diameter 9.75
Kitchen, **Cabinet**, Pantry 140.00
Kitchen, **Camphor Glass**, Jar, Barber, Antiseptic & Red Cross, 10 In. 10.00
Kitchen, **Canister**, Oriental Design, Tin, Wood Knob, 4 1/2 Sq. X 6 3/4 .... 5.00
Kitchen, **Cherry Pitter**, Twin 8.00
Kitchen, **Chopper**, Food, Handwrought, Semicircular Blade 8.50
Kitchen, **Chopper**, Universal, 1899 .... 6.00
Kitchen, **Churn**, Barrel, Wooden, Table Model, 16 In.High, 13 In.Diameter 37.50
Kitchen, **Churn**, Butter, Glass, Crank Apparatus On Top .... 8.00 To 10.00
Kitchen, **Churn**, Butter, Metal, Wood Dasher 15.00
Kitchen, **Churn**, Butter, Wooden, Carved, Vertical, Top & Dasher 50.00
Kitchen, **Churn**, Butter, Wooden, Round 37.00
Kitchen, **Churn**, Daisy 14.00
Kitchen, **Churn**, Dazey, No.40 .... 8.50
Kitchen, **Churn**, Hardwood Turbine Dasher, Glass Jar, Nickel Screw Cap 5.75
Kitchen, **Churn**, Pine 22.50
Kitchen, **Churn**, Wooden, Green Paint, Black Iron Hoops, Corseted 105.00
Kitchen, **Churn**, Wooden, Pennsylvania Dutch 25.00
Kitchen, **Cleaver**, Meat, 10 X 5 1/2 In.Blade 12.00
    Kitchen, **Coffee Grinder, see also Coffee Grinder**
Kitchen, **Coffee Grinder**, Arcade, Crystal 10.50
Kitchen, **Coffee Grinder**, Transparent Hopper, Glass Cup, Hand Crank 12.50
Kitchen, **Coffee Grinder**, Wall Type 15.00
Kitchen, **Coffee Mill**, Wood, Metal Hopper 10.00
Kitchen, **Colander**, Rolled Handle, Marked Kreamer 9.00
Kitchen, **Cookie Board**, Penna.Dutch, Gingerbread Man, Woman, 20 In.Long, Pair 25.00
Kitchen, **Cookie Cutter**, Horse, Pennsylvania Dutch, 6 1/2 X 5 1/2 In. 4.00
Kitchen, **Cookie Cutter**, Rabbit, Running, Pennsylvania Dutch, 6 1/2 X 3 In. 4.00
Kitchen, **Cookie Cutter**, Reindeer With Antlers, Pennsylvania Dutch 6.00
Kitchen, **Cookie Cutter**, Teddy Bear, Separate Arms, Pennsylvania Dutch 3.00
Kitchen, **Cookie Press**, Four Designs, Wooden, 11 3/4 X 2 1/4 In. 15.00
Kitchen, **Cork Screw**, Bone & Brass 20.00
Kitchen, **Cream Separator**, Holder, 1906, 6 1/4 X 4 In. 17.50
Kitchen, **Crimper**, Pastry, Brass 5.00
Kitchen, **Cutter**, Cabbage, Pennsylvania Dutch, Heart At Top 40.00
Kitchen, **Cutter**, Slaw, Box, 50 In. 30.00
Kitchen, **Dough Trough**, 41 X 15 X 5 1/2 In. 85.00
Kitchen, **Doughnut Cutter**, Wooden 5.00
Kitchen, **Dryer**, Vegetable, Wood & Screen 3.00
Kitchen, **Eggbeater**, Dover, Iron & Tin, Patent 1873-1888-1891 .... 11.00
Kitchen, **Eggbeater**, Wire 1.25
Kitchen, **Firkin**, Mince Meat, Staved, Label, Hoops 10.00
Kitchen, **Fork**, Barley, Four Tines, 6 In.Long 15.00
Kitchen, **Fork**, For Toasting Over Fire, Iron, 27 In.Long 5.00
Kitchen, **Freezer**, Ice Cream, Dated 1923 .... 12.50
Kitchen, **Freezer**, Ice Cream, Tin 22.00
Kitchen, **Funnel**, For Sap, Hewn Maple, One Piece, 4 1/2 In.Diameter 38.00
Kitchen, **Grater**, Climax, Glass Plunger 5.00
Kitchen, **Grater**, Food, Handmade, Iron Frame, Brass Grater, Copper Rivets 45.00
Kitchen, **Grater**, Nugmeg, Crank Handle, Moves In Circle Over Pierced Tin 5.00
Kitchen, **Grater**, Pierced Tin, Wood Back, 18 In. 27.50
Kitchen, **Grater**, Pierced, Tin, On Pine Board, Circa 1830, 16 In.Long 35.00
Kitchen, **Grinder**, Food, Clamp On Table 5.50
Kitchen, **Grinder**, Meat, Iron, Footed, Wood Handle, Black Paint, 12 In. Long ... 15.00
Kitchen, **Grinder**, Meat, Wooden Handle, Iron, Footed, Black, 12 In.Long 15.00
Kitchen, **Hook**, Pot, Wood & Iron, To Handle Hot Pot 17.50

Kitchen, Iron & Trivet, Swan, Miniature	49.00
Kitchen, Iron, Chinese, C.1850, Handle End Has Ivory & Jade	32.50
Kitchen, Iron, Coleman, Gas Heated, Blue Enameled	15.00
Kitchen, Iron, Fluting, Hand, Dated 1866	15.00
Kitchen, Iron, Fluting, Hinged	12.50
Kitchen, Iron, Gas, Blue Enamel	5.00
Kitchen, Iron, Narrow Sleeve, Removable Handle	3.95
Kitchen, Iron, Square End *Illus*	15.00
Kitchen, Jar, Butter, Wooden Lid	14.00

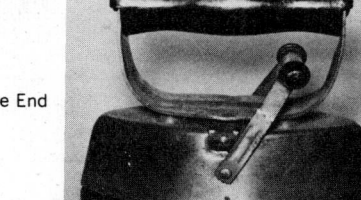

Kitchen, Iron, Square End

Kitchen, Juice Press	2.50
Kitchen, Knife & Fork, Carving, Wood Handles	3.50
Kitchen, Kraut Cutter, Wooden, 23 X 9 In.	10.00
Kitchen, Ladle, Brass, 15 In.Handle, 6 1/2 In.Diameter	4.95
Kitchen, Lemon Squeezer, Wooden	8.50
Kitchen, Masher, Potato	6.50
Kitchen, Match Holder, Wall, Iron, Openwork	9.95
Kitchen, Meat Block	175.00
Kitchen, Mold, Butter, Fern Leaves, Square, Wooden	25.00
Kitchen, Mold, Butter, Glass, Signed Bower, Pat.Applied, Plumes	30.00
Kitchen, Mold, Butter, Pineapple, Round, 1 Pound	12.50
Kitchen, Mold, Butter, Plunger Type, Triangle Design	15.00
Kitchen, Mold, Butter, Rectangular	3.00
Kitchen, Mold, Butter, Round, Flower Design	14.00
Kitchen, Mold, Butter, Strawberry, 3 In.Diameter	23.50
Kitchen, Mold, Butter, Swan, Wood, Plunger Type	18.00
Kitchen, Mold, Butter, Swiss	15.00
Kitchen, Mold, Butter, Wood, Barrel Shape, Pewter Bands, Opossum Design	75.00
Kitchen, Mold, Butter, Wooden, Plunger, Acorn Design, 6 X 3 3/4 In.	20.00
Kitchen, Mold, Butter, Wooden, Round, One Pound	12.50
Kitchen, Mold, Butter, Wooden, Strawberry Print	17.50
Kitchen, Mold, Candle, Pottery, Wood Frame, 24 Tubes, New York State	385.00
Kitchen, Mold, Candle, see also Tin, Mold, Candle	
Kitchen, Mold, Candle, 12 Tube	25.00 To 30.00
Kitchen, Mold, Chocolate, Girl With Bow *Illus*	7.50
Kitchen, Mold, Cookie, Tin, Fish, Elliptical Shape	8.00
Kitchen, Mold, Cookie, Tin, Rocking Horse	10.00
Kitchen, Mold, Gray Pottery, Oval, Geometric Design	7.00
Kitchen, Mold, Maple Sugar	5.00
Kitchen, Mold, Melon, Tin, Lid With Ring Handle	10.00
Kitchen, Mold, Pudding, Melon	11.00
Kitchen, Mold, Pudding, Swirled, Handled	22.00
Kitchen, Mold, Pudding, Tin, Oval, Ear Of Corn, Fluted	9.00
Kitchen, Mold, Pudding, Turk's Head *Illus*	18.00
Kitchen, Mold, Pudding, Turk's Head, Brown Pottery	10.00
Kitchen, Mold, Stove, Metal Bound, Lid	5.00
Kitchen, Mortar & Pestle, Walnut Handle, Ceramic	15.00
Kitchen, Noggin, American, Maple, Sided, One Piece, 8 In.High	125.00
Kitchen, Noodle Roller, Wooden	15.00

Kitchen, Mold, Chocolate, Girl With Bow
See Page 273

Kitchen, Mold, Pudding, Turk's Head
See Page 273

Kitchen, **Oven Tool**, Like Right Angled Peel	7.50
Kitchen, **Pan**, Breadstick, 12 Sections	5.50
Kitchen, **Pan**, Corn Stick, Iron, For Seven Sticks	4.00
Kitchen, **Pan**, Fry, Rattailed, Long	27.50
Kitchen, **Pea Sheller**	19.50
Kitchen, **Peeler**, Apple, Iron, Patent 1871, 11 In.Long	15.00
Kitchen, **Peeler**, Apple, Pat.'82, Iron	8.50
Kitchen, **Peeler**, Potato, Screw To Table, Crank, Painted	5.00
Kitchen, **Pie Lifter**, Two Prongs, Adjusts To Size	4.50
Kitchen, **Pie Lifter**, Two Prongs, Wooden Handle	2.75
Kitchen, **Pie Lifter**, Wire	6.50
Kitchen, **Pitter**, Cherry, Iron	8.50
Kitchen, **Pot**, Stew, For Hearth, 3 Legs, 7 3/4 In.	12.50
Kitchen, **Potato Masher**, Wooden	4.95
Kitchen, **Press**, Butter, Cow, Miniature	38.00
Kitchen, **Pressing Board**, Turned Knob, 9 X 24 In.	7.50
Kitchen, **Rack**, Plate Drying	25.00
Kitchen, **Rack**, Plate Drying, Pine, 42 In.Wide, 49 In.High	50.00
Kitchen, **Ravioli Maker**, Advertising, Royal Baking Powder, Heart Shape	3.00
Kitchen, **Roasting Jack**, Brass, Salter 40, 19th Century	52.00
Kitchen, **Roller**, To Make Cookies, Corrugated Wood	9.00
Kitchen, **Rolling Pin & Cookie Cutter**, End Pushout Doughnut Cutter, Wooden	10.00
Kitchen, **Rolling Pin**, Cherry, Figured, Scrimshaw Mounts	140.00
Kitchen, **Rolling Pin**, Commemorative Brass Plate	10.00
Kitchen, **Rolling Pin**, Dough Tray, Biscuit Board, Buckeye Wood, Circa 1840	100.00
Kitchen, **Rolling Pin**, Glass, Clear, 14 In.Long	10.00
Kitchen, **Rolling Pin**, Glass, Hollow With Place Inside For Ice	4.98
Kitchen, **Rolling Pin**, Hand Whittled, Ball Ends, Hardwood, 20 In.Long	10.00
Kitchen, **Rolling Pin**, Maple, Bird's-Eye	5.00
Kitchen, **Rolling Pin**, Maple, Flat Knob Ends, 17 In.	6.00
Kitchen, **Rolling Pin**, Noodle	12.00
Kitchen, **Rolling Pin**, Tiger Maple, Miniature, 8 In.	8.00
Kitchen, **Rolling Pin**, Wood, 20 In.Long	3.50
Kitchen, **Rolling Pin**, Wooden, One Piece	3.75
Kitchen, **Sadiron**, Double, Enterprise Mfg., Pat.1867-1877	3.95
Kitchen, **Sadiron**, Hand Fluter, Geneva, Pat.1866	8.95
Kitchen, **Sadiron**, Removable Clamp On Top To Insert Heated Iron	6.00
Kitchen, **Sadiron**, Removable Handle, Double Pointed, Colebrookdale Iron Co.	3.95
Kitchen, **Sadiron**, Removable Handle, Double Pointed, Marked Sensible No.90	3.95
Kitchen, **Sadiron**, Removable Wooden Handle	3.00
Kitchen, **Sadiron**, Solid Handle	3.00
Kitchen, **Salt Tub**, Crockery, Wooden Lid	18.00
Kitchen, **Scoop**, Apple Butter	32.00
Kitchen, **Scoop**, Apple Butter, Burl & Tiger, Maple, Heart Design Carved	115.00

Kitchen, Scoop, Cranberry, Red Paint, Stencil 55.00
Kitchen, Scoop, Grain, Metal, Iron Handle 6.00
Kitchen, Seeder, Cherry 8.00
Kitchen, Sheller, Pea, Bean, Iron, Table Clamp, 8 In.High 7.50
Kitchen, Sieve, Temse, Plaid Horsehair 27.50
Kitchen, Sifter, Flour, Wooden, Dated 1861 .... *Illus* 38.00

Kitchen, Sifter, Flour, Wooden, Dated 1861

Kitchen, Sifter, Wood Frame, Fine Screen, 5 X 11 1/2 In. 6.50
Kitchen, Skillet, 3 Legs, Handle, 9 1/2 In. 25.00
Kitchen, Sleeve Iron, Marked B&d With Star 4.75
Kitchen, Smokestack, Iron, Charcoal 11.75
Kitchen, Spoon, Hand Carved, Wooden, 18 In.Long 9.00
Kitchen, Spoon, Horn, American, 6 In. 12.00
Kitchen, Spoon, Horn, 9 1/2 In.Long 8.00
Kitchen, Squeezer, Lemon, Fry 15.00
Kitchen, Squeezer, Lemon, Wood 8.50
Kitchen, Stamp, Butter, Knob Handle, Pear With Leaves 22.50
Kitchen, Stove, Miniature 65.00
Kitchen, Stove, Raised Decor, Reservoir, Circa 1880, Iron 75.00
Kitchen, Teapot, Terra-Cotta, Wicker Handle, Dragons, 8 1/2 In. 15.00
Kitchen, Temse, Wood Framed, Woven Plaid Mesh Of Hair 27.50
Kitchen, Timer, Egg, Sand, Decorated, 4 In.High 22.00
Kitchen, Toaster, Hearth, Hand Forged, Iron, 18th Century, Rotating 75.00
Kitchen, Toaster, Two Clover-Shape Wire Prongs, Wooden Handle, 15 In.Long 5.00
Kitchen, Tongs, Food, Fork & Spoon, D.Baleen, Ivory 20.00
Kitchen, Waffle Grill, Patent, 1922, Cast Iron 15.00
Kitchen, Waffle Iron, Heart Shape Design, Alfred Andersen Co., Minneapolis 7.00
Kitchen, Waffle Iron, Stove Top 4.50
Kitchen, Waffle Iron, Stove, Stand, 2 Piece 4.50
Kitchen, Warmer, Foot, Brass Closure, Gray, Blue Lettering, Henderson, 1912 .... 15.00
Kitchen, Washboard, Brass 2.50
Kitchen, Washboard, Glass 4.50
Kitchen, Wringer, Clothes, Lovell Manufacturing Co. 5.75
Kloster Veilsdorf, Bowl, Covered, Landscape, Figures, C.1765 .... 225.00
Kloster Veilsdorf, Figurine, Woman In Flight, Nightcap, C.1755, 5 In.High 200.00
    Knowles, Taylor & Knowles, see Lotus Ware, KTK
Koch, Bowl, Berry, Grape Design, Scalloped Edge, Gold 35.00
Koch, Bowl, Grape Design, 9 In.Diameter 45.00
Koch, Bowl, Leaves & Currants, Green, Yellow, Gold Trim, Signed, 6 In. 37.50
Koch, Dish, Grapes & Berries, Pinched, Oval, Signed 25.00
Koch, Plate, Cake, Grape Design, Green, Brown, Open Handle, Signed 55.00
Koch, Plate, Dark Green & Tan, Grapes Decoration, Signed, 8 1/2 In. 22.50
Koch, Plate, Fruit & Water Scene, Signed A.Koch, J.C.Bavaria, 7 1/2 In. 25.00
Koch, Plate, Fruits, 8 1/2 In. 18.50
Koch, Plate, Grapes & Blackberries, Hand-Painted, 8 5/8 In. 35.00
Koch, Plate, Grapes, Leaves, Bavaria, 8 1/2 In. 17.50
Koch, Plate, Green & Brown, Apples, Louise, Bavaria, 8 1/2 In. 22.50
Koch, Plate, Purple & White Grapes, Autumn Leaves, Signed, 6 3/4 In. 14.00

Kornilow, Tea Set, Puce & Gold, St.Petersburg, C.1880, Blossoms, 28 Piece 300.00

KPM is part of one of the marks used about 1723 by the Meissen Factory
Konigliche Porzellan Manufaktur. Other later firms using the letters
include the Royal Manufactory of Berlin, Germany, that worked from 1832
to 1847. A factory in Scheibe, Germany, used the mark in 1928. The mark
was also used in Waldenburg, Germany, and other German cities during the
twentieth century.

KPM, Bowl, Fruit, Pastel With Roses, 10 In.	18.00
KPM, Cheeseboard, Hole To Hang, Rose & Leaf Garland Border, Marked	10.00
KPM, Cup & Saucer, Hunting Scene, Filigree, 18th Century	145.00
KPM, Cup, Winged Warrior Resting, Classic Style, Blue Mark	75.00
KPM, Dish, Cherub Holds Grapes On Cover, Floral, Butterflies, Mark	90.00
KPM, Germany, Tea Set, Marked, White, Floral Bands, 3 Piece	30.00
KPM, Painting On Porcelain, Cherub, By F.M.Beetz, Frame, 16 X 14 In.	550.00
KPM, Painting On Porcelain, Mother, Baby, On Bed, Frame, 14 X 18 In.	650.00
KPM, Painting On Porcelain, Nude, Signed Wagner, 17 1/2 X 22 1/2 In.	900.00
KPM, Painting On Porcelain, Oval, 2 Girls, Signed Walther, Marked Kpm	840.00
KPM, Painting On Porcelain, Young Girl, Frame, Oval, 9 X 7 In.	600.00
KPM, Picture, Porcelain, Girl In Religious Pose, 'the Ascension'	500.00
KPM, Picture, Porcelain, Girl, Mauve Ribbon In Hair, Frame, Gold	550.00
KPM, Picture, Porcelain, Gypsy Boy, 7 X 5 In.	325.00
KPM, Plaque, Boy, Peddling Beets, Huge Eyes, Tattered Clothes	585.00
KPM, Plate, Cake, Floral	5.00
KPM, Urn, Cobalt & Gilt, Floral, Cherubs, Covered, Pair	150.00
KTK, Cup, Tree Of Life	5.00
KTK, Plate, Dinner, Tree Of Life	4.00
KTK, Plate, Luncheon, Tree Of Life	3.00
KTK, Teapot, Stark White	95.00
Ku Klux Klan, Ring, Woman's	40.00
Ku Klux Klan, Sword, Hooded Man On Cross On Guard	100.00

Kutani Ware is a Japanese porcelain made after the mid-seventeenth
century. Most of the pieces found today are nineteenth century.

Kutani, Bowl, Enameled In Yellow, Green, & Puce, 6 Character Mien Hao	50.00
Kutani, Bowl, Orange, Circa 1810, 5 In.Diameter	57.00
Kutani, Jar, Rose, Double Cover	18.00
Kutani, Tea Set, Blue, Gold Encrusted & Enamel, Medallions, 18 Piece	145.00
Kutani, Vase, Beige, Floral, Mark, 19th Century, Pair	35.00
Kutani, Vase, Long Neck, Red & Gold Design	25.00

Lalique Glass was made by Rene Lalique's Factory in Paris, France,
from 1860 to 1945. The glass was molded, pressed, and engraved. Many of the
most familiar designs were clear or with a bluish-tinged glass molded into
birds, animals, or foliage.

Lalique, Bowl, Branches & Leaves, Footed, 8 In.Wide, 3 1/2 In.High	37.50
Lalique, Bowl, Floral Design, Signed, 6 In.Diameter	42.00
Lalique, Bowl, Floral, Footed, 10 In.Across	130.00
Lalique, Bowl, Green Jade, Signed	28.00
Lalique, Bowl, Signed Block Signature, Clear, Swirled Hobnail, Bluish	50.00
Lalique, Bowl, Water Lilies, Raised, Rippled Base, 10 In.Diameter, 5 In.Deep	80.00
Lalique, Box, Camphor Satin Ground, Raised Floral, Leaves, Twig Finial	65.00
Lalique, Box, Powder, 4 Angels On Cover, Signed In Block Letters	32.00
Lalique, Cup, Punch, Camphor Satin Ground, Etched & Cut Pattern, Signed	18.00
Lalique, Dish, Fish Design, Signed, C.1925, 11 In.Diameter	85.00
Lalique, Dish, Silver Rim, Gray, Footed With Cherubs	32.00
Lalique, Knife Rest, Knob End, Signed, Pair	21.50
Lalique, Knife Rest, Signed, Embossed Ends	12.00
Lalique, Ornament, Hood, Frosted Woman's Head, Flowing Hair, Signed	325.00
Lalique, Paperweight, Frosted Buffalo On Clear Base, France, 3 1/2 In.Tall	125.00
Lalique, Paperweight, Frosted, Thistle, Signed	18.00
Lalique, Pendant, Cross Shape, Leaf Design, Round Top, 2 In.Wide, 1 7/8 In.	65.00
Lalique, Perfume, Signed, Clear, Black Enamel, 1920, 5 In.Tall	20.00
Lalique, Perfume, Stopper Of Pair Of Birds In Flight, Signed	55.00
Lalique, Pin, Signed, Camphorey, Gold, Daisies	35.00
Lalique, Pitcher, Water, Signed R.Lalique, Leaves, 8 1/2 In.Tall	140.00

Lalique, Plate, Chop, Camphor Satin Ground, Raised Nude Dancing Figures 55.00
Lalique, Plate, France In Script, Clear, Sailing Ship In Bottom, 8 1/2 In. 45.00
Lalique, Plate, Opalescent Swirl, 11 In. 32.50
Lalique, Plate, Opaque Black, Embossed Leaf, 11 In. 28.00
Lalique, Plate, Shell Pattern, Signed R.Lalique, Round, 10 1/2 In. 75.00
Lalique, Plate, Shell Pattern, Signed, Round, Opalescent Ends Form Feet 75.00
Lalique, Plate, Shell, Opalescent, Footed, Signed, 10 1/2 In.Diameter 75.00
Lalique, Plate, Wheat, 12 In.Diameter 50.00
Lalique, Ring Tree, Frosted Bird, Tail Holds Rings, Attached Tray 35.00
Lalique, Tumbler, Signed R.Lalique, Leaves 30.00
Lalique, Tumbler, Signed, Footed, Scroll Collar 20.00
Lalique, Vase, Berries, Leaves, Raised, Iridescent, Signed, 7 In.Tall 95.00
Lalique, Vase, Blue, Bulbous, Fruit Pattern, Signed 125.00
Lalique, Vase, Clear, Wide Frosted Band Of Petals, Signed, 5 In.High 55.00
Lalique, Vase, Frosted Birds, 6 In.Tall 15.00
Lalique, Vase, Frosted, Allover Design, Bulbous, Signed, 7 In.Tall 75.00
Lalique, Vase, Gray, Thistles, Leaves, High Relief Base, 9 In.Tall 125.00
Lalique, Vase, Ladies, Faces, Frosted, Signed, 6 In.Tall 50.00
Lalique, Vase, Molded, Clear, Signed, 8 In.Tall 145.00
Lalique, Vase, Ovoid, Relief Nude Male Archers, Birds, 10 1/2 In.High, Signed 200.00
Lalique, Vase, Plums, Leaves, Berries, Short Neck, Singed, 6 1/2 In.Tall 85.00
Lalique, Vase, Signed R.Lalique, Ovoid, Peacock With Feathers 95.00
Lamp, Aladdin, Brass, Red Shade, 23 1/4 In.High 48.50
Lamp, Aladdin, Brass, White Milk Glass, Shade, Swirl Design, 23 1/4 In.High 48.50
Lamp, Aladdin, Calcite 40.00
Lamp, Aladdin, Clear Glass, Ribbed Milk Glass Shade 18.50
Lamp, Aladdin, Electrified 30.00
Lamp, Aladdin, Embossed Off-White Shade 57.50
Lamp, Aladdin, Green Milk Glass, Electrified 35.00
Lamp, Aladdin, Hanging 47.50
Lamp, Aladdin, Ivory Font 47.50
Lamp, Aladdin, Lemon 49.50
Lamp, Aladdin, Lincoln·Drape 33.00
Lamp, Aladdin, Milk Glass 26.00
Lamp, Aladdin, Pink 18.00
Lamp, Aladdin, Red, Ribbed Pattern, Pair 160.00
Lamp, Aladdin, Ribbed Green Shade, 10 In. 24.50
Lamp, Angel, Double, Brass Plated 69.50
Lamp, Angel, Double, Nickel Plated 69.50
Lamp, Applique, Louis XV Style, Ormolu, 3 Arms, Floral Nozzles, Pair 750.00
Lamp, Argand, Bronze, Cut Glass, Cox, N.Y., C.1825, Pair .... *Illus* 525.00
Lamp, Art Deco, Nudes 27.50
Lamp, Art Glass, Parrot, Life Size On Perch, Green & Orange 55.00
Lamp, Art Nouveau, Metal, Figure Of Girl Standing On Leaf, Red Glass Shade 80.00
Lamp, Art Nouveau, Painted Metal, Nude Female Holding Glass Ball Shade 50.00
Lamp, Art Nouveau, Table, Pewter Female Holding 2 Jeweled Brass Shades 125.00
Lamp, Astral, Brass, 24 In.High 45.00

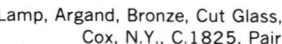
Lamp, Argand, Bronze, Cut Glass,
Cox, N.Y., C.1825, Pair

Lamp, **Astral**, Dome Globe, 8 Prisms, Marble Base, Brass Column & Feet 130.00
Lamp, **Astral**, Sandwich, Marble Base, Impressed 'e.P.Dodge, Boston' 400.00
Lamp, **Aurene**, Gold, Iridescent, Shade, Brass Base 55.00
Lamp, **Banquet**, Ball Shade, Pink Roses, 20 In. 97.50
Lamp, **Banquet**, Open Brass Work, Onyx Stem, Ball Shade, Stag Scene, 36 In. 295.00
Lamp, **Banquet**, Openwork Font, Onyx Column, Rococo Legs, Ball Shade, Honeycomb 85.00
Lamp, **Banquet**, Sandstone, Yellow Shade, Gold Fleur-De-Lis, Brass Parts 125.00
Lamp, **Banquet**, Silver, Winged Cherubs, Children, Flowers 185.00
Lamp, **Banquet**, The Hunter, Black Marble Base, 35 In.Tall 125.00
Lamp, **Banquet**, The Violin Player, Inscribed Lulli Enfant, 38 In.Tall 395.00
Lamp, **Banquet**, Three Tiers, Floral, Acorn Feet, Bristol, 17 1/2 In.High 155.00
Lamp, **Bedroom**, Brass, Red Silk Shade, Porcelain Fitting, 1903, 11 In.High 5.00
Lamp, **Betty**, Brass, Tin Base, 9 1/2 In.High 20.00
Lamp, **Betty**, Crusie, Double, Iron 12.00
Lamp, **Betty**, Iron, Pennsylvania, Pick & Hook 85.00
Lamp, **Betty**, Iron, Wick Pick, Hook, Cover 135.00
Lamp, **Betty**, Iron, Wrought Iron Hook 50.00
Lamp, **Betty**, Miner's, Iron 24.00
Lamp, **Betty**, Oil Spout, Side Spout, Iron Hook On Top, Brass, 5 In.Long 40.00
Lamp, **Betty**, Tin, Pick & Hook 40.00
Lamp, **Bicycle**, Carbide, Brass 10.00
Lamp, **Black**, Acid Cut, Flowers, Butterfly, Umbrella Shade, White 125.00
Lamp, **Blown Glass**, Clear, 4 1/2 In.High 35.00
Lamp, **Bottle**, Seltzer, English, Double Ball Shape, Pewter Top, Pair 50.00
Lamp, **Bouillotte**, Louis Xvi Ormolu Candlestick, Tole Shade, C.1750, Pair 400.00
Lamp, **Bracket**, China, Hand-Painted Flowers 15.00
Lamp, **Bracket**, Clambroth 22.00
Lamp, **Bracket**, Mercury Reflector 32.50
Lamp, **Brass & Marble Base**, Paper Shade, 14 In.High, Pair 150.00
Lamp, **Brass & Marble**, 12 In.High, Pair 45.00
Lamp, **Brass Stem**, Marble Base, Red & White Overlay, Crystal Prisms 22.50
Lamp, **Brass With Overlay**, Chimney, 12 In.High 18.50
Lamp, **Brass**, Argand, Font, J.& I.Cox, N.Y., C.1830, Pair 450.00
Lamp, **Brass**, Bracket 45.00
Lamp, **Brass**, Columnar, Pierced Tripod Base, Paper Shade, 25 In.High, Pair 90.00
Lamp, **Brass**, Glass, Marble Base, Electrified 65.00
Lamp, **Brass**, Table, Ribbed White Shade 17.50
Lamp, **Brass**, Turkish, Hall, Hanging, Colored Stones, 15 In.High 30.00
Lamp, **Bridal**, Twin Clambroth Fonts, Milk Glass Base, Blue Cup 550.00
Lamp, **Bridge**, Metal, Pleated Shades, Grooved Column, Adjustable, Pair 70.00
Lamp, **Bristol**, Banquet, Double Step, Green, Gold, Brass Base, 33 In.High 22.50
Lamp, **Bronze**, Frog Base, 8 Stones Eyes On Shade, 13 In.Tall 600.00
Lamp, **Caboose**, Wall, Tin 35.00
Lamp, **Cameo**, Base, Signed Devez 59.00
Lamp, **Cameo**, Green, Frosted, Pyramid Scene, Signed Beaute, 20 In.Tall 185.00
Lamp, **Camphene**, Brass, Handled, Signed Dyott, Philadelphia, 4 1/2 In. 65.00
Lamp, **Candle**, Hand-Painted Floral, Squat Base, Milk Glass, Wired, 10 1/2 In. 125.00
Lamp, **Candlestick**, Adam Style, Silver Plate, Wood Base, 11 1/2 In.High, Pair 30.00
Lamp, **Candlestick**, Blue Satin Glass 65.00
Lamp, **Candlestick**, Brass, Green Glass Peg Light Inserts, 16 In.High, Pair 60.00
Lamp, **Candlestick**, Silver Plate, Grooved Stem, Round Base, Mounted, Pair 100.00
Lamp, **Candlestick**, Teardrop In Stem & Shade, Clear Prisms On Frosted, Pair 155.00
Lamp, **Cased Glass Shade**, Floral Panels, Bronze Base, Two Lights, Pairpoint 400.00
Lamp, **Ceiling Fixture**, Brass, Frosted & Crystal Shade, Flower Design 8.00
Lamp, **Chandelier**, Brass, Hanging, Studded With Colored Stones, Square 70.00
Lamp, **Chandelier**, Five Branches, Lead, Hand Cut, Crystal, Waterford Style 300.00
Lamp, **Chandelier**, George III, Brass, 18th Century, S Scroll Arms, Pair 3750.00
Lamp, **Chandelier**, Georgian, Brass, 8 Light, 18th Century 1100.00
Lamp, **Chandelier**, Gilt Metal & Carved Gilt Wood, Faceted Drops, C.1850 .... 425.00
Lamp, **Chandelier**, Italian, Carved & Gilt Wood, 3 Arms, 37 In.High 70.00
Lamp, **Chandelier**, Louis XV Style, Gilt Metal & Cut Glass, Cartouche Outline 375.00
Lamp, **Chandelier**, Louis XV Style, Gilt Metal & Cut Glass, Scrolled 325.00
Lamp, **Chandelier**, Tiffany Type, Bluish White Stripes, Bronze, Pair 275.00
Lamp, **Chandelier**, Tiffany Type, Floriform, Mottled Ocher & White 225.00
Lamp, **Chandelier**, Tiffany Type, Iridescent Amber, Wirework, Foliate Motifs 125.00
Lamp, **Chandelier**, Victorian, Brass, Three Yellow Art Glass Globes 80.00

Lamp, Chandelier, Victorian, Brass, 4 Arm, Quezal Glass Globes 375.00
Lamp, Chandelier, Victorian, Cast Bronze Arms, Custard Shades, 39 In.High 600.00
Lamp, Chandelier, Victorian, Oil Lamp, Hanging, Pink Glass Shade, Prisms 280.00
Lamp, China, White, Jardiniere, Covered, 25 In.High 20.00
Lamp, Clear Glass, Marble Base, 8 In.High 12.50
Lamp, Clear Glass, Panel Side, 7 1/2 In.High 6.00
Lamp, Coach, Octagon Glass, Ornate Brass Rims, Eagle On Top, 29 In. 52.50
Lamp, Cone Shape, Burner, Chimney, Brass, 4 X 7 In. 10.00
Lamp, Cone Shape, Tube Burner, Brass, 4 X 4 In. 9.00
Lamp, Coolidge, Clear 35.00
Lamp, Cosmos, Miniature, Painted 34.00
Lamp, Cox, Frame Of Metal Trees Form Silhouettes Against Glass 195.00
Lamp, Cranberry Glass, Birds In Stippled Panels 95.00
Lamp, Cresolene, Miniature, Milk Glass Chimney, Marked 15.00
Lamp, Crusie, Double, Tin, Flower Cut Out 10.00
Lamp, Crystal Art, Prisms, Pair 50.00
Lamp, Cut Glass, Prisms, Tulip & Butterfly, Shade 12 1/2 In.Diameter, 20 In. 750.00
Lamp, Desk, Emerald, Signed & Dated, Oblong Shape, Square Base 35.00
Lamp, Desk, Tiffany Type, Brass Base .... 27.50 To 32.50
Lamp, Desk, Two Deer On Base, Bronze, Grape Shade, 19 1/2 In.High 225.00
Lamp, Desk, Two Green Feathered Art Glass Shades, 14 In.High 90.00
Lamp, Dome, Hanging, Tiffany Type, Panes Of Fruits, 22 In. .... 275.00 To 300.00
Lamp, Double Step, Marble Base, Clear Glass Ball Font, 11 In.High 40.00
Lamp, Double, Brass, Copper, Shades, Oil, Marked, 20 In. 65.00
Lamp, Druggist's, Forms Of Scale, Pierced Gilded Shape, Cutouts, 29 In.High 30.00
Lamp, Durand Type, Glass & Bronze Metal, Amber Iridescent, Cherubs, 16 In. 70.00
Lamp, Durand, Lacy Gold Threading, 5 Point Star In Top, 13 In.Tall 275.00
Lamp, Empire, Bronze & Tortoiseshell, Raw Silk Shade, Octagon Base, Pair 250.00
Lamp, Empire, Columnar, Shade, Brass Banded & Rosettes 100.00
Lamp, English, Cameo, Miniature, Raisin Color, White Butterflies, Flowers 395.00
Lamp, Fairy, Blue Satin Glass Shade, Enamel Floral, Clarke Cricklite 185.00
Lamp, Fairy, Burmese, Signed Acid Queens, Applied Yellow Wafer Base 450.00
Lamp, Fairy, Clarke, Cobalt, Marked 37.50
Lamp, Fairy, Cobalt Blue 11.25
Lamp, Fairy, Cranberry, Nailsea, Marked Clarke Base, 3 Part 195.00
Lamp, Fairy, Cricklite, Epergne, Silver Plate Stand, 16 1/2 In.Tall 125.00
Lamp, Fairy, Diamond Point, Amber.Clear Base, Signed 25.00
Lamp, Fairy, Diamond Point, Blue, Signed Clarke, 3 In.High 30.00
Lamp, Fairy, Eyewinker, Sapphire Blue Satin 9.00
Lamp, Fairy, Hobnail, Orange 9.50
Lamp, Fairy, Lighthouse Shape, Amber, 6 1/2 In.Tall 40.00
Lamp, Fairy, Marked Clarke, Clear, Diamond Point Top 22.50
Lamp, Fairy, Marked Clarke, Cobalt Blue, Diamond Point Top, Clear Base 27.50
Lamp, Fairy, Opalescent Shade, Ruffled, Applied Vaseline Petals 85.00
Lamp, Fairy, Owl .... Illus 55.00
Lamp, Fairy, Owl, Signed Clarke 125.00
Lamp, Fairy, Pale Green Satin Glass, White Swirls & Pull Up, Applied Pink 275.00
Lamp, Fairy, Pink Satin, Opalescent Swirl, Signed Clarke 275.00

Lamp, Fairy, Owl

Lamp, Fairy, Pyramid Shape, Swirled Cranberry Globe, Marked Clarkes	40.00
Lamp, Fairy, Rose Satin Glass, 3 Part, 2 Part Base, Marked U.S.Patent, 1886	85.00
Lamp, Fairy, Sandwich, Triple Overlay, Pink To White To Clear, Gold, Pewter	525.00
Lamp, Fairy, Satin Glass, Pinks, White, Signed Clarke, Matching Skirt	300.00
Lamp, Fairy, Satin Glass, Signed Pantin Deposse, Castle Shape, 7 In.	157.50
Lamp, Fairy, Satin Glass, Standard Base, Pale Green With White	275.00
Lamp, Fairy, Shell Shape Shade, Marked Clarke, 4 In.Tall	45.00
Lamp, Fairy, Signed Clarke, Citron Nailsea, Matching Bowl	285.00
Lamp, Fairy, Signed Clarke, Cobalt Blue, Diamond Point, Grooved Top	17.50
Lamp, Fairy, Signed Clarke, Rose Nailsea, Matching Bowl	285.00
Lamp, Fairy, Vaseline Glass, Hobnail, 4 5/8 In.Tall	5.95
Lamp, Fairy, Vaseline, Hobnail, Pair	25.00
Lamp, Fairy, Verre Moire, White Threads In Pulled Pattern On Blue, Signed	225.00
Lamp, Fairy, Webb, Burmese, Enameled Leaves & Berries, Clarke's Base	195.00
Lamp, Fat, Oval Top With Oil Filling Space, Two Burners, Tin, 7 In.High	60.00
Lamp, Fat, Oval Top With Oil-Filling Space, Two Burners, Tin, 7 In.High	60.00
Lamp, Fat, Tin, 7 In.High, 2 Round Burners	60.00
Lamp, Fat, Two Burners, Oil Space, 7 In.High	60.00
Lamp, Fat, Wrought Iron, Pentagonal Pan, Hanging Hook	65.00
Lamp, Finger, Clear Glass, Spiral Base & Chinmey, Wire Handle, 1 X 3 In.	27.00
Lamp, Finger, Frosted Yellow Font, Flower, Clear Base, 5 1/2 In.	19.50
Lamp, Floor, Brass, Dated 1910	37.50
Lamp, Floor, Victorian, Brass, Stamped V.Hillingswood, Boston, Patent 1885	110.00
Lamp, Fluid, Brass, Saucer Base, Marked Delavan & Brother, 19th Century, Pair	175.00
Lamp, Fluid, Sandwich Glass, Cobalt Blue & White, C.1820, Acanthus Leaf, Pair	350.00
Lamp, French Patent, To Stand Or Hang, Signed, Brass, 3 X 10 In.	19.00
Lamp, Frosted Etched Glass, Black Marble Base, 12 In.High, Pair	30.00
Lamp, Gas Light, Ceiling, Double Burner, Frosted Ball Shades	30.00
Lamp, Gas Light, Ceiling, Single Burner, Frosted Ball Shade	12.50
Lamp, Gas Light, Garden, Life Size Woman, Lead Alloy, France, C.1860	1000.00
Lamp, Gas Light, Hanging, Brass, Chains Turn Off & On	3.00
Lamp, Gas Light, Welsbach, Reflex, Patent 1903, Brass, 11 In.High	15.00
Lamp, Gimbal, Brass, Electrified, Pair	75.00
Lamp, Gimbal, Silver, Base Is Horn With Sterling Silver Fish Mounts, 7 In.	600.00
Lamp, Glass, Turkeyfoot Pattern, Milk Glass, Shade, 18 In.High, Electrified	18.75
Lamp, Glory, Brass, Marked, Handle, 22 In.	95.00
Lamp, Gone With The Wind, Blue, Green, Milk Glass, Bulbous Panels, 10 In.	120.00
Lamp, Gone With The Wind, Blue, Morning Glories, Buds, Twigs, Butterfly	55.00
Lamp, Gone With The Wind, Camel, Arabs Scene, 24 In.Tall	345.00
Lamp, Gone With The Wind, Dark To Light Green, Pink Orchid	75.00
Lamp, Gone With The Wind, Floral, Burgundy, Pink, White, 25 In.Tall	155.00
Lamp, Gone With The Wind, Flowers, Yellow, Fuchsia, Electric, 24 In.Tall	150.00
Lamp, Gone With The Wind, Frosted Ball Shade, Footed, Brass, 26 In.Tall	125.00
Lamp, Gone With The Wind, Hand-Painted Pansies, Burnt Rose Ground	165.00
Lamp, Gone With The Wind, Kissing Figures, Red Satin Glass, Wired, 25 In.	265.00
Lamp, Gone With The Wind, Lions' Heads & British Colonial Scenes	205.00
Lamp, Gone With The Wind, Morning Glories, Orange, Yellow, White, 24 In.Tall	125.00
Lamp, Gone With The Wind, Roses White, Apricot, 8 1/2 In.High, Pair	110.00
Lamp, Gone With The Wind, Roses, Pink, White, 23 In.Tall	165.00
Lamp, Gone With The Wind, Satin Glass, Red, Metal Burner Ring	265.00
Lamp, Gone With The Wind, Satin Glass, Red, 4 Puffed Sections, Brass	40.00
Lamp, Gone With The Wind, White Satin Glass, Beaded Drape, 18 In.Tall	95.00
Lamp, Gone With The Wind, Yellow & White Chrysanthemums On Yellow & Pink	245.00
Lamp, Goofus, Miniature, Painted	27.00
Lamp, Grease, Brown Pottery, Drip Saucer Base, 3 1/4 In.High	15.00
Lamp, Grease, Hanging, Hook At Top, Iron, 4 1/2 In.Diameter	22.00
Lamp, Grease, Iron, Chicken Finial, Hanging Hook	35.00
Lamp, Grease, Iron, Handle	15.00
Lamp, Grease, Pan, Four Channel, Iron, 18 In.Tall	95.00
Lamp, Grease, Tin, Conical Base, Reflector, Hanging Hook	7.50
Lamp, Grease, Wrought Iron, Duck Bill, Hanging Hook	15.00
Lamp, Grease, Wrought Iron, Duck Bill, Hook & Pick	17.50
Lamp, Hall, Cranberry, Pointed Hobnail Shade, 6 3/4 In.High	40.00
Lamp, Hall, Green, Beaded Swirl Panels	95.00
Lamp, Hall, Hanging, Adjustable, Etched Cylindrical Frosted Globe, Brass	15.00
Lamp, Hall, Hanging, Cranberry, Swirls, Wired	175.00

Lamp, Hall, Pierced Brass, Tiffany Type Shade, Blue, Green, Amber, Bull's-Eye 275.00
Lamp, Hall, Ribbed, Cranberry 95.00
Lamp, Hand, Blue & Opalescent 40.00
Lamp, Hand, Brass Burner, Glass, Etched Spray 45.00
Lamp, Hand, Brass, Squatty, Dated 1910, 5 1/2 In.Diameter 10.00
Lamp, Hand, Copper 6.75
Lamp, Hand, Etched Glass, Camphene Burner 45.00
Lamp, Hand, Glass, Handle 4.50
Lamp, Hand, Ring Handle, Turkeyfoot Pattern 7.50
Lamp, Hand, Union Shield 15.00
  Lamp, Handel, see Handel, Lamp
Lamp, Hanging, Art Glass Shade, Prisms 350.00
Lamp, Hanging, Brass, Signed Steuben 476, 4 Tiffany Style Shades 50.00
Lamp, Hanging, Candle, Glass, Frosted, Ball Shade, 14 In.Tall 125.00
Lamp, Hanging, Canopy, Bull's-Eye Inserts, Milk Glass Shade, Brass Frame 225.00
Lamp, Hanging, Cast Iron Frame, Milk Glass Shade, 38 In.Long 95.00
Lamp, Hanging, Enamel Flowers, White, Gold, Pink, Opaline, French 300.00
Lamp, Hanging, Flare Shade, Blue Flowers, Jeweled Frame, Pattern Glass Base 150.00
Lamp, Hanging, Hall, Beaded Swirled Pan 110.00
Lamp, Hanging, Hall, Candy Stripe Ball, Pink & Rose 150.00
Lamp, Hanging, Hall, Frosted, Enameled Flowers 110.00
Lamp, Hanging, Hall, Green, Embossed Pictures Around Lamp 110.00
Lamp, Hanging, Hall, Melon Rib, Rose Amber 200.00
Lamp, Hanging, Hall, Ruby Swirled 200.00
Lamp, Hanging, Oriental, Open Pierced Work, 16 In.High 30.00
Lamp, Hanging, Roses, Enamel, White, Blue, Opaline, French 300.00
Lamp, Hanging, Store, Glass Kerosene Font 24.00
Lamp, Hanging, Store, Milk Glass Font, Tin Shade 24.00
Lamp, Hanging, Synagogue, Brass .... Illus 85.00
Lamp, Hanging, Victorian, Iron 69.00
Lamp, Hanging, White Bristol Shade, Font, Smoke Bell, Brass, Wired, France 45.00
Lamp, Holder, Hurricane, Williamsburg 12.00
Lamp, Hurricane, Satin Finish, Gold, Blue, Pink, 10 In.High 90.00
Lamp, Inspection, Marked Ceag, Barnsley, York, England, 8 1/2 In.High 70.00
Lamp, Kennear Patent, Tin, Ufford, Lard, 6 1/2 In.Tall 85.00
Lamp, Kerosene, Cast Iron Wall Bracket, Mercury Reflector 25.00
Lamp, Kerosene, Charleston Font 20.00
Lamp, Kerosene, Copper Base, Frosted Pattern Glass Font, Beaded Chimney 55.00
Lamp, Kerosene, Cranberry Glass, Handle, 11 In.Tall 50.00
Lamp, Kerosene, Cut Glass, Hobstar, Fan, Crosshatching, Marked, 8 In.Tall 75.00
Lamp, Kerosene, Emerald Green, Frosted Bowl, Wild Rose Design 33.00
Lamp, Kerosene, Etched Font, 8 In. 15.00
Lamp, Kerosene, Etched Font, 12 In. 30.00

Lamp, Hanging, Synagogue, Brass

Lamp, Kerosene, Glass Font, Store, Hanging 24.00
Lamp, Kerosene, Glass Font, Tin Wall Sconce 12.50
Lamp, Kerosene, Greek Key Pattern, Large Font, 7 In.Diameter, 9 In.Tall 35.00
Lamp, Kerosene, Green, Upright 45.00
Lamp, Kerosene, Hanging, Brass 54.00
Lamp, Kerosene, Japanese, Copper Font, Carved Wood Base, 21 In.Tall 38.00
Lamp, Kerosene, Metal Base & Tank, By Perkins & House, 22 In.Tall 60.00
Lamp, Kerosene, Milk Glass Base, Clear Tank, 16 In.Tall 30.00
Lamp, Kerosene, Pedestal Base, Urn Font, Electric, Signed, Pair 190.00
Lamp, Kerosene, Princess Feather, Chimney 20.00
Lamp, Kerosene, Purple To Rush, Brass Filigree Base, 18 In.Tall 68.00
Lamp, Kerosene, Roman Key On Bowl, Egg In Sand Base 33.00
Lamp, Kitchen, Green Glass, Brass 6.00
Lamp, Lalique, Hanging, Frosted Amber, Dahlias, 12 In.Diameter 200.00
Lamp, Lard Oil, Tin, Ring Handle Saucer Base, 7 In.Tall 65.00
Lamp, Lard Oil, Tin, Round Base, Big Handle 75.00
Lamp, Lard Oil, Tin, 7 1/2 In.Tall 75.00
Lamp, Lincoln Drape Base, White 30.00
Lamp, Little Buttercup, Miniature, Cobalt 33.00
Lamp, Little Dutchess, Burner & Chimney, Cobalt 22.00
Lamp, Loomlight, Taper, Rushlight Holder, 14 In.Long 175.00
Lamp, Louis XV Style Candelabra, Ormolu, Henry Dasson & Co., 1891 .... 1400.00
Lamp, Louis XV Style Candlestick, Carved Foliage, Tole Shade, Pair 250.00
Lamp, Louis XV Ormolu, Bouillotte, 18th Century, 3 Scrolling Candle Arms 725.00
Lamp, Lucerne, Brass, Snuffer, Tweezers, Pick, 20 In.Tall 79.00
Lamp, Majolica Vase, Roses, 14 In.High 12.50
Lamp, Mandarin, Chinese, Red Dragon Handles, Ornate Brass Mounts, Pair 78.50
Lamp, Marriage, Cups On Sides, Brass, 18 In.Tall 35.00
Lamp, Metal Bottom & Top, Glass Globe 7.50
Lamp, Metal, Base, Mythological Figures & Branch Design, 14 In.High, Pair 12.00
Lamp, Mickey Mouse, Bank, Telephone, Metal & Wood, Green, Red, 8 In.High 18.00
Lamp, Milk Glass Base, 18 In. 22.50
Lamp, Milk Glass, Cranberry, Satin Finish, Brass Frame 129.00
Lamp, Milk Glass, Dresser, Shades, 21 In.High, Pair 70.00
Lamp, Milk Glass, Embossed, Painted Cosmos 19.50
Lamp, Milk Glass, Miniature, Frosted Chimney, 7 3/4 In.High 15.00
Lamp, Milk Glass, Miniature, Matching Shade, Electrified, Pair 45.00
Lamp, Milk Glass, Nutmeg 25.00
Lamp, Milk Jug, 18 In.High, Pair 35.00
Lamp, Miner's Hat, Date, Name 9.00
Lamp, Miner's, Betty, Iron 24.00
Lamp, Miner's, Brass, Carbide, Hook For Hanging, Handle For Carrying 14.50
Lamp, Miner's, Burns Fat, Tin, Hook On 20.00
Lamp, Miner's, Cap Light, Carbide 4.50
Lamp, Miner's, Carbide, Brass .... 5.00 To 8.00
Lamp, Miner's, Carbide, Iron 10.00
Lamp, Miner's, Carbide, Iron, Pint Size, Spout 16.00
Lamp, Miner's, Coal, Tin, Patent 1901 .... 9.50
Lamp, Miner's, Safety, Wolf's Patent 15.00
Lamp, Miner's, Welsh, Safety, Miniature, Brass, Riveted Bonnet & Hook 18.00
Lamp, Miniature, Camphor Glass, Swirl Pattern, Chimney, Clear & Frosted 18.50
Lamp, Miniature, Clear Fish Scale Pattern, Chimney, 5 In.High 35.00
Lamp, Miniature, Clear Glass, Pressed Flowers On Base & Globe, 8 1/2 In. 20.00
Lamp, Miniature, Clear, Swirl Pattern, Straight Chimney, 9 In.High 10.00
Lamp, Miniature, Copper, Acorn 15.00
Lamp, Miniature, Cranberry To Clear, Royal Ivy 175.00
Lamp, Miniature, Cresolene, Clear Glass Base 2.00
Lamp, Miniature, Flemish, Spout, Brass, 10 1/4 In.High 37.50
Lamp, Miniature, Greek Key 15.00
Lamp, Miniature, Handy, Burner 18.50
Lamp, Miniature, Hobnail, 4 5/8 In.High 4.00
Lamp, Miniature, Lincoln Drape, Red 26.00
Lamp, Miniature, Little Banner, Clear Glass 3.50
Lamp, Miniature, Marked Glow Night Lamp, Pat.'08 .... 18.00
Lamp, Miniature, Milk Glass, Fleur-De-Lis 58.00
Lamp, Miniature, Milk Glass, Ribbed, Blue 35.00

Lamp, Miniature, Nutmeg, Cobalt Blue, Wire Handle 37.50
Lamp, Miniature, Nutmeg, Shade, Milk Glass 37.50
Lamp, Miniature, Octagon, Panels, Green & Gold Decor, Chimney, Milk Glass 40.00
Lamp, Miniature, Oil, Clear Glass, Painted Flowers, Burner & Chimney 10.00
Lamp, Miniature, Pattern Glass, Bull's-Eye Around Font, Inverted Ovals Base 18.50
Lamp, Miniature, Pink Satin Base, Drapery Pattern 40.00
Lamp, Miniature, Ribbed, Red Decor In Base, Cone-Shape Shade, Milk Glass 55.00
Lamp, Miniature, Roman Key, Plain Chimney 8.50
Lamp, Miniature, Satin Glass, Red, 8 1/4 In. 110.00
Lamp, Miniature, Twinkle, Clear Handled Base, Ruby Globe Shade 42.50
Lamp, Miniature, Vapo-Cresolene 15.00
Lamp, Molded, Clear, Applied Handle, Pewter Collar & Burner 45.00
Lamp, Mueller Freres, Signed, Desk, Ormolu Metal, Embossed Figure Of Lady 57.00
Lamp, Nailsea Type, Amethyst Iridescence, Grayish Loopings, Mushroom Shade 145.00
Lamp, Nickel Over Brass Foot, Green Font, 13 In.High 14.50
Lamp, Night Glow, Fluted Base, Ruby Shade, U.S.A.Pat.1896, Clear Fluted Base 20.00
Lamp, Night, Figural, Castle, Light Shows Through Windows, Alabaster 25.00
Lamp, Northwood, Vintage, Clear, Signed N, Handle, 13 In.Tall 55.00
Lamp, Nutmeg, Cobalt 25.00
Lamp, Oil, Banquet, Yellow Cased, Gold Enameled Fleur-De-Lis, 28 In.Tall 185.00
Lamp, Oil, Beige Glass, Hand-Painted, Brass Fittings 25.00
Lamp, Oil, Beige, White, Flowers, Leaves, Glass Font, 9 1/4 In.Tall 19.50
Lamp, Oil, Brass & Glass, Electrified 27.50
Lamp, Oil, Brass & Glass, Painted Globe, 18 In.High 12.50
Lamp, Oil, Brass Connectors, Milk Glass Base, 9 1/2 In.Tall 30.00
Lamp, Oil, Brass, Collapsible Handle 35.00
Lamp, Oil, Brass, Hanging, Milk Glass, Shade, 14 In.High 35.00
Lamp, Oil, Brass, 7 1/4 In.High 15.00
Lamp, Oil, Bristol Base, Blue, Brass, 21 In.High 22.50
Lamp, Oil, Candlestick, Brass & Glass, Electrified, 23 In.High 30.00
Lamp, Oil, China, Raised Floral, 19 In.High 15.00
Lamp, Oil, Clear, Flint Font, Brass Stem, Iron Base 16.00
Lamp, Oil, Copper, Handmade, Loop Handle, 2 In.Deep, 4 1/2 In.Diameter 30.00
Lamp, Oil, Double Step, Brass & Marble Base, Clear Pressed Glass 40.00
Lamp, Oil, Egyptian Pattern, Cleopatra Form Shaft, Frosted Font 115.00
Lamp, Oil, Empire, Black Marble, Bronze, Ormolu, Boat Shape, 19th Century, Pair 550.00
Lamp, Oil, Frosted Embossed Glass Font, Blue Pedestal, Butterflies, 18 In. 17.50
Lamp, Oil, Frosted Font, Patent July 2, 1872, Iron Base, Brass Connectors 75.00
Lamp, Oil, Glass, Lion Pattern 90.00
Lamp, Oil, Glass, 5 1/2 In.High .... .50
Lamp, Oil, Goofus, Glass Pedestal, Floral, Embossed, Shade, 10 1/2 In.Tall 25.00
Lamp, Oil, Graphite Pontil, Ribbed Blue Opalescent, 12 In.Tall 39.50
Lamp, Oil, Handle, 8 In.High, Pair 17.50
Lamp, Oil, Hexagonal, Clear, Marble Base, 10 In.High 10.00
Lamp, Oil, Milk Glass, Brass Fittings, Chimney, 15 1/2 In.High 15.00
Lamp, Oil, Pink & White Overlay, Brass Stem, Black Painted Base, 14 In.High 55.00
Lamp, Oil, Pressed Glass, Fine Cut & Diamond Point 30.00
Lamp, Oil, Resembles Inkwell, Figural Sea Horse Handle & Sphinx Cover 15.00
Lamp, Oil, Sawmill Yard Light, Reflecting Mirrors, Circa 1878 .... 60.00
Lamp, Oil, Tall Chimney, Pedestal Base 40.00
Lamp, Oil, Tin, Reflector, Handle 10.00
Lamp, Oil, Victorian, Caramel Slag Shade, Electrified 165.00
Lamp, Oil, Victorian, China & Brass, Columnar, Painted Country Winter Scene 100.00
Lamp, Oil, Victorian, Red & White Overlay, Onyx Base, Electrified 90.00
Lamp, Oil, Wall, Iron Base, Clear Font, Mercury Glass Reflector 148.00
Lamp, Oil, Wrought Iron Hanging Basket, Yellow Globe, 26 In.High 35.00
Lamp, Opaque Canary Stem, Floral, Butterfly, Brass Connection, 14 In. 35.00
Lamp, Orange, White, Ribbed, Molded Shade, Satin Glass, 20 In.High 250.00
Lamp, Overlay, White Cut To Turquoise Blue, Double Step Marble Base 250.00
Lamp, Pairpoint, Shade & Base Signed, Red Shade, 23 In.High 475.00
Lamp, Pan, Hand-Forged, American, 17 In.Long 125.00
Lamp, Paperweight, St.Clair Glass Co., Pair 950.00
Lamp, Parade, Swinging Handle, Tin, 4 1/2 X 5 In. 20.00
Lamp, Parlor, Coleman, White, Ribbed Shade, 20 In.Tall 35.00
Lamp, Pattern Glass, Cobalt 75.00
Lamp, Peacock Feather, 8 In. 20.00

Lamp, Peg, Amber, Ribbed Font, Etched Ball Shade 25.00
Lamp, Peg, Bronze Base, Maple Pedestal, Drop Burner, 7 In.Tall 160.00
Lamp, Peg, Colorless Glass, Pair 40.00
Lamp, Peg, Cut Glass, Brass Collar, Pair 45.00
Lamp, Peg, Frosted Ground, Gold Decoration 22.50
Lamp, Peg, Satin Glass Top, Brass Base, Yellow, Blue, 19 1/2 In.Tall 132.00
Lamp, Peg, Satin Glass, Pink, Ribbed, Matching Font & Shade, Wired, 19 1/2 In. 190.00
Lamp, Peg, Slight Frosting, Enameled Scrolls & Pink & Green Floral 28.50
Lamp, Peg, Yellow, Swirl Leaf Satin, 17 1/4 In. 150.00
Lamp, Peg, 10-Panel Globe, Tin & Cork Drop Burner 35.00
Lamp, Pewter, American, 7 1/4 In.High, Pair 320.00
Lamp, Pewter, English, Weighted Base, 9 In.High, Pair 65.00
Lamp, Phonograph, Made For Capitol, By Burns Pollock Electrical Co. 700.00
Lamp, Piano, Scrolled Iron Legs, Brass Font, Openwork Holder 95.00
Lamp, Polychrome Floral, Butterflies, Hand-Painted, White, Opalescent, 12 In. 64.00
Lamp, Pottery, Gourd Shape, White, 36 In.High 4.00
Lamp, Pressed Glass Bottle, Imprinted Juliet 1830, Napoleon Finial 90.00
Lamp, Pressed Glass Font, Fern Pattern, Finger Grip, Etched Shade 17.50
Lamp, Pressed Glass, Blue Half-Moon Shade, 7 In.Tall 20.00
Lamp, Pressed Glass, Cable Pattern, Stepped Base, 9 In.High 5.00
Lamp, Pressed Glass, Diamond Pattern, 6 In.Tall, Pair 12.50
Lamp, Pressed Glass, Fluted Base, Diamond & Eye Bowl, 7 1/2 In.High 5.00
Lamp, Pressed Glass, Oil, Fern Pattern, 9 In.High 12.50
Lamp, Pressed Glass, Oil, Fluted Base, Ribbed Bowl, 10 In.High 8.00
Lamp, Punty & Star, Flint 50.00
Lamp, Rail, Victorian, Ornamental Iron, White Marble Base, Paper Shade, Pair 35.00
Lamp, Rayo Type, Green Overlay Shade, Electrified 17.50
Lamp, Rayo, Brass, White Bristol Shade 48.00
Lamp, Rayo, Burnished Brass, Lacquered, Wired, White Shade 40.00
Lamp, Rayo, Electrified 35.00
Lamp, Rayo, Milk Glass Shade, Brass Base 47.50
Lamp, Red & White Overlay, Painted White Enamel, Paper Shade, 15 In.High 40.00
Lamp, Rock Crystal & Ormolu, Hexagon Stem, Globe Terminal, Pair 1000.00
Lamp, Rush, Penny Base, Spring Control, Footed, 13 In. 115.00
Lamp, Rushlight, Twisted Stem, Pad Feet 125.00
Lamp, Rushlight, Wood Base, Hand Forged, 10 In. 65.00
Lamp, Sanctuary, Silver Plate, Pierced, Applied Cartouches, C.1720 .... 100.00
Lamp, Sandwich Glass, see also Sandwich Glass, Lamp
Lamp, Sandwich Glass, Clear, Flint, 10 1/2 In.High 35.00
Lamp, Sandwich Glass, Hexagonal, Marble Base, Brass, Column, 10 In.High 17.50
Lamp, Sandwich Glass, Mold Blown, Hand, Dated 1870, Clear, Flint 15.00
Lamp, Sandwich Glass, Stepped Base, 11 In.High 35.00
Lamp, Sandwich, Canary, 9 1/2 In.High 225.00
Lamp, Sandwich, Overlay, White Cut To Clear Font, Blue Stem, Marble Base 250.00
Lamp, Satin Glass, Orange To Apricot, Drape Pattern, Brass Burner, Collar 125.00
Lamp, Sconce, Empire, Ormolu, 3 Light, Drum Shape Bracket, C.1850, Pair 400.00
Lamp, Shade Panel, Patriotic American Carved, Translucent Cow Horn 395.00
Lamp, Shade, Conical, Mottled Blue & Green Glass, Bronze, Bigelow & Kinnard 150.00
Lamp, Shade, Student, Brass Fittings, Dated 1873, Fluted, Etched, Pair 32.00
Lamp, Shade, Tiffany Style, Leaded, 8 Oval Panels, 17 In.Diameter 60.00
Lamp, Shade, Tiffany Type, Iridescent Amber To Yellow, Wave Motifs 210.00
Lamp, Sparking, Bull's Eye 45.00
Lamp, Spoke, Wagon Wheel, Painted 22.50
Lamp, St.Clair, Paperweight, Lavender On White, Milk Glass Base, Pair 50.00
Lamp, Store, Hanging, Brass Font 22.50
Lamp, Student, Acorn, Brass, Double 325.00
Lamp, Student, Brass, Yellow Overlay Shade 350.00
Lamp, Student, Double Brass, Hand-Painted, Stork Motif 275.00
Lamp, Student, Double, Clear Cut Fonts, Green Overlay Shades 400.00
Lamp, Student, Single Light, Signed Miller 170.00
Lamp, Swirled Base & Chimney, Burner, Wire Handle, 6 In.High 14.00
Lamp, Table, Autumn Scene, Metal Base, Signed Pairpoint Mfg.Co., 21 In.High 85.00
Lamp, Table, Leaded Shade, Allover Floral, Blue, Green, Red, Yellow 300.00
Lamp, Table, Reverse Painting, Trees, Streams, Gold, Orange, & Brown 34.50
Lamp, Table, Rock Crystal & Ormolu, Swags On Lion's Paw Feet, Pair 2200.00
Lamp, Table, Satin Finish, Roses, Fleur De Lis 65.00

Lamp, Teardrop With Eyewinkers, Clear Font, 10 In. 20.00
   Lamp, Tiffany, see Tiffany
Lamp, Tiffany Type, Hanging, 22 In.Panels, Caramel & Green 250.00
Lamp, Tiffany Type, Hanging, 3 6 In.Shades, 6 Panels, Caramel & Green 95.00
Lamp, Tiffany Type, Hanging, 8 22 In.Panels, Caramel & Green 250.00
Lamp, Tiffany Type, Iridescent Amber, Bronze Base, Leaf Devices 150.00
Lamp, Tiffany Type, Wisteria, Stained Glass, 30 In.High 1900.00
Lamp, Tin Sconce, Orange Painted Base, 12 1/2 In. .... Illus   15.00

Lamp, Tin Sconce, Orange Painted Base, 12 1/2 In.

Lamp, Torch, Miner's, Brass, Alcohol, German 11.50
Lamp, Torch, Tin, Brass Tube Burner, 5 X 5 In. 10.00
Lamp, Urn Shape, White, Mottled, Frosted Shade, 17 In.High 4.00
Lamp, Victorian, Clear, Finger Grips, Pair 15.00
Lamp, Victorian, Frosted Glass, China & Brass Base, 22 In.High 20.00
Lamp, Victorian, Oil, Red & Frosted, Pear Font, Electrified 100.00
Lamp, Wall Light, Blown Glass & Brass, 19th Century, 2 Branch, Pair 525.00
Lamp, Wall Light, Louis XVI, Provincial, Oval Glass Beads, 18th Century, Pair 550.00
Lamp, Wall Light, Ormolu & Rock Crystal, 31 In.High, Pair 700.00
Lamp, Wall, Kerosene, Reflector, Chimney, Tin, Brass Finial 40.00
Lamp, Wall, Reflector & Globe, Glass Font, Cast Iron Holder 25.00
Lamp, Wall, Shell Design, Clear Glass, Brass Holder, Brass Trim, Pair 50.00
Lamp, Wedding, Crystal, 7 In.Tall 35.00
Lamp, Whale Oil, Black Wrought Iron, Gothic Spires, Zodiac Signs 75.00
Lamp, Whale Oil, Blown Glass, Pewter Top 25.00
Lamp, Whale Oil, Brass Saucer Base, Electrified 22.50
Lamp, Whale Oil, Brass, American, Lemon Font, C.1800, 8 In.High 85.00
Lamp, Whale Oil, Brass, Chimney 35.00
Lamp, Whale Oil, Brass, Dolphins, Pair 75.00
Lamp, Whale Oil, Brass, Saucer Base, Fluted Column, Dolphin Handle, 8 1/2 In. 45.00
Lamp, Whale Oil, Brass, 6 In.High 15.00
Lamp, Whale Oil, Brass, 7 In.High 15.00
Lamp, Whale Oil, Brass, 8 In.High 15.00
Lamp, Whale Oil, Bull's-Eye, Marble Base, 9 1/2 In.High 55.00
Lamp, Whale Oil, Clear Glass, American Shield, Brass & Marble Base 17.50
Lamp, Whale Oil, Clear Terraced Base, Blown Elongated Font, 11 In.High 45.00
Lamp, Whale Oil, Clear, Ribbed Step Base, Pewter Collar & Burner 35.00
Lamp, Whale Oil, Crimped Saucer Base, Cone Shape Font, Tin Handle, Brass Top 16.00
Lamp, Whale Oil, Excelsior Pattern, Two Pronged, Clear, Flint, 11 1/4 In.Pair 225.00
Lamp, Whale Oil, Fishing, Tin, Three Spout, Curved Shield 50.00
Lamp, Whale Oil, Flint, Waffle & Thumbprint, 10 1/2 In.High 65.00
Lamp, Whale Oil, Hexagon Pestle Stem & Base, Octagon Font, 9 In. 37.00
Lamp, Whale Oil, Lyre Pattern 42.00
Lamp, Whale Oil, Night, Reflector 95.00
Lamp, Whale Oil, Pewter, American, C.1810 .... Illus 250.00
Lamp, Whale Oil, Pewter, Pedestal, 7 1/2 In.Tall 115.00
Lamp, Whale Oil, Pewter, Pedestal, 8 1/2 In.Tall 150.00
Lamp, Whale Oil, Sandwich Glass, Blue & White Swirl, Brass & Marble Base 60.00
Lamp, Whale Oil, Sandwich Glass, Hexagonal, Knob Stem, 8 In.High 15.00
Lamp, Whale Oil, Sandwich Glass, Pewter Rim, 9 In. 62.50

Lamp, Whale Oil, Pewter, American, C.1810
See Page 285

Lamp, Whale Oil, Sandwich Globe, Pierced Tin Top, Bail	75.00
Lamp, Whale Oil, Sandwich, Three Mold, Loop Pattern, Pewter Collar, 4 In.Tall	48.00
Lamp, Whale Oil, Sawtooth Motif, Flint, Sandwich	52.50
Lamp, Whale Oil, Sawtooth, Clear, Sandwich, Flint, 10 1/2 In.Tall	135.00
Lamp, Whale Oil, Signed American Pewter, Capen & Molineux, N.Y., C.1825-50	245.00
Lamp, Whale Oil, Tole, Green Paint, Gold Lines, 10 1/2 In.High	90.00
Lamp, Whale Oil, Vaseline, Opalescent Flint Base, Arch Font, Pewter Burner	70.00
Lamp, Whale Oil, Waffle, Thumbprint, Font, Base, 8 In.	37.00
Lamp, Whale Oil, Wick, Shield, Embossed Lamb, 22 In.	39.50
Lamp, Wick Guard, Brass, 4 1/2 X 4 1/2 In.	10.00
Lamp, Wooden Pitcher, Paper Shade, 10 1/2 In.High	15.00
Lantern, Barn, Clear Globe	6.50
Lantern, Bicycle, Kerosene, Three Red Reflectors, Neverout Safety, 6 In.	27.00
Lantern, Brass, Bell Bottom, Clear Globe, Mc In Raised Letters	40.00
Lantern, Brass, Bell Bottom, Dl&w In Raised Letters On Globe	40.00
Lantern, Brass, NYO&W Bell Bottom, NYO&W Etched On Globe	40.00
Lantern, Brass, Folding, Chinese Junk, Bail Hook, 12 In.High	27.50
Lantern, Brass, Hanging, Cone Shape, Animal Figures, 22 In.High	35.00
Lantern, Brass, Hanging, Frosted Globe, 32 In.High	17.50
Lantern, Brass, Hanging, Multicolored Panes	40.00
Lantern, Brass, Holder At Side, 11 In.High	45.00
Lantern, Brass, Porters Sons, N.Y., Pat.Date 1882, Clear Globe	75.00
Lantern, Candle, Folding, Isinglass Windows	18.00
Lantern, Candle, Folding, Stonebridge, 1900	14.00
Lantern, Candle, Folding, Three Windows, Handle, Stonebridge, Pat.1900, Tin	20.00
Lantern, Candle, Folds	65.00
Lantern, Candle, Four Sided, Wide Bail, Curved Bands	55.00
Lantern, Candle, Hand Pierced, Tole, Cylinder	85.00
Lantern, Candle, Tin, Drum Shape, Handles, Clip, & Chain	20.00
Lantern, Candle, Tin, Glass, 10 In.High	10.00
Lantern, Candle, Tin, Green & Salmon Paint	55.00
Lantern, Candle, Tin, Pierced	65.00
Lantern, Candle, Tin, Punched Top, Three Glass Panes	12.50
Lantern, Candle, Tin, Punched, Half Cylindrical, Glass Front, Guard	200.00
Lantern, Candle, Tin, Punched, Scalloped Arched Openings, Gilded	35.00
Lantern, Candle, Tin, Punched, Triple Arch Pane, Applied Angels, Cream & Gilt	55.00
Lantern, Candle, Tin, 6 Sided, Punched Top	20.00
Lantern, Candle, Tole	19.00
Lantern, Candle, Wooden, Four Glass Panes, 12 In.Tall	45.00
Lantern, Copper, Brass Fittings, Red Globe, 21 In.High	225.00
Lantern, Crown Top, Wire Guards, Oil & Candle Burner	17.50
Lantern, Dietz, Blizzard, Farm, Cobalt Chimney, 14 In.	15.00
Lantern, Dietz, Comet, Clear Globe	6.00
Lantern, Dietz, Junior, Brass	15.00
Lantern, Dietz, No.2, Blizzard, Clear Globe	8.00
Lantern, Dietz, Traffic Yard, Red Iron, Red Swirled Globe, Electrified	10.0
Lantern, Dietz, Wagon, Colored Shade, Bull's-Eye, Reflector, Pair	19.00

Lantern, Farm, Dietz, Monarch, U.S.A, Red Globe, 13 1/2 In. 15.00
Lantern, Kerosene, Dark Room, Red Glass 13.00
Lantern, Miniature, Super Baby, Tin, Made In Germany 10.00
Lantern, Onion, Tin Star, Pierced Top & Bottom 65.00
Lantern, Peaked Roof, Isinglass Windows, Signed Stonebridge, Tin 18.00
Lantern, Pull-Up Type, Candle, Wire Bail, Bull's-Eye, Wooden, Paint Worn 27.50
Lantern, Railroad, B&M On Frame, Clear Globe 20.00
Lantern, Railroad, Brass Top, Whale Oil, Pat.1869 .... 50.00
Lantern, Railroad, NYCS On Top, Dietz Vesta, Red Globe 10.00
Lantern, Railroad, Porters Sons, N.Y.Pat.1882, Clear Globe, Brass 75.00
Lantern, Railroad, Rayo, No.39, Clear Globe 15.00
Lantern, Railroad, Red Globe, Marked C.H.& D. 30.00
Lantern, Railroad, Star Headlight Co., No.3297, Etched Red Globe 50.00
Lantern, Railroad, Whale Oil, Brass, Clear Globe, Pat.1869 .... 50.00
Lantern, Road, Pennsylvania, Highway, 2 .... 4.00
Lantern, Scout, Dietz, Tin, Pat.Date, 8 In. 15.00
Lantern, Ship, Copper, 16 In., Pair 228.00
Lantern, Ship's, Red Globe 17.50
Lantern, Signal Light, Boat, Fluid Burner 14.00
Lantern, Skater Type, Brass, 7 In. 14.00
Lantern, Skater, Tin 12.50
Lantern, Skater's 10.00
Lantern, Square Sides, Cut Star, Points, Flat Handle, Tin, Circa 1870 .... 71.50
Lantern, Switch, Colored Lens, Kerosene Fonts 35.00
Lantern, Tin & Glass, 10 In.High 10.00
Lantern, Tin, Carrying, Kerosene Burner, Reflector 12.50
Lantern, Tin, Crown Top 7.50
Lantern, Tin, Painted .... *Illus* 125.00

Lantern, Tin, Painted

Lantern, Tin, Pierced 55.00
Lantern, Tin, Square, Mustard Paint, To Be Mounted On Wall 115.00
Lantern, Tin, Wire Guard, Crown Top 17.50
Lantern, Torch, Kerosene, Locomotive Engineer's, Brass, Copper, 16 1/2 In. 24.50
Lantern, Whale Oil, Pierced Tin Top & Bottom, Bulbous Globe, Bail, 13 In. 42.50
Lapis Lazuli Bottle, Snuff, Blue, Gold Flecks 135.00
Lapis Lazuli, Casket, Russian, Steel Mounted, Rectangular, Tula, C.1850 .... 600.00
Laszlo Ispanky, Figurine, Dolphins 750.00
Laszlo Ispanky, Figurine, Horse 300.00
Laszlo Ispanky, Figurine, Reverie 350.00
Laurel & Hardy, Plate, Pair 30.00
Lawrence Welk, Tray, Lawrence & Alice Dancing 15.00
Lawrence Welk, Tray, Lawrence & Lennon Sisters 15.00
Lawrence Welk, Tray, Lawrence & Orchestra 15.00
Lawrence Welk, Tray, Lawrence, Alice, 1914 Dodge 15.00

Le Gras is a name that appeared on French Cameo Glass of the late
nineteenth and early twentieth centuries.
Le Gras, Bowl, Peacock Design, Flowers, Yellow, Orange, Blue, Marked, 8 1/4 In. 95.00
Le Gras, Bowl, Rose, Cameo, Red Flowers, Leaves, Stems 110.00

Le Gras, Bowl, Rose, Signed, 4 1/2 In.Diameter, 4 1/2 In, High	55.00
Le Gras, Bowl, Rose, Winter Scene, Crimped Top, Signed, 5 In.Diameter, 7 In.	85.00
Le Gras, Box, Winter Scene, Cover, Signed, 4 1/2 In.Diameter, 3 In.High	60.00
Le Gras, Compote, Lavender Ground, Chestnuts, Cameo, 13 X 3 1/2 In.High	135.00
Le Gras, Vase, Boat, Trees, Orange, 12 3/4 In.Tall	98.50
Le Gras, Vase, Cameo Cut, Signed	125.00
Le Gras, Vase, Cameo, Acid Cut, Purples, Gold Enamel, Signed, C.1865	95.00
Le Gras, Vase, Cameo, Enamel, Signed, 7 3/4 In.Tall	135.00
Le Gras, Vase, Cameo, French, Summer Scene, Square, Signed, 8 In.High	97.50
Le Gras, Vase, Cameo, Ovoid, Beige & Coral, Coral & Shells, Signed, 6 1/2 In.	100.00
Le Gras, Vase, Cameo, Tall, Swelling, Gray & Ocher Dogwood On Frosted Green	100.00
Le Gras, Vase, Cameo, White, Pink, Red, Frosted, Leave, Berry, 9 In.High	250.00
Le Gras, Vase, Forest Scene, Cameo Cut, Orange, Green, Signed, 7 1/4 In.Tall	155.00
Le Gras, Vase, Sunset Scene, Boat, Ocean, Acid Cut, Cameo, Square Shape, 9 In.	145.00
Le Gras, Vase, Trees, Bridge, Stream, Signed, 4 In.Tall	45.00
Le Gras, Vase, Wheel Cut, Scenic, Signed, Six Color, 4 In.	175.00
Le Gras, Vase, Yellow & Orange, Blue, 9 In.	225.00
Le Verre Francais, Bowl, Geometric Designs	55.00
Le Verre Francais, Chalice, Cameo, Flowers, Yellow, Brown, Pink, 5 In.	125.00
Le Verre Francais, Compote, Signed Charder, Orange, Cameo	195.00
Le Verre Francais, Lamp, Cameo, Signed Charder, Orange, Blue, & Lavender	425.00
Le Verre Francais, Vase, Cameo Cut, Reddish Orange To Wine Coloring	350.00
Le Verre Francais, Vase, Cameo, Cat Motif, Signed, 11 In.High	235.00
Lead, Bust, Satyr & Nymph, C.1750, Pair	300.00
Lead, Figurine, Donkey Pulling Cart, 3 In.Long	6.00
Leather, Case, For High Silk Hat	22.50
Leather, Collar, Horse	5.00
Leather, Cuff, Cowboy's, Tooled, Cheyenne, Wyo., Pair	15.00
Leather, Gloves, Man's, Horsehide, Patent Date 1908, Engraved Horses, Pair	5.00
Leather, Pouch, On Pole, Church Collection	10.00
Leather, Shoes, Bog, Pattens For Horse, Pair	25.00
Leather, Vessel, Drinking	75.00

*Leeds Pottery was made at Leeds, Yorkshire, England, from 1774 to 1878.
Most Leeds Ware was not marked. Early Leeds pieces had distinctive
twisted handles with a greenish glaze on part of the creamy ware. Later ware
often had blue borders on the creamy pottery.*

Leeds, Bowl, Blue Decoration, Reserves Of Chinese Scenes	100.00
Leeds, Cup & Saucer, Handleless, Swirled, Brown Border, Polychrome Sprig	37.50
Leeds, Plate, Green Feather Edge, Basket Of Flowers Center	185.00
Leeds, Platter, Blue Feather Edge, 19 In.	27.50
Leeds, Platter, Oval, White, Blue Border, 10 X 14 In.	14.00
Leeds, Strainer, Cheese, Creamware, Tiered Mold	75.00
Leeds, Tureen, Soup, Ladle, Cover, Cream Glaze, Ruins In Forest Scene, Gold	50.00

*Lenox China was made in Trenton, New Jersey, after 1906. The firm
also makes a porcelain similar to Belleek.*
  Lenox, see also Belleek

Lenox Belleek, Dish, Salt, Artist's Palette, 3 Gold Feet, Signed	6.00
Lenox, Bird, 3 1/4 In.Long, Green Wreath Mark	14.00
Lenox, Bowl, Cereal, Princess	3.00
Lenox, Cup & Saucer, Princess	1.00
Lenox, Cup & Saucer, Sterling Silver Holder & Saucer, Set Of 8	165.00
Lenox, Figurine, Nude With Greyhound At Her Side, Dated '37, 13 In.Tall	35.00
Lenox, Liner, Demitasse, Script L In Laurel Wreath	15.00
Lenox, Mug, King Neptune Scene, Gold, 3 1/2 In.High	35.00
Lenox, Plate, Autumn Pattern, Basket Of Fruit Center, 1910, 10 1/2 In., 6	75.00
Lenox, Plate, Boehm Bird, Wood Thrush, 10 1/2 In.Diameter	75.00
Lenox, Plate, Bread & Butter, Princess	5.00
Lenox, Plate, Cattail, Gold Wreath, 9 In., 8	50.00
Lenox, Plate, Dinner, Princess	5.80
Lenox, Plate, Fuchsia Border Encrusted With Gold, 10 1/2 In., 12	60.00
Lenox, Plate, Hand-Painted Floral, Signed	30.00
Lenox, Plate, Ming, 8 1/4 In., Belleek	15.00
Lenox, Plate, Salad, Princess	4.65
Lenox, Plate, Service, Cream, Double Gold Band, 10 1/2 In.Diameter, 5	30.00

Lenox, Plate, Soup, Lenox Rose 8.50
Lenox, Relish, Princess 8.00
Lenox, Salt & Pepper, Princess, Mill 15.00
Lenox, Salt Dip, Belleek 5.00
Lenox, Salt, Swan, Master, Pink 12.50
Lenox, Sugar & Creamer, Princess 12.00
Lenox, Swan, 2 3/4 In.High, Green Wreath Mark 6.50
Lenox, Swan, 5 In. 12.00
Lenox, Tea Set, Belleek, Footed, Hand-Painted Portraits, Gold, 3 Piece 75.00
Lenox, Teapot, Brown, Silver Filigree 25.00
Lenox, Teapot, Sterling Floral Overlay, Green Wreath Mark 22.50
Lenox, Vegetable, Princess 14.00
    Lighting Devices, see Candleholder, Candlestick, Lamp, etc.

*Lightning Rod Balls are collected for their variety of shape and color.
These glass balls were at the center of the rod that was attached to the
roof of a house or barn to avoid lightning damage.*
Lightning Rod, Ball, Ceramic, White 2.50
Lightning Rod, Ball, Fluted, Turquoise Blue 5.50
Lightning Rod, Ball, Milk Glass, Blue, Plain 5.00
Lightning Rod, Ball, Milk Glass, Green, Plain, Round 12.50
Lightning Rod, Ball, Milk Glass, White, Moon & Star 15.00
Lightning Rod, Ball, Milk Glass, White, Plain, Round 5.00
Lightning Rod, Ball, Plain, Round, Clear 10.00
Lightning Rod, Ball, Plain, Round, Ruby Red 12.50
Lightning Rod, Ball, Plain, Round, Sun Colored Amethyst 5.00
Lightning Rod, Metal Fitting 3.00
Li'l Abner, Paper Dolls, 1951 .... 12.50

*Limoges Porcelain has been made in Limoges, France, since the
mid-nineteenth century. Fine porcelains were made by many factories, including
Haviland, Ahrenfeldt, Guerin, Pouyat, Elite, and others.*
Limoges, see also Haviland
Limoges, Atomizer, Perfume, Pearl Luster, Hand-Painted Medallions 15.00
Limoges, Basket, Flowers, Gold, Signed Buisson, 4 1/2 In.Long 45.00
Limoges, Bouillon Cup & Saucer, Pink Poppy, Green Stem 4.25
Limoges, Bowl, Center, Venice Pattern, Dated 1898 .... 20.00
Limoges, Bowl, Deep, Vignaud, Molded Handle 7.00
Limoges, Bowl, Fruit, Fruit Decoration, Artist-Signed, 9 In. 17.00
Limoges, Bowl, Grape Leaf, Gold, Dvc, France, R.Deliveries & Co., Limoges 20.00
Limoges, Bowl, Marked Cfh Over Gdm, France, Blue Carnations, Pink Flowers 4.00
Limoges, Bowl, Mayonnaise, Depose, Attached Saucer, Pink Roses, Gold, T & V 17.50
Limoges, Bowl, Orange Poppies Outlined In Black, Coronet, 9 3/4 In. 17.50
Limoges, Bowl, Punch, Hand-Painted, Signed D.C.France, 2 Piece 125.00
Limoges, Bowl, Soup, Gold Band, Yellow & Pink Roses, Marked M 6928, T & V 7.00
Limoges, Box, Barbotine Cobalt, Round, Covered, 2 Nudes On Cover 30.00
Limoges, Box, Enamel, Lake Scene 40.00
Limoges, Box, Flowers, Hand-Painted, Blue, Gold, Hinged, 10 In.Across, 2 1/2 In 275.00
Limoges, Box, Pill, Hand-Painted, Hinged 22.00
Limoges, Box, Powder, Floral On Lid, Hand-Painted, Footed, 3 In.Diameter 10.00
Limoges, Brooch, Portrait, 1 1/2 In.Square 4.75
Limoges, Butter Pat, Autumn Leaf 3.50
Limoges, Butter Pat, Gold Band, Yellow & Pink Roses, Marked M 6928, T & V 2.50
Limoges, Butter Pat, Roses, Gold Trim 2.50
Limoges, Butter, Covered, Pansy Decor 30.00
Limoges, Candlestick, Enamel, Square Cluster Column, Gilt Mounts, Pair 450.00
Limoges, Chamberstick, White, Violets, Gold Handle & Edge, 7 In.Diameter 32.50
Limoges, Chocolate Pot, Cream Shaded To Pink, Gold Trim .... 36.00 To 40.00
Limoges, Chocolate Pot, Flowers, Pink, Green, Hand-Painted, France, 10 In. 18.50
Limoges, Chocolate Pot, Green Floral, Gold Trim 32.50
Limoges, Chocolate Set, Roses, Leaves, Pink, Green, Gold 87.50
Limoges, Coffee Set, Pouyat, Oriental Designs, 3 Piece 40.00
Limoges, Creamer, Violet Decoration 15.00
Limoges, Cup & Saucer, American Eagle, Gold, Footed, Demitasse 7.50
Limoges, Cup & Saucer, Black-Eyed Susans & Birds, 8 1/2 In. Plate, Set 25.00
Limoges, Cup & Saucer, Blue, Buff Border, Multicolor Sprigs 3.00

Limoges, Cup & Saucer, Bouillon, Gold Band, Yellow & Pink Roses, Marked 15.00
Limoges, Cup & Saucer, Bouillon, Gold Handle, Haviland, Set C*i* 8 .... 45.00
Limoges, Cup & Saucer, Chocolate, Pastel, Swirled Side, Gold Handle, 4 .... 20.00
Limoges, Cup & Saucer, Demitasse 6.50
Limoges, Cup & Saucer, Demitasse, Floral, Set Of, 6 ....: 36.00
Limoges, Cup & Saucer, Demitasse, Green & Pink Rose, White & Gold Border, 12 .... 150.00
Limoges, Cup & Saucer, Demitasse, White, Etched Gold Border 50.00
Limoges, Cup & Saucer, Demitasse, White, Purple & Gold Bands, Gold Leaves, 12 .... 150.00
Limoges, Cup & Saucer, Floral Design, Gold, Purple, Cylinder Cup, Set Of 6 .... 150.00
Limoges, Cup & Saucer, Flower Design, White, Blue, Gold Edge, Signed, Dated 30.00
Limoges, Cup & Saucer, Gold Band 5.00
Limoges, Cup & Saucer, Peach, Green, Birds 9.50
Limoges, Cup & Saucer, Pink Clover, Black Birds, 8 1/2 In.Plate, Set 25.00
Limoges, Cup & Saucer, Pink, Apple Blossoms; Butterflies, 8 1/2 In.Plate, Set 25.00
Limoges, Cup & Saucer, Tea Roses, Yellow, Pink, Marked 7.50
Limoges, Cup & Saucer, Wedding Band, Panel Side, 12 .... 84.00
Limoges, Dessert Set, Pink Roses, Gold, J.Pouyat, Limoges, 6 Piece 32.50
Limoges, Dish, Bone, Floral Design, Pink, Gold, Set Of 6 .... 36.00
Limoges, Dish, Butter, Flowers, Gold, Hand Painted 15.00
Limoges, Dish, Butter, Pink, Flowers, Gold, Six Pats, Set 30.00
Limoges, Dish, Pancake, White, Blue, Pink, Roses, Gold, Scrolls, Cover 25.00
Limoges, Dish, Ramekin, Floral Design, Pink, Gold 15.00
Limoges, Dish, Serving, Three Sections, Handle, White, Gold, Pink Floral, Birds 75.00
Limoges, Dish, Vegetable, Cover, Pink Poppies, Beading, Handles, Haviland, Pair 30.00
Limoges, Dish, Vegetable, Footed, Oval, Pink Flowers, Green, Gold, T & V, France 26.00
Limoges, Eggcup, Blue & White, France, 5 .... 12.95
Limoges, Fish Set, Hand-Painted, Gold Rococo Border 195.00
Limoges, Fish Set, Hand-Painted, Yellow, Platter, Ten Plates, Signed 145.00
Limoges, Fish Set, Marked Limoges, France, Lavender Ground, Floral, 10 Piece 115.00
Limoges, Ice Cream Set, J.Pouyat Limoges, Pink Roses, Gold Platter 52.00
Limoges, Jar, Cookie, Coronet, Pink Roses, Gold Handles & Finial 35.00
Limoges, Jar, Cracker, Flowers, Pink, Gold, Scrolls, Two Handle 23.50
Limoges, Jar, Cracker, Multicolor Floral, Gold On Handles & Finial 75.00
Limoges, Jar, Pomade, Hand-Painted, Pastel, 2 1/2 In. 6.50
Limoges, Jar, Powder, Green, Hand-Painted Pink & White Roses, Green Leaves 18.00
Limoges, Jar, Tobacco, Profile Of Indian, Gold Pipe Forms Handle On Lid 30.00
Limoges, Mug, Hand-Painted, Gold Handle, Signed, Black Bird Ogalala Sioux 30.00
Limoges, Mug, Purple Berries, White Floral, Green & Gold Borders, Set Of 6 .... 75.00
Limoges, Mug, Scenic, Gold Dragon Handle, Artist-Signed, 6 1/2 In.Tall 18.00
Limoges, Pitcher, France, Bird, Berries & Flowers, Signed Gay Palmer 67.50
Limoges, Pitcher, People Design, Gold, 18th Century, 1 1/2 In.Tall 4.00
Limoges, Pitcher, Tankard Shape, Hand-Painted Purple Grapes, 11 In.High 70.00
Limoges, Pitcher, Tankard, Hand-Painted, Signed, 15 In.Tall 97.50
Limoges, Plate, Blue, Buff Border, Multicolor Sprigs 2.00
Limoges, Plate, Bread & Butter, Embossed Gold Band, Tracery 9.50
Limoges, Plate, Cake, Allover Strawberry Design, 9 In. 25.00
Limoges, Plate, Chrysanthemum Pattern, 7 1/2 In.Diameter 8.00
Limoges, Plate, Coronet, Yellow, Pink, Green, Roses, Signed, 8 3/4 In.Diameter 18.00
Limoges, Plate, Cupid, Limoges, T & V France, 10 1/2 In. 20.00
Limoges, Plate, Dinner, Embossed Gold Band, Tracery 9.50
Limoges, Plate, Ducks, Hand-Painted, Scalloped, Signed Coudert, 10 3/4 In. 125.00
Limoges, Plate, Elite Pattern, Scalloped Gilt Edge, Floral Center, 9 In. 5.00
Limoges, Plate, Fish, Hand-Painted, Signed Max, 9 1/2 In. 18.00
Limoges, Plate, Fish, Scalloped, Signed, 9 In. 16.00
Limoges, Plate, Flambeau Bird, Ribbed Edge, Signed, Gray, 10 1/2 In. 75.00
Limoges, Plate, Floral, Foliage, Gold, Orange, 8 3/4 In.Diameter 10.00
Limoges, Plate, Flowers, Yellow, Blue, Fluted Border, Signed Bell, 7 1/2 In. 3.00
Limoges, Plate, Flowers, Yellow, Gold, Iridescent, Eight Sided, Handle 18.00
Limoges, Plate, Fruit, Plum & Blossoms, Hand-Painted, 8 1/2 In.Diameter 12.50
Limoges, Plate, Fruit, Scalloped, Gold Trim, Signed, 10 In. 16.00
Limoges, Plate, Game Bird, Hand-Painted, Scalloped Edge, Set Of 6 .... 155.00
Limoges, Plate, Game, Cobalt Rim, Gold Trim, Artist Ludov, 9 1/2 In.Diameter 45.00
Limoges, Plate, Game, Hand-Painted, Gold Scalloped Border, 9 In. 25.00
Limoges, Plate, Game, Hand-Painted, Scalloped, 10 In. 48.00
Limoges, Plate, Game, Mallard Duck, Pink, Signed Max 55.00
Limoges, Plate, Game, Pheasant, Gold Rococo Border, Signed Max, 10 In. 43.00

Limoges, Plate, Oyster, Half Shells, 8 3/4 In.	35.00
Limoges, Plate, Oyster, White, H.& Co.	8.50
Limoges, Plate, Pheasant, Gold Rim, Signed, 10 In.Diameter	45.00
Limoges, Plate, Pink Morning Glories, Bassett, Austria, 6 In.	2.00
Limoges, Plate, Pink Morning Glories, Bassett, Austria, 7 1/2 In.	3.00
Limoges, Plate, Pink Morning Glories, Bassett, Austria, 8 1/2 In.	4.00
Limoges, Plate, Raised Gold Design, 2 Open Handles, Haviland, France	10.00
Limoges, Plate, Sparrow, Branch, Berries, Red, Gold, 7 1/2 In.Diameter	12.00
Limoges, Plate, Swimming Duck, 10 In.	48.00
Limoges, Plate, T & V, Hand-Painted, Wide Gold Band On Green, Dogwoods	30.00
Limoges, Plate, Tulips, Turquoise & Green Foliage, Lavender Center, Pair	15.00
Limoges, Plate, Two Birds In Flight, Spray Of Iris, Gold Trim	55.00
Limoges, Plate, Two Birds, Green Ground, Gold Border, Artist Laney, 8 1/2 In.	45.00
Limoges, Plate, White & Gold Edge, Gold Floral Border, T & V, France	24.00
Limoges, Plate, White House, Harrison 1892, T & V France Decorated	80.00
Limoges, Platter, Blue Border, Roses, Gold Acanthus Leaves, Marked T & V	20.00
Limoges, Platter, Fish, Elite Pattern, Scalloped Gilt Edge, Floral Center	25.00
Limoges, Platter, Floral Design, Yellow, Pink, Marked, 13 In.Diameter	15.00
Limoges, Platter, Gold Band, Yellow & Pink Roses, Marked M 6928, T & V	15.00
Limoges, Platter, Green & Pink Floral, Gold, Theodore Haviland, Limoges	20.00
Limoges, Platter, Pink Floral Garland Border, Embossed Handles, 18 3/4 In.	28.00
Limoges, Portrait, Lady, Signed L.Dubois 1900, Wood Frame, 6 1/2 In.Square	200.00
Limoges, Powder Box, Hand-Painted .... *Illus*	20.00

Limoges, Powder Box, Hand-Painted

Limoges, Ramekin, Underplate, Pink Roses, Gold Rim, Set Of 12	75.00
Limoges, Sauce, Blue Bachelor Buttons, Chas.Field, Haviland Limoges, France	3.00
Limoges, Sauce, Blue Flowers, Gold Trim	3.00
Limoges, Sauceboat & Underplate, Elite Pattern, Scalloped Gilt Edge, Floral	10.00
Limoges, Shaker & Tray, Talc, Hand-Painted Gold On Eggshell, Footed	37.50
Limoges, Shaving Mug, Name, Dated 1905, Dark Blue Flowers On Light Green	18.00
Limoges, Soup, Embossed Gold Band, Tracery	9.50
Limoges, Sugar & Creamer, Autumn Leaves, Red & Green Marks, Cover	25.00
Limoges, Sugar & Creamer, Violets, Gold	25.00
Limoges, Sugar, Pitcher, & Dish, Shell Shape, Miniature	20.00
Limoges, Tea Set, Floral, Lavender, Pink, Brown, Gold.Sugar, Creamer, Cover	45.00
Limoges, Tea Set, Hand-Painted, Gold	39.00
Limoges, Tea Set, Roses, White, Pink, Gold, Creamer, Sugar, Six Cup & Saucer	37.50
Limoges, Gea Set, Tressemakes & Vogt, Limoges, Marguerite, Patent 7/1/84	35.00
Limoges, Teapot, Morning Glories, Green, White, Pink, Creamer, Sugar, Set	47.50
Limoges, Tray, Bread, Flowers, Purple, Blue, Gold Edge, 14 X 6 1/2 In.	10.00
Limoges, Tray, Celery, Lavender & Yellow Floral, Scalloped	17.50
Limoges, Tray, Celery, Six Matching Salts, Circa 1842	40.00
Limoges, Tray, Dresser, Floral Design, Blue, Pink, Hand-Painted, Signed	17.00
Limoges, Tray, Floral & Apple Design, Pink, Marked, Oval, 14 X 16 In.	65.00
Limoges, Tray, Pin, Blossoms, Pink, Fluted Edge, Signed	10.00
Limoges, Tray, Sandwich, Handled. 10 In.	12.00
Limoges, Tureen, Roses	25.00
Limoges, Tureen, Soup, Hand-Painted Pink Flowers & Wheat, Lid, Mark 1875	38.00
Limoges, Tureen, Soup, Twisted Rope Design Handles & Finial, Gold Outline	75.00
Limoges, Vase, Bud, Enameled, Woman, Signed Vibert, 4 In.Tall	150.00
Limoges, Vase, Flowers, Gold, Signed Buisson, Pair	50.00
Limoges, Vase, Rainbow Colors, Bud Shape, Signed, 4 1/4 In.Tall	75.00

Limoges, Vegetable, Covered, Oval, Scalloped	20.00
Limoges, Wash Set, 6 Piece	145.00

Lithophanes are porcelain pictures made by casting clay in layers of various thicknesses. When a piece is held to the light, a picture of light and shadow is seen through it. Most lithophanes date from the 1825 to 1875 period. A few are still being made.

Lithophane, Pitcher, Puzzle, Victorian Scene, Nude Lady On Bottom	75.00
Lithophane, Plaque, Scene, Children At Play, Leaded Glass Frame, 6 X 7 In.	45.00
Lithophane, Plaque, Scenic, People, Animals, Pierced For Hanging, 4 X 5 In.	22.50
Lithophane, Stein, Negro Boy, 5 In.High	135.00
Lithophane, Stein, Regimental	110.00
Lithophane, Tea Warmer, Four Panels, Brass Frame, Hinged Handle	95.00
Lithophane, Tea Warmer, Scenic Panels, Nickel Plated Holder	50.00
Little Orphan Annie, Decoder, 1936	17.00
Little Orphan Annie, Paper Dolls, Junior Commandos, 1942	25.00
Little Orphan Annie, Stove, Utensils	17.00
Little Orphan Annie, Tumbler, Bettleware, Green	17.50
Little Orphan Annie, Wristwatch, Leather Band	35.00

Liverpool, England, has been the site of several pottery and porcelain factories from 1716 to 1785. Some Earthenware was made with transfer decorations, Sadler and Green made print-decorated wares from 1756. Many of the pieces were made for the american market and featured patriotic emblems such as eagles, flags, and other special-interest motifs.

Liverpool, Mug, Odd Fellows, Dated 1832, Cream, Black Transfer	110.00

Loetz Glass was made in Austria in the late nineteenth century. Many pieces are signed Loetz, Loetz-Austria, or Austria, and a pair of crossed arrows in a circle. Some unsigned pieces are confused with Tiffany Glass.

Loetz, Creamer, Threaded Effect, Applied Green Decoration On Clear	30.00
Loetz, Dish, Shell, Gold, Iridescent, Applied Design, Mark	150.00
Loetz, Inkwell, Swirl Design, Blue	75.00
Loetz, Rose Bowl, Aqua Blue, Pinched Sides	27.50
Loetz, Rose Bowl, Scalloped, Tree Bark, Emerald Color, Pewter Handles	70.00
Loetz, Vase, Applied Butterflies, Ruffled Top, 7 3/4 In.High	90.00
Loetz, Vase, Blue, Green, Gray, Slender, Unsigned, 7 In.Tall	37.50
Loetz, Vase, Bud, 7 1/2 In.High, Pair	45.00
Loetz, Vase, Feather Design, Gold, Blue, Iridescent, Unsigned, 12 In.Tall	125.00
Loetz, Vase, Four Panels, Swirled, Dimpled, Gold Floral Decor, 11 In.	45.00
Loetz, Vase, Green With Gold Iridescence	45.00
Loetz, Vase, Ivorine, Gold Pebbly Base, Applied Green Strands At Top	145.00
Loetz, Vase, Light To Dark Green & Purple, Flared Top, 7 In.High, Pair	85.00
Loetz, Vase, Melon Rib, Squatty	50.00
Loetz, Vase, Pinecone, Metal Stand, Signed	85.00
Loetz, Vase, Purple To Green, Iridescent	30.00
Loetz, Vase, Raindrop Pattern, Blue To Purple To Green, Unsigned, 11 In.	65.00
Loetz, Vase, Ruffled Top, Blue Iridescent Swirls, Light Blue Inside	45.00
Loetz, Vase, Signed Loetz, Austria, 2 Handles, Rainbow Hues, Gold Mottling	300.00
Loetz, Vase, 8 1/2 In. *Illus*	95.00
Lone Ranger, Bullet, Silver	7.00
Lone Ranger, Button, Pin, Multicolor	2.50
Lone Ranger, Pedometer	15.00
Longton Hall, Plate, Strawberry, Birds, C.1754, 9 In.Diameter	275.00
Longton Hall, Sauceboat, White Scroll Handle, Littler's Blue Ground, C.1755	375.00

Lotus Ware was made by the Knowles, Taylor & Knowles Company of East Liverpool, Ohio, from 1890 to 1900.

Lotus Ware, Bowl, Fishnet Decoration, Artist Initials	250.00
Lotus Ware, Creamer, Undecorated	97.50
Lotus Ware, Dish, Decorated, 8 In. *Illus*	250.00
Lotus Ware, Tea Set, Fishnet & Blue Enamel Decor	425.00
Lotus Ware, Vase, Reticulated Ends, Artist Signed	185.00
Lowestoft, see Chinese Export	
Ludwigsburg, Bowl, Gilt Rim, Basket-Weave Border, C.1760, Deutsche Blumen	250.00
Ludwigsburg, Coffeepot, Pear Shape, 3 Scroll Feet, Bouquets, C.1765	30.00

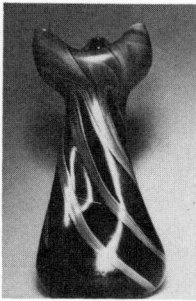

Loetz, Vase, 8 1/2 In.
See Page 292

Lotus Ware, Dish, Decorated, 8 In.
See Page 292

Ludwigsburg, Jug, Milk, Tripod, Cylindrical, Scroll Handle & Spout, C.1765-70	70.00
Ludwigsburg, Sucrier, Covered, Harbor Scenes, C.1765	375.00
Ludwigsburg, Teapot, Painted Flowers, Ovoid Shape, Scroll Handle, C.1760-65	120.00
Luneville, Bowl, Oriental Scene, Red, Blue, Yellow, 9 In.Diameter	22.50
Luneville, Pitcher, Cobalt To White, Jeweled, 6 1/2 In.	20.00
Luneville, Plate, Peach Design, Signed O.Bert, 8 3/4 In.Diameter	30.00
Luneville, Plate, Pink Green Gold, Roses, Marked, 10 In.	15.00
Luneville, Plate, Plum, Obert K & G	20.00
Luneville, Vase, Geometrically Cut, Gold, Signed, 8 In.Tall	325.00
Luneville, Vase, Natives, Desert, Yellow, Blue, France, 10 1/2 In., Pair	20.00

Lusterware was meant to resemble copper, silver, or gold. It has been used since the sixteenth century. Most of the Luster found today was made during the nineteenth century.

Luster Art, Shade, Gas, Signed	25.00
Luster, Blue, Creamer, Dark Blue Ground, Chinese Reserves	20.00
Luster, Blue, Pitcher, Embossed Babies, 7 1/2 In.High	20.00
Luster, Canary, Mug, Child's, Brown Transfer, Circa 1815	160.00
Luster, Canary, Pitcher, Black Transfer Medallions Of Hope & Faith	400.00
Luster, Copper, Bowl, Blue Band, 5 1/2 In.Diameter	27.50
Luster, Copper, Bowl, Blue Band, 6 1/4 In.Diameter	25.00 To 35.00
Luster, Copper, Bowl, Butterflies, Red, Green, White, 5 1/4 In.Diameter	30.00
Luster, Copper, Bowl, Floral, Raised Design, Blue, 5 1/2 In.Diameter, 3 In.	65.00
Luster, Copper, Bowl, Tan Band, 6 1/4 In.Diameter	27.50
Luster, Copper, Creamer, Blue Band, Luster Design, 3 In.	35.00
Luster, Copper, Creamer, Mustard Glass, Band	50.00
Luster, Copper, Creamer, Rockingham Band	29.00
Luster, Copper, Cup & Saucer, Blue Band	48.00
Luster, Copper, Cup & Saucer, Handleless, Vine-Like Copper Luster Trim	37.50
Luster, Copper, Goblet	68.00
Luster, Copper, Goblet, Blue Band, 4 1/4 In.High	22.50
Luster, Copper, Goblet, Raised Band Of Flowers, Cone Shape, Blue Band	22.50
Luster, Copper, Mug, Beaded Design, Pink, White, Applied Handle	32.00
Luster, Copper, Mug, Child's	9.00
Luster, Copper, Mug, Child's, Sanded Center, 2 3/4 In.	15.00
Luster, Copper, Mug, Green Band, 3 7/8 In.High	27.50
Luster, Copper, Mug, Purple Luster Band, Leaf Decoration	15.00
Luster, Copper, Pitcher, Blue & Mustard Bands, 5 1/2 In.High	15.00
Luster, Copper, Pitcher, Blue & White Band, House Pattern Decoration	40.00
Luster, Copper, Pitcher, Blue Band	25.00
Luster, Copper, Pitcher, Blue Band, Marked Allerton, England, 4 In.High	25.00
Luster, Copper, Pitcher, Blue Band, 5 1/2 In.High	35.00
Luster, Copper, Pitcher, Blue Design, 2 1/2 In.High	12.00
Luster, Copper, Pitcher, Children At Play, Blue Band, Ringed Body, 3 1/2 In.	26.00
Luster, Copper, Pitcher, Cream, Floral, Raised Design, Blue Band, 3 1/2 In.	48.50
Luster, Copper, Pitcher, Dancers, Blue Trim, Diamond Device On Bottom	42.00

Luster, **Copper**, Pitcher, Embossed Blue Medallions, Octagonal 95.00
Luster, **Copper**, Pitcher, Embossed Flowers, 7 1/2 In.High 30.00
Luster, **Copper**, Pitcher, Embossed, Staffordshire, C.1850 .... *Illus* 120.00
Luster, **Copper**, Pitcher, Enamel Decor, 3 1/2 In. 25.00
Luster, **Copper**, Pitcher, Enameled Floral Decoration, 4 1/2 In.High 55.00
Luster, **Copper**, Pitcher, Figures Dancing, Raised, 6 In.Tall 35.00
Luster, **Copper**, Pitcher, Floral Design, Blue, Green, Swan Neck, 7 1/2 In.Tall 45.00
Luster, **Copper**, Pitcher, Flowers, Hand-Painted, 6 In.Tall 40.00
Luster, **Copper**, Pitcher, Green, Floral Design, 5 1/2 In. 45.00
Luster, **Copper**, Pitcher, Masked Spout, Blue Band, Embossed Child & Animal 40.00
Luster, **Copper**, Pitcher, Melon Shape, Embossed Flower Bands At Bottom, 6 In. 48.50
Luster, **Copper**, Pitcher, Pink Sanded Band, 2 1/2 In.High 20.00
Luster, **Copper**, Pitcher, Raised Figures, 7 1/2 In.High 12.50

Luster, Copper, Pitcher, Embossed,
Staffordshire, C.1850

Luster, **Copper**, Pitcher, White Bands, Pink Luster Decoration, 5 1/2 In.High 55.00
Luster, **Copper**, Pitcher, Yellow Band, 5 1/2 In.High 30.00
Luster, **Copper**, Pitcher, Yellow Luster Band, 4 1/2 In.High 45.00
Luster, **Copper**, Pitcher, 2 Blue Bands 25.00
Luster, **Copper**, Pitcher, 5 1/4 In.High 22.50
Luster, **Copper**, Salt, Footed, Blue Band 22.00
Luster, **Copper**, Salt, Pink-White Band, Footed 18.00
Luster, **Copper**, Sugar, Open, Allerton's, C.1895, Blue Band 30.00
    Luster, **Copper**, Tea Lleaf, see Ironstone, Tea Lleaf
Luster, **Copper**, Teapot, English, 9 1/2 In.Long 10.00
Luster, **Copper**, Vase, Miniature, 2 In.High 8.00
Luster, **Copper**, Yellow Band, 5 1/2 In.High 30.00
Luster, **German**, Sugar, Lilies Of The Valley, Roses, Open Handles, 3 Feet 15.00
Luster, **Gold**, Chocolate Set, Grapes, M.W.& Co., Germany, 9 Piece 25.00
Luster, **Orange**, Tea Set, Czechoslovakia, Mother-Of-Pearl Lining 25.00
Luster, **Pine**, Cup, Handleless, Black Transfer Of Birds & Flowers 6.00
Luster, **Pink**, Bowl, Bird Of Paradise Transfer, 6 1/2 In.Diameter 55.00
Luster, **Pink**, Bowl, Flaring, Footed, C.1820, Sunderland 150.00
Luster, **Pink**, Bowl, Floral Decoration, Footed, 5 1/2 In.Diameter, 2 1/8 In. 35.00
Luster, **Pink**, Bowl, Pink Bands, Transfer Printed, 19th Century, Staffordshire 350.00
Luster, **Pink**, Bowl, Transfer Printed, Constitution & Java, 1797, Sunderland 160.00
Luster, **Pink**, Creamer & Sugar 50.00
Luster, **Pink**, Creamer, House, Old Castle, England 7.50
Luster, **Pink**, Cup & Saucer, Butterflies Band, English 22.00
Luster, **Pink**, Cup & Saucer, Carnation Pattern 10.00
Luster, **Pink**, Cup & Saucer, Encrusted Gold Decor 8.00
Luster, **Pink**, Cup & Saucer, Flowers, Leaves 25.00
Luster, **Pink**, Cup & Saucer, Footed, Gilt Beading, Scalloped Top 15.00
Luster, **Pink**, Cup & Saucer, German, Reserve Of Ludington Harbor 10.00
Luster, **Pink**, Cup & Saucer, Handleless 22.50
Luster, **Pink**, Cup & Saucer, Mustache, Raised Blue, Gold Trim 19.50
Luster, **Pink**, Cup Plate, Purple Luster House Decoration 20.00
Luster, **Pink**, Gravy Boat, House Pattern 50.00

Luster, **Pink**, Mug, Child's 37.50
Luster, **Pink**, Mustache Cup & Saucer, Applied Gold Rose 27.50
Luster, **Pink**, Mustard Set, 4 Pieces 12.50
Luster, **Pink**, Pitcher, Schoolhouse, C.1830-40, Bulbous 125.00
Luster, **Pink**, Plate, Dessert, Kittens In Card Game 20.00
Luster, **Pink**, Plate, Floral Decoration, 7 1/2 In.Diameter 12.50
Luster, **Pink**, Plate, House, 19th Century, 7 1/2 In. 28.00
Luster, **Pink**, Plate, Marked Charles Allerton & Sons, England, 6 7/8 In. 11.00
Luster, **Pink**, Plate, Mottled, 7 1/4 In.Diameter 17.50
Luster, **Pink**, Plate, 6 In.Diameter 10.00
Luster, **Pink**, Plate, 6 5/8 In. 12.50
Luster, **Pink**, Teapot, Rebecca-At-The-Well Raised Design 45.00
Luster, **Pink**, Washbowl & Pitcher, Greek Key Bands, Black Handle 35.00
Luster, **Purple**, Bowl, Bird-Of-Paradise Transfer, 6 1/2 In.Diameter 55.00
Luster, **Purple**, Plate, King's Rose Type Decoration, Purple Luster Border 42.50
Luster, **Purple**, Plate, Picket Fence, Goodwins & Harris Impressed, 6 1/2 In. .. 15.00
Luster, **Silver**, Bowl, 5 1/2 In.Diameter 20.00
Luster, **Silver**, Creamer, Dolphin Handle, 4 1/2 In.Long 12.50
Luster, **Silver**, Creamer, 19th Century, Festoon & Shell Motifs, 5 In.High 60.00
Luster, **Silver**, Goblet, 4 3/4 In.High 10.00
Luster, **Silver**, Pitcher, Flower Design, Collard Base, 5 In.High 22.50
Luster, **Silver**, Tea Set, 4 Piece 35.00

> *Lustres are mantel decorations, or pedestal vases, with many hanging glass*
> *prisms. The name really refers to the prisms, and it is proper to refer to a*
> *single glass prism as a lustre. Either spelling luster or lustre, is correct.*

Lustres, **Black**, Enameled Flowers, 14 In., Pair 119.50
Lustres, **Brass**, Ribbed Shades, Crystal Pendants, Steuben, 13 In., Pair 150.00
Lustres, **Light Green**, Heavy Prisms, 11 In. 115.00
Lustres, **Ruby**, Crystal Prisms, 14 In. 59.50
Lustres, **Sapphire Blue**, Triangular Crystal, 14 In.High, Pair 100.00

> *Lutz Glass was made in the 1870s by Nicholas Lutz at the Boston and*
> *Sandwich Company. He made a delicate and intricate threaded glass of*
> *several colors. Other similar wares are referred to as Lutz.*

Lutz, **Bowl**, Finger, Cherub Heads Applied, Blue 85.00
Lutz, **Bowl**, Finger, Matching Plate, Threaded, Set Of 7 .... 119.00
Lutz, **Bowl**, Plate, Cranberry, Applied Amber Threads, Blown, Ruffled 40.00
Lutz, **Bowl**, Threaded, Ruffled Top, Apricot, 4 1/2 In.Diameter 42.50
Lutz, **Dish**, White Threaded Latticinio, 4 1/2 In.Square 60.00
Lutz, **Plate**, Threaded, Ruffled Edge, Rubena Verde Coloring, 6 In.Diameter ... 75.00
Lutz, **Vase**, Brown To Gold Iridescent, Orange, Purple, Blue At Top, 7 1/2 In. ... 250.00
Lutz, **Vase**, White & Pink, Narrower Neck, Pedestal Base, 6 In. 35.00
Magazine, **Arthur's Home Magazine**, June & November 1864, 2 .... 4.00
Magazine, **Cosmopolitan**, 1907-1917, 60 Issues 25.00
Magazine, **Delineator**, The, December, 1909 .... 2.00
Magazine, **Designer**, The, October, 1912, Kewpie Kutouts .... 1.50 To 4.00
Magazine, **Godey's Lady's Book**, Vol.39040, July, 1847-June 1850 .... 50.00
Magazine, **Good Housekeeping**, 1920 .... 4.00
Magazine, **Harper's Monthly**, Dec.1887-May 1888 .... 4.00
Magazine, **Ladies' World**, The, January, 1912 .... 1.25
Magazine, **Ladies' Home Journal**, The, July, 1903, Maxfield Parrish 3.00
Magazine, **People's Home Journal**, The, July, 1912, O'neill Ad 1.25
Magazine, **People's Home Journal**, The, May, 1912, Coca-Cola Ad 1.25
Magazine, **Ladies' Home Journal**, The, September, 1903 .... 2.25
Magazine, **Ladies' Home Journal**, 1913 .... 4.00
Magazine, **Life**, 1904 .... 3.00
Magazine, **Modern Priscilla**, 1917 .... .50
Magazine, **Peterson's**, 1874-1877, 5 .... 6.00
Magazine, **Playboy**, 1953-1970, Complete Run 695.00
Magazine, **Saturday Evening Post**, The, April 23, 1938, Rockwell 2.50
Magazine, **Saturday Evening Post**, The, April 24, 1915 .... .75
Magazine, **Saturday Evening Post**, The, February 19, 1938, Rockwell 2.00
Magazine, **Saturday Evening Post**, The, November 12, 1904 .... .70
Magazine, **Saturday Evening Post**, The, 1885 .... 2.00
Magazine, **Woman's Home Companion**, March, 1906 .... 1.25

Magic Lantern, 12 Slides, Boxed	45.00
Maize, Bowl, John Locke, Libbey, 4 In.High, 9 In.Diameter	85.00

Majolica is any pottery glazed with a tin enamel. Most of the Majolica found today is decorated with leaves, shells, branches, and other natural shapes and in natural colors. It was a popular nineteenth century product.

Majolica, Bowl, Fruit, Pebbly White Center, Green Leaves, Scalloped, 10 In.	18.00
Majolica, Bowl, Leaves, Green, Orange, Blue, White, Dated 1878, 11 In.	47.50
Majolica, Bowl, Punch, Shell Shape, Blue & Amber, 13 In.Diameter	50.00
Majolica, Box, Sardine, Separate Tray, Lavender, J.Jones & Sons	37.50
Majolica, Box, Sardine, Tray Attached, Brown Basket Weave, V.P.Co.	30.00
Majolica, Box, Tobacco, 6 In. .... *Illus*	22.00
Majolica, Butter Chip, Green With Gray Fish Head	5.00
Majolica, Butter, Shells & Seaweed Base, Mottled	26.00
Majolica, Cake Stand, Pink, Panels, Evergreen Trees, Finial On Cover	85.50
Majolica, Candlestick, Green, Pyramid Of 3 Monkeys, Signed, 9 In.High	57.50
Majolica, Compote, Card, Etruscan	24.00
Majolica, Compote, Sunflower, Marked G.S.H., 9 In. X 5 1/2 In.High	50.00
Majolica, Creamer, Shell & Seaweed, Etruscan .... *Illus*	70.00

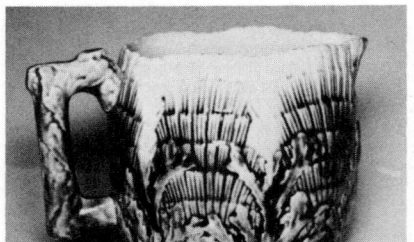

Majolica, Creamer, Shell & Seaweed, Etruscan

Majolica, Box, Tobacco, 6 In.

Majolica, Creamer, Yellow, Lily Flowers, Aqua, Brown Rope Handle	17.50
Majolica, Cup & Saucer, Mustache, Cosmos Pattern, Lavender Lining	100.00
Majolica, Dish, Flower & Leaf Design, Dated 1870, 9 X 14 In.	165.00
Majolica, Dish, Hen With Chicks Under Her, Ladle Is Half-Egg Bowl	90.00
Majolica, Dish, Leaf Shape, Etruscan, 9 In.	14.00
Majolica, Dish, Leaf Shape, Pink, Green, White, 12 X 9 In.	25.00
Majolica, Dish, Shell, Lavender Lining	18.00
Majolica, Ewer, Cobalt With Floral Center, 14 In.Tall, Pair	100.00
Majolica, Ewer, Cobalt, Floral Center, Pair	125.00
Majolica, Holder, Match, Fat Jolly Man Sitting, Beer Barrel, Doulton Lambeth	39.00
Majolica, Holder, Match, Shaggy Dog, Brown, Yellow, 5 1/4 In.Tall	28.00
Majolica, Humidor, Green, Pink Floral On Corners, Brown Leaf On Base	19.50
Majolica, Humidor, Pug Dog Head	65.00
Majolica, Jar, Tobacco, Covered, Figure Of Young Man, 5 1/2 In.High	6.00
Majolica, Jug, Syrup, Signed Etruscan, Bamboo Pattern, Pewter Top	55.00
Majolica, Jug, Syrup, Yellow Corn, Leaves	26.00
Majolica, Jug, Toby, Fat Man Head, Smiling, Hat Forming Spout	75.00
Majolica, Pitcher, Barrel Shape, Rosebud Decoration, 8 1/2 In.High	17.50
Majolica, Pitcher, Brown Basket Weave, Cream, Raised Pink Floral, Green	4.00
Majolica, Pitcher. Chrysanthemums, Blue, Amber, Scallop Base, Signed, 8 1/4 In	21.00
Majolica, Pitcher, Cream, Shell & Seaweed, 3 1/2 In.	55.00
Majolica, Pitcher, Figural, Fish, Charcoal, Green, Cream, Brown, Rose Interior	45.00
Majolica, Pitcher, Fish, 12 In.High	17.50
Majolica, Pitcher, Water, Fish & Shells, Pink, 6 1/2 In.Tall	35.00
Majolica, Pitcher, Woman's Head, Crown, Blue, Signed, 8 In.Tall	90.00
Majolica, Pitcher, Yellow Base, Taupe Top, Pink Rose, Green Leaves, 5 1/4 In.	12.00

Majolica, Plate, Blue Background, Leaves, Roses	15.00
Majolica, Plate, Blue Ground, Embossed Berries, Leaves, 6 In.	10.00
Majolica, Plate, Double Pear	4.00
Majolica, Plate, Etruscan, Shell & Seaweed	22.00
Majolica, Plate, Fish, Charcoal, Cream, Gold, Brown, Turquoise	45.00
Majolica, Plate, Flowers, 7 In.	12.00
Majolica, Plate, Green Leaf Center, Yellow Basket Edge, Signed Etruscan	19.50
Majolica, Plate, Green, White, Yellow, Leaf, Fern, Floral, 7 1/2 In.Diameter	8.00
Majolica, Plate, Leaf Pattern, 10 In.Diameter	18.00
Majolica, Plate, Portrait, Young Girl, French, C.1850, Green	20.00
Majolica, Plate, Seashell Shape, Signed, C.1864, Pair	185.00
Majolica, Plate, Stippled Yellow Ground, Pink Edge, Green Leaves, Germany	8.50
Majolica, Plate, Strawberry Design, Red, Gold, 7 1/2 In.Diameter	18.00
Majolica, Platter, Etruscan, Shell & Seaweed, Scalloped	125.00
Majolica, Platter, Leaves, Berries, Raised, Cream, Green, Red, 9 X 12 In.	22.50
Majolica, Platter, Oak Leaf, Stem & Acorn Handle, 12 X 9 In.	25.00
Majolica, Platter, Oval, On Vase, Leaf Pattern, Zigzag Trim, Handles, Pair	55.00
Majolica, Platter, Oval, 11 1/2 In.Long	16.00
Majolica, Platter, Shell & Seaweed, Etruscan	45.00
Majolica, Salt & Pepper, Fish, Standing, Blue & Tan	7.50
Majolica, Spittoon, Mums, Lavender Lined	35.00
Majolica, Sugar, Cauliflower	30.00
Majolica, Sugar, Etruscan, Covered, Pink Lining, Yellow, Lily Flowers	19.50
Majolica, Tea Set, Flowers, Blue, Rose, Yellow, Teapot, Creamer, Sugar	80.00
Majolica, Tea Tile, Footed Square, Wire Frame	15.00
Majolica, Teapot On Plate, Sugar, Creamer, Pond Lilies, Gray Blue	23.50
Majolica, Teapot, Cabbage Leaf Pattern	8.00
Majolica, Teapot, Shell & Seaweed, Etruscan, 6 1/2 In.High	85.00
Majolica, Vase, Figural, Rooster, Green & Cream Color	22.00
Majolica, Vase, Fisherman With Net, 10 In.	12.00
Majolica, Vase, Flowers, Pink, Brown, Handles, 12 In.Tall	35.00
Majolica, Vase, Mulberry, Green, Maize Flower, Maize Inside, Two Handles	12.50
Majolica, Vase, Raised Floral Vine, 3 Feet	20.00
Majolica, Vase, Raised Rose, 5 1/2 In.High	18.00
Majolica, Vase, Rooster, Green Foliage, 5 In.	25.00
Majolica, Vase, Sanded, Applied Decoration, Bulbous, 2 Handles, Green, Yellow	13.50
Majolica, Vase, Sanded, Ewer Shape, Cream, White, Autumn Hues	13.50
Majolica, Vase, Seashell, Pedestal, Gray & White Conch Shell, Pink Interior	35.00
Majolica, Vase, Village Scene, Forest Scene Reverse, Signed Munay, Pair	49.50
Majorelle, Vase, Iridescent Red, Wrought Iron Collar, Handles, Signed	130.00

Marbles of glass were made during the nineteenth century. Venetian swirl, clear glass, sulfides, and marbles with frosted white animal figures embedded in the glass were popular. Handmade clay marbles were made in many places, but most of them came from the pottery factories of Ohio and Pennsylvania. Occasionally, real stone marbles of onyx, carnelian, or jasper can be found.

Marble, Bennington Type, Blue, 1 In.Diameter	4.00
Marble, Bennington Type, Blue, 1 1/4 In.Diameter	5.00
Marble, Bennington Type, Medium Brown, 1 In.Diameter	5.00
Marble, Bennington Type, Medium Brown, 1 1/4 In.Diameter	5.00
Marble, Candy Stripe	10.00
Marble, Candy Swirl, Blue, Orange, & Yellow	6.00
Marble, Medium Brown, Cat's-Eye	5.00
Marble, Medium Brown, Smoky, 3/4 In.Diameter	4.00
Marble, Multicolored, Swirled Pattern, 1 1/2 In.Diameter	16.00
Marble, Sandwich, Inside Swirl	2.50
Marble, Sulfide, Bear, 1 1/2 In.Diameter	24.00
Marble, Sulfide, Fish In Center, 2 In.	37.50
Marble, Sulfide, Fish, 1 7/8 In.Tall	34.00
Marble, Sulfide, Goat, 2 In.Diameter	28.00
Marble, Sulfide, Lamb	19.00
Marble, Sulfide, Lion, 1 1/2 In.Diameter	22.00
Marble, Sulfide, Rabbit	26.75
Marble, Sulfide, Running Deer, Headless, 2 In.Tall	25.00
Marble, Sulfide, Sheep, 1 3/4 In.	30.00
Marble, Sulfide, Sitting Dog, 1 1/4 In.	25.00

Marble, Swirl, Red, Green, & White Core, Yellow Outside Stripes, 7 In.	50.00
Marble, Swirl, 1 7/8 In.	15.00
Marblehead, Vase, Green, 5 In.High	22.00

Mary Gregory Glass is identified by a characteristic white figure painted on dark glass. It was made from 1870 to 1910. The name refers to any glass decorated with a white silhouette figure and not just the sandwich glass originally painted by Miss Mary Gregory.

Mary Gregory, Ale Glass, Panels, White Enamel Girl, Tinted Face	22.00
Mary Gregory, Basket, Bride, Cranberry, Girl, Flower Spray, Footed, 7 1/2 In.	135.00
Mary Gregory, Bell, Cobalt Blue	7.00
Mary Gregory, Bell, Cranberry	12.50
Mary Gregory, Bottle, Barber, Amethyst, Girl Sitting On Bench	68.00
Mary Gregory, Bottle, Barber, Amethyst, White, Boy, Foliage	65.00
Mary Gregory, Bottle, Barber, Girl With Racket, Cobalt Blue, 8 1/4 In.Tall	55.00
Mary Gregory, Bottle, Barber, Girl, Flowers, White, Pewter Top	65.00
Mary Gregory, Bottle, Barber, Green, Boy With Butterfly Net, 7 1/2 In.	60.00
Mary Gregory, Bottle, Barber, White Girl, Amethyst	75.00
Mary Gregory, Bottle, Blue .... *Illus*	95.00

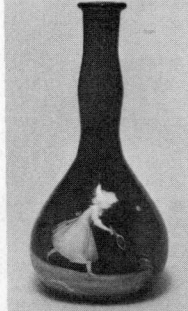

Mary Gregory, Bottle, Blue

Mary Gregory, Bottle, Perfume, White Enameled Boy, Foliage, Blown	42.00
Mary Gregory, Bottle, White Enamel Girl Holds Butterfly Net, Stopper	40.00
Mary Gregory, Bottle, White Enameled Girl, Foliage, Green Paneling	60.00
Mary Gregory, Box, Cranberry, Girl & Foliage, Crimped Edge, Cover, 6 In.	95.00
Mary Gregory, Box, Girl, Bird, Flowers, Hinged Cover, Cobalt Blue	200.00
Mary Gregory, Box, Jewel, Boy With Butterfly, Green	125.00
Mary Gregory, Box, Jewel, Garnet Block, White Boy With Sailor Hat, Footed	125.00
Mary Gregory, Butter, Covered, Cobalt, Boy Riding Bicycle	29.50
Mary Gregory, Carafe, Green, White Girl & Trees, 7 In.Tall	75.00
Mary Gregory, Creamer & Sugar, Green, White Enamel, Girl & Boy	65.00
Mary Gregory, Creamer, Cranberry Glass, White Enamel Child, 3 5/8 In.Tall	35.00
Mary Gregory, Decanter, Blue	85.00
Mary Gregory, Decanter, Figure Of Girl, White, Clear, Stopper, 9 In.Tall	75.00
Mary Gregory, Ewer, Cranberry, Boy In White Gold, Pedestal Base	75.00
Mary Gregory, Goblet, Blue, Gold, Enamel, Footed	75.00
Mary Gregory, Jar, Powder, Cobalt, Hinged Cover, Three Brass Feet	55.00
Mary Gregory, Juice, Boy Figure, Cranberry	10.00
Mary Gregory, Lamp, Black Amethyst, White Enamel Girl, Butterflies	165.00
Mary Gregory, Mug, Amber, White Enamel Elves, Applied Handle	35.00
Mary Gregory, Mug, Girl Reaching For Birds, Says Mildred 1892, Clear Handle	95.00
Mary Gregory, Pitcher, Blue, White Enamel Boy, Flowers, 10 In.	85.00
Mary Gregory, Pitcher, Boy, Butterfly, Green, Enamel, Gold, White, 6 1/2 In.	48.00
Mary Gregory, Pitcher, Boy, White, Blue Handle, Olive To Amber, Bulbous, 12 In	145.00
Mary Gregory, Pitcher, Cupid Design, Green, White, Applied Handle, 7 In.	85.00
Mary Gregory, Pitcher, Emerald Green, Blown, Enameled	20.00
Mary Gregory, Pitcher, Girl With Twig, Applied Reeded Handle	65.00
Mary Gregory, Pitcher, Girl, Flowers, Clear To Cranberry, Enamel, 12 1/2 In.	95.00
Mary Gregory, Plate, Boy & Girl Playing, Amethyst, 8 1/2 In.Diameter	75.00
Mary Gregory, Shaker, Salt, Boy, Clear With White, Tinted Face	37.50

Mary Gregory, Stein, Boy, Green, White, Blown 30.00
Mary Gregory, Stein, Girl, Green, White, Blown 30.00
Mary Gregory, Tumbler, Baby Thumbprint, Boy Blowing Bubbles, Amber, Blue 37.50
Mary Gregory, Tumbler, Blue, White Enamel Boy, Inverted Thumbprint 50.00
Mary Gregory, Tumbler, Boy With Twig, Cranberry 50.00
Mary Gregory, Tumbler, Boy, Girl, Ruby & Gold, Pair 18.50
Mary Gregory, Tumbler, Boy, Olive To Amber, Gold Rim, Paneled Body 40.00
Mary Gregory, Tumbler, Girl, Topaz 34.00
Mary Gregory, Tumbler, Green, Boy 32.50
Mary Gregory, Tumbler, Green, Girl 32.50
Mary Gregory, Tumbler, Lemonade, Blue, Handled 37.50
Mary Gregory, Tumbler, On Frame, Blue, Mary Playing Harp 15.00
Mary Gregory, Tumbler, Sapphire Blue, Ribbed 27.50
Mary Gregory, Tumbler, White Enameled Girl, Sapphire Blue 28.00
Mary Gregory, Tumbler, Woman Holding Wheat, White, Turquoise, Ribbed 35.00
Mary Gregory, Vase, Black Amethyst, White Enamel Girl, Flowers, 10 In.Tall 60.00
Mary Gregory, Vase, Blue To Amber, Girl Holding Flowers, 7 In. 65.00
Mary Gregory, Vase, Blue, Applied Crystal Petals, White Enamel Boy 75.00
Mary Gregory, Vase, Boy & Girl, Amethyst, Scalloped, 11 In.Tall 85.00
Mary Gregory, Vase, Boy With Flowers, White Enamel, Green, 7 In. 55.00
Mary Gregory, Vase, Bud, Clear, All White Girl 30.00
Mary Gregory, Vase, Bud, Girl With Bird, Cranberry, Silver Holder, 6 1/2 In. 110.00
Mary Gregory, Vase, Cranberry, Boy In White, 3 1/4 In.High 52.50
Mary Gregory, Vase, Cranberry, Satin, Couple In Colonial Costume 95.00
Mary Gregory, Vase, Custard, Girl Arranging Flowers In Holder, 12 In.Tall 85.00
Mary Gregory, Vase, Man, Woman, Colonial Dress, Bulbous, Cranberry, 10 In.Tall 145.00
Mary Gregory, Vase, Marigold, Boy In White, 5 1/2 In.Tall 65.00
Mary Gregory, Vase, Shaded Pink Satin, Molded, 5 1/2 In.High, Pair 30.00
Mary Gregory, Vase, Stick, Green, Boy 25.00
Mary Gregory, Vase, Vaseline, Boy In White, 4 In.Tall 57.50
Mary Gregory, Water Set, Boy & Girl Design, Clear, 7 Piece .... 100.00 To 245.00

*Masonic Shrine Glassware was made from 1893 to 1917. It is occasionally
called Syrian Temple Shrine Glassware. Most pieces are dated.*
Masonic, Album, Souvenir, Penna.Meeting Places, 1920 .... 5.00
Masonic, Chain, Watch, Elk Tooth, Enamel, Yellow Charm 15.00
Masonic, Chalice, Footed, Syria Shrine, 1908, St.Paul 40.00
Masonic, Champagne, Horseshoe, Emblem, Syria Shrine, 1909, Louisville, Ky. 40.00
Masonic, Champagne, Rochester, New York, 1911, Man On Camel 60.00
Masonic, Champagne, St.Paul, Minnesota, 1908, Ruby, Gold, Black Base 60.00
Masonic, Champagne, Syria Shrine, Souvenir, New Orleans, 1910, Emblem 40.00
Masonic, Champagne, Tobacco Leaf, Louisville, 1909, Set Of 6 .... 300.00
Masonic, Charm, Symbols In Circle, Elaborate Chasing, Gold, England 12.50
Masonic, Cuff Links, Onyx & Gold 10.50
Masonic, Cup & Saucer, Date, Emblem, Syria Shrine, 1906, Los Angeles 40.00
Masonic, Cup, Niagara Falls, 1905, Loving, Three Handle, Porcelain Insert 65.00
Masonic, Cup, Punch, Clear, Pittsburgh Commandry No 1 Kt 6.50
Masonic, Cup, Shriner, 1908, Cranberry, Pedestal 38.00
Masonic, Glass, Toasting, 1860 .... 28.50
Masonic, Goblet, May 22, 1900, Pittsburgh, 5 1/2 In. 25.00
Masonic, Goblet, Pittsburgh, Syria .... Illus 35.00
Masonic, Goblet, Washington, D.C., May 22, 1900, 5 1/4 In. 25.00
Masonic, Hand Monitor 5.00
Masonic, Master's Jewels, Gold 65.00
Masonic, Mug, Atlantic City, 1904, Silver Fish Handle 60.00
Masonic, Mug, Fish Handle, Syria Shrine, 1904, Atlantic City 40.00
Masonic, Mug, Glass, Lady, Fish Handle, Gold 32.00
Masonic, Mug, Indian Chief, 1906 .... 45.00
Masonic, Mug, Shriner, 1903, Indian 35.00
Masonic, Mug, Three Handles, Pictures, Syria Shrine, 1905, Niagara Falls 35.00
Masonic, Paperweight, Blown, Round, Floral & Masonic Emblem 25.00
Masonic, Paperweight, Camel, Metal, Dated 1922 .... 10.00
Masonic, Pin, Lapel, Lilies, 8 In. 5.00
Masonic, Pitcher, Cream, Green Leaves & Acorns, Branch Handles 30.00
Masonic, Plate, Commandry, China, Dated 1906, Red Border 8.50
Masonic, Shaving Mug, Square & Compass, T & V Limoges, France, Gold Bands 22.00

Masonic, Stein, Shriner Insignia, Marked A.A.O.N.M.S. 5.95
Masonic, Sugar, Open, Colorado, Clear, Asgalon·Commandry No.59 K T Pitts. 15.00
Masonic, Toothpick, Masonic Temple, Chicago, Custard Glass, Gold Ghost Weeds 25.00
Masonic, Tray, Porcelain, Oval, Dated 1915 .... 9.00
Match Holder, Cardboard, Decorated In Tole Manner, Green, Red & Yellow 145.00
Match Holder, Pocket, Silver, Fleur-De-Lis 4.00
Match Holder, Rabbit, Clear Glass 25.00
Match Holder, Tin, Painted .... *Illus* 18.50

Masonic, Goblet, Pittsburgh, Syria
See Page 299

Match Holder, Tin, Painted

Match Safe, Striker Bottom, Embossed, Hallmarked 12.00
Match Safe, Striker Bottom, Oval, Hallmarked 12.00

McCoy Pottery is made in Roseville, Ohio. Art Pottery has been made
since the firm started in 1910.
McCoy, Basket, Leaves, Berries, Green, Brown, Red, Handle, 9 1/2 In. 10.00
McCoy, Planter, Birds, Nest, Green, Cream, 2 1/2 In.High 5.50
McCoy, Planter, Deer Scene, Beige, 4 In.High, 5 In.Wide, Pair 12.00
McCoy, Planter, Gondola Shape 5.00
McCoy, Planter, Pheasant 10.00
McCoy, Planter, Turtle 5.00
McCoy, Sugar & Creamer, Raised Posies, Flesh Green Ground 8.00
McCoy, Vase, Bird, Berries, Raised, 8 1/2 In.High 7.00
McCoy, Vase, Pair 10.00
McCoy, Vase, Shaded Green, Bird & Berry, 8 In. 7.50
McCoy, Wishing Well .... 4.00 To 7.50
Meakin, Butter Pat, Mycasa Pattern, Gold, Green, Set Of 6 .... 35.00
Meakin, Plate, Gold, Blue, Flowers, Crown Mark, 10 1/2 In. 12.00
   Mechanical Bank, see Bank, Mechanical

Meerschaum Pipes and other carved pieces of Meerschaum date from the
nineteenth century to the present time.
Meerschaum, Holder, Cigar, Head Of Boxer Dog, Amber Eyes, Black Stem 55.00
Meerschaum, Holder, Cigar, Locust Shape, Yellow Stem 75.00
Meerschaum, Holder, Cigar, Pipe Shape, Shakespearean Female Head 65.00
Meerschaum, Holder, Pipe, Carved Deer 25.00
Meerschaum, Pipe, Amber Bit, Gold Crown, Case 30.00
Meerschaum, Pipe, Carved, Rip Van Winkle 14.50
Meerschaum, Pipe, Dogs, Rat, Carved, Amber Stem 45.00
Meerschaum, Pipe, Face Of Old Man, Case 32.00
Meerschaum, Pipe, Fox Stealing The Goose, Case, 6 1/2 In. 48.00
Meerschaum, Pipe, Hand-Carved, Anchor, Cornucopia, Barrels, Case 25.00
Meerschaum, Pipe, Horse, 4 In.Long, Case 22.00

Meerschaum, Pipe, In Case, Amber Stem .... *Illus*	125.00
Meerschaum, Pipe, Two Dogs, Carved, Amber Stem, Box	35.00

Meissen is a town in Germany where porcelain has been made since 1710.
Any china made in that town can be called Meissen, although the famous
Meissen Factory made the finest porcelains of the area.

Meissen, see also Dresden, Onion

Meissen, Basket, Gold & White, Openwork, 12 1/2 In.	30.00
Meissen, Beaker, Armorial, Landscape, Farmhouse, C.1735	150.00
Meissen, Beaker, Covered, Reserve Oval Panels, Harbor Scenes, C.1730	375.00
Meissen, Bowl, Cobalt Blue, Gold, White, Crossed Swords Mark ....75.00 To	100.00
Meissen, Bowl, Covered, Double Handled, Chinoiserie Panels, C.1730	900.00
Meissen, Bowl, Covered, Purpurmalerei, Landscape & River Views, C.1740	225.00
Meissen, Bowl, White, Applied Flowers, Gilt Inside, C.1740, Crossed Swords	700.00
Meissen, Bowl, White, Gold Trim, Cross Sword Mark, 12 In.	100.00
Meissen, Box, Grape, Bluish To Lavender, C.1775, 3 In.High, Pair	1150.00
Meissen, Box, Snuff, Romantic Scene, Blue Crossed Sword Mark	115.00
Meissen, Box, Sugar, Covered, Oval, Oriental Figures, Rabbit Finial, C.1730-35	170.00
Meissen, Coffeepot, Pear Shape, Stalk Handle, Hunting Scenes, Marcolini	100.00
Meissen, Coffeepot, Pear Shape, Twig Handle, Birds In Flight, C.1775-60	60.00
Meissen, Coffeepot, Turquoise, Pear Shape, Scroll Handle, Scenes, C.1730-35	150.00
Meissen, Compote, Onion Pattern, Open Lacework, 9 In.Tall, Pair	350.00
Meissen, Cup & Saucer, Coffee, Bouquets, Insects, Scroll Handle, C.1750	140.00
Meissen, Cup & Saucer, Coffee, Relief Of Fruiting Vines, Birds, C.1765	100.00
Meissen, Cup & Saucer, Coffee, Watteau Scenes, Gilt Scroll Border, C.1740-45	90.00
Meissen, Cup & Saucer, Demitasse, Floral, Cobalt & Gold Border, Signed	32.00
Meissen, Cup & Saucer, Kakiemon, Puce, Red, C.1735 .... *Illus*	375.00

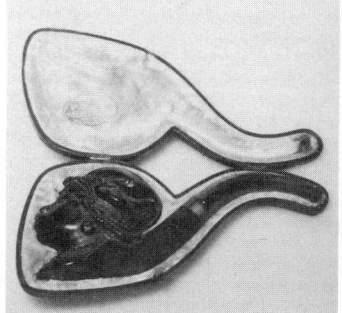

Meerschaum, Pipe, In Case, Amber Stem   Meissen, Cup & Saucer, Kakiemon, Puce, Red, C.1735

Meissen, Dish, Landscape Vignette, Figures & Sheep, C.1720-25	525.00
Meissen, Dish, Peony, Pink Center, Stalk Handle, 7 In.Long, Dot Period	275.00
Meissen, Ecuelle, Cover, & Stand, Scenes, Shepherds, Landscape, Figures	70.00
Meissen, Figure, Kingfisher, Perched On Tree Stump, Brown, Black, White	140.00
Meissen, Figurine, Bear, Crossed Swords & Modeler, 'a.Gaul'	85.00
Meissen, Figurine, Boy With Basket Of Flowers, Circa 1740, Augustus Rex	350.00
Meissen, Figurine, Burghermaster, Stein In Hand	310.00
Meissen, Figurine, Cat, Gray, White, Circa 1850, 3 1/4 In.High, 5 1/2 In.Long	-95.00
Meissen, Figurine, Cupid, Marcolini Period, Yellow Drapery, 5 3/4 In.High	30.00
Meissen, Figurine, Eagle	375.00
Meissen, Figurine, Flower Girl, Crossed Swords Mark	40.00
Meissen, Figurine, Harlequin, C.1760, 5 In. .... *Illus*	450.00
Meissen, Figurine, Harlequin, Masked, C.1760, 5 In. .... *Illus*	500.00
Meissen, Figurine, Italian Comedy Harlequin	295.00
Meissen, Figurine, Lion & Lioness, Stoneware, Artist A.Gaul, Circa 1920	225.00
Meissen, Figurine, Monk, Standing, Brown Habit, C.1750-55, 6 In.High	250.00
Meissen, Figurine, Owl, 1 1/2 In.Tall	30.00
Meissen, Figurine, Owl, 2 In.Tall	35.00
Meissen, Figurine, Owl, 3 In.Tall	65.00

Meissen, Figurine,
Harlequin, C.1760, 5 In.
See Page 301

Meissen, Figurine,
Harlequin, Masked,
C.1760, 5 In.
See Page 301

Meissen, Figurine, The Rape Of Proserpine, Crowned Figure, Female, C.1750 .... 350.00
Meissen, Figurine, The Sense Of Touch, Allegorical Statuette, C.1760 .... 200.00
Meissen, Figurine, Victory, Allegorical Group, C.1755, Crossed Swords Mark 300.00
Meissen, Figurine, Youth, Basket, Flowers, Mark Augustus Rex, 5 1/2 In. 350.00
Meissen, Jar, Powder, Apple & Flower Design, Gold Trim, Sword Mark 20.00
Meissen, Jug, Landscape, Pear Shape, Scroll Handle, Gilt Spout, C.1740-45 .... 175.00
Meissen, Mug, F.O.E., Eagle Emblem, Brown & Tan, Crossed Swords, Warwick Mark 15.00
Meissen, Plate, Floral Design, Blue, Gold, Pierced Edge, Cross Sword, Pair 52.50
Meissen, Plate, Kakiemon, Petal Rim, Phoenix Perched On Tree, C.1740 .... 260.00
Meissen, Plate, Leaf Design, White, Gold, Circa 1800, 11 1/2 In.Diameter 135.00
Meissen, Plate, Leaf Shape, Lettuce Leaves Overlapping, Kakiemon, 1740 .... 425.00
Meissen, Plate, Molded Garlands Rim, Birds & Floral Panels, Dot Period, Pair 100.00
Meissen, Plate, White, Reticulated Border, Crossed Swords, 8 In.Diameter 28.00
Meissen, Sauceboat, Double Handled, Kakiemon Decor, 4 Scroll Feet, C.1735 .... 125.00
Meissen, Saucer, Oriental Style, Johann Ehrenfried Stadler, C.1725-30 .... 260.00
Meissen, Saucer, Quatrefoil Decor, Burnished Gold, Landscape Scenes, C.1745 .... 230.00
Meissen, Server, Cheese, Hand-Painted Floral, Marked, C.1900 .... 65.00
Meissen, Shoe, Bedroom Slipper, Floral, Underglaze Blue Crossed Swords 50.00
Meissen, Sucrier, Covered, Apple Green, Quay Scene, Figures, C.1730-35 .... 1300.00
Meissen, Sugar, Covered, Polychrome Figures, Gardens, Watteau Style, C.1760 .... 40.00
Meissen, Tea & Coffee Service, Floral Bouquets, Marcolini Period, 5 Piece 150.00
Meissen, Tea Caddy, Covered, Panels Of Quay Scenes, Rectangular, C.1725-30 .... 650.00
Meissen, Tea Caddy, Quay Scenes, Iron Red Camaieu, C.F.Herold, C.1735 .... 600.00
Meissen, Tea Service, Puce Scale Border, Flowers, C.1750-1760, 5 Piece 125.00
Meissen, Tea Set, Miniature, Marcolini, 1744-1814, Birds, Floral, 13 Piece 170.00
Meissen, Teabowl & Saucer, Augsburg Decorated, Hunting Scene, C.1730 .... 225.00
Meissen, Teabowl & Saucer, Augsburg Gilded Decor, Chinoiserie, C.1730 .... 350.00
Meissen, Teacup & Saucer, Harbor Views, Flowering Plants, C.1740-50 .... 160.00
Meissen, Teacup & Saucer, Italian Comedy Decor, Dot Period 90.00
Meissen, Teacup & Saucer, Puce Camaieu, Indianische-Blumen, Marcolini 90.00
Meissen, Teacup & Saucer, Yellow, River Scenes, Medallions Inside, C.1740 .... 350.00
Meissen, Teapot, Baluster Shape, Painted Oriental Figures, C.1722-25 .... 325.00
Meissen, Teapot, C.1713, 6 1/2 In. .... *Illus* 3500.00
Meissen, Teapot, Chinoiserie Figures, Johann Gregor Hoeroldt, C.1725 .... 4200.00
Meissen, Teapot, Dragon Spout, Floral, Crossed Swords Mark, 9 1/2 In.High 92.50
Meissen, Teapot, Flower Design, Gold Trim, Bronze Finial, Mark, 5 1/2 In. 35.00
Meissen, Teapot, Grayish Celadon Glaze, Ovoid, Wishbone Handle, C.1750 .... 100.00
Meissen, Teapot, Hausmaler, Gallant & A Lady, Ovoid, C.1745-50 .... 650.00
Meissen, Teapot, Painted Relief Bouquets, Globular, Gilt, C.1713-1719 .... 3500.00
Meissen, Teapot, Quay Scene Panels, Pear Shape, Grotesque Mask Spout, C.1725 ...... 2100.00
Meissen, Vase, Miniature, Blue & White, Ovoid, Insects, Flowers, C.1725, Pair 50.00
Meissen, Vase, Miniature, Ormolu Mounted, J.J.Kaendler, C.1745, Pair 625.00

*Mercury, or Silvered, Glass was first made in the 1850s. It lost favor
for a while but became popular again about 1910. It looks like a piece of
silver.*

Mercury Glass, Candleholder, White Painted Swan, 11 In.	5.50
Mercury Glass, Candlestick, 4 In.High, Pair	17.00
Mercury Glass, Compote, Flowers, Birds, Gold Lining	35.00
Mercury Glass, Mug, For My Good Boy, 3 1/2 In.Tall	27.50
Mercury Glass, Reflector	4.25 To 5.50
Mercury Glass, Salt, Master, Footed	7.00
Mercury Glass, Tieback, Curtain, Pair	21.50
Mercury Glass, Toothpick, Red Flower, Footed	15.50
Mercury Glass, Vase, Flower Decoration, 12 In.Tall, Pair	22.00
Mercury Glass, Vase, Footed, 3 Double Rows Of Ribbing Above Base, Center	10.50
Mercury Glass, Vase, Leaf Design, Gold, Bulbous, 7 In.Tall	16.00
Metal, Statue, Blacksmith, 14 In.Tall, Pair	34.50
Metal, Statue, Day & Night, 14 In.Tall, Pair	39.50
Metal, Statue, Figure, On Pottery Base, 21 In.Tall, Pair	49.50
Metal, Statue, Fishing, 11 In.Tall, Pair	32.00
Metal, Statue, Hunting & Fishing, 18 In.Tall, Pair	59.50
Metal, Statue, Man With Horse, 14 In.Tall	24.50
Metal, Statue, The Night, Figure On Eagle, 19 In.Tall	19.00
Metal, Statue, Woman With Scythe, 18 In.Tall	22.00

*Mettlach, Germany, is a city where the Villeroy and Boch Factories
worked. Steins from the firm are known as Mettlach Steins. They date
from about 1842.*

Mettlach, Bowl, Fruit, No.2414, White, Blue, Brown Leaves, Pair Vases	395.00
Mettlach, Bowl, Silver Rim, No.1322, 9 In.Diameter, 4 In.Deep	135.00
Mettlach, Clock, No.292-3, Bonn, Blue, White, Floral, Matching Pair Vases	325.00
Mettlach, Compote, No.2895, Etched, Art Nouveau, Blue, Tan, White	85.00
Mettlach, Cup, Egg, No.131, Relief Decor, In Pedestal Holder, Silver Luster, 6	95.00
Mettlach, Cup, Punch, Pug, Colored Fruits, Nuts, White Ground, Set Of 12	150.00
Mettlach, Dish, Candy, No.269, Silver Luster Relief Decor, Stand, Lid	45.00
Mettlach, Dish, Leaf Shape, Gray, Silver Veins, 7 In.	45.00
Mettlach, Mug, No.1028, 1/2 Liter, Relief, Tree Trunk, Hops, Grapes	40.00
Mettlach, Mug, No.1044, Dresden Bruhlsche Terrasse, 12 1/4 In.	110.00
Mettlach, Mug, No.1044, Hamburg Jungfernstieg, 12 1/4 In.	110.00
Mettlach, Mug, No.1044, Nurnberg Schloss, 12 1/4 In.	110.00
Mettlach, Mug, No.2140, 1/2 Liter, Monk Drinking From Stein, Hand-Painted	60.00
Mettlach, Mug, No.3095, Hires Root Beer, Baby With Mug, Circa 1914	34.50
Mettlach, Pitcher & 5 Beakers, No.2893	250.00
Mettlach, Pitcher Stein, No.1025	225.00
Mettlach, Pitcher, No.1028 *Illus*	265.00
Mettlach, Plaque, Green Water, White Swans, Glazed 13 In.Diameter	55.00
Mettlach, Plaque, No.1024, Mercury Mark, Pied Piper	50.00
Mettlach, Plaque, No.1044-20, Pug, Floral, Butterflies, Basket Border	35.00
Mettlach, Plaque, No.1044-303, Pug, Women Gather Shellfish, 14 In.Diameter	100.00
Mettlach, Plaque, No.1044, Oriental Scene, 12 In.Diameter	95.00
Mettlach, Plaque, No.1285-26, Flamingo, Floral, Etched, 17 3/4 In.Diameter	275.00
Mettlach, Plaque, No.1405, 10 1/2 In.Diameter	160.00
Mettlach, Plaque, No.2322, Etched, 14 1/2 In.	425.00
Mettlach, Plaque, No.2361	400.00
Mettlach, Plaque, No.2362	400.00

Meissen, Teapot,
C.1713, 6 1/2 In.
See Page 302

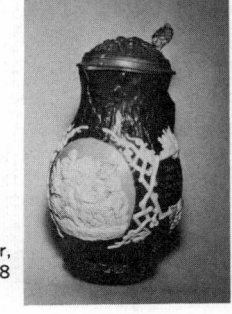

Mettlach, Pitcher,
No.1028

Mettlach, Plaque, No.24269, Pug, Port Scene, Dutch Mill, Ship, 12 In.Diameter 55.00
Mettlach, Plaque, No.2541, C-M, Signed R.Thevenin, 16 In.Diameter 395.00
Mettlach, Plaque, No.2591, Etched 375.00
Mettlach, Plaque, No.2596, Etched 375.00
Mettlach, Plaque, No.2621, Castle Mark, 7 1/2 In. 91.00
Mettlach, Plaque, No.2801-470, Pug, Winter Scene, Mill, Mountains, 8 1/2 In. 25.00
Mettlach, Plaque, No.2874 .... 425.00
Mettlach, Plaque, No.3047, Pug, Elk Head In Shades Of Green, 12 In.Diameter 30.00
Mettlach, Plaque, No.3130, Pug, Dutch Windmill, Road, Trees, 9 In.Diameter 45.00
Mettlach, Plaque, No.3131, Pug, Dutch Windmill, Stream, Trees, 9 In.Diameter 45.00
Mettlach, Plaque, No.3147-7, Pug, River Scene, Deer, Fawn, Duck, Trees, 1i In. 85.00
Mettlach, Plaque, No.3166, Pug, Evening Scene, Windmills, River, Boat, 1i In. 55.00
Mettlach, Plaque, No.3167, Pug, Evening Scene, Church, River, Women, 1i In. 55.00
Mettlach, Plaque, No.3183, Etched, 17 1/4 In. 425.00
Mettlach, Plaque, No.5171, Pug, Waterfront Scene, Dutch Women, Delft Blue 100.00
Mettlach, Plaque, No.7036 .... 425.00
Mettlach, Plaque, Pug, Scene, Castle, Rider On Horse, 12 In.Diameter 50.00
Mettlach, Plate, Blue & White Jasper, Embossed Children, Castle Mark 120.00
Mettlach, Plate, Pug, Ship Scene, Blue 35.00
Mettlach, Stein, No.6, 2 Liter 175.00
Mettlach, Stein, No.6, 3 Liter, Blue Gray 295.00
Mettlach, Stein, No.280, 1/2 Liter, Pug, Dwarf Motif, V&b Mark ....85.00 To 115.00
Mettlach, Stein, No.435, 2 Liter, Geschutz 200.00
Mettlach, Stein, No.485, 1 Liter 245.00
Mettlach, Stein, No.625, 2 Liter 175.00
Mettlach, Stein, No.675, 1/2 Liter, Glazed 110.00
Mettlach, Stein, No.1027, 1/2 Liter, Castle Mark 135.00
Mettlach, Stein, No.1028, Pitcher Type 225.00
Mettlach, Stein, No.1028, 1/2 Liter, Relief 120.00
Mettlach, Stein, No.1146, 1/2 Liter, Drinking Scene, Silver Lid .... 120.00 To 250.00
Mettlach, Stein, No.1163, 1/2 Liter, Etched, Signed Worth 270.00
Mettlach, Stein, No.1266, 1/2 Liter, Star In Top 150.00
Mettlach, Stein, No.1266, 1/4 Liter, Relief .... 100.00 To 110.00
Mettlach, Stein, No.1394, 1/2 Liter, Etched 240.00
Mettlach, Stein, No.1395, 1/2 Liter, Castle Mark 235.00
Mettlach, Stein, No.1396, 1/2 Liter, Etched, Cherub, Fish, Cat, Silver Lid 235.00
Mettlach, Stein, No.1403, 1/2 Liter, Incised, Signed Wirth 250.00
Mettlach, Stein, No.1431, 'oppo' 55.00
Mettlach, Stein, No.1526-1212, 1 Liter, Pug, Old Man Bowling 125.00
Mettlach, Stein, No.1526-599, 1 Liter, Pug, Cavalier Blowing Horn 125.00
Mettlach, Stein, No.1526, 1/2 Liter 55.00
Mettlach, Stein, No.1526, 1/2 Liter, Hand-Painted Crest Of Heidelberg 75.00
Mettlach, Stein, No.1526, 1 Liter, Plain 50.00
Mettlach, Stein, No.1536, 1/2 Liter, Tapestry, Bearded Man Drinks From Stein 175.00
Mettlach, Stein, No.1650, Mountain Climber, Castle Mark, 8 In.Tall 240.00
Mettlach, Stein, No.1675, 1/2 Liter, Etched, City Of Heidelberg 235.00
Mettlach, Stein, No.1727, 1/2 Liter, Relief, Wreath Of Shells, Shell On Lid 170.00
Mettlach, Stein, No.1756, 1 Liter 145.00
Mettlach, Stein, No.1909, 1/2 Liter 110.00
Mettlach, Stein, No.1909-942, 102 Liter, Pug 130.00
Mettlach, Stein, No.1909-1108, 1/2 Liter, Pug, Harpist, Cat, Fish, Monkey 95.00
Mettlach, Stein, No.1934, 1/2 Liter 290.00
Mettlach, Stein, No.1941, No Lid 295.00
Mettlach, Stein, No.1947, 1/2 Liter, Etched 255.00
Mettlach, Stein, No.1997, 1/2 Liter, George Ehret, Etched, Inlaid .... 195.00 To 225.00
Mettlach, Stein, No.1998, 1/2 Liter, Cavalier, Etched, Inlaid Lid .... 275.00 To 285.00
Mettlach, Stein, No.1999, 1/2 Liter, Gnome Thumb Rest, Signed Hein 245.00
Mettlach, Stein, No.2001 .... 300.00
Mettlach, Stein, No.2001b, 1/2 Liter 325.00
Mettlach, Stein, No.2001k, 1/2 Liter 325.00
Mettlach, Stein, No.2002, Mark L.Castle 250.00
Mettlach, Stein, No.2002, 1/2 Liter, Etched, Munich, Pewter Lid .... 235.00 To 250.00
Mettlach, Stein, No.2007, 1/2 Liter 275.00
Mettlach, Stein, No.2025, 1/2 Liter 255.00
Mettlach, Stein, No.2025, 3/10 Liter, Incised 185.00
Mettlach, Stein, No.2054, 1/2 Liter 235.00

Mettlach, Stein, No.2057, 1/2 Liter, Etched 250.00
Mettlach, Stein, No.2076, 2 1/2 Liter, Relief, German Eagle, Owls 150.00
Mettlach, Stein, No.2076, 3 Liter 275.00
Mettlach, Stein, No.2077 .... 110.00
Mettlach, Stein, No.2085, 1/2 Liter 255.00
Mettlach, Stein, No.2086, 1/4 Liter, Relief, Dancing Figures, Red Terra-Cotta 95.00
Mettlach, Stein, No.2086, 1/2 Liter, Relief 115.00
Mettlach, Stein, No.2089, 1/2 Liter, Etched 270.00
Mettlach, Stein, No.2090, 1/2 Liter, Club Stein, Etched, Inlaid Lid 285.00
Mettlach, Stein, No.2140-790, 1/2 Liter, Pug, Regimental 150.00
Mettlach, Stein, No.2176/1055, 3 Liter 225.00
Mettlach, Stein, No.2181, 1/4 Liter, Castle Mark 110.00
Mettlach, Stein, No.2182, 1/2 Liter, Relief, Bowling Figures .... 125.00 To 135.00
Mettlach, Stein, No.2184, 1/2 Liter 185.00
Mettlach, Stein, No.2219, 3 Liter .... 275.00 To 285.00
Mettlach, Stein, No.2231, 1/2 Liter, Etched, Inlaid Lid, Castle Mark 250.00
Mettlach, Stein, No.2235, 1/2 Liter, Music Box, My Old Kentucky Home 320.00
Mettlach, Stein, No.2277, 3/10 Liter 235.00
Mettlach, Stein, No.2348-1022, 3 Liter, Pug, Coffeepot Shape, Man, Girl 175.00
Mettlach, Stein, No.2382, 1/2 Liter, Der Durstige Ritter .... 295.00 To 365.00
Mettlach, Stein, No.2428, 4 Liter, Etched 525.00
Mettlach, Stein, No.2557, 1/2 Liter 195.00
Mettlach, Stein, No.2792-6137, 1/4 Liter, Pug, Man, Plumed Hat, Stein 115.00
Mettlach, Stein, No.2800, 1/2 Liter, Etched, Hop Blossoms, Green, Brown 200.00
Mettlach, Stein, No.2813, 1/2 Liter .... *Illus* 165.00
Mettlach, Stein, No.2833b, C-M, 1/2 Liter 235.00
Mettlach, Stein, No.2833d, C-M, 3/10 Liter 195.00
Mettlach, Stein, No.2833f, 1/2 Liter, Etched 240.00
Mettlach, Stein, No.2878, 1/2 Liter, Tapestry, Tyrolean, Man & Woman 180.00
Mettlach, Stein, No.2880, 1/2 Liter 225.00
Mettlach, Stein, No.2893, 3 Liter, Fisherman & Young Lass .... 150.00 To 235.00
Mettlach, Stein, No.2934, 1/2 Liter, Etched, Wheat, Hops, Geometric Forms 215.00
Mettlach, Stein, No.2935, Hops Decoration, 1/2 Liter 220.00
Mettlach, Stein, No.2936, 1/2 Liter, Etched 270.00
Mettlach, Stein, No.2939, 1/2 Liter, Etched 150.00
Mettlach, Stein, No.3003, 1/2 Liter, Etched, Musician 235.00
Mettlach, Stein, No.3004, 1/2 Liter, Etched, Man In Balloon Britches 235.00
Mettlach, Stein, No.3078, 1/2 Liter, Green, Triangles, Glazed 125.00
Mettlach, Stein, No.3078-403, 1/2 Liter, Green Triangles, Green Body, Glazed 125.00
Mettlach, Stein, No.3136, 3 Liter, Etched, Art Nouveau, Green & Cream 265.00
Mettlach, Stein, No.3239, 1/2 Liter, Geometric Design, German Words, Etched 190.00
Mettlach, Stein, No.3243, 1/2 Liter, Green & White Stripes, Etched 180.00
Mettlach, Stein, No.3246, 1/2 Liter, Green & White Stripes, Etched 180.00
Mettlach, Stein, 6 1/2 In. .... *Illus* 75.00
Mettlach, Tile, No.19-2, Bird Portrait, Signed V & B Mettlach, Wood Frame 30.00
Mettlach, Tile, No.19-3, Bird Portrait, Signed V & B Mettlach, Wood Frame 30.00
Mettlach, Tumbler, Beer, 1/4 Liter, Man Drinking, Villeroy & Boch 39.00

Mettlach, Stein,
No.2813, 1/2 Liter

Mettlach, Stein, 6 1/2 In.

Mettlach, Vase, Blue, Green Gray, White Grapes, Mermaids, Fish, 13 In., Pair	237.50
Mettlach, Vase, Incised Decor, Beige, Gray, Yellow, Black, Castle Mark, 11 In.	86.00
Mettlach, Vase, No.11, Tan Bark Like Body, Applied Leaves, Grapes, Relief	75.00
Mettlach, Vase, No.11x, Brown & White Geometric, Handles, 1i In.Tall	75.00
Mettlach, Vase, No.28, Silver Luster, Relief Decor, 5 In.Tall	35.00
Mettlach, Vase, No.1336, Castle Mark, Jeweled Decor, 11 In.Tall	150.00
Mettlach, Vase, No.1806, Mosaic Relief, Red, Silver, Brown, Blue, Tan, Geometric	95.00
Mettlach, Vase, No.1988, Geometric, Floral, Etched	175.00
Mettlach, Vase, No.2462, Etched Green Leaves, Floral, Brown Ground, 5 In.	95.00
Mettlach, Vase, No.2913, Blue Flowers On Beige Panels, Gold, 13 3/4 In.High	95.00
Mettlach, Vase, No.2915, Etched, Art Nouveau, Blue, Tan, White, 13 In.Tall	55.00
Mettlach, Vase, No.3358, Etched, Art Nouveau, Blue, Black, White, 12 In.Tall	55.00
Mettlach, Vase, No.5029, Pug, Three Connected Vases, Floral	55.00
Mettlach, Vase, Tan Body, Silver Luster, 12 3/4 In.Tall	75.00
Mickey Mouse, Aeroplane, Airmail	12.00
Mickey Mouse, Aeroplane, Friction, Green, Pictures Of Mickey & Friends	12.50
Mickey Mouse, Bank, Plastic, 19 In.Tall	20.00
Mickey Mouse, Bank, 18 In.High, C.1932-35	85.00
Mickey Mouse, Book, Big Little Books, Mickey Mouse & Pluto	3.00
Mickey Mouse, Book, Walt Disney, 1944	3.00
Mickey Mouse, Bowl & Tumbler, Plastic, Pictures Of Disney Characters	2.50
Mickey Mouse, Card, Trade	1.95
Mickey Mouse, Cookie Cutter, Aluminum	12.00
Mickey Mouse, Doll, Talking	10.00
Mickey Mouse, Doll, 10 In.Tall	4.00
Mickey Mouse, Drum, Tin, Mid-1930s	10.00
Mickey Mouse, Figurine, 2 In.Tall	1.00
Mickey Mouse, Fork, Stainless Steel	4.50
Mickey Mouse, Jar, Cookie, Minnie Mouse, Signed, Turnabout, 13 In	10.00 To 15.00
Mickey Mouse, Magazine, Feb., 1937	4.50
Mickey Mouse, Puppet, Hand	6.00
Mickey Mouse, Radio, Mickey Playing Instruments	175.00
Mickey Mouse, Rubber, 10 In.Tall, Molded Shorts & Gloves	16.00
Mickey Mouse, Shade, Light, Frosted Glass	15.00
Mickey Mouse, Spoon	3.50 To 5.00
Mickey Mouse, Toy, Mickey In Fire Truck, Donald Duck Riding, Rubber	15.00
Mickey Mouse, Toy, Tumbling, 15 In.Wood Frame	25.00
Mickey Mouse, Tractor, Rubber, Marked	15.00
Mickey Mouse, Truck, Fire Department, Hard Rubber, 6 1/4 In.	15.00
Mickey Mouse, Tumbler	5.00
Mickey Mouse, Watch, Ingersoll, 1951	30.00
Mickey Mouse, Watch, Ingersoll, 1953	35.00 To 65.00
Mickey Mouse, Watch, Wrist	45.00

Milk Glass was named for its milky white color. It was first made in England during the 1700s. The height of its popularity in the United States was from 1870 to 1880. It is now correct to refer to some colored glass as Blue Milk Glass, Black Milk Glass, etc.

Milk Glass, see also Cosmos

Milk Glass, Banana Boat, Pink, Footed		18.00
Milk Glass, Basket, Blue, 3 1/2 In.Tall	*Illus*	35.00
Milk Glass, Basket, Dated 1874		18.00
Milk Glass, Battleship, Covered, Wheeling		43.00
Milk Glass, Bell, Smoke		4.50
Milk Glass, Bottle, Barber, Stopper		9.00
Milk Glass, Bottle, Barber, White, Lady's Leg, Stopper		14.00
Milk Glass, Bottle, Dresser		10.00
Milk Glass, Bottle, Figural, Bird, 10 In.Tall		12.00
Milk Glass, Bottle, Painted Decoration	*Illus*	37.50
Milk Glass, Bottle, Pinch, Green, Mushroom Stopper, 9 1/2 In.High		75.00
Milk Glass, Bottle, Pinch, Mint Green, Stopper		65.00
Milk Glass, Bottle, Statue Of Liberty Base, 10 In.		45.00
Milk Glass, Bowl, Atterbury, Ruffled Edge		35.00
Milk Glass, Bowl, Cathedral, Red Top, 5 In.		12.50
Milk Glass, Bowl, Daisy Pattern With Floral, Open Edge, 8 In.		56.00
Milk Glass, Bowl, Lattice Sides, Floral Center, 9 1/2 In.Diameter		10.00

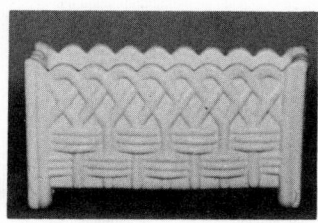

Milk Glass, Basket,
Blue, 3 1/2 In.Tall
See Page 306

Milk Glass, Bottle, Painted Decoration
See Page 306

Milk Glass, **Bowl**, Lattice, Oval	25.00
Milk Glass, **Bowl**, Low Pedestal, White, Lacy Edge, 10 In.	30.00
Milk Glass, **Bowl**, Openwork, Lace Edge, 8 1/4 In.Diameter	25.00
Milk Glass, **Bowl**, Rose, Black, Footed, 4 1/2 In.Tall	22.00
Milk Glass, **Bowl**, Sugar, Acorn Pattern, Green Leaves, Acorn Finial	37.50
Milk Glass, **Box**, Jenny Lind, Cover, Round	27.50
Milk Glass, **Box**, Jenny Lind, Oblong, Cover	22.50
Milk Glass, **Box**, Jenny Lind, Round, Cover, Large	45.00
Milk Glass, **Box**, Trinket, Raised Roses, Oval	12.00
Milk Glass, **Butter Chip**, Buckingham Palace & Queen Victoria Memorial	7.00
Milk Glass, **Butter**, Admiral Dewey Bust In Center, Battleship Maine	48.00
Milk Glass, **Butter**, Blackberry, Cover	35.00
Milk Glass, **Butter**, Versailles, Painted, Covered	30.00
Milk Glass, **Cake Stand**, Hand-Painted Wildflowers, 9 In.Diameter	20.00
Milk Glass, **Cake Stand**, Lacy Edge & Foot, Tripod Stem, 4 1/2 X 11 In.	27.50
Milk Glass, **Cake Stand**, Pink Flowers	18.50
Milk Glass, **Candlestick**, Black, Column, 8 In., Pair	17.50
Milk Glass, **Candlestick**, Blue, Curtain Style, Ring Handle, Gold, Pair	60.00
Milk Glass, **Candlestick**, Blue, 9 In.	175.00
Milk Glass, **Candlestick**, Climbing Rose	9.00
Milk Glass, **Candlestick**, Crucifix, Sandwich Type	30.00
Milk Glass, **Cat**, On Coarse Ribbed Base, Marked Westmoreland, 5 1/2 In.	9.50
Milk Glass, **Cat**, On Coarse Ribbed Base, Numbered	12.00
Milk Glass, **Chicken On Nest**, Blue, White, Ribbed	10.00
Milk Glass, **Child's Set**, Sunburst Pattern, 4 Piece	18.00
Milk Glass, **Compote**, Atterbury, Atlas	70.00
Milk Glass, **Compote**, Green, Cherries, Oak Leaves, Rippled Edge	27.00
Milk Glass, **Compote**, Lacy Basket Weave, Blue, 7 X 9 In.	60.00
Milk Glass, **Compote**, Lid, Footed	65.00
Milk Glass, **Compote**, Openwork, 9 In.Diameter	45.00
Milk Glass, **Compote**, Scroll Pattern, Knot Stem, Flint, 7 1/2 In.Diameter	75.00
Milk Glass, **Condiment Set**	20.00
Milk Glass, **Condiment Set**, Butterflies On Yellow, Hartford Silver Holder	47.50
Milk Glass, **Condiment Set**, Wild Rose, 4 Piece	18.50
Milk Glass, **Creamer & Sugar**, Pink, Fruit	12.00
Milk Glass, **Creamer**, Covered	21.00
Milk Glass, **Creamer**, Grape, White	30.00
Milk Glass, **Creamer**, Paneled Wheat, Ringed Base	25.00
Milk Glass, **Creamer**, Reeded Handle	25.00
Milk Glass, **Creamer**, Toby, Federal	4.50
Milk Glass, **Cruet**, English Hobnail, Stopper, 3 In.High	10.00
Milk Glass, **Cruet**, Flowers, Enamel, Blue, Pink, Stopper, 3 In.Tall	16.50
Milk Glass, **Cruet**, Hobnail, 4 1/2 In.Tall	6.00
Milk Glass, **Cup & Saucer**, Banded Raindrop	12.50
Milk Glass, **Cup & Saucer**, Candlewick	12.50
Milk Glass, **Cup**, Egg, Chick	7.50
Milk Glass, **Cup**, Egg, Double, Basket Weave, Dated	9.00
Milk Glass, **Decanter**, Gold Design, Scrollwork, 3 1/2 In.Square	50.00
Milk Glass, **Dish**, American Hen, Cover	45.00
Milk Glass, **Dish**, Blue, Covered Swan	6.00
Milk Glass, **Dish**, Camel	55.00

Milk Glass, Dish, Cannon, Flaccus .... *Illus*   35.00
Milk Glass, Dish, Cat Shape, Cover 40.00
Milk Glass, Dish, Cat Top, Blue, White 25.00
Milk Glass, Dish, Cat, Signed Mckee 100.00
Milk Glass, Dish, Chick & Eggs, White, Atterbury, Cover, Dated 1889 ....   145.00
Milk Glass, Dish, Chicken On Nest, Painted Base .... *Illus*   55.00
Milk Glass, Dish, Dog .... *Illus*   35.00

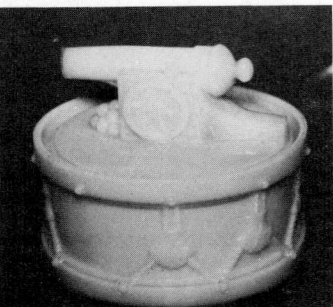

Milk Glass, Dish, Cannon, Flaccus

Milk Glass, Dish,
Chicken On Nest, Painted Base

Milk Glass, Dish, Dog

Milk Glass, Dish, Dolphin Cover 32.50
Milk Glass, Dish, Duck Covered, Blue, Atterbury 120.00
Milk Glass, Dish, Duck Covered, White, Atterbury 95.00
Milk Glass, Dish, Duck, Swimming, Covered, Blue, Oval Base 24.50
Milk Glass, Dish, Fish On Lid 50.00
Milk Glass, Dish, Hen Covered, Blue, White Head, 5 In. 50.00
Milk Glass, Dish, Hen Covered, Blue, 5 In. 35.00
Milk Glass, Dish, Hen Covered, White, 5 In. .... 15.00 To 18.00
Milk Glass, Dish, Hen On Basket, Handled, 4 X 5 In. 40.00
Milk Glass, Dish, Hen On Lacy Base, White, Blue, Atterbury .... 135.00 To 145.00
Milk Glass, Dish, Hen On Nest, Blue, 4 1/2 In.Long, 4 1/2 In.High 22.00
Milk Glass, Dish, Hen, Blue, White Head & Base 35.00
Milk Glass, Dish, Hen, Glass Eyes 45.00
Milk Glass, Dish, Lion Cover, Lacy Edge Base, Pat.Aug.6, 1889 .... 65.00 To 75.00
Milk Glass, Dish, Mustard, Upright Dolphin, Small Fish On Lid 22.50
Milk Glass, Dish, Openwork Border, 10 In.Long, 2 ....   10.00
Milk Glass, Dish, Owl Head Covered, White, Split Ribbed Base .... 160.00 To 175.00
Milk Glass, Dish, Robin On Nest, Cover 34.50
Milk Glass, Dish, Rooster Covered, Blue, White Head, 5 In. 50.00

Milk Glass, Dish, Rooster, Standing, Covered, French 29.50
Milk Glass, Dish, Ruffled, Relief, Paint, 10 1/2 In. 12.00
Milk Glass, Dish, Setting Hen, 5 1/2 In.Long 5.00
Milk Glass, Dish, Setting Hen, 8 In.Long 7.50
Milk Glass, Dish, Sleigh, Santa Claus Lid 35.00
Milk Glass, Dish, Spaniel, Oblong Base, By Boston & Sandwich Glass Co. 145.00
Milk Glass, Dish, Squirrel, Cover 75.00
Milk Glass, Dish, Strawberry, Leaves, Snail On Cover 48.00
Milk Glass, Dish, Swan Cover, 5 1/2 In.Long, 6 In.High 35.00
Milk Glass, Dish, Swan, Signed Mckee, Open Neck 95.00
Milk Glass, Dish, Sweetmeat, White, Basket Weave, Covered, Handled, Pedestal 45.00
Milk Glass, Dish, The American Hen, Covered, White 45.00
Milk Glass, Dish, Trinket, Covered, Oval, Raised Roses 15.00
Milk Glass, Dish, Trinket, White, Covered, Heart Shape 15.00
Milk Glass, Dish, Uncle Sam Battleship Cover .... 22.75 To 32.50
Milk Glass, Dish, White, Lacy Base, Atterbury 85.00
Milk Glass, Duck On Wavy Base, White 65.00
Milk Glass, Easter Egg, Hand-Painted, Flowers, 6 In.Long 15.00
Milk Glass, Egg, Easter 7.00
Milk Glass, Eggcup, Basket Weave, Dated 1874, Double 15.50
Milk Glass, Eggcup, Open Rose 12.50
Milk Glass, Flask, Blue Zigzag Overlay 100.00
Milk Glass, Flowerpot, Green 2.00
Milk Glass, Goblet, Fruit Panel, Gold Decoration, Blue 28.00
Milk Glass, Goblet, Honeycomb Pattern 15.00
Milk Glass, Goblet, Loop Pattern 12.00
Milk Glass, Hat, Blue, Ribbed, Stove Pipe Style 12.00
Milk Glass, Hat, Opalescent, Pointed Hobnail 15.00
Milk Glass, Jar, Apple Blossom 16.50
Milk Glass, Jar, Drum With Sitting Pig On Top, Cover 17.50
Milk Glass, Jar, Mustard, Bull's Head 40.00
Milk Glass, Jar, Mustard, Floral, Silver Top 6.50
Milk Glass, Jar, Mustard, Horse's Head 9.00
Milk Glass, Jar, Pineapple, 3 Feet, French 17.50
Milk Glass, Jar, Powder, Square, Souvenir Willsburg 9.00
Milk Glass, Jar, Powder, White, Covered, Gold 8.00
Milk Glass, Jug, Syrup, Blue, Grape & Leaves, Applied Handle, Spring Lid 75.00
Milk Glass, Lamp Base, Leaf Pattern, Frosted & Cut To Clear, 11 In.High 38.00
Milk Glass, Lamp Base, Oil, Blackberry Pattern, 11 In.High 48.00
Milk Glass, Lamp, American Coin, Kerosene 300.00
Milk Glass, Lamp, Hexagonal Base 30.00
Milk Glass, Lamp, Nutmeg 24.00
Milk Glass, Lamp, Oil, Glass Chimney, Brass Fittings, 15 1/2 In.High 15.00
Milk Glass, Match Holder, Kettle Shape, 2 1/2 In.Tall 8.50
Milk Glass, Match Holder, Man's Face .... Illus   22.00
Milk Glass, Match Holder, Souvenir, U.S.Government Building, Raised 5.00
Milk Glass, Mug, Rope, Peacock Feathers, White, 4 In.High 15.00
Milk Glass, Pitcher, Syrup, Floral Design, White, 6 1/2 In.High 21.00
Milk Glass, Pitcher, Syrup, Pink Flowers 17.50
Milk Glass, Pitcher, Water, Beaded, Reverse Drape, Pink Flowers 79.50
Milk Glass, Pitcher, Water, Floral Design, White, Applied Handle, 9 In.Tall 32.50

Milk Glass, Match Holder, Man's Face

Milk Glass, Pitcher, Water, Indented Red Stripes	85.00
Milk Glass, Pitcher, Water, Lacy Dew Drop	25.00
Milk Glass, Pitcher, Water, Netted Ground, Acorn & Leaf, Bulbous, Blue Top	85.00
Milk Glass, Pitcher, Water, Tankard, Scroll, Opaque White	55.00
Milk Glass, Plate, Angel & Harp	18.00
Milk Glass, Plate, Black, Hand-Painted Floral, 7 1/4 In.Square	9.00
Milk Glass, Plate, Black, Lacy Edge, 7 In.	8.00
Milk Glass, Plate, Bread, 'give Us This Day Our Daily Bread, ' 10 X 12 In.	25.00
Milk Glass, Plate, Columbus	24.00
Milk Glass, Plate, Columbus, Club Border, 9 3/4 In.Wide	34.00
Milk Glass, Plate, 'Columbus 1892 Expo,' 91/2 In.Diameter	37.50
Milk Glass, Plate, Diamond & Shell, White, 6 In.Diameter	6.00
Milk Glass, Plate, Diner, Fleur-De-Lis, Gold Trim, 7 1/2 In.Diameter	10.00
Milk Glass, Plate, Easter Chicks, Yellow, Green, Gilt Border	19.00
Milk Glass, Plate, Embossed Dahlia, Openwork Border	12.00
Milk Glass, Plate, Fan & Circle, Blown	40.00
Milk Glass, Plate, Fisheye, 7 In.Diameter	12.50
Milk Glass, Plate, Flag, Eagle, Fleur-De-Lis, Star Border, Dated 1903	20.00
Milk Glass, Plate, Fleur-De-Lis, Flag & Eagle, 7 In.	15.00
Milk Glass, Plate, Forget-Me-Not Border, 7 1/2 In.	6.00
Milk Glass, Plate, Hand-Painted Flowers, Gold Trim, 7 1/4 In., Fair	6.00
Milk Glass, Plate, Hand-Painted Flowers, Leaves, Pink, Green, 8 1/4 In.	18.00
Milk Glass, Plate, Lacy Edge, 8 1/2 In.Diameter	5.00
Milk Glass, Plate, Lacy Lattice, White, 11 In.Diameter	50.00
Milk Glass, Plate, Lacy, Blue, 8 In.Diameter	17.50
Milk Glass, Plate, Lattice Edge, Basket Weave, Circa 1876, Blue, 8 1/2 In.	18.00
Milk Glass, Plate, Owl Design, Patent 1901	15.00 To 22.50
Milk Glass, Plate, Owls, Tree, Moon, 7 1/2 In.Diameter	12.00
Milk Glass, Plate, Pig, 8 1/4 In.	12.00
Milk Glass, Plate, Rabbits In Center, 6 In, Diameter	15.00
Milk Glass, Plate, Scroll, Eye Lacy Border, White, 8 In.Diameter	29.00
Milk Glass, Plate, Statue Of Liberty In Center, Pierced Border	18.50
Milk Glass, Plate, Three Bears, 7 In.Diameter	12.50 To 22.50
Milk Glass, Plate, 3 Wise Owls Painted In Gold, Gold Lattice Edge, 1901	20.00
Milk Glass, Platter, Blue	8.00
Milk Glass, Platter, Retriever	60.00
Milk Glass, Platter, White, John Hancock	150.00
Milk Glass, Pocketbook, Blue, Sowerby, 3 1/2 In. *Illus*	35.00
Milk Glass, Rabbit On Nest, White	35.00
Milk Glass, Relish, Blackberry, Oblong	22.50
Milk Glass, Robin On Nest, Blue	42.50
Milk Glass, Salt & Pepper, Blue Basket-Weave Pattern Lower Part	5.00
Milk Glass, Salt & Pepper, Blue, Bulging Petal, Set	25.00
Milk Glass, Salt & Pepper, Lime Green, Forget-Me-Nots	35.00
Milk Glass, Salt & Pepper, Little Grape, Tray, Brass Top On Salt	24.50
Milk Glass, Salt & Pepper, Raised Flowers, Set	23.00
Milk Glass, Salt & Pepper, Refrigerator *Illus*	18.00

Milk Glass, Pocketbook, Blue, Sowerby, 3 1/2 In.

Milk Glass, Salt & Pepper, Refrigerator

Milk Glass, Salt & Pepper, Shape Of Fan, Set	4.00
Milk Glass, Salt & Pepper, Tin Top, Set	4.00
Milk Glass, Salt Shaker, Satin Finish, Palmer Cox Brownies	22.50
Milk Glass, Salt Shaker, White, Ear Of Corn	10.00
Milk Glass, Salt, Green, Cord & Tassel	8.00
Milk Glass, Salt, Master, Basket Weave, Dated 1874, 2 Handles	15.50
Milk Glass, Salt, Master, Blackberry	18.00
Milk Glass, Salt, Pepper, Mustard, Tray, Wild Rose	25.00
Milk Glass, Salt, White, Cone	6.50
Milk Glass, Salt, Zigzag, Brass Top, Pair	12.50
Milk Glass, Santa On Sleigh	55.00
Milk Glass, Shade, Dark Green Overlay Outside, Scalloped Edge, 5 In.High	17.00
Milk Glass, Shade, Flower & Leaf Motif, 6 In.High, 4 In.Diameter	20.00
Milk Glass, Shade, White, Miniature	4.75
Milk Glass, Shaker, Blue, Forget-Me-Not	15.00
Milk Glass, Shaker, Salt, Aqua, Swirl	7.50
Milk Glass, Shaker, Salt, Blue, Lily-Of-The-Valley Decor, Square	8.50
Milk Glass, Shaker, Salt, Clematis & Scroll, Blue, Tin Top	12.00
Milk Glass, Shaker, Salt, Creased Bale, White	15.00
Milk Glass, Shaker, Salt, Dice	8.00
Milk Glass, Shaker, Salt, Green, Cosmos Band	10.00
Milk Glass, Shaker, Salt, Pink, White, Feather Panel, Opalescent	28.00
Milk Glass, Shaker, Salt, Raised Scrollwork & Daisy	8.50
Milk Glass, Shaker, Salt, Ruffled Skirt	9.00
Milk Glass, Shaker, Salt, Shell & Seaweed, Pewter Top	8.00
Milk Glass, Shaker, Salt, Strawberry & Leaf, Creased Neck, Silver Lid	7.00
Milk Glass, Shaker, Sugar, Beading, Swirls, Spoke Bottom, Concave Sides	25.00
Milk Glass, Shaker, Sugar, Birds, Oriental, Multicolor	20.00
Milk Glass, Shaker, Sugar, Blue, Forget-Me-Not	38.00
Milk Glass, Shaker, Sugar, Flowers, Red	20.00
Milk Glass, Shaker, Sugar, Rosebud, Pink, Green, Blue, Hand-Painted	23.00
Milk Glass, Shaving Mug, Black, Gold Trim	9.00
Milk Glass, Slipper, Blue, Bow, 5 3/4 In.	15.00
Milk Glass, Slipper, Daisy & Button	14.00
Milk Glass, Spooner, Birch Leaf, Flint	27.50
Milk Glass, Spooner, Blackberry	15.00
Milk Glass, Spooner, Painted Pansies, Scalloped Edge, Green Trim	18.50
Milk Glass, Spooner, Pink Roses, Blue Edge & Feet	36.50
Milk Glass, Spooner, Royal Oak	17.00
Milk Glass, Spooner, Waffle	15.00
Milk Glass, Sugar & Creamer, Child's, Sunburst Pattern	8.00
Milk Glass, Sugar, Beaded Circle, Open	18.50
Milk Glass, Sugar, Blackberry	12.50
Milk Glass, Sugar, Cover, Pink Roses, Blue Trim	57.50
Milk Glass, Sugar, Creamer, Open, Spooner, Ribbed, Lacy Edges	45.00
Milk Glass, Sugar, Pink, Rose In Snow, Round, 5 In.	4.00
Milk Glass, Sugar, Twin Horn	16.00
Milk Glass, Sweetmeat, Basket Weave, Atterbury, Footed, Cover, 7 In.High	45.00
Milk Glass, Syrup, Beaded Swirl, Flower	45.00
Milk Glass, Syrup, Corn Pattern	37.50
Milk Glass, Syrup, Hand-Painted Floral Around Bottom, Metal Top	19.00
Milk Glass, Syrup, Raised Blossoms & Leaves, Bulbous, Yellow, Green	27.50
Milk Glass, Syrup, Raised Tulip & Leaf Design, Paneled Neck	22.50
Milk Glass, Syrup, Spider Web, Flowers	21.00
Milk Glass, Syrup, Tree Of Life, Turquoise	50.00
Milk Glass, Syrup, White, Honeycomb Melon Rib, Enameled Floral	35.00
Milk Glass, Toothpick, Basket	6.50
Milk Glass, Toothpick, Blue Enamel Floral, Bow At Top	15.00
Milk Glass, Toothpick, Blue, Flared Top, Beaded Edge, Souvenir	7.00
Milk Glass, Toothpick, Embossed Pansy, Lattice, White, Pink	19.00
Milk Glass, Toothpick, Indian Head, Divided	12.00
Milk Glass, Toothpick, Pipe, Flowers, Gold	10.00
Milk Glass, Tray, Blue, 5 1/2 X 4 1/2 In.	11.50
Milk Glass, Tray, Chrysanthemum, 8 X 4 1/2 In.	9.50
Milk Glass, Tray, Dresser, Gold Trim	10.00
Milk Glass, Tray, Dresser, Jenny Lind, Large	37.50

Milk Glass, Tray, Dresser, White, Gold, 12 In.	10.00
Milk Glass, Tray, Gold Decor, 5 X 9 In.	8.00
Milk Glass, Tray, Pin, Blue, Raised Design, Open Handles, 7 1/2 In.Long	15.00
Milk Glass, Tray, Pin, Jenny Lind	15.00 To 25.00
Milk Glass, Tray, Pink, Snowflake Pattern, 6 Compartments	8.00
Milk Glass, Tray, Pink, White, Grape & Leaf Decor, Beaded Edge, Gilt	8.50
Milk Glass, Tumbler, Acorn & Oak Leaf, Green Top	25.00
Milk Glass, Tumbler, Beaded Swag, Flower Decoration	17.50
Milk Glass, Tumbler, Colored Leaf Decoration	20.00
Milk Glass, Tumbler, Louisiana Purchase	10.00
Milk Glass, Tumbler, Scroll Pattern, Opaque, Blue	22.50
Milk Glass, Tumbler, Scroll, Blue	9.50 To 22.50
Milk Glass, Tumbler, Spanish Fern, Black	50.00
Milk Glass, Tumbler, St.Louis World's Fair	13.50
Milk Glass, Tumbler, Waffle	12.00
Milk Glass, Vase, Light Brown, Canary In Center, 11 In.Tall	18.00
Milk Glass, Vase, Portrait, Sitting Bull, 7 1/2 In.Tall	17.00
Milk Glass, Vase, Roses, Embossed, 5 In.High	12.00
Milk Glass, Vase, Stork In Pond, Tulips, 10 In.	18.00
Milk Glass, Vase, Swan, Reeds, 6 In., Pair	35.00
Milk Glass, Vase, White, Replica, Cleopatra's Needle Obelisk, 10 1/4 In.	195.00

Millefiori means many flowers. It is a type of glasswork popular in paperweights. Many small flower-like pieces of glass are grouped together to form a design.

Millefiori, see also Paperweight

Millefiori, Creamer, 2 In.High	12.50
Millefiori, Lamp, Boudoir, 10 1/2 In.High, Egg Shape Shade	110.00
Millefiori, Vase, Miniature, Applied Handles, Frilled Top, 3 In.High	39.00

Miniature, see also Picture, Miniature

Miniature, Bed & Mattress, Brass, 7 In.	7.50
Miniature, Bowl, Rose, Pressed Glass, Hobstars	15.00
Miniature, Coach & Horses, Silver, 5 In.Long	90.00
Miniature, Dog, China, Japanese, Pre-1930	.50
Miniature, Figurine, Dog, Sitting, Glass	6.00
Miniature, Figurine, Mule, Glass	6.00
Miniature, Figurine, Rooster, Glass	6.00
Miniature, Iron, Handled Trivet, Cast Iron	15.00
Miniature, Monkey, China, Japanese, Pre-1930	.50
Miniature, Mortar & Pestle, Brass, 1 In.	8.50
Miniature, Mug, Green Glass, Stippled & Clear, Trees, Deer	13.00
Miniature, Napoleon, Full Dress, Ivory Base, Signed Isabey, Oval	225.00
Miniature, Tea Set, Pewter, Sugar, Creamer, Teapot, 2 Cup & Saucer	12.00
Miniature, Teakettle, Copper, 4 In.	12.00
Miniature, Teapot, Copper, Tin Lined, Goose Spout, 3 In.Diameter	25.00

Minton China has been made in England from 1793 to the present time.

Minton, Bottle, Perfume, Pear Shape, Enameled Lilies Of The Valley, C.1830	60.00
Minton, Bowl, Blue & Red Copper Luster, 8 In.Diameter, 4 In.High	50.00
Minton, Bowl, Dessert, Floral, Lavender Border, Marked Tiffany & Co., 6	35.00
Minton, Caisse A Fleurs, Sevres Style, Ornithological, Blue, C.1835, Pair	170.00
Minton, Candlestick, Flower Design, Blue, Gold, Enamel Base, Mark, 3 1/2 In.	18.00
Minton, Chamber Pot, Child's, Cover	150.00
Minton, Coffeepot, Footed, Tiffany & Co., Bands Of Gold, Green Laurel	20.00
Minton, Cup & Saucer, Demitasse	6.00
Minton, Dessert Set, Leaf Shape Dishes, Pattern No.7365, C.1840, 7 Piece	100.00
Minton, Dish, Leaf Design, Cherub Handle, 12 3/4 In.Long	85.00
Minton, Dish, Soup, Vine Of Green Leaves, 7 3/4 In.Diameter, Set Of 12	18.00
Minton, Plate, Blue & Gold Border, Tiffany & Co., 10 In.Diameter	7.50
Minton, Plate, Cream, Narrow Gold Band Border, 10 In.Diameter, 12	108.00
Minton, Plate, Dinner, Norwich Pattern, 10 In., Set Of 9	55.00
Minton, Plate, Dinner, White With Blue & Gold Band Of Grapes, 12	108.00
Minton, Plate, Fruit & Butterfly Decoration In Gold, Impressed Minton	10.00
Minton, Plate, Terra-Cotta Design, White Ground, Marked 1875, 8 In., Set Of 4	15.00
Minton, Vase, Tulip, Reclining Cupid On Base, Salt Glaze, 7 In.	20.00

Mirror, see Furniture, Mirror

Mocha Ware is an English-made product that was sold in America during the early 1800s. It is a heavy pottery with pale coffee and cream coloring. Designs of blue, brown, green, orange, or black or white were added to the pottery.

Mocha, Bowl, Blue, Brown & White Snakes Inside, Leaves Outside	700.00
Mocha, Bowl, Marbleized, Blue Band, 6 In.Diameter	175.00
Mocha, Bowl, Marbleized, Terra-Cotta & Brown, Green Rim Band	175.00
Mocha, Bowl, Moss Decoration Inside	40.00
Mocha, Bowl, Red Ground, Snake Decoration, 6 1/4 In.Diameter	225.00
Mocha, Bowl, Swiggly Decoration In Green, Brown, Blue, & White	150.00
Mocha, Bowl, Terra-Cotta Ground, Seaweed, Green Rim Band, 8 3/4 In.Diameter	300.00
Mocha, Bowl, Yellow, White, Blue, Stripe, Seaweed, 13 In.Diameter	60.00
Mocha, Coffeepot, Yellow Ground, Balloon Decoration	1100.00
Mocha, Creamer, Marbleized, Green Rim, 3 1/2 In.High	200.00
Mocha, Creamer, Tan Ground, Seaweed Decoration, 3 3/4 In.High	35.00
Mocha, Cup, Custard, Yellow Ground, Seaweed Decoration	105.00
Mocha, Flowerpot, Blue, Cat's-Eyes, 2 Piece	175.00
Mocha, Holder, Spill, Blue, White & Terra-Cotta Bands, Seaweed, Pair	300.00
Mocha, Jug, Blue & White, Leaf Ends Handle, Bulbous, 6 1/2 In.High	35.00
Mocha, Mug, Blue Moss	27.50
Mocha, Mug, Blue With Black Tree	60.00
Mocha, Mug, Blue With White Panels, 6 In.High	50.00
Mocha, Mug, Gold Ground, Snake Decoration, 6 In.High	250.00
Mocha, Mug, Marbleized, 6 1/2 In.High	175.00
Mocha, Mug, Seaweed Pattern, Black On Cream Band, 3 1/2 In.High	50.00
Mocha, Mug, 6 1/2 In. ... *Illus*	65.00

Mocha, Mug, 6 1/2 In.

Mocha, Pitcher, Bands Of Shades Of Brown	30.00
Mocha, Pitcher, Blue & Pale Green Bands, Black Decoration	55.00
Mocha, Pitcher, Blue Ground, Snake & Cat's-Eye Decoration, Brown & Green	120.00
Mocha, Pitcher, Brown Band With Wavy Lines, Mustard Bands, Cat's-Eyes	300.00
Mocha, Pitcher, Orange-Tan Ground, Rayed Brown & Blue Balloon Design	200.00
Mocha, Pitcher, Pale Blue With Green & Black Bands	30.00
Mocha, Pitcher, 4 Color Bands & White Locking Circles	205.00
Mocha, Pot, Handled, Blue Bands With Cat's-Eyes, Brown Bands	100.00
Mocha, Pot, Handled, Mustard Band With Snake Decoration	200.00
Mocha, Pot, Mustard, Handle, Cover, Geometric Design, Green, Terra-Cotta, Black	100.00
Mocha, Pot, Mustard, Lid, Yellow-Tan Ground, Seaweed Decoration	225.00
Mocha, Pot, Pepper, Blue Banded	25.00
Mocha, Pot, Pepper, Blue Ground, Earthworm Decoration	500.00
Mocha, Pot, Pepper, Blue Stripes, Earthworm Decoration	80.00
Mocha, Pot, Pepper, Gray Ground, Vine Decoration, Bands	145.00
Mocha, Pot, Pepper, Striped, Blue Ground, Cat's-Eye Decoration	155.00
Mocha, Pot, Pepper, Terra-Cotta Ground, Seaweed Decoration	115.00
Mocha, Pot, Pepper, Yellow Ground, Seaweed	100.00
Mocha, Salt, Master, Open, Blue Ground, Seaweed Decoration	150.00
Mocha, Salt, Open, Yellow Ground, Seaweed Decoration	120.00
Mocha, Sugar, Covered, Terra-Cotta, Green, & Tan, Seaweed, Beehive Finial	300.00

Mocha, Tea Caddy, Marbleized, Shades Of Brown, Green Band, 4 1/2 In.High 400.00
Mocha, Teapot, Cylindrical, Marbelized, Brown & Blue, 5 1/4 In.High 75.00
Mocha, Tureen, Soup, Blue Ground, Seaweed Decoration, Snake Decoration Lid 325.00
   Mold, Candle, see Tin, Mold, Candle
   Mold, Ice Cream, see Pewter, Mold
   Mold, see Kitchen, Weapon, Pewter, Tin, etc.

Moorcroft Pottery was founded in Burslem, England, in 1914 by William
Moorcroft. The earlier wares are similar to those made today, but color and
marking will help indicate the age.
Moorcroft, Ashtray, Floral Center, Green, Yellow, Purple, Signed, 4 1/2 In. 35.00
Moorcroft, Bottle, Barber, Blue, Pomegranate Decor, Signed, Burslem, England 57.50
Moorcroft, Bowl, Fruit, Orchids, Pink, Green, 10 In.Diameter 30.00
Moorcroft, Bowl, Pansies, Red, Purple, Yellow, Silver Rim, Green Mark 49.00
Moorcroft, Box, Cigarette, Blossoms, Yellow, Red, Cover, Marked 25.00
Moorcroft, Box, Covered, Flowers On Cobalt, Signed, Paper Label 20.00
Moorcroft, Box, Floral Design, Green, Orange, Signed, Cover 39.00
Moorcroft, Candlestick, Blue, Yellow, Floral Decoration 22.50
Moorcroft, Candlestick, Floral Design, Cobalt Blue, Paper Label, 3 1/4 In. 32.50
Moorcroft, Compote, Fruit & Leaf Design, Blue, Red, Yellow, Green, 7 In.Tall 75.00
Moorcroft, Cup & Saucer, Flowers, Blue, Gray 16.00
Moorcroft, Dish, Candy, Blue, Fruit Decoration, 5 1/2 X 1 1/2 In. 23.00
Moorcroft, Dish, Candy, Cobalt, Fruit Decoration, 5 1/2 In. 20.00
Moorcroft, Vase, Blue Ground, Fruits, Berries, 6 1/2 In. 45.00
Moorcroft, Vase, Blue, Burgundy & Blue Floral, Signed W.M., 6 3/4 In. 55.00
Moorcroft, Vase, Blue, White, Art Nouveau Design, Signed, 10 In. 95.00
Moorcroft, Vase, Blues & Rust, Mark, 3 1/2 In.Diameter, 3 In.High 20.00
Moorcroft, Vase, Cobalt Blue, Floral Decoration, 4 In. 15.00
Moorcroft, Vase, Cobalt Blue, Rose & Blue, Yellow & Blue Flowers, Marked 55.00
Moorcroft, Vase, Cobalt To Blue-Green, Pink-Purple Pansies, Signed 15.00
Moorcroft, Vase, Dark Blue, Pomegranates, Script-Signed 30.00
Moorcroft, Vase, Floral Design, Bulbous, Cobalt Blue, Paper Label, 8 In. 35.00
Moorcroft, Vase, Floral, Blue, Narrow Opening, Signed, 9 In.Tall 50.00
Moorcroft, Vase, Fruit Design, Script Signature, 6 3/8 In.High 47.50
Moorcroft, Vase, Globular, Green With Orchids, Script Signature, 4 1/2 In. 40.00
Moorcroft, Vase, Grapes, Purple, Yellow, Green, Blue, 8 In.Tall, 4 1/2 In. 30.00
Moorcroft, Vase, Green Ground, Pink & Green Floral, 4 1/2 In.Tall 15.00
Moorcroft, Vase, Green, Peach, Floral Decor, 4 In. 18.00
Moorcroft, Vase, Miniature, Dark Green, Floral Decor, 2 In. 14.00
Moorcroft, Vase, Plums, Purple, Yellow, Blue, 9 1/2 In.Tall, 6 In.Diameter 38.00
Moorcroft, Vase, Trumpet, Brown, Yellow, 9 In. 12.50
Moorcroft, Vase, Urn Shape, Blue, Orange & Green Leaves, Purple Floral 47.50
Moorcroft, Vase, White, Cobalt Spatter, 6 In. 14.00
Moorcroft, Vase, Yellow, Green, Red, Floral, 8 In. 35.00
Morgantown, Pitcher, Lemonade, White, Footed, Matching Tumblers, Set 200.00

Moser Glass was made by Kolomon Moser in the early 1900s. The Art
Nouveau type classware had detailed exotic enamel designs.
Moser, Bottle, Clear To Blue, Intaglio Cut, Flowers Leaves, Signed, 6 In.Tall 75.00
Moser, Bowl, Flower, Gold, Enamel, Chartreuse Background, Signed, Footed 500.00
Moser, Bowl, Gold Design, Ruffled Rim, Green, Mark, 8 In.Diameter 145.00
Moser, Bowl, Gold Water Lily Decoration, Footed, Carlsbad 95.00
Moser, Bowl, Green, Signed, Enameled Bugs & Dragonflies 85.00
Moser, Bowl, Mayonnaise, Underplate, Spoon, Gold Engraved Bands, Amber 65.00
Moser, Bowl, 7 In.Wide, Signed 65.00
Moser, Box, Amber, Enameled Fish & Flora, Cover, 3 In.Diameter 15.00
Moser, Box, Candy, Warriors On Horses, Gold Band, Purple, Unsigned 95.00
Moser, Box, Glass, Amber, Cameos, Marked, Round, 5 1/2 In.Diameter, 3 In.Tall 95.00
Moser, Compote, Roman Figures, Paneled Amethyst, Cameo Cut, Signed, 6 In. 110.00
Moser, Cruet, Amethyst To Clear, Gold Band, Enameled 45.00
Moser, Decanter, Yellow To Clear, Intaglio Morning Glories, Triangular 150.00
Moser, Glass, Cocktail, Paperweight Base, Signed 42.50
Moser, Goblet, Amethyst, Gold Trim, Signed, 7 In. 85.00
Moser, Jar, Biscuit, Applied Brass Bees, Cranberry, Silver Lid, Signed 200.00
Moser, Ring Tree, Daisies, Gold Design, White, Mark 75.00
Moser, Rose Bowl, Lemon Yellow, Gold Leaf & Enamel, Signed 485.00

Moser, Vase, Amber-Peach, Cut Panels, Signed, 7 1/2 In.High 125.00
Moser, Vase, Amethyst To Clear, Gold Leaves, Butterfly, Applied Acorns 45.00
Moser, Vase, Amethyst, Gold Decoration, Scalloped Top, 9 3/4 In.High 325.00
Moser, Vase, Art Deco, Sapphire Blue, Goblet Form, Frieze Of Elephants 230.00
Moser, Vase, Bottle Form, Pink Opalescent, Gold, Blue, & Yellow Arabesques 225.00
Moser, Vase, Clear To Amethyst, Intaglio Cut Flowers, Signed Moser, Carlsbad 80.00
Moser, Vase, Dutch Maiden Silhouette, Rock Crystal, Gold, Blue, White, Signed 225.00
Moser, Vase, Elephants, Palm Trees, Cameo, Gold, Amber, Signed, 11 1/2 In.Tall 275.00
Moser, Vase, Green & Gold Decor, Signed 95.00
Moser, Vase, Paneled, Amber, Acid Cut Frieze Of Gilded Elephants, Signed 180.00
Moser, Vase, 10 In., Pair .... *Illus* 300.00

Moser, Vase, 10 In., Pair

Moss Rose China was made by many firms from 1808 to 1900. It refers to
any china decorated with the Moss Rose flower.
Moss Rose, Box, Covered, Oval, 6 1/2 In. 12.50
Moss Rose, Coffeepot, Royal Ironstone, A.Meakin 25.00
Moss Rose, Dish, Vegetable, Royal Ironstone, A.Meakin, Covered, Oblong 25.00
Moss Rose, Gravy Boat, Turquoise Trim, Rope Handle, Attached Tray 10.00
Moss Rose, Plate, Bread & Butter 3.00
Moss Rose, Plate, Dinner .... 5.00 To 10.00
Moss Rose, Plate, Luncheon 4.00
Moss Rose, Plate, Salad 3.00
Moss Rose, Plate, 7 1/2 In. 2.75
Moss Rose, Platter 26.00
Moss Rose, Platter, Ironstone, Cook & Hancock, 7 1/2 X 11 1/2 In. 8.50
Moss Rose, Sauce 2.00
Moss Rose, Shaving Mug, Scuttle 12.50
Moss Rose, Soup .... 2.00 To 10.00
Moss Rose, Sugar, Covered 25.00
Moss Rose, Tea Set, Child's, Signed Queen China, 16 Piece 20.00
Moss Rose, Teapot .... 15.50 To 25.00
Moss Rose, Teapot, Haviland 32.00
Moss Rose, Tray, Dresser, 7 1/2 X 10 In. 12.00

Mother-of-pearl, or Pearl Satin, Glass was first made in the 1850s in
England and in Massachusetts. It was a special type of mold-blown satin
glass with air bubbles in the glass, giving it a pearlized color.
Mother-of-Pearl, see also Pearl
Mother-Of-Pearl, Basket, Diamond-Quilted, Raspberry Shading To White 245.00
Mother-Of-Pearl, Bottle, Flower & Acorn, White, 5 In.Tall 300.00
Mother-Of-Pearl, Pitcher, Pink & Blue, Applied Camphor Handle, 9 1/2 In. 795.00
Mother-Of-Pearl, Toothpick, Ruffled Top, Pink 90.00
Mother-Of-Pearl, Tumbler, Diamond-Quilted, Blue Mica Cased 35.00
Mother-Of-Pearl, Tumbler, Diamond-Quilted, Floral, Blue 50.00
Mother-Of-Pearl, Tumbler, Pink To Cranberry Top, Herringbone 55.00
Mother-Of-Pearl, Tumbler, Pink, Diamond-Quilted, Melon Ribbed 22.50
Mother-Of-Pearl, Tumbler, Rainbow, Diamond Crisscross, White, Pink, Apricot 175.00
Mother-Of-Pearl, Vase, Blue To White Shading, Rivulet, Off-White Casing 160.00
Mother-Of-Pearl, Vase, Blue To White, Bulbous, Short Neck, 3 3/4 In.High 160.00

Mother-Of-Pearl, Vase, Blue To White, Bulbous, Short Neck, 5 In.High 160.00
Mother-Of-Pearl, Vase, Blue, Six-Cloved Body, Elliptical Teardrop Pattern 100.00
Mother-Of-Pearl, Vase, Cased, Pulled Rim, Yellow, 7 In. 100.00
Mother-Of-Pearl, Vase, Diamond-Quilted, Shaded Blue To White, 5 In.Tall 130.00
Mother-Of-Pearl, Vase, Diamond-Quilted, Pink, 6 1/4 In.High 110.00
Mother-Of-Pearl, Vase, Pink To White, Fluted Top, Satin Glass 110.00
Mother-Of-Pearl, Vase, Rose Color, Moire Pattern, Camphor Handles 125.00
Mother-Of-Pearl, Vase, Rose To Pink, Diamond-Quilted, Camphor Edge 225.00
Mother-Of-Pearl, Vase, Sink Satin, Ruffled Top 125.00
Mother-Of-Pearl, Vase, Spot Pattern, Blue, Satin Glass, Scalloped, 8 1/2 In. 75.00
Mother-Of-Pearl, Vase, Yellow Satin, Pair 150.00
       Moustache Cup, see Mustache Cup
Mt.Joye, Bowl, Rose, Cameo, Green Acid Ground, Gold Flowers, Leaves, Stems 125.00
Mt.Joye, Bowl, Rose, Green & Gold Enameling, Cameo 145.00
Mt.Joye, Vase, Cameo, Emerald Frosted Tree Bark Ground, Leaves, Stems, Cosmos 93.00
Mt.Joye, Vase, Cameo, Flowers, Leaves, Green, Gold, Signed, 8 In.Tall 90.00

       Mt.Washington Glass was made at the Mt.Washington Glass Co.
       located in New Bedford, Massachusetts. Many types of Art Glass were
       made there from 1850 to the 1890s.
Mt.Washington Glass, see also Burmese
Mt.Washington, Bowl, Cameo, White, Pink, Lady's Head On Both Sides 250.00
Mt.Washington, Bowl, Rose, Floral Design, Frosted, Gold, Signed, 7 1/2 In.Tall 175.00
Mt.Washington, Bowl, Rose, Lilies, Gold Green, Verona 50.00
Mt.Washington, Hair Receiver, Hand-Painted 25.00
Mt.Washington, Jar, Biscuit, Pairpoint, Scenic, Rustic Cottage, Pink, Cover 400.00
Mt.Washington, Jar, Cookie, Decoration Like Crown Milano, Signed In Cover 230.00
Mt.Washington, Jar, Cracker, Melon Rib, Enamel Scrolls, Floral 150.00
Mt.Washington, Jar, Cracker, Pastel Floral, Lusterless, Silver Lid, Rim, Bail 78.00
Mt.Washington, Peachblow, Ewer, Rose To Pale Pink, Enamel Decor, 10 In.Tall 125.00
Mt.Washington, Pear, Pink .... *Illus* 450.00

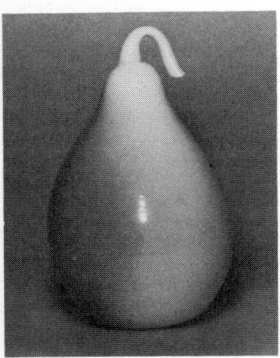

Mt.Washington, Pear, Pink

Mt.Washington, Planter, Floral, Blue, White, Footed, Miniature, Numbered 55.00
Mt.Washington, Plaque, Floral, Bouquet Of 13 Flowers, Enclosed In Clear 3800.00
Mt.Washington, Plate, Carnations, Hand-Painted, 10 In.Diameter 8.00
Mt.Washington, Plate, Day Lilies, Beige, Blue, Gold Trim, 7 1/2 In.Diameter 65.00
Mt.Washington, Plate, Flowers, Hand-Painted, 10 In.Diameter 25.00
Mt.Washington, Plate, Hand-Painted, Apple Blossoms, Acid Finish, 2 Children 25.00
Mt.Washington, Plate, Roses, Hand-Painted, Fluted, Crimped, 12 In.Diameter 35.00
Mt.Washington, Plate, White, Lusterless, Hand-Painted Pink Roses, Dated 18-8 .... 35.00
Mt.Washington, Salt & Pepper, Daisy Design, Yellow, Pink 75.00
Mt.Washington, Salt & Pepper, Fig, Forget-Me-Nots, Blue, Lavender 100.00
Mt.Washington, Salt & Pepper, Floral Design, Blue To White, 4 In.Tall 135.00
Mt.Washington, Salt & Pepper, Hand-Painted Flowers, Melon Rib 29.50
Mt.Washington, Salt & Pepper, Melon Ribbed, White, Flowers, Holder 59.00
Mt.Washington, Salt, Egg Shape, Flowers 25.00
Mt.Washington, Salt, Egg, Hand-Painted, Flat Bottom 23.50
Mt.Washington, Salt, Fig, Pale Blue, Apricot Florals, Pewter Top 20.00

Mt.Washington, Shaker, Salt, Blue Satin, World's Fair 1893 .... 30.00
Mt.Washington, Shaker, Salt, Blue To Yellow, Robin On Branch 20.00
Mt.Washington, Shaker, Salt, Blue, Yellow, Enamel, Pair 40.00
Mt.Washington, Shaker, Salt, Lusterless White, Purple Pansies, Ribbed 25.00
Mt.Washington, Shaker, Salt, Opaline, Pewter Top 22.50
Mt.Washington, Shaker, Sugar, Egg Shape 135.00
Mt.Washington, Shaker, Sugar, Egg Shape, Enameled Berries, Leaves, Label 150.00
Mt.Washington, Shaker, Sugar, Fig, Roses, Pink, Violet, Green, Brown, Enamel 250.00
Mt.Washington, Shaker, Sugar, Floral Design, Blue To White, 4 1/2 In.Tall 135.00
Mt.Washington, Shaker, Sugar, Forget-Me-Nots, Blue, Pink, Egg Shape, Pair 150.00
Mt.Washington, Shaker, Sugar, Leaves, Melon Ribbed, Yellow, Blue, Red 110.00
Mt.Washington, Shaker, Sugar, Melon Shape, Holly Decor, Resilvered Top 145.00
Mt.Washington, Shaker, Sugar, Pansies Design, Egg Shape 135.00
Mt.Washington, Toothpick, Bristol, White, Embossed Top Beading 10.00
Mt.Washington, Tumbler, White Satin, Acorn & Leaf Decoration 75.00
Mt.Washington, Vase, Bud, White, Lusterless, 8 In.Tall 35.00
Mt.Washington, Vase, Mums, Rose, White, Gold, Verona 100.00
Mt.Washington, Vase, Rose To Pink, Ruffled Edge, Applied Camphor, 8 In.Tall 75.00
Mueller Freres, Bowl, Silveria, Amber, Green, Blue, Pedestal, Signed, 3 1/2 In. 135.00
Mueller Freres, Lamp, Hanging Dome, Orange To Brown At Top, Signed, 8 In. 69.50
Mueller Freres, Light, Night, Beetle, Luneville, 6 In.Long 250.00
Mueller Freres, Vase, Cameo, Cylindrical, Green Marbleized, Iris, Signed 160.00
Mueller Freres, Vase, Cameo, Tan, Green, Black, 3 Cutting, Signed, 5 3/4 In. 210.00
Mueller Freres, Vase, Cameo, Translucent, Yellow To Green, Insects, Plants 425.00
Mueller Freres, Vase, Shepherd, Sheep, Yellow, Brown, Cameo, 9 In.Tall 195.00
Mueller Freres, Vase, Trumpet, Cameo, Black, Orange, Signed, 14 In.Tall 315.00
Muffineer, Clear, Glass, Sterling Silver Top 20.00
Muffineer, Cut Top & Base, Green 27.00
Muffineer, Green Cased Glass 25.00
Muffineer, Red Roses, Hand-Painted 14.25
Muffineer, Ruby Panel, Single Hole Top 37.50

*The Phonograph, invented by Thomas Edison in the 1880s, has been made by
many firms.*

Music, Accordion, Arion, Made In Germany 35.00
Music, Accordion, Horners, Self-Playing 700.00
Music, Accordion, Novitat, Handmade Reeds 15.00
Music, Banjo, Automatic, Encore, In Case 8995.00
Music, Banjo, Jas.Morrison, Patent 1892, Mother-Of-Pearl Inlay, 5 String 95.00
Music, Banjo, Wood Frame, 7 In.Diameter 10.00
Music, Book, A New Method For The Pianoforte, 1929, James Bellak 1.00
Music, Box, Aureophone In Gold Letters, Gold Stenciling, 1 Paper Roll 75.00
Music, Box, Bell, Baker-Troll, 4 Section, Three Cylinders 1995.00
Music, Box, Bird In Gilded Cage, Red Bird, Swiss, Handmade 49.00
Music, Box, Bremond, Inlaid Wood, Mirrored Niches, Swiss Cylinder 3995.00
Music, Box, Burl Walnut, Six Bells, Brass Plate, Dated 1869, 8 Tunes 485.00
Music, Box, Calliope, Bell, 25 1/4 In.Discs, Ornate Case 1995.00
Music, Box, Calliope, Disc, 8 Ft.10 In.High 3495.00
Music, Box, Calliope, Ten Records, Man & Woman Dancing Inside 250.00
Music, Box, Calliope, 12 Records 375.00
Music, Box, Cuff, Capital, Six Cuffs, Stayle A, Picture Under Cover 700.00
Music, Box, Cylinder, Hidden Drum & Bell, Decal On Lid, 6 Tunes 500.00
Music, Box, Drum & Bells, 8 Tune Cylinder 450.00
Music, Box, Edison, Cylinder, Model B, Morning Glory Horn 165.00
Music, Box, French, Hand Turn, Plaisirs Montmartrois & Marion Valse 45.00
Music, Box, Hand Crank, Paper Rolls, Dated 1871 .... 250.00
Music, Box, Imperator, Disc, Bells, Ornate Cabinet 1995.00
Music, Box, Key Wind, Cylinder, Four Tunes, Inlay Cover 375.00
Music, Box, Mahogany, Brass Corners, Euphonia, 11 Tin Disc Records 275.00
Music, Box, Mermod Freres, Cylinder, Coin Operated, 8 Moving Dolls 1750.00
Music, Box, Mermod Freres, Piccolo, C.1885, Matching Table, Cylinder 1995.00
Music, Box, Miniature Organ, Rosewood, Turned Spool Legs, 2 Inkwells 70.00
Music, Box, Nicole Freres, Brass Bedplate, C.1860, 10 Tune, Key Wind 995.00
Music, Box, Nicole Freres, C.1860, Brass Bedplate, 10 7/8 In.Cylinder 695.00
Music, Box, Nicole Freres, Key Wind, C.1845, 4 Tune Brass Bedplate 795.00
Music, Box, Nonopol, Upright, Coin Operated, 10 17 1/4 In.Discs 1150.00

Music, Box, Orchestra, Ami Rivenc, Switzerland, Cylinder 5995.00
Music, Box, Orchestra, Paillard, 24 Note Organ Section, 2 Drawers 4995.00
Music, Box, Orchestra, 20 Note Reed Organ, Drums, & Bells 1495.00
Music, Box, Paillard, Bell, 15 1/4 In.Cylinder 1295.00
Music, Box, Polyphone, Automatic Disc Changing, Bells 2995.00
Music, Box, Polyphone, Upright, Coin Operated 1595.00
Music, Box, Polyphone, Upright, Walnut 1995.00
Music, Box, Regina, Coin Operated, Oak Case, 6 Discs 695.00
Music, Box, Regina, Coin Operated, Table Model 450.00
Music, Box, Regina, Desk, Oak Cabinet 2495.00
Music, Box, Regina, Double Comb, Oak Case, Coin Operated 700.00
Music, Box, Regina, Folding Top 1295.00
Music, Box, Regina, Parlor Model, Automatic Disc Changer, Oak Cabinet 2495.00
Music, Box, Regina, Sublima .... *Illus* 900.00
Music, Box, Regina, Table Model, Glass Top, 27 In. 800.00
Music, Box, Regina, Table Model, Mahogany Cabinet 1149.00
Music, Box, Regina, Table Model, Mahogany, Style 26, 25 In.Discs 1350.00
Music, Box, Regina, Table Model, Style 11, Storage Base 1295.00
Music, Box, Regina, Table Model, Style 12, Storage Drawer 1195.00
Music, Box, Regina, Table Model, 12 In.Discs, Ornate 700.00
Music, Box, Regina, Table Model, 20 3/4 In.Disc, Oak Cabinet 1495.00
Music, Box, Regina, Upright 1295.00
Music, Box, Regina, 12 Tunes, 20 3/4 In.Diameter .... *Illus* 2250.00

Music, Box, Regina, Sublima

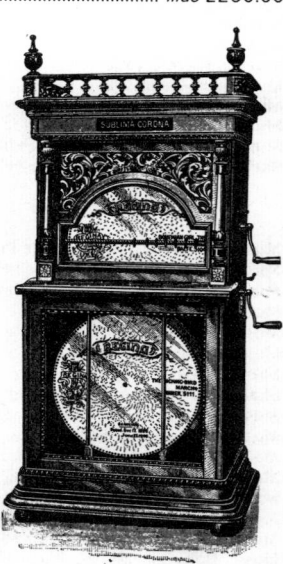

Music, Box, Regina, 12 Tunes, 20 3/4 In.Diameter

Music, Box, Regina, 15 1/2 In., 10 Discs 430.00
Music, Box, Reginaphone, Combination Disc Music Box & Phonograph 1295.00
Music, Box, Reginaphone, Style 246, Floor Model, Mahogany, Combination 1295.00
Music, Box, S.Troll Fils, Geneva, Burl Cabinet, Inlaid Brass, Cylinder 4995.00
Music, Box, Sirion, Disc Shifting, Shifting Center Spindle 1495.00
Music, Box, Swiss Orchestra, Butterfly Bell, Drums, Castanets 450.00
Music, Box, Swiss, Christmas Tree Holder, Disc, Winding 250.00
Music, Box, Swiss, Floral Marquetry Case, 12 Tunes 250.00
Music, Box, Swiss, Floral Marquetry Case, 8 Tunes, 19 In.Long 270.00
Music, Box, Swiss, Matching Table, 3 8 Tune Cylinders, Drawer 1495.00
Music, Box, Swiss, Paillard, 8 Tune, Inlaid, Rosewood Case, Repeater Switch 400.00
Music, Box, Swiss, Waltz Tunes, Repeater Switch, Inlaid Top & Front 800.00
Music, Box, Symphonion, Base Cabinet 2295.00
Music, Box, Symphonion, Bell, Upright, Matching Cabinet 1995.00
Music, Box, Symphonion, Bells, Upright, Ornate Cabinet 1295.00

Music, Box, Symphonion, C.1880, 13 Discs	500.00
Music, Box, Symphonion, Four Bells, 7 1/2 In.Disc	295.00
Music, Box, Table Model, Cylinder, 6 Bell Chorus, 97 Tooth Forks	475.00
Music, Box, Table Model, Regina, Mark No.56837	1000.00
Music, Box, Wurlitzer 146, Metal Chimes	5000.00
Music, Calliope, Model No.2, 26 1/2 In.Wide, 52 In.Long, 250 Lbs.	2295.00
Music, Calliope, Table Model, 10 9 1/4 In.Discs	350.00
Music, Calliope, Tangley, 43 Note, Automatic	5200.00
Music, Calliope, Tangley, 43 Note, Automatic & Manual, Gasoline Motor	5800.00
Music, Calliope, Tangley, 43 Note, Hand Play, Gasoline Motor	4000.00
Music, Case, Violin, Casket Type, Wood	27.50
Music, Coinola, Jr., Coin Operated	1950.00
Music, Cylinder For Music Box, Pinned, 12 3/4 In.Long, 2 1/4 In.Diameter, 3	60.00
Music, Disc Player, Standard, Model A	150.00
Music, Disc, Regina, 15 1/2 In., 8	25.00
Music, Drum, American Military, 1820-40, Tiger Stripe Grain, Curly Maple	125.00
Music, Drum, C.1880, Civil War Musician, Inlaid Wood, Metal Fastening	135.00
Music, Fotoplayer, American Photoplayer Co., Style 20, , 88 Note Rolls	4995.00
Music, Gramophone, Columbia, Patent 1905, Brass & Tin Horn	185.00
Music, Gramophone, Edison, 30 Records	150.00
Music, Graphophone, Columbia, Type B	125.00
Music, Harmonica, Wilheim Thie, Wein, 1875, Brass Plates, 8 In.Keys	15.00
Music, Harmonicon, Mahogany Oblong Case, 12 Graduated Glasses, C.1830	150.00
Music, Harp, Regency, Lacquered & Gilt Wood, 19th Century, Carved	700.00
Music, Harp, Swiss, Gold & Enamel, Miniature, 2 1/2 In.High, 19th Century	1100.00
Music, Horn, Victrola, Scalloped, Green, Red Roses, Needs Repainting	35.00
Music, Hurdy-Gurdy, Faventa, Made In Spain	300.00
Music, Juke Box, Bing Crosby Jr.	22.00
Music, Jukebox, Seeburg K.T.Special, Serial No.162883, 3 Rolls	5995.00
Music, Jukebox, Seeburg, Model Lpc-1, 1963, Plays 33 1/3 & 45 R.P.M.	550.00
Music, Jukebox, Wurlitzer, 1960, 45 R.P.M., Model No.2400, Holds 200 Records	275.00
Music, Mandolin Zither, Overture, Paillard, 13 In.Cylinder, Inlaid Brass	1000.00
Music, Mandolin, Leather Case	45.00
Music, Mandolin, Porrazo & D'agostino, Patent 1883	30.00
Music, Melodeon, Refinished Case, Plays	400.00
Music, Melodeon, Wm.A.Prince, Buffalo, N.Y.	400.00
Music, Melodeon, 73 Note, Rosewood	200.00
Music, Melodeon, 1846, 61 Note, Rosewood	125.00
Music, Metronome, Patent 1899, Wood, Brass, Theodore Presser Label	20.00
Music, Nickelodeon Piano, Western Electric, Selectra B, Oak, Art Glass	2495.00
Music, Nickelodeon, Cremona, Keyboard Type	1150.00
Music, Nickelodeon, Cremona, Style D, Art	1700.00
Music, Nickelodeon, Cremona, Style G, Full Rank Of Flute Pipes	3200.00
Music, Nickelodeon, Mills, Double Violin Violano Virtuoso, 8 Rolls	3750.00
Music, Nickelodeon, Mills, Racehorse, Horses Run While Music Plays	2300.00
Music, Nickelodeon, Nelson Wiggins	1200.00
Music, Nickelodeon, O-Roll, Custom Built, 25 Cent Slot, 6 Ft.Tall	2600.00
Music, Nickelodeon, Seeburg Junior, Keyboard Type	1150.00
Music, Nickelodeon, Seeburg, Style E, Art Glass	2900.00
Music, Orchestra, Decap, Jazz, 74 Key, Percussion & Accordion, Europe	4000.00
Music, Orchestra, Piano & Mandolin, Regina, Sublima, Spring Wound	2495.00
Music, Orchestra, Popper & Co., Salon, Flickering Torches On Front	9975.00
Music, Orchestrion, Player, Roll, Art Glass, Snare, Triangle, Castanets	3200.00
Music, Orchestrion, Roland, The Giant, German, Barrel, Coin Operated	1695.00
Music, Orchestrion, Symphonion, Bells, German, Ornate Cabinet	2495.00
Music, Orchestrion, Symphonion, Bells, New Jersey, C.1890, Oak Cabinet	2495.00
Music, Orchestrion, Weight Operated Barrel, Coin Operated Bar, Europe	1595.00
Music, Orchestrion, Welte, 11 Ft.6 In.High	9975.00
Music, Orchestrion, Western Electric, Rolls	5495.00
Music, Organ, Band, Wurlitzer, No.125, 13 Brass Pipes	3000.00
Music, Organ, Barrel, Casali, 1895, 10 Tunes, Front Crank, 43 In.High	475.00
Music, Organ, Casket, 1 Roll	50.00
Music, Organ, Celestina Roller, Denmark, 6 Rolls	195.00
Music, Organ, Concert, Roller, 10 Rolls	325.00
Music, Organ, Concert, Roller, 21 Rolls, C.Borden Co., Patent 5/31/87	250.00
Music, Organ, Decap, Dance Hall, 74 Key, Pipes, Drums, Accordion	5500.00

Music, Organ, Decap, Street, 7 Ft.High, 8 Ft.Wide, Book Operated 4000.00
Music, Organ, Electronic Univox On Counter Melody, 121 Key 8000.00
Music, Organ, Estey, Parlor, Ebony Finish 300.00
Music, Organ, Estey, Walnut, 1861 .... 500.00
Music, Organ, Estey, 2 Manual & Pedal, Reed, Style T, 10 Rank, 15 Stops 700.00
Music, Organ, Jos.Bursens & Co., 68 Key, Inlaid Veneer 7750.00
Music, Organ, Mason & Hamlin, Pump, Stool 1500.00
Music, Organ, Melodeon, Estey, Made In Battleboro, Vt., 1857 .... 1800.00
Music, Organ, Mohler, Theatre, Console & Pipe Chest, 8 Ranks 2450.00
Music, Organ, Mortier Electronic Univox, Book Operated 3200.00
Music, Organ, Mortier, 101 Key, Europe 7500.00
Music, Organ, Mortier, 80 Key, Holland, Street 8000.00
Music, Organ, Parlor, Cherry 175.00
Music, Organ, Player, Symphonia, Hand Crank, Wilcox & White, C.1895 .... 450.00
Music, Organ, Portable, By Ferrand & Doty, Date 1874, 24 In. 195.00
Music, Organ, Pump, Reed, Walnut 400.00
Music, Organ, Pump, Vocalion, Fake Front Pipes 150.00
Music, Organ, Ruth Carrousel, Book Operated 2500.00
Music, Organ, Seraphone, Roller, Europe 70.00
Music, Organ, Street, Dutch, 80 Key, Gillet, 5 Moving Figures, Carved 8550.00
Music, Organ, Street, Electronic, Amsterdam 6500.00
Music, Organ, Walnut, 1888, Stool 240.00
Music, Organ, Wurlitzer, Lodge, 2 Manual 3 Rank, Pennsylvania 895.00
Music, Organ, Wurlitzer, No.125, Band, 13 Brass Pipes 3000.00
Music, Organ, Wurlitzer, 150, Decorated Glass Mirrored Front 4590.00
Music, Perforator, Roll, Pierre Eich Factory, Belgium, Keyboard Operated 1495.00
Music, Phonograph, Busy Bee, Cylinder 98.00
Music, Phonograph, Busy Bee, Horn, 3 Records 130.00
Music, Phonograph, Cabinet, Disc 20.00
Music, Phonograph, Columbia, Grand Type Ab, Horn, Stand, 2 Records 500.00
Music, Phonograph, Columbia, Key Wind 85.00
Music, Phonograph, Columbia, Type Ab, Grand 400.00
Music, Phonograph, Edison Triumph, C.1905, Morning Glory Horn, Floor Crane 345.00
Music, Phonograph, Edison, Combination Type, Cygnet Horn 195.00
Music, Phonograph, Edison, Concert Model, For Bar Room Use 350.00
Music, Phonograph, Edison, Cylinder, Amberola Console 130.00
Music, Phonograph, Edison, Cylinder, Morning Glory Horn 150.00
Music, Phonograph, Edison, Cylinder, Morning Glory Horn, 20 Cylinders 250.00
Music, Phonograph, Edison, Home, Morning Glory Horn 150.00
Music, Phonograph, Edison, Home, Suitcase, Type A 125.00
Music, Phonograph, Edison, Home, 14 In.Horn, Records 117.50
Music, Phonograph, Edison, Standard 135.00
Music, Phonograph, Edison, Standard, 14 In.Horn, Records 111.50
Music, Phonograph, Edison, Triumph, Type E, Model O, Wooden Oak Cygnet Horn 400.00
Music, Phonograph, Edison, Wax Cylinder, Wooden Horn, 2 Cylinder 138.00
Music, Phonograph, Table Model, Metal Morning Glory Horn, Standard Model A 85.00
Music, Phonograph, Wonder Talking Machine Co., Disc, 42 Records 125.00
Music, Phonograph, Talking Machine, Gold Labeled Cherubs On Side 125.00
Music, Phonograph, Talking Machine, Victor, Type Ii, Morning Glory Horn 150.00
Music, Photoplayer, Wurlitzer, Style G, 25 Cent Slot 3600.00
Music, Piano Roll, Polish Song 1.50
Music, Piano, Ampico, Haines, Upright 395.00
Music, Piano, Ampico, Upright, Marshall & Wendall 495.00
Music, Piano, Baby Grand, Signed F.O.Smith, New York, N.Y. 6500.00
Music, Piano, Barrel, Coin Operated, Europe 2100.00
Music, Piano, Chickering, Ampico, Grand, 5 Ft.8 1/2 In. 1900.00
Music, Piano, Coin Operated, Player, Art Glass 2100.00
Music, Piano, English, Steward's Patent, Euphonicon, F.Beale & Co. 1500.00
Music, Piano, Erard French, Concert Grand, 18th Century 1300.00
Music, Piano, Gerhard, Player, Electrified, 30 Rolls 495.00
Music, Piano, Grand, Art Deco, Walnut, C.1937, Serial No.288935 .... 2400.00
Music, Piano, Grand, Fisher, Ampico 795.00
Music, Piano, Grand, Parlor, Rosewood, Weber Of New York & London, 1863 .... 2500.00
Music, Piano, Grand, Steinway, Square, Rosewood, 1873 .... 950.00
Music, Piano, H.C.Bayes, Upright, Player 500.00
Music, Piano, International, No.18064, Ludwig & Co., Carved Design, Canada 510.00

Music, Piano, Kimberlin Recordo, Upright, 42 In.High 700.00
Music, Piano, Knabe, Ampico A, 15 Rolls 1750.00
Music, Piano, Kuhl & Klath, 10 Multitune Rolls, Coin Operated, Belgium 560.00
Music, Piano, Nickelodeon, Standard, Beveled Long Oval Glass Front 650.00
Music, Piano, Orchestrelle, Aeolian, 12 Aeolian Grand Rolls 950.00
Music, Piano, Player, Coin Operated, Coin Slot, Art Glass 2100.00
Music, Piano, Player, Cremona, Nickelodeon, Dated 1925 .... 2300.00
Music, Piano, Player, Electric, Ampico, Baby Grand, William Knabe, 75 Rolls 900.00
Music, Piano, Player, Lindeman, 300 Rolls 295.00
Music, Piano, Player, Mendenhall, Cabinet Grand, 50 Rolls 200.00
Music, Piano, Player, Seeburg .... *Illus* 695.00

Music, Piano, Player, Seeburg

Music, Piano, Player, Seeburg, Art Glass, Coin Slot 1250.00
Music, Piano, Player, Seeburg, Coin Operated, Keys 2100.00
Music, Piano, Regina, Sublima, Oak Case, Electric 2495.00
Music, Piano, Schoenhut, Baby Grand, Brown, Ornate Legs, 15 X 15 3/4 X 10 In. 40.00
Music, Piano, Schoenhut, 20 X 8 In. 10.00
Music, Piano, Singer, Upright, Steel Harp, Mahogany 600.00
Music, Piano, Steck, Duo-Art, Reproducing, Grand 1085.00
Music, Piano, Street, Norrerto Gia, 50 Key, 4 Bells 600.00
Music, Piano, Stroud, Upright, Duo-Art, Reproducing 395.00
Music, Piano, Upright, Kimberlin, Reproducing & Recording, New England 775.00
Music, Piano, Upright, Welte, Reproducing, Germany 795.00
Music, Piano, Walnut Case, Upright, Edward Jules 425.00
Music, Piano, Welte, Mignon, Grand, Player 5500.00
Music, Piano, Welte, Mignon, Grand, Player 5500.00
Music, Piano, Welte, Mignon, Reproducing, Seiler, Model 98, 24 Rolls 800.00
Music, Piano, Welte, Reproducing, Cabinet Style, Keyboardless 1695.00
Music, Piano, William Bourne, Rosewood, Grande, Carved Legs 3500.00
Music, Piano, Wurlitzer Pianino, Coin Slot, 5 Tune Roll 1000.00
Music, Piano, Wurlitzer Pianino, 44 Note, Player, Coin Slot 1000.00
Music, Pianoforte, Regency, Inlaid Mahogany, Astor & Company, London, C.1815 .... 175.00
Music, Pianola, Aeolian, Player, Pushup 100.00
Music, Polyphone, Carved Walnut, Coin Operated, 4 Discs, 7 Ft.3 In.High 2400.00
Music, Polyphone, Storage Space Base, Coin Operated, 19 1/2 In.Disc 1250.00
Music, Record, Cylinder, Edison & Columbia, 5 In., Set Of 24 .... 350.00
Music, Record, Cylinder, Thomas A.Edison, Black Bakelite 1.00
Music, Record, Disc, Edison, Thick .... .60
Music, Record, Edison, Blue Amberole, Fourth Of July Patrol 1.50
Music, Record, Edison, Blue Amberole, Old Comrades 1.50
Music, Record, Edison, Blue Amberole, She Was Bred In Old Kentucky 1.50
Music, Record, 78 Rpm, New, 30 .... 15.00
Music, Recording System, Edison, 1906, Floor Stand, Brass Horn, Floor Crane 750.00
Music, Roll, Burssens, 88, Orchestrion 8.00
Music, Roll, Dienst, Mezon 8.00
Music, Roll, North Tonawanda & Artisan, 45 Key 10.00

Music, Roll, Red Welte 100	5.00
Music, Roll, Weber Solea	25.00
Music, Roll, Wilcox & White, Organ	2.50
Music, Saxophone, Leather Case	15.00 To 30.00
Music, Sheet Music, Civil War, Tell Mother I Die Happy	8.00
Music, Sheet Music, Mckinley & Hobart Grand March, By J.W.Turner, 1896	6.50
Music, Sheet Music, Slav Song, Wake Nicodemus	8.00
Music, Sheet, Absent, 1913, F.E.Hathaway	.50
Music, Sheet, As Long As The World Rolls On, 1907, Witmark	.25
Music, Sheet, Bring Back The Golden Days, 1919, Huntzinger & Dilworth	.25
Music, Sheet, Dande Of The Demon, 1906, Remich	.35
Music, Sheet, Elaborate Border, For Piano & Vocal, Four Sheets	2.00
Music, Sheet, Eventide, 1918, Mckinley Music Co.	.25
Music, Sheet, Good-Bye Sweetheart Good-Bye, 1923, Mr.Amelia Jonas	.25
Music, Sheet, Hand Printed, Handmade Linen Paper, Movable Treble Clef, 1780	8.00
Music, Sheet, Hearts Of The World, 1918, Echo Music Co.	.25
Music, Sheet, Hindustan, 1918, Forester Music, Inc.	.25
Music, Sheet, I Never Had A Mammy, Berlin, 1923	2.00
Music, Sheet, In The Glooming, 1919, Forester Music, Inc.	.25
Music, Sheet, In Virginia, 1913, F.J.Zeisberg	.25
Music, Sheet, I've Got The Mumps, 1909, Leo Feist, Inc.	.25
Music, Sheet, My Dear Old Kentucky Home, 1909, Old Glory Co.	.25
Music, Sheet, Nearer My God To Thee, 1908, Eclipse Pub.Co.	.25
Music, Sheet, Poodles & Pugs, 1906, Monroe Pub.Co.	.25
Music, Sheet, Promise Me, 1913, F.E.Hathaway Music Pub., Co.	.50
Music, Sheet, Shadows, 1901, Frederick Harris Co.	.25
Music, Sheet, Song Of The Tramp, 1926, Tri-City Music Co.	.25
Music, Sheet, That Grandest Song Of All, 1894, Old Glory Pub.Co.	.25
Music, Sheet, The Lost Chord, 1905, Eclipse Pub.Co.	.25
Music, Sheet, There Are Tears In Your Dear, Dear Eyes, 1917, Perrins	.25
Music, Sheet, They Say, 1920, Boosey & Co.	.25
Music, Sheet, Till The Sands Of The Desert Grow Cold, 1911, M.Witmark	.25
Music, Sheet, What Are You Going To Do To Help The Boys, 1918, Uncle Sam	2.00
Music, Sign, Rosa Ponselle, Columbia, Paper, 34 X 24 In. *Illus*	125.00

Music, Sign, Rosa Ponselle, Columbia, Paper, 34 X 24 In.

Music, Tanzabar, Paper Roll Activated Accordion, For Dancing Bears	400.00
Music, Tool, Piano Tuner's, 2 Headed, Wood Handle, C.1900	15.00
Music, Una-Fon, Deagan, Electric, 49 Note, For Carnivals	749.00
Music, Vibraharp, Automatic, Resotone, C.1910, Rolls, In Case	6995.00
Music, Victrola, Brunswick, Plays Thick Edison Records	25.00
Music, Victrola, Edison, Disc Horn, 35 Records	68.00
Music, Victrola, Small Baby Grand, Dated 1908	450.00
Music, Victrola, Table Model, 1904, 78 Rpm Disc Player, Oak	100.00

Music, Violano, Mill's, Virtuoso 3100.00
Music, Violin, Carlo Bergonzi Model, Case 75.55
Music, Violin, Wooden Case 17.50
Music, Xylophone, Balangi, 18 1/2 X 41 In. 300.00
Music, Xylophone, Rosewood, 24 Note, Reiterating 275.00
Music, Xylophone, Wurlitzer, 49 Notes, Aluminum Bars With Resonators 350.00
Music, Zither, Painted Case .... 10.00 To 50.00

Mustache Cups were popular from 1850 to 1900. A ledge of china or silver held the hair out of the liquid in the cup.

Mustache Cup & Saucer, China, Scalloped Saucer, Hand-Painted Florals, Gold 22.50
Mustache Cup & Saucer, Church Scene, Germany 22.00
Mustache Cup & Saucer, Cobalt Blue, Gold Decoration 40.00
Mustache Cup & Saucer, Cobalt, Gold Floral, Germany 37.00
Mustache Cup & Saucer, Floral & Leaves, Pink 23.00
Mustache Cup & Saucer, Floral Design, Cobalt Blue, Gold, White 38.00
Mustache Cup & Saucer, Floral Design, White, Gold Rim 18.00
Mustache Cup & Saucer, Floral Design, White, Gold, 'forget-Me-Not' 25.00
Mustache Cup & Saucer, Floral, Pink, Green, Blue, E.S.& Depon 24.75
Mustache Cup & Saucer, Flower, Beading, Forget-Me Not, Yellow Luster 25.00
Mustache Cup & Saucer, Flowers, Foliage, Gold Bands, Think Of Me, Porcelain 16.00
Mustache Cup & Saucer, Forget-Me-Not Pattern 15.00
Mustache Cup & Saucer, German, Old Fort Burial Hill, Bunker Hill, Gold 16.00
Mustache Cup & Saucer, Gold, 'present' 27.50
Mustache Cup & Saucer, Hand-Painted 22.00
Mustache Cup & Saucer, Lavender Pansies 17.00
Mustache Cup & Saucer, Left Hand 125.00
Mustache Cup & Saucer, Marked Burslem, Roses & Vines 25.00
Mustache Cup & Saucer, Melon Rib, Figures, Underplate, Signed Shunko, Japan 40.00
Mustache Cup & Saucer, Merry Christmas, Flowers 27.50
Mustache Cup & Saucer, Papa 36.00
Mustache Cup & Saucer, Pink & Yellow Roses, Porcelain 22.50
Mustache Cup & Saucer, Pink Luster, Gold, Beaded Separation, Floral 25.00
Mustache Cup & Saucer, Pink, Flowers 35.00
Mustache Cup & Saucer, Pink, White, Gold, Center Medallion, Man, Woman 47.00
Mustache Cup & Saucer, Remember Me, Hand-Painted Flowers, Gold Trim 19.00
Mustache Cup & Saucer, Rose Design, Yellow, Red 18.50
Mustache Cup & Saucer, Rosebuds, Pink, Scalloped Edge, Footed, Signed 45.00
Mustache Cup & Saucer, Soldiers' Home, Tilton, New Hampshire 28.00
Mustache Cup & Saucer, Turquoise, Burgundy, Gold, Signed A.Kauffmann 57.00
Mustache Cup & Saucer, Violets 31.00
Mustache Cup & Saucer, White, Gold Trim, British Crest 17.00
Mustache Cup & Saucer, White, Gold, Pink Floral, Scalloped Edges 39.00
Mustache Cup, Floral, White, Aqua, Pink, 'love The Giver' 16.00
Mustache Cup, Flower & Leaf Design, Lavender, Gold Rim 20.00
Mustache Cup, Flowers, Berries, White, Red, 'forget Me Not', Hand-Painted 16.00
Mustache Cup, Pink Luster, Two Ladies On Medallion Front, Crown, Bavaria 18.00
Mustache Cup, 'remember Me' 31.50
Mustache Cup, White, Pink Luster Band, Blue Floral, Forget-Me-Not 20.00

Nailsea Glass was made in the Bristol District in England from 1788 to 1873. Many pieces were made with loopings of colored glass as decorations.

Nailsea, Bell, Crystal Ground, White Loopings, Crystal Clapper & Handle 85.00
Nailsea, Bottle, Looping, Clear, Pink, White, 9 In.Tall 90.00
Nailsea, Bowl, Rose, Satiny Citron Background, White Loopings, 6 In.Diameter 110.00
Nailsea, Bowl, Rose, White Loopings, Ruffled Top, 6 1/2 In.Diameter 105.00
Nailsea, Cruet, Cobalt Swirl 20.00
Nailsea, Cruet, Stopper, 8 3/4 In.Tall 15.00
Nailsea, Epergne, Cranberry, White, Large & Three Small Vase, Set 350.00
Nailsea, Flask, Reclining, Purple & White Loopings, Cork Stopper 50.00
Nailsea, Lamp, Fairy, White Shade, Blue Loops, Clear Insert, Base, Pat.1886 .... 150.00
Nailsea, Rolling Pin, Red & White Loops, 12 In.Long 54.00
Nailsea, Vase, Pink, White, Handles, 6 In. 100.00
Nailsea, Vase, Yellow, Green, Blue, White, Looping, Bulbous, 3 3/4 In.Tall 70.00
Nailsea, Witch Ball, Clear, Pink & White Loopings, 6 In. 50.00
Nailsea, Witch Ball, Red, White, Looping, 18th Century, 5 In.Diameter 75.00

Nailsea, Witch's Ball, Clear Blue 35.00

> *Nakara is a trade name for a white glassware made around 1900 that was*
> *decorated in pastel colors. It was made by the C.F.Monroe Company of*
> *Meriden, Connecticut.*

Nakara, Box, Jewel, Orchids, Hand-Painted, Olive Green, Signed, Octagon Shape 138.00
Nakara, Box, Jewel, Relief Enamels In Mosaics, Pink-Rose Ground, Hinged Lid 195.00
Nakara, Fernery, Orchids, Hand-Painted, Olive Green, Signed 169.00

> *Nanking China is a blue-and-white porcelain made in China for export*
> *during the eighteenth century.*

Nanking, Platter, Blue, White, Landscape, Circa 1780, 12 In. 75.00
Nanking, Platter, Blue, White, Orange Peel Texture, 8 1/8 X 7 1/8 In. 85.00
Nanking, Platter, Blue, White, Orange Peel Texture, 9 1/4 X 8 1/8 In. 95.00

> *Napkin Rings were popular from 1869 to about 1900.*

Napkin Ring, Appended Bloom & Leaf 26.75
Napkin Ring, Bird On Tree Branch, Etched Floral, Silver 21.00
Napkin Ring, Book Shape, Silver Plate 18.00
Napkin Ring, Boy, China 6.50
Napkin Ring, Bulldog, Silver Plate 35.00
Napkin Ring, Carved Ivory, Dragons, 1 1/4 In.Wide 28.00
Napkin Ring, Clear, Pressed Glass, Initial F, Raised Blocks 16.00
Napkin Ring, Diamond Pattern, Horseshoe Shape, Glass 30.00
Napkin Ring, Dog, Jumping, Engraved Anna 8-20-05 .... 15.00
Napkin Ring, Dragon & Medallion Design, Ivory, Carved, Oriental 10.00
Napkin Ring, Engraved Name, 14k Gold, Pair 50.00
Napkin Ring, Engraved Woman's Head, Emma Buchanan, 1 In.Wide 30.00
Napkin Ring, Engraved, Nora, Birds, Silver Plate 4.00
Napkin Ring, Figural, Antelope, Meriden Co., Pair 95.00
Napkin Ring, Figural, Barrel On Twigs 13.00
Napkin Ring, Figural, Barrel Supported On Cradle, Silver Plate 22.50
Napkin Ring, Figural, Butterfly, Japanese Fans 22.00
Napkin Ring, Figural, Butterfly, Open Wings Hold Ring, Embossed 40.00
Napkin Ring, Figural, Chair, Formed By Branches 40.00
Napkin Ring, Figural, Cupid 55.00
Napkin Ring, Figural, Cupid Blowing Flute, Name Estella, Rogers & Bro. 32.00
Napkin Ring, Figural, Cupid, Wings & Butterfly, Victor Silver Co. 70.00
Napkin Ring, Figural, Dog, Green Eyes, Silver Plate 32.50
Napkin Ring, Figural, Eagles, Engraved Name, Resilvered 25.00
Napkin Ring, Figural, Fox 23.00
Napkin Ring, Figural, Gloved Hand Holds Posies, Silver Plate 12.00
Napkin Ring, Figural, Goat Pulling Ring On Wheel 80.00
Napkin Ring, Figural, Kitten Upright Beside Ring, 1 1/2 In.Tall 32.50
Napkin Ring, Figural, Parrot, Resting, Oak Leaf 40.00
Napkin Ring, Figural, Ring On Back Of Lion, Silver Plate 22.50
Napkin Ring, Figural, Ring On Saucer, Loop Handle, Flower, Silver Plate 22.50
Napkin Ring, Figural, Robin With Chain On Neck, Meriden Silver 70.00
Napkin Ring, Figural, Rooster, Shovel, Meriden On Base, Silver Plate 51.00
Napkin Ring, Figural, Squirrel .... *Illus* 40.00
Napkin Ring, Figural, Victorian Chair 25.00
Napkin Ring, Figural, Wishbones Straddling Triangular, Silver Plate 22.50
Napkin Ring, Grape Leaves & Twigs 25.00
Napkin Ring, Hallmarked Silver, Cutout Shamrocks 10.50
Napkin Ring, Lamb At Side, Silver 24.50
Napkin Ring, Oval, Flowers, Birds, Grandparents'names, Pair 6.00
Napkin Ring, Parrot On Side, Removable Head For Salt Cellar, Silver 19.00
Napkin Ring, Plated 1904, Glasgow 5.00
Napkin Ring, Porcelain, Babies On Sides 8.50
Napkin Ring, Purple Daisies, Greenery, Artist-Signed, Porcelain, 1915 .... 15.00
Napkin Ring, Scene Of Cherub With Bow & Arrow, Running Dog, Silver Plate 2.75
Napkin Ring, Setting Hen, Engraved, Meriden Silver 27.50
Napkin Ring, Sterling Silver, Double Rolled Edge 10.00
Napkin Ring, Sterling Silver, 1 In Ring, Marked Sterling 950 .... 40.00
Napkin Ring, Sterling Silver, 1 1/2 In.Wide, Engraved 35.00
Napkin Ring, Victorian, Lacy, Beaded, Red & Blue 4.00

Napkin Ring, Figural, Squirrel
See Page 324

*Nash Glass was made in Corona, New York, by Arthur Nash and his
sons after 1919. He had worked at the Webb Factory in England and for
the Tiffany Glassworks in the United States.*

Nash, Bowl, Chintz Pattern, Stripes, Dots, Green, Purple, Shallow, Pair 185.00
Nash, Bowl, Conical, 4 1/2 In.Diameter 50.00
Nash, Bowl, Pedestal, Chintz Pattern, Copper Color Cobweb On Blue Green 185.00
Nash, Stemware, Pale Rose, Golden Cup, Three Sided Stem 65.00
Nash, Vase, Floriform, Gold Iridescence At Rim, Silvery Iridescent Inside 180.00
Needlework, see Textile, Picture

*Netsuke are small ivory, wood, metal, or porcelain pieces used as the button on
the end of a cord holding a japanese money pouch. The earliest date from the
sixteenth century.*

Netsuke, Chestnuts Inside Carved Worm, Ivory, C.1820 .... 75.00
Netsuke, Child Crawling, Ball In Arms, Ivory, Signed, 1 3/4 X 1 1/2 In. 35.00
Netsuke, Chrysanthemum & Leaves, Antler, Circa 1820 .... 60.00
Netsuke, Cicada, Beetle, Ivory, C.1840-1860 .... 45.00
Netsuke, Cicada, Beetle, On Cord With Cinnabar Bead, White Jade, Circa 1900 .... 165.00
Netsuke, Cock On Bamboo Shoot, Ivory, Circa 1870 .... 80.00
Netsuke, Conqueror On Devil, Ivory, C.1840-1860 .... 50.00
Netsuke, Dejected Warrior, Ivory, 2 1/2 In.High 45.00
Netsuke, Dog & Fortune Ball, Ivory, C.1840-1860 .... 45.00
Netsuke, Eight Turtles On Mat, Ivory, 3 In.Long 120.00
Netsuke, Evil Demon, Rosewood, Signed Bizarre, 1 1/2 In. 15.00
Netsuke, Figurine, Chinese Man, Ivory, Hand Carved, High Forehead 15.00
Netsuke, Figurine, God Lohan, Ivory, 19th Century 40.00
Netsuke, Fish, Lobster Clinging To Him, Signed 17.00
Netsuke, Foo Dog, Ivory, 1 1/4 In.High 55.00
Netsuke, Foo Dog, Mad, Ivory 60.00
Netsuke, Fukurokiji, God Of Wisdom, Ivory, C.1840-1860 .... 55.00
Netsuke, Gnomes Holding Ball, Ivory, 1 In.Long 60.00
Netsuke, God Of Great Strength, Ivory, C.1760-80 .... 115.00
Netsuke, God Of Wisdom, Peachwood, C.1840-1860 .... 135.00
Netsuke, Gourd, Ivory, C.1760-80 .... 85.00
Netsuke, Hotel, Ivory, C.1840-1860 .... 60.00
Netsuke, Hoti Seated With Bag, Ivory, 1 In.High 50.00
Netsuke, Inro, Laquer, 3-Section, Malachite Bead, Ivory Lion 135.00
Netsuke, Inro, 5-Section, Cinnabar Melon Bead, Temple Bell 225.00
Netsuke, Lion Standing Holding Buckle, Ivory, 3 In.High 90.00
Netsuke, Lying Horse Box, Wood, C.1840-1860 .... 85.00
Netsuke, Magician With Frog, Ivory, C.1840-1860 .... 60.00
Netsuke, Magician With Gourd, Ivory, C.1840-1860 .... 60.00
Netsuke, Man On Bamboo Sprout, Ivory, C.1840-1860 .... 65.00
Netsuke, Man With Ivory Tusk On Back, Ivory, 1 1/2 In.High 45.00
Netsuke, Mask, Girl's Face, Nut, Circa 1820 .... 95.00
Netsuke, Monkey In Costume, Standing, Movable Head, Circa 1900 .... 135.00
Netsuke, Monkey, Carved Soapstone, 1 3/4 In. 6.00
Netsuke, Mouse On Ear Shell, Ivory, C.1840-1860 .... 60.00
Netsuke, Nude Man Protecting Basket, Ivory, 1 In.High 45.00

Netsuke, Pair Temple Dogs Wrestling, Ivory 45.00
Netsuke, Reclining Deer, Ivory, 2 In.Long 40.00
Netsuke, Samurai Warrior, Ivory, C.1840-1860 .... 50.00
Netsuke, Seated Man With Gourd, Ivory 40.00
Netsuke, Seated Sage With White Beard, Ivory 45.00
Netsuke, Small Child Seated, Ivory, 1 1/2 In.High 40.00
Netsuke, Snake Coiled Atop Skull, Signed, 1 1/4 In. 30.00
Netsuke, Standing Man With Bundle, Ivory 40.00
Netsuke, Temple Dogs Wrestling, Pair, Ivory, C.1840-1860 .... 45.00
Netsuke, Temple Lion Head, Mouth Opens, Circa 1900 .... 130.00
Netsuke, Traveling Man, Ivory, C.1840-1860 .... 45.00

*Newcomb Pottery was founded by Ellsworth and William Woodward at
Sophie Newcomb College, New Orleans, Louisiana, in 1896. The work
continued through the 1940s. Pieces of this art pottery are marked with the
letter N inside the letter C.*

Newcomb, Bowl, Dark Blue, Incised Geometric Design, Signed Sadie Irvine 65.00
Newcomb, Bowl, Pink, Cream, Floral, Signed Irene Keep, 6 In.Diameter 110.00
Newcomb, Vase, Blue To Purple To Pink, Geometric, Signed Sadie Irvine 75.00
Newcomb, Vase, Blue, Moon & Trees, Cylindrical, Artist A.F.S. 90.00
Newcomb, Vase, Oak Trees, Mountains, Artist-Signed J.M., Label 130.00
Newcomb, Vase, Raised Design, Orange, Gray, Signed, Handles, 4 1/2 In.Tall 25.00
Newcomb, Vase, Sassafras Trees, Blue, Signed, Original Label, 12 In.High 110.00
Newcomb, Vase, Signed, Cherubs, 6 In. 25.00
Newcomb, Vase, Trees With Hanging Moss, Blue, Artist-Signed 100.00
Newcomb, Vase, White Glaze, Applied Cupid, Dove, Bows, & Flowers, 8 1/4 In. 150.00
Newhall, Bowl & Saucer, Rose, Puce, & Green, Laurel Festoons, C.1790 .... 20.00
Newhall, Cup & Saucer, Handleless, Open Window Pattern 38.00
Newhall, Cup & Saucer, Oriental Decoration, Wishbone Handle, Hand Painted 35.00
Newhall, Mug, Sairey Gamp & Mr.Bubble, 4 1/2 In. 10.00
Niderviller, Coffee Set, Miniature, Cornflower Sprigs, C.1775, 6 Piece 110.00
Niderviller, Vase, Ovoid Form, Bouquets, C Mark In Blue, C.1760 .... 100.00
Niloak, Candlestick, Black, 1910-1942, Pair 40.00
Niloak, Creamer, Miniature, Green 2.00
Niloak, Dish, Swan 6.00
Niloak, Ewer, Eagle & Star, Green, 10 In.High 12.00
Niloak, Ewer, Rose To Blue, 8 In. 15.00
Niloak, Vase, Lamp Base, 12 In. 35.00
Niloak, Vase, Marbleized, Cream, Red, Brown, Blue, 8 In.Tall .... 21.00 To 23.00
Niloak, Vase, Marbleized, Marked, 3 3/4 In.High 15.00
Niloak, Vase, Marbleized, 4 1/4 In.High 5.00
Niloak, Vase, Marbleized, 4 1/2 In.High 12.00
Niloak, Vase, Marked, 3 3/4 In.High 15.00
Niloak, Vase, Missionware, Signed, 5 In. 12.00

Nippon-Marked Porcelain was made in Japan after 1891.

Nippon, Bowl, Berry, Black, White Prunus, 10 In., Six Matching Dishes 23.00
Nippon, Bowl, Berry, 7 Piece, Pink, Gold, Floral, Hand-Painted, M In Wreath 35.00
Nippon, Bowl, Birds' Heads, Orange Luster .... *Illus* 12.00

Nippon, Bowl, Birds' Heads,
Orange Luster

Nippon, Bowl, Blackberry Design, Scalloped Rim, M Mark, 8 In. 25.00
Nippon, Bowl, Center, Pastoral Scene, Gold Edge, 10 In.Diameter 38.00
Nippon, Bowl, Cottage On Shore, Yellow, Orange, Green, Green Mark, Signed 12.00
Nippon, Bowl, Floral Design, White, Gold, M Mark, Footed, Ladle 12.00
Nippon, Bowl, Flowers, Pink, Gold, Mark Green M Wreath, 9 1/2 In. 15.00
Nippon, Bowl, Hand-Painted Coreopsis, Orange, Yellow & Green, Artist-Signed 14.00
Nippon, Bowl, Hand-Painted Green & Gold Scrolling, Black Border, Handles 12.50
Nippon, Bowl, Hand-Painted Pagoda Silhouettes, Trees, Birds, Greek Key 10.00
Nippon, Bowl, Hand-Painted Sailboat Scene, Oval, Gold Pierced Handles 8.50
Nippon, Bowl, Hand-Painted Scene, Gold Ribbing, 3 Scroll Legs, Black Border 12.00
Nippon, Bowl, Hand-Painted Scene, Water & Trees, M In Wreath, Handle 18.00
Nippon, Bowl, Hand-Painted White Flowers On Orange, Yellow & Blue, Gold 12.50
Nippon, Bowl, Handled, Lake Scene, Gold Bands, Marked 15.00
Nippon, Bowl, Handled, Poppies, Gold Trim, Marked, 8 In. 15.00
Nippon, Bowl, Nut, Geishas, Gold, Footed, 5 1/2 In.Diameter 8.50
Nippon, Bowl, Nut, Hand-Painted Violets & Gold, 3 Curved Feet, Fluted 5.00
Nippon, Bowl, Nut, Red Floral Spray, Gold, Hand-Painted, M In Wreath 5.50
Nippon, Bowl, Peanuts Design, Raised, Footed, 5 1/2 In.Diameter 20.00
Nippon, Bowl, Pink, Gold, Green, Roses, 9 3/4 In. 15.00
Nippon, Bowl, Pink, Green, Yellow, Blue, Roses, Gold Trim, 8 3/4 In. 12.00
Nippon, Bowl, Scalloped, Hand-Painted Acorns, Autumn Colors, M In Wreath 12.00
Nippon, Bowl, Square, Blue Lake, White Swans, 6 In., Signed 15.00
Nippon, Bowl, Square, White, Gold, Hand-Painted Flowers, Nippon Green Mark 17.50
Nippon, Bowl, Swans On Lake, Hand-Painted, Green Mark, 8 In.Diameter 12.00
Nippon, Bowl, Underplate, Footed, Gold Trim, 2 1/2 In.Tall 12.50
Nippon, Bowl, Yellow, Gold, Open Handle, Square, 8 In. 9.00
Nippon, Box, Powder, Hand-Painted Red Roses, Cobalt Blue, Gold, White 8.50
Nippon, Butter, Floral Design, Raised Gold Rim, Cover 15.00
Nippon, Butter, Tub, Underplate & Liner, Hand-Painted Pink Flowers, Gold 14.00
Nippon, Butter, 4 Piece, Yellow Flowers, Gold Trim, Marked 12.50
Nippon, Cake Set, Open Handles, Gold Border, Orange Flowers, 6 Piece 20.00
Nippon, Cake Set, Roses, Leaves, Pink, Gold, Four Servers, 10 1/2 In.Plate 30.00
Nippon, Cake Set, Roses, Pink, Lavender, Plate, Five Sauce, Handled 25.00
Nippon, Cake Set, Water Scene, Sailboat, Trees, Six Plates 20.00
Nippon, Candy Set, Hand-Painted Sailing Scene, 8 Piece 20.00
Nippon, Castor, Jam, Underplate, Gold Jeweling, Green Inserts 35.00
Nippon, Celery Set, Hand-Painted Scenic, Shape Of Canoe, 7 Piece 30.00
Nippon, Celery Set, Tree In Meadow, Purple, Tray & 6 Salts 13.50
Nippon, Celery, Green, Pink, Gold, Roses, Four Salts, Tray, Set 10.00
Nippon, Chocolate Pot, Blue Cobalt Trim, Flower Decoration 25.00
Nippon, Chocolate Pot, Floral, Gold, Mark 7, Wreath, Straight Sided 20.00
Nippon, Chocolate Pot, Gold, Flowers, Scalloped Base 32.00
Nippon, Chocolate Pot, Three Cups & Saucers, Gold Bands, Gold Beading 30.00
Nippon, Chocolate Set, Green, Red, Flowers, Flared Pot, Five Cups 35.00
Nippon, Chocolate Set, Hand-Painted Sailboat Scene On White, 11 Piece 47.50
Nippon, Chocolate Set, Hand-Painted, Raised Beading In Gold, 15 Piece 50.00
Nippon, Chocolate Set, Hold, Hand-Painted, 5 Piece 15.00
Nippon, Chocolate Set, Rising Sun, Flowers, Blue 65.00
Nippon, Chocolate Set, 11 Piece, Hand-Painted Pink & Blue Flowers, Gold 45.00
Nippon, Chocolate Set, 5 Pieces, Hand-Painted Pink Flowers, Gold Trim 38.00
Nippon, Chocolate Set, 7 Pieces, Hand-Painted Bouquets Of Pink Flowers 40.00
Nippon, Chocolate Set, 7 Pieces, Hand-Painted Pink Roses, Gold Trim, Marked 48.00
Nippon, Compote, Black Landscape, Gold Rim, Pedestal, Handles, 7 In.Diameter 25.00
Nippon, Creamer, Bluebirds, Hand-Painted, Marked 4.50
Nippon, Creamer, Hand-Painted Black Design, Gold Paneled & Edged, 3 Feet 7.00
Nippon, Creamer, Hand-Painted Bluebird On Apple Blossom, Gold, M In Wreath 10.00
Nippon, Cup & Saucer, Chocolate, Gold Beaded Border, Ribbons, Marked 6.50
Nippon, Cup & Saucer, Floral 5.50
Nippon, Cup & Saucer, Oriental Scene, Blue, White 6.00
Nippon, Cup & Saucer, Violets 5.00
Nippon, Cup & Saucer, Winter Scene, Raised Beading, Blue, Gold, Yellow 15.00
Nippon, Dish, Autumn-Colored Acorns & Leaves, Hand-Painted, Green Mark 15.00
Nippon, Dish, Basketlike, Hand-Painted Floral, Gold Trim, M In Wreath 12.00
Nippon, Dish, Candy, Gold Handle, Hand-Painted Floral 6.00
Nippon, Dish, Candy, Hand-Painted Scene, 3 Ball Feet, 6 Bulbous Ribs 7.50
Nippon, Dish, Carnations, Pink, Yellow, Open Handle, 6 3/4 In.Diameter 7.50

Nippon, Dish, Celery, Black & Pink Flowers, Gold Trim, Open Handle	9.00
Nippon, Dish, Celery, Gold On White, 12 1/2 In.	10.00
Nippon, Dish, Cheese & Cracker, Blue, Gold, Pink, Roses, 9 In.Diameter	20.00
Nippon, Dish, Cheese & Cracker, Hand-Painted Floral, Gold, M In Wreath	10.00
Nippon, Dish, Cheese, Slant Top, Blue, Gold Trim, Pink Flowers, Green, Marked	30.00
Nippon, Dish, Flowers, Gold, Hand-Painted, Cover	19.00
Nippon, Dish, Heart Shape, White, Yellow Border, Pink Flowers, 4 1/2 In.	4.95
Nippon, Dish, Mustard, Flowers, Leaves, Coral, Green, Attached Sauce, M Mark	14.00
Nippon, Dish, Nut, Individual	1.75
Nippon, Dish, Nut, Jeweled Handles, Marked	25.00
Nippon, Dish, Nut, Rosebud, Gold Bands & Beading, Marked	3.00
Nippon, Dish, Oval, Footed, Hand-Painted	3.50
Nippon, Dish, Pancake, Hand-Painted Gold Garlands Around Pink Flowers	16.00
Nippon, Dish, Square, Handled, Gold, Roses	5.00
Nippon, Dish, Sunrise-Sunset, Hand-Painted, N In Wreath	15.00
Nippon, Dresser Set, Hand-Painted Pink Blossoms, Gold, Rising Sun Mark	30.00
Nippon, Dresser Set, Hand-Painted Scenic, 4 Pieces	20.00
Nippon, Dresser Set, Pink & Gold Coloring, 8 Piece	45.00
Nippon, Dresser Set, Round Tray, Pink Apple Blossom, Gold, Signed, 5 Piece	28.50
Nippon, Ewer, Blue & Pink Roses, White Ground	55.00
Nippon, Fernery, Country Scene, Hand-Painted, Footed, Handles	18.00
Nippon, Gravyboat, Multicolor, Flowers, Gold Trim, Tray	18.50
Nippon, Hair Receiver, Flowers, Leaves, Raised Gold Beading	11.00
Nippon, Hair Receiver, Gold & Floral	12.50
Nippon, Hair Receiver, Hand-Painted Blue Morning Glories, 6-Sided	10.00
Nippon, Hair Receiver, Hand-Painted, Beaded Trim	15.00
Nippon, Hair Receiver, Hand-Painted, Spotted With China Jewels, Round	16.00
Nippon, Hair Receiver, Red Flowers, Gold, Scenic, Signed	7.50
Nippon, Hair Receiver, Roses, Pink, Green, Gold, Marked, 3 In.Diameter	12.50
Nippon, Hatpin Holder, Hand-Painted, Open Top, Rising Sun Mark, 7 In.High	7.50
Nippon, Hatpin Holder, Hand-Painted, Rising Sun Mark, 7 In.High	7.50
Nippon, Hatpin Holder, Open Top, Ornate, Marked	8.25
Nippon, Hatpin Holder, Pink Flowers, Open Top	9.00
Nippon, Hatpin Holder, White, Hand-Painted Violets, Gold Trim	10.00
Nippon, Humidor, Charging Indian On Horseback, Blown Out Relief, Browns	55.00
Nippon, Humidor, Horse, Two Dogs, Marbleized, Jeweled Effect	58.00
Nippon, Humidor, Marble Effect, Dogs At Top, 5 In.High	50.00
Nippon, Jar & Plate, Jam, Covered, Hand-Painted Flowers, Gold	18.00
Nippon, Jar, Cookie, Dragon Design, Melon Shape, Gray, White, Underplate	65.00
Nippon, Jar, Cookie, Melon Shape, Footes, Hand-Painted Purple Pansies, Signed	35.00
Nippon, Jar, Cookie, Purple Pansies, Gold, Melon Shape, Cover, Footed	45.00
Nippon, Jar, Cracker, Flowers, Blue, Gold, Six Sided, Marked	16.50
Nippon, Jar, Cracker, 2 Handles, Blue, Gold Trim, Pink Flowers, Marked	15.00
Nippon, Jar, Jelly, Flowers, Gold, Hand-Painted, Underplate, Cover	22.00
Nippon, Jar, Lid, Hand-Painted Roses	6.00
Nippon, Match Holder, Island Scene, Ships, Green M Wreath Mark, 2 1/4 In.	5.75
Nippon, Mayonnaise Set, Cranes, Ocean, Pink, White, Mark 13, 3 Piece	22.00
Nippon, Mayonnaise Set, Floral Design, Red, Bowl.Plate, Ladle, Hand-Painted	9.00
Nippon, Mayonnaise Set, Hand-Painted Flowers, Gold, 3 Piece	15.00
Nippon, Mayonnaise Set, Hand-Painted Medallions Of Pink Flowers, 3 Piece	15.00
Nippon, Mayonnaise Set, Pink, Mauve, Gold, Oval, 2 Piece	18.00
Nippon, Mustard Pot, Two Handles, Rose Design, Marked	3.95
Nippon, Mustard, Hand-Painted Pink Flowers, Ladle	6.50
Nippon, Mustard, Hand-Painted, Ladle, Gold Trim	6.00
Nippon, Mustard, Rose Sprays, Green Lid, Ladle	6.00
Nippon, Nappy, Leaf Shape, Single Gold Handle	18.50
Nippon, Nappy, Pink, Roses, Gold Trim, Triangular Shape	12.00
Nippon, Nappy, Roses, Leaf Garland, Gold Trim, Square, Marked	1.50
Nippon, Nut Set, Floral, 7 Piece	25.00
Nippon, Nut Set, 6 Piece, Hand-Painted Gold Band & Pink Flowers, Footed	35.00
Nippon, Pickle, Hand-Painted Medallions Of Pink Roses, Green, Gold	8.50
Nippon, Pitcher & Plate, Syrup, Hand-Painted Gold Decor	20.00
Nippon, Pitcher, Lemonade, Hand-Painted Violets, Six Handled Mugs	55.00
Nippon, Pitcher, Syrup, Brown, Tan, Yellow, Cover, Mark M	8.50
Nippon, Pitcher, Winter Scene, 4 In.	7.50
Nippon, Plaque, Raised Boat Scene, 10 In.Diameter	65.00

Nippon, Plaque, Whimsical Owl, Branch, 24 Lima Mark, 9 3/4 In.Diameter	42.00
Nippon, Plate, Azalea, Hand-Painted, 6 1/4 In.	7.50
Nippon, Plate, Cake, Green, Gold, Two Handles, 10 In. Diameter	12.00
Nippon, Plate, Cake, Roses, Tulips, Embossed Gold Border, 11 In.	9.50
Nippon, Plate, Flowers, Blue, Gold Rim, 7 1/2 In.Diameter	3.00
Nippon, Plate, Flowers, Yellow, Purple, 6 In.Diameter	5.00
Nippon, Plate, Green, Burgundy, White, Gold, Wide Border, 10 In.	16.00
Nippon, Plate, Hand-Painted Brown Floral, 8 In.	9.50
Nippon, Plate, Hand-Painted Pink & Green Roses, Gold, Set Of 6	30.00
Nippon, Plate, Hand-Painted Red & White Flowers, Gold Beading, Handles	14.00
Nippon, Plate, Hanging, 8 In., Owl On Bough, Signed M.H.P.	25.00
Nippon, Plate, Maroon & Gold, 10 In.	28.50
Nippon, Plate, Pancake, Cover, White, Green & Gold Border With Roses	10.50
Nippon, Plate, Parrot On Rosebush, Butterfly, Roses, Marked	8.50
Nippon, Plate, Pierced For Hanging, Hand-Painted Sky, River & Trees	12.00
Nippon, Plate, Pink, Green, Roses, Mark M	5.00
Nippon, Plate, Pink, Primrose, Hand Painted, 10 In.	9.00
Nippon, Plate, Raised Dragons, Turquoise, 10 In.	10.00
Nippon, Plate, Roses, Pink, Green, Gold Trim, 8 1/2 In.Diameter	8.50
Nippon, Pot, Mocha, Octagonal Shape, Cobalt Trim, Gold Beading, Pink Roses	55.00
Nippon, Pot, Mustard, Hand-Painted, Green, Gold & Yellow	7.00
Nippon, Relish Server, Three Piece, Bowl, Plate, Spoon, Apple Blossoms, Gold	18.00
Nippon, Relish, Hand-Painted Pink Wild Roses, Pierced Handles, Beading	6.00
Nippon, Ring Tree, Flowers, Yellow, Gold, Hand-Painted, Mark	12.00
Nippon, Salt & Pepper Shaker, Hand-Painted Blue Butterfly & Flowers, Set	12.00
Nippon, Salt & Pepper, Floral Design, Gold Trim, M Mark, Handle	12.00
Nippon, Salt & Pepper, Flowers & Trees	14.00
Nippon, Salt & Pepper, Gold Flowers, Tankard Shape, Handles, Marked	8.00
Nippon, Salt & Pepper, Green House Scene	6.00
Nippon, Salt & Pepper, Hand-Painted, Marked, Pair	9.00
Nippon, Salt Dip, Pink, Flowers, Gold, Footed, Hand-Painted	2.00
Nippon, Salt Dip, Signed	6.00
Nippon, Salt, Gold & Floral, 6	18.00
Nippon, Salt, Master, Hand-Painted, Footed	6.25
Nippon, Shaker, Sugar, Gold Flowers, Marked	12.00
Nippon, Shaker, Sugar, Satsuma Style Figures & Coloring	12.50
Nippon, Shaker, Sugar, 6 Sided, Pink Flowers, Gold Scrolls, Marked	15.00
Nippon, Strainer, Tea, Hand-Painted, Gold, Matching Holder	30.00
Nippon, Sugar & Creamer, Blue Birds, Marked	20.00
Nippon, Sugar & Creamer, Cottage Scene, Lake, Trees, Bridge, Hand-Painted	38.00
Nippon, Sugar & Creamer, Gray-Blue Eye Dragon	6.50
Nippon, Sugar & Creamer, Hand-Painted Pink Roses, Blue At Top, Gold	7.50
Nippon, Sugar & Creamer, Lavender Matte Finish, Cottage Scene, Beaded	25.00
Nippon, Sugar & Creamer, Oval, Gold, Pink, & Blue Flowers, Marked	13.50
Nippon, Sugar & Creamer, Pink, Gold, Roses, Cover	16.00
Nippon, Sugar & Creamer, River, Trees, Amethyst, Beaded Handles, Cover	25.00
Nippon, Sugar & Creamer, Roses, Blue, Pink, White, Gold	11.00
Nippon, Sugar & Creamer, Tulips, Leaves, Gold Handles & Bands, Footed	28.50
Nippon, Syrup & Underplate, Hand-Painted Sunset Scene, Gold	12.00
Nippon, Tea Set, Blue, Gold Trim, Pink Flowers, Marked, 9 Piece	20.00
Nippon, Tea Set, Child's, Gold Band Pattern, Hand-Painted, Marked, 11 Piece	15.00
Nippon, Tea Set, Hand-Painted Pink Flowers, 11 Piece	50.00
Nippon, Tea Set, Hand-Painted, Roses, Gold Trim, 17 Piece	38.00
Nippon, Tea Set, Lithophane, Japanese Lady's Head, Red & Gold, 15 Piece	25.00
Nippon, Tea Set, Roses, Gold, Sugar, Creamer, Six Cup & Saucer	48.00
Nippon, Teapot, Bird Design, Blue, Green, White	9.00
Nippon, Teapot, Hand-Painted, Band Of Roses	7.50
Nippon, Teapot, Ivory Band, Gold Enamel	5.00
Nippon, Teapot, Melon Shape, Footed, Pink Roses, Gold Trim, Marked	15.00
Nippon, Toothpick, Hand-Painted, Blue Flowers, Green M In Wreath Mark, Blue	6.00
Nippon, Toothpick, Horse Scene	13.50
Nippon, Toothpick, Six Sided, Ornate, Marked	6.00
Nippon, Toothpick, Two Handles, Gold Beading & Trim, Marked	6.00
Nippon, Tray, Celery, Pattern 90, Marked	20.00
Nippon, Tray, Dresser, Pink, Yellow, Flowers, Oval	8.00
Nippon, Tray, Dresser, Roses, Pink, Gold Border, Marked, 13 1/2 In.Long	18.00

Nippon, Tray, Gold Bows, Tiny Flowers, Gold Edge	18.75
Nippon, Tray, Hand-Painted Orchid Roses & Green Leaves, Black Border	8.50
Nippon, Tray, Hand-Painted Scene, Water & Sailboats, M In Wreath, Handled	20.00
Nippon, Vase, Birds, Handled, 8 In.	14.00
Nippon, Vase, Blue Bottom, Red Around Top, Hand-Painted Floral, 10 In., Pair	60.00
Nippon, Vase, Cream Ground, Pink Floral, Gold Trim, Hand-Painted, Two Handles	49.00
Nippon, Vase, Enameled Swans In Water, Water Lilies, Four Handles	15.50
Nippon, Vase, Farm Scene, Urn Shape, Handle, Hand-Painted, 5 In.Tall, Pair	35.00
Nippon, Vase, Floral, Cream, Yellow, Blue, Gold Trim, Two Handle, 5 1/2 In.	8.95
Nippon, Vase, Floral, Gold, 8 In.High	28.00
Nippon, Vase, Flowers, Beaded, Gold, Hand-Painted, Two Handle, 11 In.Tall	35.00
Nippon, Vase, Gold & Floral, Handled, 7 In.	13.50
Nippon, Vase, Green, Gold Cranes & Trim, 9 In.	35.00
Nippon, Vase, Hand-Painted Floral, 5 In., M In Wreath	8.50
Nippon, Vase, Hand-Painted Flowers, Applied Floral Slip, Gold	30.00
Nippon, Vase, Hand-Painted Outdoor Scene, 11 1/2 In.High	28.00
Nippon, Vase, Hand-Painted Scene, 2 Handled, Gold Trim, Bisque Finish	25.00
Nippon, Vase, Hand-Painted White Dogwoods, Yellow Centers, Gold, Handles	16.00
Nippon, Vase, Hand-Painted White Irises, Pink Centers, Gray & White Blocks	12.50
Nippon, Vase, Iris, Brown, Orange, 11 In.Tall	17.50
Nippon, Vase, Lake & Flowers, Gold Trim, 9 1/2 In.High, 6 1/2 In.Diameter	28.00
Nippon, Vase, Lavender Floral, Gold Handles, Hand-Painted, 7 In.High	18.00
Nippon, Vase, Leaves, Flowers, Beaded Trim, Green Mark	17.00
Nippon, Vase, Lilacs, Purple, Hand-Painted, 9 In.Tall, Pair	35.00
Nippon, Vase, Peacocks, Flowers, Paneled, Hand-Painted, 12 1/2 In.	32.50
Nippon, Vase, Pink Flowers, 5 In.	7.00
Nippon, Vase, Purple, Gold *Illus*	30.00
Nippon, Vase, Roses, Leaves, Green, Pink, Six Sided, Gold Trim, 10 1/4 In.Tall	30.00
Nippon, Vase, Scene, Floral, Gold Handles & Trim, Hand-Painted, 9 In.	25.00
Nippon, Vase, Scene, Oriental, Lake, Gold Trim, 9 1/2 In.High	25.00
Nippon, Vase, Square, Lake Scene On Pale Green, Gold Handles & Trim, Signed	17.50
Nippon, Vase, Water Scenes, Orange Poppies, Gold, Hand-Painted, 8 1/2 In.	14.00
Nippon, Vase, Wisteria Decoration *Illus*	35.00

*Nodders or Nodding Figures, or Pagods, are porcelain figures with heads
and hands that are attached to wires. Any slight movement causes the parts to
move up and down. They were made in many countries during the eighteenth and
nineteenth centuries.*

Nodder, Hippopotamus, Bisque, Gray, 3 1/4 In.Long	22.00
Nodder, Man, Oriental, Droopy Black Mustache, Porcelain	35.00
Nodder, Man, Oriental, Seated, Embossed Shawl, Tassels, Collie Hat, Metal	35.00
Nodder, Man, Oriental, Seated, Holds Fan & Pipe, Bisque	32.00
Nodder, Woman, Man, Typists *Illus*	65.00
Nodder, Oriental, Bisque, Pair	150.00

*Noritake-Marked Porcelain was made in Japan after 1904 by Nippon
Toki Kaisha.*

Noritake, Bowl, Console, Cherry Tree, Parrot, Footed, Green Mark, 8 1/2 In.	25.00
Noritake, Bowl, Gold Border, Open Handles, Flowers, Butterflies	7.50
Noritake, Bowl, Gold, Black, Hand-Painted	3.00
Noritake, Bowl, Hand-Painted, Rolled Edge	6.00
Noritake, Bowl, Hunt Scene, 9 In.	10.00
Noritake, Bowl, Large Roses, Hand-Painted	10.00
Noritake, Bowl, Scenic, Handles, 10 In.	7.00
Noritake, Butter, Orange, Blue Bird Finial	9.50
Noritake, Cake Set, Gold & Yellow Border, Six Small Plates	18.00
Noritake, Cake Set, Hand-Painted Floral & Scroll Pattern, 7 Piece	10.00
Noritake, Celery Set, Flower Pattern, 5 Piece	15.00
Noritake, Chocolate Pot, Pink, Roses, Six Cups, Set	46.00
Noritake, Condiment Set	6.00
Noritake, Creamer, Gray, Green, White, Dragon, Swirls	7.00
Noritake, Cruet, Vinegar, Azalea	3.00
Noritake, Cup & Saucer, Gold Design, Ivory Band, M Mark	6.00
Noritake, Cup & Saucer, The Flamingo, Red, Green, Mark	2.50
Noritake, Dish, Candy, Hand-Painted Roses	5.00
Noritake, Dish, Cookie, Hand-Painted, Center Handle, 10 1/4 In.	10.00

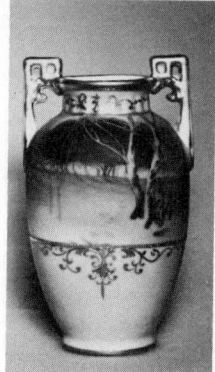

Nippon, Vase, Purple, Gold
See Page 330

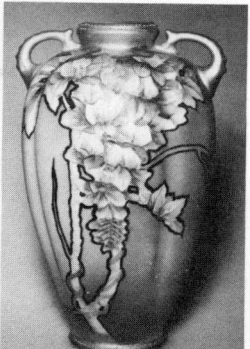

Nippon, Vase, Wisteria Decoration
See Page 330

Nodder, Woman, Man, Typists
See Page 330

Noritake, Dish, Handled, Gold & Cream Coloring	4.50
Noritake, Dish, Lemon-Shaped, Hand-Painted Yellow Lemons, Red M Mark	6.00
Noritake, Dish, Mark 20, Octagon, White, Floral, Gold, Handled	12.50
Noritake, Dish, Relish, Pink, Rose, Blue, Flowers	6.00
Noritake, Easter Egg, 1971	10.00 To 50.00
Noritake, Easter Egg, 1972	10.00 To 11.00
Noritake, Jar, Mustard, Cover, Hand-Painted Scenic, Red Mark	5.00
Noritake, Mustard, Orange & Black, Green Bill, Spoon	5.00
Noritake, Pitcher, White, Yellow, Mark M Wreath, Sugar, 2 1/2 In., Set	6.00
Noritake, Plate, Cake, Azalea Pattern, Open Handles, Gold, Marked No.19322	10.00
Noritake, Plate, Flower, Bird, Gold Edge, 8 1/2 In.Diameter, Set Of 6	55.00
Noritake, Plate, Handles, Hand-Painted Scene, 5 1/2 In.Diameter	5.00
Noritake, Plate, Mark 6, Roses, Gold Trim, 2 Handled, 9 1/2 In.Diameter	10.00
Noritake, Plate, Nude On Lily, 9 In.	5.00
Noritake, Plate, Ridgewood, 6 In.	2.00
Noritake, Plate, White, Yellow, Gold, Wreath Mark, 6 1/4 In.Diameter	6.00
Noritake, Platter, Deer In Stream, Oval, 13 1/2 X 10 1/4 In.	25.00
Noritake, Salt Dip, Butter Tub Shape	2.00
Noritake, Salt Dip, Hand-Painted	7.50
Noritake, Shaker, Sugar, Lake Scene, Blue, 7 In.	11.00
Noritake, Sugar & Creamer, Azalea, Gold Finial On Lid	3.00
Noritake, Sugar & Creamer, Azalea, Green Mark	12.50
Noritake, Sugar & Creamer, Cover, Rosedale Pattern, Gold Trim	15.00
Noritake, Sugar & Creamer, Gold, Green, Raised, Ivory Band, M Mark	18.00
Noritake, Sugar & Creamer, Lake Scene	10.00
Noritake, Sugar & Creamer, Scenic, Beading	17.50
Noritake, Sugar, Lake & Swan Scene, Pink, Blue, Green, Cover, Mark	10.00
Noritake, Tea Set, Child's, Blue Flower On Cream, 23 Piece	32.00
Noritake, Tray, Celery, Hand-Painted Scene	7.50
Noritake, Vase, Hand-Painted Desert Scene, Blue, Gold, White Interior, Pair	37.50
Noritake, Vase, Hold Handles, Brown To Blue, Hand-Painted Orange & White	16.00

*Northwood Glass Company worked in Martins Ferry, Ohio, from 1888.
They marked some pieces with the letter N in a circle. Many pieces of
Carnival Glass were made by this company.*

Northwood, see also Carnival Glass

Northwood, Banana Boat, Two Fruits, Marigold	65.00
Northwood, Basket, Bushel, Cobalt Blue	47.50

Northwood, Berry Set, Holly, Opalescent Ring, Red Berries, Green, 6 Piece	75.00
Northwood, Bowl, Berry, Umbrella Leaf, Blue Overlay, 8 In.Diameter	60.00
Northwood, Bowl, Jeweled Heart, Opalescent, Pair	18.00
Northwood, Bowl, Leaf & Beads, Green, Footed, Signed, 8 In.Diameter	32.00
Northwood, Bowl, Marked	18.00
Northwood, Bowl, Primrose Design, Shells, Footed, Green, Signed	25.00
Northwood, Bowl, Strawberry, Basket Weave, Marked, 9 In.	40.00
Northwood, Compote, Jelly, Scroll With Acanthus, Green Opalescent, Footed	22.50
Northwood, Creamer, Alaska, Vaseline	47.50
Northwood, Creamer, Blue Opalescent, Fluted Scroll	22.50
Northwood, Creamer, Book Pattern, Green, Gold, Rose	39.50
Northwood, Cruet, Intaglio, White, Clear Ball Stopper	45.00
Northwood, Dish, Bonbon, Butterfly Pattern, Green, Two Handle	28.00
Northwood, Dish, Candy, Fluted Top, Paneled Base, Purple, 3 1/2 In.Tall	16.50
Northwood, Dish, Vaseline To Opalescent, Fluted Scrolls, Footed, 3 Sided	19.00
Northwood, Hatpin Holder, Grape & Cable	50.00
Northwood, Hatpin Holder, Grape, Green, Footed	60.00
Northwood, Pitcher, Water, Cherries, Blue, Hand-Painted	60.00
Northwood, Pitcher, Water, Grape & Cable, Purple	98.50
Northwood, Pitcher, Water, Maple Leaf, Gold	175.00
Northwood, Pitcher, Water, Raspberry, 6 Glasses, Set	225.00
Northwood, Pitcher, Water, Royal Ivy	75.00
Northwood, Sauce, Grape & Thumbprint, Signed	23.00
Northwood, Shade, Tulip Shape, Marigold, Pair	25.00
Northwood, Spooner, Alaska, Vaseline	37.50
Northwood, Spooner, Enamel Decor On Colorless Glass, 4 In.High	18.00
Northwood, Sugar & Creamer, Green, Gold Trim, Signed N	45.00
Northwood, Sugar, Alaska.Vaseline, Cover	52.50
Northwood, Sugar, Covered, X Ray, Emerald Green	35.00
Northwood, Table Set, Blue To Opalescent, Sugar, Creamer, Butter, Spooner	165.00
Northwood, Tumbler, Cherries, Purple, Gold, Hand-Painted, Set Of 5	100.00
Northwood, Tumbler, Geneva Pattern, Custard	50.00
Northwood, Tumbler, Green, Floral, Hand-Painted, Signed	15.00
Northwood, Tumbler, Holly, Clear, Berries, Leaves	14.00
Northwood, Tumbler, Maple Leaf	47.50
Northwood, Tumbler, Oriental Poppy, Green, Gold	16.00
Northwood, Tumbler, Peach, Emerald Green, Gold	18.00
Northwood, Vase, Plum, Marigold, Mark N	42.50
Northwood, Water Set, Dandelion, Marigold, 7 Piece	450.00
Nymphenburg, Cup & Saucer, Coffee, Girl In Red Skirt, C.1760	40.00
Nymphenburg, Jar, Drug, Cover, Bell Shape, Puce Outlined Cartouche, C.1765	150.00
Nymphenburg, Sauceboat, Double Handle, Puce Outlined Scrollwork, C.1775	300.00
Nymphenburg, Sucrier, Covered, Chintz Pattern, Green, Puce, & Blue, C.1770	150.00
Nymphenburg, Tea Caddy, Covered, C.1765 Illus	325.00
Nymphenburg, Tea Caddy, Covered, Rectangular, Painted Meissen Style, C.1765	325.00
Nymphenburg, Teapot, Covered, Yellow, Blue, C.1765 Illus	175.00

Occupied Japan is the mark used on pieces of pottery and porcelain made during the American Occupation of Japan after World War II.
Collectors are now buying these pieces. The items were made for export to the United States.

Occupied Japan, Baby Buggy, Bird On Side, Blue & Red, 4 In.	5.00
Occupied Japan, Box, Jewel	12.00
Occupied Japan, Butter, Clear Glass, Embossed White Figure, Covered	10.00
Occupied Japan, Cake Set, Hand-Painted, Open Handles, Blue Border, 7 Piece	12.50
Occupied Japan, Cigarette Lighter, Silver Spur	4.00
Occupied Japan, Coffeepot, Sugar, & Creamer	8.50
Occupied Japan, Cup & Saucer, Child's, Blue Willow	5.00
Occupied Japan, Cup & Saucer, Says Father, Gold Trim, Large Size	8.00
Occupied Japan, Cup & Saucer, Sunset Lake Scene	1.25
Occupied Japan, Cup & Saucer, White, Gold Band, Signed Yamaka	2.50
Occupied Japan, Doll, Negro, China, Dressed, 4 In.Tall	5.00
Occupied Japan, Figurine, Blue Boy, 7 1/2 In.Tall	5.00
Occupied Japan, Figurine, Bug Musicians, Mean Looking, 4	9.50
Occupied Japan, Figurine, Chinese Made, Girl & Man, 5 1/2 In.High, Pair	5.00
Occupied Japan, Figurine, Girl, 4 In. Illus	5.00

Nymphenburg, Teapot, Covered, Yellow, Blue, C.1765
See Page 332

Nymphenburg, Tea Caddy, Covered, C.1765
See Page 332

Occupied Japan, Figurine, Girl, 4 In.
See Page 332

Occupied Japan, Figurine, Man, French Dandy, Signed Paulaux, 8 In.High	9.00
Occupied Japan, Figurine, Man, Spanish, 9 In.High	4.00
Occupied Japan, Figurine, Old-Fashioned Girl, 10 1/2 In.High	7.50
Occupied Japan, Figurine, 18th Century Costumed Man, Woman, 6 In.High, Pair	10.00
Occupied Japan, Holder, Flower, Duck, Open Wings	5.00
Occupied Japan, Holder, Toothbrush, Three Little Pigs, Walt Disney	18.00
Occupied Japan, Lamp, Colonial Figures, 10 In.High	10.00
Occupied Japan, Lighter, Cigarette, China, Form Of Candle Light	4.00
Occupied Japan, Monkeys, Hear No Evil, See No Evil, Speak No Evil	3.00
Occupied Japan, Ornament, Christmas, Box Marked, 12	1.00
Occupied Japan, Pitcher, Toby, White, 8 In.High	5.00
Occupied Japan, Plate, Blue Willow, 7 In.	3.00
Occupied Japan, Plate, Dinner, Pink & Yellow Flowers, Marked Gold China	5.00
Occupied Japan, Plate, White, Painted Figures In Center, 12	156.00
Occupied Japan, Salt & Pepper, Black Figures, 4 In., Set	3.50
Occupied Japan, Statue, Boy Mailman, Reads 'american Children, Mailman'	8.00
Occupied Japan, Tea Set, Child's, 15 Piece	6.00
Occupied Japan, Tea Set, Miniature, 10 Piece	4.95
Occupied Japan, Tea Set, Toy, 9 Piece	7.50
Occupied Japan, Toothpick, Loving Cup, Handled, Metal	3.50
Occupied Japan, Vase, Bucket Shape, Bar Handle Across Top, Landscapes	60.00
Occupied Japan, Vase, Square, Raised Figure, 9 1/2 In.High	15.00
Occupied Japan, Vase, White, Basket Shape, Applied Paste Dragon	10.00

*Old Ivory China was made in Silesia, Germany, at the end of the
nineteenth century. It is often marked with a crown and the word Silesia.
The pattern numbers appear on the base of each piece.*

Old Ivory, Berry Set, No.75, 7 Piece	125.00
Old Ivory, Bowl, No.Xvi, 9 1/2 In.	65.00
Old Ivory, Bowl, No.16, 9 1/2 In.Diameter	35.00
Old Ivory, Bowl, No.73, 9 In.	52.00
Old Ivory, Bowl, Roses, Pink, Ohme Mark, 9 1/2 In.Diameter	40.00
Old Ivory, Chocolate Pot, Clairon Xv	125.00
Old Ivory, Chocolate Set, Pot, Lid, Two Cup & Saucer	105.00
Old Ivory, Chocolate Set, Yellow Rose Decor, Signed, 9 Piece	185.00
Old Ivory, Creamer, No.202	18.50
Old Ivory, Creamer, No.84	27.00
Old Ivory, Cup & Saucer, Demitasse, No.Xv	35.00
Old Ivory, Plate, Cake, No.28, Open Handled, Ohme, Silesia, 9 1/2 In.	18.00

Old Ivory, Plate, Cake, Open Handled, 11 In.Diameter	37.50
Old Ivory, Plate, No.202, 8 1/2 In.	25.00
Old Ivory, Plate, 6 1/4 In.	8.25
Old Ivory, Sauce, No.Xvi	8.50
Old Ivory, Sauce, No.15	14.00
Old Ivory, Sugar & Creamer	29.00
Old Ivory, Sugar & Creamer, No.75, Covered	97.00
Old Ivory, Sugar, Covered, German, Pink, White Dogwood, Violets	12.50
Old Ivory, Vase, Floral, Portrait Of Two Children, 9 1/2 In.High	55.00
Onion, Bowl, Soup, Blue, Flow Blue	6.00
Onion, Cup & Saucer, Meissen	16.00
Onion, Eggcup, Meissen	7.50
Onion, Knife Rest, Blue, Metal Ends	22.50
Onion, Plate, Blue, Signed & Reg.Number, 9 3/4 In.	18.00
Onion, Plate, Dinner, Blue, Meissen, Crossed Swords	18.50
Onion, Plate, Lattice, Meissen, 6 In.	20.00
Onion, Plate, Meissen, Crossed Swords Mark, 7 3/4 In.	18.50
Onion, Plate, Meissen, 8 In.	12.00
Onion, Plate, 10 In. .... *Illus*	11.00
Onion, Platter, Meissen, 18 In.Long	22.50
Onion, Saltbox .... *Illus*	45.00

Onion, Plate, 10 In.

Onion, Saltbox

Onion, Teapot, Meissen, Crossed Swords Mark, 5 1/4 In.Tall	95.00
Onion, Tureen, Gravy, Attached Tray, Cover, Crossed Sword Mark, Meissen	58.00
Onion, Tureen, Meissen, Three Quart Size	300.00

*Opalescent Glass is translucent Glass that has the bluish-white tones of
the opal gemstone. It is often found in pressed glasware made in victorian
times. Some dealers use the terms opaline and opalescent for any of the
bluish-white translucent wares.*

Opalescent, Basket, Hobnail, Clear Handle, 6 In.	9.00
Opalescent, Berry Set, Ribbed, 7 Piece	50.00
Opalescent, Bowl, Hobnail, Ruffled	5.00
Opalescent, Bowl, Leaf & Beads, Flint, N Mark	18.00
Opalescent, Bowl, Loops, 8 In.	13.00
Opalescent, Bowl, Rose, White Swirl	10.00
Opalescent, Bowl, Spool, Collar Base	13.00
Opalescent, Bowl, Tricornered, Astro Pattern, Flint	17.50
Opalescent, Compote, Spool, Blue	25.00
Opalescent, Cruet, Blue, Swirl, 7 In.Tall	21.00
Opalescent, Dish, Argonaut, Low Base, 7 X 6 X 3 In.	10.00
Opalescent, Dish, Candy, White, Footed, 3 Mold	17.00
Opalescent, Dish, Covered, White, Hobnail, 6 In., Pair	8.50
Opalescent, Epergne, Blue, Hobnail, 3 Lily	26.50
Opalescent, Epergne, Green, Silver Plate, Base, 8 In.High	35.00
Opalescent, Hat, Blue, Hobnail, Duncan Miller	17.50
Opalescent, Pitcher, Clear, Handled, Ribbed, 3 In.Tall	22.00
Opalescent, Pitcher, Water, Clear, White, Ruffled Top, Coin Spot	62.50

Opalescent, Pitcher, Water, Flower, Leaf, White, 9 3/4 In.Tall 49.00
Opalescent, Pitcher, Water, Green To Pink, Threaded Opalescent Handle 65.00
Opalescent, Pitcher, Water, Green, Thumbprint 45.00
Opalescent, Pitcher, Water, Swirl, Blue, 9 In.Tall 67.50
Opalescent, Plate, Amethyst, Water Lily & Cattails, 11 1/2 In. 18.00
Opalescent, Rose Bowl, Swirl, White 18.00
Opalescent, Salt, Blue, Swirl 12.00
Opalescent, Salt, Bubble, Blue 7.00
Opalescent, Shade, Blue, Swirl, Ruffled Edge, 6 In., Pair 22.00
Opalescent, Spooner, Blue 22.50
Opalescent, Sugar & Creamer, Pale Green, Covered 40.00
Opalescent, Toothpick, Rib 10.00
Opalescent, Tumbler, Hobnail, Blue 35.00
Opalescent, Tumbler, Hobnail, Clear ....22.00 To 35.00
Opalescent, Tumbler, Regal, N Mark 8.00
Opalescent, Tumbler, Ribbed, Paneled, Pale Blue, 5 .... 21.00
Opalescent, Vase, Blue, Hobnail, Fan 12.50
Opalescent, Vase, Blue, Hobnail, Ruffled, 4 1/2 In.High 28.00
Opalescent, Vase, Blue, 10 1/2 In.Tall 18.00
Opalescent, Vase, Clear, Bluish Opalescence, 12 In. 8.00
Opalescent, Vase, Green, Footed, Scalloped Top, Opalescent Teardrops 17.50
Opalescent, Vase, Green, Opalescent Loops & Ruffles, 12 In. 8.00
Opalescent, Vase, Palisades 11.00

Opaline Glass, or Opal Glass, was made in white, apple green, and other
colors. The glass had a matte surface and a lack of transparency. It was
often gilded or painted. It was a popular mid-nineteenth century european
glassware.

Opaline, Basket, White, Gold Trim, Heavy, Satin Lining 95.00
Opaline, Bobeche, Pink, 3 In., Pair 12.50
Opaline, Bowl, Blue 18.00
Opaline, Bowl, Rose, Violets, Yellow, Pulled Effect, 3 1/4 In.Tall 65.00
Opaline, Compote, White, Ruffled, Fluted & Scalloped, Painted Roses 25.00
Opaline, Perfume, White, Facet & Star Cut, Stopper, 3 1/4 In.Tall, Pair 38.00
Opaline, Pitcher, Water, Jeweled Heart, Clear 45.00
Opaline, Pitcher, Water, Pink, Decorated 115.00
Opaline, Rose Bowl, Pink 12.50
Opaline, Rose Bowl, Pink, Crimped Edges 12.50
Opaline, Rose Bowl, Pink, Crimped Top 12.50
Opaline, Syrup, Hobstar, Green 38.50
Opaline, Tumbler, Oriental Design, Orange, Yellow, White, Green, Blue 15.00
Opaline, Vase, Applied Leaf & Rose, Amber, Pink, White, Ruffled Top, 3 In.Tall 40.00
Opaline, Vase, Cherub, Leafy Sprays, Brown, Pink 32.00
Opaline, Vase, Enamel Floral Decor, 8 1/2 In.High 27.50
Opaline, Vase, Hand, Victorian, Rough Pontil, Blue, 8 1/2 In.Tall 14.00
Opaline, Vase, Pink Opalie Cut To Clamwater, Overlay, Footed, Pair 45.00
Opaline, Vase, Pink, Melon Ribbed, Ruffled Top, 4 1/2 In.High 12.00
Opera Glasses, Enamel, Colmont, Paris, Carmen & Figaro, Mother-Of-Pearl 125.00
Opera Glasses, Lemaire, Paris, Mother-Of-Pearl, Gold Plate, Bumblebee Mark 16.00
Opera Glasses, Marchand, Paris, No Handle 9.50
Opera Glasses, Mother-Of-Pearl ....22.50 To 34.50
Opera Glasses, Mother-Of-Pearl & Brass, Long Handled 12.50
Opera Glasses, Mother-Of-Pearl & Brass, 19th Century, Marked Paris, Case 30.00
Opera Glasses, Mother-Of-Pearl, Brass Frames, Made In France 37.50
Opera Glasses, Mother-Of-Pearl, Colmont, Paris 35.00
Organ, see Music, Organ
Ormolu, Ornament, Desk, Signed C.H.Lebanc A Paris, 1850 .... *Illus* 550.00
Ormolu, Ornament, Desk, Signed Lebanc, 19th Century .... *Illus* 275.00
Orphan Annie & Sandy, Bisque, Japan 35.00
Orphan Annie, Doll, Composition, 8 In.Tall 35.00
Orphan Annie, Mug, Orphan Annie & Sandy 12.00
Orphan Annie, Mug, Ovaltine, Beetleware ....6.00 To 9.50
Orphan Annie, Music, Song Sheet, Ovaltine, 1931, Annie & Sandy Cover 7.50
Orphan Annie, Range, Electric, Marx, Orphan Annie & Dog Transfer 25.00
Orphan Annie, Stove, Tin 25.00
Orrefors, Bowl, Rose, Intaglio Swordfish, Bubbles, Seaweed, Signed, Date 1915 .... 165.00

Ormolu, Ornament, Desk,
Signed C.H.Lebanc A Paris, 1850
See Page 335

Ormolu, Ornament, Desk,
Signed Lebanc, 19th Century
See Page 335

*Owens Pottery was made in Zanesville, Ohio, from 1891 to 1928. The
first Art Pottery was made after 1896. Utopian Ware, Cyrano, Navarre,
Feroza, and Henri Deux were made. pieces were usually marked with a form
of the name Owens. About 1907 the firm began to make tile and gave up the
art pottery wares.*

Owens, Mug, Utopian, Cherries & Green Leaves, Right & Left Handed, Pair	75.00
Owens, Vase, Artist-Signed, Utopian, Brown, Pansy Decor, 8 In.Tall	55.00
Owens, Vase, Marked, 16 In.High, Straw Color	28.00
Owens, Vase, Signed, Blue To Brown, Wild Rose Decor, Artist-Signed, No.1118	45.00
Owens, Vase, Utopian, Leaf Pattern, Green, Orange, Signed, 6 In.Tall	45.00
Painting, see also Picture, Print	
Painting, Enamel On Porcelain, Young Lady, Oval Gilt Frame, Philadelphia	85.00
Painting, Enamel On Porcelain, Young Man, Oval Gilt Frame, Philadelphia	70.00
Painting, Fraktur, Bucks County, Pennsylvania, Dated 1808, Cherry Frame	575.00
Painting, Fraktur, Dutch, Dated 1829, Pennsylvania, Frame	40.00
Painting, Fraktur, Eagle Book Store, Dated 1861, Color, Maple Frame	35.00
Painting, Fraktur, Irrgarten, Blumen, Allentown, Black Frame	25.00
Painting, Fraktur, John Ritter, Reading, Dated 1829, Frame	30.00
Painting, Fraktur, Pennsylvania, Basket Of Flowers, Hex Symbol, Walnut Frame	250.00
Painting, Fraktur, Pennsylvania, Capital Letters, Baskets Of Flowers, Hex	250.00
Painting, Fraktur, Pennsylvania, Circlet Of Flowers, Michael Dornmeier, 1849	70.00
Painting, Fraktur, Pennsylvania, Dated 1814, Heart Cartouche, Birds	600.00
Painting, Fraktur, Pennsylvania, Northamton Co., 1806	800.00
Painting, Fraktur, Pennsylvania, Printed By D.P.Lange, 1822, Red Ink, Frame	85.00
Painting, Fraktur, Pennsylvania, Printed By D.P.Lange, 1829, Walnut Frame	20.00
Painting, Fraktur, Pennsylvania, Printed By D.P.Lange, 1882, Red Ink, Pine	85.00
Painting, Fraktur, Pennsylvania, Printed By John Ritter, Dated 1806, Frame	45.00
Painting, Fraktur, Pennsylvania, Printed By Peters, 1829, Hand Colored, Frame	35.00
Painting, Fraktur, Pennsylvania, Spray Of Tulips, Maria Cetch, 1848	145.00
Painting, Fraktur, Pennsylvania, Tulip Tree With Bird, Johannes Traup	350.00
Painting, Fraktur, Pennsylvania, 2 Bust Portraits, Dated 1836	1750.00
Painting, Fraktur, Peter Jaufman, Canton, Ohio	20.00
Painting, Fraktur, Pinprick, Heart Cartouche, Dated 1834, Reeded Frame	750.00
Painting, Fraktur, Pinprick, Roosters & Flowers, Dated 1834	750.00
Painting, Fraktur, Printed By Peters, 1829, Hand Colored, Frame	35.00
Painting, Fraktur, Printed, Ritter & Co., Reading, Pennsylvania, 1810	30.00
Painting, George Washington, C.1810, 40 X 35 In.	650.00
Painting, Miniature, French Lady, Gold & Green Frame	35.00
Painting, Miniature, Ivory, Henry Viii & 6 Wives, Signed, Silver Frame, 7	400.00
Painting, Miniature, Madonna & Child, Oval Gold & Black Frame	25.00
Painting, Miniature, On Ivory, Napoleon, Josephine, Frames, Pair	125.00
Painting, Miniature, On Ivory, Woman Wearing Ermine, Brass Frame	25.00
Painting, Miniature, On Ivory, Young Girl, Dore Bronze Frame, Diamond Shape	65.00
Painting, Miniature, On Ivory, 17th Century Queen, Brass Frame	55.00

Painting, Miniature, Porcelain, Carved Frame .... *Illus*	45.00
Painting, Miniature, Young Girl, Lemlite, 1851, Signed I.L.	40.00
Painting, Miniature, Young Man & Woman, Black Lacquer Frame, Brass Liner	35.00
Painting, Miniature, 19th Century Girl, Signed Bonet	75.00
Painting, Oil On Board Panel, Thames River, London, Signed W.Eric Thorp	295.00
Painting, Oil On Canvas, Basket Of Apples, Levi Wells Prentice	2000.00
Painting, Oil On Canvas, Girl With Basket Of Flowers, American, Primitive	275.00
Painting, Oil On Canvas, Lady, Walnut Shadowbox Frame	70.00
Painting, Oil On Canvas, Landscape, Gilded Frame	35.00
Painting, Oil On Canvas, Man, Gilt Frame, 34 X 39 In.	70.00
Painting, Oil On Canvas, Moose In Forest, Signed T.Wood, Mahogany Frame	125.00
Painting, Oil On Canvas, Oceana At The Banks, John Orne Johnson Frost, 1868	500.00
Painting, Oil On Canvas, Snow Scene, Gathering Wood In Winter, F.S.Coburn	1400.00
Painting, Oil On Ivory, American, Gentleman, C.1820, Frame	95.00

Painting, Miniature, Porcelain, Carved Frame

Painting, Oil On Ivory, American, 3 Children, Primitive, Framed	400.00
Painting, Oil On Ivory, Framed, Signed, Miniature	35.00
Painting, Oil On Ivory, Lady, E.K.Hess	110.00
Painting, Oil On Tin, Balloon, Bird's-Eye Maple Frame, J.Carrau	65.00
Painting, Oil On Velvet, Pennsylvania Dutch Distelfink & Tulips, Frame	35.00
Painting, Oil On Wood Panel, Portraits, Zedekiah Belknap, 1820, Pair	1500.00
Painting, Oil On Wood, Barnyards, A.Derhosesen, Gilt Frame, Pair	750.00
Painting, Oil, Girl Selling Vegetables, Signed Stanley Middleton, Frame	450.00
Painting, Oil, Master Ship, Stormy Sea, Frame, 16 X 20 In.	450.00
Painting, Oil, Sailing Ship, Signed Adolphus Kuell, Dated 1879, Pair	350.00
Painting, Oil, Woman, Mule, Walking, Signed Hartwich, Dated 1884	225.00
Painting, Oil, Young Girls, Signed, 1877, Frame, 19 X 23 In.	75.00
Painting, On Board, Seascape, C.1860, 16 X 10 1/2 In.	35.00
Painting, On Bone, Persian, Miniature, Hunting Party Scene, Framed	15.00
Painting, On French Porcelain, Cherubs, Woodland Scene, Brass Frame	195.00
Painting, On Glass, Birds & Flowers In Marsh, Chinese, Teak Frame	300.00
Painting, On Glass, Checkerboard, Framed	65.00
Painting, On Glass, Portrait, George & Martha Washington, C.1850, Pair	75.00
Painting, On Ivory, Marie Louise, Embossed & Beaded Frame, 4 In.	75.00
Painting, On Ivory, Miniature, Elegant Lady, Frame, Signed	80.00
Painting, On Ivory, Miniature, Two Children	140.00
Painting, On Ivory, Miniature, Young Girl, Signed Phillips, C.1900, Oval	85.00
Painting, On Ivory, Portrait, Framed	85.00
Painting, On Ivory, Portrait, Mr.& Mrs.Preston, 1816, Gilt Frame, Pair	190.00
Painting, On Ivory, Sister Of Louis Xvi, Frame, 5 1/2 X 4 1/2 In.	85.00
Painting, On Porcelain, Christ, Red Velvet Case, Brass Enclosures, 1860	65.00
Painting, On Porcelain, Lady's Head, Miniature	58.00
Painting, On Porcelain, Man Plays Musical Instrument, Woman, Frame	750.00
Painting, On Porcelain, Oval, Girl Watching Bird In Flight, Kpm	525.00
Painting, On Porcelain, Plaque, Winged Child, Gold Border, Frame	15.00
Painting, On Porcelain, Victorian Ladies, 9 X 7 1/4 In., Pair	275.00
Painting, On Porcelain, Whispering Girls, Hold Candle,,Frame	695.00
Painting, On Silk, Flowers, C.1880, 14 X 8 In.	12.00
Painting, On Tin, Cart, Man, Woman, Baby, China, Frame, 8 X 12 In., Pair	25.00

Painting, **Pen & Ink & Watercolor**, Flowers, Charles Bohn, Jr., 1806 & 07, Pair 160.00
Painting, **Pen & Ink & Watercolor**, King Of The Beasts, Felix Dogherty, 1810 .... 575.00
Painting, **Portrait**, Porcelain, Madame Elizabeth, Signed, Gold, Wood Frame 70.00
Painting, **Reverse On Glass**, George & Martha Washington, Gilt Frame, Pair 140.00
Painting, **Reverse On Glass**, House, Mountains, Lade, Boat, Signed Brienzer 40.00
Painting, **Reverse On Glass**, Prince Poniatowski, Black Frame 100.00
Painting, **Theorem**, Flowers, Reeded Frame, On Paper 85.00
Painting, **Theorem**, On Velvet, Blackened Colors, Gilt Frame 12.50
Painting, **Theorem**, On Velvet, Landscape & Castle, Framed 40.00
Painting, **Theorem**, Watercolor, Flowers, Pine Frame 12.50
Paintint, **Watercolor On Ivory**, Portrait, 18th Century, Brass Frame, 4 .... 175.00
Painting, **Watercolor**, A Bouquet, Jacob Lorn, Dated 1819 .... 170.00
Painting, **Watercolor**, American Marine, Artist Charles R.Watson, Frame 38.00
Painting, **Watercolor**, Angels With Musical Instruments, Signed Baynes, Pair 50.00
Painting, **Watercolor**, Bride & Groom, Pennsylvania, Leaf & Floral Border 700.00
Painting, **Watercolor**, Brother & Sister, American, C.1840, 9 1/2 X 12 1/2 In. 150.00
Painting, **Watercolor**, Civil War Volunteer, Blue Uniform, Frame, 15 X 19 In. 55.00
Painting, **Watercolor**, Farm Landscape, Robert Schnitzler, Dated 1884 .... 625.00
Painting, **Watercolor**, Man On Prancing Horse, Pennsylvania 275.00
Painting, **Watercolor**, On Silk, Girl, Flower, Eunice Pinney, Conn., C.1810-20 .... 275.00
Painting, **Watercolor**, Portrait, American, Signed A.Dayton, Pair 250.00
Painting, **Watercolor**, The Biddle House, Miss Allen, C.1860 .... 175.00
Painting, **Watercolor**, Tulips & Other Flowers, Youngstown, Ohio, Pine Frame 45.00
Painting, **Watercolor**, Winter Woods, K.Krishitzky 50.00
Painting, **Watercolor**, Yellow Twisted Pedestal Urns, Bremen, 1811 .... 50.00

Pairpoint Corporation was a silver and glass firm founded in New
Bedford, Massachusetts, in 1880.
Pairpoint, **Candleholder**, Cut Stem Prisms, Electrified, C.1910, 18 In., Pair 150.00
Pairpoint, **Candlestick**, Black Amethyst, Clear Bubble Stem 125.00
Pairpoint, **Candlestick**, Brass Color, Flared Octagon Base, Signed, Pair 15.00
Pairpoint, **Candlestick**, Brass, Marked, Pair 57.50
Pairpoint, **Candlestick**, Cobalt Blue, Clear Air Bubble, 11 In.Tall, Pair 60.00
Pairpoint, **Chalice**, Green & Clear, Etched Pattern 59.00
Pairpoint, **Compote**, Amethyst, Clear Air Bubble, 6 X 6 1/2 In. 37.50
Pairpoint, **Compote**, Green, Clear, Bubble Stem 125.00
Pairpoint, **Creamer & Sugar**, Wild Rose, Silver Plate, Spooner, Set 37.50
Pairpoint, **Goblet**, Amethyst Base, Color Swirl On Stem, 6 .... 150.00
Pairpoint, **Goblet**, Engraved, Signed Boda, 4 .... 60.00
Pairpoint, **Lamp**, Apple Blossom Orchard Scene, Signed, 20 In.Shade 650.00
Pairpoint, **Lamp**, Boudoir, Green, Cut Glass Stem, Prisms, Signed, Pair 135.00
Pairpoint, **Lamp**, Butterfly & Flowers, Signed, Table, 14 In.High 500.00
Pairpoint, **Lamp**, Garden Scene, Red & White, Heavy Glass 350.00
Pairpoint, **Lamp**, Puffy, Butterfly & Flower, Signed, 22 In.High 750.00
Pairpoint, **Lamp**, Table, Flowers, Green, Globe Shade, Signed 550.00
Pairpoint, **Match Safe**, Owl, Silver Plate 9.50
Pairpoint, **Peachblow**, Wine, Signed, 5 1/2 In.Tall 18.50
Pairpoint, **Perfume**, Crystal, Bird Top 22.00
Pairpoint, **Pitcher**, Water, Floral Design, Beaded Edge, Quadruple Plate, 10 In 35.00
Pairpoint, **Vase**, Flowers, Bubbly Glass, Enamel 46.00
Pairpoint, **Vase**, Garland Pattern, 8 In. 95.00
Palmer Cox, **Brownie**, Plate, 6 In., China 25.00
Palmer Cox, **Brownie**, Tray, Ice Cream, Advertising 25.00
Palmer Cox, **Calendar**, Brownies, 1894 .... 6.00
Palmer Cox, **Plate**, Brownies In Different Poses, 7 In. .... 20.00 To 25.00
Palmer Cox, **Platter**, Brownie, Oval 35.00
Pantin, **Vase**, Cameo, Red, 6 In.High 150.00
Paper, **Bookmark**, C.1880 .... 5.00
Paper, **Calendar**, Cornell, 1912 .... 3.00
Paper, **Calendar**, Fairy Tale Prints By Jessie Wilcox Smith, 1916 .... 5.00
Paper, **Calendar**, Maxfield Parrish, 'contentment, ' 1928, Edison 20.00
Paper, **Certificate**, Elgin Watch Stock, 1920s 1.25
Paper, **Certificate**, Stock, Pierce-Arrow Motor Car Co., 1917 .... 2.50
Paper, **Check**, First National Bank Of Bangor, Me., 1900-01, 5 .... 1.00
Paper, **Comics**, Deadwood Dick, Cover Illustrated 5.00
Paper, **Map**, New York, 1676, 10 X 15 In. 1.25

Paper, Pamphlet, Sights, Scenes & Wonders At The World's Fair, 1904 .... 4.00
Paper, Pass, Streetcar, Pittsburgh, 1931, Weekly 1.50
Paper, Plate, Pressed Cardboard, Scene Of Gladstone, Windsor Castle, 1878 .... 7.50
Paperweight, Abraham Lincoln, Signed St.Clair 20.00
Paperweight, Advertising, Dutch Boy, Dated 1898 .... 10.00
Paperweight, Advertising, Romanoff Caviar, Fish Shape, Metal, 6 In.Long 20.00
Paperweight, Advertising, Schoenecker Boot & Shoe 8.00
Paperweight, American Crystal, First Flight, 1st Issue ....: 60.00
Paperweight, American, New England Fruit, Pears, Cherries, Latticinio 275.00
Paperweight, American, Scrambler Millefiori Canes, Opaque Ribbon Twists 45.00
Paperweight, Anvil, Cast Iron, Detroit Stove Works Incised On Sides 10.00
Paperweight, Apple, Red, Yellow, Moretti 20.00
Paperweight, Apple, Ruby, Small, Moretti 20.00
Paperweight, Art Glass, Swirl 12.50
Paperweight, Atlas Crystal Works, Snowball, Aeroplane Inside 19.00
    Paperweight, Baccarat, see Baccarat, Paperweight
Paperweight, Ball, Red & White Wheels, Flowers, Sandwich Glass 30.00
Paperweight, Barker, Orange Double Clematis, Leaves, Purple Flash, Faceted 125.00
Paperweight, Barker, Pink Clematis & Bud On Stem, Green, Faceted, Cane 145.00
Paperweight, Barker, Snake On Branch, Green Leaves, Signed 145.00
Paperweight, Barker, Two Flowers On Stem, Green Leaves, Amber Ground 165.00
Paperweight, Barker, White Flower, Amethyst Flashed Ground 145.00
Paperweight, Bear Holding International Harvester Tractor, Aluminum 7.50
Paperweight, Bell, Advertising, Cornell University, Cobalt 20.00
Paperweight, Bell, Advertising, Gold Letters, Cornell University, Cobalt 24.00
Paperweight, Bell, Advertising, Gold Letters, New York Telephone, Cobalt 24.00
Paperweight, Bell, Advertising, 'it Pays To Use Yellow Pages, ' Cobalt 24.00
Paperweight, Bell, Advertising, New York Telephone, Cobalt 20.00
Paperweight, Bell, Advertising, Yellow Pages, Cobalt 20.00
Paperweight, Bird, Crystal, Multicolor, Swirl Interior 5.00
Paperweight, Blue Overlay, Concentric Circle Canes, Italian 15.00
Paperweight, Blue, Geometric, Signed M.E.Flegal 14.50
Paperweight, Bohemian, Ruby, Frosted Etching, 3 In.Diameter 65.00
Paperweight, Bust Of Lincoln, Sulfide, Blue To White To Clear, Italian 25.00
Paperweight, Bust Of Washington, Para Stone 1.00
Paperweight, Bust, Inscribed General Douglas Macarthur, America's Hero 30.0
Paperweight, Cambridge, C.1920, K.K.K.Wafer 10.00
Paperweight, Camel. Resting Position, Iron 12.50
Paperweight, Cherries, Ruby, Small, Moretti 20.00
Paperweight, Choko, Lizard 150.00
Paperweight, Choko, Salamander 150.00
Paperweight, Clear, Glass, Controlled Bubbles, Turtle Inside, 3 In.Diameter 33.00
Paperweight, Clear, Glass, Red, White, Blue, Spatter, Teardrops 31.00
Paperweight, Clear, Red Maltese Cross, Dated 1898 .... 25.00
Paperweight, Clichy, C Scroll, Canes Around Concentric Circles 400.00
Paperweight, Clichy, C Scroll, Pink Canes Around Green Florette 375.00
Paperweight, Clichy, Chequer, Concentric Canes, Lace Tubes, Pink, Green, White 375.00
Paperweight, Clichy, Concentric Circle 200.00
Paperweight, Clichy, Concentric Millefiori, Turquoise Ground, Rose Center 485.00
Paperweight, Clichy, Florette, Rows Of Canes, Wine Ground 500.00
Paperweight, Clichy, Napoleon, Sulfide, Signed Andreau 200.00
Paperweight, Clichy, Scattered Millefiori, Canes 250.00
Paperweight, Clichy, Three Cane Nosegay, Rose Center 290.00
Paperweight, Colored Glass, Engraved, Dated July 8, 1875 .... 35.00
Paperweight, Crystal, 1970 .... 180.00
Paperweight, Crystal, 1971 .... 200.00
Paperweight, Cut Glass, Triangular Shaped Facets, 2 1/2 In.Diameter 18.00
Paperweight, D'Albret, Albert Schweitzer, Sulfide, Blue Overlay, Cut 60.00
Paperweight, D'Albret, Astronauts With Shepard, 4 In. ....: 80.00
Paperweight, D'Albret, F.D.Roosevelt .... 55.00 To 62.00
Paperweight, D'Albret, F.D.Roosevelt Overlay 160.00
Paperweight, D'Albret, General Douglas Macarthur, Overlay 160.00
Paperweight, D'Albret, General Douglas Macarthur, Sulfide 62.00
Paperweight, D'Albret, Hemingway 62.00
Paperweight, D'Albret, J.F.Kennedy, Overlay 160.00
Paperweight, D'Albret, King Gustavus VI Of Sweden, Sulfide .... 40.00 To 62.00

Paperweight, **D'Albret**, Leonardo Da Vinci, Sulfide	62.00
Paperweight, **D'Albret**, Mark Twain, Sulfide	62.00
Paperweight, **D'Albret**, Mark Twain, Sulfide, Overlay	160.00
Paperweight, **D'Albret**, Moon Astronauts, Sulfide	62.00 To 80.00
Paperweight, **D'Albret**, Moon Astronauts, Sulfide, Overlay	160.00 To 180.00
Paperweight, **D'Albret**, Paul Revere, Sulfide	62.00
Paperweight, **D'Albret**, Prince Charles, Overlay	160.00
Paperweight, **D'Albret**, Prince Charles, Sulfide	62.00
Paperweight, **D'Albret**, Robert Kennedy, Sulfide, Overlay	160.00
Paperweight, **D'Albret**, Schweitzer, Sulfide	62.00
Paperweight, **D'Albret**, Schweitzer, Sulfide, Overlay	160.00
Paperweight, **Daghenhardt**, C.1930, Speckled Ground, Bubble & Flowers	10.00
Paperweight, **Daghenhardt**, Red & White Flower	20.00
Paperweight, **Daghenhardt**, Speckled Design	12.50
Paperweight, **Doorstop**, Five Petal Flower	40.00
Paperweight, **Doorstop**, Four Bubbles	40.00
Paperweight, **Double Buggy**, Marked, Patent Feb., 1876, 1 1/8 In.	12.75
Paperweight, **Eagle Silver Dollar Copy**, Certificate 1, By M.R.Erlacher	175.00
Paperweight, **Faceted Bouquet**, Ruby Ground, Signed W	350.00
Paperweight, **Figural**, Polar Bear, Signed Maleras Alexandrite	25.00
Paperweight, **Figural**, Sturgeon, Advertises Romanoff Russian Caviar, Metal	22.00
Paperweight, **Floral Canes**, D.E.Bottomfield, 3 1/2 In.Diameter	50.00
Paperweight, **Floral Canes**, Mollie Bottomfield, 3 1/2 In.Diameter	50.00
Paperweight, **Flower**, Red Ground, Faceted	40.00
Paperweight, **Four Stacked Iridescent Balls**	24.00
Paperweight, **Francis Whittemore**, Christmas Candle, Faceted, Signed W	400.00
Paperweight, **Gentile**, Butterfly	6.50
Paperweight, **Gentile**, Glass, Maroon Flower, Speckled Base	12.50
Paperweight, **Gentile**, Glass, Orange Flower & Bubbles	15.00
Paperweight, **Gentile**, Glass, Speckled Yellow, White, & Green Flowers	17.50
Paperweight, **Gentile**, Green & White Flower, Signed	25.00
Paperweight, **Gentile**, Red & Yellow Snake On Green, Window	40.00
Paperweight, **Gentile**, Signed, Christmas	12.00
Paperweight, **Gentile**, Signed, Pearl Harbor	12.00
Paperweight, **Gentile**, Three Green Lilies	20.00
Paperweight, **H.Stone**, 3 White Flowers & Bubbles	10.00
Paperweight, **Hacker**, Black Octopus On Blue Ground, Seashells	300.00
Paperweight, **Hacker**, Butterfly, Signed	15.00
Paperweight, **Hacker**, Cobra	425.00
Paperweight, **Hacker**, Green Snake, Striped Markings, Red & White Ground	200.00
Paperweight, **Hacker**, Hunting Dog, White Ground, Signed	30.00
Paperweight, **Hacker**, Turtle, Faceted, Tortiseshell Colored Glass	75.00
Paperweight, **Hand Painting Of A Covered Bridge**	10.00
Paperweight, **Hansen**, Bouquet, Faceted, Signed	45.00
Paperweight, **Hansen**, Flower & Buds On Blue, H In Center Of Flowers	45.00
Paperweight, **Hansen**, Flower, Cobalt Ground, Faceted, Etched Signature	45.00
Paperweight, **Hansen**, Orange Rose, Miniature, Signed	50.00
Paperweight, **Hansen**, Poinsettia, Blue Ground, 1967, Faceted, Signed	55.00
Paperweight, **Hansen**, Purple Flower, Faceted, Etched Signature	45.00
Paperweight, **Hansen**, Red Flower, Footed, Signed	50.00
Paperweight, **Hansen**, Red Poinsettia, White Ground, Green Leaves	100.00
Paperweight, **Hansen**, Rose, Faceted, Footed, Signed	45.00
Paperweight, **Hansen**, Three Flowers, Yellow, Turquoise, & Lavender, Green, Red	100.00
Paperweight, **Hansen**, Upright Bouquet, Red, Green, & Blue Flowers, Red, Faceted	195.00
Paperweight, **Hansen**, White Flowers & Leaves On Cobalt, Faceted, Signed	55.00
Paperweight, **Hansen**, Yellow Flower, Green, Cane At Base, Yellow Buds	185.00
Paperweight, **'Home Sweet Home' In White Over Red**, Blue, & Green Canes	35.00
Paperweight, **Iron**, Nickel Plate Brass Plate At Top Says Peerless Granite	4.95
Paperweight, **Iron**, Shape Of Iron Pipe, Says Attalla, Ala., Pipe & Fdry.Co.	6.00
Paperweight, **Ivory**, Carved Reclining British Lion	35.00
Paperweight, **Kaziun**, Flower, Gold Speckled Ground, Pedestal	165.00
Paperweight, **Kaziun**, Millefiori	345.00
Paperweight, **Kaziun**, Pansy, Blue & Purple, Topaz Ground, Gold Bee	480.00
Paperweight, **Kaziun**, Pedestal	145.00
Paperweight, **Kaziun**, Sandwich Rose, Amethyst Ground, Pedestal	270.00
Paperweight, **Kaziun**, Yellow Rose, Cane Signature, 1 1/4 In.	275.00

Paperweight, **Kosta**, Father's Day, 1971 .... 21.00
Paperweight, **Kosta**, Mother's Day.1970 .... 20.00
Paperweight, **Labino**, Cow Jumped Over Moon, Iridescent, Green 100.00
Paperweight, **Labino**, Free-Form Flower, Gold & Rust, Iridescent Gold, Green 100.00
Paperweight, **Labino**, Free-Form Striped Snake, Gold With Rosy Hue 125.00
Paperweight, **Labino**, Tulip, Pink To White Petals, Iridescent Gold, Clear 150.00
Paperweight, **Labino**, 4 Kite Like Objects Floating In Opalescent 100.00
Paperweight, **Leaves**, Strands, 3 In.Diameter 25.00
Paperweight, **Lewis**, Red Rose With Green Leaves On Mica Flecked Ground 150.00
Paperweight, **Locomotive**, Cast Iron, Black, 4 1/2 In.Long 1.95
Paperweight, **Lutz**, Sandwich Morning Glory, Blue Jasper Ground 300.00
Paperweight, **Mailbox**, Metal, Incised U.S.Mail, Shiny, Tubular 7.00
Paperweight, **Mayflower**, Whitefriars, Signed 125.00
Paperweight, **Millefiori**, Canes, Red, Yellow, White, Blue, 2 In.Diameter 35.00
Paperweight, **Millefiori**, Eggshaped 10.50
Paperweight, **Miniature Nosegay**, New England 140.00
Paperweight, **Moretti**, Flame, Signed 40.00
Paperweight, **Mortar & Pestle**, Brass 17.00
Paperweight, **Moses In Bulrushes**, Frosted Center, Oval 45.00
Paperweight, **Odd Fellows Insignia**, Round 12.50
Paperweight, **Orange Cone**, Bubbles, Engraved Top 12.50
Paperweight, **Orange**, White, Canes, Butterfly 40.00
Paperweight, **Pairpoint**, Glass, Flat, Bubbles 15.00
Paperweight, **Pear**, Crystal, Large, Moretti 60.00
Paperweight, **Pear**, Red, Yellow, Moretti 20.00
Paperweight, **Perthshire**, Crown, Red & White Spiral, Latticinio Threads, 1969 .... 135.00
Paperweight, **Perthshire**, Dragonfly, Ring Of Canes, Marked P 1970 .... 100.00
Paperweight, **Perthshire**, Faceted Pansy, Millefiori Canes, Signed P.1971 .... 145.00
Paperweight, **Perthshire**, Faceted Patterned Millefiori, Star Cut Base, 1971 .... 40.00
Paperweight, **Perthshire**, Flower In A Basket, 1972 .... 75.00
Paperweight, **Perthshire**, Millefiori 9.50
Paperweight, **Perthshire**, Millefiori, Translucent Color, Star Cut Base 15.00
Paperweight, **Perthshire**, Patterened Millefiori On Translucent, Star Cut 17.50
Paperweight, **Perthshire**, Ribbon, Canes Rising To Central Flower, Signed 85.00
Paperweight, **Perthshire**, Scattered Millefiori On Lace, Amethyst Base, 1971 .... 45.00
Paperweight, **Perthshire**, Scattered Millefiori On Lace, Green Base, 1971 .... 45.00
Paperweight, **Perthshire**, Scattered Millefiori On Lace, White Base, 1971 .... 45.00
Paperweight, **Perthshire**, Scrambled Millefiori With A P 1971 Cane 37.50
Paperweight, **Perthshire**, Swirl, Cane Center 17.50
Paperweight, **Petaled Flower On Lattice Ground** 150.00
Paperweight, **Pete Lewis**, Crimped Red Rose In Clear Crystal, 2 1/4 In. 150.00
Paperweight, **Picture Of William Mckinley**, Oval 8.00
Paperweight, **Pink & White Canes With Lace**, Italian 15.00
Paperweight, **Pittsburgh Exposition**, Oval, Red Flashed 18.00
Paperweight, **Plymouth Rock**, Inscribed Base, Dated 1876 .... 30.00
Paperweight, **Poland**, Signed, Green, Bubbles, Hand-Cut Top 25.00
Paperweight, **Polished**, Blue, Bubbles, Hand-Cut Top 17.50
Paperweight, **Ravenna**, Friendship, Arrow-Pierced Hearts 15.00
Paperweight, **Red Rose**, Standard .... 25.00 To 40.00
Paperweight, **Red**, Swirls, Clear, Magnifying, 3 1/2 In.Diameter 20.00
Paperweight, **Rock Ledge Hotel**, Poppam Beach, Maine, 4 X 2 1/2 In. 3.75
Paperweight, **Ron Ray**, Yellow Crimped Rose, Blue Foot, 1 1/2 In. 75.00
Paperweight, **Round**, Crystal, Coral, Large 50.00
Paperweight, **Royale**, Crystal, 1970 .... 180.00
Paperweight, **Royale**, Crystal, 1971 .... 200.00
Paperweight, **Ruby Flash**, Says Papa From Eddie 12.00
Paperweight, **Schneider**, Red & White Swirls, French, Signed 40.00
Paperweight, **Simulated Stack Of Coins**, Lincoln, Eagle, Metal 8.50
Paperweight, **Six Bubbles**, Clear, 3 1/2 In.Diameter 12.50
Paperweight, **Snake On Lattice Ground** 195.00
Paperweight, **Snowball**, House & Trees Inside 9.50
Paperweight, **Souvenir**, Washington, D.C. 6.50
Paperweight, **St.Clair**, Abraham Lincoln 20.00
Paperweight, **St.Clair**, Crimp 11.50
Paperweight, **St.Clair**, James Garfield 20.00
Paperweight, **St.Clair**, John Kennedy 20.00

Paperweight, St.Clair, William Mckinley	20.00
Paperweight, St.Louis, Dahlia, Signed Sl, Dated 1939	140.00
Paperweight, St.Louis, Dahlia, Signed Sl, Dated 1970	140.00
Paperweight, St.Louis, Faceted Flower, Dark Blue Ground, 1970	140.00
Paperweight, St.Louis, Flat Bouquet, Red, Blue, & Yellow Flowers, 1971	140.00
Paperweight, St.Louis, Fruit, 2 Pears, Apple, 3 Cherries, Latticinio Basket	700.00
Paperweight, St.Louis, King Of France, Commemorative, Sulfide, 1967	225.00
Paperweight, St.Louis, Marbrie, Center Cane Signed S.L.1971	70.00
Paperweight, St.Louis, Millefiori In Star Shape, Faceted, 1971	120.00
Paperweight, St.Louis, Mushroom, Overlay, Signed Sl, Dated 1969	210.00
Paperweight, St.Louis, Mushroom, Overlay, Signed Sl, Dated 1970	210.00
Paperweight, St.Louis, Nosegay, 4 Cane Bouquet, Faceted	400.00
Paperweight, St.Louis, Pears & Cherries On Swirling Latticinio, 1953	185.00
Paperweight, St.Louis, Pinwheel In Five Colors, 1971	140.00
Paperweight, St.Louis, Pinwheel, Blue & White	70.00
Paperweight, St.Louis, Pinwheel, Blue & White, 1971	140.00
Paperweight, St.Louis, Poinsettia, Signed Sl, Dated 1969	140.00
Paperweight, St.Louis, Poinsettia, Signed Sl, Dated 1970	140.00
Paperweight, St.Louis, Red Cherries On Branch, Latticinio Ground, 1952	185.00
Paperweight, St.Louis, Yellow Flower, 1970	140.00
Paperweight, Star Shape, Picture Magnifying Type	8.50
Paperweight, Stone, 3 Green & White Flowers With Bubbles	10.00
Paperweight, Strathearn, Magnum, Blue Flower & Lace, S Cane	35.00
Paperweight, Strathearn, Panels Of Canes & Lace	25.00
Paperweight, Strathearn, Pink Striped Ground, Cones Of Candy Ends	15.00
Paperweight, Strathearn, Red Flower, Blue To Clear, Faceted, 1970	65.00
Paperweight, Sulfide, Bismarck, 2 ½ X 1 ¼ In.	40.00
Paperweight, Sulfide, Lafayette Surrounded With Circle Of Canes, Faceted	110.00
Paperweight, Swirl Design, Pink, Gold, 2 3/4 In.Tall	30.00
Paperweight, Teapot Shape	7.50
Paperweight, Toadstool, Green & Yellow, 4 In.Tall	3.50
Paperweight, View Of Detroit Harbor, 4 X 2 1/2 In.	3.75
Paperweight, Waterfowl, By E.Frank Adams, Miniature, Paper Label, Pair	100.00
Paperweight, Whitefriars, Millefiori, Concentric Circle, Signed & Dated	40.00
Paperweight, Whitefriars, Millefiori, Diamond Cut Faceting	50.00
Paperweight, Whittemore, Blue Rose, White-Tipped Petals, Footed Pedestal	150.00
Paperweight, Whittemore, Cobalt Ground, Yellow Rose, Green Leaves	400.00
Paperweight, Whittemore, Lavender Rose, Standard, Signed	105.00
Paperweight, Whittemore, Yellow Rose, Pedestal, Signed	85.00
Paperweight, Wm.Drew, C.1925, 5 Flowers	20.00
Paperweight, Woman's Picture, Oval	30.00
Paperweight, Ysart, Three Flowers, Pink, Blue, & Lavender, Millefiori Canes	255.00
Paperweight, Zimmerman, Blue Butterfly On White Glass	20.00
Paperweight, Zimmerman, Blue Jay On Red Ground, Signed	45.00
Paperweight, Zimmerman, Glass, Pink & White Double Flowers	17.50
Paperweight, Zimmerman, Pink Crocus, Footed	35.00
Paperweight, Zimmerman, Pink Water Lily, Green Base, Faceted, Footed	20.00
Paperweight, Zimmerman, Three Mustard Colored Roses, Bubble	25.00
Paperweight, Zimmerman, Yellow Crocus, Footed	45.00
Paperweight, 8 Pointed Star, Signed B	12.50

Papier-Mache is a decorative form made from paper mixed with glue, chalk, and other ingredients, then molded and baked. It becomes very hard and can be decorated. Boxes, trays, and furniture were made of Papier-Mache. Some of the early nineteenth century pieces were decorated with mother-of-pearl.

Papier-Mache, see also Furniture

Papier-Mache, Bowl, Dull Reds, Gold, 9 In.	6.50
Papier-Mache, Box, Chinese Decorated, 2 Pewter Tea Caddies	60.00
Papier-Mache, Box, Collar, Round Center For Button, Black, Silver Dragon	8.00
Papier-Mache, Box, Footed, Black, Nacre Inlay, 7 In.Wide	17.50
Papier-Mache, Box, Music, Lacquered, Mother-Of-Pearl, 19th Century	150.00
Papier-Mache, Box, Snuff, Brass Shield On Lid	9.50
Papier-Mache, Box, Snuff, Silver Decor, 3 In.	8.50
Papier-Mache, Box, Snuff, Silver Decor, 4 1/2 In.	15.00
Papier-Mache, Dish, Soap, Black, Gold Oriental Figures, Pagoda, Trees	8.50
Papier-Mache, Dog, R.C.A.Victor, 14 In.	35.00

Papier-Mache, Doll, Shadowbox Painting, Blue Boy 50.00
Papier-Mache, Egg, Easter, Russian, Lacquer, Resurrection, N.Lukutin, C.1880 .... 400.00
Papier-Mache, Plate, Footed, Black, Chinese Decoration, Gilt, 11 1/4 In. 12.50
Papier-Mache, Sheep, Black Face, 6 In.High 9.00
Papier-Mache, Tray, Bird, Flowers, Mother-Of-Pearl Inlay 150.00
Papier-Mache, Tray, Gilded, 18th Century, Shepherd & Sheep, Stamped Illidge 225.00
Papier-Mache, Tray, Tea, Constitution & Guerriere, 1850 .... *Illus* 650.00

Papier-Mache, Tray, Tea,
Constitution & Guerriere, 1850

*Parian is a fine-grained, hard-paste porcelain named for the marble it
resembles. It was first made in England in 1846 and gained in favor in the
United States about 1860. Figures, tea sets, vases, and other items were
made of Parian at many English and American factories.*

Parian, Box, Blue & White Lions In Relief 20.00
Parian, Bust, Abraham Lincoln, 5 1/2 In. 45.00
Parian, Bust, Apollo, 11 In.Tall 75.00
Parian, Bust, Lady, 12 In.High 45.00
Parian, Bust, Longfellow, Marked R&I, 7 3/4 In.High 40.00
Parian, Bust, Marie Antoinette, Signed A.Carrier, 17 1/2 In. 500.00
Parian, Bust, Mozart 17.50
Parian, Bust, Shakespeare, 6 In. 35.00
Parian, Bust, Sir Walter Scott, 9 In. 37.50
Parian, Bust, Venus, 6 In. 35.00
Parian, Figurine, Child Kneeling, Minton, 'Hope,' Signed John Bell, C.1847 .... 100.00
Parian, Figurine, Marianne, Rifle, Commemorates Revolution, David Jongen 175.00
Parian, Figurine, Pekingese, Molded Ribbon Neck, 5 In.Long 10.00
Parian, Figurine, Smith Working On Sword 17.50
Parian, Figurine, Woman, Grape Garland, Basket, Vines, 10 1/2 In.Tall 50.00
Parian, Figurine, Young Man & Lady, 9 In.High, Pair 15.00
Parian, Jug, Syrup, Bulbous, Panels, Ovals, Stripes, Silver Lid & Handle 45.00
Parian, Match Holder, 2 Owls On Branch, 8 In.High 65.00
Parian, Pitcher, English, Embossed Punch, Scenes, Lavender 55.00
Parian, Pitcher, Water, Cupids, Grape, Leaves, 6 In. At Base, 9 In.Tall 225.00
Parian, Vase, Dolphins 45.00
Parian, Vase, Eagles, Pair 100.00
Parian, Vase, Hands With Fan, Pair 65.00
Parian, Vase, Man & Woman Sitting Playing Cards 17.50
Parian, Vase, Wheat Pattern With Grapes, 7 In.High 25.00
Paris, Incense Burner, Form Of Lady Playing Mandolin, C.1830 .... 30.00
Paris, Saucepan, Covered, Wood Handle, Bouquets, Crown C.P.Mark, C.1850, Pair 150.00
Paris, Tea & Coffee Set, Blue Bands, White & Gold Borders, C.1830, 9 Piece 90.00
Pate De Verre, Basket, Green, Cherubs 135.00
Pate De Verre, Chick, Pale Yellow, Green Base, Signed Walter, 4 In.High 380.00
Pate De Verre, Figurine, Buddha, White To Green, Signed A.Walter, Nancy, Pair 250.00
Pate De Verre, Figurine, Chick, Yellow, Green Base, Signed Walter, 4 In.High 380.00
Pate De Verre, Inkwell, Penholder Stand, Signed A.Walter-Nancy, Berge, S.C. 525.00
Pate De Verre, Liquor, Translucent Gray Ground, Blue Floral, Argy-Rousseau 110.00
Pate De Verre, Tray, Pin, Leaf Shape, Green Forsted, Signed A.Walter, Nancy 200.00

Pate De Verre, Vase, Gray, Red, Poppies, Signed G.A.R., 7 In. 425.00
Pate De Verre, Vase, Signed G.Argy-Rousseau 365.00

*Pate Sur Pate means paste on paste. The design was made by painting
layers of slip (which see) on the piece until a relief decoration was formed.
The method was developed at the Sevres Factory in France about 1850.
It became even more famous at the English Minton Factory about 1870.*
Pate Sur Pate, Box, Blue, White, Angelic Figure Playing Instrument, Limoges 69.50
Pate Sur Pate, Cachepot, Minton, Signed Schenck, 5 1/2 X 6 In.Diameter 450.00
Pate Sur Pate, Vase, Covered, Potpourri, Inverted Ball Shape, C.1880, Dresden 375.00
Paul Revere, Bowl, Blue Semigloss, Hand-Formed Body, Marked Ink Prp 42.00
Paul Revere, Bowl, Blue, Handled, Prp Mark 35.00
Paul Revere, Bowl, White, Paul On Horseback Impressed Mark 15.00
Paul Revere, Candleholder, Green, Artist-Signed & Dated 27.50
Paul Revere, Cup & Saucer, Slate Blue, Signed 38.50
Paul Revere, Jar, Covered, Pink With Decorated Stripes, Beige, Blue 22.00
Paul Revere, Plate, John's, Green Ground, Dog, House, Tree, Marked 45.00
Paul Revere, Plate, White, Paul On Horseback Impressed Mark 12.50
Paul Revere, Tile, Round, Ships Decoration, Artist-Signed & Dated 25.00
Paul Revere, Vase, Wall, Hanging, Green, Artist-Signed & Dated 35.00

*Peachblow Glass originated about 1883 at Hobbs, Brockunier and Company
of Wheeling, West Virginia. It is a glass that shades from yellow to
peach. It was lined in white. New England Peachblow is a one-layer
glass with a lining shading from red to white. Mt.Washington Peachblow
shades from pink to blue. Reproductions of peachblow have been made, but they
are of a poor quality and can be detected.*
Peachblow, see also Gunderson, Peachblow
Peachblow, Apple, New England 185.00
Peachblow, Basket, Deep Pink To Bluish White, Amber Glass Legs & Handle 32.50
Peachblow, Bowl, Bride's, Pink To White, Inner Caramel To Yellow, Frilly 170.00
Peachblow, Bowl, Frilled Top, New Martinsville, 5 In.Diameter 95.00
Peachblow, Bowl, New Martinsville, Ruffled Top, 10 In.Diameter 100.00
Peachblow, Bowl, New Martinsville, Scalloped & Ribbed, Iridescent 125.00
Peachblow, Bowl, Rose, Sandwich, 3 1/2 X 4 In. 49.50
Peachblow, Bowl, Rose, World's Fair 1893, New England 195.00
Peachblow, Bowl, Three Corners, New England 400.00
Peachblow, Bride's Basket, Pink To Cream, New Martinsville, Plated Holder 175.00
Peachblow, Cup, Punch, Wheeling Drape, White To Dark Pink ....65.00 To 140.00
Peachblow, Dish, New Martinsville, Ruffled Edge 40.00
Peachblow, Jar, Pickle, Mum Design, Rose Color, Cover, 8 1/2 In.Tall 95.00
Peachblow, Mustard Pot, Wheeling 275.00
Peachblow, Pear, New England 95.00
Peachblow, Pear, Wheeling, Marked Hobbs, Brockunier & Co. 95.00
Peachblow, Pitcher, Wheeling Drape, Cased, 5 1/2 In.High 200.00
Peachblow, Pitcher, Wheeling, Amber, Square Mouth, 5 In.High 850.00
Peachblow, Salt & Pepper, Glossy 325.00
Peachblow, Salt & Pepper, Glossy Finish, Original Caps, Wheeling 245.00
Peachblow, Tumbler, New England .... 200.00 To 275.00
Peachblow, Tumbler, Wheeling .... 195.00 To 325.00
Peachblow, Vase, Crimped, Ruffled, Ribbed, Pink To Light Pink 148.00
Peachblow, Vase, Fish Scale Pattern, Red, Yellow, Bulbous, Wheeling, 10 In. 475.00
Peachblow, Vase, Lily, Three Petals, Acid, New England, 9 In.High 500.00
Peachblow, Vase, New England, 9 1/2 In.High 250.00
Peachblow, Vase, Pink, Caramel Iridescent, Acid Finish 175.00
Peachblow, Vase, Shiny Finish, Mt.Washington 875.00
Peachblow, Vase, Teardrop, Mahogany To Lemon, Wheeling, 8 3/4 In.High 550.00
Peachblow, Vase, Wheeling, Overlay, Pink Liner, Applied Amber Feet & Fruit 110.00
Peachblow, Vase, Wheeling, Rose Top, Yellow Bottom, Crinkle Edge, 7 In. 265.00
Peachblow, Vase, Wheeling, Stick, 8 1/2 In.High 400.00
Peachblow, Vase, Wheeling, 4 1/4 In.High 435.00
Peachblow, Vase, White Cased, Deep Rose To Pink To White, 4 1/2 In.Wide 125.00
Pearl, Dish, Lap, Inlay, Compartments 29.00
Pearl, Knife, Dinner, Handles, Sterling Ferrules, Carved, Set Of 6 .... 30.00
Pearl, Knife, Luncheon, Set Of 12 .... 60.00
Pearl, Pen, Ink, 5 5/8 In.Long 2.75

Pearl, Tatting Shuttle 6.00

*Peking Glass is a Chinese Cameo Glass of the eighteenth and
nineteenth centuries.*
Peking, Bottle, Flower Design, Carnelian Stopper, Kwang-Hsu 1876-1908 .... 700.00
Peking, Bottle, Snuff, Carved Coral 80.00
Peking, Bottle, Snuff, Oriental Design, Yellow, Hand Carved, 3 In.Tall 100.00
Peking, Bowl, Azure Blue, Marked China 21.50
Peking, Bowl, Cameo, Red Cut To White, Butterflies & Floral, Standard 150.00
Peking, Bowl, Deep Blue 50.00
Peking, Bowl, Fish, Flower, Blue, White, Cameo 145.00
Peking, Bowl, Raspberry, Transparent, 6 In.Diameter, 3 In.High 65.00
Peking, Bowl, 18th Century, Pair 750.00

*Peloton Glass is european glass with small threads of colored glass rolled
onto the surface of clear or colored glass. It is sometimes called spaghetti
or shredded coconut glass.*
Peloton Glass, Pitcher, Water, Enameled Floral, Applied Pastel Glass 130.00
Peloton Glass, Syrup, Purple Threads, Silver Plate Cover & Handle 35.00
Pen, see Store, Pen
Perthshire, Bottle, Translucent Overlay, Purple & Amethyst, Millefiori 175.00

*Pewter is a metal alloy of tin and lead. Some of the Pewter made after
about 1840 has a slightly different composition and is called britannia metal.*
Pewter & Brass, Dish, Sideboard, Paw Supports, Caldwell & Co., N.Y., Pair 400.00
Pewter, Basin, English, 18th Century, Hallmarked, 13 In.Diameter 75.00
Pewter, Basin, Love, Philadelphia, 11 1/2 In.Diameter 450.00
Pewter, Basket Tray, Tulip Handle, Kayserzinn, No. 4308, 11 1/2 In.Diameter 55.00
Pewter, Basket, Marked Kayserzinn, Handled, Openwork Edge, Floral, 10 In. 37.50
Pewter, Beaker, English, Charles Ii, Engraved, Oval Cartouches, C.1680, Pair 500.00
Pewter, Beaker, English, Charles Ii, I.Z.Mark, C.1680 .... 350.00
Pewter, Beaker, Unpolished 15.00
Pewter, Bed Warmer, Hole For Tumbler 30.00
Pewter, Bedpan, English 95.00
Pewter, Bowl, Baptismal, Scottish, 8 In.Diameter 75.00
Pewter, Bowl, Footed 8.50
Pewter, Bowl, Monteith, Scalloped Rim, 19th Century 275.00
Pewter, Bowl, Round, Hand Hammered, Footed, 9 1/2 In. 12.50
Pewter, Bowl, Round, Sheffield, Hand Hammered, Footed 6 In. Diameter 12.50
Pewter, Box, Snuff, Spoon 28.00
Pewter, Candelabra, Two Candle, Marked, 10 In.Tall, 11 In.Wide 12.00
Pewter, Candlestick, English, 7 5/8 In.High, Pair 80.00
Pewter, Candlestick, English, 8 1/2 In.High, Pair 85.00
Pewter, Candlestick, English, 10 1/2 In.High, Pair 100.00
Pewter, Candlestick, Inverted Bowl Base, 5 1/2 In.High, Pair 155.00
Pewter, Candlestick, Kayserzinn, Bell Bottom, Embossed Flowers, Signed, Pair 30.00
Pewter, Candlestick, Pricket, Triform Base, Marked I.T.W., Dated 1782, Pair 160.00
Pewter, Candlestick, Pricket, Triform Base, Paw Feet, C.1800, Pair 85.00
Pewter, Candlestick, Swirled Pedestal, Norway, 7 3/4 In.Tall 30.00
Pewter, Castor Set, Elks' Heads Around Body 125.00
Pewter, Castor Set, Signed R.Dunham, Bottles With Pewter Tops 130.00
Pewter, Chalice, Bell Shape Bowl, Peter Young, New York, C.1784, Pair 5250.00
Pewter, Charger, American, Thomas Boardman, Hartford, Double Marked 350.00
Pewter, Charger, English, Engraved Crest & Hunting Scene, Bewdely, C.1780 .... 200.00
Pewter, Charger, English, 16 1/2 In.Diameter, Pair 140.00
Pewter, Charger, London, 12 In.Long 15.00
Pewter, Charger, Louis Xvi, Center Medallion Chased King, Etched 125.00
Pewter, Charger, Mark Dim, 13 1/2 In. 130.00
Pewter, Charger, Samuel Hamlin, Hartford & Providence, C.1800 .... 200.00
Pewter, Charger, Stamped 'len Bri, '15 In.Long 30.00
Pewter, Charger, 13 1/2 In.Diameter 80.00
Pewter, Charger, 16 1/2 In.Diameter 40.00
Pewter, Chocolate Pot, Continental, 10 1/2 In.High 50.00
Pewter, Coffee Set, Sugar, Creamer, Marked Pilgrim, Pot 10 In.Tall 38.00
Pewter, Coffeepot, American, I.C.Lewis 225.00
Pewter, Coffeepot, Cylindrical, Branch Handle, 11 1/2 In.High 40.00

Pewter, **Coffeepot**, J.Dixon & Son, 8 In. 68.00
Pewter, **Coffeepot**, Leonard Reed & Barton, Mass., C.1825 .... *Illus* 150.00
Pewter, **Coffeepot**, No.3400, Leonard, Reed & Barton, 1837-47 .... 125.00
Pewter, **Coffeepot**, Pear Shape, S Spout, Japanned Handle, American, C.1825 .... 80.00
Pewter, **Coffeepot**, Porcelain Lined, Statue Of Liberty 55.00
Pewter, **Coffeepot**, Unmarked, Early 19th Century, 11 In.Tall 105.00
Pewter, **Coffeepot**, Urn Shape, Leonard Reed & Barton, Mass., C.1825 .... 90.00
Pewter, **Coffeepot**, Wood Handle & Finial, Footed, Mark Reed & Barton 60.00
Pewter, **Container**, Food, Continental, Etched Sides 15.00
Pewter, **Creamer & Sugar**, Hand Hammered 9.00
Pewter, **Creamer**, Broadhead-Atkins, Helmet 17.50
Pewter, **Creamer**, Sugar, Tray, Flagg & Homan 35.00
Pewter, **Cruet Stand**, Israel Trask, Mass., C. 1830, Sandwich .... *Illus* 250.00

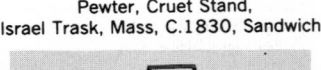

Pewter, Cruet Stand,
Israel Trask, Mass, C.1830, Sandwich

Pewter, Coffeepot,
Leonard Reed & Barton, Mass., C.1825

Pewter, **Cup**, Collapsible, Tin Case, N.Filley & Sons, Philadelphia 4.75
Pewter, **Cup**, Covered, Charles Ii, 2 Handles, Engraved Armorials, C.1680 .... 450.00
Pewter, **Cup**, English, Covered, Dixon & Sons 30.00
Pewter, **Cup**, Loving, Marked Kayserzinn, 3 Handles, Butterfly Decor, 8 In. 42.50
Pewter, **Cup**, Presentation For Baby, Engraved 15.00
Pewter, **Dish**, American, Raised Sides, Joseph Danforth, 18th Century 275.00
Pewter, **Dish**, Bread, Signed Plymouth, Handled, 14 In.Long 20.00
Pewter, **Dish**, Deep, Hammered Booge, Henry Will, New York, C.1760 .... 850.00
Pewter, **Dish**, Raised Cherries, Mark Kayserzinn, 5 1/4 In.Diameter 20.00
Pewter, **Dish**, Raised Flowers, Mark Kayserzinn, 4 1/2 In.Diameter 15.00
Pewter, **Dish**, Shallow Round, Handles, 6 In. 18.00
Pewter, **Dish**, 4 In., 1/2 In.Flat Rim, 1/2 In.Deep 25.00
Pewter, **Figure**, Baseball Player, C.1890, American, Copper Base, Gas Jet Light 64.50
Pewter, **Figurine**, Puck, Painted, Woodward Chaoone & Co., Oct.12, 1869 .... 50.00
Pewter, **Flagon**, Continental, Baluster, Ram's Head Finial, 19th Century 110.00
Pewter, **Flagon**, Continental, 3 Mask Supports, Dolphin Finial 40.00
Pewter, **Inkstand**, Desk, 5 Quill Holes 40.00
Pewter, **Inkstand**, Treasury, Rectangular Casket Shape, Marked King, C.1800 .... 110.00
Pewter, **Inkstand**, Well On Flat Plate, 5 Holes For Quills, English, C.1840 .... 45.00
Pewter, **Inkstand**, Well On Flat Plate, 6 Holes For Quills, English, C.1850 .... 55.00
Pewter, **Inkwell**, Blown Glass Bowl, Saucer Base, Embossed Top, Hinged 28.00
Pewter, **Inkwell**, Figural, Oriental Shoe, Brass Floral & Symbol Inlay 30.00
Pewter, **Inkwell**, Owl, 4 In.High, 9 1/2 In.Long 85.00
Pewter, **Inkwell**, Owl, 5 In.High 65.00
Pewter, **Jar**, Tobacco, Knob Top, Circa 1820 .... 67.50
Pewter, **Ladle** 22.50
Pewter, **Ladle**, Ashberry, 12 1/2 In. 45.00
Pewter, **Lamp**, Double Crusie, Hanging Spike, Wick Pick On Chain 85.00

Pewter, Measure, Circa 1820, Polished, England, Set Of 6	300.00
Pewter, Measure, English, Quart To 1/4 Gill, Set Of 6	200.00
Pewter, Measure, English, Quart, Pair	30.00
Pewter, Measure, English, 1/2 Gill	20.00
Pewter, Measure, English, 1/4 Gill	15.00
Pewter, Measure, Flared Base, 1/2 Pint	30.00
Pewter, Measure, Half Gill, Pear Shape, George Iv, English, 2 5/8 In.Tall	25.00
Pewter, Measure, 1/2 Gill, England, Crown & E.R.Mark	22.00
Pewter, Mold, Butter, Log Cabin	225.00
Pewter, Mold, Ice Cream	7.00
Pewter, Mold, Ice Cream, American Flag	18.00
Pewter, Mold, Ice Cream, Angel With Cross	24.00
Pewter, Mold, Ice Cream, Apple	11.50
Pewter, Mold, Ice Cream, Apple, E.& Co.	11.50
Pewter, Mold, Ice Cream, Apple, S.& Co.	6.50
Pewter, Mold, Ice Cream, Asparagus Bunch	6.50
Pewter, Mold, Ice Cream, Asparagus, Single	9.00
Pewter, Mold, Ice Cream, Automobile	14.00
Pewter, Mold, Ice Cream, Banana	11.50
Pewter, Mold, Ice Cream, Banana, E.& Co.	11.50
Pewter, Mold, Ice Cream, Basket, Three Piece	11.50
Pewter, Mold, Ice Cream, Battleship	15.00
Pewter, Mold, Ice Cream, Bear, Standing	11.50
Pewter, Mold, Ice Cream, Bell	10.00 To 11.50
Pewter, Mold, Ice Cream, Bell, E.& Co.	11.50
Pewter, Mold, Ice Cream, Bicyclist, Man Riding	20.00
Pewter, Mold, Ice Cream, Boat With Sailor	18.00
Pewter, Mold, Ice Cream, Boy On Bike	25.00
Pewter, Mold, Ice Cream, Bride	12.00
Pewter, Mold, Ice Cream, Buddha	11.50
Pewter, Mold, Ice Cream, Bull	15.00
Pewter, Mold, Ice Cream, Bunch Of Grapes	6.50
Pewter, Mold, Ice Cream, Bunch Of Grapes, E.& Co.	11.50
Pewter, Mold, Ice Cream, Calla Lily	10.00
Pewter, Mold, Ice Cream, Calla Lily, Three Piece, S.& Co.	11.50
Pewter, Mold, Ice Cream, Candlestick	15.00
Pewter, Mold, Ice Cream, Cannon	10.00
Pewter, Mold, Ice Cream, Carnation	9.00
Pewter, Mold, Ice Cream, Carnation With Stem	11.50
Pewter, Mold, Ice Cream, Cat Sitting	11.50
Pewter, Mold, Ice Cream, Chick Head Coming Out Of Egg	11.50
Pewter, Mold, Ice Cream, Chick, Standing, E.& Co.	11.50
Pewter, Mold, Ice Cream, Chicks In Basket	16.00
Pewter, Mold, Ice Cream, Chinaman, Yum Yum	13.50
Pewter, Mold, Ice Cream, Christmas Tree	13.00
Pewter, Mold, Ice Cream, Chrysanthemum	11.50
Pewter, Mold, Ice Cream, Church Window, Centerpiece	25.00
Pewter, Mold, Ice Cream, Clown	19.00
Pewter, Mold, Ice Cream, Cluster Of Strawberries, 3	11.50
Pewter, Mold, Ice Cream, Corn In Husk	13.00
Pewter, Mold, Ice Cream, Cotton Bale	9.00 To 11.00
Pewter, Mold, Ice Cream, Cupid	12.00
Pewter, Mold, Ice Cream, Cupid, E.& Co.	11.50
Pewter, Mold, Ice Cream, Daisy, E.& Co.	11.50
Pewter, Mold, Ice Cream, Daisy, S.& Co.	11.50
Pewter, Mold, Ice Cream, Diamond Ring	10.00
Pewter, Mold, Ice Cream, Dog Sitting	11.50
Pewter, Mold, Ice Cream, Donkey	15.00
Pewter, Mold, Ice Cream, Drinking Glass, Three Piece, S.& Co.	11.50
Pewter, Mold, Ice Cream, Drum, 3 Piece	20.00
Pewter, Mold, Ice Cream, Eagle	25.00
Pewter, Mold, Ice Cream, Eagle With Cannon	25.00
Pewter, Mold, Ice Cream, Ear Of Corn	11.50
Pewter, Mold, Ice Cream, Easter Lily	10.00
Pewter, Mold, Ice Cream, Easter Lily, Three Piece	11.50
Pewter, Mold, Ice Cream, Egg	9.00

Pewter, Mold, Ice Cream, Egg, E.& Co. 11.50
Pewter, Mold, Ice Cream, Egg, Goose, S.& Co. 11.50
Pewter, Mold, Ice Cream, Egg, Mallard Duck 11.50
Pewter, Mold, Ice Cream, Elk Head, S.& Co., 3 Piece 11.50
Pewter, Mold, Ice Cream, Elk's Head 12.00
Pewter, Mold, Ice Cream, Engagement Ring With Diamond 11.50
Pewter, Mold, Ice Cream, Fish 14.00
Pewter, Mold, Ice Cream, Football Player 15.00
Pewter, Mold, Ice Cream, Frog Standing 11.50
Pewter, Mold, Ice Cream, George Washington, Hinged, Crossed Flags On Shield 18.00
Pewter, Mold, Ice Cream, George Washington, Martha Washington, Pair 32.00
Pewter, Mold, Ice Cream, Gold Piece 20.00
Pewter, Mold, Ice Cream, Golf Ball, E.& Co. 6.50
Pewter, Mold, Ice Cream, Hatchet, George Washington Initials .... 12.00 To 16.00
Pewter, Mold, Ice Cream, Heart With Cupid 14.00
Pewter, Mold, Ice Cream, Hen, Setting 12.00
Pewter, Mold, Ice Cream, Horn Of Plenty, S.& Co. 11.50
Pewter, Mold, Ice Cream, Horse & Jockey 18.00
Pewter, Mold, Ice Cream, Indian Chief 22.00
Pewter, Mold, Ice Cream, Jack O'lantern 15.00
Pewter, Mold, Ice Cream, Kiwanis Club Emblem, E.& Co. 11.50
Pewter, Mold, Ice Cream, Leaf 9.00
Pewter, Mold, Ice Cream, Lemon, S.& Co. 11.50
Pewter, Mold, Ice Cream, Lion, S.& Co. 11.50
Pewter, Mold, Ice Cream, Maltese Cross 11.50
Pewter, Mold, Ice Cream, Masonic Square & Compass, E.& Co. 11.50
Pewter, Mold, Ice Cream, Miss Columbia 18.00
Pewter, Mold, Ice Cream, Morning Glory 11.50
Pewter, Mold, Ice Cream, Mushroom 12.50
Pewter, Mold, Ice Cream, Mystic Shrine Emblem, Crescent With Sphinx Face 11.50
Pewter, Mold, Ice Cream, Napoleon 20.00
Pewter, Mold, Ice Cream, New Year Baby 18.00
Pewter, Mold, Ice Cream, Oak Leaf With Acorns 11.50
Pewter, Mold, Ice Cream, Peach .... 8.00 To 11.50
Pewter, Mold, Ice Cream, Peach Half With Stone, S.& Co. 11.50
Pewter, Mold, Ice Cream, Pear .... 9.00 To 11.50
Pewter, Mold, Ice Cream, Pig .... *Illus* 16.50

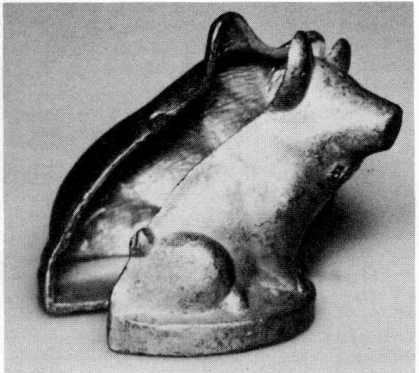

Pewter, Mold, Ice Cream, Pig

Pewter, Mold, Ice Cream, Pig, Sitting 11.50
Pewter, Mold, Ice Cream, Pineapple 11.50
Pewter, Mold, Ice Cream, Pineapple, E.& Co. 11.50
Pewter, Mold, Ice Cream, Pond Lily 11.50
Pewter, Mold, Ice Cream, Poppy, S.& Co. 11.50
Pewter, Mold, Ice Cream, Pumpkin .... 9.00 To 11.50
Pewter, Mold, Ice Cream, Pumpkin, E.& Co. 11.50
Pewter, Mold, Ice Cream, Pumpkin, S.& Co. 11.50
Pewter, Mold, Ice Cream, Rabbit, Running, S.& Co. 11.50

Pewter, Mold, Ice Cream, Rooster .... 15.00 To 16.00
Pewter, Mold, Ice Cream, Rose, American Beauty .... 10.00 To 11.50
Pewter, Mold, Ice Cream, Rose, E.& Co. 11.50
Pewter, Mold, Ice Cream, Rotary Club Emblem, E.& Co. 11.50
Pewter, Mold, Ice Cream, Santa Claus .... 13.50 To 16.00
Pewter, Mold, Ice Cream, Santa In Wreath 14.00
Pewter, Mold, Ice Cream, Seashell 6.50
Pewter, Mold, Ice Cream, Shamrock 12.00
Pewter, Mold, Ice Cream, Slipper 9.00
Pewter, Mold, Ice Cream, Slipper, Three Piece 6.50
Pewter, Mold, Ice Cream, Snowman 12.00
Pewter, Mold, Ice Cream, Soldier, National Guard 18.00
Pewter, Mold, Ice Cream, Spade Shape, For Cards, E.& Co. 11.50
Pewter, Mold, Ice Cream, Squirrel 6.50
Pewter, Mold, Ice Cream, Stork & Baby, E.& Co. 11.50
Pewter, Mold, Ice Cream, Sunflower, E.& Co. 11.50
Pewter, Mold, Ice Cream, Sweet Pea Flower 11.50
Pewter, Mold, Ice Cream, Telephone, Wall 25.00
Pewter, Mold, Ice Cream, Three Pears, Triple Mold 11.50
Pewter, Mold, Ice Cream, Tiger, S.& Co., 3 Piece 11.50
Pewter, Mold, Ice Cream, Tomato, E.& Co. 11.50
Pewter, Mold, Ice Cream, Tomato, S.& Co. 11.50
Pewter, Mold, Ice Cream, Triple, Daisy 11.50
Pewter, Mold, Ice Cream, Triple, Small Pears, 3 .... 11.50
Pewter, Mold, Ice Cream, Turkey 10.00
Pewter, Mold, Ice Cream, Turkey, Centerpiece, 3 Piece 45.00
Pewter, Mold, Ice Cream, Turkey, E.& Co. 11.50
Pewter, Mold, Ice Cream, Turkey, Roast 11.50
Pewter, Mold, Ice Cream, Turkey, Roast, E.& Co. 11.50
Pewter, Mold, Ice Cream, Watermelon With Slice Out, S.& Co. 11.50
Pewter, Mold, Ice Cream, Watermelon, Slice 9.00
Pewter, Mold, Ice Cream, Wedding Ring 11.50
Pewter, Mold, Ice Cream, Wild Rose 11.50
Pewter, Mold, Spoon 220.00
Pewter, Mug, English, Pint 20.00
Pewter, Mug, English, Quart, 7 In.High 45.00
Pewter, Mug, English, Side Spout, Engraved Wreath & Initials 80.00
Pewter, Mug, Irish Hallmark 40.00
Pewter, Penknife, English, C.1850 .... 12.00
Pewter, Pitcher, American, Baluster, Harp Shape Handle, Boardman & Hart, 1830 .... 220.00
Pewter, Pitcher, Britannia 35.00
Pewter, Pitcher, Cream, Flag & Hoffman, 4 In.Tall 25.00
Pewter, Pitcher, Helmet Shape, Round Base, Grecian Handle 30.00
Pewter, Pitcher, Marked Crescent Pewter 1506, 7 1/4 In.High 22.00
Pewter, Pitcher, Marked Salem Pewter, 7 1/2 In.Tall 25.00
Pewter, Pitcher, 8 In.Tall 28.50
Pewter, Plate, American, Austin, Charlestown, Mass. 305.00
Pewter, Plate, American, Boardman Eagle Touch Mark, 9 1/4 In.Diameter 325.00
Pewter, Plate, American, Marked Love, 13 In.Diameter 295.00
Pewter, Plate, American, Roswell Gleason, 10 In.Diameter 390.00
Pewter, Plate, American, S.Danforth, 8 In.Diameter .... 175.00 To 265.00
Pewter, Plate, American, Samuel Kilbourn, Baltimore, 8 In.Diameter 200.00
Pewter, Plate, Colonial, Townsen & Compton, 7 3/4 In.Diameter 35.00
Pewter, Plate, English, Made By Curtis, 8 In.Diameter 25.00
Pewter, Plate, English, 8 1/4 In.Diameter 22.50
Pewter, Plate, English, 8 3/4 In.Diameter 40.00
Pewter, Plate, English, 13 1/2 In.Diameter 45.00
Pewter, Plate, Hammered Booge, Cornelius Bradford, New York, C.1750 ..... 850.00
Pewter, Plate, Hot Water, James Dixon, Sheffield, Pair 60.00
Pewter, Plate, Initials W.A., Robert Dawe, Exeter, C.1680, Pair 130.00
Pewter, Plate, Mark L.H.Vaughn, Taunton, 9 In.Diameter 55.00
Pewter, Plate, Marked Insico Pewter, Anchor, 12 In., Deep 30.00
Pewter, Plate, Marked L.H.Vaughn, Taunton, 7 1/8 In. 8.75
Pewter, Plate, 9 1/2 In. 30.00
Pewter, Platter, Fish, Embossed Crabs, Fish, Snails, Seahorses, Kayserzinn 50.00
Pewter, Porringer, Crown Handle, New England, C.1800 .... 175.00

Pewter, Porringer, Lee Type Handle, American, 19th Century	180.00
Pewter, Porringer, New England, C.1800, 5 1/2 In. .... *Illus*	175.00
Pewter, Pot, Mustard, Spoon	58.00
Pewter, Salt & Pepper, Marked Federal Soild Pewter, 2 3/8 In.Tall	2.50
Pewter, Salt Dip, Viking Ship	7.50 To 8.50
Pewter, Salt, Master, English, Footed	18.50
Pewter, Sauceboat, Marked Kayserzinn, Attached Base, Embossed Flowers	35.00
Pewter, Spoon, Soup, Lovers Embossed On Handle Ends, Wooden Holder, Set Of 6	75.00
Pewter, Spoon, 6 1/4 In.	4.00
Pewter, Stick, Altar, Church, 18th Century, 40 In., Pair	348.00
Pewter, Sugar, Raised Shell Design, Gadroon Rim, Footed, Oval, Cover, Mark	35.00
Pewter, Syrup, Footed, Acorn Finial	32.00
Pewter, Tankard, English, William & Mary, Engraved, R.S.Crowned, C.1690	1900.00
Pewter, Tankard, French, C.1780	78.00
Pewter, Tankard, Pint, By James Yates, 1840, 5 In.Tall	37.50
Pewter, Tankark, Musical, C.1920, Marked Hale, England, 2 Operatic Arias	40.00
Pewter, Tappit Hen, Irish, 18th Century	65.00
Pewter, Tea Set, Kayzerzinn, Floral Design, Embossed, Sugar, Creamer, Teapot	95.00
Pewter, Tea Set, Miniature, Dollhouse, Creamer, Sugar, 2 Cup & Saucer, Tray	12.00
Pewter, Teapot, American, A.Griswold, Meriden, Conn., Mark J.154	150.00
Pewter, Teapot, American, Baluster, Boardman & Hart, N.Y., C.1830	110.00

Pewter, Porringer, New England, C.1800, 5 1/2 In.

Pewter, Teapot, American, Baluster, Wood Scroll Handle, Daniel Curtiss, 1840	210.00
Pewter, Teapot, American, Bordman & Hall, Philadelphia	290.00
Pewter, Teapot, American, E.Smith, Beverly, Mass.	150.00
Pewter, Teapot, American, G.Richardson	285.00
Pewter, Teapot, American, H.Yale & Co., Wallingsford, Mark J.296	225.00
Pewter, Teapot, American, L.J.Curtis	125.00
Pewter, Teapot, American, Octagonal	175.00
Pewter, Teapot, American, T.D.& S.B., Hartford, Conn.	275.00
Pewter, Teapot, Broadhead, Round, Squatty	37.50
Pewter, Teapot, By E.B.Manning, 1862, 7 1/2 In.	24.75
Pewter, Teapot, Chinese, Engraved, Woman, Flowers, Scrolls	48.50
Pewter, Teapot, Creamer, Sugar, Tray, England, Circa 1821, Marked F In Circle	150.00
Pewter, Teapot, Dixon, Octagon, Wood Handle, 10 In.Tall	59.50
Pewter, Teapot, Dixon, Smith, Boat Shape	45.00
Pewter, Teapot, English, Dixon & Sons	37.50
Pewter, Teapot, English, Pineapple Finial, James Dixon & Son	55.00
Pewter, Teapot, Footed, By James Dixon & Sons, 10 1/2 In.Tall	65.00
Pewter, Teapot, Grape Finial, Morey & Ober, Boston	165.00
Pewter, Teapot, Grooved & Paneled Sides, Wood Handle, 8 1/2 In.High	17.50
Pewter, Teapot, Hound Handle On Cover	22.00
Pewter, Teapot, Marked Ive	40.00
Pewter, Teapot, Pear Shape, Black Wood Handle, Footed Marked	45.00
Pewter, Teapot, Pear Shape, Blossom & Leaf Finial, 8 In.Tall	55.00

Pewter, Teapot, Pigeon Breasted, Fluted, By Taunton Britannia, 12 In.Tall 85.00
Pewter, Teapot, R.Dunham 135.00
Pewter, Teapot, Squatty Bulbous 15.00
Pewter, Teapot, Two Cup, Dixon & Sons 37.50
Pewter, Teapot, Wood Handle 17.00
Pewter, Teaspoon, Marked Libertas, Germany, Eagle Head, Pair 6.00
Pewter, Tray, Chinese, Brass & Copper Inserts, Birds & Men, 12 1/2 In.Long 55.00
Pewter, Trophy, Shooting, Silver Finish, Kneeling Soldier, 1792-1892 .... 59.50
Pewter, Tumbler, Slender 7.50
Pewter, Tureen, Marked Kayserzinn, Covered, Round, Raised Vintage Pattern 75.00
Pewter, Urn, Chestnut, Regency, Decorated, C.1815, Ring Handles, Pair 250.00
Pewter, Vase, Art Nouveau, Woman, Floral, 4 In. 7.50
Pewter, Vase, Kayserzinn, Boar's Head Embossed On One Side, Hound On Other 43.50
Pewter, Vase, Kayserzinn, Embossed Leaves, Berries, Fish, 7 In. 70.00
Pewter, Whistle, 2 1/4 In.Long, Cord 4.75
Pewter, Wine Taster, 3 In. 5.00
Phantom, Figure, Presswood, King Features, 1944, 5 In. 35.00

> *Phoenix Glass Company was founded in 1880 in Pennsylvania. The firm
> made commercial products such as lampshades, bottles, glassware. Collectors
> today are interested in the sculptured glassware made by the company from the
> 1930s until the mid-1950s.*

Phoenix Type, Vase, White, Molded Fern On Satin Finish, Wide Mouth 38.00
Phoenix, Bowl, Diving Girl, Blue, Oval, 14 In.Long 45.00
Phoenix, Bowl, Frolicking Nudes, Flat 60.00
Phoenix, Bowl, Reverse, Pale Frosted Blue, Fish & Swirls, Flared Top 155.00
Phoenix, Candlestick, Pink, Edelweiss Decor, Pair 15.00
Phoenix, Cup & Saucer, Bird 3.50
Phoenix, Pitcher, Green & Clear Swirl, 7 1/2 In. 37.50
Phoenix, Plate, Bird, 6 In. 1.50
Phoenix, Plate, Bird, 7 1/2 In. 2.50
Phoenix, Plate, Green Swirl, 8 1/2 In. 8.00
Phoenix, Shade, Gas, Ruffled, 4 In. 30.00
Phoenix, Vase, Blossoms, Green, Frosted, Panels, 8 In.Tall, Pair 85.00
Phoenix, Vase, Bluebirds 55.00
Phoenix, Vase, Cameo Ferns, Blue, Green, White 60.00
Phoenix, Vase, Fern, Sculptured Cameo, Yellow, 7 In.High 30.00
Phoenix, Vase, Ferns, Leaves, Blue, Green, White, Original Label, 7 In.Tall 50.00
Phoenix, Vase, Fish Design, Orange, Green, 9 In.Tall 75.00
Phoenix, Vase, Freesia Style, Grasshopper Motif, Clear, 8 In.High 40.00
Phoenix, Vase, Green, Pink, Birds 45.00
Phoenix, Vase, Green, 7 In.   *Illus*   35.00
Phoenix, Vase, Herringbone, Blue, Satin Glass 95.00
Phoenix, Vase, Leaves, Birds, Green, Peach, Opal 50.00
Phoenix, Vase, Lovebirds, Blossoms, Blue, White, Bulbous, 10 1/2 In.Tall 65.00
Phoenix, Vase, Rectangular, Raised Gold Birds & Floral, Pair 35.00
Phoenix, Vase, Sculptured, White, Crystal Overlay, 2 Birds On Each Side 42.50

Phoenix, Vase, Green, 7 In.

Phoenix, Vase, White, Dogwood Pattern, Bulbous 39.50
 Phonograph, see Music, Phonograph
Photography, Album, Art Leather, Black, Embossed Statue Of Liberty, 1930 .... 5.00
Photography, Album, Brown Suede, Embossed Colored Pansies, Minnie, Minn. 12.00
Photography, Album, Cardboard Box, Reversible Collar Co., Boston, 1870 .... 5.00
Photography, Album, Celluloid Cover, Off-White, 10 X 8 In. 9.50
Photography, Album, Easel, Gold Velvet, Metal Deer & Half-Moon 14.50
Photography, Album, Gibson Girl Paddling Canoe, Empty 32.50
Photography, Album, Leather, Maroon Plush, 10 X 8 In. 12.50
Photography, Album, Leather, Tooled, Metal Trim, 10 X 8 In. 12.50
Photography, Album, Leather, Tooled, White Bead Trim, 4 1/2 X 5 1/2 In. 6.50
Photography, Album, Leather, Tooled, 5 X 4 In. 6.50
Photography, Album, Miniature, Tintype, Red Leather, Gold Embossing 15.00
Photography, Album, Velvet 4.00
Photography, Album, Woman On Cover 5.00
Photography, Ambrotype, Confederate Officer Portrait 54.50
Photography, Camera, Brownie, Box, Model C 8.50
Photography, Camera, Brownie, Box, No.2, Model B 6.50
Photography, Camera, Bull's-Eye, Model D, Box, Pat.1894, Wood Inside 37.50
Photography, Camera, Folding, Kodak, No.3, Model F, Patent 1909, Case 7.50
Photography, Camera, Kodak, Autographic, Vest Pocket, Portrait Lens, Leather 14.00
Photography, Camera, Kodak, Box, Miniature 13.50
Photography, Camera, Kodak, Cine, Movie, 1934 .... 16.50
Photography, Camera, Kodak, No.2a, Folding, Pocket, Brownie, 1909 .... 7.50
Photography, Camera, Sereco, Portrait, C.1900, Ivory Gauge Plates, Brass 90.00
Photography, Daguerreotype Case, Black, Basket Of Flowers, Two Gilt Frames 32.50
Photography, Daguerreotype Case, Gutta-Percha, Beehive, Brown 30.00
Photography, Daguerreotype Case, Gutta-Percha, Civil War, Black 55. 0
Photography, Daguerreotype Case, Gutta-Percha, Dated 1858, Embossed Scenes 32.50
Photography, Daguerreotype Case, Gutta-Percha, Lattice Shield & Scrolls 10.00
Photography, Daguerreotype Case, Gutta-Percha, Signed F.Goll, Brown 69.00
Photography, Daguerreotype Case, Gutta-Percha, Three Children, Toys, Trees 52.50
Photography, Daguerreotype Case, Hard Case, Man & Lady Playing Chess 43.00
Photography, Daguerreotype, Baby In Carriage, Velvet Lined Case 8.00
Photography, Daguerreotype, Boy In Civil War Suit, Sword, Gold Frame 8.00
Photography, Daguerreotype, Double, Mother & Child, Two Positions 11.50
Photography, Daguerreotype, Lady, Cameo Pin On Dress, Velvet Lined Case 12.00
Photography, Daguerreotype, Man & Woman, Velvet Lined Case 10.00
Photography, Daguerreotype, Man, Woman, House, Trees, Oval Case 7.00
Photography, Daguerreotype, Small Boy 4.50
Photography, Flasher, Tin Trough, Wooden Handle, Trigger, Paper Caps 8.00
Photography, Magic Lantern Slides, Winter Scenes, Santa, Schoolroom, 4 .... 10.00
Photography, Magic Lantern, Kerosene, Tin, 18 Slides 47.50
Photography, Magic Lantern, Wood Case, 235 Slides, 19 X 16 In. 275.00
Photography, Magic Lantern, 10 Slides, Color, 11 In. .... *Illus* 30.00
Photography, Paper Photograph, U.S.Grant 3.00
Photography, Photograph, Funeral Of Lincoln, '65 .... 20.00
Photography, Photograph, General Fitz John Porter & Staff, July 16, 1862 .... 40.00
Photography, Projector, Postcard, Dated 1912, Clear Pointed Bulbs 15.00
Photography, Reel, Century Of Progress, Chicago, 1933, 35mm. 10.00
Photography, Slide, Indians, 16 Pieces, Glass, Color 16.00
Photography, Slide, Magic Lantern, C.1932, 1 Mickey Mouse, 12 .... 4.25
Photography, Slide, Paramount Pictures, Charley Ray, 'the Family Skeleton' 4.50
Photography, Slide, Select Pictures, Constance Talmadge, 'the Honeymoon' 4.50
Photography, Slide, Uncle Tom's Cabin, Glass, 7 .... 12.00
Photography, Slide, Votes For Women, 1912, Glass 5.00
Photography, Tintype, Child, Horse, Buggy, 2 .... 2.00
Photography, Tintype, Civil War Soldier, Canteen In Lap 35.00
Photography, Tintype, Infantry Private, Oval Gilt Frame 22.50
Photography, Tintype, Oval Gold Leaf Frame, 2 .... 30.00
Photography, Tintype, Two Little Girls Playing, Brother, Tinted Cheeks 4.00
Photography, Tintype, Union Infantryman, Fatigue Jacket 32.50
Photography, Tintype, Union Soldier, Standing, Sword, Colt, Cavalry Jacket 45.00
Photography, Tintype, Union Soldier, U.S.Buckle, Bayonet 60.00
 Piano, see Music, Piano

Photography, Magic Lantern, 10 Slides, Color, 11 In.
See Page 352

Pickard China was started in 1898 by Wilder Pickard. Hand-painted china was a featured product. The firm is still working in Antioch, Illinois.

Pickard, **Bowl**, Berries & Leaves, Orange To Brown, Gold Band, 9 3/4 In. 80.00
Pickard, **Bowl**, Hand-Painted Poppies & Daisies, Artist Signed Gasper 65.00
Pickard, **Bowl**, Roses, Red, Yellow, Green, Hand-Painted, 6 In.Diameter 37.50
Pickard, **Celery**, Hand-Painted Formal Border ....
Pickard, **Creamer & Sugar**, Floral Design, Oblong Shape, Gold Handles 22.50
Pickard, **Creamer**, Allover Embossed Design, Gold, 2 1/2 In.Tall 10.00
Pickard, **Cup & Saucer**, Demitasse, Gold Encrusted Allover Design 10.00
Pickard, **Cup & Saucer**, Gold Encrusted Allover Design 15.00
Pickard, **Dish**, Bonbon, Daisy Design, Hand-Painted, Handle, 7 In.Diameter 35.00
Pickard, **Dish**, Candy, Handles, Signed Efdon, 1910 .... 22.50
Pickard, **Jar**, Jam, Gold Encrusted Allover Design, Open Handles, Underplate 22.50
Pickard, **Jar**, Jam, White Ground, Orange Tree, Gold Trim, Underplate 22.50
Pickard, **Plate**, Floral, Gold Etched Band, 8 In. 20.00
Pickard, **Plate**, Floral, Pink, Green, Cream, Gold, Artist-Signed, 8 1/2 In. 35.00
Pickard, **Plate**, Gold, Marked Hand-Painted, W.A.Pickard, 5 In. 15.00
Pickard, **Plate**, Travel Building, Chicago, 1833-1933, Square 6.00
Pickard, **Plate**, Violets, Purple, Initial P.G., 1912, 6 In.Diameter 12.50
Pickard, **Plate**, White Water Lilies On Green To Yellow, Artist Keates 35.00
Pickard, **Relish**, Oval, Open Handles, Gold Center, Water Lilies, Artist James 32.50
Pickard, **Salt & Pepper**, Fuchsia, Purple, Pink, Gold Top, Mark 10.00
Pickard, **Sugar & Creamer**, Gold Etched 20.00
Pickard, **Sugar & Creamer**, Gooseberries, Leaves, Mahogany To Cream, Signed 79.00
Pickard, **Sugar & Creamer**, Squat, Covered, Hand-Painted Flowers, Gold, 1912-19 .... 27.50
Pickard, **Tea Set**, Art Nouveau Design, Gold, Platinum, Signed 50.00
Pickard, **Tray**, Hand-Painted Flowers In Center, Gold Trim, 5 In. 5.00
Pickard, **Vase**, Floral Design, Signed W.Lemke, 8 1/4 In.High 65.00
Pickard, **Vase**, Flower Design, Pink, Gold, Signed Simond, 1938, 5 In.Tall 20.00
Pickard, **Vase**, Fruit Design, Enamel, Gold, Black, Hand-Painted, 8 In.Tall 65.00
Pickard, **Vase**, Poinsettias, Red, Pearlized, Signed N.R.Gifford, 1898 .... 80.00
    Picture, see also Print, Painting
Picture, **Applique**, Bird, Natural Feather, Pair 10.00
Picture, **Artist Proof**, F.Remington, Evening On A Canadian Lake, Frame 14.50
Picture, **British Man O'war**, Carved & Painted, C.1850 .... 225.00
Picture, **Charcoal Drawing**, Landscape, Building, Sandpaper, Gilt Frame 15.00
Picture, **Cross Stitched**, Floral, Blue Ribbon Swimmers, Pair 30.00
Picture, **Cut Paper**, Bucolic Scene, Shepherds, 18th Century, Shadowbox Frame 30.00
Picture, **Hair Wreath**, Octagonal Box Frame, 27 In.Square 300.00
Picture, **Needlework On Silk**, Girl With Milk Pan, C.1800, Black & Gilt Frame 300.00
Picture, **Needlework On Silk**, Memorial, Lovicy Collins, Aged 15 Yrs, 1809 .... 300.00
Picture, **Needlework**, Memorial, Narcissa Botsford, Made In 1806, Conn. 650.00
Picture, **Pen & Ink**, Landscape, Signed A.B.Frost, 6 X 9 In., Framed 150.00
Picture, **Pencil Drawing**, Stone Mason & Woman With Broom, Frame, Pair 60.00

Picture, Plaque, Birds On Branch, Roses, Victoria Austria	48.00
Picture, Porcelain, Child's Face Resting On Hands, Res, Gold Frame, 5 X 6 In	150.00
Picture, Porcelain, Woman Kissed By Cupid, Frame, 13 3/4 X 18 3/4 In.	950.00
Picture, Portrait Of Jennie Lind, White Gown, Roses	750.00
Picture, Portrait Of Low Dog, Sioux Chief, By R.Spires, Frame	550.00
Picture, Portrait On Copper, Man, 4 3/4 In.X 6 3/4 In.	450.00
Picture, Portrait On Ivory, Woman In Period Costume, Brass Insert, Frame	60.00
Picture, Ship, Gloucester Schooner, U.S.Flag, Full Sail	180.00
Picture, Ship, Mary L.Skilling, Freeport, Maine, Wood, Painted, C.1815	275.00
Picture, Silhouette, Children Picking Apples, Dog, By K.Kaskeline, Frame	25.00
Picture, Silhouette, Joseph W.King, Aged 15, 1829, Ohio, Frame	60.00
Picture, Silhouette, Lady, Highlights Penciled In Gold	40.00
Picture, Silhouette, Lady, Penciled White & Gold, Frame	110.00
Picture, Silhouette, Lady, Rosewood Frame	40.00
Picture, Silhouette, Man, Oval Black Frame	55.00
Picture, Silhouette, Man, Under Convex Glass In Oval Brass Bezel, 1800	30.00
Picture, Silhouette, Painted, The Gurney Sisters Of Eartham, M.A.S., Pair	45.00
Picture, Silhouette, Sir John Wrottesley, Phila., C.1778 .... *Illus*	650.00
Picture, Silhouette, Wm.White, Kellogg, Maple Frame, 10 X 15 In.	48.00
Picture, Silhouette, Woman, Full Skirt, Fancy Bonnet, C.1835, 14 X 11 In.	55.00
Picture, Silhouette, Young Lady, Real Applied Hair, Mahogany Frame	115.00
Picture, Silk & Chenille Embroidery, Farm Folk, C.1800, Framed	70.00
Picture, Silk Embroidery, Banqueting Scene, C.1810, Framed	90.00
Picture, Silkwork, American, Fanny Winsor, R.I., 1801, Vase Of Wild Flowers	600.00
Picture, Silkwork, Regency, Pheasant On Tree Branch, Duck, 19th Century	190.00
Picture, Stumpwork Cushion, Solomon Greeting Queen Of Sheba, Frame	200.00
Picture, Theorem, Stencil On Velvet, Floral	25.00
Picture, Theorem On Velvet, Fruit On Table, Dishes, Knife, Gold Leaf Frame	1200.00
Picture, Tinsel In Black Frame, Ivanhoe On Horse, 8 X 9 1/2 In.	35.00
Picture, Tinsel In Black Frame, Sir Brian On Horse, 9 X 10 In.	35.00
Picture, Tinsel, Floral Urn, American, C.1820, Framed, Pair	275.00
Picture, Wax, Lady Hamilton, 6 1/2 X 8 In. .... *Illus*	125.00
Picture, Wax, Old Woman & Man Smoking Cigar, 19th Century	40.00

Picture Frame, see Furniture, Frame

Picture, Silhouette, Sir John Wrottesley,
Phila., C.1778

Picture, Wax, Lady Hamilton, 6 1/2 X 8 In.

Pigeon Blood, see Ruby, Cranberry
Pink Slag, see Slag
Pipe, Briar, Sterling Silver Rim, Marked Kaldenberg, N.Y. 3.00
Pipe, Carved Bone, Porcelain Bowl, Brass Chains, Gruss Aus Wien, Germany 94.50
Pipe, Carved, Porcelain Bowl, Gruss Aus Wien, 19th Century 94.50
Pipe, Clay, Marked Stoke On Trent 1.75
Pipe, French Briar, Amber Bit, Gold Grown, Case 20.00
Pipe, Indian, Catlinite Bowl, Wood Stem 65.00
Pipe, Meerschaum, see Meerschaum, Pipe
Pipe, Opium 12.00
Pipe, Wood Stem, China Bowl 9.00
Plaster Of Paris, Plaque, Wall, Victorian, Round, Female Figure, Gilded, Pair 5.00
Plaster, Bust, Hiawatha 85.00
Plaster, Plaque, Madonna & Child, Held With Human Hair, 18th Century 25.00
Plate, see under special types such as ABC, Calendar, christmas
Plated Silver, see Silver Plate

*Plique a jour is an enameling process. The enamel was laid between thin
raised metal lines and heated. The finished piece has transparent enamel
held between the thin metal wires.*
Plique A Jour, Box, Round, Royal Blue Enamel On Gilded Silver Frame 265.00
Plique A Jour, Spoon, Gold, Transparent Colors 100.00
Plique A Jour, Viking Boat, 3 X 2 1/2 In. 500.00
Plymouth, Figurine, Putto On Stump, Wreath Of Flowers, White, C.1770, Pair 375.00
Political Campaign, Badge, Black & White Picture Of Alton B.Parker 15.00
Political Campaign, Badge, Bryan & Kern, Pictures, 7/8 In. 10.00
Political Campaign, Badge, Bryan & Sewall Pictures, 7/8 In. 15.00
Political Campaign, Badge, Bryan For President, Silver, Free Coinage 30.00
Political Campaign, Badge, First Voters Bryan Club, 7/8 In. 8.50
Political Campaign, Badge, Our Next President, Roosevelt, Picture 8.00
Political Campaign, Badge, Picture Of Teddy Roosevelt On Gold 5.75
Political Campaign, Badge, Pictures Of Teddy Roosevelt & Fairbanks 10.00
Political Campaign, Badge, Sepia Pictures Of Taft & Sherman, 1908 .... 18.00
Political Campaign, Badge, W.H.Taft For President, Brown Ground 8.00
Political Campaign, Bandana, T.Roosevelt, 1910 .... 25.00
Political Campaign, Bank, Goldwater, Plastic, 1964 .... 2.50
Political Campaign, Bank, Johnson, Plastic, 1964 .... 2.50
Political Campaign, Blotter, Nathan L.Miller, Governor Of N.Y. .... .50
Political Campaign, Boat, P.T., JFK, 1960, Metal, Silver Color, On Card 9.00
Political Campaign, Book Mark, Tin, Roosevelt, 1902, Portrait 25.00
Political Campaign, Book, Song, Townsend Plan 7.00
Political Campaign, Box, Match, Feltcovered, Vote Democratic, Donkey, 1960 .... .75
Political Campaign, Brick Paperweight, L.B.J. 2.00
Political Campaign, Bumper Strip, Another Democrat For Nixon .... .50
Political Campaign, Bumper Strip, H.H.H. .... .10
Political Campaign, Bumper Strip, H.H.Humphrey .... .25
Political Campaign, Bumper Strip, Johnson, Humphrey .... .50
Political Campaign, Bumper Strip, Johnson, Humphrey For The USA .... .50
Political Campaign, Bumper Strip, Kennedy 5.00
Political Campaign, Bumper Strip, Kennedy In 1968 .... 1.00
Political Campaign, Bumper Strip, LBJ For The Usa .... .50
Political Campaign, Bumper Strip, Nixon, Agnew .... .25
Political Campaign, Bumper Strip, Paulsen For President .... .25
Political Campaign, Bumper Strip, Women For Nixon .... .35
Political Campaign, Button, A Square Deal All Around, T.R., 1912 .... 6.00
Political Campaign, Button, A Winning Team, Stevenson, Kefauver, Picture 75.00
Political Campaign, Button, A.E.Smith, Democratic Candidate, Picture 10.00
Political Campaign, Button, Adlai, Rectangular, Blue, White 1.00
Political Campaign, Button, Adlai, Red Bug .... .25
Political Campaign, Button, Al Smith And Bob Wagner 6.00
Political Campaign, Button, America Needs Goldwater, Jugate, Picture, Oval 1.00
Political Campaign, Button, America Needs Stevenson 1.50
Political Campaign, Button, American Needs Kennedy, Johnson, Jugate 3.00
Political Campaign, Button, Breckinridge, Lane, Ferrotype 65.00
Political Campaign, Button, Bryan, Picture 5.00
Political Campaign, Button, Bryan, Picture, 'i Gave My Dollar, Did You, ' Tan 18.00

Political Campaign, Button, Bryan, Picture, Silver Border	18.00
Political Campaign, Button, Bryan, Red, White, & Blue	5.00
Political Campaign, Button, Button, Smith, Picture	1.00
Political Campaign, Button, Carry On FDR	1.50
Political Campaign, Button, Carry On With Roosevelt, Picture	2.00 To 3.95
Political Campaign, Button, Cleaver For President, Picture	2.00
Political Campaign, Button, Coolidge And Dawes	1.50 To 5.00
Political Campaign, Button, Courage Confidence And Coolidge	3.00
Political Campaign, Button, Cox	12.00 To 45.00
Political Campaign, Button, Cox, Roosevelt	17.00
Political Campaign, Button, Coxsure	25.00
Political Campaign, Button, Dewey	1.75
Political Campaign, Button, Dewey And Warren, Jugate	5.00
Political Campaign, Button, Dewey And Warren, Picture	2.50
Political Campaign, Button, Dewey For President, Celluloid, Black & White	1.00
Political Campaign, Button, Dewey, Bricker	17.00
Political Campaign, Button, Dewey, Warren, 'i'm On The Team'	1.00
Political Campaign, Button, Dewey, Warren, Lithograph	1.00
Political Campaign, Button, 'don't Send A Boy---, ' Nixon	6.00
Political Campaign, Button, Earle, Greenfield, Picture, Pennsylvania	5.00
Political Campaign, Button, Eisenhower Party Press, Celluloid, Red, White	1.00
Political Campaign, Button, Eisenhower, Picture, Natural Color, Celluloid	1.50
Political Campaign, Button, FDR & Wallace, Jugate, 7/8 In.	2.00
Political Campaign, Button, FDR For President, Picture	3.00
Political Campaign, Button, FDR Independent Voter	1.50
Political Campaign, Button, For Congress, James S.Sherman, Picture	5.00
Political Campaign, Button, For First Lady, Edith Willkie, Picture	6.00
Political Campaign, Button, For President, Adlai E.Stevenson, Celluloid	2.00
Political Campaign, Button, For President, Alfred E.Smith, Picture	17.00
Political Campaign, Button, For President, Calvin Coolidge, Picture	60.00
Political Campaign, Button, For President, Charles E.Hughes	9.00 To 11.00
Political Campaign, Button, For President, Dewey, Black & White, Celluloid	1.00
Political Campaign, Button, For President, Franklin D.Roosevelt, Picture	2.00
Political Campaign, Button, For President, Henry A.Wallace, Picture	5.00
Political Campaign, Button, For President, Herbert C.Hoover, Picture	18.00
Political Campaign, Button, For President, Hoover	6.00
Political Campaign, Button, For President, John F.Kennedy	5.00
Political Campaign, Button, For President, John F.Kennedy, Celluloid	3.00
Political Campaign, Button, For President, John F.Kennedy, Picture	4.00
Political Campaign, Button, For President, Lar Daly, America First Party	2.00
Political Campaign, Button, For President, Robert F.Kennedy, Picture	1.00
Political Campaign, Button, For President, Stevenson	1.50
Political Campaign, Button, For President, Thomas E.Dewey, Black & White	3.00
Political Campaign, Button, For President, Thomas E.Dewey	1.50 To 3.00
Political Campaign, Button, For President, Warren G.Harding, Picture	4.50
Political Campaign, Button, For President, Wendell Willkie	3.00
Political Campaign, Button, For President, Wendell Willkie, Picture	3.00
Political Campaign, Button, For President, Wm.J.Bryan, Picture	6.00
Political Campaign, Button, For U.S.Senator, Franklin D.Roosevelt, Picture	13.00
Political Campaign, Button, Garner For President, Picture	9.00
Political Campaign, Button, George Wallace, 1 In., 'stand Up For America'	.20
Political Campaign, Button, 'Go Forward With Stevenson, ' Sparkman, Jugate	6.00
Political Campaign, Button, 'Go Bless America, ' Dewey, 1944-1948, Picture	6.00
Political Campaign, Button, Goldwater, 6 In.	2.00
Political Campaign, Button, Grant-Colfax, Jugate, Ferrotype	80.00
Political Campaign, Button, Harding And Coolidge	2.00
Political Campaign, Button, Harding, Picture	1.00 To 5.00
Political Campaign, Button, Harding, Picture, 1 1/4 In.	5.00
Political Campaign, Button, Harrison	7.00
Political Campaign, Button, Harrison, Morton, 1889	9.00
Political Campaign, Button, Hearst For President, Picture	5.00
Political Campaign, Button, Henry A.Wallace For President, Picture	8.00
Political Campaign, Button, Hoover And Curtis	4.00
Political Campaign, Button, Hoover And Tobey	4.00
Political Campaign, Button, Hoover For President	4.00
Political Campaign, Button, Hoover, Glenn, Small	5.00

Political Campaign, Button, Hoover, Loyal Republican 7.00
Political Campaign, Button, Hoover, Picture .... 1.00 To 12.00
Political Campaign, Button, Hoover, Picture, Al Smith, 1 1/4 In. 5.00
Political Campaign, Button, Hughes 5.00
Political Campaign, Button, I Like Ike, Celluloid 1.00
Political Campaign, Button, I Like Ike, Vote For Stevenson 3.00
Political Campaign, Button, I Like Stevenson 3.00
Political Campaign, Button, 'I Told You So, ' J.F.Kennedy 2.00
Political Campaign, Button, 'I Want Roosevelt Again, ' Lithograph 3.50
Political Campaign, Button, 'I Want Roosevelt Again, ' Picture 3.00
Political Campaign, Button, 'I'm For Goldwater For V.P., ' Celluloid 2.50
Political Campaign, Button, 'I'm For Nixon In '64' 2.00
Political Campaign, Button, 'If I Were 21 I'd Vote For Kennedy' 1.50
Political Campaign, Button, 'Ike, Dick, They're For You, ' Jugate 4.00
Political Campaign, Button, Ike, Inauguration, 1953, Flasher, Ribbon 1.00
Political Campaign, Button, Independent Party, 1908, Thomas L.Hisgen 35.00
Political Campaign, Button, J.F.Kennedy, Picture, Dark Blue 2.00
Political Campaign, Button, JFK, 'I Told You So, ' Picture, Celluloid 2.00
Political Campaign, Button, John F.Kennedy For President, Celluloid .... .20
Political Campaign, Button, John F.Kennedy For President, Picture 5.00
Political Campaign, Button, John Kennedy Our Next President 3.00
Political Campaign, Button, Johnson, Humphrey, Democrats Are We, Jugate 1.00
Political Campaign, Button, Joshua Levering, Picture 22.00
Political Campaign, Button, Keep Coolidge, Picture .... 4.00 To 9.00
Political Campaign, Button, Kennedy & Johnson, Jugate 2.50
Political Campaign, Button, Kennedy For President, Jfk .... .35
Political Campaign, Button, Kennedy For President, Lithograph 2.00
Political Campaign, Button, Kennedy For President, Picture, Jfk 1.50
Political Campaign, Button, Kennedy For President, Picture, 2 1/2 In. 2.50
Political Campaign, Button, Kennedy For President, Picture, 3 1/2 In. 2.50
Political Campaign, Button, Kennedy For President, Picture, 4 In. 2.50
Political Campaign, Button, Kennedy For President, 1968, Picture 1.00
Political Campaign, Button, Kennedy, Johnson, America's Men For The '60s 4.00
Political Campaign, Button, Kennedy, Johnson, Jugate, New Leadership 4.00
Political Campaign, Button, Kennedy, Man For The '60s, Flasher, 3 In. 3.00
Political Campaign, Button, Kennedy, Man For The '60s, Flasher, 3 1/2 In. 3.00
Political Campaign, Button, La Follette For President, Picture 20.00
Political Campaign, Button, La Follette, Wheeler 5.00
Political Campaign, Button, Landon 3.00
Political Campaign, Button, Landon, And Knox 3.00
Political Campaign, Button, Landon, Deeds Not Deficits' 3.00
Political Campaign, Button, Landon For President, Picture 9.00
Political Campaign, Button, Landon, Knox, Brass 2.00
Political Campaign, Button, Landon, Picture 2.00
Political Campaign, Button, Lapel, Cox, 'i Will Crow In Nov., ' Rooster 25.00
Political Campaign, Button, LBJ For President, 1964, Picture, 6 In. 3.00
Political Campaign, Button, LBJ, HHH, Celluloid, Jugate, Pictures 1.00
Political Campaign, Button, LBJ, 6 In. 4.50
Political Campaign, Button, LBJ, 9 In. 5.50
Political Campaign, Button, Lemke, O'brien, Union Party, Picture 18.00
Political Campaign, Button, Let's Back Ike, ' Lithograph 1.00
Political Campaign, Button, 'Life Begins In '40 With Willkie' 4.00
Political Campaign, Button, Lindsay '72 .... .25
Political Campaign, Button, Lowden For President 3.00
Political Campaign, Button, MacArthur For America, 1948 .... 3.00
Political Campaign, Button, Make Hoover President .... 3.00 To 6.00
Political Campaign, Button, Make The White House The Dwight House 3.00
Political Campaign, Button, Mamie For First Lady, Celluloid 3.00
Political Campaign, Button, Mamie For First Lady, 3 1/2 In.Diameter 2.00
Political Campaign, Button, McCarthy In '72 .... .25
Political Campaign, Button, McKinley, Picture 7.00
Political Campaign, Button, Member Will County Willkie Club 3.00
Political Campaign, Button, New Deal Waste Basket, Willkie 5.00
Political Campaign, Button, Nixon 2.00
Political Campaign, Button, Nixon For Governor, Picture 5.00
Political Campaign, Button, Nixon Plus Spiro Equals Zero .... .25

Political Campaign, Button, Nixon, Agnew, Jugate, 1968 .... 2.00
Political Campaign, Button, Nixon, Lodge, Jugate 4.00
Political Campaign, Button, Nixon, 6 In. 2.00
Political Campaign, Button, No Third Term, The Constitutionalists 1.50
Political Campaign, Button, No Third Term, Willkie 1.50
Political Campaign, Button, Oregon For Kennedy, JFK 4.00
Political Campaign, Button, Our Next President, Adlai Stevenson, Picture 2.00
Political Campaign, Button, Parker For President, Picture, Blue Border 12.00
Political Campaign, Button, Parker, Picture, White Ground 12.00
Political Campaign, Button, Peace & Prosperity With Eisenhower 1.00
Political Campaign, Button, Peace In America, God Bless Wilson 5.00
Political Campaign, Button, President Harding, Monument Fund, Picture 8.00
Political Campaign, Button, President Harry S.Truman, Picture .... 2.50 To 7.00
Political Campaign, Button, Re-Elect Our President, Franklin D.Roosevelt 5.00
Political Campaign, Button, Reagan For Governor .... .25
Political Campaign, Button, Ritchie, Picture 5.00
Political Campaign, Button, Roosevelt For Humanity 1.50
Political Campaign, Button, Roosevelt, Garner, Brass 2.00
Political Campaign, Button, Roosevelt, Labor's Non-Partisan League, Picture 4.00
Political Campaign, Button, Roosevelt, Mead, Picture 12.00
Political Campaign, Button, Roosevelt, Picture .... 2.00 To 3.00
Political Campaign, Button, Roosevelt, The American, Picture 7.00
Political Campaign, Button, Roosevelt, Wallace, Lithograph 6.00
Political Campaign, Button, Roosevelt, 1912 .... 3.00
Political Campaign, Button, Senior Citizens For Kennedy, JFK .... .50
Political Campaign, Button, Senior Citizens For Kennedy, JFK, Red & Gold .... .50
Political Campaign, Button, Seymour, Picture 7.50
Political Campaign, Button, Smile, Harding And Coolidge, 1920, A.P.T.L., N.Y. 18.00
Political Campaign, Button, Smith & Robinson, Lithograph .... 2.00 To 2.50
Political Campaign, Button, Smith For President, Picture 6.00
Political Campaign, Button, Sound Money, Flat 5.00
Political Campaign, Button, Stevenson For President 1.50
Political Campaign, Button, Stevenson, Kefauver, Lithograph 1.25
Political Campaign, Button, Stevenson, Picture 1.50
Political Campaign, Button, Stevenson, Picture, 3/4 In. 2.25
Political Campaign, Button, Stevenson, 1960 .... 1.50
Political Campaign, Button, Students For Kennedy, Picture, JFK 2.00
Political Campaign, Button, Switch & Fight .... .25
Political Campaign, Button, T.Roosevelt, Picture, Gold Ground 8.00
Political Campaign, Button, T.Roosevelt, Picture, Tan 6.00
Political Campaign, Button, T.Roosevelt, Stand Pat, Picture, Hand Of Cards 25.00
Political Campaign, Button, Taft For President, Picture .... 1.50 To 9.00
Political Campaign, Button, Taft, Picture 1.00
Political Campaign, Button, Taft, Picture, Black & White 5.00
Political Campaign, Button, Team With Roosevelt 3.00
Political Campaign, Button, Ted Kennedy For Senator, 1970 .... .25
Political Campaign, Button, Teddy Roosevelt, Picture 1.00
Political Campaign, Button, Teddy Roosevelt, Rough Rider, 1898, Penna. 15.00
Political Campaign, Button, Teddy, 1970 .... .25
Political Campaign, Button, The Last Act, Willkie 2.00
Political Campaign, Button, They're For You, Ike, Dick, Picture 2.00
Political Campaign, Button, Truman .... 5.00 To 8.00
Political Campaign, Button, Truman For Me, Picture 9.00
Political Campaign, Button, Truman, Picture 12.00
Political Campaign, Button, Vote For President Barry Goldwater, Celluloid 2.50
Political Campaign, Button, Vote Socialist, Thomas Maurer 6.00
Political Campaign, Button, Vote Straight Democratic, Stevenson, Sparkman 75.00
Political Campaign, Button, Vote Truman For President 8.00
Political Campaign, Button, Wallace For Governor, 1970 .... .25
Political Campaign, Button, Wallace For President, Picture, 3 In. 2.00
Political Campaign, Button, Wallace, Lemay, 1 In. .... .25
Political Campaign, Button, Welcome Roosevelt, May 25th, 1903, Red Ribbon 6.50
Political Campaign, Button, Welcome T.Roosevelt, Picture, Tan, Red Ribbon 15.00
Political Campaign, Button, William J.Bryan, Picture 5.00
Political Campaign, Button, Willkie, 'ring It Again' 2.00
Political Campaign, Button, Wilson 3.00

Political Campaign, Button, Wilson And Marshall, Picture	14.00
Political Campaign, Button, Wilson For Me And Mine	4.00
Political Campaign, Button, Wilson, Marshall, Jugate	17.50
Political Campaign, Button, Win With Willkie Volunteers	1.50
Political Campaign, Button, Win With Willkie, Picture	2.50
Political Campaign, Button, Wm.McKinley, Picture	1.50 To 3.00
Political Campaign, Button, 'won't You Be My Teddy Bear'	10.00
Political Campaign, Button, Work With Wallace	3.50
Political Campaign, Button, 'You Lose Franklin'	2.50
Political Campaign, Card, McCarthy	.25
Political Campaign, Card, RFK Headquarters	.25
Political Campaign, Card, Willkie Workers League Member	.50
Political Campaign, Clicker Bug, Nixon, 2 In.	2.00
Political Campaign, Coupon, Goldwater	.25
Political Campaign, Doll, Soap, William Jennings Bryan	23.00
Political Campaign, Dollar, Bryan, 'We Don't Think, Sixteen To One, ' Metal	17.00
Political Campaign, Envelope, Robert F.Kennedy	.25
Political Campaign, Envelope, William H.Taft & James S.Sherman Pictures	5.00
Political Campaign, Ferrotype, Stephen A.Douglas, 1860, Herschel Johnson	65.00
Political Campaign, Figurine, Uncle Sam Hat, Taft, Sherman, Milk Glass	22.50
Political Campaign, Flag, American, Harrison & Morton, Silk	15.00
Political Campaign, Flag, Auto, Hoover For President, Tin, Black On Yellow	5.00
Political Campaign, Flag, Auto, Repeal 18th Amendment, Tin, Black On Orange	5.00
Political Campaign, Flag, Auto, Roosevelt For President, Tin, White On Green	5.00
Political Campaign, Flannel Monogram, LBJ	.50
Political Campaign, Handbill, LBJ For The USA	.25
Political Campaign, Handbill, See, Hear, Meet, Senator Robert F.Kennedy	.75
Political Campaign, Handbill, Senator Robert F.Kennedy	.75
Political Campaign, Hanger, Doorknob, Ike	.50
Political Campaign, Hanger, Doorknob, R.F.K	3.00
Political Campaign, Hat, T.Roosevelt & McKinley, Rough Riders, Bronze	30.00
Political Campaign, Invitation, Inaugural, Nixon's	8.50
Political Campaign, Jugate, Bryan & Kerr, Gold Frame	15.00
Political Campaign, Jugate, Bryan & Kerr, Picture	15.00
Political Campaign, Jugate, Bryan, Stevenson, Silver, Red, White, & Blue	20.00
Political Campaign, Jugate, McKinley & Tanner, Illinois	20.00
Political Campaign, Jugate, Parker, Davis, Flag Between Candidates	20.00
Political Campaign, Jugate, Parker, Davis, Gold Ground	20.00
Political Campaign, Jugate, Stickpin, Grant & Colfax, Brass, Glass	75.00
Political Campaign, Jugate, Taft & Sherman, Blue Ground, Picture	15.00
Political Campaign, Jugate, Willkie & Mcnary, Color	30.00
Political Campaign, Landon & Knox	2.00
Political Campaign, Landon And Knox, Young Republicans	2.00
Political Campaign, Lapel Stud, Harding, Gold-Colored, Picture	5.00
Political Campaign, License Plate, Metal, Landon & Knox, Elephant, Sunflower	7.50
Political Campaign, License Plate, 1965 Presidential Inauguration	6.75
Political Campaign, Medal, Roosevelt & Garner, 1936, Jugate	3.75
Political Campaign, Medal, William H.Taft	5.00
Political Campaign, Mug, Bust Profile Of William McKinley, Slogan	22.00
Political Campaign, Mug, Ike & Mamie, Eggshell Color, Pair	22.50
Political Campaign, Music, Sheet, Andrew Johnson	6.00
Political Campaign, Napkin, Paper, Alf Landon, Song	4.00
Political Campaign, Napkin, Sunflower	7.00
Political Campaign, Necktie, Eisenhower & Wallace	2.00
Political Campaign, Needle Packet, Hoover, Curtis	10.00
Political Campaign, Pt Boat, 'Kennedy For President, ' On Card	12.00
Political Campaign, Pamphlet, Anti-Nixon, 1968	.25
Political Campaign, Pamphlet, Humphrey Vs.Nixon	.25
Political Campaign, Pamphlet, Landon	2.00
Political Campaign, Pamphlet, McCarthy For President	.50
Political Campaign, Pamphlet, Richard Nixon	.25
Political Campaign, Pamphlet, Rocky	.25
Political Campaign, Paperweight, Brick, L.B.J.	2.00
Political Campaign, Paperweight, McKinley Sepia Picture	8.00 To 8.50
Political Campaign, Pennant, Ike, Felt, 52 Ft.	7.00
Political Campaign, Photograph, John F.Kennedy, Black & White, 2	25.00

Political Campaign, Photograph, John F.Kennedy, Cardboard, Metal Rim	.75
Political Campaign, Photograph, John Garner, Signed	14.50
Political Campaign, Photograph, Mckinley, 1900, Miniature	.50
Political Campaign, Picture, Jfk, Civil Rights	2.00
Political Campaign, Picture, Vote Democratic, Picture Of Donkey	2.00
Political Campaign, Plaque, Mckinley, Roosevelt, Picture, 1 3/4 In.	6.00
Political Campaign, Plate, Bumper, Wallace, Goldwater, Metal	2.00
Political Campaign, Plate, Mckinley, Hobart, Portrait, Sepia, Dresden	30.00
Political Campaign, Plate, Theodore Roosevelt, Elephant, Bear, Donkey, Wagon	35.00
Political Campaign, Poster, For Governor Woodrow Wilson	12.50
Political Campaign, Poster, For President Thomas E.Dewey, Bricker, V.P.	8.50
Political Campaign, Poster, Forward With Roosevelt	19.00
Political Campaign, Poster, Hoover	5.00
Political Campaign, Poster, Humphrey, Muskie, Plastic, 20 X 30 In.	.50
Political Campaign, Poster, Jim M.Cox, Democratic Nominee For President	27.00
Political Campaign, Poster, Kennedy, 28 X 20	12.00
Political Campaign, Poster, President Wendell L.Willkie, McNary For Vp	8.50
Political Campaign, Poster, See, Hear, Meet, Senator Robert F.Kennedy	1.00
Political Campaign, Ring, Al Smith, 1928, Brass Color, Donkey's Head	6.00
Political Campaign, Ring, Metal, Al Smith	7.50
Political Campaign, Scarf, Win With Ike For President, Red	12.00
Political Campaign, Sign, Teddy Roosevelt, Standing, 13 X 20 In., 1903	15.00
Political Campaign, Sticker, Brooks, Willkie, Green, Paper	.50
Political Campaign, Sticker, Goldwater, 1964, Paper	1.00
Political Campaign, Sticker, Humphrey, Muskie, Satin	.25
Political Campaign, Sticker, Kennedy For President, Paper	3.50
Political Campaign, Sticker, Landon, Knox, Sunflower	4.00
Political Campaign, Sticker, LBJ, Paper, Shape Of Hat	.25
Political Campaign, Sticker, Willkie, Elephant	1.00
Political Campaign, Sticker, Win With Goldwater, Paper	.25
Political Campaign, Sticker, Win With Johnson & Humphrey, Paper	.25
Political Campaign, Stud, Black & White Picture Of McKinley, 7/8 In.	5.00
Political Campaign, Stud, M.S.Quay, Republican, Hopeful From Penna., 1896	25.00
Political Campaign, Stud, Protection 96, Sepia Of McKinley	5.00
Political Campaign, Stud, Teddy Roosevelt, Blue & White	3.50
Political Campaign, Theodore Roosevelt, Brass Hat, Framed Pin, Both	20.00
Political Campaign, Token, Lincoln, 1860	12.00
Political Campaign, Tray, Pin, Theodore Roosevelt & Fairbanks, 5 X 3 In.	12.50
Political Campaign, Tumbler, McKinley, Protection & Plenty	15.00
Political Campaign, Umbrella, McKinley & Hobart	100.00
Political Campaign, Watch Fob, Coolidge, Metal, Celluloid Insert	60.00
Political Campaign, Wallace-Lemay, 1 In.	.25
Political Campaign, Watch Fob, Moose, Progressive Party	8.50
Political Campaign, Watch Fob, Taft, Sherman	8.00 To 18.50
Political Campaign, Watch Fob, Wilson, Lock To White House, 1912	32.00
Political Campaign, Watch Fob, Wilson, Metal	4.00
Political Campaign, Watch, T.Roosevelt Day, Elgin, Pocket	18.00

Pomona Glass is clear with a soft amber border decorated with pale blue or rose-colored flowers and leaves. The colors are very, very pale. The background of the glass is covered with a network of fine lines. It was made from 1885 to 1888 by the New England Glass Company.

Pomona, Bowl & Plate, Green	72.50
Pomona, Bowl, Cornflowers, Clear, Scalloped, Footed, 4 In.High	450.00
Pomona, Bowl, Rose, Very Little Stain, First Grind, Three Legs	65.00
Pomona, Castor, Pickle, First Grind	250.00
Pomona, Castor, Pickle, Second Grind	200.00
Pomona, Celery, Blue Cornflower Decor, First Grind	190.00
Pomona, Cup, Punch, Etched, Scalloped Rim, Amber Handle, New England	88.00
Pomona, Cup, Punch, First Grind	35.00
Pomona, Glass, Lemonade, Cornflowers, Applied Clear Handle, 5 3/4 In.High	450.00
Pomona, Pitcher, Butterfly & Wheat Decor, First Grind, 12 In.High	1750.00
Pomona, Pitcher, Water, Amber Satin, Bulbous, 4 Corner Top, 7 In.Tall	265.00
Pomona, Pitcher, Water, Amber, Bulbous, First Grind, 7 In.High	285.00
Pomona, Toothpick, Flowers & Leaves, Lavender, 2 1/2 In.Tall	65.00
Pomona, Tumbler, Acanthus Leaf Decor, Diamond Quilted, First Grind	125.00

Pomona, Tumbler, Blue Cornflower, Second Grind 90.00
Pomona, Tumbler, Cornflowers, Diamond Quilted, Second Ground 95.00
Pomona, Tumbler, Daisy & Fern Decor, Enameled 45.00
Pomona, Tumbler, Fern & Floral Design, Enamel 45.00
Pomona, Tumbler, Inverted Thumbprint, First Grind 75.00
Pomona, Tumbler, Pansy & Butterfly Decor, Diamond Quilted, Second Ground 165.00
   Pontypool, see Tole
Popeye, Paint Set, 1933 .... 6.50
   Porcelain, see also Bow, Copeland, Nippon, RS Prussia, etc.
Porcelain, Blotter, Rocker, Hand-Painted Pink Flowers, Royal Blue 35.00
Porcelain, Boot, Red, White, Blue 5.00
Porcelain, Bowl & Pitcher, Cream & Yellow, Red Cherries, Green Leaves 29.50
Porcelain, Bowl & Pitcher, Ivory Background, Yellow & Red Flowers 32.00
Porcelain, Bowl & Pitcher, Ivory Background, Yellow Buttercups, Blue, Black 32.00
Porcelain, Bowl & Pitcher, Ivory, Pink, Yellow, & Blue Roses, Brown Ribbon 32.00
Porcelain, Bowl & Pitcher, Lavender, Wide Band Of Flowers & Leaves, Tan 29.50
Porcelain, Bowl & Pitcher, Pink Trim, Flowers 32.00
Porcelain, Bowl & Pitcher, Pink, Black Trim, Red Roses 32.00
Porcelain, Bowl & Pitcher, Raised White Floral, Gold Trimmed Black Squares 32.00
Porcelain, Bowl & Pitcher, Shaded Blue, Marked Bungolow, England, 4 .... 32.50
Porcelain, Bowl & Pitcher, White Background, Tan, Brown, Red, & Blue Flowers 32.00
Porcelain, Bowl & Pitcher, White Ground, Blue Star Shape Decor, Roses 45.00
Porcelain, Bowl & Pitcher, White, Black Lattice, Pink Roses & Violets 32.00
Porcelain, Bowl & Pitcher, White, Blue Band, Yellow, White, Blue, & Pink 32.00
Porcelain, Bowl & Pitcher, White, Blue Flowers 22.00
Porcelain, Bowl & Pitcher, White, Gray-Blue Flowers & Leaves 32.00
Porcelain, Bowl & Pitcher, White, Pink & Blue Flowers, Green Leaves, Black 27.50
Porcelain, Bowl & Pitcher, White, Pink Apple Blossoms, Green Leaves, Blue 34.50
Porcelain, Bowl & Pitcher, White, Pink Ribbons, Pink Roses, Green Leaves 32.00
Porcelain, Bowl & Pitcher, White, Pink Roses, Green Leaves 32.00
Porcelain, Bowl & Pitcher, Yellow Outside, White Inside 22.00
Porcelain, Bowl & Pitcher, Yellow, Black Handles & Squares, White Centers 22.00
Porcelain, Bowl & Pitcher, Yellow, Pink & White Background, Flowers 31.00
Porcelain, Bowl & Pitcher, Yellow, Pink Roses, Blue Ribbon 32.00
Porcelain, Bowl, Blue Willow Pattern, Blue, Gold, Shallow, 8 In.Diameter 38.00
Porcelain, Bowl, Blue, Hand Painted, Russian, Marked 55.00
Porcelain, Bowl, Blue, Red, Hand Painted, Russian, Marked, 7 In. 55.00
Porcelain, Bowl, Cereal, Child's, Hand-Painted Scene, Winnie-The-Pooh Party 35.00
Porcelain, Bowl, Four Petal Shape, Autumn Scene, Swans, Farm, Hand-Painted 25.00
Porcelain, Bowl, Fruit, Open Latticework, Footed, Gold Band, 9 In.High 35.00
Porcelain, Bowl, Fruit, 3 Crown Mark, 9 In.Diameter 10.00
Porcelain, Bowl, German, Three Crown, Gold, Red & Pink Roses 13.00
Porcelain, Bowl, Pink Star Pattern, Impressed Kh Mark 35.00
Porcelain, Bowl, Shell Shape, Pastel Colors 30.00
Porcelain, Bowl, Violets, Hand-Painted, Gold Trim, 7 1/2 In.Diameter 28.00
Porcelain, Bowl, White Floral, Pastel, 7 In.Diameter 80.00
Porcelain, Box & Pin Tray, Covered, Leaf Shape, Austrian 10.00
Porcelain, Box, Food, Chinese, Blue, White, Two Tier, Dome Cover, 19th Century 175.00
Porcelain, Box, Powder, Shape Of Girl, Pink, Flowers 8.00
Porcelain, Box, Stamp, Floral, Cottage, Three Compartment, Austria 10.50
Porcelain, Cake Set, Peach, Sweet Peas, P.M., Austria, Pierced Handle 45.00
Porcelain, Cask, Jewel, Scenes, Cobalt Ground, Gold Decor, Marked Jbh, France 125.00
Porcelain, Celery, Germany, Green, Shaded White, Yellow, & Cream, Roses 15.00
Porcelain, Chocolate Pot, French, Gold Decoration, 8 1/2 In.High 12.50
Porcelain, Chocolate Pot, Oriental, Japanese Ladies 12.00
Porcelain, Chocolate Pot, Rust & Pink Flowers, Gold, Straight Sides 17.50
Porcelain, Chocolate Set, Bird-Of-Paradise, White, Green, German 120.00
Porcelain, Chocolate Set, German, Tan & Green, Fruit, Birds, 9 Piece 32.50
Porcelain, Chocolate Set, Oriental Design, Red, Eight Cup & Saucer 150.00
Porcelain, Creamer, Animals, Alphabet, Pink, White, Marked, Germany 12.00
Porcelain, Creamer, Czechoslovakia, Cow Sitting, Orange, Brown, 4 1/2 In. 10.00
Porcelain, Creamer, French, Cover, Gold Trim, Blue-Green Ground 20.00
Porcelain, Creamer, Germany, Cow 12.00
Porcelain, Creamer, Hand-Painted Roses On White 4.50
Porcelain, Creamer, M.Z.Austria, Red & White Roses, Green, Gold 6.50
Porcelain, Creamer, Rose Design, Pink, White, Hand Painted, 3 In.High 4.50

Porcelain, Creamer, Strawberry Shape, Leaf Spout, Green Luster, 3 1/2 In.	6.50
Porcelain, Cup & Saucer, Coffee, Germany, Inscribed To My Mother	16.00
Porcelain, Cup & Saucer, Demitasse, Robin's-Egg Blue, Johnson Bros., England	4.50
Porcelain, Cup & Saucer, Demitasse, Victoria, Czechoslovakia	
Porcelain, Cup & Saucer, Germany, 2 Pigs Dressed In Coats & Top Hats	8.75
Porcelain, Cup & Saucer, Handleless, Blue Flower & Vine Decoration	10.00
Porcelain, Cup & Saucer, Handleless, Gaudy Red & Blue Bleeding Hearts	32.50
Porcelain, Cup & Saucer, Pink, Roses, Victoria	5.00
Porcelain, Cup & Saucer, Wedding, German Letters, Gold Band, Hands Clasped	25.00
Porcelain, Cup Plate, Oriental Scene, Dark Blue	17.50
Porcelain, Cup, Chocolate, Think Of Me	4.00
Porcelain, Cup, Nut, Gardiner, St.Vladimir Service, 18th Century	250.00
Porcelain, Cuspidor, Lady's, Pink, Yellow Lilies, Scalloped Inverted Rim	62.50
Porcelain, Dish, C.S.Bavaria, Grapes, Gold, Open Handles	15.00
Porcelain, Dish, Cheese, Black & Gold Top, Red Floral, Matching Plate, Melbar	19.00
Porcelain, Dish, German, B.R.S.Moliere, Pink Flowers	12.00
Porcelain, Dish, Hairpin, Hand-Painted Roses, Blue Ground, 2 Gold Handles	5.00
Porcelain, Dish, J.R.Bavaria, Peaches Decor, Green Ground, Open Handles	12.00
Porcelain, Dish, Leaf Shape, Dark Blue, Riley's Semi China, Pair	30.00
Porcelain, Dish, Lobster, Victoria, Austria, Green, Gold Lobster & Edge	42.50
Porcelain, Dish, Powder, Covered, Brass At Top, 3 Feet, Pink Canterbury Bell	15.00
Porcelain, Dish, Sardine, Marked Bonn Rhein, Attached Plate, Florals	17.00
Porcelain, Dish, Soap, Marked Orchid, Royal Vitreous, England, Cover	100.00
Porcelain, Dish, Soap, Oval	3.50
Porcelain, Dish, Soap, Rectangular	3.50
Porcelain, Dish, Warwick China, Yellow & Pink Roses	16.00
Porcelain, Dresser Set, Hand-Painted Daisies, White, Red, Gold, 6 Piece	38.00
Porcelain, Dresser Set, Pale Yellow, Gold Trim & Beading, 4 Piece	9.00
Porcelain, Dresser Set, White, Pink, Roses, Tray, Ring Tree, Bottle, 3 Dishes	18.00
Porcelain, Egg, Easter, Russian Imperial, Maria Feodorovna, 19th Century	120.00
Porcelain, Figure, Girl With Swan, English, Label 'rw, ' Cream Tones	30.00
Porcelain, Figurine, Boy & Girl Riding Goats, German, 5 1/2 In.Tall, Pair	60.00
Porcelain, Figurine, Farmer, Cow, Plow, Teplitz, 14 In.Long, 11 In.High	275.00
Porcelain, Figurine, Lady, Purple Dress, 10 In.High, Pair	40.00
Porcelain, Figurine, Oriental, Lady & Man, 9 In.High, White, Pair	12.00
Porcelain, Figurine, Vienna, Lippizzaner Horse, Capriole, 12 1/2 In.High	150.00
Porcelain, Font, Wall, Gray Well, Raised Blue Dolphin Pewter Spout	40.00
Porcelain, Gravy Boat, White, Blue Trim, F.Sons, Burslem	5.00
Porcelain, Hair Receiver, Carnegie Library, Oklahoma City, Oklahoma Terr.	15.00
Porcelain, Hair Receiver, Floral, Turquoise, Gold, Square	9.50
Porcelain, Hair Receiver, German, Pink Roses, Raised Gold	8.50
Porcelain, Hatpin Holder, White, Pink & White Roses, Scalloped Base	16.00
Porcelain, Hatpin Holder, White, Reads 'hat Pins'	10.00
Porcelain, Holder, Pin, Housefly, Wings Raise, Reveal Cavity, Hand-Painted	8.00
Porcelain, Holder, Stickpin, Pedestal Type On Saucer, Hand-Painted Floral	24.50
Porcelain, Holder, Toothbrush, Covered, Decorated ...:......................	4.50
Porcelain, Holder, Toothbrush, Flowers	3.50
Porcelain, Holder, Toothbrush, Roses On Front & Back, Round, White Ground	8.50
Porcelain, Invalid Feeder, White, Japan	5.00
Porcelain, Jar, Biscuit, Crown China, Hunting Scene, Octagonal	15.00
Porcelain, Jar, Biscuit, Germany, Roses	25.00
Porcelain, Jar, Biscuit, Orchid Primroses, Nickel Over Brass Bail, Lid	32.00
Porcelain, Jar, Cracker, Handles, White & Beige Ground, Grapes, Scalloped	8.00
Porcelain, Jar, Cracker, Marked Germany, Scalloped Upper Rim & Bottom, Roses	16.00
Porcelain, Jar, Cracker, Marked Mz, Austria West, Handles, Pink Roses	18.00
Porcelain, Jar, Cracker, Squatty, Handles, White To Pale Blue Ground, Fruit	15.00
Porcelain, Jar, Leaf & Floral, Marked Es, French, Cover, 6 In.Tall	20.00
Porcelain, Jar, Mustard, White, Pink Handle, Embossed Pink Flower & Vine	15.00
Porcelain, Jar, Rose, Kutani, Liner, Cover, Oriental Signature	8.50
Porcelain, Jar, Talcum, Marked Vienna, Austria, Hand-Painted Pink Roses, Gold	8.00
Porcelain, Knife, Fruit, Blue & White, Brass Blade, Mark Bohemia	7.50
Porcelain, Match Holder, Baggy Pants, Toonerville Trolley Co., Germany	12.00
Porcelain, Match Holder, Blue & White, Hanging, Violets	12.50
Porcelain, Match Holder, Floral Design, Marked Victoria, Austria	15.00
Porcelain, Match Holder, Naughty Dog, White Tail, Basket, Striker Base	29.00
Porcelain, Match Holder, Pink & White, Hanging, Double, Etched Bird In Gold	15.00

Porcelain, Match Holder, Striker, White, Union Porcelain Works 15.00
Porcelain, Mortar & Pestle, Germany, Miniature 10.00
Porcelain, Mug, A Present From The Isle Of Man 5.00
Porcelain, Mug, Car .... *Illus* 12.00
Porcelain, Mug, Child's, Marked French, White, Black Houses & Scenes 5.75
Porcelain, Mug, Floral Design, Enamel, Blue, Applied Handle, Pair 75.00
Porcelain, Mug, Iridescent Gold .... *Illus* 12.00

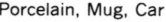

Porcelain, Mug, Car

Porcelain, Mug,
Iridescent Gold

Porcelain, Mush Set, English 17.50
Porcelain, Mustard, Germany, Pink Pig With Two Green Toothpick Holders 25.00
    Porcelain, Napkin Ring, see also Napkin Ring
Porcelain, Napkin Ring, Hand-Painted 10.50
Porcelain, Pickle, German, Violets, Gold 9.00
Porcelain, Pitcher, Baroque, Blue Flowers, 5 In.High 7.50
Porcelain, Pitcher, Blue, Gray, German No.798 .... 250.00
Porcelain, Pitcher, Cream Color, Cobalt Band, Embossed Flowers 12.50
Porcelain, Pitcher, Cream, German, Pink Chrysanthemums, Marked Kamla 10.00
Porcelain, Pitcher, Hand-Painted Multicolored Rose & Purple Flowers, Gold 25.00
Porcelain, Pitcher, Made In England, Figural, Granny Type, Blue, Green 23.00
Porcelain, Pitcher, Roses, Pink, Red, Tankard, Marked Germany, 12 In.Tall 50.00
Porcelain, Pitcher, Wedgwood Blue Ground, Embossed Flowers, 4 In.High 20.00
Porcelain, Pitcher, Wood's Hotel, Ripon, Wisc., English Registry Date, 1878 .... 16.00
Porcelain, Plaque, French, Light To Dark Blue, Antlered Moose 40.00
Porcelain, Plate, Admiral Dewey, 11 In., Gold 12.00
Porcelain, Plate, Artist's Palette In Center, Crimped, 8 1/2 In. 12.50
Porcelain, Plate, Austrian, Scalloped Edge, 7 1/2 In.Diameter, Pair 7.00
Porcelain, Plate, Baby, Fairy Queen, Flower Carriage, Bird, Luster Glaze 8.00
Porcelain, Plate, Bread, Hand-Painted, 'give Us This Day, ' Pink Roses 7.50
Porcelain, Plate, Brown & White, Adelaide's Bower, 8 In., Scalloped 5.00
Porcelain, Plate, Cake, Austrian, Cutout Handles, Oval Medallions, Gold, Roses 15.00
Porcelain, Plate, Cake, Germany, Scalloped Edge, Lilac Design 10.00
Porcelain, Plate, Cake, Hand-Painted, Roses, Pink, Green, Rust 14.50
Porcelain, Plate, Cake, Queen Victoria, Dated 1837, Crown & Coat Of Arms 23.50
Porcelain, Plate, Cake, Rose Decor, Open Handles 6.00
Porcelain, Plate, Child, See Saw Marjorie Daw, Green, Clear, Divided, 8 In. 12.00
Porcelain, Plate, Chop, 3 Crown, Germany, White Ground, Multicolor Daisies 22.00
Porcelain, Plate, Crown Over N Mark, Decal Portrait Of Marechal Lefebure 22.50
Porcelain, Plate, Cup, American Eagles, Blue, Circa 1812, 4 In.Diameter 25.00
Porcelain, Plate, Dinner, Tree Of Life, Taylor & Knowles 4.00
Porcelain, Plate, Dresden Type, Pierced Rim, Floral Decoration, 7 1/2 In. 10.00
Porcelain, Plate, English, Painted Flowers & Cavetto, C.1815, 4 .... 125.00
Porcelain, Plate, George Washington, Sepia On White, From Stuart Painting 10.00
Porcelain, Plate, Grapes, Pansies, Hand-Painted, 10 In.Diameter, Pair 30.00
Porcelain, Plate, Grecian Pattern, Sterling Overlay, Marked, 7 In. 4.00
Porcelain, Plate, Hand-Painted Daisies, 8 1/2 In. 12.00
Porcelain, Plate, Homer Laughlin, Betsy Ross Showing First Flag, Pink 13.50
Porcelain, Plate, Leuchtenburg, Germany, Open Handles, Robin On Branch 12.50
Porcelain, Plate, Hand-Painted Daisies, 8 1/2 In. 12.00
Porcelain, Plate, Homer Laughlin, Betsy Ross Showing First Flag, Pink 13.50
Porcelain, Plate, Leuchtenburg, Germany, Open Handles, Robin On Branch 12.50

Porcelain, Plate, M.Z.Austria, Blackberries, Blossoms, Artist M.W.Poole 15.00
Porcelain, Plate, M.Z.Austria, Hand-Painted Yellow Daisies, Green, Gold Edge 8.50
Porcelain, Plate, Oyster, Pink On White, Bronze Trim, High Luster 35.00
Porcelain, Plate, Oyster, Victoria, Austria, Blue Flower In Each Section 12.50
Porcelain, Plate, Shell Design Border, Lady Disguised As Rose 20.00
Porcelain, Plate, Violets, Gold, Scalloped 13 In.Diameter 34.00
Porcelain, Plate, White To Green, Scallop Edge, Flowers, Windmill Scene 12.00
Porcelain, Platter, Oval, Japanese Garden Scene, A.W.& Company, 16 In.Long 15.00
Porcelain, Platter, Turkey, Flowers, Leaves, Yellow, Brown, 20 X 16 In. 16.00
Porcelain, Platter, Wall, Victorian, Floral, Scalloped, 18 X 10 In. 38.00
Porcelain, Rack, Toast, English, Space For Marmalade & Butter, Yellow, Floral 6.00
Porcelain, Rack, Toast, White, 4 Slices, Loop Handle 12.50
Porcelain, Rose Bowl, Vienna, Austria, 3 Gold Feet, Hand-Painted Pink Roses 20.00
Porcelain, Salt & Pepper, Leafy Scroll, Pair 10.50
Porcelain, Salt Dip, Painted Flowers, 6 .... 22.00
Porcelain, Salt Dip, Princess Louise, Austria, Footed 4.50
Porcelain, Salt Dip, Swan Shape, Feathers, Embossed, Gold, Spoon, Set 9.00
Porcelain, Salt, Master, Pink, Silver Plate Rim, Mark Epns, 2 1/2 In. 16.00
Porcelain, Shaker, Sugar, Hand-Painted Daisies 25.00
Porcelain, Shoe, Baby Doll, Strap, Rose 6.00
Porcelain, Shoe, Baby's, White, Blue Bow, Blue Ruffled Top, Open Eyelets 7.50
Porcelain, Shoe, Embossed Flowers, Gold Decor, 5 In. 12.00
Porcelain, Shoe, Japan, Red, White, Blue 5.00
Porcelain, Shoe, Marked Germany, Halifax, Nova Scotia, High Heel, Gold 10.00
Porcelain, Shoe, White, Blue, Hand-Painted Flowers, Dutch 6.00
Porcelain, Silpper, Baby Boots, Green, Pink, Bow, Eyelets 8.00
Porcelain, Slipper, Applied Roses, Forget-Me-Nots, Bisque 10.00
Porcelain, Slipper, Blue, Forget-Me-Nots 6.50
Porcelain, Slipper, Embossed Bow, Gold, 3 In. 2.50
Porcelain, Slipper, Fancy, Blue, Applied Rose 6.50
Porcelain, Slipper, Gold, Japan 4.50
Porcelain, Slipper, Hand-Painted, Pink, Flowers 8.50
Porcelain, Slipper, High Heel, Gold Decor 6.50
Porcelain, Slipper, High Heeled, Yellow, Blue, Pink, Rose, Turned-Up Toe 8.50
Porcelain, Slipper, Lace Trim, Pansies 7.00
Porcelain, Slipper, Pink, Blue, Gold, Tassels 10.00
Porcelain, Slipper, Portrait Josephine In Beaded Medallion, Gold, White 15.00
Porcelain, Slipper, Portrait Marie Louise In Beaded Medallion, Gold, White 15.00
Porcelain, Slipper, Salt Glaze, Crocheted 8.00
Porcelain, Slipper, Yellow, Gold Decor, Bow, Flowers, 5 In. 8.00
Porcelain, Spittoon, Ladies, Flowers, Yellow, Hand-Painted, 6 In.Tall 32.50
Porcelain, Statue, Neptune, English, 1800, 13 In.High 70.00
Porcelain, Strainer, Tea, Hand-Painted, Floral, Loop Handle, 4 1/2 In. 10.00
Porcelain, Sugar & Creamer, Germany, Rose, Footed 10.00
Porcelain, Sugar & Creamer, Gold Filigree Design, Embossed, Signed 65.00
Porcelain, Sugar & Creamer, Japanese, Covered, Gold Enamels 23.00
Porcelain, Sugar & Creamer, Lefton, Covered, Hand-Painted Roses, Lavender 22.50
Porcelain, Sugar & Creamer, Miniature, 22k Gold, Flowers & Leaves 12.50
Porcelain, Sugar, Flowers, Covered 40.00
Porcelain, Sugar, Sprig Decorated, 3 1/2 In.High 5.00
Porcelain, Syrup, Country Scene, Gold Outline, Pewter Cover 35.00
Porcelain, Tea Set, Austrian, Figured Segments, Blue & Gold, 15 Piece 45.00
Porcelain, Tea Set, Child's, Germany, White, Green & Gold Bands, 17 Piece 20.00
Porcelain, Tea Set, Child's, Oriental, 3 Piece 15.00
Porcelain, Tea Set, Child's, White, Blue Bands, Pink & Blue Floral, 19 Piece 45.00
Porcelain, Tea Set, Germany, White Ground, Fruit, Ornate Handles, 3 Piece 27.50
Porcelain, Tea Set, Light Green, Raised White Flowers, 3 Piece 12.50
Porcelain, Tea Set, Miniature, 'tea For Two, ' Gold Trim 45.00
Porcelain, Tea Set, White, Gold Leaf Scroll, Paneled Sides, 27 Piece 80.00
Porcelain, Teakettle, Roses, Pink, Green, Luster, Marked Victoria, Austria 35.00
Porcelain, Teapot, Creamer, Sugar, Cover, Hexagon, Pink & White Floral, Gold 25.00
Porcelain, Teapot, Gardiner, Scroll Handle, Seminude Female, 19th Century 70.00
Porcelain, Teapot, Italian, Flowered 8.50
Porcelain, Teapot, Oriental Flower Design, Cream Color, Cover, 5 In.Tall 12.00
Porcelain, Teapot, Sugar, Creamer, Tray, Four Cups, Saucers, Red, Gold, Russia 495.00
Porcelain, Teapot, Transfer Flowers, Wire Bail Handle 6.00

Porcelain, Teapot, Underplate, Gardiner, Russia 100.00
Porcelain, Toothpick, England, Gullane, 3 Handles, Golfer 3.50
Porcelain, Toothpick, Germany, Two Pink Pigs & Trough 8.50
Porcelain, Tray, Dresser, Decorated 4.50
Porcelain, Tray, Dresser, German, Green Edge, Roses, 9 1/2 X 6 1/2 In. 7.50
Porcelain, Tray, Grapes, Leaves, Gold, Hand-Painted, 15 1/2 X 12 In. 32.50
Porcelain, Tray, Pin, Perry & Sailors In Rowboat, Put-In-Bay 12.00
Porcelain, Tray, Pipe, German 5.00
Porcelain, Tray, Victoria, Austria, Scalloped, Ladies & Men Eating 27.00
Porcelain, Trinket Set, Shaded Yellow, Peach, & White, Roses, Beige, 6 Piece 50.00
Porcelain, Tumbler, Portrait, Queen Alexandra & King Edward VII, White, 1902 ..... 25.00
Porcelain, Urn, English, 19th Century, Decorated, Green & Gold, Pair 400.00
Porcelain, Urn, Lake Success In Medallion, Black & Gold, Covered, Pair 25.00
Porcelain, Vase, Bird Design, Hand-Painted, Artist Denbo, 13 In.Tall 45.00
Porcelain, Vase, Bud, Daisies, Leaves, Blue, Green, Enamel 20.00
Porcelain, Vase, Bud, M-Z Austria, White, 6 In.Tall, Pair 19.00
Porcelain, Vase, Floral Design, Man, Woman, Dog, Artist Signed, Austrian, 9 In. 35.00
Porcelain, Vase, Florentine, Blue, White Enameled Boy On Water Lily 70.00
Porcelain, Vase, Flower, Leaf, Pink, Green, Raised, French, 15 In.Tall, Pair 250.00
Porcelain, Vase, Girl, Bonnet, Boy, Hat, Kate Greenaway Type 35.00
Porcelain, Vase, Hand Holds Vase, Floral, Translucent, Marked 1056, 3 1/2 In. 15.00
Porcelain, Vase, Lady's Portrait, Orange, Germany, 8 In.Tall 15.00
Porcelain, Vase, Paris, Mounted As Lamp, Ovoid, Peasants, 19th Century, Pair 225.00
Porcelain, Vase, Poppy, Black Paint Inside, Decoration In Relief, 8 1/2 In. 8.50
Porcelain, Vase, Russian Imperial, 2 Scroll Handles, Peasant Scenes, 1761-96 ..... 250.00
Porcelain, Wash Set, Brown Chinese Transfer Design, Date 1850, 2 Piece 45.00
Portland, Bowl, Finger, Maiden's Blush 30.00
Portrait, Plate, Admiral Dewey, Lacy, Clear, Open Keyhole Border 6.00
Portrait, Plate, Austrian, Green & Gold Border, 9 In.Diameter, Pair 20.00
Portrait, Plate, Beehive, Signed L.Jaickl, Dark Blue Ground, Gold, 10 In. 165.00
Portrait, Plate, Broken Arm, Sioux Chief, A.Kuntson & Co., Portland, Ore. 25.00
Portrait, Plate, Constance, Head & Shoulders, Gold Border 39.00
Portrait, Plate, Inscribed Oude Loosdrecht, Sepia Medallion, C.1775 ..... 60.00
Portrait, Plate, Lady In Center, Green Border With Pink Roses 45.00
Portrait, Plate, Lady's Portrait, Victoria, Austria, Cobalt & Gold 37.50
Portrait, Plate, Lindbergh, 1927, Porcelain 12.00
Portrait, Plate, Queen Louise 25.00
Portrait, Plate, Queen Victoria, Lace Gown & Veil, 8 In.Diameter 24.00
Portrait, Plate, Queen Victoria, Clear Glass, Dated 1887, 10 In. 20.00
Portrait, Plate, Woman, Green Border, Gold, GDA France, 10 In. 38.50
Portrait, Tray, Celery, Hand-Painted, Woman, Flowing Hair, Beehive Mark 35.00
Portrait, Vase, Lady In Empire Gown, Signed Klutzon, 2 1/2 In.Tall 35.00
Portrait, Vase, Woman, Maroon, Gold, Signed, Beehive Mark, 10 In. 45.00
  Postcard, see also Album
Postcard, Abraham Lincoln, Set Of 15 ..... 2.00
Postcard, Al McCoy, Boxer, 1921, Black & White 1.00
Postcard, America's Famous Men, J.I.Austen, 24 ..... 10.00
Postcard, American Indian, Copyright 1912, Color, 40 In Book Shape Box 18.00
Postcard, Arizona, State Capitol & Seal, Embossed, Color ..... .75
Postcard, Barnum & Bailey Circus, Advertising, 1896 Duryea Wagon, Color ..... .35
Postcard, Baseball, Mordecai Brown, 1907 ..... 1.00
Postcard, Battleship Britton & Rey, Color ..... .25
Postcard, Battleship U.S.Alabama, Color ..... .25
Postcard, Battleship U.S.Ohio, Color ..... .25
Postcard, British Views, 100 ..... 11.50
Postcard, Budweiser Beer, Fold Over 1.00
Postcard, Busy Bears, Color, Series 79, Set Of 7 ..... 21.00
Postcard, California Views, 300 In Album 20.00
Postcard, Captain, U.S.Cavalry, S.Langsdorf, No.12 ..... 1.00
Postcard, Caribbean, South, & Central America, 100 ..... 12.50
Postcard, Carl Morris, Boxer, 1921, Black & White 1.00
Postcard, Christmas, Santa, Set Of 25 ..... 35.00
Postcard, Christmas, Signed, Embossed ..... .35
Postcard, Christmas, 100 In Album 15.00
Postcard, Clock, Era 1906-1920, 50 ..... 10.00
Postcard, Columbus Baseball Team, 1906 ..... 1.00

Postcard, **Comic**, Alligator After Bait	1.00
Postcard, **Comic**, Babies, Children, 22	2.00
Postcard, **Courthouses**, 17	1.00
Postcard, **Cowboy Scene**, Color, 1902	1.50
Postcard, **Detroit**, 15	1.00
Postcard, **E.Nister**, Punishment Series, Color, 3	3.00
Postcard, **Easter Greetings**, Little Susie Sunbonnet	3.00
Postcard, **Easter**, Birthday, Christmas, 100	12.00
Postcard, **European**, Black & White, Colored, Used & Unused, Per Thousand	75.00
Postcard, **Ford V-8**, Tudor Sedan, 1936, Advertising, Black & White	1.50
Postcard, **Fourth Of July Series No.1**, Color, 6	3.00
Postcard, **Fourth Of July Series No.5**, E.Nash, Color, 6	5.00
Postcard, **Fourth Of July**, Cannon, Eagle, Stars, Unused, Set Of 4	3.00
Postcard, **Fourth Of July**, E.Nash Series J-6, Color, 2	1.00
Postcard, **Fourth Of July**, E.Nash Series J-8, Color, 6	6.00
Postcard, **Fourth Of July**, 3	1.80
Postcard, **Freddie Walsh**, Boxer, 1921, Black & White	1.00
Postcard, **Gelatin Coated**, 100 In Album	25.00
Postcard, **German American Novelty Art Co.**, Floral, Signed Mary Golay, 3	1.80
Postcard, **German-American Novelty Art**, 24	5.75
Postcard, **Greeting**, The Twenty-Third Psalm, Signed C.Klein, Color	.50
Postcard, **Greetings**, Assorted, 100	5.00
Postcard, **Hands Across The Sea**, Fredrick Peterson, Sweden, Color	.50
Postcard, **Happy Thought**, Advertising Chewing Tobacco, Color, 3	1.50
Postcard, **Humorous**, Family Type, 25	2.00
Postcard, **In Memory Of Centennial Anniversary Of Abraham Lincoln**, 3	3.75
Postcard, **Indian Chief**, Black Eagle, E.C.Kropp No.272, Color	1.00
Postcard, **Indian Portrait**, Chase In The Morning, F.A.Rinehart, 1903, Color	1.25
Postcard, **Indian Scenes**, Signed Frank Teller, Valentine & Son, Color, 2	.50
Postcard, **Indian**, 1907, 10	1.00
Postcard, **Irish Views**, 100	11.50
Postcard, **Italian**, 1940s, 16	1.00
Postcard, **J.I.Case Steam Roller**, Advertising, Color	.50
Postcard, **James Jeffries**, Boxer, 1921, Black & White	1.00
Postcard, **James John Corbett**, Boxer, 1921, Black & White	1.00
Postcard, **Jamestown Exposition**, 1907, Color, No.9	1.25
Postcard, **Jamestown Exposition**, 1907, Color, No.10	1.25
Postcard, **Jamestown Exposition**, 1907, Color, No.12	1.25
Postcard, **Jamestown Exposition**, 1907, Color, No.13	1.25
Postcard, **Jamestown Exposition**, 1907, Color, No.17	1.25
Postcard, **Jamestown Exposition**, 1907, Color, No.20	1.25
Postcard, **John L.Sullivan**, Boxer, 1921, Black & White	1.00
Postcard, **Kewpie**, Santa Claus, Rose O'neill Signed, Used	3.00
Postcard, **Korn Kinks**, Advertising, Negro Children, Color	.35
Postcard, **Kornelia Kinks**, Negro Girl & Verse, Unused	2.50
Postcard, **Lady**, 1910-1911, 2	.35
Postcard, **Leather**	.35
Postcard, **Leather**, Comic & Christmas, 2	.70
Postcard, **Leather**, Comic, 6	2.75
Postcard, **Lewis & Clark Centennial Exposition**, 1905, Lincoln Homestead	2.00
Postcard, **Lincoln The Martyr**, H.M.Rose, Color, Embossed	1.25
Postcard, **Lincoln's Birthday**, International Art Series 51658, C.Chapman, 6	7.50
Postcard, **Lord's Prayer**, Our Father, Who Art In Heaven, Series 7070	1.00
Postcard, **Lord's Prayer**, P.F.B.Series 7066, Embossed, Color, 8	8.00
Postcard, **Lord's Prayer**, Series 7070, Set Of 8	10.00
Postcard, **Louisiana Purchase Exposition**, Souvenir	2.50
Postcard, **Maps Of U.S.**, Set Of 50	12.50
Postcard, **Mechanical**, Santa Claus	4.75
Postcard, **Mechanical**, Your Fortune Teller, Charles Gerlach, 1910	.75
Postcard, **National Cupid Series No.75**, Ullman Co., Canada, Color	.75
Postcard, **National Girls In Native Costume**, Country Seal, Austria, Color	1.00
Postcard, **National Girls In Native Costume**, Country Seal, Germany, Color	1.00
Postcard, **Negro Melodies**, R.Tuck, No.2398, Color	1.50
Postcard, **Negro**, Linen, 20	4.25
Postcard, **New England View**, Early 1900s, 50	4.00
Postcard, **New Year's**, Babies & Children, 10	1.00

Postcard, Pan American Exposition, 1901, Color 6.00
Postcard, Perry's Flagship, The Niagara, 1913, 2 .... 1.50
Postcard, Photo-Type, Babies & Children, 67 .... 4.00
Postcard, Photo, Susquehanna Silk Mills, Sunbury, Pa., Delivery Truck 1.00
Postcard, Pope, Signed, 1903, 12 .... 18.00
Postcard, Postmarked 1903-08, 100 .... 10.00
Postcard, Pre-1920, 100 .... 7.50
Postcard, Railroad, Chrome Colored, Locomotives, 30 .... 3.50
Postcard, Railroad, Chrome, Locomotives, Steam, Diesel, U.S.& Canada, 31 .... 3.50
Postcard, Railroad, Trains, Bridges, Stations, 27 .... 3.00
Postcard, Roosevelt Bears, Color 1.50
Postcard, Ruins Of World War I, 100 .... 12.50
Postcard, Santa Claus, Pre-1920, 16 .... 8.50
Postcard, Santa Claus, 1905-20, Color, Embossed, 3 .... 2.00
Postcard, Santa Claus, 6 .... 5.00
Postcard, Santa, Full Length 1.50
Postcard, Scandinavian, 100 .... 11.50
Postcard, Sheridan's Ride, Blue Background 1.50
Postcard, Signed H.C.Christy 1.00
Postcard, Signed Harrison Fisher 1.50
Postcard, Signed Philip Boileau, Dated 1907 .... 1.25
Postcard, Signed Philip Boileau, Dated 1908 .... 1.25
Postcard, Silk Picture, Rms Lusitania, W.H.Grant & Co., Coventry 18.50
Postcard, Sohio Oil, Advertising, Color, 8 .... 1.20
Postcard, St.Louis Exposition, R.Tuck, No.6024, Color 2.50
Postcard, St.Louis Exposition, R.Tuck, No.6025, Color 2.50
Postcard, St.Louis World's Fair, 1904, Bridge On The Lagoon 2.00
Postcard, St.Louis World's Fair, 1904, Buxton & Skinner 3.00
Postcard, St.Louis World's Fair, 1904, Corner Palace Of Varied Industries 2.50
Postcard, St.Louis World's Fair, 1904, German Pavilion, Color 1.50
Postcard, St.Louis World's Fair, 1904, Machinery Building 2.00
Postcard, St.Louis World's Fair, 1904, Mines & Metallurgy Building 2.00
Postcard, St.Louis World's Fair, 1904, Palace Of Liberal Arts 1.50
Postcard, St.Louis World's Fair, 1904, Palace Of Mines & Metallurgy 1.50
Postcard, Sunbonnet, Embossed, H.I.Robbins, Boston, Unused, Set Of 7 .... 75.00
Postcard, Talking Cat, Color, Cat Squeal, Set Of 12 .... 2.75
Postcard, Talking, Squeeze & Squeal, Kittens, 12 .... 2.50
Postcard, Teddy Bears & Little Girl, M.Grenier, Color 2.00
Postcard, Thanksgiving, Turkey, Era 1906-1920, 40 .... 10.00
Postcard, Train, Signed .... .35
Postcard, Trans Mississippi & International Exposition, 1898 .... 7.50
Postcard, Transportation, Ships, Trains, Trolleys, 100 In Album 20.00
Postcard, Tuck Greetings & Views, 100 In Album 25.00
Postcard, Tuck Oilette Manila Series 2506, Set Of 4 .... 1.00
Postcard, U.S., Pre-1945, 50 .... 3.00
Postcard, U.S.Battleship Wisconsin, Edward H.Mitchell No.1275, Color .... .35
Postcard, U.S.Presidents Collector's Series, Bowman Gum Co., 1952, 7 .... .75
Postcard, U.S.Street Scenes, Pre-1925, 50 .... 5.50
Postcard, U.S.Street Scenes, 1940s, 70 .... 3.00
Postcard, Ullman Series, Comic, 3 .... .75
Postcard, Ullman, Busy Bears Series No.79, Wednesday, Color 2.50
Postcard, Union Oil, 1939, 37 .... 10.00
Postcard, Valentine .... .15
Postcard, Victorian, Silk, Panel, S.S.Celtic, Gold Frame, Embossed Border 7.50
Postcard, Votes For Woman, Picture Of Mrs.T.Billington-Creig, Sepia 1.50
Postcard, Washington's Birthday, E.Nash Series W-14, Color .... .75
Postcard, Washington's Birthday, Julius Bien Series 760, Color, 3 .... 1.45
Postcard, Washington's Birthday, S.Garre Series 51766, R.Veenfliet, 6 .... 6.00
Postcard, Washout Of Erie Canal, July 30, 1907, 3 .... .75
Postcard, Women's Suffrage, Political 2.00
Postcard, Wooden, 'well, Pigs Is Pigs' 1.00
Postcard, World War Ii, Comic, 12 .... 1.00
Postcard, Woven Silk, R.M.S.Saxonia, Stevens 20.00
Poster, Circus, Yankee Robinson, Black & White, Elephant, Airship, 1909 .... 25.00
     Pottery, see also Buffalo Pottery, Staffordshire, Wedgwood, etc.
Pottery, Bird Watering Station, Slip Glazed, American, W.B.& Co., Ohio, 1855 .... 40.00

Pottery, Bowl, Connecticut, Shallow, 9 In.Diameter	30.00
Pottery, Cup & Saucer, Mercer Pottery, Trenton, N.H., Rose Floral	20.00
Pottery, Dish, Hen Covered, Tan, Signed P.V.2277	18.00
Pottery, Figure, English Lion, Light Blue, Orange Mane, 6 In.High	25.00
Pottery, Holder, Pipe, Duck, Art Nouveau	7.50
Pottery, Jar, Apothecary, Covered, Set Of 4 Graduated	50.00
Pottery, Jar, Miniature, Marked C.Price, Bristol	10.00
Pottery, Jug, Water, Drinking Spout, White Clay, Brown Slip	4.00
Pottery, Matchbox, Terra-Cotta Color, Raised Eagle & Scrolls, Striker In	25.00
Pottery, Mold, Cake, Turk's Head, Tan & Green Glaze	10.00
Pottery, Mold, Plum Pudding, Grape Cluster Top, Fluted Sides, England	23.00
Pottery, Pitcher, Green & Brown, North State Pottery Co.	20.00
Pottery, Pitcher, Yellow Glaze, 4 In.High	12.50
Pottery, Pot, Handmade, Black Interior Glaze, 16 In.Diameter	25.00
Pottery, Tankard & Six Tumblers, Luster Finish, Harker Pottery, 1890, 9 In.	50.00
Pottery, Teapot, Chinese, Brown, Foo Dog Finial	7.50
Pottery, Tub, Foot, Ohio, Oval, 15 X 21 1/2 In.	5.00
Pottery, Tub, Shenandoah, Green, Cream, & Brown Slip, 3 3/4 In.Diameter	50.00
Pottery, Tureen, Shape Of Turkey, Green With Brown, Quart Size, Signed	8.00
Pottery, Vase, Clifton, Newark, N.J., Incised Four-Mile-Ruin, Arizona	35.00
Pottery, Vase, Korean, Monkey In Relief, Impressed Mark, 12 In.High	20.00
Pottery, Vase, Light Brown Tones, 7 In.High, Impressed Red Wing 751	3.00
Pottery, Vase, Signed Clement Massier, Iridescent, 5 In.Tall	45.00

Powder Horn, see Weapon, Powder Horn

*Pratt Ware means two different things. It was an early Staffordshire
Pottery, cream-colored with colored decorations, made by Felix Pratt
during the late eighteenth century. There was also Pratt Ware made with
transfer designs during the mid-nineteenth century.*

Pratt, Bowl, Pedestal, Signed J.Austin	250.00
Pratt, Box, Covered, Room In Which Shakespeare Was Born	33.00
Pratt, Figure, Ceres Holding Cornucopia, C.1780-90, David Wilson, Hanley	95.00
Pratt, Jar, Blue, 4 In. *Illus*	18.00
Pratt, Jug, Bacchanalians At Play, Purple, Green, & Blue, Fenton	48.00
Pratt, Kid, Ironstone, Advertising, J.B.Thorn, Chemist, London	10.00
Pratt, Lid, Albert Memorial, Master Of The Hounds, Jars, Pair	80.00
Pratt, Lid, Fording The Stream	35.00
Pratt, Lid, Sailing Vessel Scene, Round	22.50
Pratt, Lid, The Enthusiast & The Game Bag, Framed	85.00
Pratt, Lid, The Wolf & The Lamb	30.00
Pratt, Pitcher, Classical Figure, Orange, Bulbous, 4 3/4 In.Tall	75.00
Pratt, Pitcher, Classical Figures, Greek Key Trim, Orange, 5 1/4 In.Tall	85.00
Pratt, Pitcher, Classical Figures, Orange, Bulbous, 6 1/4 In.Tall	100.00
Pratt, Pitcher, Lord Wellington In Relief, Black, Browns, Oranges, & Blue	125.00
Pratt, Plate, Boys Playing, Mother, Children, Acorn & Leaves, Signed, 9 1/2 In	95.00
Pratt, Plate, Cattle & Ruins, Key Edge, Orange, 7 In.Diameter	50.00

Pratt, Jar, Blue, 4 In.

Pratt, Plate, Penseroso, White, Red, 7 In.Diameter 45.00
Pratt, Plate, Red Bull Inn, Green Border, Gold, 8 1/2 In. 35.00
Pratt, Plate, Roman Coliseum Center, 8 1/2 In.Diameter 20.00
Pratt, Plate, The Poultry Woman, Yellow, Gold, 7 In.Diameter 45.00
Pratt, Plate, The Village Wedding, Rasberry, Key Edge, 7 In.Diameter 45.00
Pratt, Plate, The Waterfall, Key Edge, Green, 7 In.Diameter 50.00
Pratt, Pot Lid, Shakespeare's Birthplace, Fenton 31.00
Pratt, Pot Lid, Uncle Toby, Fenton 31.00
Pratt, Sauceboat, Fox Head, Red, Yellow & Green Leaves, C.1790 .... 140.00
Pratt, Toby Mug, Man, Seated, Blue Coat, Yellow Pants, C.1785 .... 170.00
     Pressed Glass, see also Cosmos, Croesus, etc.
Pressed Glass, Basket, Daises & Hobstars, Footed 10.00
Pressed Glass, Bell, Deer & Pine, Blue 12.00
Pressed Glass, Berry Set, Daisy & Button, Green, Clover Shape Bowl, 6 Piece 35.00
Pressed Glass, Berry Set, Daisy & Oval Panel, Gold, 7 Piece 37.50
Pressed Glass, Berry Set, Herringbone, 5 Piece 30.00
Pressed Glass, Berry Set, Hobnail, 5 Piece 12.50
Pressed Glass, Berry Set, Shell & Tassel, Oval, 7 Piece, Square Sauces 72.50
Pressed Glass, Berry Set, Texas, Scalloped Edges, 7 Piece 50.00
Pressed Glass, Berry Set, Toy, Lacy Daisy, 7 Piece 27.50
Pressed Glass, Boat, Daisy & Button, Blue, 14 In.Long 15.00
Pressed Glass, Boat, Relish, Banded Portland, Pastel Yellow, 9 In.Long 14.00
Pressed Glass, Boat, Rose, Blue 50.00
Pressed Glass, Bobeche, Clear, Cranberry Edge, Ruffled, Pair 13.50
Pressed Glass, Boot, Baby, Daisy & Button, Sapphire Blue, Eyelet Holes 24.00
Pressed Glass, Bootie, Daisy & Button, Blue 5.00
Pressed Glass, Bottle, Castor, Bull's-Eye, Shaker Top, Flint 5.00
Pressed Glass, Bottle, Water, Banded Portland, Clear 27.50
Pressed Glass, Bottle, Water, Etched Stork, Cut Stopper 25.00
Pressed Glass, Bowl, Alabama, 7 1/4 X 5 1/4 In. 8.50
Pressed Glass, Bowl, Banana, Delaware, Green, 12 In. 30.00
Pressed Glass, Bowl, Banana, Thousand Eye, Apple Green, Open, 8 In.Square 48.00
Pressed Glass, Bowl, Beaded Grape, Clear, Rectangular 10.00
Pressed Glass, Bowl, Berry, Bar & Diamond, Six Sauces, Set 30.00
Pressed Glass, Bowl, Berry, Block & Fan, Clear, 8 In.Diameter 10.00
Pressed Glass, Bowl, Berry, Bull's-Eye, Ruby Flashed Eyes, Gold, Scalloped 35.00
Pressed Glass, Bowl, Berry, Cane, Blue, Three Panel, Footed 22.50
Pressed Glass, Bowl, Berry, Colorado, Clear, Footed, 5 Small, 1 Large, Set 57.50
Pressed Glass, Bowl, Berry, Dewey, Green, Greentown 21.00
Pressed Glass, Bowl, Berry, Empress, Gold 45.00
Pressed Glass, Bowl, Berry, Festoon, 9 1/4 In. 9.50
Pressed Glass, Bowl, Berry, Frisco 15.00
Pressed Glass, Bowl, Berry, Hairpin 17.50
Pressed Glass, Bowl, Berry, Heart & Thumbprint 22.50
Pressed Glass, Bowl, Berry, Honeycomb 14.00
Pressed Glass, Bowl, Berry, Kansas, 8 1/2 In. 15.00
Pressed Glass, Bowl, Berry, Moon & Star, Footed 20.00
Pressed Glass, Bowl, Berry, Moon & Star, 7 In. 15.00
Pressed Glass, Bowl, Berry, Paneled Daisy 16.00
Pressed Glass, Bowl, Berry, Paneled Thistle, Footed 5.00
Pressed Glass, Bowl, Berry, Sawtooth 14.00
Pressed Glass, Bowl, Berry, Stippled, Clear 12.50
Pressed Glass, Bowl, Berry, Torpedo 15.00
Pressed Glass, Bowl, Bird & Strawberry, Oval, Footed 37.50
Pressed Glass, Bowl, Block, Flint, 8 In.Diameter 19.00
Pressed Glass, Bowl, Blue, Grape & Cherry, Blue, Square, Ruffled Edge, 9 In. 17.50
Pressed Glass, Bowl, Broken Column, 8 1/2 In.Diameter, 3 1/2 In.Deep 27.50
Pressed Glass, Bowl, Bulb, Lilies, Frosted, Silver Overlay, Flint 45.00
Pressed Glass, Bowl, Butter, Swan, 5 In.Diameter 10.00
Pressed Glass, Bowl, California, Square 12.50
Pressed Glass, Bowl, Candlewick, Cover 16.00
Pressed Glass, Bowl, Colorado, Green, Gold Trim, Flared, Footed .... 22.50 To 38.00
Pressed Glass, Bowl, Console, Imperial Jewels, Blue, 12 In.Diameter 17.50
Pressed Glass, Bowl, Cord & Tassel, Oval 7.50
Pressed Glass, Bowl, Daisy & Button, Blue, 7 In.Diameter 10.00
Pressed Glass, Bowl, Delaware, Banana Shape, Silver Frame 95.00

Pressed Glass, Bowl, Delaware, Emerald Green & Gold, 10 In. 32.50
Pressed Glass, Bowl, Delaware, Fluted, Green, Gold, 10 In.Diameter 32.50
Pressed Glass, Bowl, Delaware, Green, Gold, Ruffled Edge, 9 3/4 In. 25.00
Pressed Glass, Bowl, Delaware, Green, Gold, 9 In. 30.00
Pressed Glass, Bowl, Delaware, Green, Round, Gold, 8 In. 30.00
Pressed Glass, Bowl, Dessert, Daisy & Button, Sapphire Blue, Square 16.00
Pressed Glass, Bowl, Dewey, Cord & Drapery, Amber, Greentown 24.00
Pressed Glass, Bowl, Diamond Quilted, Blue, 9 1/2 In.Diameter 17.00
Pressed Glass, Bowl, Esther, Clear, Etched, 9 In. 24.00
Pressed Glass, Bowl, Etched Grasshopper, Footed 8.00
Pressed Glass, Bowl, Feather & Fine Cut, Oval 7.50
Pressed Glass, Bowl, Finger, Chandelier 18.75
Pressed Glass, Bowl, Finger, Daisy & Button 12.00
Pressed Glass, Bowl, Finger, Inverted Thumbprint, Blue 22.50
Pressed Glass, Bowl, Finger, Opalescent Coin Dot 22.50
Pressed Glass, Bowl, Flat, Bellflower, Scallop & Point Edge, Flint 110.00
Pressed Glass, Bowl, Flute, Scalloped, Flint 19.50
Pressed Glass, Bowl, Frosted Hidalgo, Square 17.50
Pressed Glass, Bowl, Frosted Maple Leaf 15.00
Pressed Glass, Bowl, Frosted, Dog In Base 60.00
Pressed Glass, Bowl, Fruit, Amberette 50.00
Pressed Glass, Bowl, Fruit, Delaware, Green, Gilt, Boat Shape .... 24.00 To 42.00
Pressed Glass, Bowl, Fruit, Heart & Thumbprint, 8 1/2 In. 17.50
Pressed Glass, Bowl, Fruit, Paneled Thistle, 8 1/2 In.Tall, 25 In.Diameter 16.50
Pressed Glass, Bowl, Fruit, Shell & Jewel, Footed, 8 1/2 In.High 28.00
Pressed Glass, Bowl, Gladstone, Circa 1870, 8 1/2 In.Diameter 24.00
Pressed Glass, Bowl, Good Luck, Pedestal, Cover, 8 In.High, 7 In.Diameter 48.50
Pressed Glass, Bowl, Grasshopper, Shallow, 10 In.Diameter 22.50
Pressed Glass, Bowl, Herringbone, Green, 7 1/2 In. 8.00
Pressed Glass, Bowl, Herringbone, Green, 9 In. 12.00
Pressed Glass, Bowl, Hobnail, Blue, Fan Top, Fern Decoration, 8 In.Diameter 12.50
Pressed Glass, Bowl, Ice Cream, Rose Point Band 2.50
Pressed Glass, Bowl, Imperial Grape, Green, Ruffled, 8 In.Diameter 25.00
Pressed Glass, Bowl, Iris & Herringbone, 9 In. 5.00
Pressed Glass, Bowl, Jacob's Ladder, 6 In. 5.00
Pressed Glass, Bowl, Jewel & Dewdrop, Kansas, 8 1/2 In.Diameter 14.00
Pressed Glass, Bowl, King's Crown, Clear, Etched, 6 In.Diam. 16.50
Pressed Glass, Bowl, Klondike, 6 In.Square 85.00
Pressed Glass, Bowl, Lafayette At Franklin's Tomb 60.00
Pressed Glass, Bowl, Manhattan, 8 1/2 In. 10.00
Pressed Glass, Bowl, Maple Leaf, Footed, Oblong, 11 In.Long 17.50
Pressed Glass, Bowl, Moon & Star, Open, Footed, 8 1/2 In.Diameter, Pair 25.00
Pressed Glass, Bowl, Moon & Star, Pedestal, 8 In. 9.50
Pressed Glass, Bowl, Moon & Star, 7 In. 9.75
Pressed Glass, Bowl, Panel Thistle, Bee Mark, 8 1/2 In.Diameter 22.50
Pressed Glass, Bowl, Paneled Grape, Round, Covered 42.50
Pressed Glass, Bowl, Paneled Grape, 7 5/8 In.Diameter 10.00
Pressed Glass, Bowl, Paneled Thistle, Footed, 8 In.Diameter 10.00
Pressed Glass, Bowl, Paneled Thistle, 9 In. 18.00
Pressed Glass, Bowl, Princess Feather Medallion, 7 1/2 In.Diameter 55.00
Pressed Glass, Bowl, Punch, Beaumont, Miniature 16.25
Pressed Glass, Bowl, Punch, Hobstars, Cane, Strawberry Diamond, 2 Quart, Stand 22.00
Pressed Glass, Bowl, Punch, Little Red Riding Hood, Clear 35.00
Pressed Glass, Bowl, Punch, Press Cut, 7 In.High 7.75
Pressed Glass, Bowl, Rose Medallion, 5 1/2 In.Diameter 55.00
Pressed Glass, Bowl, Rose Sprig, 9 In.Diameter 12.00
Pressed Glass, Bowl, Salad, Fleur-De-Lis, 9 In.Diameter 15.00
Pressed Glass, Bowl, Shell & Tassel, Oval, 12 In. 24.50
Pressed Glass, Bowl, Shoshone, Footed 12.00
Pressed Glass, Bowl, Stippled Bar 7.00
Pressed Glass, Bowl, Stippled Cherry, Clear 12.50
Pressed Glass, Bowl, Texas Star, 9 In.Diameter 22.50
Pressed Glass, Bowl, Thumbprint, Shallow, Flint 30.00
Pressed Glass, Bowl, Torpedo, Flat, 8 1/2 In.Diameter 20.00
Pressed Glass, Bowl, Vera, Frosted, 10 In.Diam. 16.00
Pressed Glass, Bowl, Waste, Etched Hidalgo 11.00

Pressed Glass, Bowl, Waste, Horseshoe 18.00
Pressed Glass, Bowl, Waste, King's No.500 .... 6.00
Pressed Glass, Bowl, Waste, Ribbon, Frosted 40.00
Pressed Glass, Box, Green, Footed, Oval, Cover, 4 1/2 X 3 In. 20.00
Pressed Glass, Box, Jewel, Clear, 4 1/2 X 3 1/2 X 2 In. 7.00
Pressed Glass, Box, Puff, Delaware, Green 35.00
Pressed Glass, Bride's Basket, Delaware, Ruby Flashed, Frame 125.00
Pressed Glass, Bride's Basket, Portland, Clear, Silver Plate Frame, Footed 37.50
Pressed Glass, Bucket, Ice, Engraved, Green 6.00
Pressed Glass, Bucket, Ice, Frosted Horses, Raised Figures 42.50
Pressed Glass, Buddha, Gillinder, Amber, Marked, 6 1/2 In.Tall 45.00
Pressed Glass, Butter Pat, Daisy & Button, Blue, Triangle 7.50
Pressed Glass, Butter, Acorn 35.00
Pressed Glass, Butter, Alaska, Opalescent Blue, 5 In.Square 10.00
Pressed Glass, Butter, Avon, Covered 20.00
Pressed Glass, Butter, Beaded Ellipse With Fan, Covered 16.50
Pressed Glass, Butter, Block 6.00
Pressed Glass, Butter, Bridal Rosette, Cover 25.00
Pressed Glass, Butter, Buckle 28.00
Pressed Glass, Butter, Carolina, Covered 17.50
Pressed Glass, Butter, Cathedral 25.00
Pressed Glass, Butter, Centennial .... *Illus* 60.00

Pressed Glass,
Butter, Centennial

Pressed Glass, Butter, Cherry 10.50
Pressed Glass, Butter, Classic 110.00
Pressed Glass, Butter, Colorado, Clear, Cover 24.50
Pressed Glass, Butter, Colorado, Clear, Cover 25.00
Pressed Glass, Butter, Colorado, Green 65.00
Pressed Glass, Butter, Colorado, Green, Covered, Gold, Footed 59.50
Pressed Glass, Butter, Cube & Fan, Covered 16.50
Pressed Glass, Butter, Cut & Pressed, Covered, Flint 32.75
Pressed Glass, Butter, Daisy & Button 25.00
Pressed Glass, Butter, Daisy & Button Crossbar, Amber, Footed, Cover 47.50
Pressed Glass, Butter, Daisy & Button With Thumbprint, Blue, Covered, Footed 40.00
Pressed Glass, Butter, Deer & Pine 60.00
Pressed Glass, Butter, Delaware, Green, Covered, Gold 75.00
Pressed Glass, Butter, Diamond, Scalloped Edge, High Dome 18.00
Pressed Glass, Butter, Egyptian, Covered 45.00
Pressed Glass, Butter, Etched Panovia, Covered 35.00
Pressed Glass, Butter, Eureka, Covered, Flint 35.00
Pressed Glass, Butter, Eyewinker, Covered 27.50
Pressed Glass, Butter, Feather, Cover .... 15.00 To 25.00
Pressed Glass, Butter, Fishscale .... 18.00 To 25.00
Pressed Glass, Butter, Fleur-De-Lis Drape, Pedestal 17.50
Pressed Glass, Butter, Flowerpot, Covered 18.50
Pressed Glass, Butter, Frosted Flower Band, Cover 52.00
Pressed Glass, Butter, Frosted Lion, Crouched Lion Finial 45.00

Pressed Glass, Butter, Frosted Ribbon, Cover .... 25.00 To 40.00
Pressed Glass, Butter, Grape & Festoon, Covered 20.00
Pressed Glass, Butter, Heart & Thumbprint, Covered 50.00
Pressed Glass, Butter, Herringbone, Green, Cover 18.00
Pressed Glass, Butter, Horn Of Plenty, Covered, 6 In.Diameter .... 60.00 To 75.00
Pressed Glass, Butter, Horn Of Plenty, Washington Head Knob On Cover 600.00
Pressed Glass, Butter, Horsemint, Cover 15.00
Pressed Glass, Butter, Iris & Herringbone, Covered 13.50
Pressed Glass, Butter, King's 500, Cobalt Blue, Gold Eyes 55.00
Pressed Glass, Butter, Klondike, Covered 130.00
Pressed Glass, Butter, Liberty Bell, Cover 42.50
Pressed Glass, Butter, Loop & Dart With Round Ornament, Covered, Flint 32.50
Pressed Glass, Butter, Loop & Pyramids, Covered 13.75
Pressed Glass, Butter, Massachusetts 25.00
Pressed Glass, Butter, Michigan 35.00
Pressed Glass, Butter, New Jersey, Covered, Gold Trim 24.00
Pressed Glass, Butter, Open Log Feet, Cover 100.00
Pressed Glass, Butter, Paneled Forget-Me-Not 18.00
Pressed Glass, Butter, Paneled Heather 13.00
Pressed Glass, Butter, Paneled Thistle With B, Covered, Square 25.00
Pressed Glass, Butter, Paneled Thistle, Bee Mark 13.75
Pressed Glass, Butter, Paneled Thistle, Cover 45.00
Pressed Glass, Butter, Paneled Wheat, Covered 28.50
Pressed Glass, Butter, Panels, Clear 24.50
Pressed Glass, Butter, Peacock Feather 22.50
Pressed Glass, Butter, Pineapple & Tan, Cover 37.50
Pressed Glass, Butter, Pointed Jewel, Covered .... 15.75 To 20.00
Pressed Glass, Butter, Regal Pattern 60.00
Pressed Glass, Butter, Roman Rosette, Cover 12.00
Pressed Glass, Butter, Rosette With Palms, Covered, Footed 25.00
Pressed Glass, Butter, Royal Ivy, Clear To Frosted, Covered 29.50
Pressed Glass, Butter, Royal, Covered, Belmont Glass Co. 25.00
Pressed Glass, Butter, Sheraton, Clear 19.50
Pressed Glass, Butter, Shrine, Covered 22.00
Pressed Glass, Butter, Snail 20.00
Pressed Glass, Butter, Spooner, Sugar, & Creamer, Red Block, Covered 150.00
Pressed Glass, Butter, Star & Pillar, Cover 13.00
Pressed Glass, Butter, Star & Pillar, Covered, Footed 18.50
Pressed Glass, Butter, Star Medallion 20.00
Pressed Glass, Butter, Stippled Dart & Balls, Covered 13.50
Pressed Glass, Butter, Stippled Ivy, Cover 28.50
Pressed Glass, Butter, Stippled Medallion, Covered, Flint 23.50
Pressed Glass, Butter, Stippled Sand Burr 28.00
Pressed Glass, Butter, Straight Ball & Swirl 14.00
Pressed Glass, Butter, Swag With Bracket, Green, Cover 45.00
Pressed Glass, Butter, Teardrop & Tassel .... 34.00 To 40.00
Pressed Glass, Butter, Teardrop & Tassel, Blue, Greentown 80.00
Pressed Glass, Butter, Teardrops, Blue, Flowered, Covered, Gold 45.00
Pressed Glass, Butter, Tidy, Covered 18.50
Pressed Glass, Butter, Tree Of Life 26.00
Pressed Glass, Butter, Twin Leaves 15.00
Pressed Glass, Butter, Two Band, Covered 12.50
Pressed Glass, Butter, Viking 34.50
Pressed Glass, Butter, Washboard, Covered 18.00
Pressed Glass, Butter, Westward Ho, Covered 30.00
Pressed Glass, Butter, Westward Ho, Covered, Standard 75.00
Pressed Glass, Butter, Wheat & Barley 17.50
Pressed Glass, Butter, Wildflower, Collared Base, Cover 25.00
Pressed Glass, Butter, Willow Oak, Amber, Cover 45.00
Pressed Glass, Buttermilk, Pressed Leaf 12.00
Pressed Glass, Cake Stand, Actress 80.00
Pressed Glass, Cake Stand, Actress, Frosted, 10 In. 72.50
Pressed Glass, Cake Stand, Beveled Diamond & Star, 9 In. 15.00
Pressed Glass, Cake Stand, Broken Column 35.00
Pressed Glass, Cake Stand, Cabbage Rose, 11 In. 22.50
Pressed Glass, Cake Stand, Child's, Zipper Pattern 10.00

Pressed Glass, Cake Stand, Cottage, 9 In.High	11.00
Pressed Glass, Cake Stand, Curtain	15.00
Pressed Glass, Cake Stand, Cut Log	20.00 To 28.50
Pressed Glass, Cake Stand, Diamond & Sunburst, Clear	12.50 To 16.50
Pressed Glass, Cake Stand, Festoon, Pedestal, 9 In.Diameter	16.00
Pressed Glass, Cake Stand, Festoon, 10 In.	16.50
Pressed Glass, Cake Stand, Fleur-De-Lis	15.00
Pressed Glass, Cake Stand, Frosted Circle 10 In.	27.50
Pressed Glass, Cake Stand, Frosted Circle, 10 1/2 In.High, Pedestal	28.00
Pressed Glass, Cake Stand, Good Luck, Clear, 8 1/2 In.Diameter	25.00
Pressed Glass, Cake Stand, Gooseberry, Clear, 9 1/2 In.Diameter	28.00
Pressed Glass, Cake Stand, Grand	9.50
Pressed Glass, Cake Stand, Hand, 10 In.	27.50
Pressed Glass, Cake Stand, Horseshoe, Footed, 10 In.Diameter	24.50
Pressed Glass, Cake Stand, Horseshoe, 9 In.	21.50 To 25.00
Pressed Glass, Cake Stand, Lotus, 11 In.	27.50
Pressed Glass, Cake Stand, Minerva, 9 In.	38.50
Pressed Glass, Cake Stand, Moon & Star, 6 In.Diameter, 9 In.High	42.50
Pressed Glass, Cake Stand, Paneled Forget-Me-Not	25.00
Pressed Glass, Cake Stand, Paneled Thistle	19.50
Pressed Glass, Cake Stand, Paneled Thistle, 10 In.Diameter	22.00
Pressed Glass, Cake Stand, Peacock Feather, Dust Particle Center	13.00
Pressed Glass, Cake Stand, Pineapple & Fan, Clear	12.00
Pressed Glass, Cake Stand, Pleat & Panel, 9 In.	14.00
Pressed Glass, Cake Stand, Pleat & Panel, 9 1/4 In.Diameter	22.00
Pressed Glass, Cake Stand, Post	40.00
Pressed Glass, Cake Stand, Quartered Block, 9 1/2 In.Diameter	15.00
Pressed Glass, Cake Stand, Raindrop, Blue, Footed, 9 1/2 In.High	10.00
Pressed Glass, Cake Stand, Romeo, 8 In.	10.50
Pressed Glass, Cake Stand, Shell & Tassel	28.00
Pressed Glass, Cake Stand, Shell & Tassel, 8 In.Square	21.50
Pressed Glass, Cake Stand, U.S.Coin Glass, Frosted, Dollars	295.00
Pressed Glass, Cake Stand, Willow Oak, Blue	28.00
Pressed Glass, Candleholder, Cornflower, 3 Branch, Low, Pair	16.00
Pressed Glass, Candleholder, Cranberry Glass Chimney, 6 Prisms, Pair	60.00
Pressed Glass, Candleholder, Iris & Herringbone, Double, Pair	9.00
Pressed Glass, Candlestick, Dolphin, Clear	95.00
Pressed Glass, Candlestick, Dolphin, Green, Marked, Pair	40.00
Pressed Glass, Candlestick, Etched, Blue	65.00
Pressed Glass, Candlestick, Excelsior, Clear	95.00
Pressed Glass, Candlestick, Grape Pattern, Green, 5 1/2 In.Tall, Pair	45.00
Pressed Glass, Candlestick, Pittsburgh, Clear, Terraced Base, Flint	40.00
Pressed Glass, Canoe, Daisy & Button, Clear, 12 In.	15.00
Pressed Glass, Canoe, Daisy & Button, Ruby Flashed	28.00
Pressed Glass, Carafe, Water, Massachusetts	28.50
Pressed Glass, Castor Set, Five Bottle, Gothic Arch, Pewter Frame	45.00
Pressed Glass, Castor, Gothic Arch, Pewter Stand, C.1865, 5 Piece	45.00
Pressed Glass, Castor, Pickle, Cupid & Venus, Silver	37.50
Pressed Glass, Castor, Pickle, Daisy & Button, Amber	85.00 To 110.00
Pressed Glass, Castor, Pickle, Daisy & Button, Clear, Hartford Silver Frame	75.00
Pressed Glass, Celery, Actress	90.00
Pressed Glass, Celery, Actress, Clear	87.50
Pressed Glass, Celery, Ashburton	55.00
Pressed Glass, Celery, Banded Portland	16.50
Pressed Glass, Celery, Barberry	*Illus* 18.50
Pressed Glass, Celery, Barberry, Clear, Oval	12.00
Pressed Glass, Celery, Barley	18.00
Pressed Glass, Celery, Beautiful Lady, Footed	12.00
Pressed Glass, Celery, Beauty Rib Swirl, Blue	58.00
Pressed Glass, Celery, Beveled Diamond & Star	10.00
Pressed Glass, Celery, Bijou	9.00
Pressed Glass, Celery, Bird & Fern, Clear, Footed	19.50
Pressed Glass, Celery, Block & Fan	18.00 To 19.50
Pressed Glass, Celery, Block & Fan, 7 In.	15.00
Pressed Glass, Celery, Bull's Eye, Scalloped Top, Flint	50.00
Pressed Glass, Celery, Bull's-Eye & Diamond Point, Flint, Pair	99.00

Pressed Glass, Celery, Barberry
See Page 373

Pressed Glass, Celery, Chandelier	18.75
Pressed Glass, Celery, Checkerboard	8.75
Pressed Glass, Celery, Checkerboard, Footed, 7 In.	12.50
Pressed Glass, Celery, Classic, Footed, 8 In.	110.00
Pressed Glass, Celery, Crystal, Flint	24.00
Pressed Glass, Celery, Cupid & Venus	27.50 To 37.50
Pressed Glass, Celery, Cut Log	18.00
Pressed Glass, Celery, Daisy & Button With V Ornament	12.00
Pressed Glass, Celery, Dakota, Flat Base	18.50
Pressed Glass, Celery, Dewdrop With Star	16.50
Pressed Glass, Celery, Diamond Block	9.00
Pressed Glass, Celery, Diamond Block & Sunburst, Pedestal Base	8.00
Pressed Glass, Celery, Diamond Thumbprint, Flint	85.00
Pressed Glass, Celery, Double Fan, Findlay	13.00
Pressed Glass, Celery, Double Frosted Ribbon	16.00
Pressed Glass, Celery, Etched Fan	9.00
Pressed Glass, Celery, Etched Snail	22.50
Pressed Glass, Celery, Fine Rib & Cut Ovals	110.00
Pressed Glass, Celery, Fishscale	16.50 To 19.00
Pressed Glass, Celery, Flattened Sawtooth & Fan, Scalloped Top	11.00
Pressed Glass, Celery, Fleur-De-Lis, 2 Handles	9.50 To 15.00
Pressed Glass, Celery, Fleur-De-Lis, 2 Handles, Greentown	17.50
Pressed Glass, Celery, Flower & Quill	14.50
Pressed Glass, Celery, Frosted Flower Band	27.50
Pressed Glass, Celery, Garfield Drape	18.00
Pressed Glass, Celery, Good Luck, Pedestal Base	24.00
Pressed Glass, Celery, Hartley	9.00
Pressed Glass, Celery, Heart, Thumbprint	16.00
Pressed Glass, Celery, Henrietta	20.00
Pressed Glass, Celery, Herringbone, Green, Two Handle	33.00
Pressed Glass, Celery, Hidalgo	18.50
Pressed Glass, Celery, Hidalgo, Frosted	18.00
Pressed Glass, Celery, High Hob	9.50
Pressed Glass, Celery, Honeycomb, 1860, Flint	30.00
Pressed Glass, Celery, Honeycomb, 8 In.High	7.50
Pressed Glass, Celery, Horn Of Plenty, Flint	77.50
Pressed Glass, Celery, Horn Of Plenty, Knob Stem, 8 1/2 In.	55.00
Pressed Glass, Celery, Horsemint	6.00
Pressed Glass, Celery, Jacob's Ladder	20.00 To 22.50
Pressed Glass, Celery, Jewel Band	12.00
Pressed Glass, Celery, Job's Tears, Clear	16.00
Pressed Glass, Celery, Lily Of The Valley	22.00
Pressed Glass, Celery, Loop, 9 3/4 In.High	15.00
Pressed Glass, Celery, Loop, 10 In.High, Pair	22.50
Pressed Glass, Celery, Marquisette	22.50
Pressed Glass, Celery, Mikado Fan	8.00 To 9.50
Pressed Glass, Celery, Minerva	20.00

Pressed Glass, Celery, Palm Leaf Fan, 6 1/2 In.	11.00
Pressed Glass, Celery, Palmette	20.00
Pressed Glass, Celery, Paneled Thistle	18.00
Pressed Glass, Celery, Parrot 1891	9.00
Pressed Glass, Celery, Pavonia	20.00
Pressed Glass, Celery, Pillar Etched	9.50
Pressed Glass, Celery, Pleat & Panel	15.00
Pressed Glass, Celery, Post, Clear	25.00
Pressed Glass, Celery, Princess Feather	23.00 To 27.50
Pressed Glass, Celery, Prism Block, 9 1/4 In.High, C.1880	20.00
Pressed Glass, Celery, Psyche & Cupid	28.00
Pressed Glass, Celery, Psyche & Cupid, Pedestal Base	42.50
Pressed Glass, Celery, Quartered Block	10.00
Pressed Glass, Celery, Regal Block	9.50
Pressed Glass, Celery, Ribbed Palm	58.00
Pressed Glass, Celery, Ribbed Palm, Flint	47.50
Pressed Glass, Celery, Ribbon	22.50
Pressed Glass, Celery, Roman Key, Frosted, Scalloped, 9 In.Tall	45.00
Pressed Glass, Celery, Rose In Snow	8.00
Pressed Glass, Celery, Rose Sprig, Standard	25.00
Pressed Glass, Celery, Rosette	15.00
Pressed Glass, Celery, Sandwich Loop, Flint, 8 1/2 In.Tall	25.00
Pressed Glass, Celery, Sawtooth	19.00
Pressed Glass, Celery, Sawtooth & Tulip	30.00
Pressed Glass, Celery, Sawtooth, Notched Edge	30.00
Pressed Glass, Celery, Star & Oval, Diamond Medallion	8.50
Pressed Glass, Celery, Stippled Star	16.00 To 17.50
Pressed Glass, Celery, Swan	18.00
Pressed Glass, Celery, Texas Blue Bell, Clear	17.00
Pressed Glass, Celery, Three Faces	15.00
Pressed Glass, Celery, Torpedo	25.00
Pressed Glass, Celery, Triangular Prism, Flint, Pair	28.00
Pressed Glass, Celery, Tulip & Sawtooth	45.00
Pressed Glass, Celery, Two Panel, Blue, 7 1/4 In.Tall	29.50
Pressed Glass, Celery, U.S.Coin, 1892 Quarters	140.00
Pressed Glass, Celery, Vernon Honeycomb, 10 In., Flint	40.00
Pressed Glass, Celery, Virginia	9.00
Pressed Glass, Celery, Waffle, Flint	39.50
Pressed Glass, Celery, Washboard	17.50
Pressed Glass, Celery, Westward Ho	18.00 To 95.00
Pressed Glass, Celery, York Herringbone	9.00
Pressed Glass, Celery, 1, 000-Eye	14.50
Pressed Glass, Center Set, Feather, 4 Piece	67.50
Pressed Glass, Center Set, Wheat & Barley, 4 Piece	68.00
Pressed Glass, Champagne, Ashburton	32.50
Pressed Glass, Champagne, Ashburton, Double Knob Stem, Flint	35.00
Pressed Glass, Champagne, Crystal, Flint	22.00
Pressed Glass, Champagne, Cut Argus	40.00
Pressed Glass, Champagne, Diamond-Quilted, Blue	18.50
Pressed Glass, Champagne, Fine Prism, Rayed Base	22.50
Pressed Glass, Champagne, Honeycomb, Flint	15.00
Pressed Glass, Champagne, Huber	12.00 To 18.00
Pressed Glass, Champagne, Magnet & Grape, Frosted Leaf, Flint	65.00
Pressed Glass, Champagne, New Jersey	18.00
Pressed Glass, Champagne, Umbilicated Sawtooth	30.00
Pressed Glass, Champagne, Waffle & Thumbprint	32.50
Pressed Glass, Champagne, Waffle & Thumbprint, Flint	37.50
Pressed Glass, Champagne, Washington, Flint	55.00
Pressed Glass, Child's Set, Embossed Woolie Sheep In Grass, 3 Piece	65.00
Pressed Glass, Child's Set, Sandwich Ivy, Flint	225.00
Pressed Glass, Claret, Ashburton	32.50
Pressed Glass, Claret, Frosted Flower, Signed 'locke Art'	75.00
Pressed Glass, Comb Case, Daisy & Button, Blue, Hanging	57.50
Pressed Glass, Compote, Actress, Clear, Cover, 8 In.High	72.50
Pressed Glass, Compote, Actress, Covered	130.00
Pressed Glass, Compote, Alabama, Open, 8 In.Tall	35.00

Pressed Glass, Compote, Apollo, Open	15.00
Pressed Glass, Compote, Ball & Swirl, Open, 5 In.Tall	13.00
Pressed Glass, Compote, Barberry, Open	22.50
Pressed Glass, Compote, Barberry, 8 1/2 In. .... *Illus*	35.00
Pressed Glass, Compote, Beaded Dart Band, Open	18.50
Pressed Glass, Compote, Beaded Grape Medallion, Cover, 8 1/4 In.Tall	42.50
Pressed Glass, Compote, Bellflower, Single Vine, Ribbed, Scalloped, Flint	35.00
Pressed Glass, Compote, Bird & Strawberry, Clear, Cover	55.00
Pressed Glass, Compote, Bird & Strawberry, Covered	30.00
Pressed Glass, Compote, Blackberry, Daisy, & Plume	45.00
Pressed Glass, Compote, Bleeding Heart, Open, Round	18.00
Pressed Glass, Compote, Bleeding Heart, Open, 7 In.	19.00
Pressed Glass, Compote, Block, Baluster Base, 6 1/2 In.Diameter	42.00
Pressed Glass, Compote, Broken Column, Covered, High Stem	24.50
Pressed Glass, Compote, Broken Column, 8 In.Diameter, 6 In.Tall	27.50
Pressed Glass, Compote, Buckle & Diamond, 10 1/2 In.Tall	25.00
Pressed Glass, Compote, Button Band	15.00
Pressed Glass, Compote, Cable	28.00
Pressed Glass, Compote, Cable, Smocking, Flint	27.50
Pressed Glass, Compote, Cameo, Open	16.50
Pressed Glass, Compote, Candy, Daisy & Leaf, Semicut, 8 In.High	17.50
Pressed Glass, Compote, Candy, Star & Button, 8 In.High	15.00
Pressed Glass, Compote, Cape Cod, Covered	35.00
Pressed Glass, Compote, Cape Cod, Open, 7 7/8 In.Diameter	35.00
Pressed Glass, Compote, Cathedral, Amber, Open	38.00
Pressed Glass, Compote, Cord Drapery, Clear, Open	32.50
Pressed Glass, Compote, Crystal Wedding, Clear	10.00
Pressed Glass, Compote, Crystal Wedding, Cover, 7 In.Tall	42.50
Pressed Glass, Compote, Crystal Wedding, Cover, 10 1/2 In.Tall	27.00
Pressed Glass, Compote, Crystal Wedding, 6 In.Tall	37.50
Pressed Glass, Compote, Cupid's Hunt	40.00
Pressed Glass, Compote, Curtain, Open, 9 In.	17.50
Pressed Glass, Compote, Curtain, 8 In.	12.00
Pressed Glass, Compote, Cut Log, 6 In.Tall	11.00
Pressed Glass, Compote, Daisy & Button With Cross Bars, Covered	35.00
Pressed Glass, Compote, Daisy & Button, Fluted, Clear, 8 In.Tall	32.50
Pressed Glass, Compote, Daisy & Button, Thumbprint, Green	30.00
Pressed Glass, Compote, Dakota, Clear, Etched, Open, 6 In.	18.50
Pressed Glass, Compote, Diamond Medallion, Open, 5 1/4 In.Tall	8.00
Pressed Glass, Compote, Diamond Point & Bull's-Eye, Clear, 3 In.Tall	36.00
Pressed Glass, Compote, Diamond Point & Bull's-Eye, Clear, 6 In.Tall	45.00
Pressed Glass, Compote, Diamond Rosette, Flint	50.00
Pressed Glass, Compote, Diamond Thumbprint	30.00
Pressed Glass, Compote, Diamond Thumbprint, 11 1/2 In.Diameter, 9 In.High	125.00
Pressed Glass, Compote, Diamond, Blue, Cover, 11 In.Tall, 8 In.Wide	49.50
Pressed Glass, Compote, Dolphin, Frosted Stand	55.00
Pressed Glass, Compote, Double Frosted Ribbon, Covered	48.50
Pressed Glass, Compote, Egyptian, 7 1/2 In. .... *Illus*	75.00
Pressed Glass, Compote, Egytian, Cover, 12 In.Tall, 8 In.Diameter	65.00
Pressed Glass, Compote, Electric, Covered	35.00
Pressed Glass, Compote, Etched Grasshopper, Covered, 9 In.	35.00
Pressed Glass, Compote, Eyewinker, Scalloped Top	60.00
Pressed Glass, Compote, Fan, Diamond, Cover, 7 1/2 In.Diameter & Tall	19.50
Pressed Glass, Compote, Feather Duster, Cover, 6 In.High	28.00
Pressed Glass, Compote, Feather, Open	15.00
Pressed Glass, Compote, Finecut, Blue, Open	45.00
Pressed Glass, Compote, Fishscale, Open	14.50
Pressed Glass, Compote, Florida Palm, Cover, 7 In.Tall	25.00
Pressed Glass, Compote, Flowered Scroll, Cover, 7 In.High	24.00
Pressed Glass, Compote, Flying Stork, Cover, 8 In.High	40.00
Pressed Glass, Compote, Frosted Etched, Open, 6 In.High, Pair	15.00
Pressed Glass, Compote, Frosted Lion, Open, Pedestal	25.00
Pressed Glass, Compote, Frosted Lion, Open, Standard, 6 In.Diameter	25.00
Pressed Glass, Compote, Frosted Lion, Oval, Footed, Rampant Lion Cover	45.00
Pressed Glass, Compote, Frosted Lion, Standard, Lion & Stump Cover	55.00
Pressed Glass, Compote, Frosted Pheasant, 101 Border	30.00

Pressed Glass, Compote, Barberry, 8 1/2 In.
See Page 376

Pressed Glass, Compote, Egyptian, 7 1/2 In.
See Page 376

Pressed Glass, Compote, Grape & Festoon, Stippled, 8 In.	36.00
Pressed Glass, Compote, Grape & Festoon, Stippled, 9 In.	40.00
Pressed Glass, Compote, Grape Festoon, Pedestal Base, Stippled, Cover	27.00
Pressed Glass, Compote, Grape, Low Stem, 8 In.	6.50
Pressed Glass, Compote, Greek Key, Green	40.00
Pressed Glass, Compote, Hand, Frosted Stem, Open, 9 In.High	37.50
Pressed Glass, Compote, Heart Stem, Covered, 7 In.Tall	27.00
Pressed Glass, Compote, Hobnail, Amber, Covered	18.00
Pressed Glass, Compote, Honeycomb & Diamond, Covered	12.50
Pressed Glass, Compote, Honeycomb, Covered, Footed, 7 1/2 In.Diameter, Flint	40.00
Pressed Glass, Compote, Honeycomb, Flint	22.50
Pressed Glass, Compote, Horn Of Plenty, Open, Horn Of Plenty In Base, 8 In.	20.00
Pressed Glass, Compote, Horn Of Plenty, Open, Horn Of Plenty In Base, 10 In.	50.00
Pressed Glass, Compote, Horn Of Plenty, Waffle Design In Base, Covered, Pair	140.00
Pressed Glass, Compote, Horn Of Plenty, Waffle Design In Base, Open, 6 In.	30.00
Pressed Glass, Compote, Horn Of Plenty, Waffle Design In Base, Open, 7 In.	30.00
Pressed Glass, Compote, Horseshoe, Cover, 8 In.High	46.00
Pressed Glass, Compote, Jacob's Ladder, Clear, Scalloped Edge, 8 1/4 In.	15.00
Pressed Glass, Compote, Jacob's Ladder, Cover	32.00
Pressed Glass, Compote, Jacob's Ladder, 10 1/2 In.High, 7 In.Diameter, Cover	25.00
Pressed Glass, Compote, Jelly, Droplet Band, Open, Stemmed	4.75
Pressed Glass, Compote, Jelly, Feather, Open	12.00
Pressed Glass, Compote, Jelly, Fish Scale, 4 1/2 In.High	10.00
Pressed Glass, Compote, Jelly, Fish Scale, Open, Stemmed	15.00
Pressed Glass, Compote, Jelly, Frosted Block, Clear	15.00
Pressed Glass, Compote, Jelly, Horsemint	9.00
Pressed Glass, Compote, Jelly, Iowa	12.00
Pressed Glass, Compote, Jelly, Maryland	8.50
Pressed Glass, Compote, Jelly, Paneled Thistle, Sawtooth Rim	15.00
Pressed Glass, Compote, Jelly, Priscilla	18.50
Pressed Glass, Compote, Jelly, States Pattern, Handle, Footed, 4 In.High	22.00
Pressed Glass, Compote, Jelly, Tennessee	15.00
Pressed Glass, Compote, Jelly, Westward Ho, 5 X 5 In.	55.00
Pressed Glass, Compote, Jubilee, Cover, 8 In.Tall	26.00
Pressed Glass, Compote, Lattice, Cover	25.00
Pressed Glass, Compote, Lincoln Drape, Flint	42.00
Pressed Glass, Compote, Lincoln Drape, 8 In.Diameter *Illus*	65.00
Pressed Glass, Compote, Lion, Frosted Lion Finial On Cover	71.50
Pressed Glass, Compote, Log Cabin	87.50
Pressed Glass, Compote, Log Cabin, Covered, Lutten's Cough Drops On Lid	75.00
Pressed Glass, Compote, Loop & Dart, Open	28.50
Pressed Glass, Compote, Loop, Footed, Open, 11 1/2 In.Diameter	20.00

Pressed Glass, Compote,
Lincoln Drape, 8 In.Diameter
See Page 377

Pressed Glass, Compote, Loop, Open, 8 In.Diameter 15.00
Pressed Glass, Compote, Maple Leaf, Covered, 9 In.Diameter 17.50
Pressed Glass, Compote, Maple Leaf, Open 25.00
Pressed Glass, Compote, Marquisette, 7 In.High, 7 In.Diameter, Open 15.00
Pressed Glass, Compote, Mascotte, Open 8.00
Pressed Glass, Compote, Mirror, Open, Standard, Flint 40.00
Pressed Glass, Compote, Missouri, 6 1/2 In. 15.00
Pressed Glass, Compote, Moon & Star, Low Footed, 6 In.Diameter 32.50
Pressed Glass, Compote, Moon & Star, Scalloped Rim, 10 In.Diameter 65.00
Pressed Glass, Compote, Nail, Clear, Etched Leaf Rim, 7 3/4 In. 19.50
Pressed Glass, Compote, New England Pineapple 50.00
Pressed Glass, Compote, New Jersey, Open, 5 In.Deep 12.50
Pressed Glass, Compote, Old Abe, Frosted Eagle, Eagle Finial On Cover 85.00
Pressed Glass, Compote, Paneled Forget-Me-Not, Cover, 7 In.High 35.00
Pressed Glass, Compote, Paneled Thistle 15.00
Pressed Glass, Compote, Paneled Thistle, Open, 8 In.Tall 25.00
Pressed Glass, Compote, Paneled, Covered, Octagonal Sides, Flint 20.00
Pressed Glass, Compote, Paneled Grape, Low, Open 20.00
Pressed Glass, Compote, Pears, Thumbprint, Open, Flint, 4 1/2 In.High 42.50
Pressed Glass, Compote, Pharaoh's Head, Open, 6 In. 12.00
Pressed Glass, Compote, Pleat Panel, 8 In.Tall 47.50
Pressed Glass, Compote, Plume, 6 1/2 In.Diameter 15.00
Pressed Glass, Compote, Plume, 7 In. .... 10.00 To 20.00
Pressed Glass, Compote, Pointed Panel Daisy & Button, Apple Green, Open 38.00
Pressed Glass, Compote, Pointed Paneled Daisy & Button, Open, Stemmed 15.00
Pressed Glass, Compote, Portland Tree Of Life, Frosted Base, Ball Stem 41.00
Pressed Glass, Compote, Portland Tree Of Life, Open, 9 In. 27.50
Pressed Glass, Compote, Princess Feather, Flint, Cover 30.00
Pressed Glass, Compote, Princess Feather, Open .... 14.00 To 15.00
Pressed Glass, Compote, Priscilla, 5 In.Tall 10.00
Pressed Glass, Compote, Psyche & Cupid, Footed 22.00
Pressed Glass, Compote, Psyche & Cupid, Open 24.00
Pressed Glass, Compote, Rayed Flower, Covered, 9 In. 25.00
Pressed Glass, Compote, Ribbon 18.00
Pressed Glass, Compote, Ribbon, Frosted, Cover, 12 In. 30.00
Pressed Glass, Compote, Rose Sprig 14.00
Pressed Glass, Compote, Rose Sprig, Open, 8 1/2 X 5 3/4 In.High 18.50
Pressed Glass, Compote, Royal, Cover, 8 In.Tall 35.00
Pressed Glass, Compote, Sawtooth Top, Tulip Base, 7 1/4 In.Tall 17.50
Pressed Glass, Compote, Sawtooth, Knob Stem, Cover, Flint 59.00
Pressed Glass, Compote, Sawtooth, Open 18.00
Pressed Glass, Compote, Seneca Loop, Flint 30.00
Pressed Glass, Compote, Seneca Loop, 8 1/2 In.Diameter, Flint 30.00
Pressed Glass, Compote, Seneca Loop, 9 1/2 In. 15.00
Pressed Glass, Compote, Shell & Tassel, Open, 8 In. 29.50
Pressed Glass, Compote, Shell & Tassel, Square, 6 1/4 In.High 25.00
Pressed Glass, Compote, Smocking, Footed, Flint 70.00

Pressed Glass, Compote, Spearhead, Covered	14.00
Pressed Glass, Compote, Sprig, Covered, 12 In.	32.50
Pressed Glass, Compote, Sprig, Open, 6 3/4 In.High	12.50
Pressed Glass, Compote, Stippled Band, Flint	12.00
Pressed Glass, Compote, Sunk Daisy	19.50
Pressed Glass, Compote, Sweetmeat, Cover, 6 In.Tall	35.00
Pressed Glass, Compote, Three Face	28.00
Pressed Glass, Compote, Thumbprint, Bakewell Pears, Open, Flint	42.50
Pressed Glass, Compote, Thumbprint, Covered, 6 In.Diameter	15.00
Pressed Glass, Compote, Thumbprint, Footed, 6 3/4 In.Diameter, Flint	25.00
Pressed Glass, Compote, Tree Of Life, Hand Stem, Low	27.50
Pressed Glass, Compote, Tulip & Sawtooth, 9 In.Diameter, Flint	40.00
Pressed Glass, Compote, U.S.Coin Glass	350.00
Pressed Glass, Compote, U.S.Coin Glass, Half Dollar, Covered, 8 In.Diameter	450.00
Pressed Glass, Compote, Utah, High Lid, 10 1/2 In.	15.00
Pressed Glass, Compote, Valencia Waffle, Blue, Cover, 12 In.Tall	80.00
Pressed Glass, Compote, Valencia Waffle, Blue, Open, 8 In.	27.50
Pressed Glass, Compote, Valencia Waffle, Clear, Open, 6 1/2 In.	12.50
Pressed Glass, Compote, Viking, Open	12.50
Pressed Glass, Compote, Waffle, Thumbprint, Footed, Flint, 7 In.Tall	30.00
Pressed Glass, Compote, Westward Ho	85.00
Pressed Glass, Compote, Westward Ho, Cover, 12 In.	65.00
Pressed Glass, Compote, Westward Ho, Cover, 14 In.	185.00
Pressed Glass, Compote, Westward Ho, Oval, 9 In.	110.00
Pressed Glass, Compote, Westward Ho, 7 3/4 In. .... *Illus*	100.00
Pressed Glass, Compote, Wildflower, Apple Green, 7 In.Diameter, 4 In.Tall	22.00
Pressed Glass, Compote, Willow Oak, Sapphire Blue	45.00
Pressed Glass, Compote, Windflower	19.00
Pressed Glass, Compote, 1, 000-Eye, Apple Green, Square, 8 In.	32.50
Pressed Glass, Compote, 1, 000-Eye, Apple Green, Turned Up Corners	38.50
Pressed Glass, Condiment Set, Child's, Hickman, Five Pieces	22.50
Pressed Glass, Cordial, Daisy & Button, Cross Bar	12.00
Pressed Glass, Cordial, Dew & Raindrop, Set Of 6	32.00
Pressed Glass, Cordial, Duchess Loop, Flint	10.00
Pressed Glass, Cordial, Feather	50.00
Pressed Glass, Cordial, Feather, Rounded Top	40.00
Pressed Glass, Cordial, Fine Cut & Block	34.50
Pressed Glass, Cordial, Flute, Knob Stem	12.00
Pressed Glass, Cordial, Hairpin, Thumbprint, Flint	20.00
Pressed Glass, Cordial, Hobnail	8.00
Pressed Glass, Cordial, Hobstar	8.00
Pressed Glass, Cordial, Pine Tree, Green	40.00
Pressed Glass, Cordial, Seneca Loop	25.00
Pressed Glass, Cornucopia, Daisy & Button, Clear, Hand Holding, 5 1/4 In.	18.50

Pressed Glass, Creamer & Sugar, see Pressed Glass, Sugar & Creamer

Pressed Glass, Compote, Westward Ho, 7 3/4 In.

Pressed Glass, Creamer, Actress 45.00
Pressed Glass, Creamer, Alhambra, Iowa City, Bubbles 95.00
Pressed Glass, Creamer, Arched Ovals 16.00
Pressed Glass, Creamer, Argus, Flint 48.00
Pressed Glass, Creamer, Austrian, Greentown 14.50
Pressed Glass, Creamer, Azalea 5.00
Pressed Glass, Creamer, Baltimore Pear 11.50
Pressed Glass, Creamer, Banded Star, Legs 12.00
Pressed Glass, Creamer, Barley Pattern 14.50
Pressed Glass, Creamer, Beaded Grape Medallion 23.00
Pressed Glass, Creamer, Bearded Man, Footed 10.00
Pressed Glass, Creamer, Bedford 18.50
Pressed Glass, Creamer, Bird & Strawberry .... 23.00 To 28.00
Pressed Glass, Creamer, Bleeding Heart, Applied Handle 35.00
Pressed Glass, Creamer, Block & Bar .... 52.00 To 65.00
Pressed Glass, Creamer, Block & Pleat 9.50
Pressed Glass, Creamer, Blue, Opalescent, Jefferson 20.00
Pressed Glass, Creamer, Broken Column, Red Notch, Applied Handle ... 75.00
Pressed Glass, Creamer, Broken Column, 4 1/4 In.High 27.50
Pressed Glass, Creamer, Buckle & English Hobnail 9.50
Pressed Glass, Creamer, Buckle, Applied Handle, Pedestal Foot 21.50
Pressed Glass, Creamer, Cameo, Classic Medallion 17.50
Pressed Glass, Creamer, Cane, Individual 8.50
Pressed Glass, Creamer, Cathedral 29.50
Pressed Glass, Creamer, Chain 17.50
Pressed Glass, Creamer, Chain & Shield 18.00
Pressed Glass, Creamer, Chain & Star .... 10.00 To 12.00
Pressed Glass, Creamer, Classic 40.00
Pressed Glass, Creamer, Classic Log, Footed 60.00
Pressed Glass, Creamer, Classic Medallion 17.50
Pressed Glass, Creamer, Clear Diagonal Band .... *Illus* 15.00
Pressed Glass, Creamer, Colorado, Green, Gold .... 35.00 To 45.00
Pressed Glass, Creamer, Columbia Coin 80.00

Pressed Glass, Creamer, Clear Diagonal Band

Pressed Glass, Creamer, Cupid & Psyche, Venus 22.00
Pressed Glass, Creamer, Cupid & Venus 17.00
Pressed Glass, Creamer, Cut Log 9.50
Pressed Glass, Creamer, Cut Log, Low Base 8.50
Pressed Glass, Creamer, Dahlia, Blue 22.00
Pressed Glass, Creamer, Daisy & Button With Crossbar, Amber, 3 In. .. 18.50
Pressed Glass, Creamer, Delaware, Clear, Gold 10.50
Pressed Glass, Creamer, Delaware, Green 37.50
Pressed Glass, Creamer, Diamond Peg, Emerald Green, Individual 15.00
Pressed Glass, Creamer, Diamond Point With Panels, Applied Handle ... 30.00
Pressed Glass, Creamer, Diamond Point, Scalloped 16.00
Pressed Glass, Creamer, Diamond, Opalescent, Miniature 35.00
Pressed Glass, Creamer, Dolphin 35.00
Pressed Glass, Creamer, Dolphin, Frosted Base 67.50
Pressed Glass, Creamer, Double Spearpoint, Pedestal, Footed 10.00
Pressed Glass, Creamer, Egyptian .... 22.00 To 24.50

Pressed Glass, Creamer, Emblem	40.00
Pressed Glass, Creamer, Empress	14.75
Pressed Glass, Creamer, Esther, Clear, Engraved 1000 Islands 1896	24.00
Pressed Glass, Creamer, Etched Mascotte, Pedestal	22.50
Pressed Glass, Creamer, Flamingo Habitat	23.00
Pressed Glass, Creamer, Forget-Me-Not, Amber, Ribbed	37.50
Pressed Glass, Creamer, Forget-Me-Not, Ribbed	22.50
Pressed Glass, Creamer, Frosted Circle	30.00
Pressed Glass, Creamer, Frosted Fan With Diamond, Footed	15.00
Pressed Glass, Creamer, Frosted Lion	25.00
Pressed Glass, Creamer, Garfield Drape	19.50
Pressed Glass, Creamer, Gibson Girl	40.00
Pressed Glass, Creamer, Good Luck, Frosted, Footed	22.50
Pressed Glass, Creamer, Green, Gold	37.50
Pressed Glass, Creamer, Heart & Thumbprint	14.00
Pressed Glass, Creamer, Heart, Circa	65.00
Pressed Glass, Creamer, Hickman	13.50
Pressed Glass, Creamer, Honeycomb, Frosted, Footed, Applied Handle	17.50
Pressed Glass, Creamer, Horn Of Plenty, Crimped Applied Handle, Footed	90.00
Pressed Glass, Creamer, Horseshoe	22.00
Pressed Glass, Creamer, Huber, Clear, Scalloped Rim	12.00
Pressed Glass, Creamer, Hummingbird	24.00
Pressed Glass, Creamer, Hummingbird, Footed	27.50
Pressed Glass, Creamer, Individual, Texas, Gold	7.50
Pressed Glass, Creamer, Inverted Fern, Applied Handle, Flint	55.00
Pressed Glass, Creamer, Inverted Fern, 6 In.Tall	45.00
Pressed Glass, Creamer, Jacob's Ladder	20.00
Pressed Glass, Creamer, Legged Banded Star	9.50
Pressed Glass, Creamer, Liberty Bell, Applied Handle	62.50
Pressed Glass, Creamer, Lily Of The Valley	25.00
Pressed Glass, Creamer, Lily Of The Valley, Footed	35.00
Pressed Glass, Creamer, Lincoln Drape	125.00
Pressed Glass, Creamer, Lincoln Drape, Flint	165.00
Pressed Glass, Creamer, Lion, Clear, Frosted Lion On Base	35.00
Pressed Glass, Creamer, Loop & Fans	10.50
Pressed Glass, Creamer, Loop, 6 In.High	17.50
Pressed Glass, Creamer, Lotus	12.00
Pressed Glass, Creamer, Manhattan, Gold	3.50
Pressed Glass, Creamer, Maple Leaf, Frosted Footed	25.00
Pressed Glass, Creamer, Minerva	28.00
Pressed Glass, Creamer, Minerva, Footed	32.50
Pressed Glass, Creamer, Moon & Star	30.00
Pressed Glass, Creamer, Moon & Star, Applied Handle	35.00
Pressed Glass, Creamer, Nailhead	16.50
Pressed Glass, Creamer, New Hampshire, Large	14.50
Pressed Glass, Creamer, New Jersey, Gold On Loops	15.00
Pressed Glass, Creamer, Open Rose	22.00
Pressed Glass, Creamer, Paneled Acorn Band, Applied Handle	30.00
Pressed Glass, Creamer, Paneled Cane	10.50
Pressed Glass, Creamer, Paneled Forget-Me-Not	16.00
Pressed Glass, Creamer, Paneled Grape, Clear	10.00
Pressed Glass, Creamer, Paneled Sunflower	15.00
Pressed Glass, Creamer, Pharaoh's Head	12.50
Pressed Glass, Creamer, Pineapple & Fan	15.00
Pressed Glass, Creamer, Pittsburgh	13.50
Pressed Glass, Creamer, Pleat & Panel	12.00
Pressed Glass, Creamer, Quilt & Flute	9.50
Pressed Glass, Creamer, Regal Pattern	27.50
Pressed Glass, Creamer, Ribbed Opal	15.00
Pressed Glass, Creamer, Ribbon, Frosted	20.00
Pressed Glass, Creamer, Roman Rosette	15.00
Pressed Glass, Creamer, Roman Rosette, Frosted, Footed	15.00
Pressed Glass, Creamer, Roman Rosette, 5 In.High	12.00
Pressed Glass, Creamer, Rose In Snow *Illus*	20.00
Pressed Glass, Creamer, Rose In Snow, Square	22.50
Pressed Glass, Creamer, Royal, Belmont Glass Co.	15.00

Pressed Glass, Creamer, Rose In Snow
See Page 381

Pressed Glass, Creamer, Smocking, Applied Handle	90.00
Pressed Glass, Creamer, Snail	22.50
Pressed Glass, Creamer, Snowflake, Ruby Flashed, Gold Trim, Pedestal Base	35.00
Pressed Glass, Creamer, Stork, Clear	20.00
Pressed Glass, Creamer, Sunburst	15.00
Pressed Glass, Creamer, Sunk Daisy	9.50
Pressed Glass, Creamer, Sunk Honeycomb, Red, Individual	16.00
Pressed Glass, Creamer, Teardrops, Blue, Flowered, Gold	45.00
Pressed Glass, Creamer, Texas	8.50 To 9.50
Pressed Glass, Creamer, Three Face	52.50
Pressed Glass, Creamer, Thumbprint, Ruby	20.00
Pressed Glass, Creamer, Torpedo	22.50
Pressed Glass, Creamer, Tree Of Life	30.00
Pressed Glass, Creamer, Two Band	8.00
Pressed Glass, Creamer, U.S.Coin, 1892 Quarters	160.00
Pressed Glass, Creamer, Victoria, Flint	110.00
Pressed Glass, Creamer, Waffle	85.00
Pressed Glass, Creamer, Waffle, Flint	90.00
Pressed Glass, Creamer, Westward Ho	50.00 To 65.00
Pressed Glass, Creamer, Wheat & Barley	10.00 To 17.50
Pressed Glass, Creamer, Wheat & Barley, Footed	27.50
Pressed Glass, Creamer, Wildflower, Blue, Decorated, 5 1/4 In.High	9.00
Pressed Glass, Creamer, Willow Oak, Amber	22.50
Pressed Glass, Creamer, Windflower	13.00
Pressed Glass, Creamer, Windflower, Footed	22.50
Pressed Glass, Creamer, Wyoming	12.00
Pressed Glass, Creamer, York Herringbone, Green, Individual	13.00
Pressed Glass, Creamer, 1, 000-Eye, Opalescent, Footed	42.00
Pressed Glass, Cruet, see also Cruet	
Pressed Glass, Cruet, Amber	44.00
Pressed Glass, Cruet, Big Button	18.50
Pressed Glass, Cruet, Block & Iris	15.00
Pressed Glass, Cruet, Button & Arches	18.00
Pressed Glass, Cruet, Challinor, Pink, Clear Stopper	65.00
Pressed Glass, Cruet, Cottage, Stopper	18.50
Pressed Glass, Cruet, Daisy & Button, Amber	24.50
Pressed Glass, Cruet, Daisy & Button, Amber, Blown, Clear Stopper	35.00
Pressed Glass, Cruet, Daisy & Cube, Amber	35.00
Pressed Glass, Cruet, Daisy & Fern, Yellow	17.50
Pressed Glass, Cruet, Deer & Pine, Amber	16.50
Pressed Glass, Cruet, Dewey, Green, Stopper, Greentown	48.00 To 65.00
Pressed Glass, Cruet, Feather	18.50
Pressed Glass, Cruet, Fernburst	9.75
Pressed Glass, Cruet, Hobstars, Diamonds, Rosettes, 5 1/2 In.Tall	11.50
Pressed Glass, Cruet, Jacob's Ladder, Maltese Cross For Stopper	65.00
Pressed Glass, Cruet, Jewel, Stopper	15.00
Pressed Glass, Cruet, Paneled Thistle	12.00

Pressed Glass, Cruet, Paneled, 7 In.High	7.00
Pressed Glass, Cruet, Peacock Feather, Pontil	15.00
Pressed Glass, Cruet, Purple, Three-Way Lip, Enamel Dot Decor, Cut Stopper	55.00
Pressed Glass, Cruet, Vinegar, Stopper	4.50
Pressed Glass, Cruet, 1, 000-Eye	15.00
Pressed Glass, Cup & Saucer, Eagle Over Panel	100.00
Pressed Glass, Cup Plate, Barberry, Oval Berries	11.50
Pressed Glass, Cup Plate, Leaf Border, Clear, Flint	14.00
Pressed Glass, Cup Plate, Rayed Center, Clear, Hexagonal Shape, Flint	9.50
Pressed Glass, Cup Plate, Snakeskin & Dot	9.00
Pressed Glass, Cup, Button Arches, Red & Clear, Mattie, Hot Springs, Arkansas	16.00
Pressed Glass, Cup, Eye, Clear, High Pedestal	2.00
Pressed Glass, Cup, Lacy Medallion, Green, Souvenir Holton, Kansas	12.00
Pressed Glass, Cup, Lion's Head, Miniature	13.00
Pressed Glass, Cup, O'hara Diamond, Red, Mug Shape	15.00
Pressed Glass, Cup, Punch, Daisy & Button, Low Side Handle	14.00
Pressed Glass, Cup, Punch, Deer & Pine Tree, Set Of 6	55.00
Pressed Glass, Cup, Punch, Delaware, Rose	18.00
Pressed Glass, Cup, Punch, Diamond & Fan, Set Of 6	18.00
Pressed Glass, Cup, Punch, Empress	8.50
Pressed Glass, Cup, Punch, Flute, Marked Pres Cut, 6	15.00
Pressed Glass, Cup, Punch, Heart & Thumbprint	7.50
Pressed Glass, Cup, Punch, Hobnail, 3 In.High	5.00
Pressed Glass, Cup, Punch, Michigan	7.50
Pressed Glass, Cup, Punch, Minnesota	3.00
Pressed Glass, Cup, Punch, Paneled Grape, 10	20.00
Pressed Glass, Cup, Punch, Pres Cut, 8	25.00
Pressed Glass, Cup, Punch, Three Fruit, Clear	5.00
Pressed Glass, Cup, Torpedo	12.50
Pressed Glass, Decanter, Bull's-Eye With Diamond Point, Green, Flint	38.00
Pressed Glass, Decanter, Bull's-Eye, Flint	30.00
Pressed Glass, Decanter, Cord & Tassel, Doughnut Stopper	15.00
Pressed Glass, Decanter, Daisy & Button With Narcissus, Clear, Stopper	30.00
Pressed Glass, Decanter, Loop, Stopper, 13 1/2 In.High	15.00
Pressed Glass, Decanter, Peacock Feather, Amethyst, Handle	32.50
Pressed Glass, Decanter, Plain Base, Rib At Neck, Rib Stopper, Flint	85.00
Pressed Glass, Decanter, Sandwich Star, Flint	35.00
Pressed Glass, Decanter, Waffle & Thumbprint, Flint, Patent Stopper, Pint	75.00
Pressed Glass, Decanter, Waffle & Thumbprint, Flint, Stopper	85.00
Pressed Glass, Decanter, Waffle & Thumbprint, Pewter Stopper, Flint	75.00
Pressed Glass, Dessert, Actress, Footed	8.50
Pressed Glass, Dish, Banana, Colorado, Clear, Footed, 7 1/4 X 5 1/4 In.	12.00
Pressed Glass, Dish, Banana, Diamond & Fan	10.00
Pressed Glass, Dish, Banana, Ladders, Miniature	12.50
Pressed Glass, Dish, Banded Portland	12.00
Pressed Glass, Dish, Basket Weave, Green, 6 1/2 In.Diameter	15.00
Pressed Glass, Dish, Block, Clear, Oblong, Upturned Sides	9.50
Pressed Glass, Dish, Boat Shape, Maidens Blush, 8 3/4 In.Diameter	17.50
Pressed Glass, Dish, Broken Column, Rectangular, 7 X 4 1/2 In.	22.50
Pressed Glass, Dish, Butter, see Pressed Glass, Butter	
Pressed Glass, Dish, Candy, Basket Weave, Green, Opalescent	10.00
Pressed Glass, Dish, Candy, Colorado, Green, Gold, Ruffled Top, 7 1/2 In.	15.00
Pressed Glass, Dish, Candy, Colorado, Tricornered, Blue, Gold	21.50
Pressed Glass, Dish, Candy, Crisscross, Blue, Fluted, Footed, 3 In.	18.00
Pressed Glass, Dish, Candy, Diamond & Fan, Flat, 8 X 8 In.	8.50
Pressed Glass, Dish, Candy, Green, Basket Weave, 5 1/4 In.Diameter, 2 3/4 In.	10.00
Pressed Glass, Dish, Candy, Heart, Triangular	5.00
Pressed Glass, Dish, Candy, Rainbow Iridescence, Clear, Covered, Pedestal	15.00
Pressed Glass, Dish, Candy, Windmill	22.50
Pressed Glass, Dish, Cheese & Cracker, Colorado, Clear	15.00
Pressed Glass, Dish, Cheese, Actress, Covered	95.00 To 175.00
Pressed Glass, Dish, Cheese, Actress, Frosted	125.00
Pressed Glass, Dish, Cheese, Owl & Pussycat	150.00
Pressed Glass, Dish, Cheese, Snail Covered	65.00
Pressed Glass, Dish, Child, Tulip & Honeycomb, Scalloped Edge	9.00
Pressed Glass, Dish, Colorado, Green & Gold, Footed, Fluted	27.50

Pressed Glass, Dish, Colorado, Green, 3 Sided, Footed, Gold 23.00
Pressed Glass, Dish, Cut Log, Rectangular 9.50
Pressed Glass, Dish, Daisy & Button, Amber, Fan Shape 6.00
Pressed Glass, Dish, Daisy & Button, Fan Shape, Blue 25.00
Pressed Glass, Dish, Dessert, Daisy & Button, Amber, 4 1/2 In.Square 5.00
Pressed Glass, Dish, Dome Rabbit, Amber, Cover 110.00
Pressed Glass, Dish, Dome Rabbit, Blue, Cover 115.00
Pressed Glass, Dish, Etched Vine, Red Flashed, Oval, Oblong Star Bottom 12.50
Pressed Glass, Dish, Fan & Fleur-De-Lis, Green, Opalescent, N Mark, 3 1/2 In. 25.00
Pressed Glass, Dish, Frosted Lion, Covered, Footed, Oval, 8 In. 20.00
Pressed Glass, Dish, Harp, Green, Deep, 6 3/4 In.Diameter, Flint 47.50
Pressed Glass, Dish, Heart Shape, Blue 15.00
Pressed Glass, Dish, Hobnail, Clear, Oblong 10.00
Pressed Glass, Dish, Honey, Ashburton, Flint 7.00
Pressed Glass, Dish, Honey, Cable, Flint 8.50
Pressed Glass, Dish, Honey, Hamilton, Flint 4.00
Pressed Glass, Dish, Honey, Horn Of Plenty, Covered, Rectangular 525.00
Pressed Glass, Dish, Honey, Horn Of Plenty, Flint .... 10.00 To 11.00
Pressed Glass, Dish, Honey, Stippled Birch Leaf, Footed 32.50
Pressed Glass, Dish, Horn Of Plenty, Open, Scalloped Edge, 7 In.Diameter 15.00
Pressed Glass, Dish, Horn Of Plenty, Oval, 10 X 6 3/4 In. 55.00
Pressed Glass, Dish, Ivy In Snow, Oval 4.50
Pressed Glass, Dish, Olive, Minnesota, Oval, Gold 5.50
Pressed Glass, Dish, Paneled Daisy & Button, Green, 3 Rounded Corners 30.00
Pressed Glass, Dish, Paneled Thistle, Rectangular, Mark Bee 18.00
Pressed Glass, Dish, Pheasant Covered 30.00
Pressed Glass, Dish, Pickle, Acorn, Footed 12.50
Pressed Glass, Dish, Pickle, Actress 30.00
Pressed Glass, Dish, Pickle, Cable & Lion, Head Forms Handles 15.00
Pressed Glass, Dish, Pickle, Daisy & Button, Clear, Footed Silver Holder 45.00
Pressed Glass, Dish, Pickle, Fleur-De-Lis, 9 3/4 In.Long 8.50
Pressed Glass, Dish, Pickle, Floral Diamond 7.00
Pressed Glass, Dish, Pickle, Loop & Jewel 6.50
Pressed Glass, Dish, Pickle, Rose In Snow 12.50
Pressed Glass, Dish, Pickle, Rose In Snow, Double, 8 In.Long, 7 In.Diameter 52.50
Pressed Glass, Dish, Pleat & Panel, Covered 25.00
Pressed Glass, Dish, Priscilla, Knob Finial, Cover, 6 In.Diameter 27.50
Pressed Glass, Dish, 'remember The Maine, ' Covered 29.00
Pressed Glass, Dish, Sawtooth, 4 In.Diameter, 4 .... 10.00
Pressed Glass, Dish, Soap, Fine Cut & Block, Apple Green 22.50
Pressed Glass, Dish, States 12.00
Pressed Glass, Dish, States, Round, Handled 22.50
Pressed Glass, Dish, Tree Of Life, Portland, Silver Plate Holder 45.00
Pressed Glass, Dish, Vegetable, Actress 60.00
Pressed Glass, Dish, Vegetable, Buckle, Open 8.50
Pressed Glass, Eggcup, Argus, Flint 18.00
Pressed Glass, Eggcup, Ashburton .... 14.00 To 18.00
Pressed Glass, Eggcup, Banded Buckle 16.75
Pressed Glass, Eggcup, Barberry 15.00
Pressed Glass, Eggcup, Bull's-Eye & Diamond Point 100.00
Pressed Glass, Eggcup, Cable, Flint .... 22.00 To 29.75
Pressed Glass, Eggcup, Colonial, Flint 7.50
Pressed Glass, Eggcup, Crystal, Flint .... 11.00 To 15.00
Pressed Glass, Eggcup, Excelsior .... 19.00 To 20.00
Pressed Glass, Eggcup, Fine Rib, Flint 21.00
Pressed Glass, Eggcup, Flute .... 7.00 To 13.50
Pressed Glass, Eggcup, Flute, 6 .... 20.00
Pressed Glass, Eggcup, Hamilton, Flint .... 19.00 To 22.00
Pressed Glass, Eggcup, Herringbone Band 8.50
Pressed Glass, Eggcup, Hexagonal Flute 15.00
Pressed Glass, Eggcup, Honeycomb 5.00
Pressed Glass, Eggcup, Horn Of Plenty, Flint .... 23.00 To 26.00
Pressed Glass, Eggcup, Horn Of Plenty, 3 3/4 In. 22.50
Pressed Glass, Eggcup, Inverted Fern, Rayed Base, Flint 18.00
Pressed Glass, Eggcup, Lincoln Drape, Flint .... 19.00 To 37.00
Pressed Glass, Eggcup, Moon & Star 15.00

Pressed Glass, Eggcup, New England Pineapple, Flint .... 16.00 To 30.00
Pressed Glass, Eggcup, Open Rose 13.50
Pressed Glass, Eggcup, Paneled Ovals, Flint 18.50
Pressed Glass, Eggcup, Pineapple, Flint 32.00
Pressed Glass, Eggcup, Raindrop, Double 10.00
Pressed Glass, Eggcup, Ribbed Ivy, Flint .... 16.50 To 20.00
Pressed Glass, Eggcup, Ribbed Palm, Flint 20.00
Pressed Glass, Eggcup, Scroll With Flowers, Double Handles 14.75
Pressed Glass, Eggcup, Umbilicated Sawtooth, Flint .... 15.00 To 16.50
Pressed Glass, Eggcup, Waffle 18.00
Pressed Glass, Eggcup, Waffle & Thumbprint .... 20.00 To 22.00
Pressed Glass, Figurine, Hat, Daisy & Button, Amber 15.00
Pressed Glass, Fly Trap, Free Blown, Applied Neck Ring, Feet, 6 1/2 In.High 135.00
Pressed Glass, Frosted Ribbon With Double Bands .... *Illus* 20.00
Pressed Glass, Glass, Bottoms Up, Caramel 25.00
Pressed Glass, Glass, Juice, Sandwich, Dark Green 1.75
Pressed Glass, Glass, Roly Poly, King's 500, Blue 25.00
Pressed Glass, Glass, Shot, Massachusetts 7.50
Pressed Glass, Glass, Shot, Pennsylvania 7.50
Pressed Glass, Glass, Shot, 'thimble, Just A Thimbleful' 7.50
Pressed Glass, Goblet, Acorn 10.50
Pressed Glass, Goblet, Actress, Clear, Footed .... 35.00 To 55.00
Pressed Glass, Goblet, Almond Thumbprint .... 7.50 To 8.00
Pressed Glass, Goblet, Apollo 15.00
Pressed Glass, Goblet, Arabesque 14.00
Pressed Glass, Goblet, Arched Fan 12.50
Pressed Glass, Goblet, Arched Grape .... *Illus* 12.50

Pressed Glass,
Frosted Ribbon With Double Bands

Pressed Glass, Goblet,
Arched Grape

Pressed Glass, Goblet, Argus, Flint .... 17.50 To 26.00
Pressed Glass, Goblet, Ashburton, Flint .... 20.00 To 25.00
Pressed Glass, Goblet, Ashman 18.50
Pressed Glass, Goblet, Austrian, Gold Top 16.50
Pressed Glass, Goblet, Baby Thumbprint 12.00
Pressed Glass, Goblet, Balder 8.00
Pressed Glass, Goblet, Ball & Swirl 9.50
Pressed Glass, Goblet, Banded Beaded Grape Medallion 9.50
Pressed Glass, Goblet, Banded Flute, Flint 13.00
Pressed Glass, Goblet, Banded Portland 24.00
Pressed Glass, Goblet, Banded Sawtooth 9.50
Pressed Glass, Goblet, Banded Stippled Starflower 8.00
Pressed Glass, Goblet, Barberry .... 7.00 To 13.50
Pressed Glass, Goblet, Barley .... 5.00 To 9.75
Pressed Glass, Goblet, Barred Forget-Me-Not 14.75
Pressed Glass, Goblet, Barred Hobnail 12.00
Pressed Glass, Goblet, Beaded Band, Clear 8.50
Pressed Glass, Goblet, Beaded Chain 7.00
Pressed Glass, Goblet, Beaded Grape Medallion .... 12.00 To 16.00

Pressed Glass, Goblet, Beaded Grape Medallion, Opaque 16.50
Pressed Glass, Goblet, Beaded Mirror .... 12.00 To 12.50
Pressed Glass, Goblet, Belcher Loop 10.00
Pressed Glass, Goblet, Bellflower With Loops, Flint 115.00
Pressed Glass, Goblet, Bellflower, Barrel, Knob Stem, Flint .... 22.00 To 30.00
Pressed Glass, Goblet, Bellflower, Coarse Rib, Flint 21.50
Pressed Glass, Goblet, Bellflower, Rayed Base, Flint 20.00
Pressed Glass, Goblet, Bellflower, Straight Sides, Rib, Flint 21.50
Pressed Glass, Goblet, Belted Worcester, Flint 21.00
Pressed Glass, Goblet, Bessimer Flute, Flint .... 14.00 To 24.00
Pressed Glass, Goblet, Bigler, Flaring, Grooved, Flint 29.00
Pressed Glass, Goblet, Bigler, Flint .... 15.00 To 27.00
Pressed Glass, Goblet, Birch Leaf 12.50
Pressed Glass, Goblet, Birds & Roses 8.00
Pressed Glass, Goblet, Birds At Fountain, Opaque 17.50
Pressed Glass, Goblet, Bismarck Star 4.50
Pressed Glass, Goblet, Blackberry Band 9.00
Pressed Glass, Goblet, Bleeding Heart .... 15.00 To 17.50
Pressed Glass, Goblet, Bleeding Heart, Opaque 14.00
Pressed Glass, Goblet, Block With Fan Border 20.00
Pressed Glass, Goblet, Block With Stars 8.50
Pressed Glass, Goblet, Block, Clear 6.50
Pressed Glass, Goblet, Boling 8.00
Pressed Glass, Goblet, Bradford Blackberry, Flint 37.50
Pressed Glass, Goblet, Brilliant, Clear, Flint 20.00
Pressed Glass, Goblet, Broken Column .... *Illus*   10.00
Pressed Glass, Goblet, Brooch Band 9.00
Pressed Glass, Goblet, Brooklyn Flute, Flint 13.60
Pressed Glass, Goblet, Brooklyn, Flint 22.50
Pressed Glass, Goblet, Buckle .... *Illus*   15.00
Pressed Glass, Goblet, Buckle, Flint .... 18.00 To 20.00
Pressed Glass, Goblet, Budded Ivy 15.00
Pressed Glass, Goblet, Bull's-Eye & Broken Column, Flint 54.00
Pressed Glass, Goblet, Bull's-Eye & Daisy, Purple & Gold Trim 22.50
Pressed Glass, Goblet, Bull's-Eye & Diamond Panels 14.50
Pressed Glass, Goblet, Bull's-Eye & Wishbone, Flint 100.00
Pressed Glass, Goblet, Bull's-Eye With Diamond Point, Clear, Flint 50.00
Pressed Glass, Goblet, Bull's-Eye With Fleur-De-Lis, Flint .... 35.00 To 45.00
Pressed Glass, Goblet, Bull's-Eye, Clear, Flint 25.00
Pressed Glass, Goblet, Bull's-Eye, Diamond Point 65.00
Pressed Glass, Goblet, Bull's-Eye, Flint .... 30.00 To 35.00
Pressed Glass, Goblet, Cabbage Rose .... 12.50 To 17.00
Pressed Glass, Goblet, Cable, Flint .... 22.50 To 45.00
Pressed Glass, Goblet, Cable, Lady's Size 80.00
Pressed Glass, Goblet, Canadian .... 16.00 To 25.00
Pressed Glass, Goblet, Cane, Amber 20.00
Pressed Glass, Goblet, Capitol Building, Acorn Design, Ribbed 10.50
Pressed Glass, Goblet, Cardinal Bird .... 21.00 To 24.00
Pressed Glass, Goblet, Chain With Star .... 9.00 To 12.50
Pressed Glass, Goblet, Chain, Opaque 7.00
Pressed Glass, Goblet, Cherry 12.50
Pressed Glass, Goblet, Cherry, Red 5.50
Pressed Glass, Goblet, Chilson, Flint .... 100.00 To 105.00
Pressed Glass, Goblet, Classic, Clear 75.00
Pressed Glass, Goblet, Coin & Dewdrop 7.50
Pressed Glass, Goblet, Colonial With Band Of Diamond Points, Clear, Flint 15.00
Pressed Glass, Goblet, Colonial, Flint .... 10.00 To 22.50
Pressed Glass, Goblet, Colonial, Jefferson .... *Illus*   6.00
Pressed Glass, Goblet, Comet, Clear, Flint .... 20.00 To 60.00
Pressed Glass, Goblet, Crazy Patch 10.00
Pressed Glass, Goblet, Creased Ashburton, Flint 29.50
Pressed Glass, Goblet, Crowfoot 25.00
Pressed Glass, Goblet, Crystal Wedding 18.50
Pressed Glass, Goblet, Crystal, Flint .... 10.00 To 16.00
Pressed Glass, Goblet, Cupid & Venus, Clear .... 27.50 To 37.50
Pressed Glass, Goblet, Currant 14.50

Pressed Glass, Goblet, Cut Argus, Flint, 5 In.Tall 28.50
Pressed Glass, Goblet, Cut Log .... 6.00 To 25.00
Pressed Glass, Goblet, Dahila, Etched 15.00
Pressed Glass, Goblet, Daisies In Oval .... *Illus* 9.00
Pressed Glass, Goblet, Daisy & Button .... 4.50 To 5.75

Pressed Glass, Goblet, Broken Column
See Page 386

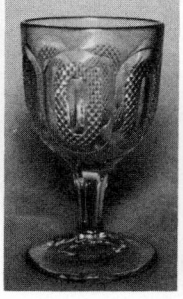

Pressed Glass, Goblet, Buckle
See Page 386

Pressed Glass, Goblet, Colonial, Jefferson
See Page 386

Pressed Glass, Goblet, Daisies In Oval

Pressed Glass, Goblet, Daisy & Button With Narcissus 8.75
Pressed Glass, Goblet, Daisy & Button, Blue, 6 In.High 5.00
Pressed Glass, Goblet, Daisy Whorl With Diamond Band .... *Illus* 11.50
Pressed Glass, Goblet, Dakota, Etched 22.50
Pressed Glass, Goblet, Dakota, Etched, Flowers 16.50
Pressed Glass, Goblet, Deer & Dog .... *Illus* 27.00
Pressed Glass, Goblet, Deer & Doe & Lily Of The Valley, Clear 17.50
Pressed Glass, Goblet, Deer & Pine 30.00
Pressed Glass, Goblet, Deer & Pine Tree 25.00
Pressed Glass, Goblet, Dewdrop Band .... 6.00 To 9.00
Pressed Glass, Goblet, Diagonal Band .... *Illus* 9.50
Pressed Glass, Goblet, Diamond Medallion .... 6.50 To 10.00
Pressed Glass, Goblet, Diamond Panels, Clear .... 5.50 To 6.50
Pressed Glass, Goblet, Diamond Point .... 10.00 To 28.00
Pressed Glass, Goblet, Diamond Point Band, Engraved Grapes & Leaves, Flint 12.50
Pressed Glass, Goblet, Diamond Point With Panels, Flint .... 22.50 To 26.00
Pressed Glass, Goblet, Diamond Point, Knop Stem, Flint 20.00
Pressed Glass, Goblet, Diamond Point, Ornate Knob Stem, Flint 9.00
Pressed Glass, Goblet, Diamond-Quilted, Blue 19.50
Pressed Glass, Goblet, Diamonds & Flowers, Scalloped 12.00
Pressed Glass, Goblet, Dickenson, Flint .... 17.50 To 19.50
Pressed Glass, Goblet, Dodo, Flint .... 16.50 To 22.50
Pressed Glass, Goblet, Dots & Dashes 8.50
Pressed Glass, Goblet, Double Disc Prisms, Flint .... 49.00 To 57.50
Pressed Glass, Goblet, Double Frosted Ribbon, Clear 12.50
Pressed Glass, Goblet, Double Loop & Dart 7.00
Pressed Glass, Goblet, Double Vine, Flint 145.00
Pressed Glass, Goblet, Dragon, Clear 30.00
Pressed Glass, Goblet, Duncan Block, Ruby Stained 17.50
Pressed Glass, Goblet, Egg In Sand 11.00
Pressed Glass, Goblet, Egyptian .... *Illus* 25.00

Pressed Glass, Goblet, Daisy Whorl With Diamond Band
See Page 387

Pressed Glass, Goblet, Deer & Dog
See Page 387

Pressed Glass, Goblet, Diagonal Band
See Page 387

Pressed Glass, Goblet, Egyptian
See Page 387

Pressed Glass, Goblet, Elongated Honeycomb, Clear, Flint	17.50
Pressed Glass, Goblet, Excelsior With Diamond, Clear, Flint	22.50
Pressed Glass, Goblet, Excelsior With Maltese Cross	32.50 To 38.50
Pressed Glass, Goblet, Excelsior, Flint	25.00
Pressed Glass, Goblet, Falcon Strawberry	9.00
Pressed Glass, Goblet, Fan Band	8.50
Pressed Glass, Goblet, Fan With Diamonds	10.50 To 12.50
Pressed Glass, Goblet, Feather	4.50 To 24.00
Pressed Glass, Goblet, Fern Burst	*Illus* 7.50
Pressed Glass, Goblet, Fern Garland	9.50
Pressed Glass, Goblet, Fine Prism, Flint	16.50
Pressed Glass, Goblet, Fine Rib, Cut Ovals, Three Rows, Flint	195.00
Pressed Glass, Goblet, Fishbone	8.50
Pressed Glass, Goblet, Flamingo Habitat	15.00
Pressed Glass, Goblet, Flamingo, Etched	17.00
Pressed Glass, Goblet, Flat Diamond	9.00
Pressed Glass, Goblet, Flattened Saw With Panels, Flint	27.50
Pressed Glass, Goblet, Fleur-De-Lis, Bull's-Eye	45.00
Pressed Glass, Goblet, Fleur-De-Lis, Clear, Flint	32.50
Pressed Glass, Goblet, Flute, Clear, Flint	10.00 To 15.00
Pressed Glass, Goblet, Flute, Double Knob Stem	8.00
Pressed Glass, Goblet, Flying Birds, Clear	20.00
Pressed Glass, Goblet, Flying Stork	12.00 To 22.50
Pressed Glass, Goblet, Framed Ovals, Flint	150.00
Pressed Glass, Goblet, Frog & Spider, Clear	40.00 To 60.00
Pressed Glass, Goblet, Frosted Artichoke	12.50
Pressed Glass, Goblet, Frosted Circle	28.00
Pressed Glass, Goblet, Frosted Flower Band	45.00
Pressed Glass, Goblet, Frosted Flower Bowl, Clear	20.00
Pressed Glass, Goblet, Frosted Leaf, Clear	25.00 To 55.00
Pressed Glass, Goblet, Frosted Lion	37.50
Pressed Glass, Goblet, Frosted Magnet & Grape, Clear, Flint	70.00
Pressed Glass, Goblet, Frosted Polar Bear	47.50 To 62.00
Pressed Glass, Goblet, Frosted Ribbon	5.00

Pressed Glass, Goblet, Frosted Ribbon With Bulging Sides, Clear 17.50
Pressed Glass, Goblet, Frosted Roman Key With Flutes, Flint 32.50
Pressed Glass, Goblet, Frosted Roman Key, Flint .... 20.00 To 30.00
Pressed Glass, Goblet, Frosted Stork, Clear 30.00
Pressed Glass, Goblet, Galloway, Clear, Flint .... 22.50 To 27.50
Pressed Glass, Goblet, Garfield Drape 18.50
Pressed Glass, Goblet, Giant Prism, Flint 45.00
Pressed Glass, Goblet, Giant Sawtooth, Clear, Flint 25.00
Pressed Glass, Goblet, Girl & Fan, Clear 22.50
Pressed Glass, Goblet, Good Luck, Knob Stem .... 12.50 To 18.50
Pressed Glass, Goblet, Gooseberry 17.50
Pressed Glass, Goblet, Gothic, Clear, Flint .... 22.50 To 35.00
Pressed Glass, Goblet, Graduated Diamond 5.00
Pressed Glass, Goblet, Grape & Festoon .... 5.00 To 13.00
Pressed Glass, Goblet, Grape & Festoon With Shield .... *Illus* 15.00
Pressed Glass, Goblet, Grape & Festoon, Stippled .... 10.00 To 15.00
Pressed Glass, Goblet, Grasshopper 5.25
Pressed Glass, Goblet, Grogan 6.50
Pressed Glass, Goblet, Grooved Bigler, Flint 35.00
Pressed Glass, Goblet, Hairpin With Rayed Base .... *Illus* 10.00
Pressed Glass, Goblet, Hairpin With Thumbprint, Flint .... 20.00 To 25.00
Pressed Glass, Goblet, Haley's Comet 12.00
Pressed Glass, Goblet, Hamilton With Frosted Leaf, Clear, Flint .... 25.00 To 30.00
Pressed Glass, Goblet, Hamilton, Flint .... 23.00 To 28.00
Pressed Glass, Goblet, Hand 25.00
Pressed Glass, Goblet, Harvard 7.50
Pressed Glass, Goblet, Hawaiian Pineapple, Flint 50.00
Pressed Glass, Goblet, Heart & Thumbprint 28.50
Pressed Glass, Goblet, Heavy Paneled, Fine Cut .... *Illus* 7.00
Pressed Glass, Goblet, Herringbone 12.00
Pressed Glass, Goblet, Herringbone Band, 4 In.High 8.00
Pressed Glass, Goblet, Herringbone Band, 6 In.Tall 8.00
Pressed Glass, Goblet, Hinoto, Flint 22.50

Pressed Glass, Goblet, Fern Burst
See Page 388

Pressed Glass, Goblet,
Grape & Festoon With Shield

Pressed Glass, Goblet, Hairpin With Rayed Base

Pressed Glass, Goblet, Heavy Paneled, Fine Cut

Pressed Glass, Goblet, Holly Leaf 15.00
Pressed Glass, Goblet, Holly, Clear 27.50
Pressed Glass, Goblet, Holly, Loop, & Dart With Round Ornaments, Clear 12.50
Pressed Glass, Goblet, Honeycomb .... 4.00 To 6.00
Pressed Glass, Goblet, Honeycomb, Barrel, Flint 14.50
Pressed Glass, Goblet, Honeycomb, Flint 16.00
Pressed Glass, Goblet, Honeycomb, Flint, Pittsburgh .... *Illus* 15.00
Pressed Glass, Goblet, Honeycomb, Footed, 4 1/2 In.High 15.00
Pressed Glass, Goblet, Honeycomb, Loop 13.00
Pressed Glass, Goblet, Hooks & Eyes 8.50
Pressed Glass, Goblet, Hops Band .... 5.00 To 9.75
Pressed Glass, Goblet, Horizontal Ribs With Diamond Point, Clear, Flint 10.00
Pressed Glass, Goblet, Horn Of Plenty .... 15.00 To 39.50
Pressed Glass, Goblet, Horn Of Plenty, 6 1/4 In. 30.00
Pressed Glass, Goblet, Horse, Rabbit, & Cat, Clear .... 55.00 To 110.00
Pressed Glass, Goblet, Horseshoe, Knobbed Stem 18.50
Pressed Glass, Goblet, Hotel Argus 5.50
Pressed Glass, Goblet, Huber, Flint 13.00
Pressed Glass, Goblet, Hunter Shooting Deer, Etched, Clear 35.00
Pressed Glass, Goblet, Iconoclast .... *Illus* 18.00
Pressed Glass, Goblet, Inverted Diamond Point, Clear, Flint 17.50
Pressed Glass, Goblet, Inverted Fern .... 18.00 To 35.00
Pressed Glass, Goblet, Inverted Fern, Buttermilk, Flint 25.00
Pressed Glass, Goblet, Inverted Thumbprint, Amber 17.00
Pressed Glass, Goblet, Ionia .... 6.50 To 9.50
Pressed Glass, Goblet, Iris & Herringbone, Clear 4.00
Pressed Glass, Goblet, Jacob's Ladder .... 29.50 To 32.50
Pressed Glass, Goblet, Jersey Swirl, Clear 12.50
Pressed Glass, Goblet, Jewel & Dewdrop 29.50
Pressed Glass, Goblet, Jewel Band, Scalloped Top 12.00
Pressed Glass, Goblet, Jeweled Drapery .... 7.00 To 8.00
Pressed Glass, Goblet, Kallbach 12.00
Pressed Glass, Goblet, King's Crown 12.00
Pressed Glass, Goblet, Kokomo 11.00
Pressed Glass, Goblet, Laminated Petals, Clear, Flint .... 20.00 To 25.00
Pressed Glass, Goblet, Lattice 6.50
Pressed Glass, Goblet, Lattice With Oval Panels, Flint 55.00
Pressed Glass, Goblet, Leaf & Dart .... *Illus* 15.00
Pressed Glass, Goblet, Lee, Clear, Flint 35.00
Pressed Glass, Goblet, Liberty Bell .... *Illus* 27.00
Pressed Glass, Goblet, Lily Of The Valley .... 7.50 To 35.00
Pressed Glass, Goblet, Lincoln Drape With Tassel, Clear, Flint .... 45.00 To 85.00
Pressed Glass, Goblet, Lincoln Drape, Flint .... 12.50 To 35.00
Pressed Glass, Goblet, Lion, Frosted 25.00
Pressed Glass, Goblet, Loop & Dart .... 12.50 To 16.50
Pressed Glass, Goblet, Loop & Dart Diamond 6.75
Pressed Glass, Goblet, Loop & Dart, Flint 22.50
Pressed Glass, Goblet, Loop & Dart, Opaque 16.50
Pressed Glass, Goblet, Loop & Moose Eye, Flint 23.50
Pressed Glass, Goblet, Loop & Petals, Flint 15.00
Pressed Glass, Goblet, Loop With Fisheye .... *Illus* 12.50
Pressed Glass, Goblet, Loop, Flint .... 5.00 To 10.00
Pressed Glass, Goblet, Loop, 6 1/2 In.High 9.00
Pressed Glass, Goblet, Louisiana .... 10.00 To 16.50
Pressed Glass, Goblet, Magnet & Grape 12.00
Pressed Glass, Goblet, Magnet & Grape With Frosted Leaf, Flint .... 30.00 To 34.50
Pressed Glass, Goblet, Mascotte, Etched 18.00
Pressed Glass, Goblet, Medallion, Sapphire Blue 17.50
Pressed Glass, Goblet, Mephistopheles 37.50
Pressed Glass, Goblet, Michigan With Gold Panels 19.50
Pressed Glass, Goblet, Mirror, Flint .... 21.00 To 26.00
Pressed Glass, Goblet, Mitered Diamond .... *Illus* 10.00
Pressed Glass, Goblet, Moon & Star, Clear .... 4.50 To 18.00
Pressed Glass, Goblet, Moon & Stork .... *Illus* 75.00
Pressed Glass, Goblet, Moose's Eye & Sand 12.00
Pressed Glass, Goblet, Morning Glory, Flint 200.00

Pressed Glass, Goblet, Nailhead 12.50
Pressed Glass, Goblet, New England Centennial 57.50
Pressed Glass, Goblet, New England Flute, Flint 20.00
Pressed Glass, Goblet, New England Pineapple, Clear, Flint .... 20.00 To 25.00
Pressed Glass, Goblet, New York, Honeycomb, Flint .... 10.00 To 12.50
Pressed Glass, Goblet, Nicotiana, Etched 15.00
Pressed Glass, Goblet, Nova Scotia Starflower 7.50
Pressed Glass, Goblet, Open Rose .... *Illus* 15.00

Pressed Glass, Goblet, Honeycomb, Flint, Pittsburgh
See Page 390

Pressed Glass, Goblet, Iconoclast
See Page 390

Pressed Glass, Goblet,
Leaf & Dart
See Page 390

Pressed Glass,
Goblet, Liberty Bell
See Page 390

Pressed Glass, Goblet,
Loop With Fisheye
See Page 390

Pressed Glass, Goblet,
Mitered Diamond
See Page 390

Pressed Glass, Goblet,
Moon & Stork
See Page 390

Pressed Glass,
Goblet, Open Rose

Pressed Glass, Goblet, Orange Peel .... *Illus* 9.50
Pressed Glass, Goblet, Ostrich Looking At Moon, Clear .... 39.00 To 60.00
Pressed Glass, Goblet, Oval Miter, Flint 18.00
Pressed Glass, Goblet, Oval Panel, Gold 9.50
Pressed Glass, Goblet, Owl & Possum, Clear .... 30.00 To 60.00
Pressed Glass, Goblet, Owl In Horseshoe, Clear 25.00
Pressed Glass, Goblet, Paisley, Purple Eyes, Gold 7.00
Pressed Glass, Goblet, Paling .... 5.00 To 6.50
Pressed Glass, Goblet, Panel 44 .... 12.00
Pressed Glass, Goblet, Paneled Acorn Band, Opaque 14.00
Pressed Glass, Goblet, Paneled Daisy 24.00
Pressed Glass, Goblet, Paneled Daisy & Button 11.50
Pressed Glass, Goblet, Paneled Daisy, Clear 12.50
Pressed Glass, Goblet, Paneled Diamond & Flowers .... *Illus* 10.00
Pressed Glass, Goblet, Paneled Flower 14.00
Pressed Glass, Goblet, Paneled Grape Band, Flint 21.50
Pressed Glass, Goblet, Paneled Jewels 8.00
Pressed Glass, Goblet, Paneled Jewels, Sapphire Blue 17.50
Pressed Glass, Goblet, Paneled Julep 12.00
Pressed Glass, Goblet, Paneled Ovals, Flint 25.00
Pressed Glass, Goblet, Paneled Sunflower .... 8.00 To 13.50
Pressed Glass, Goblet, Paneled Thistle .... 7.00 To 29.50
Pressed Glass, Goblet, Paneled Thistle, Flared 12.50
Pressed Glass, Goblet, Parrot 20.00
Pressed Glass, Goblet, Parrot With Fan 18.50
Pressed Glass, Goblet, Pear 16.00
Pressed Glass, Goblet, Pendleton, Clear, Flint 17.50
Pressed Glass, Goblet, Pigs & Corn, Clear .... 55.00 To 90.00
Pressed Glass, Goblet, Pillar & Bull's-Eye, Flint 20.00
Pressed Glass, Goblet, Pittsburgh Centennial, Clear 17.50
Pressed Glass, Goblet, Pleat & Panel .... 5.00 To 12.00
Pressed Glass, Goblet, Plume 5.75
Pressed Glass, Goblet, Pointed Jewel 7.50
Pressed Glass, Goblet, Polar Bear 59.50
Pressed Glass, Goblet, Popcorn, Clear 27.50
Pressed Glass, Goblet, Powder & Shot, Flint .... 20.00 To 32.50
Pressed Glass, Goblet, Pressed Leaf 8.50
Pressed Glass, Goblet, Pressed Leaf, Flint 17.50
Pressed Glass, Goblet, Prism & Flattened Sawtooth 31.00
Pressed Glass, Goblet, Rail Fence Band 8.50
Pressed Glass, Goblet, Recessed Ovals 10.00
Pressed Glass, Goblet, Red Block 28.50
Pressed Glass, Goblet, Rexford .... *Illus* 9.50
Pressed Glass, Goblet, Ribbed Grape, Flint .... 24.00 To 35.00
Pressed Glass, Goblet, Ribbed Ivy 20.00
Pressed Glass, Goblet, Ribbed Ivy, Flint .... 22.00 To 22.50
Pressed Glass, Goblet, Ribbed Palm, Flint .... 17.50 To 30.00
Pressed Glass, Goblet, Ribbon 22.50
Pressed Glass, Goblet, Ringed Frame Ovals, Flint 50.00
Pressed Glass, Goblet, Rising Sun, Purple & Gold Trim 12.50
Pressed Glass, Goblet, Roanoke Star 4.50
Pressed Glass, Goblet, Roman Cross .... *Illus* 9.50
Pressed Glass, Goblet, Roman Key, Clear 10.50
Pressed Glass, Goblet, Roman Key, Flint 28.00
Pressed Glass, Goblet, Roman Key, Frosted, Flint 27.50
Pressed Glass, Goblet, Roman Rosette 22.50
Pressed Glass, Goblet, Rose In Snow, Clear .... 15.00 To 20.00
Pressed Glass, Goblet, Rose Leaves .... 6.50 To 8.00
Pressed Glass, Goblet, Rose Sprig 10.50
Pressed Glass, Goblet, Round Thumbprint, Flint 19.50
Pressed Glass, Goblet, Running, Reclining, & Standing Deer, Clear 30.00
Pressed Glass, Goblet, Sage Brush 12.00
Pressed Glass, Goblet, Sandwich Loop, Flint 18.50
Pressed Glass, Goblet, Sawtooth, Knop Stem, Flint 20.00
Pressed Glass, Goblet, Scalloped Lines 11.00
Pressed Glass, Goblet, Scarab, Flint 65.00

Pressed Glass, Goblet, Scroll 7.00
Pressed Glass, Goblet, Scroll With Flowers .... *Illus* 10.00
Pressed Glass, Goblet, Seneca Loop .... 8.00 To 12.50
Pressed Glass, Goblet, Seneca Loop, Flint 14.00
Pressed Glass, Goblet, Sexton Flute, Flint 13.00

Pressed Glass, Goblet, Orange Peel
See Page 392

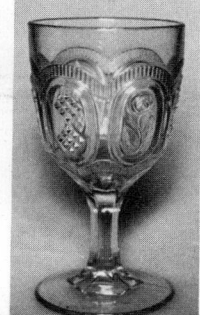

Pressed Glass, Goblet,
Paneled Diamond & Flowers
See Page 392

Pressed Glass,
Goblet, Rexford
See Page 392

Pressed Glass, Goblet, Roman Cross
See Page 392

Pressed Glass, Goblet, Scroll With Flowers

Pressed Glass, Goblet, Shell & Tassel, Clear 25.00
Pressed Glass, Goblet, Shield 25.00
Pressed Glass, Goblet, Shield & Anchor, Clear 75.00
Pressed Glass, Goblet, Shovel .... 5.00 To 7.00
Pressed Glass, Goblet, Shrine 28.00
Pressed Glass, Goblet, Skilton 18.50
Pressed Glass, Goblet, Smocking, Flint .... 39.50 To 45.00
Pressed Glass, Goblet, Snake Drape 12.50
Pressed Glass, Goblet, Spanish Coin, Clear, Gold 17.50
Pressed Glass, Goblet, Sprig In Mitered Blocks, Sapphire Blue 27.50
Pressed Glass, Goblet, Square Panes, Clear 3.00
Pressed Glass, Goblet, Squirrel, Clear 65.00
Pressed Glass, Goblet, Star & Palm 10.00
Pressed Glass, Goblet, Star Rosetted 10.00
Pressed Glass, Goblet, Stars & Stripes 9.00
Pressed Glass, Goblet, States 18.00
Pressed Glass, Goblet, Stedman, Flint .... 14.00 To 16.00
Pressed Glass, Goblet, Stippled 6.50
Pressed Glass, Goblet, Stippled & Dotted Rosettes, Clear 10.00
Pressed Glass, Goblet, Stippled Festoons, Clear 12.50
Pressed Glass, Goblet, Stippled Fuchsia .... 10.00 To 15.00
Pressed Glass, Goblet, Stippled Grape & Festoon 16.00
Pressed Glass, Goblet, Stippled Loop & Dart 13.00

Pressed Glass, Goblet, Stippled Starflower 7.00
Pressed Glass, Goblet, Stork, Clear .... 27.50 To 39.00
Pressed Glass, Goblet, Sunburst 7.50
Pressed Glass, Goblet, Sunburst Medallion 7.00
Pressed Glass, Goblet, Swimming Swan 28.00
Pressed Glass, Goblet, Tandem Bicycle 10.50
Pressed Glass, Goblet, Tandem Diamonds With Thumbprint .... *Illus* 10.00
Pressed Glass, Goblet, Tape Measure .... 12.00 To 14.00
Pressed Glass, Goblet, Texas Bull's-Eye 8.50
Pressed Glass, Goblet, Thistle 21.50
Pressed Glass, Goblet, Three Face 45.00
Pressed Glass, Goblet, Three Face, Etched 40.00
Pressed Glass, Goblet, Tic-Tac-Toe 9.00
Pressed Glass, Goblet, Tile Band 15.00
Pressed Glass, Goblet, Torpedo 25.00
Pressed Glass, Goblet, Tree Of Life, Clear 20.00
Pressed Glass, Goblet, Tree Of Life, Flint, Signed Pg Co. 35.00
Pressed Glass, Goblet, Triple Triangle, Ruby Stained 24.50
Pressed Glass, Goblet, Tulip & Sawtooth, Knob Stem, 7 In.High .... 8.00 To 24.00
Pressed Glass, Goblet, Tulip With Ribs, Flint 27.00
Pressed Glass, Goblet, U.S.Thumbprint 8.50
Pressed Glass, Goblet, Umbilicated Sawtooth, Flint 22.00
Pressed Glass, Goblet, Valentine, Clear 25.00
Pressed Glass, Goblet, Waffle & Thumbprint, Clear, Flint .... 14.50 To 17.50
Pressed Glass, Goblet, Washington Centennial 15.00
Pressed Glass, Goblet, Water Lily 15.00
Pressed Glass, Goblet, Water, Iris & Herringbone, Clear 10.00
Pressed Glass, Goblet, Waterflower With Serpent's Head, Clear 30.00
Pressed Glass, Goblet, Wedding Ring, Clear, Flint 17.50
Pressed Glass, Goblet, Westward Ho, Frosted .... 32.00 To 55.00
Pressed Glass, Goblet, Wheat & Barley .... 14.50 To 22.50
Pressed Glass, Goblet, Wildflower 9.50
Pressed Glass, Goblet, Wildflower, Amber 17.50
Pressed Glass, Goblet, Wildflower, Apple Green 30.00
Pressed Glass, Goblet, Wildflower, Blue 27.50
Pressed Glass, Goblet, Wildflower, Vaseline .... *Illus* 22.00
Pressed Glass, Goblet, Willow Oak 16.50
Pressed Glass, Goblet, Worcester, Flint 18.00
Pressed Glass, Goblet, Yoke Band 5.00
Pressed Glass, Goblet, Yoked Loop 14.00
Pressed Glass, Goblet, Yoked Loop, Flint 17.50
Pressed Glass, Goblet, Yuma Loop 10.00
Pressed Glass, Goblet, Zipper 13.50
Pressed Glass, Goblet, 1, 000-Eye .... 6.00 To 18.50
Pressed Glass, Goblet, 1000 Eye, Green 32.00
Pressed Glass, Hat, Cubed, Green 14.00
Pressed Glass, Hat, Daisy & Button, Clear, 6 In.Tall, 8 In.Across 18.00
Pressed Glass, Holder, Match, Daisy & Button 8.00
Pressed Glass, Holder, Match, Daisy & Button, Sapphire Blue, Half Canoe 55.00
Pressed Glass, Holder, Match, New Hampshire, Gold 6.00
Pressed Glass, Holder, Spill, Sawtooth, Octagonal 18.00
Pressed Glass, Ice Cream Set, Daisy & Button, Blue, Amber & Canary 85.00
Pressed Glass, Jam, Westward Ho, Cover 65.00
Pressed Glass, Jar, Cookie, Broken Column, Covered 26.00
Pressed Glass, Jar, Cracker, Nickel Plate Top & Bail, Star Pattern 25.00
Pressed Glass, Jar, Jam, Burred Hobnail, Cover 15.00
Pressed Glass, Jar, Jam, Cupid & Venus, Covered 48.00
Pressed Glass, Jar, Jam, Diagonal Band, Clear 12.25
Pressed Glass, Jar, Jam, Flamingo, Covered 25.00
Pressed Glass, Jar, Jam, Frosted Lion .... 27.00 To 60.00
Pressed Glass, Jar, Jam, Good Luck, Cover 45.00
Pressed Glass, Jar, Jam, Tiny Lion, Nose Of Lion On Lid 21.00
Pressed Glass, Jar, Pomade, Sawtooth, Covered, Flint 24.00
Pressed Glass, Jug, Syrup, Galloway, Nickel Plate Top 17.00
Pressed Glass, Knife Rest, Barbell Shape 3.50
Pressed Glass, Knob, Drawer, Rib, Swirl, Blown, Circa 1820, Set Of 8 .... 18.00

Pressed Glass, Lamp Base, U.S.Coin, Square Bowl, Clear, 8 1/2 In.High	175.00
Pressed Glass, Light, Christmas, Diamond Pattern, Amber	9.50
Pressed Glass, Light, Christmas, Diamond Pattern, White	12.00
Pressed Glass, Marmalade Jar, Jumbo *Illus*	225.00
Pressed Glass, Mug, Beaded Swirl	7.50
Pressed Glass, Mug, Bird & Harp, Clear	15.00
Pressed Glass, Mug, Bird, Amber, 2 1/2 In.	10.00
Pressed Glass, Mug, Bleeding Heart	17.50
Pressed Glass, Mug, Bleeding Heart, Opaque	19.00
Pressed Glass, Mug, Child, Two Dogs With Bird	28.00
Pressed Glass, Mug, Child's, A Good Boy, Amber	15.00
Pressed Glass, Mug, Cut Log	8.50
Pressed Glass, Mug, Dewdrop, Applied Handle, 4 In.High	7.50
Pressed Glass, Mug, Dewey, Amber, Greentown	25.00
Pressed Glass, Mug, Extended Thumbprint, 4 In.High	7.00
Pressed Glass, Mug, Flute, Flint, Applied Handle	18.00
Pressed Glass, Mug, Forget-Me-Not, Ribbed, Handle	18.50
Pressed Glass, Mug, Garfield, Portrait, Memorial, Dated 1881	25.00
Pressed Glass, Mug, Grape & Festoon With Shield, Cobalt Blue	13.00
Pressed Glass, Mug, Honeycomb	12.00
Pressed Glass, Mug, Horn Of Plenty, Applied Handle, 3 In.	100.00
Pressed Glass, Mug, Jewel With Dewdrop, 3 1/2 In.High, 5 In.Diameter	8.75
Pressed Glass, Mug, Liberty Bell, Miniature, 2 In.High	55.00
Pressed Glass, Mug, Lyre	22.00
Pressed Glass, Mug, Martyr's	39.00
Pressed Glass, Mug, Medallion	11.00
Pressed Glass, Mug, Minnesota, Gold, Handled	9.50
Pressed Glass, Mug, Monkey	50.00
Pressed Glass, Mug, Paneled Palm	6.50
Pressed Glass, Mug, Paneled St.Louis, 1/2 Pint	25.00
Pressed Glass, Mug, Robin, Blue *Illus*	18.50

Pressed Glass, Goblet, Tandem Diamonds With Thumbprint
See Page 394

Pressed Glass, Goblet,
Wildflower, Vaseline
See Page 394

Pressed Glass,
Mug, Robin, Blue

Pressed Glass,
Marmalade Jar, Jumbo

Pressed Glass, Mug, Root Beer, Rochester, Clear, Name In Raised Letters 9.00
Pressed Glass, Mug, Rosette Star, Clear, Ribbed, Molded Handle 10.00
Pressed Glass, Mug, Tennessee 20.00
Pressed Glass, Mug, Thumbprint, Clear 5.50
Pressed Glass, Mug, Thumbprint, Cobalt Blue 5.50
Pressed Glass, Mug, Thumbprint, Ruby 5.50
Pressed Glass, Mug, Wheat & Barley 14.50
Pressed Glass, Mug, Whiskey, Diamond Point, Handle 80.00
Pressed Glass, Mustard, Panel & Star, Yellow, Metal Top 10.00
Pressed Glass, Nappy, Beaded Dewdrop, Handle 15.00
Pressed Glass, Nappy, Bird & Strawberry, Round, Footed 18.00
Pressed Glass, Nappy, Paneled Thistle, 5 1/2 In. 14.50
Pressed Glass, Nappy, Ribbon, Square, Flat 7.50
Pressed Glass, Nappy, Sunflower, Green, Flint 25.00
Pressed Glass, Nappy, Wisconsin, Beaded Edge, Two Handle, 5 1/2 In.Round 13.50
Pressed Glass, Parfait, Paneled Grape 6.00
Pressed Glass, Pickle, Daisy & Button 7.50
Pressed Glass, Pickle, Delaware, Clear, Gold Edge, 8 In. 10.00
Pressed Glass, Pickle, Diamond Block, Pink, Handled, 6 1/2 In. 6.50
Pressed Glass, Pickle, Double Frosted Ribbon 14.50
Pressed Glass, Pickle, Emblem, Eagle Handles 26.00
Pressed Glass, Pickle, Hawaiian Lei 7.50
Pressed Glass, Pickle, Rosette 6.00
Pressed Glass, Pickle, X Logs, Flat 5.00
Pressed Glass, Pitcher, Aberdeen, Clear, Applied Handle 30.00
Pressed Glass, Pitcher, Actress .... *Illus* 37.50
Pressed Glass, Pitcher, Ale, Mephistopheles, Frosted & Clear, Applied Handle 45.00
Pressed Glass, Pitcher, Barberry 42.50
Pressed Glass, Pitcher, Bellflower, Double Vine, Mold Blown, Flint, 1835 .... 250.00
Pressed Glass, Pitcher, Bull's-Eye & Daisy, Green 28.00
Pressed Glass, Pitcher, Button & Arches, Ruby Stained, White Rock, S.D. 75.50
Pressed Glass, Pitcher, Chain & Shell .... *Illus* 15.00
Pressed Glass, Pitcher, Checkerboard 22.00
Pressed Glass, Pitcher, Coin Dot, Green, Ruffled Top, Applied Handle 65.00
Pressed Glass, Pitcher, Cupid & Venus 52.50
Pressed Glass, Pitcher, Cupid & Venus, 12 In. 25.00
Pressed Glass, Pitcher, Daisy & Button, X Bar, Clear 25.00
Pressed Glass, Pitcher, Dakota, Tankard Type 30.00
Pressed Glass, Pitcher, Deer & Oak Tree 25.00
Pressed Glass, Pitcher, Delaware Rose, 9 1/2 In. .... *Illus* 58.50
Pressed Glass, Pitcher, Delaware, Green, Water 67.50
Pressed Glass, Pitcher, Dewey, Clear, 9 1/2 In.High 35.00
Pressed Glass, Pitcher, Emerald Buckle 18.50
Pressed Glass, Pitcher, Garfield Drape 37.50
Pressed Glass, Pitcher, Grasshopper 27.50
Pressed Glass, Pitcher, Guttate Pattern, Pink, Clear Handle, 5 In.Tall 41.00
Pressed Glass, Pitcher, Herringbone, Frosted Flower Band, 8 In. 35.00
Pressed Glass, Pitcher, Inverted Thumbprint, Amber 65.00
Pressed Glass, Pitcher, Jewel & Dewdrop 24.50
Pressed Glass, Pitcher, Lemonade, Delaware, Green 40.00
Pressed Glass, Pitcher, Lemonade, Nail, Etched 25.00
Pressed Glass, Pitcher, Lotus, Clear, Applied Handle, 11 In.Tall 65.00
Pressed Glass, Pitcher, Milk, Actress 100.00
Pressed Glass, Pitcher, Milk, Beaded Dewdrop 35.00
Pressed Glass, Pitcher, Milk, Beaded Loop 17.50
Pressed Glass, Pitcher, Milk, Bowtie 20.00
Pressed Glass, Pitcher, Milk, Cane, Tankard Shape, 8 In. .... 14.00 To 16.50
Pressed Glass, Pitcher, Milk, Cottage 18.00
Pressed Glass, Pitcher, Milk, Cupid & Venus, 7 3/4 In. .... 26.00 To 35.00
Pressed Glass, Pitcher, Milk, Dahlia .... 5.00 To 14.00
Pressed Glass, Pitcher, Milk, Daisy & Button With Crossbar 20.00
Pressed Glass, Pitcher, Milk, Daisy & Button With Crossbar, Amber 25.00
Pressed Glass, Pitcher, Milk, Egg In Sand 18.00
Pressed Glass, Pitcher, Milk, Fan, Diagonal Band, 8 In. 25.00
Pressed Glass, Pitcher, Milk, Lily Of The Valley 65.00
Pressed Glass, Pitcher, Milk, Louisiana 17.50

Pressed Glass, Pitcher, Actress
See Page 396

Pressed Glass, Pitcher, Chain & Shell
See Page 396

Pressed Glass, Pitcher, Delaware Rose, 9 1/2 In.
See Page 396

Pressed Glass, Pitcher, Milk, Paneled Forget-Me-Not 24.50
Pressed Glass, Pitcher, Milk, Primrose 26.00
Pressed Glass, Pitcher, Milk, Ruby Thumbprint, Applied Handle 25.00
Pressed Glass, Pitcher, Milk, Tree Of Life, 7 In.High 25.00
Pressed Glass, Pitcher, Milk, Westward Ho, 8 In. 197.50
Pressed Glass, Pitcher, Milk, Willow Oak .... 18.50 To 22.50
Pressed Glass, Pitcher, Milk, Wyoming 28.00
Pressed Glass, Pitcher, Ramsey Grape 30.00
Pressed Glass, Pitcher, Ribbed Palm, Flint, 9 In.Tall 95.00
Pressed Glass, Pitcher, Ruffled Eye, Amber, Greentown 75.00
Pressed Glass, Pitcher, Shell & Jewel .... 15.00 To 17.50
Pressed Glass, Pitcher, Shell & Tassel, Round 22.00
Pressed Glass, Pitcher, Sleepy Eye, Signed Monmouth, Quart 29.00
Pressed Glass, Pitcher, Stippled Double Loop 22.50
Pressed Glass, Pitcher, Striped, Yellow & White, Flint Handle, Pair 80.00
Pressed Glass, Pitcher, Syrup, Cane, Metal Top, Rough Pontil 21.50
Pressed Glass, Pitcher, Syrup, Falcon Strawberry, Dome Lid 27.00
Pressed Glass, Pitcher, Syrup, Hobstar, Pewter Top 21.50
Pressed Glass, Pitcher, Syrup, Rexford 15.00
Pressed Glass, Pitcher, Tankard, Ball & Swirl, Clear 17.50
Pressed Glass, Pitcher, Thistle 40.00
Pressed Glass, Pitcher, Torpedo, Clear, Tankard Type 30.00
Pressed Glass, Pitcher, Two Panel, Blue, 6 In.Tall 25.00
Pressed Glass, Pitcher, Water, Aberdeen, Clear, Applied Handle 30.00
Pressed Glass, Pitcher, Water, Actress 130.00
Pressed Glass, Pitcher, Water, Admiral Dewey, Clear .... 35.00 To 50.00
Pressed Glass, Pitcher, Water, Almond Thumbprint 16.00
Pressed Glass, Pitcher, Water, Anthemion 27.50
Pressed Glass, Pitcher, Water, Basket Weave, Blue 30.00
Pressed Glass, Pitcher, Water, Basket Weave, Honey Amber 18.50
Pressed Glass, Pitcher, Water, Beaded Band .... 21.50 To 27.50
Pressed Glass, Pitcher, Water, Beaded Tulip, 8 In.High 35.00
Pressed Glass, Pitcher, Water, Bent Buckle 24.00
Pressed Glass, Pitcher, Water, Bevel Diamond With Star 20.00
Pressed Glass, Pitcher, Water, Broken Column 55.00
Pressed Glass, Pitcher, Water, Bull's-Eye & Daisy, Gilt Rim & Eyes 25.00
Pressed Glass, Pitcher, Water, Bull's-Eye With Fan, Emerald Green & Gold 30.00

Pressed Glass, Pitcher, Water, Cane, Apple Green	35.00
Pressed Glass, Pitcher, Water, Carnation	22.50
Pressed Glass, Pitcher, Water, Chain With Shield	19.50
Pressed Glass, Pitcher, Water, Chandelier	35.00
Pressed Glass, Pitcher, Water, Colorado, Green	95.00
Pressed Glass, Pitcher, Water, Columbia Coin, Gold	140.00
Pressed Glass, Pitcher, Water, Crow & Fox, Purple Tinge	95.00
Pressed Glass, Pitcher, Water, Crusader Cross	10.50
Pressed Glass, Pitcher, Water, Cupid & Venus, 9 1/2 In.	32.50
Pressed Glass, Pitcher, Water, Dahlia	9.00 To 16.50
Pressed Glass, Pitcher, Water, Daisy & Button With Almond Band	17.50
Pressed Glass, Pitcher, Water, Daisy & Button With Fine Cut Panels	17.50
Pressed Glass, Pitcher, Water, Daisy & Button With V Ornament	12.00
Pressed Glass, Pitcher, Water, Daisy & Button, Clear, Scalloped	12.50
Pressed Glass, Pitcher, Water, Daisy & Button, Grooved Handle, 8 3/4 In.High	24.00
Pressed Glass, Pitcher, Water, Deer & Oak Tree	48.00
Pressed Glass, Pitcher, Water, Delaware, Green	60.00
Pressed Glass, Pitcher, Water, Dew & Raindrop	18.50
Pressed Glass, Pitcher, Water, Dewey	32.50 To 37.50
Pressed Glass, Pitcher, Water, Dewey, Clear, 9 1/2 In.High	35.00
Pressed Glass, Pitcher, Water, Dewey, Lindsey	25.00
Pressed Glass, Pitcher, Water, Diagonal Band	16.50
Pressed Glass, Pitcher, Water, Diagonal Band With Fan	16.50
Pressed Glass, Pitcher, Water, Diamond In Diamond	19.50
Pressed Glass, Pitcher, Water, Diamond Medallion	16.00
Pressed Glass, Pitcher, Water, Diamond Thumbprint, Flint	160.00
Pressed Glass, Pitcher, Water, Diamonds In Diamonds, Applied Handle	10.00
Pressed Glass, Pitcher, Water, Double Arch, Green, Gold	85.00
Pressed Glass, Pitcher, Water, Doyle's Shell, Tankard Shape	13.50
Pressed Glass, Pitcher, Water, Egg In Sand, Clear	36.50
Pressed Glass, Pitcher, Water, Egyptian	115.00
Pressed Glass, Pitcher, Water, Empress, Green, Four Tumbler, Set	165.00
Pressed Glass, Pitcher, Water, Eyewinker	42.50
Pressed Glass, Pitcher, Water, Feather	18.00 To 19.50
Pressed Glass, Pitcher, Water, Feather & Block	12.50
Pressed Glass, Pitcher, Water, Feather Duster, Green	24.00
Pressed Glass, Pitcher, Water, Festoon	29.50
Pressed Glass, Pitcher, Water, Fickle Block	18.00
Pressed Glass, Pitcher, Water, Fine Cut & Feather, Clear	17.50
Pressed Glass, Pitcher, Water, Fine Cut With Block	23.50
Pressed Glass, Pitcher, Water, Fish Scale	16.50
Pressed Glass, Pitcher, Water, Garfield Drape, Applied Handle, Bulbous	35.00
Pressed Glass, Pitcher, Water, Geneva, Green, Gold Trim, Greentown	75.00
Pressed Glass, Pitcher, Water, Giant Thumbprint	30.00
Pressed Glass, Pitcher, Water, Herringbone, Green	39.50
Pressed Glass, Pitcher, Water, Hidalgo, Applied Handle	25.00
Pressed Glass, Pitcher, Water, Hidalgo, Etched	23.50
Pressed Glass, Pitcher, Water, Hobnail, Amber	25.00
Pressed Glass, Pitcher, Water, Hobnail, Bull's-Eye Base	25.00
Pressed Glass, Pitcher, Water, Hobnail, Golden Amber	25.00
Pressed Glass, Pitcher, Water, Honeycomb, Gillinder	50.00
Pressed Glass, Pitcher, Water, Horn Of Plenty, Cherries	25.00
Pressed Glass, Pitcher, Water, Horsemint	14.00
Pressed Glass, Pitcher, Water, Hummingbird, 8 In.Tall	22.00
Pressed Glass, Pitcher, Water, Inverted Thumbprint, Blue, Gold & Enamel	40.00
Pressed Glass, Pitcher, Water, Iris & Herringbone, Clear, Rayed Base	8.00
Pressed Glass, Pitcher, Water, Jewel With Moon & Star	40.00
Pressed Glass, Pitcher, Water, King's Curtain	12.50
Pressed Glass, Pitcher, Water, Kokomo	19.50
Pressed Glass, Pitcher, Water, Laverne	25.00
Pressed Glass, Pitcher, Water, Loop With Dewdrop	26.50
Pressed Glass, Pitcher, Water, Loop, Applied Handle	35.00
Pressed Glass, Pitcher, Water, Majestic, Red, Clear	38.00
Pressed Glass, Pitcher, Water, Michigan	35.00
Pressed Glass, Pitcher, Water, Minerva	50.00
Pressed Glass, Pitcher, Water, Narcissus Spray	16.00

Pressed Glass, Pitcher, Water, Overshot, Blue, Amber Handle 75.00
Pressed Glass, Pitcher, Water, Overshot, Clear, 7 In.High 75.00
Pressed Glass, Pitcher, Water, Pan Thistle 30.00
Pressed Glass, Pitcher, Water, Paneled Forget-Me-Not 23.50
Pressed Glass, Pitcher, Water, Paneled Grape 20.00
Pressed Glass, Pitcher, Water, Pleat & Panel .... 35.00 To 40.00
Pressed Glass, Pitcher, Water, Pleated Medallion 16.00
Pressed Glass, Pitcher, Water, Polar Bear 125.00
Pressed Glass, Pitcher, Water, Popcorn With Line Ears 35.00
Pressed Glass, Pitcher, Water, Portland Tree Of Life 18.50
Pressed Glass, Pitcher, Water, Primrose 25.00
Pressed Glass, Pitcher, Water, Prism Arc 18.50
Pressed Glass, Pitcher, Water, Quaker Lady 45.00
Pressed Glass, Pitcher, Water, Queen 23.50
Pressed Glass, Pitcher, Water, Romeo 15.00
Pressed Glass, Pitcher, Water, Rose In Snow, Clear 53.50
Pressed Glass, Pitcher, Water, Rosette 17.50
Pressed Glass, Pitcher, Water, Rosette With Palms 22.50
Pressed Glass, Pitcher, Water, Scalloped Lines, Applied Handle, Bulbous 32.50
Pressed Glass, Pitcher, Water, Sedan 16.50
Pressed Glass, Pitcher, Water, Serrated Bands, Flared Top 14.50
Pressed Glass, Pitcher, Water, Shell & Jewel .... 12.50 To 18.50
Pressed Glass, Pitcher, Water, Shrine, Clear .... 27.50 To 40.00
Pressed Glass, Pitcher, Water, Snakeskin & Dot 25.00
Pressed Glass, Pitcher, Water, Spiraled Ivy 17.50
Pressed Glass, Pitcher, Water, Star & Bars 21.50
Pressed Glass, Pitcher, Water, Stippled Cherry 22.50
Pressed Glass, Pitcher, Water, Teardrop & Tassel, Blue 47.50
Pressed Glass, Pitcher, Water, Teardrop & Tassel, Clear 42.00
Pressed Glass, Pitcher, Water, Tidy, Applied Handle 15.00
Pressed Glass, Pitcher, Water, Tiny Lion 27.50
Pressed Glass, Pitcher, Water, Waffle, Thumbprint, Flint, 9 1/2 In.High 150.00
Pressed Glass, Pitcher, Water, Wedding Bells, Gold, Tankard Shap .... 16.00 To 26.50
Pressed Glass, Pitcher, Water, Westward Ho 65.00
Pressed Glass, Pitcher, Water, Wheat & Barley, Clear 22.50
Pressed Glass, Pitcher, Water, Wildflower, Blue 30.00
Pressed Glass, Pitcher, Water, Wildflower, Clear 22.50
Pressed Glass, Pitcher, Water, Zipper Pattern, Amber 29.00
Pressed Glass, Pitcher, Water, 44 Pattern, Silver Top 45.00
Pressed Glass, Pitcher, Wildflower, Yellow, 9 In.Tall 38.00
Pressed Glass, Pitcher, Willow Oak 25.00
Pressed Glass, Plate, Admiral Dewey 14.00
Pressed Glass, Plate, Azalea, 7 1/2 In. 3.00
Pressed Glass, Plate, Basket Weave, Handled 11.00
Pressed Glass, Plate, Battleship Maine, Clear, Lacy Edge, 5 1/2 In.Diameter 15.00
Pressed Glass, Plate, Beaded Loop, Oval 7.00
Pressed Glass, Plate, Birds In Frame, 10 In.Square 15.00
Pressed Glass, Plate, Bopeep 16.50
Pressed Glass, Plate, Bread, Actress .... 32.50 To 60.00
Pressed Glass, Plate, Bread, Barley 9.00
Pressed Glass, Plate, Bread, Beehive 50.00
Pressed Glass, Plate, Bread, Birds, Double, Stippled & Beaded Border, Handles 25.00
Pressed Glass, Plate, Bread, Columbus 22.50
Pressed Glass, Plate, Bread, Cupid & Venus, Clear, 11 In. 18.00
Pressed Glass, Plate, Bread, Cupid & Venus, Handles 17.50
Pressed Glass, Plate, Bread, Cupid & Venus, 10 1/2 In. 22.50
Pressed Glass, Plate, Bread, Daisy & Button With Crossbar, Amber 35.00
Pressed Glass, Plate, Bread, Deer & Pine Tree, Amber 37.50
Pressed Glass, Plate, Bread, Deer & Pine Tree, Clear 22.50
Pressed Glass, Plate, Bread, Deer & Pine Tree, Green 37.50
Pressed Glass, Plate, Bread, Dewdrops, Points 13.00
Pressed Glass, Plate, Bread, Diagonal, Green 17.50
Pressed Glass, Plate, Bread, Egyptian, Cleopatra Center .... 22.50 To 27.50
Pressed Glass, Plate, Bread, Eureka, Clear 20.00
Pressed Glass, Plate, Bread, Festoon 17.50
Pressed Glass, Plate, Bread, Flowerpot 20.00

Pressed Glass, Plate, Bread, Garfield Memorial .... 18.50 To 22.50
Pressed Glass, Plate, Bread, Garfield, Dated 1881 .... 24.00
Pressed Glass, Plate, Bread, 'give Us This Day, Milk Glass Center 75.00
Pressed Glass, Plate, Bread, Good Luck 27.00
Pressed Glass, Plate, Bread, Grant Memorial, Clear 24.75
Pressed Glass, Plate, Bread, Grant, Peace, Blue 38.00
Pressed Glass, Plate, Bread, Heroes Of Bunker Hill 30.00
Pressed Glass, Plate, Bread, Horseshoe, Clear, Oval 22.50
Pressed Glass, Plate, Bread, Horseshoe, Horse Handles 25.00
Pressed Glass, Plate, Bread, Horseshoe, 13 In.Long, 9 In.Wide 28.00
Pressed Glass, Plate, Bread, In Remembrance, Washington, Lincoln, Garfield 42.50
Pressed Glass, Plate, Bread, Last Supper, Frosted Center, 'give Us This Day' 45.00
Pressed Glass, Plate, Bread, Leo Xiii 27.50
Pressed Glass, Plate, Bread, Liberty Bell, With Signers .... 37.50 To 45.00
Pressed Glass, Plate, Bread, Lion, Clear 28.00
Pressed Glass, Plate, Bread, Lotus, 'give Us This Day' 28.50
Pressed Glass, Plate, Bread, Merry Christmas, Clear 30.00
Pressed Glass, Plate, Bread, Mccormick Reaper, Oval 50.00
Pressed Glass, Plate, Bread, Mulberry 26.50
Pressed Glass, Plate, Bread, Pleat & Panel 15.00
Pressed Glass, Plate, Bread, Pleat & Panel, Open Handle .... 16.00 To 20.00
Pressed Glass, Plate, Bread, Pope Leo 20.00
Pressed Glass, Plate, Bread, Rosette, 9 In.Diameter 15.00
Pressed Glass, Plate, Bread, Saxon, 12 In. 10.00
Pressed Glass, Plate, Bread, Sheaf Of Wheat .... 14.00 To 25.00
Pressed Glass, Plate, Bread, Sheaf Of Wheat Center 11.50
Pressed Glass, Plate, Bread, Sheaf Of Wheat, Clear, Motto .... 17.00 To 18.00
Pressed Glass, Plate, Bread, Three Presidents 20.00
Pressed Glass, Plate, Bread, U.S.Grant, Clear, Square .... 25.00 To 32.00
Pressed Glass, Plate, Bread, 'we Mourn Our Nation's Loss' 35.00
Pressed Glass, Plate, Bread, Wildflower, Clear, Cut Corners, 10 In. 11.00
Pressed Glass, Plate, Bread, 101 Motto 40.00
Pressed Glass, Plate, Bread, 101, 'Give Us This Day Our Daily Bread, ' Round 25.00
Pressed Glass, Plate, Broken Column, 8 In.Diameter 28.00
Pressed Glass, Plate, Cake, Ball & Swirl 22.00
Pressed Glass, Plate, Cake, Cottage 7.00
Pressed Glass, Plate, Cake, Dahlia, Clear, Closed Handles, 8 1/2 In. 12.50
Pressed Glass, Plate, Cake, Dahlia, Handles, 9 In.Diameter 18.00
Pressed Glass, Plate, Cake, Daisy & Button, Square, 9 In. 12.50
Pressed Glass, Plate, Cake, Daisy & Button, Thumbprint, Blue 17.50
Pressed Glass, Plate, Cake, Diamond Medallion 7.00
Pressed Glass, Plate, Cake, Good Luck, 9 In. 29.00
Pressed Glass, Plate, Cake, Illinois, Pedestal, 10 3/4 In.Square 32.50
Pressed Glass, Plate, Cake, Jacob's Ladder, Maltese Cross, Footed, 11 In. 18.00
Pressed Glass, Plate, Cake, Minerva, Pedestal, 9 In. 42.00
Pressed Glass, Plate, Cake, Ribbon 17.50
Pressed Glass, Plate, Cake, Stippled Star, Footed, 8 1/4 In.Diameter 12.50
Pressed Glass, Plate, Campbell Kids, Baby's 15.00
Pressed Glass, Plate, Child's, Hey Diddle Diddle, 6 1/2 In. 18.00
Pressed Glass, Plate, Child's, This Little Pig Went To Market .... 15.00 To 18.00
Pressed Glass, Plate, Chop, Heart & Thumbprint 27.50
Pressed Glass, Plate, Chop, Minerva, Mulberry, 10 1/2 In. 15.00
Pressed Glass, Plate, Classic Warrior, Signed Jacobus 95.00
Pressed Glass, Plate, Classic Warrior, 11 1/2 In.Diameter 95.00
Pressed Glass, Plate, Cube & Fan, Square 5.00
Pressed Glass, Plate, Cupid & Venus .... 19.50 To 22.00
Pressed Glass, Plate, Dewdrop With Star, 5 1/2 In. 5.75
Pressed Glass, Plate, Dewdrop With Star, 8 1/4 In. 12.50
Pressed Glass, Plate, Diamond Medallion, 10 In.Diameter 9.50
Pressed Glass, Plate, Dolphin, Amber 22.50
Pressed Glass, Plate, Egg, Dewdrop, Clear, Fluted Rim, Place For 15 Eggs 6.50
Pressed Glass, Plate, Elaine, Frosted Center, Plain Border, 9 In. 38.00
Pressed Glass, Plate, Elaine, Frosted, Birds Border 35.00
Pressed Glass, Plate, Etched Battleship Maine, 101 Border, 5 In. 12.00
Pressed Glass, Plate, Faith, Hope & Charity 30.00
Pressed Glass, Plate, Feather, 10 In.Diameter 22.50

Pressed Glass, Plate, Feathers & Rosette, Opalescent, Fluted, 8 3/4 In.	18.00
Pressed Glass, Plate, Fine Cut, Canary, 10 In.	18.00
Pressed Glass, Plate, Fleur-De-Lis, Square	12.50
Pressed Glass, Plate, Floral Ovals, 7 1/4 In.Square	12.50
Pressed Glass, Plate, Fruit, Peach & Berries, Scalloped, 8 In.Diameter	2.50
Pressed Glass, Plate, Fruit, Pears & Berries, Scalloped, 8 In.Diameter	2.50
Pressed Glass, Plate, Garfield Drape	32.50
Pressed Glass, Plate, Garfield Drape, Frosted Edge, 10 1/2 In.Diameter	7.50
Pressed Glass, Plate, Garfield, Frosted Portrait, Border Of 13 Stars	20.00
Pressed Glass, Plate, General Grant	23.00
Pressed Glass, Plate, Good Luck, Round, 10 In.	9.00
Pressed Glass, Plate, Good Luck, 8 In.	28.50
Pressed Glass, Plate, Grape, 6 In.	6.50
Pressed Glass, Plate, Late Thistle, 10 1/2 In., New Cut	13.50
Pressed Glass, Plate, Lattice, 6 In.Diameter	4.00
Pressed Glass, Plate, Lattice, 10 In.Diameter	7.50
Pressed Glass, Plate, Liberty Bell, Round, Handles, Signed Names Of Colonies	35.00
Pressed Glass, Plate, Loop & Dart, Round, Flint	22.50
Pressed Glass, Plate, Loop & Dart, 6 In.	25.00
Pressed Glass, Plate, Manhattan	15.00
Pressed Glass, Plate, Maple Leaf, Blue, Grant Peace	27.50
Pressed Glass, Plate, Maple Leaf, Vaseline, 11 In.	35.00
Pressed Glass, Plate, Maple Leaf, 10 In.	9.00
Pressed Glass, Plate, Nailhead, Square	8.00
Pressed Glass, Plate, Nailhead, 9 1/4 In.Diameter	10.50
Pressed Glass, Plate, New Jersey, 11 In.	10.00
Pressed Glass, Plate, Paneled Daisy, 9 In.Square	14.00
Pressed Glass, Plate, Paneled Daisy, 9 1/4 In.	15.00
Pressed Glass, Plate, Paneled Thistle, 10 In.	22.50
Pressed Glass, Plate, Pillow & Sunburst, 10 1/4 In.	12.00
Pressed Glass, Plate, Pleat & Panel, 7 In.	7.00
Pressed Glass, Plate, Pleat & Panel, 7 In.Square	9.50
Pressed Glass, Plate, Primrose, Amber, 7 In.	19.00
Pressed Glass, Plate, Primrose, Blue, 6 In.	7.40
Pressed Glass, Plate, Primrose, Blue, 7 In.	8.25 To 22.00
Pressed Glass, Plate, Primrose, Clear, 7 In.	13.00
Pressed Glass, Plate, Primrose, Light Blue, 6 In.	14.81
Pressed Glass, Plate, Primrose, Light Blue, 7 In.	16.72
Pressed Glass, Plate, Primrose, Round, 2 Handles	9.50
Pressed Glass, Plate, Priscilla, Findlay, 10 In.Diameter, 2 In.High	18.50
Pressed Glass, Plate, Priscilla, 8 3/4 In.Diameter	16.00
Pressed Glass, Plate, Rose In Snow, 7 1/4 In.Diameter	22.50
Pressed Glass, Plate, Rose In Snow, 9 1/2 In.Diameter	10.00
Pressed Glass, Plate, Salem Swirl, Santa Claus Bust Picture	7.00
Pressed Glass, Plate, Scalloped Loop Variant, Blue, Fluted Rim, 8 1/2 In.	27.50
Pressed Glass, Plate, Thistle, 7 In.Square	8.50
Pressed Glass, Plate, Triple Triangle, Clear, 11 In.	16.50
Pressed Glass, Plate, Warrior	100.00
Pressed Glass, Plate, 101, 8 In.	11.50
Pressed Glass, Plate, 1, 000-Eye, Amber, 10 In.Square	20.00
Pressed Glass, Plate, 1, 000-Eye, Blue, Square, 8 In.	16.00
Pressed Glass, Plate, 1, 000-Eye, 6 In.Diameter	10.00
Pressed Glass, Plate, 1, 000-Eye, 8 In.Diameter	14.00
Pressed Glass, Platter, Beaded Loop, Oval	18.50
Pressed Glass, Platter, Bread, Arched Leaf	11.00
Pressed Glass, Platter, Bread, Bunker Hill, Prescott & Stark	40.00
Pressed Glass, Platter, Bread, Centennial	45.00
Pressed Glass, Platter, Bread, Constitution, Clear	25.00
Pressed Glass, Platter, Bread, Continental Hall	31.00
Pressed Glass, Platter, Bread, Cupid & Venus	18.00
Pressed Glass, Platter, Bread, Cupid's Hunt, Portrait Of Woman In Center	20.00
Pressed Glass, Platter, Bread, Dahlia	13.00
Pressed Glass, Platter, Bread, Daisy & Button	12.00
Pressed Glass, Platter, Bread, Deer & Pine, Amber	40.00
Pressed Glass, Platter, Bread, Dewdrop In Points	10.00
Pressed Glass, Platter, Bread, Dewdrop, Sheaf Of Wheat	13.00

Pressed Glass, Platter, Bread, Double Ribbon, Frosted 18.00
Pressed Glass, Platter, Bread, Egyptian 35.00
Pressed Glass, Platter, Bread, Eureka 22.50
Pressed Glass, Platter, Bread, Fine Cut, Panels 13.00
Pressed Glass, Platter, Bread, Forget-Me-Not, Stippled Kitten 45.00
Pressed Glass, Platter, Bread, Frosted Lion With Cable, Oval, Handles 28.00
Pressed Glass, Platter, Bread, Golden Rule 13.00
Pressed Glass, Platter, Bread, Good Luck 35.00
Pressed Glass, Platter, Bread, Horseshoe, 'give Us This Day' 22.50
Pressed Glass, Platter, Bread, Horseshoe, 'give Us This Day, ' Double Handle 24.50
Pressed Glass, Platter, Bread, Jeweled Band 15.00
Pressed Glass, Platter, Bread, Kansas, 'our Daily Bread' 35.00
Pressed Glass, Platter, Bread, Lattice, Clear, 'waste Not, Want Not' 40.00
Pressed Glass, Platter, Bread, Lotus 15.00
Pressed Glass, Platter, Bread, Minerva 25.00
Pressed Glass, Platter, Bread, Primrose 13.00
Pressed Glass, Platter, Bread, Rock Of Ages 40.00
Pressed Glass, Platter, Bread, Roman Rosette 18.00
Pressed Glass, Platter, Bread, Scroll, Flowers 10.00
Pressed Glass, Platter, Bread, Sheaf Of Wheat 15.00
Pressed Glass, Platter, Bread, Theodore Roosevelt, Frosted 45.00
Pressed Glass, Platter, Bread, Three Presidents 30.00
Pressed Glass, Platter, Bread, Three Presidents, Frosted 39.00
Pressed Glass, Platter, Bread, Three Presidents, Stippled 29.50
Pressed Glass, Platter, Bread, Two Bands 10.00
Pressed Glass, Platter, Deer & Pine Tree, Handled, 9 X 15 In. 40.00
Pressed Glass, Platter, Double Frosted Ribbon 45.00
Pressed Glass, Platter, Double Horseshoe, Handles, 10 X 14 In. 42.50
Pressed Glass, Platter, Fruit & Flower, 16 1/4 In.Long 95.00
Pressed Glass, Platter, Garden Of Eden 24.00
Pressed Glass, Platter, George Washington, 1776-1876, Bear Paw Handles 110.00
Pressed Glass, Platter, Good Luck, Anchor Handles 25.00
Pressed Glass, Platter, Jacob's Ladder, Maltese Cross 35.00
Pressed Glass, Platter, Liberty Bell, Signers 45.00
Pressed Glass, Platter, Lion, Frosted, Oval 35.00
Pressed Glass, Platter, Mckinley Memorial ....20.00 To 36.00
Pressed Glass, Platter, Peerless, Oval 11.00
Pressed Glass, Platter, Pinafore 46.00
Pressed Glass, Platter, Sheaf Of Wheat 25.00
Pressed Glass, Platter, Sheaf Of Wheat, Rim Turned Under 30.00
Pressed Glass, Platter, Stork, Frosted 42.00
Pressed Glass, Platter, Three Presidents, Clear 35.00
Pressed Glass, Platter, Westward Ho, Flint 45.00
Pressed Glass, Pressed Glass, Plate, Block & Fan, 6 3/4 In.Diameter 9.50
Pressed Glass, Punch Set, Honeycomb, Miniature, 7 Piece 35.00
Pressed Glass, Punch Set, Nortec, Pres Cut, 8 Piece 95.00
Pressed Glass, Punch Set, Sunburst, Child's, 7 Piece 50.00
Pressed Glass, Relish, Baltimore Pear 8.00
Pressed Glass, Relish, Actress, Clear, Rectangular ....25.00 To 27.50
Pressed Glass, Relish, Baltimore Pear, 8 In. 9.00
Pressed Glass, Relish, Bleeding Heart 10.00
Pressed Glass, Relish, Colorado, Clear, Footed, 5 X 7 In. 14.50
Pressed Glass, Relish, Comet, Square 12.00
Pressed Glass, Relish, Dewey, Green, Greentown 29.00
Pressed Glass, Relish, Dewey, Serpentine 15.00
Pressed Glass, Relish, Double Snail, 8 In. 12.50
Pressed Glass, Relish, Egyptian ....10.00 To 12.00
Pressed Glass, Relish, Floral Diamond, Gold 5.00
Pressed Glass, Relish, Frosted Daisy & Leaf 12.50
Pressed Glass, Relish, Frosted Daisy & Leaf, 2 Handles, 10 In.Diameter 25.00
Pressed Glass, Relish, Good Luck, 9 X 5 In. 8.00
Pressed Glass, Relish, Grape & Festoon 15.00
Pressed Glass, Relish, Jacob's Ladder ....6.00 To 13.00
Pressed Glass, Relish, Kentucky, Green 10.50
Pressed Glass, Relish, Narcissus Spray, Clear 4.50
Pressed Glass, Relish, New Hampshire 7.50

Pressed Glass, Relish, Paneled Holly, Clear, Oblong 35.00
Pressed Glass, Relish, Pillow Encircled, Green 8.00
Pressed Glass, Relish, Pleat & Panel, Open Handles, 8 1/2 X 5 In. 11.00
Pressed Glass, Relish, Priscilla, Three-Leaf Clover Shape 12.00
Pressed Glass, Relish, Raindrop, Amber, Oblong 13.50
Pressed Glass, Relish, Roman Rosette, Oval 10.00
Pressed Glass, Relish, Seashell, Footed, 3 Compartment, 9 In. 22.00
Pressed Glass, Relish, Stippled Peppers 7.50
Pressed Glass, Relish, Strawberry 7.00
Pressed Glass, Relish, Tennessee, Oval 7.50
Pressed Glass, Relish, Thumbprint, Ruby, Oblong 25.00
Pressed Glass, Relish, Wildflower, Clear 10.00
Pressed Glass, Rose Bowl, Amethyst, Flint, 4 In.Diameter 25.00
Pressed Glass, Rose Bowl, Block & Fan, 4 1/2 X 3 In. 12.50
Pressed Glass, Rose Bowl, Double Snail, 7 In. 35.00
Pressed Glass, Rose Bowl, Framed Jewel 11.50
Pressed Glass, Rose Bowl, Leaf & Beads, Twig Feet, Flint 28.00
Pressed Glass, Rose Bowl, Paneled Thistle .... 7.00 To 16.50
Pressed Glass, Rose Bowl, Pineapple & Fan, 4 1/2 In. 6.00
Pressed Glass, Rose Bowl, Priscilla .... 8.00 To 15.00
Pressed Glass, Rose Bowl, Priscilla, 3 In.High 6.00
Pressed Glass, Rose Bowl, Wyoming 25.00
Pressed Glass, Salt & Pepper, Banded Fleur-De-Lis, Pair 10.00
Pressed Glass, Salt & Pepper, Broken Column, Set 13.00
Pressed Glass, Salt & Pepper, Cornucopia, Clear, 2 In.High 8.00
Pressed Glass, Salt & Pepper, Empress, Green, Gold Decorated, Pair 35.00
Pressed Glass, Salt & Pepper, Galloway .... 8.00 To 15.00
Pressed Glass, Salt & Pepper, Klondike 90.00
Pressed Glass, Salt & Pepper, Leaf Palm, Blue, 2 3/4 In.High 25.00
Pressed Glass, Salt & Pepper.1, 000-Eye, Amber, Pair 12.50
Pressed Glass, Salt & Pepper, Zigzag, Pair 7.50
Pressed Glass, Salt Dip, Chicken On Nest, Green .... .75
Pressed Glass, Salt Dip, Daisy & Button, Apple Green, Canoe 11.00
Pressed Glass, Salt Dip, Squirrel 15.00
Pressed Glass, Salt Dip, Swan, Individual 13.50
Pressed Glass, Salt Shaker, Acorn, Blue 17.50
Pressed Glass, Salt Shaker, Arrowhead In Oval, Pewter Lid 4.00
Pressed Glass, Salt Shaker, Atlas, Tin Top 4.50
Pressed Glass, Salt Shaker, Block & Fan 6.50
Pressed Glass, Salt Shaker, Christmas Panel, Amber 10.00
Pressed Glass, Salt Shaker, Curlicue, Metal Top 6.50
Pressed Glass, Salt Shaker, Curtain 12.50
Pressed Glass, Salt Shaker, Delaware, Cranberry, Clear 14.00
Pressed Glass, Salt Shaker, Double Diamond, Flint 12.50
Pressed Glass, Salt Shaker, Baby Thumbprint, Blue 19.00
Pressed Glass, Salt Shaker, Butterfly Handles, Pewter Top 9.00
Pressed Glass, Salt Shaker, Fine Cut, Apple Green, Pewter Top 7.00
Pressed Glass, Salt Shaker, Foggy Bottom, Metal Top 9.50
Pressed Glass, Salt Shaker, Frosted Circle 10.00
Pressed Glass, Salt Shaker, Galloway, Tin Top 7.50
Pressed Glass, Salt Shaker, Googley Eyed, Metal Top 5.00
Pressed Glass, Salt Shaker, Inverted Thumbprint, Blue 10.00
Pressed Glass, Salt Shaker, Harp, Flint 16.50
Pressed Glass, Salt Shaker, Heavy Drape, Tin Top 4.50
Pressed Glass, Salt Shaker, Hundred Eye, Metal Top 5.00
Pressed Glass, Salt Shaker, Ladder With Diamond, Tin Top 6.25
Pressed Glass, Salt Shaker, Leaf, Footed, Master 12.50
Pressed Glass, Salt Shaker, Maine 12.50
Pressed Glass, Salt Shaker, Manhattan, Bottle Shape, Lid 8.50
Pressed Glass, Salt Shaker, Marsh, Pink, Square 8.50
Pressed Glass, Salt Shaker, National's Eureka, Tin Top 6.00
Pressed Glass, Salt Shaker, Paneled Thistle 12.50
Pressed Glass, Salt Shaker, Peacock Feather 18.50
Pressed Glass, Salt Shaker, Pineapple & Fan, Pewter Top 6.00
Pressed Glass, Salt Shaker, Priscilla, Lid 20.00
Pressed Glass, Salt Shaker, Strawberry, Master, Footed 17.50

Pressed Glass, Salt Shaker, Three Face	10.00
Pressed Glass, Salt Shaker, Two Band, Metal Top	6.50
Pressed Glass, Salt Shaker, Wheat & Barley, Blue	9.50
Pressed Glass, Salt, Bull's-Eye	20.00
Pressed Glass, Salt, Heart & Thumbprint	25.00
Pressed Glass, Salt, Horn Of Plenty, Oval	45.00
Pressed Glass, Salt, Master, Bellflower, Ribbed	18.00
Pressed Glass, Salt, Master, Buckle	12.00
Pressed Glass, Salt, Master, Bull's-Eye, Flint	18.00
Pressed Glass, Master, Daisy & Button	15.00
Pressed Glass, Salt, Master, Giant Sawtooth	9.00
Pressed Glass, Salt, Master, Jacob's Ladder	14.50
Pressed Glass, Salt, Master, Jersey Swirl, Spitton Shape	12.50
Pressed Glass, Salt, Master, King's Crown	14.00
Pressed Glass, Salt, Master, Loop	12.00
Pressed Glass, Salt, Master, Loop With Diamond Ornaments	7.50
Pressed Glass, Salt, Master, Open Rose	12.00
Pressed Glass, Salt, Master, Squirrel	22.00
Pressed Glass, Salt, Master, Star Band	7.50
Pressed Glass, Salt, Master, Straw Hat, Clear	12.00
Pressed Glass, Salt, Master, U.S.Coin, Lion Mask, Paw Feet, Circa 1845, Pair	148.00
Pressed Glass, Salt, Prism & Diamond Point, Footed	9.50
Pressed Glass, Salt, Tepee	8.00
Pressed Glass, Salt, Two Panel, Miniature	3.00
Pressed Glass, Salt, Utah	8.50
Pressed Glass, Sauce Set, Delaware, 7 Piece, Cranberry Flowers, Gold Trim	125.00
Pressed Glass, Sauce, Actress, Flat, 4 1/2 In.	15.00
Pressed Glass, Sauce, Actress, Footed	15.50
Pressed Glass, Sauce, Alabama	4.00
Pressed Glass, Sauce, Ball & Swirl, Pedestal Base	6.50
Pressed Glass, Sauce, Beaded Grape, Clear, 7 3/8 In.Square	15.00
Pressed Glass, Sauce, Beaded Grape, Square, 4 In.	4.00
Pressed Glass, Sauce, Beaded Swirl, Green, Round, 3 Feet, Gold, 4 In.	13.00
Pressed Glass, Sauce, Bearded Man, Footed, 4 In.	6.00
Pressed Glass, Sauce, Bellflower, Flint	3.00
Pressed Glass, Sauce, Bleeding Heart	6.00
Pressed Glass, Sauce, Block & Fan, Footed	5.75
Pressed Glass, Sauce, Buckle .... 5.00 To 5.75
Pressed Glass, Sauce, Canadian, Footed	6.50
Pressed Glass, Sauce, Cardinal, Flat	12.00
Pressed Glass, Sauce, Cathedral, Flat	5.00
Pressed Glass, Sauce, Chain With Star	5.75
Pressed Glass, Sauce, Chrysanthemum Leaf	6.50
Pressed Glass, Sauce, Classic, Log Feet	28.50
Pressed Glass, Sauce, Colorado, Clear, Flared Rim, Footed	10.50
Pressed Glass, Sauce, Colorado, Green, Footed, 5 In.Diameter .... 11.00 To 17.50
Pressed Glass, Sauce, Colorado, Green, Ruffled, 5 In.Diameter	15.00
Pressed Glass, Sauce, Cupid & Venus, Footed .... 4.00 To 7.00
Pressed Glass, Sauce, Cupid's Hunt, Footed, 4 In.	16.00
Pressed Glass, Sauce, Curtain, Footed, 4 1/2 In.Diameter	1.00
Pressed Glass, Sauce, Cut Log, Footed, 4 1/2 In.	10.00
Pressed Glass, Sauce, Daisy & Button, Blue, 4 In.Diameter	10.00
Pressed Glass, Sauce, Daisy & Button, Clear, Heart Shape	5.00
Pressed Glass, Sauce, Daisy & Button, Green, Clover Shape	8.25
Pressed Glass, Sauce, Daisy & Button, Panel, Set Of Six	22.00
Pressed Glass, Sauce, Diagonal Band With Fan, Footed	5.00
Pressed Glass, Sauce, Diamond-Quilted, Bull's-Eye Border, Flint	6.50
Pressed Glass, Sauce, Egyptian, 4 1/2 In.Diameter	10.00
Pressed Glass, Sauce, Etched Grasshopper	4.50
Pressed Glass, Sauce, Feather, Footed	10.00
Pressed Glass, Sauce, Florida, Clear, Flat, 4 1/4 In.	5.00
Pressed Glass, Sauce, Flowered Scroll	4.50
Pressed Glass, Sauce, Frosted Artichoke	12.50
Pressed Glass, Sauce, Frosted Circle	6.00
Pressed Glass, Sauce, Frosted Crystal, Flat, 4 1/2 In.	5.00
Pressed Glass, Sauce, Frosted Lion, Crouched Lion On Base	10.00

Pressed Glass, Sauce, Frosted Stork, 101 Border, Iowa City, 4 In. 29.00
Pressed Glass, Sauce, Grape & Festoon 5.00
Pressed Glass, Sauce, Grape, Flint 3.00
Pressed Glass, Sauce, Hartley, Blue, Footed 9.75
Pressed Glass, Sauce, Herringbone, Green 6.00
Pressed Glass, Sauce, Horn Of Plenty, Flat, 4 1/2 In.Diameter 12.50
Pressed Glass, Sauce, Horn Of Plenty, Rayed Center, Scalloped Edge 17.50
Pressed Glass, Sauce, Ivy In Snow, Frosted, 3 3/4 In. 6.25
Pressed Glass, Sauce, Jacob's Ladder, 4 1/2 In. 2.00
Pressed Glass, Sauce, Jewel With Dewdrop, Flat 8.50
Pressed Glass, Sauce, Kentucky, Blue, Footed, 4 1/4 In. 12.50
Pressed Glass, Sauce, Kentucky, Green, Flat, 4 1/2 In. 7.50
Pressed Glass, Sauce, Klondike, Scalloped Top, Frosted, Amber Band 26.00
Pressed Glass, Sauce, Klondike, 4 In.Square 40.00
Pressed Glass, Sauce, Lace Band, Flat 3.75
Pressed Glass, Sauce, Loop & Pyramid, Gilt, Flat 4.00
Pressed Glass, Sauce, Louise, Flat, 4 In.Diameter 5.50
Pressed Glass, Sauce, Mascotte, Footed 6.00
Pressed Glass, Sauce, Morning Glory 88.50
Pressed Glass, Sauce, Nail, Footed, 4 In. 6.50
Pressed Glass, Sauce, New Jersey, Gold, 5 In. 5.00
Pressed Glass, Sauce, Nursery Tales 6.00
Pressed Glass, Sauce, Panel Cherry 12.00
Pressed Glass, Sauce, Paneled Daisy & Button 4.00
Pressed Glass, Sauce, Paneled Grape 4.00
Pressed Glass, Sauce, Paneled Grape With Thumbprint 2.50
Pressed Glass, Sauce, Paneled Thistle, Footed 6.25
Pressed Glass, Sauce, Paneled Wheat, Clear, Flat, 4 1/4 In. 5.00
Pressed Glass, Sauce, Peacock Eye, Flint 7.00
Pressed Glass, Sauce, Peacock Feather, Clear 4.00
Pressed Glass, Sauce, Plume & Waffle, Square, Footed, Set Of 4 .... 28.00
Pressed Glass, Sauce, Plume, Footed 9.50
Pressed Glass, Sauce, Pointed Hobnail 7.00
Pressed Glass, Sauce, Rib, Straight 22.00
Pressed Glass, Sauce, Ribbed Sawtooth 3.50
Pressed Glass, Sauce, Roman Rosette, Lacy, Flint 11.00
Pressed Glass, Sauce, Rose In Snow, 4 In.Diameter .... 4.00 To 6.50
Pressed Glass, Sauce, Sedan, Flat 2.50
Pressed Glass, Sauce, Shell & Tassel, Handle, 4 1/2 In., Set Of 4 .... 25.00
Pressed Glass, Sauce, Snail, Flat 6.75
Pressed Glass, Sauce, Squirrel, Footed 12.50
Pressed Glass, Sauce, Star Medallion, Set Of F 10.00
Pressed Glass, Sauce, Teasel, Footed 7.50
Pressed Glass, Sauce, Transverse Ribs 4.50
Pressed Glass, Sauce, Two Panel Oval, Clear, Flat 3.50
Pressed Glass, Sauce, Valencia Waffle 4.50
Pressed Glass, Sauce, Viking 6.00
Pressed Glass, Sauce, Viking, Footed, 4 1/2 In. 10.00
Pressed Glass, Sauce, Westward Ho 16.25
Pressed Glass, Sauce, Wreath & Shell, Clear To Opalescent, Footed 6.50
Pressed Glass, Sauce, 101 .... 4.00
Pressed Glass, Sauce, 1, 000-Eye, Green 10.25
Pressed Glass, Saucer, Dew & Raindrop, 4 In.Diameter 4.50
Pressed Glass, Saucer, Diamond Point, Flint 7.50
Pressed Glass, Saucer, Paneled Daisy, Amber, 5 1/4 In.Diameter 9.75
Pressed Glass, Shade, Diamond Pattern, Opalescent, Bell Shape, 4 1/2 In. 15.00
Pressed Glass, Shaker, Sugar, Beaded Rib, Tin Top 22.00
Pressed Glass, Shaker, Sugar, Frosted Royal Ivy 37.50
Pressed Glass, Shaker, Sugar, Moon & Star, Clear, Silver Lid 10.00
Pressed Glass, Shaker, Sugar, Swirl, Tin Cover 4.50
Pressed Glass, Shaker, Sugar, Three Face 35.00
Pressed Glass, Shaker, The States, Tin Top 7.50
Pressed Glass, Shaker, Tiny Block, Tin Top 4.00
Pressed Glass, Shaker, Zipper Slash, Red Flashed 12.00
Pressed Glass, Sherbet, Bee In Bottom 5.25
Pressed Glass, Sherbet, Cupid's Hunt, Footed 10.00

Pressed Glass, Sherbet, 44 Pattern, Stemmed, Silver Top	8.00
Pressed Glass, Sherry, Bull's-Eye	30.00
Pressed Glass, Shoe, Cane, Amber, Side Button, Impressed Bouquet	24.00
Pressed Glass, Shoe, Cane, Sapphire Blue, Side Button, Impressed Bouquet	29.00
Pressed Glass, Shoe, Gillinder Centennial *Illus*	22.00
Pressed Glass, Slipper, Daisy & Button, Clear, 7 In.	15.00
Pressed Glass, Slipper, Daisy & Button, On Roller Skates	6.50
Pressed Glass, Spill, Bucket	11.00
Pressed Glass, Spill, Bull's-Eye, Variant, Flint	22.00
Pressed Glass, Spill, Diagonal Band	8.50
Pressed Glass, Spill, Diamond & Thumbprint, Clear, Flint	22.50
Pressed Glass, Spill, Diamond Point & Panels, Flint	18.00
Pressed Glass, Spill, Diamond Point, Flint	10.00
Pressed Glass, Spill, Framed Ovals With Thumbprints	30.00
Pressed Glass, Spill, Framed Ovals, Flint	35.00
Pressed Glass, Spill, Horn Of Plenty	25.00
Pressed Glass, Spill, Prism, Flint	19.50
Pressed Glass, Spill, Sandwich Star	22.00
Pressed Glass, Spill, Sawtooth	22.00
Pressed Glass, Spill, Sawtooth, Flint	18.50
Pressed Glass, Spill, Umbilicated Sawtooth	14.00
Pressed Glass, Spooner, Actress, Footed, 5 1/2 In.	27.50
Pressed Glass, Spooner, Baltimore Pear	17.00
Pressed Glass, Spooner, Banded Buckle	19.00
Pressed Glass, Spooner, Barley	12.50 To 13.50
Pressed Glass, Spooner, Beaded Dewdrop	10.50
Pressed Glass, Spooner, Bellflower	12.00 To 16.00
Pressed Glass, Spooner, Bellflower, Flint	16.00
Pressed Glass, Spooner, Bellflower, Footed, Scalloped, Flint	25.00
Pressed Glass, Spooner, Bellflower, Single Vine	15.00 To 24.00
Pressed Glass, Spooner, Blackberry	2.00
Pressed Glass, Spooner, Bleeding Heart	17.00
Pressed Glass, Spooner, Block, Ruby Flashed	20.00
Pressed Glass, Spooner, Bouquet	20.00
Pressed Glass, Spooner, Broken Column	19.00
Pressed Glass, Spooner, Buckle	7.50 To 14.00
Pressed Glass, Spooner, Buckle, Clear, Scalloped Edge	18.00
Pressed Glass, Spooner, Buckle, Flint	25.00
Pressed Glass, Spooner, Budded Ivy	15.00
Pressed Glass, Spooner, Bull's-Eye, Diamond Point, Gold Band Top	50.00
Pressed Glass, Spooner, Cabbage Rose	7.50
Pressed Glass, Spooner, Cable	21.50
Pressed Glass, Spooner, Cable, Flint	22.50 To 28.50
Pressed Glass, Spooner, Cameo	11.00 To 18.00
Pressed Glass, Spooner, Cardinal Bird *Illus*	8.00
Pressed Glass, Spooner, Cathedral	10.00 To 16.50
Pressed Glass, Spooner, Chain & Star	15.00
Pressed Glass, Spooner, Chain With Shield	15.00
Pressed Glass, Spooner, Chandelier	10.00
Pressed Glass, Spooner, Colorado, Green	45.00
Pressed Glass, Spooner, Cottage	7.50
Pressed Glass, Spooner, Curtain *Illus*	8.00
Pressed Glass, Spooner, Daisy & Button, Amber	18.00 To 45.00
Pressed Glass, Spooner, Daisy & Button, Amber, Scalloped Edge	28.00
Pressed Glass, Spooner, Daisy & Button, Amber, Stipe	38.50
Pressed Glass, Spooner, Daisy & Button, Clear, 5 In.High	17.50
Pressed Glass, Spooner, Daisy & Button, Narcissus	10.00
Pressed Glass, Spooner, Daisy & Button, Yellow, V Ornament	27.00
Pressed Glass, Spooner, Daisy In Diamond	8.00
Pressed Glass, Spooner, Daisy, Amber Panel	35.00
Pressed Glass, Spooner, Dakota	12.00
Pressed Glass, Spooner, Dart	15.00
Pressed Glass, Spooner, Delaware, Clear	25.00
Pressed Glass, Spooner, Delaware, Green	39.50
Pressed Glass, Spooner, Diamond Point, Loop	10.00
Pressed Glass, Spooner, Diamond Point, Flint	24.00

Pressed Glass, Shoe, Gillinder Centennial
See Page 406

Pressed Glass,
Spooner, Cardinal Bird
See Page 406

Pressed Glass, Spooner, Curtain
See Page 406

Pressed Glass, Spooner, Diamond Point, Footed, Flint	25.00
Pressed Glass, Spooner, Diamond Point, Gold Band, Flint	29.50
Pressed Glass, Spooner, Diamond Point, Scalloped	15.00
Pressed Glass, Spooner, Diamond Rosettes, Flint	14.00
Pressed Glass, Spooner, Double Frosted Ribbon, Pedestal Base, Scalloped Rim	16.50
Pressed Glass, Spooner, Draped Fan	6.50
Pressed Glass, Spooner, Fickle Block	6.00
Pressed Glass, Spooner, Flattened Diamond	12.50
Pressed Glass, Spooner, Fleur-De-Lis & Drape	9.00
Pressed Glass, Spooner, Flying Stork	17.00
Pressed Glass, Spooner, Forget-Me-Not In Scroll	12.50
Pressed Glass, Spooner, Frosted Circle	17.50
Pressed Glass, Spooner, Frosted Lion	12.00
Pressed Glass, Spooner, Garfield Drape	7.50
Pressed Glass, Spooner, Good Luck	12.00
Pressed Glass, Spooner, Grape & Festoon	12.00
Pressed Glass, Spooner, Grape & Festoon, Clear Leaf, Stippled Background	10.00
Pressed Glass, Spooner, Hairpin & Thumbprint, Flint	22.00
Pressed Glass, Spooner, Hamilton	15.00
Pressed Glass, Spooner, Herringbone	15.00
Pressed Glass, Spooner, Holly	37.50
Pressed Glass, Spooner, Honeycomb	16.50
Pressed Glass, Spooner, Honeycomb, Flint	12.50
Pressed Glass, Spooner, Hops Band	12.50
Pressed Glass, Spooner, Horn Of Plenty, 4 1/2 In.	18.33
Pressed Glass, Spooner, Hummingbird, Blue	22.50
Pressed Glass, Spooner, Inverted Fern, Flint	16.50 To 18.00
Pressed Glass, Spooner, Inverted Thumbprint, Amber	4.75
Pressed Glass, Spooner, Jacob's Ladder	15.00
Pressed Glass, Spooner, Klondike	125.00

Pressed Glass, Spooner, Ladders, 2 3/4 In.High	10.00
Pressed Glass, Spooner, Leaf & Dart	10.50
Pressed Glass, Spooner, Lily Of The Valley	10.50 To 16.50
Pressed Glass, Spooner, Lion	22.50
Pressed Glass, Spooner, Log Cabin	45.00
Pressed Glass, Spooner, Loop & Dart, Clear	15.00
Pressed Glass, Spooner, Loop & Fans	10.00
Pressed Glass, Spooner, Loop, 5 In.Long	10.00
Pressed Glass, Spooner, Louisiana	7.50
Pressed Glass, Spooner, Magnet & Grape	9.00
Pressed Glass, Spooner, Magnet & Grape With Stippled Leaf	15.00
Pressed Glass, Spooner, Mascotte, Etched	18.00
Pressed Glass, Spooner, Massachusetts	9.00
Pressed Glass, Spooner, Minerva	16.00
Pressed Glass, Spooner, Moon & Star, Flint	35.00
Pressed Glass, Spooner, New England Pineapple, Flint	22.50
Pressed Glass, Spooner, New Jersey, Gold Trim	14.00
Pressed Glass, Spooner, Open Rose	12.00 To 14.50
Pressed Glass, Spooner, Paneled Grape Band, Flint	18.50
Pressed Glass, Spooner, Paneled Wheat, Round	11.50
Pressed Glass, Spooner, Pennsylvania, Ruby Top	25.00
Pressed Glass, Spooner, Pleat & Panel	7.00 To 12.00
Pressed Glass, Spooner, Pointed Jewel, Clear	15.00
Pressed Glass, Spooner, Powder & Shot	22.50
Pressed Glass, Spooner, Pressed Leaf	12.00
Pressed Glass, Spooner, Princess Feather	11.00 To 18.50
Pressed Glass, Spooner, Psyche & Cupid	21.00
Pressed Glass, Spooner, Queen Anne	20.00 To 25.00
Pressed Glass, Spooner, Ribbed Grape	25.00
Pressed Glass, Spooner, Ribbed Grape, Scalloped Rim, Flint	25.00
Pressed Glass, Spooner, Ribbed Ivy	24.00
Pressed Glass, Spooner, Ribbed Palm, Flint, 5 In.High, Pair	17.50
Pressed Glass, Spooner, Ribbon, Frosted	15.00
Pressed Glass, Spooner, Ripple	13.50
Pressed Glass, Spooner, Rose In Snow	15.00
Pressed Glass, Spooner, Royal Ivy, Frosted	12.00
Pressed Glass, Spooner, Ruby Flashed, Clear	24.00
Pressed Glass, Spooner, Ruby To Clear	20.00
Pressed Glass, Spooner, Sandwich Star, Flint	17.00
Pressed Glass, Spooner, Sheraton, Clear	9.00
Pressed Glass, Spooner, Smocking	18.00
Pressed Glass, Spooner, Snail	18.00
Pressed Glass, Spooner, Snowflake, Ruby Flashed, Pedestal Base	30.00
Pressed Glass, Spooner, Star Medallion	13.00
Pressed Glass, Spooner, Stippled Grape & Festoon	9.50
Pressed Glass, Spooner, Stippled Medallion, Flint	17.50
Pressed Glass, Spooner, Stippled Star	20.00
Pressed Glass, Spooner, Swan	14.50
Pressed Glass, Spooner, Teardrop, Cobalt Blue	35.00
Pressed Glass, Spooner, Thistle	10.50
Pressed Glass, Spooner, Three Panel	8.50 To 18.00
Pressed Glass, Spooner, Thumbprint, Scalloped Top, Flint	19.00
Pressed Glass, Spooner, Tokyo	13.50
Pressed Glass, Spooner, Triangular Prism, Flint	16.00
Pressed Glass, Spooner, Triple Triangle, Ruby Flashed	25.00
Pressed Glass, Spooner, U.S.Coin	95.00 To 120.00
Pressed Glass, Spooner, Viking	12.00
Pressed Glass, Spooner, Waffle & Thumbprint	25.00
Pressed Glass, Spooner, Washboard	7.50
Pressed Glass, Spooner, Westward Ho	55.00
Pressed Glass, Spooner, Windflower, Clear	11.00
Pressed Glass, Spooner, Wisconsin	16.50
Pressed Glass, Spooner, 1, 000-Eye	16.00 To 17.00
Pressed Glass, Sugar & Creamer, Baltimore Pear	16.00
Pressed Glass, Sugar & Creamer, Cable & Ring	105.00
Pressed Glass, Sugar & Creamer, Cable, Cover	130.00

Pressed Glass, Sugar & Creamer, Crystal Wedding, Cover, Spooner, Set 65.00
Pressed Glass, Sugar & Creamer, Dakota 40.00
Pressed Glass, Sugar & Creamer, Dakota, Pedestal, Open 32.00
Pressed Glass, Sugar & Creamer, Diamond & Sunburst, Squatty 8.00
Pressed Glass, Sugar & Creamer, Diamond, Amber, Cover 60.00
Pressed Glass, Sugar & Creamer, Green, Delaware, Gold Metal Collars, Handles 75.00
Pressed Glass, Sugar & Creamer, Iris & Herringbone, Clear 8.00
Pressed Glass, Sugar & Creamer, Lacy, Daisy 12.50
Pressed Glass, Sugar & Creamer, Maiden's Blush, Pink Flashed 54.50
Pressed Glass, Sugar & Creamer, Maple Leaf, Covered 68.00
Pressed Glass, Sugar & Creamer, Minerva, Footed 20.00
Pressed Glass, Sugar & Creamer, Portland Tree Of Life, Marked P.G.Co., ... 65.00
Pressed Glass, Sugar & Creamer, Portland, Individual 11.00
Pressed Glass, Sugar & Creamer, Ribbed Grape 25.00
Pressed Glass, Sugar & Creamer, Ribbed, Gold Trim, Square 7.50
Pressed Glass, Sugar & Creamer, Roman Rosette .... *Illus* 35.00

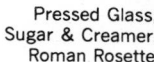

Pressed Glass,
Sugar & Creamer,
Roman Rosette

Pressed Glass, Sugar & Creamer, Rose In Snow, Cover, Square 47.50
Pressed Glass, Sugar & Creamer, Stippled Star, Open 30.00
Pressed Glass, Sugar & Creamer, Three Face 25.00
Pressed Glass, Sugar & Creamer, Westward Ho 150.00
Pressed Glass, Sugar, Acorn, Open 10.00
Pressed Glass, Sugar, Arched Leaf, Covered, Flint 57.50
Pressed Glass, Sugar, Ashburton, Open, Flint .... 22.50 To 30.00
Pressed Glass, Sugar, Azalea, Covered 5.00
Pressed Glass, Sugar, Balder, Covered 18.50
Pressed Glass, Sugar, Baltimore Pear, Clear 6.00
Pressed Glass, Sugar, Banded Buckle, Open 22.00
Pressed Glass, Sugar, Barberry, Covered 29.50
Pressed Glass, Sugar, Barred Forget-Me-Not, Cover 19.00
Pressed Glass, Sugar, Beaded Band, Footed 9.50
Pressed Glass, Sugar, Beaded Band, Open 17.50
Pressed Glass, Sugar, Beaded Dewdrop, Cover 22.00
Pressed Glass, Sugar, Beaded Grape Medallion, Open 16.50
Pressed Glass, Sugar, Beaded Grape, Covered 16.75
Pressed Glass, Sugar, Beaded Mirror, Open 13.50
Pressed Glass, Sugar, Bellflower, Flint, Cover 57.50
Pressed Glass, Sugar, Bleeding Heart 19.00
Pressed Glass, Sugar, Bleeding Heart, Open 15.00
Pressed Glass, Sugar, Block, Red, Covered 25.00
Pressed Glass, Sugar, Block, Ruby Flashed, Covered, Double Handles 25.00
Pressed Glass, Sugar, Blue, Opalescent, Jefferson, Cover 25.00
Pressed Glass, Sugar, Buckle, Cover, Flint .... 40.00 To 45.00
Pressed Glass, Sugar, Buckle, Open .... 10.00 To 20.00
Pressed Glass, Sugar, Bull's-Eye & Daisy, Pink, Open 14.00
Pressed Glass, Sugar, Bull's-Eye, Frosted Pedestal, Hexagon, Open, Flint 34.50
Pressed Glass, Sugar, Bull's-Eye, Pedestal, Open, Flint, 4 1/2 In.High 35.00
Pressed Glass, Sugar, Cable & Lion 20.00

Pressed Glass, Sugar, Cable & Ring, Open, Flint 25.00
Pressed Glass, Sugar, Cable, Cover, Flint 52.00
Pressed Glass, Sugar, Cardinal Bird, Covered 45.00
Pressed Glass, Sugar, Cathedral, Open 14.50
Pressed Glass, Sugar, Chain With Star, Covered 19.50
Pressed Glass, Sugar, Cherry, Covered 15.00
Pressed Glass, Sugar, Chocolate Cactus, Greentown 27.50
Pressed Glass, Sugar, Church Windows, Open, Color 23.00
Pressed Glass, Sugar, Classic, Covered 45.00
Pressed Glass, Sugar, Classic, Log Footed, Cover 65.00
Pressed Glass, Sugar, Classic, Open, Log Feet 110.00
Pressed Glass, Sugar, Colorado, Green, Cover 55.00
Pressed Glass, Sugar, Colorado, Green, Gold, Covered 59.50
Pressed Glass, Sugar, Colossus, Cover 14.00
Pressed Glass, Sugar, Columbia Co-Op, Open, Gold 15.00
Pressed Glass, Sugar, Corner Medallion, Open 6.00
Pressed Glass, Sugar, Creamer, & Butter, Canadian, Covered 89.00
Pressed Glass, Sugar, Creamer, & Butter, Iris & Herringbone, Clear 12.50
Pressed Glass, Sugar, Creamer, & Butter, Stippled Double Loop, Cover 37.00
Pressed Glass, Sugar, Creamer, & Spooner, Colonial Variant, Red Tops 45.00
Pressed Glass, Sugar, Creamer, & Spooner, Maryland, Ruby Loops 50.00
Pressed Glass, Sugar, Creamer, & Tray, Heart & Thumbprint, Individual 35.00
Pressed Glass, Sugar, Creamer, Butter, & Spooner, Star Band 48.00
Pressed Glass, Sugar, Cupid & Venus, Lid 20.00
Pressed Glass, Sugar, Cupid & Venus, Open 16.50
Pressed Glass, Sugar, Cut Log, Low Base 35.00
Pressed Glass, Sugar, Daisy & Button With Crossbar, Amber, 4 In.Diameter 7.50
Pressed Glass, Sugar, Daisy & Button, Amber, Cover 37.00
Pressed Glass, Sugar, Dakota, Plain, Covered .... 20.00 To 23.50
Pressed Glass, Sugar, Dart & Leaf, Open 15.00
Pressed Glass, Sugar, Delaware, Clear, Covered 17.50
Pressed Glass, Sugar, Diamond-Quilted, Cover 18.00
Pressed Glass, Sugar, Diamond Point 65.00
Pressed Glass, Sugar, Diamond Point With Panels, Flint, Cover 57.50
Pressed Glass, Sugar, Diamond Thumbprint, Flint, Open 35.00
Pressed Glass, Sugar, Dolphin, Frosted Base, Cover 87.50
Pressed Glass, Sugar, Drapery, Open 7.00
Pressed Glass, Sugar, Edgerton, Covered 10.00
Pressed Glass, Sugar, Egyptian Pattern, Open 15.00
Pressed Glass, Sugar, Etched Bull's-Eye & Diamond Point, Covered 15.00
Pressed Glass, Sugar, Etched Mascotte, Cover 23.50
Pressed Glass, Sugar, Excelsior, Maltese Cross, Flint, Cover 57.50
Pressed Glass, Sugar, Fan With Diamonds, Covered, Pedestal 18.50
Pressed Glass, Sugar, Feather, Covered 23.50
Pressed Glass, Sugar, Festoon, Covered 27.50
Pressed Glass, Sugar, Fine Rib, Lid 45.00
Pressed Glass, Sugar, Four Petals, Flint, Cover 45.00
Pressed Glass, Sugar, Frosted Lion, Lid 35.00
Pressed Glass, Sugar, Galloway, Covered .... 13.00 To 19.75
Pressed Glass, Sugar, Giant Sawtooth, Open 35.00
Pressed Glass, Sugar, Heart & Thumbprint, Green, Handles 12.50
Pressed Glass, Sugar, Heart & Thumbprint, 2 1/2 In.Tall 7.00
Pressed Glass, Sugar, Henrietta, Cover 18.00
Pressed Glass, Sugar, Herringbone, Green, Open 12.00
Pressed Glass, Sugar, Hexagonal Bull's-Eye, Open 6.50
Pressed Glass, Sugar, Hinoto, Covered, Flint .... 45.00 To 57.50
Pressed Glass, Sugar, Horn Of Plenty, Flint, Open 25.00
Pressed Glass, Sugar, Horn Of Plenty, Steeple Cover 65.00
Pressed Glass, Sugar, Horseshoe 20.00
Pressed Glass, Sugar, Horseshoe, Open 9.50
Pressed Glass, Sugar, Inverted Fern, Covered, Flint .... 42.50 To 50.00
Pressed Glass, Sugar, Inverted Strawberry, Open 18.50
Pressed Glass, Sugar, Jacob's Ladder, Maltese Cross, Open, 6 In.Tall 12.00
Pressed Glass, Sugar, Job's Tears, Covered 19.50
Pressed Glass, Sugar, Klondike, Covered 150.00
Pressed Glass, Sugar, Klondike, Open 45.00

Pressed Glass, Sugar, Lee	70.00
Pressed Glass, Sugar, Legged Band Star, Covered	25.00
Pressed Glass, Sugar, Liberty Bell, Covered, 9 In.	45.00
Pressed Glass, Sugar, Loop & Dart With Round Ornament, Covered, Flint	35.00
Pressed Glass, Sugar, Loop & Dart With Round Ornament, Open	16.50
Pressed Glass, Sugar, Loop & Dart, Flint, Open	18.50
Pressed Glass, Sugar, Loop & Moose Eye, Flint, Open	61.50
Pressed Glass, Sugar, Louisiana, Cover	13.50
Pressed Glass, Sugar, Massachusetts, Cover	13.00
Pressed Glass, Sugar, Moon & Star	27.50 To 30.00
Pressed Glass, Sugar, New England Pineapple, Covered, Flint	52.50
Pressed Glass, Sugar, New Hampshire, Cover	18.00
Pressed Glass, Sugar, Open Rose, Open	12.50
Pressed Glass, Sugar, Paneled Heather, Covered	15.00
Pressed Glass, Sugar, Paneled Dewdrop, Open	9.00
Pressed Glass, Sugar, Petticoat, Covered	10.00
Pressed Glass, Sugar, Pillow & Sunburst, Cover, Oval	7.00
Pressed Glass, Sugar, Pioneer Victoria, Covered	15.00
Pressed Glass, Sugar, Pointed Hobnail, Covered, Ball Feet	37.50
Pressed Glass, Sugar, Powder & Shot, Flint, Open	32.00
Pressed Glass, Sugar, Princess Feather, Cover	33.00
Pressed Glass, Sugar, Priscilla, Covered	45.00
Pressed Glass, Sugar, Psyche & Cupid	20.00
Pressed Glass, Sugar, Psyche & Cupid, Open	25.00
Pressed Glass, Sugar, Queen Anne, Open	13.50
Pressed Glass, Sugar, Red Block, Cover	25.00
Pressed Glass, Sugar, Regal Pattern, Cover	30.00
Pressed Glass, Sugar, Ribbed Palm, Open, Flint	16.00 To 26.00
Pressed Glass, Sugar, Ribbon Candy, Footed	7.00
Pressed Glass, Sugar, Rosette, Covered	19.50
Pressed Glass, Sugar, Sandwich Loop, Covered, Flint	47.50
Pressed Glass, Sugar, Sawtooth & Honeycomb, Open	7.50
Pressed Glass, Sugar, Scroll With Flowers, Covered	26.50
Pressed Glass, Sugar, Scroll With Flowers, Open	7.50
Pressed Glass, Sugar, Sheraton, Blue, Cover	35.00
Pressed Glass, Sugar, Smocking	40.00
Pressed Glass, Sugar, Snowflake	2.50
Pressed Glass, Sugar, Star & Punty, Flint, Cover	75.00
Pressed Glass, Sugar, Star & Punty, Flint, Open	22.00
Pressed Glass, Sugar, Stippled Chain, Covered	19.75
Pressed Glass, Sugar, Stippled Double Loop, Covered	18.50
Pressed Glass, Sugar, Stippled Grape & Festoon, Clear Leaf, Open	15.00
Pressed Glass, Sugar, Stippled Leaf, Covered	25.00
Pressed Glass, Sugar, Stippled Sandburr, Covered	16.00
Pressed Glass, Sugar, Stippled Star, Covered, 8 1/2 In.High	7.50
Pressed Glass, Sugar, Stork, Clear, Covered	32.50
Pressed Glass, Sugar, Sunburst Medallion, Covered	13.50
Pressed Glass, Sugar, Sunk Daisy, Cover	14.50
Pressed Glass, Sugar, Thistle, Cover	16.00
Pressed Glass, Sugar, Three Face, Open	37.50
Pressed Glass, Sugar, Thumbprint, Flint, Open	20.00
Pressed Glass, Sugar, Torpedo, Cover	30.00
Pressed Glass, Sugar, Triangular Prism, Covered, Flint	45.00
Pressed Glass, Sugar, Two Band, Covered	10.00
Pressed Glass, Sugar, U.S.Coin, Frosted, Half Dollar	200.00
Pressed Glass, Sugar, Viking, Cover	22.00 To 28.50
Pressed Glass, Sugar, Viking, Open	9.00
Pressed Glass, Sugar, Waffle & Thumbprint, Cover, Flint	60.00
Pressed Glass, Sugar, Westward Ho, Covered	55.00 To 65.00
Pressed Glass, Sugar, Wheat & Barley, Covered	17.50 To 19.50
Pressed Glass, Sugar, Wheat & Star, Handle, 4 1/4 In.High	6.00
Pressed Glass, Sugar, Yoked Loop	35.00
Pressed Glass, Sugar, Yoked Loop, Open, Flint	15.00
Pressed Glass, Sugar, Zipper, Open	7.00
Pressed Glass, Sugar, 1, 000-Eye, Cover	21.50
Pressed Glass, Syrup, Amazon, Clear, Metal Top	12.50

Pressed Glass, Syrup, Bennet, Blue Floral, Pink, Gold Trim, Pewter Cover	22.50
Pressed Glass, Syrup, Diagonal Thumbprint, Amber, Dated, Tin Lid	45.00
Pressed Glass, Syrup, Feather, Pewter Top	15.00
Pressed Glass, Syrup, Heart & Thumbprint	27.50
Pressed Glass, Syrup, Heart & Thumbprint, Pewter Top, Dated '72	32.50
Pressed Glass, Syrup, Inverted Thumbprint, Blue, Pewter Top, Patent 1884	60.00
Pressed Glass, Syrup, Loop With Dewdrop, Hinged	20.00
Pressed Glass, Syrup, Manhattan	24.00
Pressed Glass, Syrup, Paneled, Clear, Pewter Lid, Hollow Handle	4.00
Pressed Glass, Syrup, Torpedo, Clear, Tin Top	19.50 To 27.50
Pressed Glass, Syrup, Wisconsin, Metal Top	25.00
Pressed Glass, The Patriot & Soldier, General Ulysses S.Grant	25.00
Pressed Glass, Toothpick, Atlas, Clear	5.00
Pressed Glass, Toothpick, Beaded Drape, Red & Clear, Willie, 1908, Beaded Top	22.00
Pressed Glass, Toothpick, Beaded Grape	9.00
Pressed Glass, Toothpick, Clear, Opal	18.00
Pressed Glass, Toothpick, Colorado, Blue, Gold	27.50
Pressed Glass, Toothpick, Colorado, Blue, Gold Trim, Footed	20.00
Pressed Glass, Toothpick, Colorado, Green, Gold	25.00
Pressed Glass, Toothpick, Cordova	8.00
Pressed Glass, Toothpick, Daisy & Button, Clear	12.50
Pressed Glass, Toothpick, Daisy & Button, Cobalt Blue, Footed	5.00
Pressed Glass, Toothpick, Daisy & Button, Uncle Sam Hat, 4 Mold	12.50
Pressed Glass, Toothpick, Delaware, Green	34.00 To 37.50
Pressed Glass, Toothpick, Delaware, Tint Of Rose & Gold	13.50
Pressed Glass, Toothpick, Duncan & Sons	8.00
Pressed Glass, Toothpick, Feather, Footed	30.00
Pressed Glass, Toothpick, Fleur-De-Lis	9.00
Pressed Glass, Toothpick, Gold Top, Three Handles	8.00
Pressed Glass, Toothpick, Honeycomb, Light Green	15.00
Pressed Glass, Toothpick, Illinois	10.00 To 13.50
Pressed Glass, Toothpick, Inverted Fan & Feather	11.50
Pressed Glass, Toothpick, Jewel & Dewdrop	25.00
Pressed Glass, Toothpick, King's Crown	5.50
Pressed Glass, Toothpick, Loop & Pillar	12.00
Pressed Glass, Toothpick, Maiden's Blush	37.50
Pressed Glass, Toothpick, Maiden's Blush, Pink Flashed	25.00
Pressed Glass, Toothpick, Manhattan	8.00
Pressed Glass, Toothpick, Minnesota	9.00
Pressed Glass, Toothpick, New Hampshire	7.50 To 10.00
Pressed Glass, Toothpick, New Hampshire, Pink Flashed	15.00
Pressed Glass, Toothpick, Oaken Bucket, Amber	8.00
Pressed Glass, Toothpick, Opalescent Ribs, Blue	25.00
Pressed Glass, Toothpick, Portland	7.50
Pressed Glass, Toothpick, Raindrop, Gold Trim	9.00
Pressed Glass, Toothpick, Serpent With Tree	10.00
Pressed Glass, Toothpick, Shoshone	8.50
Pressed Glass, Toothpick, Thompson 77, Ruby	12.00
Pressed Glass, Toothpick, Thumbprint, Ruby & Clear	11.50
Pressed Glass, Toothpick, Wedding Bells, Footed	6.00
Pressed Glass, Toothpick, Wisconsin	10.00
Pressed Glass, Toothpick, 1, 000-Eye, Pointed Hobnail	6.50
Pressed Glass, Tray, Bread, see Pressed Glass, Plate, Bread	
Pressed Glass, Tray, Celery, California, Green, Flat	27.50
Pressed Glass, Tray, Celery, Kentucky, Flat	12.50
Pressed Glass, Tray, Celery, Shimmering Star	12.00
Pressed Glass, Tray, Currier & Ives, Balky Mule, 9 In.Round	24.50
Pressed Glass, Tray, Daisy & Button With Narcissus, Clear, 10 1/2 In.	10.00
Pressed Glass, Tray, Daisy & Button, Amber, Open Handles	15.00
Pressed Glass, Tray, Deer & Pine, Clear	28.00
Pressed Glass, Tray, Deer & Pine, Yellow	32.00
Pressed Glass, Tray, Dresser, Delaware, Green, Gold	28.00
Pressed Glass, Tray, Fan	12.50
Pressed Glass, Tray, Frosted Fruits, Stippled, Scalloped, Handles	18.00
Pressed Glass, Tray, 'give Us This Day, Liberty & Freedom 1776, ' Oval	25.00
Pressed Glass, Tray, Hobnail, Clear, Round, 11 In.	10.00

Pressed Glass, Tray, Ice Cream, Tree Of Life 14.00
Pressed Glass, Tray, Jewel & Dewdrop, Oblong 6.50
Pressed Glass, Tray, Liberty Bell, 1776-1876 .... 32.00
Pressed Glass, Tray, Pin, Set Of 4 .... 6.00
Pressed Glass, Tray, Relish, Broken Column, Red Notch, Flat 38.50
Pressed Glass, Tray, Relish, Liberty Bell, Centennial, Oval, Twig Handles 25.00
Pressed Glass, Tray, Sheraton, 8 Sided 8.00
Pressed Glass, Tray, Water, Columbia Coin 150.00
Pressed Glass, Tray, Water, Egg In Sand 7.50
Pressed Glass, Tray, Water, Hobs, Clear, 12 In.Diameter 15.00
Pressed Glass, Tray, Water, Pointed Hobnail, 11 1/2 In.Diameter 18.00
Pressed Glass, Tray, Water, Wildflower, Blue 25.00
Pressed Glass, Tub, Ice, Cube, Insert 22.50
Pressed Glass, Tumbler, Acanthus Scroll 6.50
Pressed Glass, Tumbler, Admiral Dewey 35.00
Pressed Glass, Tumbler, Ashburton 37.50
Pressed Glass, Tumbler, Ashburton, Emerald Green, Footed, Flint 25.00
Pressed Glass, Tumbler, Austrian, Clear, Greentown 15.00
Pressed Glass, Tumbler, Beaded Grape, Green 18.75
Pressed Glass, Tumbler, Beaded Swirl & Disc .... 7.00 To 12.00
Pressed Glass, Tumbler, Bellflower 55.00
Pressed Glass, Tumbler, Bellflower, Banded 55.00
Pressed Glass, Tumbler, Belted Worcester, Footed, Flint 15.00
Pressed Glass, Tumbler, Bird & Strawberry .... 18.50 To 19.50
Pressed Glass, Tumbler, Blue Opalescent, Jefferson 10.00
Pressed Glass, Tumbler, Bottoms Up, Coaster 8.00
Pressed Glass, Tumbler, Broken Column 25.00
Pressed Glass, Tumbler, Broken Column With Red Dots 39.50
Pressed Glass, Tumbler, Bull's-Eye & Broken Column, Footed, Flint 35.00
Pressed Glass, Tumbler, Bull's-Eye & Daisy, Gilt Eyes 6.50
Pressed Glass, Tumbler, Bull's-Eye & Daisy, Green Eyes 8.50
Pressed Glass, Tumbler, Bull's-Eye, Diamond Panel 15.00
Pressed Glass, Tumbler, Bumper To The Flag, Flint 65.00
Pressed Glass, Tumbler, Button Arch, Clear 8.50
Pressed Glass, Tumbler, Cathedral, Red Flashed 15.00
Pressed Glass, Tumbler, Civil War, Flint, 4 3/4 In.Tall 72.00
Pressed Glass, Tumbler, Coin, Blue Opalescent 16.50
Pressed Glass, Tumbler, Colorado, Green 17.00
Pressed Glass, Tumbler, Columbia Coin 75.00
Pressed Glass, Tumbler, Crystal, Footed, Flint 30.00
Pressed Glass, Tumbler, Cut Log 20.00
Pressed Glass, Tumbler, Daisy & Button With Thumbprint, Blue 17.50
Pressed Glass, Tumbler, Dakota, Etched 25.00
Pressed Glass, Tumbler, Dewey .... 27.50 To 34.00
Pressed Glass, Tumbler, Dewey, Lindsey 30.00
Pressed Glass, Tumbler, Diamond Filled Ovals, Flint 16.00
Pressed Glass, Tumbler, Diamond Point 35.00
Pressed Glass, Tumbler, Diamond Point, Paneled, Footed, Flint .... 16.00 To 22.50
Pressed Glass, Tumbler, Diamond Thumbprint, 3 1/2 In.Tall 35.00
Pressed Glass, Tumbler, Diamond Thumbprint, 3 7/8 In. 80.00
Pressed Glass, Tumbler, Diamond With Sunburst 10.00
Pressed Glass, Tumbler, Double Arch, Green, Gold 20.00
Pressed Glass, Tumbler, Double Wedding Ring, Footed 22.00
Pressed Glass, Tumbler, Drapery, Red Cased 45.00
Pressed Glass, Tumbler, Etched Dakota 24.50
Pressed Glass, Tumbler, Etched Mascotte 10.00
Pressed Glass, Tumbler, Etched Nail 10.00
Pressed Glass, Tumbler, Etched Pavonia 11.00
Pressed Glass, Tumbler, Eureka, Footed, Flint 15.00
Pressed Glass, Tumbler, Excelsior, 3 In. 25.00
Pressed Glass, Tumbler, Festoon 12.50
Pressed Glass, Tumbler, Fine Rib 35.00
Pressed Glass, Tumbler, Flute, Footed 18.00
Pressed Glass, Tumbler, Frosted Hidalgo With Stars 9.50
Pressed Glass, Tumbler, Frosted Leaf & Flower 12.50
Pressed Glass, Tumbler, Garfield, Lindsey 40.00

Pressed Glass, Tumbler, God & Home 140.00
Pressed Glass, Tumbler, Good Luck 10.00
Pressed Glass, Tumbler, Grogan 15.00
Pressed Glass, Tumbler, Heart & Thumbprint 22.50
Pressed Glass, Tumbler, Heart & Thumbprint, Gold 22.00
Pressed Glass, Tumbler, Herringbone, Green 11.00
Pressed Glass, Tumbler, Hobnail, Amber 15.00
Pressed Glass, Tumbler, Honeycomb, Amber 11.50
Pressed Glass, Tumbler, Honeycomb, Flint 16.00
Pressed Glass, Tumbler, Horn Of Plenty .... 10.00 To 55.00
Pressed Glass, Tumbler, Horn Of Plenty, 3 3/4 In. 40.00
Pressed Glass, Tumbler, Hummingbird 14.50
Pressed Glass, Tumbler, Hummingbird, Amber 13.50
Pressed Glass, Tumbler, Hummingbird, Blue 15.50
Pressed Glass, Tumbler, Imperial Lace 4.00
Pressed Glass, Tumbler, Inverted Fan & Feather 12.50
Pressed Glass, Tumbler, Inverted Strawberry 12.00
Pressed Glass, Tumbler, Inverted Thumbprint, Blue 23.00
Pressed Glass, Tumbler, Inverted Thumbprint, Green, 3 1/2 In.High 7.50
Pressed Glass, Tumbler, Jeweled Heart 7.00
Pressed Glass, Tumbler, Klondike 100.00
Pressed Glass, Tumbler, Lacy Medallion, Green 16.50
Pressed Glass, Tumbler, Leaf & Dart .... .50
Pressed Glass, Tumbler, Leaf & Fern With Etched Honeycomb 6.00
Pressed Glass, Tumbler, Massachusetts 7.50
Pressed Glass, Tumbler, Memphis, Marked N 10.00
Pressed Glass, Tumbler, Michigan .... 9.75 To 15.00
Pressed Glass, Tumbler, Nail, Clear, Etched Leaf Rim 10.00
Pressed Glass, Tumbler, New England Pineapple 65.00
Pressed Glass, Tumbler, New Jersey, Gold Band .... 8.50 To 29.00
Pressed Glass, Tumbler, Oregon, Ruby 17.50
Pressed Glass, Tumbler, Pan Heather, Pink, Gold 11.50
Pressed Glass, Tumbler, Paneled Daisy 24.00
Pressed Glass, Tumbler, Paneled Strawberry 9.00
Pressed Glass, Tumbler, Paneled Strawberry, Gold 12.50
Pressed Glass, Tumbler, Peacock Feather 10.00
Pressed Glass, Tumbler, Pittsburgh Eight Panel, Clear 15.00
Pressed Glass, Tumbler, Pittsburgh Eight Panel, Peacock Green, 3 1/4 In. .. 85.00
Pressed Glass, Tumbler, Pittsburgh Six Panel, Aqua, 3 3/4 In.High 17.50
Pressed Glass, Tumbler, Pittsburgh, Paneled Base, Handle 8.00
Pressed Glass, Tumbler, Pointed Hobnail, Amber 15.00
Pressed Glass, Tumbler, Poppy, Clear, Mark N 10.00
Pressed Glass, Tumbler, Portland, Gold 9.50
Pressed Glass, Tumbler, Priscilla, Findlay 18.00
Pressed Glass, Tumbler, Red Block .... 16.00 To 20.00
Pressed Glass, Tumbler, 'remember The Maine' 20.00
Pressed Glass, Tumbler, Roman Rosette 5.50
Pressed Glass, Tumbler, Rose & Gold, Clear, Delaware 15.00
Pressed Glass, Tumbler, Rose Band, Green 6.50
Pressed Glass, Tumbler, Rose In Snow 32.50
Pressed Glass, Tumbler, Rose In Snow, In Remembrance 20.00
Pressed Glass, Tumbler, Royal Ivy, Rose & Canary 25.00
Pressed Glass, Tumbler, S-Repeat, Clear 8.50
Pressed Glass, Tumbler, Scroll & Cane, Yellow Flashed 5.00
Pressed Glass, Tumbler, Shell & Jewel .... 8.00 To 12.50
Pressed Glass, Tumbler, Skilton, Red Flashed 25.00
Pressed Glass, Tumbler, Spirea Band, Amber 13.00
Pressed Glass, Tumbler, Star & Circle, Footed, Flint 30.00
Pressed Glass, Tumbler, Star Band 8.00
Pressed Glass, Tumbler, Stippled Star, 4 In.High 5.00
Pressed Glass, Tumbler, Stork In Rushes 9.50
Pressed Glass, Tumbler, Stork In Rushes, Blue 18.00
Pressed Glass, Tumbler, Sunken Buttons, Blue 10.00
Pressed Glass, Tumbler, Teardrop & Tassle, Clear 25.00
Pressed Glass, Tumbler, Thistle 14.00
Pressed Glass, Tumbler, Thistle, Gold Band 8.50

Pressed Glass, Tumbler, Three Panel, Amber 13.50
Pressed Glass, Tumbler, Thumbprint, Red 24.00
Pressed Glass, Tumbler, Torpedo, Ruby Top 18.50
Pressed Glass, Tumbler, Triple Triangle 15.00
Pressed Glass, Tumbler, Truncated Cube, Clear With Red 12.50
Pressed Glass, Tumbler, Tulip With Sawtooth 40.00
Pressed Glass, Tumbler, Tulip With Sawtooth Variant 25.00
Pressed Glass, Tumbler, U.S.Coin 150.00
Pressed Glass, Tumbler, U.S.Coin Bottom, Clear 70.00
Pressed Glass, Tumbler, U.S.Coin, Dated 1879 .... 150.00
Pressed Glass, Tumbler, Vesta, Opalescent 17.00
Pressed Glass, Tumbler, Waffle & Thumbprint 35.00
Pressed Glass, Tumbler, Whiskey, Ashburton 45.00
Pressed Glass, Tumbler, Whiskey, Bull's-Eye & Rosette, Flint 28.50
Pressed Glass, Tumbler, Whiskey, Hinoto, Footed, Flint 20.00
Pressed Glass, Tumbler, Whiskey, Horn Of Plenty, 3 In. .... 50.00 To 65.00
Pressed Glass, Tumbler, Whiskey, Ribbed Ivy 37.50
Pressed Glass, Tumbler, Whiskey, Smocking 60.00
Pressed Glass, Tumbler, Wildflower, Apple Green 21.50
Pressed Glass, Tumbler, Wildflower, Blue 14.00
Pressed Glass, Tumbler, Wildflower, Canary 15.00
Pressed Glass, Tumbler, Willow Oak 10.00
Pressed Glass, Tumbler, 1, 000-Eye, Amber 14.50
Pressed Glass, Tumbler, 1, 000-Eye, Blue 11.50
Pressed Glass, Tureen, Soup, Leaves & Thumbprint, 16 In.High 47.50
     Pressed Glass, Vase, Celery, see Pressed Glass, Celery
Pressed Glass, Vase, Curtain, 10 In. 10.50
Pressed Glass, Vase, Daisy & Button, Apple Green, Hand Holding Cornucopia 25.00
Pressed Glass, Vase, Diamond Block 7.00
Pressed Glass, Vase, Fleur-De-Lis, Footed, 10 In.Tall 7.50
Pressed Glass, Vase, Heart & Thumbprint, 9 1/2 In.Tall 22.50
Pressed Glass, Vase, Heart & Thumbprint, 10 In. 22.00
Pressed Glass, Vase, Iris & Herringbone, Clear 5.00
Pressed Glass, Vase, Iris & Herringbone, 9 In. 7.50
Pressed Glass, Vase, Klondike, Clear, 8 In. 15.00
Pressed Glass, Vase, Maiden's Blush, Pink Flashed, 5 1/2 In.Tall 25.00
Pressed Glass, Vase, Massachusetts, 9 3/4 In. 16.50
Pressed Glass, Vase, Moonstone, Clear, 5 In., Pair 8.00
Pressed Glass, Vase, Paneled Dewdrop, Footed, 9 1/2 In.Tall 25.00
Pressed Glass, Vase, Paneled Thistle, Scalloped Top 17.00
Pressed Glass, Vase, Pineapple & Fan, Footed, 9 In. 7.50
Pressed Glass, Vase, Teasel, Footed 5.00
Pressed Glass, Vase, Texas Pattern 11.00
Pressed Glass, Vase, Trumpet,, Viking, 8 In.High 16.50
Pressed Glass, Vase, Tulip, Daisy & Button, 9 In.Tall 20.00
Pressed Glass, Vase, Tulip, Octagonal Paneled, Clear, Trumpet Base 50.00
Pressed Glass, Vase, 1, 000-Eye, 8 In.Tall 30.00
Pressed Glass, Vase, 1, 000-Eye, 8 1/4 In.Tall 18.00
Pressed Glass, Wagon, Conestoga, Amber 45.00
Pressed Glass, Water Set, Frosted Crystal, Ruby Flashed, Gold, 6 Piece 69.00
Pressed Glass, Water Set, Gothic Arch, Pitcher 12 Glasses 60.00
Pressed Glass, Water Set, Inverted Thumbprint, Blue, 3 Piece 40.00
Pressed Glass, Water Set, Iris & Herringbone, Clear, 7 Piece 25.00
Pressed Glass, Water Set, Palm Rosette, 5 Piece 25.00
Pressed Glass, Water Set, Thumbprint, Pink, 5 Piece 15.00
Pressed Glass, Wheelbarrow, Barley, Clear, Metal Wheel 35.00
Pressed Glass, Whiskey Taster, Ribbed Opal 10.00
Pressed Glass, Whiskey, Crystal, Handled, Flint 35.00
Pressed Glass, Whiskey, Diamond Block, Panelled 6.00
Pressed Glass, Whiskey, Diamond Point, Flint 16.00
Pressed Glass, Wine Set, Daisy & Button With Narcissus, 8 Piece 45.00
Pressed Glass, Wine Set, Decanter & 6 Wines, Sunk Honeycomb, Ruby 90.00
Pressed Glass, Wine, Ashburton .... 22.50 To 25.00
Pressed Glass, Wine, Ashburton, Double Knob Stem, Flint 27.00
Pressed Glass, Wine, Balder 12.50
Pressed Glass, Wine, Barred Forget-Me-Not 18.50

Pressed Glass, Wine, Beaded Dewdrop	18.50
Pressed Glass, Wine, Beaded Tulip	11.50
Pressed Glass, Wine, Bird & Strawberry	21.50
Pressed Glass, Wine, Bird & Strawberry, Clear	9.00
Pressed Glass, Wine, Bull's Eye & Diamond, Flint	110.00
Pressed Glass, Wine, Bull's-Eye & Diamond Point	110.00
Pressed Glass, Wine, Cable, Flint, Footed	22.00
Pressed Glass, Wine, Cadmus	7.50
Pressed Glass, Wine, Chain & Star	10.00
Pressed Glass, Wine, Checkerboard	8.00
Pressed Glass, Wine, Colorado, Clear	7.50
Pressed Glass, Wine, Cord & Tassel	11.50
Pressed Glass, Wine, Currant	15.00
Pressed Glass, Wine, Cut Log	10.00 To 12.00
Pressed Glass, Wine, Dahlia	28.00
Pressed Glass, Wine, Daisy & Button With Narcissus	9.50 To 12.50
Pressed Glass, Wine, Dew & Raindrop	5.00 To 7.00
Pressed Glass, Wine, Diagonal Block Band	6.50
Pressed Glass, Wine, Diamond Point	20.00
Pressed Glass, Wine, Diamond Point, Banded	9.00
Pressed Glass, Wine, Diamond, Horseshoe	9.00
Pressed Glass, Wine, Etched Atlas	18.50
Pressed Glass, Wine, Fan Band	12.50
Pressed Glass, Wine, Fans With Diamonds	17.00
Pressed Glass, Wine, Feather	20.00
Pressed Glass, Wine, Feather, Scalloped Top	16.50
Pressed Glass, Wine, Fernburst	7.00
Pressed Glass, Wine, Fine Cut, Emerald Green	10.00
Pressed Glass, Wine, Fine Cut & Panel, Amber	14.00
Pressed Glass, Wine, Floral Oval	7.95
Pressed Glass, Wine, Galloway, Clear	15.00
Pressed Glass, Wine, Heart & Thumbprint, Emerald Green	14.00
Pressed Glass, Wine, Heart & Thumbprint Footed, Gold	17.25
Pressed Glass, Wine, Honeycomb With Pillar	6.00
Pressed Glass, Wine, Horn Of Plenty	17.50
Pressed Glass, Wine, Horn Of Plenty, Flint	50.00
Pressed Glass, Wine, Horn Of Plenty, Knob Stem, 5 1/4 In.	27.50
Pressed Glass, Wine, Iris & Herringbone, Clear	4.50 To 6.00
Pressed Glass, Wine, Ivy In Snow	22.50
Pressed Glass, Wine, Jacob's Ladder	9.00 To 20.00
Pressed Glass, Wine, Jeweled Moon & Star	40.00
Pressed Glass, Wine, King's Crown	6.50 To 7.00
Pressed Glass, Wine, Late Buckle	15.00
Pressed Glass, Wine, Lattice	13.00
Pressed Glass, Wine, Liberty	7.00
Pressed Glass, Wine, Loop & Noose	7.50
Pressed Glass, Wine, Marigold Iris & Herringbone	5.00
Pressed Glass, Wine, Melrose, Leaf Etching	12.50
Pressed Glass, Wine, Milton	7.00
Pressed Glass, Wine, Nailhead	12.50
Pressed Glass, Wine, Overall Lattice	6.00
Pressed Glass, Wine, Petal, Knob Stem, Flint	10.50
Pressed Glass, Wine, Prism & Bull's Eye, Flint	29.00
Pressed Glass, Wine, Prism Band	5.00
Pressed Glass, Wine, Red Block	26.50
Pressed Glass, Wine, Red Flash, Souvenir Ackley, Iowa	13.00
Pressed Glass, Wine, Reed Stem, Flute	12.50
Pressed Glass, Wine, Ribbed Palm, Flint	30.00
Pressed Glass, Wine, Rising Sun	14.00
Pressed Glass, Wine, Rose On Basket Weave, Ruby Top, 3	16.50
Pressed Glass, Wine, Round Thumbprint, Flint, 4 In.Tall	13.50
Pressed Glass, Wine, Sawtooth	16.00
Pressed Glass, Wine, Sawtooth, Flint, Knob Stem	15.50
Pressed Glass, Wine, Smocking	38.50
Pressed Glass, Wine, Stars & Stripes	8.00 To 9.00
Pressed Glass, Wine, States	16.00

Pressed Glass, Wine, Texas Bull's-Eye 7.50
Pressed Glass, Wine, The States, Flared, Tilted 13.00
Pressed Glass, Wine, Thumbprint & Block, Clear, Flint 15.00
Pressed Glass, Wine, Thumbprint With Lined Band, Round, 4 In., Flint 13.50
Pressed Glass, Wine, Tree Of Life, Portland 27.50
Pressed Glass, Wine, Tulip & Sawtooth .... 9.00 To 17.50
Pressed Glass, Wine, Two Panels, Green 26.50
Pressed Glass, Wine, Waffle & Thumbprint 35.00
Pressed Glass, Wine, 1, 000-Eye, Blue 35.00
Print, A Rising Family, Louis Maurer, On Stone, Hand-Colored Lithograph 350.00
Print, Aboriginal Portfolio, 72 Hand-Colored Lithographs, J.O.Lewis, 1835 .... 2600.00
Print, American Child, Maud Humphrey, Dated 1889, Chromolithograph 15.00
Print, American Scene, Bartlett, C.1842, Engraving On Steel 5.00
Print, Anchor & Liberty, Home Of Brave, Verse, Color, Framed 17.50
Print, Andersonville Stockade, Half Margins, 24 X 16 In. 75.00
Print, Aries-1912, Love Lake Bridges-1913, Trowbridge, Mezzotint, Pair 30.00
Print, B.Franklin Of Philadelphia, James Mcardell, 1761, Mezzotint 190.00
Print, Battle Of The Big Horn, Louis Kurz, Lithograph, C.1876 .... 175.00
Print, Battle Of The Thames, John Dorival, C.1834 .... 550.00
Print, Bird's-Eye View Of Philadelphia, G.Matter, Hand-Colored Lithograph 600.00
Print, Birds, Published 1844, Color, 11 X 8 In. 3.50
Print, Canvassing For A Vote, Claude Regnier, Lithograph, C.1853 .... 1000.00
Print, City Of Detroit, Michigan, William James Bennett, C.1837, Aquatint 1500.00
Print, Colonial Maiden, Gold Liner, Walnut Frame, 7 3/4 X 5 3/4 In., Pair 15.00
    Print, Currier & Ives, see Currier & Ives
Print, Custer's Last Chance, Feodor Fuchs, C.1876, Lithograph 900.00
Print, Custer's Last Charge, 1876, Lithograph .... Illus 900.00

Print, Lithograph, Custer's Last Charge, 1876

Print, Custer's Last Fight, Otto Becker, C.1896, Chromolithograph 160.00
Print, Custer's Last Rally, Christian Fabronius, C.1876, Lithograph 150.00
Print, Detroit In 1820, View Of Walk-In-The-Water, Corries Detroit, C.1872 .... 250.00
Print, Detroit In 1820, View Of Walk-In-The-Water, M.A.Tryon, C.1819 .... 4500.00
Print, Dr.Syntax In A Court Of Justice, Rowlandson, 1820, Color 6.50
Print, Ducks At Play On Pond, Frank Benson, Etching 45.00
Print, Fisherman, Coneo, Campfire, Philip R.Goodwin, Color 2.00
Print, Flapper Shooting, By H.Aitken, 6 X 9 In., Set Of 4 .... 85.00
Print, Floral, 19th Century, Frame, Pair 35.00
Print, Game Bird, A.Pope, Jr., Engraving, Colored, 6 .... 240.00
Print, Game Bird, Dupont, Copyright 1917, Lynn Bogue Hunt 1.00

Print, George Washington, Master Of His Lodge, Black & White, Framed	175.00
Print, Godey, Americanized Parish Fashions, 1847, Frame, 1¼ X 10 In.	8.00
Print, Godey, Fashion Plates, 1855	15.00
Print, Godey, Signed, Framed, Pair	12.50
Print, Great Western Steamship Leaving Bristol, Reeve, Aquatint	225.00
Print, Haarlem, Signed Sir David Young Cammeron, 1893, Etching	120.00
Print, Hoar Frost, Otto Matthael Rauhreif, Colored	35.00
Print, Houses Along Canal, Trowbridge, Mezzotint, Colored	12.50
Print, Howard Chandler Christy, Black & White, C.1900	1.50
Print, Hunter, Bark Canoe, Moose In Lake, Philip R.Goodwin, Color	2.00
Print, Hunting, King's Great Western Powder Co., Ohio, Lithograph, Pair	600.00
Print, Inauguration Of George Washington, 1789, Color, C.1840	165.00
Print, Kellogg & Thayer, Rival Charms, C.1860	12.50
Print, Kellogg, Elmer Ellsworth, 1861, Color, Lithograph	20.00
Print, Kellogg, George Washington, Small Folio, Cherry Frame	25.00
Print, Kellogg, Martin Van Buren, Silhouette, 1844, Lithograph	75.00
Print, Kellogg, Silas Wright, Brown's Silhouettes, Frame	12.50
Print, Kellogg, William Henry Harrison's Silhouette, 1844, Lithograph	75.00
Print, Lady, Nicolas Delaunay, 1770, Engraving, Frame	250.00
Print, Lake George, Appleton & Co., 1873, Lithograph	2.50
Print, Le Serment D'amour, Color, French, Inlaid Frame	40.00
Print, Le Tortelet, Signed Francoise Deberdt, Color, Lithograph	35.00
Print, Lewis & Clark Exposition, Signed Caughey, 1903, Lithograph	25.00
Print, Map, World, 1826, 20 X 32 In.	25.00
Print, Maxfield Parrish, Daybreak, 12 X 15 In.	3.00
Print, Maxfield Parrish, Daybreak, 1924, Color, 18 X 30 In.	40.00
Print, Maxfield Parrish, Daybreak, 23 X 34 In.	15.00
Print, Maxfield Parrish, Lights Of Welcome, Framed	12.00
Print, Maxfield Parrish, Mazada	5.00
Print, Maxfield Parrish, Three Women, By Lake With Mandolins	25.00
Print, Maxfield Parrish, Tranquility, 4 X 5 In.	1.00
Print, Mckenney & Hall, Indians, Hand Colored, 1855	25.00
Print, Miss Muffet's Christmas Party, Maud Humphrey, Lithograph	7.50
Print, Moss Covered Tree, Alfred Hutty, Engraving, Black & White	10.00
Print, Mount Shasta, Appleton & Co., 1873, Lithograph	2.50
Print, Nantucket, The Shipowner, Black Frame	19.00
Print, Nativity Scene, Frame, 10 3/4 X 7 3/4 In.	5.00
Print, New York From Governors Island, John Hill, 1820-28, Aquatint	725.00
Print, New York, C.Mottram, 1855, Hand Colored, Engraving & Aquatint	225.00
Print, New York, Winter Scene In Broadway, P.Girardet, 1857, Aquatint	300.00
Print, Newport, R.I., In 1730, J.P.Newell, Hand-Colored Lithograph	675.00
Print, North Country, Snow, Mountains & Deer, Korry Ely, Engraving	25.00
Print, Nutting, August In The Meadows, Frame, 17 1/4 X 11 In.	13.00
Print, Nutting, Concord Banks, Framed, 14 X 16 In.	14.00
Print, Nutting, Concord, Banks, 1920	6.50
Print, Nutting, On Worcester Hills, Framed	7.00
Print, Old Mcintosh, Oak Tree In Winter, Ella Tillmore Lille, Etching	20.00
Print, Owl, Hand Colored, 1871	18.00
Print, Paris Book Mart, F.T.Simon, Engraving, Colored	45.00
Print, Peterson's, Fashion, Color	2.00
Print, Philadelphia Centennial, 1876, Framed	100.00
Print, Picnic On The Beach, By Harrison Fisher, 10 1/2 X 16 1/2 In.	5.00
Print, Pond With Swans, Lattnay, Engraving, Colored, Large Folio	150.00
Print, Portrait, James Oglethorpe, Esq., Thomas Burford, Mezzotint	375.00
Print, Prang, Wildflowers, Color, 10 X 7 In.	3.50
Print, Proclamation Of Emancipation, N.Y., 1864, Demnick, Lithograph	47.50
Print, Prohibition Movement, Signed F.Graetz, Lithograph, Framed	15.00
Print, Quebec, Dated 1874, Color, Matted & Framed	17.50
Print, Quick Flight Of Quail, Walter E.Bohl, Engraving	35.00
Print, Regatta Of New York Yacht Club, 1854, The Start, Charles Parsons	700.00
Print, Remington, His First Lesson, Lithograph, Oak Frame	100.00
Print, Remington, The Shadows At The Water Hole, Color	15.00
Print, Rural Landscape, Fred Millar, Colored, Mezzotint	15.00
Print, Sadanobu, Landscape, Circa 1850	40.00
Print, Saint Michael, Pattison, Colored, Mezzotint	25.00
Print, Scene On The Delaware River, Haskell & Allen, 1845, Lithograph	50.00

Print, So Nice, Baxter, Shadowbox Frame, 9 X 11 In.	52.50
Print, St.Germain-Des-Pres, Initialed B.B., Etching, Frame	47.50
Print, St.Mary & Michilimakinac, Map, Hand Colored, C.1761	125.00
Print, Steam Train Engine, C.1895, Lithograph	5.00
Print, Steamships, Harbor, Town, St.Charles, Missouri, Lithograph, Hand Color	30.00
Print, The Antelope Hunter, Peter Hurd, Hercules Powder Co., 1955	20.00
Print, The Battle Of Bunker's Hill, J.Muller, 1798, Engraving	450.00
Print, The Cotillion, By Howard Chandler	5.00
Print, The Country Election, Sartain, 1854, Color .... *Illus*	750.00

Print, The Country Election, Sartain, 1854, Color

Print, The Fleecy Charge, G.Shepheard, 1796, Engraving, Colored	70.00
Print, The Highwayman, Signed In Pencil, P.E.Waller, 1855, Etching	7.50
Print, The Jolly Flat Boat Men, Thomas Doney, Mezzotint, C.1847	650.00
Print, The Market, Skrimpshire, Engraving, Colored	60.00
Print, The Old Violin, William Michael Harnett, Chromolithograph, 1881	325.00
Print, The Upper Yellowstone Falls, Appleton & Co., 1873, Lithograph	2.50
Print, The Warrior's Last Ride, Remington	12.50
Print, The Washington Family, Edward Savage, 1798, Stipple Engraving	200.00
Print, Three Strikes & The Bases Full, Gibson	7.00
Print, Uncle Sam, Poster, Black & White, 10 X 15 In.	1.50
Print, U.S.Frigate Constitution, William Marsh, Jr., Colored, Lithograph	500.00
Print, U.S.Ship Pennsylvania, William James Bennett, 1839, Aquatint	900.00
Print, Versailles & Fontainebleau, Dated 1674, French, Framed, Pair	70.00
Print, View From Gowanus Heights, Brooklyn, By W.H.Bartlett, 1837	10.00
Print, View Of Falls On The Passaick, Governor Pownal, 1768, Engraving	90.00
Print, View Of Water Celebration On Boston Common, B.F.Smith, Jr., 1848	110.00
Print, Volunteer Refreshment Saloon, Phila., 1861, W.Boell, Lithograph	27.50
Print, Warne, Ferns, Color, 9 X 6 In.	3.00
Print, Welcome Soap, Under Glass, Curtis Davis Co.17 X 31 In.	85.00
Print, William McKinley Memorial, 1904, Framed	22.50
Print, Winter Pastime, F.F.Palmer, 1855, Hand-Colored Lithograph	425.00
Print, Yacht America, G.W.Lewis, Hand-Colored Lithograph, 1851	160.00
Print, Yellowstone National Park, 1904, Lithograph, Oak Frame	185.00
Purple Slag, see Slag	
Quartz, Figurine, Cat & Kitten, Rose Color	35.00

Quezal Glass was made from 1901 to 1920 by Martin Bach, Sr. He made iridescent glass of the same type as Tiffany.

Quezal, Dish, Nut, Signed	60.00
Quezal, Glass, Juice, Iridescent, Threaded Decoration	75.00
Quezal, Lamp, Hanging, Glass & Metal, Opalescent White, Iridescent Gold	100.00
Quezal, Salt, Gold, Signed	57.50
Quezal, Shade, Feather Motif, Gold, Unsigned	32.50
Quezal, Shade, Feather, Signed	42.50
Quezal, Shade, Gold Iridescent, Feather, Green Edged, 14 1/2 In.Diameter	300.00
Quezal, Shade, Green Feather, Signed, 7 In.	40.00
Quezal, Shade, Hurricane, Calcite, Gold Interior, Gold Feathers, Pair	52.00
Quezal, Shade, Lamp, Gold, Paneled, Signed, 5 In.High	30.00
Quezal, Shade, Light, Signed, Green Feathers Outlined In Gold Over Calcite	45.00
Quezal, Shade, Paneled Motif, Gold, Signed, 5 In.Tall	30.00
Quezal, Shade, Wavy White, Gold & Green Feathers, Yellow Interior	29.00
Quezal, Vase, Cabinet, Iridescent, White & Green, Signed	400.00
Quezal, Vase, Flower Form.Gold Ground, Green Feathers, Peacock Eye	125.00
Quezal, Vase, Iridescent, Ovoid, Green Striations, Ivory Ground, Quezal C833	525.00
Quezal, Vase, Leaf Design, Green, Gold, Luster, Signed, Lily, 7 1/4 In.Tall	525.00
Quezal, Vase, Scalloped Top, Iridescent, Signed, 7 1/4 In.High	450.00
Quezal, Vase, Signed, Baluster Shape, Green Feathers Outlined In Gold	375.00
Quezal, Vase, Snowflaking, Blue, Iridescent, Signed, 4 1/2 In.High	375.00
Quezal, Vase, White & Gold Calcite, Signed	175.00
Quilt, see Textile, Quilt	

Quimper Pottery was made in Finistere, France, after 1900. Most of the pieces found today were made during the twentieth century. A Quimper factory has worked in France since the eighteenth century.

Quimper, Bell, With Lady, Signed	16.50
Quimper, Bowl, Mixing, Yellow, Orange, Blue, Stripes, Man, 11 5/8 In.Diameter	28.00
Quimper, Bowl, Pink, Woman, Flowers, Handles, Signed, Pair	11.00
Quimper, Coffeepot, Signed H.Quimper, Girl & Floral Decor, 7 In.High	35.00
Quimper, Creamer, Peasant Boy, Signed, 4 1/4 In.Tall	12.50
Quimper, Cup, Saucer, Eggcup, Porringer, & Plate, Man's, Marked HB, France	30.00
Quimper, Cup, Saucer, Porringer, & Plate, Woman's, Marked HB, France	30.00
Quimper, Knife Rest, French Faience, Man & Woman, Pair	36.00
Quimper, Matchbox Holder	*Illus* 22.50
Quimper, Plate, Peasant Lady, Flowers, 6 3/4 In., Pair	15.00
Quimper, Plate, Peasant Scene, Men, Women, 8 1/2 In.Diameter	10.00
Quimper, Plate, Sailboats, Fish Border, Artist J.Louchard, 9 1/4 In.	6.50
Quimper, Vase, Floral Design, Tub Shape, Green, Blue, Yellow, Black Rim, Signed	7.00
Radio, Aeriola Sr. Receiver, Wd 11 Tubes	85.00

Quezal, Vase, Cabinet, Iridescent, White & Green, Signed

Quimper, Matchbox Holder

Radio, Aircraft, Plug In Coils	40.00
Radio, Appelby, Model X, Horn Type Speaker	25.00
Radio, Atwater-Kent, Breadboard, Tubes	225.00
Radio, Atwater-Kent, Horn Type Speaker, Model M	37.50
Radio, Atwater-Kent, Model 30	37.50
Radio, Atwater-Kent, Model 35	42.50
Radio, Atwater-Kent, 4 Prong Type	22.50
Radio, Badge, Coco Wheats	12.50
Radio, De Forest, T 200, Multiwave Tuner, 1920	225.00
Radio, Fada, Cathedral Type, Serial No.15562-B, Built In Electric	32.50
Radio, Freed-Eisemann, Model Nr-20, No.262c, Gold Trim	65.00
Radio, Magnavox Speaker, R3, Label	50.00
Radio, Magnavox, Model 25, Cabinet	55.00
Radio, Magnavox, Type 20, 16 X 9 1/2 X 10 In.	27.50
Radio, Microphone, Electro Voice, Chrome Casting, 1929, Table Model	22.50
Radio, Peerless Reproducer Speaker, Cathedral Type	21.50
Radio, Philco, Cathevical Type, Model 66, 16 In.Tall	32.50
Radio, Philco, Cathevical Type, Type 91, 19 In.Tall	32.50
Radio, Philco, Cathevical Type, 16 1/2 In.Tall	19.75
Radio, Philco, Cathevical Type, 17 1/2 In.Tall	32.50
Radio, Philco, Table, Electric, Model 37 610, Wooden Cabinet	22.50
Radio, Radiola Iii, Box Shape, Earphones, Bakelite Top, 1924	16.00
Radio, Radiola, Electric, No.18	40.00
Radio, Radiola, No.16 Tubes	55.00
Radio, Radiola, No.3a Tubes	50.00
Radio, Radiola, 100a, Speaker	19.00
Radio, Rca Radiola 33, Model 784, Metal Case, Floor Model	65.00
Radio, Riders, No.1 Volume	17.50
Radio, Spark Gap, Beenwood Spark Wheel, U.S.Navy Helix, 1919	225.00
Radio, Stewart Warner, Table, Model 300, 1925, S Shaped Horn, Walnut Case	60.00
Radio, Tube, Audion De Forest, Type 426, A-C Filament Amplifier	4.50
Radio, Tube, Concertmaster Deluxe Radio Tube, X-201	4.50
Radio, Tube, Majestic 27	4.50
Radio, Tube, No.80	2.80
Radio, Tube, Wd	10.75
Radio, Ware Music Master, 4 Tubes, Slant Front	85.00
Railroad, Ax & Brush Cutter, B & M R.R., For Track Crews	15.00
Railroad, Basket, Cake, Marked Santa Fe, Super Chief, Oval, Fluted	49.50
Railroad, Bell, Brass, Steam Engine	295.00
Railroad, Bell, From Locomotive, 12 In.High, Stand 21 In.High, 17 In.Opening	400.00
Railroad, Bell, Iron, 100 Lbs., 17 In.Diam., 24 In.High, Bracket	225.00
Railroad, Bell, Locomotive, Brass, 56 Lbs.	125.00
Railroad, Bell, Locomotive, Stand, 17 In.Opening	400.00
Railroad, Bowl, China, B.& O., Blue	9.00
Railroad, Bowl, Salad, Pink, Traveler, The Milwaukee Road	28.00
Railroad, Bowl, Soup, Baltimore & Ohio, Shenango, Dated 1827-1927	10.00
Railroad, Bowl, Sugar, Covered, Hinged Lid, 'nyc, ' Silver	30.00
Railroad, Bowl, Sugar, Lid, Pennsylvania Railroad Monogram	25.00
Railroad, Bowl, Sugar, Marked 'Seaboard' On Front, Silver	25.00
Railroad, Bowl, Sugar, "PRR, ' Hollow Ware, Keystone, Covered, Silver	25.00
Railroad, Butter Pat, Baltimore & Ohio, Shenango, Dated 1827-1927	3.00
Railroad, Calendar, P.R.R., 1930s	11.00
Railroad, Cap Emblem, Brass, Says S.P.Co.Freight Conductor, 3 1/2 In.	14.00
Railroad, Cap, Conductor, Milwaukee Road	15.00
Railroad, Certificate, Stock, Boston, Worcester, 1840s	3.00
Railroad, Certificate, Stock, Boston, Worcester, 1870s	3.00
Railroad, Certificate, Stock, Southwestern, 1860s	2.50
Railroad, Certificate, Stock, Southwestern, 1890s	2.50
Railroad, Certificate, Stock, Western, 1830s	3.00
Railroad, Certificate, Stock, Western, 1850s	3.00
Railroad, Coffeepot, 'NYC' On Top, 14 Oz., Silver	25.00 To 35.00
Railroad, Coffeepot, 'PRR," Hollow Ware, 14 Oz., Keystone, Silver	35.00
Railroad, Coffeepot, PRR Monogram, Silver, 14 Oz.	25.00 To 35.00
Railroad, Coffeepot, Silver, Pennsylvania Railroad Raised On Front	35.00
Railroad, Cover, Dome, Burlington Route Monogram, Silver	12.50
Railroad, Creamer, Covered, Hinged Lid, 'NYC,' Silver	3.00

Railroad, Creamer, Lid, Pennsylvania Railroad Monogram	25.00
Railroad, Creamer, 'PRR,' Hollow Ware, Covered, Keystone, Silver	25.00
Railroad, Creamer, Silver, Marked Santa Fe Super Chief	25.00
Railroad, Cup & Saucer, China, B.& O., Blue	8.00
Railroad, Cup & Saucer, Coffee, Baltimore & Ohio, Shenango, Dated 1827-1927	12.00
Railroad, Cup & Saucer, Wild Rose, Chicago & Northwestern	25.00
Railroad, Cup, Bouillon, Great Northern R.R., Pedestal, Handles, Silver	25.00
Railroad, Date Nail, Copper, Milwaukee, 1930, Indented	2.00
Railroad, Date Nail, From 1906-1972, Round, Square, Indent, Etc., 50	7.00
Railroad, Date Nail, Southern Pacific, 1928-1951, 20	5.00
Railroad, Date Nail, Square Indent, No.1	2.25
Railroad, Date Nail, Square Indent, No.2	2.25
Railroad, Date Nail, Square Indent, No.3	2.25
Railroad, Date Nail, Square Indent, No.4	2.25
Railroad, Date Nail, Square, Raised, No.22	.55
Railroad, Date Nail, Square, Raised, No.23	.55
Railroad, Date Nail, Square, Raised, No.24	.55
Railroad, Date Nail, Steel, 15	2.00
Railroad, Date Nail, 1917-1931	10.00
Railroad, Date Nail, 1921	.50
Railroad, Date Nail, 1922	.50
Railroad, Date Nail, 1923	.50
Railroad, Date Nail, 1927	.20
Railroad, Date Nail, 1959	.20
Railroad, Date Nail, 1960	.50
Railroad, Date Nail, 1961	.20
Railroad, Date Nail, 1962	.20
Railroad, Date Nail, 1963	.20
Railroad, Date Nail, 1964	.20
Railroad, Date Nail, 1965	.20
Railroad, Date Nail, 1966	.20
Railroad, Date Nail, 1967	.20
Railroad, Date Nail, 1969	.50
Railroad, Dish, Celery, China, B.& O., Blue	10.00
Railroad, Dish, Oatmeal, China, B.& O., Blue	5.50
Railroad, Dish, Vegetable, Baltimore & Ohio, Shenango, Dated 1827-1927	7.50
Railroad, Dish, Vegetable, China, B.& O., Blue	5.00
Railroad, Dish, Vegetable, The Pullman Company, Oval, Silver	15.00
Railroad, Emblem, Cap, Brass, S.P.Co., Freight Brakeman	8.50
Railroad, Emblem, Cap, Brass, S.P.Co., Freight Conductor	8.50
Railroad, Fork, Marked Nyc	5.00
Railroad, Fork, Pennsylvania, Silver	5.00
Railroad, Glass, Juice, Blown, P.R.R., Keystone Insignia, Locomotive In Red	4.50
Railroad, Gravy Boat, China, B.& O., Blue	8.00
Railroad, Holder, Menu & Pencil, Pennsylvania R.R. Monogram, Silver	15.00
Railroad, Key, Switch, For Turning Gas Lights Off & On In Coaches, Brass	6.00
Railroad, Key, Switch, Penn Central, Brass	2.50
Railroad, Knife, Crumb.Mark Seaboard, Silver Plate	10.00
Railroad, Knife, Fruit, Mark Seaboard, Silver Plate	6.00
Railroad, Knife, Marked NYC	5.00
Railroad, Knife, Pennsylvania, Silver	5.00
Railroad, Lamp, Aladdin, Union Pacific, Brass, White, Orange Milk Glass	50.00
Railroad, Lantern, see also Lantern, Railroad	
Railroad, Lantern, Brass, Conductor's, Porters Sons, N.Y., Pat.Date 1882	75.00
Railroad, Lantern, Brass, Pat.1869, Clear Globe, Whale Oil	50.00
Railroad, Lantern, Chicago & Northwestern, Red	8.00
Railroad, Lantern, Chicago, Milwaukee, St.Paul & Pacific, Adlake 250, Red	8.00
Railroad, Lantern, Dietz Stand.No.39, Clear Etched Globe, CRR Of NJ	20.00
Railroad, Lantern, Dressel, Crr Of NJ On Clear Globe, Marked Frame	20.00
Railroad, Lantern, Frame & Globe Signed P.R.R.	12.50
Railroad, Lantern, GR & Trunk Western, Clear	8.00
Railroad, Lantern, Keystone The Casey, Pat.1902, B&S Etched On Clear Globe	30.00
Railroad, Lantern, Marked I.C.R.R., Chimney	7.00
Railroad, Lantern, Marked S.P.Co.	15.00
Railroad, Lantern, PRR	8.00
Railroad, Lantern, Rayo, No. 39WB, Clear Globe	15.00

Railroad, Lantern, Rock Island Line 12.50
Railroad, Lantern, Rock Island, Clear Globe 8.00
Railroad, Lantern, Southern Pacific Company, Red 6.50
Railroad, Lantern, Star Headlight Co., Roch., N.Y., No.3294, Wm On Frame 50.00
Railroad, Lantern, Union Pacific 12.50
Railroad, Light, Switch Stand, Pennsylvania, 4 Amber & Green Lenses 45.00
Railroad, Lock & Key, Adlake R.R. 10.00
Railroad, Lock, Key, Iron With Trap Door Over Keyhole, Marked D.L.& W. 8.00
Railroad, Map, N.P.R.R., 1936, U.S.A.Rail Lines, 3 X 5 Ft. 22.00
Railroad, Martini Set, Glass Pitcher & 2 Glasses, Union Pacific Shield 25.00
Railroad, Menu, California Zephyr 5.00
Railroad, Menu, Denver Zephyr 5.00
Railroad, Menu, Union Pacific, Aug.6, 1929 .... .35
Railroad, Mustard Pot, Marked Made For Santa Fe, Cover 15.00
Railroad, Padlock, Chain & Brass Key, Union Pacific, Switch, Bronze 15.00
Railroad, Padlock, Key, American Express 12.00
Railroad, Pass, 1851, Cardboard 2.00
Railroad, Pass, 1886, Cardboard 2.00
Railroad, Pencil, Seaboard Coast Line, 12 .... 2.25
Railroad, Pitcher, China, B.& O., Blue, 12 Oz. 8.00
Railroad, Pitcher, Cream, B.& O.R.R., Shenango Pottery, 10 Oz. 11.00
Railroad, Pitcher, Cream, Baltimore & Ohio, 12 Oz., Shenango, Dated 1827-1927 ...... 10.00
Railroad, Plate, Bread & Butter, Baltimore & Ohio, Shenango, Dated 1827-1927 .... 8.00
Railroad, Plate, Bread & Butter, Rio Grande, Syracuse China 9.00
Railroad, Plate, Dinner, Baltimore & Ohio, Shenango, 1827-1927 .... 8.00 To 12.00
Railroad, Plate, Dinner, Rio Grande, Syracuse China 14.00
Railroad, Plate, Service, Dinner, Rio Grande 13.00
Railroad, Plate, Union Pacific, Streamliner 13.00
Railroad, Platter, China, B.& O., Blue, 10 In. .... 8.00 To 10.00
Railroad, Platter, Meat, Marked Santa Fe, Oval, Gadroon Edge 22.50
Railroad, Platter, Meat, Santa Fe, 12 In. 22.50
Railroad, Platter, Rio Grande, Syracuse China 17.00
Railroad, Playing Cards, Santa Fe, Beautiful Trains, Box 7.00
Railroad, Server, Coffee, Nickel Silver, 'Pullman' On Front, Hinged Lid 15.00
Railroad, Server, Coffee, Nickel Silver, Thermos, 'Pullman' On Front 27.50
Railroad, Server, Coffee, 'Pullman' On Front, Nickel Silver, 16 Oz. 27.50
Railroad, Spoon, Runcible, Mark Seaboard, Silver Plate 6.50
Railroad, Spoon, Soup, Marked NYC 5.00
Railroad, Spoon, Soup, Pennsylvania, Silver 5.00
Railroad, Sugar & Creamer, Silver, Pennsylvania Railroad Raised On Front 50.00
Railroad, Sugar, China, B.& O., Blue 8.00
Railroad, Sugar, Hinged Lid, Santa Fe, Fluted Pattern, Silver 40.00
Railroad, Sugar, Lid, C.B.& O.R.R., Burlington Route On Front, Silver 35.00
Railroad, Sugar, Silver, Marked Santa Fe Super Chief, Covered 40.00
Railroad, Sugar, U.P.R.R., International Silver Co. 6.50
Railroad, Teapot, California Zephyr, White Ceramic, Silver Lid .... 15.00 To 25.00
Railroad, Teapot, California Zephyr, White Ceramic, Silver Handle, 'C/Z' 25.00
Railroad, Teaspoon, Marked NYC 5.00
Railroad, Teaspoon, Pennsylvania, Silver 5.00
Railroad, Ticket, 1885, Conductor's Hand Stanp 1.00
Railroad, Ticket, 1886, Conductor's Hand Stamp 1.00
Railroad, Tongs, Sugar, Silver Plate, Atlantic Coast Line 5.00
Railroad, Tongs, Sugar, Silver Plate, R.F.& P. 5.00
Railroad, Tongs, Sugar, Silver Plate, Seaboard 5.00
Railroad, Tongs, Sugar, Silver, Atlantic Coast Line 3.95
Railroad, Torch, Kerosene, Brass, Inspector's 30.00
Railroad, Tray, Bread, Atlantic Coast Line, Oval, Silver .... 20.00 To 25.00
Railroad, Tray, Bread, Marked, Silver Plate, Oval, 11 In. 20.00
Railroad, Tray, Bread, Seabord, Oval, Scalloped, Silver 20.00
Railroad, Tray, Oval, Silver, Marked Santa Fe Super Chief, 12 In. 22.50
Railroad, Tureen & Tray, Seaboard On Front, Handles, Silver 35.00
Railroad, Tureen, Handles, Underliner, Seaboard, Silver Plate 35.00
Railroad, Tureen, 3-Piece, Silver, Marked Santa Fe, Fluted Pattern 49.50
    Rainbow, see Satin Glass
Rauenstein, Tea & Coffee Service, Dutch View & Inscription, C.1790, 9 Piece 125.00
Redware, Bowl, Miniature 20.00

Redware, Bowl, Pennsylvania, Shallow, 9 In.Diameter	27.50
Redware, Bowl, Pensylvania, Brown Splotched Decoration, 12 1/4 In.Diameter	10.00
Redware, Bowl, Yellow, Green, & Brown Slip Decoration, 12 1/2 In.Diameter	55.00
Redware, Creamer & Sugar, Two Handle	65.00
Redware, Crock, Interior Glaze, Signed John Bell, Waynesburg	40.00
Redware, Crock, Pennsylvania, Interior Glaze	10.00
Redware, Figurine, Animal Group, Monkey Riding Dog, Penna., C.1850, 7 In.	110.00
Redware, Figurine, Cat, White Glaze, Applied Green Glass Eyes, France	22.50
Redware, Flask, Glazed With Manganese Splotches, 7 In.Tall	29.00
Redware, Jar, Ovoid, Interior Mustard Glaze	10.00
Redware, Jar, Pennsylvania, Green & Yellow Slip Decoration	40.00
Redware, Mold, Cake, Pennsylvana, Dutch, 5 1/2 In.Diameter, Pair	100.00
Redware, Mold, Cake, Pennsylvania Dutch, 5 1/2 In.Diam., 2	100.00
Redware, Mold, Cake, Pennsylvania Dutch, 5 1/2 In.Diameter, Pair	100.00
Redware, Mold, Pudding, Swirl Ribs, Open Cone Shape Center	18.00
Redware, Pan, Milk, Inside Glaze, 12 X 2 In.	60.00
Redware, Pitcher, Milk, Penna.Dutch, 3 3/4 In. X 5 1/2 In.Diameter	100.00
Redware, Pitcher, Pennsylvania, Miniature, 3 1/2 In.High	25.00
Redware, Plate, Pie, Indian Chief's Head, Word National	25.00
Redware, Pot, Bean, Pennsylvania, Red Glaze	35.00
Redware, Pot, Pennsylvania, Handle, Interior Glaze	12.50
Redware, Pot, Two Handles, 8 In.Diameter	12.00
Redware, Salt, Master, High Standard, Cream Glaze	75.00
Redware, Teapot, English	8.00
Revolutionary War, Box, Cartridge, British, To Fit Waist, Leather, Wood, Iron	155.00
Ridgewood, Plate, Venetian Scene, 9 In.Diameter	5.00

Ridgway Pottery has been made in the Staffordshire District in England since 1808 by a series of companies with the name Ridgway. The transfer-design dinner sets are the most widely known product. They are still being made.

Ridgway, Bowl, Coaching Days & Ways, Silver Border, 9 1/2 In.	20.00
Ridgway, Bowl, Coaching Days, 8 In.Diameter *Illus*	30.00
Ridgway, Bowl, Oriental Pattern, Blue, White, Staffordshire, 1o In.Diameter	39.00
Ridgway, Compote, Black Transfer, 1877	35.00
Ridgway, Creamer, Brown, Coaching Day Scenes, Bulbous, 3 3/4 In.High	25.00
Ridgway, Cup & Saucer, Handleless, Wm.Ridgway Co., C.1834, Tyrolean, Lavender	25.00
Ridgway, Cup Plate, Port Scene	16.00
Ridgway, Dish, Bone, Brown & White Floral & Birds, Marked, Pair	9.00
Ridgway, Jug, Bacchus, Faces On Sides, Tan, Salt Glaze, Circa 1840, 11 1/4 In.	85.00
Ridgway, Jug, Tam O' Shanter, Beige, Salt Glaze, Dated 1835	38.00
Ridgway, Mug, Coaching Days & Ways, Brown, Silver Rim & Handle	22.00 To 32.00
Ridgway, Mug, Coaching Days & Ways, Titled Scenes	17.00
Ridgway, Mug, Coaching Days & Ways, 4 In.Tall	22.50
Ridgway, Pitcher & Bowl, White, Blue, Columbian Star, Staffordshire	150.00
Ridgway, Pitcher, Brown, Twisted Rope Handle	22.00
Ridgway, Pitcher, Coaching Days, Brown, 7 In. *Illus*	25.00

Ridgway, Bowl,
Coaching Days, 8 In.Diameter

Ridgway, Pitcher, Coaching Days, Brown

Ridgway, Pitcher, Water, Oriental Design, Green 18.50
Ridgway, Pitcher, White, Flowers, Pink, Green, Bell Shape, 8 1/2 In. 80.00
Ridgway, Pitcher, White, Pink, Green, Bell Shape, 6 1/2 In. 60.00
Ridgway, Pitcher, White, Pink, Green, Bell Shape, 7 1/2 In. 70.00
Ridgway, Plate, A Duel On Putney Heath, 9 In. 23.50
Ridgway, Plate, Bulldog, Brown, Silver Band, 9 In.Diameter 16.00
Ridgway, Plate, Coaching Days, A Christmas Visitor, 11 In. 22.00
Ridgway, Plate, Grecian Pattern, Scenic, Blue, Staffordshire, 10 1/3 In. 9.50
Ridgway, Plate, Landing Of Pilgrims, Rolled Border, 10 In. 14.50
Ridgway, Plate, Morro Castle, Brown Luster, 6 3/4 In.Diameter 6.50
Ridgway, Plate, Oriental, Blue, Gold Rim, 9 In.Diameter 8.00
Ridgway, Plate, Oriental, Blue, White, 8 In.Diameter 6.00
Ridgway, Plate, Oriental, Blue, 10 In.Diameter 10.00
Ridgway, Platter, Asiatic Place, Blue & White, 15 In.Long 20.00
Ridgway, Platter, Blue, Pennsylvania Hospital, 18 1/2 In. 425.00
Ridgway, Platter, Tyrolean, Staffordshire, Blue, 14 X 18 In. 25.00
Ridgway, Pot, Blue, Flowers, Dragon Spout, C.1850, Marked 50.00
Ridgway, Sauce Boat, Boston State House, Blue 125.00
Ridgway, Stein, Coaching Ways & Days, Silver Luster Handle & Rim, 5 In.High 22.50
Ridgway, Sugar, Covered, 1794-1859 Mark, Brown Transfer Print, Gold 38.50
Ridgway, Tankard, Coaching Days & Ways, Brown, Signed, 10 1/4 In. 45.00
Rock Crystal, Cup, Standing, Carved Form Of Sea Monster & Shell, Jewels 1300.00

Rockingham in the United States is a brown glazed pottery with a tortoiseshell-like glaze. It was made from 1840 to 1900 by many american potteries. The mottle brown Rockingham Wares were first made in England at the Rockingham Factory. Other wares were also made by the english firm.

Rockingham, Bottle, Laced Shoe 47.50
Rockingham, Bowl, Footed, 5 In.Diameter 35.00
Rockingham, Bowl, Mixing, Mottled, 12 3/4 In.Diameter 45.00
Rockingham, Bowl, Mottled, 10 1/2 In.Diameter 30.00
Rockingham, Cup & Saucer, Red, Marked, Gold Trim, Brown 150.00
Rockingham, Cuspidor, Molded Leaves, 4 In.Tall, 9 In.Across 17.00
Rockingham, Cuspidor, Mottling, 4 1/4 X 7 1/2 In.Diameter 43.00
Rockingham, Cuspidor, Shell Pattern, Mottled Brown, 8 In.Diameter 18.00
Rockingham, Dessert Set, Cobalt Blue, Polychrome Flowers, C.1835, 21 Piece 510.00
Rockingham, Dish, Baking, Bennington Type, Oblong, 11 X 13 In. 45.00
Rockingham, Dish, Baking, Bennington Type, Oval 17.50
Rockingham, Figurine, Turk, Sitting, Green, Pink, Blue, Brown, Gold, Circa 1830 .... 95.00
Rockingham, Inkwell, Sanded Surface, Pastel, Mother Bird On Nest, Snake 52.50
Rockingham, Jar, Sugar, Mottled, No Lid, 2 .... 50.00
Rockingham, Mold, Cake, Mottled, 9 1/4 In.Diameter 20.00
Rockingham, Mug, Mottled, 3 3/4 In.High 22.50
Rockingham, Pitcher, Acanthus Leaf Lip & Handle Ends, Circa 1850, 5 In.High 25.00
Rockingham, Pitcher, Acanthus Leaf, 5 1/4 In.Tall 18.00
Rockingham, Pitcher, Allover Decor, Grapes, Leaves, Brown Ground, 10 In.High 30.00
Rockingham, Pitcher, Anchor Design, 8 In.Tall 50.00
Rockingham, Pitcher, Deer Attacking Dog, Brown, Hound Handle 65.00
Rockingham, Pitcher, Embossed Tulips, Brown & Yellow 16.50
Rockingham, Pitcher, Hound Handle, Embossed Deer & Dog Scene, Ohio Mark 275.00
Rockingham, Pitcher, Toby, 6 In.High 12.50
Rockingham, Plate, Floral, Transfer Printed Basket Weave, Gray, C.1830, 6 .... 40.00
Rockingham, Shoe, Baby's, Brown Glaze, 3 3/4 X 2 In.High 15.00
Rockingham, Spaniel, C.1820 .... *Illus* 75.00
    Rogers, see John Rogers
Rogers Type, Figurine, Henneke's Florentine Statuary .... *Illus* 125.00

Rookwood Pottery was made in Cincinnati, Ohio, from 1880 to 1960. All of this art pottery is marked, most with the famous flame mark. The R is reversed and placed back to back with the letter P. Flames surround the letters.

Rookwood, Bookend, Crow Design, Blue, Dated 1920, Pair 40.00
Rookwood, Bookend, Crow Design, Turquoise, Dated 1945, Pair 40.00
Rookwood, Bookend, White, Rooks On Branch, 1940, 6 1/2 In., Pair 40.00
Rookwood, Bowl, Blue, Matte Glaze, 3 In.High, 5 1/2 In.Diameter 8.00

Rockingham, Spaniel, C.1820
See Page 425

Rogers Type, Figurine, Henneke's Florentine Statuary
See Page 425

Rookwood, Bowl, Bulbous, Dated 1929, Signed, 5 3/4 In.	95.00
Rookwood, Bowl, Dark Green, Dated 1942	12.00
Rookwood, Bowl, Floral Design, Green, Purple, Spider, Signed S.T., 4 1/2 In.	45.00
Rookwood, Bowl, Revere Shape, White, Turquoise, 9 3/4 In.Wide, 4 3/4 In.Tall	50.00
Rookwood, Bowl, Rose To Green, Raised Blossoms, 6 In.Diameter, 1914	10.00
Rookwood, Bowl, Rose Vellum, Greek Key Decor, 1909, 6 1/2 X 3 In.	15.00
Rookwood, Bowl, Stippled Red Glazed Exterior, Stippled Brown In, 1922	30.00
Rookwood, Bowl, White, Turquoise Lining, Dated 1921, 9 3/4 In.Diameter	50.00
Rookwood, Box, White Matte, Floral, Marked Xxxvii	25.00
Rookwood, Candleholder, Aqua, Low, Pair	26.50
Rookwood, Candlestick, Green To Plum, Signed Hicks, 1907, 8 1/2 In.High	24.50
Rookwood, Chamberstick, Yellow, Artichoke, 1927	20.00
Rookwood, Creamer, Dated 1887, Signed Sallie Twooie, Butterfly Handle	165.00
Rookwood, Creamer, Footed, Yellow, Rose, C.Steinle, 1899, 4 In.	110.00
Rookwood, Creamer, Yellow, Flowers, Butterfly, Signed, Dated 1887, 2 In.Tall	160.00
Rookwood, Cup & Saucer, Blue Ships	24.50
Rookwood, Cup & Saucer, Pink To Green Gray, Virginia Creeper, Wilcox, 1888	225.00
Rookwood, Ewer, Cream With Wild Rose Decoration, Dated 1892, Artist-Signed	85.00
Rookwood, Ewer, Floral, Josephine E.Zettle, Artist, 1899	175.00
Rookwood, Ewer, Fluted Top, Floral, Signed Eth, 1899	225.00
Rookwood, Ewer, Pyriform, Yellow Blossoms, Dated 1899, 9 1/4 In.	90.00
Rookwood, Ewer, Signed Ccl, Shape 606b, 1899	175.00
Rookwood, Figurine, Collie, Standing, 6 In.High, 6 In.Long	75.00
Rookwood, Figurine, Dog, Tan, Dated 1946, 5 In.Tall	37.00
Rookwood, Figurine, Pelican, Dated 1932, Paper Label	22.00
Rookwood, Holder, Flower, Green Porcelain Glaze, Satyr On Rock, 1922	55.00
Rookwood, Humidor, Cream Color, Coat-Of-Arms Finial, Marked, Dated 1936	35.00
Rookwood, Jug, Sage Color, Mouse On Ear Of Corn, Signed Valentien, 8 In.	275.00
Rookwood, Jug, Swallow Flying Over Foliage, Signed Arv, Dated 1884	235.00
Rookwood, Paperweight, Elephant, White	35.00
Rookwood, Paperweight, Open Book Shape, White	37.50
Rookwood, Paperweight, Rook, Gunmetal	35.00
Rookwood, Paperweight, Rooster, White, Red, Green, Signed Macdonald, 1943	42.50
Rookwood, Paperweight, Seated Nude, White	35.00
Rookwood, Paperweight, Signed, Dated 1900, Bird On Square Base	32.00
Rookwood, Pitcher, Albert Valentien, 1888	265.00
Rookwood, Pitcher, Brown To Green, Floral Spray, Artist Sadie Markland, 1898	130.00
Rookwood, Pitcher, Maple Leaves, Winged Seed, Artist, Mary Nourse, 9 1/4 In.	225.00
Rookwood, Pitcher, Water, Clover Design, Signed H.R.S., 6 In.	135.00
Rookwood, Pianter, Medieval Countryside Scene, Signed Conant, 8 In.Diameter	140.00
Rookwood, Plaque, Lorinda Epply, Evening Scene, 9 X 12	275.00
Rookwood, Plate, Floral Decoration, Pink, 1889, H.E.W., 9 1/2 In.Diameter	135.00
Rookwood, Rose Bowl, Blue, Pink Roses, Green,Leaves, White Border, 1908, E.N.	95.00
Rookwood, Stein, Dated 1896, Signed William P.Macdonald, Pewter Lid	1900.00
Rookwood, Teapot, Ship Design, Blue	35.00

Rookwood, Tile, Footed, Basket Of Flowers, Butterflies, 1930 .... 22.50
Rookwood, Tile, Molded Pattern, Dove, Floral, Eight Small Feet, 1928 .... 38.00
Rookwood, Tray, Lyre Shape, Sitting Satyr Playing Flute, Ivory On Olive 22.50
Rookwood, Vase, Blackberry Flowers, Laura E.Lindeman Artist, 1902, Signed 116.25
Rookwood, Vase, Blue Gray, C.1922, 3 ½ In. High 14.00
Rookwood, Vase, Blue Matte, Hand-Painted Floral, Charles Stewart Todd 60.00
Rookwood, Vase, Blue, Festoon Vine, Purple Flowers, Signed C.S.T. 48.00
Rookwood, Vase, Blue, Fluted, Four-Leaf Clover Shape Top, 1927, 6 1/2 In. 15.00
Rookwood, Vase, Blue, Yellow Lining, Dated 1922, 9 1/2 In.Tall 35.00
Rookwood, Vase, Blue, 1919, 5 In. 22.00
Rookwood, Vase, Brown, Blackberries, Laura E.Lindeman Artist, 1902 .... 99.50
Rookwood, Vase, Cabinet Size, Holly, Artist-Signed, Dated 1902 .... 110.00
Rookwood, Vase, Chalice, Green Matte, Floral, Marked Mcmcxx 50.00
Rookwood, Vase, Clover Decor, Bees On Blossom 250.00
Rookwood, Vase, Cream, Green, Leaves, Signed E.B., S Mark, 7 In. 50.00
Rookwood, Vase, Cylindrical, Poppies On Brown & Orange, Edith R.Felten, 1901 .... 120.00
Rookwood, Vase, Dark To Pale Blue, Bulbous, Dated Xvii, 11 In.Tall, 7 In. 65.00
Rookwood, Vase, Deep Blue-Gray, 1926, 6 1/2 In.Tall 25.00
Rookwood, Vase, Dragonfly Design, Tan, Dated 1922, 7 In.Tall 30.00
Rookwood, Vase, Edward Diers, 1904, Green, Mistletoe, Pink Berries, 6 In, ... 275.00
Rookwood, Vase, Elizabeth Lincoln, 1902, Brown, Autumn Leaves, 6 1/2 In. 275.00
Rookwood, Vase, Elizabeth Lincoln, 1908, Vellum, Pink Poppies, 8 In. 125.00
Rookwood, Vase, Elizabeth Lincoln, 1928, Matte Vellum, Roses, Leaves 150.00
Rookwood, Vase, Floral Design, Green, Glossy, 6 1/2 In.Tall 22.50
Rookwood, Vase, Floral Rim, Blue To Pink, Signed C.S., Dated 1913, 6 In. 50.00
Rookwood, Vase, Floral, Signed Ads, 1899, Shape 583f 140.00
Rookwood, Vase, Flowers, Butterflies, Purple To Rose, Signed Lnl 1921, 13 In. 85.00
Rookwood, Vase, Flowers, Paneled, Yellow, Tan, 7 1/2 In.Tall 30.00
Rookwood, Vase, Gorham Silver Overlay, Hand-Painted Flowers, Signed Coyne 275.00
Rookwood, Vase, Grapes, Mauve-Colored, Signed, 1908, 7 1/2 In. 58.00
Rookwood, Vase, Gray Blue Forest Scene, Indians On Horseback, 1911, E.D. 95.00
Rookwood, Vase, Gray To Pink, Matte, 1925, 3 1/2 In. 8.00
Rookwood, Vase, Green To Yellow, Artist-Signed Amelia B.Sprague, 1890 .... 145.00
Rookwood, Vase, Green, Signed C.A.D., 1908, 5 In.High 18.00
Rookwood, Vase, Handles, Yellow, Orange, & Brown, Signed Ks, Shape 639c, 1892 .... 195.00
Rookwood, Vase, High Glaze, Rose To Beige, 1946, 8 In.High 15.00
Rookwood, Vase, Jens Jensen, 1929, Matte Vellum, Cherries, Leaves, Green Lined 130.00
Rookwood, Vase, Leaves, Flowers, Rose Color, Signed Weh, Dated 1929, 5 1/4 In. 55.00
Rookwood, Vase, Lorinda Epply, 1914, Scenic, Beige, Brown, Blue, Green, Cream 225.00
Rookwood, Vase, Melon Rib, Green, Yellow Lining, Cover, 15 In.High 195.00
Rookwood, Vase, Misty Glaze Over Red Cherry Blossoms, 1922 .... 125.00
Rookwood, Vase, Pink Poppy, Pods, Cream Ground, 1901, 7 In.Tall 125.00
Rookwood, Vase, Pink, Dated 1927, 9 In.High 35.00
Rookwood, Vase, Purple, Blue, Green, & Yellow, Artist Lincoln, Signed, 1920 .... 95.00
Rookwood, Vase, Raised Floral Design, Blue, Dated 1919 .... 28.00
Rookwood, Vase, Ribbed, Yellow & Brown Decor, Artist Carrie Steinle, 1894 .... 150.00
Rookwood, Vase, Rook Decor, Five Sided, 1912, 6 In. 10.00
Rookwood, Vase, Rose & Petals, Signed Ley, 6 In.Tall 55.00
Rookwood, Vase, Sailboats, Signed Sallie E.Coyne, Vellum Glaze, 1913 .... 275.00
Rookwood, Vase, Sallie Coyne, 1914, Blue, Leaves, Berries, Wax Fat Vellum 150.00
Rookwood, Vase, Signed R R V 1883 .... *Illus* 325.00

Rookwood, Vase, Signed R R V 1883

Rookwood, Vase, Signed Wilhelmine Rehm, 1930, Brown Tones, Flowers 70.00
Rookwood, Vase, Signed, Dated 1898, Artist, Ed Dier, Brown Glaze 60.00
Rookwood, Vase, Stick, Cecil A.Duell, 1908, Dull Red Finish 55.00
Rookwood, Vase, Vellum, Birds Flying Through Trees, Mark X, 9 In.High 90.00
Rookwood, Vase, Vellum, Marine Scene, Sallie Coyne, Dated 1912, 8 1/2 In.High 195.00
Rookwood, Vase, Vellum, Pink & Green, White Daisies, E.N., 1908, 7 1/4 In. 75.00
Rookwood, Vase, Violets, Leaves, Rose To Green, Bulbous, 5 In.Tall 27.50
Rookwood, Vase, Wax Matte, Light Blue, Blue & Green Floral, Signed Cstodd 65.00
Rookwood, Vase, Yellow, Three Handles At Top, 1925 .... 15.00

*Rosaline Glass is a rose-colored jade glass that was made by the Steuben
Glass Works in Corning, New York.*
Rosaline, Sherbet & Plate, Steuben 145.00

*Rose Bowls were popular during the 1880s. Rose petals were kept in the
open bowl to add fragrance to a room. The glass bowls were made with crimped
tops, which kept the petals inside. Many types of Victorian Art Glass
were made into rose bowls.*
Rose Bowl, see also under special types of Art Glass
Rose Bowl, Blue Shading To White, Acid Finish, 6 In.High, 6 1/2 In.Diameter 75.00
Rose Canton, Plate, Dinner, 10 In.Diameter 35.00

*Rose Medallion China was made in China during the nineteenth and
twentieth centuries. It is a distinctive design picturing people, flowers,
birds, and butterflies. They are colored in greens, pinks, and other colors.*
Rose Medallion, Bowl, Canton, Red & Green Flowers & Birds 375.00
Rose Medallion, Bowl, Circa 1820, 7 1/4 In. 45.00
Rose Medallion, Bowl, Gold Ground, Figures, Birds, Floral, C.1820 .... 250.00
Rose Medallion, Bowl, Punch, Footed, Famille Rose, Domestic Scenes, C.1820 .... 350.00
Rose Medallion, Bowl, Punch, Gold Ground, Oriental Family Scenes, C.1820 .... 700.00
Rose Medallion, Bowl, Punch, 15 3/4 In. 348.00
Rose Medallion, Bowl, Punch, 5 In.High, 11 1/2 In.Diameter 265.00
Rose Medallion, Bowl, Punch, 7 In.High, 16 In.Diameter 550.00
Rose Medallion, Bowl, Rice, Cover, On Stand 38.50
Rose Medallion, Bowl, Rice, Four Panels, 6 In.Diameter 24.00
Rose Medallion, Bowl, Stand, Reticulated, Famille Rose, C.1830 .... 225.00
Rose Medallion, Bowl, Tea, Matching Saucer 23.00
Rose Medallion, Bowl, Underplate, Reticulated Sides & Edges, Marked China 125.00
Rose Medallion, Bowl, 16 In.Diameter, Matching Bottle, Lid, Finial, 16 In. 675.00
Rose Medallion, Box, Brush, Two Compartments, 7 1/2 In.Long, 2 3/4 In.Tall 100.00
Rose Medallion, Box, Lid, 4 5/8 In.High, 3 7/8 In.Diameter 95.00
Rose Medallion, Box, Soap, Cover, 4 1/2 X 5 1/2 In. 65.00
Rose Medallion, Brush Pot, Circa 1850, 6 In.High 110.00
Rose Medallion, Butter & Strainer, Polygonal, Family Scenes, C.1820, Pair 225.00
Rose Medallion, Candlestick, Butterflies & Figures, 7 In., Pair 75.00
Rose Medallion, Creamer, Three Legs, 2 3/4 In.Tall, 3 1/4 In.Across Body 20.00
Rose Medallion, Cup & Saucer .... 20.00 To 30.00
Rose Medallion, Cup & Saucer, Bouillon, Covered 19.00
Rose Medallion, Cup & Saucer, Bouillon, Covered, Marked China 15.00
Rose Medallion, Cup & Saucer, Continuous Scene, C.1820, 11 .... 225.00
Rose Medallion, Cup & Saucer, Figural Scene, C.1820, 12 .... 200.00
Rose Medallion, Cup & Saucer, Marked China 10.00
Rose Medallion, Cup & Saucer, 8 .... 140.00
Rose Medallion, Dish, Kidney Shape, Oriental Figures, C.1820, 2 .... 150.00
Rose Medallion, Dish, Serving, Medallions
Rose Medallion, Dish, Serving, 'touch Not The Cat But The Clove' 200.00
Rose Medallion, Dish, Shell Shape, Center Man Bowing, Women, C.1820 .... 125.00
Rose Medallion, Dish, Shell Shape, Gold Ground, Central Medallion, C.1820 .... 130.00
Rose Medallion, Dish, Vegetable, Cover 135.00
Rose Medallion, Dish, Vegetable, Covered, Oval, Gilt Ground, C.1820, Pair 350.00
Rose Medallion, Dish, Vegetable, Covered, Rectangular, Gold, C.1820, Pair 325.00
Rose Medallion, Dish, Vegetable, Covered, Square, Figural, Birds, C.1825 .... 125.00
Rose Medallion, Dish, Vegetable, Covered, 8 X 9 In. 105.00
Rose Medallion, Dish, Vegetable, Rectangular, C.1820, Pair 150.00
Rose Medallion, Ecuelle, Covered, Continuous Figural Scenes, C.1820, Pair 225.00
Rose Medallion, Jar, Peach Finial, Circa 1850, Cover, 3 In.Tall 40.00

Rose Medallion, Mug, Cylindrical, Gold Ground, Figures, C.1820, 5 .... 225.00
Rose Medallion, Pitcher, Helmet, 1000 Butterfly 50.00
Rose Medallion, Pitcher, No Mark, Helmet, 5 In.Tall, 6 In.Diameter 75.00
Rose Medallion, Pitcher, Water, Ovoid, Strap Handle, Ornithological, C.1830 .... 180.00
Rose Medallion, Plate, China, 8 1/2 In.Diameter 20.00
Rose Medallion, Plate, Court Scene Center, Bats, Birds, Floral, C.1820, 18 .... 350.00
Rose Medallion, Plate, Deep Bowl, 7 1/4 In.Diameter, 3 .... 70.00
Rose Medallion, Plate, Deep, 9 In.Diameter 18.85
Rose Medallion, Plate, Famille Rose Oriental Court Scenes, C.1820, 10 .... 180.00
Rose Medallion, Plate, People, Roses, Birds, Enamel Decor, 9 3/4 In. 22.50
Rose Medallion, Plate, Reticulated, 8 1/2 In. 39.50
Rose Medallion, Plate, Scalloped Edge, 8 1/2 In.Diameter, 5 .... 100.00
Rose Medallion, Plate, Soup, Teahouse Scene, Man In Window 38.00
Rose Medallion, Plate, 6 In.Diameter 10.00
Rose Medallion, Plate, 9 1/2 In.Diameter 15.00
Rose Medallion, Plate, 9 3/4 In. 23.50
Rose Medallion, Platter, Circa 1850, 14 3/4 X 12 In. 110.00
Rose Medallion, Platter, Deep, Fluted Edge, 11 X 9 In. 90.00
Rose Medallion, Platter, Footed, Gravy Wells, 11 X 15 In. 80.00
Rose Medallion, Platter, Meat, Center Oriental Figures, Fish, C.1820, Pair 300.00
Rose Medallion, Platter, Orange Peel Back, 11 1/2 X 14 1/2 In. 125.00
Rose Medallion, Platter, Oval 65.00
Rose Medallion, Platter, Oval, Deep Bowl, 14 1/2 In.Long 110.00
Rose Medallion, Platter, 18 In.Diameter .... 120.00 To 135.00
Rose Medallion, Platter, 7 X 9 In. 45.00
Rose Medallion, Pot, Bough, Covered, Figural Panels, C.1820, Pair 700.00
Rose Medallion, Sauce, Figures In Window 22.00
Rose Medallion, Saucer, Medallion Of Oriental Figures, C.1820, 7 .... 110.00
Rose Medallion, Seat, Garden, Barrel Shape, Pierced, Famille Rose, C.1820, 2 .... 1350.00
Rose Medallion, Soup, 10 In. 30.00
Rose Medallion, Stand, Fluted, Oval, 8 5/8 In.Long, C.1820, Pair 120.00
Rose Medallion, Stand, Fruit, Lozenge Shape, Gold Ground, Scrolls, C.1820 .... 130.00
Rose Medallion, Sugar, Covered 45.00
Rose Medallion, Tea Set, Wicker Case, 4 Piece 90.00
Rose Medallion, Teapot .... Illus 42.00

Rose Medallion, Teapot

Rose Medallion, Teapot, Cylindrical Sides, 7 In.High 50.00
Rose Medallion, Teapot, Cylindrical, Double-Twist Handle, C.1820 .... 40.00
Rose Medallion, Teapot, Double Wire Handle, 4 3/4 In.High 45.00
Rose Medallion, Teapot, Fills From Bottom 80.00
Rose Medallion, Teapot, Miniature, 2 3/4 In.High .... 35.00 To 42.50
Rose Medallion, Teapot, Miniature, 3 In.Tall 50.00
Rose Medallion, Teapot, Puzzle 75.00
Rose Medallion, Teapot, Twisted Handle, Berry Finial, C.1800 .... 75.00
Rose Medallion, Teapot, Wicker Caddy 75.00
Rose Medallion, Teapot, Wire Handle, 5 1/2 In.Tall 65.00
Rose Medallion, Tureen & Stand, Sauce, Covered, C.1820 .... 275.00
Rose Medallion, Tureen, Covered, Oval, Famille Rose, Domestic Scenes, C.1830 .... 500.00
Rose Medallion, Tureen, Covered, Oval, Strap Handles, Court Scene, C.1820 .... 675.00
Rose Medallion, Tureen, Soup, Covered, Oval, C.1820 .... 700.00

Rose Medallion, Vase, Cylindrical, 19th Century, 10 1/2 In.High ... 95.00
Rose Medallion, Vase, Figures & Flowers, 12 In.High, Pair ... 100.00
Rose Medallion, Vase, Gold Dragons In Relief At Top, Flowers, Birds, Pair ... 150.00
Rose Medallion, Vase, Gourd Shape, 9 In. ... 85.00
Rose Medallion, Vase, 6 3/4 In.High, Pair ... 35.00
   Rose O'Neill, see Kewpie
Rose Quartz, Figurine, Bear, 3 In.High ... 37.50
Rose Quartz, Figurine, Rabbit, 3 1/2 In.Long ... 55.00

    Rose Tapestry Porcelain was made by the Royal Bayreuth Factory of Germany during the late nineteenth century. The surface of the ware feels like cloth.
Rose Tapestry, Box, Pin, Oval, Blue Mark, Cover ... 108.00
Rose Tapestry, Creamer & Sugar ... 245.00
Rose Tapestry, Creamer, Fighting Fowl, Royal Bayreuth ... 45.00
Rose Tapestry, Creamer, Pinched Spout, Blue Mark ... 195.00
Rose Tapestry, Creamer, Pinched Spout, Red Mark, Royal Bayreuth ... 95.00
Rose Tapestry, Creamer, Pinched Spout, Scenic, 4 In., Royal Bayreuth ... 90.00
Rose Tapestry, Creamer, Pinched Spout, 3 1/2 In., Royal Bayreuth ... 110.00
Rose Tapestry, Creamer, Roses, Dark To Light Pink, Pinched Lip, Blue Mark ... 155.00
Rose Tapestry, Creamer, Tavern Scene, Signed Dixon, Royal Bayreuth ... 135.00
Rose Tapestry, Creamer, 3 1/4 In.Tall ... 105.00
Rose Tapestry, Dish, Berry, Three Colors, Embossed Rim, Blue Mark ... 75.00
Rose Tapestry, Dish, Pickle, Blue Mark ... 155.00
Rose Tapestry, Frame, Pink Roses, 6 X 8 In. ... 400.00
Rose Tapestry, Hair Receiver, Pink, White, Yellow Roses, Three Gold Feet ... 87.50
Rose Tapestry, Hair Receiver, Powder Box, Set ... 185.00
Rose Tapestry, Hair Receiver, 3 Color Roses, Blue Mark, Royal Bayreuth ... 89.00
Rose Tapestry, Hatpin Holder, Openwork Base, Blue Mark ... 175.00
Rose Tapestry, Jar, Dresser, Blue Mark, Cover ... 89.00
Rose Tapestry, Jar, Powder, Pink & Yellow Roses, Royal Bayreuth ... 145.00
Rose Tapestry, Pitcher, Corset Shape, 3 Color Roses, Blue Mark, Bayreuth ... 90.00
Rose Tapestry, Plate, Four Shell, Blue Mark, 7 1/2 In.Diameter ... 95.00
Rose Tapestry, Plate, Royal Bayreuth, Green Mark, 6 In. ... 80.00
Rose Tapestry, Rose Bowl, Summer Scene, Winter Scene, Gobelins ... 140.00
Rose Tapestry, Salt Shaker, 3 in. ... *Illus* 75.00
Rose Tapestry, Shoe, Oxford ... 195.00
Rose Tapestry, Toothpick, Hunting Scene, Two Handles, Royal Bayreuth, Mark ... 90.00
Rose Tapestry, Tray, Dresser, Pink Roses, Blue Mark, Royal Bayreuth ... 150.00
Rose Tapestry, Tray, Dresser, Sterling Silver Roses, Royal Bayreuth ... 225.00
Rose Tapestry, Tray, Dresser, 3 Colors Of Roses, 11 X 8 In. ... 165.00
Rose Tapestry, Tray, Handles ... 135.00
Rose Tapestry, Tray, Pastoral Scene, Green, Blue, White, 8 X 11 In. ... 150.00
Rose Tapestry, Tray, Trinket, Cover ... 135.00
Rose Tapestry, Vase, Blue Mark, 7 In. Tall ... 185.00
Rose Tapestry, Vase, Bulbous, Blue Mark, 3 1/2 In.Tall ... 155.00
Rose Tapestry, Vase, Castle Landscape Scene, 4 1/2 In. ... 75.00
Rose Tapestry, Vase, Royal Bayreuth, 4 In.Tall ... 110.00
Rose Tapestry, Vase, Swans Swimming, 4 1/2 In. ... 75.00
Rose Tapestry, Vase, Three Colors, Royal Bayreuth, Blue Mark, 4 1/2 In.Tall ... 110.00
Rosenburg, Cup & Saucer, Art Nouveau, 2 1/4 In.High ... *Illus* 275.00

    Rosenthal Porcelain was established in Sels, Bavaria, in 1880. The german factory still continues to make fine-quality tableware and figurines.
Rosenthal, Bowl, Rose, White, Ripple Rim, Signed, 18 In.Diameter ... 25.00
Rosenthal, Bowl, Soup, King's Rose ... 2.50
Rosenthal, Candleholder, 3 Candles, Hand-Painted Dresden Flowers, Gold ... 20.00
Rosenthal, Hatpin Holder ... 10.00
Rosenthal, Jar, Cracker, Rose Design, Green, White, Marked ... 35.00
Rosenthal, Plaque, Lady On Lion ... 75.00
Rosenthal, Plate, Aida Pattern, 7 1/8 In., Marked Bahnor Selb, Germany ... 7.00
Rosenthal, Plate, Aida Pattern, 9 3/4 In., Marked Bahnor Selb, Germany ... 9.00
Rosenthal, Plate, Hand-Painted Violets, 2 Handled ... 15.00
Rosenthal, Plate, Hanging, Delft, Canal Scene, Urn & Pipes Mark, 9 1/2 In. ... 25.00
Rosenthal, Platter, Aida Pattern, 14 1/2 In., Marked Bahnor Selb, Germany ... 15.00
Rosenthal, Platter, Ivory, Floranada, 15 In. ... 12.50

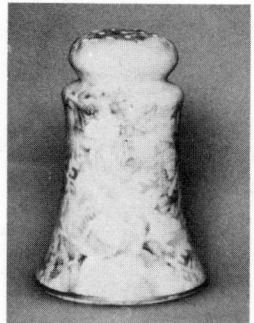

Rose Tapestry, Salt Shaker, 3 In.
See Page 430

Rosenburg, Cup & Saucer,
Art Nouveau, 2 1/4 In.High
See Page 430

Rosenthal, Teapot, Gold, Blue, Red, Flowers, Creamer, Set 10.00

Roseville Pottery Company was established in 1891 in Zanesville, Ohio.
Many types of pottery were made, including flower vases.

Roseville, Base, Bulbous, White Flowers, Green Leaves, 12 1/2 In.Tall 35.00
Roseville, Basket, Apple Blossoms, Twig Handle, Shaded Pink To Rose 16.00
Roseville, Basket, Floral Design, Blue, Green, Red, Handle, 8 1/2 In.Tall 12.50
Roseville, Basket, Handle, Green, Pink, Yellow Floral 20.00
Roseville, Basket, Hanging, Blue Magnolia 18.00
Roseville, Basket, Magnolia Pattern, Blue, 7 1/4 In.Tall 18.00
Roseville, Basket, Pink, Turquoise Handle, Blue Foliage Decor 18.00
Roseville, Basket, Reddish Tan, Green Lining, Tree Branch Handle, Floral 17.00
Roseville, Bookend, Blue Columbine, Pair 24.00
Roseville, Bowl & Frog, Green Corinthian, 8 In. 18.00
Roseville, Bowl, Beneda Line, Paper Label, 7 3/4 In. 15.00
Roseville, Bowl, Centerpiece, Green Ground, White & Purple Flowers 30.00
Roseville, Bowl, Lily, Zephyr, Orange, 2 In.High 7.00
Roseville, Bowl, Mock Orange On Pink, Footed, Signed 10.00
Roseville, Bowl, Mostique, Gray, Rough Texture, Arrowhead Shape Decor 12.00
Roseville, Bowl, Pinecone 22.50
Roseville, Bowl, Rose, Black, Grapes, Mark, 3 1/2 In. 18.00
Roseville, Bowl, Snowberry, Pink, Double Handle, Signed 12.00
Roseville, Bowl, White Brown, Peach, Snowberry, Open Handle, 11 In.Diameter 13.00
Roseville, Bowl, White Rose, 10 In.Diameter 13.00
Roseville, Candleholder, Signed, 2 In.High, Pair 8.00
Roseville, Candlestick, Balsam Cone, Tree, Ives, Green, 2 1/2 In.Tall, Pair 12.00
Roseville, Candlestick, Blue, Pink, White, Flowers, Leaves, 4 1/4 In.Tall, Pair 15.00
Roseville, Console Set, Dark Blue To Light, Raised Grapes & Leaves, Marked 15.00
Roseville, Cuspidor, Open Flared Top, Brown, Marked R.R.P.C.O.Roseville, O. 25.00
Roseville, Dish, Brown, Green, Yellow, Marked R, 3 In.High 10.00
Roseville, Dish, Child's, Rabbit Decoration, Mark, 1918-1935 .... 10.00
Roseville, Ewer, Blossoms, Foliage, Blue, White, Green, Raised Design, 11 In. 26.50
Roseville, Holder, Cigarette, Green & Beige, Pinecone & Needles, 3 In.High 12.00
Roseville, Jar, Cookie, Magnolia, Green, 8 In.Tall 45.00
Roseville, Jar, Cookie, Yellow Lilies, Side Handles, Cover, 10 1/2 In.Tall 27.50
Roseville, Jardiniere, Donatello, Marked, 6 1/2 In.High, 8 In.Wide 25.00
Roseville, Jardiniere, Magnolia Line, Burnt Orange Ground, Floral 18.00
Roseville, Jardiniere, Tan To Green, White Floral, Two Handles, 9 In. 16.00
Roseville, Jardiniere, Urn Shape, Blue, Cream, Flower Decor, 8 In.High 18.00
Roseville, Jug, Brown 3.00
Roseville, Planter, Apple Blossoms, Twig Handle, Blue, 10 In. 8.50
Roseville, Planter, Green Gardenia, Handled, 10 In. 12.50

Roseville, Planter, Green, Embossed Florals, 2 Handles 12.50
Roseville, Planter, Orange, Green, Brown, Berries, Leaves, 8 1/2 In.Tall 30.00
Roseville, Planter, Pinecone Pattern, Blue, 10 1/2 X 4 In. 10.00
Roseville, Pot, Flower, Brown, White Fern Shadings, R.R.P.Co. 7.00
Roseville, Sugar & Creamer, Open, Poinsettias 17.50
Roseville, Tea Set, White Rose Pattern, Aqua, Teapot, Creamer, Sugar 45.00
Roseville, Vase, Art Deco Style, Cinnamon, Label, 6 In.Tall 18.00
Roseville, Vase, Basket, Handle Over Top, Blue 14.00
Roseville, Vase, Beneda Line, Paper Label, 6 In. 15.00
Roseville, Vase, Blue Snowberry, Handled, 6 In. 15.00
Roseville, Vase, Brown To Tan, 2 Handles, 8 In. 15.00
Roseville, Vase, Brown, Green, Tan Flowers, Bark-Like Finish, Two Handles 12.00
Roseville, Vase, Bud, 2 Handles, Leaf & Cherry Decor, Blue Ground, 7 1/2 In. 9.00
Roseville, Vase, Carnelian, Rose, Gray, Unmarked, 4 In.Tall 5.00
Roseville, Vase, Cornucopia, Green Freesia, 7 In. 12.50
Roseville, Vase, Cornucopia, Green, Brown, Ivory Flowers 12.00
Roseville, Vase, Double Floral Design, Rozane, 10 In.High 55.00
Roseville, Vase, Double Handle, Signed, 6 1/2 In.High 9.00
Roseville, Vase, Florentine, 6 In., R.V.Mark 15.00
Roseville, Vase, Flower Design, Blue, 7 1/2 In.Tall 6.25
Roseville, Vase, Fuchsia Design, Green, Purple, White, Handle, 9 In.Tall 26.50
Roseville, Vase, Glazed Finish, 12 In.High 12.00
Roseville, Vase, Green With Raised Flower Decor, 2 Handles, 7 1/2 In. 9.50
Roseville, Vase, Green, Magnolia, 6 In. 8.50
Roseville, Vase, Green, Pinecone, 10 In.Tall 15.00
Roseville, Vase, Handle, Green, White, Flowers, 1940, 6 In. 5.00
Roseville, Vase, Hanging, Flowers, Blue, Yellow, 9 In.Diameter 20.00
Roseville, Vase, Iris Pattern, Handled 4.00
Roseville, Vase, Iris, Pastel, 9 In.Tall 12.00
Roseville, Vase, Light To Dark Blue, Embossed Flowers, Marked, 6 1/2 In. 15.00
Roseville, Vase, Magnolias On Green-Brown Ground, 4 1/2 In.High 12.50
Roseville, Vase, Marked Rozane Pottery, 8 In.High 17.00
Roseville, Vase, Pinecone & Needles, Brown, Tan, Two Handles 3.95
Roseville, Vase, Pinecone, Blue, Twig Handles, 7 In.Tall 10.50
Roseville, Vase, Pink, Green, White Wild Roses, Two Handles, 1i In. 25.00
Roseville, Vase, Rozane, Signed Dunlavy, Orchard Leaves, Brown, Tan, 15 In. 98.00
Roseville, Vase, Rust Peony, Handled, 4 In. 9.50
Roseville, Vase, Side Handles, Blue, Lily Of The Valley Decor, 9 1/2 In.Tall 6.00
Roseville, Vase, Side Handles, Brown, Green Inside, Dogwood & Leaves, 7 In. 4.00
Roseville, Vase, Tan Ground, Green Leaves, Berries, Green Handles, 8 In.Tall 15.00
Roseville, Vase, Tan To Green, Embossed Floral, Handle, 7 1/2 In. 16.00
Roseville, Vase, Thorn Apple, Rose With Green Leaves & Apples, 4 In.Tall 15.00
Roseville, Vase, Urn, Floral Design, Green, Yellow, Red, Handle, 6 1/2 In.Tall 10.00
Roseville, Vase, Wall, Mum Decoration, Yellow, Green, Brown, Handle, 8 1/2 In. 10.00
Roseville, Vase, Wall, Mum Design, Yellow, Brown, Handle, 8 1/2 In.Tall 10.00
Roseville, Vase, Wild Roses, Two Handles, 8 1/2 In. 8.50
Roseville, Vase, Yellow Green Pink, Poppies, 3 3/5 In.Tall 10.00
Roseville, Vase, 2 Handled, Flesh Color, Wild Roses, Green, Signed 27.50
Roseville, Vase, 2 Handled, Peach To Salmon Ground, Poppy Flowers 18.00
Royal Austria, Bowl, Vegetable, Rose & Leaf, 11 In.High, 5 In.High, Cover 7.50
Royal Austria, Holder, Hatpin, Ivory Ground, Floral, Gold Top, Signed 12.00
Royal Austria, Plate, Hand-Painted Rose, Scalloped Gold Border 15.00
Royal Austria, Platter, Pheasant 14.00
Royal Austria, Sugar & Creamer, O & Eg, Orange Iridescent 9.00

Royal Bayreuth Porcelain was made in Germany during the late
nineteenth and twentieth centuries. Many types of wares were made.
Royal Bayreuth, see also Rose Tapestry, Sunbonnet Babies
Royal Bayreuth, Ashtray, Arab, Horses, 5 In. ......30.00 To 32.50
Royal Bayreuth, Ashtray, Blue Mark 22.50
Royal Bayreuth, Ashtray, Clown Holds Hat, Blue Mark 45.00
Royal Bayreuth, Ashtray, Red Devil, Blue Mark 38.00
Royal Bayreuth, Ashtray, White With Pink Roses, 4 In.Diameter 18.00
Royal Bayreuth, Bowl, Cherry Clusters, Red, Green, Blue Mark, 10 1/2 In. 85.00
Royal Bayreuth, Bowl, Cherry, Grape Design 55.00
Royal Bayreuth, Bowl, Lobster, Mark 85.00

Royal Bayreuth, **Bowl**, Nut, 6 Nut Cups, Decorated 50.00
Royal Bayreuth, **Bowl**, Orange, Black Mark, 7 X 8 In. 125.00
Royal Bayreuth, **Bowl**, Roses, Blue Mark, 11 In.Diameter 65.00
Royal Bayreuth, **Bowl**, Scene, Dutch Boy, Girl, Wharf, Ship, Water, Buoy, 6 In. 28.50
Royal Bayreuth, **Bowl**, Tomato, Blue Mark, Cover, 4 In.Diameter .... 19.00 To 22.00
Royal Bayreuth, **Box**, Match, Clown Design, Hanging 45.00
Royal Bayreuth, **Box**, Pillow, Blue Mark 22.50
Royal Bayreuth, **Box**, Pin, Little Miss Muffet, Oblong, 2 Piece, Blue Mark 75.00
Royal Bayreuth, **Box**, Tapestry Cover, Rose, Pink, Yellow, Blue Crest Mark 58.00
Royal Bayreuth, **Box**, Trinket, Floral Design, Pink, White, Green Mark 28.00
Royal Bayreuth, **Butter Chip**, Blue Mark, Peach Leaves & Pink Blossoms 20.00
Royal Bayreuth, **Candlestick**, Black Corinthian, 4 In.Tall 55.00
Royal Bayreuth, **Chamberstick**, Clown, Mother-Of-Pearl, Blue Mark 65.00
Royal Bayreuth, **Cigarette & Match Set**, Musician Decor, Blue Mark 55.00
Royal Bayreuth, **Coffeepot**, Pink, Gold Trim, Roses, 6 1/2 In. 37.50
Royal Bayreuth, **Compote**, Blue Mark, Pastoral Scene, Goats & Mountains 20.00
Royal Bayreuth, **Creamer**, Allover Leaf Design, Rust, Green, Pointed Spout 30.00
Royal Bayreuth, **Creamer**, Apple, Red 37.50
Royal Bayreuth, **Creamer**, Black Crow, Blue Mark 35.00
Royal Bayreuth, **Creamer**, Black, Corinthian, Blue Mark 65.00
Royal Bayreuth, **Creamer**, Boy & Donkeys, Red, Gray, Blue, Gold Handle, 4 In. 65.00
Royal Bayreuth, **Creamer**, Chicken Figural 95.00
Royal Bayreuth, **Creamer**, Conch Shell, Pearlized, Blue Mark, 4 In.Tall 50.00
Royal Bayreuth, **Creamer**, Conch Shell, Pearlized, 4 1/2 In. 32.50
Royal Bayreuth, **Creamer**, Corinthian, White Classical Figures On Black 22.00
Royal Bayreuth, **Creamer**, Corset Shape, Peasant Musicians, 4 3/4 In. 50.00
Royal Bayreuth, **Creamer**, Cows Grazing, Pinch Spout 30.00
Royal Bayreuth, **Creamer**, Devil & Cards, Blue Mark .... 45.00 To 58.00
Royal Bayreuth, **Creamer**, Devil & Cards, Green Mark 44.00
Royal Bayreuth, **Creamer**, Elk .... 29.00 To 35.00
Royal Bayreuth, **Creamer**, Figural, Eagle, Gray To Beige, Blue Mark 75.00
Royal Bayreuth, **Creamer**, Figural, Elk, Blue Mark 39.00
Royal Bayreuth, **Creamer**, Figural, Parrot, Blue Mark 69.00
Royal Bayreuth, **Creamer**, Figural, St-Bernard, Unsigned 55.00
Royal Bayreuth, **Creamer**, Girl, Basket, Goose, Handles, Blue Mark 95.00
Royal Bayreuth, **Creamer**, Goose Girl, Blue Mark 48.00
Royal Bayreuth, **Creamer**, Gray Cat, Signed Deponiert 29.00
Royal Bayreuth, **Creamer**, Hunting Scene, Yellow, Green, Blue Mark, 4 In.Tall 32.50
Royal Bayreuth, **Creamer**, Lady Hunter, Dogs, Blue Mark 35.00
Royal Bayreuth, **Creamer**, Legal Advice, Lawyer, Clients, Signed V.Venner 75.00
Royal Bayreuth, **Creamer**, Lemon, Blue Mark 55.00
Royal Bayreuth, **Creamer**, Little Boy Blue, Blue Mark 65.00
Royal Bayreuth, **Creamer**, Little Jack Horner 45.00
Royal Bayreuth, **Creamer**, Lobster Over Cabbage Leaf, Claw Makes Handle 35.00
Royal Bayreuth, **Creamer**, Man In Stream With Hunting Dogs 45.00
Royal Bayreuth, **Creamer**, Morning Glory, Watermelon Spout 65.00
Royal Bayreuth, **Creamer**, Mountain Goat Scene 42.50
Royal Bayreuth, **Creamer**, Parrot Figural 90.00
Royal Bayreuth, **Creamer**, Poppy 50.00
Royal Bayreuth, **Creamer**, Scenic, Lady With Basket, Sea Gull, Houses, Mark 32.00
Royal Bayreuth, **Creamer**, Sitting Hound, Blue Mark, 4 In.Tall 40.00
Royal Bayreuth, **Creamer**, Tomato, Leaf Handle & Spout, Red, Green 28.00
Royal Bayreuth, **Creamer**, Tomato, Signed 27.50
Royal Bayreuth, **Creamer**, Yellow, Blue, Goats In Pasture, 4 1/2 In.Tall 15.00
Royal Bayreuth, **Cup & Saucer**, Conch Shell, Blue Mark 35.00
Royal Bayreuth, **Cup & Saucer**, Greek Key Border, Blue Mark 22.50
Royal Bayreuth, **Cup & Saucer**, Happifat 22.50
Royal Bayreuth, **Cup & Saucer**, Jack Horner, Blue Mark 42.00
Royal Bayreuth, **Cup & Saucer**, Rose Design, Orange Trim, Green Mark 18.00
Royal Bayreuth, **Cup & Saucer**, Tomato, Leaf, Demitasse 17.50
Royal Bayreuth, **Cup & Saucer**, Tomato, Pair 35.00
Royal Bayreuth, **Cup**, Nut, Green, Brown, Ruffled, Mark, Set Of 6 .... 18.00
Royal Bayreuth, **Cup**, Nut, Roses, Blue Mark 65.00
Royal Bayreuth, **Cup**, Soup, Boy & Donkeys, No Handle 35.00
Royal Bayreuth, **Dish**, Candy, Figural, Elk, Blue Mark 31.00
Royal Bayreuth, **Dish**, Candy, Lobster, Handle, 4 1/2 In.Long 22.50

Royal Bayreuth, Dish, Candy, Mark	36.00
Royal Bayreuth, Dish, Candy, Tomato, Underplate, Cover, Ring Handle	32.50
Royal Bayreuth, Dish, Child's, Little Miss Muffet, Blue Mark	52.50
Royal Bayreuth, Dish, Condiment, Tomato Shape, Green Leaf Base, Signed	32.00
Royal Bayreuth, Dish, Feeding, Little Bopeep, Blue Mark	55.00
Royal Bayreuth, Dish, Heart Shape, Hunting Scene, Horse, Dog, 5 1/4 In.Long	28.50
Royal Bayreuth, Dish, Little Miss Muffet, Blue Mark, 4 1/2 In.Long	55.00
Royal Bayreuth, Dish, Nut, Wavy Edge, Roses	28.00
Royal Bayreuth, Dish, Oak Leaf, Handled, Pearlized, 8 In.Diameter	47.00
Royal Bayreuth, Dish, Pin, Roses, Swirl Design, Yellow, Orange, Blue Mark	28.00
Royal Bayreuth, Dish, Relish, Tomato Shape, Red, Green, Leaf Base, Blue Mark	34.00
Royal Bayreuth, Figurine, Cat, Black	65.00
Royal Bayreuth, Figurine, Parrot	75.00
Royal Bayreuth, Hair Receiver, Hunt Scene, Green Gold, Footed	50.00
Royal Bayreuth, Holder, Card, Queen Of Hearts, 6 In.Tall, 3 3/4 In.Wide	50.00
Royal Bayreuth, Holder, Card, Red Devil With Cover, Blue Mark	75.00
Royal Bayreuth, Holder, Hatpin, Poppy, Satin Finish, Gold Trim, 4 1/2 In.Tall	110.00
Royal Bayreuth, Jar, Mustard, Apple	22.50
Royal Bayreuth, Jar, Mustard, Tomato, Spoon	27.00
Royal Bayreuth, Mug, Devil & Cards, Blue Mark, 5 3/4 In.Tall	60.00
Royal Bayreuth, Mustard, Leaf Spoon, Poppy	42.50
Royal Bayreuth, Mustard, Lobster	42.00
Royal Bayreuth, Mustard, Tomato On Leaf, Spoon, Cover	30.00
Royal Bayreuth, Mustard, Tomato, Blue Mark, Spoon, Cover	37.50
Royal Bayreuth, Pin Tray, Scene, Bulls In Field, Mountains, Spruces, Octagon	25.00
Royal Bayreuth, Pitcher, Arab & Horses, Blue Mark, 6 1/2 In.	42.50
Royal Bayreuth, Pitcher, Brittany Girl, Double Handle, Blue Mark, 3 1/2 In.	45.00
Royal Bayreuth, Pitcher, Carriage House, People, Blue Mark, 2 1/2 In.Tall	45.00
Royal Bayreuth, Pitcher, Child's, Pumpkin *Illus*	75.00
Royal Bayreuth, Pitcher, Children & Dog Down Hill, Blue Mark, Pinched Spout	45.00
Royal Bayreuth, Pitcher, Conch Shell, Blue Mark, 3 1/2 In.	45.00
Royal Bayreuth, Pitcher, Corinthian, Orange Band, Grecian Figures, 5 In.	75.00
Royal Bayreuth, Pitcher, Devil & Cards, 4 1/2 In. *Illus*	58.00
Royal Bayreuth, Pitcher, Devil & Cards, 8 In.Tall ....65.00 To 115.00	
Royal Bayreuth, Pitcher, Elk, Signed	25.00
Royal Bayreuth, Pitcher, Etruscan, 5 1/2 In.	59.00
Royal Bayreuth, Pitcher, Figural, Arab On Horse, 4 1/2 In.Tall	38.00
Royal Bayreuth, Pitcher, Figural, Black Crow, Orange Beak, Mark, 5 In.Tall	65.00
Royal Bayreuth, Pitcher, Little Boy Blue	42.50
Royal Bayreuth, Pitcher, Milk, Cows Grazing, Birch Trees, White, 7 1/2 In.	78.50
Royal Bayreuth, Pitcher, Milk, Hunt Scene, 7 In.High	37.50
Royal Bayreuth, Pitcher, Milk, Storks, Yellow, Blue Mark, 6 1/2 In.Tall	45.00
Royal Bayreuth, Pitcher, Milk, Two Troubadors, Green Bottom, 4 1/4 In.Tall	35.00
Royal Bayreuth, Pitcher, Moose	14.00
Royal Bayreuth, Pitcher, Orange, Green, Signed Dixon, 6 In.	59.50
Royal Bayreuth, Pitcher, Three Beach Babies Running, Blue Mark, 4 In.	85.00
Royal Bayreuth, Pitcher, Water, Arabs, Blue Ground, Blue Mark	32.50
Royal Bayreuth, Pitcher, Women, Basket, Bird, Blue Mark, 4 In.Tall	37.50
Royal Bayreuth, Pitcher, Water, Arabs, Blue Mark	32.50
Royal Bayreuth, Plate, Beach Baby, Blue Mark, 8 1/4 In.Diameter	85.00
Royal Bayreuth, Plate, Blue Mark, Green, Red Tomatoes	19.00
Royal Bayreuth, Plate, Cake, Open Handles, 10 1/2 In.	42.00
Royal Bayreuth, Plate, Children Playing Ring-Around-The-Rosy, Blue Mark	35.00
Royal Bayreuth, Plate, Farmer, Turkeys, Blue Mark, 7 1/2 In.Diameter	22.50
Royal Bayreuth, Plate, Floral, Gold Scallops, 9 In.Diameter	12.50
Royal Bayreuth, Plate, Floral, Red, Blue, Gold Rim, 6 In.	5.00
Royal Bayreuth, Plate, Jack & Jill, 7 1/2 In. ....35.00 To 45.00	
Royal Bayreuth, Plate, Jack & The Beanstalk, 7 1/2 In.	35.00
Royal Bayreuth, Plate, Little Bopeep, 7 1/2 In.	45.00
Royal Bayreuth, Plate, Little Miss Muffet, 7 1/2 In.	45.00
Royal Bayreuth, Plate, Ring-Around-The-Rosy, 6 In.	55.00
Royal Bayreuth, Plate, Rose Design, Hand-Painted, High Luster, 6 1/2 In.	8.00
Royal Bayreuth, Plate, Snow Baby, Blue Mark, 8 1/4 In.Diameter	85.00
Royal Bayreuth, Plate, Sunbonnet Babies, Blue Mark, 6 In.	69.50
Royal Bayreuth, Plate, Tapestry, Desert Scene, Arab, Horses, 11 1/4 In.	175.00
Royal Bayreuth, Salt & Pepper, Cluster Of Grapes, Mother-Of-Pearl Satin	13.00

Royal Bayreuth, Salt & Pepper, Elk	27.00
Royal Bayreuth, Salt & Pepper, Farm Scene, Blue Mark	57.50
Royal Bayreuth, Salt Shaker, Washing Woman, Marked	62.50
Royal Bayreuth, Sauce, Pink Roses On White, Green Trim, Scrolled Edge	60.00
Royal Bayreuth, Saucer, Sunbonnet Babies, Mopping & Washing Windows	35.00
Royal Bayreuth, Shoe, High Top, Black, Beige, Blue Mark	55.00
Royal Bayreuth, Sugar & Creamer, Conch Shells .... *Illus*	55.00

Royal Bayreuth, Pitcher, Child's, Pumpkin
See Page 434

Royal Bayreuth, Pitcher,
Devil & Cards, 4 1/2 In.
See Page 434

Royal Bayreuth, Sugar & Creamer,
Conch Shells

Royal Bayreuth, Sugar & Creamer, Covered, 2 Handles, Openwork Legs	50.00
Royal Bayreuth, Sugar & Creamer, Figural, Strawberry, Blue Mark	65.00
Royal Bayreuth, Sugar & Creamer, Grape Cluster, Leaf Handle, Cover, Signed	82.00
Royal Bayreuth, Sugar & Creamer, Hunting Scene, Blue Mark, Cover	69.00
Royal Bayreuth, Sugar & Creamer, Moose, Double-Headed Sugar	45.00
Royal Bayreuth, Sugar & Creamer, Pink Roses, Gold, Blue Mark	35.00
Royal Bayreuth, Sugar & Creamer, Tomato, Cover	35.00
Royal Bayreuth, Sugar, Lobster Cover, Blue Mark	45.00
Royal Bayreuth, Sugar, Lobster, Cover, 5 In.Long, 5 In.High	35.00
Royal Bayreuth, Sugar, Tomato, Covered, Blue Mark, 4 In.Diameter	20.00
Royal Bayreuth, Sugar, Tomato, Covered, Green Mark	18.00
Royal Bayreuth, Sugar, Tomato, 2 Handles, 3 1/2 In.High	20.00
Royal Bayreuth, Tea Set, Tomato, Leaf Plates, Creamer & Sugar	125.00
Royal Bayreuth, Tea Set, Tomato, Sugar, Creamer, Teapot	65.00
Royal Bayreuth, Teapot, Conch Shell, Mother-Of-Pearl, Blue Mark	85.00
Royal Bayreuth, Teapot, Orange Blossoms, Orange, Footed, Blue Mark	75.00
Royal Bayreuth, Toothpick, Doe & Deer, Three Handle, Blue Mark	10.00
Royal Bayreuth, Toothpick, 3 Handles, 2 Musicians, Gray Brown, Blue Mark	40.00
Royal Bayreuth, Tray, Cabbage Leaf, Flat	10.00
Royal Bayreuth, Tray, Woman Floating On Water, Sides Of Tray Are Waves	125.00

Royal Bayreuth, Vase, Bottle Shape, Girl On Stairway With Candle 67.09
Royal Bayreuth, Vase, Boy With Donkeys, Marked, 5 In. 28.00
Royal Bayreuth, Vase, Brown To Gray, Flowers, Ducks, Blue Mark, 7 In. 85.00
Royal Bayreuth, Vase, Bud, Ring-Around-The-Rosy, Flared Sterling Rim 75.00
Royal Bayreuth, Vase, Candle Shape, Girl On Stair With Candle, Buff 67.09
Royal Bayreuth, Vase, Cavalier, Maroon, Gold, Tettau Mark, 7 1/2 In.Tall 75.00
Royal Bayreuth, Vase, Desert Scene, Blue, Gold, Blue Mark, 5 1/2 In. 42.50
Royal Bayreuth, Vase, Fighting Cock Scene, Green, 2 Handle, Blue Mark, 7 In. 72.50
Royal Bayreuth, Vase, Gay Cavalier, Small Neck, Round, 4 In.Diameter 35.00
Royal Bayreuth, Vase, Hunter, Dog, Ducks, Blue Mark, 6 In.Tall 49.00
Royal Bayreuth, Vase, Landscape, Mountains, Cows, Blue Mark 45.00
Royal Bayreuth, Vase, Lavender, Cavaliers .... *Illus* 78.00

Royal Bayreuth, Vase, Lavender, Cavaliers

Royal Bayreuth, Vase, Pasture Scene, 4 1/4 In. 29.00
Royal Bayreuth, Vase, Portrait, Couple, Handles 55.00
Royal Bayreuth, Vase, Red Corinthian, Classical Figures, Two Handles 58.00
Royal Bayreuth, Vase, Scene, Swans, Water, Sky, Trees, Yellow Ground, 7 1/4 In. 57.00
Royal Bayreuth, Vase, Scenic, Woman On Horse, Couple With Butterfly Net 38.00
Royal Bonn, Dish, Celery, Mehlein, Gold Edges, Red & Yellow Roses 9.50
Royal Bonn, Dish, Cheese, Covered, Floral 20.00
Royal Bonn, Dish, Cheese, Covered, Green, Pink Roses 16.00
Royal Bonn, Plate, Fish, Shell Border, Pair 12.50
Royal Bonn, Vase, Gold & White Ground, Floral, 14 In.High 55.00
Royal Bonn, Vase, Gold & White, Ornate Decor, 11 In.High 50.00
Royal Bonn, Vase, Pink, Green, Brown, Flowers, Gold Trim, 2 Handle, 10 3/4 In. 36.00
Royal Bonn, Vase, White Ground, Floral, Gold, 14 In.High 55.00
Royal Bonn, Vase, White, Decorated, Gold Trim, 11 In.High 50.00
Royal Cauldon, Plate, England, The Meet, Brown On White Scene 12.50

*Royal Copenhagen Porcelain and Pottery has been made in Denmark since
1772. It is still being made. One of their most famous wares is the
Christmas Plate Series.*
    Royal Copenhagen, see also Collector plate
Royal Copenhagen, Bowl, Handle, Flora Danica Decoration, Shallow 50.00
Royal Copenhagen, Bowl, Triangular, Flora Danica Decoration, Standard 95.00
Royal Copenhagen, Butter Chip, Blue, White, Openwork Border, 3 In.Diameter, 8 .... 25.00
Royal Copenhagen, Candlestick, Blue Decoration, Embossed Lion Heads, Pair 10.00
Royal Copenhagen, Coaster, Old Cars Decorated, 6 .... 12.00
Royal Copenhagen, Coffeepot, 1897 .... 60.00
Royal Copenhagen, Creamer, Floral Decor, Mark, 3 1/4 In.Tall 8.50
Royal Copenhagen, Figurine, Fawn, Raven, 6 3/4 In.Tall 115.00
Royal Copenhagen, Figurine, Scholar & Child 80.00
Royal Copenhagen, Figurine, Two Foxes Lying Together, 7 X 9 In.Long 185.00
Royal Copenhagen, Pipe, Porcelain 25.00
Royal Copenhagen, Plate, Botany Decoration, Pierced Edge 20.00
Royal Copenhagen, Pot, Sauce, Flora Danica Decoration, Applied Flowers 40.00
Royal Copenhagen, Teapot, Raised Basket Weave Decor, Cornflowers, 10 In. 18.00
Royal Copenhagen, Vase, Narcissus, White, Blue, Green, Ogee Shape, 9 In. 38.00
Royal Copenhagen, Vase, Sailing Boat In Reserve, 6 1/2 In.High 20.00

Royal Crown Derby Company LTD. was established in England in 1876.

Royal Crown Derby, see also Crown Derby

Royal Crown Derby, Creamer, Water Lilies	20.00
Royal Crown Derby, Cup & Saucer, Demitasse, Floral, Circa 1945	4.00
Royal Crown Derby, Jar, Flower Design, Beige, Gold, Round, Cover, 6 In.Tall	32.00
Royal Crown Derby, Vase, Cobalt & Gold, 4 1/2 In.	75.00
Royal Crown Derby, Vase, Gold On Red Ground, 10 In.High	12.50
Royal Crown Derby, Vase, 2 Handles, Roses With Floral Reserve	40.00

Royal Doulton was the name used on pottery made after 1902. The Doulton Factory was founded in 1815. Their wares are still being made.

Royal Doulton, see also Doulton

Royal Doulton, Berry Set, Under The Greenwood Tree, 5 Piece	45.00
Royal Doulton, Bird, Bluebird, Pedestal, 4 In.Marked Hn137	12.00
Royal Doulton, Bottle, Man In Black Cape	35.00
Royal Doulton, Bowl, Alice In Wonderland, 'alice & Duchess'5 5/8 In.	21.00
Royal Doulton, Bowl, Barkis, Little Nell, Alfred Jingle, 6 1/2 In.	42.50
Royal Doulton, Bowl, Cereal, Bumpkins	5.50
Royal Doulton, Bowl, England, Blue Fish Scale, Floral, Pheasants Center	35.00
Royal Doulton, Bowl, Fruit, Yellow, Scalloped, Crown Mark, 9 1/2 In.Diameter	29.00
Royal Doulton, Bowl, Incised Leaf Pattern On Mottled Ground, Signed	35.00
Royal Doulton, Candlestick, Dickensware, Sam Weller, Tony Weller, Pair	55.00
Royal Doulton, Child's Set, Bunnykins, Signed Barbara Vernon, 3 Pieces	35.00
Royal Doulton, Chocolate Pot, Floral Decor, Beige Ground	42.00
Royal Doulton, Chocolate Pot, Under The Greenwood Tree	45.00
Royal Doulton, Creamer, Dickens Scene, Brown Colors, Signed	10.00
Royal Doulton, Creamer, 2 1/2 In.High	12.50
Royal Doulton, Cup & Saucer, Demitasse, Arcadia Pattern	4.00
Royal Doulton, Cup & Saucer, Demitasse, Multicolored Flowers, Brown Trim	5.00
Royal Doulton, Cup & Saucer, Watchman Series, Beige, Blue Figures	14.50
Royal Doulton, Cup, Coronation, 1911	15.00
Royal Doulton, Dish, Leeds Spray, Cover, 8 In.Diameter	25.00
Royal Doulton, Dish, Serving, Rustic England, 6 Sided, Artist Signed Grace	20.00
Royal Doulton, Ewer, Tapestry Decorated, Signed, Pair	65.00
Royal Doulton, Figurine, Autumn Breezes	35.00
Royal Doulton, Figurine, Baby	22.00
Royal Doulton, Figurine, Belle Of The Ball	52.50 To 85.00
Royal Doulton, Figurine, Blithe Morning	35.00
Royal Doulton, Figurine, Bumble, 4 In.	8.50
Royal Doulton, Figurine, Captain Cuttle, 4 In.	8.50
Royal Doulton, Figurine, Churchill Toby, 8 In.	55.00
Royal Doulton, Figurine, Dickens's Bumble, 4 In.	8.95
Royal Doulton, Figurine, Dickens's Captain Cuttle, 4 In.	8.95
Royal Doulton, Figurine, Dickens's Fagin, 4 In.	5.95
Royal Doulton, Figurine, Dickens's Little Nell, 4 In.	8.95
Royal Doulton, Figurine, Dickensware, Tony Weller, 4 In.	18.00
Royal Doulton, Figurine, Doberman Pinscher, 6 In Tall	18.50
Royal Doulton, Figurine, English Bulldog	22.50 To 25.00
Royal Doulton, Figurine, Fagin, 7 In.	8.50
Royal Doulton, Figurine, Jane	*Illus* 50.00
Royal Doulton, Figurine, Janet, Marked Rd778640, 4 In.Tall	20.03
Royal Doulton, Figurine, Little Nell, 4 In.	8.50
Royal Doulton, Figurine, Little Pig	27.00
Royal Doulton, Figurine, Memories	35.00
Royal Doulton, Figurine, Puppies In Basket, 3 In.High	19.50
Royal Doulton, Figurine, Robin, Kneeling Boy, 2 1/2 In.High	8.50
Royal Doulton, Figurine, To Bed	18.00
Royal Doulton, Figurine, Toymaker, 6 In.	45.00
Royal Doulton, Jug, Hunt, Irish Silver Cover, Dublin, Edward Power, 1832	148.00
Royal Doulton, Jug, Milk, Dickensware, Sam Weller, Signed Noke	50.00
Royal Doulton, Jug, Stoneware, Mushroom Shape, Scrollwork & Seaweed, Marked	55.00
Royal Doulton, Jug, Viking Ship Decor, Brown To Beige Ground, 7 1/2 In.High	68.00
Royal Doulton, Jug, Whiskey, Viking Ship Special Highland	20.00
Royal Doulton, Mug & Plate, Child's, Bunnykins	17.00
Royal Doulton, Mug, Annual, 1971	32.50
Royal Doulton, Mug, Coaching Scene, 3 1/4 In.	15.00

Royal Doulton, Figurine, Jane
See Page 437

Royal Doulton, Mug, Cobalt Blue Bottom, Gray Top, 6 1/4 In.	25.00
Royal Doulton, Mug, Queen Victoria Jubilee, 4 In.High	35.00
Royal Doulton, Mug, 3 Handles, Embossed Hunt & Drinking Scenes, Silver Rim	105.00
Royal Doulton, Nutcup, Canary Luster, Set Of 4	10.00
Royal Doulton, Pitcher, Auld Mac, Large	38.00
Royal Doulton, Pitcher, Cavalier, 3 In.Tall	12.50
Royal Doulton, Pitcher, Don Quixote, Signed Noke, 9 In.High	35.00
Royal Doulton, Pitcher, Embossed Drinking & Hunting Scenes, Blue Top, Tan	55.00
Royal Doulton, Pitcher, Footed, Blue Decoration Of Sailing Galleys	35.00
Royal Doulton, Pitcher, Milk, 'Watchman, What Of The Night'	40.00
Royal Doulton, Pitcher, Old London, Dickens Scenes	65.00
Royal Doulton, Pitcher, Old London, 1949, Embossed Scenes, Rectangular	52.50
Royal Doulton, Pitcher,Old Moreton Hall, Bulbous Base, Oval, 4 5/8 in.	22.00
Royal Doulton, Pitcher, Oliver Twist, Rectangular	55.00
Royal Doulton, Pitcher, Raised Decoration, Initialed, 11 In.Hihg	35.00
Royal Doulton, Pitcher, Shakespeare Series, 'Katherine,' 4 1/4 In.High	25.00
Royal Doulton, Pitcher, Squire, Signed Noke, 7 In.High	28.00
Royal Doulton, Pitcher, Toby, Old Charley, 3 1/2 In. 24.50 To	27.50
Royal Doulton, Pitcher, 'Under The Greenwood Tree'	20.00
Royal Doulton, Pitcher, 'Watchman, What Of The Night, ' 9 In.High	45.00
Royal Doulton, Pitcher, Water, Sunset Scene, Rope Handle	50.00
Royal Doulton, Plate, 'An Open Door May Tempt A Saint, ' 10 1/4 In.	25.25
Royal Doulton, Plate, Balanced Rock, 9 In.Diameter	27.00
Royal Doulton, Plate, Battle Of The Nile	22.50
Royal Doulton, Plate, Canterbury Pilgrims, Dates 1335-1399, 10 1/2 In.	23.00
Royal Doulton, Plate, Coach Scene, 8 In.Diameter	15.00
Royal Doulton, Plate, Cottage, Country Setting, 10 1/2 In.Diameter	16.00
Royal Doulton, Plate, Country Setting, Pastel Colors, 10 1/2 In.Diameter	19.50
Royal Doulton, Plate, Dutch Scene, Signed Noke, 9 1/2 In.Diameter	12.00
Royal Doulton, Plate, Falconer, 10 1/2 In.	19.00
Royal Doulton, Plate, Falstaff, Polychrome, 8 1/2 In.Diameter	17.50
Royal Doulton, Plate, Flowers, 7 In.	3.50
Royal Doulton, Plate, Hanging, Artful Dodger, Noke, 13 1/2 In.	75.00
Royal Doulton, Plate, 'I Be All The Way From Zummerset, ' Black Mark	37.50
Royal Doulton, Plate, Indian Chief, 10 1/2 In.Diameter	34.00
Royal Doulton, Plate, Jester, 10 1/2 In.	19.00
Royal Doulton, Plate, Man Sitting In Front Of Cobbler's Store	37.50
Royal Doulton, Plate, Monk Fishing, Tomorrow Will Be Friday, Signed Noke	30.00
Royal Doulton, Plate, Mt.Vernon, 10 In.	20.00
Royal Doulton, Plate, 'Of Recreation There Is None So Free As Fishing'	42.50

Royal Doulton, Plate, Pheasant, Floral Border, 9 1/2 In., Set Of 6 .... 32.00
Royal Doulton, Plate, "Pride Goeth Before A Fall', Skating Scene 15.00
Royal Doulton, Plate, Red Roses, Yellow, Purple, Blue Floral, 10 1/2 In., 6 .... 125.00
Royal Doulton, Plate, The Admiral 37.50
Royal Doulton, Plate, The Bookworm 22.00
Royal Doulton, Plate, The Bookworm, 10 In.Diameter 20.00
Royal Doulton, Plate, The Doctor, 10 1/2 In. 20.00
Royal Doulton, Plate, The Jester 37.50
Royal Doulton, Plate, The Mayor 37.50
Royal Doulton, Plate, The Squire, 10 1/2 In. 20.00
Royal Doulton, Plate, Washington's Mansion, Mt.Vernon, 10 In. 15.00
Royal Doulton, Plate, 'when I Last Saw Him He Was A Venerable Old Man' 42.50
Royal Doulton, Platter, Flowers, Geometric Design, Blue, 13 X 10 In. 27.50
Royal Doulton, Shaving Mug, Scuttle, Blue & Gold 24.00
Royal Doulton, Sugar & Creamer, Country Scene, Windmill, Tan, Brown 47.50
Royal Doulton, Sugar & Creamer, Dickensware, Bill Sykes & Poor Jo 60.00
Royal Doulton, Sugar & Creamer, Watchman Series, Beige, Blue Figures 48.00
Royal Doulton, Tankard, 1971 .... 35.00
Royal Doulton, Teapot, Dickensware, Little Nell 60.00
Royal Doulton, Teapot, Under The Greenwood Tree, 5 3/4 In.Tall 37.50
Royal Doulton, Toby Mug, Auld Mac, 4 In. 14.50
Royal Doulton, Toby Mug, Auld Mac, 7 In. 24.50
Royal Doulton, Toby Mug, Captain Henry Morgan, 3 1/2 In. 10.00
Royal Doulton, Toby Mug, Captain Hook 16.50
Royal Doulton, Toby Mug, Cavalier, 3 1/4 In. 25.00
Royal Doulton, Toby Mug, Churchill, Full Body, Seated, 5 1/2 In.Tall 36.00
Royal Doulton, Toby Mug, Churchill, Full Body, Seated, 8 1/2 In.High 55.00
Royal Doulton, Toby Mug, Dated 1946 .... 15.00
Royal Doulton, Toby Mug, Dick Turpin, 3 1/4 In. 25.00
Royal Doulton, Toby Mug, Dick Turpin, 7 In. 19.50
Royal Doulton, Toby Mug, Falconer, 2 3/4 In. 8.75
Royal Doulton, Toby Mug, Falstaff, 4 In.Tall 15.00
Royal Doulton, Toby Mug, Falstaff, 7 In. 19.50
Royal Doulton, Toby Mug, Granny, 2 3/4 In. 12.50
Royal Doulton, Toby Mug, Granny, 4 In. 14.50
Royal Doulton, Toby Mug, Granny, 7 In. 23.50
Royal Doulton, Toby Mug, Happy John, Full Figure, 8 1/2 In. 22.50
Royal Doulton, Toby Mug, Jester, 3 1/4 In. 32.00
Royal Doulton, Toby Mug, John Peel, Large .... 45.00 To 47.50
Royal Doulton, Toby Mug, John Peel, 2 1/2 In.High 15.00
Royal Doulton, Toby Mug, John Peel, 5 1/4 In. 45.00
Royal Doulton, Toby Mug, Lawyer, 2 3/4 In. 8.75
Royal Doulton, Toby Mug, Lawyer, 4 In. 11.50
Royal Doulton, Toby Mug, Lord Nelson, Salt Glaze 175.00
Royal Doulton, Toby Mug, Mad Hatter 15.00
Royal Doulton, Toby Mug, Merlin, 4 In. 11.50
Royal Doulton, Toby Mug, Mine Host, 7 In. 19.50
Royal Doulton, Toby Mug, North American Indian 35.00
Royal Doulton, Toby Mug, Old Charley, 2 3/4 In. 12.50
Royal Doulton, Toby Mug, Old Charley, 4 In. 14.50
Royal Doulton, Toby Mug, Old Charley, 5 1/2 In. 20.00
Royal Doulton, Toby Mug, Old Charley, 7 In. 24.50
Royal Doulton, Toby Mug, Old King Cole, Miniature, England 15.00
Royal Doulton, Toby Mug, Paddy, 2 1/4 In. 22.00
Royal Doulton, Toby Mug, Poacher, 7 In. 17.50
Royal Doulton, Toby Mug, Robinson Crusoe, 7 In. 18.50
Royal Doulton, Toby Mug, Sairey Gamp, 2 1/4 In. 8.50
Royal Doulton, Toby Mug, Sairey Gamp, 2 3/4 In. 12.50
Royal Doulton, Toby Mug, Sairey Gamp, 3 In.High 8.00
Royal Doulton, Toby Mug, Sairey Gamp, 7 In. .... 24.00 To 24.50
Royal Doulton, Toby Mug, Sam Weller, 5 1/4 In. 55.00
Royal Doulton, Toby Mug, The Huntsman 58.00
Royal Doulton, Toby Mug, Tony Weller, 2 1/4 In. 8.50
Royal Doulton, Toby Mug, Viking, 3 1/4 In.Tall 15.00
Royal Doulton, Toby Mug, Winston Churchill, 8 1/2 In. 24.00
Royal Doulton, Toothpick, Robin Hood 15.00

Royal Doulton, Tray, Dresser, Candlesticks, Flower Garlands In Basket Decor 24.00
Royal Doulton, Tray, Hand-Painted Gibson Type Woman & Child, Farm Scene 80.00
Royal Doulton, Tumbler, Alice In Wonderland, King & Hatter, 3 1/4 In. 18.00
Royal Doulton, Vase, Dickensware, Old Peggotty, 4 1/4 In. 29.00
Royal Doulton, Vase, English Secnes, The Cleaners, 7 In. 25.00
Royal Doulton, Vase, Floral, Cobalt, White, Gold, Warwick 35.00
Royal Doulton, Vase, Green & Blue Raised Decor On Brown Mottled Ground 30.00
Royal Doulton, Vase, Heubach, Gray, Bird Flying, Attached Handles, Fan Sign 47.50
Royal Doulton, Vase, Onion Skin, Orange, Iridescent, Small Neck, 4 X 3 1/2 In 40.00
Royal Doulton, Vase, Red, Art Nouveau Sterling Overlay, 6 In. 65.00
Royal Doulton, Vase, Rustic England, Artist Signed Grace, 7 In. 23.00
Royal Doulton, Vase, Transfer Of Santa, Sleigh, Embossed Holly, Berries 20.00
Royal Doulton, Vase, Under The Greenwood Tree 25.00
Royal Doulton, Vase, Veined Flambe, 5 3/4 In.Tall 47.50
Royal Doulton, Vase, Witch, 5 In. 16.50

*Royal Dux is a Czechoslovakian pottery made at the turn of the twentieth
century. Unfortunately reproductions are now appearing on the market.*
Royal Dux, Figurine, Bust, Pair 750.00
Royal Dux, Figurine, Lioness, Stalking, 15 In.Long, 7 In.High 150.00
Royal Dux, Figurine, Parakeets, Yellow, Rose, Pink, On Perch, 7 1/2 In.Tall 45.00
Royal Dux, Figurine, Robed Girl Holding Pitcher, Pink Triangle Mark 55.00
Royal Dux, Figurine, Stalking Lioness, Bohemia, 15 In.Long, Beige 150.00
Royal Dux, Figurine, Stalking Lioness, Oval Base, Bohemia, Beige, 7 In.Tall 150.00
Royal Dux, Figurine, Venus, Conch Shell, Rust, Gold, Green, Doves, Marked 150.00
Royal Dux, Figurine, Woman, Leaves, Mask, Dagger, Pink Mark, 8 1/2 In. 125.00
Royal Dux, Planter, Maiden, Pink Mark, Green, Ivory, Gold Highlights 45.00
Royal Dux, Ring Tree, Cream & Gold, Pink Triangle Mark 35.00
Royal Dux, Vase, Olive Green Base, Tan Goat & Wagon, Green, 8 In.Tall 175.00
Royal Dux, Vase, Raised Floral, Sawtooth Gold Edge, 12 1/2 In.Tall 65.00

*Royal Flemish Glass was made during the late 1880s in New Bedford,
Massachusetts, by the Mt.Washington Glass Works. It is a colored
satin glass decorated in dark colors with gold designs.*
Royal Flemish, Bowl, Pansies, Frosted, Melon Ribbed, Gold & Silver Edge 285.00
Royal Flemish, Jar, Cookie, Frosted, Melon Rib, Pansies, Mt.Washington, No Lid 285.00
Royal Flemish, Jar, Cookie, Raised Bail On Cover, 9 3/4 In.High 1650.00
Royal Flemish, Jar, Cracker, Mt.Washington, Signed J.W.In Lid 700.00
Royal Flemish, Vase, Covered, Light Colors .... *Illus* 2250.00
Royal Lace, Plate, Cobalt, 8 1/2 In.Diameter 11.00
Royal Munich, Plate, Cake, Open Handle, Roses, Gold Border 25.00
Royal Munich, Plate, Cake, Roses 25.00
Royal Munich, Sugar & Creamer, Pink Roses 27.50
Royal Rudolstadt, Bowl, Square, Floral On Light Ground, Gold 12.00
Royal Rudolstadt, Cake Set, Poppies, Yellow, Hand-Painted, Four Plates 68.00
Royal Rudolstadt, Creamer, Satin Finish, Floral Spray On Cream Ground 15.00
Royal Rudolstadt, Holder, Hatpin, White & Blue Ground, Roses, Signed Hahn 26.50
Royal Rudolstadt, Jar, Cracker, Green Ferns, Red Rosebuds, Cover 22.00
Royal Rudolstadt, Jar, Powder, Rose Border, White, Red, Cover, 4 1/2 In. 22.00
Royal Rudolstadt, Jar, Rose, Lily, Violets, Yellow, Cream 32.50
Royal Rudolstadt, Plate, Four Petal Shape, Pastel Roses, Gold Edge 15.00
Royal Rudolstadt, Plate, General Grant, Black & White, Gold Rim, 9 1/2 In. 26.00
Royal Rudolstadt, Plate, General Sherman, Black & White, Gold Rim, 9 1/2 In. 26.00
Royal Rudolstadt, Plate, Hand-Painted Scene, Gold Scalloped, Signed 29.00
Royal Rudolstadt, Plate, Hand-Painted Yellow Roses, Signed, 1o In.Diameter 23.00
Royal Rudolstadt, Plate, Hand-Painted, Beige, Pink, Gold, Signed 8.00
Royal Rudolstadt, Plate, Pink Roses, Gold Band, 12 1/2 In. 18.00
Royal Rudolstadt, Relish, Hand-Painted, Star Base, 9 In.Long 22.00
Royal Rudolstadt, Sugar & Creamer, Kewpie, Signed Rose O'Neill, Large 150.00
Royal Rudolstadt, Vase .... *Illus* 45.00
Royal Rudolstadt, Vase, Flowers, Gold Trim, Germany, 6 In.Tall 20.00
Royal Rudolstadt, Vase, Flowers, Purple, Gold 30.00
Royal Rudolstadt, Vase, Footed, Handle 48.00
Royal Rudolstadt, Vase, Swan Shape, Lavender, Beak In Wing, 6 1/2 In.High 46.75
Royal Vienna, Comport, Red, Cobalt, & Gold, Beehive Mark, Circular Base 26.50
Royal Vienna, Creamer, Hand-Painted Floral, Fish Scale, Beehive Mark, 3 In. 48.00

Royal Flemish, Vase,
Covered, Light Colors
See Page 440

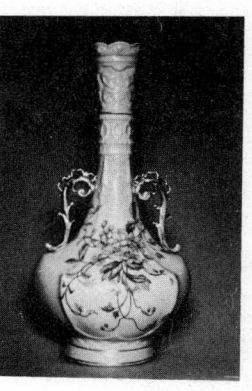

Royal Rudolstadt, Vase
See Page 440

Royal Vienna, Cup & Saucer, Floral Design, Blue, Red, Luster Trim, Mark	12.50
Royal Vienna, Figurine, Camel, Pincushion Insert, 3 1/2 X 4 1/2 In.Long	85.00
Royal Vienna, Figurine, Fox, Pen Wiper Insert, 4 In.High, 7 1/2 In.Long	85.00
Royal Vienna, Holder, Toothbrush, Bird, Yellow, Red, Marked	25.00
Royal Vienna, Jar, Rose Petal, Cobalt, Portrait In Medallion, Beehive Mark	68.00
Royal Vienna, Pitcher, Satyr's Mask	65.00
Royal Vienna, Plate, Green, Gold, Mythological Figures, Beehive Mark, 10 In.	25.00
Royal Vienna, Plate, Lady's Portrait, Brown Hair	55.00
Royal Vienna, Plate, Portrait, Signed Wagner, Titled Reflexion, Brown Hair	195.00
Royal Vienna, Plate, The Gleaners, Signed, Beehive	150.00
Royal Vienna, Stein	550.00
Royal Vienna, Sugar & Creamer	28.00
Royal Vienna, Urn, Beehive, Blue Medallion, Cover	27.50
Royal Vienna, Urn, Mythological Painting, Gold, Jeweled Maroon Piping	75.00
Royal Vienna, Vase, 2 Handles, Cupid & Aphrodite, Signed Kauffmann, Beehive	37.50
Royal Winton, Jar, Tobacco, Rural Street Scene	17.50
Royal Winton, Pitcher, Summertime, 3 1/2 In.Tall	15.00

*Royal Worcester Porcelain and Pottery was made in England from 1862
to the present time. The factory was founded in 1751 but a different name
was used.*

Royal Worcester, see also Worcester

Royal Worcester, Basket, Beige Ground, Gold Decor, Mark	30.00
Royal Worcester, Bowl, Berry, Woven Basket, Cream, Matching Saucer	65.00
Royal Worcester, Bowl, Bird Decor, 1901, 3 In.	32.50
Royal Worcester, Bowl, Blue To White, Signed Grainger & Co.7 In.Diameter	75.00
Royal Worcester, Bowl, Locke, Yellow To Pale Peach, Garlands Of Blossoms	35.00
Royal Worcester, Bowl, Rose, Miniature, Bird Decor, 2 3/4 In.High	32.00
Royal Worcester, Box, Cover, Cream Ground, Floral, 2 3/4 In.Diameter	25.00
Royal Worcester, Candleholder, Molded Design, Wedge Shape, White, Dated 1888	35.00
Royal Worcester, Candlesnuffer, Brown Owl Wears White Hood, Gold Tassel	60.00
Royal Worcester, Cup & Saucer, Blue & Gold Border, Flowers, Purple Mark	12.00
Royal Worcester, Cup & Saucer, Cream Ground, Floral	32.00
Royal Worcester, Cup & Saucer, Demitasse, Cream Color, Rust Flowers	12.00
Royal Worcester, Cup & Saucer, Demitasse, Cromwell Pattern, Circa 1937	4.00
Royal Worcester, Cup & Saucer, Dessert Plate, Hand-Painted Floral, Mark	30.00
Royal Worcester, Cup & Saucer, Fern & Flowers, Blue, White, Set Of 6	110.00
Royal Worcester, Cup & Saucer, Floral, 1892	45.00
Royal Worcester, Dessert Set, Hand-Painted Pink Rose Medallion, Gold	75.00
Royal Worcester, Dish, Enameled Floral, Green Crown & Circle Mark	20.00
Royal Worcester, Dish, Relish, Matte Finish, Purple Floral Decor	50.00
Royal Worcester, Egg Coddler, Hand-Painted Flowers, Metal Lid, Ring Handle	5.50

Royal Worcester, Ewer, Cream Ground, Blue Floral Spray, Gold Handle, 6 In.	35.00
Royal Worcester, Ewer, Orchid Roses, 12 In.	68.50
Royal Worcester, Ewer, Pink & Blue Flowers, Gold, Ivory, 9 In.High	45.00
Royal Worcester, Figurine, Anne Boleyn, Frederick Gertner, 1917, 8 1/4 In.	100.00
Royal Worcester, Figurine, Boy Sitting, Tree Trunk, 4 In.Diameter, 6 1/2 In.	150.00
Royal Worcester, Figurine, Bridget, 1969, Victorian Ladies Series, Croquet	100.00
Royal Worcester, Figurine, British Friesian Bull, Doris Linder, 8 1/2 In.	200.00
Royal Worcester, Figurine, Caroline, 1960, Victorian Ladies Series	100.00
Royal Worcester, Figurine, Charlotte & Jane, Ruth Van Ruyckevelt, 1968	400.00
Royal Worcester, Figurine, Deer, Head Erect, 4 3/8 In.Long	65.00
Royal Worcester, Figurine, Duke Of Edinburgh On Polo Pony, Doris Lindner	500.00
Royal Worcester, Figurine, Elizabeth, 1967, Victorian Ladies Series	150.00
Royal Worcester, Figurine, Entitled Betty, Signed	35.00
Royal Worcester, Figurine, Little Girl, Skinny-Dipping, Black Mark, August	37.50
Royal Worcester, Figurine, Marion, 1968, Victorian Ladies Series, Tennis	175.00
Royal Worcester, Figurine, Mary Queen Of Scots, Frederick Gertner, 1916	150.00
Royal Worcester, Figurine, Melanie, Ruth Van Ruyckevelt, 1964, 1880s Dress	150.00
Royal Worcester, Figurine, Owl, Gold, Mark, 4 1/2 In.	125.00
Royal Worcester, Figurine, Parakeet, White, Gold, Roses, 7 1/4 In.High	37.50
Royal Worcester, Jar, Biscuit, Pale Blue, Cream Colored Leaves, Silver Top	55.00
Royal Worcester, Jar, Cookie, Melon Rib Body, Enamel Floral, Underplate	125.00
Royal Worcester, Jar, Floral, Ivory Satin, Gold Trim, Cover, 4 1/2 In.Tall	50.00
Royal Worcester, Jardiniere, Flowers, Cream, Purple Mark	87.50
Royal Worcester, Jug, Matte Finish, Floral, England, Dated 1896, 4 3/4 In.	55.00
Royal Worcester, Pitcher, Cream Ground, Hand-Painted Floral, Gold, 5 1/2 In.	40.00
Royal Worcester, Pitcher, Floral, Ribbed Handle, Helmet Shaped, 6 1/2 In.	38.00
Royal Worcester, Pitcher, Floral, Yellow Black, Hand-Painted, Mark Purple	52.00
Royal Worcester, Pitcher, Floral, 5 In.	30.00
Royal Worcester, Pitcher, Pink, Gold, Purple Mark, 5 1/2 In.Tall	35.00
Royal Worcester, Pitcher, White, Purple	49.00
Royal Worcester, Plate, Blue Willow Pattern, 8 In.	9.50
Royal Worcester, Plate, Chamberlain, Circa 1810, Pair	148.00
Royal Worcester, Plate, Floral, Gold Border, 7 In.	12.50
Royal Worcester, Plate, Hanging, Blackberries, Leaves, 10 In.	5.00
Royal Worcester, Plate, Lunch, Lille	6.25
Royal Worcester, Plate, Purple Flowers, Purple Mark & Register, 9 1/4 In.	15.00
Royal Worcester, Plate, Purple Mark, Beige To Pink Ground, Hand-Painted	18.00
Royal Worcester, Platter, Bread, Cream Ground, Turquoise, Gold, Bread Motto	55.00
Royal Worcester, Shaker, Sugar, Locke & Co., Beige Background, Silver Top	30.00
Royal Worcester, Teapot, Cream, Marsh Flowers	27.50
Royal Worcester, Teapot, Creamer, Sugar, Floral, Gold Handles, Spout, Finials	150.00
Royal Worcester, Thimble, Flowers, Hand-Painted	9.00
Royal Worcester, Tureen, Melon Shape, Brown Leaf On Lid, Purple Mark	48.00
Royal Worcester, Tureen, White, Turquoise	65.00
Royal Worcester, Urn, Acorn & Leaves, Raised Base, Cover, 14 In. High	350.00
Royal Worcester, Vase, Beige Background, Floral, Pedestal Base, Gold Trim	55.00
Royal Worcester, Vase, Beige, Gold Owl Stands In Front Of Vase	120.00
Royal Worcester, Vase, Beige, Gold, Handles, Marked, Date 1902, 8 1/2 In.	60.00
Royal Worcester, Vase, Floral, Leaves, Pierced Panels Around Collar	35.00
Royal Worcester, Vase, Enameled Floral, Gold & Cream Ground, 9 3/4 In.High	80.00
Royal Worcester, Vase, Floral & Fern Design, Purple Mark, 3 1/4 In.Tall	40.00
Royal Worcester, Vase, Floral, Beige, Gold Trim, 6 In.	35.00
Royal Worcester, Vase, Floral, Crackle Top, 8 In.Tall	20.00
Royal Worcester, Vase, Hand-Painted Floral, Gold Base, Handles, 7 In.Tall	65.00
Royal Worcester, Vase, Hand-Painted Orange Poppies, Reg.Mark 1896	65.00
Royal Worcester, Vase, Matte Finish, Floral, England, Dated 1896, 3 In.High	40.00
Royal Worcester, Vase, Purple Mark, C.1900, Pheasant Decor, Signed	48.50
Royal Worcester, Vase, Shell, C.1876 _Illus_	75.00
Roycroft, Ashtray, Signed, 4 1/2 In.Diameter	12.00

RS Germany Porcelain was made at the factory of Rheinhold Schlegelmilch after 1869 in Tillowitz, Germany. It was sold both decorated and undecorated.

RS Germany, see also RS Prussia

Rs Germany, Ashtray, Poppies, Orange	15.00
Rs Germany, Basket, Hand-Painted Floral, Gold Border & Handle, Signed	20.00

Royal Worcester, Vase, Shell, C.1876
See Page 442

RS Germany, **Basket**, Rainbow, Iridescent, Blue	30.00
RS Germany, **Basket**, Rose Design, Pink, White, Octagonal4 In.Tall	40.00
RS Germany, **Berry Set**, Peonies, Pink, White, Four Sauce	35.00
RS Germany, **Bonbon**, Winter Scene, Handle, Elliptical Shape, Gold Edge	47.50
RS Germany, **Bowl**, Black Mark, Green With Lavender Sprays, Gold Edge	20.00
RS Germany, **Bowl**, Calla Lilies, Green Mark, 5 1/2 In.Diameter	4.00
RS Germany, **Bowl**, Dessert, Orange Ground, Pink Floral, Pair	12.00
RS Germany, **Bowl**, Easter Lilies, Green To Gray, Handles, Green Mark	27.50
RS Germany, **Bowl**, Farm Scene, Paneled, Cream, Gold, 11 In.Diameter	45.00
RS Germany, **Bowl**, Fruit, Camelias, White, Green, Gold Trim, Signed	28.50
RS Germany, **Bowl**, Fruit, Daisies, Sheaves Of Wheat, 10 In.Diameter	22.50
RS Germany, **Bowl**, Fruit, Iridescent, Lavender, Turquoise, , Floral	25.00
RS Germany, **Bowl**, Greens, Gold Rim, White Phlox Inside, 3 Ball Feet, Signed	19.75
RS Germany, **Bowl**, Poppies, 7 1/2 In.Diameter	15.00
RS Germany, **Bowl**, Poppy, Flowers, Raspberries, Black, Blue, 9 In.	22.00
RS Germany, **Bowl**, Red, Pink, Yellow Roses, Two Handles, Green Mark	20.00
RS Germany, **Bowl**, Rose Design, 10 In.	35.00
RS Germany, **Bowl**, Roses, Red, Green Mark, 5 1/2 In.Diameter	4.00
RS Germany, **Bowl**, S & T Steeple Mark, Floral, Gold Trim, 9 In.	39.00
RS Germany, **Bowl**, Salad, Tea Roses, Green Mark, 10 1/2 In.Diameter	25.00
RS Germany, **Bowl**, Yellow Poppies, Hand-Painted, Footed, 2 1/4 In.Diameter	12.00
RS Germany, **Box**, Dresser, Pearl Luster, Gold Trim, 5 1/2 In.Square	10.00
RS Germany, **Box**, Powder, Pink & White Tulips, Gold Trim	50.00
RS Germany, **Chocolate Pot**, Pastel, Roses, Leaves, Gold, Tillowitz	51.00
RS Germany, **Chocolate Set**, Green Mark, 10 Piece, Pink Roses, Gold Tracery	42.50
RS Germany, **Creamer**, Blue Sweetpeas, Orange Poppy, Mark	11.00
RS Germany, **Creamer**, Poppies, Red	8.00
RS Germany, **Creamer**, White To Green, Purple, Flowers, Scallop Edge, 2 3/4 In.	10.00
RS Germany, **Cup & Saucer**, Demitasse, Green Decor, Lavender Flowers	5.00
RS Germany, **Cup & Saucer**, Roses, White, Green, Gold, Mark Blue Wreath & Star	15.00
RS Germany, **Cup & Saucer**, White Floral, Green Leaves, Leaf Handle	10.00
RS Germany, **Cup**, Nut, Footed, Gold Trim	
RS Germany, **Dish**, Candy, Roses, Two Handles, 5 3/4 In.Square	18.00
RS Germany, **Dish**, Double Deck, Tulips, Gold, Green, Hand-Painted	20.00
RS Germany, **Dish**, Mayo, White, Gold Edge, Undertray, Blue Mark	13.50
RS Germany, **Dish**, Oval, Gold Trim, White & Green, Orange Floral	6.50
RS Germany, **Dish**, Pastry, Orchid Ground, Pink Floral, Open Handles	15.00
RS Germany, **Dish**, Triangular, Gray Border, Roses In Corners	10.00
RS Germany, **Dresser Set**, Autumn Design, Tray, Jar, Hatpin Holder	67.50
RS Germany, **Gravyboat**, Flowers, Blue, Gold, Under Plate	20.00
RS Germany, **Hair Receiver**, Floral	15.00
RS Germany, **Hair Receiver**, Flowers, Gold Trim, Round, 4 1/2 In.Diameter	15.00
RS Germany, **Hair Receiver**, Roses, Pink, Yellow, White, Gold Trim, 4 1/2 In.	20.00
RS Germany, **Hair Receiver**, White & Beige Ground, Roses	27.50
RS Germany, **Hatpin Holder**, Calla Lilies, Green, White, Green Mark	22.50
RS Germany, **Hatpin Holder**, Calla Lily Decoration, Blue Mark	22.00

RS Germany, **Hatpin Holder**, Green Mark, Green To White, Pink Roses 27.50
RS Germany, **Hatpin Holder**, Green, Hand-Painted Yellow Jonquils, Signed 24.00
RS Germany, **Hatpin Holder**, Hand-Painted Blue Flowers, 4 1/2 In. 22.00
RS Germany, **Hatpin Holder**, Pale Green, Pink & White Roses 18.50
RS Germany, **Hatpin Holder**, Pink Roses, Blue Forget-Me-Nots, Dome Shape Top 22.50
RS Germany, **Hatpin Holder**, Pond Lily 18.00
RS Germany, **Hatpin Holder**, Rose Design, Pink, White, Green, Artist Signed 27.50
RS Germany, **Hatpin Holder**, Roses, Pink, Marked 18.50
RS Germany, **Hatpin Holder**, White To Beige, Cluster Pink & White Flowers 13.75
RS Germany, **Jar**, Biscuit, Roses 25.00
RS Germany, **Mustard**, Covered, Pink Roses On Green 19.50
RS Germany, **Mustard**, Lacy Gold & Dubonnet Borders, Ladle, Open Handle 14.00
RS Germany, **Mustard**, Pink Rose 22.50
RS Germany, **Perfume**, Roses, Pink, Orange To Gold, Stopper, 7 In.Tall 40.00
RS Germany, **Pitcher & Tray**, Gravy, Gold Trim On Pearly Finish ....,.................. 15.00
RS Germany, **Plate**, Apple Blossoms, Green Ground 6.50
RS Germany, **Plate**, Blue Floral Pattern, 6 In.Diameter 3.50
RS Germany, **Plate**, Bread, Pheasants, Artist Hornlein, Green Mark, Handles 40.00
RS Germany, **Plate**, Cake, Green-Gray Ground, Gold & White Floral, Handles 25.00
RS Germany, **Plate**, Cake, Handled, Pink Roses, 9 1/2 In.Diameter 18.00
RS Germany, **Plate**, Cake, Purple & White Magnolia, Green Mark, 2 Handle, 10 In 40.00
RS Germany, **Plate**, Cake, Rose Design 19.00
RS Germany, **Plate**, Carnation Design, Pink, Signed, Blue Mark, 10 In.Diameter 35.00
RS Germany, **Plate**, Chop, Browns, White Dogwood Flowers, Green Mark 40.00
RS Germany, **Plate**, Dessert, Green, Sweet Peas, Blue Mark, Set Of 5 .... 20.00
RS Germany, **Plate**, Floral, 6 1/2 In.Diameter 9.00
RS Germany, **Plate**,Lilies, White, Green, 8 1/2 in Diameter 28.00
RS Germany, **Plate**, Orchid Pattern, Scalloped Edge, 6 1/2 In.Diameter 5.00
RS Germany, **Plate**, Pale Blue, White Tulips, Foliage, Pierced Handles 18.00
RS Germany, **Plate**, Pink Floral, Gray To Pink Ground, 8 In. 10.00
RS Germany, **Plate**, Poppies, Orange, 6 In.Diameter 4.50
RS Germany, **Relish**, Lily Design, Mark Blue, Tillowitz, Green 13.50
RS Germany, **Sauce**, Flowers, Purple, Gold, Scallop, Mark 4.50
RS Germany, **Sauce**, Scalloped, Pink Roses, Green Leaves, Gold Tracery, 6 .... 25.00
RS Germany, **Sauce**, Sweet Pea Design, Green, Blue Mark, 6 In., Set Of 5 .... 22.50
RS Germany, **Sauce**, Tulips, Set Of 5 .... 20.00
RS Germany, **Sugar & Creamer**, Art Nouveau Decor, Artist-Signed, 1915 .... 15.00
RS Germany, **Sugar & Creamer**, Azaleas, Leaves, Green Gold, White, Bulbous 40.00
RS Germany, **Sugar & Creamer**, Blue, Gray, Iridescent, Blue Mark 14.50
RS Germany, **Sugar & Creamer**, Floral, Gold Trim, Green Mark 25.00
RS Germany, **Sugar & Creamer**, Orchid Ground, Pink Floral, Hand-Painted 28.50
RS Germany, **Sugar**, Covered, Blue With Floral, Gold Trim, Openwork Handles 15.00
RS Germany, **Sugar**, Covered, Green Leaves On White, Pink, Gold Band & Trim 16.00
RS Germany, **Sugar**, Leaves, Green, White, Cover, 3 1/2 In.High 6.50
RS Germany, **Sugar**, Lily, White, Green 12.00
RS Germany, **Toothpick**, Two Handles, Daffodils 15.00
RS Germany, **Tray**, Celery, Roses, Yellow, Gold, Blue Mark, 11 In.Long 25.00
RS Germany, **Tray**, Pin, Roses, Yellow, Green Mark, Handle, 5 In.Long 12.50
RS Germany, **Tray**, Pin, Tea Roses, Pink, Green Mark, Oblong, 5 In. 12.50
RS Germany, **Tray**, Relish, Lilies 18.00
RS Germany, **Vase**, Butterfly, Fuchsia To Blue, Green, Yellow, Wall, 7 In.Tall 40.00
RS Germany, **Vase**, Green, Tan, Gold, Green Mark, 5 1/2 In. Tall 14.50

*RS Prussia Porcelain was made at the factory of Rheinhold
Schlegelmilch after 1869 in Tillowitz, Germany. The porcelain was sold
decorated or undecorated.*
RS Prussia, see also RS Germany
RS Prussia, **Basket**, Candy, Floral Design, Apricot, Gold, Open Handle 12.00
RS Prussia, **Basket**, Gold Floral, Rolled Edge, Mark 17.00
RS Prussia, **Basket**, Pink Floral, Footed, Red Mark 145.00
RS Prussia, **Berry Set**, Cobalt Blue, White, Irises, Unsigned, 7 Piece 125.00
RS Prussia, **Berry Set**, White Roses, Red Lion & Prussia Mark, 7 Piece 45.00
RS Prussia, **Bowl**, Basket Of Flowers Design, 10 In. 87.50
RS Prussia, **Bowl**, Cabbage Leaf 250.00
RS Prussia, **Bowl**, Calla Lilies, Green Trim, Satin Finish, Red Mark 95.00
RS Prussia, **Bowl**, Calla Lilies, Ives, Beige, Red Mark, 9 1/2 In.Diameter 50.00

RS Prussia, Bowl, Carnations, Red Mark, 10 1/4 X 3 In. 80.00
RS Prussia, Bowl, Christmas Holly, 9 In.Diameter 160.00
RS Prussia, Bowl, Floral Design, Gold Trim, 11 In.Diameter 85.00
RS Prussia, Bowl, Floral, Raised Gold Floral On Border, Red Mark, 10 1/2 In. 29.00
RS Prussia, Bowl, Floral, Scalloped, White, Red Mark, 10 In.Diameter 51.00
RS Prussia, Bowl, Flowers, White, Pink, Gold Trim, Red Mark, 10 In.Diameter 80.00
RS Prussia, Bowl, Fluted, Red Roses, Green Leaves, Scalloped Base, Red Mark 85.00
RS Prussia, Bowl, Fruit, Yellow Ground, Floral, Octagonal, Red Star 60.00
RS Prussia, Bowl, Jewels & Garland Border, 10 In., Pair 95.00
RS Prussia, Bowl, Leaves, Green, Gold, Brown Tone, Red Mark, 9 In.Diameter 56.00
RS Prussia, Bowl, Lilies, Foliage, Orange, Yellow, Green, Scalloped, 10 In. 65.00
RS Prussia, Bowl, Mush, Child's, Green, White, Leaves, Creamer, Set 45.00
RS Prussia, Bowl, Panels, Embossed Edges, Pink Roses, Green Garlands, 10 In. 65.00
RS Prussia, Bowl, Panels, Yellow Roses, Lavender, Green, Gold Tracery 55.00
RS Prussia, Bowl, Pastel Floral, Gold Trim, Red Mark, 10 1/2 In.Diameter 85.00
RS Prussia, Bowl, Pink & White Roses, Molded Flower Edges, 10 In., Red Mark 75.00
RS Prussia, Bowl, Pink Roses Center, Gold Clover & Floral Around Edge 85.00
RS Prussia, Bowl, Pink, White, Yellow, Roses 55.00
RS Prussia, Bowl, Poppies, Blue, Pink, White, Gold, Fluted Edge, 10 In.Diameter 58.00
RS Prussia, Bowl, Red Mark, Pansies, Shell Pink 25.00
RS Prussia, Bowl, Red Mark, Water Lilies, 9 In. 58.00
RS Prussia, Bowl, Red Mark, Yellow Roses, Blue Flowers, Scalloped Edge 25.00
RS Prussia, Bowl, Rose, Daisy, Red Mark, 10 1/4 X 3 In. 80.00
RS Prussia, Bowl, Roses, Footed, 6 In. 40.00
RS Prussia, Bowl, Roses, Gold, Beige, Red Mark & Star, Jeweled 88.50
RS Prussia, Bowl, Sugar, Garland Rim, 9 In. 125.00
RS Prussia, Bowl, Vegetable, Roses, Pink, Gold Trim, Ruffled Edge 125.00
RS Prussia, Bowl, White, Pink, & Yellow Mums Inside, Rim Like Open Flowers 37.50
RS Prussia, Bowl, Yellow, White, Gold, Forget-Me-Nots, Red Mark, 11 In. 70.00
RS Prussia, Box, Portrait, Chocolate Girl, Irises, Cover, Star Mark 125.00
RS Prussia, Cake Plate, Pastel Apricot Double Roses, White Ground, Gilt 57.40
RS Prussia, Celery Dish .... *Illus* 215.00

RS Prussia, Celery Dish

RS Prussia, Celery, Open Handles, Pink & White Roses On White Ground 36.00
RS Prussia, Celery, White & Tan, Yellow Roses 45.00
RS Prussia, Centerpiece, Pink, Yellow, Roses, Scallop Top, 10 X 5 In. 85.00
RS Prussia, Chocolate Pot, Four Cups & Saucers, Dogwood Pattern, Red Mark 185.00
RS Prussia, Chocolate Pot, Gold Tracery, Petal Floral, Footed, Red Mark 120.00
RS Prussia, Chocolate Pot, Lake & Swans, Satin 80.00
RS Prussia, Chocolate Pot, Pink To Yellow, Tulips Leaves, Red Mark 125.00
RS Prussia, Chocolate Pot, Red, Green, Red Mark 75.00
RS Prussia, Chocolate Pot, Roses, Lilacs, Morning Glory Shape, Red, White 130.00
RS Prussia, Chocolate Pot, Roses, Pink, Green, White, Cover 76.00
RS Prussia, Chocolate Pot, Roses, Red, White, Satin Finish 125.00
RS Prussia, Chocolate Pot, Sculptured Tulip Pattern, No Mark 95.00
RS Prussia, Chocolate Pot, Slender Spout, Red Mark 125.00
RS Prussia, Chocolate Pot, White & Purple, Lilies 85.00
RS Prussia, Chocolate Set, Hand-Painted Roses, Signed Roth, Gold 225.00
RS Prussia, Chocolate Set, Roses, Pink, Green, Red Mark, Five Cup & Saucer 195.00
RS Prussia, Coffee Set, Floral Design, Red Mark, Four Cup & Saucer, 9 1/2 In 250.00

RS Prussia, **Creamer**, Roses, Pink, Yellow, Pedestal Base, 4 In.Tall 22.50
RS Prussia, **Cup & Saucer**, Chocolate, Floral & Leaf, Red Mark 25.00
RS Prussia, **Cup & Saucer**, Chocolate, Red Mark, White With Pink Flowers 17.50
RS Prussia, **Cup & Saucer**, Chocolate, Red, Green, Red Mark 25.00
RS Prussia, **Cup & Saucer**, Chocolate, Roses, Octagon, Red Mark 20.00
RS Prussia, **Cup & Saucer**, Demitasse, Melon Boy, Red Mark 85.00
RS Prussia, **Cup & Saucer**, Iridescent, Gold Trim, Roses, Signed 28.50
RS Prussia, **Cup & Saucer**, Leaf Design, Gold, Footed 25.00
RS Prussia, **Cup & Saucer**, Roses, Gold, Red Mark .... 25.00 To 30.00
RS Prussia, **Cup**, Chocolate, Canterbury Bells, Set Of 6 .... 115.00
RS Prussia, **Cup**, Floral Decoration 20.00
RS Prussia, **Cup**, Floral, Four Pedestal, Signed 20.00
RS Prussia, **Dish**, Candy, Rope Design, Green, Footed, Red Mark, 6 1/2 In. 41.00
RS Prussia, **Dish**, Celery, Rose Design, Pink, Red Mark, Open Handle, 12 In. 49.00
RS Prussia, **Dish**, Pickle, Green Ground, Red Roses, Red Mark 32.50
RS Prussia, **Dish**, Relish, Lilies, Scalloped, Embossed, Pink, Yellow, Handled 45.00
RS Prussia, **Dish**, Relish, Red Star Mark, Pierced Handle, 9 In.Long 30.00
RS Prussia, **Dish**, Sauce, Poppies, Scalloped Edge, Gold, Red Mark 18.00
RS Prussia, **Dish**, Sauce, Red Mark 15.00
RS Prussia, **Fernery**, Poppy Design, Footed, 8 In. 95.00
RS Prussia, **Hair Receiver**, Cottage Scene, Footed, Unmarked 24.50
RS Prussia, **Hair Receiver**, Footed, Flower Decor 55.00
RS Prussia, **Hair Receiver**, Roses, Octagon, Red Mark 32.00
RS Prussia, **Hair Receiver**, Roses, 2 Piece, Red Mark 75.00
RS Prussia, **Jar**, Biscuit, Roses, Footed, Red Mark 85.00
RS Prussia, **Jar**, Cookie, Flowers, Gold, Red Star Mark, Footed, 5 In.Tall 75.00
RS Prussia, **Jar**, Cookie, Red Mark, Octagonal, Pink, White, & Yellow Roses 185.00
RS Prussia, **Jar**, Cracker, Floral Design, Green, White, Gold, Red Mark 85.00
RS Prussia, **Jar**, Cracker, Pheasants, Peacock, Tall Trees 350.00
RS Prussia, **Jar**, Cracker, Rose Shading, Embossed Floral, Gold Outline 175.00
RS Prussia, **Jar**, Powder, Covered, Rose Decoration, 5 In.High 39.00
RS Prussia, **Jar**, Tobacco, Gray & Black, Heart, Diamond, Club & Spade 35.00
RS Prussia, **Nappy**, Scenic Mill Wheel 37.50
RS Prussia, **Pickle**, Red Mark, End Handles, Pastels 45.00
RS Prussia, **Pitcher**, Hand-Painted Red & Yellow Roses, Green Mark 32.50
RS Prussia, **Plate**, Cake, Canterbury Bell, Open Handle, 10 In.Diameter 42.00
RS Prussia, **Plate**, Cake, Green, White, Floral, Gold Border, Tillowitz 55.00
RS Prussia, **Plate**, Cake, Leaf Festoons, Rm & Star Mark 28.00
RS Prussia, **Plate**, Cake, Panels, Pink Roses, Scalloped, White Center, Mark 21.50
RS Prussia, **Plate**, Cake, Pink & White Water Lilies, Blue Pond, Handles 125.00
RS Prussia, **Plate**, Cake, Rose Design, Pink, Embossed, Red Mark, 10 In. 59.00
RS Prussia, **Plate**, Cake, Roses, Gold Trim 48.00
RS Prussia, **Plate**, Cake, Roses, Pink, Yellow, Green, Scalloped Edge, Red Mark 50.00
RS Prussia, **Plate**, Cake, Violets, Pedestal Base, Handles, 10 In.Diameter 58.00
RS Prussia, **Plate**, Dessert, Pink & Green Floral, Red Mark, Set Of 8 .... 100.00
RS Prussia, **Plate**, Duck, Forest, Red Mark, 6 In.Diameter 95.00
RS Prussia, **Plate**, Embossed Floral, Blue, Gold, Mark, 8 1/2 In. 58.00
RS Prussia, **Plate**, Flowers, Gold, Scalloped Rim, Red Mark, 7 In.Diameter 20.00
RS Prussia, **Plate**, Flowers, Pink, White, Red Mark, 7 1/2 In.Diameter 26.00
RS Prussia, **Plate**, Gold Festoons, Rose Garlands, Fluted, Red Mark 40.00
RS Prussia, **Plate**, Hand-Painted Roses, Signed Roth, Pierced Handles, Gold 85.00
RS Prussia, **Plate**, Mill Scene, 6 In. 37.50
RS Prussia, **Plate**, Pink, Green, White, Gold, Flower, Red Mark, 8 1/2 In. 125.00
RS Prussia, **Plate**, Red Mark, Brown With Pink Carnations, 8 In. 35.00
RS Prussia, **Plate**, Roses, Fleur-De-Lis, Red Mark, 8 In.Diameter 39.00
RS Prussia, **Plate**, Roses, 6 In. 15.00
RS Prussia, **Pot**, Mustard, Floral Design, Pearlized, Gold Trim, Red Mark 39.50
RS Prussia, **Relish**, Flower Sprays, White, Green, Scalloped, Handle, 9 In.Long 37.50
RS Prussia, **Relish**, Marked Tillowitz, Cream & Gold Filigree, Flowers 7.00
RS Prussia, **Relish**, Roses, Pink, Lavender, Green, 9 1/2 In.Long 35.00
RS Prussia, **Sauce**, Fruit Design In Bottom, Scalloped Rim, Red Mark 15.00
RS Prussia, **Sauce**, Violets 5.00
RS Prussia, **Shaker**, Sugar, Rose Design, Pink, Ribbed, Red Mark, 3 3/4 In.Tall 75.00
RS Prussia, **Shaving Mug**, Embossed Yellow Fleur-De-Lis, Blue To Yellow 82.50
RS Prussia, **Shaving Mug**, Golden Hues, Floral, Gold, Red Star Mark 90.00
RS Prussia, **Shaving Mug**, Lady, White, Gold, Strawberries 47.00

RS Prussia, Shaving Mug, Rose Design, Soap Shelf, Footed, Red Mark 68.00
RS Prussia, Sugar & Creamer, Chrysanthemum Decoration 85.00
RS Prussia, Sugar & Creamer, Floral Design, Footed 27.50
RS Prussia, Sugar & Creamer, Ivy Leaves, Green, Gold Trim, Footed, Red Mark 14.50
RS Prussia, Sugar & Creamer, Lavender, Green, Red Mark, Cracker Jar, Set 135.00
RS Prussia, Sugar & Creamer, Multicolor Chrysanthemums, Pedestal, Red Mark 85.00
RS Prussia, Sugar & Creamer, Pink Roses, Gold, Footed On Maple Leaves 95.00
RS Prussia, Sugar & Creamer, Portrait, Red Mark 135.00
RS Prussia, Sugar & Creamer, Red Mark, Apple Blossoms 85.00
RS Prussia, Sugar & Creamer, Rosebuds, Pink, Pedestal Base, Cover 65.00
RS Prussia, Sugar & Creamer, Water, Swans, Lilies, Pearlized Finish 75.00
RS Prussia, Sugar, Cover, Pink Roses, Red Mark 35.00
RS Prussia, Sugar, Pink, Roses, Gold, Mark Red, Cover 35.00
RS Prussia, Sugar, Red Mark, 5 1/2 In.High 30.00
RS Prussia, Tea Set, Roses, Gold, Green Trim, Red Mark, Cover, Creamer Sugar 135.00
RS Prussia, Tea Set, 3 Piece 170.00
RS Prussia, Teapot, Lily Of The Valley, Satin Finish 75.00
RS Prussia, Teapot, Satin Finish, Roses, Rose Finial, Red Mark 85.00
RS Prussia, Toothpick, Pink & Green Floral, 3 Handles 32.50
RS Prussia, Toothpick, Pink Roses, Handles, Cream To Green Background 82.50
RS Prussia, Toothpick, Three Handle 95.00
RS Prussia, Tray, Bread, Rose Design, Lavender, Handles, 13 1/2 In.Long 85.00
RS Prussia, Tray, Celery, Roses, Daisies, Gold, 7 X 13 1/2 In., Red Mark 50.00
RS Prussia, Tray, Dresser, Snowballs, 8 1/4 X 11 1/4 In. 45.00
RS Prussia, Tray, Pickle, Red Mark, Roses, 10 In. 55.00
RS Prussia, Tray, Relish, Blue, Gold, Open Work, Black Mark 42.50
RS Prussia, Tray, Sailboat On Lake, Open Handles, 9 In. 50.00
RS Prussia, Tray, Scalloped Edge, Rectangular .... *Illus* 89.50

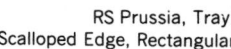

RS Prussia, Tray,
Scalloped Edge, Rectangular

RS Prussia, Vase, Church, Boy, Lake, Boat, 4 1/2 In.Tall 95.00
RS Prussia, Vase, Cottage Scene 125.00
RS Prussia, Vase, Dark Green To Yellow, Snowballs, Daisies, Roses, 6 In. 78.50
RS Prussia, Vase, Floral, Green To Yellow, Red Mark, 5 1/4 In. 75.00
RS Prussia, Vase, Gray, Brown, Pansies, Leaves, 9 In., Pair 200.00
RS Silesia, Bowl, Candy, Tulips, Butterfly, Pink, Blue 12.00
RS Silesia, Bowl, Dogwood Design, Green To White, Blue Mark, 9 1/2 In. 24.00

*Rubena Verde is a victorian glassware that was shaded from red to green.
It was first made by Hobbs, Brockunier and Company of Wheeling, West
Virginia, about 1890.*
Rubena Verde, Bowl, Frosted, Hobnail, Silver Standard, 10 In.Diameter 145.00
Rubena Verde, Castor, Pickle, Insert With Enamel 75.00
Rubena Verde, Compote, Green Swag Pattern, Ruffled, Silver Pedestal Base 65.00
Rubena Verde, Cruet, Hobnails, Opalescent 125.00
Rubena Verde, Cup, Punch, Inverted Thumbprint, Enamel Flower, Handle 75.00
Rubena Verde, Epergne, Center Lily Shades From Green To Red At Top 85.00
Rubena Verde, Epergne, Mirrored Base, Cut Border, Applied Crystal Leaves 135.00
Rubena Verde, Pitcher, Tankard Shape, Paneled, Applied Crystal Handle 45.00

Rubena Verde, Pitcher, Thumbprint, Ruffled Top, Clear, Applied Handle	175.00
Rubena Verde, Rose Bowl, Enamel Floral	115.00
Rubena Verde, Rose Bowl, Threaded Glass, 4 1/2 In.Diameter, 3 3/4 In.High	58.00
Rubena Verde, Tumbler, Baby Thumbprint, Vaseline To Cranberry	42.00
Rubena Verde, Tumbler, Hobbs Brockunier, Wheeling, W.Va., Decorated	75.00
Rubena Verde, Tumbler, Inverted Thumbprint	48.00
Rubena Verde, Vase, Clear To Red, Ruffle At Top, Enamel Design, 7 3/4 In.	25.00
Rubena Verde, Vase, Cylindrical, Ribbed, Enameled Floral, 9 1/2 In.High	55.00
Rubena Verde, Vase, Goblet Shape, Art Nouveau, 10 In.High	100.00
Rubena Verde, Vase, Red To Green Base, Applied Leaf-Shape Feet, Blown	45.00
Rubena Verde, Wine Inverted Thumbprint, Stem	55.00

Rubena is a glassware that shades from red to clear. It was first made by George Duncan and Sons of Pittsburgh, Pennsylvania, about 1885.

Rubena, Bowl, Rose, Cranberry To Clear, Ribbed, Crimped Top, 4 In.Diameter	48.00
Rubena, Castor, Pickle, Caroline Flowers	175.00
Rubena, Castor, Pickle, Decorated	150.00
Rubena, Castor, Pickle, Frosted, Etched	140.00
Rubena, Decanter, Wine, Red To Rubena, Stopper	50.00
Rubena, Salt & Pepper, Royal Ivy	55.00
Rubena, Shaker, Sugar, Cut, Silver Plate Cover	60.00
Rubena, Syrup, Opalescent Coin Spot, Metal Cap & Pouring Spout	45.00
Rubena, Vase, Enameled Flowers, Cranberry Shading To Clear, 13 3/8 In.Tall	85.00
Rubena, Vase, Overshot, Melon Ribbed, Footed	35.00
Rubena, Vase, Ribbed, Footed, Etched 'made In England, ' 5 In.High	25.00

Ruby Glass is a dark red color. It was a victorian and twentienth-century ware. The name means many different types of red glass.

Ruby Glass, see also Cranberry Glass

Ruby Glass, Bowl, Berry, Block & Fan	20.00
Ruby Glass, Bowl, 7 1/2 In.Diameter, Scalloped Top, Ribbed	8.00
Ruby Glass, Carafe & Tumbler, Flashed, Cut Panels, Outlined In Gold	50.00
Ruby Glass, Castor, Pickle, Decorated	140.00
Ruby Glass, Compote, Moon & Stars, Footed, Cover	35.00
Ruby Glass, Compote, Scalloped Top, Biedermeier, 6 X 6 In.	35.00
Ruby Glass, Creamer, Thumbprint	20.00
Ruby Glass, Creamer, Thumbprint, 3 In.Tall	18.00
Ruby Glass, Cup, Punch, Handleless	9.00
Ruby Glass, Goblet, Thumbprint	28.50
Ruby Glass, Jar, Jam, Ornate Holder	47.50
Ruby Glass, Knife Rest, Arched Shank, Taped Ends	30.00
Ruby Glass, Mug, Flashed, Clear Base, Beaded Scallops, Etched Mankato	9.00
Ruby Glass, Mug, Handled, Souvenir	13.00
Ruby Glass, Mug, Miniature, 'Gettysburg, 1863, 8' 1 3/4 In.High	14.00
Ruby Glass, Nappy, Thumbprint, Handle	18.50
Ruby Glass, Pitcher, Inverted Hearts, 4 In.Tall	12.00
Ruby Glass, Pitcher, Tankard, Pillow Encircled Pattern, 13 1/4 In.High	55.00
Ruby Glass, Pitcher, Turncoat Cube, 3 In.	12.00
Ruby Glass, Pitcher, Water, Block & Fan	25.00
Ruby Glass, Salt & Pepper, Octagon	22.00
Ruby Glass, Salt, Master, Clear Rigaree, Footed Silver Holder	40.00
Ruby Glass, Shaker, Sugar, Flashed	45.00
Ruby Glass, Toothpick, Flashed, Clear Base, Beaded Scallops	12.00
Ruby Glass, Toothpick, Thumbprint	18.50
Ruby Glass, Tray, Pin, Flashed, Heart Shaped, Stockton, Ill.	15.00
Ruby Glass, Tumbler, Barrel, Cut To Clear, 1, 000-Eye	27.50
Ruby Glass, Tumbler, Thumbprint	24.00
Ruby Glass, Tumbler, Thumbprint, Etched Vintage Grape	20.00
Ruby Glass, Tumbler, Thumbprint, Vintage, Etched	25.00
Ruby Glass, Vase, Flower Form, Art Nouveau, Blown, Circa 1900, 7 In.Tall	18.00
Ruby Glass, Vase, 6 1/2 In.High, Pair	6.00
Ruby Glass, Water Set, Double Swirl Design, 7 Piece	18.00
Rug, see Textile, Rug	
Russian Enamel, Cup & Saucer, Green, Gold, Korajeloffe Brothers, Circa 1827	90.00
Russian Enamel, Spoon, Serving, Signed E.H., No.84	235.00
Russian Enamel, Spoon, Tea	70.00

Sabino, Figurine, Two Birds, Glass Cluster, Opalescent	48.00
Sabino, Light, Wall, Art Deco, Female Mascaron, Signed, 10 In.High	90.00

Salopian Ware was made by the Caughley Factory of England during the eighteenth century. The early pieces were in blue and white with some colored decorations. Many of the pieces called Salopian are elaborate, color-transfer decorated tablewares made during the late nineteenth century.

Salopian, Bowl, Blue & White, Transfer Printed Pagoda Pattern, C.1780	70.00
Salopian, Cup & Saucer, Blue & White Chintz Pattern	45.00
Salopian, Dish, Square, Transfer Printed, Blue, Fisherman Pattern, C.1755	180.00
Salopian, Plate, Polychrome, Bird & Floral Decoration, 7 In.Diameter, Pair	330.00
Salopian, Sugar, Covered, Deer & Thatched Cottage	200.00
Salt and Pepper, see Pressed Glass, Porcelain, etc.	

Salt Glaze is a hard, shiny glaze that was developed for pottery during the eighteenth century. It is still being made.

Salt Glaze, Figurine, King, Queen, White, France, 7 1/2 In.High, Pair	20.00
Salt Glaze, Jug, Julius Caesar	75.00
Salt Glaze, Pitcher, Apostle, Reg.March 17, 1842 By Charles Meigh, Hanley	125.00
Salt Glaze, Pitcher, Bust Of Washington, Crossed Flags & Independence, 1776	50.00
Salt Glaze, Pitcher, Classical Design, Embossed, Signed, 4 3/4 In.	40.00
Salt Glaze, Pitcher, Cream Ground, Embossed Classical Figure, 5 1/2 In.High	22.50
Salt Glaze, Pitcher, Embossed Rebecca At Well, Pewter Lid, Marked Arabic	65.00
Salt Glaze, Pitcher, English, Light Green, Swans, 8 1/2 In.High	12.50
Salt Glaze, Pitcher, Pewter Lid, Marked Booth Hanley, 9 In.Tall	50.00
Salt Glaze, Pitcher, Pewter Lid, Raised Leaf & Ribbon, 19th Century	60.00
Salt Glaze, Pitcher, Rope Handle, Green, Dated 1835, 8 In.Tall	35.00
Salt Glaze, Pitcher, Staffordshire, 19th Century, Classical Battle Scene	60.00
Salt Glaze, Pitcher, Syrup, Raised Design, Pewter Lid, 7 In.Tall	35.00
Salt Glaze, Pitcher, Water, Gray-Blue, Scene, The Cup Tosser, Man, Woman	65.00
Salt Glaze, Plate, Cheese, Domed Cover, Basket Weave, Circa 1850, 11 1/2 In.	55.00
Salt Glaze, Stein, Figural, Shepherd's Flute, Bacchus, Pewter Lid, 10 In.	165.00
Salt Glaze, Teapot, Apple Blossoms, Birds, Blue, Footed, 8 In.Tall	50.00
Salt Glaze, Teapot, Embossed Racing On Donkeys Scene, Pewter Lid, Hanley	40.00
Salt Glaze, Teapot, Relief Scrolls, Eight Sided, Blue, 4 1/2 In.Tall, Pair	95.00
Salt Glaze, Teapot, Ribbing, Hunting Scene, Stoneware, Circa 1760	65.00
Salt Glaze, Toothpick, Puppy Sitting On Lily Pad, Holder Beside Him	6.00
Salt Glaze, Vase, Blue Gray	26.00
Sampler, see Textile, Sampler	
Samson, Plate, Floral Design, Paris 1875, Octagonal	38.00

Sandwich Glass is any one of the Myriad types of glass made by the Boston and Sandwich Glass Works in Sandwich, Massachusetts, between 1825 and 1888. It is often very difficult to be sure whether a piece was really made at the Sandwich Factory because so many types were made there and similar pieces were made at other glass factories.

Sandwich Glass, see also Pressed Glass, etc.	
Sandwich Glass, Bottle, Bar, Petal & Loop, Bar Lip, Ground Pontil, 9 In.High	30.00
Sandwich Glass, Bottle, Blue, Green, Blown, No Stopper, 4 In.Tall	32.50
Sandwich Glass, Bottle, Perfume, Blue, Flint	38.00
Sandwich Glass, Bottle, Perfume, Fiery Opal, Flint	30.00
Sandwich Glass, Bottle, Scent, Blue, Pewter Cap	43.00
Sandwich Glass, Bowl, Industry, 6 1/4 In.	110.00
Sandwich Glass, Bowl, Pint To White, Clear Bull's-Eyes, 5 In.Diamater	40.00
Sandwich Glass, Bowl, Rayed Peacock Eye, 5 1/2 In.	45.00
Sandwich Glass, Bowl, Shell & Tassel, Handle Oval	60.00
Sandwich Glass, Bowl, Tulip & Acanthus Leaf, 6 1/4 In.Serration	38.00
Sandwich Glass, Butter, Bellflower, Clear, Beaded Edge, Cover, 5 In.Tall	65.00
Sandwich Glass, Butter, Circle Pattern, Clear	75.00
Sandwich Glass, Candlestick, Canary	40.00
Sandwich Glass, Candlestick, Clambroth, Speckled Finish, Pair	110.00
Sandwich Glass, Candlestick, Loop Base, Petal Socket, Pair	65.00
Sandwich Glass, Candlestick, Petal & Loop, Clear, Flint, Pair	80.00
Sandwich Glass, Candlestick, Petal Hex, Pair	34.00
Sandwich Glass, Candlestick, Sandwich Glass Factory, Clear, Pair	150.00
Sandwich Glass, Candlestick, Single Canary	50.00

Sandwich Glass, **Celery**, Gothic Arch, Thumbprint, Flint, Scalloped Rim, 10 In. 75.00
Sandwich Glass, **Celery**, Tulip Shape, Clear, Pedestal, 10 In.Tall, Pair 125.00
Sandwich Glass, **Compote**, Open, Diamond Point, Flint, 10 1/4 X 9 1/4 In.Tall 75.00
Sandwich Glass, **Compote**, Petal & Loop 120.00
Sandwich Glass, **Compote**, Rayed Peacock Eye, C.1830 .... *Illus* 185.00
Sandwich Glass, **Creamer**, Lacy 115.00
Sandwich Glass, **Cruet**, Star, Vaseline To Clear, Blown, Stopper 40.00
Sandwich Glass, **Cup Plate**, 'Bunker Hill Battle Fought June 17, 1775' 25.00

Sandwich Glass, Compote,
Rayed Peacock Eye, C.1830

Sandwich Glass, **Cup Plate**, Fan & Star, Flint 15.00
Sandwich Glass, **Cup Plate**, Fiery Opalescent, L&r No.465I 35.00
Sandwich Glass, **Cup Plate**, Hairpin Loop, Flint 27.00
Sandwich Glass, **Cup Plate**, Heart Border, Diamond & Stippled Center 10.00
Sandwich Glass, **Cup Plate**, L&r No.271 .... 14.00
Sandwich Glass, **Cup Plate**, L&r No.447 .... 9.00
Sandwich Glass, **Cup Plate**, L&r No.467b 9.00
Sandwich Glass, **Cup Plate**, L&r No.641a 15.00
Sandwich Glass, **Cup Plate**, Lacy, 3 .... 15.00
Sandwich Glass, **Cup Plate**, Lacy, 13 Heart 10.00
Sandwich Glass, **Cup Plate**, Log Cabin 40.00
Sandwich Glass, **Cup Plate**, Melrose, 1845 .... 8.00
Sandwich Glass, **Cup Plate**, Opalescent, 13 Hearst, 52 Scallops 52.00
Sandwich Glass, **Cup Plate**, Oval Loop Border, Waffle Pattern Center 10.00
Sandwich Glass, **Cup Plate**, Sandwich Star, Flint 9.00
Sandwich Glass, **Cup Plate**, Shell, Flint 14.00
Sandwich Glass, **Cup Plate**, Stars, Forget-Me-Nots, Scalloped Edge 12.00
Sandwich Glass, **Decanter**, Arch & Fern, Blown Molded, Quart 110.00
Sandwich Glass, **Decanter**, Fern Design, Stopper, 13 In.High 22.50
Sandwich Glass, **Dish**, Gothic, Oblong, 5 1/4 X 7 In. 48.00
Sandwich Glass, **Dish**, Lacy Pattern, Flint, Oval 165.00
Sandwich Glass, **Dish**, Peacock Eye, Oval 75.00
Sandwich Glass, **Dish**, Peacock's Eye Pattern, Lacy, 9 In.Diameter 65.00
Sandwich Glass, **Dish**, Princess Feather Pattern, Lacy, 8 1/2 In. 20.00
Sandwich Glass, **Dish**, Sauce, Oak Leaf 14.00
Sandwich Glass, **Dish**, Star Medallion Center, Feather Border, Lacy, 5 1/4 In. 26.50
Sandwich Glass, **Dish**, Sweetmeat, Riffled Edge, Opalescent, 4 1/2 X 3 1/2 In. 25.00
Sandwich Glass, **Drawer Pulls**, Opalescent, 2 3/8 In., Pair 18.00
Sandwich Glass, **Globe**, Snakeskin, Ribbed Rim, 6 1/4 X 4 In.High 85.00
Sandwich Glass, **Goblet**, Argus, Clear, Flint 29.00
Sandwich Glass, **Goblet**, Magnet & Grape, Clear, Flint 35.00
Sandwich Glass, **Holder**, Spill, Star 38.50
Sandwich Glass, **Knife Rest**, Frosted Baby's Head 32.00
Sandwich Glass, **Lamp**, see also Lamp
Sandwich Glass, **Lamp**, Whale Oil, Star Pattern 60.00
Sandwich Glass, **Paperweight**, Scrambled, Canes, Dated 1852 .... 125.00
Sandwich Glass, **Peachblow**, Bride's Basket, Maroon, Ivory, Blue, Silver Holder 225.00
Sandwich Glass, **Pitcher**, Crackle, Cranberry, Applied Handle, French 275.00
Sandwich Glass, **Pitcher**, Cranberry, Overshot, Tankard Shape, Applied Handle 65.00
Sandwich Glass, **Pitcher**, Lily Of The Valley, Cobalt Blue, 7 1/2 In., Pair 65.00

Sandwich Glass, Pitcher, Milk, Bellflower, Double Vine, Clear, Flint, 9 In. 275.00
Sandwich Glass, Pitcher, Milk, Overshot, Clear Applied Handle 35.00
Sandwich Glass, Pitcher, Miniature, 2 In.Tall 45.00
Sandwich Glass, Pitcher, Mint Green To Clear Base, Reeded Handle, Blown 60.00
Sandwich Glass, Pitcher, Overshot, Sapphire Blue, Applied Amber Handle 75.00
Sandwich Glass, Plate, Beehive, Lacy, Octagonal, 9 3/4 In.Diameter 68.50
Sandwich Glass, Plate, Cake, Harps, Scalloped Rim, Gold, 10 In.Diameter 125.00
Sandwich Glass, Plate, Cake, Tulip Spray, Hobnail, 9 In.Square 18.00
Sandwich Glass, Plate, Lacy, Clear, Lyre Panels, 12 Sided, 6 In.Diameter 12.50
Sandwich Glass, Plate, Lacy, Clear, Octagonal, Thistle Center, Acanthus 55.00
Sandwich Glass, Plate, Lacy, Flint, 6 In. 22.00
Sandwich Glass, Plate, Peacock Eye, Flint, 7 1/2 In.Diameter 50.00
Sandwich Glass, Plate, Purple 65.00
Sandwich Glass, Plate, Rayed, Loop Border, 6 In., Clear, Flint 21.00
Sandwich Glass, Plate, Ribbed Grape 15.00
Sandwich Glass, Plate, Shield & Pine Tree, 6 In. 50.00
Sandwich Glass, Salt, Amethyst, Pair 65.00
Sandwich Glass, Salt, Inverted Thumbprint, Amber, Flowers 28.00
Sandwich Glass, Salt, Lacy, Deep Blue 80.00
Sandwich Glass, Salt, Master, Flattened Sawtooth, Pedestal 7.00
Sandwich Glass, Salt, Master, Lacy, 6 Sided 2.75
Sandwich Glass, Salt, Master, Punty, Hexagonal Rim, Footed, Flint, 3 1/2 In. 17.00
Sandwich Glass, Salt, Master, Shape Of Anvil, Daisy & Button 12.00
Sandwich Glass, Salt, Open, Ribbed Partway, Round Feet, 3 In. 10.00
Sandwich Glass, Salt, Open, Ribbed, Clear, Footed, 3 In.Diameter 9.00
Sandwich Glass, Sauce, Nectarine, Lacy, Flint 18.00
Sandwich Glass, Sauce, Oak Pattern, Lacy, Set Of 8 .... 80.00
Sandwich Glass, Sauce, Plume, Clear 9.50
Sandwich Glass, Saucer, Stippled Heart 16.00
Sandwich Glass, Spooner, Horn Of Plenty 22.50
Sandwich Glass, Sugar & Creamer, Ivy 90.00
Sandwich Glass, Sugar, Opalescent, Gothic Arch, 4 3/4 In.Diameter 20.00
Sandwich Glass, Tieback, Opalescent, Pewter Shank, 3 In.Diameter, Flint 12.50
Sandwich Glass, Tieback, Opalescent, Pewter Shank, 4 1/2 In.Diameter, Flint 15.00
Sandwich Glass, Tray, Card, Blue Hob, In Wire Basket 22.50
Sandwich Glass, Tray, Oblong, Snakeskin Loop, 10 In.Long 45.00
Sandwich Glass, Tray, Peacock Eye, 5 X 6 1/2 In. 23.00
Sandwich Glass, Tray, Pin, Milk Glass, Beaded, Lacy, Scroll, Sawtooth, Flint 13.75
Sandwich Glass, Tumbler, Lemonade, Cranberry Threading, Handle, Set Of 6 .... 150.00
Sandwich Glass, Tumbler, Snakeskin, 3 3/8 In.High 45.00
Sandwich Glass, Tureen, Lacy, Miniature, Cover, Platter 145.00
Sandwich Glass, Vase, Applied Icicles, Amber, 5 1/2 In.Tall 95.00
Sandwich Glass, Vase, Birds, Moon, Roses, White, Green, 10 In.Tall, Pair 65.00
Sandwich Glass, Vase, Canary, 7 1/4 In. 150.00
Sandwich Glass, Vase, Canary, 11 1/2 In.High, Pair 500.00
Sandwich Glass, Vase, Cased Sandwich Red, Yellow Ruffled Top 35.00
Sandwich Glass, Vase, Cranberry, Overshot, Blown-Out Teardrops 45.00
Sandwich Glass, Vase, Flowers, Leaves, Clear, White, 15 In.Tall 85.00
Sandwich Glass, Vase, Overshot, Blown Out & Teardrops, 6 1/2 In. 45.00
Sandwich Glass, Vase, Tulip, Blue, Mounted On Marble Base, 6 Panels, Pair 275.00
Sandwich Glass, Wine, Bellflower, Single Vine, Ribbed 27.50
Sandwich Glass, Wine, Overshot, Casket, Six Glasses, 8 1/2 In.Tall, Set 65.00

Sarreguemines Pottery was first made in Lorraine, France, about 1770.
Most of the pieces found today date from the late nineteenth century.
Sarreguemines, Plate, Dinner, Floral, 8 In.Diameter 8.00
Sarreguemines, Toby, Man's Head, Bloodshot Nose 27.50

Satin Glass is a late nineteenth-century art glass. It has a dull finish
that is caused by a hydrofluoric acid vapor treatment. Satin Glass was made
in many colors and sometimes had applied decorations.
Satin Glass, Basket, Blue, Green Lining, Camphor Handle, Pontil 150.00
Satin Glass, Basket, Brown, 5 In.High 75.00
Satin Glass, Basket, Herringbone, Pink, Mother-Of-Pearl 750.00
Satin Glass, Basket, Overlay, White Out, Red To Lemon In, Thorn Handle, Ribs 150.00
Satin Glass, Bell, Quilted Mother-Of-Pearl 18.50

Satin Glass, Bottle, Cologne, Flowers & Gilt, Hand Painted, Stopper	85.00
Satin Glass, Bottle, Cologne, Lizard Chasing Fly	100.00
Satin Glass, Bottle, Figural, Negro Waiter, Black Head, Sheared Neck	150.00
Satin Glass, Bowl, Blue, Stretch	25.00
Satin Glass, Bowl, Bride's, Pink, White, Crimped, Fluted, 10 In.Diameter	75.00
Satin Glass, Bowl, Plaid, Ruffled Top, Frosted Applied Feet, Signed 'tartan'	275.00
Satin Glass, Bowl, Powder, Fenton, Peach Color, White Inside	25.00
Satin Glass, Bowl, Rainbow Cased, Overlay, Four Feet, Swirled Ribs, Gold	225.00
Satin Glass, Bowl, Rainbow, Ruffled Edge, Pink, Blue, Yellow, & White, Enamel	300.00
Satin Glass, Box, Ring, White, Hand-Painted Victorian Lady On Lid	29.50
Satin Glass, Candleholder, Cardinals Decor, Black Amethyst, Pair	25.00
Satin Glass, Candlestick, Green, Twisted, 8 1/2 In.Tall	18.00
Satin Glass, Castor, Pickle, Amber, Frosted, Decorated	150.00
Satin Glass, Castor, Pickle, Orange, Frosted, Decorated	145.00
Satin Glass, Castor, Salt & Pepper, Rose Color	42.50
Satin Glass, Compote, Swirls, Crimped Edge, Brass Pedestal Base	45.00
Satin Glass, Cruet, Blue	45.00
Satin Glass, Cup, Egg, White, Hand Painted	7.50
Satin Glass, Ewer, Blue, Enamel Floral, Camphor Handles, 7 In., Pair	95.00
Satin Glass, Ewer, Enamel Decor, Thorn Handle, 10 1/4 In.High	65.00
Satin Glass, Ewer, Flower Design, Blue, Enamel, 9 In.Tall, Pair	135.00
Satin Glass, Ewer, Green, Opaque, Enameled Iris, Melon Ribbed, Clear Handle	85.00
Satin Glass, Ewer, White, Bluebirds, Branches, Ball Shape Base, 10 In., Pair	125.00
Satin Glass, Goblet, Shaded Pink, Diamond-Quilted Bowl, 7 1/4 In.High	25.00
Satin Glass, Inkwell, Shaded Pink, Covered, Swirled	50.00
Satin Glass, Jar, Biscuit, Blue, Ribbed, Swirled, Covered	95.00
Satin Glass, Jar, Biscuit, Enameled, Camphor Background, Hand-Painted Floral	42.00
Satin Glass, Jar, Biscuit, Hand-Painted Florals, Silver Cover & Bail Handle	45.00
Satin Glass, Jar, Cookie, Pink, Quilted, Tufted, Silver Plated Top	125.00
Satin Glass, Jar, Cracker, White, Blubous, Melon Shape, 'so Good'	165.00
Satin Glass, Jar, Sweetmeat, Pink, White, Daisies, Silver Rim, Lid, Handle	75.00
Satin Glass, Perfume, Horses	2.00
Satin Glass, Pitcher, Apricot, Bulbous, Footed, Ribbed Edge, 7 In.	125.00
Satin Glass, Pitcher, Diamond-Quilted, Blue, 9 In.High	200.00
Satin Glass, Pitcher, Floral Design, White, Gold, Ewer Shape, Frosted, 6 In.	32.50
Satin Glass, Pitcher, Pink, Shaded, Mother-Of-Pearl, Raindrop Pattern	160.00
Satin Glass, Plate, Fleur-De-Lis, Flowers, Gold, 7 1/2 In.Diameter	15.00
Satin Glass, Rose Bowl, Bird, Flowers, Green, Red, Egg Shape, Hand-Painted	55.00
Satin Glass, Rose Bowl, Blue	35.00
Satin Glass, Rose Bowl, Blue, Crimp Rim, 5 In.	42.50
Satin Glass, Rose Bowl, Blue, White Casing, Raised Enamel Decor, Footed	80.00
Satin Glass, Rose Bowl, Blue, Fluted Rim, White Casing, 3 1/2 In.High	39.50
Satin Glass, Rose Bowl, Blue, Herringbone, Bubbles, Coralene Trim	75.00
Satin Glass, Rose Bowl, Cobalt Blue, White Enameled Dogwood	75.00
Satin Glass, Rose Bowl, Crimped Top, Blue, White Lining	58.00
Satin Glass, Rose Bowl, Dark Blue To Light Blue, Crimped	52.00
Satin Glass, Rose Bowl, Deep Pink, Shaded To White, 3 1/2 In.Tall	45.00
Satin Glass, Rose Bowl, Light Blue, Herringbone Pattern, Bubbles, Coralene	75.00
Satin Glass, Rose Bowl, Light To Deep Pink, White & Yellow Flowers	45.00
Satin Glass, Rose Bowl, Orange To Salmon Color, Enameled Floral, Crimped	85.00
Satin Glass, Rose Bowl, Pale To Dark Pink, Crimp Top	55.00
Satin Glass, Rose Bowl, Pink	30.00 To 50.00
Satin Glass, Rose Bowl, Pink, Crimped Opening	45.00
Satin Glass, Rose Bowl, Pink, Shell & Seaweed	70.00
Satin Glass, Rose Bowl, Pink, 4 1/2 In.Diameter	20.00
Satin Glass, Rose Bowl, Pink, 5 In.Wide X 4 1/2 In.High	75.00
Satin Glass, Rose Bowl, Quilted Mother-Of-Pearl	12.50
Satin Glass, Rose Bowl, Rose Cased In White	35.00
Satin Glass, Rose Bowl, Shaded Blue, Wide Swirls, Enameled Pansies	85.00
Satin Glass, Rose Bowl, Shaded Pink, Raised Shell Decor, Enameled Floral	85.00
Satin Glass, Rose Bowl, Shell & Seaweed, Yellow To White, 5 In.Tall	175.00
Satin Glass, Rose Bowl, Violet Design, Purple, White, 6 In.Diameter	65.00
Satin Glass, Rose Bowl, Yellow, Egg Shape	35.00
Satin Glass, Rose Bowl, Yellow, Enameled Floral Around Top Edge	75.00
Satin Glass, Rose Bowl, Yellow, Swirl Pattern, Enamel Floral	58.50
Satin Glass, Rose Bowl, Yellow, 6 In.Diameter	25.00

Satin Glass, Salt & Papper, Pink, Diamond-Quilted	75.00
Satin Glass, Salt & Pepper, Flowers, Green, Coral, Melon Rib, Silver Tops	38.50
Satin Glass, Salt & Pepper, Melon Rib, Yellow, Enamel Floral	68.00
Satin Glass, Salt & Pepper, White, Flowers, Little Apple	48.00
Satin Glass, Salt & Pepper, Yellow, Flower Spray, Tomato	65.00
Satin Glass, Salt Shaker, Loop & Daisy, Lid	14.00
Satin Glass, Salt, Pink, Overlapping Shell	12.00
Satin Glass, Shaker, Sugar, Drapery Pattern, Pink	85.00
Satin Glass, Shaker, Sugar, Pink, Overlapping Leaf Design, 4 In.Diameter	38.50
Satin Glass, Shaker, Sugar, Yellow To Cream, Enameled Floral, Silver Top	105.00
Satin Glass, Swan, Open, Clear, 9 In.Long	25.00
Satin Glass, Toothpick, Pink	12.50
Satin Glass, Toothpick, Quilted Mother-Of-Pearl	12.50
Satin Glass, Tray, Dresser, White, 8 1/2 X 11 In.	10.00
Satin Glass, Tray, Pin, White, Embossed Floral	4.00
Satin Glass, Tumbler, Citron, Enameled Decoration Of Norderney Seestag	12.00
Satin Glass, Tumbler, Herringbone, Fuchsia To White	85.00
Satin Glass, Tumbler, Pale Green, Swirled	22.50
Satin Glass, Tumbler, Pink Cased, Florette	40.00
Satin Glass, Tumbler, Pink, Bulging Petal, Gold Leaf Centers	50.00
Satin Glass, Tumbler, Pink, Raised Enamel Floral	30.00
Satin Glass, Tumbler, Rose Spray, Yellow, Hand-Painted	75.00
Satin Glass, Tumbler, Yellow To White, Blue, White, Flowers, Vines	85.00
Satin Glass, Vase, Blue Mother-Of-Pearl, Melon Sectioned	87.50
Satin Glass, Vase, Blue To Sapphire, Copper Casing, Birds	95.00
Satin Glass, Vase, Blue, Mother-Of-Pearl, Herringbone Pattern, Ruffled, Pair	225.00
Satin Glass, Vase, Bud, Pink, Pontil, Slender Neck, Three Flares At Top, 7 In.	35.00
Satin Glass, Vase, Bulbous, Folded Top, White Drapery On Blue Ground	55.00
Satin Glass, Vase, Butterscotch, Raindrop, Fluted Top, 7 In.Tall	125.00
Satin Glass, Vase, Crackle Finish, Red, Double Pontil, White Lining, English	165.00
Satin Glass, Vase, Dark To Pale Pink, White Enameled Flowers, English, Pair	97.50
Satin Glass, Vase, Diamond-Quilted, Blue Green, 5 In.High	20.00
Satin Glass, Vase, Diamond-Quilted, Pink, Tall	57.00
Satin Glass, Vase, Diamond-Quilted, Mother-Of-Pearl, Blue, 2 Bursted Bubbles	60.00
Satin Glass, Vase, Diamond-Quilted, Peach Color, Long Neck, Flat Ball Type	20.00
Satin Glass, Vase, Floral Design, White, Lilac	125.00
Satin Glass, Vase, Herringbone, Yellow, 10 In.Tall	110.00
Satin Glass, Vase, Light Blue, Bubbles, Diamond Pattern, 6 3/4 In.High	60.00
Satin Glass, Vase, Mother-Of-Pearl, Pinched Top, Maize Ribbon Stripe	115.00
Satin Glass, Vase, Overlay, Yellow, Floral & Butterfly Decoration In Enamel	70.00
Satin Glass, Vase, Pink, Diamond-Quilted, 4 1/4 In.High	20.00
Satin Glass, Vase, Pink, Enameled Flower & Leaves, 11 In.	45.00
Satin Glass, Vase, Pink, Gilt Decoration, 8 1/2 In.High	150.00
Satin Glass, Vase, Pink, Gold Decor, Gold Butterfly, Uncased	48.00
Satin Glass, Vase, Pink, White Pull-Up Decoration, Inverted Saucer Base	55.00
Satin Glass, Vase, Poppies, Bulbous, Black	62.50
Satin Glass, Vase, Rainbow Mother-Of-Pearl *Illus*	685.00
Satin Glass, Vase, Raindrop, Blue, Red, Pontil	125.00
Satin Glass, Vase, Raindrop, White, 6 In.Tall	65.50
Satin Glass, Vase, Shaded Pink, Overlay, Raindrop Pattern In Relief	135.00
Satin Glass, Vase, Shaded Pink, Overlay, Ribbed Handle	95.00
Satin Glass, Vase, Stick, Pink, Shaded	55.00
Satin Glass, Vase, Stick, Ruffled Top, Wafer Base, Black, Red, 10 In.Tall	37.50
Satin Glass, Vase, Stick, Shaded Pink, 7 1/4 In.High	55.00
Satin Glass, Vase, Yellow, 7 In.	35.00
Satin Glass, Wine, Pedestal, Blue, Elue Enameled Flowers, Gold Rim	15.00

Satsuma is a Japanese Pottery with a distinctive creamy beige crackled glaze. Most of the pieces were decorated with blue, red, green, orange, or gold. Almost all the Satsuma found today was made after 1860. Japanese faces are often a part of the decorative scheme.

Satsuma Type, Figurine, Girl, Cat, 6 1/2 In. *Illus*	32.50
Satsuma, Box, Cricket, Decorated, Reticulated Lid, 5 1/2 In.	150.00
Satsuma, Button, Flowers, Butterflies, Crackle Buff Ground, Set Of 4	22.00
Satsuma, Coffeepot, Sugar, Creamer, Four Cups & Saucers, Millefiori, Marked	175.00

Satsuma, Cup & Saucer, Demitasse, Floral, Leaves, Birds, Gold Handle	15.00
Satsuma, Cup & Saucer, Thousand Faces Pattern, Signed	15.00
Satsuma, Dish, Candy, Floral Spray, Blue To Gray, Oval, Footed	15.00
Satsuma, Dish, Olive, Water Scene, Kimono Clad Figures, Gold	8.50
Satsuma, Figurine, Woman Seated On Tree Trunk, Enameled, 6 1/2 In.	300.00
Satsuma, Jar, Wine, Bulbous, Birds, Floral, Gold, 11 In.High, Stopper	40.00
Satsuma, Plate, Figures In Garden, Gold, 6 In.Diameter	40.00
Satsuma, Rose Bowl, 6 In.	25.00
Satsuma, Salt & Pepper, Squat, Ribbed, Set	20.00
Satsuma, Teapot, Cover, Wicker Handle	29.00
Satsuma, Teapot, Small .... *Illus*	75.00

Satin Glass, Vase, Rainbow Mother-Of-Pearl
See Page 453

Satsuma Type,
Figurine, Girl, Cat, 6 1/2 In.
See Page 453

Satsuma, Teapot, Small

Satsuma, Teapot, Teahouses, Women, Trees, Gold Serpent Spout & Handle	60.00
Satsuma, Vase, Allover Figures Of Ladies & Scholars, 2 1/4 In.Tall	32.50
Satsuma, Vase, Bud, Geishas, Cobalt Blue, Gold, 4 3/4 In.High	125.00
Satsuma, Vase, Chickens & Bamboo, Marked, 5 In.High	80.00
Satsuma, Vase, Court Scene, Cobalt & Gold, 8 In.	55.00
Satsuma, Vase, Crackle Cream Ground, Bamboo Design, 7 In.High	45.00
Satsuma, Vase, Cream Ground, Lacy Gold Encrusting, Teak Base, 3 3/4 In.High	20.00
Satsuma, Vase, Double Gourd, Polychrome & Gilt Floral, Reserve Scenes	70.00
Satsuma, Vase, Floral, Bird, Oriental, Pink, Green, Signed, 12 1/4 In.	25.00
Satsuma, Vase, Four Panel, Pedestal, Cobalt Blue, Geishas, Landscapes, Signed	55.00
Satsuma, Vase, Green Bamboo, Tan Background, 10 In., Pair	100.00
Satsuma, Vase, Green, Warriors, 7 1/4 In.	60.00
Satsuma, Vase, Ladies & The Warriors, Cobalt Blue, Gold, 6 Sided, Marked	65.00
Satsuma, Vase, Landscape Scene, Signed, Stand, 3 1/2 In.High	45.00
Satsuma, Vase, Light & Dark Blue, Black Ground, Floral Overlay, 13 In.High	25.00
Satsuma, Vase, Signed, 15 In., Pair	50.00
Satsuma, Vase, Thousand Faces, Cobalt Blue	16.00
Satsuma, Vase, Warriors, Mounted, Rust, Green, Crackled Glaze, 9 1/2 In., Pair	85.00
Satsuma, Vase, Women, Panels Of Birds & Floral, Browns, Blue, Gold, Signed	65.00

Scale, Analytical, Mahogany Base, Glass Top, Metal Pans, Weights 85.00
Scale, Cherry Frame, Glass Sides, Burnished Pans, Pat.1885, Springer Torsion 160.00
Scale, Egg, Measures Small, Medium, Large, Extra Large 6.50
Scale, For Weighing Gold, Two Brass Pans, Marked W&t Avery, 6 In.Long 14.75
Scale, Gold, Brass, Tin Box, Hinged 75.00
Scale, Hanging, Brass Front, 24 Lb., P.S.&w. Co. 5.00

Schneider Glass is an Art Nouveau Glass made in France.
Schneider, Bowl, Center, Smoky Amber, Stippled Background, Cut Bottom 55.00
Schneider, Bowl, Three Sided, Green, Signed, 4 In.Diameter 45.00
Schneider, Compote, Blue Shades, Wrought Iron Base, Signed, 14 In.Diameter 95.00
Schneider, Compote, Orange Bowl, Amethyst Base, Signed, 4 1/2 In. 125.00
Schneider, Ewer, Applied Handle, Tan To Cobalt Blue 150.00
Schneider, Pitcher, Purple, Blue, Spattered, Signed, 5 1/2 In.Tall 95.00
Schneider, Plate, Signed, Deep Blue To Lemon Yellow, Mottled, 8 1/4 In. 100.00
Schneider, Ring Tree, Mottled Orange, Yellow, Wine, Black Glass Stem, Signed 42.00
Schneider, Tazza, Green, Amethyst Base, Signed, 5 In.High, 8 In.Diameter 125.00
Schneider, Vase, Art Deco, Sapphire Blue, Acid Cut Back Floral, Signed 130.00
Schneider, Vase, Blown, Pink, Mauve Swirl, Signed, 6 1/2 In.High 60.00
Schneider, Vase, Elongated Bell Shape Bowl, Mottled Green, Red Interior 60.00
Schneider, Vase, Orange, White, Bulbous, Narrow Top, Pinched Opening, 19 In. 170.00

*Scrimshaw is bone or ivory or whale's teeth carved by sailors and others for
entertainment during the sailing ship days. Some Scrimshaw was carved as
early as 1800.*
Scrimshaw, Carved Sperm Whale Tooth, Female Figure, 'justice, ' C.1860 .... 140.00
Scrimshaw, Carved Whale Tooth, Female Figure, 'liberty, ' Shield, C.1860 .... 165.00
Scrimshaw, Carved Whale Tooth, Young Woman, Elizabethan Costume, C.1840 .... 225.00
Scrimshaw, Horn, Cow, Carved Man, Woman, Flowers, & Birds 25.00
Scrimshaw, Naval Officer On Horseback, Reverse, Boy & Girl 80.00
Scrimshaw, Powder Horn, Engraved Map Of Passawamagoosic River, Dated 1802 .... 375.00
Scrimshaw, Powder Horn, Map Of Lake Ontario & Champlain, N.Y., Dated 1786 .... 900.00
Scrimshaw, Shell, Ship Design, The Great Easterly 40.00
Scrimshaw, Skull, Walrus, Ivory Tusks 175.00
Scrimshaw, Toothpick, Carved 15.00
Scrimshaw, Walrus Tusk, Carved 3 Vignettes, American, 19th Century 550.00
Scrimshaw, Walrus Tusk, R.I., C.1850, Eagle, 25 In. .... *Illus* 650.00
Scrimshaw, Walrus Tusk, R.I., C.1850, Man, Birds .... *Illus* 1000.00
Scrimshaw, Whale Tooth, American, 18th Century, 6 In. .... *Illus* 550.00
Scrimshaw, Whale Tooth, Sailing Ship & Men In Boat Harpooning Whale 90.00
Scrimshaw, Whale Tooth, Sailing Ship, Addie Fuller, 1861 .... 75.00
Scrimshaw, Whale, Whalebone, Mahogany Plaque 250.00
    Scuttle Mug, see Shaving Mug

*Sevres Porcelain has been made in Sevres, France, since 1769. Many
copies of the famous ware have been made. The name originally referred to
the works of the Royal Factory. The name now includes any of the wares
made in the town of Sevres, France.*
Sevres, Bowl, Turquoise Ground, Birds, Landscape Settings, 1769 .... 700.00
Sevres, Box, Portrait, Man & Woman, Red, Oval, Footed, Hinged, 8 In.Tall 185.00
Sevres, Cachepot, Turquoise Ground, Birds, Oak Leaf Swags, 1769 .... 300.00
Sevres, Clock, Enamel Numerals Fitted On China Scroll 95.00
Sevres, Compote, Portrait, Man & Woman, Hand-Painted, Gold, Blue, 11 In.Wide 250.00
Sevres, Cup & Saucer, Birds, Roses, Pink, Gold, Mark 47.50
Sevres, Cup & Saucer, People, Flowers, Blue, Gold, Medallion Border 75.00
Sevres, Dish, Mounted In Bronze Ormolu, Blue Lattice Design, Pink, C.1771 .... 165.00
Sevres, Jug, Milk, Bulbous, Rustic Handle, Blue Du Roi Band, Gilt, C.1750 .... 80.00
Sevres, Plate, Armorial, Gilt Entrelac-De-Rubans Border, Dated 1785, Pair 40.00
Sevres, Plate, Blue Border, Scene, Flowers, Hand-Painted, Marked 1869, Pair 170.00
Sevres, Plate, Classical Empire Figures, Marble Border, Gold, 1830 .... 145.00
Sevres, Plate, Cream, Green & Gold Border, Tulip & Butterflies, 8 .... 96.00
Sevres, Plate, Dinner, Painted Garden Flowers, Gold, 18th Century, 11 .... 150.00
Sevres, Plate, Dinner, Rococo Floral, Painted Floral Center, C.1750, 27 .... 350.00
Sevres, Plate, Soup, Apple Green, Floral Medallions, C.1844, 12 .... 325.00
Sevres, Pot De Creme, Baluster Form, Roses, Gilt, Blue, Dated 1788 .... 25.00
Sevres, Saucer, Blue Celeste, Patriotic Decor, C.1802, 5 In.Diameter 100.00

Scrimshaw, Walrus Tusk, R.I., C.1850, Eagle, 25 In.
See Page 455

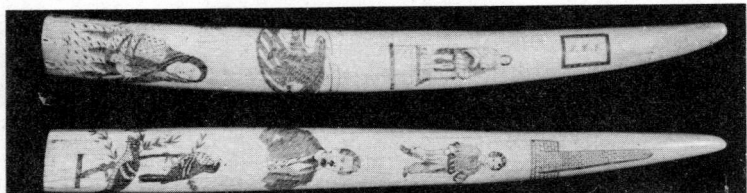

Scrimshaw, Walrus Tusk, R.I., C.1850, Man, Birds
See Page 455

Scrimshaw, Whale Tooth, American, 18th Century, 6 In.
See Page 455

Sevres, Tea Set, Cobalt Blue, Gold, 10 Cup & Saucer, Creamer & Sugar, Mark	450.00
Sevres, Teapot, White, Pink, Roses, Signed	17.50
Sevres, Tray, Breakfast, Quatrefoil Shaped, Cupids, Stamp & Mark 1846	125.00
Sevres, Tray, Receiving, White	35.00
Sevres, Tray, Turquoise Ground, Lozenge Shape, Rustic Landscape, 1762	450.00
Sevres, Urn, Biscuit, Rinceau Band, Upright Handles, Floral, C.1750	400.00
Sevres, Urn, Bleu De Roi, Covered, Bronze Mounted, C.1756, Entwined L's	500.00
Sevres, Urn, Bleu De Roi, Louis XVI, Pair	9500.00
Sevres, Urn, Bleu De Roi, Revolving Body, 35 In.Tall	700.00
Sevres, Urn, Napoleon I After-Battle Scene, Signed H.Desprez, 1806	850.00
Sevres, Vase, Cobalt & White, Painted Decor, 34 In.Tall	650.00
Sevres, Vase, Green, Gold, Leaf Body, Floral, White Porcelain	500.00
Sewer Tile, Poodle, Ohio, 5 In.High	30.00
Sewer Tile, Stump, Ohio, Anchor & Cross, Impressed F.W., 7 In.High	10.00
Sewing Tool, Bird, Brass, Dated	17.50
Sewing Tool, Bird, Embossed Brass, 2 Cushions	17.50
Sewing Tool, Bird, Red Cushion	24.75
Sewing Tool, Bird, 2 Cushions	25.00
Sewing Tool, Box & Spool Holder, Victorian, Painted	20.00
Sewing Tool, Box, 100 Years Old	10.00
Sewing Tool, Buttonhole Cutter, Leaf Shape, Brass, Iron Handle, Adjusted	18.00
Sewing Tool, Case, Needle, Carved Ivory, 4 In.Long	15.00
Sewing Tool, Case, Needle, Wood Barrel, Top Rotates	9.50
Sewing Tool, Crochet Hook, Bone	5.00
Sewing Tool, Cutter, Buttonhole, Brass, Leaf Shape Plate	18.00
Sewing Tool, Cylinder With Thread, Needles, & Thimble, Brass	4.00
Sewing Tool, Darner, Cranberry Glass, End Of Day, 6 1/2 In.Long	30.00
Sewing Tool, Darner, Glove, Dumbbell Shape	5.00
Sewing Tool, Darner, Sock, Handle, 5 In.Long	6.00

Paperweights. (1) Prob. Gilliland, (2) New England, (3) facet cut, Gilliland.

Paperweights. (1) New England Glass Works, (2) St. Louis, (3) New England.

Log-cabin lamp, 1840.

Pomona glass pitcher. American, 1886.

Carnival glass pitcher, grape and cable design.

Stoneware jar, Alexandria, Va., 1823–1843. Marked "H. C. Smith Alexa."

Art Pottery 1900–1910. (1)
European pottery vase, (2)
Van Briggle Pottery, Colorado
Springs, Colo., (3) Rookwood
Pottery, Cincinnati, Ohio.

Jar, Union Glass Co., 1905, Somerville,
Mass.

Silver plated candlestick. English,
ca. 1785.

Cobalt blue candlesticks.
Sandwich, 1835–1840.

Pewter communion flagons.
American, nineteenth century.

Coffeepot, John Adams, Jr.
Alexandria, Va., 1800–1843.

Candle mold, New England.

American Renaissance Gothic
bureau with mirror, ca. 1880.

Chest, cottage furniture.
Victorian, American.

Desk by Donn & Co., Washington, D.C., ca. 1840.

Chairtable. North English, mid-seventeenth century from Story house.

Tilt-top table. New England, 1790–1810.

Fancy painted American armchair.

Chair in cast iron. Marks cast on
back above lyre "J. B. Moery,"
and below, "Wm. Adams & Co."

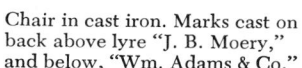

Papier-mâché chair. Puerto Rico;
nineteenth century.

Farmhouse bedroom, stenciled walls, 1820.

Chamber of Richard Dole house, Massachusetts, 1670.

Sewing Tool, Darner, Sock, Red Glass, Open End, Bulbous 22.00
Sewing Tool, Darning Egg, Wood, Handle 2.75
Sewing Tool, Darning Egg, 11 Laminated Layers 4.00
Sewing Tool, Holder, Clamp Type, Iron 8.75
Sewing Tool, Holder, Needle, Souvenir, World's Fair, 1904, Orangewood 3.00
Sewing Tool, Holder, Spool, Beaded Top & Bottom, Sterling Silver 12.00
Sewing Tool, Holder, Spool, Iron, Christmas Tree Shape, 12 In.Tall 22.50
Sewing Tool, Holder, Thimble, Barrel Shape, Sterling Silver 15.00
Sewing Tool, Machine, Child's, Made In Germany 15.00
Sewing Tool, Machine, Child's, Singer 7.00
Sewing Tool, Machine, Hand, Red Floral Design, Germany, 6 In.Tall 18.00
Sewing Tool, Machine, White, Table Model, Hand Crank 12.50
Sewing Tool, Niddy Noddy, To Wind Skein Yarn 7.50
Sewing Tool, Scissors, Brass Handles, Ornate Brass Guard Fits Over Blades 15.00
Sewing Tool, Scissors, Buttonhole, Howe & Hulbert 4.50
Sewing Tool, Scissors, Figural, Stork, In Case 5.00
Sewing Tool, Seamstress Caddy, Pegs, Pincushion, Drawer, Walnut, Cherry, 1890 .... 60.00
Sewing Tool, Sewing Bird, Pincushion, Brass, Dated 1863 .... 32.00
Sewing Tool, Sewing Machine, Gloria 10.00
Sewing Tool, Sewing Machine, Sears, 1901 .... 34.00
Sewing Tool, Tailor's Goose, Iron 12.50
Sewing Tool, Tatter, Celluloid 1.25
Sewing Tool, Thimble, Gold, Chester 1901 Hallmark 22.00
Sewing Tool, Thimble, No.8, Signed With An Anchor 19.00
Sewing Tool, Thimble, Persian, Gold, 14k, Handmade, Carved 27.50
Sewing Tool, Thimble, Persian, Gold, 14k, Jewels, Handmade, Carved 34.50
Sewing Tool, Thimble, Persian, Silver, Handmade, Carved 3.75
Sewing Tool, Thimble, Persian, Sterling Silver, Hand Carved 4.50
Sewing Tool, Thimble, Persian, 14k Gold, Handmade & Carved 27.50
Sewing Tool, Thimble, Persian, 14k Gold, Handmade & Carved, Jewels 34.50
Sewing Tool, Thimble, Ruffled Edge, Engraved, Hallmarked, Sterling Silver 9.00
Sewing Tool, Thimble, Silver, 3/4 Gold, Hand Engraved Bessie 2.50
Sewing Tool, Thimble, Sterling Silver .... 4.00 To 4.25
Sewing Tool, Thimble, Sterling Silver, Lily-Of-The-Valley Border, Size 9 .... 16.00
Sewing Tool, Thimble, Sterling, Pat.1889 .... 2.95
Sewing Tool, Thimble, Wide Band, 14k Gold, Size 10 .... 23.00
Sewing Tool, Yarn Reel, Upright 42.50

Shaving Mugs were popular from 1860 to 1900. Many types were made,
including occupational mugs featuring pictures of the man's job. There were
scuttle mugs, silver-plated mugs, glass-lined mugs, and Others.
shaving mug, berry, leaf, white, gold, scalloped rim 18.00
Shaving Mug, Bisque, Egyptian Head, Brush Inside .... *Illus* 35.00
Shaving Mug, Black, White Stencil Of Poolroom Scene 25.00
Shaving Mug, Blue & White Forget-Me-Nots, Crimped Edge 8.50
Shaving Mug, Blue, Orange, Tree, Carnival 35.00

Shaving Mug, Bisque,
Egyptian Head, Brush Inside

Shaving Mug, **Cherubs**, Ornate, Silver, Liner	35.00
Shaving Mug, **Cobalt**, Hand-Painted Flowers, Leaves, Name	10.00
Shaving Mug, **Daisies**, Hand-Painted	12.00
Shaving Mug, **F.A.Allen**	22.50
Shaving Mug, **Face Cards**, Initials, Impressed Mercer & Globe, Square	45.00
Shaving Mug, **Floral Decoration**, Gold, Red, Green, Germany	12.50
Shaving Mug, **Floral Decoration**, Soap Rest	15.00
Shaving Mug, **Floral Design**, Pink, White, Gold, 'think Of Me'	15.00
Shaving Mug, **Floral Design**, White, Porcelain, English	22.00
Shaving Mug, **Floral**, Bavarian	16.00
Shaving Mug, **Floral**, China, Soap Rest	15.50
Shaving Mug, **Floral**, Germany	16.00
Shaving Mug, **Floral**, S Over L, D.& C.Co.	20.00
Shaving Mug, **Flower Design**, Iridescent, Gold Trim	24.00
Shaving Mug, **Flowers**, Small	15.00
Shaving Mug, **Gold Leaves**, Blue Flowers, Front Pocket, 6 In.High	22.00
Shaving Mug, **Gold**, Ribbon, Wreath, Peter Smith, 4 In.High	8.50
Shaving Mug, **Hand-Painted Daisies**	12.00
Shaving Mug, **Ironstone**, White To Green, Dog's Head, Marked Germany	12.00
Shaving Mug, **Ironstone**, White, Scroll Handle	5.00
Shaving Mug, **Little Tommy Tucker**, Ridgway, 1924	15.00
Shaving Mug, **Man In Two Horse Drawn Buggy**	55.00
Shaving Mug, **Maroon & Green**, 7 In.	8.00
Shaving Mug, **Maroon & White**, Hand-Painted, Gold Lettering & Trim, D & C Co.	15.00
Shaving Mug, **Milk Glass**, Gold	17.50
Shaving Mug, **Milk Glass**, White	4.98
Shaving Mug, **Mustache**, Left Handed, Cream Color, Dated 1890	30.00
Shaving Mug, **Narrow Bands**, Gold Name	15.00
Shaving Mug, **Occupational**, Actor, F.Dose *Illus*	69.50
Shaving Mug, **Occupational**, Baseball & Bats	80.00
Shaving Mug, **Occupational**, Farmer Driving Wagon	65.00
Shaving Mug, **Occupational**, Gentleman Driving Coach	65.00
Shaving Mug, **Occupational**, Head Of Steer & Name Mj Jones, Hand-Painted	40.00
Shaving Mug, **Occupational**, Hunter, A.R.Owen, Hunter & Dog Landscape	85.00
Shaving Mug, **Occupational**, Hunting Scene	75.00
Shaving Mug, **Occupational**, Jeweler	75.00
Shaving Mug, **Occupational**, Mason, Signed Berninghaus	60.00
Shaving Mug, **Occupational**, Pharmacist	57.00
Shaving Mug, **Occupational**, Plumber's Tools, Hammer & Pliers Are Crossed	65.00
Shaving Mug, **Occupational**, Sportsman, Hand-Painted On White, Gold	60.00
Shaving Mug, **Occupational**, Two-Wheel Bicycle	70.00
Shaving Mug, **Occupational**, Woman In Bed, Doctor Pours Medicine In Spoon	65.00
Shaving Mug, **Openwork Scroll Handle**, Pewter, James Dixon & Sons, 1840	150.00
Shaving Mug, **Orange Tree**, Carnival Glass, Marigold, Prismatic Handle	15.00
Shaving Mug, **Panels**, Clear Glass	3.75
Shaving Mug, **Peter Piper**, Doulton, 1902	15.00
Shaving Mug, **Pink Floral**, Rest	10.00
Shaving Mug, **Porcelain**, Violets	8.50
Shaving Mug, **Scuttle Type**, Bird On Tree	10.00
Shaving Mug, **Scuttle**, Floral	19.00
Shaving Mug, **Scuttle**, Marked Union Shaving Mug, Pat.1870	11.95
Shaving Mug, **Scuttle**, White, Roses	20.00
Shaving Mug, **Silver Plate**, Milk Glass Insert	22.50
Shaving Mug, **Silver Plate**, Milk Glass Insert, Brush Rest	9.95
Shaving Mug, **Silver**, Engraved, Soap Tray, 1881	22.00
Shaving Mug, **Souvenir Of Wales**, Ladies, White, Gold, 3 In.Tall	17.50
Shaving Mug, **Tin**, Side Compartment, Strap Handle	17.50
Shaving Mug, **Two Wide Gold Bands**, Monogram	20.00
Shaving Mug, **White**, Gold Bands	5.95
Shaving Mug, **White**, Shaving Mug In Gold Script	5.50
Sheffield, see Silver, Sheffield	
Ship, Box, Strong, 1860s, Royal Mint Crown Cast In Lid, Ocean Freight	275.00
Ship, Chest, Medicine, Rosewood, C.1850-60, Brass Binding, Bottles, Cups	195.00
Ship, Eagle, Pilot House, Carved & Gilded Pine, American, 19th Century	225.00
Ship, Light, Red, Horizontally Ribbed Glass, Electrified	17.00
Ship, Model *Illus*	110.00

Shaving Mug, Occupational, Actor, F.Dose
See Page 458

Ship, Model
See Page 458

Ship, Model, Frigate, 18-Gun, Three Masted, Fully Rigged	500.00
Ship, Model, Manager, Steamer, Half Hull, Dated 1908, Robert Palmer & Son	200.00
Ship, Model, Twin Screw Tug, Waterman, 33 In.Long	150.00
Ship, Quadrant, Navigation, C.1820, Black Ebony, Brass, Ivory Inlaid	84.50
Ship, Saw, Gallery, Embossed	12.50
Ship, Telescope, Sea Captain's, Presentation, Leather Cover, Brass, 1847	89.50
Ship, Wheel, Brass, 35 In.Diameter, Oak Handles	110.00
Ship, Whistle, Bos'n's, British Navy, Brass, Engraved	37.50

Shirley TempleDishes, Blue Glassware, and any other souvenir-type objects with her name and picture are now collected.

Shirley Temple, Baby & Buggy	150.00
Shirley Temple, Book, Captain January & The Little Colonel	5.00
Shirley Temple, Book, Coloring, No.1717	5.00
Shirley Temple, Book, Shirley Temple And The Screaming Specter, C.1946	3.00
Shirley Temple, Book, The Littlest Rebel	5.00
Shirley Temple, Bowl & Mug, Cereal	20.00
Shirley Temple, Bowl, Cereal, Blue Glass	12.50
Shirley Temple, Creamer, Blue	5.00
Shirley Temple, Doll, Bisque, Statue, 4 In.Tall	10.00
Shirley Temple, Doll, Composition, Marked Head & Body, 13 In.Tall	35.00
Shirley Temple, Doll, Composition, 22 In.Tall	17.00
Shirley Temple, Doll, Cutout, Clothes Set	5.00
Shirley Temple, Doll, Marked, 12 In.Tall	35.00
Shirley Temple, Doll, Marked, 18 In.Tall	35.00
Shirley Temple, Doll, Paper, No.4490, Saalfield, Dresses, 1960, Folder	5.00
Shirley Temple, Doll, Paper, Stand-Up, No.304, Samuel Gabriel Sons, 1959	10.00
Shirley Temple, Doll, Paper, 4 Pages	5.25
Shirley Temple, Doll, Vinyl, 11 In.Tall	25.00
Shirley Temple, Doll, Vinyl, 12 In.Tall	10.00
Shirley Temple, Doll, Vinyl, 17 In.Tall, Dressed	15.00
Shirley Temple, Doll, Vinyl, 18 In.Tall, Dressed, Flirty Eyes	26.00
Shirley Temple, Doll, Vinyl, 19 In.Tall	18.00
Shirley Temple, Doll, 18 In.Tall, Marked, Wig	18.00 To 37.50
Shirley Temple, Doll, 25 In.Tall, Marked, Flirty Eyes	75.00
Shirley Temple, Fan, Royal Crown Cola	5.00
Shirley Temple, Jug, Milk, Blue, 5 In.Tall	7.00
Shirley Temple, Pitcher, Blue Glass	6.00 To 8.50
Shirley Temple, Pitcher, Bowl, Set, Blue Glass	13.50 To 15.00
Shirley Temple, Pitcher, Picture, 4 1/2 In.	7.50
Shirley Temple, Playing Cards, Little Colonel	10.00
Shirley Temple, Playing Cards, 1930	10.00

Shirley Temple, Ring, Adjustable	2.25
Shirley Temple, Shirt	25.00
Shirley Temple, Vinyl, 15 In.Tall	15.00
Silesia, Berry Set, Pink Roses, Green Luster, P.& K.Silesia, 5 Piece	30.00
Silesia, Bowl, Jack-In-The-Pulpits, Pink, White, Gray Ground, Gold Border	22.50
Silesia, Bowl, Pink & Yellow Flower Design, R.S.Silesia	21.00
Silesia, Cake Set, Roses, Pink, Green, Six Plates, Hand-Painted	85.00
Silesia, Chocolate Pot, Pale Green, White, Pink & Coral Roses	22.50
Silesia, Dish, Hand-Painted, Gold Handles, Signed, Pansies, Shallow, 6 3/4 In.	10.00
Silesia, Hair Receiver, Beading, Floral	9.50
Silesia, Plate, Hand Painted, Rainbow Border, Scalloped Edge, Open Handle	18.50
Silesia, Plate, Hand-Painted Acorns & Oak Leaves, 7 1/2 In.	11.00
Silesia, Plate, Hand-Painted Floral, 8 1/4 In.	12.50
Silesia, Plate, Ivory Ground, Red Strawberries, Green Leaves, Gold Edge	10.00
Silesia, Plate, Octagonal, Blossoms, Pink	40.00
Silesia, Plate, Open Handles, Three Roses, 9 1/2 In.	18.00
Silesia, Plate, White House Portrayed, 10 In.	10.00
Silesia, Plate, White House, 10 In.	12.00
Silesia, Sauceboat & Underplate, Green Mark, Oval	16.00
Silesia, Sugar & Creamer, Footed, Mother-Of-Pearl Rim, Orange, Signed	15.00
Silesia, Sugar, R.S.Tillowitz, Covered, White Floral On Green & Brown, G3ld	16.00
Silhouette, see Picture, Silhouette	

Silver Deposit Glass was made during the late nineteenth and early twentieth centuries. Solid sterling silver was applied to the glass by a chemical method so that a cutout design of silver metal appeared against a clear or colored glass.

Silver Deposit, Base, Bud, Etched Flowers & Leaves	10.00
Silver Deposit, Bonbon, Pink Glass	8.00
Silver Deposit, Bottle, Perfume, Clear Glass, 2 3/4 In.Tall	9.50
Silver Deposit, Bowl, Fruit, Flared, 11 1/2 In.	25.00
Silver Deposit, Compote, Green, 7 In.High	9.00
Silver Deposit, Creamer & Sugar, Silver Flower, Leaves	15.00
Silver Deposit, Creamer & Sugar, 3 1/4 In.	15.00
Silver Deposit, Decanter & Six Glasses, Brandy, Emerald Green	45.00
Silver Deposit, Decanter, Amethyst, Sterling Silver, 5 Shot Glasses	25.00
Silver Deposit, Decanter, Blue, 8 1/2 In.	36.00
Silver Deposit, Dish, Candy, Wavy, Coral, 6 In.Diameter	6.00
Silver Deposit, Inkwell, Gorham, Square Base, Flower Design, Initials	55.00
Silver Deposit, Pitcher, Green, Applied Handle, Pint	6.00
Silver Deposit, Pitcher, 9 3/4 In.	30.00
Silver Deposit, Plate, Cake, Flowers, Leaves, '25th Anniversary, ' Handled	12.50
Silver Deposit, Sugar & Creamer, Clear	15.00
Silver Deposit, Tumbler, Flared, Narrow Flutes On Bottom	5.00
Silver Deposit, Vase, Amethyst *Illus*	37.50
Silver Deposit, Vase, Bud, Art Nouveau Silver Design, 6 In.High	13.00
Silver Deposit, Vase, Clear, Silver Roses & Border, 10 In.Tall	12.00
Silver Deposit, Vase, Squatty, Striped Design, Leaves & Flowers	15.00

Silver Deposit, Vase, Amethyst

Silver Deposit, Water Set, Amber, 5 Piece, Butterfly Design 25.00
Silver Deposit, Wine, Emerald Green, Footed, Flaring 7.50
Silver Mesh, Handbag, Baked Enamel Finish 14.50
Silver Overlay, Basket, Sterling, Applied Handle, 3 1/2 In.High 28.00
Silver Overlay, Dresser Set, Bulbous Cruets, Topaz, Swirled Handled, 3 Piece ... 60.00
Silver Overlay, Jar, Powder, Girl Figurine On Top 7.50
Silver Overlay, Vase, Dark Green, Birds, Squiggles 30.00
Silver Overlay, Vase, Green, Floral, 5 In.High 15.00
Silver Plate, Basket, Cake, Homan, Quadruple, Grape Clusters, Vines 25.00
Silver Plate, Basket, Cake, Movable Handle, Peacock Center 35.00
Silver Plate, Bowl, Finger, Footed, Set Of 6 .... 47.50
Silver Plate, Box, Hinged, Heart Shape, Victorian, Floral, Scrolls, Pairpoint ... 12.00
Silver Plate, Butter, Cow Finial, Footed 25.00
Silver Plate, Butter, Glass Insert 8.00
Silver Plate, Butter, Liner, Knife Holder 25.00
Silver Plate, Butter, Swan Finial, Footed 22.00
Silver Plate, Candelabra, Leaf & Grape, 11 In.Wide, Low, Pair 22.50
Silver Plate, Candelabra, 5 Branch, Victor Quadruple Plate, 17 In.High 50.00
Silver Plate, Candelabrum, Five Branches, Forbes 22.50
Silver Plate, Candleholder, Leaf & Vine, 15 In.High, Pair 45.00
Silver Plate, Candleholder, 3 Arm, Homan Mfg.Co., Floral 5.00
Silver Plate, Candlesnuffer 25.00
Silver Plate, Candlestick, Chamber, Handle, Three Feet 12.50
Silver Plate, Candlestick, Column, 8 1/2 In.High, Pair 30.00
Silver Plate, Candlestick, Raised Figures, 4 1/2 In.High, Pair 10.00
Silver Plate, Candlesticks, Poppies, Stems, Leaves, Meriden, Conn., 8 In., Pair ... 25.00
Silver Plate, Case, Card, Lady's, Filigree Work, Book Shape 18.00
    Silver Plate, Castor, see Castor
Silver Plate, Chocolate Pot, Pairpoint, Quadruple, Ebony Handle 40.00
Silver Plate, Coffeepot, English Flower Engraving, Quadruple Plate 14.50
Silver Plate, Coffeepot, Teapot, Creamer, Sugar, Tray, International, Wilcox ... 195.00
Silver Plate, Compote, International, Wilcox, 6 3/4 X 6 1/4 In.Tall 12.50
Silver Plate, Container, Muffin, Dome Top 50.00
Silver Plate, Cooler & Stand, Water, Pairpoint, Signed, Dated Sept.30, 1885 ... 65.00
Silver Plate, Cooler, Wine, On Copper, Urn Shape, Gadroon Top & Bottom, Pair ... 35.00
Silver Plate, Creamer, St.Francis Hotel, Reed & Barton 6.00
Silver Plate, Cup, Loving, Engraved Sheaf Of Wheat, Quadruple, James W.Tufts ... 18.00
Silver Plate, Dish, Butter, English Flower Engraving, Quadruple Plate 12.00
Silver Plate, Dish, Butter, Lid, Glass Liner, 6 In. 7.50
Silver Plate, Dish, Butter, Reed & Barton, Waterford Insert 25.00
Silver Plate, Dish, Nut, Quadruple, Footed, Van Bergh 15.00
Silver Plate, Dish, Nut, Squirrel, Leaves, Acorns, Marked, 12 In. 40.00
Silver Plate, Epergne, Cherub Holding Iridescent Green Glass Lily 125.00
Silver Plate, Epergne, Swans Hold Red, Blue, Yellow & Purple Glass Lilies ... 125.00
Silver Plate, Fish Set, Knives & Forks, Fluted Handles, Set Of 24 ...... 120.00
Silver Plate, Flatware Set, Child's, Girl & Doll, Boy & Boat, Rogers, 3 Piece ... 10.00
Silver Plate, Fork, Child's, Embossed Handle 2.00
Silver Plate, Fork, Olive, Long Handle 5.00
Silver Plate, Frame, Picture, 6 In.Square, Raised Egrets, Stream, & Trees ... 10.00
Silver Plate, Goblet, Raised Head On Coin Decor, Initial, Rogers, Pair ... 37.50
Silver Plate, Holder, Spoon, English Flower Engraving, Quadruple Plate ... 8.00
Silver Plate, Holder, String, Lacy Filigree Dome, 12 In. 15.00
Silver Plate, Jar, Cookie, Helmschmit, 6-Cornered, Signed H, Hand-Painted ... 65.00
Silver Plate, Kettle, Alcohol Burner, English Flower Engraving, Quadruple ... 27.00
Silver Plate, Knife Rest, Footed, Wheels With Daisies & Bee 6.50
Silver Plate, Knife Rest, Pheasants 22.50
Silver Plate, Knife Rest, Tennis Raquet Ends 5.00
Silver Plate, Mirror, Hand, Woman's Head, Carnations, Marked 17.50
Silver Plate, Mirror, Hand, Woman's Head, Flowers, Vines, Simpson H.M. & Co. ... 12.00
Silver Plate, Mug, Wynken, Blynken, & Nod, 1 3/4 In. 40.00
    Silver Plate, Napkin Ring, see Napkin Ring
Silver Plate, Pitcher & Plate, Syrup, Forbes 18.00
Silver Plate, Pitcher, Cream, English Flower Engraving, Quadruple Plate ... 8.00
Silver Plate, Pitcher, Syrup, Marked Meriden & 189, Ornate 18.00
Silver Plate, Pitcher, Syrup, Underplate, English Flower Engraving 11.50
Silver Plate, Platter, Bead Rim, Oval, 14 In. 8.50

Silver Plate, Purse, Embossed Design, Child's, On Chain	8.00
Silver Plate, Rack, Toast, 6 Slice, Scalloped, Beaded	7.50
Silver Plate, Salt & Pepper, Vintage Pattern, Copper Tray, Footed, Sheffield	26.50
Silver Plate, Salt, Cobalt Insert, 2 1/4 In.Diameter, Pair	18.00
Silver Plate, Salt, Lion Head, Footed, Blue Liner, Spoon	55.00
Silver Plate, Salt, Master, Pair	25.00
Silver Plate, Sheffield, Mustard Pot, Cobalt Liner, Spoon, Mark, Circa 1868	30.00
Silver Plate, Spoon, Souvenir, see Souvenir Spoon	
Silver Plate, Spoon Rack Sugar Bowl, Bird Finial, Squirrels In Handles	40.00
Silver Plate, Spoon Warmer, Scrolls & Fish, Engraved, Snail Shape	50.00
Silver Plate, Spoon, Child's, Embossed Handle	2.00
Silver Plate, Spoon, Serving, Embossed Handle	2.50
Silver Plate, Strainer, Tea, Handled	8.00
Silver Plate, Strainer, Tea, Open Flower Shape, Handle Shape Of Leaf	10.00
Silver Plate, Strainer, Tea, Round Serrated Bowl, Wide Bent Handle	11.00
Silver Plate, Strainer, Tea, Tetley	3.25
Silver Plate, Sugar & Creamer, Engraved Scroll Design, 5 In.High	8.00
Silver Plate, Sugar & Creamer, Rockford Silver Co., E.P.N.S., Etched	18.00
Silver Plate, Sugar Crusher	2.00
Silver Plate, Sugar, Spoon Holders & Tongs, Meriden Co., Glass Insert	45.00
Silver Plate, Tea Caddy, Repousse Tavern Scene, Sailboat & Windmill On Lid	30.00
Silver Plate, Tea Set, Bow & Garland Design, Initial W, Cream, Sugar	30.00
Silver Plate, Tea Set, Quadruple, 4 Piece	15.00
Silver Plate Tea Set, Van Bergh Of Rochester, 1898, 4 Piece	47.50 To 85.00
Silver Plate, Teapot, English Flower Engraving, Quadruple Plate	13.50
Silver Plate, Teapot, Greek Key Pattern, Rogers & Smith Co., Hartford, 7 In.	45.00
Silver Plate, Teapot, Reed & Barton .... *Illus*	25.00

Silver Plate, Teapot, Reed & Barton

Silver Plate, Teapot, RM Co., Adams Design	18.50
Silver Plate, Toast Rack, Footed, Handle On Top, England	12.00
Silver Plate, Toothpick, Barrel Shape, Cocker Spaniel At Side	22.00
Silver Plate, Toothpick, Derby, Embossed Flowers	15.00
Silver Plate, Toothpick, Dolphin Handle, Footed	15.00
Silver Plate, Toothpick, Forbes Silver Co., Meriden, Conn., Circa 1890	4.95
Silver Plate, Toothpick, Urn Shape, Chicken & Wishbone At Side	20.00
Silver Plate, Toothpick, Victorian, Figural, Chick On Wishbone	15.00
Silver Plate, Toothpick, Wishbone, Chick At Side, Rogers	12.00
Silver Plate, Tray, Card, Footed	25.00
Silver Plate, Tureen, Soup, Footed, Victor Silver Co.	40.00
Silver Plate, Urn, Hot Water, Beaded Border, Loop Handles, Square Base	80.00
Silver Plate, Urn, On Platform, Double Handled, 8 In.High	22.50
Silver Plate, Vase, Bud, Pierced Rim, 6 1/2 In.Tall	6.50
Silver Plate, Wine Cooler, 19th Century, Pair	300.00
Silver, American, Basket, Cake, Garret Eoff, N.Y., Boat Shape, Pedestal, Coin	1200.00
Silver, American, Basket, Cake, Gilt, Oval, Black, Starr & Frost, C.1900	225.00
Silver, American, Basket, Sweetmeat, Boat Shape, Engraved, Gale & Willis, 1850	100.00
Silver, American, Basket, Sweetmeat, C.1860, Boat Shape, Engraved Swags	200.00

Silver, American, Basket, Sweetmeat, Oval, Repousse, S.Kirk & Son Co., 1903-24 .... 120.00
Silver, American, Basket, Sweetmeat, William Gale & Son, N.Y., Boat Shape 155.00
Silver, American, Basket, William Gale & Sons, N.Y., C.1923, Open Wire Body 250.00
Silver, American, Beaker, Cylindrical, Engraved M.C., David Greenleaf, C.1800 .... 475.00
Silver, American, Beaker, Cylindrical, Engraved Maj.Sill, Lewis Feueter, 1775 .... 550.00
Silver, American, Beaker, Ebenezer Moulton, Newburyport, Mass., 4 Oz., Coin 500.00
Silver, American, Beaker, Footed, Engraved, Thomas Richards, N.Y., C.1820 .... 180.00
Silver, American, Beaker, Thomas Richards, N.Y., Inscribed Adrian Onderdonk 375.00
Silver, American, Beaker, Young & Veal, Columbia, S.C., Footed, Coin 400.00
Silver, American, Boat, Pap, Engraved, William I.Tenney, N.Y., C.1840 .... 225.00
Silver, American, Bowl, Engraved, John David, Jr., Phila., C.1785 .... 1100.00
Silver, American, Bowl, Joseph Lownes, Philadelphia, C.1790, Footed 700.00
Silver, American, Bowl, Shell Shape, Daffodil Handle, John H.Welsh, 7 In. 12.50
Silver, American, Box, Upright Cylindrical, Engraved, Edmund Milne, C.1790 .... 275.00
Silver, American, Butter, Covered, William Gale & Son., N.Y., C.1860, Engraved 80.00
Silver, American, Can, Baluster, Double Scroll Handle, William Taylor, C.1780 .... 1000.00
Silver, American, Can, Baluster, Engraved, Joel Sayre, N.Y., C.1810 .... 450.00
Silver, American, Can, Baluster, Engraved, John David, Phila., C.1780 .... 1100.00
Silver, American, Can, Baluster, Engraved, Lewis & Smith, Phila., C.1805 .... 350.00
Silver, American, Can, Baluster, Engraved, Robert Wilson, N.Y., C.1810 .... 500.00
Silver, American, Can, Baluster, Engraved, Thomas Sheilds, Phila., C.1780 .... 700.00
Silver, American, Can, Cylindrical, Engraved Initials, William Jones, C.1720 .... 600.00
Silver, American, Can, Engraved E.R., John & Peter Targee, N.Y., C.1810 .... 675.00
Silver, American, Can, Engraved Eliza Bacon, Joseph Rice, Baltimore, C.1800 .... 150.00
Silver, American, Can, Miniature, Scroll Handle, Elias Pelletreau, C.1780 .... 375.00
Silver, American, Can, Reeded Border, Engraved, John & Peter Targee, C.1810 .... 425.00
Silver, American, Coffee Set, S.Kirk & Son, 1880-1924, Repousse, 3 Piece 275.00
Silver, American, Coffeepot, J.E.Caldwell & Co., Philadelphia, Repousse 500.00
Silver, American, Coffeepot, Vase Shape, Chased, C.1830 .... 275.00
Silver, American, Coffeepot, 19th Century, Vase Shape, Square Pedestal Foot 400.00
Silver, American, Communion Set, Chased, Engraved, Welles & Gelston, C.1829 .... 1800.00
Silver, American, Compote, Boat Shape, Engraved, The Gorham Co., C.1869 .... 110.00
Silver, American, Compote, Pedestal, Key Border, Tiffany & Co., C.1854 .... 250.00
Silver, American, Compote, Strawberry Vine, Tiffany & Co., C.1854 .... 250.00
Silver, American, Creamer, B.Pitman, Providence, Circular, Gold Wash 425.00
Silver, American, Creamer, Elias Pelletreau, N.Y., C.1770, Pear Shape, Footed 1700.00
Silver, American, Creamer, John Owen, Philadelphia, C.1815, Rectangular 150.00
Silver, American, Creamer, Philip Garrett, Phila., Square, 4 Ball Feet, Coin 400.00
Silver, American, Cup, Braverman & Levy, San Francisco, Applied Scroll Bands 125.00
Silver, American, Cup, C.Bard & Son, Phila., Cylindrical, 4 Oz., Coin 135.00
Silver, American, Cup, Camp, Joseph Anthony, Jr., Phila., C.1780, Set Of 6 .... 2300.00
Silver, American, Cup, Communion, J.B.Jones & Co., Boston, C.1833, Pair 350.00
Silver, American, Dish, Entree, Cover, The Gorham Co., C.1871, Oval, Set Of 4 .... 800.00
Silver, American, Dish, Entree, Covered, A.Rogers, Boston, C.1867, Oval, Pair 525.00
Silver, American, Ewer, Ball, Black & Co., 1860 .... *Illus* 250.00
Silver, American, Ewer, Baluster, Embossed, S.W.& Co., C.1850 .... 150.00
Silver, American, Ewer, Samuel Kirk, Baltimore, 1830-46, Helmet, Engraved 800.00
Silver, American, Fish Slice, Fiddle Thread, George Gelston, Albert Coles 125.00
Silver, American, Fish Slice, Olive, William Gale & Son, N.Y.C., Engraved 45.00
Silver, American, Fish Slice, Oval Thread, Squire & Lander, N.Y.C., Engraved 45.00
Silver, American, Fish Slice, Pierced Blade, Engraved, Fiddle Handle, C.1810 .... 60.00
Silver, American, Flagon, Sharp, Bailey & Co., C.1850 .... *Illus* 425.00
Silver, American, Fork, Blynn & Baldwin, Mark Coin 1855, Set Of 8 .... 42.00
Silver, American, Fork, Brinsmaid, Burlington, C.1830, Coin, 4 .... 39.75
Silver, American, Fork, Cold Meat, Duhme, C.1848, 4 Prong, Cut 29.00
Silver, American, Fork, Dinner, Fiddle End, A.C.Benedict & Co., N.Y.C., 6 .... 100.00
Silver, American, Fork, Dinner, Fiddle End, Alexander Troup, Jr., Halifax, 4 .... 65.00
Silver, American, Fork, Dinner, William I.Tenney, N.Y., C.1831, Coin, 10 .... 89.75
Silver, American, Fork, Dinner, William N.J., Read, Phila., C.1830, Coin, 3 .... 26.75
Silver, American, Fork, Engraved, Bailey & Co., Phila., Coin 10.00
Silver, American, Fork, Engraved, William Gale, Jr., N.Y.C., Marked Sterling, 2 .... 25.00
Silver, American, Fork, Fiddle Thread, B.Gardiner, Phila., Coin, 4 .... 45.00
Silver, American, Fork, Fiddle Thread, Bailey & Co., Phila., Coin, 6 .... 100.00
Silver, American, Fork, Fiddle Thread, G.E.Adams, Coin, 12 .... 225.00
Silver, American, Fork, Fiddle Thread, Hyde & Goodrich, New Orleans, Pair 35.00
Silver, American, Fork, Fiddle Thread, J.E.Caldwell & Co., Phila., Coin, 6 .... 100.00

Silver, American, Ewer, Ball, Black & Co., 1860
See Page 463

Silver, American, Flagon, Sharp, Bailey & Co., C.1850
See Page 463

Silver, American, Fork, Olive, Farr & Thompson, Coin	5.00
Silver, American, Fork, Olive, R.Ferris, Coin, 6	55.00
Silver, American, Fork, Oval Thread, Platt & Bros., C.1825, Coin, 10	75.00
Silver, American, Fork, Serving, Farrington & Hunnewell, C.1850, Coin	30.00
Silver, American, Fork, Serving, Openwork, Grecian Head In Medallion, Coin	12.00
Silver, American, Fork, Twisted Shaft, Engraved Top, Name, C.1815, Coin, 5	6.50
Silver, American, Fork, Victorian Pattern, O.S.Jennings, N.Y.C., Coin, 12	85.00
Silver, American, Fork, Wood & Hughes, N.Y., C.1845, Coin, 5	37.50
Silver, American, Goblet, William Forbes, N.Y., C.1850, Bell Shape, Repousse	160.00
Silver, American, Jug, Hot Water, Scroll Handle, Harris & Stanwood, C.1835	140.00
Silver, American, Kettle On Lampstand, Hot Water, John C.Moore, N.Y., C.1850	525.00
Silver, American, Knife, Butter, Brinsmaid's, Burlington, C.1830, Coin	9.95
Silver, American, Knife, Butter, C.Hervey, C.1850, Coin	9.95
Silver, American, Knife, Cheese, Engraved Blade, Wood & Hughes, Coin	12.75
Silver, American, Knife, Fruit, Pocket, Mark F, Eagle Touchmark, Coin	7.95
Silver, American, Ladle, Beaded Oval End, William Gale & Son, N.Y.C., Coin	80.00
Silver, American, Ladle, Chased Design, Dexter & Haskins, Coin	125.00
Silver, American, Ladle, Coffin Handle, T.Sargeant, Mass., 1798-1800, Coin	35.00
Silver, American, Ladle, Fiddle End, Samuel M.Hopper, Phila., Coin	75.00
Silver, American, Ladle, Gravy, Beaded Oval, W.Gale & Son, N.Y.C., Marked	22.00
Silver, American, Ladle, Gravy, Coffin Corner, Curtis, 6 1/2 In.Long, Coin	35.00
Silver, American, Ladle, Gravy, Engraved Newell Harding, Boston, Gold Wash	35.00
Silver, American, Ladle, Gravy, Olive, Mulford & Wendell, Albany, N.Y., Coin	25.00
Silver, American, Ladle, Mayonnaise, I.C.H.Huntington, 1830-35, 6 1/4 In.	15.00
Silver, American, Ladle, Mustard, William F.Ladd, N.Y., C.1830, Coin	6.95
Silver, American, Ladle, Olive, Gilbert, N.Y.C., Shell Bowl, Coin	80.00
Silver, American, Ladle, Olive, Platt & Brother, N.Y.C., Fluted Bowl, Coin	50.00
Silver, American, Ladle, R.& W.Wilson, Phila., Coin	95.00
Silver, American, Ladle, Raised Border Design, Albert Coles, 13 In.Long	90.00
Silver, American, Ladle, Sauce, Engraved, Abraham Gerritze Forbes, N.Y., 1790	125.00
Silver, American, Ladle, Sauce, Fiddle, G.Baker, Providence, Coin	25.00
Silver, American, Ladle, Sauce, Fiddle, L.B.Candee & Co., Woodbury, Conn.	25.00
Silver, American, Ladle, Sauce, Fiddle, Munger & Pratt, Ithaca, N.Y., Coin	20.00
Silver, American, Ladle, Sauce, Fiddle, Willard & Hawley, Syracuse, N.Y.	25.00
Silver, American, Ladle, Sauce, Francis Curtis, Woodbury, Conn., Coin	25.00
Silver, American, Ladle, Soup, Coffin End, Henry Farnam, Boston, C.1800	110.00
Silver, American, Ladle, Soup, Engraved Crest, William W.Gilbert, N.Y., C.1770	450.00
Silver, American, Ladle, Soup, Joseph Anthony, Jr., Phila., C.1780	250.00
Silver, American, Ladle, Thread Pattern, N.W.Galt & Bro., C.1830, 7 In.	24.75
Silver, American, Ladle, Two Lip Bowl, Beaded Decor., E.A.Tyler, 11 1/2 In.	75.00

Silver, American, Mug, Medallions, Albert Coles, N.Y., C.1840	98.00
Silver, American, Mug, Octagonal, Engraved, Francis W.Cooper, N.Y., C.1840	120.00
Silver, American, Pitcher, Covered, Embossed Foliage, Wood & Hughes, C.1847	220.00
Silver, American, Pitcher, Helmet Form, Engraved, Peter L.Krider, Phila., 1870	150.00
Silver, American, Pitcher, Milk, Covered, George Sharp For Bailey & Co.	300.00
Silver, American, Pitcher, Water, Baluster, Repousse, Peter L.Krider, C.1870	200.00
Silver, American, Pitcher, Water, Engraved, Ball, Tompkins & Black, C.1850	500.00
Silver, American, Pitcher, Water, San Francisco, C.1860, Inverted Pear Shape	300.00
Silver, American, Pitcher, Water, The Gorham Co., New York, Vase Shape	180.00
Silver, American, Porringer, Cover, 19th Century, Keyhole Handle, Dated 1856	70.00
Silver, American, Salt Cellar, William Gale & Son, N.Y., C.1850, Pair	100.00
Silver, American, Salt, S.Kirk & Son, Footed, Ribbed Band At Top & Base	35.00
Silver, American, Salver, Chased, Edward Lownes, Phila., C.1830	200.00
Silver, American, Salver, Circular, Ball, Tompkins & Black, N.Y., C.1840	250.00
Silver, American, Server, Pie, Engraved, Farrington & Hunnewell, Boston, Coin	45.00
Silver, American, Server, Pie, Engraved, Marked Coin	35.00
Silver, American, Server, Pie, Engraved, O.S.Jennings, N.Y.C., Pierced, Coin	45.00
Silver, American, Server, Pie, Engraved, Sphinx, Krider & Biddle, Phila., Coin	35.00
Silver, American, Server, Pie, Olive, William Wise, Brooklyn, Engraved, Coin	35.00
Silver, American, Sifter, Jones, Low, Ball, Boston, 1839, 7 In.Long, Coin	38.00
Silver, American, Snuffbox, Albert Cole, N.Y., C.1860, Rectangular, Dated 1869	60.00
Silver, American, Spoon, Basket Of Flowers, Appollos Moore, Albany, N.Y., 6	175.00
Silver, American, Spoon, Basket Of Flowers, F.S.In Rectangle, Lion Head, 6	350.00
Silver, American, Spoon, Basket Of Flowers, Peter P.Hayes, N.Y., Coin, 3	175.00
Silver, American, Spoon, Bright Cut, A.& C.Brandt, Phila., Coin, Pair	45.00
Silver, American, Spoon, Bright Cut, Bernard Wenman, N.Y.C., Coin .... 20.00 To	25.00
Silver, American, Spoon, Bright Cut, John Boutier, N.Y.C., Coin	30.00
Silver, American, Spoon, Bright Cut, John David, Jr., Phila., Coin	35.00
Silver, American, Spoon, Bright Cut, John Sayre, N.Y.C., & Cohoes, N.Y., Coin	25.00
Silver, American, Spoon, Bright Cut, Joseph Moulton, Newburyport, Mass., 5	175.00
Silver, American, Spoon, Bright Cut, Joseph Shoemaker, Phila., Coin	30.00
Silver, American, Spoon, Bright Cut, Stephen Williams, Providence, Coin	45.00
Silver, American, Spoon, Bright Cut, Tunis D.Dubois, N.Y., Coin	55.00
Silver, American, Spoon, Bright Cut, William V.Brady, N.Y.C., Coin	15.00
Silver, American, Spoon, Bright Cut, Z.Owen, Phila., Coin.3	80.00
Silver, American, Spoon, Burr Co., Coin	4.50
Silver, American, Spoon, Coffee, N.Freeborn, Newport, R.I., 1810, Set Of 6	55.00
Silver, American, Spoon, Coffin End, Shephard & Boyd, Albany, N.Y., Coin	35.00
Silver, American, Spoon, Coffin End, William Roe, Albany, Kingston & Troy, 6	100.00
Silver, American, Spoon, Coffin, Plain, I.R.In Shaped Cartouche, Coin	30.00
Silver, American, Spoon, Coffin, Plain, Juday Hart, Norwich, Conn., Coin	25.00
Silver, American, Spoon, Coffin, Plain, Samuel Babcock, Middletown & Saybrook	35.00
Silver, American, Spoon, Coffin, William Simes, Portsmouth, N.H., Coin	10.00
Silver, American, Spoon, Crest On Handle, Dated 1866, N.Harding & Co., 11	55.00
Silver, American, Spoon, D.Smith, Phila., 18th Century, Coin	9.00
Silver, American, Spoon, Dessert, Coffin End, John Bedford, Fishkill, N.Y.	35.00
Silver, American, Spoon, Dessert, Fiddle & Shell, Cleveland & Post, Conn., 5	95.00
Silver, American, Spoon, Dessert, Fiddle & Shell, Frederick Marquand, 1822, 2	75.00
Silver, American, Spoon, Dessert, Fiddle End, A.Hewes, Jr., Boston, Coin	10.00
Silver, American, Spoon, Dessert, Fiddle End, B.Pitman, Providence, Coin, 6	75.00
Silver, American, Spoon, Dessert, Fiddle End, R.& W.Wilson, Phila., Coin	10.00
Silver, American, Spoon, Dessert, Fiddle End, R.M.Bailey, Vermont, Coin	18.00
Silver, American, Spoon, Dessert, Fiddle End, Wheeler & Son, Coin, Pair	25.00
Silver, American, Spoon, Dessert, Fiddle Thread, S.Hoyt & Co., N.Y., Coin	20.00
Silver, American, Spoon, Dessert, Fiddle, Plain, J.Hall, Albany, N.Y., Coin	10.00
Silver, American, Spoon, Dessert, Fiddle, Plain, J.Moulton, Newburyport, Mass.	18.00
Silver, American, Spoon, Dessert, Fiddle, Plain, Thomson & Evans, Coin	10.00
Silver, American, Spoon, Dessert, Oval End, William Gilbert, N.Y.C., Coin	75.00
Silver, American, Spoon, Eagle Touchmark, Coin	3.95
Silver, American, Spoon, Engraved C.C.M., Rattail Back, Akerly & Briggs, 12	59.75
Silver, American, Spoon, Engraved C.C.M., Squire & Brothers, C.1846, Coin, 6	29.75
Silver, American, Spoon, Engraved C.S.M., Bacon, John Coney, C.1700, Coin	1000.00
Silver, American, Spoon, Engraved, Farrington & Hunnewell, Boston, Coin, 6	85.00
Silver, American, Spoon, Fiddle End, A.Sanborn, Lowell, Mass., Coin	10.00
Silver, American, Spoon, Fiddle End, D.K.Benjamin, Coin	10.00
Silver, American, Spoon, Fiddle End, J.E.Parker, Shell Back, Coin, Pair	25.00

Silver, American, Spoon, Fiddle End, J.Hollister, Oswego, N.Y., Coin 18.00
Silver, American, Spoon, Fiddle End, W.M.Root, Pittsfield, Coin 10.00
Silver, American, Spoon, Fiddle Thread, Bailey & Co., Phila., 6 .... 70.00 To 75.00
Silver, American, Spoon, Fiddle Thread, Brown & Anderson, N.C., Dated 1852, 6 .... 75.00
Silver, American, Spoon, Fiddle Thread, Coin, 8 .... 75.00
Silver, American, Spoon, Fiddle Thread, F.A.& Co., Galveston, Texas, Coin 35.00
Silver, American, Spoon, Fiddle Thread, Jones, Ball & Poor, Boston, Coin, 6 .... 65.00
Silver, American, Spoon, Fiddle Thread, W.S.Smith, Coin, 6 .... 65.00
Silver, American, Spoon, Fiddle Thread, William Wise, Brooklyn, Coin 6.00
Silver, American, Spoon, Fiddle Thread, Wood & Hughes, N.Y.C., Coin, 8 .... 75.00
Silver, American, Spoon, Fiddle, Abraham Fellows, Troy, N.Y., Coin 25.00
Silver, American, Spoon, Fiddle, Albert Coles, N.Y.C., Coin 5.00
Silver, American, Spoon, Fiddle, B.B.Wood, Boston, Coin, 4 .... 20.00
Silver, American, Spoon, Fiddle, B.K.Twambly, Coin, Pair 10.00
Silver, American, Spoon, Fiddle, Bailey & Bowers, Phila., Coin, 6 .... 30.00
Silver, American, Spoon, Fiddle, Benoni B.Forman, Albany & Troy, N.Y., Coin, 4 .... 35.00
Silver, American, Spoon, Fiddle, Farrington & Hunnewell, Boston, Coin 5.00
Silver, American, Spoon, Fiddle, H.W.Bessac, Hudson, N.Y., Coin 10.00
Silver, American, Spoon, Fiddle, Hotchkiss & Schreuder, Syracuse, N.Y., Coin, 2 .... 10.00
Silver, American, Spoon, Fiddle, I.Reed & Son, Phila., Coin, 6 .... 40.00
Silver, American, Spoon, Fiddle, John Bedford, Fishkill, N.Y., Coin, Pair 60.00
Silver, American, Spoon, Fiddle, Joseph Moulton, Newburyport, Mass., Coin 25.00
Silver, American, Spoon, Fiddle, Lowell & Senter, Portland, Me., Coin, Pair 25.00
Silver, American, Spoon, Fiddle, Marked H & S Coin 6.00
Silver, American, Spoon, Fiddle, Marked Utica, Coin 8.00
Silver, American, Spoon, Fiddle, N.Cornwell, Danbury, Conn., Coin 35.00
Silver, American, Spoon, Fiddle, Newell Matson, Oswego, N.Y., Coin 5.00
Silver, American, Spoon, Fiddle, Palmer & Batchelder, Boston, Coin, 2 .... 10.00
Silver, American, Spoon, Fiddle, Plain, A.Rasch & Co., Phila., Coin 18.00
Silver, American, Spoon, Fiddle, Plain, Beers & Pond, Coin, 6 .... 27.50
Silver, American, Spoon, Fiddle, Plain, Clark, Coin 6.00
Silver, American, Spoon, Fiddle, Plain, Colin V.G.Forbes, N.Y.C., Coin.3 .... 25.00
Silver, American, Spoon, Fiddle, Plain, Erastus Cook, Rochester, N.Y., Pair 35.00
Silver, American, Spoon, Fiddle, Plain, G.W.Byll, Farmington, Conn., Coin, 3 .... 18.00
Silver, American, Spoon, Fiddle, Plain, George B.Appleton, Salem, Mass., Coin 15.00
Silver, American, Spoon, Fiddle, Plain, George W.King, N.Y.C., Shell Back, Pair 25.00
Silver, American, Spoon, Fiddle, Plain, H.Goodwin, Hartford, Conn., Coin, 3 .... 15.00
Silver, American, Spoon, Fiddle, Plain, H.S.Bradley, Utica, N.Y., Coin, 4 .... 25.00
Silver, American, Spoon, Fiddle, Plain, Hall & Hewson, Albany, N.Y., Coin 4.50
Silver, American, Spoon, Fiddle, Plain, Henry B.Mumford, Providence, Coin 15.00
Silver, American, Spoon, Fiddle, Plain, Henry Salisbury, N.Y.C., Coin 12.50
Silver, American, Spoon, Fiddle, Plain, J.M.Barrows, Tolland, Conn., Coin 15.00
Silver, American, Spoon, Fiddle, Plain, J.R.Hobby, N.Y., Coin 5.00
Silver, American, Spoon, Fiddle, Plain, Jaccard & Co., St.Louis, Coin 15.00
Silver, American, Spoon, Fiddle, Plain, James M.Ford, Coin, Pair 30.00
Silver, American, Spoon, Fiddle, Plain, John Beck, Phila., Coin, 6 .... 75.00
Silver, American, Spoon, Fiddle, Plain, Joseph Moulton Iv, Newburyport, Mass. 20.00
Silver, American, Spoon, Fiddle, Plain, L.Odell, N.Y.C., Shell Back, Coin 10.00
Silver, American, Spoon, Fiddle, Plain, L.W.Clark, Utica, N.Y., Coin, 6 .... 30.00
Silver, American, Spoon, Fiddle, Plain, Palmer & Batchelder, Boston, Coin, 2 .... 24.00
Silver, American, Spoon, Fiddle, Plain, R.& W.Wilson, Phila., Coin 12.00
Silver, American, Spoon, Fiddle, Plain, R.H.Bailey, Vermont, Coin 15.00
Silver, American, Spoon, Fiddle, Plain, R.M.Bailey, Vermont, Coin 18.00
Silver, American, Spoon, Fiddle, Plain, Rogers & Cole, Coin, 4 .... 20.00
Silver, American, Spoon, Fiddle, Plain, Seitz, Coin, Pair 35.00
Silver, American, Spoon, Fiddle, Plain, Theosophilus Bradbury Ii, Mass.2 .... 16.00
Silver, American, Spoon, Fiddle, Plain, Thomas Fletcher & Sidney Gardiner 6.00
Silver, American, Spoon, Fiddle, Plain, W.Kimball, Coin, 4 .... 20.00
Silver, American, Spoon, Fiddle, Plain, W.Thomson, N.Y., Coin, 6 .... 60.00
Silver, American, Spoon, Fiddle, Plain, William Simes, Portsmouth, N.H., Pair 15.00
Silver, American, Spoon, Fiddle, Pseudo Hallmarks, Star, S.Eagle, Coin 5.00
Silver, American, Spoon, Fiddle, Samuel Brown, N.Y., Coin 35.00
Silver, American, Spoon, Fiddle, R.& W.Wilson, Phila., Coin, 5 .... 25.00
Silver, American, Spoon, Fiddle, Richards & Williamson, Phila., Coin, Piar 25.00
Silver, American, Spoon, Fiddle, S.Richard, Phila., Coin, Pair 20.00
Silver, American, Spoon, Fiddle, W.M.Root, Pittsfield, Dated 1862, Coin, 3 .... 16.00

Silver, American, Spoon, Fiddle, W.Pitkin, E.Hartford, Conn., Coin, 5 .... 25.00
Silver, American, Spoon, Geo.Baker, Providence, R.I., 1811, Coin, Pair 18.00
Silver, American, Spoon, Henry B.Stanwood, Initials, C.1835, Coin 3.95
Silver, American, Spoon, Initial, Henry B.Stanwood & Co., C.1850, Coin 3.95
Silver, American, Spoon, J.Moulton The 4th, Mass., Coin 10.00
Silver, American, Spoon, Jelly, Fiddleback, Leonard & Hall, Marked Coin 9.50
Silver, American, Spoon, Jones, Ball & Co., Initials, C.1850, Coin, 5 .... 24.75
Silver, American, Spoon, K & L, Coin 4.50
Silver, American, Spoon, King's, William B.North, New Haven & N.Y., Coin, Pair 35.00
Silver, American, Spoon, Kirkham, Initials Kew, Coin 4.75
Silver, American, Spoon, M.Root & Bros., Engraved, C.1850, Coin 3.95
Silver, American, Spoon, Marked C.Thayer, Coin, 4 .... 20.00
Silver, American, Spoon, Marked Coin-N.G.Wood, Boston, 3 .... 17.00
Silver, American, Spoon, Master Salt, Vancott Polhamus, Coin 5.50
Silver, American, Spoon, Master Salt, William F.Ladd, N.Y., C.1830, Coin 5.95
Silver, American, Spoon, Mustard, Fiddle Thread, F.A.Co., Galveston, Texas 18.00
Silver, American, Spoon, Mustard, Fiddle Thread, John B.Ginocchio, N.U.C. 12.50
Silver, American, Spoon, Mustard, Fiddle, Ginocchio, N.Y.C., Coin 10.00
Silver, American, Spoon, Mustard, Fiddle, Oliver B.Cooley, Utica, N.Y., Coin 15.00
Silver, American, Spoon, N.Harding, Boston, 1796-1862, Coin 5.00
Silver, American, Spoon, Olive, N.E.Crittenden, Cleveland, Ohio, Coin 5.00
Silver, American, Spoon, Olive, N.Harding & Co., Boston, Coin, 4 .... 25.00
Silver, American, Spoon, Olive, S.Hoyt & Co., N.Y.C., Coin 10.00
Silver, American, Spoon, Oval End, Christian Wiltberger, Phila., Coin 20.00
Silver, American, Spoon, Oval End, John Martin, Phila., Coin, 3 .... 65.00
Silver, American, Spoon, Oval End, Joseph Antgony, Jr., Phila., Coin, Pair 75.00
Silver, American, Spoon, Oval End, Thomas Purse, Winchester, Va., & Baltimore 50.00
Silver, American, Spoon, Oval End, William Gilbert, N.Y.C., Coin 35.00
Silver, American, Spoon, Oval Thread, B.D.Haskell, Boston, Coin, 6 .... 45.00
Silver, American, Spoon, Oval Thread, Bigelow & Kennard, Boston, Coin, Pair 25.00
Silver, American, Spoon, Oval Thread, Coin, 7 .... 40.00
Silver, American, Spoon, Oval Thread, P.L.Taylor, Brooklyn, Coin 8.00
Silver, American, Spoon, Pitkin, Initials Aam, Coin 4.75
Silver, American, Spoon, Plain Handle, Nathan Hobbs, C.1820, Coin, 4 .... 20.00
Silver, American, Spoon, Pointed End, Abner Reeder, Phila.& Trenton, Coin, 5 .... 135.00
Silver, American, Spoon, Pointed End, D.Osborn, Coin 25.00
Silver, American, Spoon, Pointed End, Daniel Rogers, Newport, R.I., Coin 25.00
Silver, American, Spoon, Pointed End, John Myers, Phila., Coin, 2 .... 75.00
Silver, American, Spoon, Pointed End, John Vernon, N.Y., Coin 60.00
Silver, American, Spoon, Pointed End, William Simes, Portsmouth, N.H., Coin 20.00
Silver, American, Spoon, Pointed End, William Whiting, Norwich, Conn., Coin 65.00
Silver, American, Spoon, Rattail, Marked J.Budd, Coin 5.00
Silver, American, Spoon, Salt, Fiddle, Round Bowl, J.B.Jones & Co., Boston 8.00
Silver, American, Spoon, Salt, Fiddle, Round Bowl, O.E, Sibley, Buffalo, Coin 8.00
Silver, American, Spoon, Salt, Fiddle, Round Bowl, Palmer & Batchelder, Boston 8.00
Silver, American, Spoon, Salt, Fiddle, Round Bowl, Thomas Stebbins, N.Y., Coin 8.00
Silver, American, Spoon, Salt, Master, Leonard & Hall, Mark Coin 8.50
Silver, American, Spoon, Serving, Beasom & Read, M.H., Coin 12.50
Silver, American, Spoon, Serving, C.Maynard, Worcester, Coin 18.00
Silver, American, Spoon, Serving, Geo.Baker, Providence, R.I., 1811, Pair 32.00
Silver, American, Spoon, Serving, Gooding Of Boston, 1833 .... 12.50
Silver, American, Spoon, Serving, Medallion, Albert Coles, N.Y.C., Pierced 65.00
Silver, American, Spoon, Serving, Olive, J.E.Caldwell & Co., Phila., Shell 25.00
Silver, American, Spoon, Serving, Pierced Shell Shape Bowl, John & James Cox 24.75
Silver, American, Spoon, Serving, Shovel Shape, Fiddle, Ball, Black, & Co. 30.00
Silver, American, Spoon, Serving, Wood & Hughes, N.Y.C., Marked Sterling 22.50
Silver, American, Spoon, Sheaf Of Wheat, Bernard Wenman, N.Y.C..Coin, 6 .... 175.00
Silver, American, Spoon, Sheaf Of Wheat, Colton & Collins, N.Y.C., Coin, 3 .... 85.00
Silver, American, Spoon, Soup, Marked M.Harding, Coin 3.00
Silver, American, Spoon, Stamped Pure Coin, Engraved Monogram 4.75
Silver, American, Spoon, Stebbins, Coin 4.75
Silver, American, Spoon, Sugar, A.Smiley, C.1850, Initials, Coin 9.95
Silver, American, Spoon, Sugar, Engraved W.F., A.Smiley & Co., Boston, Coin 9.95
Silver, American, Spoon, Thread & Leaf, Albert Coles, N.Y.C., 6 .... 40.00 To 65.00
Silver, American, Spoon, Twist Stem, E.& D Kinsey, Cincinnati, Ohio, Coin 10.00
Silver, American, Spoon, Twist Stem, R.& W.Wilson, Phila., Coin, 3 .... 35.00

Silver, American, Spreader, Engraved, Farrington & Hunnewell, Boston, Coin	10.00
Silver, American, Spreader, Olive With Medallion, Albert Coles, N.Y.C., Coin	15.00
Silver, American, Spreader, Olive, George B.Appleton, Salem, Mass., Coin	10.00
Silver, American, Spreader, Olive, R.& W.Wilson, Phila., Engraved Blade, Coin	18.00
Silver, American, Spreader, Thread & Leaf, Albert Coles, N.Y.C., Coin, 2	24.00
Silver, American, Spoon, Trefid, Engraved C.S.M., Bacon, John Coney, C.1700	1000.00
Silver, American, Stand, Decanter, Samuel Kirk, Baltimore, 1830-46, 3 Bottles	400.00
Silver, American, Sugar & Creamer, Covered Bowl, Oval, Isaac Hutton, C.1810	350.00
Silver, American, Sugar & Creamer, Covered, Abraham Dubois, Phila., C.1790	1700.00
Silver, American, Sugar & Creamer, Covered, Chased, Pardon Miller, R.I., 1810	200.00
Silver, American, Sugar & Creamer, Covered, Gale, Wood & Hughes, N.Y., C.1830	375.00
Silver, American, Sugar & Creamer, Covered, H.Mahler, N.C., C.1840, Vase Shape	300.00
Silver, American, Sugar Shell, Beaded Olive, A.C.Benedict, N.Y.C., Coin	12.50
Silver, American, Sugar Shell, Engraved Name, Farrington & Hunnewell, C.1835	10.95
Silver, American, Sugar Shell, Farrington & Hunnewell, Boston, C.1835, Coin	10.95
Silver, American, Sugar Shell, Palmer & Batchelder, Mark M, Coin	12.00
Silver, American, Sugar Shell, Plain, Engraved M., Palmer & Batchelder, Coin	12.00
Silver, American, Sugar Shell, S.& F., N.Y., Pear Shape, Applied Flowers, Coin	125.00
Silver, American, Sugar, Covered, John Sayre, N.Y., 1810 *Illus*	400.00
Silver, American, Sugar, Covered, Octagonal, Engraved, Harvey Lewis, C.1810	475.00
Silver, American, Sugar, Covered, Oval Boat Shape, Isaac Hutton, N.Y., C.1795	800.00
Silver, American, Sugar, Covered, Oval, 19th Century, Federal Style	170.00
Silver, American, Sugar, Covered, Pedestal, Engraved, Curry & Preston, C.1830	150.00
Silver, American, Tablespoon, Basket Of Flowers, Abraham Fellows, 1826, Coin	50.00
Silver, American, Tablespoon, Engraved Italic H.H., Paul Revere, C.1795	900.00
Silver, American, Tablespoon, Henry & Edward Kelley, Nantucket Island, Mass.	9.95
Silver, American, Tablespoon, Joseph Richardson, Philadelphia, 1711-1784	45.00
Silver, American, Tablespoon, Marked Jn.B.Mcfadden, C.1840, Coin	15.00
Silver, American, Tablespoon, Plain Turn Down Handle, N.Harding, 1830, Coin	9.50
Silver, American, Tablespoon, Sheaf Of Wheat, Fiddle, Samuel C.Brown, C.1825	60.00
Silver, American, Tankard, Barrel, Monogram, S Scroll Handle, John Burt, 1740	5000.00
Silver, American, Tankard, Flat Top, S Scroll Handle, Thauvet Besley, C.1730	7500.00
Silver, American, Tea & Coffee Set, Engraved, Tiffany & Co., 7 Piece	2000.00
Silver, American, Tea & Coffee Set, John Mcmullin, Phila., C.1805, 5 Piece	3600.00
Silver, American, Tea & Coffee Set, Nicholas J.Bogert, C.1819, 4 Piece	1800.00
Silver, American, Tea Caddy, Rectangular, Applied Floral, Tiffany & Co., 1880	175.00
Silver, American, Tea Set, Charles L.Boehme, Baltimore, 1774-1868, 3 Piece	1800.00
Silver, American, Tea Set, Eoff & Howell, N.Y., 1805, 4 Piece, Monogram Ew	1800.00
Silver, American, Tea Set, R.& W.Wilson, Philadelphia, C.1830, 5 Piece	1000.00
Silver, American, Tea Set, S.Kirk & Son, Co., Baltimore, 1903-24, 5 Piece	1700.00
Silver, American, Tea Set, Tapered Form, William Adams, N.Y., C.1830, 4 Piece	400.00
Silver, American, Tea Set, William Adams, N.Y., Applied Leaf Banding, 3 Piece	975.00
Silver, American, Teakettle, On Lampstand, N.Y., C.1840, Inverted Pear Shape	425.00
Silver, American, Teapot & Coffeepot, Applied Shields, The Gorham Co., 1870	300.00
Silver, American, Teapot & Mug, Child's, Dated 1847, Pedestal	120.00
Silver, American, Teapot & Sugar, Covered, Bulbous, Engraved, Dated 1832	180.00
Silver, American, Teapot, Bulbous Oblong, Pedestal, Leaves & Palmettes, 1825	170.00
Silver, American, Teapot, Bulbous, Abijah B.Warden, Phila., C.1840	135.00
Silver, American, Teapot, Edward Rockwell, N.Y., C.1810 *Illus*	350.00
Silver, American, Teapot, Inverted Pear Shape, Pedestal, S.Hildeburn, C.1825	175.00
Silver, American, Teapot, John & Peter Targee, N.Y., Engraved Cartouche	550.00
Silver, American, Teapot, Robert Monteith, Baltimore, Engraved Floral Band	950.00
Silver, American, Teapot, S.Kirk & Son, Baltimore, 1903-24, Repousse	500.00
Silver, American, Teapot, Scrolling Foliage, Howard & Co., New York, C.1900	90.00
Silver, American, Teaspoon, A.Cutler, Boston, 1842, Coin	5.00
Silver, American, Teaspoon, Coffin End, Engraved, David Smith, N.Y., C.1810, 6	40.00
Silver, American, Teaspoon, Feather Edges, Birds, John Le Telier, C.1780, 4	40.00
Silver, American, Teaspoon, Finless Fiddle Pattern, Nathaniel Vernon, 1820, 6	130.00
Silver, American, Teaspoon, M.M.Fredericks, Marked Coin, 12	75.00
Silver, American, Teaspoon, Pointed End, Cut Ovals, Joseph Dubois, C.1790, 6	130.00
Silver, American, Tongs, Aaron Dikeman, N.Y., Round Bowl, Coin	20.00
Silver, American, Tongs, J.E.Caldwell, C.1840, 5 In., Coin	18.00
Silver, American, Tongs, Mulford & Wendell Co., Pierced Shell Bowl, Coin	60.00
Silver, American, Tongs, N.Harding, Boston, Claw End, Coin	25.00
Silver, American, Tongs, Squire & Brother, N.Y.C., Shell Bowl, Coin	15.00
Silver, American, Tongs, Sugar, Marked I.P., C.1790, Sunbursts On Grips	70.00

Silver, American, Sugar, Covered,
John Sayre, N.Y., 1810
See Page 468

Silver, American, Teapot,
Edward Rockwell, N.Y., C.1810
See Page 468

Silver, **American**, Tray, Tea, Oval, Beaded Border, Handles, The Gorham Co., 1860 ...... 850.00
Silver, **American**, Tongs, Sugar, T.Sargeant, Mass., C.1750, Bright Cut, Coin 35.00
Silver, **American**, Tray, Tea, Oval, Engraved, Tiffany & Co., C.1910 .... 500.00
Silver, **American**, Tureen, Sauce, Cover, Stamped Sterling, Boston, 1867, Pair 475.00
Silver, **American**, Tureen, Soup, A.Rogers, Boston, C.1867, 15 1/2 In.Long 750.00
Silver, **American**, Tureen, Soup, A.Rogers, Boston, C.1867, 16 1/2 In.Long 600.00
Silver, **American**, Urn, Coffee, Presentation From Monroe To Howe, C.1808 .... 2500.00
Silver, **American**, Urn, Hot Water, Vase Shape, Andrew E.Warner, Jr., C.1870 .... 800.00
Silver, **American**, Urn, Hot Water, W.Gale & Son, C.1855 .... *Illus* 500.00
Silver, **American**, Urn, Tea, S.Kirk & Son, Baltimore, C.1850, Repousse 950.00
Silver, **American**, Waiter, Engraved, Gale & Hughes, N.Y., C.1850, Pair 200.00
Silver, **American**, Waiter, Jones, Ball & Co., Boston, C.1850, Oval, Engraved 140.00
Silver, **American**, Wine Cooler, Tiffany, C.1865, Pair .... *Illus* 1300.00
Silver, **Australian**, Egg, Emu, Carved, C.1870 .... *Illus* 300.00
Silver, **Chinese**, Basket, Mesh, Panels, Cloisonne Medallion, Enameled Handle 125.00

Coin Silver was made in America before 1860. Coin Silver was made
from melted currency and usually has a silver content of about 800 or 900 parts
silver. Sterling Silver is 925 parts silver with 75 parts copper. Most
coin silver spoons are thin, handmade pieces.
Silver, **Coin**, see also Silver, American
Silver, **Coin**, Case, Calling Card, Engraved, Circa 1830 .... 12.75
Silver, **Coin**, Cup, Marked S.F., Coin, Engraved Cartouche, 2 Oz. 50.00
Silver, **Coin**, Cup, Repousse Flowers, Leaves & Scrolls, Pear-Shaped, 4 Oz. 95.00
Silver, **Coin**, Fork, Serving, Openwork, Grecian Head In Medallion 12.00
Silver, **Coin**, Fork, Twisted Shaft, Engraved Top, Name, Circa 1815, Set Of 5 .... 6.50
Silver, **Coin**, Knife, Pocket, Fruit, Mark F, Eagle Touchmark 7.95
Silver, **Coin**, Ladle, Sauce, Fiddle Thread, Marked F T & S In Rectangles 18.00
Silver, **Coin**, Ladle, Soup, Leaf, Flower, Engraved, Oval Bowl, 4 X 12 In. 65.00
Silver, **Coin**, Server, Pie, Engraved, Marked Coin 35.00
Silver, **Coin**, Spectacle Frames, American, Box 10.00
Silver, **Coin**, Spoon, Dessert, Rounded Handle, B Engraved, Set Of 6 .... 55.00
Silver, **Coin**, Spoon, Fiddle & Shell, Chinese Export, C.G.In Rectangle 60.00
Silver, **Coin**, Spoon, Master Salt, 'jennie, ' England 8.50
Silver, **Coin**, Spoon, Salt, Fiddle 8.00
Silver, **Coin**, Spoon, Salt, Fiddle, Pseudo Hallmark, D, Crown, Pair 15.00
Silver, **Coin**, Spoon, Salt, Fiddle, Round Bowl, B.& M M.Swan 8.00
Silver, **Coin**, Spoon, Serving, Fluted, Scalloped, Gold Wash Bowl, Olive Leaves 30.00
Silver, **Coin**, Spreader, Fiddle & Shell, Chinese Export, Pseudo Hallmarks 70.00
Silver, **Coin**, Tablespoon, Initials J.G.A.S., Marked, Set Of 5 .... 50.00
Silver, **Coin**, Tablespoon, King Pattern, By J.&i.C. & C.1825 To 1835 .... 12.75
Silver, **Coin**, Tea Set, Engraved Butterfly, Squatty, Round, C.1870 .... 300.00

Silver, Coin, Tongs, Claw Ends	15.00
Silver, Coin, Tongs, Shell Ends, Circa 1830	22.00
Silver, Continental, Beaker, Parcel Gilt, Cylindrical, Engraved, C.1600	175.00
Silver, Continental, Figurine, Pheasant, Hinged Wings, Standing, C.1900, Pair	100.00
Silver, Continental, Mug, Three Ring Band At Top, Etched M Felipa Mol G	90.00
Silver, Continental, Nef, Late 19th Century, 25 In.High .... *Illus*	1050.00

Silver, American, Urn,
Hot Water, W.Gale & Son, C.1855
See Page 469

Silver, American,
Wine Cooler, Tiffany, C.1865, Pair
See Page 469

Silver, Australian,
Egg Emu, Carved, C.1870
See Page 469

Silver, Continental,
Nef, Late 19th Century, 25 In.High

Silver, Dutch, Basket, Cake, Pierced, Engraved, Ring Handles, 1903	170.00
Silver, Dutch, Cup, Covered, Gilt, Standing, Fursterhaupt Dammerval, 1840	1000.00
Silver, Dutch, Sconce, Wall, S Scroll Branches Form, C.1870, Pair	240.00
Silver, English, Basket, Sweetmeat, George III, Langford & Sebille, 1763	170.00
Silver, English, Basket, Sweetmeat, George III, Michael Plummer, 1796	150.00
Silver, English, Basket, Sweetmeat, London, 1893, Boat Shape, Pair	125.00

Silver, English, Biggin, Coffee, George III, William Bateman, 1810 .... 550.00
Silver, English, Bowl, Covered, Thomas Glaswin, London, 1719, Monogram A 325.00
Silver, English, Box, Thomas Henning, London, 1744, Raised March Flowers 250.00
Silver, English, Butter Shell, George II, Crests, Edward Aldridge, 1744, Pair 400.00
Silver, English, Butter Shell, George III, Crest, Burrage Davenport, 1772, 3 .... 335.00
Silver, English, Butter Shell, George III, Engraved Crest, London, 1786, 4 .... 400.00
Silver, English, Butter Shell, George III, John King, London, 1793, Pair 250.00
Silver, English, Butter Shell, Victorian, Robinson, Edkins & Aston, 1838, 3 .... 200.00
Silver, English, Cake Basket, London, 1742 .... *Illus* 1150.00
Silver, English, Can, Engraved Crest, Hallmarks Of Stephen Walsh, Dated 1766 .... 400.00
Silver, English, Candelabra, 2 Light, George III, Style, London, 1903, Pair 500.00
Silver, English, Candlestick, Chamber, George III, J.Edwards, London, 1792 .... 170.00
Silver, English, Candlestick, George III, Adam Style, John Waston, 1778, Pair 450.00
Silver, English, Candlestick, Georgian, John & Thomas Settle, 1796, Pair 325.00
Silver, English, Candlestick, Queen Anne, Jame Gould, London, 1738, Pair 4500.00
Silver, English, Candlestick, Table, George II, James Gould, 1731, Pair 1300.00
Silver, English, Candlestick, Table, 19th Century Style, Crichton & Co., Pair 60.00
Silver, English, Castor, C.1733, Urn Finial, Round Base, Monogrammed I S M 150.00
Silver, English, Castor, George II, Baluster Shape, Samuel Wood, London, 1752 .... 130.00
Silver, English, Castor, George III, Baluster Form, J.Delmester, London, 1766 .... 210.00
Silver, English, Castor, George III, Baluster Form, Pierced, I.D., I.M., 1770 .... 150.00
Silver, English, Castor, George III, Baluster Shape, Hester Bateman, 1780 .... 275.00
Silver, English, Castor, George III, Baluster, Thomas Daniel, London, 1778 .... 110.00
Silver, English, Castor, George III, Engraved, George Giles, 1790 .... 120.00
Silver, English, Castor, George III, R.Peaston, London, 1763, Pair 200.00
Silver, English, Castor, London, 1746 .... *Illus* 225.00
Silver, English, Castor, Pepper, C.1757, Marked I.D.M., Gadroon Band, Pair 225.00
Silver, English, Castor, Samuel Wood, London, 1758, Baluster Form 180.00
Silver, English, Centerpiece, Stand, Benjamin Smith, 1823 .... *Illus* 2700.00
Silver, English, Chamberstick, George III, Crouch & Hannam, 1755 .... 300.00
Silver, English, Coaster, Wine, George III, William Burwash, 1812, Pair 250.00
Silver, English, Coffeepot, Cylindrical, Engraved Armorials, Dated 1705 .... 200.00
Silver, English, Coffeepot, George I, Seth Lofthouse, London, 1716, Octagonal 2300.00
Silver, English, Coffeepot, George II, Armorials, George Boothby, 1742 .... 750.00
Silver, English, Coffeepot, George II, Pear Shape, Crest, Fuller White, 1850 .... 475.00
Silver, English, Coffeepot, George II, Pear Shape, W.C., London, 1761 .... 625.00
Silver, English, Coffeepot, 18th Century Style, Octagonal, Lighthouse Shape 250.00
Silver, English, Creamer, Cow, John Schuppe, London, 1763 .... *Illus* 2600.00
Silver, English, Creamer, George II, Helmet Shape, Edward Wakelin, 1758 .... 180.00
Silver, English, Creamer, George III, Chased, Hester Bateman, London, 1776 .... 250.00
Silver, English, Creamer, George III, Engraved Borders, Loop Handle, 1781 .... 130.00
Silver, English, Creamer, George III, Engraved, Andrew Fogelberg, 1789 .... 70.00
Silver, English, Creamer, George III, Helmet Form, Engraved Vine Collar, 1799 .... 90.00
Silver, English, Creamer, George III, Scroll Handle, Robert Hennell, 1776 .... 90.00
Silver, English, Cup, Caudle, Miniature, William III Style, London, 12 .... 110.00
Silver, English, Cup, George I, 2 Handles, Embossed, Nathaniel Gulliver, 1723 .... 100.00
Silver, English, Cup, George II, 2 Handles, William Shaw & Priest, 1756 .... 170.00
Silver, English, Cup, George III, Bell Shape, Edward Fennell, 1788 .... 90.00
Silver, English, Cup, George Unite, Birmingham, 1876, Single Handle, Embossed 150.00
Silver, English, Cup, Paul Storr, London, 1795, 8 Oz., 2 Handles 625.00
Silver, English, Cup, William IV, Floral, Vines, I.W., London, 1834, Pair 260.00
Silver, English, Cup, 1771, Pair .... *Illus* 325.00
Silver, English, Cup, 1810, 5 In., Pair .... *Illus* 450.00
Silver, English, Dish, Entree, Cover, George III, Crest, Paul Storr, 1810, Pair 825.00
Silver, English, Dish, Entree, George III, Rectangular, Paul Storr, 1803 .... 400.00
Silver, English, Dish, Entree, Paul Storr, 1816 .... *Illus* 2750.00
Silver, English, Dish, Meat, George III, Octagonal, Paul Storr, 1801, Pair 3250.00
Silver, English, Dish, Paul Storr, 1816 .... *Illus* 1600.00
Silver, English, Dish, Strawberry, Georgian, William Tant, London, 1785, Pair 550.00
Silver, English, Egg Cruet, London, 1805 .... *Illus* 350.00
Silver, English, Flatware, Dessert, Victorian, George W.Adams, 1870, 24 Piece 275.00
Silver, English, Fork, Armorial Handles, Samuel Hennel, London, 1812, 12 .... 150.00
Silver, English, Fork, Dinner, Georgian, Wallace & Hayne, London, 1813, 6 .... 50.00
Silver, English, Funnel, Wine, George III, John Emes, London, 1807, Reeded Rim 100.00
Silver, English, Inkstand, George III, Rectangular, William Plummer, 1790 .... 350.00
Silver, English, Inkstand, Treasury Style, Crichton Bros., London 180.00

Silver, English, Cake Basket, London, 1742
See Page 471

Silver, English, Centerpiece,
Stand, Benjamin Smith, 1823
See Page 471

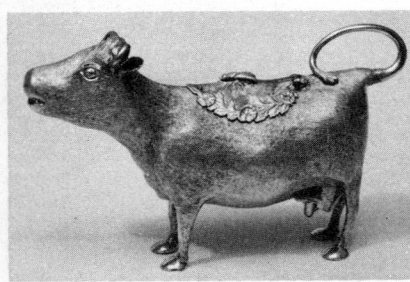

Silver, English, Creamer, Cow,
John Schuppe, London, 1763
See Page 471

Silver, English,
Castor, London, 1746
See Page 471

Silver, English,
Cup, 1771, Pair
See Page 471

Silver, English, Cup,
1810, 5 In., Pair
See Page 471

Silver, English, Dish, Entree,
Paul Storr, 1816
See Page 471

Silver, English, Dish, Paul Storr, 1816
See Page 471

Silver, English,
Egg Cruet, London, 1805
See Page 471

Silver, English, Inkwell, Paul Storr, London, 1808, Scroll Feet, Beaded	800.00
Silver, English, Jug, Coffee, Paul Storr, 1807 .... *Illus*	1600.00
Silver, English, Jug, Coffee, Paul Storr, 1817 .... *Illus*	1100.00
Silver, English, Jug, Hot Water, George III, Cylindrical, London, 1815	130.00
Silver, English, Kettle On Lampstand, Hot Water, Waste Bowl & Strainer, 1812	260.00
Silver, English, Knife Rest, 3 In.Knob End, Pair	10.00

Silver, English, Jug,
Coffee, Paul Storr, 1807

Silver, English, Jug,
Coffee, Paul Storr, 1817

Silver, English, Ladle, Engraved Crest, Peter & Ann Bateman, 1799, 13 1/2 In.	175.00
Silver, English, Ladle, Plain Handle, Peter & William Bateman, 1808, 13 In.	175.00
Silver, English, Ladle, Punch, Georgian, Samuel Hennel, London, 1810	45.00
Silver, English, Ladle, Sauce, Georgian, Thomas Northcote, London, 1784, Pair	55.00
Silver, English, Ladle, Soup, George III, Peter & Ann Bateman, London, 1795	250.00
Silver, English, Ladle, Toddy, Twisted Horn Handle, London, 1807, 10 In.Long	125.00
Silver, English, Mug, George II, Jonathan Swift, London, 1749	200.00
Silver, English, Mug, London, 1762 .... *Illus*	190.00
Silver, English, Mustard Jar, Raised Feet, Cobalt Liner	24.00
Silver, English, Plate, Dinner, George II, Engraved, Edward Wakelin, 1759, 4	650.00

Silver, English, Plate, Dinner, George III, Armorial, Pitts & Preedy, 1792, 12	....	2000.00
Silver, English, Plate, Dinner, III, III, Armorial, Smith & Sharpe, 1785, 12	....	2600.00
Silver, English, Plate, George III, Engraved Crest, Paul Storr, 1808	....	200.00
Silver, English, Plate, George III, Engraved Crest, Wakelin & Garrard, 1796, 4	....	600.00
Silver, English, Plate, Soup, George III, Armorial, Williams Simmons, 1802, 12	....	2000.00
Silver, English, Plate, Soup, George III, Crests, Wakelin & Taylor, 1788, Pair	....	190.00
Silver, English, Pot, C.1684, Ribbed Sides, Marked Nb, Rose Finial	....	375.00
Silver, English, Pot, John Moore, London, 1801, Ball Wire Band Finial	....	300.00
Silver, English, Pot, Mustard, George III, Boat Shape, Andrew Fogelberg, 1799	....	140.00
Silver, English, Salt Boat, Georgian, Steven Adams, London, 1805, Glass, Pair	....	100.00
Silver, English, Salt Cellar, George III, Monogram, Paul Storr, 1808, 4	....	650.00
Silver, English, Salt Cellar, George III, Pierced, R.& D.Hennel, 1768, Pair	....	100.00
Silver, English, Salt Cellar, George IV, Armorials, Applied Leaves, 1827, Pair	....	210.00
Silver, English, Salt Celler, George III, D.& R.Hennel, London, 1763, 3	....	180.00
Silver, English, Salt, Ann Robertson, New Castle, 1801, Gadroon Edge, 4	....	200.00
Silver, English, Salver, George II, Armorial, William Peaston, London, 1753	....	1200.00
Silver, English, Salver, George II, Hoof Supports, William Justus, 1751	....	370.00
Silver, English, Salver, George II, Piecrust, Engraved Scrolls & Floral, 1736	....	130.00
Silver, English, Salver, George III, Oval, Armorials, Crouch & Hannam, 1798	....	475.00
Silver, English, Salver, George III, Rectangular, Crest, William Bateman, 1812	....	600.00
Silver, English, Salver, George III, Round, Joseph Heriot, London, 1784	....	370.00
Silver, English, Salver, 1822, 18 1/2 In.Diameter	.... *Illus*	900.00
Silver, English, Sauceboat, George II, Engraved, Samuel Laundry, 1729	....	525.00
Silver, English, Sauceboat, George III, W.B., London, 1805	....	325.00
Silver, English, Sauceboat, Victorian, Mortimer & Hunt, London, 1842, Chased	....	540.00
Silver, English, Sauceboat, Victorian, Pearce & Burrows, London, 1847	....	275.00
Silver, English, Sauceboat, 18th Century Style, Gadroon Rim, Birmingham, Pair	....	120.00
Silver, English, Scoop, Marrow, George III, Smith & Smith & Fearn, 1780, 2	....	100.00
Silver, English, Serving Trowel, 12 In.	.... *Illus*	70.00

Silver, English,
Mug, London, 1762
See Page 473

Silver, English, Salver,
1822, 18 1/2 In.Diameter

Silver, English, Serving Trowel, 12 In.

Silver, English, Shovel, Salt, London, C.1793, 4 .... 90.00
Silver, English, Skewer, Hester Bateman 285.00
Silver, English, Skewer, Joseph Wilson, London, 1821 .... 80.00
Silver, English, Snuffbox, George III, Rectangular, Engraved, John Shaw, 1811 .... 100.00
Silver, English, Snuffbox, George IV, Foliate Borders, Joseph Willmore, 1826 .... 90.00
Silver, English, Snuffbox, Samuel Pemberton, Birmingham, 1814, Engraved 80.00
Silver, English, Snuffbox, Thomas Shaw, Birmingham, 1826, Raised Rabbit 140.00
Silver, English, Spoon, Basting, 1799-1800, Plain Bowl & Shank 50.00
Silver, English, Spoon, Salt, Fiddle, Gilt Bowl, Wm.Elliott, London, 1818, Pair 35.00
Silver, English, Spoon, Stuffing, Crested, Wm.Sutton, London, 1793, 11 In.Long 110.00
Silver, English, Stand, Cruet, George II, 2 Bottle, Samuel Wood, 1741 .... 140.00
Silver, English, Stand, Teapot, George III, Rectangular, R.& S.Hennell, 1805 .... 60.00
Silver, English, Standish, Georgian, Thomas Watson, 1797 .... 200.00
Silver, English, Strainer, George III, Gadroon Rim, London, 1767 .... 100.00
Silver, English, Strainer, London, 1765 .... *Illus* 225.00
Silver, English, Sugar & Creamer, George III, Engraved Armorials, 1771 .... 130.00
Silver, English, Sugar & Creamer, Victorian, Engraved, R.Hennel, 1866 .... 90.00
Silver, English, Sugar Nip, George Washington Family, Robert Cox, C.1755 .... 3750.00
Silver, English, Sugar, Double Handled, Footed, Scalloped Rim, Oval Base 60.00
Silver, English, Sugar, George III, Fluted, Gilt Interior, John Robins, 1802 .... 120.00
Silver, English, Tablespoon, Engraved Crest, Geo.Smith, London, 1778 .... 52.50
Silver, English, Tablespoon, Rattail, C.1730 .... 25.00
Silver, English, Tankard, George I, Engraved Armorials, Philip Elliott, 1724 .... 1200.00
Silver, English, Tankard, George II, Samuel Thompson, Newcastle, 1751 .... 700.00
Silver, English, Tankard, George III, Sheap Shearing Scene, W.Cripps, 1763 .... 375.00
Silver, English, Tankard, Hester Bateman, Monogrammed, 1782, 11 Troy Oz. 2900.00
Silver, English, Tankard, London, 1752, Floral Embossed, Coat Of Arms 475.00
Silver, English, Tankard, William III, Armorials, Pierre Platel, 1701 .... 3500.00
Silver, English, Taperstick, George II, London, 1754 .... 210.00
Silver, English, Taperstick, London, 1769 .... *Illus* 350.00

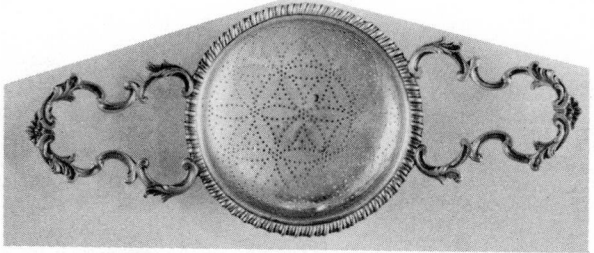

Silver, English, Strainer, London, 1765

Silver, English, Taperstick, London, 1769

Silver, English, Tea Caddy, George II, Repousse, Samuel Taylor, 1756, Pair 225.00
Silver, English, Teapot & Stand, George I, Christopher Canner, London, 1717 .... 2600.00
Silver, English, Teapot & Stand, George III, Armorials, Robert Salmon, 1798 .... 375.00
Silver, English, Teapot, George II, Engraved, Gurney & Cook, London, C.1735 .... 400.00
Silver, English, Teapot, George III, Oval, Beaded, I.R., London, 1780 .... 100.00
Silver, English, Teapot, George III, Oval, Fluted, William Vincent, 1781 .... 260.00
Silver, English, Teapot, George IV, Engraved Armorials, William Elliot, 1821 .... 230.00
Silver, English, Tray, Chippendale, William Peaston, London, 1746, Pair 600.00
Silver, English, Tray, Oval, Footed 275.00
Silver, English, Tray, Tea, Chippendale, Plated, Scalloped Open Work Rim 175.00
Silver, English, Tray, Thumb Grip, William Cafe, London, 1761, Kidney 525.00
Silver, English, Trophy, Racing, George IV, Gilt, J.E.Terry & Co., London, 1822 .... 450.00
Silver, English, Tureen, Sauce, Cover, George III, Burwash & Sibley, 1807, Pair 900.00
Silver, English, Tureen, Soup, Covered, George II, Peter Archambo, London, 1744 .... 4000.00

Silver, English, Urn, Tea, George III, Armorials, Daniel Pontifex, 1802 .... 1000.00
Silver, English, Vase, Covered, Gilt, Chased, Marked W.F., London, C.1680, Pair 1900.00
Silver, English, Vinaigrette, Leaf & Floral, Samuel Pemberton, 1809 .... 75.00
Silver, English, Waiter, George II, Armorial, William Peaston, London, 1753 .... 400.00
Silver, English, Waiter, George II, Chippendale Rim, John Tuite, 1733 .... 325.00
Silver, English, Waiter, George II, Engraved Crest, R.Rew, London, 1756 .... 160.00
Silver, English, Waiter, George II, Engraved, Robert Abercromby, 1739 .... 140.00
Silver, English, Waiter, George III, Engraved Name, Edward Capper, 1769 .... 110.00
Silver, English, Waiter, George III, Oblong, Crest, William Bateman, 1820 .... 375.00
Silver, English, Waiter, George III, Oval, Engraved Crest, Marked T.B., 1799 .... 230.00
Silver, English, Waiter, George III, Oval, Pierced, Makepeace & Carter, 1777 .... 260.00
Silver, English, Waiter, George III, Round, Pierced, J.Swift, London, 1777 .... 400.00
Silver, English, Waiter, George III, William Bateman, London, 1812, Pair 575.00
Silver, English, Wash Set, George III, Monogram, J.E.Terry, 1818, 2 Piece 1900.00
Silver, French, Bowl, Spirally Fluted, Cherub's Heads, Floral, C.1850 .... 140.00
Silver, French, Candlestick, Empire, Table, J.P.Viveron, Paris, 1798-1809, Pair 400.00
Silver, French, Chocolate Pot, Gilt, Cylindrical, Embossed Festoons, C.1900 .... 120.00
Silver, French, Dish, Conserve, Covered, Blue Glass Bowl, Paris, C.1800 .... 130.00
Silver, French, Ewer, Gilt, Jean-Baptiste-Claude Odiot, Paris, 1819-38 .... 2700.00
Silver, French, Pot, Bointa Buret, Paris, 10 Oz., Wood Handle, Embossed 80.00
Silver, French, Snuffbox, Oval, Embossed Head Of Caesar, Fruit, Shields 80.00
Silver, French, Urn, Covered, Paris, 1765, Ribbon Handles, 4 Paw Feet 275.00
Silver, French, Wine Taster, Chased Grapevine, Snake Handle, 1772 .... 220.00
Silver, French, Wine Taster, Louis XV, Engraved Initials, Ring Handle, 1762 .... 200.00
Silver, German, Beaker, Covered, Parcel Gilt, 1700 .... Illus 1050.00
Silver, German, Beaker, Parcel Gilt, Marked E.B.F., Nuremberg, 18th Century 275.00
Silver, German, Bell, Figural, Woman, Long Gown, Arms Held Out, 3 In.High 65.00
Silver, German, Figurine, Equestrian, Parcel Gilt, Knights, C.1850, Pair 1150.00
Silver, German, Shears, Grape, Grape Design On Handle, Marked 24.00
Silver, Irish, Candlestick, Table, George Iii, Engraved, John Lloyd, 1780, Pair 1000.00
Silver, Irish, Castor, George II, Pierced, Engraved, Dublin, C.1750 .... 110.00
Silver, Irish, Creamer, George II, Helmet Shape, Double Scroll Handle, C.1750 .... 110.00
Silver, Irish, Creamer, George III, Helmet Shape, Pedestal, Dublin, C.1760 .... 200.00
Silver, Irish, Cup, C.1814, 2 Handles, Embossed Flowers & Ribbon Scrolls 175.00
Silver, Irish, Dish, Sweetmeat, Octagonal, Gadroon Border, Dublin, 1798, 4 .... 160.00
Silver, Irish, Fork, Serving, Crested, M.Keating, Dublin, 1801 .... 100.00
Silver, Irish, Salt Cellar, George III, Rectangular, James Scott, 1807, 4 .... 340.00
Silver, Irish, Sauceboat, George II, Oval, Engraved Crest, John Wilne, C.1750 .... 210.00
Silver, Irish, Sauceboat, George III, Embossed Shepherds, Matthew West, 1780 .... 120.00
Silver, Irish, Sauceboat, George III, Oval, Joseph Jackson, Dublin, 1796 .... 130.00
Silver, Irish, Spoon, Dessert, Dublin, Circa 1800 .... 38.00
Silver, Irish, Spoon, Mutton, Fiddle Handle, John Power, Dublin, 1862, 1o In. 150.00
Silver, Irish, Spoon, Stuffing, Dublin, Dated 1782 .... 185.00
Silver, Italian, Coffeepot, Vase Shape, Horn Handle, Ossani Francesco, C.1810 .... 350.00
Silver, Italian, Lamp, Sanctuary, Baluster, Repousse, Chased, Marked P.C., 1750 .... 225.00
Silver, Italian, Plate, Dinner, Rome, C.1775, Engraved Armorials 120.00
Silver, Japanese, Tea Set, Applied Dragons, Arthur & Bond, Yokohama, 7 Pieces 750.00
Silver, Oriental, Casket, Jewel, Cabinet Form, Lacquer, Engraved 180.00
Silver, Oriental, Tea & Coffee Set, Hand-Engraved Palm Trees, 5 Piece 200.00
Silver, Peruvian, Pitcher, Water 85.00
Silver, Portuguese, Chamberstick, Reeded Border, V.A.D., Lisbon, C.1830, Pair 100.00
Silver, Portuguese, Toothpick, Amphitrite, Gilt, C.1855 .... Illus 140.00
Silver, Portuguese, Toothpick, Atlas, C.1830 .... Illus 180.00
Silver, Portuguese, Toothpick, Birds At Fountain, Oporto, C.1850 .... 210.00
Silver, Portuguese, Toothpick, Birds On Flower Spray, F.D.G., 1830 .... 250.00
Silver, Portuguese, Toothpick, Classical Shepherdess, I.J.V.A., 1850 .... 140.00
Silver, Portuguese, Toothpick, Greek, Oporto, C.1870 .... 140.00
Silver, Portuguese, Toothpick, In Renaissance Dress, C.R.A., C.1855 .... 180.00
Silver, Portuguese, Toothpick, Indian, I.J.V.A., C.1850 .... 140.00
Silver, Portuguese, Toothpick, Peacock On Globe, C.1850 .... Illus 180.00
Silver, Portuguese, Toothpick, Peasant Boy With Flute, A.P.L., 1855 .... 160.00
Silver, Portuguese, Toothpick, Poodle, C.1860 .... Illus 170.00
Silver, Russian, Basket, Cake, Parcel Gilt, Oval, St.Petersburg, 1840 .... 170.00
Silver, Russian, Beaker, Chased Birds On Rococo Ornament, Moscow, 1769 .... 130.00
Silver, Russian, Candlestick, Repousse, C Scrolls, Tula, 1856, Pair 225.00
Silver, Russian, Case, Cigarette, Gilded, Translucent Enamel, C.1900 .... 500.00

Silver, German, Beaker, Covered, Parcel Gilt, 1700
See Page 476

Silver, Portuguese, Toothpick,
Amphitrite, Gilt, C.1855
See Page 476

Silver, Portuguese,
Toothpick, Atlas, C.1830
See Page 476

Silver, Portuguese, Toothpick,
Peacock On Globe, C.1850
See Page 476

Silver, Portuguese,
Toothpick, Poodle, C.1860
See Page 476

Silver, Russian, Case, Cigarette, Rectangular, Enamel Flag Of Navy, C.1900 .... 80.00
Silver, Russian, Garniture, Desk, Green Onyx, Ral & Co., St.Petersburg, C.1850 .... 125.00
Silver, Russian, Knife, Fruit, Gilded, Mother-Of-Pearl Handle, C.1880, 12 .... 170.00
Silver, Russian, Kovsh, Gilded, Enamel, Eleventh Artel, Moscow, C.1900 .... 750.00
Silver, Russian, Kovsh, Gilded, Enamel, G.P.Gratchev, 19th Century 3400.00
Silver, Russian, Kovsh, Imperial Presentation, Parcel Gilt, Moscow, 1749 .... 2300.00
Silver, Russian, Kovsh, Parcel Gilt, Russian Imperial Eagle, C.1900 .... 325.00
Silver, Russian, Kovsh, Presentation, Gilded, Boat Shape, Medallion, 1689-1725 .... 4800.00
Silver, Russian, Ladle, Incised Scrolling Foliage, Moscow, 1858 .... 110.00
Silver, Russian, Ladle, Soup, 12 In.Long, St.Petersburg, 1896 .... 125.00
Silver, Russian, Salt, Ball Feet, 2 In.Diameter 12.00
Silver, Russian, Salt, Circular, 3 Shaped Legs, Pad Feet, St.Petersburg 30.00
Silver, Russian, Salt, Engraved, Three Ball Feet, Dated 1895, Pair 50.00
Silver, Russian, Snuffbox, Gilded, Niello, Feodor Bushkovski, 1822 .... 140.00
Silver, Russian, Spoon, Enamel, Stamped C K, Red, White & Blue, 6 .... 250.00
Silver, Russian, Spoon, Gilded, Enamel ....
Silver, Russian, Spoon, Serving, Niello Work On Gilt Bowl, Dated 1841, 7 In. 86.00
Silver, Russian, Tazza, Gilded, Blue & Red Enamel, G.P.Gratchev, C.1850 .... 1300.00
Silver, Russian, Teaspoon, Mark 84 .... 6.00
Silver, Scottish, Snuff Mull, Engraved Crest, John Young, Sadler, C.1770 .... 210.00
Silver, Scottish, Tablespoon, Two-Part Construction, Edinburgh, 1815, Pair 40.00
Silver, Scottish, Tray, Tea, George III, W.& P.Cunningham, Edinburgh, 1814 .... 500.00
Silver, Sheffield, Basket, Openwork, C.1790, 5 3/8 In.Diameter 35.00
Silver, Sheffield, Candelabra, 2 Branch, Plated, C.1810, Vase Shape Stem 100.00
Silver, Sheffield, Candelabra, 2 Branch, Urn Finials, C.1800, Pair 325.00
Silver, Sheffield, Candelabra, 3 Branch, Floral, Leaf, Silver On Copper, Pair 450.00
Silver, Sheffield, Candelabra, 5 Branch, Grooved Border, Gadroon Edging, Pair 180.00
Silver, Sheffield, Candlestick, Chamber, Shell & Foliate Border, C.1820, Pair 100.00

Silver, Sheffield, Candlestick, Table, George III, John Green & Co., 1800, 6	650.00
Silver, Sheffield, Chamberstick, George IV, T.J.& N.Creswick, 1827, Pair	375.00
Silver, Sheffield, Coaster, Overlapping Gadroon Rim, Pair	80.00
Silver, Sheffield, Coaster, Wine, Gadroon Border, Engraved, C.1810, 4	170.00
Silver, Sheffield, Coaster, Wine, Pierced & Engraved, C.1790, 2 Pair	225.00
Silver, Sheffield, Coaster, 19th Century, 7 1/2 In.Diameter	20.00
Silver, Sheffield, Condiment Set, Stand, Crystal Containers, 4 Piece	27.50
Silver, Sheffield, Dish, Vegetable, Oval, Covered, Armorials, C.1800, Pair	325.00
Silver, Sheffield, Epergne, Cut Glass Bowls, Paw Feet, C.1820	110.00
Silver, Sheffield, Ewer, Vase Shape, Reeded Border, Ball Finial, C.1790	150.00
Silver, Sheffield, Flask, Drinking, James Dixon, Incurved Sides	8.00
Silver, Sheffield, Inkwell, Standing Elk, 2 Wells, Sterling Lids	75.00
Silver, Sheffield, Knife, Pocket, Pearl Handle, Les 1886 Mark On Blade	55.00
Silver, Sheffield, Muffineer, Merrin & Web, Engraved, 7 1/2 In.Tall	45.00
Silver, Sheffield, Salt, Master, Cobalt Liner, Pair	20.00
Silver, Sheffield, Salver, Oval, Engraved Armorials, Beaded Rim, C.1780	250.00
Silver, Sheffield, Salver, Oval, Reeded Rim, Four Panel Supports, C.1790	120.00
Silver, Sheffield, Sauceboat, Thomas Bradbury & Sons, Pair	180.00
Silver, Sheffield, Saucepan, Covered, Pierced Dome, Wood Handle, C.1800	90.00
Silver, Sheffield, Stand, Decanter, George III, 2 Cut Glass Bottles, 1802	250.00
Silver, Sheffield, Tankard, Engraved Crest, Scroll Handle, C.1770	130.00
Silver, Sheffield, Tea Dispenser, Plunger Handle	12.00
Silver, Sheffield, Teapot, Batchelor's, George IV, John & Thomas Settle, 1820	130.00
Silver, Sheffield, Tray, Brainard Lemon, C.1810, Chased Center, 29 In.	100.00
Silver, Sheffield, Tray, Galleried, Footed, Shell Decorated, 8 In.Wide	35.00
Silver, Sheffield, Tray, Tea, Oval, Engraved Center Armorials, Pierced, C.1790	300.00
Silver, Sheffield, Tray, Tea, Oval, Engraved Center Crest, Wood Base, C.1800	225.00
Silver, Sheffield, Tray, Well, Footed, Vintage Border	45.00
Silver, Sheffield, Trolley, Decanter, Wood Base, Ivory Wheels, C.1835	170.00
Silver, Sheffield, Tureen, Ribbon Handles, Knob & Sunburst Finial	700.00
Silver, Sheffield, Urn, Engraved Peacock, Scrolls, & Daisy Vine	90.00
Silver, Sheffield, Urn, Spirit Lamp, C.1790, Brainard Lemon	175.00
Silver, Sheffield, Wine Cooler, Deus Providebet Motto, Gadroon Edge, Pair	450.00
Silver, Sheffield, Wine Cooler, 2 Handles, Engraved Armorials, C.1820	200.00
Silver, Spoon, Round Bowl, Curved Handle, Motts, N.Y., 1789, 5 In.	12.00

Sterling Silver is made with 925 parts of silver out of 1, 000 parts of metal. The word sterling is a quality guarantee used in the United States after about 1860.

Silver, Sterling, Basket, Openwork With Scroll	18.00
Silver, Sterling, Basket, Openwork, Embossed Rose Garlands, Continental	175.00
Silver, Sterling, Basket, Pierced Border, 6 1/2 In.Diameter	7.50
Silver, Sterling, Basket, Repousse, Hinged Handle	85.00
Silver, Sterling, Basket, Sugar, Footed, Cobalt Blue Liner, 3 1/2 In.	30.00
Silver, Sterling, Basket, Sugar, Mark Gorham, Handle, Initial E.B.A., 3 In.	28.00
Silver, Sterling, Bell, Woman Peeks Out Of Shawl On Head, Peruvian, 6.85 Oz.	17.50
Silver, Sterling, Bookmark, Embossed	4.50
Silver, Sterling, Bookmark, Gold Wash, George	8.00
Silver, Sterling, Bookmark, Gold Wash, Jim	8.00
Silver, Sterling, Bottle, Perfume, Round, Amethyst On Lid, Funnel	16.50
Silver, Sterling, Bowl, Fruit, Scalloped Rococo Edge, Shreve, Crump, & Lowe	15.00
Silver, Sterling, Bowl, Nursery Rhyme & Picture, Engraved Billie, Handle	15.00
Silver, Sterling, Bowl, Punch, Reed & Barton, Swirled Handles	350.00
Silver, Sterling, Bowl, Serving, Reed & Barton, Wide Rim With Floral Design	100.00
Silver, Sterling, Box, Cigarette, Cedar Lined, Marked, 2 1/2 X 3 1/2 X 1 In.	27.00
Silver, Sterling, Box, Match, Ornate	10.00
Silver, Sterling, Box, Raised Floral Design On Lid, 3 In.Diameter	15.00
Silver, Sterling, Box, Signed Tiffany & Co., 2 Compartments, Embossed	45.00
Silver, Sterling, Box, Soap, Raised Scroll & Roses	18.50
Silver, Sterling, Box, Thread Spool, Woman, Cherub, Embossed	30.00
Silver, Sterling, Brush, Clothes, Lady's, Embossed	5.00
Silver, Sterling, Brush, Hair, Art Nouveau, Lady's Head, Flowers, Birds	27.00
Silver, Sterling, Buckle, Belt, Gilt, Cutout Flowers	12.00
Silver, Sterling, Butter, Engraved, Holly, Flowers, Handles, Drain Plate	25.00
Silver, Sterling, Butter, Simpson Hall, Cow Lid, Handles, Liner, Cover	85.00
Silver, Sterling, Butter, Victorian	12.00

Silver, Sterling, Butterpat, Scalloped Edge, Beaded, Set Of 4 .... 14.50
Silver, Sterling, Buttonhook, Glove .... 4.75 To 8.00
Silver, Sterling, Buttonhook, Shoehorn 13.50
Silver, Sterling, Candlestick, Garland Design, 10 1/4 In.Tall Pair 125.00
Silver, Sterling, Candlestick, Hurricane Shade, Etched Grapes, Vines, Pair 35.00
Silver, Sterling, Cane Head, Etching Of Civil War Soldier 10.00
Silver, Sterling, Card Case, Floral Design, Monogram, Chain, 3 3/4 X 2 1/2 In 20.00
Silver, Sterling, Case, Cigarette, Woman, Enamel, Black, White, 2 X 3 In. 75.00
Silver, Sterling, Case, Eyeglass, Engraved, Green Velvet Lining, Snap Shut 12.00
Silver, Sterling, Case, Eyeglass, Filigree, Chain To Hang From Belt 35.00
Silver, Sterling, Case, Glasses, Hand Chased On Front, Blue Sapphire Catch 20.00
Silver, Sterling, Castor, Pickle, Etched Inserts, Double, Matching Forks 85.00
Silver, Sterling, Chalice, Drinking, Gorham, 2 Staghead Handles, 8 1/2 In. 165.00
Silver, Sterling, Clip, Napkin, Rogers, Lunt & Bowlen Mark 6.00
Silver, Sterling, Coffeepot, S.Kirk & Son, Co., Cone Shape, Embossed Ruins 300.00
Silver, Sterling, Coffeepot, Tiffany & Co., Cone Shape, Trefoils 100.00
Silver, Sterling, Creamer & Sugar, Diamond Shaped, Coffee Server, Set 225.00
Silver, Sterling, Creamer, Beaded Rim, 2 1/2 In.High 10.00
Silver, Sterling, Cup & Saucer, Demitasse, Lenox Inserts, Set Of 4 .... 90.00
Silver, Sterling, Cup & Saucer, Engraved, Relief, Signed Gorham 25.00
Silver, Sterling, Cup & Saucer, Lenox Liners, Overwork Side, Set Of 12 .... 150.00
Silver, Sterling, Cup, Baby's 25.00
Silver, Sterling, Cup, Child's, Applied Enamel Mickey Mouse, 2 1/2 In. 40.00
Silver, Sterling, Cup, Collapsible .... 7.50 To 10.00
Silver, Sterling, Cup, Shape Of Funnel, With Bottle Opener, Corkscrew, Case 7.95
Silver, Sterling, Curler, Mustache 6.50
Silver, Sterling, Dish, Nut, Victorian Design, Pair 18.00
Silver, Sterling, Dresser, Hairbrush, Powder, Mirror, Nail Brush 100.00
Silver, Sterling, Eraser, Desk 1.75
Silver, Sterling, Fork, Oyster, Engraved Rosebud, 10 .... 55.00
Silver, Sterling, Fork, Pickle, Floral, J.W.Perry 7.50
Silver, Sterling, Frame, Easel Back, Lacy Scroll Border, 2 1/4 In.Diameter 9.00
Silver, Sterling, Frame, Picture, Oval 14.00
Silver, Sterling, Game Set, 6 Piece, China 35.00
Silver, Sterling, Glove Mender 12.00
Silver, Sterling, Glove Stretcher, Pair 12.50
Silver, Sterling, Goblet, Water, Walls Of Troy Border, Base, Gorham, 6 In., 6 .... 240.00
Silver, Sterling, Holder, Cigarette, Amber, Engraved, Case 20.00
Silver, Sterling, Holder, Pipe 7.50
Silver, Sterling, Inkwell, English, Round, C.1905-10 .... 42.50
Silver, Sterling, Inkwell, Mark Birmington 28.00
Silver, Sterling, Knife Rest, Horses, Grass, Fence, Pair 58.00
Silver, Sterling, Knife, Butter, Pearl Handle, Set Of 6 .... 18.00
Silver, Sterling, Knife, Pocket, Two Blades, Nail File 4.50
Silver, Sterling, Knife, Royal Danish, International 8.00
Silver, Sterling, Ladle, Gold Wash Bowl, 4 7/8 In.Long 5.95
Silver, Sterling, Ladle, Mustard, 4 3/4 In.Long 6.95
Silver, Sterling, Ladle, Punch, Gilt Bowl, Audubon Pattern, Hennegan & Bates 64.00
Silver, Sterling, Ladle, Punch, Louis Xv, Gold Washed Bowl, Monogram G 75.00
Silver, Sterling, Letter Clip, Lady's, Ornate, Small Amethyst 12.75
Silver, Sterling, Letter Opener, Monogrammed 20.00
Silver, Sterling, Letter Opener, Ornate Handle, Monogram, Late 19th Century 20.00
Silver, Sterling, Match Holder, Pocket 20.00
Silver, Sterling, Match Safe, Dragon Design, Striker Bottom 24.50
Silver, Sterling, Match Safe, Embossed Dolphins 12.00
Silver, Sterling, Match Safe, Embossed Fishing Scene, 2 Men, Woods 15.00
Silver, Sterling, Match Safe, Etched Florals 8.00
Silver, Sterling, Match Safe, Floral 16.00
Silver, Sterling, Match Safe, Hunter, Dog, Raised 28.00
Silver, Sterling, Match Safe, Ornate Floral Embossed 15.00
Silver, Sterling, Match Safe, Snakeskin, Striker On Bottom, Gorham 7.50
Silver, Sterling, Matchbox Holder, Monogrammed H.T.A. 4.50
Silver, Sterling, Mirror, Hand, Lilies-Of-The-Valley, Monogram 20.00
Silver, Sterling, Muffineer, Fluted, England, Circa 1909-10, 7 In.Tall 75.00
Silver, Sterling, Mustard Pot, Oval, English Mark, Blue Insert, Spoon 24.00
Silver, Sterling, Mustard Pot, Spoon, Lid, Cutout Decor, Cobalt Insert 15.00

Silver, Sterling, Napkin Ring, see also Napkin Ring.

Silver, Sterling, Napkin Ring, Eagles & Ring, Signed Meriden	30.00
Silver, Sterling, Opener, Bottle, Staghorn	12.00
Silver, Sterling, Pitcher, Cream, H.S.Kirk & Son, 2 3/4 In.	95.00
Silver, Sterling, Pitcher, Water, Tiffany & Co., Melon Sides, Roses, Leaves	275.00
Silver, Sterling, Platter, Oval, 18 X 12 1/2 In.	275.00
Silver, Sterling, Pot, Mustard, Engraved	35.00
Silver, Sterling, Rattle, Baby's	5.00
Silver, Sterling, Rattle, Baby's, With Mother-Of-Pearl Teething Ring	7.50
Silver, Sterling, Salt & Pepper, Figural, Chinese Junks	25.00
Silver, Sterling, Salt & Pepper, Form Of Bird, Pair	38.50
Silver, Sterling, Salt & Pepper, Form Of Buddhas	35.00
Silver, Sterling, Salt, Open, Embossed, Rams' Heads, Footed, Pair	75.00
Silver, Sterling, Salt, Oval, Pedestal Base	12.50
Silver, Sterling, Salt, Round, Pedestal Base	8.00
Silver, Sterling, Scoop, Ornate, By Gorham, Pat.1900	12.75
Silver, Sterling, Server, Cheese, Mother-Of-Pearl Handle, 5 1/2 In.	10.00
Silver, Sterling, Server, Ice Cream, Victorian, Monogram, Flowers, Scrolls	14.00
Silver, Sterling, Server, Pie, Rosette, Gorham, 1868	25.00
Silver, Sterling, Server, Tomato, Lancaster Rose Pattern, Flower Design	22.00
Silver, Sterling, Shears, Grape, Mark Germany, 6 1/4 In.	30.00
Silver, Sterling, Shoehorn, Hand Hammered, Monogrammed, 6 1/8 In.Long	25.00
Silver, Sterling, Shoehorn, Monogrammed, 4 1/2 In.Long	15.00
Silver, Sterling, Spoon, Baby's, Curved Handle, Pennant W Mark	7.50
Silver, Sterling, Spoon, Berry, Charter Oak	15.00
Silver, Sterling, Spoon, Berry, Fleur-De-Lis, Reed & Barton	55.00
Silver, Sterling, Spoon, Demitasse, Case, 6	22.50
Silver, Sterling, Spoon, Demitasse, Gold Washed Bowl, 8	22.00
Silver, Sterling, Spoon, Fruit, Gold Wash Bowl	10.00
Silver, Sterling, Spoon, Nut, L.Kimball, Son	9.00
Silver, Sterling, Spoon, Olive, 11 Stars, Grace On Handle	4.00
Silver, Sterling, Spoon, Salt, Signed W For Webster	5.00
Silver, Sterling, Spoon, Serving, Empire, Reed & Barton, Gold Wash Bowl	22.50
Silver, Sterling, Spoon, Serving, George W. Webb, Engraved Decor	7.50

Silver, Sterling, Spoon, Souvenir, See Souvenir Spoon

Silver, Sterling, Spoon, Sugar, By Gorham, Pat.1911	6.95
Silver, Sterling, Spoon, Sugar, Shell Shape	8.00
Silver, Sterling, Spoon, Turkey Stuffing, C.1800, 12 In.	50.00
Silver, Sterling, Strainer, Tea, Cherubs, Flowers, Birds	8.95
Silver, Sterling, Stretcher, Glove, Pair	12.50
Silver, Sterling, Sugar & Creamer, European Mark	32.50
Silver, Sterling, Sugar, Bird Finial, Squirrel Handle, 12 Spoon Holders	38.00
Silver, Sterling, Sugar, Engraved, Glowers, Footed, Blue Insert, Cover	95.00
Silver, Sterling, Tablespoon, Hallmarked, Pat.June 9-08, Monogram T	4.00
Silver, Sterling, Tea Ball, Kettle Shape, Matching Plate	11.50
Silver, Sterling, Tea Caddy, Gadroon Trim, Slanted Lid, English, 3 1/2 In.	48.00
Silver, Sterling, Tea Dispenser, Spoon Shape	8.00
Silver, Sterling, Tea Set, P.S.Co., 3 Piece	165.00
Silver, Sterling, Teapot, Allover Scenes, Samuel Kirk	225.00
Silver, Sterling, Teapot, Chinese Decor, Cream & Sugar, Set	150.00
Silver, Sterling, Teapot, Three-Cup, Matching Tray	50.00
Silver, Sterling, Teaspoon, Holly	12.00
Silver, Sterling, Teaspoon, Violet Design, 6	20.00

Silver, Sterling, Thimble, See Sewing Tool, Thimble

Silver, Sterling, Thimble Holder, Hinged Cover	20.00
Silver, Sterling, Tongs, Perforated Shell Shapes At Outside, Filigree, 6 In.	18.00
Silver, Sterling, Tongs, Sugar, Marked R.W.& S., Roses, Claw End	9.00
Silver, Sterling, Toothbrush, Art Nouveau, Full-Length Lady, Celluloid	18.00
Silver, Sterling, Tray, Card, Engraved, Shell Border	15.00
Silver, Sterling, Tray, Sugar, Cube, 5 7/8 In.Long	15.00
Silver, Sterling, Trophy, Regatta, 1909, 1910, Pierced Edge Bowl, Pair	15.00
Silver, Sterling, Tureen, Soup, Claw Feet, Signed Frisbie, 11 1/2 In.Long	350.00
Silver, Sterling, Vase, Embossed Cherubs, Dated 1899, 7 1/4 In.High	55.00
Silver, Sterling, Vase, Theodore B.Starr, C.1880	450.00
Silver, Sterling, Vase, Trumpet	40.00
Silver, Sterling, Whistle, Bosun's, Nautical	35.00

Silver, Sterling, Wine Set, Footed Pitcher, 6 Goblets 100.00
Silver, Swedish, Dish, Shell, Parcel Gilt, Gustaf Folcker, Stockholm, 1834, 4 .... 600.00
Silver, Tiffany, Cup, Presentation From Mckinley To Jules Cambon, C.1898 .... 1200.00
Silver, Tiffany, Cup, Presentation, C.1898 .... *Illus* 1200.00
Silver, Tiffany, Pitcher, Water, Helmet Shape, Shells, Scrolls, & Strapwork 190.00
Silver, Tiffany, Sugar & Creamer, Helmet Pitcher 100.00
Silver, Tureen, Soup, Cover, The Gorham Co., C.1871, Oval 500.00
Silver, Viennese, Horn, Ceremonial, Enamel, Allegorical, 19th Century 1600.00
Sinclaire, Vase, Cut & Engraved, Silver Rim & Bottom Rim, Signed In Silver 125.00
Skull, Human, Prehistoric 50.00

> *Slag Glass is streaked with several colors. There were many types made
> from about 1880. Caramel or Chocolate Glass was made by the Indiana
> Tumbler and Goblet Company of Greentown, Indiana, from 1900 to 1903.
> Pink Slag was an american victorian product of unknown origin. Purple and
> Blue Slag were made in American and English factories. Red Slag is
> a very late victorian product. Other colors are known, but are of less
> importance to the collector.*

Slag, Amber, Figurine, Bust Of Dewey, Greentown 85.00
Slag, Blue, Cornucopia, 3 1/2 In.High 65.00
Slag, Blue, Dish, Hen Covered 7.50
Slag, Blue, Plate, Basket Weave, Loop Edge, 8 3/4 In.Diameter 18.50
Slag, Blue, Vase, Basket Weave, Loop Edge, Incurving Top, 3 3/4 In.Tall 10.00
Slag, Brown, Salt & Paper, Silver Top, Five Sided, 3 1/2 In.Tall 7.00
Slag, Brown, Tea Set, Child's, 15 Piece 35.00
Slag, Caramel, Bowl, Fruit, Shell Pattern, Large 67.50
Slag, Caramel, Bowl, Fruit, Shell Pattern, Round 67.50
Slag, Caramel, Butter, Cover, Leaf Bracket, Greentown 55.00
Slag, Caramel, Butter, Shell Pattern, Cover 87.50
Slag, Caramel, Creamer, Cactus .... 45.00 To 60.00
Slag, Caramel, Creamer, Shell Pattern .... 57.50 To 60.00
Slag, Caramel, Cruet 12.50
Slag, Caramel, Cruet, Matching Stopper 18.00
Slag, Caramel, Cruet, Shell Pattern, Stopper 125.00
Slag, Caramel, Dolphin, Greentown .... *Illus* 200.00
Slag, Caramel, Light Fixture, Hanging, Brass Trim 50.00
Slag, Caramel, Match Holder, Footed, 3 3/4 In.High 12.00
Slag, Caramel, Nappy 35.00
Slag, Caramel, Nappy, Leaf Bracket, Handle, Tri-Corner 29.00
Slag, Caramel, Pitcher, Syrup, Cactus, Dewey Cover 38.00
Slag, Caramel, Pitcher, Water, Cactus 125.00

Silver, Tiffany, Cup, Presentation, C.1898

Slag, Caramel, Dolphin, Greentown

Slag, Caramel, Pitcher, Water, Wild Roses	85.00
Slag, Caramel, Plate, Cactus Pattern, Scalloped Edge, 7 1/2 In.	25.00 To 38.00
Slag, Caramel, Sauce, Cactus	27.50
Slag, Caramel, Sauce, Shell Pattern	35.00
Slag, Caramel, Spooner, Embossed Swans' Heads, 4 1/2 In.High	55.00
Slag, Caramel, Spooner, Shell Pattern	50.00
Slag, Caramel, Sugar, Leaf Bracket, Open	37.50
Slag, Caramel, Sugar, Shell Pattern, Cover	60.00 To 67.50
Slag, Caramel, Syrup, Cactus Pattern	65.00
Slag, Caramel, Syrup, Cord Drapery	68.00
Slag, Caramel, Toothpick, Cactus Pattern	30.00
Slag, Caramel, Tumbler, Cactus	25.00 To 39.50
Slag, Caramel, Tumbler, Fleur-De-Lis	22.50
Slag, Caramel, Tumbler, Shell Pattern	39.50
Slag, Caramel, Tumbler, Uneeda Biscuit	40.00 To 55.00
Slag, Caramel, Tumbler, Uneeda Milk Biscuit, 5 3/4 X 3 1/2 In.	55.00 To 150.00
Slag, Chocolate, Toothpick, Cactus	20.00
Slag, Green, Basket	27.50
Slag, Green, Box, Bronze Floral Filigree, Beaded Edge	45.00
Slag, Green, Match Holder, Cornucopia	3.50
Slag, Green, Toothpick, Flared Top, Footed, Mark	9.00
Slag, Green, Vase, Nude Motif, Triangular, 8 1/2 In.High	45.00
Slag, Orange, Candlestick, 8 1/2 In.High, Pair	135.00
Slag, Pink, Cruet, 4 In.High	250.00
Slag, Pink, Pitcher, Water	900.00
Slag, Pink, Sauce, Footed, Inverted Fern Pattern, 4 1/2 In.High	175.00 To 225.00
Slag, Pink, Tumbler	*Illus* 325.00
Slag, Purple, Bowl	70.00
Slag, Purple, Butter, Shell & Coral, Finial	35.00
Slag, Purple, Cake Stand, 11 In.Diameter	75.00
Slag, Purple, Candlestick, Circa 1840, Pair	58.00
Slag, Purple, Candlestick, Ribbed Foot, Dolphins, 7 In.Tall	75.00
Slag, Purple, Candlestick, 8 In., Pair	22.50
Slag, Purple, Castor, Pickle	160.00
Slag, Purple, Compote, Cover, Low	65.00
Slag, Purple, Compote, Jelly, Standard	15.00
Slag, Purple, Compote, Signed Stourbridge, 5 1/4 In.High	37.50
Slag, Purple, Compote, Standard, Jenny Lind Bust, 8 1/2 In.Diameter	70.00
Slag, Purple, Creamer & Sugar, Shell & Coral	38.00
Slag, Purple, Creamer, Embossed Pattern, 4 In.Tall	28.50
Slag, Purple, Cruet, Pressed Pattern, Blown In Mold, Stopper	27.50
Slag, Purple, Dish, Bee Finial, Cover	75.00
Slag, Purple, Dish, Berry	50.00
Slag, Purple, Dish, Lion Cover, Lacy-Edge Bowl, Dated Aug.6, 1889	59.00
Slag, Purple, Mug, Raised Bird Design	14.50
Slag, Purple, Plate, Bread, Oval	30.00
Slag, Purple, Platter, Oval, 13 In.	60.00
Slag, Purple, Spooner, 4 1/2 In.High, Pair	65.00
Slag, Purple, Swan-Covered Dish, Basket-Weave Nest	24.50
Slag, Purple, Turkey-Covered Dish, Basket-Weave Nest	24.50
Slag, Purple, Vase, Embossed Woman Picking Apples From Tree, 5 1/2 In.	95.00
Slag, Red, Bowl, Flared, 8 In. X 3 1/2 In.High	42.50
Slag, Red, Bowl, Rose, Ruffled, Satin Finish, Imperial, Open	35.00
Slag, Red, Candleholder, Bowl, Set, Northwood	225.00
Slag, Red, Candleholder, Fenton, 8 1/2 In.Tall, Pair	60.00
Slag, Red, Vase, Chinese Red, 12 In.	50.00
Slag, Red, Vase, Dark Red, 6 1/2 In.	40.00

Sleepy Eye Pottery was made to be given away with the flour products of the Sleepy Eye Milling Co., Sleepy Eye, Minnesota, from about 1893 to 1952. It is a heavy stoneware with blue decorations, usually the famous profile of an indian.

Sleepy Eye, Pitcher, White, Blue, Unsigned	45.00
Sleepy Eye, Vase, Signed	55.00
Sleigh, Cutter, Black, Red Velvet Lined	220.00
Sleigh, One Horse, Red Under Carriage, Decorated, Eagle, Date 1776	400.00

Slip is a thin mixture of clay and water, about the consistency of sour cream, that is applied to the pottery for decoration. If the pottery is made with red clay, the Slip is mixed with yellow clay.

Slipware, Bowl, Pennsylvania, Shallow, 7 In.Diameter	65.00
Slipware, Bowl, Red Clay, Yellow Decoration, 8 1/2 In.Diameter	75.00
Slipware, Bowl, Yellow Decoration, Miniature, 3 3/4 In.Diameter	30.00.
Slipware, Charger, Red Clay, Yellow, Green Slip Decoration, 13 In.Diameter	110.00
Slipware, Flowerpot, Cream & Chocolate Slip, Signed Solomon Bell	25.00
Slipware, Jar, Cylindrical, Pennsylvania Red Clay, Brown Glaze	80.00
Slipware, Plate, Inscribed In Yellow Cheap Ware, Pennsylvania	200.00
Slipware, Plate, Pie, Reddish Brown, Yellow Slip, Penna.C.1850	200.00
Slipware, Whistle, Bird, Bird On Branch, Smaller Birds, American, C.1850	180.00
Smilin Jack, Book, Coloring, 1945	6.50

Smith Brothers Glass was made after 1878. The owners had worked for the Mt.Washington Glass Company in New Bedford, Massachusetts, for seven years before going into their own shop. Some of the designs were similar.

Smith Brothers, Bowl, Pansies, Melon Ribbed, Gold, White, 3 1/2 In.Across	120.00
Smith Brothers, Bowl, Rose, Daisy Design, Beaded Top	75.00
Smith Brothers, Box, Melon Ribs, Floral Decor, Signed, 4 In.High	195.00
Smith Brothers, Creamer, Prunus Blossoms, Melon, Gold, Squatty	100.00
Smith Brothers, Fernery, Violet Design, Purple, Melon Ribbed, Signed, Insert	275.00
Smith Brothers, Humidor, Shasta Daisy, Metal Lid, Signed	185.00
Smith Brothers, Jar, Cookie, Jeweled Decor, Signed	325.00
Smith Brothers, Jar, Cookie, Pansy Design, Lion Sign	165.00
Smith Brothers, Jar, Cracker, Daisy Design, Blue, Green, S.B.In Cover	256.00
Smith Brothers, Salt, Flower Design, Beading, Blue, Pink, Melon Shape, Open	35.00
Smith Brothers, Salt, Open, Pale Blue, Enamel Red & Green, Beaded Edge	25.00
Smith Brothers, Shaker, Sugar, Daisy Decor, Silver Top	150.00
Smith Brothers, Shaker, Sugar, Ribbed Opal, Pink To Yellow, Wild Rose	135.00
Smith Brothers, Vase, Pinched Shape, Decor Like Crown Milano, Signed	385.00
Smith Brothers, Vase, Rose Bowl Shape, Signed	220.00
Smith Brothers, Vase, Signed, Enameled Flowers, Swirled	145.00
Smith Brothers, Vase, Stork Decor, Pink & White, Mt.Washington	26.50
Smith Brothers, Vase, Swirls, Enameled Floral, Signed, 7 In.	145.00
Snow Baby, 2 In.High *Illus*	45.00

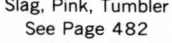

Slag, Pink, Tumbler
See Page 482

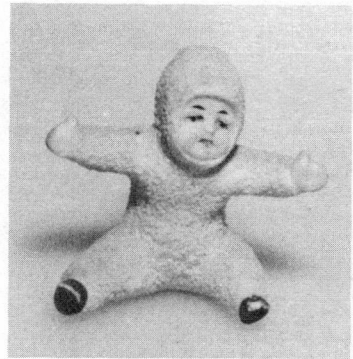

Snow Baby, 2 In.High

Snuff Bottle, see Bottle, Snuff

Snuffbox, Enamel, Turkey, Cartouche Shape, C.1770, Metal Mounts	675.00
Snuffbox, Rectangular, Enamel, Double Opening, Figures, Rural Scenes, C.1770	150.00
Snuffbox, Rectangular, Enamel, Latticework, South Staffordshire, C.1770	120.00
Snuffbox, Rectangular, Enamel, Puce Landscape, Metal Mounts, C.1770	275.00
Snuffbox, Rectangular, Enamel, Transfer Music, South Staffordshire, C.1770	180.00
Snuffbox, Rectangular, Enamel, Transfer Printed, Painted, C.1760	260.00
Snuffbox, Rectangular, Gold, Wavy Pattern, Engraved, Paris, 1819-38	375.00

Snuffbox, Rectangular, Mother-Of-Pearl, Mounted En Cage, 18th Century 100.00
Snuffbox, Swiss, Gold & Enamel, Oval, Harbor Scenes, C.1810 .... 850.00
Snuffbox, Swiss, Gold & Enamel, Oval, Set With Miniature, Lady, C.1750 .... 1000.00

Soapstone is a mineral that was used for foot warmers or griddles because of
its heat-retaining properties. Chinese Soapstone Carvings of the
nineteenth and twentieth centuries are found in many antique shops.

Soapstone, Basket, Grotesque, Gray & Cream, Carved Monkeys, Bats, & Flowers 50.00
Soapstone, Bookends, Foo Dog, Beige, Hand Carved, 7 1/2 In.Tall 85.00
Soapstone, Charm, Carved Elephant 5.00
Soapstone, Cigarette & Match Holder, Carved, Monkeys & Birds 16.00
Soapstone, Cup, Wine, Green, Cylindrical, 2 1/4 In.Tall, Set Of Four 38.00
Soapstone, Figurine, Bird & Flowers, Gray & Brown 22.00
Soapstone, Figurine, Bird At Urn, Leaves, Vines, 3 1/2 X 4 1/2 In. 14.00
Soapstone, Figurine, Elephant, Green, 4 In.Long 12.00
Soapstone, Figurine, Monkeys, Carved, Rust & Gray, 5 X 5 In. 19.75
Soapstone, Figurine, Monkeys, Gray, 5 X 10 In. 22.00
Soapstone, Figurine, Temple Dog, Foo, Teeth Bared, 3 In.Tall, 4 In.Long 30.00
Soapstone, Foot Warmer, Slab, Bail Handle .... 3.00 To 4.00
Soapstone, Match Holder, Ornate, 3 1/2 X 3 In.High 12.50
Soapstone, Monkey, Carved, Hear Not, See Not, Speak Not, 3 .... 16.00
Soapstone, Teapot, Bird Finial, Tan To Green, Cover, Unmarked, 7 In. 70.00
Soapstone, Toothpick, Three Monkeys, 3 In.Tall .... 7.00 To 15.00
Soapstone, Trinket,Holder, Double Floral, 9 in. Across 25.00
Soapstone, Vase & Bowl, 2 Monkeys, Deer & Bird 25.00
Soapstone, Vase & Bowl, 3 Monkeys & 5 Birds 35.00
Soapstone, Vase, Black Base, Gray & Brown, 5 X 9 In. 17.50
Soapstone, Vase, Bud, Leaves Climbing, Footed, 6 In.Tall, Pair 25.00
Soapstone, Vase, Carved Water Lilies, Pair 10.00
Soapstone, Vase, Carved, 4 1/2 In.High 9.00
Soapstone, Vase, Tan, Black, Flowers, Leaves, Hand Carved 35.00
Soapstone, Vase, Terra Cotta, Floral, Carved 22.00
Soapstone, Vase, 4 In.High .... *Illus*   25.00

Soapstone, Vase, 4 In.High

Soft Paste, Cachepot, English, Sevres Type Decoration, Floral, C.1810, Pair 90.00
Soft Paste, Creamer, Sprig Pattern, American, 4 In.High 30.00
Soft Paste, Cup & Saucer, Eagle With Pennant, Handleless, Staffordshire 90.00
Soft Paste, Cup & Saucer, Handleless, Blue, White, Transfer, Cherubs 38.00
Soft Paste, Dessert Set, English, C.1820, Flowers, Gilt, Blue, 20 Piece 575.00
Soft Paste, Dish, Leaf, Green Edge, Leeds, 5 1/4 In. 65.00
Soft Paste, Dish, Sweetmeat, Leaf Shape 12.00
Soft Paste, Figurine, Couple, Staffordshire, 4 1/4 In.High 115.00
Soft Paste, Mug, Roses & Morning Glories, Puce, Yellow, & Green, C.1760 .... 90.00
Soft Paste, Pitcher, Queen's Rose, Raised Leaves At Bottom, Staffordshire 55.00
Soft Paste, Plate, King's Rose, Pink Luster Rim, 6 1/4 In.Diameter 40.00
Soft Paste, Plate, Red Rose Center, Polychrome Raised Border 55.00
Soft Paste, Plate, Rose Center, 7 3/4 In.Diameter 35.00

Soft Paste, Plate, Rose Center, 10 In.Diameter	45.00
Soft Paste, Plate, Strawberry, 8 In.Diameter	40.00
Soft Paste, Platter, Gaudy Decoration On Red, Green, & Blue, Staffordshire	50.00
Soft Paste, Sugar, Covered, English, 1820, Painted Spring Flowers	40.00
Soft Paste, Tea Set, Steuberville, Ohio, Miniature, 3 Piece	50.00
Soft Paste, Teapot, Strawberry	95.00
Souvenir, Anvil, Philadelphia, 1876, Embossed, Bronze, Miniature, 3 1/2 In.	12.50
Souvenir, Ashtray, Nevada Resort, Carnival Glass, Marigold	7.50
Souvenir, Ashtray, State Capitol, Columbus, Ohio, Clear Glass, 3 Wells	2.50
Souvenir, Banner, Welcome Lindbergh, Wall	3.50
Souvenir, Book, World's Fair, 1933	4.00
Souvenir, Bookmark, Christopher Columbus, Discoverer Of America, Silk	20.00
Souvenir, Bookmark, Columbian Exposition, Sterling Silver	5.50
Souvenir, Bracelet, 1933, Century Of Progress, Chicago	2.50
Souvenir, Button, Spirit Of St.Louis	2.50
Souvenir, Canoe, Chicago, Ill., Clambroth	7.50
Souvenir, Canoe, Hartland, Wis., Clambroth	7.50
Souvenir, Canoe, Potter, Wis., Clambroth	7.50
Souvenir, Cookie Tin, New York World's Fair, 1939, Map	6.50
Souvenir, Creamer, Chambersburg, Pa., Court House, China	7.50
Souvenir, Creamer, Red Flashed Glass, Martinsville, Ind.	16.50
Souvenir, Creamer, World's Fair, 1893, Cora St.John	15.50
Souvenir, Creamer, 1897, Red Flashed Glass, Petoskey, Mich.	14.50
Souvenir, Cup, Boston, German Porcelain, Pink Pig In Cup	14.00 To 15.00
Souvenir, Cup, Button Arch, Green, Name, Dated 1931	10.00
Souvenir, Cup, Crescent Athletic Club, Brooklyn, N.Y., April 23, 1910	35.00
Souvenir, Cup, Punch, Ruby, Elizabeth, 1905, 2 X 3 In.	12.00
Souvenir, Cup, Punch, Ruby, Martell, Wis., Sprig & Leaves	13.50
Souvenir, Cup, World's Fair, St.Louis, 1904, Enameled	6.00
Souvenir, Dish, Dresser, Niagara Falls, Cat Handle, Gold, Cover, 5 In.Long	5.00
Souvenir, Dish, Nut, Frying Pan Shape, Pan-American Exposition, 1904	3.00
Souvenir, Flag, Silk, International Exposition, 1916, Buildings	20.00
Souvenir, Flag, Silk, Pan Pacific Exposition, 1915, Tower Of Jewels	20.00
Souvenir, Glass, Water, Springfield, Mass., Thumbprint Base, Ruby Flashed	12.00
Souvenir, Goblet, Buffalo, S.D., Gold & Ruby Flashed	18.50
Souvenir, Goblet, Ware, Mass., Ruby Flashed, King's Crown	10.00
Souvenir, Grip Check, Columbian Exposition, 1893	8.50
Souvenir, Guidebook, World's Fair, 1939	3.50
Souvenir, Handkerchief, Silk, Chicago, 1933	4.25
Souvenir, Key Ring & Light, World's Fair, 1939, Pen-Lite	5.00
Souvenir, Letter Opener, Queen Elizabeth, Dated June 2, 1953, Sheffield	5.00
Souvenir, Match Cover, World's Fair, 1939, Matches	2.00
Souvenir, Match Safe, Celluloid Inserts, Pan Am Exposition, Buffalo 1901	10.00
Souvenir, Match Safe, Pan American Exposition, Lady, Falls, Nickel On Brass	12.50
Souvenir, Match Safe, Pocket, Crystal Palace, N.Y., Nickel Plate	15.50
Souvenir, Match Safe, Pocket, Mid-Winter Fair, San Francisco, 1894, Nickel	8.00
Souvenir, Match Safe, St.Louis Exposition	7.00
Souvenir, Medal, Autumn Festival, Chicago, 1899, Red Silk Ribbon	7.50
Souvenir, Medal, Gar 27 National Encampment, 1893, Indianapolis	5.00
Souvenir, Medal, Grand Army Of The Republic, 1866	15.00
Souvenir, Medal, Michigan, World's Columbian Exposition, 1893	5.00
Souvenir, Medal, Omaha Exposition, 1898, Indian Congress, Bronze	17.50
Souvenir, Medal, Police, Honor, Robert Kennedy	3.00
Souvenir, Mug, Alma, 1914, Colorado, Green	5.00
Souvenir, Mug, Elk, Bpoe, Clock, Cobalt, Gold, Marked Brunt Art Ware	11.00
Souvenir, Mug, Juneau, Wis., Inverted Heart, Clear, Gold Handle, 3 1/2 In.	15.00
Souvenir, Mug, Oliver, 1917, Miniature, Red Flashed	4.50
Souvenir, Mug, Pan American Exposition, 1901, Glass, 3 1/2 In.	10.00
Souvenir, Mug, Travel Building, A Century Of Progress, 1934, Copper	7.50
Souvenir, Paperweight, Pan-Pacific Exposition, 1925, Bronze	5.00
Souvenir, Paperweight, St.Louis	10.00
Souvenir, Perfume, Chicago, Century Of Progress, 1933, Miniature	8.00
Souvenir, Paperweight, World's Fair, 1893, Ferris Wheel	10.00
Souvenir, Pinback, Pioneer Jubilee, Salt Lake City, 1897, Celluloid	5.00
Souvenir, Pinback, Studebaker	3.00
Souvenir, Pipe, Norwalk, Wis., Clambroth	5.00

Souvenir, Pitcher, Gettysburg 1863, Ruby, Clear, Miniature	10.00
Souvenir, Pitcher, Pan American Exposition, Buffalo, 1901, 7 In.Tall	24.00
Souvenir, Pitcher, World's Fair 1893, Red Flashed, 2 1/4 In.	18.50
Souvenir, Plate, Detroit, Mich., English, Blue, 7 3/4 In.Diameter	10.00
Souvenir, Plate, Footed, Lodge Of Perfection, Jan.29, 1921, Sterling	15.00
Souvenir, Plate, Fort Pitt Block House, Victoria, Austria, 8 1/2 In.Diameter	5.00
Souvenir, Plate, Frash Bros., Wakarusa, Ind., 7 In., Red & Pink Roses, Green	8.00
Souvenir, Plate, J.F.Kennedy, Signed L.S.Hudson, 8 3/8 In.Diameter	5.00
Souvenir, Plate, Library Of Congress, Blue With White	6.50
Souvenir, Plate, Missouri, Pacific, Engine Center, States & Flowers Border	18.00
Souvenir, Plate, New City Hospital, Cincinnati, Ohio, China, Hole For Hanging	7.50
Souvenir, Plate, Portrait, Queen Elizabeth Ii, Tin, 10 In.	10.00
Souvenir, Plate, Providence, R.I., Old Man Of Mountain, English, Blue & White	9.00
Souvenir, Plate, Rockland, Maine, Blue & White China	4.50
Souvenir, Plate, St.Mary's Hospital, Rochester, Minn., Rose Trim	5.50
Souvenir, Plate, World's Fair, 1939, Potters	7.00
Souvenir, Platter, Boston Mails, 12 X 15 In.	20.00
Souvenir, Pocketbook, Columbian Exposition, 1893	8.00
Souvenir, Program, Chicago World's Fair	5.00
Souvenir, Ribbon, Gar Representative, Mich., Benton Harbor, 1893	4.00
Souvenir, Salt & Pepper, G.B.Wildwood, 1905, Ruby Flashed, Pair	15.00
Souvenir, Salt & Pepper, Trylon & Perisphere	5.00
Souvenir, Salt, Pepper & Toothpick Set, Wisconsin Dells	10.00
Souvenir, Seat, Cane That Folds Into Seat, Kan-O-Seat, N.Y.World's Fair	17.50
Souvenir, Silk, World's International & Cotton Centennial, 1884-85	20.00
Souvenir, Skillet, Child's, Iron, S.T.Keys Furn.Co., 1899	4.00
Souvenir, Slipper, Lady's, 1893 Exposition	7.50
Souvenir, Spoon, Actress, Gloria Swanson, Silver Plate	3.75
Souvenir, Spoon, Actress, Norma Talmadge, Silver Plate	3.75
Souvenir, Spoon, Baby, Gerber, Silver Plate	1.50
Souvenir, Spoon, Banner Buggy, Silver Plate	9.00
Souvenir, Spoon, Battle Of Manila, Silver Plate	2.50
Souvenir, Spoon, Battleship Olympia, Admiral Dewey, 1898, Silver Plate	2.00
Souvenir, Spoon, Belgium, Silver Plate	2.00 To 2.50
Souvenir, Spoon, Campbell, Girl, Silver Plate	1.50
Souvenir, Spoon, Century Of Progress Exposition, Chicago, 1933, Silver Plate	2.50
Souvenir, Spoon, Century Of Progress, Chicago, 1933, Enamel On Brass	10.00
Souvenir, Spoon, Charlie Mccarthy	5.50
Souvenir, Spoon, Chicago, Administration Bldg., East View, Embossed Handle	3.00
Souvenir, Spoon, Chicago, Administration Bldg., Embossed Handle	3.00
Souvenir, Spoon, Chicago, Century Of Progress, 1934, Silver Plate	2.50
Souvenir, Spoon, Chicago, General Exhibits Group, Embossed Handle	3.00
Souvenir, Spoon, Chicago, Hall Of Science, Embossed Handle	3.00
Souvenir, Spoon, Chicago, Masonic Temple	18.50
Souvenir, Spoon, Chicago, Science Court, Embossed Handle	3.00
Souvenir, Spoon, Chicago, World's Fair, 1933, Silver Plate	2.50
Souvenir, Spoon, Christiania, Norway, 1908	20.00
Souvenir, Spoon, Columbian Exposition World's Fair, 1893	6.50
Souvenir, Spoon, Columbus, Chicago Fair, 1893	12.00
Souvenir, Spoon, Demitasse, St.Louis Fair, 1904	7.75
Souvenir, Spoon, Dennis The Menace, Silver Plate	2.50
Souvenir, Spoon, Dionne Quintuplet	7.00
Souvenir, Spoon, Dionne Quintuplet, Marie	6.50
Souvenir, Spoon, District Of Columbia, Silver Plate	2.50
Souvenir, Spoon, Douglas Fairbanks, Silver Plate	2.50
Souvenir, Spoon, Douglas Fairbanks, Sr.	10.00
Souvenir, Spoon, Eisenhower, Bust Design	20.00
Souvenir, Spoon, Eisenhower, Chapel Design	2.00
Souvenir, Spoon, Fisheries Building, Silver Plate	2.50
Souvenir, Spoon, Flagship Olympia	6.50
Souvenir, Spoon, Fort Snelling, Silver Plate	2.50
Souvenir, Spoon, General Joffre, Beaver, Silver Plate	2.50
Souvenir, Spoon, Golden Gate	12.00
Souvenir, Spoon, Harding, Silver Plate	2.50
Souvenir, Spoon, Hibbing, Minnesota, Washington School, Easter Lily	8.25
Souvenir, Spoon, Howdy Doody	5.50

Souvenir, Spoon, Hub Of Boston, Old South Church In Bowl 15.00
Souvenir, Spoon, Iowa, Wm.Rogers 2.75
Souvenir, Spoon, John Adams, President, Silver Plate 2.50
Souvenir, Spoon, John Adams, Second President 2.50
Souvenir, Spoon, John F.Kennedy, Silver Plate 2.50
Souvenir, Spoon, Machinery Hall, Columbian Exposition .... 2.50 To 2.75
Souvenir, Spoon, Maine, 1915, Wm.Rogers 2.50
Souvenir, Spoon, Maryland, Wm.Rogers .... 2.50 To 2.75
Souvenir, Spoon, Massachusetts, Wm.Rogers .... 2.50 To 2.75
Souvenir, Spoon, Minnesota, Wm.Rogers 2.75
Souvenir, Spoon, Montreal, Canada, 1920 .... 20.00
Souvenir, Spoon, Mr.Peanut 5.50
Souvenir, Spoon, New Hampshire 2.50
Souvenir, Spoon, New Hampshire, 1915, Wm.Rogers 2.50
Souvenir, Spoon, New Jersey, 1915, Wm.Rogers 2.50
Souvenir, Spoon, New York, Wm.Rogers 2.75
Souvenir, Spoon, Ohio, Wm.Rogers 2.75
Souvenir, Spoon, Ottawa, Enameled Maple Leaf, Silver Plate 2.50
Souvenir, Spoon, Pennsylvania, Wm.Rogers 2.75
Souvenir, Spoon, Pinocchio, Silver Plate 2.50
Souvenir, Spoon, Queen Elizabeth Ii 2.50
Souvenir, Spoon, Queen Elizabeth Ii, Silver Plate 2.50
Souvenir, Spoon, Skyline Of New York, Grant's Tomb In Bowl 20.00
Souvenir, Spoon, Soda, Niagara Falls Silver Co., 1877, 7 1/2 In.Long 2.50
Souvenir, Spoon, South Carolina, Wm.Rogers .... 2.50 To 2.75
Souvenir, Spoon, Sterling Silver, Atlantic City 8.00
Souvenir, Spoon, Sterling Silver, Brattleboro, Vt. 8.50
Souvenir, Spoon, Sterling Silver, Chanute, Kansas, Church In Bowl 10.00
Souvenir, Spoon, Sterling Silver, Chautauqua, Texas, Star, Wreath, Steer, Miner 8.50
Souvenir, Spoon, Sterling Silver, Cincinnati, Ohio 5.00
Souvenir, Spoon, Sterling Silver, Cleveland, Ohio 5.00
Souvenir, Spoon, Sterling Silver, Cobdon Canada, Enamel Handle 4.50
Souvenir, Spoon, Sterling Silver, Columbus, Gold Wash Bowl 14.00
Souvenir, Spoon, Sterling Silver, Council Grove, Kansas, Cottage In Bowl 10.00
Souvenir, Spoon, Sterling Silver, Council Grove, Kansas, Floral Handle 7.50
Souvenir, Spoon, Sterling Silver, Cutout Skyline, Pittsburgh, Pennsylvania 6.50
Souvenir, Spoon, Sterling Silver, Famous Point, 3 Rivers, Gold Wash Bowl 8.50
Souvenir, Spoon, Sterling Silver, Flatiron Bldg., N.Y., Gold Wash Bowl 8.50
Souvenir, Spoon, Sterling Silver, Galveston, Texas, Sea Wall, Steer, Star 12.50
Souvenir, Spoon, Sterling Silver, Indianapolis, Soldier Monument 10.00
Souvenir, Spoon, Sterling Silver, Iowa, Indian Hawkeye 7.00
Souvenir, Spoon, Sterling Silver, Jacksonville 12.00
Souvenir, Spoon, Sterling Silver, Jacksonville, Florida, Alligator Handle 9.50
Souvenir, Spoon, Sterling Silver, Kansas City, Kansas, Wallace Irving Handle 10.00
Souvenir, Spoon, Sterling Silver, Kansas Seal, Capitol 10.00
Souvenir, Spoon, Sterling Silver, London, England 5.00
Souvenir, Spoon, Sterling Silver, Louisiana, Capitol 10.00
Souvenir, Spoon, Sterling Silver, Louisiana, Enamel Handle 4.50
Souvenir, Spoon, Sterling Silver, Marion, Kansas, State Seal, Sunflower 12.50
Souvenir, Spoon, Sterling Silver, Mary B.Eddy 30.00
Souvenir, Spoon, Sterling Silver, Missouri, Gold Washed Bowl 7.50
Souvenir, Spoon, Sterling Silver, Missouri, Union Station In Bowl 8.00
Souvenir, Spoon, Sterling Silver, Monroe City, Mo. 8.00
Souvenir, Spoon, Sterling Silver, Mrs.Potter Palmer Of Chicago 12.50
Souvenir, Spoon, Sterling Silver, Nampa, Idaho 8.75
Souvenir, Spoon, Sterling Silver, New Orleans, Louisiana 8.00
Souvenir, Spoon, Sterling Silver, New York Skyline 15.00
Souvenir, Spoon, Sterling Silver, Niagara Falls 5.50
Souvenir, Spoon, Sterling Silver, Nigra Ciuta, Enamel Handle 4.50
Souvenir, Spoon, Sterling Silver, Oshkosti, Figure Of Indian 9.00
Souvenir, Spoon, Sterling Silver, Pan-American, Demitasse 6.00
Souvenir, Spoon, Sterling Silver, Paul Revere, Gold Wash Bowl 12.00
Souvenir, Spoon, Sterling Silver, Petoskey, Michigan 8.00
Souvenir, Spoon, Sterling Silver, Philipsburg, Montana, Enamel Handle 4.50
Souvenir, Spoon, Sterling Silver, Pittsburgh, Pa., Gold Wash Bowl 8.50
Souvenir, Spoon, Sterling Silver, Portland, Oregon 7.50

Souvenir, Spoon, Sterling Silver, River Front, Detroit, Mich. 8.50
Souvenir, Spoon, Sterling Silver, Rochester, Falls, Indian 9.00
Souvenir, Spoon, Sterling Silver, Saltair, Utah, Tabernacle, Eagle, Gate 12.50
Souvenir, Spoon, Sterling Silver, Santa Ana In Handle 7.50
Souvenir, Spoon, Sterling Silver, Springfield, Mo., 'Show Me, Mule' In Bowl 12.50
Souvenir, Spoon, Sterling Silver, St.Paul, Minn. 4.50
Souvenir, Spoon, Sterling Silver, State Capitol, Denver, Colorado 8.50
Souvenir, Spoon, Sterling Silver, Statue Of Liberty 15.00
Souvenir, Spoon, Sterling Silver, Summit Of Pikes Peak, Columbine Handle 10.00
Souvenir, Spoon, Sterling Silver, Sycamore, Illinois, Floral Handle 10.00
Souvenir, Spoon, Sterling Silver, Tennessee, Enameled Handle 4.50
Souvenir, Spoon, Sterling Silver, The Capitol, Washington, D.C., Gold Wash 8.50
Souvenir, Spoon, Sterling Silver, The Graduate, Male, Stanford, Penn. 13.00
Souvenir, Spoon, Sterling Silver, The Hub, Boston 6.00
Souvenir, Spoon, Sterling Silver, Toronto 10.00
Souvenir, Spoon, Sterling Silver, Toronto Exposition, Enamel Handle, 1911 .... 4.50
Souvenir, Spoon, Sterling Silver, Trenton, N.J., State Flower, Monument 7.50
Souvenir, Spoon, Sterling Silver, Trinidad, Colorado, Floral Handle 10.00
Souvenir, Spoon, Sterling Silver, Unitarian Church, Brattleboro, Vt. 8.50
Souvenir, Spoon, Sterling Silver, Utah, State Seal On Handle 12.00
Souvenir, Spoon, Sterling Silver, Vinton, Iowa, Courthouse In Bowl 7.50
Souvenir, Spoon, Sterling Silver, Yellowstone, Elk, Bear 15.00
Souvenir, Spoon, Sterling, Los Angeles, Embossed, Demitasse 4.50
Souvenir, Spoon, Sterling, Mckinley, Picture On Handle 10.50
Souvenir, Spoon, Sunny Jim, Golf Club, Silver Plate 2.50
Souvenir, Spoon, Sunny Jim With Golf Club 2.50
Souvenir, Spoon, Texas, Wm.Rogers 2.75
Souvenir, Spoon, University Of Illinois, Nut Spoon 5.00
Souvenir, Spoon, War Declared April 16, 1917, Silver Plate 2.50
Souvenir, Spoon, Washington Bicentennial, Rogers, Silver Plate 1.50
Souvenir, Spoon, Washington, D.C., Wm.Rogers 2.75
Souvenir, Spoon, Wisconsin, Wm.Rogers 2.75
Souvenir, Spoon, Women's Building, Silver Plate 2.50
Souvenir, Spoon, World's Fair, Columbian, 1892, Silver Plate 2.50
Souvenir, Stickpin, California Midwinter Exposition, 1894, Brass 6.50
Souvenir, Teaspoon, Norma Shearer 2.50
Souvenir, Thermometer, Chicago, Century Of Progress, 1933 .... 3.50
Souvenir, Ticket, Philadelphia Centennial, 1876 .... 1.50
Souvenir, Token, Metal, Century Of Progress, Chicago, Ford, 1934 .... 8.00
Souvenir, Token, St.Louis World's Fair, Majestic Ranges, First Prize 4.00
Souvenir, Token, 1940 Penny, Good Luck, Stork Club 3.00
Souvenir, Toothpick, Red, Colorado, 1899 .... 25.00
Souvenir, Toothpick, World's Fair, 1893, King's Crown, Ruby Flashed 18.00
Souvenir, Tray, Bread, Philadelphia, 1776-1876, Patent Dated, July 6, 1875 .... 47.50
Souvenir, Tray, Chicago, 1893, Silver 7.50
Souvenir, Tray, Pin, Quincy, Ill., China 4.00
Souvenir, Tray, Pin, St.Louis Fair, 1904, Illinois Building, Brass Corners 6.00
Souvenir, Tray, World's Fair, 1939 .... 6.50
Souvenir, Tub, Bath, Grand Rapids, Green Glass, Legs 6.00
Souvenir, Tumbler, Alaska Pacific Steamship Company 15.00
Souvenir, Tumbler, Chicago World's Fair 9.50
Souvenir, Tumbler, Memphis, Emerald Green, Gold, Northwood 14.50
Souvenir, Tumbler, Mother, World's Fair, 1893, Dresden, King's Crown, Ruby 15.00
Souvenir, Tumbler, Ridgetown, Canada, Button & Arches, Clambroth 13.00
Souvenir, Tumbler, Shore View, Glen Cove, Long Island, Porcelain 5.50
Souvenir, Tumbler, St.Louis Exposition, Clear 9.00
Souvenir, Tumbler, St.Louis Exposition, Scenes In Relief 10.00
Souvenir, Tumbler, Washington, D.C., Library Of Congress 3.75
Souvenir, Tumbler, White House Before Renovation, Victoria, Austria 25.00
Souvenir, Tumbler, World's Fair, Food Building, 1939 .... 5.00
Souvenir, Vase, State Fair 1921, Clear, Floral, 13 In.Tall 18.00
Souvenir, Vase, World's Fair, 1934, Amethyst, 5 In.Tall 6.00
Souvenir, Vase, 1900, Red Flashed Glass, Bellaire 12.50
Souvenir, Viewer, Peephole, World's Fair, 1939 .... 7.50

Spangle Glass is multicolored glass made from odds and ends of colored glass rods. It includes metallic flakes of mica covered with gold, silver, nickel, or cooper. Spangle Glass is usually cased glass with a thin layer of clear glass over the multicolored layer.

Spangle Glass, Basket, Gold Mica Flakes On Opalescent Ground, Amber Handle	39.00
Spangle Glass, Basket, Hat Shape, Orange, Red, Green, 7 X 4 In.	52.00
Spangle Glass, Bowl, Rose, Light Rose To Deep Rose, Bulbous, 5 1/4 In.High	175.00
Spangle Glass, Box, Trinket, Applied Glass Design, Clear, Red Green	25.00

Spanish Lace is a Victorian glass pattern that seems to have white lace on a colored background. Blue, yellow, cranberry, and clear glass was made with this distinctive white pattern.

Spanish Lace, Barber Bottle	*Illus*	27.50
Spanish Lace, Bottle, 19th Century, Slender Neck, Pair		36.00
Spanish Lace, Bowl, Bride, Ruffled, Cranberry, 10 1/2 In.Diameter		40.00

Spanish Lace, Barber Bottle

Spanish Lace, Bride's Basket, Cranberry, Resilvered Holder	100.00
Spanish Lace, Mug, Coin, Clear, Gold Decorated	25.00
Spanish Lace, Pitcher, Opalescent Floral, Blown Molded, Ringed Base	75.00
Spanish Lace, Pitcher, Water, Applied Handle	85.00
Spanish Lace, Pitcher, Water, Cranberry, Clear Reeded Handle	85.00
Spanish Lace, Pitcher, Water, Crimped Top, Ground Pontil, Opalescent Blue	48.00
Spanish Lace, Rose Bowl, Cranberry Opalescent	35.00
Spanish Lace, Rose Bowl, Opalescent, Blue, 4 In.	28.00
Spanish Lace, Salt, Opalescent, Vaseline	14.00
Spanish Lace, Syrup, Blue	52.00
Spanish Lace, Tumbler, Coin, Clear, Gilded Coins	40.00
Spanish Lace, Tumbler, Electric Blue, Opalescent, Fern Pattern	18.50
Spanish Lace, Water Set, Clear To Cranberry, Pitcher & Four Tumbler	165.00
Spanish Lace, Water Set, Opalescent	55.00

Spatter Glass is a multicolored Glass made from many small pieces of different colored glass.

Spatter Glass, Basket, Cased, Pink, Orange, Yellow, Crimped Edge, Thorn Handle	68.50
Spatter Glass, Basket, Red, Pink, Yellow, Blue, Clear, Handle, 5 X 6 In.	75.00
Spatter Glass, Bottle, Liqueur, Blue & White Spatters, Crystal Stopper	30.00
Spatter Glass, Bottle, Wine, Pink, Green, White Spatters, Crystal Stopper	30.00
Spatter Glass, Bowl, Green & White, 9 In.Diameter, 4 In.Tall	25.00
Spatter Glass, Bowl, Rose, Allover Cranberry & White Spatters	45.00
Spatter Glass, Candlestick, Custard Color Ground, Pink, Blue, White, Pair	40.00
Spatter Glass, Cruet, Green Ground, Multicolor Spatters, Crystal Stopper	40.00
Spatter Glass, Cup & Saucer, Handleless, Rainbow Red & Blue, C.1840	100.00
Spatter Glass, Floral, Green Yellow, Blue, White Lining, Bulbous, 8 In.Tall	65.00
Spatter Glass, Pitcher, Pink, White, Melon Rib, Clear Handle	30.00
Spatter Glass, Plate, Blue, Bull's-Eye Effect, 9 1/4 In.	40.00
Spatter Glass, Plate, Mulberry, Octagonal, 9 1/2 In.	30.00
Spatter Glass, Tumbler, Blue With Custard Splashes	18.00

Spatter Glass, Tumbler, Pink, Leaf Umbrella	35.00
Spatter Glass, Tumbler, Pink, Yellow, White, Royal Ivy	35.00
Spatter Glass, Vase, Aqua, Brown, Ruffled Edge, Clear Handle, 6 3/4 In.	45.00
Spatter Glass, Vase, Ribbed, Swirled, Crystal Thorn Handles, 6 In.Tall	28.00
Spatter Glass, Vase, Yellow, Red, Amethyst, Ruffled Top, Bulbous, 5 1/2 In.	30.00

Spatterware is a creamware or soft-paste dinnerware decorated with spatter designs. The earliest pieces were made during the late eighteenth century, but most of the wares found today were made from 1800 to 1850. The Spatterware dishes were made in the Staffordshire District of England for sale in the american market.

Spatterware, Bowl, Blue, Peafowl Decoration, 4 1/4 In.Diameter	75.00
Spatterware, Bowl, Blue, Red Flower, 6 1/2 In.Diameter	100.00
Spatterware, Bowl, Stick, Inscribed 'keep The Home Fires Burning, ' Etc.	15.00
Spatterware, Bowl, Stick, Vine Band In Black, Red Flower, Green Vine	35.00
Spatterware, Creamer, Peafowl, Green, 2 5/8 In.High	160.00
Spatterware, Creamer, Red, Peafowl Decoration, 3 3/4 In.High	225.00
Spatterware, Cup & Saucer, & Plate, Child's, Blue, Brown Vine Decoration	55.00
Spatterware, Cup & Saucer, Blue, Peafowl Decoration	125.00
Spatterware, Cup & Saucer, Brown, Handleless, Deep Saucer	90.00
Spatterware, Cup & Saucer, Handleless, Brown, Cock's Comb Decoration	145.00
Spatterware, Cup & Saucer, Handleless, Green, Peafowl Decoration	175.00
Spatterware, Cup & Saucer, Handleless, Rooster, Penna.Dutch	100.00
Spatterware, Cup & Saucer, Peafowl On Branch Of Green Leaves	90.00
Spatterware, Cup & Saucer, Purple & Red Rainbow, Peafowl	145.00
Spatterware, Cup & Saucer, Red Sponge Decorated, Flower In Center	25.00
Spatterware, Cup Plate, Blue, Peafowl Decoration, 4 In.Diameter	150.00
Spatterware, Jug, Milk, Blue, Beige, Tankard Shape	35.00
Spatterware, Mug, Staffordshire	22.50
Spatterware, Plate, Blue, Six Petal Flower Decoration, 8 In.Diameter	225.00
Spatterware, Plate, Pink & Blue Rainbow Edge, Starflower Center	150.00
Spatterware, Plate, Pink, Tulip Decoration, 7 1/2 In.Diameter	170.00
Spatterware, Plate, Purple, Peafowl Decoration	175.00
Spatterware, Plate, Red, Peafowl Decoration, Tail Goes To Rim	175.00
Spatterware, Plate, Stick, 9 In.Diameter	30.00
Spatterware, Sugar, Covered, Blue, Octagonal, Peafowl Decoration	250.00
Spatterware, Tea Caddy	60.00
Spatterware, Teapot, Pink, 6 In.High	15.00
Spatterware, Washbowl, Stick, Green, Brown, Blue, & Purple Decoration	25.00

Spelter is a white metal often used to make decorative figures and statues. The spelter is sometimes coated with bronze. It was used in the late Victorian period and after.

Spelter, Figurine, French, Boys, Pair, 14 In.	32.50
Spelter, Figurine, Two Dogs Playing With Turtle, Bronze Finish	40.00
Spelter, Fishing, Pair	27.50
Spelter, Le Power, Le Force, Pair	27.50
Spelter, Warriors On Horses, Pair, 18 In.	47.50
Spinning Wheel, see Tool, Spinning Wheel	

Spode Pottery, Porcelain, and Bone China were made by the Stoke-on-Trent Factory of England founded by Josiah Spode about 1770. The firm became Copeland and Garrett from 1833 to 1847, then W.T.Copeland or W.T.Copeland and Sons until the present time. The word spode appears on many pieces made by the Copeland Factory. Most antique dealers included all the wares under the more familiar name of Spode.

Spode, see also Copeland	
Spode, Bell, Christmas, 1971	25.00
Spode, Bust, Winston Churchill, White, Matte Finish, 1965, 1st Edition	20.00
Spode, Candlestick, Applied Bands Of Beading, Enamels, C.1820, Pair	70.00
Spode, Compote, Blue, Gothic Castle Pattern, Circa 1810, 12 X 9 1/4 In.	78.00
Spode, Cup & Saucer, Blue Scenic	17.50
Spode, Cup & Saucer, Demitasse, Tree Of Life	8.50
Spode, Cup & Saucer, Giant, Pink, Camellia, 'Auld Lang Syne' In Cup	12.00
Spode, Cup & Saucer, Prince Of Wales, Feathers, White, Blue, Marked	6.00
Spode, Cup & Saucer, Scenic, Blue	17.50

Spode, Cup, Mountain Scene, Mark 15.00
Spode, Dessert Set, Hexagonal Plates, Floral, Lavender, C.1814, 19 Piece 350.00
Spode, Dessert Set, Stone China, Famille Rose Style, C.1816, 24 Piece 450.00
Spode, Dish, Oval, Claret Ground, Bouquets, Scroll Handles, C.1815, Pair 100.00
Spode, Pitcher, Blue & White Hunting Scene, C.1850, Copeland 75.00
Spode, Plate, Cream Color, Cluster Of Fruit Center, Blue & Gold, 12 .... 96.00
Spode, Plate, Dinner, Dark Blue Greek Classic Center, Greek Key Band, 12 .... 216.00
Spode, Plate, Floral, 5 1/2 In. 3.50
Spode, Plate, Ivory, Floral Cluster Of Autumn Flowers, 12 .... 72.00
Spode, Plate, Lucano, Blue & White, Impressed Spode, C.1805 .... 22.00
Spode, Plate, Seasons, November, Blue & White, 9 In., Copeland 15.00
Spode, Plate, Soup, Ivory, Sprigs Of Small Flowers Center & Border, 12 .... 48.00
Spode, Plate, St.Thomas Becket, No.236, Red & Gold 50.00
Spode, Plate, White, Rose Center, Green Border, 9 In.Diameter, 12 .... 96.00
Spode, Platter, Blue & White, Canal Scene, Floral Border, 18 In.Long 30.00
Spode, Platter, Tiber, Circa 1815, 15 In.Long 48.00
Spode, Stand, Oval, Central Floral Panel, Beige Border, C.1815, Pair 70.00
Spode, Sucrier, Cover, Stand, Floral, Gilt Scroll Handles, C.1830, Pair 110.00
Spode, Tea Set, Gilt Fruit & Leaves, Wine Borders, C.1825, 20 Piece 100.00
Spode, Tea Set, Pattern No.9080, Floral Outlined In Gilt, C.1854, 20 Piece 250.00
Spode, Urn, Tower Pattern, Finial On Cover, Dark Blue, 13 In.High, Pair 145.00
Spode, Vase, Investiture, Charles, Prince Of Wales, 1969, No.149 .... 65.00

Spongeware is very similar to Spatterware in appearance. The designs
were applied to the ware by daubing the color. Many dealers do not
differentiate between the two wares and use the names interchangeably.

Spongeware, Bowl, Batter, Green & White 25.00
Spongeware, Bowl, Blue, Cream, Brown, 7 1/2 In.Diameter 20.00
Spongeware, Bowl, Blue, 10 In.Diameter 4.00
Spongeware, Bowl, Cake, Blue, Gray & Rust, 'it Pays To Mix With Zimmerman's' 35.00
Spongeware, Inkwell, Blue, Square, Slant Front, 2 1/2 In.High 15.00
Spongeware, Jug, Blue, 9 In. 45.00
Spongeware, Mug, Blue & Brown On Cream Ground, Handle 25.00
Spongeware, Pitcher, Blue, Brown, Red, 8 1/2 In.Tall 45.00
Spongeware, Potty, Blue 15.00
Spongeware, Spittoon, Blue & White, 6 1/2 In.Diameter 23.00
Spongeware, Spittoon, Pennsylvania Dutch, Spatter Blue & Gray 28.00

Staffordshire is a district in England where pottery and porcelain have
been made since the 1900s. Thousands of types of pottery and porcelain have
been made in the hundreds of factories that worked in the area. Some of the
most famous factories have been listed separately. See Royal Doulton,
Royal Worcester, Spode, Wedgwood, and others.

Staffordshire, see also Flow Blue
Staffordshire, Inkwell, see also Inkwell
Staffordshire, Bank, Still, Cottage Series 55.00
Staffordshire, Basket, Cutout Sides, Blue & White 65.00
Staffordshire, Basket, Stand, Oval, Pierced, Twig Handle, C.1790, Pair 275.00
Staffordshire, Bookends, Couple Seated On Deacon Bench 16.00
Staffordshire, Bowl & Pitcher, Purple, Olympic Games, T.Mayer 125.00
Staffordshire, Bowl, Blue, 6 1/2 In.Diameter 22.50
Staffordshire, Bowl, Brush Polychrome Decor, C.1800-1835, Yellow 195.00
Staffordshire, Bowl, Dancing Ladies, Urn, Flowers, Blue, White, Mark 22.50
Staffordshire, Bowl, Dark Blue, Cherubs Dancing, 6 1/2 In.Diameter 17.50
Staffordshire, Bowl, Dark Blue, Colonial Pattern, Mckee Bros., Scalloped 30.00
Staffordshire, Bowl, Fruit, Stand, Lafayette At Castle Garden, 1824, Clews 500.00
Staffordshire, Bowl, Gaudy Marbleized Decoration, 5 1/4 In.Diameter 12.50
Staffordshire, Bowl, Historical, Dark Blue, Boat Shape, Landing Of Lafayette 275.00
Staffordshire, Bowl, Return Of Fisherman, Lion Head Handles, Oval 19.00
Staffordshire, Bowl, Sugar, Covered, Gaudy Blue Decoration 45.00
Staffordshire, Box, Man Feeding Child, 3 1/4 X 4 1/2 In. 18.50
Staffordshire, Box, Pin, Covered, Bird On Lid 15.00
Staffordshire, Box, Pin, Covered, Cat & Mouse 20.00
Staffordshire, Box, Pin, Covered, Children Eating 22.50
Staffordshire, Box, Pin, Covered, Red Riding Hood 10.00
Staffordshire, Box, Puppy Dogs, 3 X 4 1/2 In. 15.00

Staffordshire, Box, Trinket, Applied Flowers, Pillow Shape, Ruffle, Gold	30.00
Staffordshire, Box, Trinket, Clock On Lid, Yellow Horns & Book	12.50
Staffordshire, Box, Trinket, Cupboard Shape, Gray Luster, Gold Trim	45.00
Staffordshire, Box, Trinket, Three Pears On Blue Lid	22.50
Staffordshire, Burner, Pastille, Cottage, Applied Moss	45.00
Staffordshire, Burner, Pastille, Swan Decor	45.00
Staffordshire, Bust, George Washington, Wearing Periwig, 19th Century	160.00
Staffordshire, Cake Stand, Gray Water Birds, Flying Birds Around Edge	19.50
Staffordshire, Candlestick, Apple Green, Pink Roses, C.1810, Pair	120.00
Staffordshire, Candlestick, Floral, Purple, Green, White, 6 In.Tall, Pair	15.00
Staffordshire, Coffeepot, Gaudy Blue Decoration	225.00
Staffordshire, Cow, Calf At Side	75.00
Staffordshire, Creamer, Gaudy Blue Decoration	15.00
Staffordshire, Creamer, Gaudy Blue Decoration, 3 1/2 In.High	40.00
Staffordshire, Creamer, Historical, Pink, Hudson River Scene	50.00
Staffordshire, Creamer, Wild Duck Shooting & Cricket, Black, White	45.00
Staffordshire, Cup & Saucer, Child's, Girl, Boy, Bird, Floral, Scrolls	9.50
Staffordshire, Cup & Saucer, Child's, Pastoral Scene, Black, White	15.00
Staffordshire, Cup & Saucer, Eagle On Urn, Clews	155.00
Staffordshire, Cup & Saucer, Farmer's Creed, Adams	8.50
Staffordshire, Cup & Saucer, Handleless, Blue, Salopian Pattern, Shepherd	55.00
Staffordshire, Cup & Saucer, Signed, Marked, 1910	10.00
Staffordshire, Cup Plate, Blue Canova	15.00
Staffordshire, Cup Plate, Historical, Blue, Battery, New York	125.00
Staffordshire, Cup Plate, Historical, Blue, Landing Of Lafayette	150.00
Staffordshire, Cup Plate, Light Blue, Clews	15.00
Staffordshire, Cup Plate, Napoleon Series, Blue	35.00
Staffordshire, Dish Drain, Sepia Transfer, Signed Morea, 12 3/4 X 9 1/2 In.	45.00
Staffordshire, Dish, Oval, Napoleon Series, 8 In.	19.00
Staffordshire, Dish, Setting Hen, Gray & Brown, Chick On Her Back	150.00
Staffordshire, Dish, Vegetable, Cover, Scenic, Brown & White Transfer, 1840	22.00
Staffordshire, Dish, Vegetable, Covered, Brown & White, Oriental, Ridgway	50.00
Staffordshire, Dish, Vegetable, Historical, Dark Blue, Washington Medallion	400.00
Staffordshire, Dog, Brown ..... *Illus*	18.50
Staffordshire, Dresser Set, Box, Lid, Ring Tree, Pair Bottles, Millefiori	42.50
Staffordshire, Eggcup, Blue Violets, Pair	8.50
Staffordshire, Figurine, Bird Group, 2 Yellow Birds, C.1770, 7 1/2 In.High	275.00
Staffordshire, Figurine, Boy & Dog ..... *Illus*	35.00

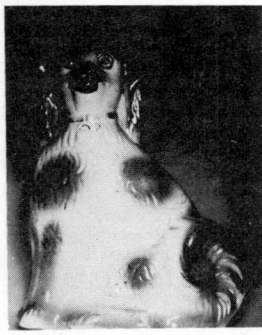

Staffordshire,
Dog, Brown

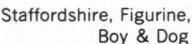

Staffordshire, Figurine,
Boy & Dog

Staffordshire, Figurine, Boy, Girl, Seated, C.1780, Pair	30.00
Staffordshire, Figurine, Calf Nursing	35.00
Staffordshire, Figurine, Camel	15.00
Staffordshire, Figurine, Castle, Rust-Orange Coloration, 6 1/4 X 7 1/8 In.	55.00
Staffordshire, Figurine, Cottage	35.00
Staffordshire, Figurine, Couple With Birdcage, Mounted As Lamp, 12 In.High	90.00
Staffordshire, Figurine, Couple, 12 3/4 In.High	40.00
Staffordshire, Figurine, Deer, White, Black, Gold, 14 In.High	35.00
Staffordshire, Figurine, Dog, Sitting, 10 In.	75.00
Staffordshire, Figurine, Dog, Spaniel, Painted Eyes, Gold Chain & Lock	28.00

Staffordshire, Figurine, Dog, Whippet, Brown, White, Black, 2 1/2 In.High		35.00
Staffordshire, Figurine, Elephant, Rider, Clock Tower Vase, 19th Century		140.00
Staffordshire, Figurine, French Poodle, Basket In Mouth, 2 1/2 X 3 In.		45.00
Staffordshire, Figurine, Girl & Goat		7.00
Staffordshire, Figurine, Girl & Lamb, 15 In.High		20.00
Staffordshire, Figurine, Girl & Reclining Sheep		30.00
Staffordshire, Figurine, Girl At Piano, Hand Raised		45.00
Staffordshire, Figurine, Girl With Basket		15.00
Staffordshire, Figurine, Hen, Bright Plumage, Bisque, 19 X 9 In.		145.00
Staffordshire, Figurine, Hound		12.50
Staffordshire, Figurine, Lamb By Tree, White, Sanded		25.00
Staffordshire, Figurine, Lovers In A Bower, With Dog, White, Gold Trim		23.50
Staffordshire, Figurine, Man Carries Urn, Lady Carries Basket, 14 In.Tall		55.00
Staffordshire, Figurine, Man, Woman, Guitar, Tambourine		29.00
Staffordshire, Figurine, Pekingese, Tan, Blue Bow, Pair		75.00
Staffordshire, Figurine, Poodle, Seated		10.00
Staffordshire, Figurine, Poodles, White, Pink, Blue Base, Sad Face, Pair		45.00
Staffordshire, Figurine, Queen Victoria, Prince Of Wales, 18 In.Tall, Pair		95.00
Staffordshire, Figurine, Rabbit		15.00
Staffordshire, Figurine, Ram, Standing, Gray Coat, C.1780, Pair		110.00
Staffordshire, Figurine, Red Riding Hood & Wolf, 10 In.High	20.00 To	35.00
Staffordshire, Figurine, Rooster & Hen		20.00
Staffordshire, Figurine, Running Deer & Dog, 11 In.High		25.00
Staffordshire, Figurine, Scotch Boy & Girl With Dog, Pair		100.00
Staffordshire, Figurine, Scotsman In Kilts, Waterfall, Bridge, 18 In.Tall		62.00
Staffordshire, Figurine, Scottish Huntsman, Mounted, Deer On Horse		49.00
Staffordshire, Figurine, Scottish Man, Woman, Kilts, Bagpipe, 14 In.		55.00
Staffordshire, Figurine, Sheep & Tree Stump		25.00
Staffordshire, Figurine, Spaniel, Red, Brown, 7 1/2 In.Tall, Pair		65.00
Staffordshire, Figurine, Two Girls With Baskets, Flowers, Clock		40.00
Staffordshire, Figurine, Uncle Tom & Eva		40.00
Staffordshire, Figurine, Whippet Dog, Rabbit, Rust, Orange, 3 3/4 In.		22.00
Staffordshire, Figurine, Zebra, Black & White, C.1830, 5 1/8 In.High		130.00
Staffordshire, Goblet, Pink, Black Transfer Of Sniper Shooting & Cursing		20.00
Staffordshire, Gravy Boat, Blue & White		27.50
Staffordshire, Group, Spaniels, Seated, White, Gold Collars, Marked		35.00
Staffordshire, Hen On Nest, Brown, Green, 8 In.Long	*Illus*	110.00
Staffordshire, Hen On Nest, Yellow, Red, Black, White, 5 1/2 In.Long, 4 In.		47.50
Staffordshire, Hen On Nest, 7 1/2 In.		75.00
Staffordshire, Hen, Bisque, Bright Plumage		145.00
Staffordshire, Inkwell, Tree Stump, Rooster & Chicken At Base, Eggs		110.00
Staffordshire, Jug, Lusterware, Mustard Color, Floral, C.1800, Pair		125.00
Staffordshire, Jug, Toby, Man Taking Snuff, Green, 8 1/2 In.High		150.00
Staffordshire, Jug, Toby, Seated Soldier, Hat & Boots, Black, 10 In.High		150.00
Staffordshire, Mantel Set, Victorian, Cupid & Venus Decor, 3 Pieces		50.00
Staffordshire, Mug, Checkered Decoration In Greenish-Gray		12.50
Staffordshire, Mug, Polychrome Transfer Of Train		35.00
Staffordshire, Mug, Red, Blue, & Green Gaudy Decoration		15.00

Staffordshire, Hen On Nest,
Brown, Green, 8 In.Long

Staffordshire, Mug, Shaving, Scuttle, Blue Roses	19.00
Staffordshire, Phrenologist's Head, Inscribed L.N.Fowler, London, C.1850	220.00
Staffordshire, Pitcher, Bluebirds In Medallions, Spout Is Man's Face	20.00
Staffordshire, Pitcher, Bologna Pattern, Green & Red	35.00
Staffordshire, Pitcher, Boston State House, J.Stubbs .... *Illus*	250.00
Staffordshire, Pitcher, Caneware, Figure Handle, High Relief	85.00
Staffordshire, Pitcher, Figural, Man's Face, Hat, Blue, Copper, Pink, 5 In.Tall	50.00
Staffordshire, Pitcher, Figural, World War I Soldier	25.00
Staffordshire, Pitcher, Historical, Blue, Boston State House, Joseph Stubbs	250.00
Staffordshire, Pitcher, Historical, Copper Luster & Yellow, C.1810	850.00
Staffordshire, Pitcher, Milk, Dog	35.00
Staffordshire, Pitcher, Red, Blue & Green Gaudy Decoration	20.00
Staffordshire, Pitcher, Rural Transfer Scene, Brown, Green, 2 In.Tall	8.00
Staffordshire, Pitcher, Water, Blue & White, Blantyre Pattern, 8 In.High	7.50
Staffordshire, Pitcher, Water, Celonese, Blue, White, Signed G.Phillips	75.00
Staffordshire, Plate, American Scene, Black, 10 In.Diameter	65.00
Staffordshire, Plate, American Villa, Deep Blue, 10 In.	65.00
Staffordshire, Plate, Blue & White Floral Border, Mohawk Indian Figure	10.00
Staffordshire, Plate, Blue & White, Bird On Nest, 6 In.Diameter	30.00
Staffordshire, Plate, Blue, British Ship, Shannon, Shell & Seaweed Border	80.00
Staffordshire, Plate, Cake, Rhode Island Arms, T.Mayer .... *Illus*	200.00
Staffordshire, Plate, Child's, 'my Childhood, ' Daisies, Mother, Child, C.1840	28.00
Staffordshire, Plate, Child's, The Order Of The Visitation Of The Sick	25.00
Staffordshire, Plate, Child's, 'the Shuttlecock, ' Children & Dog	28.00
Staffordshire, Plate, Cupid Imprisoned, Blue, Wood Mark, 9 1/2 In.	125.00
Staffordshire, Plate, Dark Blue, Barrington Hall, A.Stevenson	40.00
Staffordshire, Plate, Dark Blue, Nahant Hotel, Boston, By R.S.W.	125.00
Staffordshire, Plate, Dark Blue, Park Theatre, N.G.Stevenson	160.00
Staffordshire, Plate, Dinner, Basketwork Ground, Cartouche, C.1825, 6	40.00
Staffordshire, Plate, Dinner, New York Arms, T.Mayer .... *Illus*	350.00

Staffordshire, Pitcher, Boston State House, J.Stubbs

Staffordshire, Plate, Cake, Rhode Island Arms, T.Mayer

Staffordshire, Plate, Dinner, New York Arms, T.Mayer

Staffordshire, Plate, Don Quixote, Knighthood Conferred, 10 In. 125.00
Staffordshire, Plate, Don Quixote, Sancho Panza & Theresa, Clews, 9 In. 95.00
Staffordshire, Plate, Dr.Franklin Maxim, Make Hay While The Sun Shines 38.00
Staffordshire, Plate, Enoch Wood's, Blue English Scenery, 9 In.Diameter 18.50
Staffordshire, Plate, European Scenery, Mark, 7 In.Diameter, Set Of 6 .... 45.00
Staffordshire, Plate, Franklin D.Roosevelt, Blue & White 22.50
Staffordshire, Plate, Franklin Maxim, Brown Transfer, 6 1/2 In.Diameter 20.00
Staffordshire, Plate, Franklin Maxim, Make Hay While The Sun Shines 30.00
Staffordshire, Plate, Green & Blue Chinoiserie Scenery, 12 .... 96.00
Staffordshire, Plate, Historic Blue, Revelation, Wood, 9 In. 35.00
Staffordshire, Plate, Historical, Blue, Arms Of Rhode Island, Thomas Mayer 300.00
Staffordshire, Plate, Historical, Blue, At Washington, Johnson Bros. 15.00
Staffordshire, Plate, Historical, Blue, City Hall, New York 85.00
Staffordshire, Plate, Historical, Blue, Harvard College, 10 In.Diameter 150.00
Staffordshire, Plate, Historical, Blue, Jackson's Waterworks, Phila. 45.00
Staffordshire, Plate, Historical, Blue, Landing Of Lafayette .... 175.00 To 225.00
Staffordshire, Plate, Historical, Dark Blue, New York Battery 225.00
Staffordshire, Plate, Historical, Dark Blue, View Of Governors Island 400.00
Staffordshire, Plate, Historical, Pink, Allegheny Scenery, Peppard & Callon 120.00
Staffordshire, Plate, Historical, Pink, Harvard College, 10 1/4 In.Diameter 60.00
Staffordshire, Plate, Italy Design, Purple, 10 In.Diameter 25.00
Staffordshire, Plate, Landing Of Pilgrims, Blue, Enoch Wood .... 75.00 To 85.00
Staffordshire, Plate, Marine Hospital, Louisville, Ky., Enoch Wood, Blue 200.00
Staffordshire, Plate, Millennium, Pink, 8 In.Diameter 30.00
Staffordshire, Plate, Missionary, Soft Paste, Circa 1840, Transfer 30.00
Staffordshire, Plate, New York Harbor, Red, 9 1/2 In.Diameter 65.00
Staffordshire, Plate, Petal Shape Rim, Sponged Treacle Center, C.1765 .... 50.00
Staffordshire, Plate, Pink, English Fishermen Scene, Hopkins & Vernon 10.00
Staffordshire, Plate, Pink, J.H.& Co., 8 In.Diameter 12.50
Staffordshire, Plate, Quincy, Ill., Courthouse, Adams 14.50
Staffordshire, Plate, Salad, Clear, Flowers, Scalloped, 6 1/4 In.Diameter 21.50
Staffordshire, Plate, Shannondale Springs, Va., 8 In. 33.00
Staffordshire, Plate, Signed, Marked, 1910, 8 In.Diameter 12.50
Staffordshire, Plate, Soup, Canova, Brown & White, 10 1/4 In. 12.00
Staffordshire, Plate, Table Rock, Niagara, Dark Blue, 10 In. 145.00
Staffordshire, Plate, The Sentinel, Blue, Miniature, 3 1/2 In.Diameter 12.50
Staffordshire, Platter, Black, Lake Como Scene, 13 In.Long 5.00
Staffordshire, Platter, Blue Willow, 17 3/4 X 14 In. 25.00
Staffordshire, Platter, Blue, Canal Scene, Rose Border, 16 In.Long 12.50
Staffordshire, Platter, Blue, Castle Garden, Battery, N.Y., Enoch Wood & Sons 525.00
Staffordshire, Platter, Blue, Floral Border & Cluster In Center, Bird 16.00
Staffordshire, Platter, Blue, Gold Coast Castle, Wood Shell Border, 18 In. 225.00
Staffordshire, Platter, Blue, Lake George, N.Y., Octagonal, Enoch Wood & Sons 200.00
Staffordshire, Platter, Blue, Shell & Seaweed, Rogers, 1815, 19 1/2 In. 375.00
Staffordshire, Platter, Castles, Sailing Ships, Signed, 15 X 18 .... 45.00
Staffordshire, Platter, Compton Verney, Blue, 10 1/2 In.Long 48.00
Staffordshire, Platter, Corinthian, Black, White, 10 X 8 In. 15.00
Staffordshire, Platter, Dark Blue, Arms Of Massachusetts 1900.00
Staffordshire, Platter, Dark Blue, British Views, 14 3/4 X 11 1/2 In. 88.00
Staffordshire, Platter, Delaware Arms, T.Mayer .... *Illus* 1600.00
Staffordshire, Platter, Hannibal Crossing Alps 50.00
Staffordshire, Platter, Historical, Dark Blue, Winter View Of Pittsfield 600.00
Staffordshire, Platter, Lafayette's Landing, Castle Garden, 17 1/2 In. 350.00
Staffordshire, Platter, North Carolina Arms, T.Mayer .... *Illus* 1800.00
Staffordshire, Platter, Pagoda Scene In Brown, Fruits & Flowers 17.50
Staffordshire, Platter, View Of Greenwich, Grapevine Border, Wood, 15 In. 85.00
Staffordshire, Salt & Pepper, Dog, White, Long Ears, Gold Bag In Mouth 10.00
Staffordshire, Sifter, Sugar, Toby, Yellow Tricorn Hat, Blue, Orange, C.1820 .... 32.00
Staffordshire, Sucrier, Cover, Cafe-Au-Lait Bands, Floral, C.1820, Pair 140.00
Staffordshire, Sugar, Cover, Dark Blue, Wander-In Boy, 6 1/2 In. 118.00
Staffordshire, Sugar, Dark Blue, Flower Basket Design, 6 1/2 In.Long 25.00
Staffordshire, Tea Set, Child's, Birds, Flowers, & Animals In Sepia, 3 Piece 17.50
Staffordshire, Tea Set, Child's, Miniature, Pink Spatterware, 15 Piece 35.00
Staffordshire, Tea Set, Strawberry Luster, C.1820, 18 Piece 250.00
Staffordshire, Teapot, Blue & White, Mother & Child In Forest Scene 22.50
Staffordshire, Teapot, Blue, Floral, 12 1/2 In.Long 30.00

Staffordshire, Teapot, Brown, Figures & Floral Urns, 10 In.High	20.00
Staffordshire, Teapot, Brown, Harvest Flowers, 10 1/2 In.Long	10.00
Staffordshire, Teapot, Flower Encrusted Lid, Signed, Marked	22.50
Staffordshire, Teapot, Miniature, Child & Dog	15.00
Staffordshire, Teapot, Ovoid, Black Ground, Floral Decor, 19th Century	25.00
Staffordshire, Toby Mug, Gentleman, Blue Coat, Ocher Pants, C.1790	70.00
Staffordshire, Toby Mug, Gentleman, Seated, Holding Jug Of Ale, C.1780	130.00
Staffordshire, Toby Mug, Man With Tricorn Hat, 18th Century, 8 In., Pair	175.00
Staffordshire, Toothpick, Dog On Pillow, Paw On Umbrella, Tall Hat On Side	9.50
Staffordshire, Tray, Pen, Apricot Ground, Bouquet Of Flowers, C.1810	120.00
Staffordshire, Tureen & Underplate, Sepia Covered, Oriental Figures	45.00
Staffordshire, Tureen, Alcock, Avon, Sepia	22.00
Staffordshire, Tureen, Oak Sprays, Acorns, Artist's Marks, 6 X 4 In.	25.00
Staffordshire, Tureen, Ridgway, Fairy Villas, Blue, England, 10 1/2 In.	55.00
Staffordshire, Vase, Arbor, Seated Man Playing Mandolin	15.00
Staffordshire, Vase, Blue & Gold Floral Decor, 2 Handles, 9 In.High, Pair	250.00
Staffordshire, Vase, Brown & Gold, 9. 1/2 In.High, Pair	30.00
Staffordshire, Vase, Cartouche On Bottom, Marked Abbey 1790, 8 In., Pair	87.50
Staffordshire, Vase, Duck's Head Handles, Flowers & Butterflies, Pair	70.00
Staffordshire, Vase, Fan Type, Hunter, Dog, Rabbit, 5 1/4 In.Tall	18.00
Staffordshire, Vase, Figural Scotsman, Plaid Attire, Stands Beside Vase	45.00
Staffordshire, Vase, Tree Trunk, Dog, Red Riding Hood	39.50
Stangl, Bird, 4 In.High *Illus*	16.00

Staffordshire, Platter,
Delaware Arms, T.Mayer
See Page 495

Staffordshire, Platter,
North Carolina Arms, T.Mayer
See Page 495

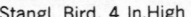

Stangl, Bird, 4 In.High

Stangl, Bluebird, Marked, Labeled	35.00
Stangl, Figurine, Bird, Dogwood Branch, Scarlet, Artist-Signed, 5 In.Tall	35.00
Stangl, Figurine, Bluejay, Foliage Perch, 8 In.High, Pair	20.00
Stangl, Figurine, Cockatoo, Pink	39.00
Stangl, Figurine, Parrot	35.00
Stangl, Figurine, Rooster, C.1940, Impressed No.3445, Artist-Signed, 10 In.	20.00
Stangl, Figurine, Two Birds, Branch Base, 10 In.Tall	49.00

Star Holly is a milk glass type of glass made by the Imperial Glass Company of Bellaire, Ohio, in 1957. The pieces were made to look like Wedgwood jasperware. White holly leaves appear against colored borders of blue, green, or rust. IG is marked on the bottom of every piece.

Star Holly, Bowl, Blue Ground, Imperial	45.00
Stein, Amber Glass, Pewter Lid, 12 In.	75.00
Stein, Amber, Jewel In Cover, Glass, 1/2 Liter, 8 In.	11.00
Stein, Beaded, Flower, Glass, 1/2 Liter, 9 In.	10.00
Stein, Blue, Gray, Cavalier, Greentown	20.00
Stein, Bowling Ball, Ten Pin, Gut Holz, German, 1 Liter	275.00
Stein, Building Scene, Munchen, Brown & Blue, 1/2 Liter, 9 In.	22.00
Stein, Child Of Munich, H.R.Engraved, 1 Liter	135.00
Stein, Clear, Paneled, Alpine Scene, Girl, Pewter Lid & Handle	47.50
Stein, Cobalt Blue, Good Luck Written In German, 1 Liter	95.00
Stein, Delft, Sailboats, Blue, White, German	10.00
Stein, Enameled Porcelain & 1897 On Cover, Jewel Center Flowers, 1/2 Liter	29.50
Stein, Etched, Don Quixote, Servant, Pewter Lid, 1 Liter, K.B.Mark, No.1088	95.00
Stein, Faience Revelers, Pewter Top, Signed Getz, Germany	45.00
Stein, Fat Monk, Mark 05I, 7 In.Tall	45.00
Stein, Flat Top, Gray, 1 Liter	9.75
Stein, German Crest, Pattern Glass, 7 In.	14.00
Stein, German, Musician & Girl Friend, Engraved, 1/2 Liter	75.00
Stein, German, Pewter Lid, Dated 1927	45.00
Stein, Germany, Elves *Illus*	55.00

Stein, Germany, Elves

Stein, Gestzlic Geschutzt, German, Dated 1896, 1/2 Liter	95.00
Stein, Getz, Germany, 1/2 Liter, Faience On Cobalt, Embossed	37.50
Stein, Glass, Augusta-Brau, Augsburg, 10 In.	22.00
Stein, Glass, Blue, Metal Top, Enamel Decoration, 6 In.	42.50
Stein, Glass, Festzell Widmann, 9 1/2 In.	15.00
Stein, Glass, Green, Stippled, 1/2 Liter, 7 In.	15.00
Stein, Glass, 1/2 Liter, Pewter Cover, Porcelain Insert, 'hockreitstein'	12.50
Stein, Glass, 1/2 Liter, Pewter Cover, Ruby Insert	12.50
Stein, Goldene Gans, Gray & Blue Leters, 1 Liter, 8 1/2 In.	11.50
Stein, Gray, Hafenbrau-Augsburg, 1 Liter, 9 In.	9.75
Stein, Gray, 1 Liter, 8 In.	9.75
Stein, Gray, 1 Liter, 9 In.	6.75
Stein, Green, Mary Gregory Girl, Pewter Lid, Glass Insert	75.00
Stein, Hoplen Und May, Gray & Blue, 1 Liter, 9 In.	19.00
Stein, Hunting Scene, Tan & Blue Background, 9 1/2 In.	29.00
Stein, Hunting Scene, 1/2 Liter, 9 In.	18.00
Stein, Incised Germany, Old Man Smoking Pipe, 1 1/2 Liter, Pewter Top	40.00
Stein, Incised Germany, 1/2 Liter, Drinking Scene, Hunters, Pewter Top	45.00
Stein, Ivory & Blue, Tavern, Dragon, Cover With Jewel, 11 In.Tall	26.00
Stein, Ivory, Dark Blue, 2 Hunters & Bar Maid In Tavern, 1 Liter	15.00
Stein, Ivory, Silver & Jeweled, 4 1/2 In.High	400.00
Stein, L.Meyer, Gray, 1 Liter, 9 In.	9.75

Stein, Ladies Face, German, Zum Wohl Herbst, 1 Liter 145.00
Stein, Lithopane, German City, Ingolstadt, 8 1/2 In. 49.00
Stein, Lodge, Mark Uhu Lulu, Nartevoluplas, Eh; Aha, German, 1/2 Liter 85.00
Stein, Man & Woman, Castle, High Relief, Germany, 1/2 Liter 35.00
Stein, Man With Gout, Signed H.B.Relief, 1 Liter 125.00
Stein, Man, Bagpipes, Mandolin, German, High Relief, 1 Liter 85.00
Stein, Mettlach, see Mettlach, Stein
Stein, Monk Holds Stein & Bible, Marked Made In Germany 65.00
Stein, Mueller, German, Pewter Top 16.50
Stein, Musterschutz, Bicycle, Lithophane 275.00
Stein, No.1335, Germany, 1/2 Liter, Lady In Blue, Man, Inscription 65.00
Stein, Oval Panels, 1/2 Liter, 9 In. 9.75
Stein, Pewter Cover, 1/2 Liter, 6 In.High 8.00
Stein, Pewter Lid, Miniature, Marked Musterschutz, 3 In.Tall 50.00
Stein, Pewter Top, Gray Pottery, 9 1/2 In. 12.50
Stein, Pewter Top, Pattern Glass, 8 1/2 In. 14.00
Stein, Pewter Top, Pattern Glass, 9 In. 14.00
Stein, Pewter Top, Picture Of Man, Hand-Painted 70.00
Stein, Picture Of Gruss Ausmittenwald, Karl Nach, 1912, 1/2 Liter, 5 1/2 In. 17.50
Stein, Pictures From Coblenz, Brown & Blue, 1/2 Liter, 9 In. 22.00
Stein, Pitcher, 3 Liters, Pewter Cover, 14 In.High 22.50
Stein, Porcelain, Red & Blue Painted Flowers 14.00
Stein, Pottery, Gray, Woman Holding A Platter, German 14.50
Stein, Rainier Ale, 'a Good Judge Knows, ' Germany, 5 1/2 In.High 10.00
Stein, Regimental, Lithopane, Pewter Lid & Finial, Circa 1880 .... 62.50
Stein, Shield, Helmet, Pewter Lid, Signed G.K., German, 5 Liter 350.00
Stein, Stoneware, Gray, Blue Art Nouveau Decor, Pewter Lid, Marked 1328 E 42.50
Stein, Stoneware, Gray, Blue, Scene, Monk, Wine Barrel, Pewter Top, 1/2 Liter 30.00
Stein, Stoneware, Pewter Lid, Says Muenchen, July 7, 1913, 8 1/2 In.High 75.00
Stein, Swedish, Pochrug, 18th Century, Medallion Of Gustavus Adolphus 250.00
Stein, Tavern Garden, Blue, 1 Liter 25.00
Stein, Tavern Scene, Brown & Blue Background, Red, Blue, White 35.00
Stein, Tavern Scene, Brown & Blue Background, Red, Blue, White, 11 1/2 In. 39.00
Stein, Tavern Scene, Brown & Blue Background, 9 1/2 In. 35.00
Stein, Tavern Scene, Brown & Blue Background, 11 1/2 In. 39.00
Stein, Tavern Scene, Tan & Blue Background, 10 In. 39.00
Stein, Tavern Scene, Tan & Blue, 11 In. 32.00
Stein, Tavern Scene, Tan & Blue, 11 1/2 In. 39.00
Stein, Tavern, People, Cottage, Leaves & Nuts, 1 Liter, 10 In. 29.50
Stein, Thumbprint, Ciugusta Brau, Augsburg, 1 Liter, 11 In. 12.50
Stein, Thumbprint, Glass, 1/2 Liter, 9 In. 9.75
Stein, Vater John, Gut Heil, 1/2 Liter 35.00
Stein, Yellow, Green & Tan Background, 10 In. 29.00

*Stereo Cards that were made for stereopticon viewers became popular after
1840. Two almost identical pictures were mounted on a stiff cardboard
backing so that, when viewed through a stereoscope, a three-dimensional picture
could be seen.*
Stereo, Card, Columbian Exposition 2.50
Stereo, Card, Comic Views, 10 .... 3.00
Stereo, Card, Doll & Carriage 1.25
Stereo, Card, Girl & Kittens 1.25
Stereo, Card, Girl At Fireplate Putting Supplies For Santa 1.25
Stereo, Card, Going To War, Set Of 12 .... 3.50
Stereo, Card, Indian 2.75
Stereo, Card, McKinley Funeral, Wilson, Roosevelt, 12 .... 27.50
Stereo, Card, Philadelphia Exposition Of 1876 .... 4.00
Stereo, Card, President & Mrs.Mckinley 2.25
Stereo, Card, President Mckinley At Desk 2.25
Stereo, Card, President T.R.& Mrs.Roosevelt, Shipboard 2.25
Stereo, Card, President T.R.Roosevelt 2.25
Stereo, Card, President T.R.Roosevelt In Connecticut 2.25
Stereo, Card, Pre-1920, 100 .... 5.50
Stereo, Card, Romance, Set Of 12 .... 3.50
Stereo, Card, Scenes Of World War I, Keystone, 147 .... 34.75
Stereo, Card, Teddy Roosevelt's Inauguration, 1905, 10 .... 5.00

Stereo, Card, Tour Of Sears Roebuck, 1900 Era, 50 .... 12.00
Stereo, Card, U.S.Views, 10 .... 2.00
Stereo, Card, World War I, Keystone View Co., 98 .... 25.00
Stereo, Card, World War I, Keystone, 62 .... 45.00
Stereo, Card, Wrecked Battleship Maine 2.25
Stereo, Card, 3 Girls With Easter Eggs & Chick 1.25
Stereo, Telebinocular, Library, Keystone, 100 Cards 35.00

*Stereoscopes, or Stereopticons, were used for viewing the stereo cards. The
hand viewer was invented by Oliver Wendell Holmes, although more
complicated table models were used before his was placed in production in 1859.*
Stereoscope, Double Type, Wooden, Made By Alex Beckers, Pat.1857 .... 69.75
Stereoscope, Folding Handle, 6 Cards 12.50
Stereoscope, Hand Type, Slide Adjustment 15.00
Stereoscope, Hand Viewer, Sliding Adjuster, 150 Stereo Cards 36.00
Stereoscope, Metal, Velvet Around Eyepiece 20.00
Stereoscope, Ornate, 150 Color Cards 20.00
Stereoscope, Wooden, 100 Cards 25.00
Stereoscope, 12 Cards In Color 16.50
Sterling Silver, see Silver, Sterling

*Steuben Glass was made at the Steuben Glass Works of Corning, New
York. The factory, founded by Frederick Carder and T.C.Hawkes,
SR., was purchased by the Corning Glass Company. They continued to
make glass called Steuben. Many types of art glass were made at Steuben.
The firm is still producing glass of exceptional quality.*
Steuben, see also Aurene, Verre De Soie
Steuben Type, Bowl, Blue Jade, Flaring, Low Foot, 10 In.Diameter 100.00
Steuben, Ashtray, Jade & Alabaster, Cable Ring Through Alabaster Loop 73.00
Steuben, Bowl, Acid Cut Back, Green Jade On Alabaster, Chinese Pattern 400.00
Steuben, Bowl, Amethyst Crystal, Stand, Signed, 10 In.Diameter 150.00
Steuben, Bowl, Calcite, Gold Luster, Ribbed Underside, 5 In., Underplate 165.00
Steuben, Bowl, Calcite, 10 1/4 In.Diameter 150.00
Steuben, Bowl, Calcite, 12 In., Pair Candlesticks, Blue 850.00
Steuben, Bowl, Centerpiece, Cobalt, Turned Down Rim, Numbered 3027 .... 35.00
Steuben, Bowl, Crystal, Clear, Applied Handles, Signed, 10 In.Diameter 30.00
Steuben, Bowl, Daffodil, Plate 185.00
Steuben, Bowl, Deep Amethyst To Clear, 4 1/2 In. X 3 1/2 In.Tall 85.00
Steuben, Bowl, Footed, Crystal, Signed, 7 In.Diameter, Pair 100.00
Steuben, Bowl, Fruit, Green Jade, Pedestal, 15 3/4 In.Diameter, Jade Frog 150.00
Steuben, Bowl, Grotesque, Cerise Ruby, 5 1/2 In.Deep 85.00
Steuben, Bowl, Grotesque, Purple To Clear, Signed, 6 X 7 1/2 In. 95.00
Steuben, Bowl, Ivory, Fluted, Square, Signed 125.00
Steuben, Bowl, Silverina, Clear, Mica Flecks, Diamond-Quilted, 14 1/2 In. 135.00
Steuben, Bowl, Topaz, Footed, Signed, 12 In. 75.00
Steuben, Bowl, Verre De Soie, 3 Feet, 10 In.Wide, 2 1/4 In.High 65.00
Steuben, Box, Signed Frederick Carder, Rosaline, Round, Covered, Alabaster 575.00
Steuben, Candlestick, Amber, Signed, 4 In.Tall, Pair 38.00
Steuben, Candlestick, Aurene, Pair .... *Illus* 95.00
Steuben, Candlestick, Clear To Cranberry, 4 Piece Construction, Signed, Pair 225.00
Steuben, Candlestick, Fleur-De-Lis, Clear To Cranberry, Signed, 14 In.Pair 225.00
Steuben, Candlestick, Green Jade, Mushroom Shape, Signed, Pair 135.00
Steuben, Candlestick, Knob Stem, Inverted Saucer Base, 10 1/2 In.High 30.00
Steuben, Candlestick, Rosaline & Alabaster, Pair 125.00
Steuben, Candlestick, Stars, Signed, Fleur-De-Lis, 9 In.Tall 25.00
Steuben, Candlestick, Swirled Ribbed, Inverted Teardrop, Blue, 10 In., Pair 125.00
Steuben, Case, Signed, Green Jade, 8 In. 175.00
Steuben, Compote, Calcite & Gold Aurene, 5 In.High 210.00
Steuben, Compote, Calcite, Opalescent White, Gold Inside 225.00
Steuben, Compote, Calcite, Ribbed, Flat, 3 In.Tall, 6 In.Diameter 95.00
Steuben, Compote, Crystal, Signed, 7 In.Diameter 90.00
Steuben, Compote, Rosaline, Alabaster Feet, Folded Over Rim, 4 In.High 65.00
Steuben, Console Set, Green Jade & Alabaster, Twisted Stems, Footed, 3 Piece 350.00
Steuben, Dessert & Underplate, Gold Aurene & Calcite 175.00
Steuben, Dish, Candy, Calcite, White, Gold Inside, Stretched Edge, Unsigned 125.00
Steuben, Figurine, Cat, Crystal, 8 3/4 In.Tall 160.00

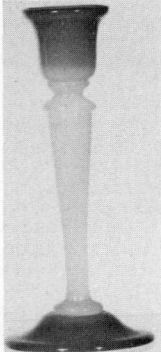

Steuben, Candlestick, Aurene, Pair
See Page 499

Steuben, **Figurine**, Songbird, 4 1/2 In.Long	65.00
Steuben, **Figurine**, Whale, Crystal, Signed, 5 In.Long	75.00
Steuben, **Goblet**, Clear, Pink Threads, Applied Stem & Foot, 8 In.High	125.00
Steuben, **Goblet**, Jade & Alabaster	65.00
Steuben, **Goblet**, Ribbed, Etched, Blue, Footed, 5 3/4 In.Tall	75.00
Steuben, **Goblet**, Warwick Pattern, Signed	75.00
Steuben, **Goblet**, Water, Melon Rib Stem & Base	10.50
Steuben, **Goblet**, Yellow Crystal, Pedestal Stem, Signed, 8 In.Tall	40.00
Steuben, **Holder**, Cigarette, Blue, Topaz Stem, 5 In.Tall	110.00
Steuben, **Lamp**, Jade, Acid Cut Back Chrysanthemums, Signed, 23 In.High	550.00
Steuben, **Lamp**, Table, Ivorene, Iridized White Ground, Green Feathers	750.00
Steuben, **Lampshade**, Calcite, Gold-Lined, 5 In.High, Set Of 5	175.00
Steuben, **Paperweight**, Bubbles, Signed	40.00
Steuben, **Paperweight**, Egg Shape, Bubbles, Clear Base, 4 1/2 In.High	97.50
Steuben, **Paperweight**, Green Basket, Blue Flower, By Thomas Boreli	95.00
Steuben, **Paperweight**, Pear Shape, 6 In.High	97.50
Steuben, **Paperweight**, Pineapple, White Swirl, 6 1/2 In.Tall	110.00
Steuben, **Paperweight**, Rosaline, 10 In.	9.50
Steuben, **Parfait**, Rosaline & Alabaster	100.00
Steuben, **Perfume**, Dubois, Gold Aurene, Rainbow Colors, 7 1/2 In.Tall	110.00
Steuben, **Perfume**, Gold Purple, Ribbed, Signed, 3 3/4 In.Tall	65.00
Steuben, **Pitcher**, Topaz, Green Handle, Signed	65.00
Steuben, **Planter**, Jade Green, Alabaster Lions' Heads At Sides	125.00
Steuben, **Plaque**, Thomas Edison, Signed	600.00
Steuben, **Plate**, Blue Jade, Depressed Center, Unsigned, 8 1/2 In.Diameter	59.00
Steuben, **Plate**, Bristol Yellow, Black Reeding, Unmarked, Set Of 3	50.00
Steuben, **Plate**, Cloverleaf Decor, Black Rim Cut To Clear, Intaglio Floral	65.00
Steuben, **Plate**, Green Jade, Unsigned, 8 In.Diameter	50.00
Steuben, **Plate**, Green, Opal Pinwheel Stripes Radiating From Pontil	25.00
Steuben, **Plate**, Oriental Poppy, Carder	235.00
Steuben, **Plate**, Rosaline, 8 In., Signed	40.00
Steuben, **Rose Bowl**, Scroll Design, Melon Rib, Amethyst, Footed, 4 1/2 In.	32.50
Steuben, **Salt**, Gold, Calcite, Pedestal	65.00
Steuben, **Salt**, Pedestal, Aurene & Calcite, Pair	95.00
Steuben, **Salt**, Pedestal, Rosaline, Signed	95.00
Steuben, **Salt**, Pedestal, Verre De Soie, Pair	60.00
Steuben, **Shade**, Calcite, Aurene Inside, Ribs, Unsigned, 4 1/2 In.Wide	25.00
Steuben, **Shade**, Gold & Green, Signed	· 45.00
Steuben, **Shade**, Gold Feather, Signed, 5 In.	47.50
Steuben, **Shade**, Ivorene Acid Cut Back, Pair	50.00
Steuben, **Shade**, Lamp, Calcite, Ribbed, Gold Inside, 5 In.High, Pair	60.00
Steuben, **Shade**, Lamp, Ruffled, Relief Ribs, Signed, 5 3/4 In.Tall	55.00
Steuben, **Shaker**, Salt, Calcite, Pedestal, Aurene	95.00
Steuben, **Sherbet & Plate**, Calcite	100.00
Steuben, **Sherbet**, Calcite, Gold Lining, 4 In.Tall, 3 3/4 In.Diameter	150.00
Steuben, **Sherbet**, Oriental Poppy, Green, Stem, Carder	195.00
Steuben, **Tazza**, Calcite, Blue, Iridescent, Opalescent, Pedestal, 6 1/2 In.	395.00

Steuben, Tazza, Purple, Clear Crystal Twisted Stem, Signed 65.00
Steuben, Tumbler, Verre De Soie, Engraved In Chrysanthemum Pattern 35.00
Steuben, Urn, Alabaster, Black Band, Black Handles, 12 X 7 1/4 In. 285.00
Steuben, Vase, Acid Cut Back, Green, Chinese Landscape Medallions, 12 In. 275.00
Steuben, Vase, Amber, Three-Pronged Thorn, Signed 95.00
Steuben, Vase, Birds, Leaves, Green To Yellow, Signed Steuben, F.Carder 750.00
Steuben, Vase, Black To Alabaster, Deep Cut, Frederick Carder 675.00
Steuben, Vase, Blue & Lavender, Signed Carder, 10 1/2 In.High 225.00
Steuben, Vase, Blue Aurene, Signed, Mirror Surface, 6 In. 105.00
Steuben, Vase, Blue, Candleholders, Three Piece Set, Carder 165.00
Steuben, Vase, Bubbly, Twisted, Red Iris, 10 In.Tall 45.00
Steuben, Vase, Calcite, Gold Lined, Footed, 4 1/2 In. 75.00
Steuben, Vase, Clear Top, Green Base, Fan Shape 25.00
Steuben, Vase, Clear, Applied Base, Signed, 6 X 4 1/4 In. 50.00
Steuben, Vase, Clear, Green Trim, Signed, 6 1/4 In. 42.00
Steuben, Vase, Clear, Two Applied Prunts, Pinched In At Waist, Signed, 6 In. 35.00
Steuben, Vase, Cluthra, Blue & White, Signed, 10 In.High, 10 In.Diameter 395.00
Steuben, Vase, Fan, Blown, Threaded Top, Pale Green Bubbles 95.00
Steuben, Vase, Fan, Bubbly, Flemish Blue, 11 In.High 165.00
Steuben, Vase, Fan, Jade Green, Alabaster Foot 75.00
Steuben, Vase, Globular, Iridescent Blue To Silver At Neck, Everted Rim 350.00
Steuben, Vase, Gold Calcite, Flare Top, 8 In.High 135.00
Steuben, Vase, Green Jade, Fan Shape, Pinched Top, Ribbed, Signed 125.00
Steuben, Vase, Green, Signed, 11 1/2 In.High 57.50
Steuben, Vase, Iridescent, Peacock Blue, Flared Top, 5 1/2 In.Tall, Signed 350.00
Steuben, Vase, Ivorene, Footed, Tulip Shape, Ribbed 38.00
Steuben, Vase, Ivory, Flared, Paper Label, 6 In. 70.00
Steuben, Vase, Ivory, 10 1/4 In.High 150.00
Steuben, Vase, Jade, Alabaster, Butterfly & Flower, 10 In. 750.00
Steuben, Vase, Jade, Green, Signed, 8 In. 10.00
Steuben, Vase, Jade, Ivorene Handle, Signed Steuben F.Carder, 9 1/2 In. 725.00
Steuben, Vase, Rosaline, Alabaster Foot, 5 In.Tall 135.00
Steuben, Vase, Signed, Green, Swirled, Fluted Top 35.00
Steuben, Vase, Signed, Paper Label, Ruffled Edge, Bulbous, 6 In.Tall 350.00
Steuben, Vase, Swirled, Amethyst, Signed, 7 In.High 135.00
Steuben, Vase, Tree Trunk, Three Sections, Green Crystal, 6 In. 85.00
Steuben, Vase, Twisted Coil Stem, Swirls, 8 In.High 65.00
Steuben, Vase, Verre De Soie, Footed, 6 1/4 In.High 70.00
Steuben, Vase, Verre De Soie, Ovoid, Paper Label, 6 3/4 In.High 85.00
Steuben, Wine, Blue Base, Clear Stem, Unsigned 20.00
Steuben, Wine, Rhine, Amber, Blue Band, Unsigned 19.50

Stevengraphs are woven pictures made like ribbons. They were manufactured
by Thomas Stevens of Coventry, England, and became popular in 1862.
Stevengraph, Full Cry, Frame, Label 115.00
Stevengraph, Landing Of Columbus 50.00
Stevengraph, The Finish 110.00
Stevengraph, The Meet, Frame, Label 115.00
Stevengraph, The Start 110.00
Stevengraph, Water Jump 110.00

Stevens & Williams of Stourbridge, England, made many types of art glass.
Stevens & Williams, Bowl, Sweetmeat, Lily Pads, Silver Plate Holder 65.00
Stevens & Williams, Ewer, Amber Leaves, Cranberry & White Flower, 5 1/2 In. 30.00
Stevens & Williams, Ewer, Melon Ribbed, Blue, Jewels, 8 In. 70.00
Stevens & Williams, Ewer, Peach, Satin Glass, Frosted Handle, 6 1/2 In. 70.00
Stevens & Williams, Ewer, Satin Glass, Apricot Color To Pink Base, Floral 52.00
Stevens & Williams, Ewer, Satin Glass, Floral, Enamel Bird, Coralene Leaves 75.00
Stevens & Williams, Ewer, Tortoiseshell, Ruffled Leaf, Flower, 7 1/2 In. 60.00
Stevens & Williams, Rose Bowl, Applied Flowers & Leaves, Pink, 5 1/2 In. 65.00
Stevens & Williams, Rose Bowl, Blue Jade, Turned-Down Lip, 3 In.High 70.00
Stevens & Williams, Rose Bowl, Flowers, Vine, Blue, Footed, Registered, 5 In. 600.00
Stevens & Williams, Rose Bowl, Pink To Rose, Flowers, Bird, Footed, 6 1/2 In. 75.00
Stevens & Williams, Rose Bowl, Pleated Top, Swirl To Chartreuse, Blue, 5 In. 145.00
Stevens & Williams, Rose Bowl, Rainbow Striped, Melon Ribbed, 6 3/4 In. 125.00
Stevens & Williams, Rose Bowl, Red To Pink, Amber, Branches, White Floral 425.00

Stevens & Williams, Rose Bowl, Ribbed, Thumbprint, Cranberry, Amber Shadows	110.00
Stevens & Williams, Rose Bowl, Rubena Threaded, Leaf & Stem, Blown	48.00
Stevens & Williams, Vase, Amber, Pink, Blue, Cranberry, Sapphire, 11 In.	95.00
Stevens & Williams, Vase, Blue Satin, Applied Camphor Edge, Hand-Painted	65.00
Stevens & Williams, Vase, Blue Satin, Applied Camphor Handles, Coralene	60.00
Stevens & Williams, Vase, Blue, White, Green, Brown, Flowers, 8 In.	55.00
Stevens & Williams, Vase, Custard Color, Applied Three Color Leaf, 5 In.	55.00
Stevens & Williams, Vase, Enamel, White To Apricot, Birds, Handles, 7 1/2 In.	60.00
Stevens & Williams, Vase, Green, Iridescent, Snake Design, Set Of 3	65.00
Stevens & Williams, Vase, Jack-In-The-Pulpit, Purple, 8 In.Tall	27.00
Stevens & Williams, Vase, Opalescent To Rose, Ribbed, Footed, 9 1/2 In.	50.00
Stevens & Williams, Vase, Pink, Ruffled, Allover Enamel Floral, White Lined	65.00
Stevens & Williams, Vase, Satin Glass, Jeweled Butterfly, Coralene Leaves	50.00
Stevens & Williams, Vase, Satin Glass, Lavender, Swirls	245.00
Stevens & Williams, Vase, Satin, Pink To Rose At Top, Hand-Painted Daisies	55.00
Stevens & Williams, Vase, Silveria, Two Handles At Top, Signed, 11 1/2 In.	850.00
Stevens & Williams, Vase, Vaseline, Pink Amber Leaves, Stems, Center Flower	45.00
Stoneware, Bottle, Tan, 4 1/2 In.High	7.50
Stoneware, Bowl, Pipe, Blue Glaze, 2 In.Long	8.50
Stoneware, Centerpiece, Glossy White, Turned-Over Edge, Ground Bottom	20.00
Stoneware, Churn, Butter, Eagle, Banner, Swan, Four Gallon	75.00
Stoneware, Crock, Apple Cider, 3 Gal., Pewter Handle & Spigot	15.00
Stoneware, Crock, Blue Decoration Of Bird Feeding, 4 Gallon	25.00
Stoneware, Crock, Blue Decoration Of Bird, New York Stoneware Co., 2 Gallon	25.00
Stoneware, Crock, Blue Decoration, E.& L.P.Norton, Bennington, Vt., 2 Gallon	35.00
Stoneware, Crock, Blue Decoration, E.Hart & Son, Sherburne	15.00
Stoneware, Crock, Blue Decoration, North Bay, 1 Gallon	15.00
Stoneware, Crock, Blue Leaf Decoration, N.A.White & Son, Utica, 2 Gallon	30.00
Stoneware, Crock, Bluebird Decoration, M.& T.Miller, Newport, 3 Gallon	25.00
Stoneware, Crock, Chocolate Glaze, E.Norton & Co., Bennington, Vt.	22.50
Stoneware, Crock, Chocolate Glaze, Signed E.E.Wallace, Choicest Butter	9.00
Stoneware, Crock, Decorated, J.& E.Norton, Bennington, Vt., 2 Gallon	45.00
Stoneware, Crock, F.H.Crowden, Harrisburg, 2 Gallon	35.00
Stoneware, Crock, Flower Decoration, Harrington & Burger, 2 Gallon	20.00
Stoneware, Crock, General Store, Manor Sta., Pa., 2 Gallon	17.50
Stoneware, Crock, Hamilton & Jones, Greensboro, Pa., 1 Gallon	9.00
Stoneware, Crock, Impressed Cow, Gardiner Stoneware Co., 5 Gallon	17.50
Stoneware, Crock, Incised Decoration, The Redwing Stoneware Co., Minn., 1889	7.50
Stoneware, Dish, Potato, Pearl, Pw & Co., Ontario	12.00
Stoneware, Humidor, Cobalt, Gray, Man Drinking, Pipe In Relief, Germany	45.00
Stoneware, Inkwell, Sprig Design, Blue, Marked	22.00
Stoneware, Jar, A.P.Donaghho, Parkersburg, W.Va., 2 Gallon	15.00
Stoneware, Jar, Handles, Ballard & Bros., Burlington, Vt., 2 Gallon	22.50
Stoneware, Jar, Ovoid, 2 Handles, Cream Glaze, 4 Gallon	7.50
Stoneware, Jar, Williams & Ruppert, Greensboro, Pa., 5 Gallon	55.00
Stoneware, Jug, Apostle, Figural Design, Marked, Dated 1843	95.00
Stoneware, Jug, Ballard, Blue Decoration	30.00
Stoneware, Jug, Bird Decoration	35.00
Stoneware, Jug, Bird Decoration, J.Norton & Co., Bennington, Vt.	60.00
Stoneware, Jug, Bird Decoration, Satterlee & Mory, 2 Gallon	20.00
Stoneware, Jug, Bird Decoration, 1 1/2 Gallon, J.A.& C.W.Underwood, N.Y.	45.00
Stoneware, Jug, Bird Decoration, 2 Gallon, A.B.Wheeler & Co., Mass.	65.00
Stoneware, Jug, Bird On Spray Of Leaves, 2 Gallon, V.& J.P.Norton, Vt.	65.00
Stoneware, Jug, Bird On Tree, J.& E.Norton, Bennington, Vt., 4 Gallon	250.00
Stoneware, Jug, Blue Decoration, Brown Glaze, 19th Century	45.00
Stoneware, Jug, Blue Decoration, Haxstun & Co., Fort Edwards, 2 Gallon	20.00
Stoneware, Jug, Blue Decoration, New York, 1 Gallon	20.00
Stoneware, Jug, Blue Decoration, Signed T.B.Norton, Worcester, Mass., Gallon	25.00
Stoneware, Jug, Blue Decoration, Somerset Potters Works, 2 Gallon	25.00
Stoneware, Jug, Blue Decoration, Stebbins & Co., Springfield	30.00
Stoneware, Jug, Blue Decoration, West Troy Pottery, 1 Gallon	25.00
Stoneware, Jug, Blue Decoration, Whites, Utica, 1 Gallon	17.50
Stoneware, Jug, Blue Flower Decoration, Cowden, Harrisburg, Pa., 1 Gallon	27.50
Stoneware, Jug, Charlestown, Marked	40.00
Stoneware, Jug, Chicken Eating Corn, New York Stone Ware Co., 4 Gallon	110.00
Stoneware, Jug, Cream, Bands Of White & Brown, Beading, Pewter Top, England	25.00

Stoneware, Jug, England, Gallon	7.50
Stoneware, Jug, England, 2 Gallon	12.00
Stoneware, Jug, Floral Decoration, Ottman Bros. & Co., N.Y., 5 Gallon	100.00
Stoneware, Jug, Flower Decoration, Impressed New York Mark In Rectangle	30.00
Stoneware, Jug, Flower Decoration, 2 Gallon, T.O.Goodwin	30.00
Stoneware, Jug, G.Thompson & Co., West Winsted, Ohio	15.00
Stoneware, Jug, Gray, Cylindrical, 9 In.	4.50
Stoneware, Jug, Incised Decor, Dragon, Snake, Martin Brothers	350.00
Stoneware, Jug, Leaf Decoration, 2 Gallon, A.K.Balla, Vt.	45.00
Stoneware, Jug, Long-Tailed Bird On Spray Of Leaves, New York, 2 Gallon	75.00
Stoneware, Jug, Ovoid, Incised Pigeon, I.Seymour, Troy, 3 Gallon	130.00
Stoneware, Jug, Parkersburg, W.Va., 1 Gallon	10.00
Stoneware, Jug, Three Birds Decoration, West Troy Pottery, 5 Gallon	225.00
Stoneware, Mug, Bird On Spray Of Leaves, 2 Gallon, F.B.Norton & Co.	60.00
Stoneware, Pitcher, Bucket Shape, Brown, 6 1/4 In.Tall	10.00
Stoneware, Pitcher, Green, Fish & Seaweed	12.50
Stoneware, Pitcher, Milk, Cows, Blue & Gray	20.00
Stoneware, Pitcher, Signed, 6 Gallon	12.50
Stoneware, Plate & Jar, Miniature, Footed	20.00
Stoneware, Pot, Applied Handles, Bust Of Woman, Brown, Blue	550.00
Stoneware, Salt & Pepper Shaker, Blue Band, Incised Decoration	100.00
Stoneware, Tea Set, Marked, Numbered, Initialed, 3 Piece	85.00
Stoneware, Vase, Cameo, Brown, Blue, Green, White, Signed, Dated 1890	95.00
Stoneware, Vase, Flying Geese, Signed Florence Barlow, 12 1/2 In.Pair	265.00
Store, see also Card, Advertising, Coffee Grinder, Tool, Scale	
Store, Badge, Coco Wheats, Radio	12.50
Store, Badge, Fire Department, Newark, N.J., Metal, 2 X 2 In.	7.50
Store, Barber Pole, Painted Wood, 53 In.Tall	325.00
Store, Barber Pole, Wood, Painted, Ball Finial, 53 In. *Illus*	325.00

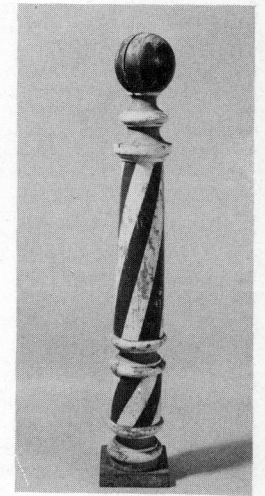

Store, Barber Pole, Wood, Painted, Ball Finial, 53 In.

Store, Barrel, Biscuit, Wooden Strapped, Huston Biscuits	12.00
Store, Barrel, Planter's Peanut, Embossed Mr.Peanut, 10 In.High	40.00
Store, Barrel, Wine, European, 10 Liters, Wood Spigot, Steel Bands	20.00
Store, Barrel, Wine, Portuguese, 50 Liters, Wood Spigot, Steel Bands	25.00
Store, Basket, Egg, Wire Mesh	2.50
Store, Basket, Grocer's	3.00
Store, Basket, Papago	4.50
Store, Basket, Shaker, Wooden Handle, Cover Slides Up Handle, Round	17.50
Store, Battery, Glass, Telephone, Lead Insert, C.1890-1900	5.00
Store, Beads, Trade, Black Glass, 100	3.00
Store, Beaker, Druggist's, Clear, 8 Oz., Footed	7.50

Store, Bench, Wat~~.........~~ .... ~ ~ak	1400.00
Store, Bit, Bridle	1.75
Store, Blackboard, Country Store, 12 X 22 In.	9.00
Store, Blatz Bartender With Glass Of Beer, Swinging Gate, Cast Aluminum	25.00
Store, Block, Butcher's, Turned Legs, Bolt Covers, 17 X 17 X 14 In.	110.00
Store, Booklet, Swan's Down Cook Booklet, 1929	.50
Store, Bootjack, Naughty Nellie	18.00
Store, Bottle Opener, E.Robinson's & Sons, Pilsener Beer, Scranton, Pa.	3.00
Store, Bottle Opener, Mechanical	.98
Store, Bowl, Embossed Diamond Crystal Shaker Salt, Glass	2.00
Store, Bowl, Punch, Sunkist Embossed, Pink Glass	50.00
Store, Box, Arbuckle's Coffee, Shipping, Wood	42.50
Store, Box, Big Load Plug Tobacco, Cardboard, Old West Letters	3.00
Store, Box, Cake, Tin, Schepp's	35.00
Store, Box, California Perfume Co., Tooth Tablet, 1906, Milk Glass, Metal Top ...	75.00
Store, Box, Cigar, Royal Champion High Standard, Wooden, Knight On Horse	2.50
Store, Box, Display, Target Cigarette Tobacco, 1933	15.00
Store, Box, Gold Dust Soap Powder, Contents	10.00
Store, Box, Kellogg's, 1922 .... *Illus*	32.00
Store, Box, Monarch Tea, Tin	5.00
Store, Box, Mother's Oats .... *Illus*	2.00

Store, **Box**, Kellogg's, 1922

Store, Box, Mother's Oats

Store, Box, Royal Gall Hoof Cure Co., Paten, Me., Tin	7.50
Store, Box, Sugar, Wooden, Bucket, Red	8.50
Store, Box, Tin, Diamond Match Co., Chip Matches That Pass In The Dark	12.50
Store, Box, Tobacco, Cardboard, Buckwheat Fine Cut	2.00 To 3.00
Store, Box, Tobacco, Cardboard, Cream De Menthe Plug	3.00
Store, Box, Tobacco, Cardboard, Dan Patch	2.00 To 3.00
Store, Box, Tobacco, Cardboard, Ojibua Fine	2.00 To 3.00
Store, Box, Tobacco, Cardboard, Peachy, C.1910, Color Picture Of Peach	4.00
Store, Box, Tobacco, Cardboard, Sweet Mist	20.00
Store, Box, Tobacco, Cardboard, Union Workman Chew, Pocket, C.1910	3.00
Store, Box, Tobacco, Cardboard, Yankee Girl, Red, White, & Blue	4.00
Store, Box, Tobacco, Nosegay, Imperial Tobacco Co., Great Britain & Ireland ...	22.00
Store, Broadside, Anheuser-Busch, Pre-1893, Color, Lithograph, 27 X 43 In.	35.00
Store, Bucket, Chocolate Cream Coffee, 5 Lbs.	18.50
Store, Bucket, Cream Brand Peanut Butter, 1 Lb.	9.00
Store, Bucket, Peaberry Texas Coffee, 3 Lb., Bucking Horse	18.50
Store, Buttonhook, Celluloid Handle	1.50 To 2.50
Store, Buttonhook, Glove, Bone Handle, Closed Hook	4.00

Store, Buttonhook, Glove, Flint & Kent, Closed Hook	4.50
Store, Buttonhook, Glove, Nickel Silver Handle	4.00
Store, Buttonhook, Glove, Steel Handle, Samter Bros.Co., Scranton, Pa.	4.00
Store, Buttonhook, Glove, Turned Bone Handle	4.50
Store, Buttonhook, Shoe, Unangst Furniture & Carpet Co., Nazareth, Pa.	4.50
Store, Buttonhook, Steele, Hats & Shoes, Providence, Pa.	5.00
Store, Button, Pinback, Sweet Caporal Cigarettes	.75
Store, Cabinet, Corticelli Spool, 3 Drawers, Glass Front	45.00
Store, Cabinet, Delaval, Oak, Embossed Tin Door	87.50
Store, Cabinet, Delaval, Wood, Tin Sign	95.00
Store, Cabinet, Dental, Pine, 8 Drawers On Each Side, China Pulls	120.00
Store, Cabinet, Dental, 2 Doors, 2 Drawers, Opalescent Pulls	20.00
Store, Cabinet, Diamond Dye, Open Doors, Black Finish, Tin, 18 X 6 X 5 In.	25.00
Store, Cabinet, Dye, Diamond, Tin Door, Painted Woman In Kitchen	50.00
Store, Cabinet, Dye, Putnam, Tin, Wood Lined	25.00
Store, Cabinet, J.P.Coats Spool, 6 Drawer	85.00
Store, Cabinet, J.P.Coats, 3 Drawer	25.00
Store, Cabinet, Medical, Mahogany, Sliding Glass Top, 10 X 12 In.	100.00
Store, Cabinet, Putnam Dye, Color Lithograph Girl, C.1920s	45.00
Store, Cabinet, Putnam Dye, Wood, Continental Soldier Leading Army	32.50
Store, Cabinet, Spool, Corticelli Silk, 4 Drawers	60.00
Store, Cabinet, Spool, Desk Type, 3 Drawers On One Side, 1 On Other	95.00
Store, Cage, Cricket	18.00
Store, Calendar, Hood's Sarsaparilla, Household, 1888	6.50
Store, Calendar, International Harvester, 1936	1.00
Store, Calendar, Pompeian Beauty Products, 1918, Mary Pickford Picture	27.50
Store, Calendar, Pompeian Beauty Products, 1921, Marguerite Clark, 1921	24.50
Store, Calendar, Western Ammunition Co., Old Hunter & His Dog Picture	16.00
Store, Can, Coffee, Breakfast Delight, Red, Gold Lettering	4.00
Store, Can, Coffee, Butternut, Paper Label, Tin, 1 Lb.	3.00
Store, Can, Coffee, Butternut, Paper Label, Tin, 3 Lb.	4.00
Store, Can, Coffee, Fiaroma, Red, Gold Lettering, Tin, 1 Lb.	8.00
Store, Can, Coffee, Montgomery Ward, Dark Blue, Cardboard	7.00
Store, Can, Coffee, Peak, Blue & Black Lithograph	2.00
Store, Can, Coffee, Pure Gold, Red, Gold, Black, 6 1/2 X 4 1/2 X 2 1/2	5.00
Store, Can, Coffee, Rob Roy, Paper Label, Dated 1919, Tin, 3 Lb.	4.00
Store, Can, Coffee, Vienna, Yellow & Black, Lithograph, Tin, 1 Lb.	7.00
Store, Can, Coffee, Yale, Blue, Red, Gold, Lettering, Tin, Lithograph	7.00
Store, Can, Cream, Bail, Gallon	7.00
Store, Can, Elephant Peanuts, Picture On Side	8.00
Store, Can, Gold Dust Scouring Powder, Contents	10.00
Store, Can, Milk, Gallon, Lid & Chain, Painted	4.00
Store, Can, Milk, 5 Gallon	6.00
Store, Can, Milk, 8 Gallon	4.50
Store, Can, Milk, 10 Gallon	2.00 To 3.50
Store, Can, Syrup, Log Cabin, Towles	18.00
Store, Canister, Campbell's Coffee, 4 Pound, Camel, Bail	15.00
Store, Canister, Campfire Marshmallows, 5 Lb.	5.00 To 7.50
Store, Canister, Coffee, Blue Paint	12.50
Store, Canister, Kibbie's Salted Jumbos	8.00
Store, Canister, Planter's Peanuts	18.00
Store, Canister, Star Maid Peanuts, White, Blue, Silver	10.00
Store, Canister, Sunshine Biscuit, Glass Top	20.00
Store, Capper, Bottle, Metal	4.00
Store, Carrier, Grapette, Metal	4.00
Store, Carrier, Ice, Topeka, Kansas	10.00
Store, Carrier, Milk, Wire, 6 Section	3.00
Store, Carrier, Pepsi, Wooden	6.50
Store, Carrier, Undertaker's, Folding, Portable, Wheels	25.00
Store, Case, Candy, Bunte Bros., 12 In.High	30.00
Store, Case, Demonstration, Nu-Way Automatic Potato Peeler, C.1930	9.50
Store, Case, Dispenser, A.W.Shelton, New York, 5 Compartments, Dated 1879	85.00
Store, Case, Display, Bonnie B.Human Hair Nets, Tin, 1921, Oak Base	55.00
Store, Case, Display, Boyemaco Curtain Fixture, Lid Lifts	48.50
Store, Case, Display, Schaffer's, Oak & Glass, Sliding Doors	35.00
Store, Case, Display, Shulmate Straight Razor, Wood & Glass, 30 Compartments	35.00

Store, **Case**, Display, Spencerian Pen, Oak & Glass, 12 Compartment, Drawer 35.00
Store, **Case**, Dyola Dye, Wooden 20.00
Store, **Case**, Esquire Boot Polish, Metal, Revolving Base 8.00
Store, **Case**, Gillette, Wooden, Hinged Glass Lid, 18 X 14 X 1 3/4 In. 12.50
Store, **Case**, Needle, Boyle, Needles & Bobbins, 17 In.Diameter 48.00
Store, **Case**, Turned Corner Posts, Glass Sides & Lid, Maple, 7 In. 42.50
Store, **Cash Register**, National, Brass 84.00
Store, **Cash Register**, National, Large 250.00
Store, **Cash Register**, National, 50 Cent Size, Wood Grained Metal, Marble 100.00
Store, **Cash Register**, Under Counter, Wood, Cast Iron Finger Pull 50.00
Store, **Chair**, Barber, Walnut, Rosewood, C.1865 .... 100.00
Store, **Check Canceller**, 1892 .... 12.00
Store, **Check Writer** 18.75
Store, **Chest**, Hardware, Chestnut, 14 Drawers, Labeled 'dec.1, 1902' 70.00
Store, **Chicken Catcher**, Wire 2.00
Store, **Clock**, St.Joseph Aspirin, Electric, Back Lighted 20.00
    Store, **Coffee Grinder, see Coffee Grinder**
Store, **Comb**, Xylonite, Patent 1869, Boxed, Pair 2.50
Store, **Container**, Straw, Soda, Tall 15.00
Store, **Cooler**, Dispensing, Mission Orange, Paper Label, Crockery & Glass 45.00
Store, **Corkscrew**, Victorian, Legged 12.50
Store, **Cover**, Cheese, Merchant's, Glass, Knob, 17 In.Diameter 38.50
Store, **Crate**, Egg, Slotted, Filters, 12 Dozen 5.00
Store, **Creamer**, Johnson's Pasteurized Milk, China, Covered 25.00
Store, **Creamer**, Kellog's Cereal, Individual .... 4.00 To 5.00
Store, **Cup & Saucer**, Dobbs Hat, Advertising 4.75
Store, **Curling Iron**, Hair, Wooden Handles, 8 In.Long 2.00
Store, **Cuspidor**, Japanned, Shallow 9.00
Store, **Cutter**, Biscuit, Rumford's 1.25
Store, **Cutter**, Cigar .... *Illus* 18.00
Store, **Cutter**, Cigar, Counter, Red Glass Trimmed, Chamber Of Commerce Cigars 49.00
Store, **Cutter**, Cigar, The Champion Automatic Match Safe & Cigar Cutter 38.00
Store, **Cutter**, Cigar, The Champion, Patent 1871 .... 18.00
Store, **Cutter**, Cheese, Counter .... 22.50 To 35.00
Store, **Cutter**, Cheese, Shape Of Horse 40.00
Store, **Cutter**, Kraut 4.75
Store, **Cutter**, Kraut, Sliding Wood Box On Top, T & D Spec.No.672 .... 10.00
Store, **Cutter**, Tobacco, American, Crank, Fluted, Patent, 1877 .... 17.00
Store, **Cutter**, Tobacco, Brown Mule 15.00
Store, **Cutter**, Tobacco, Brunhoff 20.00
Store, **Cutter**, Tobacco, Happy Thoughts, Round Blade 37.50
Store, **Cutter**, Tobacco, Imp, Thumbing Nose, Mounted On Pine 45.00
Store, **Cutter**, Tobacco, Lorillard's Climax Plug, Red, Tin, Tag 22.50
Store, **Cutter**, Tobacco, Perfection 15.00
Store, **Cutter**, Tobacco, Queen 15.00
Store, **Cutter**, Tobacco, Standard 15.00
Store, **Cutter**, Tobacco, Star 15.00
Store, **Cutter**, Tobacco, Star, Save The Tags 15.00
Store, **Desk**, Counter, Victorian, Walnut, Country Store 105.00
Store, **Dish**, Planter's Peanut, Tin, Set Of 5 .... 5.00
Store, **Dish**, Soap, Wire, Coil Spring Handle 1.00
Store, **Dispenser**, Syrup, Fowler's Root Beer 38.00
Store, **Drawer**, Cash, Counter, Finger Springs 10.00
Store, **Dryer**, Seed Corn 2.75
Store, **Eagle**, Bronzed Pressed Wood, National Eagle Whiskey, 24 In.High 35.00
Store, **Eight Horse Beer Wagon**, Painted In 8 Colors, 36 In.Long 59.95
Store, **Fan**, Cardboard, General Putnam Dyes, Dragoons 1.50
Store, **Fan**, Electric, 6 Brass Blades, 3 Speeds, 18 In. 20.00
Store, **Fan**, Moxie, Cardboard, Copyright 1923, Girl With Brown Hair 17.50
Store, **Fan**, Planter's Peanut, Cardboard, Wood Handle 6.00
Store, **Fan**, T.Eaton Co., Ltd., Toronto, Cardboard, Wood Handle 6.00
Store, **Foot Warmer**, Carpeted, Charcoal 12.00
Store, **Foot Warmer**, Henderson, Dated 1912 .... 6.50
Store, **Foot Warmer**, Metal, Carpet, Coal 10.00
Store, **Foot Warmer**, Signed & Dated, Angola, N.Y., Folding, Lantern 75.00
Store, **Foot Warmer**, Tin, Wood, 9 In.Long .... *Illus* 32.00

Store, Cutter, Cigar
See Page 506

Store, Foot Warmer, Tin, Wood, 9 In.Long
See Page 506

Store, Freezer, Ice Cream, Salesman's Sample, Wood Case, Iron, Dated 1891	28.00
Store, Glass, Coors Beer	2.00
Store, Glass, Moxie	6.00
Store, Glass, Pilsener, Cobalt, Clear Pedestal, 14 Oz., 8	62.00
Store, Glass, Shot, Calvert Reserve	2.00
Store, Glass, Welch's Grape Juice	1.00
Store, Grinder, Cheese, Iron, Tin, Glass, Crank Handle, Plunger Clamp	13.50
Store, Gum Machine, see Store, Machine, Gumball	
Store, Hammer, Los Ramos, The Cigar You Can Inhale, Richman-Neville Co.	5.00
Store, Handbag, Tobacco, Foster & Hilson Company, Wood	15.00
Store, Hat Stand, Lady's, Glass, Swirled Design, 12 In.High, Turning Purple	18.00
Store, Heads, Shooting Gallery, Carved & Painted Wood, Grotesque Face, Pair	260.00
Store, Heinz Pickle, 1 In.Long	1.25
Store, Holder, Broom, Wood, Floor Mount, Fold-Up	5.00
Store, Holder, Change, Glass, Benbey	8.00
Store, Holder, Paper Roll, 12 In.Wide	8.50
Store, Holder, Paper, 26 In.	5.00
Store, Holder, Pepsi, Tin	3.00
Store, Holder, String, Beehive, Tin Cap	22.50
Store, Holder, String, Bronze, Table Model, Embossed	10.00
Store, Holder, String, Corn Flakes, 1910	25.00
Store, Holder, String, Hanging, Iron, 4 1/2 In.Tall	9.00
Store, Holder, String, Post Toasties, 1910	25.00
Store, Holder, String, Shaped Like 3 Legged Iron Kettle, Use Jaxon Soap	16.50
Store, Holder, String, Tin, Revolves, Postum, Health First	16.00
Store, Holder, String, With Cone Of String	12.00
Store, Holder, Wrapping Paper	22.00
Store, Humidor, Cinco Tobacco	4.00
Store, Humidor, Cremo Cigars, 6 X 15 In.	22.50
Store, Humidor, Glass, La Palina Cigars, Embossed Lettering	12.00
Store, Ice Chipper, Iron	2.50
Store, Ice Cream, Dipper, Iron	2.50
Store, Jar, Berg's Leetonia Pretzels, Enameled	22.00
Store, Jar, Cigar, Tin Lid	12.50
Store, Jar, Clear Glass, 2 Gallon	8.50
Store, Jar, La Reforma Cigars, Glass, Oval, C.1895	30.00
Store, Jar, Planter's Peanut, 6 Sided, Peanut Finial On Lid	20.00
Store, Jar, Prince Albert Tobacco, Labels, 1910 Stamp	6.75
Store, Jar, Tobacco, Turbaned Arab, Bisque	42.50

Store, Jar, Weyman's Snuff, 6 In.Tall	12.50
Store, Juicer, Marked Sunkist, Clear	7.00
Store, Juicer, Milk Glass, Marked Sunkist	2.50
Store, Keg, Dupont Powder, Paper Label, Pat.1893	17.50
Store, License, Liquor, From Saloon, Cardboard, 24 X 27 In.	15.00
Store, Light Bulb, Pointed-Tip, Burned Out, 12	1.00
Store, Lunch Pail, Painted Black	5.00
Store, Machine, Al Jolson Sings, Used In English Pub In 1920s	2000.00
Store, Machine, Bear & Hound, Coin, Amusement	35.00
Store, Machine, Candy, Hershey 1 Cent	22.50
Store, Machine, Cube Steak, Hand Operated, Cast Iron	45.00
Store, Machine, Football, Kicker & Catcher, Key Missing	150.00
Store, Machine, Gumball *Illus*	45.00
Store, Machine, Matchbook Vendor, 1 Cent	10.00
Store, Machine, Mutoscope, French, Charlie Chaplin Movies On Flip Cards	350.00
Store, Machine, Peanut & Popcorn, Electric	300.00
Store, Machine, Peanut, Hog, 1920s	40.00
Store, Machine, Peanut, Penny, Iron	12.50
Store, Machine, Penny Gum Ball, Arcade	50.00
Store, Machine, Penny Gum Vendor, Pulver, Key	70.00
Store, Machine, Penny Pack	175.00
Store, Machine, Penny, Add Your Score	125.00
Store, Machine, Penny, Baby Vendor Slot Machine, Key Missing	125.00
Store, Machine, Penny, Cigarette Slot Machine, Lock Missing	95.00
Store, Machine, Penny, Japanese Ball, Glass On Top Missing	95.00
Store, Machine, Penny, Pop-Up Baseball, Back Missing	125.00
Store, Machine, Penny, Sandy's Horses, Key Missing	125.00
Store, Machine, Penny, The Target, Key Missing	65.00
Store, Machine, Penny, Try-Your-Skill Football, Key Missing	150.00
Store, Machine, Penny, Zoom, Wood, Iron & Glass Front, Lever Type, 25 In. High	50.00
Store, Machine, Pinball, Coin Operated	150.00
Store, Machine, Pinball, Five Cents, Vending, Key Missing	150.00
Store, Machine, Roulette Wheel, Mahogany, Metal, Painted *Illus*	200.00
Store, Machine, Slot, Counter Top, 10 Cents, 1933	
Store, Machine, Slot, Las Vegas Type	325.00
Store, Machine, Soda & Malt	25.00
Store, Machine, Strength Tester, Amusement Park, Penny *Illus*	800.00
Store, Machine, Ultraviolet Ray	12.00
Store, Machine, Vending, Match, 1010, Box For 5 Cents, 13 In.Tall	62.50
Store, Machine, Vending, Peanut, 1 Cent, Columbus, Cast Iron Base, Glass Globe	25.00
Store, Machine, Vending, Penny, Cast Iron Base, Glass Globe	25.00 To 40.00
Store, Mail Sorter, Wood, Half Circle, 2-Tier, Many Compartments	15.00
Store, Mannequin, Female Modeling Corset, P.N.Practical Front	35.00
Store, Mannequin, Milliner's, Gilded, Carved Wood, 15 In.Tall	18.50
Store, Match Holder, Lady's Slipper, Cinderella Stoves & Ranges, Striker	28.00
Store, Matchbox, Pocket, Blatz Beer	14.00
Store, Measuregraph, Cloth Used On Counter Of Drygoods Store	15.00
Store, Milk Fever Outfit, Wood Dovetailed Box	17.50
Store, Mill, Cane, Horsepower, Ballencamp Fdr.Hardware Co., Ky., 1899	150.00
Store, Mill, Cider, No.D8-Fj, 2 Tubs, Iron & Steel, Positive Force-Feed	52.22
Store, Mirror, Anderson Candy, Gem Stones	8.00
Store, Mirror, Berry Bros., Varnish, Toy Cart, Dog, & Children	6.00
Store, Mirror, Copper Clad Stove, Oval	8.00
Store, Mirror, Curtis Collars, Tailor Made, Art Nouveau Lady, Metal	16.00
Store, Mirror, Dr.A.C.Daniel's Veterinary Medicines	17.50
Store, Mirror, Dr.Hebra's Viola Cream	5.00
Store, Mirror, Gavitt's System Regulator Pills	1.25
Store, Mirror, Grinnell Bros., Detroit Michigan	5.00
Store, Mirror, Hays Cash Shoe Store, Adrian, Michigan	5.00
Store, Mirror, Kleinert's Shields, Picture Of Girl, 2 In.Diameter	6.50
Store, Mirror, Loomis Co., Boots, Shoes, Findlay, Ohio	5.00
Store, Mirror, Nature's Remedy	4.00
Store, Mirror, Pabst Blue Ribbon, Tin Frame, 18 X 12 In.	12.50
Store, Mirror, Palmer Candy Co.	5.50
Store, Mirror, Pomona Perfume, Picture Of Girl, Oval	27.50
Store, Mirror, Queen Quality Shoes, Diana	14.00

Store, Machine, Gumball
See Page 508

Store, Machine, Strength Tester,
Amusement Park, Penny
See Page 508

Store, Machine, Roulette Wheel,
Mahogany, Metal, Painted
See Page 508

Store, Mirror, Sperm Whale Oil, New Bedford, Chas.Morgan	25.00
Store, Mirror, Studebaker, Oblong	10.00
Store, Mirror, Toasted Butter Crackers	10.00
Store, Model, Artist's, Wood, Form Of Horse, Articulated, 23 In.	550.00 To 950.00
Store, Mold, see also Tin, Mold	
Store, Mold, Chocolate, Nickel Plate On Iron, 40 1 In.Squares, La Marquise	4.00
Store, Mold, Chocolate, Nickel Plate On Iron, 40 1 In.Squares, Rosemarie	4.00
Store, Mold, Cigar Press	20.00
Store, Mold, Maple Sugar, Quebec	18.00
Store, Mold, Mother's Oats, Metal, Ring	3.00
Store, Mold, Walter Baker Chocolate, 6 X 4 1/2 In.	23.00
Store, Mortar & Pestle, Ball Type Handles, 5 In.Diameter	30.00
Store, Mortar & Pestle, Brass, Square Handles	30.00
Store, Mortar & Pestle, Brass, 4 1/4 In.Diameter	25.00
Store, Mortar & Pestle, Bronze, Weighs 7 1/4 Pounds	47.50
Store, Mortar & Pestle, Burl & Maple	20.00
Store, Mortar & Pestle, Pottery, Coor's, U.S.A.	12.00
Store, Mortar & Pestle, Pottery, Signed	15.00
Store, Mortar & Pestle, Stoneware, Marked H.M.Co., 2 1/4 In.Diameter	6.95
Store, Mortar & Pestle, Wooden, 7 1/2 In.Tall, 6 In.Diameter	28.00
Store, Mortar & Pestle, Wooden, 8 In.Diameter, 8 In.High	45.00
Store, Mug, Armour's Bouillon Cubes, Hand-Painted Flowers, Silesia	10.00
Store, Mug, Blatz Beer, 6	37.00
Store, Mug, Hire's Root Beer, Made By Mettlach	14.00 To 20.00
Store, Mug, Ovaltine, Dated 1924, Uncle Wiggily Wants His Ovaltine	9.00
Store, Mug, Rochester Root Beer, Clear Glass	8.00
Store, Mug, Store Ad, Maker Of Good Goods Only *Illus*	20.00
Store, Mustache Curler, Scissors Type	10.00
Store, Mustache Curler, Sterling Silver Handle	22.50
Store, Opener, Bottle, Brass, Face Of Laughing Negro Man	16.50
Store, Opener, Letter, Bronzed Indian, C.1910	12.00
Store, Pack, Cigarette, Salome, Cardboard	3.00
Store, Package, Lydia E.Pinkham's Pills For Constipation	3.00

Store, **Pail**, Lunch, U.S.Marine, Cut Plug, Tin	5.00
Store, **Pail**, Nigger Hair Tobacco, Lunch Box	45.00
Store, **Pail**, Planter's Peanuts, Handle, 5 In.	10.00
Store, **Pail**, Sultana Peanut Butter, 1 Lb.	9.50
Store, **Paperweight**, Smith Bros., Iron, Looks Like Black Cough Drop	10.50
Store, **Pearson's Red Top Snuff**	3.50
Store, **Pen**, Fountain, Blue Plastic .... *Illus*	25.00
Store, **Pen**, Fountain, Silver Mount .... *Illus*	25.00
Store, **Pen**, Fountain, Waterman's	2.00
Store, **Pen**, Fountain, Waterman's, Engraved, Sterling Silver	20.00
Store, **Pencil Sharpener**, Car, 1920s, Germany	5.00
Store, **Pencil Sharpener**, Hand Crank	9.00
Store, **Pencil Sharpener**, Metal, Dated 1872	4.00
Store, **Pencil Sharpener**, Midget	6.00
Store, **Pencil**, Maine Ax Factory, Nickel Tip, 12	1.50
Store, **Pestle**, Glass, Clear Knob, 5 In.Long	2.25
Store, **Phrenologist Head**, Gilded .... *Illus*	180.00

Store, Mug, Store Ad,
Maker Of Good Goods Only
See Page 509

Fountain Pen, Blue Plastic

Fountain Pen, Silver Mount

Store, Phrenologist Head, Gilded

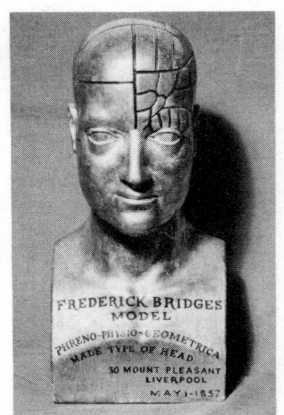

Store, **Picture**, Gypsy, Cardboard, Framed	25.00
Store, **Pipe**, Trade, Clay, Face	5.00
Store, **Plate**, Anheuser-Busch, 1905, Tin, Lady With Flowing Hair, 10 In.	25.00
Store, **Plate**, Cake, Calumet Baking Powder, Tin	10.00
Store, **Plate**, Campbell Kid, Handles, 7 In.	12.50
Store, **Plate**, Campbell Kids, Feeding	7.50
Store, **Plate**, Hershey Chocolate Factory, 7 In.	25.00
Store, **Plate**, Soup, Campbell, China, Recalled	5.00
Store, **Press**, Cork, Counter, Pharmacist's, To Compress Bottle Corks	15.00
Store, **Pump**, Beer Barrel, 2	18.00
Store, **Pump**, Pitcher Spout, Leather Plunger	7.50
Store, **Puzzle**, Victor Talking Machine Co., 1908, Movie Stars	12.00
Store, **Rack With Pen & Pencil**, Standing, Child's, Metal, 4 1/2 In.High	5.00

Store, Razor & Strop, Drawer Type Case, For Travel	12.50
Store, Razor Strop & Hone, Superior	5.00
Store, Razor, Elk Carved On Handle	7.50
Store, Razor, For Women, Curvfit, Boxed	5.00
Store, Razor, Harmar, Boxed	2.00
Store, Razor, Straight, Keen Kutter, Simmons Hdwe Co., Inc., Germany Made	8.50
Store, Reel, Fishing, Wood & Brass	7.50
Store, Register, Trolley, New England Trolley, Brass	65.00
Store, Riveting Machine, National	7.50
Store, Roller, Pill, Brass, Wood	24.50
Store, Sack, Canvas Coffee, Cuban Coffee Mills	1.50
Store, Sack, Cornmeal, Cloth, Negro Boy Eating Ear Of Corn, 25 Lbs.	10.00
Store, Sack, Matanzas Sugar Estates, Inc., Cuba, Red Star	6.00
Store, Saddle, Wooden, Pack	37.50
Store, Saw, Butcher's, Meat, 28 In.Blade	5.00
Store, Scale, Brass, Hanging, Two 10 In.Diameter Pans	42.00
Store, Scale, Butcher, Marble Weighing Base	100.00
Store, Scale, Cast Iron, Balance	12.00
Store, Scale, Chatillon	7.00
Store, Scale, Cylinder	9.00
Store, Scale, Druggist, Marble Top, Walnut Case	25.00
Store, Scale, Fairbanks, Brass Scoop, 'sacker'	40.00
Store, Scale, Family, 1908	7.00
Store, Scale, Gold Miner's, Depose, Trays, Brass, 1860	18.00
Store, Scale, Gold, Walnut Case, Drawer, Set Of Weights	45.00
Store, Scale, Hanging, 18th Century, 9 In.Diameter, 22 In.Long	32.50
Store, Scale, Howe, Brass Pan, Iron Weights, 10 Lbs.	39.00
Store, Scale, Pharmacy, Wood Base, Weights	11.00
Store, Scale, Pocket Prescription	4.00
Store, Scale, Pull, Brass	2.50
Store, Scale, Toledo, Calculatine, Dated 1902	50.00
Store, Scales, Gold Assayer's, Wood & Glass, Plumb Bob-Drawer, 2 Weights	125.00
Store, Scales, Jeweler's, C.1820-40, Brass, Mahogany Base	115.00
Store, Scales, Round·Face Dial, Penn.Scale Mfg.Co., 40 Lbs.	12.00
Store, Sharpener, Razor Blade, Bruecker Bladedger, Boxed	1.00
Store, Shell Crimper, Iron & Wood	4.50
Store, Shopping Bag, Moxie, 1905	1.50
Store, Sign, Advertising, Babbitt's Baking, Girl In Net, Glass Frame, 10 In.	15.00
Store, Sign, Anheuser-Busch, Western Scene, Framed, 11 1/2 X 20 In.	15.00
Store, Sign, Baker's Cocoa, Circa 1905, 17 X 23	85.00
Store, Sign, Barbershop, Enameled, Half Round, 18 X 24 In.	17.50
Store, Sign, Bartel's Beer, Upper Pa., Brewing Co., Tin, Lithograph	10.00
Store, Sign, Beer, Lawson Wood, Tin	30.00
Store, Sign, Between The Acts Cigars, 14 X 18 In.	17.50
Store, Sign, Blacksmith's, Cast Iron & Brass, Gloucester Forge, Shield Form	350.00
Store, Sign, Blacksmithing, Gray Paint, 'in God We Trust, ' 1891	350.00
Store, Sign, Braem's Bitters, Paterson, N.J., Metal, Color, 7 X 13 In.	7.50
Store, Sign, Buckeye Beer, Tin, C.1934, 3 X 13 In.	3.00
Store, Sign, Buckeye Beer, Tin, Multicolor, C.1934, 16 X 20 In.	20.00
Store, Sign, Bulldog Suspenders, Tin, Wall, 10 In.	24.00
Store, Sign, C.L.Centlivre Brewing Co., Color, Lithograph, C.1900	25.00
Store, Sign, Canadian Club 5 Cent Cigar, Cardboard, Round, Maple Leaf	2.50
Store, Sign, Canadian Club 5-Cent Cigar, Maple Leaf, Cardboard, Oval, 7 In.	3.00
Store, Sign, Carling's Nine Pints Of The Law, Carling's, London, Ont., 1881	25.00
Store, Sign, Castle Hall Twins Cigars, The New Arrivals	3.00 To 5.00
Store, Sign, Centlivre Tonic, Cardboard, Multicolor, Lithograph, C.1905	10.00
Store, Sign, Centlivre's Nickel Plate Bottled Beer, Lithograph, C.1900	5.00
Store, Sign, Chew Cash Value Chewing Tobacco, Tin	12.50
Store, Sign, Chew Only The Best-Hamilton's Bulldog Tobacco, Paper	1.25
Store, Sign, Coffee Grinder	*Illus* 15.00
Store, Sign, Columbian Beer, C.1900, Tin, Embossed, Color, Chain Hanging	17.00
Store, Sign, Cook's Beer, Man With Dog, Hunting, 21 X 25 In.	15.00
Store, Sign, Cook's Beer, Tin, Negro Servant Rushing Tray Of Beer	47.50
Store, Sign, Coon Cigar, Paper	2.00
Store, Sign, Cooper Boot, Bootmaker's, 22 In.High	170.00
Store, Sign, Courage Tobacco, Lithograph	15.00

Store, Sign, Crescent Beverages, Tin, 27 In. 4.50
Store, Sign, Dan Patch, Horse's Head, Round 4.50
Store, Sign, Dan Patch, International Stock Food Co., Horse & Driver 150.00
Store, Sign, Davis Tobacco, Lithograph 15.00
Store, Sign, Devilish Good 5 Cent Cigar, Tin, Multicolor, C.1910, 10 X 14 In. 13.00
Store, Sign, Dimsdale Hotel & Bar, Entrance, Brass, Shield, 32 In.High 150.00
Store, Sign, Diorama, Butcher's, Painted Wood, 19th Century, 19 1/2 In.Long 250.00
Store, Sign, Diorama, Fishmonger's, Painted Wood, Glazed Vitrine, C.1850 .... 625.00
Store, Sign, Dolly Madison Cigar, Tin, Red & Black On Yellow, 6 X 20 In. 3.00
Store, Sign, Dr.Hall's Catarrh Remedy, Lithograph, Paper, Black, Blue & White 10.00
Store, Sign, Drink Braem's Bitters, C.1910, Shows Bottle 4.00
Store, Sign, Drink Moxie, Cardboard, Shape Of Palette, Color 4.50
Store, Sign, Drink Orchard Queen, Tin, C.1920, 4 X 6 In. 4.00
Store, Sign, Duffee's Cough Syrup, Tin, Yellow & Black, C.1920, 9 X 13 In. 6.00
Store, Sign, Duffee's Laxative, Tin, Yellow & Black, C.1920, 9 X 13 In. 5.00
Store, Sign, Duke's Smoking Tobacco, Paper, 27 X 20 In. .... *Illus* 150.00
Store, Sign, E & O Pilsener & Lager Beer, Tin, Lithograph, C.1935 .... 10.00
Store, Sign, Egyptian Straights, Girl On Front, 18 X 16 In. 40.00
Store, Sign, Fatima Turkish Blend Cigarettes 15.00
Store, Sign, Fishmonger's, Painted Wood, P.Mcintyre, Fish & Poultry 650.00
Store, Sign, Frank Fehr Brewing Co., Tin.26 X 33 In. .... *Illus* 165.00

Store, Sign, Coffee Grinder
See Page 511

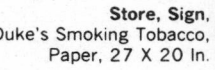

Store, Sign,
Duke's Smoking Tobacco,
Paper, 27 X 20 In.

Store, Sign,
Frank Fehr Brewing Co.,
Tin.26 X 33 In.

Store, Sign, Fremlin's Family Ale & Stout Depot, English, C.1850, Metal 130.00
Store, Sign, Glovemaker's Shop, Red Gloved Hand, Ruffled Cuff, Metal 450.00
Store, Sign, Gold Label Beer, The Prosecutor, By Peter Hurd, Color 12.00
Store, Sign, Gravley's Golden Rule Cigar, Tin 4.00
Store, Sign, Green River Whiskey, Tin, Horse, Jug & Rider 75.00
Store, Sign, Harvester 5 Cent Cigar, Dolores Del Rio, Tin, Oval 7.00
Store, Sign, Henry Arthur Boot & Shoe, 27 X 19 In. .... *Illus* 135.00
Store, Sign, Honeymoon Tobacco, Tin, Embossed, 7 X 10 In. .... 12.00 To 18.00
Store, Sign, Hotel, Brass, Shield Form, Dimsdale Hotel & Bar, Entrance 250.00

Store, Sign, Humphrey's 77 For Grip, Metal 17.50
Store, Sign, Imperial Club 5 Cent Cigar, Tin, C.1910, 10 X 14 In .... 7.50 To 12.00
Store, Sign, Infallible, Hercules Powder Co., Cardboard, C.1918 .... 25.00
Store, Sign, It Keeps A Nocken, The Hammer Cigars Costs 5 Cent .... 6.00 To 8.50
Store, Sign, J.H.Moulton, 1848, Wooden, Green Ground, Yellow Decoration, Iron 170.00
Store, Sign, J.Kimmey, Theatrical & Masquerade Costumer, Glass 350.00
Store, Sign, J.P.Alley's Hambone Sweets, 5-Cent Cigar, Cardboard, Oval, 7 In. 3.50
Store, Sign, Jacob Hoffman Brewing Co., N.Y., Vase Of Roses, Hips, Barley 8.00
Store, Sign, James Lewis Clear Havana Filter 5-Cent Cigar, Aluminum 3.00
Store, Sign, Just The Thing, Tobacco, Lithograph 15.00
Store, Sign, Kelly Tires, Lady Driving Car, Tin, 24 In.Diameter 165.00
Store, Sign, Kidneywort-A Purely Vegetable Remedy, Tin, Red & Black 3.50
Store, Sign, King Oscar Coffee, Glass & Metal, 6 X 18 In. 22.50
Store, Sign, Knife Sharpener's, Jacknife Form, Four Blades, Painted Wood 250.00
Store, Sign, Manitou Table Water, Color, Lithograph, C.1895, 20 X 24 In. 30.00
Store, Sign, Marine Recruitment, Christy .... *Illus* 45.00
Store, Sign, Matrozen Shag, Tin, Picture Of Sailors, 14 X 9 In. 23.50
Store, Sign, Men's Fashions For All Seasons, 1890, Color 40.00
Store, Sign, Moxie, Drink Moxie, 100 Percent 15.00
Store, Sign, Munsingwear, Tin, 38 X 25 In. .... *Illus* 375.00
Store, Sign, Napoleon Cigars, Cardboard, Color, 10 X 30 In. .... *Illus* 4.00
Store, Sign, Northern Grown Seeds, 33 X 25 In. .... *Illus* 50.00
Store, Sign, Oh Boy Gum, Boy, Tin, 1925, 7 1/2 X 15 1/2 In. 25.00

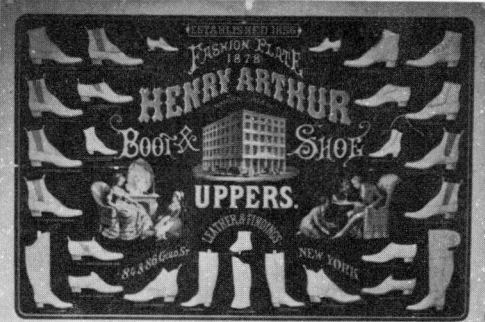

Store, Sign,
Henry Arthur Boot & Shoe, 27 X 19 In.
See Page 512

Store, Sign,
Marine Recruitment, Christy

Store, Sign, Munsingwear,
Tin, 38 X 25 In.

Store, Sign, Northern Grown Seeds, 33 X 25 In.

Store, Sign, Old Reliable Consumer's Beer, Ask Father, Metal 8.00
Store, Sign, Old Shay Ale, Glass, Figural, Bulb In Back, 10 X 10 In. 20.00
Store, Sign, Old Style Beer, Oil Print On Canvas, Musketeer, Framed 30.00
Store, Sign, Old Style Lager, Canvas, 35 X 22 In. .... *Illus* 45.00
Store, Sign, Old Virginia Cheroots, Cloth, 20 X 36 In. 20.00
Store, Sign, Orange Crush, Tin, 1932 .... 8.00
Store, Sign, Oysters, Cardboard, 28 X 20 In. .... *Illus* 225.00
Store, Sign, Pepsi, Negro Girl Holding Phone & Bottle, Oval 4.50
Store, Sign, Peter's Shoes, Diamond Brand, Brass, For Window Display 4.00
Store, Sign, Pink Pills For Pale People, Wooden, 20 In. .... *Illus* 150.00
Store, Sign, Pioneer Baskets, Color, Lithograph, Wall Hanger, 16 X 12 In. 8.50
Store, Sign, Poster Depicting Men's Fashions, 1890 Era, Tin, 18 X 28 In. 40.00
Store, Sign, Poulterer's, Carved Wood, Rooster, W.Kinstler, Penna., C.1850 .... 300.00
Store, Sign, Propert's Leather & Saddle Soap, Tin, Man On Horse 2.50
Store, Sign, R.G.Sullivan's Cigar, Metal, Porcelain, 12 X 30 In. 10.00
Store, Sign, R.G.Sullivan's 7-20-4 Cigar, Color, Enamel 17.50
Store, Sign, Ramon's Co-Tabs, Cold Tablets, Tin, Blue & White 1.25
Store, Sign, Recruiting, C.1895, Canvas Back 75.00
Store, Sign, Red Goose Shoes, Tin, Color, C.1930, 13 X 16 In. 6.00
Store, Sign, Red Goose Shoes, Tin, Yellow, Red, & Black, C.1930 .... 6.00 To 14.00
Store, Sign, Rooming House, Marked Rooms, Wood & Metal .... *Illus* 180.00
Store, Sign, Rough On Rats, Color, 30 In. 12.50
Store, Sign, Royal Baking Powder, Free Fairy Book, Lithograph, C.1923 .... 12.00
Store, Sign, Royal Crown Cola, Tin, 25 In.Tall 6.00
Store, Sign, S S 5 Cent Cigar, Hand Made, Cardboard, Lithograph, 1904 .... 85.00
Store, Sign, Satin Skin Powder, Satin Skin Cream, Color, Lithograph, 1903 .... 9.00
Store, Sign, Schlitz Beer, Metal, Soldier Holding Bottle & Glass 37.50
Store, Sign, Scottish Guard, Steel Helmet, Kilts, 57 1/2 In.Tall 500.00
Store, Sign, Seminola Cigar, Indian Girl, Frame, 13 1/2 X 17 In., 1906 .... 25.00
Store, Sign, Sharples Tubular Cream Separator, Tin, 1900s 115.00
Store, Sign, Shoplifter's, Cash Register, 10 X 15 In. 1.25
Store, Sign, Sleepy Eye, Paper, 38 X 50 In. .... *Illus* 150.00
Store, Sign, Smoke The White Label 5-Cent Cigar, Tin, 9 3/4 X 13 3/4 In. 9.00
Store, Sign, Star Tobacco 10 Cents, Tin 14.00
Store, Sign, Star Tobacco, Color, Cardboard 4.00
Store, Sign, Stoneware, 13 X 19 In. .... *Illus* 30.00
Store, Sign, Swan's Down Complexion Soap, Girl, On Canvas, C.1900 .... 30.00
Store, Sign, Theater, Goo Goo Girl, Isle Of Spice, C.1905 .... 8.00
Store, Sign, Thompson Bros., Clothiers, Bath., Tin, Embossed, C.1900 .... 1250.00
Store, Sign, Tobacconist's Counter, Wood, Sailor Holding Snuff, 24 In.High 800.00
Store, Sign, U.S.Seal 5 Cent Cigar, Aluminum 5.00
Store, Sign, Umbrella Shop, Arm Holding Unfurled Umbrella, Metal 425.00
Store, Sign, Uncle John's, Cardboard, Lithograph, 18 X 12 In. 5.00
Store, Sign, Union Standard Tobacco, Color, Cardboard 4.00
Store, Sign, V.J.David & Co., Oil Dealer, Ship's Chandler, Wood, C.1850 .... 160.00
Store, Sign, Velvet & Piedmont Smoking Tobacco, Metal, 2 Sided 20.00
Store, Sign, Vintner's, Wood, Carved Cluster Of Grapes, Gilded, 20 In.Long 70.00
Store, Sign, Watchmaker's Shop, Painted Metal Watch, Gillet On Dial 325.00
Store, Sign, Water Street Hotel By W.Davis, Painted Wood, Oval 250.00
Store, Sign, We Sell Foss' Pure Extracts, Color, Enamel 12.00
Store, Sign, We Sell Star Tobacco, Color, Enamel 17.50
Store, Sign, Welcome Nugget, Tobacco, Lithograph 15.00
Store, Sign, Western Union Telegraph & Cable, Porcelain, 12 X 24 In. 15.00
Store, Sign, White Label 5 Cent Cigars, Tin, C.1910, 10 X 14 In. 10.00
Store, Sign, Winner, Tobacco, Lithograph 15.00
Store, Sign, World's Champions & Past Greats Of The Prize Ring 10.50
Store, Sign, Wunder Beer, Cardboard, Color, C.1915, 6 X 8 In. 3.00
Store, Silk, Cigarette, Indian Chief 2.95
Store, Slate, School 4.00
Store, Slate, Schoolboy's 5.00
Store, Sleigh, Cutter, Black, Lined In Red Velvet 220.00
Store, Stamp, Notary Public, Form Of Lion's Head, 1904 .... 15.00
Store, Stand, Gum, Teaberry, Clark 18.00
    Store, Stereoscope, see Stereoscope
Store, Stove Polish, Rising Sun, 1 1/2 Oz.Cake 1.00

Store, Sign, Old Style Lager,
Canvas, 35 X 22 In.
See Page 514

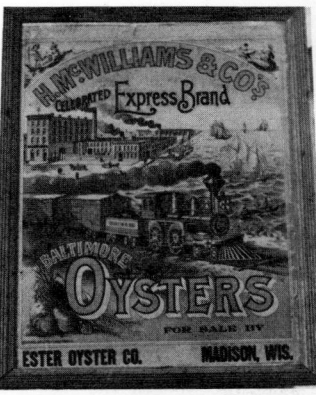

Store, Sign, Oysters,
Cardboard, 28 X 20 In.
See Page 514

Store, Sign,
Pink Pills For
Pale People,
Wooden, 20 In.
See Page 514

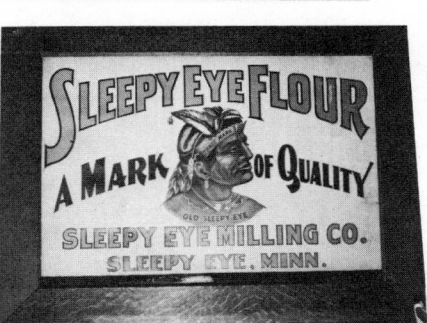

Store, Sign, Stoneware, 13 X 19 In.
See Page 514

Store, Sign, Sleepy Eye, Paper, 38 X 50 In.
See Page 514

Store, Sign, Rooming House, Marked Rooms, Wood & Metal
See Page 514

Store, Stretcher, Glove, Sterling Handle, Patent, Feb.15, 1898	22.50
Store, Surveying Instrument, Dietzgen, 1913, Case & Tripod	175.00
Store, Telegraph Key & Sounder, Western Electric	15.00
Store, Thermometer, Boschee's German Syrup, Brass Case	12.00
Store, Thermometer, Pepsi, Tin, 24 In., Girl With Straw In Bottle	16.50
Store, Thermometer, Pepsi, 7 X 27 In., Yellow, Embossed Cap	12.00
Store, Thermometer, Tin, Camel Cigarettes, Bold Relief, 13 X 5 3/4 In.	16.00
Store, Tin, A&p Coffee, Bank	2.50
Store, Tin, Adams California Fruit Chewing Gum, Gray	20.00
Store, Tin, American Powder Mills, Drum Type, Labels	30.00
Store, Tin, Arbuckle's Tea, 1/4 Lb.	8.50
Store, Tin, Arm & Hammer Baking Soda	2.00
Store, Tin, Atwood Coffee	5.95
Store, Tin, Bagley's Red Band Scrap Tobacco, White, Blue, & Gold	95.00
Store, Tin, Bagley's Wild Fruit Tobacco, Lunch Box	22.00
Store, Tin, Belfast Cut Plug	6.00
Store, Tin, Bellwood Smoking Tobacco	4.00
Store, Tin, Between The Acts, Little Cigars, Embossed, Lettering	6.50
Store, Tin, Big Ben, Horse, Pocket	3.00
Store, Tin, Blue Tiger	75.00
Store, Tin, Blue Tiger, Lunchbox	10.00
Store, Tin, Bond Street Pipe Tobacco, Pocket	3.50
Store, Tin, Boston Coffee _Illus_	9.50
Store, Tin, Briggs, Pocket	2.00
Store, Tin, Buckingham Tobacco, Pocket	7.00
Store, Tin, Bucklin Salve	1.00
Store, Tin, Buffalo Brand Fancy Salted Peanuts	15.00
Store, Tin, Bunte Diana Candy, 5 Lbs. 6.50 To	10.00
Store, Tin, Bunte Candy, Imitation Glass Front	6.50
Store, Tin, Cake Tobacco	6.00
Store, Tin, Camel, Pocket	3.00
Store, Tin, Cascarets Laxative, Miniature	2.00
Store, Tin, Castile Cream Harness Dressing	1.50
Store, Tin, Plug, Central Union, Red, Gold, 3 X 6 1/4 X 3 3/4 In.	3.50
Store, Tin, Chase & Sanborn Coffee, 17 In.Tall	55.00
Store, Tin, Chesterfield, Flat Fifties 2.50 To	3.00
Store, Tin, Cigar, Between The Acts, Small	2.00
Store, Tin, Cigar, La Palina	2.00
Store, Tin, Cigar, 25 Bankers Handmade	5.00
Store, Tin, Cigarette, Chesterfield, Cream & Gold	4.00
Store, Tin, Cigarette, Lucky Strike, Green, Flat 50's	3.50
Store, Tin, Cinco, Lunch Box	8.50
Store, Tin, Climax Tobacco, Small Tin	4.00
Store, Tin, Coffee, Historical Scene, Wooden Knob	10.00
Store, Tin, Colebrookdale	6.50
Store, Tin, Courtland Coffee, Cardboard, Tin Top & Bottom, 5 Lbs	14.00
Store, Tin, Crimson Rambler Syrup, Label, Dated 1919	5.00
Store, Tin, Culture Crush Cut Smoking Tobacco, Black, Green, & Yellow, Pocket	1.50
Store, Tin, Dan Patch _Illus_	12.00
Store, Tin, Deane's Mustard Plasters, Yonkers, N.Y., Gold, Red, Green	5.50
Store, Tin, Derby, Pocket	8.00
Store, Tin, Dill's Best Cut Plug Tobacco, Pocket 3.50 To	4.50
Store, Tin, Dill's Best 5-Inch Cylinder	12.00
Store, Tin, Dixie Kid Tobacco, Lunch Box	35.00
Store, Tin, Dixie Queen Plug Cut, Lunch Box	12.50
Store, Tin, Dixie Queen Tobacco, Lady, Lunch Box	35.00
Store, Tin, Dr.Korinek's Dip, Labels, Full	4.50
Store, Tin, Droste Harlem Candy, Oval	3.00
Store, Tin, Dunhill's Cakes	5.00
Store, Tin, Dy-O-La Dye, Door, Bins Inside, Black Letters	30.00
Store, Tin, Edgemont Crackers	3.50
Store, Tin, Edgeworth	12.50
Store, Tin, Edgeworth Pipe Tobacco	3.00
Store, Tin, Edgeworth Plug Tobacco	3.95
Store, Tin, Edgeworth, Pocket	1.00
Store, Tin, Edgeworth, Small Size 4.50 To	5.00

Store, Tin, Boston Coffee
See Page 516

Store, Tin, Dan Patch
See Page 516

Store, Tin, Egyptian Cigar	2.50
Store, Tin, Elephant Peanuts, Red Elephant	25.00
Store, Tin, Eve, Pocket	7.00
Store, Tin, Fashion Tobacco, Lunch Box	45.00
Store, Tin, Fashion Sexy, Lunch Box	42.00
Store, Tin, Ferndell Tea	3.75
Store, Tin, Five Brothers, Red, Black Lettering, Dated 1890	3.00
Store, Tin, Garcia Tobacco	2.00
Store, Tin, Golden Leaf	6.00
Store, Tin, Golden Squarecut	6.00
Store, Tin, Granulated 5 Cent Tobacco, Pocket	4.00
Store, Tin, Granulated 54, Free Sample	9.00
Store, Tin, Grease, Americo, American Oil Company	17.50 To 28.00
Store, Tin, George Washington Cut Plug, Round	6.50
Store, Tin, Griffin Shoe Polish, Orange	2.00
Store, Tin, H&p Holiday	25.00
Store, Tin, Half & Half, Telescopic	3.00 To 5.00
Store, Tin, Handbag Cut Plug	35.00
Store, Tin, Hercules Blasting Caps, Miniature	3.00
Store, Tin, Hershey's Chocolate & Cocoa, 12 In.	9.95
Store, Tin, Hi-Plane, Airplane, Pocket	7.00
Store, Tin, Hills Bros.Coffee, Red Ground	20.00
Store, Tin, Holstads Coffee, Orange & Red, 5 Lbs., Bail Handle	12.50
Store, Tin, Holtzman's, Tin-Tite, Pretz-Sticks, 3 Gallon	3.00
Store, Tin, Honey Bee Snuff, 3 In., Paper Label	5.00
Store, Tin, Humo Cigars	5.00
Store, Tin, Hunt Scene, Fox & Rabbit Border, Biscuit, 7 1/2 X 12 1/2 In.	30.50
Store, Tin, Huntley Palmer, Horse Drawn Carriage, Lady, Horsemen	28.00
Store, Tin, Huntley Palmer, Syrian Table	38.00
Store, Tin, Huntley Palmer, 6 Farm Scenes	22.50
Store, Tin, Imperial Ginger	3.50
Store, Tin, In-B-Tween	5.00
Store, Tin, Ivin's Biscuits, Lunch Box, Wire Handle, Yellow, Red, White, Black	12.00
Store, Tin, Just Suits Cut Plug, Lunch Box	7.50 To 12.50
Store, Tin, Kentucky Club, Pocket	3.00
Store, Tin, Kenway Mild Havana 10 Cent Blunts, Round	3.00
Store, Tin, Lafayette Mixture	6.00
Store, Tin, Laflin & Rand, Hercules Powder Co., 1 Lb.	10.00
Store, Tin, Licoree Lozenges, Glass Window In Front, National Licorice Co.	17.50
Store, Tin, Light, Sweet, Burley Tobacco	20.00 To 22.00
Store, Tin, Little Tom Cigars	5.00
Store, Tin, Log Cabin	14.00
Store, Tin, Lucky Green, Pocket	3.00
Store, Tin, Lucky Strike, Flat Fifties	3.00 To 4.00
Store, Tin, Lucky Strike, Free Sample	9.00

Store, Tin, Lucky Strike, Green, 6 In.	9.00
Store, Tin, Lucky Strike, Green & Red, Hinged Cover	7.50
Store, Tin, Mainsprings, Hasker, Marcuse Co.	5.00
Store, Tin, Mainsprings, Somer's Bros.	5.00
Store, Tin, Mayo's Cut Plug, Lunch Box	10.00 To 14.00
Store, Tin, Melichrino 100's Cigarettes	3.00
Store, Tin, Mellomints Pure Sugar Confection, 5 Lbs.	4.50
Store, Tin, Mellomints, Miniature	1.00
Store, Tin, Meltis Chocolates, Coronation, Miniature Of Elizabeth	10.00
Store, Tin, Mentholatum	2.00
Store, Tin, Monarch Tea	2.50
Store, Tin, Nature's Remedy	1.00
Store, Tin, Nursery Candies, United Cigar Emblem, Blue, Lunch Box	12.00
Store, Tin, Nut Brown Tobacco, English	13.00
Store, Tin, Old English Curvecut	6.00
Store, Tin, Old English, Pocket, Contents	3.50
Store, Tin, Old Velvet Tobacco	7.00
Store, Tin, Orcico Cigars	25.00
Store, Tin, P.Lorillard & Co., Rose Leaf Chewing Tobacco, 1878	15.00
Store, Tin, Packer's Tar Soap	3.50
Store, Tin, Pail & Ax Navy Tobacco, Small Tin	10.00
Store, Tin, Pastime Tobacco, Store Tin, Lunch Box	25.00 To 32.00
Store, Tin, Pat Hand, Pocket	10.00
Store, Tin, Patterson's Seal Cut Plug, Yellow Backet Weave	6.00 To 14.00
Store, Tin, Patterson's Seal Tobacco, Trunk	5.00
Store, Tin, Patterson's Tuxedo, Canister	12.00
Store, Tin, Peachy Tobacco, Pocket	3.50 To 5.00
Store, Tin, Peak-Freen Biscuits, English, Round, Gold & Green	22.00
Store, Tin, Pedro, Lunchbox	25.00
Store, Tin, Pepsin Mints, Gold, Miniature	1.50
Store, Tin, Philadelphia Cigars	5.00
Store, Tin, Philip Morris, Pocket	2.50
Store, Tin, Piper Heidsieck	10.00
Store, Tin, Piper Heidsieck, Pocket	2.00 To 4.00
Store, Tin, Player's Cut Plug, Cream, Black, & Red, Yang-Yin Symbol	4.00
Store, Tin, Plowboy, Lunch Box	7.50
Store, Tin, Plug, Sensible Sliced, White, Gold Lithograph	7.00
Store, Tin, Polar Bear, Picture On Ends, 18 X 14 X 12 In.	125.00
Store, Tin, Portage	2.00
Store, Tin, Possum Cigars	25.00
Store, Tin, Possum, 1 1/2 In.High Illus	20.00
Store, Tin, Postmaster Smokers	12.00
Store, Tin, Postmaster, 2 For 5 Cents	7.50
Store, Tin, Prince Albert, Pocket	1.00
Store, Tin, Prince Albert, 6 In.	5.00
Store, Tin, Quaker Maid Syrup, Red With White Lettering	7.00
Store, Tin, Queen Elizabeth Ii, Biscuit	2.00
Store, Tin, Ramon's, Pictures Of Little Boy & Doctor, Aspirin Size	1.50
Store, Tin, Red Jacket Tobacco, Pocket	3.00 To 4.00
Store, Tin, Red Tiger Chewing Tobacco, Lunch Box	12.00 To 18.50
Store, Tin, Revelation Tobacco, Pocket	2.00 To 4.00
Store, Tin, Richmond Mixture	6.00
Store, Tin, Richmond Mixture, Green, Gold Lighograph, Dated 1876	15.00
Store, Tin, Ricoro Operas, Pocket	3.00
Store, Tin, Riley's Toffee, Blue, Raised Mane	20.00
Store, Tin, Rose Dainties, Miniature	2.00
Store, Tin, Sawyer's Electric Cough Drops, Red	22.50
Store, Tin, Say-So Cigars	6.00
Store, Tin, Seidlitz Powders	4.00
Store, Tin, Sensible	7.00
Store, Tin, Snuff, Filled, Dated 1874, Paper Label	4.50
Store, Tin, Solitaire Coffee, Morey Mercantile Denver Co., 3 Lbs.	7.50
Store, Tin, Square Snuff, Lunch Box	2.00
Store, Tin, Stag, Elk, Pocket	7.00
Store, Tin, Square Snuff, Lunchbox	2.00
Store, Tin, Standard Separator Oil	2.50

Store, Tin, Possum, 1 1/2 In. High
See Page 518

Store, Tin, Sterling Tobacco, Cylindrical, Gold	17.00
Store, Tin, Sterling Tobacco, Cylindrical, Green	17.00
Store, Tin, Sterling Tobacco, Hinged Lid, Round	25.00
Store, Tin, Sterling Tobacco, Plaid, Round, 5 Lbs.	13.00 To 17.50
Store, Tin, Sunset Trail Cigars	25.00
Store, Tin, Swee-Touch-Nee Tea, Chest	4.50 To 6.50
Store, Tin, Sweet Burley, Red, Round	30.00
Store, Tin, Sweet Burley, Yellow, Round	20.00
Store, Tin, Sweet Cuba, Bin	38.00
Store, Tin, Sweet Cuba, Brown, Round	20.00
Store, Tin, Sweet Mist, Round	21.00 To 45.00
Store, Tin, Taiwan Tea, Animal Pictures	5.00
Store, Tin, Tea, Black, Gold, Black Knob	2.00
Store, Tin, Tea, English, White & Blue Wedgwood Design	12.00
Store, Tin, Tea, Japanese, Round	3.50
Store, Tin, Tea, Three Compartment Lids	42.50
Store, Tin, Tea, Ridgway, Souvenir 1915 San Francisco Exposition	8.00
Store, Tin, Temple Bar	4.00
Store, Tin, Three Crow Mustard	2.50
Store, Tin, Three Merry Widows-Agnes, Mable, & Beckie, Aluminum, Miniature	7.00
Store, Tin, Tiger, Round	18.00
Store, Tin, To Simulate Shelves Of Books	35.00
Store, Tin, Tobacco Girl Cigars	12.00
Store, Tin, Tobacco, Nigger Hair, Pail Type	65.00 To 85.00
Store, Tin, Tone Brothers Red Berry Coffee	9.50
Store, Tin, Triangle Club Black Pepper, Hinged Top, Green, Red, White	13.50
Store, Tin, Tuxedo, Pocket	3.00
Store, Tin, U.S.Marine Tobacco, Lunch Box	8.50 To 11.00
Store, Tin, Union Leader Tobacco, Lunch Box	9.00
Store, Tin, Union Leader Tobacco, Red, Gold Eagle	4.00
Store, Tin, Union Leader, Gold	12.00
Store, Tin, Union Leader, Poinsettia, Lunch Box	14.00
Store, Tin, Union Leader, Round, 6 In.	4.00
Store, Tin, Union Leader, Uncle Sam, Pocket	11.00
Store, Tin, Velvet Pipe Tobacco, Red & Gold, Knob On Top	3.95
Store, Tin, Velvet, Round, 6 In.	8.00
Store, Tin, Velvet, 1926, Tax Stamp, Pocket	1.00
Store, Tin, Walter Baker & Co., Breakfast Cocoa, Embossed	5.00
Store, Tin, Wishbone, Picture, Round, 4 Lb.	20.00
Store, Tin, White Ash, Man's Face, Round, 6 In.	9.00
Store, Tin, Whiz Auto Top Dressing, Lithograph Of 1910 Auto	7.50
Store, Tin, Whiz Saddle Soap	1.50
Store, Tin, Whiz Top Patching Outfit, Round	3.50
Store, Tin, Winner, Lunch Box	32.50
Store, Tin, Yale, 3 Oz.	6.50
Store, Tobacco Jar, Blue Boar *Illus*	50.00
Store, Tobacco, Cardboard, Tiger Chewing, 5 Cent	39.00
Store, Token, Brass, J.H.Butler Bengal, Indian Territory, 1 Dollar	7.50

Store, Tobacco Jar, Blue Boar
See Page 519

Store, Token, Fort D.A., Russell, Wyoming	15.00
Store, Token, Good For 1 Pt.Milk, W.C.Wharton, Marysville, Ohio	.50
Store, Token, Green River Whiskey, Brass, Negro Standing By Packhorse	4.50
Store, Token, Hoquiam, Washington, 1939, Wooden, 25 Cents	4.00
Store, Token, Moxie, Good For 5 Cents	5.00
Store, Token, Nevada, Gaming, 2 Dollars & 50 Cents	7.00
Store, Tongs, Ice	5.00
Store, Tongs, Ice, Topeka, Kansas, Icehouse	14.50
Store, Tongs, Mechanical, Metal	1.00
Store, Top, Cracker Jack, Tin	5.00
Store, Tray, Admiral Dewey, Change, Color Portrait	30.00
Store, Tray, Anheuser-Busch, 1915	15.00
Store, Tray, Arrow Beer	24.00
Store, Tray, Beer, Fehr's, F.F.X.L.Beers, Louisville, 1910, 13 In.Round	40.00
Store, Tray, Beer, Kaier Brewing Co., Mahandy City, 1905, 13 1/2 X 16 1/2 In.	60.00
Store, Tray, Blatz Old Heidelberg Beer, European Men Sitting At Table	37.50
Store, Tray, Bravo Beer	35.00
Store, Tray, Burkhardt's, Akron, Ohio, 12 In.Diameter	20.00
Store, Tray, C.Feigenspan Brewing Co., Dated 1910, Girl	22.50
Store, Tray, Change, Arcadia Brewing Co., Round	9.50
Store, Tray, Change, Eagle Brewing Co., Utica, N.Y., Eagle In Center	24.00
Store, Tray, Change, Fairy Soap, 4 In.Diameter .... 18.50 To	22.50
Store, Tray, Change, Iroquois Brewery, Buffalo, Indian Head In Center	10.00
Store, Tray, Change, King's Puremalt, Oval, C.1915-20	35.00
Store, Tray, Change, Leather & Felt, Erbanco Cigars	4.00
Store, Tray, Change, Mascot Tobacco, Mountain & Lake Scene	5.00
Store, Tray, Change, Mellowwood Whiskey, Round	9.50
Store, Tray, Change, Miller High Life Beer, Men On Coach	11.50
Store, Tray, Change, Miller, 1951	5.00
Store, Tray, Change, Moxie, Blonde Holding Glass, Round, 6 In. .... 45.00 To	55.00
Store, Tray, Change, Ruppert's Beer, No.3	7.50
Store, Tray, Change, Signed I.Sacke, Lithograph	9.50
Store, Tray, Change, William Jennings Bryan, Oval	16.50
Store, Tray, Chero Cola	30.00
Store, Tray, City Cousins, 1908, Square	75.00
Store, Tray, Corona Victoria Beer, Tin, Woman Wearing Sombrero, 13 In.Round	2.00
Store, Tray, Corona Victoria, Mexico, Woman, Aztec Pyramids, Tin	2.00
Store, Tray, Cream Top Lager, 1905, Lykens, Pa., Oval, Girl, Horse, Rose	28.00
Store, Tray, Evervess Sparkling Water, Product Of Pepsi-Cola	2.50
Store, Tray, Girl Holding 6 Beer Mugs, Tin, 13 In.Round	2.00
Store, Tray, Green River Whiskey _Illus_	75.00
Store, Tray, Hadley Beer, Bulldog	11.00
Store, Tray, Home Beer, Round, Picture Of Beer Bottle	16.50
Store, Tray, Hudepohl, Cincinnati, Decidedly The Best, Black, Yellow	13.00
Store, Tray, Ice Cream, Green & Red, De Courtes In White Letters	7.50
Store, Tray, Knickerbocker Beer	6.00
Store, Tray, Lily Neer Beer, C.1926	3.50
Store, Tray, Mcbride Hardware, Cranbrook, Building & Printing, Round, Metal	8.00

Store, Tray, Green River Whiskey
See Page 520

Store, Tray, Miller High Life Beer, Oval, Girl Sitting On Moon 17.50
Store, Tray, Nugrape, Hand Holding Bottle, Rectangular 19.50
Store, Tray, Old Bohemian, Cooper Brewing Co., York, Pa., Girl 18.00
Store, Tray, Olde Towne Fine Beer & Ale, Round, Lamplighter Picture 18.00
Store, Tray, Orange Crush 8.00
Store, Tray, Red Head Girl, Tin, 13 In.Round 2.00
Store, Tray, Scheidt's Beer, Rectangular, Washington At Valley Forge 29.00
Store, Tray, Schlitz, World On Back 4.75
Store, Tray, Senorita Being Serenaded, Tin, 13 In.Round 2.00
Store, Tray, Superior Beer, Blonde Girl, Tin, 13 In.Round 2.00
Store, Tray, Tara's Hall Straightest Whiskey, Jos.Dudenhoefer Co., 1905 .... 26.00
Store, Tray, Two Xx Doz.Equis Beer, Cold Bottle Of Beer, Tin, 13 In.Round 2.00
Store, Tray, Valley Forge Beer, Washington's Headquarters Picture 1778 .... 15.00
Store, Tray, Western Brewing Co., Picture Of Stag, Round 17.50
Store, Tray, Woman's Head, Horse, 1908, Oval 75.00
Store, Tub, Piggin Handle, Staved, Buttonhole Hoops 85.00
Store, Tumbler, Moxie 8.75
Store, Typewriter, Oliver 15.00
Store, Typewriter, Simplex, 1920, Model A 12.00
Store, Veterinary Dental Equipment, Dated 1912, For Horses 25.00
Store, Wig Stand, Turned, 15 1/2 In.High 22.50
Store, Wooden Shoe, Heineken's Beer, Marked Holland, Yellow 5.00
Store, Yo-Yo, Life Savers 5.00
  Strawberry, see Soft Paste
Suhl, Salt, Pink, Gold, Roses, Oval, Green Mark 8.00
Sulfide, Bust Of Voltaire, Black Frame 145.00
  Sulfide, Marble, see Marble, Sulfide
  Sulfide, Paperweight, see Paperweight, Sulfide

Sunbonnet Babies were first introduced in 1902 in the Sunbonnet Babies
Primer. The stories were by Eulalie Osgood Grover, illustrated by
Bertha Corbett. The children's faces were completely hidden by the
sunbonnets, and had been pictured in black and white before this time. The
color pictures in the book were immediately successful. The Royal
Bayreuth China Company made a full line of children's dishes decorated
with the Sunbonnet Babies.

Sunbonnet Babies, Bell, 'washing' 85.00
Sunbonnet Babies, Book, Grover 10.00
Sunbonnet Babies, Book, Sunbonnet Babies In Holland, 1915 .... 48.00
Sunbonnet Babies, Bowl, Footed 48.50
Sunbonnet Babies, Bowl, Ironing, Blue Mark, 6 In.Diameter .... 75.00 To 90.00
Sunbonnet Babies, Card, Baby Mailing Letter, Wall's 5.00
Sunbonnet Babies, Card, Saturday, Ullman's 3.00
Sunbonnet Babies, Card, Saying Grace, U.Co. 3.00
Sunbonnet Babies, Card, Set Of 7 Days Of Week, Ullman's .... 42.00 To 55.00
Sunbonnet Babies, Card, Spetember, Ullman's 6.00
Sunbonnet Babies, Creamer 98.50

Sunbonnet Babies, **Creamer**, Mending, 2 1/2 In.Tall, Royal Bayreuth	78.00
Sunbonnet Babies, **Creamer**, Royal Bayreuth .... *Illus*	235.00
Sunbonnet Babies, **Cup & Saucer**, Sweeping & Mending, Royal Bayreuth	95.00
Sunbonnet Babies, **Dish**, Candy, Beach, Gold Handles, Ruffled, Blue Mark	75.00
Sunbonnet Babies, **Dish**, Washing & Ironing, Heart Shape, Blue Mark	65.00
Sunbonnet Babies, **Paper Dolls**, Uncut Page From Magazine, June, 1909	60.00
Sunbonnet Babies, **Picture**, Nursery Rhymes, Framed, Red Dresses	18.50
Sunbonnet Babies, **Picture**, Scrubbing Day, Signed Corbett, 6 X 8 In.	20.00
Sunbonnet Babies, **Picture**, Wash Day, Corbett, Dated 1904, Frame, 8 X 16 In.	17.50
Sunbonnet Babies, **Pitcher**, Milk, Washing & Hanging Clothes, Royal Bayreuth	115.00
Sunbonnet Babies, **Plaque**, Rain, Rain Go Away, Owens Bros., Boston	18.00
Sunbonnet Babies, **Plate**, Cleaning, Royal Bayreuth, 6 In.Diameter	65.00
Sunbonnet Babies, **Plate**, Ironing, Royal Bayreuth, 6 In.	85.00
Sunbonnet Babies, **Plate**, Two Girls, Two Geese, Dog, Gold Edge, 6 1/2 In.	28.00
Sunbonnet Babies, **Relish**, Fishing	75.00
Sunbonnet Babies, **Sugar & Creamer**, Flow Blue, Royal Bayreuth	110.00
Sunbonnet Babies, **Tray**, Dresser, Girls Hanging Wash, 9 1/2 X 10 In.	165.00

Sunderland Luster is a name given to a characteristic pink luster made by Leeds, Newcastle, and other english firms during the nineteenth century. The luster glaze is metallic and glossy and sometimes appears to have bubbles as a decoration.

Sunderland, **Jug**, Bridge, River, Verse, Spout, Handle, Luster, Liverpool, 7 In.	275.00
Sunderland, **Cup & Saucer**, Pattern Inside Cup	45.00
Sunderland, **Plate**, Luster, 6 In.	7.50

Swansea Pottery was made at the Cambrian Pottery in Glamorganshire, Wales. It was founded in 1765 and worked until 1870. The early wares were of a fine-quality soft paste. All types of Staffordshire Wares were also made.

Swansea, **Urn**, Biscuit, Campana Shape, Applied Flowers, C.1815, Incised Mark	250.00
Sword, see Weapon, Sword	
Syrup Pitcher, see Pressed Glass, Pitcher, Syrup;Pewter, etc.	
Taffeta Glass, see Carnival Glass	
Tapestry, Porcelain, see Rose Tapestry	
Tarzan, **Book**, Tarzan Of The Apes, Copyright, Great Britain, June, 1914	50.00
Tea Caddy, see Furniture, Tea Caddy	
Tea Leaf, see Ironstone	
Tea Leaf, see Luster, Copper	
Telephone, **Candlestick Stand**, Upright, Black & Nickel .... 19.00 To 37.50	
Telephone, **Denmark**, Model S, 1908, No Dial	15.00
Telephone, **Desk**, French-Style, Magneto, Black & Nickel, Gold Trim	37.50
Telephone, **English**, Dial	8.00
Telephone, **National Cash**, Handset, Pushbuttons, Drawer, Gray-Black Metal	27.50
Telephone, **Oak**, Magneto, Ringer Box	12.50
Telephone, **Oak**, Wall, Picture Frame Front, Long Stem	55.00
Telephone, **Platform**, Gooseneck	40.00
Telephone, **Wall Type**, Hotel Room, The Edward Pat.'07	35.00
Telephone, **Wall**, Oak, Apartment Size	30.00
Telephone, **Western Electric**, Wood	78.00
Telephone, **1928** .... *Illus*	21.00
Telescope, **Mariner's**, Black Enamel, Brass Ends, 16 In.Open	19.50
Teplitz, **Compote**, Amphora, Gray, Pink, Green, Black, Brown, Enamel, Austria	37.50
Teplitz, **Figurine**, Amphora, Boy, Wine Cask, Austria, 1889, 6 1/2 In.Tall	52.00
Teplitz, **Figurine**, Camel & Driver, Amphora, Austria .... *Illus*	125.00
Teplitz, **Jar**, Cracker, Hand-Painted, Angel Figural Cover	39.00
Teplitz, **Urn**, Amphora, Austria, Enameled, Gold Bird On Brown & Green, Pink	42.50
Teplitz, **Vase**, Amphora, 8 1/2 In. .... *Illus*	125.00
Teplitz, **Vase**, Child's Portrait, Blue, Gold, Signed, Handles, 13 1/2 In.	45.00
Teplitz, **Vase**, Green, Gold, Red, Floral Decor, Handle, 8 3/4 In.	14.00
Teplitz, **Vase**, Hand-Painted Poinsettia, Gold, 8 In.High	45.00
Teplitz, **Vase**, Marked Amphora, Grecian Motif, 2 Handles, 10 In.Tall	30.00
Teplitz, **Vase**, Purple, Iridescent, Jewels In Neck, 6 1/2 In.High	30.00
Teplitz, **Vase**, Roses, Leaves, Amphora, Brown, Yellow, Green, 4 Handle, 9 In.	45.00
Teplitz, **Vase**, Scenic, Art Nouveau, 17 In.Tall	55.00
Terry & The Pirates, **Book**, Coloring, 1945	6.50

Sunbonnet Babies,
Creamer, Royal Bayreuth
See Page 522

Telephone, 1928
See Page 522

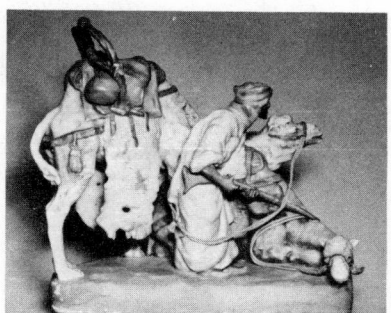

Teplitz, Figurine,
Camel & Driver, Amphora, Austria
See Page 522

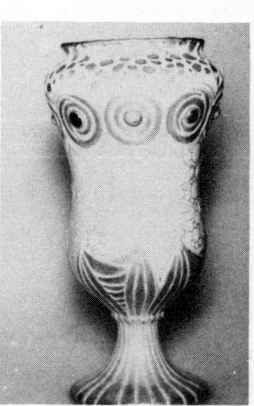

Teplitz,
Vase,
Amphora,
8 1/2 In.
See Page 522

Textile includes all types of table linens and household linens such as coverlets, quilts, fabrics, etc.

Linen or Wool Coverlets were made during the eighteenth century. Most of the coverlets date from 1800 to 1850. Four types were made, the double woven, jacquard, summer and winter, and overshot.

Samplers were made in the United States during the early 1700s. The best examples were made from 1790 to 1840. Long narrow samplers are usually older than the square ones. Early samplers just had stitching or alphabets. The later examples had numerals, borders, and pictorial decorations. Those with mottoes are mid-victorian.

Textile, Afghan, Dark Red & Blue Geometric	100.00
Textile, Afghan, Handmade, Blue Willow Pattern, 56 In. X 65 In.	125.00
Textile, Afghan, Rose & Wine Shades, Hairpin Lace Pattern	15.00
Textile, Altar Cloth, Russian, Gold Embroidered Velvet, Orange, 19th Century	120.00
Textile, Apron, Laced, Ankle Length	5.00
Textile, Bag, Camel, Oriental, Flat, Woven, Turkey Red	60.00
Textile, Bag, Flower Design, Beaded, Green, Yellow, Pink, Chain Handle	12.95
Textile, Bag, Horse Feeding, Canvas, 1944	4.50
Textile, Banquet Cloth, Damask Linen, Chrysanthemums, 2 X 4 Yards	25.00
Textile, Banquet Cloth, Damask Linen, Roses, 2 X 3 Yards, 12 Napkins	33.00
Textile, Basket, Crocheted, Party Favors, White Cotton, 1930	5.00
Textile, Bedspread, Blue & White, White Squares Diagonally Across	90.00

Textile, **Bedspread**, Chintz, Eagles In Brown, Swags Of Multicolor Floral 450.00
Textile, **Bedspread**, Federal Period, Scalloped Valance, Fringe 600.00
Textile, **Bedspread**, Hand Crocheted 70.00
Textile, **Bedspread**, Hand Crocheted, Octagon Popcorn, Off-White 35.00
Textile, **Bedspread**, Multicolor, Homespun, Geometric Flowers 200.00
Textile, **Bedspread**, Patchwork, Green & Red Floral 70.00
Textile, **Bedspread**, Seersucker, White 5.00
Textile, **Bedspread**, White, Candlewick, Adam & Eve Pattern, C.1825 .... 350.00
Textile, **Bell Pull**, Embroidery On Linen, 50 In.Long, Pair 35.00
Textile, **Blanket**, Homespun, American, Red, Geometric Decoration 125.00
Textile, **Bonnet**, Lady's, Black Silk 6.00
Textile, **Boot**, Carriage, Lady's, Black Velvet, Tie Ribbon, Fur Trim, Pair 7.00
Textile, **Carpet**, Aubusson, Central Medallion, 13 Ft.4 In.X 9 Ft.4 In. 1500.00
Textile, **Carpet**, Bessarabian, Corridor, Blue Green Field, 12 Ft.X 5 Ft.5 In. 800.00
Textile, **Carpet**, Chinese Design, Tufted, Sapphire Blue Field, 25 Ft.X 24 Ft. 850.00
Textile, **Carpet**, Chinese, Beige Field, Vines, Lotus, 12 X 11 Ft.3 In. 600.00
Textile, **Carpet**, French Design, Hand Tufted, Beige, Cornucopias, 14 X 12 Ft. 450.00
Textile, **Carpet**, Indian, French Design, Floral Medallion, 14 X 9 Ft.10 In. 450.00
Textile, **Carpet**, Indian, Silk & Gold, Woven, 13 Ft.3 In.X 9 Ft.9 In. 2300.00
Textile, **Carpet**, Kashan, Beige Field, 21 Ft.6 In.X 11 Ft.3 In. 3100.00
Textile, **Carpet**, Kashan, Medallion, Beige Field, 11 Ft.5 In.X 8 Ft.3 In. 3750.00
Textile, **Carpet**, Kerman, Ivory Field, Medallions, 15 Ft.4 In.X 12 Ft.6 In. 1200.00
Textile, **Carpet**, Kerman, Ivory, Flowers, Animals, Birds 1500.00
Textile, **Carpet**, Kerman, Medallion, 21 Ft.10 In.X 15 Ft.9 In. 600.00
Textile, **Carpet**, Needlepoint, Beige Field, Medallions, 12 X 9 Ft. 1200.00
Textile, **Carpet**, Needlework, Beige Floral, 10 X 8 Ft. 550.00
Textile, **Carpet**, Tabriz, Wine Field, Leaf Scrolls, 18 Ft.6 In.X 11 Ft.2 In. 2000.00
Textile, **Carpet**, Turkish, Plum Ground, Rosettes & Leaves In Ivory & Blue 500.00
Textile, **Chasuble**, French, 18th Century, Embroidered Flowers 40.00
Textile, **Coat**, Man's, Prince Albert, 1860 .... 15.00
Textile, **Comforter**, Crazy Quilt, 70 X 70 In. 30.00
Textile, **Costume**, Baby's, Chinese, One-Year-Old, Red Jacket, Embroidery 20.00
Textile, **Coverlet**, Blue & White, Handwoven 18.00
Textile, **Coverlet**, Blue & White, 2 Piece, N.Y., 1842 .... 160.00
Textile, **Coverlet**, Callimanco, Rose Red Color, Linsey-Woolsey Lined 550.00
Textile, **Coverlet**, Double Woven, One Side Red, Other Blue, 75 X 78 In. 75.00
Textile, **Coverlet**, Marseilles Type, Eagles 75.00
Textile, **Coverlet**, Red, Blue, & Yellow, Samuel Meily, Mansfield, Ohio, 1842 .... 25.00
Textile, **Coverlet**, Red, Pink, Green, Quilted, Signed, 1852 .... *Illus* 400.00
Textile, **Coverlet**, Tomato Red, Deep Blue, & White 55.00
Textile, **Coverlet**, Uncut, Red, White, Blue, & Green 425.00
Textile, **Coverlet**, White, Red, & Blue, B.Lichty, Bristol, O., 1852 .... 65.00
Textile, **Coverlet**, Wool & Linen Crewelwork, Floral, Insects 150.00
Textile, **Coverlet**, Wool, Linen Crewelwork .... *Illus* 150.00
Textile, **Crazy Quilt**, German, Silk & Velvet, Embroidered, Appliqued 65.00
Textile, **Dress**, Baby's, Long, Circa 1865 .... 5.98
Textile, **Dress**, C.1920, Beige Chiffon, Heavily Beaded 10.00
Textile, **Dress**, Lady's, Chiffon Velvet, Size 18, Red, Gray & Black, 1926 .... 10.00
Textile, **Embroidery**, Seal Of N.Y.City, Framed 17.50
Textile, **Flag**, American, 48 Stars, Made In 1912 .... 25.00
Textile, **Flag**, 46 Star, Sewn Stripes, 33 X 61 In. 20.00
Textile, **Handbag**, Lady's, C.1920, Opera, Clutch, Brocaded Gold & Green 12.00
Textile, **Handbag**, White Silk, Seed Pearls, Gold Frame & Chain 18.00
Textile, **Handkerchief**, Admiral Dewey, Red, White & Blue, Silk 22.00
Textile, **Handkerchief**, Gone With The Wind, 1930s, Floral, Rhett & Bonnie 2.50
Textile, **Kokoshinik**, Russian, Gold Embroidered, Silk, Purple, Floral, C.1850 .... 50.00
Textile, **Needlework Silhouette On Velvet**, Napoleon 175.00
Textile, **Nightgown**, Ladies', White, Tatting Lace, Size 12 .... 2.00
Textile, **Panel**, Needlework, Red Background, Floral & Green Overlay 12.50
Textile, **Piece**, Crewel, Connecticut, 18th Century, 51 X 76 In. 2000.00
Textile, **Pillow Case**, Handmade, Tatted Edge, Pair 3.00
Textile, **Pillow Cover**, World War I Era, Military Figures, Fringe, Satin 15.00
Textile, **Pillow Sham**, 25 In.Square, White, Red Embroidery, Pair 8.00
Textile, **Quilt**, Applique, Urn Of Flowers & Berries, Green & Red 185.00
Textile, **Quilt**, Child's, Applique 10.00
Textile, **Quilt**, Cotton, Brownies In Action, Palmer Cox, Pat.1895, 76 X 80 In. 70.00

Textile, Coverlet, Red, Pink,
Green, Quilted, Signed, 1852
See Page 524

Textile, Coverlet, Wool, Linen Crewelwork
See Page 524

Textile, Quilt, Flowerpot Design, Hand Stitched	45.00
Textile, Quilt, Hand Pieced, Pink, Tan, 4 1/2 In.Block, 72 X 80 In.	27.00
Textile, Quilt, Handmade, Red & White, 72 X 72 In.	35.00
Textile, Quilt, Homespun Wool, Stuffed, Hand-Quilted	25.00
Textile, Quilt, Homespun, Blue & White, 2 Sides, Signed 'rd'	100.00
Textile, Quilt, Patchwork, Color Strips, Woolen, 52 X 72 In.	20.00
Textile, Quilt, Patchwork, Featherstitch, White Background, 80 In.Square	35.00
Textile, Quilt, Patchwork, Pink Ground, 75 X 88 In.	25.00
Textile, Quilt, Patchwork, Shades Of Pink & Red, 82 X 87 In.	35.00
Textile, Quilt, Patchwork, Stripes Of Printed Blocks	60.00
Textile, Quilt, Patchwork, Yellow Border, 80 X 92 In.	35.00
Textile, Quilt, Red, Pink, Green, Floral, Eliza E.Hamilton, 1852	400.00
Textile, Quilt, Red, White, Blue, Green, American	950.00
Textile, Quilt, Red, White, Green, Appliqued	425.00
Textile, Quilt, Silk, Handmade, Briarstitched, 80 X 65 In.	25.00
Textile, Quilt, Tumbling Block	20.00
Textile, Robe, Buggy	15.00
Textile, Robe, Chinese, Forbidden Stitch, Black, Multicolors	100.00
Textile, Robe, Lap, Automobile, Plaid, Fringed Ends, Chase & Co. Label	23.00
Textile, Robe, Lap, Horsehair, Brown, Red & Green	22.00
Textile, Robe, Lap, Plaid, Fringed Ends	22.00
Textile, Rug, Afghan Bokhara, Oriental, 4 Ft.2 In.X 5 Ft.4 In.	70.00
Textile, Rug, Afghan Bokhara, Oriental, 3 Ft.1 In.X 4 Ft.4 In.	55.00
Textile, Rug, Afghan Bokhara, 25 In.X 3 Ft.	55.00
Textile, Rug, Afghan Bokhara, 5 Ft.4 In.X 6 Ft.9 In.	175.00
Textile, Rug, Anatolian, Silk, 21 X 38 In.	20.00
Textile, Rug, Anatolian, 3 Ft.1 In.X 5 Ft.4 In.	45.00
Textile, Rug, Belouch, Browns & Plum, 5 Ft.7 In.X 9 Ft.	375.00
Textile, Rug, Belouch, Turkoman Design, 5 Ft.5 In.X 9 Ft.6 In.	400.00
Textile, Rug, Beluchistan, 2 Ft.9 In.X 4 Ft.9 In.	45.00
Textile, Rug, Beluchistan, 3 Ft.X 4 Ft.11 In.	40.00
Textile, Rug, Beluchistan, 3 Ft.1 In.X 5 Ft.4 In.	60.00
Textile, Rug, Bergama, Blue Beads & Shells, 3 Ft.3 In.X 3 Ft.	200.00
Textile, Rug, Bijar, Camel's Hair, 24 Ft.X 32 In.	50.00

Textile, Rug, Bijar, Oriental, Red, Gray Squares, Blue & Green Rosettes 1100.00
Textile, Rug, Bijar, Oriental, 4 Ft.6 In.X 7 Ft.2 In. 135.00
Textile, Rug, Bokhara, Afghan, 7 Ft.2 In.X 10 Ft.5 In. 950.00
Textile, Rug, Bokhara, Red Field With Rosettes, 3 Ft.8 In.X 4 Ft.11 In. 225.00
Textile, Rug, Bokhara, 4 Ft.10 In.X 7 Ft.12 In. 125.00
Textile, Rug, Bokhara, 3 Ft.4 In.X 4 Ft.4 In. 60.00
Textile, Rug, Cabistan, 3 Ft.7 In.X 5 Ft.3 In. 125.00
Textile, Rug, Cabistan, Oriental, 3 Ft.2 In.X 4 Ft.5 In. 130.00
Textile, Rug, Camel's Hair, 3 Ft.4 In.X 10 Ft. 75.00
Textile, Rug, Chinese, Blue & Rust, Oval, 6 Ft.X 8 Ft.8 In. 70.00
Textile, Rug, Daghestan, Red Medallion On White, 9 Ft.2 In.X 15 Ft.5 In. 700.00
Textile, Rug, Daghestan, 3 Ft.4 In.X 4 Ft. 55.00
Textile, Rug, Daghestan, 4 Ft.2 In.X 4 Ft.10 In. 85.00
Textile, Rug, Embroidery On Linen, 23 X 4 Ft.9 In. 17.50
Textile, Rug, Embroidery On Linen, 27 X 8 Ft.4 In. 20.00
Textile, Rug, Feraghan, Blue & Rose, Geometric Fish, 3 Ft.8 In.X 13 Ft.4 In. 80.00
Textile, Rug, French, Needlework, Beige, Floral, Birds, 5 Ft.4 In.X 4 Ft.6 In. 100.00
Textile, Rug, Gorovan, Oriental, 4 Ft.X 6 Ft.6 In. 85.00
Textile, Rug, Hamadan, Blue & Orange, 5 Ft.9 In.X 9 Ft.4 In. 400.00
Textile, Rug, Hamadan, Black & Red Floral, 3 Ft.7 In.X 5 Ft.9 In. 100.00
Textile, Rug, Hamadan, Blue Field, Allover Pattern, 3 Ft.7 In.X 6 Ft.8 In. 45.00
Textile, Rug, Hamadan, Camel's Hair, 3 Ft.5 In.X 5 Ft.9 In. 70.00
Textile, Rug, Hamadan, Geometric Fish, 3 Ft.9 In.X 6 Ft.3 In. 150.00
Textile, Rug, Hamadan, Midnight Blue Field, 6 Ft.9 In.X 4 Ft.7 In. 475.00
Textile, Rug, Hamadan, Tan, Pole Medallion, Blue & Green 175.00
Textile, Rug, Hamadan, 3 Ft.5 In.X 6 Ft.10 In. 70.00
Textile, Rug, Hamadan, 4 Ft.1 In.X 6 Ft.2 In. 80.00
Textile, Rug, Hamadan, 4 Ft.1 In.X 7 Ft.9 In. 95.00
Textile, Rug, Hamadan, 4 Ft.3 In.X 4 Ft. 175.00
Textile, Rug, Hamadan, 4 Ft.8 In.X 12 Ft. 80.00
Textile, Rug, Hooked, Cream Ground, Geometric Pattern 12.50
Textile, Rug, Hooked, Floral Design On Ecru, 7 Ft.X 4 Ft.8 In. 210.00
Textile, Rug, Hooked, Flowers & Oak Leaves, 26 X 52 In. 150.00
Textile, Rug, Hooked, Home Sweet Home, 31 X 62 In. 25.00
Textile, Rug, Hooked, New England, Shirred, Mass., 1828, 6 Ft.X 4 Ft.4 In. 575.00
Textile, Rug, Horsehide, Felt Backed, Old Dobbin 25.00
Textile, Rug, Isfahan, Blue Field, 44 1/2 X 16 In. 475.00
Textile, Rug, Kabistan, Oriental, Brown, Geometric Figures & Rosettes 550.00
Textile, Rug, Kabistan, Oriental, 3 Diamond Medallions, Tan & Ivory On Blue 275.00
Textile, Rug, Karabagh, Browns, 4 Ft.10 In.X 11 Ft.7 In. 450.00
Textile, Rug, Karaja, 3 102 Ft.X 5 Ft.3 In. 50.00
Textile, Rug, Kashan, Silk, Medallion, 6 X 4 Ft. 3600.00
Textile, Rug, Kashan, Weeping Willows, 4 X 7 Ft. 400.00
Textile, Rug, Kazak, Animals, Birds, Muslim Date 1331, 4 Ft.10 In.X 12 Ft. 475.00
Textile, Rug, Kazak, Birds 3 Animals, 3 Ft.4 In.X 7 Ft.5 In. 155.00
Textile, Rug, Kazak, Cloud Band, 7 Ft.9 In.X 4 Ft.5 In. 190.00
Textile, Rug, Kazak, Warriors, 4 Ft.9 In.X 9 Ft.10 In. 225.00
Textile, Rug, Kazak, 2 Ft.11 In.X 3 Ft.9 In. 50.00
Textile, Rug, Kazak, 3 Ft.9 In.X 6 Ft. 175.00
Textile, Rug, Kazak, 4 Ft.11 In.X 7 Ft.10 In. 75.00
Textile, Rug, Kazak, 5 Ft.4 In.X 7 Ft.7 In. 500.00
Textile, Rug, Kerman, Dark Blue, 8 Trees & Flowering Shrubs 850.00
Textile, Rug, Kerman, Ivory, Flowers, Blue, Red, & Brown 525.00
Textile, Rug, Kerman, Ivory, 8 Equestrians, Deer, Bowmen, Floral 65.00
Textile, Rug, Kerman, 3 Ft.X 5 Ft. 205.00
Textile, Rug, Kerman, 4 Ft.X 7 Ft. 550.00
Textile, Rug, Kerman, 4 Ft.4 In.X 6 Ft.10 In. 125.00
Textile, Rug, Kurdistan, Camel's Hair, Beige Field, Diamond Medallion 160.00
Textile, Rug, Kurdistan, Mustard Color Medallion, 6 Ft.9 In.X 6 Ft.3 In. 250.00
Textile, Rug, Kurdistan, Oriental, Tan, Diamond Medallions In Blue & Red 200.00
Textile, Rug, Laver Kerman, 6 Ft.9 In.X 4 Ft.4 In. 300.00
Textile, Rug, Lillihan, Oriental, 2 Ft.7 1/2 In.X 4 Ft.8 1/2 In. 32.50
Textile, Rug, Mosul, Red & Blue Ground, Fish & Floral Motif 100.00
Textile, Rug, Navajo, Blue With White Birds In Flight & 4 Capital E's 250.00
Textile, Rug, Navajo, Dark Blue With Ducks In Flight 360.00
Textile, Rug, Navajo, Geometric Design, 4 1/2 Feet X 9 Feet 500.00

Textile, Rug, Navajo, Gray With Blue, Black, White, & Yellow Diamonds 270.00
Textile, Rug, Navajo, Horizontal Lines Of Red, Light Blue, & Yellow 100.00
Textile, Rug, Navajo, Maroon With Diamonds In Black, Olive, Green, & Orange 140.00
Textile, Rug, Navajo, Red & Black Diamonds With White Separations 200.00
Textile, Rug, Navajo, Red & White Bands With Yellow & Blue Pine Trees 360.00
Textile, Rug, Navajo, Red Diamonds In White, Black, & Green 90.00
Textile, Rug, Navajo, Red With Black & White Diamonds 90.00
Textile, Rug, Navajo, Rose With Black & White & Blue & White Diamonds 230.00
Textile, Rug, Navajo, Seven Colors, Swastika Design, 6 Ft.9 In.X 4 Ft.9 In. 1500.00
Textile, Rug, Navajo, Wool, Diamond Design, 5 X 3 Ft. 35.00
Textile, Rug, Needlepoint & Beadwork, Victorian, C.1845, 7 Ft.2 In.X 6 Ft. 250.00
Textile, Rug, Needlepoint, Beige Field, 8 Ft.6 In.X 6 Ft. 500.00
Textile, Rug, Needlework, English, Tiles, Floral, 3 Ft.2 In.X 5 Ft.5 In. 400.00
Textile, Rug, Needlework, Tile Pattern, 7 Ft.7 In.X 5 Ft.1 1/2 In. 350.00
Textile, Rug, Persian, Animals, Birds, Fowls, & Trees, 8 Ft.Long 400.00
Textile, Rug, Prayer, Anatolian, Beige Mihrab, 5 Ft.9 In.X 4 Ft.4 In. 375.00
Textile, Rug, Prayer, Anatolian, Silk, C.1890, 44 X 62 In. 175.00
Textile, Rug, Prayer, Anatolian, 3 1/2 Ft.X 5 Ft.4 In. 40.00
Textile, Rug, Prayer, Beluchistan, 33 X 53 In. 100.00
Textile, Rug, Prayer, Beshir, 26 In.X 4 Ft. 130.00
Textile, Rug, Prayer, Bokhara, Princess, 4 Ft.4 In.X 5 1/2 Ft. 375.00
Textile, Rug, Prayer, Cabistan, Mihrab & Geometric Floral, 4 Ft.5 In.X 4 Ft. 80.00
Textile, Rug, Prayer, Cabistan, 4 Ft.5 In.X 3 Ft.5 In. 140.00
Textile, Rug, Prayer, Daghestan, Oriental, Brown, Red, Blue & Ivory 850.00
Textile, Rug, Prayer, Daghestan, Oriental, Red, Green Niche 225.00
Textile, Rug, Prayer, Daghestan, 3 Ft.X 4 Ft.9 In. 350.00
Textile, Rug, Prayer, Kazak, Red & Blue Webbing, 3 Ft.3 In.X 4 Ft. 90.00
Textile, Rug, Prayer, Kazak, 3 Ft.X 5 Ft. 75.00
Textile, Rug, Prayer, Ladik, 5 Ft.6 In.X 3 Ft.8 In. 225.00
Textile, Rug, Prayer, Mudjar, 42 X 65 In. 120.00
Textile, Rug, Prayer, Turkish, Silk, 5 Ft.5 In.X 3 Ft.11 In. 325.00
Textile, Rug, Prayer, Wabashay, Indian God, Hand Woven 350.00
Textile, Rug, Prayer, Yuruk, Greens, 3 Ft.3 In.X 6 Ft. 325.00
Textile, Rug, Sarouk, 2 Ft.X 4 Ft. 40.00
Textile, Rug, Sarouk, 2 Ft.5 In.X 5 Ft.5 In. 60.00
Textile, Rug, Sarouk, 3 Ft.5 In.X 4 Ft.10 In. 110.00
Textile, Rug, Sarouk, 3 Ft.6 In.X 4 Ft.9 In. 165.00
Textile, Rug, Sarouk, Oriental, 4 Ft.7 In.X 4 Ft.11 In. 80.00
Textile, Rug, Sarouk, Pillars Of A Mosque, Floral Border, 6 Ft.5 In.X 7 Ft. 550.00
Textile, Rug, Sarouk, Red Ground, Tree Of Life, Oak Leaf Border 60.00
Textile, Rug, Sehna Kilim, Light Greens, 4 Ft.6 In.X 7 Ft.4 In. 60.00
Textile, Rug, Sehna Kilim, Silk Warp, 53 X 81 In. 110.00
Textile, Rug, Sehna Kilim, 4 Ft.X 5 Ft.9 In. 65.00
Textile, Rug, Sehna, 55 X 78 In. 10.00
Textile, Rug, Serabend, Oriental, 4 Ft.9 In.X 6 Ft.3 In. 190.00
Textile, Rug, Serabend, Red Background, Fish Motif, 4 Ft.4 In.X 9 Ft.5 In. 250.00
Textile, Rug, Shiraz, Oriental, Black Rectangle With Bird, 4 Ft.2 In.X 6 Ft. 120.00
Textile, Rug, Shiraz, Oriental, 3 Ft.6 In.X 5 Ft.2 In. 95.00
Textile, Rug, Shiraz, Oriental, 4 Ft.3 In.X 7 Ft. 95.00
Textile, Rug, Shiraz, Paisley Pattern, 4 Ft.5 In.X 5 Ft.5 In. 225.00
Textile, Rug, Shirvan, 3 Ft.5 In.X 4 Ft.11 In. 35.00
Textile, Rug, Shirvan, 3 Ft.8 In.X 4 Ft.7 In. 55.00
Texyile, Rug, Shirvan, 3 Ft.10 In.X 4 Ft.9 In. 40.00
Textile, Rug, Shirvan, 6 Ft.X 3 Ft.9 In. 250.00
Textile, Rug, Tabriz, Yellow Medallion On Blue Floral Trellis, 6 X 5 Ft. 150.00
Textile, Rug, Turkoman Bokhara, Orange & Dark Blue, 8 Ft.8 In.X 13 Ft.7 In. 1000.00
Textile, Rug, Turkoman Bokhara, Saryk Turkomans Pattern, 8 Ft.9 In.X 12 Ft. 750.00
Textile, Rug, Turkoman, Yellow & Brick Red, 7 Ft.4 In.X 17 Ft.4 In. 600.00
Textile, Rug, Yomud, 1 Ft.6 In.X 3 Ft.6 In. .... 80.00 To 90.00
Textile, Rug, Yomud, 2 Ft.3 In.X 3 Ft.6 In. 130.00
Textile, Rug, Yuruk, Red, Blue, & White, 4 Ft.7 Ft.10 In. 300.00
Textile, Runner, Caucasian, 3 Ft.X 15 Ft.2 In. 105.00
Textile, Runner, Hamadan, Rose, Diamond Medallions, Brown 325.00
Textile, Runner, Lillihan, 30 1/2 In.X 22 Ft.4 In. 50.00
Textile, Runner, Red & Black, 3 Ft.10 In.X 8 Ft.2 In. 275.00
Textile, Saddle Bag, Shiraz 10.00

Textile, **Saddle Bag**, Turkoman	5.00
Textile, **Saddle Piece**, Bokhara	250.00
Textile, **Sampler**, Abc's, Floral, By Hannah Fisher, Aged Eleven, 1818, Frame	50.00
Textile, **Sampler**, Alphabet, Numbers, Worked By Six-Year-Old In 1825	35.00
Textile, **Sampler**, Alphabet, 1844	65.00
Textile, **Sampler**, Ann Roe, Standfrod, 1810, 18 In, Square	70.00
Textile, **Sampler**, By Sophia Sarle Wall, 1926, New Berlin, N.Y., Frame	65.00
Textile, **Sampler**, C.1840, 22 X 28 In.	37.50
Textile, **Sampler**, Della Margeret Warron, April 21, 1835, Frame	40.00
Textile, **Sampler**, Embroidery, Berries, Floral, American, Dated 1809	60.00
Textile, **Sampler**, In Memory Of Lee, 1879, 11 1/2 X 13 1/2 In.	7.50
Textile, **Sampler**, Mahogany Ogee Frame, Nancy Krauss, 1853, Rosebush	55.00
Textile, **Sampler**, Mary Thomson, Poem On Virtue, House, Trees, & Flowers	105.00
Textile, **Sampler**, Needlework, American, 'wrought By Mary H.White, 1825'	325.00
Textile, **Sampler**, Needlework, Silk On Linen, Flowers, 19th Century	65.00
Textile, **Sampler**, Sarah Jane Rockwell, Hewington, Conn., 1831	45.00
Textile, **Scarf**, Linen, 5 In.Hand Crocheted Endpieces, Floral Embroidery	10.00
Textile, **Shawl**, Paisley Chiffon, 54 X 94 In.	25.00
Textile, **Shawl**, Silk, Lace, Black, Scalloped, Flower, Leaf, 82 In.Long	18.00
Textile, **Shawl**, Spanish, Black Silk, Roses, Leaves, Fringe, 54 In.	25.00
Textile, **Shawl**, Triangular, Black, Scalloped Edge	40.00
Textile, **Shawl**, White Silk, Embroidered, Wide Fringe	20.00
Textile, **Shoe**, High Top, Lady's, Laced, Black, Pair	5.00
Textile, **Silk**, Embroidered Prunus Blossoms, Birds, Oriental	16.00
Textile, **Skirt**, Chinese Mandarin, Silk, Embroidered	200.00
Textile, **Spats**, Gray	2.00
Textile, **Tablecloth**, Damask, Fringed, Stripes, White, Red, 6 X 12 Ft.	50.00
Textile, **Tablecloth**, Hand Crocheted, White, 58 X 77 In.	12.00
Textile, **Tablecloth**, Hand Woven, Red, Blue, Fringed Edge, 66 X 66 In.	25.00
Textile, **Tablecloth**, Handmade, Battenburg, 58 In.Diameter	25.00
Textile, **Tablecloth**, Handmade, Needlepoint, Lilies, Dragons, Square, 60 In.	45.00
Textile, **Tablecloth**, Linen, Hand-Embroidered, Pond Lilies, Lily Pads, 53 In.	21.50
Textile, **Tablecloth**, Red & White, Fringe, 84 X 54 In.	5.00
Textile, **Tablecloth**, Red, White, Fringe, Floral Border, 58 X 38 In.	21.00
Textile, **Tapestry**, Flemish, Gentleman, Dog, Figures, C.1600	200.00
Textile, **Tapestry**, Flemish, Historical, Queen, 3 Figures, C.1650	500.00
Textile, **Tapestry**, Flemish, Verdure, Birds, Cottage, Fruit, Flowers, C.1700	850.00
Textile, **Tapestry**, Flemish, Verdure, Cottage Scene, Gold, Blue, & Ivory, 1750	950.00
Textile, **Tapestry**, Flemish, Verdure, 18th Century *Illus*	900.00
Textile, **Tapestry**, French, Apollo Chasing Daphne, C.1880	400.00
Textile, **Tapestry**, French, Central Floral Bouquet Medallion, C.1750	250.00
Textile, **Tapestry**, Peasants Going To Market, Lilli Teniers, 18th Century	4000.00
Textile, **Tent Decoration**, Bokhara, 14 X 51 In.	55.00
Textile, **Throw**, Paisley, Red, Blue, 65 In.Square, Fringe	47.50
Textile, **Towel**, Linen, Red Edges, Fringe, 3	19.00
Textile, **Towel**, Red Embroidery, Fringe	3.50 To 5.00
Textile, **Towel**, Yellow Border, Fringe	3.00
Textile, **Uniform**, U.S.Artillery Sergeant's, War Of 1898, Cotton, Tan	84.50
Textile, **Uniform**, Wisconsin National Guard, 1875, Brass Buttons	39.50
Textile, **Vest**, Child's, Velvet, Flowered, Beaded Trim	4.50
Textile, **Vest**, Floral, River Boat Gambler's	10.00
Textile, **Wall Motto**, Embroidered On Perforated Paper, Hand Carved Frame	30.00

Tiffany Glass was made by Louis Comfort Tiffany, the american glass designer who worked from about 1879 to 1933. His work included iridescent glass, art nouveau styles of design, and original contemporary styles. He was also noted for his stained glass windows, his unusual lamps, and his bronze work.

Tiffany **Type, Chandelier**, Bowl Form, Iridescent Blue Stripes, Bronze, 4	50.00
Tiffany **Type, Chandelier**, Domical Shade, Leaf Panels, Birds, Metal	500.00
Tiffany **Type, Chandelier**, Domical Shade, Pearly Iridescent Tiles	170.00
Tiffany **Type, Lamp**, Domical Shade, Lavender Tiles, Green, Bronze Base	170.00
Tiffany **Type, Vase**, Bottle Shape, Iridescent Green, Red, & White, Bronze	50.00
Tiffany **Type, Vase**, Ivory, Amber, Iridescent *Illus*	140.00
Tiffany, **Ashtray**, Matchbox Holder, Bronze, Zodiac Sign, Signed	50.00
Tiffany, **Back Bar**, 11 Panels Leaded Glass, Carved Wood, Mirror, 14 Ft.Long	3600.00
Tiffany, **Basket**, Gold, Iridescent, Brass Handle, Signed, 8 1/4 In.	575.00

Tiffany, Blotter Ends, Zodiac, 18 In.	31.00
Tiffany, Blotter, 5 1/2 In.Long, Signed	75.00
Tiffany, Bonbon, Flared Rim, Pink Opalescent Body, Red Edge	58.50
Tiffany, Bowl & Plate, Finger, Signed L.C.T.	175.00
Tiffany, Bowl, Brass, Pebbly Design, Gold Wash, 9 In., Shallow	22.50
Tiffany, Bowl, Console, Blue Iridescent, Signed, 10 In.	275.00
Tiffany, Bowl, Diamond Pattern, White To Aqua, Original Label, Signed, 6 In.	275.00
Tiffany, Bowl, Favrile, Signed L.C.T., 6 1/4 In.	145.00
Tiffany, Bowl, Finger, Signed & Numbered, Peacock Blue, Ribbed, Scalloped	180.00
Tiffany, Bowl, Floral Intaglio Cut, Signed L.C.Tiffany, Favrile	275.00
Tiffany, Bowl, Flower, Iridescent Blue At Rim To White At Top, Favrile	210.00
Tiffany, Bowl, Flower, Purple, 11 1/2 In.Diameter *Illus*	375.00

Textile, Tapestry, Flemish, Verdure, 18th Century
See Page 528

Tiffany Type, Vase,
Ivory, Amber, Iridescent
See Page 528

Tiffany, Bowl, Flower, Purple,
11 1/2 In.Diameter

Tiffany, Bowl, Gold & Blue Iridescent, Ribbed, Crimped Rim, Signed, 6 In.	185.00
Tiffany, Bowl, Gold & Blue Iridescent, Ribbed, Scalloped, Signed, 6 3/4 In.	225.00
Tiffany, Bowl, Iridescent Amber, Ribs, Crimped Serpentine Rim, L.C.T.	300.00
Tiffany, Bowl, Iridescent Gold Blue Highlights, Scalloped Swirl, 10 In.	275.00
Tiffany, Bowl, Iridescent, Violet, Green, Scalloped, Signed, 4 In.Diameter	195.00
Tiffany, Bowl, Miniature, Bulbous, Handles, Translucent Amber, 1 In.High	70.00
Tiffany, Bowl, Nut, Ribbed, Ruffled Rim, Iridescent, Gold, Signed	67.50
Tiffany, Bowl, Pastel, Opalescent Rays & Rim, Paper Label, 9 3/4 In.Diameter	120.00
Tiffany, Bowl, Punch, Sterling Silver, Holloware, 15 In.Ladle	500.00
Tiffany, Bowl, Radially Ribbed, Iridescent Blue, Inscribed L.C.T.Favrile	170.00
Tiffany, Bowl, Silver On Bronze, Ship Decor	95.00
Tiffany, Bowl, Spiral Ribbing, Scalloped Rim, Iridescent Amber, Favrile	120.00

Tiffany, Box & Ashtray, Gold Finish, Signed	30.00
Tiffany, Box, Brass, Signed, Dated 1918, 3 X 5 In.	75.00
Tiffany, Box, Pill, Silver	35.00
Tiffany, Candelabra, Floriform Handle, 6 Arms, Bronze Sockets, Green Inserts	725.00
Tiffany, Candlestick, Bronze & Green Glass, Signed, 18 In.High, Pair	450.00
Tiffany, Candlestick, Bronze, Green Glass Neck, Signed, 18 In.Tall, Pair	500.00
Tiffany, Candlestick, Bronze, Iridescent, Gold, Signed	475.00
Tiffany, Candlestick, Bronze, Urn Form Socket, Inscribed Tiffany Studios	150.00
Tiffany, Candlestick, Enameled Bronze, Blue, Louis C.Tiffany Furnaces, Pair	175.00
Tiffany, Candlestick, Gilded Bronze, Urn Form Socket, Tiffany Studios, Pair	175.00
Tiffany, Candlestick, Swirl Ribbed, Iridescent, Gold, Blue, Signed L.C.T.	95.00
Tiffany, Card Holder, Calling, Sterling, Signed Tiffany & Co., Art Nouveau	55.00
Tiffany, Chalice, Silver On Bronze, Ship Decor	95.00
Tiffany, Champagne, Green, Hollow Stem, 5 1/2 In.High	175.00
Tiffany, Champagne, Iridescent Silvery Amber, Twist Stem, L.C.T., 11, Case	825.00
Tiffany, Champagne, Pink, Green Teardrop Stem, Opalescent, Signed, 6 1/4 In.	295.00
Tiffany, Chandelier, Conical, Dogwood Blossoms, Bronze, Tiffany Studios	3800.00
Tiffany, Chandelier, Inverted Dome, Mottled Yellow Tiles, Tiffany Studios	1700.00
Tiffany, Coffee Set, George Ii Style, Sterling, 3 Piece	225.00
Tiffany, Compote, Bronze	56.00
Tiffany, Compote, Gold, Blue, Signed, 5 In.Tall	155.00
Tiffany, Compote, Green Pastel, Optic Rib, Signed, Label	325.00
Tiffany, Compote, Signed L.C.Tiffany Favrile & X, Blue Iridescent, Footed	240.00
Tiffany, Cordial, Dimpled, Iridescent, Signed & Numbered	85.00
Tiffany, Cordial, Iridescent, Gold, Lily Pads, Signed, 1 3/4 In.High	125.00
Tiffany, Cover, Matchbox, Bronze, Signed, Zodiac Pattern	20.00
Tiffany, Cup, Punch, Gold, Iridescent, Applied Lily Pads, Signed	150.00
Tiffany, Desk Set, Bronze, Zodiac Decoration, Tiffany Studios, 10 Piece	325.00
Tiffany, Desk Set, Filigree Bronze Over Caramel Slag, Signed, 7 Piece	250.00
Tiffany, Desk Set, Glass & Bronze, Pine Motifs, 6 Piece	160.00
Tiffany, Desk Set, Mottled Glass, Pinecone Pattern, Bronze, 8 Piece	250.00
Tiffany, Desk Set, Mottled Green Glass, Bronze, Favrile, 6 Piece	200.00
Tiffany, Desk Set, Signed, Brass, Blotter Ends, Note Pad, Calendar, Pen, Tray	180.00
Tiffany, Desk Set, Zodiac Pattern, Patina Finish, Ten Piece	425.00
Tiffany, Desk Set, Zodiac, Bronze, 3 Piece, Signed	30.00
Tiffany, Dialer, Telephone, Sterling Silver	12.00
Tiffany, Dish, Candy, Iridescent Gold, Signed L.C.T., 5 In.Diameter	225.00
Tiffany, Dish, Feather, Blue, Footed, 2 In.High, 4 1/2 In.Diameter	225.00
Tiffany, Dish, Gold, Mother-Of-Pearl Inserts Around Edge, Signed	240.00
Tiffany, Dish, Nut, Flared Rim, Ribbed, Ground Pontil, Gold, Blue, Signed Lct	85.00
Tiffany, Dish, Pink To Clear, Radial Pattern Of Opaque Stripes, Favrile	170.00
Tiffany, Fork, Bird Of Paradise, Engraved Davis, Dated 1871, Set Of 12	220.00
Tiffany, Fork, Bread Server, Sterling, Initials, 1892	22.00
Tiffany, Glass, Shot, Gold, Iridescent, Set Of 6	750.00
Tiffany, Goblet, Gold Iridescent, Pulled Leaf Decor, Nos.08100 & 08095, Pair	400.00
Tiffany, Goblet, White, Pink To Cranberry Bowl, Green Stem, Signed	190.00
Tiffany, Holder, Calling Card, Cherub & Floral Decor, Sterling Silver	48.00
Tiffany, Holder, Matchbox, Bronze, Liner, Signed, 4 In.High	58.00
Tiffany, Inkwell, Bronze, Signed	85.00
Tiffany, Inkwell, Gold & Ivory, C.1900	*Illus* 1300.00
Tiffany, Inkwell, Indian Pattern, Bronze, Signed	55.00 To 90.00
Tiffany, Inkwell, Pen Tray, Zodiac, Bronze	68.00
Tiffany, Inkwell, Round, Marbled Green Glass, Bronze Grapevines, Inscribed	110.00
Tiffany, Inkwell, Zodiac Center, Bronze	41.00 To 65.00
Tiffany, Lamp Base, Roman Oil Lamp Form, Baluster Stem, Tiffany Studios, 4	325.00
Tiffany, Lamp, Acorn, Oil Font, Green Ground, Electrified, Signed, 16 In.	895.00
Tiffany, Lamp, Apple Blossom, Dome Shade, Bronze, 21 In.High, Tiffany Studios	1700.00
Tiffany, Lamp, Apple Blossom, 16 1/2 In.	*Illus* 7250.00
Tiffany, Lamp, Black-Eyed Susan, Yellow On Green Domed Shade, Bronze	3100.00
Tiffany, Lamp, Bridge, Iridescent Paneled Amber Shade, Bronze, 52 In.High	425.00
Tiffany, Lamp, Bridge, Mother-Of-Pearl Domical Shade, Bronze Scroll Base	375.00
Tiffany, Lamp, Bronze Foo Dog Base, Mother-Of-Pearl Conch Shell Shade	2800.00
Tiffany, Lamp, Candle, Gold & Red Shade, Footed, Signed, 17 In.Tall	300.00
Tiffany, Lamp, Candle, Shade, Gold, Signed, 13 In.Tall	295.00
Tiffany, Lamp, Cobra, Bronze Base, Gold Shade, Signed	290.00
Tiffany, Lamp, Daffodil, Bronze, Yellow & Green, 27 In.High, Impressed	4800.00

Tiffany, Lamp, Daffodil, 19 In. .... *Illus* 3800.00
Tiffany, Lamp, Desk, Bronze Base & Filigree Shade, Glass Panels, Signed 525.00
Tiffany, Lamp, Desk, Bronze Base, Glass Shade, Bronze Finial, 17 In.High 650.00
Tiffany, Lamp, Desk, Bronze Filigree, Amber Glass, Signed, Six Sided, 17 In. 400.00
Tiffany, Lamp, Desk, Bronze, Slag Glass, Signed 400.00
Tiffany, Lamp, Desk, Domical Shade, Swags In Green & Blue, Bronze, L.C.T. 375.00
Tiffany, Lamp, Desk, Iridescent Amber Domical Shade, Gilt Metal Base 350.00
Tiffany, Lamp, Desk, Iridescent Gold Waves On Green Domed Shade, Bronze 375.00
Tiffany, Lamp, Desk, Iridescent Green & Ocher, Bronze Base, Wave Pattern 225.00
Tiffany, Lamp, Dogwood, Conical Shade, Bronze, Scrolled Feet, 22 In.High 4300.00
Tiffany, Lamp, Dome Shade, Green Tiles, Bronze, 22 In.High, Favrile 1800.00
Tiffany, Lamp, Dome Shade, Irises, Leaves, Mottled Ocher & Green, Bronze 1000.00
Tiffany, Lamp, Domical Shade, Mottled Green Tiles, Bronze, 21 1/2 In.High 800.00
Tiffany, Lamp, Domical Shade, Mottled Yellow Panels, Ivy, Bronze, 18 In.High 800.00
Tiffany, Lamp, Dragonfly, Mottled Blue & Red Conical Shade, Bronze Base 4500.00
Tiffany, Lamp, Dragonfly, Signed Favrile, Bronze, Designed By Clara Driscoll 3200.00
Tiffany, Lamp, Floor, Cantilever, Bronze Shade, Signed 400.00
Tiffany, Lamp, Floor, Domical Shade, Ocher & Yellow Panels, Bronze 4000.00
Tiffany, Lamp, Floor, Green, Shade, Footed, Gold, Signed, 56 In.Tall 475.00
Tiffany, Lamp, Floor, Iridescent Green Shade, Bronze, Wave Pattern 325.00
Tiffany, Lamp, Floor, Peony, Domical Shade, Mottled Yellow, Favrile 7000.00
Tiffany, Lamp, Floor, 6 Ft.6 In. .... *Illus* 7000.00

Tiffany, Inkwell,
Gold & Ivory, C.1900
See Page 530

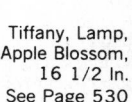

Tiffany, Lamp,
Apple Blossom,
16 1/2 In.
See Page 530

Tiffany, Lamp, Daffodil, 19 In.

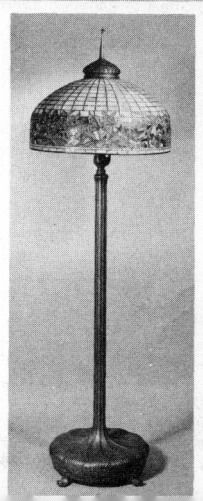

Tiffany, Lamp,
Floor, 6 Ft.6 In.

Tiffany, Lamp, Green Leaves On Iridescent Yellow, Cylindrical Base, Pair 1700.00
Tiffany, Lamp, Jonquil, 28 1/2 In High, Leaded Shade, 20 1/2 In.Diameter 4500.00
Tiffany, Lamp, Lily, Gold Iridescent Shade, Three Light, Signed .... 525.00 To 650.00
Tiffany, Lamp, Paneled Shade, Drapers, Bronze, Tiffany Studios, 21 In.High 1000.00
Tiffany, Lamp, Peony, Domical Shade, White & Green On Mottled Yellow, Bronze 4100.00
Tiffany, Lamp, Peony, Mottled Green Ground, Impressed Tiffany Studios 3100.00
Tiffany, Lamp, Spider In Web, Green, White, Signed, 15 In.Diameter, 18 In. 2150.00
Tiffany, Lamp, Table, Bronze Art Nouveau, Peacock Feather Shade, Signed 375.00
Tiffany, Lamp, Table, Candelabra, Six Arm, Gold, Iridescent, Globes, 17 In. 1250.00
Tiffany, Lamp, Table, Candlestick Base, Swirls, Gold Shade, Feather Decor 365.00
Tiffany, Lamp, Table, Chinese Design, Signed, 34 In.High 3000.00
Tiffany, Lamp, Table, Daffodil, Conical Shade, Blue Green Ground, Bronze 4300.00
Tiffany, Lamp, Table, Dogwood, 32 In.High, Leaded Shade, 20 1/2 In. 3800.00
Tiffany, Lamp, Tulip Pattern 6000.00
Tiffany, Nut Basket, Handle, Sterling Silver, Signed, 4 In. 28.00
Tiffany, Paperweight, Bronze 95.00
Tiffany, Paperweight, Bronze, Chinese Style 40.00
Tiffany, Paperweight, Lion, Couchant, Gilded Bronze, 5 In.Long, Impressed 225.00
Tiffany, Parfait, Pastel Blue, Signed Lct Favrile, 5 3/8 In.High 295.00
Tiffany, Pencil, Opens, Sterling Silver Slide, 12 In. 65.00
Tiffany, Pin, Scarab, Green Iridescent Center, 14k Gold 295.00
Tiffany, Pitcher, Iridescent Amber, Loop Handle, L.C.Tiffany Favrile 225.00
Tiffany, Plaque, Round, Iridescent Mauve, Center Blue & Amber Rosette 600.00
Tiffany, Plate, Brass, Mottled Finish, Signed Tiffany Studios, 1736, 9 In. 60.00
Tiffany, Plate, Stippled Finish, Embossed Floral Design Border, Brass 36.00
Tiffany, Plate, Vintage Pattern, Bronze, 10 1/2 In.Diameter 65.00
Tiffany, Salt, Blue Highlights, Ruffled Edge, L.C.T. 75.00
Tiffany, Salt, Blue, Scalloped, Signed Tiffany, L.C.T. 95.00
Tiffany, Salt, Favrile, Gold, Fluted Rim, Signed L.C.T. 70.00
Tiffany, Salt, Gold Iridescent, Ruffled 62.00
Tiffany, Salt, Gold, Signed, Ribbed, 3 X 1 In. 70.00
Tiffany, Salt, Gold, Signed 55.00
Tiffany, Salt, Master, Footed, C.1848 .... 68.00
Tiffany, Salt, Round, Crimped Rim, Iridescent Silvery Amber, L.C.T., 11 .... 575.00
Tiffany, Salt, Round, Iridescent Amber, Convex Sides, Swirled Crimps, 9 .... 500.00
Tiffany, Salt, Ruffled, Gold Iridescence, Signed, L.C.T. 72.00
Tiffany, Salt, Ruffled, Iridescent, Blue, Footed 87.50
Tiffany, Salt, Thorn Pattern, Signed, Gold Iridescent, 1 1/4 In.High 55.00
Tiffany, Shade, Hammered Effect, Iridescent, Signed, Pair 195.00
Tiffany, Shade, Iridescent Green, Etched Flowers In Pink, Blue, & Yellow 18.00
Tiffany, Shade, Lime Green, 3 In.High 28.00
Tiffany, Shaker, Salt, Master, Footed, Signed, Crimped Top 90.00
Tiffany, Sherbet, Blue, Radial Ribs, Low Foot, Crimped Rim, L.C.T.Favrile 300.00
Tiffany, Sherbet, Opaque White Bowl, Yellow Interior & Stem, Favrile 130.00
Tiffany, Spoon & Fork, Salad, Vermeil Bowls, Wave Edge, Sterling Silver 80.00
Tiffany, Spoon, Berry, Serving, Gold Wash Bowl, Shell Decor On Handle, Pair 82.00
Tiffany, Sprinkler, Rose Water, Serpentine Neck, Iridescent Bluish Amber 1000.00
Tiffany, Stand, Calendar, Bronze, Zodiac Pattern 75.00
Tiffany, Tazza, Colloidal Vines, Blue, Scalloped, Footed, Signed, 7 3/4 In. 255.00
Tiffany, Tazza, Iridescent Amber, Cameo Cut, Vines, Favrile, Pair 300.00
Tiffany, Tazza, 4 Cabriole Legs, Gilded Bronze, Tiffany Studios, Pair 70.00
Tiffany, Tile, Raised Center, 4 In.Square 18.00
Tiffany, Toothpick, Bronze, Marked 47.50
Tiffany, Toothpick, Gold, Blue, Iridescent, Pinch 90.00
Tiffany, Toothpick, Iridescent Gold, Signed L.C.T. 105 .... 115.00
Tiffany, Toothpick, Pale Gold To White Iridescence, Applied Lily Pad Decor 38.00
Tiffany, Toothpick, Signed L.C.T., Swirls, Gold Iridescent, Blue, Pink 155.00
Tiffany, Tray, Pen, Zodiac, Bronze .... 25.00 To 26.00
Tiffany, Vase, Baluster Shape, Green To Yellow Green At Base, Ivy Vines 525.00
Tiffany, Vase, Baluster Shape, Iridescent Amber, Green Zigzag, Favrile 325.00
Tiffany, Vase, Baluster Shape, Iridescent Blue & Purple, Silver Ivy, Vines 700.00
Tiffany, Vase, Baluster Shape, Pale To Deep Iridescent Blue At Base, Ribs 400.00
Tiffany, Vase, Baluster, Iridescent Green To Purple Neck, L.C.Tiffany 650.00
Tiffany, Vase, Blue, 8 1/4 In.High, Signed 275.00
Tiffany, Vase, Bulbous, Cylindrical Neck, Iridescent Amber To Violet 250.00
Tiffany, Vase, Bulbous, Ribbed, Iridescent Blue & Amber, Favrile 225.00

Tiffany, **Vase**, Bulbous, Ribbed, Iridescent Green To Blue To Lavender 300.00
Tiffany, **Vase**, Cabinet, Amber To Pale, Inscribed L.C.T. .... *Illus* 350.00
Tiffany, **Vase**, Cabinet, Floriform, Iridescent Blue, Green Leaves, Favrile 500.00
Tiffany, **Vase**, Cabinet, Paperweight, Pyriform, Marbleized Purplish Blue 350.00
Tiffany, **Vase**, Clear With Chartreuse & White Decor, No.208 L.C.Favrile 265.00
Tiffany, **Vase**, Conical, Ribbed, Iridescent Amber, Opalescent Loops, Favrile 60.00
Tiffany, **Vase**, Cypriote, Iridescent Silver On Mottled Yellow, Favrile 700.00
Tiffany, **Vase**, Elongated Oval, Ribbed, Iridescent Blue To Gold, L.C.Tiffany 400.00
Tiffany, **Vase**, Favrile, Aquamarine .... *Illus* 225.00

Tiffany, Vase, Cabinet,
Amber To Pale, Inscribed L.C.T.

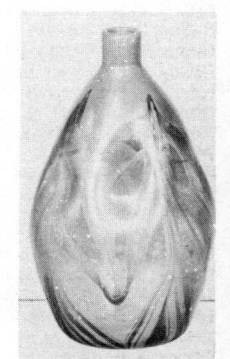

Tiffany, Vase,
Favrile, Aquamarine

Tiffany, **Vase**, Flaring, Iridescent Green, Silver Carnations, Favrile 425.00
Tiffany, **Vase**, Floriform, Collar Of Gold Green Striated Leaves, Amber Foot 550.00
Tiffany, **Vase**, Floriform, Green, Gold, & White, Signed 'I.C.T.1872' 450.00
Tiffany, **Vase**, Floriform, Iridescent Amber, Ribbed, L.C.Tiffany, Favrile 250.00
Tiffany, **Vase**, Floriform, Iridescent Amber, Slender Stem, Domed Foot, L.C.T. 475.00
Tiffany, **Vase**, Floriform, Iridescent Amber, Vertical Ribs, Favrile 350.00
Tiffany, **Vase**, Floriform, Opalescent White Conical Bowl, Green Collar 300.00
Tiffany, **Vase**, Floriform, Opalescent White To Green, L.C.Tiffany, Favrile 170.00
Tiffany, **Vase**, Floriform, Semiopaque White, Green Feathers, Inscribed L.C.T. 375.00
Tiffany, **Vase**, Floriform, Triangular Body, Signed, 12 1/2 In.Tall 450.00
Tiffany, **Vase**, Gold Iridescent, Green Flecks, Signed, 12 In.Tall 295.00
Tiffany, **Vase**, Gold, Green, Leaves, Vines, Fish Shape, Signed, 4 1/2 In. 375.00
Tiffany, **Vase**, Gourd Shape, Gold Iridescent, L.C.T.Favrile 7003, Label 400.00
Tiffany, **Vase**, Gourd Shape, Pale To Deep Blue At Base, Ribbed, L.C.T. 400.00
Tiffany, **Vase**, Iridescent Blue, Ribbed Base, Signed & Numbered, 11 In.High 450.00
Tiffany, **Vase**, Iridescent Gold, Blue Hues In Base, Ribbed, L.C.T. 300, Label 350.00
Tiffany, **Vase**, Iridescent Gold, Signed & Numbered, 5 1/2 In.Tall 225.00
Tiffany, **Vase**, Iridescent Grayish Blue, Asymmetrical Design Of Blossoms 575.00
Tiffany, **Vase**, Iridescent Pottery, Paper Label, 4 In.High 105.00
Tiffany, **Vase**, Leaf, Green Tones, Dore Acorn Holder 240.00
Tiffany, **Vase**, Leaves, Flowers, Gold, Green, White, Signed L.C.Tiffany, Favrile 795.00
Tiffany, **Vase**, Leaves, Vines, Purple, Gold, Unsigned, 12 In.Tall 195.00
Tiffany, **Vase**, Miniature, Baluster, Iridescent Amber, Applied Teardrop Motif 110.00
Tiffany, **Vase**, Miniature, Bottle Form, Carved Fleurette Panels, Favrile 180.00
Tiffany, **Vase**, Miniature, Bulbous, Iridescent Amber, Inscribed L.C.T. 70.00
Tiffany, **Vase**, Miniature, Bulbous, Yellow Neck, Opalescent & Green Leafage 300.00
Tiffany, **Vase**, Miniature, Fluted, Bluish, Gold, Signed & Numbered, L.C.T. 125.00
Tiffany, **Vase**, Miniature, Gold Iridescent, 3 In. 95.00
Tiffany, **Vase**, Miniature, Ovoid, Iridescent Amber, Ribs, Inscribed Favrile 170.00
Tiffany, **Vase**, Miniature, Ovoid, Opalescent Ivory, Inscribed Favrile 140.00
Tiffany, **Vase**, Miniature, Urn Shape, Iridescent Purple, Amber Fan Motifs 400.00
Tiffany, **Vase**, Miniature, Urn Shape, Iridescent Red, Zigzag Swirls On Collar 675.00
Tiffany, **Vase**, Miniature, Urn Shape, Yellow, Iridescent Leafage, L.C.Tiffany 280.00
Tiffany, **Vase**, Ocher To Transparent Amber At Base, Pair 70.00
Tiffany, **Vase**, Ovoid, Aquamarine, Pink Blossoms, Inscribed Favrile 200.00
Tiffany, **Vase**, Ovoid, Cameo Cut, White Blossoms, Green Leaves, Favrile 1600.00
Tiffany, **Vase**, Ovoid, Flared Neck, Iridescent Amber, L.C.Tiffany, Favrile 130.00
Tiffany, **Vase**, Ovoid, Iridescent Purple, Amber, & Green, Favrile 350.00

Tiffany, Vase, Ovoid, Iridescent Silvery Amber, White Millefiori Blossoms	525.00
Tiffany, Vase, Ovoid, Pale To Deep Iridescent Blue At Base, Label	275.00
Tiffany, Vase, Pale To Deep Blue At Base, Ribbed, Inscribed L.C.T.	350.00
Tiffany, Vase, Paperweight, Baluster Shape, Iridescent Amber, White Floral	400.00
Tiffany, Vase, Paperweight, Baluster Shape, Petaled Blossoms & Green Leaves	525.00
Tiffany, Vase, Paperweight, Brown Marble, Ocher & Brown Trellis Pattern	1500.00
Tiffany, Vase, Paperweight, Iridescent Mottled Green, Ocher Swirls, Favrile	1700.00
Tiffany, Vase, Paperweight, Ovoid, Opalescent Reddish, Green Leaf Motifs	725.00
Tiffany, Vase, Peacock, Blue, Signed 1994m L.C.Tiffany Favrile, 19 1/2 In.	1200.00
Tiffany, Vase, Peacock, Green, Blue, Gold, Iridescent, Signed L.C.T., 5 In.	795.00
Tiffany, Vase, Pottery, Green, Glazed, Signed, 4 3/4 In.	165.00
Tiffany, Vase, Ribbed, Gold Iridescent, Green Leaves, 9 1/2 In.	425.00
Tiffany, Vase, Striated Zigzags, Iridescent, Squat, Inscribed Favrile	175.00
Tiffany, Vase, Swelling, Iridescent Amber, Green & White Leaves, Favrile	325.00
Tiffany, Vase, Swelling, Iridescent Green & Amber, Mottled Brown Leaf Motif	300.00
Tiffany, Vase, Tapering, Blue, Iridescent Neck, Striated Zigzags, Favrile	650.00
Tiffany, Vase, Tapering, Iridescent Amber, Cameo Cut Leafage, Favrile	475.00
Tiffany, Vase, Transparent Green, Pyriform Shape, Iridescent, Favrile	325.00
Tiffany, Vase, Trumpet Shape, Iridescent Amber, Bronze, Feather Devices	175.00
Tiffany, Vase, Trumpet Shape, Iridescent Amber, Inscribed L.C.T.Favrile	150.00
Tiffany, Vase, Trumpet Shape, White Striations, Yellow Interior, Favrile	120.00
Tiffany, Vase, Trumpet, Bronze, Enameling Around Base	165.00
Tiffany, Vase, Trumpet, Gold, Green, Feather Design, Signed, 15 In.	290.00
Tiffany, Vase, Trumpet, Signed Lct, Favrile, Gold Iridescent, 19 In.High	250.00
Tiffany, Vase, Tulip Shape, Iridescent Amber, Ribbed, L.C.Tiffany, 8 In.	200.00
Tiffany, Vase, Urn Form, Incised Vertical Ribs, L.C.Tiffany, Inc., Favrile	160.00
Tiffany, Vase, Urn Shape, Blue, Vertical Ribs, Inscribed L.C.Tiffany Favrile	370.00
Tiffany, Vase, Urn Shape, Handles, Iridescent Blue, Horizontal Striations	400.00
Tiffany, Vase, Urn Shape, Iridescent Greenish Amber, Concentric Bandings	525.00
Tiffany, Vase, White Pottery, Sculptured Leaves & Vines, Signed L.C.T.	185.00
Tiffany, Watch, Repeater, 1/4 Hour, In Case	350.00
Tiffany, Wine, Gold Iridescent, Signed	95.00
Tiffany, Wine, Swirl Design, Cut Stem, Gold, Green, Signed	110.00
Tiffin, Bowl, White Iridescent, Stretch Surface	32.50
Tiffin, Compote, Tomato, Flared Rim	58.00
Tiffin, Rose Bowl, Poppy Pattern, Satin Glass, 5 In.	15.00
Tiffin, Vase, Tangerine, Footed, 9 In.Tall	54.00
Tiffin, Vase, 5 Leaf Flowers In Relief, Black	35.00
Tiffin, Vase, 5 Leaf Flowers In Relief, Pink	30.00
Tile, Ashtray, Mosaic Tile Co., Figural, Birddog	25.00
Tile, Beige, Brown, 'old Hancock House, ' 6 X 6 In.	18.00
Tile, Blue & White, Mosaic Tile Co., Lincoln	20.00
Tile, Blue, White, Priscilla & John Alden, Wedgwood, 6 X 6	15.00
Tile, Calendar, Bunker Hill, 'dedicated June 17, 1842, ' Wedgwood	18.00
Tile, Calendar, 1896, Trinity Church, Wedgwood, Color	18.00
Tile, Calendar, 1907	27.50
Tile, Calendar, 1910	27.50
Tile, Calendar, 1911	27.50
Tile, Calendar, 1912, Cunard Line Dock, Wedgwood	25.00
Tile, Calendar, 1913	27.50
Tile, Calendar, 1914, Jones, Mcduffee & Stratton, Commonwealth Docks	32.50
Tile, Calendar, 1915	27.50
Tile, Calendar, 1915, Jones, Mcduffee, & Stratton, Boston Custom House	32.50
Tile, Calendar, 1917, Section Of United States Navy Yard, Boston, Wedgwood	25.00
Tile, Daisies & Buttercups, Round, Green, Yellow, White, 6 1/2 In.	12.00
Tile, Dewey, Milk Glass	10.00
Tile, Esmerelda, Madison Square Theatre, 1882, Signed Elihu Vedder	85.00
Tile, Floral Design, Pink, Green, 6 In.Round	5.75
Tile, Green, Hand-Painted, 18th Century	75.00
Tile, Indian Chief Portrait, Lavender Edge	13.50
Tile, Man With Axe, 8 X 4 1/2 In.	55.00
Tile, President Grover Cleveland, 6 X 4 1/2 In.	58.00
Tile, Profile Of Grecian Woman, 'dedication A.E, Tile Works, April 1892'	35.00
Tile, Profile, Woman With Hat, 6 In.Square	35.00
Tile, Roof, Carp, Brown & Green, China, 11 In.High X 9 In.	50.00
Tile, Sea Serpent, 6 In.Square	24.00

Tile, **Spring & Autumn**, Blue, Chelsea, Dated 1885, 4 X 6 In., Pair 98.00
Tile, **Tea**, Pink, White, Wild Roses Profusion 10.00
Tile, **Tea**, Portrait, Girl, Gold Ruffled Edge, Circa 1910, Bavaria 17.50
Tile, **Tea**, Round, Hand-Painted Cherry Leaves 5.00
Tile, **Zanesville**, Bust Of Lincoln In Relief, 8 1/2 In. 38.00
    Tin, see also Store
Tin, **Bed Warmer** 75.00
Tin, **Bee Box**, 2 Glass Windows, Double, 3 X 6 In. 27.00
Tin, **Boiler**, Wash, Child's 10.00
Tin, **Box**, Document, Black, Envelopes Dated 1890 .... 12.00
Tin, **Box**, Oval, Japanese, 10 1/2 In.High 12.50
Tin, **Box**, Snuff 4.00
Tin, **Box**, Spice, Rectangular, 6 Smaller Inside Boxes, Grater 25.00
Tin, **Box**, Tea, Hallers, Pettit I, Brass Hinges 35.00
Tin, **Box**, To Carry Military Hat, Owned By A Major 12.50
Tin, **Bread Riser**, Cover 12.00
Tin, **Bucket**, Lunch, Man's 9.50
Tin, **Cabinet**, Spice, Hanging, Four Oval Drawers, Knobs, Paint Worn 55.00
Tin, **Can**, Milk, Handmade, Handle, Cover 12.50
Tin, **Can**, Oil, Copper Bottom, 3 .... 3.75
Tin, **Candle Light**, Shaped Like Street Lantern 60.00
Tin, **Candleholder**, Round, Tinderbox, 4 1/4 In.Diameter 145.00
Tin, **Candlestick**, Oval Base, Gallery Type, Step Lift, Handle, 7 1/2 In.Tall 45.00
Tin, **Candlestick**, Push-Up 8.00
Tin, **Candlestick**, Saucer Type, Whale Oil, 8 1/2 In.High 12.50
Tin, **Candlestick**, Square Weighted Base, Scalloped Flange, Leaf Designs 25.00
Tin, **Case**, Comb, Mirror, Tin Comb 12.50
Tin, **Chamberstick**, Pair 9.00
Tin, **Chandelier**, Candle, 6 Branch 45.00
Tin, **Chandelier**, Double Tier With 7 Branches, 18th Century 5250.00
Tin, **Coffee Roaster**, Round, Long Handle 45.00
Tin, **Coffeepot**, Circa 1860 .... 6.98
Tin, **Coffeepot**, Circular Floral Painting, Conn., C.1800 .... 500.00
Tin, **Coffeepot**, Painted, Oliver Filley, Conn., C.1800 .... *Illus* 625.00
Tin, **Coffeepot**, Punched, Inscribed 'June 3rd, 1830, Liberty & Independence' 2000.00
Tin, **Coffeepot**, Punched, Penn., C.1800, 12 In. .... *Illus* 550.00
Tin, **Coffeepot**, Tapering, Sprays Of Flowers & Leaves, 11 In.High 350.00
Tin, **Comb Case**, Match Holder, & Mirror 12.00
Tin, **Cover**, Dome, Pair 30.00
Tin, **Cover**, Food, 9 In.Diameter 5.00
Tin, **Cup**, Baking, 2 In.Tall, 3 In.Diameter 1.50

Tin, Coffeepot, Punched, Penn., C.1800, 12 In.

Tin, Coffeepot, Painted, Oliver Filley, Conn., C.1800

Tin, **Cup**, Shaving	5.00
Tin, **Cutter**, Cookie, Camel Shape	9.00
Tin, **Cutter**, Cookie, Horse	18.00
Tin, **Cutter**, Doughnut, Double Ring	2.00
Tin, **Cutter**, Doughnut, Rolling	3.00
Tin, **Dishes**, Doll's, 24 Piece	15.00
Tin, **Dustpan**, Handmade	10.00
Tin, **Foot Warmer**, Pierced	23.00
Tin, **Foot Warmer**, Pierced Decor, Wire Handle, Red Paint	25.00
Tin, **Grater**, Nutmeg, Flat, Sliding Wood Nutmeg Holder, 4 In.	9.00
Tin, **Grater**, Snuff	34.00
Tin, **Holder**, Taper, Hanging	25.00
Tin, **Horse**, Dappled Paint, Red Harness, 8 In.Long, 6 In.High	10.00
Tin, **Ladle**, For Pouring Wax Into Candle Mold, Conical Shape	14.50
Tin, **Lantern**, Candle, Round, 7 Panes	110.00
Tin, **Light**, Candle, Springs Hold Chimney In Place	15.00
Tin, **Light**, Torch, Handle, Bale	10.00
Tin, **Match Holder**, Wall, Embossed Matches, Striker Lift Lid	6.00
Tin, **Mold**, Bread, Log Shaped, 2 Pieces	9.00
Tin, **Mold**, Candle, Single	4.95
Tin, **Mold**, Candle, Single, Cathedral, Round Well, 19 In.	70.00
Tin, **Mold**, Candle, 2 Tube, Handle, 10 In.Long	38.00
Tin, **Mold**, Candle, 5 Tube	40.00
Tin, **Mold**, Candle, 6 Tube	20.00 To 24.50
Tin, **Mold**, Candle, 8 Tube	9.00 To 25.00
Tin, **Mold**, Candle, 12 Tube	12.50 To 35.00
Tin, **Mold**, Candle, 12 Tube, Handle	*Illus* 35.00
Tin, **Mold**, Candle, 12 Tube, Ring & Strap Handle	125.00
Tin, **Mold**, Candle, 12 Tube, Strap Handle	33.00
Tin, **Mold**, Chocolate, Lamb	5.00 To 10.00
Tin, **Mold**, Chocolate, Rabbit	6.00
Tin, **Mold**, Chocolate, Rabbit, 4 1/2 In.	8.00
Tin, **Mold**, Chocolate, Turkey, Two Pieces	10.00
Tin, **Mold**, Egg	12.00
Tin, **Mold**, Fish, Carved	9.50
Tin, **Mold**, Heart	*Illus* 15.00
Tin, **Mold**, Heart Shape, Individual, Fluted, England, Set Of 8	6.00
Tin, **Mold**, Maple Sugar, Heart Shape, 8 On Tin Frame	60.00
Tin, **Mold**, Melon Shape	7.00
Tin, **Mold**, Melon Shape, Cover, Handles	5.00
Tin, **Mold**, Melon, Fluted, Two Pieces, 6 1/2 In.Long	3.75
Tin, **Mold**, Melon, Fluted, Two Pieces, 7 1/2 In.Long	4.75
Tin, **Mold**, Narrow, Center Tube, Fluted, 10 In.	4.00
Tin, **Mold**, Plum Pudding, Fluted, Center Tube, Friction Lid	12.50
Tin, **Oven**, Dutch	30.00
Tin, **Oven**, Warming, Wrought Iron Legs, Penny Feet, Red Paint	35.00
Tin, **Pan**, Angel Cake, Fluted, 9 1/2 In.	4.50
Tin, **Plate**, Christmas, Victorian Child In Red	18.00
Tin, **Roaster**, Apple, Reflector, Double Trough	15.00
Tin, **Rocker**, Miniature, 10th Wedding Party, 6 In.	45.00
Tin, **Roly-Poly**, Singing Waiter	*Illus* 150.00
Tin, **Roly-Poly**, Storekeeper	*Illus* 150.00
Tin, **Ruler**, Light Green, Gold Lettering, Lithograph, 5 1/2 X 6 3/4 In.	10.00
Tin, **Salt Shaker**, 29 In.	37.50
Tin, **Sander**, Cylindrical	9.00 To 16.00
Tin, **Sconce**, Candle, American, C.1830, Crimped Top, 13 1/2 In.Tall	75.00
Tin, **Sconce**, Candle, American, Crimped Top, 6 X 14 In.	32.50
Tin, **Sconce**, Wall, Glass Kerosene Font	12.50
Tin, **Sconce**, Wall, Milk Glass Insert Font	12.50
Tin, **Sconce**, Whale Oil, Cylindrical Font	50.00
Tin, **Shade**, Lamp, Green Enamel Back, White Enamel Front, 8 In.Diameter	.30
Tin, **Skimmer**, Cream	6.50
Tin, **Spittoon**, Red Paint, Floral Decoration	10.00
Tin, **Spoon**, Ice Cream, Heart On Handle, 3 1/2 In.	1.25
Tin, **Strainer**, Cheese, Heart Shape	30.00
Tin, **Teakettle**	*Illus* 22.50

Tin, Mold,
Candle, 12 Tube, Handle
See Page 536

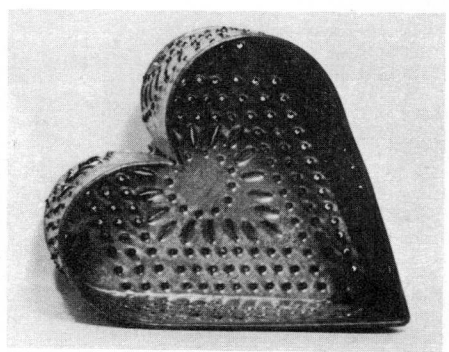

Tin, Mold, Heart
See Page 536

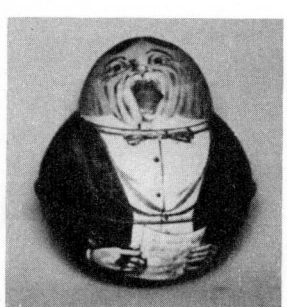

Tin, Roly-Poly,
Singing Waiter
See Page 536

Tin, Roly-Poly,
Storekeeper
See Page 536

Tin, Teakettle
See Page 536

Tin, Teapot, Gooseneck Spout, 11 In.High	22.50
Tin, Teapot, Straight Spout	20.00
Tin, Thermometer, Shape Of Bottle, 16 In.Tall	8.50
Tin, Tray, Advertising, Czar Of Russia Caviar, Paneled Decor, 18 1/2 In.	7.00
Tin, Tray, Decorated, Pie Crust Rim, 22 1/2 In.	17.50
Tin, Tray, Knife, Oval	15.00
Tin, Tray, Tavern Drinking Scene, Stencil, Oval, 15 X 12 In.	4.00
Tin, Tray, Zodiac, Horoscope, 14 In.	4.00
Tin, Washtub & Board Set, Child's	4.50

Toby Mugs have been made since the seventeenth century.

Toby Mug, see also Royal Doulton
Toby Mug, Betsy Prigg, Porcelain, Miniature, Marked Germany 7.50
Toby Mug, Christmas, 1925, White, Gold Trim .... *Illus* 125.00
Toby Mug, Little Dorrit, Porcelain, Miniature, Marked Germany 7.50
Toby Mug, Seated With Pitcher In Hand, Brown, 8 1/2 In.Tall 25.00
Toby Mug, Sitting Woman, German, C.1860 .... 250.00
Toby Pitcher, George Washington, Parian, 2 In.Tall 10.00
Toby Teapot, Double Faced, Marked Shorter, England, 3 1/2 In. 17.50
Tole, Bath Tub, Oval, Two Handles, Tin, 20 1/2 X 14 In. 6.50
Tole, Bin, Cream City Flour, Black Tin, Sifter, 10 1/2 In.Diameter, 23 In. 58.50
Tole, Box, Book Form 15.00
Tole, Box, Document, Floral Decoration .... 250.00 To 300.00
Tole, Box, Document, Miniature, White Band With Red & Green Decoration 55.00
Tole, Candleholder, Attached Conical Snuffer & Shade, Red 80.00
Tole, Canister, Tea, Red Paint 25.00
Tole, Case, Knitting Needle, 9 In.Long 35.00
Tole, Chamberstick, Blue, Deep Saucer 25.00
Tole, Coffeepot, Black, Red Flowers 300.00
Tole, Coffeepot, Red Paint 70.00
Tole, Coffeepot, Side Spout 45.00
Tole, Coffeepot, Side Spout, Apple Decoration 300.00
Tole, Coffeepot, Yellow Apple Decoration 400.00
Tole, Food Carrier, Green Basket Weave, Strap Handles 12.00
Tole, Jar, Biscuit, English, Portraits Of Ladies, Pair 15.00
Tole, Jardiniere, Regency, Pontypool, Grape Design, 19th Century, Pair 200.00
Tole, Mug, Japanned Ground, Red & Yellow Flowers, 5 3/4 In.High 450.00
Tole, Mug, Lip, Black, Red Flower, Green & Yellow Leaves 125.00
Tole, Sander, Decorated, Mark, 1830, 3 In.Diameter, 3 In.High 25.00
Tole, Sander, 1930, Decorated, 3 In.High, Marked On Bottom 25.00
Tole, Sconce, Candle, Red Flower Decoration 100.00
Tole, Tea Caddy, Lid, Red, Yellow, & Green Decoration 80.00
Tole, Tea Caddy, Red, Lid 45.00
Tole, Tea Caddy, Victorian, Painted, Sarcophagus Shape, Roses, C.1850 .... 170.00
Tole, Teapot, Oval, Black Ground, Red Flowers 85.00
Tole, Tray, Basket Of Fruit, 8 Sided, 22 1/2 In.Long 30.00
Tole, Tray, Bird & Trees Decorated, 18 In. 25.00
Tole, Tray, Chippendale, Basket Of Fruit Decor, Gilded Edge 160.00
Tole, Tray, Scalloped, Stenciled Floral & Peacock, 24 In.Long 30.00
Tole, Tray, Stencil, 11 1/2 In. 15.00
Tole, Tray, Stenciled Decoration Of Train, 16 1/2 In.X 22 1/2 In. 175.00
Tole, Tray, Train, Trees, Man, Woman, Child, Stenciled Border, Black, Tin 185.00
Tole, Urn, Black, Pontypool, 19th Century, Pair .... *Illus* 375.00
Tole, Urn, Chestnut, Regency, Black Japanned, 19th Century, Gilt Leaf, Pair 190.00
Tole, Warmer, Milk, Handle, Side Vents, Hinged Door, Oil Lamp Inside, Stencil 20.00
Tom Mix, Ring, Ralston, Straight Shooter's 45.00
Tool, see also Kitchen, Store, Wooden, Iron, Tin
Tool, Adze, Cooper's .... 15.00 To 17.50
Tool, Adze, Hand, Cooper's, Wide Curved Blade 15.00
Tool, Adze, Shipwright's, Curved Handle 25.00
Tool, Adze, Shipwright's, Turned Up Blade Edge 17.50
Tool, Auger, Tap, Cooper's, Twisted Cutting Tip, 4 In.Blade 7.50
Tool, Ax, Broad 9.50
Tool, Ax, Broad, Shapleigh Day & Co., 11 In.Wide Blade 50.00
Tool, Ax, Goosewing 600.00
Tool, Bed Jack, Tightens Ropes On Beds 7.50
Tool, Bed Warmer, Iron Handles, Brass Lid 25.00
Tool, Bee Box, Wood Slide & Glass Front, 5 In.High 8.00
Tool, Bee Smoker, Tin, Wood, & Leather 5.00
Tool, Bit Brace, One Piece, Colonial American, 16 In.Long 75.00
Tool, Blade, Sawmill, 30 In.Diameter 8.50
Tool, Blueberry Picker, New England, Wood, Tin Fittings, J.F.V. 28.00
Tool, Boring Machine, Tilts To Bore At Angles 20.00
Tool, Box, Carpenter's, Hand Grip, Pine, 19 In.Long, 11 In.Wide, 9 In.High 10.50
Tool, Broadax, Beveled Edge, Woodsman's 40.00
Tool, Broadax, 100 Years Old 16.00

Toby, Mug, Christmas, 1925, White, Gold Trim
See Page 538

Tole, Urn, Black, Pontypool, 19th Century, Pair
See Page 538

Tool, Bucksaw, Handwrought, 25 In.	25.00
Tool, Buttress, Farrier's	7.50
Tool, Carder, Wool, Sharp Spikes, 5 X 22 In.	8.50
Tool, Carpet Beater, Batwing	2.50
Tool, Chisel, Pinking, Sawtooth Edge, 1/2 In.	4.00
Tool, Comb, Flax	12.50
Tool, Comb, Flax, Cover, Thick Base	50.00
Tool, Cranberry Picker, Long Handle	30.00
Tool, Driver, Spinning Wheel, Slim	2.00
Tool, Flail, Wooden	8.50
Tool, Flax Hetchel, Double Row, Long Toothed	17.00
Tool, Froe, Handwrought, For Making Boards Or Shingles	6.50
Tool, Gauge Rod, Cooper's, Brass Tip, Measures Capacity	5.00
Tool, Gauge, Marking, Carpenter's, Brass Trim & Screw	3.50
Tool, Gimlet, Wood Handle	1.25
Tool, Grass Stripper, R.C.King, Dec.14, 1889, Blue Paint	27.50
Tool, Hame, Harness, Brass Knob On Top	2.75
Tool, Hame, Ox, Leather Covered	6.75
Tool, Hammer, Stone Mason's, 12 Blades	9.00
Tool, Hane, Brass Tips, Pair	3.00
Tool, Hatchet, Flax, Dated 1811	27.50
Tool, Holder, Gophering Iron, Polished Steel	12.50
Tool, Hook, For Crates, Cord Wrapped Handle	5.00
Tool, Hook, Hay, Handwrought	3.50
Tool, Knife For Stripping Corn	4.00
Tool, Knife, Chamfering, Cooper's	15.00
Tool, Lathe, Jeweler's, 13 Collets, 9 Turning Gravers	160.00
Tool, Lather Stick, For Horse, Brass Band, Wood Grips	7.50
Tool, Level, Stanley, Wooden, 30 In.	4.00
Tool, Line Spreader, For Harness, White Celluloid Rings, Pair	12.50
Tool, Loom, Rug	35.00
Tool, Mallet, Burl	20.00
Tool, Mallet, Holbrook No.4	4.00
Tool, Mallet, Shooting Stick, Printer's, To Tighten Type	15.00
Tool, Marker, Carpenter's, For Planing	3.50
Tool, Measurer, Inside, Carpenter's	7.50
Tool, Measurer, Lumber, Wood & Brass	10.00
Tool, Microscope, Brass, Monocular, 19th Century	75.00
Tool, Mortise	37.50
Tool, Nail, Square Cut, 1 Lb.	.75
Tool, Pitch Boat, For Boat Caulker	25.00
Tool, Plane, Handmade, Wooden, Circa 1891, 26 In.Long	29.00

Tool, Plane, Jointer, Wooden, 27 In.	7.50
Tool, Plane, Molding *Illus*	15.00
Tool, Plane, Molding, Wooden	2.50
Tool, Plane, Molding, Wooden, 9 1/2 In.	7.00
Tool, Plane, Sun, 21 X 5 1/2 In.	50.00
Tool, Pleating Board, Metal Strips, 13 In.	10.00
Tool, Saw, Hand, Stillman Patent, 1848	7.50
Tool, Saw, Keyhole, Tapered Blade, Wood Handle	2.00
Tool, Saw, Log, 1 Man, Long	6.50
Tool, Saw, Log, 2 Man, 5 Ft.	4.50
Tool, Spade, Boat, Whaling, Hand Forged Iron, 17 In., Wood Pole	94.50
Tool, Spinning Wheel, Flax, Spin Indicator	40.00
Tool, Spiral Tip, Lumberman's, Logging Pole	5.00
Tool, Spoke Shave, Central Shavings Tunnel	9.00
Tool, Stock, Bit, Mushroom Handle, Egg Center Grip, Bond	12.50
Tool, Surveyor's Chain, C.1800, Brass Handles & Measuring Bobs	60.00
Tool, Surveyor's Chain, W.& L.E.Gurley's, Troy, N.Y., Brass Handles	25.00
Tool, Tongs, Pipe, Handmade, Toggle Extension	75.00
Tool, Trammel, Chimney, Sawtooth Adjustments	35.00
Tool, Trap, Bear, Drag Chain, 44 In.	95.00
Tool, Trap, Bear, No.6	150.00
Tool, Trap, Bear, No.15, Oneida, Crossed Teeth, Double Spring, 32 In.Long	110.00
Tool, Trap, Deer, Wire Foot Pan	7.50
Tool, Trap, Double Spring	2.00
Tool, Trap, Double Spring, Jump Bait Pan	7.50
Tool, Trap, Mole, Spiked, Spring Action	15.00
Tool, Trap, Mouse, Cage	12.50
Tool, Trap, Rat, Wire, 17 In.	12.00
Tool, Trap, Single Spring	10.00
Tool, Trap, Wolf, 14 In.	12.00
Tool, Tweezers, Watchmaker's, Hand Forges, 4 1/2 In.	5.00
Tool, Vise, Wooden, 16 In.Diameter	10.00
Tool, Wheelwright's Spoke Rounder	12.50
Tool, Whip, Buggy, Woven Leather Strips	12.50
Tool, Wrench, For Wagons, Wooden, Hand Hewn	12.50
Tool, Yarn Winder, Four Arms, Freestanding	45.00
Tool, Yarn Winder, From Mill *Illus*	6.00

Toothpick Holders are sometimes called Toothpicks by collectors. The variously shaped containers made to hold the small wooden toothpicks are of glass, china, or metal. Most of the toothpicks are victorian.

Toothpick, see also other categories such as Bisque, Slag, etc.

Toothpick, Basket, Storefront, Colby Bros., Plainville, Kan.	6.50
Toothpick, Bird Holding Eggshell, Caramel, Signed Porteaux	22.00
Toothpick, Bird Moves, Metal *Illus*	3.50
Toothpick, Bird On Wishbone	22.00
Toothpick, Bird, Wishbone, Silver, Best Wishes	8.75
Toothpick, Blue, Colorado	27.50
Toothpick, Boot Shape, 2 1/4 In.	3.75
Toothpick, Butterflies, Sunflowers, Silver, Cranberry Glass	45.00
Toothpick, Button Arches, Ruby Top, Delaware	10.50
Toothpick, Cameo, White, Glass Dome Cover	20.00
Toothpick, Carnival Flute, Amethyst, Rayed Star Bottom	78.00
Toothpick, Clear Glass Urn, Sterling Rim At Top	10.00
Toothpick, Coin Spot, Blue, Pedestal Base	10.00
Toothpick, Colorado, Green, Gold	13.00
Toothpick, Cupid Next To Pink Heart, Blue Trim, Porcelain	9.50
Toothpick, Daisy & Button, Blue, Shape Of Chair	12.50
Toothpick, Forget-Me-Nots, Yellow, Hand-Painted, Footed	10.00
Toothpick, Galloway	6.00
Toothpick, Gatling Gun, Blue	32.50
Toothpick, Green Clematis, Profuse Sprays, Intaglio & Relief Gold Floral	48.00
Toothpick, Green Opaque, Harvard Tarentum	16.50
Toothpick, Green To Opalescent, Iris & Meander	15.00
Toothpick, Green, Glass, Inverted Thumbprint, Ground Base	15.00
Toothpick, Harvard, New London, 1903	25.00

Tool, Plane, Molding
See Page 540

Tool, Yarn Winder, From Mill
See Page 540

Toothpick, Bird Moves, Metal
See Page 540

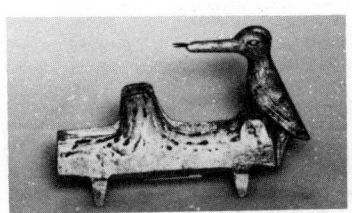

Toothpick, Hat, Raindrop Pattern, Clear Glass	21.50
Toothpick, Indian, White, Metal	10.00
Toothpick, Iris With Meander, Blue	23.00
Toothpick, Maiden's Blush, Banded Portland	22.00
Toothpick, Maiden's Blush, Ruby	14.00
Toothpick, Minnesota, Three Handles	9.50
Toothpick, Monkey Beside Hat On Platform	18.50
Toothpick, Monkey On Stump, Blue	25.00
Toothpick, Nippon, Floral, Hand Painted, Six Sided	3.75
Toothpick, Paneled Thistle, Footed	30.00
Toothpick, Roses, Yellow, Brown, Rs Poland, Red Mark	22.00
Toothpick, Roses, Yellow, Gold, Three Handle, Signed Germany	12.50
Toothpick, Ruby Flashed, Clear, Ribbed Base, Marked Fair 1903	10.00
Toothpick, Ruby Flashed, Dated 1906	10.00
Toothpick, Ruby Flashed, May Jones 1910	15.00
Toothpick, Ruby Flashed, Sawtooth Top, Marked Marie 1903	10.00
Toothpick, Ruby Flashed, Zipper Slash, Grandma, 1899	18.50
Toothpick, Ruby, Bohemian	1.00
Toothpick, Scalloped Swirl	15.00
Toothpick, Silver Plate, Engraved 'i'm Your Match, ' Ball Feet	8.50
Toothpick, Silver Plate, Engraved 'take Your Pick, ' Ball Feet	8.50
Toothpick, Star, Clear, Fluted Top	6.50
Toothpick, Texas, Footed	9.50
Toothpick, Three Dolphins On Tails	16.50
Toothpick, Three Handled, Pressed, Gold Edge	12.00
Toothpick, Top Hat, Blue Threaded Glass	7.50
Toothpick, Tree Trunk, Acorns, Squirrel, Clear Glass	32.50
Toothpick, Winged Cherub Sits Atop Eggshell, Silver Plate, Derby	21.00
Toothpick, Wishbone, Chick	18.00

Tortoiseshell Glass was made during the 1880s and after by the Sandwich Glass Works of Massachusetts and some firms in Germany. Tortoiseshell has been reproduced.

Tortoiseshell Glass, Compote, Amber Feet	*Illus*	85.00
Tortoiseshell Glass, Pitcher, Sandwich, Enameled Floral Decoration		160.00
Tortoiseshell Glass, Tumbler		18.00

Tortoiseshell Glass, Compote, Amber Feet
See Page 541

Tortoiseshell, **Case**, Cigar, Lacquered Flowering Trees & Herons, 5 In.Long	45.00
Tortoiseshell, **Comb**, Mantilla, Egyptian Decoration	2.00
Tortoiseshell, **Tea Caddy**, Regency, Ivory Border, Rectangular, 19th Century	60.00
Toy, see also **Doll, Tin, Wooden, Card, Marble**	
Toy, **Aero Swing**, Chein	24.00
Toy, **Airplane**, Biplane, Glow Plug Engine	19.50
Toy, **Airplane**, Brass, Handmade	8.00
Toy.**Airplane**, Cast Iron, 'lindy, ' 4 In.Long	15.00
Toy, **Airplane**, Movable Propeller & Wheels, Iron	9.50
Toy, **Airplane**, Pot Metal, Hubley	4.00
Toy, **Airplane**, Tin, Gear Drive	2.00
Toy, **Airplane**, Tin, Windup, The Sky Writer, No.87, Katz Toys	6.00
Toy, **Airplane**, Windup, Tin, C.1930, 8 1/2 In.Long	25.00
Toy, **Animal**, Circus.Schoenhut, Horse, Saddle, Bridle	13.00
Toy, **Animal**, Farm, Rubber, Set Of 6	15.00
Toy, **Auto**, Coup, Running Board, Tin, Orange, 13 In.Long	35.00
Toy, **Auto**, Man At Wheel, Windup, Tin, 1910	9.00
Toy, **B.O.**, Sparkle Plenty, Windup	20.00
Toy, **B.O.Holding Sparkle Plenty**, Tin, Windup, Marx	15.00
Toy, **Badge**, Police, Tootsie Toy	2.00
Toy, **Ball & Cup**, Chinese, Carved, 7 In.Long	15.00
Toy, **Bathroom**, Tin, 3 Walls, Hanging Water Closet, Tub, Mirror	15.00
Toy, **Bathtub**, Porcelain, Salesman's Sample	9.00
Toy, **Bathtub**, Tootsie Toy	6.00
Toy, **Bear With Drum**, Mechanical	15.00
Toy, **Bear**, Stuffed, Standing, 6 In.Tall	6.50
Toy, **Bear**, Windup, Walking, Blown Eyes, Black Fur Fabric	27.50
Toy, **Bed**, Doll's, C.1865	22.00
Toy, **Bed**, Doll's, Four-Poster, Hardwood	15.00
Toy, **Bed**, Doll's, Four-Poster, Spool, C.1900	40.00
Toy, **Bed**, Doll's, 1930s, Head & Foot Board, 6 In.	4.00
Toy, **Bed**, Oak, Mattress, Pad, Pillow, Doll's	21.50
Toy, **Bed**, Tootsie Toy	6.00
Toy, **Bell**, Pair Wheels, Heart Design, Gong Bell Co., 1880s, Cast Iron	40.00
Toy, **Bell**, Pull, Heart Wheels, Horse & Rider, Patent 1915	75.00
Toy, **Bell**, Pull, Horse & Rider, Pulling Bell	50.00
Toy, **Bell**, S Curved Wheels, Gong Bell Co., 1890s, Cast Iron	50.00
Toy, **Bicycle, see also Bicycle**	
Toy, **Bicycle**, High Wheeled, Victorian, Wire, 6 1/2 In.Tall, 9 In.Long	15.00
Toy, **Bird**, Mechanical, Dated 1929	6.00
Toy, **Bird**, Mechanical, Pecking, Velour Body, Windup	16.00
Toy, **Bird**, Tin, Ges Gesch, Germany *Illus*	22.50
Toy, **Bird**, Windup, Germany, Tin, 3 1/2 X 3 1/2 In.	7.50
Toy, **Bird**, Windup, Tin, 1927	12.00
Toy, **Bizzy Andy Jr.**, No.58, Automatic, Marble Toy By Wolverine	4.00
Toy, **Blocks**, Little Black Sambo, Cardboard	12.00

Toy, Bird, Tin, Ges Gesch, Germany
See Page 542

Toy, Blocks, Picture, Wood, Children In Victorian Costumes	7.50
Toy, Blocks, Wooden, Covered With Paper Letters, Animals, Set Of 12	10.00
Toy, Blocks, Wooden, Red & Blue, Letters, Pictures, 1 3/4 In.Cubes, 32	9.00
Toy, Boat, Ferry, Lindstrom, Windup, 8 1/2 In.Long, 5 In.High	20.00
Toy, Boat, Motor, Windup, Chein, Tin, 15 In.Long	6.50
Toy, Bomb, Cap, Dog's Head, Patent, Cast Iron	45.00
Toy, Bomb, Cap, Washington, Cast Iron	45.00
Toy, Bomb, Cap, Yellow Kid With Sayai, Cast Iron	30.00
Toy, Bomber, B-29, Marx, Tin, Windup, 1940, 18 In.Wings	15.00
Toy, Bomber, B29, Marx, Tin, Windup, 1940	10.00
Toy, Bombo The Monk, Tin, Windup	18.50
Toy, Bubble Blowing Boy, Windup, Tin, 8 In.High	14.50
Toy, Buggy, Doll's, Rattan, Handmade Spoke Wheels	16.00
Toy, Builder Set, American Model, No.3, 1914, 250 Piece	25.00
Toy, Bus, Iron, Made In England, Dinky Toy Co., 4 In.	3.00
Toy, Bus, Made By Wolverine, 1942, Tin, 14 In.Long X 4 In.Tall	35.00
Toy, Busy Mike, Chein	5.00
Toy, Butterfly, Pull, Long Stick	13.50
Toy, Cab, Arcade, Yellow, 9 In.Long	125.00
Toy, Cabinet, Dish, Child's, Two Shelves, Mirror Top, Glass Doors, Maple	15.00
Toy, Cabinet, Kitchen, Tootsie Toy	6.00
Toy, Cabinet, Set Of Dishes, Child's, Pine, Wall	6.00
Toy, Camel, Felt, Iron Wheels, Humphrey, 10 In.Long, 8 In.High	12.50
Toy, Cannon & Soldier, World War I, Tin	10.00
Toy, Cannon, Caisson, Seven Men, Four Horses, Circa 1915	62.50
Toy, Cannon, Repeating Carbide, Iron, Dated 1932	28.00
Toy, Cannon, Tin, 15 In.Long	8.00
Toy, Cannon, Wooden, Legs, Cork Shooter, Metal, 7 X 9	15.00
Toy, Captain Video Space Fleet	10.00
Toy, Car, Gold Paint	10.00
Toy, Car, Hansom Cab, Hubley, C.1920	200.00
Toy, Car, Iron, Brown, Green Roof	17.50
Toy, Car, Model A, Arcade, Cast Iron, Blue, 4 Rubber Wheels	14.00
Toy, Car, Model A, Tootsie, 1939	4.00
Toy, Car, Model T Ford, Cast Iron	12.00
Toy, Car, Race, Driver, Tin, Windup, 5 In., Yed, Yellow, Marx Toys	9.00
Toy, Car, Racing, Cast Iron, Paint	62.00
Toy, Car, Rubber, 1938	2.00
Toy, Car, Stock, Tin, C.1930, 4 3/4 In.Long	12.50
Toy, Car, Tootsie Toy, 1939	3.00
Toy, Car, Train, Cast Iron	5.00
Toy, Car, Transport, Cast Iron, Red & Green Paint	45.00
Toy, Car, Windup, Tin, Lehmann, Patent May 12, 1903, Horn, Man	75.00
Toy, Carriage, Doll's, Reed, Wooden Wheels	45.00
Toy, Cart, Child's, Wood & Leather, Painted, Upholstered Seat, 19th Century	120.00
Toy, Cart, Sleigh Shape, Upholstered Leather, Red Wheels, 19 In.Long	45.00
Toy, Cart, Wooden, Dated 1895	12.00

Toy, Castor Set, Four Bottles, Round Stand, Doll's	25.00
Toy, Cement Mixer, Buddy L, Wheels, 18 X 14 In.	65.00
Toy, Chair, Doll's, 1930s, 5 In.	3.75
Toy, Chair, Side, Doll's, 1930s, 4 In.	3.00
Toy, Chair, Tootsie Toy	6.00
Toy, Chamber Pot, Doll's, 1 3/4 In.Diameter	1.00
Toy, Charlie Chaplin, Swings Cane, Windup	65.00
Toy, Chest, Doll, Oak, Four Drawers, 4 In.High	16.00
Toy, Chest, Doll's, C.1865	.
Toy, Chest, Three Drawers, Spooled, Grooved, Pulls, Walnut, 9 In.	28.00
Toy, Chest, Drawer At Top, Two Doors At Bottom, Porcelain Pulls, Victorian	85.00
Toy, Circus Wagon, Polar Bear & Trainer Inside, Bear Moves, Wooden, 14 In.	47.00
Toy, Clock, Doll's, Iron	10.00
Toy, Clown & Jo Jo In Car, Unique Arts	7.00
Toy, Clown On Cart Pulled By Donkey, Windup, 1905, Germany	95.00
Toy, Clown On Mule, Windup, Tin	15.00
Toy, Clown, Tin, Mechanical, Stands On Hands	5.00
Toy, Coach & Horses, Coronation, Ben Bros., England, 4 1/2 In.	10.00
Toy, Coffee Grinder, Lap Style, Marked Daisey	45.00
Toy, Couch, Doll's, Tapestry Cover, Bolster Arms, 25 1/2 In.Long	75.00
Toy, Coupe, Cast Iron	18.00
Toy, Cowboy On Horse, Wyandotte	4.00
Toy, Cradle, Doll's, Folds, Pine, 10 X 17 1/2 In.	15.00
Toy, Cradle, Doll's, Hooded, Sponge Decor, 28 In.Long	100.00
Toy, Cradle, Round Headboard, Doll's, 7 1/2 In.Tall	18.00
Toy, Crane, Sand, Wolverine, Automatic, Patent 1915-16, Tin, Engineer, Box	20.00
Toy, Creamer, Sugar, Butter, Covers, Child's, Acorn Pattern, Boy, Girl, Dog	65.00
Toy, Cupboard, Doll's, Walnut, Porcelain Knobs, 19th Century, 30 In.	35.00
Toy, Dancing Couple, Mechanical, Tin, Marked F.M.Paris, 7 1/2 In.Tall	125.00
Toy, Desk, Roll Top, Chair, 5 1/2 In.High Illus	45.00
Toy, Dinner Set, Doll's, 21 Piece	65.00
Toy, Dishes, Doll, Windmill Design, German	14.00
Toy, Dishes, Doll's, Pink, Blue & Gold On White, 21 Pieces, Boxed	12.00
Toy, Dishes, Doll's, White Metal, Embossed Design, 11 Piece	10.00
Toy, Dishes, Multifloral, Gold Rim, 12 Piece	22.50
Toy, Dog, 'sparky, ' Doghouse, Lithograph, Tin	5.00
Toy, Doghouse, Swiss, Musical, Fido	20.00
Toy, Dogpatch, Windup, Tin, 1945, 4 In.	40.00
Toy, Doll, see Doll	
Toy, Dollhouse, Folding, Mcloughlin Bros.	65.00
Toy, Donkey, Mohair, Nods, Tiny Wheels On Hoofs, 10 In.Long	35.00
Toy, Dresser, Doll's, C.1865	.
Toy, Dresser, Salesman's Sample, Refinished	65.00
Toy, Dresser, Three Velvet Lined Drawers, Salesman's Sample, 7 X 7 In.	35.00
Toy, Drum, Chein, Military Decor, 12 In.	3.50
Toy, Drummer, Windup, Chein, Tin, 9 In.	8.00
Toy, Duck, Chein, 4 In.	3.00
Toy, Duck, Friction, Tin, 8 1/4 In.Long	38.00
Toy, Dump Wagon, Two Horses & Driver, Says Sand & Gravel, Iron	37.50
Toy, Dutch Boy, Mechanical, Windup, Painted, 6 In.	17.50
Toy, Easter Egg, Papier-Mache Illus	15.00
Toy, Elephant, Iron, Trunk Up, 4 In.High	4.75
Toy, Engine, Fire, Driver, Painted, Cast Iron	23.00
Toy, Engine, Ives, No.1100, Three Coaches	10.00
Toy, Engine, Ives, No.3241, Three Coaches, Wide Gauge, Track	335.00
Toy, Engine, Steam, Weeden, Horizontal	50.00
Toy, Erector Set, Electric Engine, 1938	20.00
Toy, Erector Set, Gilbert No.7, Wooden Box	25.00
Toy, Erector Set, Ives Struktiron, Miniature Railways, 1914, 175 Piece	25.00
Toy, Express Wagon, Iron, Red, Blue, 8 In. Illus	47.50
Toy, Farm Wagon, Horse, Driver, Tin, 12 In.Long	32.50
Toy, Felix The Cat, Wooden, Jointed, 8 1/2 In.	50.00
Toy, Felix, Schoenhut, Wood, Dated 1922	28.00
Toy, Felix, Tin, Cat, Sullivan, Paint, 1922	28.50
Toy, Ferdinand The Bull, Branded Ferdinand On Hip, Walt Disney Enterprises	9.00
Toy, Ferdinand The Bull, Disney, Hard Rubber	8.00

Toy, Desk, Roll Top,
Chair, 5 1/2 In.High
See Page 544

Toy, Easter Egg, Papier-Mache
See Page 544

Toy, Express Wagon,
Iron, Red, Blue, 8 In.
See Page 544

Toy, Ferdinand The Bull, Marx, Windup, Tin, Walt Disney, 1938, Painted	15.00
Toy, Figures, Christmas, Religious, Musical, German, Tin	10.00
Toy, Fire Chief, Tin, Windup	2.75
Toy, Fire Engine, Boiler, Air Tank, Gold Color Smokestack, 12 1/2 In.Long	38.00
Toy, Fire Engine, Cast Iron, 2 Horses, 2 Men, Red Wagon, Yellow Wheels, White	75.00
Toy, Fire Engine, Iron, Aluminum Wheels, 3 3/4 In.	9.50
Toy, Fire Engine, Marx, Friction, Patent March 15, 1927, 9 X 9 In.	25.00
Toy, Fire Engine, Tender, Tin & Iron, 18 3/4 In.Long, 4 3/4 In.High	38.00
Toy, Fire Station, Tin, Red, C.1890, Windup, Doors Fly Open, Bell Rings	37.50
Toy, Fire Truck, Red, Yellow Wheels, Driver, Marked Kenton, Iron, 8 1/2 In.	50.00
Toy, Fire Wagon, Horse Pulling, Cast Iron	15.00
Toy, Foxy Grandpa Hat Party, Selchow & Richter, Pin The Hat On Grandpa	12.00
Toy, Furniture, Chein Metal, 4 Pieces	15.00

Toy, Furniture, Doll, Lawn Swing, Glass, Tin Canopy	95.00
Toy, Furniture, Doll's, Red Paint, Yellow Decoration, 4 Pieces	60.00
Toy, Furniture, Dresser, Oak, Mirror, 3 Drawer, 7 1/2 In.Tall	18.00
Toy, Game, see Game	
Toy, Gas Range, Marked Royal, Iron	8.75
Toy, Grinder, Food	12.50
Toy, Grinder, Meat, Child's	7.00
Toy, Gun, Cap, Big Bill	7.50
Toy, Gun, Cap, Cast Iron, 5 In., Echo	5.00
Toy, Gun, Cap, Kilgore, Iron	4.00
Toy, Gun, Me & My Buddy, Clicker Pistol, Metal, Wyandotte	10.00
Toy, Gun, Propello-Pistol, 3 Propellers, Metal, Midwest Industries	4.00
Toy, Gypsy With Barrel Organ, Chained Dancing Bear, Timpo, England	8.00
Toy, Helicopter, Streamline, Metal, Push, Wyandotte	5.00
Toy, Hen, Cackles & Lays Eggs, Tin	6.00
Toy, Highchair, Doll's, Converts To Playpen, On Rollers	135.00
Toy, Hobbyhorse, Child's, Carved, Painted, White & Gray, American, C.1850	210.00
Toy, Hobbyhorse, English	33.00
Toy, Hobbyhorse, Rocking, Natural Hide Covered, 42 In.High	200.00
Toy, Hobbyhorse, Wood, Carved, Painted, American, C.1850 .... *Illus*	210.00

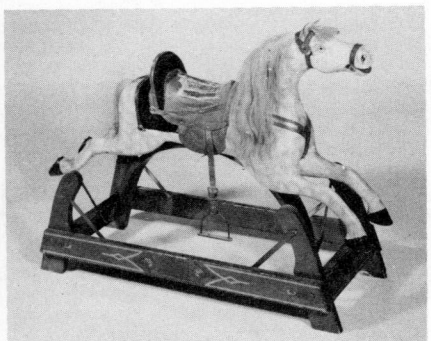

Toy, Hobbyhorse, Wood, Carved,
Painted, American, C.1850

Toy, Horse & Rider On Iron Frame, Ives, C.1910, Cast Iron	65.00
Toy, Horse, Composition, On Rockers, 10 In.Long	28.00
Toy, Horse, Mechanical, Celluloid, Occupied Japan, Indian Boy	6.50
Toy, Horse, Mechanical, Tin, Painted, 31 In.High	45.00
Toy, Horse, Mobo, Tin, Made In England, Press Stirrups & He Moves	95.00
Toy, Horse, Wooden, Platform, Iron Wheels, Horsehair Mane, Leather Pull Strap	95.00
Toy, Horse, Wooden, Saddle, Stirrup, Mane, Tail, Wheeled Platform, 13 In.Long	35.00
Toy, Horseshoe Set, Lone Ranger, Rubber	5.00
Toy, House, Doll's, New England Colonial, 2 Story, Furnished, Electric Lights	3500.00
Toy, House, Doll's, Pennsylvania Dutch, 14 In.Long, 11 In.Wide, 11 In.High	125.00
Toy, House, Lithograph, Tin, 1914	10.00
Toy, Hutch, Doll's, Open, Painted Blue, Wooden, 9 In.High	7.50
Toy, Ice Chest, Oak, 12 3/4 In.Tall, 7 1/2 In.Across	35.00
Toy, Ice Cream Set, Dollhouse, Tray, Four Plates	28.00
Toy, Ice Skates, Clamp-On, Iron	3.00
Toy, Ice Skates, 1880s	5.00
Toy, Ice Truck, Blue, Iron, 6 3/4 In.	16.00
Toy, Iron, Doll's, Mini Swan	4.00
Toy, Ironing Board, Child's, Wood	5.00
Toy, Ironing Board, Folding, Wood, 21 In.High	10.00
Toy, Jazzbo, Jum Strauss, Dancer On Roof, Tin, 1921 .... 60.00 To	85.00
Toy, Jenny The Balking Mule, Strauss, 11 In.	14.00
Toy, Jockey On Horse, 1910, Painted, Cast Iron	75.00
Toy, Jumbo Bumbo Peanut Clown, 18 In.Tall	10.00
Toy, Jumping Jeep	7.00
Toy, Kitchen Cabinet, Cast Iron, Glass Doors, White Paint	35.00
Toy, Knock-Out, Strauss, 1921, Windup, Tin	22.00

Toy, **Lead Soldier**, General Pershing On Horse, Marked, Gold	3.00
Toy, **Liberty Blocks**, Copyright 1918, Patriotic Instructor, Boxed	10.00
Toy, **L'il Abner Band**, Tin, Windup	20.00
Toy, **Limousine**, Cast Iron, 5 In.	12.50
Toy, **Locomotive**, Tender, 'hill Climber, ' C.1900, Friction, 20 In.Long	60.00
Toy, **Locomotive**, Tin, Red, Gold, Friction Drive, 14 1/2 In.Long	22.50
Toy, **Lone Ranger & Silver**, Windup, Marx, 1938	32.50
Toy, **Make A Toy**, Wood, Teach Tot Toy, Educational	10.00
Toy, **Mammy**, Dancing, Tin, Windup	17.50
Toy, **Man On Pig**, Lehmann, Dated 1903	48.00
Toy, **Man**, Standing, Spin Toy, 5 In.High	15.00
Toy, **Marionette**, Mouseketeer, Disney	8.00
Toy, **Meccano Set**, Made In Wurtemberg, Pat.1929	20.00
Toy, **Mechanical**, Bird, Windup, Tin, Dated 1927	9.50
Toy, **Mechanical**, Chinese Man, Pulling Cart, Marked Carter Toy	50.00
Toy, **Mechanical**, Ham & Sam, Windup	65.00
Toy, **Mechanical**, Hen, Clucking, Tin	4.00
Toy, **Merry-Go-Round**, Tin, Windup, C.1900, Children Riding, Germany	35.00
Toy, **Merry-Go-Round**, Tin, 14 In.High	85.00
Toy, **Merrymakers**, Drummer, Dancer At Piano, Marx	95.00
Toy, **Mickey Mouse, see Mickey Mouse**	
Toy, **Mohair Donkey Pulls Cart**, Iron Wheels	25.00
Toy, **Monkey On Stick**, Folk Art, C.1830, Wood, 17 In.Long	35.00
Toy, **Monkey**, Mechanical, Strums Harp, Papier-Mache Head Turns	750.00
Toy, **Motor**, Sand, C.1910, Tin, Paint	16.50
Toy, **Motorcycle & Rider**, Cast Iron, C.1925, 6 1/2 In., Battery Operated	23.00
Toy, **Motorcycle**, Tin, Friction, 3 1/2 In.	6.50
Toy, **Motorcycle**, Tin, Windup, 5 In.	9.50
Toy, **Mouse In Clock**, Chein	3.00
Toy, **Musical**, Crank In Top, Religious Christmas Figures, Germany	10.00
Toy, **Oil Well**, Drake's, Working Model	150.00
Toy, **One-Arm Bandit**, Potluck, Karson Mfg.Co.	14.50
Toy, **Ostrich**, Pull, Head Wobbles, 4 In.Long	15.00
Toy, **Parasol**, Child's, Pink, Lace, Tree Bark Ring Handle	7.00
Toy, **Parasol**, Child's, Silk	4.00
Toy, **Peanut Man**, Peanut Butter Maker	6.50
Toy, **Phone**, Tin, Wall, 2 X 5 1/2 In.	17.50
Toy, **Phonograph**, Child's, Hand Crank, Baby, The Garford Mfg.Co., Elyria	28.00
Toy, **Piano**, Doll's, Upright, Glass Backing, Movable Keys	37.50
Toy, **Piano**, Schoenhut, Doll Size, Gold Lettering & Stencil	25.00
Toy, **Piano**, Schoenhut, 13 X 8 1/2 X 7 1/4 In.	40.00
Toy, **Pig**, Fur Covered, Musical, Glass Eyes, White, German, 7 In.Long	40.00
Toy, **Pile Driver**, Railroad, Cast Iron, 12 In.Long, 9 In.High	60.00
Toy, **Pipe**, Bubble, Tin, C.1865, St.Johnsbury, Vt.	2.00
Toy, **Pistol**, Cap, Animated, Butting Match, Pre-1900, Cast Iron 135.00 To	200.00
Toy, **Pistol**, Cap, Animated, Dolphin, Stevens, 1875-95, Cast Iron	300.00
Toy, **Pistol**, Cap, Animated, Humpty-Dumpty, 2 Headed, Cast Iron	300.00
Toy, **Pistol**, Cap, Animated, Monkey On Log, Stevens, 1880s-90s, Cast Iron	275.00
Toy, **Pistol**, Cap, Animated, Moonface, Cast Iron	500.00
Toy, **Pistol**, Cap, Animated, Shoot The Hat, 1890s, Cast Iron	275.00
Toy, **Pistol**, Cap, Animated, The Chinese Must Go, 1880s, Cast Iron	225.00
Toy, **Pistol**, Cap, Bunker Hill	10.00
Toy, **Pistol**, Cap, Cannon On Barrel	325.00
Toy, **Pistol**, Cap, Detective	3.50
Toy, **Pistol**, Cap, Figural, Sambo, Pat.1887, Cast Iron	55.00
Toy, **Pistol**, Cap, Scout, 1917	9.00
Toy, **Pistol**, Cap, Single Shot, Marked S And W, Iron, 5 3/4 In.Long	8.75
Toy, **Pistol**, Cap, Texas, Hubley	3.50
Toy, **Pistol**, Cast Iron, Cap, Big Bill, 6 In.Long	8.50
Toy, **Pistol**, Dnya-Mite, With Caps	5.00
Toy, **Pistol**, Liquid, Usa, Pat'd June 30, 1896, Cast Iron, Nickel Plate	20.00
Toy, **Pistol**, Repeater, Cap, National, Pat.1909, Iron	8.75
Toy, **Popeye**, Music Box, Mechanical	25.00
Toy, **Popeye**, Windup, Tin, Carrying Suitcases	26.00
Toy, **Projector**, Postcard, Electric, Tin, C.1915, Red & Gold	23.00
Toy, **Pump**, Painted *Illus*	45.00

Toy, Pump, Tin, Red & Green Paint	25.00
Toy, Punch Set, Child's, 7 Piece	35.00
Toy, Punch Set, Fan Pattern, Bowl, Six Cups, Doll's	35.00
Toy, Purse, Doll's, Drawstring, Mirror On Bottom, White Silk	3.00
Toy, Puzzle, Mcloughlin Bros.1887, The Dissected Map Of The U.S.	5.00
Toy, Rabbit Pulling Wagon, Chein	6.00
Toy, Rabbit, Tin, J.Chein & Co. .... Illus	3.00
Toy, Racer & Driver, Austin, Red, Cast Iron, Steel Wheels	17.50
Toy, Racer, Cast Iron, 4 Rubber Wheels, 2 Drivers	10.00
Toy, Racer, Hubley, Metal, 7 In.	80.00
Toy, Racer, Marx, Tin, Windup, Driver, Painted, 16 In.Long	18.00
Toy, Racing Horses On Double Track, C.1900, Jeu De Course, M.J.& Cie, France	125.00
Toy, Railway Express, Buddy L Toy, Butterfinger Ad On Side, 22 In.	45.00
Toy, Range, Play, Metal, Wolverine, Skillet & Mixing Bowl	5.00
Toy, Rattle, Baby	7.00
Toy, Rattle, Tin Can	3.00
Toy, Refrigerator, 2 Doors, Tin, Wolverine, 13 X 8 In.	7.00
Toy, Reindeer, Fur Covered, Metal Horns, Saddle, Bridle, Germany, 11 In.Tall	15.00
Toy, Roadster, M.G., Tin	4.00
Toy, Roadster, Tootsie Toy	15.00
Toy, Rocks & Rings Bell, Cast Iron, Brass Bell, U.S.Shield Impressed, C.1875	40.00
Toy, Rooster, Papier-Mache .... Illus	30.00
Toy, Rub Board, Child's	5.00
Toy, Sadiron, Child's, Dated 1900 .... 3.50 To 10.00	
Toy, Sadiron, Child's, Iron, 3 In.	6.00
Toy, Sand Toy, Tin Children On Hobbyhorses, J.Chein	10.00
Toy, Sedan, Desoto, Tin	4.00
Toy, Sedan, Tin, C.1930, 4 3/4 In.Long	12.50
Toy, Seesaw, Courtland, Tin, Windup	15.00
Toy, Settee, Dollhouse, Cast Iron, Gray Paint	16.50
Toy, Sewing Machine, Cast Iron, Marked Singer	17.00
Toy, Sewing Machine, Electric	14.00
Toy, Sewing Machine, Germany .... Illus	16.00

Toy, Pump, Painted
See Page 547

Toy, Rabbit, Tin, J.Chein & Co.

Toy, Rooster, Papier-Mache

Toy, Sewing Machine, Germany
See Page 548

Toy, Sewing Machine, Little Comfort, Smith & Egge Mfg.	20.00
Toy, Sewing Machine, Little German Sewing Machine	18.00
Toy, Sewing Machine, Reliable Mfg., Wood Case, 8 In.	18.00
Toy, Sewing Machine, Singer	18.00
Toy, Sewing Machine, Singer, Clamp On Type	9.00
Toy, Ship, Wooden, Ocean Liner, 10 In.Long	4.00
Toy, Shocking Machine, Knapp, Electric Thriller, Wooden Box	16.00
Toy, Shooting Gallery, Hopalong Cassidy, Mechanical, Tin	15.00
Toy, Shovel, Sand, Structo, Tin, Side Lever, Cab, 4 Wheels, 16 In.High	10.00
Toy, Sink, Tin, Wolverine, 12 X 11 In.	12.00
Toy, Siren, Bicycle, Tin, Fire Chief Painted On Front, 48	16.00
Toy, Slate, Child's, Wooden Frame, 10 X 14 In.	14.00
Toy, Slate, Training, Wooden Frame, Child's	4.50
Toy, Sleigh, Doll's, Pewter, 4 1/2 In.	16.00
Toy, Sleigh, Driver, Hubley, 1906, 1 Horse, Cast Iron	150.00
Toy, Sleigh, Horse Drawn, Cast Iron, Painted	95.00
Toy, Sleigh, Hubley, C.1920, Cast Iron, 1 Reindeer	150.00
Toy, Slot Machine, Japanese, Battery Operated, One-Arm-Bandit Type	8.95
Toy, Smokey The Bear, Ideal	8.00
Toy, Snowshoes, Pair	10.00
Toy, Sofa & Two Chairs, Doll's, Bamboo, Cane Seats	8.00
Toy, Sofa, Two Armchairs, Table, Doll's, Wicker, Made In China, Label	50.00
Toy, Soldier, British, Lead, 11	60.00
Toy, Soldier, Lead, 2 In., 15	10.00
Toy, Soldier, Lead, 3 In.	1.50
Toy, Soldier, Metal, British, Hand-Painted, Action Soldier, 13	12.50
Toy, Soldier, Metal, British, Hand-Painted, Cowboys & Indians, 21	23.50
Toy, Soldier, Metal, British, Hand-Painted, Cowboys, 6	7.50
Toy, Soldier, Tin, Pvt., Recruit Little Cigars, 3 In.	3.50
Toy, Soldier, World War Ii, Metal	1.50
Toy, Spectacles, Doll's, Tortoise Frame	3.00
Toy, Speedboat, Tin, Lindstrom Co.	10.00
Toy, Stagecoach, Victorian, Wire, 10 In.Long, 5 1/2 In.High	20.00
Toy, Steam Engine, Brass, Wooden, Electric	95.00
Toy, Steam Engine, Tootsie, Pennsylvania On Cab	6.00
Toy, Steam Shovel, Keystone Toy	37.50
Toy, Steam Shovel, 13 In. .... Illus	25.00
Toy, Steamer, Doll's, McGraw Junior Globe Trotter	17.00
Toy, Stove, Child's, Electric, Looks Like Oil Stove	12.00
Toy, Stove, Child's, Gas, Iron, Yellow & Black, 2 Iron Kettles	25.00
Toy, Stove, Child's, Iron	2.00
Toy, Stove, Cook, Child's, Champion, Cast Iron & Nickel Plate	95.00
Toy, Stove, Dolly's Favorite, Kettle, Skillet, Pans, 14 In.Tall	225.00
Toy, Stove, Electric, C.1930, Tin, Mottled Green Granite	10.00
Toy, Stove, Electric, Pat'd 1924	15.00
Toy, Stove, Prize, Utensils, 12 In.High .... Illus	35.00

Toy, Steam Shovel, 13 In.
See Page 549

Toy, Stove, Prize, Utensils, 12 In.High
See Page 549

Toy, Stove, Stars On Oven Door & Lids, 3 1/2 X 3/4 In.	12.00
Toy, Stove, Stationary Lids, Oven Door Opens, Iron, Nickel Plated, Mark Star	15.00
Toy, Stove, Tin, Mechanical Sparks	6.00
Toy, Stove, Tin, Porcelain Knobs, Six Burners, Six Kettles, Teakettle	42.50
Toy, Stove, Tin, 2 Ovens, Hooks, Embossed 1895, 7 X 8 In.	12.00
Toy, Stroller, Doll's, Leather, Collapsible, Rubber Tires, Dated 1907	65.00
Toy, Sulky, Pre-1912, Painted, Cast Iron	45.00
Toy, Surrey, Two Horses, Stanley, Cast Metal, 11 1/2 In.Long	33.00
Toy, Surrey, Victorian Lady In Back Seat, Gent In Front, Black Horses, Iron	30.00
Toy, Sweeper, Child's, Bissell	5.00
Toy, Table & Chairs, Doll's, Bentwood, Four Pieces	14.00
Toy, Table Set, Pressed Glass, Tray, Cruet, Salt, Pepper, Stopper	23.50
Toy, Table Setting, Child's, Sugar, Creamer, & Spooner, Purpled Glass	30.00
Toy, Table, Doll's	6.50
Toy, Table, Doll's, Drop Leaf, Chair, Red Paint, 6 In.Tall	5.00
Toy, Table, Doll's, Parlor, Marble Top, 4 X 2 7/8 In.	15.00
Toy, Table, Ice Cream, Four Chairs, Heart Backs, Handmade, 2 1/8 In.	28.50
Toy, Tank, Fighter, Midget, Climbing, Tin, Windup, Marx	12.00
Toy, Tank, Tin, Marx, Man Rises & Shoots	35.00
Toy, Taxi, Lupor, Tin, Windup	2.75
Toy, Tea Set, Doll's, Blue Majolica Type, 8 Piece	13.50
Toy, Teakettle, Tin, Strap Handle, No Lid, 2 In.Tall	6.00
Toy, Teapot, Creamer, Sugar, Four Cups, Saucers, Child's, Blue Willow	15.00
Toy, Tel A Tot, Wood, Teach Tot Toy, Educational	10.00
Toy, Tin, Mixing Lady, Windup Illus	18.00
Toy, Top, Push Handle, Tin, Chein	3.50
Toy, Top, Walt Disney Enterprises, Spinning, Metal	15.00
Toy, Town Post Office, Copy.1910, Milton Bradley, Boxed	4.00
Toy, Tractor & Trailer, Buddy L Toy, Allied Van Lines, 30 In.	65.00
Toy, Tractor & Trailer, Stake Bed, Rubber Wheels, Wyandotte	15.00
Toy, Tractor & Trailer, Van Lines, Rubber Wheels, Wyandotte	15.00
Toy, Tractor, Fordson, Cast Iron, Driver	65.00
Toy, Tractor, International Arcade, Cast Iron, Red	25.00
Toy, Tractor, International, Cast Iron, Red, Steel Wheel, 4 In.	20.00
Toy, Train Car, Gondola, Keystone, Rubber Wheels, Brake Wheel	40.00
Toy, Train Car, Lionel, Green, 8 In. Illus	10.00
Toy, Train, American Flyer, 3250, Cars No.1116, 3017 & Wrecker Car	40.00
Toy, Train, Carved Wood, Locomotive, Tender, & 5 Cars, American	325.00
Toy, Train, Cast Iron, Wilkins, Engine & 3 Cars	160.00
Toy, Train, Cast Iron, 4 In.Long	5.00
Toy, Train, Engine & Car, Cast Iron	35.00
Toy, Train, Engine, Tender, Four Cars, 1880	365.00
Toy, Train, Engine, Tender, Iron, 6 In.Long	25.00
Toy, Train, H.O., Gauge 31036, Track, Transformer	10.50
Toy, Train, Ives, No.3250, Cars No.65, 66, &551	25.00

Toy, Tin, Mixing Lady, Windup
See Page 550

Toy, Train Car, Lionel, Green, 8 In.
See Page 550

Toy, Train, Ives No.3258, Original Box	50.00
Toy, Train, Lionel, American Flyer, No.293	18.00
Toy, Train, Lionel, American Flyer, No.300, A.C.	18.00
Toy, Train, Lionel, American Flyer, No.310	20.00
Toy, Train, Lionel, American Flyer, No.312	20.00
Toy, Train, Lionel, Diesel, No.1055	10.00
Toy, Train, Lionel, Diesel, Switcher, No.370, Plastic	15.00
Toy, Train, Lionel, Engine, No.21085, Plastic	10.00
Toy, Train, Lionel, Engine, With Tender, No.221, Torpedo Block, Metal	25.00
Toy, Train, Lionel, Engine, With Tender, No.224, Metal	22.50
Toy, Train, Lionel, Engine, With Tender, No.229, Metal	22.50
Toy, Train, Lionel, Engine, With Tender, No.301, Metal	8.00
Toy, Train, Lionel, Engine, With Tender, No.303, Metal	8.00
Toy, Train, Lionel, Engine, With Tender, No.307, Metal	8.00
Toy, Train, Lionel Engine, With Tender, No.1110, Metal	8.00
Toy, Train, Lionel, Engine, With Whistle Tender, No.736, Metal	45.00
Toy, Train, Lionel, Engine, With Tender, No.1654, Metal	10.00
Toy, Train, Lionel, Engine, With Tender, No.1666, Metal	22.50
Toy, Train, Lionel, Engine, With Tender, No.1668, Torpedo Block, Metal	25.00
Toy, Train, Lionel, Engine, With Tender, No.1684, Metal	15.00
Toy, Train, Lionel, Engine, With Tender, No.1688, Metal, Torpedo Gray	22.50
Toy, Train, Lionel, Engine, With Tender, No.2016, Metal	22.50
Toy, Train, Lionel, Engine, With Tender, No.2025, Metal	25.00
Toy, Train, Lionel, Engine, With Tender, No.2026, Metal	22.50
Toy, Train, Lionel, Engine, With Tender, No.2037, Metal	22.50
Toy, Train, Lionel, Engine, With Whistle Tender, No.1688-E, Torpedo Gray	30.00
Toy, Train, Lionel, Standard Gauge, No.8	70.00
Toy, Train, Marx, Mechanical, Tin, Windup, Steel Wheels	3.25
Toy, Train, Windup, Five Cars, Original Box	65.00
Toy, Train, Wyandotte, Hofner, Windup, 4 Piece	10.00
Toy, Tricycle, Tin, 4 X 6 In.	6.00
Toy, Trolley Car, No.1, Lionel	375.00
Toy, Trolley, Toonerville, Glass	95.00
Toy, Trolley, Windup, Tin, St-Auss	35.00
Toy, Truck, Arcade, Cast Iron, Green Railing, 4 Rubber Wheels	12.50
Toy, Truck, Arcade, Ton, Cast Iron, 4 Rubber Wheels, Red Paint	12.50
Toy, Truck, Bell Service, Cast Iron, C.1937	199.00
Toy, Truck, Bell Telephone	12.50
Toy, Truck, Buddy L Toy, Wrigley Spearmint Gum Ad On Side, 15 In.	35.00
Toy, Truck, Buddy L Van, 1929	40.00
Toy, Truck, Coke, Electric	7.90
Toy, Truck, Dairy, Tootsie Toy, Tractor With 2 Trailers	32.00
Toy, Truck, Delivery, Wooden, Tin Wheels	12.50
Toy, Truck, Dump Bed, Buddy L	65.00
Toy, Truck, Dump, Cast Iron, Green & Red Paint	12.50

Toy, Truck, Dump, Metal, Rubber Wheels, 19 1/2 In.Long, Wyandotte	10.00
Toy, Truck, Dump, Tin, 8 1/2 In.Long	22.50
Toy, Truck, Fire, Cast Iron, Marked Kenton, Yellow Wheels, Driver	50.00
Toy, Truck, Fire, Cast Iron, 5 In.	12.50
Toy, Truck, Fire, Hook & Ladder, Tin, Kingsbury, Windup, 18 In.Long, C.1930	17.00
Toy, Truck, Fire, Pressed Steel, Chemical, Hose, Rubber Tires	75.00
Toy, Truck, Fire, Pumper, Tin	22.50
Toy, Truck, Fire, Red, Yellow Wheels, Kenton, Iron, 8 1/2 In.Long	50.00
Toy, Truck, Fire, Rubber	3.00
Toy, Truck, Friction Drive, 14 In.Long	7.75
Toy, Truck, Hubley, No.505 Log Truck, Orange Cab, 5 Logs	16.00
Toy, Truck, Hubley, No.506 Carryall, Orange Flatbed, Round Scraper	16.00
Toy, Truck, Hubley, No.509 Dump Truck, Green Cab, Red Dump Body	16.00
Toy, Truck, Ladder, Two Drivers, Cast Iron, 5 In., White Rubber Wheels	25.00
Toy, Truck, Marx, Royal Van Co., C.1935	10.00
Toy, Truck, Pickup, Cast Iron, Arcade, 9 In.Long	35.00
Toy, Truck, Pickup, Tin, C.1930, 4 1/2 In.Long	12.50
Toy, Truck, Tin, Rapid Delivery *Illus*	38.00
Toy, Trunk, Doll's, C.1860	24.00
Toy, Trunk, Doll's, Dome Top, Lift Out Tray, Key, Lock, Leather Handles	20.00
Toy, Trunk, Doll's, Red, Clothing	45.00
Toy, Trunk, Doll's, Tray & Hatbox Compartments, 12 X 7 In.	22.00
Toy, Trunk, Doll's, 8 X 14 In.	6.00
Toy, Tub, Victorian, Tin, 4 1/2 In.Long, 2 In.Tall	12.00
Toy, Twist N Turns, Wood, Teach Tot Toy, Educational	10.00
Toy, Typewriter, Simplex, 1911	10.00
Toy, Union Flyer, Tootsie Toy, 3 Pieces	10.00
Toy, Van, Moving, Metal, Rubber Tires, Wyandotte, 8 In.	4.00
Toy, Village, Cardboard, Painted, Carved Animals, People, & Tree	18.50
Toy, Wagon, Aluminum	8.00
Toy, Wagon, Bear, Royal Circus, Hubley, 1920, 12 In.Long	65.00
Toy, Wagon, Borden's Milk, Wood & Tin, C.1930	30.00
Toy, Wagon, Child's, Tin & Wood, Wire Wheels, Horse Stencil, 18th Century	45.00
Toy, Wagon, Child's, Wagon Seat, Red Paint, Green Bed	90.00
Toy, Wagon, Coal, Hubley, 1906, Colored Man Driver, Painted	165.00
Toy, Wagon, Express, 1 Horse, Kenton, 1920, Cast Iron	100.00
Toy, Wagon, Milk, Hubley, 1920, Driver, Painted	85.00
Toy, Wagon, Two Horses, One, Driver, Signed Hubley	75.00
Toy, Wagon, 3, Wagon Master, & Scout, Budgie, England	10.00
Toy, Waiting Room, Tin, For Train Station	5.50
Toy, Washer, Automatic, Metal, Wolverine	5.00
Toy, Washer, Ringer Type, Metal, Wolverine, 12 In.High	5.00
Toy, Washer, Wringer, Three Little Pigs, Tin, Chein, 8 In.	15.00
Toy, Washing Machine, Sunny Suzy *Illus*	15.00
Toy, Washstand, Wringer Attached, Metal Bands On Tub, Wood Scrubboard	18.00
Toy, Washtub & Wringer	8.25
Toy, Whale, Blows Tiny Ball, Windup, Tin	3.00
Toy, Whistle, Shape Of Bird, Water	16.00
Toy, Windmill, Sand, Tin, T.Conn.	3.00
Toy, World Globe With Time Indicator, Precision, Reefloogle, 12 In.	3.50
Trap, see Tool, Trap	
Treen, Bowl, Footed, Black Paint & Stencil Decoration, 5 In.Diameter	55.00
Treen, Cup, Salt, Standard, Swirled Lid, Pair	45.00
Treen, Hand Holding Cup, Carved, 5 1/2 In.High	12.50
Treen, Matchbox, 4 In. *Illus*	6.50
Treen, Sugar, Covered, Red & Black Decoration, 5 In.High	45.00
Treen, Vase, Bird's-Eye Maple, 4 In.High	3.00

Trivets are now used to hold hot dishes. Most of the late nineteenth and early twentieth century trivets were made to hold hot irons. Iron or brass reproductions are being made of many of the old styles.

Trivet, Brass, Collapsible, 12 In.High	5.00
Trivet, Brass, Cutouts In Top Plate	25.00
Trivet, Brass, Urn With Fern	26.00
Trivet, Cast Iron, Enterprise	5.00
Trivet, Cathedral, Handle, Iron	5.95

Toy, Truck, Tin, Rapid Delivery
See Page 552

Toy, Washing Machine,
Sunny Suzy
See Page 552

Treen, Matchbox, 4 In.
See Page 552

Trivet, China, Marked Germany 244, Flowers	2.50
Trivet, Colt, Made In 1890 By Colt Firearms Co.	15.00
Trivet, Double Heart	6.50
Trivet, English, Penny Feet, Brass Top, 13 In.High	85.00
Trivet, Enterprise E, Iron	3.95
Trivet, Fender, Iron, British, Adjustable Clamp	15.00
Trivet, Footed, Iron	5.00
Trivet, George Washington, Iron	30.00
Trivet, Heart Shape, Brass, Footed	9.95
Trivet, Horseshoe Shape, Good Luck To All Who Use This Stand	9.95
Trivet, Howell H, Iron	4.95
Trivet, I Want U Comfort Iron, Iron	3.95
Trivet, Iron, Horseshoe, Hands, Heart, Star, Good Luck	8.00
Trivet, Iron, S.F.& Co., St.Louis, Mo., Roped Edge, Openwork Heart	15.00
Trivet, Iron, Tree Of Life	4.00
Trivet, Lacy Urn, Iron	4.75
Trivet, Openwork Design, Brass, Footed, Marked China	3.75
Trivet, Pattern Of Keys, Iron	4.50
Trivet, Pot Flowers, Handle, Miniature, Iron	5.00
Trivet, Pot Of Flowers Pattern, Footed, Iron	7.00
Trivet, Royal W, Iron	5.95
Trivet, Says Colt	14.00
Trivet, Spider Web, Iron	3.95
Trivet, Star, Sunburst, Cleveland Foundry Co., Iron	4.95
Trivet, The Peerless W, Double Pointed	5.95
Trivet, Triangular, Plain, Three Legs, Handle	40.00
Trivet, Twelve Squares Within A Square	7.50
Trivet, U Need It, Rosenbaum Mfg. Co., Iron	4.95
Trivet, Wrought Iron, Hinged Brace, Wavy Lines, Painted Black	25.00
Trivet, Wrought Iron, Penny Feet, Wooden Handle	10.00
Trivet, Wrought Iron, Triangular	5.00
Trivet, 5-Pointed Star In Circle	17.50
Trunk, Brass Buttons	40.00

Trunk, Camelback .... 25.00 To 40.00
Trunk, Child's, Wood, Painted Red Picture Of Priscilla & Bear 8.00
Trunk, Dome Top, Grained, Green Banding, 30 In.Wide 95.00
Trunk, Dome Top, Wooden, Paper Cover, 1824, 22 1/2 X 11 X 10 In. 25.00
Trunk, Grained Dome Top, 28 1/2 In.Wide 80.00
Trunk, Stagecoach, Cube Shape, 16 X 16 X 17 In. 25.00
Tucker, Pitcher, Gold & Polychrome Flowers & Leaves, 7 3/4 In.High 298.00
Tuthill, Chalice, Butterfly Pattern, Zigzag Chain Of Hobstars, Rayed Base 150.00
Tuthill, Compote, Intaglio Primroses, Strawberry Diamonds, Fluted Stem 195.00
Tuthill, Vase, Intaglio Cut, Flared Rim, 6 In. 95.00
Typewriter, Corona, Portable, Case, Circa 1930 .... 30.00
Typewriter, Hammond, Greek & English Type .... *Illus* 20.00

Typewriter, Hammond, Greek & English Type

Typewriter, Oliver, No.3, 1898 .... 15.00
Typewriter, Oliver, No.5 .... 35.00
Umbrella, Sterling Silver Chubby Cupid Handle 12.50
Val St.Lambert, Bottle, Cameo Cut, Signed, Cranberry Flowers On Frosted 45.00
Val St.Lambert, Bottle, Cologne, Feathered Ground, Cranberry Relief Flowers 45.00
Val St.Lambert, Bottle, Perfume, Cameo, Frosted Ground, Cut Floral, 6 In.Tall 45.00
Val St.Lambert, Box, Cameo, Flower, Berries, Leaf Ormolu Lid & Rim, Signed 175.00
Val St.Lambert, Box, Covered, Signed, 3 1/2 In.Diameter 25.00
Val St.Lambert, Box, Round, Green Glass, Infant & Mother, Intaglio Cut 60.00
Val St.Lambert, Compote, Polished Pontil, Gold, Ruby, Clear Stem, Signed 80.00
Val St.Lambert, Dish, Crescent, Cut Glass, Signed 8.00
Val St.Lambert, Dish, Violets, Leaves, Swirls, Frosted, Blue, Cameo 68.00
Val St.Lambert, Glass, Juice, Feather Ground, Cranberry Floral In Relief 30.00
Val St.Lambert, Inkwell, Silver Top, Feather Ground, Cranberry Floral 75.00
Val St.Lambert, Plate, Feathered Ground, Cranberry Floral In Relief 27.50
Val St.Lambert, Sugar & Creamer, Signed, Diamond Pattern, Panels On Upper 45.00
Val St.Lambert, Vase, Bud, Cameo, Signed, 6 1/2 In.High 75.00
Val St.Lambert, Vase, Cameo, Bottle Shape, Enameled Pattern In Purple 175.00
Vallerystahl, Bowl, Centerpiece, Upright Dolphin Base, Milk Glass 55.00
Vallerystahl, Bowl, Covered, Blue, Dog On Blanket, Flowers In Relief 49.50
Vallerystahl, Bowl, Raised Grapes, Leaves, Open, Deep, Signed 34.50
Vallerystahl, Boy On Elephant, Green 175.00
Vallerystahl, Dish & Saucer, Ice Cream, Signed, Amber 35.00
Vallerystahl, Dish, Butter, Cow, Marked, Oval 145.00
Vallerystahl, Dish, Candy, Irish Setter On Cover 75.00
Vallerystahl, Dish, Duck Shape, Blue, Cover, Signed 40.00
Vallerystahl, Dish, Fish Shape 65.00
Vallerystahl, Dish, Robin On Round Nest 75.00
Vallerystahl, Dish, Three Dolphin Footed, Blue Milk Glass, Shells Decor 32.50
Vallerystahl, Flowerpot, Cobalt Blue, Embossed Vintage, Signed 12.50
Vallerystahl, Hen On Nest, Miniature, Signed, Pair 28.00
Vallerystahl, Hen On Nest, White, Signed, 7 X 5 1/2 In. 50.00
Vallerystahl, Honey Pot, Raised Bees On Ribbed Base, Cover, Ball Finial 42.00
Vallerystahl, Mouse On Cabbage 75.00
Vallerystahl, Plate, Amber, Signed France, Small 16.00
Vallerystahl, Salt, Basket-Shaped, Blue 12.00
Vallerystahl, Snail On Strawberry 50.00
Vallerystahl, Squirrel On Acorn 65.00

Vallerystahl, Tub, Cover, Blue Milk Glass, Handle 15.00

Van Briggle Pottery was made by Artus Van Briggle in Colorado
Springs, Colorado, after 1901. Mr.Van Briggle had been a decorator at
the Rockwood Pottery of Cincinnati, Ohio, and he died in 1904. His
wares were original and had modeled relief decorations with a soft dull glaze.

Van Briggle, Bowl, Green, Dragonflies, Artist C.Lo Sypes, 9 1/2 In. 18.00
Van Briggle, Bowl, Petal Shape, Purple 10.00
Van Briggle, Bowl, Rose, Green Moth, Brown, 3 In. 10.00
Van Briggle, Centerpiece, Pedestal, Turquoise, Oak Leaves, Acorn Holder 30.00
Van Briggle, Jar, Persian Rose, 4 1/4 In. 16.00
Van Briggle, Sugar & Creamer, Plum Color, 2 1/2 In.Tall 22.00
Van Briggle, Toothpick, Handled, Signed 25.00
Van Briggle, Vase, Alpine Horn, Signed 12.50
Van Briggle, Vase, Blue, Signed Van Briggle C.L.Springs 17.50
Van Briggle, Vase, Butterfly On Side, Green 14.00
Van Briggle, Vase, Cabinet, Turquoise & Blue, Signed 15.00
Van Briggle, Vase, Decanter Type, Blue, 11 In.High, Pair 18.00
Van Briggle, Vase, Green & Brown, 3 1/2 In. 6.00
Van Briggle, Vase, Indian Heads, Blue, Green, Colorado Springs .... 35.00 To 40.00
Van Briggle, Vase, Lorelei, Figure Of Woman, Water, Blue, Dated 1919 .... 65.00
Van Briggle, Vase, Maroon Red To Blue Green, Bulbous Body, Dated 1905 .... 45.00
Van Briggle, Vase, Maroon, 6 In. 10.00
Van Briggle, Vase, Persian Rose, 9 1/2 In. 15.00
Van Briggle, Vase, Plum Design, Signed, 5 In.Tall 15.00
Van Briggle, Vase, Reddish Brown To Dark Blue, Raised Floral, 7 In. 18.00

Vasa Murrhina is the name of a glassware made by the Vasa Murrhina
Art Glass Company of Sandwich, Massachusetts, about 1884. The
glassware was transparent and was embedded with small pieces of colored glass
and metallic flakes. Some of the pieces were cased. The same type of glass
was made in England. Collectors often confuse Vasa Murrhina Glass
with Aventurine, Spatter, or Spangle Glass. There is much confusion
about what actually was made by the Vasa Murrhina Factory.

Vasa Murrhina, Basket, Ruffled, Cased White, Yellow Overlay, Silver Flecks 30.00
Vasa Murrhina, Bowl, Bride's, Blue, Crimped Edge, Silver Mica, Ormolu Holder 70.00
Vasa Murrhina, Bowl, Fruit, Raspberry To Pink, Mica Flecks, Silver Holder 125.00
Vasa Murrhina, Bowl, Rose, Deep Gold Color, 3 1/2 In.Tall, 2 In.Across Mouth 67.00
Vasa Murrhina, Dresser Set, Pink, Gold Mica Flecks, 4 Piece 28.50
Vasa Murrhina, Pitcher, Globular, Ruffled Rim, Red & Silver Mottling, Pink 60.00
Vasa Murrhina, Pitcher, Pink, Green, White & Apricot, Hand-Painted 35.00
Vasa Murrhina, Spooner, Cranberry, White 49.00
Vasa Murrhina, Tumbler, Cranberry Splashed With White, Green & Vaseline 18.00
Vasa Murrhina, Vase, Cranberry Ground, Allover Gold Mica, Swirls, 9 In.Tall 48.00
Vasa Murrhina, Vase, Ewer Type, Cased, Rose, Mica Flecks, Crimped Top 37.50
Vasa Murrhina, Vase, Fluted, Gold Flecks, Rose 35.00
Vasa Murrhina, Vase, Mica Crystal, Orange, Red, Yellow, Gold, 10 In., Pair 210.00
Vasa Murrhina, Vase, Multicolored, Gold Mica, Bulbous Base, 7 In. 35.00
Vasa Murrhina, Vase, Pink, Wide Pedestal Base, White Lining, 10 In. 38.00
Vasa Murrhina, Vase, White Striped, Ruffled Edge, Silver Mica, Peace 70.00
Vasart, Vase, Mottled Orange Flaring Top, Mottled White Below, Label 65.00

Vaseline Glass is a greenish yellow glassware resembling petroleum jelly.
Some Vaseline Glass is still being made in old and new styles. Pressed
Glass of the 1870s was often made of vaseline-colored glass. The old glass
was made with uranium, but the reproductions are being colored in a different
way. See Pressed Glass for more information about patterns that were also
made of vaseline-colored glass.

Vaseline Glass, Basket, Wishbone, Button, Beaded, Opalescent 25.00
Vaseline Glass, Basket, 2 1/2 X 6 X 2 In. 12.00
Vaseline Glass, Berry Set, Daisy & Button With Thumbprint Band, 6 Pieces 57.50
Vaseline Glass, Bottle, Inverted Panels, Bird, Insect, Enamel, Cleat, Stopper 40.00
Vaseline Glass, Bottle, Perfume, Cut & Etched Floral, Blue Stopper 25.00
Vaseline Glass, Bowl, Berry, Wreath & Shell, Footed, Six Sauces, Set 90.00
Vaseline Glass, Bowl, Daisy & Button, Three Cornered 22.00
Vaseline Glass, Bowl, Fruit, Daisy & Button, Footed, Scalloped, 7 In.Tall 57.50

Vaseline Glass, Bowl, Green, 4 In.High, 5 In.Diameter	15.00
Vaseline Glass, Bowl, Maple Leaf, Footed, 10 In.	32.50
Vaseline Glass, Bowl, Opalescent, Ruffled Edge, 9 X 5 In.	20.00
Vaseline Glass, Bowl, Rose, Opaline Swirl, Footed, Fluted	35.00
Vaseline Glass, Bowl, Shell & Tassel, Oval	28.50
Vaseline Glass, Candlestick, Apron Bottom, 8 1/2 In.Tall, Pair	14.00
Vaseline Glass, Candlestick, Petal Hex, Round, Pair	80.00
Vaseline Glass, Candlestick, Sandwich Glass Factory, Pair	150.00
Vaseline Glass, Candlestick, White, Enamel Ring, 6 In.Tall, Pair	55.00
Vaseline Glass, Candlestick, 3 In.Tall, Pair	12.00
Vaseline Glass, Castor, Pickle, Daisy & Button With V Ornament	100.00
Vaseline Glass, Castor, Pickle, Daisy & Button, Silver Holder & Tongs	80.00
Vaseline Glass, Celery, Canoe, 13 1/2 In.	25.00
Vaseline Glass, Celery, Cross Bar & Daisy Pattern	35.00
Vaseline Glass, Celery, Daisy & Button	24.50
Vaseline Glass, Celery, Diamond-Quilted	42.50
Vaseline Glass, Celery, Jacob's Ladder	97.50
Vaseline Glass, Celery, Rose Sprig	25.00
Vaseline Glass, Compote, Fine Cut & Panel, Shallow, 10 In.Diameter	30.00
Vaseline Glass, Compote, Jelly, Intaglio, Opalescent	22.50
Vaseline Glass, Compote, Opalescent, Beaded Pattern, 5 1/2 In.High	25.00
Vaseline Glass, Compote, Rose Sprig, Open, 7 In.	32.50
Vaseline Glass, Creamer, Alaska, Opalescent	31.00
Vaseline Glass, Creamer, Everglades, Opalescent	32.50
Vaseline Glass, Creamer, Palm Beach, Opaline	27.50
Vaseline Glass, Cruet, Hobnail	22.50
Vaseline Glass, Cruet, Inverted Rib, Opalescent, Stopper	40.00
Vaseline Glass, Cruet, Spanish Fern	14.50
Vaseline Glass, Cup, Punch, Daisy & Button	14.50
Vaseline Glass, Dish, Candy, Green, Opalescent, Cover	75.00
Vaseline Glass, Epergne, Lily, Magenta Edge, Diamond-Quilted	10.00
Vaseline Glass, Epergne, Opalescent, Lily Shaped, Ruffled Base, 17 In.	105.00
Vaseline Glass, Goblet, Daisy & Button With Thumbprint .... *Illus*	15.00

Vaseline Glass, Goblet, Daisy & Button With Thumbprint

Vaseline Glass, Goblet, Oval Panels	22.00
Vaseline Glass, Goblet, Panels Of Diamond Points, Canary	15.00
Vaseline Glass, Goblet, Wildflower	27.50
Vaseline Glass, Knife Rest, 4 Sides, Square Ends, Shank Fluted	30.00
Vaseline Glass, Pitcher, Rough Pontil	15.75
Vaseline Glass, Pitcher, Water, Basket Weave, 8 1/2 In.Tall	32.50
Vaseline Glass, Pitcher, Water, Daisy & Button With Crossbar	37.50
Vaseline Glass, Pitcher, Water, Daisy & Button, Pointed Panel	37.50
Vaseline Glass, Plate, Bread, Pleat & Panel	32.00
Vaseline Glass, Plate, Fine Cut, 10 1/4 In.	25.00
Vaseline Glass, Plate, Maple Leaf, 9 In.Diameter	20.00
Vaseline Glass, Plate, Swirl Border, 8 In.	5.00
Vaseline Glass, Plate, 1, 000-Eye, Square, 8 In.	16.00
Vaseline Glass, Platter, Daisy & Button, Oval, Open Handle	29.50
Vaseline Glass, Platter, Maple Leaf	22.00

Vaseline Glass, Salt Dip, Bird With Berry 7.50
Vaseline Glass, Salt, Fluted, Signed N, Individual 28.00
Vaseline Glass, Salt, Inverted Diamond, Pewter Top 9.00
Vaseline Glass, Salt, Wildflower, Blue, 2 1/2 X 3 1/4 In. 22.50
Vaseline Glass, Sauce, Daisy & Button 15.00
Vaseline Glass, Sauce, Three Panel, Footed 12.50
Vaseline Glass, Sauce, Wreath & Shell, Opalescent 12.50
Vaseline Glass, Shoe, Daisy & Button 22.50
Vaseline Glass, Shoe, Daisy & Button, Without Vamp 22.00
Vaseline Glass, Spooner, Inverted Thumbprint 18.50
Vaseline Glass, Spooner, Opalescent, Crimped Top 15.50
Vaseline Glass, Spooner, Opalescent, Fern 30.00
Vaseline Glass, Spooner, Opalescent, Paneled, 4 1/2 X 4 1/2 In. 35.00
Vaseline Glass, Sugar, Belmont 17.00
Vaseline Glass, Sugar, Cathedral, Open 18.00
Vaseline Glass, Sugar, Everglades, Opalescent, Cover 45.00
Vaseline Glass, Sugar, Open, Three Panels 14.00
Vaseline Glass, Tray, Clark's Teaberry Gum, Advertising, Stemme .... 13.50 To 22.50
Vaseline Glass, Tray, Hobnail, 14 X 10 In. 65.00
Vaseline Glass, Tumbler, Opalescent, Coin Spot, 4 In.Tall 32.50
Vaseline Glass, Vase, Allover Vine Decor, Sunburst On Bottom, 9 In. 18.00
Vaseline Glass, Vase, Car, Holder 18.00
Vaseline Glass, Vase, Flowers, Pink, Black Band, 8 In.Tall 10.00
Vaseline Glass, Vase, Vaseline To Opalescent 25.00

Venetian Glass has been made near Venice, Italy, from the thirteenth to
the twentieth century. Thin, colored glass with applied decorations is favored,
although many others types have been made.
Venetian Glass, Bowl, Finger, Blown, Applied Gargole Handles, C.1750 .... 35.00
Venetian Glass, Cornucopia, Blue, Gold, White, Serpent Around Body, On Stand 60.00
Venetian Glass, Cup & Saucer, Punch, Green To Clear, Gold Lacy Design 17.50
Venetian Glass, Goblet, Topaz, Green & Crystal, With Prunties, 8 In. 50.00
Venetian Glass, Salt, Swan, Amber, Gold 12.50
Venetian Glass, Vase, Footed, Pink & White Swirls, Blue Rim, Knop Stem 12.50
Venetian Glass, Vase, Hobnail, Pink Luster, 200 3/4 In.Hobs, Pair 3000.00
Venetian, Vase, Flowers, Fluted Top, Lime, White, 9 1/2 In. 20.00

Verlys Glass was made in France after 1931. Verlys was also made in the
United States. The glass is either blown or molded. The american glass
is signed with a diamond-point-scratched name, but the french pieces are marked
with a molded signature.
Verlys, Bowl, Centerpiece, Flying Birds Make Footrest, Fish, Signed 48.00
Verlys, Bowl, Fruit, Wheat Pattern, France, 11 1/2 In. 42.00
Verlys, Bowl, Pinecone Pattern, Signed, 6 In.Diameter 10.00
Verlys, Bowl, Poppies, Frosted, Signed, 13 1/2 In.Diameter 55.00
Verlys, Bowl, Shallow, Birds, Beer, & Deer, 11 1/2 In.Diameter 125.00
Verlys, Bowl, Signed, Clear, Frosted Cupid In Bottom, Hearts 48.50
Verlys, Bowl, Signed, Frosted Pinecone, 6 In. 15.00
Verlys, Box, Rectangular, 2 Birds Flying On Frosted 45.00
Verlys, Box, Round, Amber Butterflies On Lid, Filigree Knob, Signed, 6 In. 72.50
Verlys, Candy, Thistle Pattern, Signed 19.00
Verlys, Planter, Frosted, Flower & Leaf Motif, 10 In., Greek Key Base, Signed 25.00
Verlys, Plaque, Signed, Raised Pattern Of 3 Fish, Iridescent 45.00
Verlys, Vase, Bulbous, Butterflies In Relief, 5 1/2 In.Tall 37.50
Verlys, Vase, Clear, Frosted, Flowers, Leaves, Signed, 9 In.High 75.00
Verlys, Vase, Dragonfly Design, Frosted, Signed, 5 1/4 In.Tall 50.00
Verlys, Vines, Berry Knobs, Frosted, Clear, 6 1/2 In.Tall, 7 In.Wide 40.00

Verre De Soie Glass was first made by Frederick Carder at the
Steuben Glass Works from about 1905 to 1930. It is an iridescent glass
of soft white or very, very pale green. The name means glass of silk, and it
does resemble silk. Other factories have made Verre De Soie, and some of
the english examples were made of different colors. Verre De Soie is an
art glass and is not related to the iridescent pressed white carnival glass
mistakenly called by its name.
Verre De Soie, see also Steuben

Verre De Soie, Barrel, Biscuit, Hand-Painted, Brass Frame, Handles, Lid	72.00
Verre De Soie, Basket, Bride, Flowers, Leaves, Gold, Yellow, Iridescent	100.00
Verre De Soie, Bottle, Perfume, 2 1/2 In.High	25.00
Verre De Soie, Bowl, Matching Underplate	38.00
Verre De Soie, Bride's Basket, Gold Leaves, Enamel Floral, Silver Holder	125.00
Verre De Soie, Compote, Wreaths & Floral, Copper Wheel Engraved, Rainbow	90.00
Verre De Soie, Epergne, Five Lilies, Ice Green, White, Gold Frame	195.00
Verre De Soie, Hair Receiver, Engraved Design, Sterling Lid, 2 1/2 In.Tall	38.00
Verre De Soie, Perfume, Floral Design, Melon Shaped Body, 7 In.Tall	165.00
Verre De Soie, Pitcher, Tumble Up, Glass Fits Inside Top, Steuben	100.00
Verre De Soie, Salt, Footed, Steuben	35.00
Verre De Soie, Sherbet, Underplate, Set Of 9	300.00
Verre De Soie, Tazza, Rainbow Colors, Fluted Edge, Twisted Stem, 6 In.Tall	75.00
Verre De Soie, Vase, Blue, Green Aurene Filigree, Flowerpot Styoe, Steuben	17.50
Verre De Soie, Vase, Bud, Floral Decor, Frosty White, Iridescent, 8 In.	16.00
Verre De Soie, Vase, Fan Shape, Twisted Stem, Flower Form, 6 In.High	175.00
Verre De Soie, Vase, Flower Form, Braided Stem, 8 In.	50.00
Vienna Art, Plate, Anheuser Busch, Dated 1905	47.50
Vienna Art, Plate, Portrait, Signed Wagner, Patent 1905	10.00
Vienna Art, Plate, 1909, Advertising On Back	36.50
Vienna Art, Tray, Coca Cola, Topless	150.00
Vienna Art, Tray, Hole For Hanging	25.00
Vienna Art, Tray, Kuntz, Remler Co., Chicago	12.00
Vienna Art, Tray, Ludwig Co., Philadelphia	37.50
Vienna Art, Tray, Redhead	7.50
Vienna Du Paquier, Beaker & Saucer, Sepia Figures, Landscapes, C.1745, Pair	210.00
Vienna Du Paquier, Beaker, Armorial, Puce Camaieu Painted, C.1725-30	400.00
Vienna Du Paquier, Beaker, Landscape, Figures, C.1730-40	500.00
Vienna Du Paquier, Coffeepot, Pear Shape, Flowering Oriental Tree, C.1720	500.00
Vienna Du Paquier, Group, Anna & Maria, C.1744-49, 9 1/2 In.Tall	600.00
Vienna Du Paquier, Plate, Sevres Style Decorated, C.1770, Pair	250.00
Vienna Du Paquier, Teabowl, Schwarzlot Decorated, C.1730	160.00
Vienna Du Paquier, Teacup & Saucer, Chinoiserie Decor, C.1780	200.00
Vieux Paris, Dessert Set, Floral Garlands, Gilt, C.1840, 29 Piece	50.00
Vieux Paris, Jardiniere, Continuous Fenced Garden, Classical Motifs, C.1825	40.00
Vieux Paris, Pot De Creme, Apple Green, Pear Shape, Scroll Handle, C.1830, 16	375.00
Vieux Paris, Tea & Coffee Set, Gold, Flowers, C.1800, 20 Piece	450.00
Vieux Paris, Tureen, Covered, Boat Shape, Applied Volute Handles, C.1830	110.00
Vieux Paris, Urn, Campana, Masks, Baskets Of Flowers, Landscapes, C.1835, Pair	525.00

Villeroy & Boch Pottery of Mettlach, Germany, was founded in 1841.
The firm made many types of pottery, including the famous Mettlach Steins.

Villeroy & Boch, see also Stein	
Villeroy & Boch, Bowl & Pitcher, Blue Decorations	37.50
Villeroy & Boch, Bowl, Punch, White, Blue, Mercury Mark, Signed	200.00
Villeroy & Boch, Cake Set, 7 Pieces, Pedestal Plate, Green, Mums	60.00
Villeroy & Boch, Pitcher, Cream, Saxony, Blue	25.00
Villeroy & Boch, Plate, Wall, Wallerfangen, 10 1/2 In.	45.00
Villeroy & Boch, Soup, Onion Pattern	8.00
Villeroy & Boch, Tile, Floral Design, Green, White	12.50
Walt Disney, Matchbox Holder, Three Pigs	5.00
Walt Disney, Mug, Three Pigs	10.00

Warwick China was made in Wheeling, West Virginia, in a pottery factory
founded in 1887.

Warwick, Mug, Gloucester Fisherman	20.00
Warwick, Platter, Cover, Squab	14.50
Warwick, Vase, Flower Spray, Brown, Red, Ivory, Handles, 12 In.Tall	30.00
Warwick, Vase, Red, Bulbous, Flaring Top, Portrait Of Lady, Artist Boehm	35.00

Watch Fobs were worn on watch chains. They were popular during victorian
times.

Watch Fob, Adam's Horse Drawn Grader	18.50
Watch Fob, Advertising, To Earn More, Learn More, No Strap	3.95
Watch Fob, Agate With Insect Intaglio, Rectangular	10.00
Watch Fob, Boston Revolver Club, Sterling, No Strap	3.95

Watch Fob, Buick	2.50
Watch Fob, Campaign, Strap, Buckle, Brass, Bryan, Kern, 1908	13.00
Watch Fob, Chicago Fair, 1933	5.50
Watch Fob, Cigar Cutter, Floral, Sterling	9.00
Watch Fob, Commemorative, Terre Haute Masonic Temple, Copper, Dated 1915	9.00
Watch Fob, Dated 1914	7.50
Watch Fob, Drink Cherry Smash	22.00
Watch Fob, Elk's Tooth	4.00
Watch Fob, Elk's Tooth, Insignia, Gold Cap	9.00
Watch Fob, Exposition, 1833-1933	6.00
Watch Fob, Fisherman In Stream, No Strap	2.75
Watch Fob, Ford	2.50
Watch Fob, Glass, Shield With Dates 1861-1865, U V L	17.50
Watch Fob, Gold Mesh, Buckle To Hang On Belt	6.00
Watch Fob, Great Seal Of U.S., No Strap	3.95
Watch Fob, Green River	12.00
Watch Fob, Hinman Milkers, Embossed, Enameled, Leather Strap	4.00
Watch Fob, Lindbergh's Flight, 1927, Compass	6.00
Watch Fob, Maxwell Velie	2.50
Watch Fob, Metal, Bust Of Lincoln	9.00
Watch Fob, Metal, We Must Cover The Earth With Atlas Paint	8.00
Watch Fob, Raised Letters B.S.A., No Strap	3.75
Watch Fob, Roosevelt-Fairbanks, 1904	18.50
Watch Fob, Safety First, Metal & Porcelain, Commercial Travelers, N.Y.	4.50
Watch Fob, Says Spirit, Mind, Body, No Strap	3.75
Watch Fob, Shape Of Stove, Sterling Ranges, Sill Stove Works, Rochester	30.00
Watch Fob, Shield Shape, Bloodstone, Gold Filled	10.00
Watch Fob, Sterling Silver, C.1900	2.50
Watch Fob, Victor Phonograph With Dog, 1904, Model I	25.00
Watch Fob, World War Veteran, A.E.F., Eagle, Strap	3.95
Watch Fob, Yellowstone Park, Deer	3.75
Watch, American Watch Co., Gold Filled Hunting Case, Lever Set	75.00
Watch, Betsy Ross, Hunting Case, Gold, 7 Jewel	75.00
Watch, Braille, Wrist, Up & Down	25.00
Watch, Burlington, Eagle On Back, Open Face	65.00
Watch, Cameo, Set As Watch Cover On Ring, Lady's	55.00
Watch, Canton, Ohio, Hunting Case, 17 Jewel, Gold	15.00
Watch, Chain Driven, Key Wind, Closed Case	15.00
Watch, Chain Driven, Key Wind, Pocket, Carved, R.Johnstone, London	45.00
Watch, Child's, Hopalong Cassidy, Good Luck From Hoppy	45.00
Watch, Chronograph, Swiss, 14k Gold & Enamel, Hunting Case, Pearl Borders	675.00
Watch, Cinderella, Walt Disney	35.00
Watch, Clock, Gold Case, Thomas Tompion, London, C.1690, Engraved, Key	425.00
Watch, Coin Silver, Jeweled, Hunting Case, Inscribed Paul Breton, Geneva	50.00
Watch, Crog Geneva, Closed Face, Silver Case	15.00
Watch, Desk, William Bond & Son, Boston, No.387-1870, Cylinder Escapement	170.00
Watch, Dueber, Hunting Case, 4 Jewel, Stem Wind	65.00
Watch, Dueber, Hunting Case, 15 Jewel	65.00
Watch, Edward Prior, London, 1845, Silver, Triple Case, Turkish Numerals	110.00
Watch, Elgin, Closed Case, Gold, Presentation, May, 1922	27.00
Watch, Elgin, Closed Gold Case, Presentation, Engraved 1928 On Back	37.50
Watch, Elgin, Gold Hunting Case, Key Wind	175.00
Watch, Elgin, Hunting Case, Coin Silver, Key Wind	35.00
Watch, Elgin, Hunting Case, Gold Filled	85.00
Watch, Elgin, Hunting Case, 15 Jewel	65.00
Watch, Elgin, Key Wind & Key Set, Size 18, No.528759, C.1877, Dueber Case	40.00
Watch, Elgin, Lady's, Hunting Case, Gold, 7 Jewel	85.00
Watch, Elgin, Lady's, Hunting Case, 14k Gold, 15 Jewel	125.00
Watch, Elgin, Lady's, Hunting Case, 7 Jewel	75.00
Watch, Elgin, Man's, Open Face, Pocket, Gold	7.50
Watch, Elgin, Octagon Case	8.50
Watch, Elgin, Open Face, 7 Jewel, South Bend, 20 Year Gold Case, Carved	35.00
Watch, Elgin, Pocket, Gold Double Case, C.1880	150.00
Watch, Elgin, Railroad, Gold Filled	135.00
Watch, Elgin, Shockmaster, Open Face, Pocket, 17 Jewel, C.1874	10.00
Watch, Elgin, Size 12, Keystone Silveroid Case, C.1926, 5 Jewels	25.00

Watch, **Elgin**, 15 Jewel, Gold Open Face Case, 1 7/8 In.Diameter 40.00
Watch, **English**, Hunting Case, Key Wind, Gold Plated, C.1815, Engraved 76.00
Watch, **F.C.A.Tiebner**, C.1800, Silver, Quarter Repeating Clock, Roman 475.00
Watch, **Fusee**, Chain Driven, Silver, Key Wind, C.1840 .... 75.00
Watch, **Fusee**, Improved Patent 17.00
Watch, **George Oram & Sons**, London, C.1850, Pocket, Chronometer, Engraved 250.00
Watch, **Gold & Enamel**, Open Face, Pocket, L'epine, Paris, C.1830 .... 200.00
Watch, **Greenwich Lever W.E.Watts**, Nottingham 15.00
Watch, **Hamilton**, Gold, Railroad .... 70.00 To 75.00
Watch, **Hamilton**, Lady's, Art Deco, 14k Gold, Classic Ornament 75.00
Watch, **Hamilton**, Man's, Open Face, Pocket, Lever Set, C.1899 .... 10.00
Watch, **Hamilton**, Man's, Open Face, Pocket, Lever Set, C.1914 .... 15.00
Watch, **Hamilton**, Man's, 1930, Art Deco, 14k White Gold, Diamonds, Square 45.00
Watch, **Hampden**, Hunting Case, Gold Plated, 17 Jewel 5.00
Watch, **Hampden**, Lady's, Hunting Case, Lever Set 65.00
Watch, **Hopalong Cassidy**, Leather Band 52.50
Watch, **Howard**, 21 Jewel, Open Face 95.00
Watch, **Hunting Case**, Gold, 15 Jewel .... 45.00 To 95.00
Watch, **Hunting Case**, Key Wind, Engraved Floral, Scroll, Steam Engine, Elgin 95.00
Watch, **Hunting Case**, Porcelain Face, Marked M.W.Co., Gold Filled, Engraved 75.00
Watch, **Hunting Case**, 15 Jewel, Lever Set 65.00
Watch, **Imperial**, Hunting Case, 15 Jewel, Gold 25.00
Watch, **Ingersoll**, Pluto 20.00
Watch, **Ingersoll**, Yankee, Dollar, C.1903 .... 28.00
Watch, **Jules Amidon**, Locle, C.1880, Gold, Open Face, Pocket, Engraved 120.00
Watch, **Jules Jurgensen**, Copenhagen, Patent 1867, 18k Gold Hunting Case 1000.00
Watch, **Lady's**, Gold Filled, Hunting Case, Illinois 42.50
Watch, **Lady's**, Hunting Case, Gold Filled, Engraved Decor, Elgin 60.00
Watch, **Lady's**, Hunting Case, Gold, 7 Jewel 75.00
Watch, **Lady's**, Hunting Case, Sterling Silver, Marked U.S.Assay, Elgin 60.00
Watch, **Lady's**, Hunting Case, Swiss Movement, Scene On Case, 14k Gold 85.00
Watch, **Lady's**, Open Face, Engraved Front & Back, Sheffield, 18k, Long Chain 100.00
Watch, **Lady's**, Open Face, Swiss Movement, Silver, Turquoise Enamel On Front 35.00
Watch, **Lady's**, Waltham, Open Face, Fleur-De-Lis In Rose Diamonds 150.00
Watch, **Lady's**, 14k Gold, Lapel, Open Face, Celtic 45.00
Watch, **Longines**, Lady's, Art Deco, 14k White Gold, Lines & Squares 50.00
Watch, **Longines**, Lady's, Hunting Case, 7 Jewel, Gold 60.00
Watch, **M.J.Tobias**, London, Silver, Key Wind, Etched Thames Scene 10.00
Watch, **Man's**, Gold, Providence, Pocket, 17 Jewels 15.00
Watch, **Man's**, Open Face, Gold Case, Waltham 22.50
Watch, **Minute Repeater**, 14k Gold, Open Face 750.00
Watch, **Musical**, Gold, Repeating, C.1810, Virgule Escapement 1200.00
Watch, **Open Face**, French, Silver, Pocket, 19th Century, Breguet A Paris 225.00
Watch, **Open Face**, Gold, Pocket, C.1830, Cylinder Movement, Chain 160.00
Watch, **Open Face**, Hinged Bezel, Floral, Order Of Garter Insignia, Gold 125.00
Watch, **Open Face**, Marked Guar.20 Years, Phila.Watch Case Co., Elgin 85.00
Watch, **Open Face**, Porcelain Face, Marked Amer.Waltham Watch Co., Pat.1879 .... 60.00
Watch, **Open Face**, Porcelain Face, Marked C.Luther, Engraved Engine & Tender 65.00
Watch, **Open Face**, Porcelain Face, Marked R.R.Special, Engraved Steam Engine 85.00
Watch, **Open Face**, Silver Case 12.00
Watch, **P.Combret**, Lyons, C.1620, Rock Crystal, Gold, & Enamel, Octagonal 4200.00
Watch, **Pair Case**, Gold & Enamel, Repeating, John Leroux, Charing Cross, 1778 .... 1300.00
Watch, **Pair Case**, Gold, Joseph Martineau, Sr., London, 1725, 5 Fables 1200.00
Watch, **Pair Case**, Gold, Pocket, Isa.Roberts, London, 1755, Verge Movement 290.00
Watch, **Pair Case**, Silver, Pocket, George Graham, London, Arabic Figures 40.00
Watch, **Pendant**, 2 Parts, Enameled Flower & Leaves, Cyclamens 250.00
Watch, **Pepine**, Paris, Key Wind, Bull's-Eye, Gold Case, Miniature Of Lady 275.00
Watch, **Pocket**, French, Gold, C.1820, Cylinder Movement, White Enamel Dial 50.00
Watch, **Pocket**, Gold, Enamel, 1788 .... *Illus* 450.00
Watch, **Pocket**, Gold, 1780 .... *Illus* 200.00
Watch, **Pocket**, Hunting, Gold, Paris, 1900 .... *Illus* 625.00
Watch, **Pocket**, Silver-Gilt, Enamel, 2 1/4 In.Diameter .... *Illus* 700.00
Watch, **Pocket**, Waltham, 17 Jewel, Gold Case, Engraved Rse 25.00
Watch, **Pocket**, 18k Gold, Minute Repeating, Patek Philippe & Co., Pa., Chain 875.00
Watch, **R.Johnstone**, London, Brass, Carved, Chain Driven, Key Wind 25.00
Watch, **Railroad**, Hunting Case, Engineer's Special Marked On Face 125.00

Watch, Pocket, Gold, 1780
See Page 560

Watch, Pocket,
Hunting, Gold, Paris, 1900
See Page 560

Watch, Pocket,
Gold, Enamel, 1788
See Page 560

Watch, Pocket, Silver-Gilt,
Enamel, 2 1/4 In.Diameter
See Page 560

Watch, Railroad, Open Face, Marked Century, U.S.A., Seth Thomas No.221109 .... 75.00
Watch, Railroad, Open Face, 21 Jewel, Chrome Case, Carved 75.00
Watch, Railroad, Open Face, 21 Jewel, Hamilton Railway Special, Gold Case 125.00
Watch, Reed & Co., Cambridge, C.1790, Gold & Enamel, Open Face 525.00
Watch, Repeating, Gold & Enamel, C.1820, Father Time Rowing Cupid On Dial 600.00
Watch, Repeating, Gold, Hunting Case, Pocket, Breguet Et Fils, C.1822 .... 1300.00
Watch, Roy Rogers & Trigger, Leather Band 62.50
Watch, Size 18, Hampden, Hunting Case, Engine Turnings, Porcelain Dial 110.00
Watch, Snow White, 1930s, Stretch Band 19.00
Watch, Stand, Carved, Wood, Folds Flat 10.00
Watch, Standard, Size 16, 15 Jewels, Defiance Goldene Case 25.00
Watch, Standard, Size 16, 7 Jewels, Goldene Case, Engraved Steam Engine 30.00
Watch, Stem Wind, 7 Jewel, Heavy 9.00
Watch, Swiss, Constantaras Freres, C.1900, Gold, Hunting Case, Pocket 500.00
Watch, Swiss, Gold, Hunting Case, Pocket, Patek Philippe & Co., Geneva, C.1881 .... 275.00
Watch, Swiss, Gold, Pearl Set, Pocket, Moulinie Freres & Cie, Geneva, C.1820 .... 800.00
Watch, Swiss, Key Wind, Silver Case 13.50
Watch, Swiss, Ryrie Bros., Toronto, Gold, Open Face, Minute Repeating, Pocket 575.00
Watch, Swiss, Schumann & Sons, N.Y., C.1890, Gold, Hunting Case, Calendar 1500.00
Watch, Swiss, Thin Gold, Enamel, Hunting Case, Pocket, Bautte & Moynier 450.00
Watch, Thos.Russell, Liverpool, Key Wind 15.00
Watch, Tiffany, Sterling, 8 Day, 11 Oz. 250.00

Watch, Tiffany, 18k Gold, Open Face	600.00
Watch, Verge, Book Form, Nicolaus Feidl-Signed, Gilt Metal, Engraved	325.00
Watch, Verge, Gilt Metal & Enamel, Scene Galante, Lnt.Vallon, Geneva, C.1800	400.00
Watch, Verge, Gold & Enamel, John Wright, London, C.1760, Roman Numerals	600.00
Watch, Verge, 4 Color Gold & Enamel, Michael Dobler, Munich, C.1780	200.00
Watch, Verge, 4 Color Gold, Bartholomy, Paris, C.1760, White Dial	180.00
Watch, Waltham, Closed Gold Case, Presentation, March, 1918	37.50
Watch, Waltham, Gold Plated, 24 Hour Enamel Dial, C.1888	43.00
Watch, Waltham, Hunting Case, Diamond, 7 Jewel	115.00
Watch, Waltham, Size 18, 17 Jewels, C.1908, Silveroid Swing-Out Case	45.00
Watch, Waltham, Stem Wind, Silver	9.00
Watch, Waterbury, Silver, Gun & Holster Leather Fob Says Redwood Highway	6.00

Waterford Type Glass resembles the famous glass made in the Waterford
Glass works in Ireland. It is a clear glass that was often cut for
decoration. Modern glass is still being made in Waterford, Ireland.

Waterford Glass, Urn, Diamond Cut, Square Base, 19th Century, 7 3/4 In., Pair	300.00
Waterford Type, Decanter, Heavy, 15 In.	49.00
Waterford Type, Decanter, Hollow Stopper	12.50
Waterford Type, Pitcher & Plate, 4 In. ...... *Illus*	125.00

Waterford Type, Pitcher & Plate, 4 In.

Wavecrest Glass is a white glassware manufactured by the Pairpoint
Manufacturing Company of New Bedford, Massachusetts, and some french
factories. It was then decorated by the C.F.Monroe Company of
Meriden, Connecticut. The glass was painted pastel colors and decorated
with flowers. The name Wavecrest was used after 1898.

Wavecrest, Basket, Shell Pink Inside, Silver Plate Bail & Rim	145.00
Wavecrest, Bell, Desk, Rose, Pink, Yellow, Brass Base, 4 1/2 In.Tall	200.00
Wavecrest, Bowl, Enameled Floral, Ormolu Collar, Handles, Red Banner Mark	75.00
Wavecrest, Bowl, Flowers, Leaves, White, Green, Brass Collar, Square, 6 1/2 In.	68.00
Wavecrest, Bowl, Green, White, Floral Panels, Footed, Signed, 5 In.Square	195.00
Wavecrest, Bowl, Open, Blue, Pink, Carnations, Signed, 5 In.	55.00
Wavecrest, Bowl, Pansies, Metal Rim, Signed, 5 1/2 In.	80.00
Wavecrest, Bowl, Salad, Fork & Spoon, Swirl Design, Blue & Cream, Rust Floral	175.00
Wavecrest, Bowl, White, Flowers, Signed, 6 1/2 In.Square	165.00
Wavecrest, Box, Aqua, Scrolls, Panels, Floral, Plain Ormolu Rim	120.00
Wavecrest, Box, Blue Enamel Floral, Hinged, Lining, 3 In.Square	65.00
Wavecrest, Box, Blue, Scrolls, Panels, Pink Flowers, Ormolu Rim	125.00
Wavecrest, Box, Collars & Cuffs, Open, Banner Mark	155.00
Wavecrest, Box, Creamy Puffed Decor, Violets, Lining, Ormolu	110.00
Wavecrest, Box, Cuff Link, Ormolu Rim, Signed, 3 1/2 In.	65.00
Wavecrest, Box, Flowers, Bulbous, Hand-Painted, Yellow, Blue, Green, Signed	70.00
Wavecrest, Box, Flowers, Pink, Yellow, Green, Signed, Cover, 7 1/2 In.Wide	275.00
Wavecrest, Box, Flowers, White, Pink, Brass Collar, Open	40.00
Wavecrest, Box, Forget-Me-Not, White, Blue, Brass Collar	55.00
Wavecrest, Box, Hand-Painted Flowers, Signed, 3 X 3 In.	85.00
Wavecrest, Box, Hinged, Lock & Key, Signed, Red Mark	185.00
Wavecrest, Box, Hinged, Raised Shell Design, Blue, Footed, Signed	195.00
Wavecrest, Box, Hinged, Swirl, Square Top, White With Pink Flowers	60.00

Wavecrest, Box, Jewel, Chrysanthemums, Blue, Ivory, Signed, Lid, 3 In.Diameter	90.00
Wavecrest, Box, Jewel, Daisies, Yellow, White, Lid, Unsigned, 4 1/2 In.Diameter	90.00
Wavecrest, Box, Jewel, Daisy, Leaves, White, Green, Cover, 3 X 2 1/2 In.Square	100.00
Wavecrest, Box, Jewel, Flowers, Blue, White, Hinged Lid, 3 In.Square	68.00
Wavecrest, Box, Jewel, Flowers, White, Pink, Blue, Yellow, Cover, 4 In.Tall	220.00
Wavecrest, Box, Jewel, Pink, Blue, Gray Flowers, Enamel, Ormolu, Hinged Lid	200.00
Wavecrest, Box, Jewel, Pink, Gray, Blue Floral, Enamel, Swirls, Signed	195.00
Wavecrest, Box, Jewel, Violets, Blue, Ivory, Paper Label, 3 In.Square	80.00
Wavecrest, Box, Jewelry, Blue, Shells & Flowers, Red Banner Mark	150.00
Wavecrest, Box, Jewelry, Shell Design, Blue, Mark Red Banner	138.00
Wavecrest, Box, Jewelry, Signed, Floral, Hinged, 7 In. Wide, 4 In.High	225.00
Wavecrest, Box, Letterholder, Puffy, Signed, 6 In.Long, 4 1/4 In.High	165.00
Wavecrest, Box, Open, Puffed, Yellow, Blue Floral, White Panels, 3 In.Square	120.00
Wavecrest, Box, Pale Green, Pink Flowers, White Scrolls Inside, Mark	95.00
Wavecrest, Box, Pansy Design, Yellow, Pink, Signed, 2 1/2 X 4 X 3 In.	225.00
Wavecrest, Box, Pink, Blue & White Forget-Me-Nots, Gray Ferns, Brass Rims	375.00
Wavecrest, Box, Raised Shell Pattern, Enameled Pansy, Lined, Signed	145.00
Wavecrest, Box, Square, White, Forget-Me-Nots	75.00
Wavecrest, Box, Swirl, Paper Label, Cream, Blue & White Flowers	140.00
Wavecrest, Box, Trinket, Flowers, Pink, Cobalt Blue, Brass Handle, Signed	60.00
Wavecrest, Box, Venetian Harbor Scene, Green, Pink Highlights, Signed	225.00
Wavecrest, Box, White Satin Finish, Puffy	100.00
Wavecrest, Cigarette Urn, Footed	145.00
Wavecrest, Dish, Flowers, Gold Rim, Handles, Fully Marked, 7 In.Diameter	200.00
Wavecrest, Dish, Hand-Painted Floral, Red Banner Mark, 3 In.Diameter	65.00
Wavecrest, Dish, Open, Brass Rim & Handles, Signed	35.00
Wavecrest, Dish, Open, Embossed Decor, Painted Floral, Brass Handles, Signed	47.00
Wavecrest, Dish, Pin, Openwork, Reliefs, Wide Ormolu Handles, Signed, 3 In.	95.00
Wavecrest, Dish, Pin, Swirl Pattern, Posies, Signed, 4 In.Wide	50.00
Wavecrest, Dish, Sweetmeat, Covered, Red Banner Mark, Silver Lid & Bail	150.00
Wavecrest, Dish, White, Flowers, Openwork Ears, Brass Top, Unsigned, 3 In.	45.00
Wavecrest, Dish, White, Raised Shell Design, Brass Top, Signed, 3 In.	55.00
Wavecrest, Dresser Piece, Open Top, Floral, Brass Rim, Signed	75.00
Wavecrest, Holder, Photo, Embossed Clover Decor, Signed	225.00
Wavecrest, Holder, Switch, Pin Tray, Signed, 4 1/2 X 4 1/2 X 9 In.Long	475.00
Wavecrest, Humidor, Roses, Pink, Blue, Signed, Lid, 6 In.High, 4 In.Diameter	200.00
Wavecrest, Humidor, Square, Cigars	250.00
Wavecrest, Jar, Biscuit, Silver Plate Lid, Signed C.F.M., Pink Blossoms	145.00
Wavecrest, Jar, Biscuit, Yellow, Floral Panels, Resilvered Lid & Bail	100.00
Wavecrest, Jar, Cookie, Signed, Hand-Painted Floral, Silver Handle	105.00
Wavecrest, Jar, Cracker, Flowers, Pink, Yellow, Silver Lid & Handle, 7 In.Tall	80.00
Wavecrest, Jar, Cracker, Made Into Lamp, Lime Green, Red Flowers	40.00
Wavecrest, Jar, Cracker, Scrolls, Flowers, Lavender, Raised	75.00
Wavecrest, Jar, Cracker, Silver Lid & Bail	85.00
Wavecrest, Jar, Sweetmeat, Flowers, Scrolls, Tan, Blue, Silver Handle & Lid	185.00
Wavecrest, Planter, Basket Weave, Floral, Foliage, Brass Liner	175.00
Wavecrest, Salt & Pepper, Enameled Erie Twist, Patent By Helmschmied, Pair	60.00
Wavecrest, Salt & Pepper, Hand-Painted Flowers	68.00
Wavecrest, Shaker, Salt & Pepper, Signed, Raised Petals, Hand-Painted, Pair	75.00
Wavecrest, Shaker, Salt, Swirled Rib, Flowers, Enamel, Pink, Unsigned	22.50
Wavecrest, Toothpick, Forget-Me-Not Design, Blue, Footed	75.00
Wavecrest, Tray, Dresser, Flowers, Pink, Grey, Blue, Signed, 4 1/2 In.Long	95.00
Wavecrest, Tray, Pin, Double Handle	36.50
Wavecrest, Vase, Apple Blossom, Green, Brown, Footed, Signed, 13 1/2 In.Tall	375.00
Wavecrest, Vase, Flowers, Red, Barss Collar, Signed, 3 In.Tall, 3 1/2 In.Wide	75.00
Wavecrest, Vase, Signed Kelva, Salmon Color Ground, White Cosmos, 13 In.	175.00
Weapon, Armor, Roman, Nickel Plate, Handmade For Movie Ben Hur	40.00
Weapon, Ax, Boarding, Csn, Southern, Dated & Hallmarked, Brooks Brothers	52.00
Weapon, Bayonet, Colonial	15.00
Weapon, Bayonet, Iron, Civil War Gun	22.00
Weapon, Bayonet, Musket Socket For M1795, U.S., Initials E.W.	37.50
Weapon, Bayonet, Saber Sword, Union, Voslyn, Iron, Scabbard, 1865	95.00
Weapon, Belt Plate, Brass, British Cross, C.1800-10, Oval, Crown, Engraved	69.50
Weapon, Blunderbuss, English, 1680-1700, Iron Barrel, Walnut Stock	425.00
Weapon, Boot, Carbine, For M1873 Or Spencer, U.S., Marked June, 1884	39.50
Weapon, Box, Cartridge, Infantry, U.S., Waters Pattern, Leather, Wood	67.50

Weapon, **Box**, Cartridge, Leather, Dated 1880	2.50
Weapon, **Box**, Patch, Agate, Scotch, Hinged, Stone On Both Sides	32.00
Weapon, **Broadax**	10.00
Weapon, **Broadsword**, Scottish Highland, Basket Hilt, C.1720-50	275.00
Weapon, **Cannon Ball**, Civil War, Small Size	20.00
Weapon, **Cannon**, Winchester, Breech Loading, 10 Gauge, Cast Iron Frame	89.50
Weapon, **Capper**, Navy, Brass, For Use With Colt 1851, Marked K.M.	44.50
Weapon, **Carbine**, Ball Patent, Civil War, .50 Caliber	325.00
Weapon, **Carbine**, Burnside, Civil War, Percussion, Silver Inlay	140.00
Weapon, **Colt Derringer**, No.3	95.00
Weapon, **Cup**, Drinking, Tin, U.S., Field, Indian Wars Era, Marked U.S.	8.50
Weapon, **Cutlass**, Naval, American, Cast Iron Grips, 19th Century	79.50
Weapon, **Dagger**, Hand, Lady's, Chinese, Enamel, 6 In.Long	15.00
Weapon, **Dagger**, Persian	35.00
Weapon, **Dagger**, Sheath, Nazi Storm Trooper's, Sa, Brown Wood Handle, Insignia	59.50
Weapon, **Diamond Edge**, 3 Blades, Stockman, Imperial	5.50
Weapon, **Dirk**, British Naval Officer's, C.1810, Brass Guard, Ivory Grips	54.50
Weapon, **Dirk**, Naval, C.1780-1800, Brass Hilt, Lion Head Pommel	295.00
Weapon, **Dirk**, Scottish Highland Military, C.1750-1780, Oak Grips, Carved	325.00
Weapon, **Flask**, Powder, Brass, American Flask & Cap Co., 10 In.Long	12.50
Weapon, **Flask**, Powder, Brass, James Dixon & Sons, 7 In.Long	12.50
Weapon, **Flask**, Powder, Brass, Shell Decoration, 8 In.Long	22.50
Weapon, **Flask**, Powder, Copper, Leaf Decoration, 7 In.Long	12.50
Weapon, **Flask**, Powder, Copper, Pheasants & Flower Decoration, 7 1/4 In.Long	20.00
Weapon, **Flask**, Powder, Copper, Scene Of Hunting Dogs, 7 1/2 In.High	15.00
Weapon, **Flask**, Powder, Copper, Shape Of Flowering Petal, 7 In.Long	20.00
Weapon, **Flask**, Powder, Copper, Stork On Each Side, 8 1/4 In.Tall	40.00
Weapon, **Flask**, Powder, Embossed Eagle, Shield, 13 Stars, Brass, 4 In.Long	40.00
Weapon, **Flask**, Powder, Embossed Flowers & Scrolls, 7 In.Long	12.50
Weapon, **Flask**, Powder, Embossed Running Deer Decoration, 7 In.Long	35.00
Weapon, **Flask**, Powder, Fluted, Brass Graduated Dispenser, 8 In.High	20.00
Weapon, **Flask**, Powder, Ribbed & Beaded, Corn Cob Shape, 8 1/4 In.Long	15.00
Weapon, **Flask**, Powder, Translucent Cow Horn, Flattened, Brass Overlay	32.50
Weapon, **Flask**, Priming, Zinc, Brass Top	22.50
Weapon, **Flint**, For Fire Gun, Circa 1820	5.00
Weapon, **Fowler**, Curly Maple, Flint Lock, Signed Ketland & Co., Brass	400.00
Weapon, **Gun**, Bb, Red Ryder	110.00
Weapon, **Gun**, Harpoon, Greener, Macy, New Bedford, Red Paint	295.00
Weapon, **Gun**, Trap, Winchester, 12 Gauge, Double Barrel, Model 21, Walnut Stock	800.00
Weapon, **Gun**, Whaling, New England	575.00
Weapon, **Halberd**, American, 18th Century, Steel Head, Wooden Handle	185.00
Weapon, **Harpoon**, Whaling, Hand Forged Iron, 19th Century, 2 Flues	145.00
Weapon, **Harpoon**, Whaling, Marked & Dated, English, 1830, Middleton	195.00
Weapon, **Helmet**, Imperial German Hussar's, Pelzmutze, Black Fur, Busby	395.00
Weapon, **Holder**, Shot, Brass, Shell Pattern	30.00
Weapon, **Holster**, Rea Express Pistol	2.25
Weapon, **Holster**, Rifle, Leather, Double Strap, Made In St.Louis, Mo.	8.00
Weapon, **Holster**, U.S., Black Leather, For Colt Single Action, Impressed U.S.	24.50
Weapon, **Horn**, Hunting, Relief Carved	300.00
Weapon, **Knapsack**, Isaac-Campbell, Leather, Linen	47.50
Weapon, **Knife**, Black Composition Handle, 5 In.Blade	6.00
Weapon, **Knife**, Black Composition Handle, 6 In.Blade	7.00
Weapon, **Knife**, Bone Handle, 1 Spear Blade	15.00
Weapon, **Knife**, Bowie, 'let Me Get Close, ' Etched On Blade, Horn Grip	15.00
Weapon, **Knife**, Bowie, Brass Guard & Butt Plate, Wood Handle, 7 In.Blade	10.00
Weapon, **Knife**, Bowie, Brass Guard & Butt Plate, Wood Handle, 9 In.Blade	12.00
Weapon, **Knife**, Bowie, Confederate, Bone Handle, Knuckle Guard, 14 In.Blade	19.50
Weapon, **Knife**, Bowie, Olson, Stag Handle, 6 In.Blade	7.00
Weapon, **Knife**, Bowie, Olson, Stag Handle, 8 In.Blade	9.00
Weapon, **Knife**, Bowie, Olson, Stag Handle, 10 In.Blade	11.00
Weapon, **Knife**, Boy Scout, Hammer Brand, New York Knife Co., Bone Handle	20.00
Weapon, **Knife**, Butcher, Green River	7.50
Weapon, **Knife**, C.Bertram, Hen & Rooster, Pearl Handle	20.00
Weapon, **Knife**, C.Bertram, Pearl Handle, Clip, Pin & File Blades	18.00
Weapon, **Knife**, Clasp, Multiblade, C.1820-30, Tools, Stag Handles	145.00
Weapon, **Knife**, Curled Tail Case	45.00

Weapon, Knife, Diamond Edge, 2 Blades, Trapper, S.S., Imperial 5.00
Weapon, Knife, Diamond Edge, 3 Blades, Imperial 4.00
Weapon, Knife, F.A.Bower Co., Germany, 4 Blade, Congress Pattern, Bone Handle 8.00
Weapon, Knife, Finn, Black Composition Handle, 4 1/4 In.Blade 6.00
Weapon, Knife, Finn, Leather Disk Handle, 4 1/2 In.Blade 6.00
Weapon, Knife, German, Bull, 3 Blade, Bone Handle 4.00
Weapon, Knife, German, Eyeball, Pearl Handle, 1 Blade 25.00
Weapon, Knife, Hunter, Folding, Ka-Bar, Olean, New York, Stag Handles, 2 Blade 30.00
Weapon, Knife, Hunting, Olson, Coca Bola Handle, Handmade, 4 1/2 In.Blade 15.00
Weapon, Knife, Hunting, Olson, Coca Bola Handle, Handmade, 5 1/2 In.Blade 15.00
Weapon, Knife, Hunting, Olson, Stag Handle 18.00
Weapon, Knife, Hunting, Stag Handle, Remington 20.00
Weapon, Knife, Imperial, Scout 1.25
Weapon, Knife, Imperial, 2 Blade, Barlow 1.25
Weapon, Knife, J.A.Henckel, 3 Blade, Stockman, Stag Handle 12.00
Weapon, Knife, KA-Bar, Leather Disk Handle 4.00
Weapon, Knife, Kinfolks, Leather Disk Handle 15.00
Weapon, Knife, Nazi Air Force, Folding, Insignia On Side 30.00
Weapon, Knife, Olson, Buffalo Pattern, Pearl Handle, 5 In.Blade 5.00
Weapon, Knife, Olson, Lock Back, Bone Handle 20.00
Weapon, Knife, Paper, Bone, Dog Head Carved On End, 10 In.Long 15.00
Weapon, Knife, Pick Solingen, Germany, Multicolor Disk Composition Handle 5.00
Weapon, Knife, Pike-Bowie, John Brown, Wooden Handle 350.00
Weapon, Knife, Pine Knot, Hawkbill, Ebony Handle 30.00
Weapon, Knife, Pocket, Case, 3 Blades 25.00
Weapon, Knife, Pocket, Fish, Blade & Scaler, Imperial, No.P2170537 & 2281782 ...... 12.00
Weapon, Knife, Pocket, Horn Handle, Made By G.Wostenholm, Sheffield, England 15.00
Weapon, Knife, Pocket, Remington, Shape Of Man's Shoe, Brass Studded, 1 Blade 35.00
Weapon, Knife, Pocket, Remington, Silver Bullet 300.00
Weapon, Knife, Pocket, Remington, 2 Blade, Signed 15.00
Weapon, Knife, Pocket, Remington, 3-Blade 17.50
Weapon, Knife, Pocket, Russell-Barlow, C.1860, 2 Blades 32.50
Weapon, Knife, Pocket, Schrade-Walden, N.Y., No.834, Stag Handle, 3 Blades 15.00
Weapon, Knife, Pocket, Wade & Butcher, Whittler, Sliding 20.00
Weapon, Knife, Pocket, Wood Handle, 2 Blades, Cattarangus No.21476 .... 12.50
Weapon, Knife, Queen, No.49, 3 Blades, Bone Handle 7.00
Weapon, Knife, Remington, Bullet, No.R4243, 4 Blades 475.00
Weapon, Knife, Remington, Dupont, Fixed Blades, Horn Scales 40.00
Weapon, Knife, Remington, Hunting, Leather Sheath, Striped Handle 23.00
Weapon, Knife, Victorian Shoe, Advertising On Side 20.00
Weapon, Knife, Wells Fargo, Stamped Maleham & Yeomans, Cutlers, Sheffield 30.00
Weapon, Knife, Whittler, Serpentine Pattern, Pearl, 3 Blades 30.00
Weapon, Lance, Bomb, C.1870, Iron & Brass, Lacquer Finish 39.50
Weapon, Lance, Whaling, 6 Ft., Hand Forged, C.1840-50, Black Paint 225.00
Weapon, Leg Guard, Mounted Artilleryman's, U.S., C.1874 .... 17.50
Weapon, Link Strap, U.S.Cavalry, C.1860, Indian War Pattern, D Shaped Buckle 9.50
Weapon, Mess Gear, U.S., C.1870-80, 2 Pieces, 3 Prong Fork, Marked U.S. 3.95
Weapon, Mold, Bullet, American, 18th Century, Brass, 4 Round 50 Caliber Balls 34.50
Weapon, Mold, Bullet, 45 G, Ideal Mfg.Co., New Haven 15.00
Weapon, Musket, Brown Bess, American 675.00
Weapon, Musket, Civil War, Percussion, .58 Caliber, Springfield, 1862 .... 225.00
Weapon, Musket, French, Flintlock, M1763 .... 650.00
Weapon, Musket, Joslyn Conversion, Civil War, .50 Caliber, Springfield, 1864 .... 250.00
Weapon, Pepperbox, Allen & Thurber, 1837 .... 85.00
Weapon, Pepperbox, Bacon Iron Frame, Spur Trigger, 6-Shot, Rosewood Grips 94.50
Weapon, Pistol, British Officer's, Percussion, C.1840-50, .57 Caliber, Pair 850.00
Weapon, Pistol, British Officer's, Silver Mounted, C.1730-40, Pair 950.00
Weapon, Pistol, Chieftain's, Flintlock, Silver Overlay 150.00
Weapon, Pistol, Colt, Frontier, Serial No.113, 4 In.Barrel 125.00
Weapon, Pistol, Derringer, Single Barrel, Percussion 50.00
Weapon, Pistol, Derringer, 7 In., Marked 'deringer-Philadela, ' .44 Caliber 795.00
Weapon, Pistol, Duel, By Le Page, Gunmaker To The King, Engraved, Case 650.00
Weapon, Pistol, Percussion, Double Barrel, Derringer Type 59.00
Weapon, Pistol, Traveling, Percussion, French, Carved, Silver Trim, Pair 290.00
Weapon, Pistol, U.S.Navy, N1843, Percussion, Brown Metal, 1845 .... 450.00
Weapon, Pistol, Volcanic, Brass Frame, Repeating, .38 Caliber 1150.00

Weapon, Pistol, Walnut Stock, Signed Rogers, Phila., Circa 1812	500.00
Weapon, Pouch, Ax, Confederate Navy, Marked	15.00
Weapon, Pouch, Cartridge, For Wheelock Rifle, European, 17th Century	225.00
Weapon, Pouch, Cartridge, Infantry, U.S., Wood Block For .50 Caliber Bullets	47.50
Weapon, Pouch, Cartridge, Infantry, U.S., Wood Block, Russet Leather	64.50
Weapon, Pouch, Fuse, U.S.Navy, Gunner's, Black Leather, Patent Oct., 1879	32.50
Weapon, Pouch, Shot, Leather, Wood Ball Top	4.00
Weapon, Powder Flask, Brass	35.00
Weapon, Powder Horn, American Naval, Scrimshaw, Designs Of 3 Masted Vessels	325.00
Weapon, Powder Horn, Birth Horn, Inscribed 1801	175.00
Weapon, Powder Horn, Black Watch Regimental, French & Indian War, Bushy Run	750.00
Weapon, Powder Horn, Brass, Deer Head, Fox & Oak Leaves, 8 In.Long	45.00
Weapon, Powder Horn, Cow, 7 In.Long	10.00
Weapon, Powder Horn, Cow, 9 1/2 In.Long	25.00
Weapon, Powder Horn, Engraved View Of Boston Massacre, 18th Century	1500.00
Weapon, Powder Horn, Flask Shape, Copper, Brass, Hunter, Dog, Gun, Pheasant	48.00
Weapon, Powder Horn, Kentucky Rifle, Masonic Symbols Carved, Ohio, 1834	90.00
Weapon, Powder Horn, Kentucky Rifle, Signed Zephinah Tubs, Carved	80.00
Weapon, Powder Horn, Kentucky Rifle, York County Horn, Screw-Off Top	75.00
Weapon, Powder Horn, Pistol, Engraving Of Animals, Dated 1817	135.00
Weapon, Powder Horn, Scrimshaw	175.00
Weapon, Powder Horn, Signed Zephinah Tubs, Carved Hope Insignia	80.00
Weapon, Powder Horn, 10 In.	10.00
Weapon, Powder Horn, 13 In.	15.00
Weapon, Rattle, Policeman's, 1880s, Wooden, 16 In.	18.00
Weapon, Revolver, Civil War, Army, Allen & Wheelock, Percussion, .44 Caliber	325.00
Weapon, Revolver, Colt M1860, Percussion, Army, .44 Caliber	875.00
Weapon, Revolver, Colt, Brevet, Navy, Engraved, C.1850, .36 Caliber	1150.00
Weapon, Revolver, French, 'apache, ' 6-Shot, .20 Caliber, German Silver Inlay	375.00
Weapon, Revolver, Iver Johnson, 7-Shot, Hammerless, Owl Head Design	45.00
Weapon, Revolver, Remington M1875 Sa Frontier, .44 Caliber	795.00
Weapon, Revolver, Smith & Wesson Model 53, Jet Magnum, .22 Caliber	125.00
Weapon, Revolver, Smith & Wesson Model, .32 Caliber, Serial No.186676	84.50
Weapon, Revolver, Whitneyville, .22 Caliber	37.50
Weapon, Rifle Loading Tool, Winchester, Patent, 1874	15.00
Weapon, Rifle, Air, .22 Caliber, Silver Presentation Medallion, 1873	70.00
Weapon, Rifle, Harpers Ferry, U.S.M1814, Half Stock, Date 1814	265.00
Weapon, Rifle, Kentucky, C.1820, .48 Caliber Bore	1450.00
Weapon, Rifle, Kentucky, Curly Maple, Brass Patch Box, 41 In.Barrel	800.00
Weapon, Rifle, Kentucky, Curly Maple, Flint Lock, Brass Patch Box	700.00
Weapon, Rifle, Kentucky, Curly Maple, Silver & Eagle Inlay, Brass Patch Box	400.00
Weapon, Rifle, Kentucky, Swivel Breech, Percussion, Brass Center Rib	850.00
Weapon, Rifle, Remington, Model 16, Auto Loading, .22 Caliber	47.50
Weapon, Rifle, Springfield, Model 1873, .45-.70 Caliber, Leather Sling	135.00
Weapon, Rifle, U.S.M1841, Mississippi, .58 Caliber, Harpers Ferry, 1851	375.00
Weapon, Rifle, U.S.Springfield M1873, 45/70 Bore	150.00
Weapon, Rifle, U.S.Springfield M1898, Krag, Gallery Practice, 1906	550.00
Weapon, Rifle, Winchester, Lo-Wall, Scheutzen Type	495.00
Weapon, Rifle, Winchester, Model 61, 22 Long	80.00
Weapon, Rifle, Winchester, Model 61, 22 Short	80.00
Weapon, Rifle, Winchester, 1873	5500.00
Weapon, Saber, Cavalry, Horseman, C.1775-1780, American, Brass Hilt	650.00
Weapon, Saber, Cavalry, M 1860, Scabbard, Leather Grips, Marked Roby, 1864	79.50
Weapon, Saber, Officer's, English, C.1790-1800, Engraved, Ebony Carved Grips	110.00
Weapon, Saber, Officer's, Silver Eagle Head Pommel Foot, Ivory, Phila., 1810	200.00
Weapon, Shield, Irish, 17th Century	55.00
Weapon, Shield, War, Persian, Rhino Hide, 18th Century, Brass Rosettes	24.50
Weapon, Shotgun, British, W.W.Greener, Hammerless, 12 Gauge	185.00
Weapon, Shotgun, Chatham Arms	20.00
Weapon, Shotgun, Cherokee, 12 Gauge, Single Barrel	51.00
Weapon, Shotgun, King Nitro, Double Barrel, Shapleigh, 12 Gauge	75.00
Weapon, Shotgun, Parker D H, 12 Gauge, 1930, 26 In.Barrel	875.00
Weapon, Shotgun, Pin Fire, 28 Gauge, Underbarrel Lever	39.50
Weapon, Shotgun, Winchester, Model 12, 12 Gauge, Pump, 28 In.Barrel	175.00
Weapon, Shoulder Strap, Frogs For Sword, Bayonet, & Musket, C.1850	67.50
Weapon, Sidearm, Colt, .36 Caliber, Navy, Civil War	290.00

Weapon, Sight Cover, Navy, Marked Ordnance Dept., U.S.Navy Yard, Wash.1872 .... 14.50
Weapon, Slug, For Air Gun, Quackenbush, Felted, Patent, 1883, 100 In Box 2.50
Weapon, Spear, African, War, 4 1/2 Ft., Wooden Shaft, Hand Forged Steel Spike 27.50
Weapon, Spear, Eel, Iron, American, 18th Century 48.00
Weapon, Spear, Obsidian, Buffalo 8.00
Weapon, Spear, Trench, Iron, Hand Forged 34.50
Weapon, Suit Of Armor, Miniature, 19th Century, 32 In.High, Handmade 450.00
Weapon, Sword Guard, Gold Inlay, Carved, Design Of God Of Wind 55.00
Weapon, Sword, American Officer's, Scabbard, C.1830-50, Brass Hilt, Engraved 84.50
Weapon, Sword, American, Lion Head Pommel, Officer's, Brass Hilt 450.00
Weapon, Sword, Broadsword Design, Blade Of Bone, Twisted Hilt, Brass, 30 In. 115.00
Weapon, Sword, Burmese, Wood Scabbard, 32 In. 16.50
Weapon, Sword, German Artillery Officer's, Scabbard, C.1890, Brass Hilt 39.50
Weapon, Sword, German, Hunting, Presentation, Stag Grip, Brass Overlaid 145.00
Weapon, Sword, Hunting, Dutch, C.1750, Brass Hilt, Bone Grips 64.50
Weapon, Sword, Officer's, Luftwaffe, Silver Finish, Swastika On Pommel 97.50
Weapon, Sword, Scabbard, British Officer's, Commemorating Egyptian Campaign 395.00
Weapon, Sword, Scabbard, Coast Guard Officer's, U.S.Revenue Marine, C.1870 .... 375.00
Weapon, Sword, Scabbard, Danish Officer's, C.1860, Brass Hilt, Iron Sheath 37.50
Weapon, Sword, Scabbard, Nazi Army Officer's, Brass Hilt, Lion Head Pommel 69.50
Weapon, Sword, Spanish Officer's, C.1800-20, Iron Hilt, Engraved Floral 59.50
Weapon, Sword, U.S.Artillery Officer's, Scabbard, 1821-40, Brass Hilt 150.00
Weapon, Sword, U.S., Eagle Head, C.1821-40, Brass Hilt, Engraved 54.50
Weapon, Sword, Wooden, Military Training, Circa 1855 .... 40.00
Weapon, Tomahawk, Handmade 20.00
Weapon, Tool, Loading, Winchester 20.00
Weapon, Tools, For M1841 Mississippi Rifle, Iron Worm & Iron Ball Remover 24.50
Weapon, Waistbelt, U.S.Artillery Issue, Frog For Sword, Buff Leather 94.50
Weather Vane, Angel Gabriel, Painted Metal, 31 In.High 225.00
Weather Vane, Auto Driver Wearing Duster, Goggles, Blue Milk Glass Ball 85.00
Weather Vane, Clipper Ship, Metal, Painted, U.S.Colors, 40 In.High 425.00
Weather Vane, Clipper Ship, Painted Metal, 20 In.High 170.00
Weather Vane, Cock, Fighting, On Orb, Copper, 6 Ft.6 In.High 300.00
Weather Vane, Cow, Copper, Three Dimensions, 48 In.Long 1700.00
Weather Vane, Cow, Copper, 47 In. .... Illus 1700.00
Weather Vane, Cow, Gold Leaf, 27 1/2 In.Long 150.00
Weather Vane, Crowing Rooster, Hollow Copper, Arrow Is 3 1/2 Ft. 600.00
Weather Vane, Deer Leaping Brush Pile, Hollow Copper, Gold Leaf 2500.00
Weather Vane, Eagle On Ball, Hollow Copper, 32 In.High 300.00
Weather Vane, Eagle, Copper, Gilded, Spread Wings, On Orb, 41 In.Long 400.00
Weather Vane, Eagle, Copper, Gold Leaf, Wingspan 48 In. 1600.00
Weather Vane, Eagle, Copper, On Orb, American, 19th Century, 50 In.Long 375.00
Weather Vane, Eagle, Copper, Painted, American, 19th Century, 7 Ft.High 325.00
Weather Vane, Eagle, Copper, Painted, Spread Wings, On Orb, 45 In.Long 250.00
Weather Vane, Eagle, Copper, Spread Wings, On Orb, 28 In.Long 700.00
Weather Vane, Eagle, Gilded Copper, Spread Wings, On Orb, 5 Ft.2 In.High 325.00
Weather Vane, Horse, Copper, American, 31 In.Long 130.00

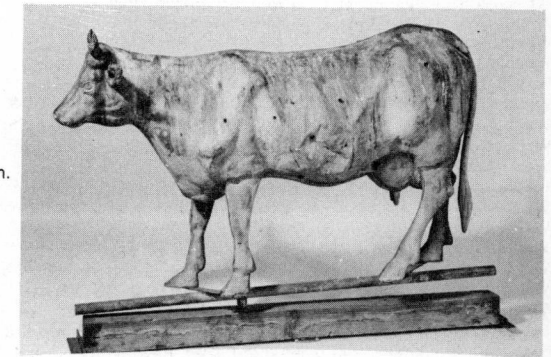

Weather Vane, Cow, Copper, 47 In.

Weather Vane, Horse, Copper, Running, 5 Ft.High 750.00
Weather Vane, Horse, Iron, Copper, Two Brass Balls, Compass, N.E.S.W., 58 In. 325.00
Weather Vane, Horse, Post & Finders, Copper, Cast Iron Head, Green Patina 275.00
Weather Vane, Jockey On Running Horse, Gilded Metal, American, C.1870 .... 650.00
Weather Vane, Mercury Silhouette, On Orb, Metal, 36 In.High 180.00
Weather Vane, Pig, Gilded Metal, Wrought Iron, American, C.1850, 28 In.Long 200.00
Weather Vane, Rooster, Copper, 34 In.High 180.00
Weather Vane, Rooster, Iron, Painted, 5 Ft.8 In.High .... *Illus* 650.00

Weather Vane, Rooster, Iron,
Painted, 5 Ft.8 In.High

Weather Vane, Running Horse, Gilded Metal, American, C.1850, 42 In.Long 400.00
Weather Vane, Running Horse, Hollow Copper, 31 In.Long 275.00

Webb Glass was made by Thomas Webb & Sons of Stourbridge, England.
Many types of art and cameo glass were made by them during the victorian era.
Webb Burmese, Bowl, Rose, Scalloped, Signed, 3 In.Diameter, 2 1/4 In.Tall 255.00
Webb Burmese, Lamp, Fairy, Colored Shade, Clarke Base, 2 3/4 In.Tall 125.00
Webb Burmese, Lamp, Fairy, Leaves, Vines, Pyramid Shade, 5 1/2 In.Diameter 325.00
Webb Burmese, Lamp, Fairy, Marked Clarke, 4 In.High 175.00
Webb Burmese, Pitcher, Juice, Ivy Vine, Green Leave, 3 In. 275.00
Webb Burmese, Rose Bowl, Miniature, Acid Finish, 2 1/2 In.High 150.00
Webb Burmese, Vase, Fairy Light, Mark, 5 In. 195.00
Webb Burmese, Vase, Flower Rim, Pink To Yellow, 3 In.Tall 175.00
Webb Burmese, Vase, Salmon Pink, Rippled Top, 3 1/8 In. 295.00
Webb Burmese, Vase, Scalloped Top, Bulbous, Signed, 3 In.Tall 235.00
Webb Burmese, Vase, Star Shape, Rolled Rim, Signed, 3 1/4 In.Tall 325.00
Webb, Candleholder, Air Bubbles, Crosshatch, Signed Webb, England 85.00
Webb, Bowl, Boat Shape, Pink, Custard Casing, Shell Feet, Strawberry Pontil 55.00
Webb, Bowl, Cameo, Carved Floral, Butterfly, Citron Yellow Ground, 5 In. 375.00
Webb, Bowl, Peachblow, Pleated Rim, One Side Folds In, Glossy, 5 In. 90.00
Webb, Bowl, Rose, Aqua, Teardrop Pattern, Crystal Shell Feet 75.00
Webb, Bowl, Rose, Ruffled Top, Signed, 2 3/4 In.Diameter 255.00
Webb, Compote, Engraved, Greek Key Border, 5 In.High 40.00
Webb, Compote, Floral & Swag Pattern, Signed Corbett, England 37.50
Webb, Compote, White, Crimped, Rose Lining, 8 1/2 In.Diameter, 7 In.High 75.00
Webb, Decanter, Cameo, Intaglio Carved, Green, Stopper, 12 In.Tall 350.00
Webb, Decanter, Emerald Green Cut To Cranberry, Flowers, Silver Neck, Chain 350.00
Webb, Goblet, Diamond, Signed, 3 3/4 In. 85.00
Webb, Lamp, Pink Satin, Acanthus Leaves & Flowers, Ruffled Shading, 12 In. 195.00
Webb, Perfume, Pocket Size, Cameo, Laydown, Red, Morning Glories, 3 3/4 In. 250.00
Webb, Pitcher, Cut Velvet, Pink, White Lining 275.00
Webb, Pitcher, White To Apricot, Flowers, Camphor Satin Handle, 7 In. 75.00
Webb, Tumbler, Cherry, Red To Pink, Hand-Painted Forget-Me-Nots, Peachblow 125.00
Webb, Vase, Amber, Acid Cut Leaves, Signed, 6 1/4 In.High 42.00
Webb, Vase, Cameo, Citron & White, 6 3/4 In., Signed 850.00
Webb, Vase, Cameo, Cut To Clear, Green, Birds, Signed, 10 In.High, Pair 425.00
Webb, Vase, Cameo, Wild Rose Blossoms, Yellow Ground, White-Cased, 4 In.High 385.00
Webb, Vase, Floral, Birds, Hand-Painted, Rose, Gold, Bulbous, 8 1/2 In.Tall 95.00

Webb, Vase, Floral, Enameled Birds, Dull Satin, 16 In., Signed Thomas Webb 450.00
Webb, Vase, Miniature, Opaque Ivory, Impressed Thomas Webb & Sons, 2 1/4 In. 300.00
Webb, Vase, Quilted, Ruffled Top, Floral, Leaves, Berries, Butterfly, 8 In. 800.00
Webb, Vase, Red, Brown, Green, Berries, Leaves, Ruffled Top, Signed 285.00
Webb, Vase, Red, White, Flowers, Leaves, Cameo, 5 In.High, 5 1/2 In.Diameter 485.00
Webb, Vase, Ribbed, Satin Glass, Blue, Gold Decoration 160.00
Webb, Vase, Satin Glass, Applied White Threads, Melon Rib Body, 4 In. 85.00
Webb, Vase, Seven Pointed, Ruffled Top, Bulbous, Signed, 3 In. 235.00
Webb, Vase, Stick, Enamel, Gold Silver, Red, 9 In.Tall, 5 1/2 In.Wide 295.00
Webb, Vase, Wine Color, White Enamel Decor, White Lining, Gold Ormolu Holder 150.00

> *Wedgwood Pottery has been made at the famous Wedgwood Factory in*
> *England since 1759. A large variety of wares has been made, including the*
> *well-known Jasperware, Basalt, Creamware, and even a limited amount of*
> *porcelain.*

Wedgwood, see also Jasperware, Basalt, Creamware
Wedgwood, Ashtray, Green & White, Marked Wedgwood, England 8.00
Wedgwood, Barrel, Biscut, Classical Figures, Blue, Silver Bail & Lid 95.00
Wedgwood, Biscuit Barrel, Blue Jasperware, Classic Figures, Silver Lid 95.00
Wedgwood, Bowl, Black Basalt, 10 In.Diameter 95.00
Wedgwood, Bowl, Blue Luster, Iridescent Lined, Fish Design, 3 1/2 In. 69.00
Wedgwood, Bowl, Boat Shape, Underplate, Pair 70.00
Wedgwood, Bowl, Cauliflower Pattern, 11 In.Round 25.00
Wedgwood, Bowl, Dragon Design, Blue, Yellow, Gold, 3 3/8 In.Diameter 105.00
Wedgwood, Bowl, Dragon, Floral, Blue, Gold, Green, Red, Marked, 5 1/2 In. 125.00
Wedgwood, Bowl, Fairyland Luster, Butterflies, Green, Orange Inside, 4 In. 145.00
Wedgwood, Bowl, Fairyland Luster, Fairies, Gnomes, Cherubs, Signed Portland 375.00
Wedgwood, Bowl, Fairyland, Butterfly, Mother-Of-Pearl, Round, 4 In. 145.00
Wedgwood, Bowl, Fairyland, Butterfly, Mother-Of-Pearl, Round, 5 In. 165.00
Wedgwood, Bowl, Fairyland, Butterfly, Orange, Gold, Blue, Round, 3 In. 135.00
Wedgwood, Bowl, Fairyland, Dragon, Butterflies, Octagon Shape, Blue 235.00
Wedgwood, Bowl, Fairyland, Fish Inside & Out, Blue, Luster, Octagon, 9 In. 325.00
Wedgwood, Bowl, Fairyland, Foo Dog, Orange, Blue, 2 1/4 In.Diameter 95.00
Wedgwood, Bowl, Fairyland, Gold Fish Design, Oriental Symbols, Green, Gold 82.50
Wedgwood, Bowl, Luster, Marbleized Orange With Gold, Portland Mark, England 125.00
Wedgwood, Bowl, Marbleized, 8 In.Diameter, Underplate, 10 In.Diameter 125.00
Wedgwood, Bowl, Mottled Blue, Gold Dragons, Pearl Luster Interior, Portland 285.00
Wedgwood, Bowl, Salad, Blue, White Classical Figures, Silver Rim 110.00
Wedgwood, Bowl, Salad, Jasperware, Leaf Decoration, Fork & Spoon, Set 165.00
Wedgwood, Box, Basalt, Black, Classical Figures, Acorns 85.00
Wedgwood, Box, Blue Mottle, Hexagon, Gold Insects On Lid, Portland Mark 124.00
Wedgwood, Box, Green Jasper, White Classic Figures, 3 In.Diameter 30.00
Wedgwood, Box, Heart Shape, Blue Mottle, Butterflies Inside, Portland Mark 132.00
Wedgwood, Box, Jasper, Blue, 2 1/2 In.Square 57.50
Wedgwood, Box, Power, Flowers & Scroll Decor, Round 67.50
Wedgwood, Box, Ruby Luster, Blue Lining, Rooster & Goat On Lid, Bird Inside 124.00
Wedgwood, Bust, Winston Churchill, Black Basalt, Arnold Machen, 1940 .... 35.00
Wedgwood, Can & Saucer, Coffee, Gray, Red, & Gold, Floral, C.1850, Marked, 10 .... 230.00
Wedgwood, Candle Shield, Classical Figures, Lithophane, White, Marked 30.00
Wedgwood, Candlestick, Three Colors, 5 In.High 10.00
Wedgwood, Comport, 3 Bird & 3 Fan Panels, Multicolor Majolica, C.1880 .... 40.00
Wedgwood, Compote, Raised Designed, Black, Basalt, Footed, 6 In.Tall 110.00
Wedgwood, Creamer, Black Basalt, Wild Rose, Harp Scrolls 60.00
Wedgwood, Creamer, Blue, Jasper, Cameo, Classical Decor, Signed 50.00
Wedgwood, Creamer, Blue, White, Bulbous, England, 2 1/2 In.High 22.00
Wedgwood, Creamer, Dark Blue Classical Figures, 4 1/2 In.High 27.50
Wedgwood, Creamer, Old Man Of The Mountain Scene, Wishbone Handle 20.00
Wedgwood, Cup & Saucer, Basalt, Hand-Painted Crest Of Bermuda, Signed 18.00
Wedgwood, Cup & Saucer, Blue & Gold 10.50
Wedgwood, Cup & Saucer, Harvard Tercentenary, 1936 .... 5.00
Wedgwood, Cup & Saucer, High Raised Figures, Sage Green, Signed 37.75
Wedgwood, Cup, Handleless, Black Basalt 30.00
Wedgwood, Cuspidor, Lady's, Black Basalt, Basket Weave, 5 In.Diameter 30.00
Wedgwood, Dessert Set, Ornithological, C.1812, Birds & Feathers, 15 Piece 2600.00
Wedgwood, Dish, Basket, Creamware, England, Oval, 7 1/2 X 9 In. 22.50
Wedgwood, Dish, Cheese, Blue & White, Cover 125.00

Wedgwood, Dish, Cheese, Blue, Classical Figures, Dome Cover .... 65.00 To 75.00
Wedgwood, Dish, Game, Birds, Pheasants, Rabbit, Cover, 6 1/2 X 8 1/2 In. 125.00
Wedgwood, Dish, Jam, Blue, White Figures, Trees, Animals, Silver Lid & Rim 48.00
Wedgwood, Dish, Jam, England, Blue, White Classical Figures, Silver Cover 40.00
Wedgwood, Dish, Pin, Dark Blue, Oval, 4 1/4 X 2 1/2 In. 32.50
Wedgwood, Dish, Shell Shape, Cream Ground, Gold & Rust Sea Flora, Portland 48.00
Wedgwood, Dish, Trinket, Blue Mottle, Gold Grasshopper, Portland Mark 78.00
Wedgwood, Dish, Vegetable, Flowers, White, Cover 27.00
Wedgwood, Fish Set, Blue & White, 7 Piece, Marked Wedgwood & Co.Ltd. 200.00
Wedgwood, Inkwell, Covered, Green, Classical Figures, England 47.50
Wedgwood, Jar, Biscuit, Blue Jasperware, White Classical Figures, Silver Lid 63.00
Wedgwood, Jar, Biscuit, Dark Blue, Classical Figures, Silver Lid & Bail 75.00
Wedgwood, Jar, Biscuit, Jasperware, Blue, Silver Lid & Bail 65.00
Wedgwood, Jar, Cookie, Blue Jasperware, England, 6 In. 100.00
Wedgwood, Jar, Cracker, Jasperware, Classical Figures, Blue, Footed, 6 1/2 In. 100.00
Wedgwood, Jar, Tobacco, Green, 6 1/4 In.High, 5 1/2 In.Diameter 150.00
Wedgwood, Jardiniere, Black Basalt, Classical Figures, Trees, Roses 125.00
Wedgwood, Jardiniere, Blue With White Roses Border, Lions, Heads, Swags 145.00
Wedgwood, Jardiniere, Blue, White Medallions, Lafayette, Franklin, Jefferson 200.00
Wedgwood, Jardiniere, Classical Figures, Grapes, Blue, White, 4 3/4 In. 60.00
Wedgwood, Jardiniere, Jasper, Blue Ground, England 50.00
Wedgwood, Jardiniere, Jasper, Green Ground, England 75.00
Wedgwood, Jug, Ale, Russo Antico, Cambridge, 4 1/2 In.Tall 45.00
Wedgwood, Jug, Ale, Russo Antico, Cambridge, 5 1/4 In.Tall 55.00
Wedgwood, Jug, Ale, Russo Antico, Cambridge, 6 3/4 In.Tall 65.00
Wedgwood, Jug, Black Basalt, England, 4 In.High 18.00
Wedgwood, Jug, Cream, Ryan Jewelry Co., Omaha, On Bottom, Impressed Mark 15.00
Wedgwood, Jug, Green, Fox Hunting Scene, Set Of Graduated Four 95.00
Wedgwood, Medallion, Bach, Black Basalt 50.00
Wedgwood, Medallion, Brass Frame, Green, White Classical Figure, 2 3/4 In. 50.00
Wedgwood, Mug, Fishing Scene, Floral Border, Blue, White 22.00
Wedgwood, Napkin Ring, Floral, Porcelain 12.50
Wedgwood, Perfume, Jasper, Green, White, Marked England, 8 1/4 In.Tall, Pair 175.00
Wedgwood, Pitcher, Apple Blossoms, White, Blue, Gold, Marked, 7 In.Tall 27.50
Wedgwood, Pitcher, Basalt, Black, Grape Band, Figures, Trees, Marked 97.50
Wedgwood, Pitcher, Black Basalt, Bulbous, Thistle, Clover, Leaves, Harp, 5 In. 80.00
Wedgwood, Pitcher, Black Basalt, Thistle, Clover, Leaves, Harp, Bulbous, 4 In. 65.00
Wedgwood, Pitcher, Blue, Classical Figures, 6 In. 45.00
Wedgwood, Pitcher, Classical Figures, Blue, White, 6 In.Tall 100.00
Wedgwood, Pitcher, Classical Figures, Light Blue, Twisted Handle, 4 In.Tall 60.00
Wedgwood, Pitcher, English, Portrait, 'For Richard Briggs,' 6 1/2 In.High 10.00
Wedgwood, Pitcher, Fallow Deer, England, 6 In.High 25.00
Wedgwood, Pitcher, Green, England, 4 In.Tall 32.00
Wedgwood, Pitcher, Green, White, Classical Figures, England, 8 In. 135.00
Wedgwood, Pitcher, Green, White, Classical Figures, Rope Handle, 5 In. 29.00
Wedgwood, Pitcher, Green, 7 In.High 125.00
Wedgwood, Pitcher, Hunt Scene, White, Hound Handle 25.00
Wedgwood, Pitcher, Jasper, Green, England, White Classical Figures, 1955 .... 32.50
Wedgwood, Pitcher, Jasperware, White On Blue, Pastoral Scene 70.00
Wedgwood, Pitcher, Jasperware, White On Blue, Sacrificial Scene 85.00
Wedgwood, Pitcher, Milk, Longfellow Portrait, Title Of Poems 55.00
Wedgwood, Pitcher, Syrup, Jasperware, Blue, Classical Figures, England, Mark 45.00
Wedgwood, Pitcher, Syrup, White, Blue, Signed, 5 In. 45.00
Wedgwood, Plaque, Harry S.Truman, Raised Silhouette, Floral Border 13.50
Wedgwood, Plaque, Kings & Queens, Black Basalt, Sterling Silver Frame 195.00
Wedgwood, Plaque, Lilac Color, 4 1/2 In. 30.00
Wedgwood, Plaque, Queen Charlotte, White On Blue, Jasperware, Oval 250.00
Wedgwood, Plate, Blue Jasperware, Mythological Figures, 7 In. 37.50
Wedgwood, Plate, Blue, 2nd Annual Dinner, Albany Chamber Of Commerce, 1904 .... 11.00
Wedgwood, Plate, Boston State House, 10 1/4 In. 16.50
Wedgwood, Plate, Boston Tea Party, 10 1/4 In. 16.50
Wedgwood, Plate, Bread & Butter, Ventnor, 1926 .... 6.00
Wedgwood, Plate, Bulfinch Pattern, Marked Wedgwood, 10 In.Diameter 18.50
Wedgwood, Plate, Cake, Flowers, Butterflies, Square, Signed & Dated 40.00
Wedgwood, Plate, Columbia College, N.Y., 7 1/2 In. 15.00
Wedgwood, Plate, Commemoration, Fairbanks House, Mass., 1904, Blu .... 11.00 To 25.00

Wedgwood, Plate, Commemorative, Boston State House, 1891	25.00
Wedgwood, Plate, Commemorative, Ft.Ticonderoga, Lake Champlain, Blue	9.00
Wedgwood, Plate, Commemorative, Old South Church, 1899	25.00
Wedgwood, Plate, Commemorative, Principia College, 1898-1948, 10 1/4 In.	30.00
Wedgwood, Plate, Creamware, Oriental Decor, Rock, Floral, Circa 1820	47.50
Wedgwood, Plate, Dark Blue, American Historical, 9 1/4 In.Diameter, 10	110.00
Wedgwood, Plate, Dinner, Etruria, Silver, Blue, Set Of 8	75.00
Wedgwood, Plate, Dinner, Fruit, Blue, Pink, Red, Marked, England, Set Of 12	75.00
Wedgwood, Plate, Dinner, Ventnor, 1926	10.62
Wedgwood, Plate, Fallow Deer, 10 In.Diameter	18.00
Wedgwood, Plate, Ferrara, Dark Blue, Wedgwood, Etruria, England, 6 In.	23.07
Wedgwood, Plate, Faneuil Hall, 10 1/4 In.	16.50
Wedgwood, Plate, Game, Birds, Pheasants, Fowl, Rabbit, Caneware	125.00
Wedgwood, Plate, Havard College Scene, Blue, 10 1/4 In.Diameter	9.50
Wedgwood, Plate, Harvard University, 1927, 12	120.00
Wedgwood, Plate, House Of Seven Gables, Blue, White, 9 1/4 In.Diameter	15.00
Wedgwood, Plate, Ivanhoe, Story To Cedric, Blue, Green, White, 8 In.	20.00
Wedgwood, Plate, Longfellow's Early Home, Portland, Me., 9 In.	15.00
Wedgwood, Plate, Longfellow's House, Cambridge, 1900, Blue, Impressed, 9 In.	22.50
Wedgwood, Plate, Melrose Public Library, Blue, White	16.00
Wedgwood, Plate, Mulberry, Ferrara, 9 1/4 In.	7.00
Wedgwood, Plate, North Church, 10 1/4 In.	16.50
Wedgwood, Plate, Pearl, 9 1/4 In.	29.00
Wedgwood, Plate, Pink, Luster, Ribbed, Mother-Of-Pearl, 9 In.	45.00
Wedgwood, Plate, Shell Shape, Cream Ground, Pink Shades	30.00
Wedgwood, Plate, Ship, Strawberry Border, Blue, Green	190.00
Wedgwood, Plate, Smith College Scene, Green, White, Dated 1932	6.75
Wedgwood, Plate, Spirit Of '76, 9 1/4 In.	15.00
Wedgwood, Plate, State House, Boston, 9 1/4 In.	15.00
Wedgwood, Plate, University Of Chicago, Queensware, Set Of 4	28.00
Wedgwood, Plate, Wall, Brown, Monochrome, Dated 1876	30.00
Wedgwood, Plate, Washington Crossing The Delaware, 9 1/4 In.	15.00
Wedgwood, Plate, Wicker Design, Creamware, Oval	48.00
Wedgwood, Platter, Oval, Grape & Shell Rim, Queensware, 11 X 16 In.	20.00
Wedgwood, Platter, Sibyl Pattern, Blue, Oval, 14 In.	15.00
Wedgwood, Platter, Ventnor, 1926, Square	35.00
Wedgwood, Ring Tree, Hand-Painted Roses, Blue Wide Band	10.50
Wedgwood, Sauce, Ventnor, 1926	4.75
Wedgwood, Sugar & Creamer, Blue Jasper	100.00
Wedgwood, Sugar & Creamer, Blue, White, England, Cover	25.00
Wedgwood, Sugar & Creamer, Classical Figures, White, Blue, Silver Band	60.00
Wedgwood, Sugar & Creamer, Green Jasperware, Squatty, England	70.00
Wedgwood, Sugar & Creamer, Jasperware, Silver Rim, White Classical Figures	60.00
Wedgwood, Sugar & Creamer, Squatty Shape, Black Basalt	65.00
Wedgwood, Sugar, Blue, White, Bulbous, Handles, England, 4 1/2 In.High	45.00
Wedgwood, Sugar, Classic Figures, Jasperware, Green, White, England	38.00
Wedgwood, Sugar, Jasper Dip Three Colors, Covered, England	35.00
Wedgwood, Tea Set, Jasper, Marked, Creamer, Sugar, Teapot, Set	140.00
Wedgwood, Teapot, Black Basalt, Circa 1820	120.00
Wedgwood, Teapot, Blue & White, 4 1/2 In.Tall, England	25.00
Wedgwood, Teapot, Blue Satiny Ground, White Leaf Border, Classical Figures	70.00
Wedgwood, Teapot, Blue, White, Bulbous, Large	75.00
Wedgwood, Teapot, Classic Figures, Tunstall, England, Mark Adams	65.00
Wedgwood, Teapot, Jasperware, Blue, White Classical Figures, White Spout	70.00
Wedgwood, Teapot, Sugar, Creamer, White Flaxman Figures, Blue	110.00
Wedgwood, Tile, Blue & White, March	45.00
Wedgwood, Tile, Boston Public Library, Blue, White, 6 X 6 In.	22.00
Wedgwood, Tile, Calendar, John Hancock House, Boston, 1900	30.00
Wedgwood, Tile, Calendar, The Home Of Washington, Black, White, 1892	30.00
Wedgwood, Tile, Mottled Brown & Green, Daisies, Marked Josiah Wedgwood	25.00
Wedgwood, Tile, 1918 Calendar	24.00
Wedgwood, Tile, 1924 Calendar	24.00
Wedgwood, Tile, 1925 Calendar	24.00
Wedgwood, Tray, Blue Satiny Ground, Medallion Center, Figures, Floral Border	60.00
Wedgwood, Tray, Jasperware, Blue, White Classical Figures, Acorns, Leaves	75.00
Wedgwood, Tray, Oval, Blue, White Flaxman Figures	60.00

Wedgwood, **Tray**, Pin, Green, White Classical Figures	28.00
Wedgwood, **Tureen**, Terra-Cotta, Relief Animals, Liner Dish	185.00
Wedgwood, **Urn**, Covered, Gray-Green, Classic Figures, 2 Handles, 7 In.	75.00
Wedgwood, **Vase**, Black Basalt, Cylindrical, 5 1/2 In.Tall	80.00
Wedgwood, **Vase**, Black Jasper, White Classical Decor, Ovoid, 5 In.High	90.00
Wedgwood, **Vase**, Blue Ground, White Figures, England, 5 1/4 In.Tall	32.00
Wedgwood, **Vase**, Bud, Blue Jasperware, White Figures, 5 In.High	65.00
Wedgwood, **Vase**, Cobalt Blue & White, Bisque, Portland, Classical Scenes	425.00
Wedgwood, **Vase**, Cylindrical, Three Colors, Wedgwood Made In England	30.00
Wedgwood, **Vase**, Fairyland Luster, Oriental Scenes, 8 1/2 In.High	295.00
Wedgwood, **Vase**, Fairyland, Hummingbirds, Orange, Blue, Bulbous, 5 In.Tall	165.00
Wedgwood, **Vase**, Fairyland Scenic Panels, Pink, Blue, Gold, Bulbous, 8 In.Tall	650.00
Wedgwood, **Vase**, Ferns, Flowers, Cylinder Shape, 8 In.Tall	90.00
Wedgwood, **Vase**, Hummingbird, Luster, Blue, Marked Z5294	220.00
Wedgwood, **Vase**, Pearl Luster Ground, Butterflies, Portland, 8 1/4 In.Tall	365.00
Wedgwood, **Vase**, Pearl Luster, Butterfly Decor, Mottled Orange Inside Rim	345.00
Wedgwood, **Vase**, Stick Neck, Green, White Classical Figures, Medallions, 6 In.	52.00
Wedgwood, **Vase**, Trumpet, Fairyland, Dragons, Pagodas, Blue, 11 In.Tall	295.00
Wedgwood, **Wash Set**, Signed & Impressed, 7 Piece	200.00
Weesp, **Dish**, Saucer, Maid & Cook Center, Landscape, Scrollwork, C.1765	175.00

Weller Pottery was made in Fultonham, Ohio, from 1873 to 1900. The most famous pottery made at the factory was art pottery that resembled Rookwood, and a type of gold metallic luster pottery.

Weller, **Basket**, Acorn & Tree Limb Shape, Green, Brown, Marked	28.00
Weller, **Basket**, Blossoms, Peach, White, Signed, 7 1/2 In.Tall	10.00
Weller, **Basket**, Flowers, Brown, Yellow, Green, Twig Handle	17.00
Weller, **Basket**, Green Matte Finish, Pink Roses, 2 Rope Handles	12.50
Weller, **Bowl**, Bulb, Green High Glaze, 8 In.Diameter	6.95
Weller, **Bowl**, Chengtu, Handled, 3 1/2 In.High, Marked	24.00
Weller, **Bowl**, Ducks' Heads .... *Illus*	8.50

Weller, Bowl, Ducks' Heads

Weller, **Bowl**, Rochelle Line, Ivy Under Glaze, Dorothy England Artist	54.50
Weller, **Bowl**, Rose, Aurelian, Crimped Top, Yellow Floral On Front, 5 In.High	43.50
Weller, **Bowl**, Rose, Palm Trees, Iridescent	85.00
Weller, **Bowl**, Rose, Pastel Blue, Cream Floral, Scalloped Opening, Signed	15.00
Weller, **Bowl**, Rose, Tulips Design, Pink, Gray, Signed D.L.	22.50
Weller, **Bowl**, Sicardo, 6 In.Diameter	115.00
Weller, **Candleholder**, Cameo Type, White, Black, Pair	7.50
Weller, **Candleholder**, Matte Green, 4 1/2 In.Diameter	8.50
Weller, **Candlestick**, Marked, Brown, 4 Sided Classical Shape, Pair	32.50
Weller, **Candlestick**, Tan Matte Finish, Grapes On Base, 9 1/4 In.	17.00
Weller, **Centerpiece**, Signed In Script, White Matte, Crackled, 3 Piece Set	25.00
Weller, **Creamer**, Zona	17.00
Weller, **Dish**, Panels, Flowers, Basket, Round, 6 1/2 In.Diameter	10.00
Weller, **Ewer**, Fruit & Nut Design, 8 In.Tall	32.00
Weller, **Ewer**, Louwelsa, Shaded Browns, Greens, Wild Rose, 9 In.	90.00
Weller, **Figurine**, Woman, White & Blue, 11 In.High	48.00
Weller, **Jar**, Tobacco, Dickens, Bearded, Turbaned Man	75.00
Weller, **Jar**, 2 Handles, Brown, Tulip Decoration, 12 1/2 In.High	17.50
Weller, **Jardinere**, Cream Color, Medallion Heads On Sides, 4 In.Square	24.50

Weller, Jardiniere, Forest, 9 In.Tall, Signed Weller In Block 40.00
Weller, Jardiniere, Lotus Pods, Pedestal, Signed Sicardo Weller, 30 In.Tall 925.00
Weller, Jardiniere, Louwelsa, Brown, Green, Orange Color Open Rose Decor 75.00
Weller, Lamp Base, Dickensware, Yellow, Artist-Signed Act, 5 Petal Flower 75.00
Weller, Lamp Base, Louwelsa, Brown Glaze, Yellow Tulip 25.00
Weller, Lamp Base, Signed Lasa Weller, 11 In.High 45.00
Weller, Mug, Dickensware, Matte Blue Ground, Incised Dragon 55.00
Weller, Mug, Indian's Head, Dickensware, 5 1/2 In.High 250.00
Weller, Pitcher, Brown Ground, Louwelsa, Artist-Signed 105.00
Weller, Pitcher, Clock Letters, Tankard, 15 In.Tall 10.00
Weller, Pitcher, Figural, Head, 5 1/2 In.High 36.50
Weller, Pitcher, Gray To White Ground, Signed Etna & Louwelsa 40.00
Weller, Pitcher, Kingfisher 47.50
Weller, Pitcher, Shape Of Lily Pad, Green, Fish Handle, Signed, 7 In.High 45.00
Weller, Pitcher, Trefoil Spout, Pansy Decor, Josephine Imlay Artist, L.W. 62.50
Weller, Pitcher, Water, Paneled, Trees, Cattails, Marked Kingfisher, 8 1/2 In. 72.50
Weller, Planter, Cream Ground, Pink Flowers, Holes For Hanging, 7 1/2 In. 20.00
Weller, Plaque, Lincoln, Signed, 4 1/2 In.Diameter 15.00
Weller, Pot, Flower, Forest In Relief 16.00
Weller, Vase, Apple, 6 In.High, Pair 35.00
Weller, Vase, Aqua To Pink Dogwood Flowers, 7 In. 7.00
Weller, Vase, Aurelian, Brown To Yellow Ground, Square, Signed E.Roberts 200.00
Weller, Vase, Basket Type, Flowers, Orange, White 8.50
Weller, Vase, Blackberry Design, Brown, 6 In.Tall 45.00
Weller, Vase, Blue Drapery, Artist Mark B 10.00
Weller, Vase, Blue Drapery, Matte Glaze, 4 1/2 In. 10.00
Weller, Vase, Blue To Light Blue, Flowers Leaves, Bulbous, 6 1/2 In. 12.00
Weller, Vase, Blue, Pink, Flowers, Robins, Signed, Ivy 45.00
Weller, Vase, Bluish-Gray, Floral Decoration, Etna Weller, 5 3/4 In. 30.00
Weller, Vase, Bonita, Two Handled, Artist Signed, 7 In.Tall 45.00
Weller, Vase, Branch Handle At Center, Pink Blossoms, Green Ground, Pair 25.00
Weller, Vase, Brown Ground, Signed E.R. 275.00
Weller, Vase, Brown Mottle, Morning Glory Decor, Green Border, 6 In. 25.00
Weller, Vase, Bud, Floretta, Gray, Pink Flower, Signed, 5 1/2 In.High 15.00
Weller, Vase, Bulbous, Apples In Relief 50.00
Weller, Vase, Burnt Wood Pattern, 7 In. .... *Illus* 30.00

Weller, Vase, Burnt Wood Pattern, 7 In.

Weller, Vase, Cameo, Bust Of Beethoven On Raised Surface, 12 In. 60.00
Weller, Vase, Chrysanthemums In Relief, Etna Weller, 10 1/2 In.High 40.00
Weller, Vase, Cornucopia, 5 1/2 In.Tall 10.00
Weller, Vase, Cylindrical, Floral, Impressed Mark, 6 In.High 40.00
Weller, Vase, Cylindrical, Lasa Weller, 8 3/4 In. 20.00
Weller, Vase, Dark Brown, Pansy Decoration, 10 1/2 In.High 20.00
Weller, Vase, Dickensware, Lady Golfer, Inscribed, Dated July 1908 .... 150.00

Weller, Vase, Dickensware, Lady Golfer, 7 1/2 In.High	140.00
Weller, Vase, Dickensware, Yellow Floral, Rust Tracery, Black Ground	47.50
Weller, Vase, Double Ardsley, Mark, 10 In.	15.00
Weller, Vase, Draped Female, White, Blue, Signed Block, 11 In.Tall	60.00
Weller, Vase, Embossed & Painted Cattails, Ardsley Line, Marked Weller	14.40
Weller, Vase, Eocean, Gray To White Ground, 6 Handles At Top, Signed	95.00
Weller, Vase, Etna, Pink Flowers On Gray To White, Signed Etna Weller, Block	40.00
Weller, Vase, Floral Design, Embossed, Bulbous, 8 1/2 In.Tall	22.00
Weller, Vase, Floral, Green, Gold, Orange, Signed, 8 1/2 In.	17.00
Weller, Vase, Floretta, Tan, Brown, Grape, 7 1/2 In.	50.00
Weller, Vase, Flower Design, Yellow, Brown Glaze, Corset Shape, 7 1/2 In.Tall	45.00
Weller, Vase, Flowers, Leaves, White, Green, Blue, Bulbous, 6 1/2 In.Tall	12.00
Weller, Vase, Fluted Top	15.00
Weller, Vase, Grape Vine Decor, Slots In Top Rim, Marked Weller	14.25
Weller, Vase, Gray, Drapery, 7 1/2 In.High	27.50
Weller, Vase, Horn Of Plenty, Blue, Marked, 6 In.Tall, Pair	35.00
Weller, Vase, Hudson, Blue To Green Ground, Signed Weller Pottery, Script	45.00
Weller, Vase, Incised & Painted Flowers, Cream Ground, Marked Weller	14.60
Weller, Vase, Incised, Baldin Pattern, Tree Bark, Peach Decor, Bulbous Bottom	30.00
Weller, Vase, Incised, Baldin Pattern, Tree Bark, Stick, Red & White, Rose	18.00
Weller, Vase, Lasa, 10 In.	155.00
Weller, Vase, Lasa, 7 In. *Illus*	95.00
Weller, Vase, Louwelsa, Long Neck, Buds & Flowers, 5 1/2 In.High	35.00
Weller, Vase, Man Golfing, Green To Brown, Dickensware, 9 In. ....65.00 To	125.00
Weller, Vase, Multicolor, Signed Weller Sicard, 6 3/4 In.Tall	89.00
Weller, Vase, Ovoid, Dark Brown, Pansy Decoration, 10 In.High	25.00
Weller, Vase, Palm Tree Decor, 11 In.High, Signed Lasa Weller	155.00
Weller, Vase, Pink Flowers, White, Signed, 6 1/4 In.High	10.00
Weller, Vase, Pink Roses On Gray, Etna Weller, 10 In.	32.00
Weller, Vase, Pink, Blue, Green, Berries, Ivy, Signed Eocean Weller, 11 In.	60.00
Weller, Vase, Pink, White & Lavender Blooms, 13 In.Tall, Weller Hudson	38.00
Weller, Vase, Rose Design, Cornucopia, White, 6 1/2 In.Tall	7.50
Weller, Vase, Rust Color To Brown, Floral, Ruffled Edge, 8 In.Tall	30.00
Weller, Vase, Sea Serpents, Blue, Dickensware, 15 In.Tall	150.00
Weller, Vase, Sicardo, Iridescent Green	125.00
Weller, Vase, Sicardo, Iridescent Purple Ground, Silver Clovers, Signed	90.00
Weller, Vase, Signed In Script, Pastel Blue, Morning Glories On Front	16.00
Weller, Vase, Signed Lasa Weller, Trees Against Sea, 7 In.High	125.00
Weller, Vase, Signed Weller Sicard, Green & Gold On Blue Iridescent Field	210.00
Weller, Vase, Silver Tone, Signed	35.00
Weller, Vase, Squirrel, 8 In.Diameter *Illus*	22.50
Weller, Vase, Tree Pattern, Turquoise, 8 In.	20.00
Weller, Vase, Tree Trunk & Apples, 8 1/2 In.Tall	22.50
Weller, Vase, Tree Trunk, Signed, 5 In. Opening, Pair	27.50
Weller, Vase, Triangular, Brown, Grapes In Relief, Floretta Weller	35.00
Weller, Vase, Two Handles, Etna Weller, 11 In.	55.00
Weller, Vase, Urn Shape, Blue, Marked, 6 1/2 In.High	5.95
Weller, Vase, Urn Style, 2 Handles, Embossed, Painted Pink Roses, Marked	16.00
Weller, Vase, Voile Pattern, 7 1/2 In.Tall	16.00
Weller, Vase, Wall, Basket, Roses, Signed, 8 1/2 X 4 In., Pair	32.50
Weller, Vase, Waterfall & Stream, Embossed, 7 1/2 In.Tall	27.50
Weller, Vase, White, Raised Lavender Flower, Two Handles, Mark	10.00
Weller, Vase, Woman's Portrait, Crescent Shape	75.00
Weller, Vase, Woodland, Block Signature, 6 3/4 In.Tall	14.00
Weller, Vase, Yellow, Brown, Bulbous, Handles, 8 In.High, Pair	22.50
Weller, Vase, Yellow, Brown, 8 In. *Illus*	10.00
Weller, Vase, Yellow, Squatty, 6 In.Tall, 8 In.Diameter	55.00
Weller, Vase, 2 Handles, Dark Blue & Copper Luster, Melon Ribbed	30.00
Weller, Vase, 2 Handles, 17 In.High	45.00
Wells Fargo, Horseshoe Pouch, Stamped Wells Fargo & Co.	45.00
Wheeling, Humidor, Dewey *Illus*	55.00
Whitefriars, Tumbler, Millefiori Base, 10 Oz., Signed & Dated	40.00
Willow, see Blue Willow	
Windowpane, Amethyst, Scrolled, 5 In.Square	5.00
Windowpane, Cathedral, Stained & Ribbed Glass, Lead Framing	45.00
Windowpane, Church, Stained Glass	50.00

Windowpane, Stained & Cobbled Glass, Triangular, Lead Framing, 2	40.00
Windowpane, Stained, Leaded, Paris, France, 6 X 3 Ft.	200.00
Wood Carving, Arms Of New York, Mahogany, Cake Board, Signed J.Conjer	1200.00
Wood Carving, Bear, Walking, Brown, 50 In.Long	700.00
Wood Carving, Bearded Man Standing Holding Frog On Shoulder	25.00
Wood Carving, Bird, Shore, Flying, Long Beak	50.00
Wood Carving, Bookend, Handcarved, Indian Profiles, Copper Trim, Pair	18.00
Wood Carving, Bust Of Man, American, 19th Century	175.00
Wood Carving, Bust, Shakespeare, Mahogany, Hand Carved, 12 3/4 In.Tall	150.00
Wood Carving, Chain, Carved From One Piece Of Wood, Anchor & Wheel At Ends	95.00
Wood Carving, Cherubs, Painted, Pair	18.00
Wood Carving, Eagle, Gilded, American, 19th Century, On Orb, 43 In.High	250.00

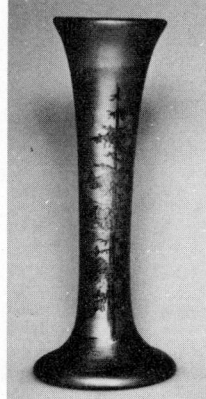

Weller, Vase, Lasa, 7 In.
See Page 574

Weller, Vase, Squirrel, 8 In.Diameter
See Page 574

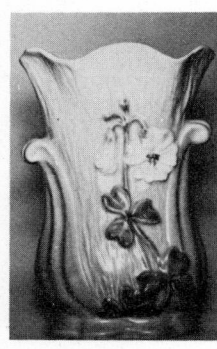

Weller, Vase, Yellow,
Brown, 8 In.
See Page 574

Wheeling, Humidor, Dewey
See Page 574

Wood Carving, Eagle, Painted, Pa., C.1850, 40 In.High .... *Illus*	250.00
Wood Carving, Elephant, Teak, Ivory Tusk & Eyes, China, 3 X 1 1/2 In.	9.00
Wood Carving, Figurehead, Ship's, Nude Nymph, Painted, Red Scarf	500.00
Wood Carving, Figurine, Bird, Hand Carved	47.50
Wood Carving, Figurine, Buddha, Hand Carved, 5 Ft.Circumference, 253 Lbs.	500.00
Wood Carving, Figurine, Oriental Fisherman, Rosewood, 20 In.	200.00
Wood Carving, Figurine, Oriental Man, Carved Stand, 9 In., Pair	85.00
Wood Carving, Figurine, Oriental, Polychrome Paint, 10 In.High	45.00
Wood Carving, Figurine, Shrine, Oriental, Traveling, C.1850, Gold Hinges	125.00
Wood Carving, Figurine, Soldier, Civil War, Movable Arms, Blue Uniform, 4 In.	8.00
Wood Carving, Figurine, Woman Holds Child, Marie Kannon, Madonna, 6 In.High	75.00
Wood Carving, Foo Dog, Gilded, 5 X 12 In.Long, Pair	90.00

Wooden, Eagle, Carved, Painted,
Penna., C.1850, 40 In.High
See Page 575

Wood Carving, **Gnome Holding Musical Instrument**, 4 1/2 In.High	25.00
Wood Carving, **Jesus & Woman At Well**, Painted	5.00
Wood Carving, **Lesser Yellowlegs**, Painted, Pair	110.00
Wood Carving, **Lion With Shield**, 11 In.High	40.00
Wood Carving, **Lion**, Holding Shield, 4 In.High	28.50
Wood Carving, **Mandarin With 2 Servants**, 8 1/2 In.High	70.00
Wood Carving, **Moose**, Mahogany, Hand Carved, Attacked By Wolf, Artist-Signed	95.00
Wood Carving, **Negro Boy**, Folk Art, Knickers & Coat, 5 In.Tall	20.00
Wood Carving, **Nude Lady Emerges From Clamshell**, Oriental, 4 In., Pair	40.00
Wood Carving, **Plaque**, Eagle, Painted, Cortland, N.Y., 19th Century	120.00
Wood Carving, **Plaque**, Eagle, Pine, Spread Wings, 38 1/2 In.Long	375.00
Wood Carving, **Robin**, American, Primitive	35.00
Wood Carving, **Squirrel**, Glass Eyes, 9 In.Tall	15.00
Wood Carving, **Statue**, Cow & Bull, Signed G.Straehli, Pair	135.00
Wood Carving, **Three Ladies Facing Outward**, 2 In.High	85.00
Wood Carving, **Totem Pole**, Cowichan Indian, Lodge House, 6 Ft. X 6 Ft., Pair	650.00
Wood Carving, **Totem Pole**, Cowichan Indian, Lodge House, 8 Ft. X 11 Ft.High	950.00
Wood Carving, **Winter Yellowlegs**, Sleeping Form, Painted	140.00
Wood Carving, **Woman**, Mountain, Signed Trygg	37.50
Wooden, see also Kitchen, Store, Tool	
Wooden, **Apple Peeler**, Bench Type, Three Legs, 33 In.Long, 17 In.Tall	35.00
Wooden, **Barber Pole**, Painted	80.00
Wooden, **Barrel**, Biscuit, English Porcelain Lined, Oak, Silver Cover	32.50
Wooden, **Basket**, Carved Grapes & Leaves	5.00
Wooden, **Beehive**, Gray Paint On Outside, Undercoat White, 12 In.Diameter	75.00
Wooden, **Birdcage**, Carved, Painted, Form Of House, C.1850-60	100.00
Wooden, **Block**, Chopping, Maple, Oval	22.00
Wooden, **Board**, Cookie, Bowed Ends, 22 1/2 X 28 In.	12.00
Wooden, **Bootjack**, Adjustable Prongs, Wooden Cleat, Maple, Pat.1859	20.00
Wooden, **Bootjack**, Lady's, On Standard, Shoe Feet	10.00
Wooden, **Bootjack**, Maple	5.00
Wooden, **Bootjack**, Oval Ends, Square Nails, 25 In.Long	7.50
Wooden, **Bootjack**, Walnut, 21 In.Long	5.00
Wooden, **Bowl**, Burl, American, Scrubbed, 15 In.Diameter, 6 In, Deep	350.00
Wooden, **Bowl**, Burl, Dark, 12 1/2 X 5 In.	17.50
Wooden, **Bowl**, Burl, Deep, Dark, 12 1/2 X 5 In.	22.50
Wooden, **Bowl**, Burl, Handcarved	16.00
Wooden, **Bowl**, Burl, Handles, 11 In.High	300.00
Wooden, **Bowl**, Burl, Handmade, 14 X 6 1/2 In.	24.50
Wooden, **Bowl**, Burl, 10 1/2 X 11 In.	70.00
Wooden, **Bowl**, Burl, 10 3/4 In.Diameter	110.00
Wooden, **Bowl**, Burl, 11 X 5 In.	29.50
Wooden, **Bowl**, Burl, 6 In.Diameter	75.00
Wooden, **Bowl**, Butter, Maple	20.00

Wooden, Bowl, Butter, 11 X 21 In. 22.50
Wooden, Bowl, Butter, 15 1/2 In.Diameter 12.50
Wooden, Bowl, Chopping, Oblong, 8 X 21 In. 35.00
Wooden, Bowl, Hand Carved, Burl 16.00
Wooden, Bowl, Handmade, Dark, 6 In.Deep, 12 X 15 In. 24.50
Wooden, Bowl, Handmade, 11 1/2 X 5 In. 12.50
Wooden, Bowl, Indian, Burl, 12 In.Diameter 70.00
Wooden, Bowl, Octagonal Shape, 11 In. 37.50
Wooden, Bowl, Oval, Hand Carved, Black, 11 X 7 X 5 In. 12.50
Wooden, Bowl, Pine, 13 In. 22.50
Wooden, Bowl, Round, 24 In.Diameter, 7 1/2 In.High 100.00
Wooden, Bowl, Sugar, Covered, Turned, Burl, American, Ring Handles 70.00
Wooden, Bowl, Sugar, Mahogany, Turned, 19th Century, 8 In.High 30.00
Wooden, Box, Burnt, Green Flowers .... *Illus*   6.50
Wooden, Box, Candle, Hangs, Slide Front, Oak 50.00
Wooden, Box, Candle, Slide Top, Dovetailed, Pine, 1i In.Long 35.00
Wooden, Box, Candle, Sliding Top, Green, Square Nails, 4 3/4 X 3 3/4 X 9 In. ... 35.00
Wooden, Box, Carved, Tray At Top, Handles, Compartments, 6 X 9 X 12 In. 14.50
Wooden, Box, Cover, Walnut, Mother Of Pearl Inlay, 5 X 9 X 12 In. 19.50
Wooden, Box, Deed, Dovetailed, Dated 1886 .... 45.00
Wooden, Box, Jewel, Carved, Ivory Inset, Red Silk Lining, 10 X 4 .... 32.00
Wooden, Box, Jewel, Owl Design, 2 1/2 In.Diameter 32.50
Wooden, Box, Pencil, Compartments, Advertising 2.95
Wooden, Box, Round Top, Burl Walnut, 5 1/2 X 7 X 10 In. 19.50
Wooden, Box, Round, 6 1/2 In.Diameter .... *Illus* 11.00

Wooden, Box, Burnt, Green Flowers

Wooden, Box, Round, 6 1/2 In.Diameter

Wooden, Box, Salt, Cover, 2 Compartment 15.00
Wooden, Box, Salt, Cover, 3 Compartment 17.50
Wooden, Box, Salt, Hand Carved, 3 Compartment 28.00
Wooden, Box, Salt, Hanging, Cover, 5 X 10 X 14 In. 14.50
Wooden, Box, Silver Inlay 7.50
Wooden, Box, Snow Scene, Hand-Painted, Signed, 5 X 3 1/2 X 2 In. 18.00
Wooden, Box, Snuff, Cover 5.00
Wooden, Box, Snuff, Cover, Black, Ebony 5.00
Wooden, Bucket, Apple Butter, Shaker, Painted Gray 25.00
Wooden, Bucket, English, Mahogany, Coopered In Brass, 19th Century, Pair 450.00
Wooden, Bucket, Ice Cream, Freezer With Bail, Fre-Zee-Zee, 1 Gallon 14.50
Wooden, Bucket, Lard, Handle, Signed C.Wilder & Son 25.00
Wooden, Bucket, Lid, Pie, Staved 22.50
Wooden, Bucket, Sugar, Cover .... 15.00 To 20.00
Wooden, Bucket, Sugar, Red Varnish 20.00
Wooden, Bucket, Sugar, 10 Lb. 12.50
Wooden, Busk, For Lady's Undergarment 5.00
Wooden, Cabinet, Smoking, Cover Lift, Double Doors, 8 X 10 X 14 In. 24.50

Wooden, Candleholder, Wall, 2 Compartments, 15 1/2 In.High	50.00
Wooden, Candlestick, Red Paint, 10 1/4 In.High, Pair	110.00
Wooden, Candlestick, White Painted Floral On Black, Carved, C.1850, Pair	80.00
Wooden, Canteen, American, Revolutionary Era, Red Paint	69.50
Wooden, Case, Lady's, Burl Veneer, Oval	17.50
Wooden, Cigar Store Indian, see also Iron, Cigar Store Indian	
Wooden, Cigar Store Indian, Brave, Feathered Headdress, 6 Ft.9 In.Tall	3600.00
Wooden, Cigar Store Indian, Carved From Solid Log, 6 Ft.Tall	275.00
Wooden, Cigar Store Indian, Chief, Feathered Headdress, 5 Ft.5 In.Tall	2200.00
Wooden, Cigar Store Indian, Hand Carved, 6 Ft.Tall	275.00
Wooden, Cigar Store Indian, Male, Feathered Headdress, 6 Ft.8 1/2 In.Tall	1900.00
Wooden, Cigar Store Indian, Princess, Feathered Headdress, 58 In.Tall	1700.00
Wooden, Cigar Store Indian, Scout Pose, Hand Carved, C.1850	2300.00
Wooden, Cigar Store Indian, Squaw, Feathered Headdress, 48 In.Tall	1700.00
Wooden, Cigar Store Indian, Squaw, Feathered Headdress, 6 Ft.5 In.Tall	1000.00
Wooden, Cigar Store Indian, Squaw, Feathered Headdress, 6 Ft.9 In.Tall	3700.00
Wooden, Cigar Store Indian, Squaw, Headdress, 6 Ft.5 In. *Illus*	1000.00
Wooden, Cigar Store Indian, Warrior, Feathered Headdress, 55 In.Tall	1500.00
Wooden, Cigar Store Indian, 6 Ft.Tall, Carved From Solid Log	275.00
Wooden, Clamp, Cabinetmaker's	8.00
Wooden, Clothespin, Hand Carved	5.00
Wooden, Coffeepot, Stave, Willow Bound, Painted Decoration	35.00
Wooden, Comb, Carved, 12 1/2 In.	20.00
Wooden, Compass	35.00
Wooden, Compote, Burl, Standard, 6 1/2 In.Diameter	500.00
Wooden, Counter, Pine Handle, Double Bag, 13 In.Long	25.00
Wooden, Decoy, Duck, Glass Eyes, Sears Roebuck	22.00
Wooden, Desk, Lap, Lady's, Blue Velvet Lining, Lock, Key, Dated 1878, Walnut	40.00
Wooden, Desk, Lap, Walnut, Lined	12.00
Wooden, Dipper, Olive, Hand Carved, 13 In.Long	9.50
Wooden, Dipper, Pickle	20.00
Wooden, Dumbbell, School, Pair	4.00
Wooden, Easel, Handcarved, 13 In.High	25.00
Wooden, Fid, Sailor's, For Splicing Rigging	5.00
Wooden, Fire Bellows, Carved, 22 In.Long	25.00
Wooden, Frame, Candle Mold, Shoe Feet, 18th Century	15.00
Wooden, Frame, Holds Saw To File Teeth, 24 X 10 In.	10.00
Wooden, Funnel, 2 1/2 X 3 In.	20.00
Wooden, Hackle, German, 40 Steel Teeth	15.00
Wooden, Harness, Shoulder, Handmade, For Two Buckets	39.00
Wooden, Hat Block, Lady's	10.00
Wooden, Hat Form	5.00
Wooden, Holder, Book, Sliding, Blue, Decals	9.50
Wooden, Holder, Plate, Folding, 8 In.	1.50
Wooden, Horse, see Carousel Horse	
Wooden, Hourglass, C.1790	50.00
Wooden, Ink Sander, Circa 1850, Maple	12.00
Wooden, Jar, Mahogany, Turned, Cylindrical, Covered, Stone Liner	5.00
Wooden, Kit, Tool, Blacksmith's, 2 Tiered	20.00
Wooden, Match Holder, Carved, Shape Of Ives, Striker On Bottom, 2 3/4 In.	6.75
Wooden, Match Holder, Design Of Tied Bundle Of Tobacco Leaves, Carved	6.75
Wooden, Match Holder, 2-Tier, For Good & Used Matches	17.50
Wooden, Matchbox, 10 X 4 In., Partition In Middle	10.00
Wooden, Measure, Stave Constructed, Handle, 6 1/2 In.Diameter	7.50
Wooden, Measure, Stave Constructed, Hickory Bound	17.50
Wooden, Measure, Stove	7.00
Wooden, Mirror, Purse Size, Advertising	2.00
Wooden, Mold, Butter, Carved Cow In Hay, 4 In.Diameter	110.00
Wooden, Mold, Butter, Fern & Leaf Pattern, Round, One Piece	14.00
Wooden, Mold, Butter, Flower & Leaf Carving, 3 3/4 In.Diameter	20.00
Wooden, Mold, Butter, Individual, Acorn & 2 Leaves, 1 1/2 In.Diameter	5.00
Wooden, Mold, Butter, Oak Leaf & Acorn, Plunger Type, 4 In.High	12.00
Wooden, Mold, Butter, Pineapple, Plunger, 3 In.	15.00
Wooden, Mold, Butter, Pineapple, Stubby	20.00
Wooden, Mold, Butter, Pineapple, 4 In.Diameter	24.50
Wooden, Mold, Butter, Rose, Thistle, Leaves	17.50

Wooden, Mold, Butter, Sheaf Of Wheat, 4 1/4 In.Diameter 18.50
Wooden, Mold, Butter, Strawberry, Leaves, 4 1/2 In.Diameter 24.50
Wooden, Mold, Butter, Swan, 4 1/2 In.Diameter 65.00
Wooden, Mold, Butter, Swan, 5 In.High, 3 In.Diameter 35.00
Wooden, Mold, Butter, Three Wheat Heads, 3 1/2 In.High, 2 1/4 In.Diameter 15.00
Wooden, Mold, Butter, Tulip Carving, Flower Carving On Handle 125.00
Wooden, Mold, Cheese 10.00
Wooden, Mold, Gingerbread .... *Illus* 12.00

Wooden, Cigar Store Indian, Squaw,
Headdress, 6 Ft.5 In.
See Page 578

Wooden, Mold, Gingerbread

Wooden, Mold, Maple Sugar, Heart Cutout, Block Of Wood 15.00
Wooden, Mold, Maple Sugar, Scalloped, Flower Center 45.00
Wooden, Mortar, American, Indian Grain 40.00
Wooden, Noggin, Maple, 4 In.Diameter, 5 In.Tall 85.00
Wooden, Noisemaker, Pine, Dovetailed 10.00
Wooden, Nutcracker, Head Of Rutherford B.Hayes, Hand Carved, 8 1/2 In.Long 35.00
Wooden, Opener, Can, Squeeze 10.00
Wooden, Ornament, Mantel, Carved, Polychrome Decoration, 20 In.High, Pair 265.00
Wooden, Paddle, Butter .... 2.50 To 5.50
Wooden, Peel, 48 In.Long 55.00
Wooden, Pegboard, Clothes, Simulates Bamboo, 33 1/2 In.Wide 30.00
Wooden, Picker, Blueberry 14.50
Wooden, Pitcher, Press Wood, Tin Hangles, Signed, Patented 3.00

Wooden, Pitcher, Tankard, Handmade, 11 In.Tall	85.00
Wooden, Plaque, Armorial Shape, Soldier Insert	10.00
Wooden, Plaque, Marquetry, Rectangular, Nude, Lounging Before Oval Mirror	60.00
Wooden, Printing Block For Fabric, American Indians, Hand Carved	7.00
Wooden, Printing Block For Fabric, Peacocks, Hand Carved	6.50
Wooden, Pump, Barrel	5.00
Wooden, Rack, Clothes, Swingout Hooks, Iron	7.50
Wooden, Rack, Hook, 24 In., Hand Forged Iron Hook	18.00
Wooden, Rack, Meat Hook, Hanging	18.00
Wooden, Rack, Meat Hook, Hanging	18.00
Wooden, Rack, Spoon, Carved Leaf Scrolls At Top & Sides, 20 In.High	35.00
Wooden, Rack, Utensil, Wrought Iron Hooks, Red	90.00
Wooden, Rattle, Child's, Form Of Rolling Pin, Decorated	10.00
Wooden, Ruler, Advertising Haskins Art Glass Co., 6 In.	.50
Wooden, Sandals, Chinese, Inlaid Ivory	20.00
Wooden, Sander, For Pounce, 2 In.	17.50
Wooden, Scoop, 10 In., Whittles, Open Knot Hole	15.00
Wooden, Scouring Board, Box, 36 In.Long	15.00
Wooden, Shovel, Snow, Patent Date 1904, 5 In.Tall, Decorated	35.00
Wooden, Showshoes	10.00
Wooden, Signature Seal, Oriental, Large	12.00
Wooden, Sled, Logging, Miniature, 1895, 17 In.	12.50
Wooden, Spigot, Curly Maple	30.00
Wooden, Spoon, Hand Carved	9.00
Wooden, Spoon, Scoop Type, Curved, 10 In.	25.00
Wooden, Spoon, Serving, Carved Head End, American	25.00
Wooden, Squeezer	5.00
Wooden, Stamp, Butter, Miniature, Carved Fish, 2 1/8 In.Diameter	75.00
Wooden, Stick, Household, 28 In.Long	5.00
Wooden, Stretcher & Blocker, Hat, 2 Part	6.00
Wooden, Sugar, Turned Cherry, Covered, Flared Foot	75.00
Wooden, Tankard, Stave, Willow Bound	20.00
Wooden, Tazza, Cake Stand, Hand-Hewn, Maple, One Piece	135.00
Wooden, Tea Caddy, Shaped Like Books, Hidden Lock, Signed	158.00
Wooden, Tea Caddy, Two Compartments, Cut Glass Jar, Mahogany	95.00
Wooden, Telephone, see Telephone	
Wooden, Tray, Pennsylvania Dutch Decoration, 11 1/2 In.Diameter	35.00
Wooden, Urn, Cylindrical Standard, 8 1/4 In.High, Pair	30.00
Wooden, Vise	20.00
Wooden, Washing Machine, Handle Works Agitator	75.00
Wooden, Whale, Flat, Black Paint	17.50
Wooden, Wheel, Ship, Brass Trim	250.00
Wooden, Wheel, Ship's, Brass Hub & Trim, 54 In.Diameter	450.00
Wooden, Whirligig, Painted, American, C.1850, 21 In.High _Illus_	650.00
Wooden, Whistle, Bird, Carved, Bark Left On	6.00
Wooden, Yoke, Ox, 36 In.	29.00
Wooden, Yoke, Ox, 40 In.	20.00
Wooden, Yoke, Shoulder, Man's	37.50
Wooden, Yoke, Shoulder, Man's, Sap, 2 Wood Bucket Hooks	25.00
Wooden, Yoke, Training	35.00
Wooden, Yoke, Wagon, Metal Band, 3 Ft.7 In.Long	6.00
Worcester, see also Royal Worcester	
Worcester, Basket, Chestnut, Covered, Blue & White, Quatrefoil, 1st Period	375.00
Worcester, Basket, Cover, Chestnut, Yellow, Bengal Tiger Pattern, 1st Period	1050.00
Worcester, Basket, Oval, Pierced Basketwork, Floral Panels, 1st Period, Pair	450.00
Worcester, Bowl, Basket Weave, Oriental Scenes In Blue, 18th Century	300.00
Worcester, Bowl, Blue & White, Landskip & Oriental Teahouse, 1st Period	70.00
Worcester, Bowl, Rose Design, Pink, Gold, Green, Mark, Cover, 6 In.High	110.00
Worcester, Bowl, Transfer Printed, First Period, Scalloped Edge	400.00
Worcester, Coffeepot, Blue & White Pear Shape, Fence Pattern, 1st Period	200.00
Worcester, Cup & Saucer, Coffee, Blue & White, St.Cloud Style, 1st Period	140.00
Worcester, Cup & Saucer, Floral Sprays, Circa 1760	37.50
Worcester, Cup & Saucer, Queen Charlotte Pattern, 1st Period	210.00
Worcester, Dessert Set, Medallion, C.1820, Flight, Barr & Barr, 30 Piece	1700.00
Worcester, Dish, Blind Earl, Scalloped Edge, Painted Flowers, 1st Period	450.00
Worcester, Dish, Chamberlain's, Jabberwocky Pattern, Oval, C.1810	80.00

Worcester, Dish, Sunburst Leaf, 10 1/4 In. .... *Illus*	450.00
Worcester, Jardiniere, Stand, Chamberlain's, Landscape, C.1810, Pair	170.00
Worcester, Jug, Cabbage Leaf, Scroll Handle, Mask Spout, 1st Period	200.00
Worcester, Mug, Hand-Painted Roses, Gold Trim, Flesh Color, 2 Handles	20.00
Worcester, Plate, Armorial, Fides In Amicitia, C.1810, Barr, Flight & Barr	60.00
Worcester, Plate, Floral Design, Red, White, Circa 1820, 11 1/2 In.Long	130.00
Worcester, Plate, Jabberwocky Pattern, Birds, 1st Period, Pair	425.00

Wooden, Whirligig, Painted, American,
C.1850, 21 In.High
See Page 580

Worcester, Dish,
Sunburst Leaf, 10 1/4 In.

†————————— Worcester, Sauceboat, 8 In., Pair ————————†

Worcester, Plate, Oriental Design, Red, Gold, Blue, Gold Band, Marked, 8 In.	90.00
Worcester, Plate, Roses, Pink, Gold Border, C, 1820, 10 In.Diameter	60.00
Worcester, Sauceboat, 8 In., Pair .... *Illus*	450.00
Worcester, Saucer, Transfer Printed Landscape In Sepia, Dr.Wall Period	50.00
Worcester, Tea & Coffee Set, Famille Rose Type Decor, 1800-10, 133 Piece	3000.00
Worcester, Tea Set, White & Gold, C.1800, 14 Piece	175.00
Worcester, Teacup & Saucer, Blue Panels, Gilt Husks, Dr.Wall Period	70.00
Worcester, Teacup & Saucer, Blue Scale, Iron Red Flowers, Dr.Wall Period	200.00
Worcester, Teacup & Saucer, Fan Pattern, Gilt, 1st Period	250.00
Worcester, Teacup & Saucer, Floral Bouquets, Famille Verte, Dr.Wall, Pair	290.00
Worcester, Teacup & Saucer, Fluted, Wheat & Floral In Kakiemon, 1st Period	150.00
Worcester, Teacup & Saucer, White Cup, Gold Outline On Saucer, C.1785, 12	85.00
Worcester, Tub, Butter, Cover, Puce Floral, Gilt, Scroll Handles, 1st Period	375.00
Worcester, Vase, Bulbous, Ribbed, Hand-Painted Floral, Gold, Locke & Co.	37.50
Worcester, Vase, Floral & Bird Decor, 1st Period, 6 1/4 In.High, Pair	1100.00
World War I, Button, Tunic, German, No.7	4.00

World War I, Canteen, German	8.50
World War I, Cap, Khaki, Soldier's	3.00
World War I, Container, Bullet, Leather, 3 Compartments, For Waist	12.00
World War I, Epaulettes, German Naval Officer's Dress, Silver Bullion	34.50
World War I, First Aid Packet, 1918, Pull Ring	6.00
World War I, Foot Powder, 1917, Infantry	1.50
World War I, Helmet, American	32.50
World War I, Helmet, German, 1917, Steel	24.00 To 32.50
World War I, Helmet, Steel, Doughboy	12.95
World War I, Iron Cross	7.00
World War I, Lock With Key, U.S.Army, C.1918	7.00
World War I, Match Case, Celluloid, Picture Kaiser Wilhelm	5.00
World War I, Medal, British, Mercantile Marine	12.00
World War I, Medal, British, Silver Service	3.00
World War I, Medal, British, Victory	2.00
World War I, Medal, British, 1914-1915, Star	2.00 To 4.00
World War I, Memento, Kaiser With Head Pierced By Sword, Metal	15.00
World War I, Mess Kit, 1917, 5 Pieces	5.00
World War I, Mirror, Steel, Case	1.25
World War I, Mug, Victory, China	11.00
World War I, Plate, 1914, 7 In.	6.00
World War I, Sampler, There'll Always Be An England, On Linen	15.00
World War I, Statue, German Infantryman, White Metal & Pewter, C.1915	97.50
World War I, Sword, Scabbard, German	30.00
World War I, Tin, Bacon, Dated 1916	2.00
World War I, Vest, Grenade, Trench, U.S., Khaki Canvas	5.95
World War II, Band, Arm, Wehrmacht	10.00
World War II, Book, Mein Kampf, Adolf Hitler, 1943	40.00
World War II, Buckle, Belt, Brass, Nazi, Emblem	14.00
World War II, Buckle, Belt, Nazi, Gott Mit Uns, Eagle, Dated 1940	10.00
World War II, Button, Lapel, Nazi, 1933, Ja	4.00
World War II, Button, Lapel, V For Victory, Metal	1.00
World War II, Button, Pin Back, Uncle Sam Hanging Hitler, Mechanical	8.00
World War II, Dagger, Nazi, Original Paper Tags	45.00
World War II, Dagger, Nazi, Scabbard	50.00 To 80.00
World War II, Dagger, Sheath, Nazi Labor Corps, Stag Grips, Urbeit Adelt	84.50
World War II, Flag, Nazi, Chefs Der Hauptamter, Silver-Gray Color, Eagle	15.00
World War II, Flag, Nazi, Swastika In Center, 2 X 3 Ft.	20.00
World War II, Flag, Nazi, 3 X 5 Ft.	15.00
World War II, Hat, Nazi Officer's	40.00
World War II, Hat, Nazi Youth's, Insignia	12.00
World War II, Helmet, Nazi Officer's, Afrika Korps, Pith, Insignia	30.00
World War II, Helmet, Nazi, 1933 Issue, Ss Decals	25.00
World War II, Knife, British Commando, Markings & Combat, 1943, Scabbard	12.00
World War II, Knife, Fork, & Spoon, Nazi, Air Force, Eagle, Swastika	18.50
World War II, Knife, German Survival, 6 1/2 In.Long, Metal Sheath	20.00
World War II, Knife, Knuckle, British, Commando, White Metal Grips, Marked	150.00
World War II, Knife, Nazi Youth, Swastika On Grip, Blood & Honor On Blade	22.00
World War II, Pin, Swastika, Red Enameled	6.00
World War II, Plaque, Ss, Skull & Crossbones, Bronze, Berlin, 1939	6.00
World War II, Plaque, Wall, Nazi, 3rd Reich, Eagle On Swastika, Aluminum	12.00
World War II, Radio Transmitter, Made For Russia, Lend-Lease	150.00
World War II, Rosettes, For Prussian Helmet, Black, White, & Red, Pair	3.50
World War II, Tag, Kit Bag, Waffen Ss, Brass, 1939, Berlin, Rzm On Back	7.00
World's Fair, Cup, Child's, Chicago, Metal, 1 3/4 In.	20.00
World's Fair, Bottle, 1939, Figural	15.00
World's Fair, Cup, 1904, Enameled	10.00
World's Fair, Flag, 1893, Chicago, Silk, Fair & Lake Michigan In Color	20.00
World's Fair, Spoon, Souvenir, 1893, Silver Plate, Administration Building	2.50
World's Fair, Spoon, Souvenir, 1893, Silver Plate, Agricultural Building	2.50
World's Fair, Spoon, Souvenir, 1893, Silver Plate, Art Palace	2.50
World's Fair, Spoon, Souvenir, 1939, Silver Plate, New York	2.50
Yellowware, Mug, Child's, Blue Checkerboard Decoration	8.50
Yellowware, Pitcher, Ohio, Blue Seaweed On White Band, 6 In.High	22.50
Yellowware, Pot, Seaweed Decoration, Ohio, 8 In.Diameter	12.50
Zanesville, Glass, Whiskey, Blown, Green With Swirls To Right, 2 5/8 In.High	175.00

Zsolnay Pottery was made in Hungary after 1855.

Zsolnay, Ewer, Art Nouveau, Mottled Gold Iridescent Green, Rope Handle 100.00
Zsolnay, Ewer, Enameled, 10 In.High 45.00
Zsolnay, Jar, Covered, Reticulated .... *Illus* 40.00
Zsolnay, Pitcher, Rose, Pewter Lid, 10 In.Tall 25.00
Zsolnay, Planter, Persian Flowers, Gold Traced, 5 1/2 X 5 1/2 In. 75.00
Zsolnay, Urn, Wine, Green, Yellow, Brown, Pink Foral, Signed, 11 1/2 In.Tall 115.00
Zsolnay, Vase, Blue Iridescent, 4 1/2 In.High 85.00
Zsolnay, Vase, Enameled, 10 In.High 45.00
Zsolnay, Vase, Reticulated & Enameled, 7 1/2 In.High 65.00
Zurich, Teapot, Bullet Shape, Serpent Spout, Rural Landscapes, C.1770 .... 310.00

/Zsolnay, Jar, Covered, Reticulated